ECHOES FROM
FORGOTTEN
MOUNTAINS

ADVANCE PRAISE FOR THE BOOK

"Tibet watchers know him as one of the most incisive and prolific commentators on the political scene, a writer with strong opinions but also the wide reading and intellectual depth to back them up, sometimes fiercely"—*International Herald Tribune*

"Jamyang Norbu La has produced a massive and brilliantly detailed panoramic view of Tibet's history. The writing is vivid, and every page reveals new observations and a fresh examination of old stories. Undoubtedly the most comprehensive narrative, it will serve as one of the most authoritative and indispensable books on Tibet"—Tsering Shakya, associate professor, University of British Columbia and author of *The Dragon in the Land of Snows* and *Fire under the Snow*

"A nation needs people who will tell its stories. Otherwise, in this world, so filled with the loud proclamations of victors or robbers, no one will hear the testimonies of the dispossessed. Jamyang Norbu is precisely such a defender and champion of Tibet. For many years, I have recognized this about him. And through our many conversations, I have come to understand his mission of both battle and bearing witness, how it permeates his entire life, and how his actions have affected me in formative yet imperceptible ways. For all this, I am deeply grateful to him. Today, Jamyang Norbu is the most prominent writer and thinker inside and outside Tibet. His writings have historical and literary value, they are a monument dedicated to the Land of Snows, which in the end cannot be destroyed by any power [Translated from Chinese]"—Tsering Woeser, author of *Forbidden Memory* and *Scarlet Ruins*

"*Echoes from Forgotten Mountains* is a magnificent gift to us all. Part oral history, part literary memoir, part critical reflection, this book is a skilful, thoughtful journey through contemporary Tibetan history. Jamyang Norbu's singular voice is simultaneously intimate and intellectual, critical and compassionate, providing detailed character sketches, insightful analyses of major events, and new, invaluable historical data. From households in Lhasa to refugee settlements in India, guerrilla army bases in Nepal to apartments in Paris, the genius of this book is in the combination of Norbu's own personal experiences and his commitment to documenting the stories of Tibetans from many walks of life. Based on decades of research, writing and action, this is the book many of us have long been waiting for. An uncompromising and brilliant tour de force!"—Carole McGranahan, professor, University of Colorado Boulder and author of *Arrested Histories: Tibet, the CIA, and Memories of a Forgotten War* and *Imperial Formations: Thinking Empire beyond Europe*

"*Echoes from Forgotten Mountains* is a masterful opus that is a must-read for any student of contemporary Tibetan history, Cold War insurgencies, India-China relations and the earliest decades of the People's Republic of China.

It adds intriguing details about Tibetan paramilitary and intelligence operations that have never before been revealed, adding important nuances to the involvement of countries like the US, India and France, to name a few. Jamyang Norbu writes as not only a scholar of the subject matter but also a direct participant in some of the operations described. Highly recommended"—Kenneth Conboy, former deputy director of the Asian Studies Center in Washington DC and author of *The CIA's Secret War in Tibet*, *Spies in the Himalayas*, *CIA Paramilitary Operations in Tibet: 1957–1974* and *Spies & Commandos*

"Jamyang Norbu, the master of the critical essay on Tibetan politics, has now turned his considerable talents to a sweeping history of the Chinese invasion of Tibet and the subsequent decades of uprisings and repressions. I have previously compared his essays favourably with those of George Orwell. Now I am compelled to compare him favourably with Aleksandr Solzhenitsyn for his skilful telling of the tragic and heroic stories of actual resistance fighters who were his comrades when he joined the Mustang guerrilla base in 1972. The result is a brilliant history of Tibetan resistance to the Chinese invasion"—Warren W. Smith Jr, author of *Tibetan Nation: A History of Tibetan Nationalism and Sino-Tibetan Relations*

"Jamyang Norbu is the preeminent and most prolific Tibetan writer in exile. Erudite, polemical, provocative and controversial, his writings over decades have tracked the vicissitudes of Tibetan politics, history and culture with wit and insight, and time and again, reflected his own passionate concern for the fate of Tibet. Now, he has written his magnum opus, a sweeping work—part autobiography, part history, and part a deeply felt portrayal of people and events—that chronicles the most turbulent period of Tibet's history, its invasion and occupation by Communist China. *Echoes from Forgotten Mountains* is a tour de force, a gripping and original work of literature that comprehensively tells the tragic story of Tibet in all its complexity and contradictions"—Tenzing Sonam, film-maker, *The Shadow Circus: The CIA in Tibet*, *A Stranger in My Native Land*, *Dreaming Lhasa* and *The Sweet Requiem*

ECHOES FROM
FORGOTTEN
MOUNTAINS

TIBET IN WAR AND PEACE

JAMYANG NORBU

PENGUIN
VIKING
An imprint of Penguin Random House

VIKING

USA | Canada | UK | Ireland | Australia
New Zealand | India | South Africa | China | Singapore

Viking is part of the Penguin Random House group of companies
whose addresses can be found at global.penguinrandomhouse.com

Published by Penguin Random House India Pvt. Ltd
4th Floor, Capital Tower 1, MG Road,
Gurugram 122 002, Haryana, India

Penguin
Random House
India

First published in Viking by Penguin Random House India 2023

Copyright © Jamyang Norbu 2023

ISBN 9780670094660

For sale in the Indian Subcontinent only

Typeset in Adobe Garamond Pro by Manipal Technologies Limited, Manipal
Printed at Replika Press Pvt. Ltd, India

This is a legitimate digitally printed version of the book and therefore might not
have certain extra finishing on the cover.

In memory of my dear mother who, from my earliest childhood to her last days in early 2005, told me stories of Tibet

"The struggle of man against power is the struggle of memory against forgetting"

—Milan Kundera

"We are the mountains. The echo from us is of thee"

—Maulana Jalaluddin Rumi

"This centre of heaven,
This core of the earth,
This heart of the world,
Fenced round by snow-mountains,
This headland of all rivers
Where the peaks are high and the land is pure,
A country so good,
Where men are born as sages and heroes,
And act according to good laws,
To this land of horses ever more speedy
He came . . ."

—A ninth-century panegyric to the land where the
first Tibetan emperor manifested himself[*]

[*] Michael Aris, trans., *Documents de Touen-houang relatifs à l'histoire du Tibet*, ed. Jacques Bacot, Frederick W. Thomas and Gustave C. Toussaint (Paris: Libraire Orientaliste Paul Geuthner, 1940).

CONTENTS

Introduction   XV

1. Origin Chronicle: Matrilineal   1
2. Origin Chronicle: Patrilineal   33
3. My Journey to Lhasa   42
4. The Ghosts of Chamdo   49
5. Seventeen Point Swindle   90
6. Requiem   104
7. Fall of the South   121
8. "Nest of Spies"   151
9. March Winds   189
10. A Crane from Lithang   206
11. The Confluence   226
12. Lithang Uprising   239
13. Wind and Wildfire   264
14. Never Return   283
15. The Man Whose Luck Dried Up   305
16. Memory Songs of Lhasa   328
17. "The Men Especially Sent by Chairman Mao"   344
18. Occupation Years   364
19. The Golden Throne   384

20. Drop Zone Tibet   406

21. Four Rivers Six Ranges   426

22. Calcutta Interlude   443

23. The Long Ride North   448

24. Primordial Playground   477

25. Lhasa Twilight   501

26. Crossing the River of Happiness   533

27. The Lhasa Uprising   550

28. Silent Struggle   590

29. Air Operations   595

30. Camp Hale, Colorado   610

31. The Great Forests of Kham   624

32. Mission to Markham   644

33. Confessions of an American Imperialist Spy   669

34. "Sea of Inhumanity"   696

35. Guerrilla Trails to Mustang   716

36. Raids into Tibet   746

37. French Connection   765

38. Mao Is Dead! Long Live Mao!   786

39. Bhusang Goes Home   803

40. High Mountain Elegy   816

Acknowledgements   833

Notes   837

Index   875

INTRODUCTION

There are only a few of them left now, but the bards, the true ones, who sang the great epic of King Gesar of Ling did so entirely from memory. They were said to be able to sing for many days, even a week or so, without repeating themselves or missing a line or a word. And it is a long poem, possibly one of the longest in the world. This feat of memory was (in one particular bardic tradition) attributed to divine inspiration, "the story descending" (*bhab-drung*) as it were, when the spirit of Gesar or one of his heroes entered the bard (in dreams and visions) and spoke through him or her.

Tibetans of the past, especially those *ur*-nomads we call *Horpa*, among whom the most accomplished Gesar singers are found, have highly accurate, archival memories. This is, of course, a quality found in many oral cultures of the past, where mythologies, cosmogonies, histories and genealogies of kings and chieftains were transmitted faithfully through many generations. In Tibet, the recitation and singing of such accounts were essential features of formal ceremonies in various tribal assemblies and courts of the once independent and semi-independent principalities in Eastern Tibet such as Gyalrong, Dergé, Chamdo, Chagla, Minyak, Nangchen, Lingtsang, Lhatö, Mili and other kingdoms on the frontiers of India and Nepal such as Ladakh, Sikkim, Mustang and Bhutan; and earlier in history the kingdoms of Choné, Ngawa and Tsongkha in Amdo.

Such a tradition, called the *molla*[1] or *molwa* (articulation), is still practised in Tibet, particularly on its western frontier where the old Tibetan empire once touched Persia and the fragmentary remains of the Greco–Indian world. To the east, on the frontiers of China, a similar tradition called the *tamgenma*[2] (ornamented speech) survives to this day.

Such oral traditions were so widespread throughout Tibet that a class of wandering beggars who majestically called themselves the "White Seed Fulfiller of Wishes", *Drekar Samphe Thundup*, performed irreverent parodies of this ritual. Their grandiose recitations ". . . interlarded with jests which cannot be said to border on the vulgar, for they are well across the line" (according to Charles Bell) have, over time, become institutionalized in New Year celebrations and wedding ceremonies. An interesting part of the Drekar's monologues are the "Origin Chronicles of Tibet" (*bhöd seepa chagpae chag-rap*), where short, pithy verses describe major towns, landmarks and religious sites in Tibet and recount their (largely) fabulous origins.[*]

The Drekar's verse on the origin of Lhasa city reflects the traditional belief that the Holy City was built around a lake, Wothang Tso, which was filled in and the Jokhang Temple built over it.

> Lhasa was not made
> Lhasa came into being
> On the surface of a lake

> *Lhasa machag*
> *Lhasa chag*
> *Lhasa tsomoe teng la chag*

---

[*] When reciting the origin chronicle of Tsethang town, the Drekar digresses on the superior quality of the *chang* ale served there: "Knocked back a bowl and got drunk/ Guzzled two and went crazy/ Couldn't tell a sheep from a calf/ Couldn't tell the mother from the bride/ Tried to mount the mother's . . . etc. (*ghang thung ni zi/ dho thung ni nyol/ lug dang peypey ngo mashen/ ama dang nama ngo mashen/ amae kup la tsezay, tsezay*)."

Even with the advent and spread of the written language, from the seventh century CE, such oral traditions have maintained their hold on Tibetan society to this day.

In early imperial Tibet, when literacy was not widespread, it appears that official records were sometimes maintained by way of memorization. The scholar F.W. Thomas tells us that around CE 670, after the Tibetan Imperial army had completed a series of conquests* in Central Asia and installed a new administration ". . . the census of various farmers was made into a song and committed to the memory of the district governors."3

Tibetans are still not a very modern people, and many of them retain their native ability to recall their past in accurate and vivid detail. I have spent a considerable period of my life interviewing people for their personal stories. My inquiries also extended to less-private areas: music, dance, opera, costumes, ceremonies, crime, jurisprudence, rituals and especially travel. I heard accounts of yak-caravan expeditions on the Northern Tea Road, which, starting from Dartsedo in the far east, headed across the vast northern grasslands to the trade centre of Jyekundo, then swung south to Lhasa; of pilgrim treks and arduous full-prostration journeys to Mount Kailash, the centre of the Bön, Hindu and Buddhist cosmos; of dangerous jungle expeditions to the sacred Pure Crystal Mountain of Tsari; of the pilgrim circuit of the high mountain caves and retreats of Lapchi Gang around the Everest range where the great yogi Milarepa meditated; and of the journey to Lhamo Latso, the lake of visions.

I also sought out stories of gods (*lha*), ghosts (*dre*), oracles (*lha-ba*), wraiths (*yidag*), witches (*dünmu*), imps (*theurang*), naiads (*lu*) and demons (*dü*). This was done out of curiosity, wonder and the love of a good story, but also with the appreciation gained through reading Lafcadio Hearn's stories of "ghostly" Japan and the great Chinese compendium of eerie tales, the *Liao Chai Chih I* of

---

*In the final "Battle of Dafei River", a Chinese army of 1,00,000 men under General Xue Rengui of the Tang dynasty was annihilated by a Tibetan force under General Gar Tridring Tsendrö, who then took control of the Tarim Basin. See Drikung Kyabgon Chetsang, *A History of the Tibetan Empire* (Dehradun: Songtsen Library, 2011).

P'u Sung-ling, that the naïve, supernatural aspects of folklore and traditional beliefs perhaps give us access to the often overlooked, and once in a while, subliminal, areas of a culture that somehow elude us in more straightforward academic studies.

Much of my search was conducted through long interviews with refugees, sometimes for documentation and intelligence work but more often for my own writing and curiosity. I would catch myself taking notes and asking follow-up questions even in casual conversations with my mother, uncles, grandaunt (who, in 1920, had her photograph taken by Sir Charles Bell[4] in Lhasa) and other relatives, friends and comrades, especially those who had fought in the Resistance. The right sort of question, I learned over time, had a way of turning casual remarks into lengthy reminiscences—which was what I was really after.

Sometimes such reminiscing took place in a small chang tavern, which in the poverty of the refugee world was often no more than the main room of a humble Tibetan family. The customers would be seated around two or three beds circling a rough-hewn square table (covered with a sheet of grimy rexine) being served home-made (and illegal) barley-ale* or chang by the lady of the house. If it was late, her little daughter might be fast asleep on the very bed the customers were seated on, warming their backs, oblivious to the talk and occasional laughter.

It was at the chang-house† by the old McLeod Ganj post office that the late editor of the *Tibetan Review*, Tsering Wangyal and I met this fierce-looking tantric priest (*ngakpa*). His eyes were bloodshot, and his long-matted hair coiled around his head in an untidy, oversized turban. He was having a drink, which, since he was a lay practitioner and not an ordained monk, he was allowed to do. He had been summoned to Dharamshala by the Religious Department of the exile government

---

*The traditional English ale, brewed from barley without the addition of hops, better describes the Tibetan chang than the term beer, which is brewed with hops.

†The place was owned by Kamikhang Chönze, one of the five members of the first underground organization in Lhasa, the "Mimang" or "People's Organization", that opposed the Chinese military occupation.

to demonstrate his skill at *tumo*, the yogic ability to raise one's body temperature at will, to a team of medical scientists from Harvard led by Dr Herbert Benson. The old priest was fairly incensed at having to perform for foreigners an activity he regarded as a profound spiritual exercise. But orders were orders—especially when they came from the Dalai Lama's administration. However, he was not averse to accepting a drink from us, and as the evening progressed, he told us his story.

Proust said that: "The only true voyage, the only bath in the fountain of youth, would be not to visit strange lands but to possess other eyes, to see the universe through the eyes of another, of a hundred others, to see a hundred universes that each of them sees, that each of them is." For someone like myself who would never know what it was to be an ascetic like Milarepa or meditate in a solitary mountain cave, to see, if only for an evening, through the eyes of someone who was making such a genuine spiritual journey, was "a true voyage" to be remembered and cherished.

There were, of course, areas in many of these accounts where you needed some experience to navigate around. Having been processed through a no-nonsense rationalist educational system, I initially tended to disregard and even argue with the narrator over the more fantastic and sometimes dubious-sounding details in some of the stories I was told. But over time, I learned to hold my peace and listen. The trick was to filter the information you were getting through the circumstances of the speaker's cultural and even personal background.

For instance, Tibetans invariably talk of fighting a "war" (*mak*) when they might mean a battle, a firefight or even a minor skirmish. Afghans also tend to do this with the generic Pashto term *jang*, probably to the confusion of journalists and the frustration of American military advisors. Also, sometimes, numbers are not used in a statistical sense but more as a literary device, as occurs in medieval European literature. Then, too, in accordance with the nature of memory, the impression of time and space gets telescoped as events become distant over the years.

But two areas of people's recollection of their homeland were unfailingly, even literally, accurate. One was in their feeling for the exquisiteness of the Tibetan landscape, for the infinite, deep blue sky, and the rippling waves of red, blue and yellow wildflowers covering the boundless mountainsides. An old woman from Kandzé told me that as a child, she would take off her *zomba* boots and run down the hillside and have a rainbow of flowers sticking out between her toes when she got to the bottom.

Such landscapes, and the images of Tibet's unique wildlife, one being vast herds of the elegant Kiang (*Equus kiang*) the Tibetan wild ass, trotting gracefully across the Great Northern Highlands (Jhangtang) have by now been reproduced so often in the pages of so many coffee-table books, as to effectively and indisputably validate the substance and accuracy of Tibetan remembrances. Such nostalgia also served to point out the condescension of certain Western travellers to the Himalayas and Tibet, writing that only outsiders like them could appreciate the beauty of the landscape, as the local people regarded their surroundings, especially the mountains, either from a superstitious, supernatural point of view or as an extra hardship in their already burdened lives.

People's accounts of their suffering under the Chinese were, in retrospect, also largely reliable. When I started my inquiries, I had been infected with the prevalent left-intellectual viewpoint that ". . . refugees' stories were always exaggerated" (especially those emanating from Communist or Communist occupied countries), which Hugh Richardson, the doyen of Tibetan Studies, reproachfully observed was ". . . a commonplace of the professionally detached observer."[5]

But when one heard, over and over, strikingly similar testimonies of "struggles", torture, executions, massacres, famine and destruction, from people of diverse origins and backgrounds, there was no way, in all intellectual integrity, one could go on cultivating such an Olympian attitude. I gradually discovered that, far from being exaggerated, most of these stories were often circumscribed by the limits of the narrator's own world and by their limited sphere of experience.

I heard stories so bizarre that I found them hard to believe. At the time, they were flatly rejected by the Western press and human rights organizations. Yet, forced blood donations, ritual cannibalism, forced abortions and sterilizations, state psychiatric persecution of political prisoners and the harvesting of transplant organs of executed prisoners, for example, which I first heard in the mid-seventies, are now all too familiar and proven crimes of the Chinese regime. The last two practices continue at this time of writing.

The recording of such reminiscences has an additional significance beyond the unquestionably valuable task of human-rights documentation. The Chinese leadership has become skilled at blurring, even erasing, disagreeable memories in China's national consciousness. One near expunged memory is the relatively recent pro-democracy uprising and massacre at Tiananmen Square in 1989, and within that greater event the celebrated image of the lone man who stood in the way of a column of advancing T59 tanks. In a 2006 Frontline documentary, a retrospective on the events of 1989, the film-maker Anthony Thomas surreptitiously shows the iconic photograph of the Tank Man to undergraduates at Beijing University, the nerve centre of the 1989 protests. None of the students recognize the man. The students appear genuinely baffled. Thomas concludes ". . . only one (student) sensed that the photo had something to do with the events of 1989, but the Tank Man meant nothing to him."[6]

"The struggle of man against power," Milan Kundera has noted, "is the struggle of memory against forgetting."

Tibetans have not forgotten. Still, I suppose one must concede that no matter how innately truthful the average person is, or how sound his memory, the process of remembering itself is not unfailing. Individual memories must always be, to some extent, suspect. Ancient societies may have learned to fix communal memories through poetry, mnemonics and ritual, but there probably was always some manipulation of narrative and history to the advantage of those in power. Still, it was certainly nowhere as efficient, all-pervasive and sophisticated as what we have in present-day China.

Remembering is a dynamic process, and there is no storehouse of inviolate memories we can delve into to retrieve pristine recollections. Every time we remember, we are, in a sense, recreating a new version of an event, modified, influenced or distorted by whatever we may have experienced up to that moment. This "Rashomon" factor of human recollection may not usually present itself dramatically as in Kurowsawa's classic film of 1950, but it serves to remind us of the inescapable relativism of human recall.

Yet, in his next film Kurosawa developed this somewhat anodyne observation on the unknowability of remembered truth into a more dynamic philosophy on memory as encomium. This celebration of affirmative remembering comes through in *Ikiru* (1952), where a petty municipal clerk, Watanabe (played by the great Takashi Shimura), dying of stomach cancer, realizes he has lived a life devoid of meaning. After a wrong turn or two, he dedicates his remaining days to an epic struggle with the hidebound municipal bureaucracy of Tokyo to create a children's playground out of a mosquito-infested cesspool in his neighbourhood. At his funeral wake, his fellow office workers in their sake-sodden reminiscences gradually come around to the realization that Watanabe, through his selfless action, had found a way to vindicate his death and, more crucially, his life. He had found out what it meant "to live"—*ikiru*.

But it is in his subsequent film, *The Seven Samurai* (1954), his own favourite work, where Kurosawa throws himself into an enthusiastic and lyrical, a full-bore celebration of men who, when called upon, are able to commit themselves to a relatively selfless and heroic course of action. The seminal *New York Times* film critic, Pauline Kael, called *The Seven Samurai* ". . . incomparable as a modern poem of force." It is set in a period of Japanese history (the strife-torn sixteenth century) where life is dominated by brutal, internecine and meaningless conflict; where the population, especially the farmers, are starving and where even the samurai generally go hungry and are quite prepared to sell their service for a bowl of rice. Only the bandits appear to be eating well. The hero of the film, the *ronin*, Kambei (also played by Takashi Shimura), puts together a band of masterless samurai, essentially mercenaries, and accepts a contract to protect a farming village against a bandit army, all on the payment of a daily meal of rice. That's all there is. That is essentially the story.

Kurosawa takes this: the mud, the rain, the blood, the cruelty, the violence, the inhumanity and the sordidness, right down to the fact of the farmers being distrustful, ungrateful and cowardly, and transforms the story into an epic that cinema will probably never be able to sufficiently equal. Donald Richie, the major Western authority on Japanese cinema, certainly thought so. "*Seven Samurai* is an epic all right—it is an epic of the human spirit because very few films indeed have dared to go this far, to show this much, . . . to dare suggest personal bravery, gratuitous action, and choice in the very face of the chaos that threatens to overwhelm."

During the early months of World War II, two profound but despairing thinkers, Frenchwomen of Jewish ethnicity, each wrote, apparently unaware of the coincidence, an essay on another and more ancient "poem of force", the Iliad.[7] These are not academic reflections on a masterwork of antiquity. Simone Weil and Rachel Bespaloff, in turning to the greatest war epic in Western literature for insight into the chaos and despair of late 1939 and the early 1940s were able— each in her own way—to discover a greater meaning than the merely intellectual, within the devastating changes that the war was effecting on themselves and their time.

Weil's essay "The Iliad or the Poem of Force" has long been regarded as the supreme anti-war manifesto, and an English translation released as a pamphlet (1957) by Quaker Publishing House in Pennsylvania, even found a place, for a while, in the reading room of the Library of Tibetan Works and Archives in Dharamshala, where I first came across it. The Dalai Lama's Secretariat had also received a copy.

Weil examines the centrality of force in human affairs and meditates on its implacable double-edged nature. Using the violent deaths portrayed by Homer, she argues that force dehumanizes those who wield it as much as those who are victims of it. Yet, Weil is not your typical anti-war pamphleteer. She sees that the Iliad, as a poem ". . . is a miracle. Its bitterness is the only justifiable bitterness, for it springs from the subjection of the human spirit to force, that is, in the last analysis, to matter. This subjection is the common lot, although each spirit will bear it differently, in proportion to its own virtue. No one in the Iliad is spared by it, as no one on earth is."

But the bleakness of her particular pacifist world view was at odds with her genuine desire to share the suffering of those fighting fascism in Spain and resisting Nazism in occupied France. It was probably what made her rethink her philosophy. In fact, the day after Hitler entered Prague in May 1939, Weil decided ". . . after a very painful inner struggle, that in spite of my pacifist inclinations it had become an overriding obligation in my eyes to work for Hitler's destruction . . . my resolve has not altered."

Bespaloff composed her own distinctive discussion of the Iliad in the midst of World War II, calling it "her method of facing the war." Her account of the Iliad brings out Homer's novelistic approach to character and the existential drama of his character's choices; it is marked, too, by a tragic awareness of how the Iliad speaks to times and places where there is no hope apart from war. For Bespaloff, the Iliad is not so much the "poem of force" as "the saga of resistance", and the noble Hector is her "resistance-hero". He is a hero because he is the defender of non-combatants, but even more, because he is "the guardian of life's perishable joys". Bespaloff rounds off her analysis with this reflection, ". . . for Homer's warrior, glory is not some vain illusion or empty boast; it is the same thing that Christians saw in the Redemption, a promise of immortality outside and beyond history, in the supreme detachment of poetry."

Perhaps that is why the old man seated in the parlour of the Amnye Machen Institute (Tibetan Center for Advanced Studies) in Dharamshala, had, in spite of scholarly advice to the contrary, insisted on writing his life story in the style of the Gesar epic. His dark, bony head stuck out of a shirt collar, a few sizes too large for him, and a cast-off, double-breasted jacket (also voluminous) draped his thin, emaciated body. His lungs were riddled with the inevitable tuberculosis of twenty years in Chinese prison and slave-labour camps. But as a young man, he had led a violent uprising against a vastly superior Chinese military force in the district of Drayab in Eastern Tibet from 1958 to 1961.

First, the resistance army he had helped create was destroyed, then his last guerrilla band was wiped out and finally he himself was captured and imprisoned for twenty years. He handed my colleague, the great scholar, Tashi Tsering, the first draft of his autobiography, written in elegant cursive, in six cheap exercise books, the kind used by schoolchildren in India. There was a sense of dignity, something of the solemnity of a rite in the way he handed over the manuscript, which appeared to me to convey an unwritten codicil: that this was not a refugee report nor the testimony of a victim, but rather the saga of a man, a hero.[8]

It must be acknowledged that in recent years, the culture of victimhood has gained a hold in exile Tibetan society, especially within the leadership, but most of the Tibetans whose lives I recorded over the years did not see themselves as victims. No matter how outnumbered or powerless, they had done something about their fate. They had not accommodated themselves to their oppressor. They had not allowed themselves to be led tamely like sheep to the labour camps or the execution grounds. They had fought, often to the last bullet and even after that, had kept up their opposition to Chinese rule in whatever way they could, even if that defiance might sometimes appear irrational or ineffectual to the progressive or the realist.

Still, you could not put these people on a pedestal without a wobble here and there. They were all too human in their shortcomings, idiosyncrasies and, in at least a couple of them—good friends of mine—self-destructive behaviour. But where it ultimately counted, when it was all that mattered at that moment, they had chosen, as the noble Hector, to be "the guardians of life's perishable joys." They were heroes, flawed heroes perhaps—a little too much of the rage and impetuosity of Achilles and not enough of the calculation, the *mētis* or "cunning wisdom" of Odysseus—but their stories, however told: in dull official reports, in self-deprecatory tales, in boastful but amusing ramblings over a drink, were all undeniably sagas. Narrative psychology, a recondite branch of the cognitive sciences, has recognized that the human brain has a natural affinity for narrative construction. It appears that seeing oneself acting in a play or a story is not merely fantasy or indulgence; it is fundamental to how people work out who they are and may become.

The need to leave behind more permanent testaments has in the last couple of decades resulted in a flowering of memoirist writing in the Tibetan language, which in turn has received considerable academic attention within the world of Tibetan Studies.[9] Biographical (*namthar*) and autobiographical (*rang-nam*) writings are respected genres in traditional Tibetan literature, though largely confined to the lives of religious and, once in a while, political figures. But some experts have noticed a more "Western style of 'testimony'" in the new writings by Tibetans in exile. A Belgian scholar, Dr Isabelle Henrion-Dourcy, in her research, has ". . . so far listed nearly a hundred such book-length autobiographies (not including biographies) about a fourth of which are written in English."[10] Two recent publications might be singled out for the exhaustive lengths to which the authors have laboured to tell their stories. There is the four-volume autobiography of the resistance commander Ratuk Ngawang[11] of Lithang, and Lhamo Tsering's eight-volume memoir/history.[12]

For most of these people, their memories are all they have of lives once lived, of homes destroyed and loved ones left behind. They are appreciative of people like me recording their accounts on tape or committing them to paper. Yet, it sometimes seemed to me that for some of them, merely possessing their memories gave them a sense of sufficiency and resurrecting them provided not just nostalgia or longing but compelling *joie de vivre* that sustained them through the drudgery and depression of refugee existence; a kind of existence that, admittedly, often reduced the rest of us to depression and cynicism. Proust observed that with age and sensitivity memory sometimes unfolded in its true richness—a richness often unperceived at the time of the actual event—a phenomenon that he called involuntary memory, a kind of epiphanic or "invading happiness".

Perhaps I am flying somewhat high here. It might be acknowledged that no matter how meaningful or rewarding, even the truest of memories must ultimately unravel and fade with age, infirmity and death. For as Buddhists, Tibetans (whether victims or heroes) are, strictly speaking, not supposed to have immortal souls—with accompanying memory banks—that can be taken with them to the next world. When the brain cells die and the neural connections blink out—then, that's that.*

Yet somehow—notwithstanding the certainty that memories will fade—the choices made, the actions taken, their effects and ramifications: the waves generated by Basho's frog jumping into that ancient pond, and all the secondary, tertiary and myriad overlapping ripples, expanding ever outwards, are never quite lost. The Buddha himself explained it in his most fundamental formulation "universal conditionality of existence" (Sanskrit, *pratitya-samutpadha*), which might loosely be called the Buddhist "Theory of Everything".[13] What remains, in the end, is not memory, identity or even self, but the results of actions and choices, of which even the most infinitesimal and incidental, contribute to creating subsequent phenomena, and the conditions for our next round of existence.

---

*On the night of his enlightenment, Buddha is said to have recalled his previous lives, over many aeons, which raises the question of whether there is another consciousness, perhaps a primordial one, where memory survives.

TIBET

EASTERN TURKESTAN

Khotan ○

JHANGTANG

Ruthok ●

LADAKH

Gegyé ●   Gertsé ●

Tsaparang
(Guge)   NGARI

Thöling ●

△ Mt. Kailash

Damshung ●

Purang ●   Drongpa ●   TSANG   LHASA

Saga ●   TÖ   Shigatsé ●   Nyemo ●   Ü ◎

Lhatsé ●

Lo Monthang   Kyirong ●   ● Sakya   LHOKA

(MUSTANG)   Gampa ●   Driguthang

Pokhara ○   Mt. Everest △

NEPAL   Dromo

○   Gangtok ●(Yatung)

KATHMANDU   ○

Lucknow ○   Darjeeling   B H U T A N

Patna ○

Benares

TIBET IN ASIA

DARJEELING, KALIMPONG AND SIKKIM

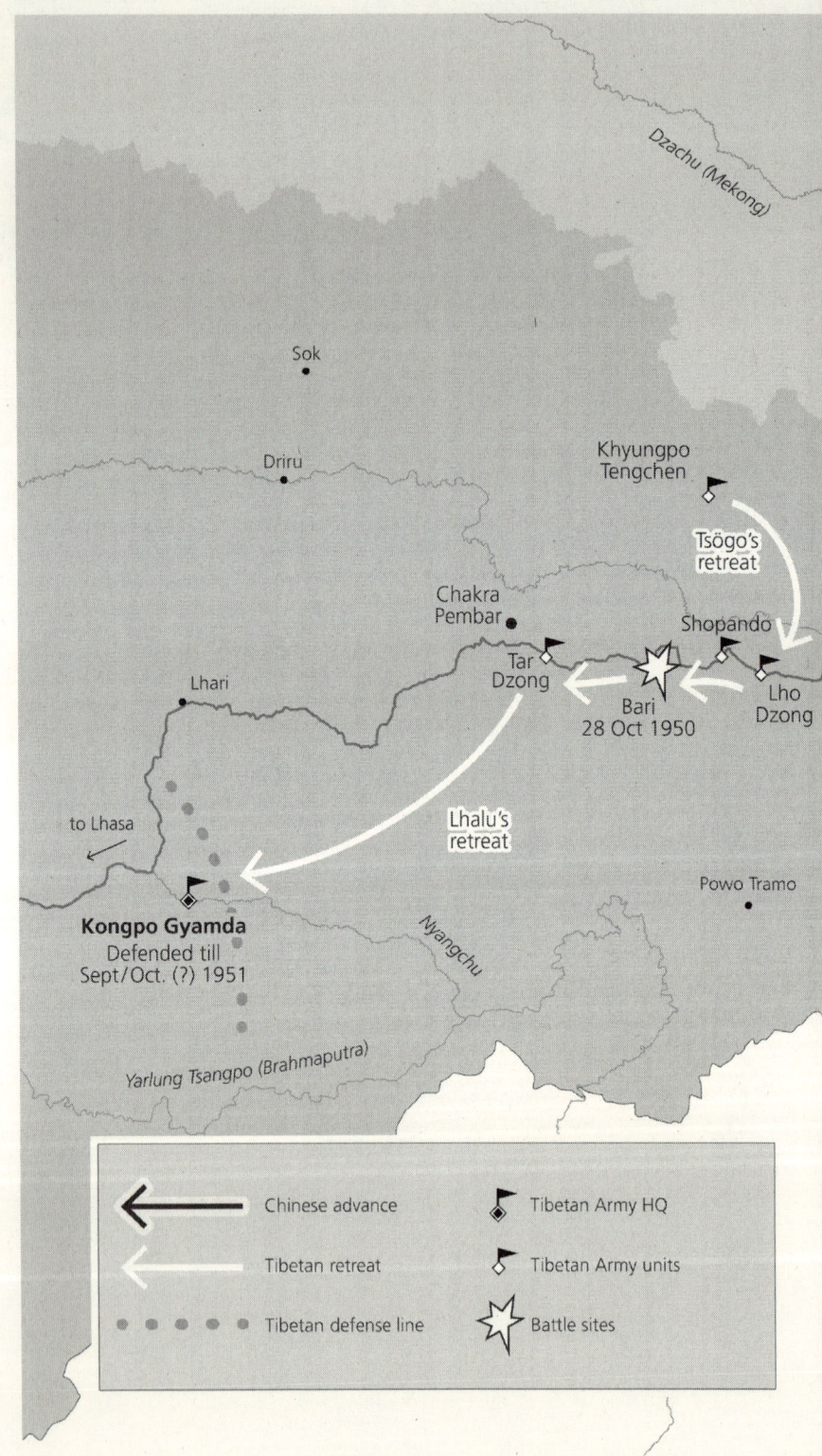

Dzachu (Mekong)

Sok

Driru

Khyungpo
Tengchen

Tsögo's
retreat

Chakra
Pembar

Shopando

Tar
Dzong

Lhari

Bari
28 Oct 1950

Lho
Dzong

to Lhasa

Lhalu's
retreat

Powo Tramo

Kongpo Gyamda
Defended till
Sept/Oct. (?) 1951

Nyangchu

Yarlung Tsangpo (Brahmaputra)

Chinese advance
Tibetan retreat
Tibetan defense line

Tibetan Army HQ
Tibetan Army units
Battle sites

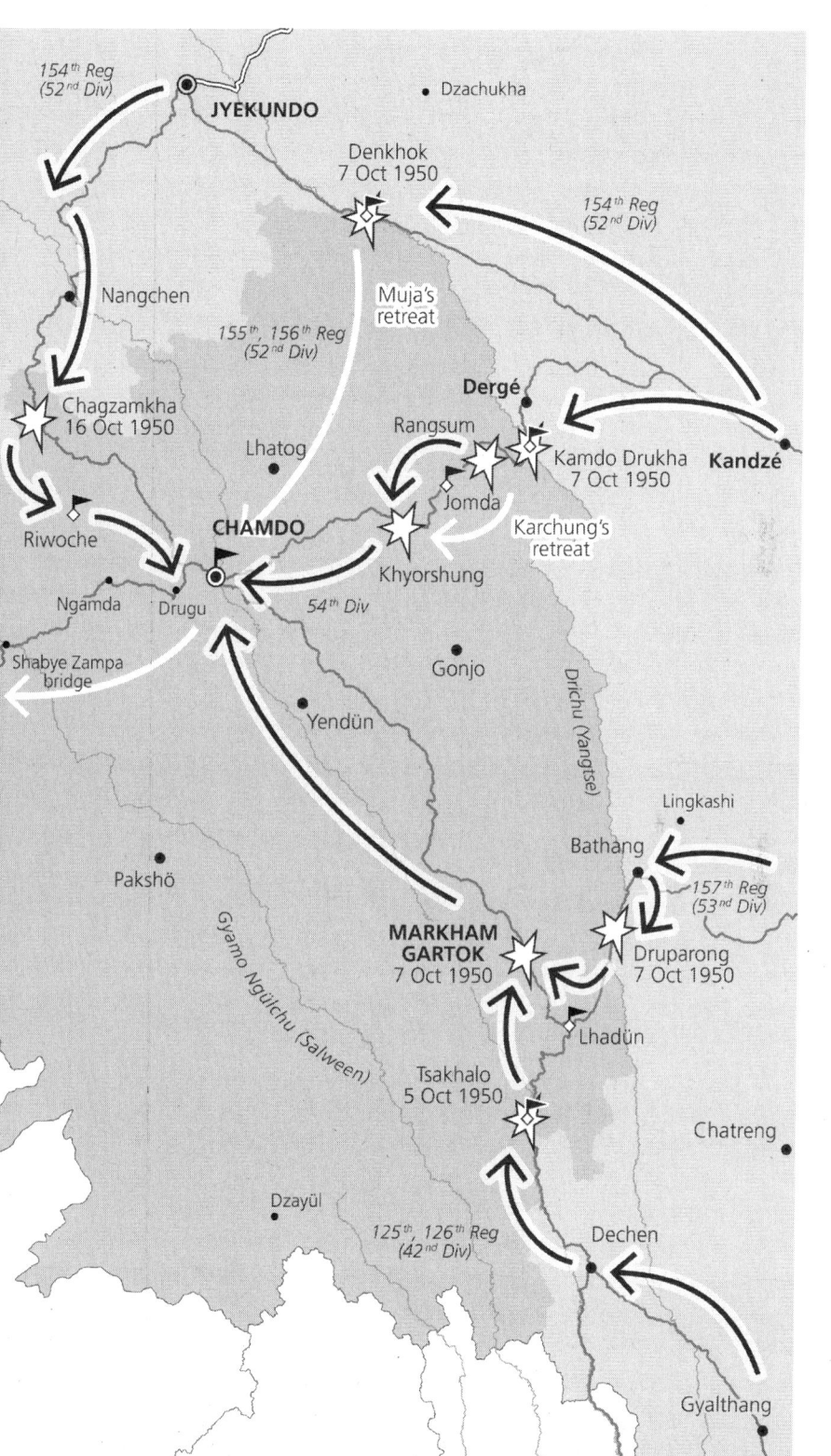

154th Reg
(52nd Div)

JYEKUNDO

Dzachukha

Denkhok
7 Oct 1950

154th Reg
(52nd Div)

Nangchen

Muja's
retreat

155th, 156th Reg
(52nd Div)

Dergé

Chagzamkha
16 Oct 1950

Lhatog

Rangsum

Kamdo Drukha
7 Oct 1950

Kandzé

Riwoche

CHAMDO

Jomda

Khyorshung

Karchung's
retreat

Ngamda

Drugu

54th Div

Shabye Zampa
bridge

Gonjo

Yendün

Drichu (Yangtse)

Lingkashi

Bathang

Pakshö

157th Reg
(53nd Div)

MARKHAM
GARTOK
7 Oct 1950

Druparong
7 Oct 1950

Gyamo Ngülchu (Salween)

Lhadün

Tsakhalo
5 Oct 1950

Chatreng

Dzayül

125th, 126th Reg
(42nd Div)

Dechen

Gyalthang

LHASA CITY AND ENVIRONS (1958–59)

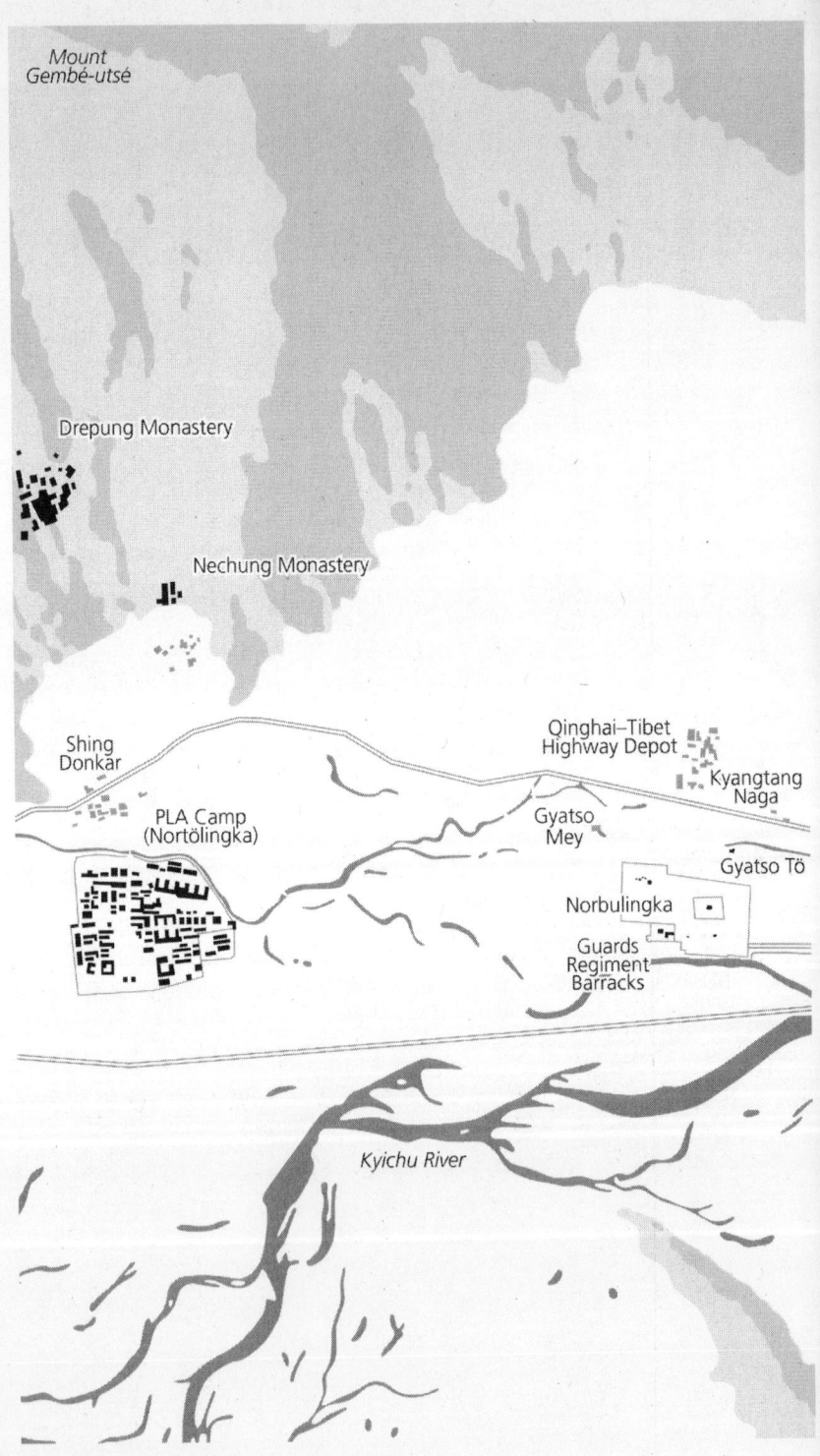

Mount
Gembé-utsé

Drepung Monastery

Nechung Monastery

Shing
Donkar

Qinghai–Tibet
Highway Depot

Kyangtang
Naga

PLA Camp
(Nortölingka)

Gyatso
Mey

Gyatso Tö

Norbulingka

Guards
Regiment
Barracks

Kyichu River

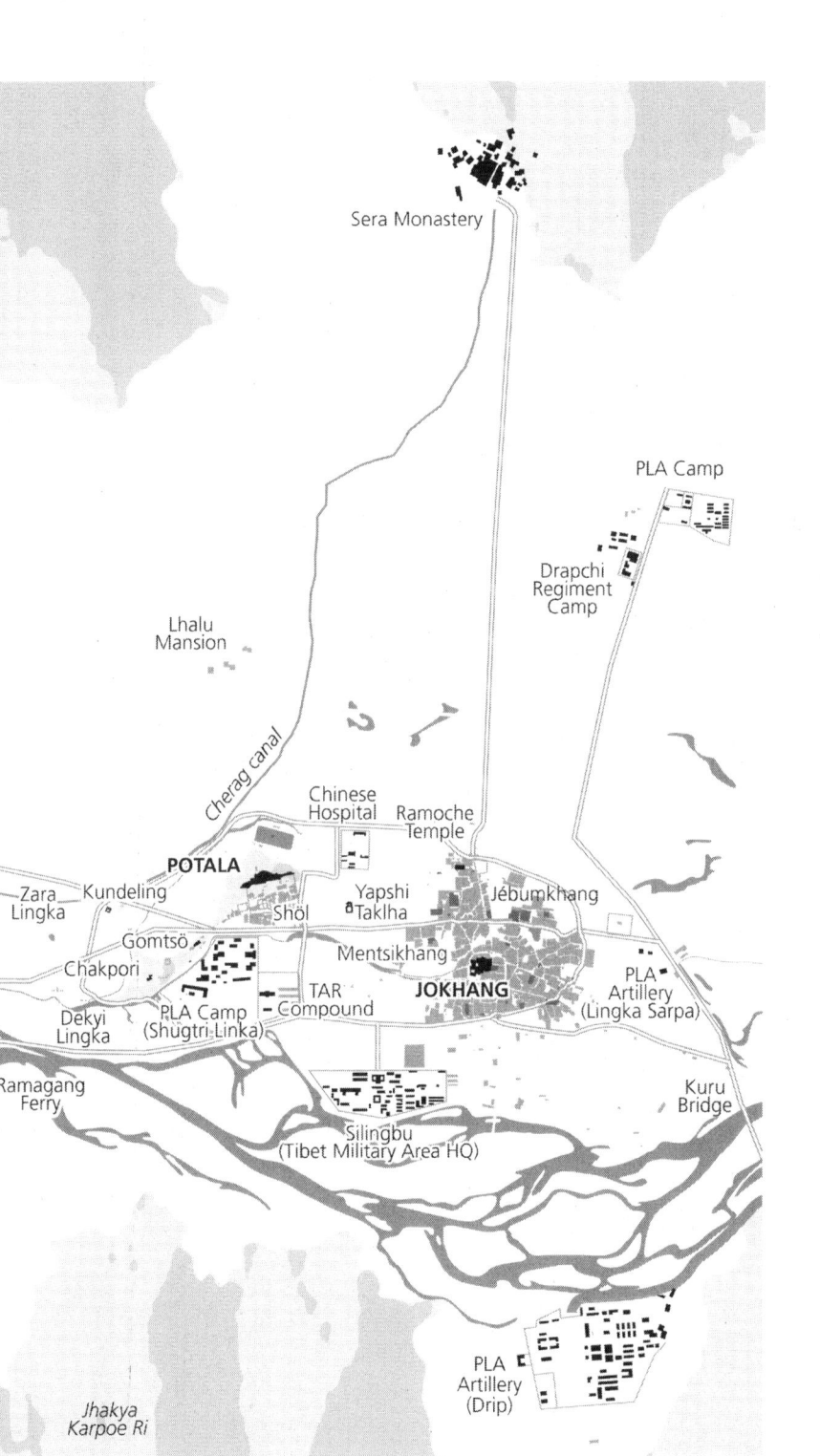

Sera Monastery

PLA Camp

Drapchi
Regiment
Camp

Lhalu
Mansion

Cherag canal

Chinese
Hospital   Ramoche
Temple

POTALA

Zara   Kundeling   Yapshi   Jébumkhang
Lingka   Shöl   Taklha

Gomtsö
Chakpori   Mentsikhang   PLA
                                                       Artillery
                        TAR   (Lingka Sarpa)
Dekyi   PLA Camp   Compound   **JOKHANG**
Lingka   (Shugtri Linka)

Ramagang   Kuru
Ferry   Bridge

                        Silingbu
                        (Tibet Military Area HQ)

                                          PLA
                                          Artillery
Jhakya   (Drip)
Karpoe Ri

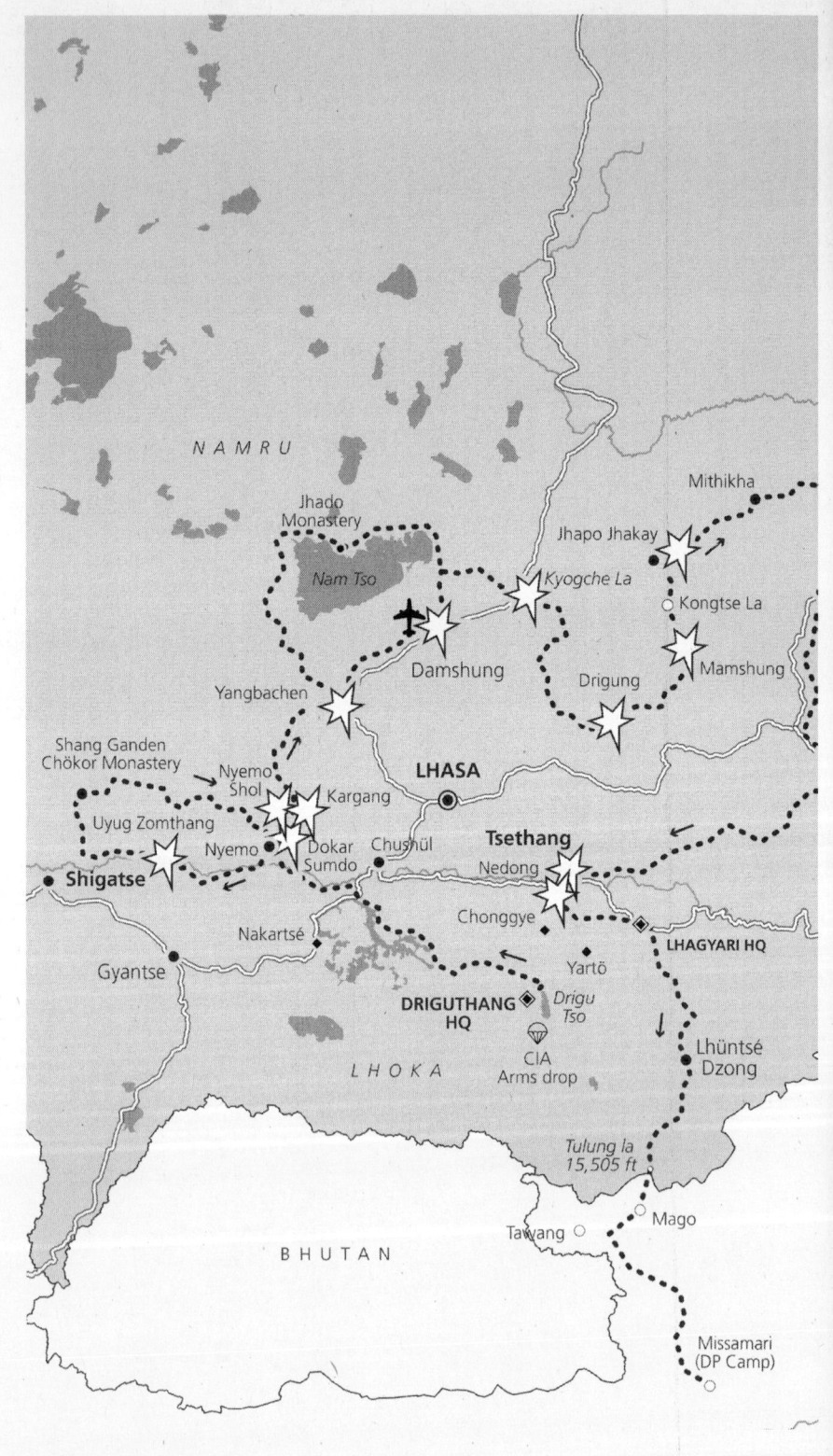

NAMRU

Jhado
Monastery

Nam Tso

Mithikha

Jhapo Jhakay

Kyogche La

Kongtse La

Damshung

Drigung

Mamshung

Yangbachen

Shang Ganden
Chökor Monastery

Nyemo
Shol

Kargang

LHASA

Uyug Zomthang

Nyemo

Dokar
Sumdo

Chushül

Tsethang

Nedong

Shigatse

Chonggye

LHAGYARI HQ

Nakartsé

Yartö

Gyantse

**DRIGUTHANG
HQ**

*Drigu
Tso*

Lhüntsé
Dzong

LHOKA

CIA
Arms drop

*Tulung la
15,505 ft*

Mago

Tawang

BHUTAN

Missamari
(DP Camp)

EASTERN TIBET (AMDO AND KHAM)

Dunhuang

Suzhou

Ganzhou

Liangzhou

Kangtsa   Semnyi   Pari

Ulan   **XINING**   Tsongkha

Gormo   Kumbum   Kamalok

Dulan   Chabcha   Thriga   Chentsa   **LANZHOU**

Mangra   Nangra

Gepa Sumdo   Rebkong   Linxia

Matö   *Amnye*   Labrang   Chone
         Machen   Tashikyil

Chumarleb   Machen   Luchu

Dritö   *GOLOK*   Gade   Machu

Niratsogen   Dzoge   Drukchu
Lake   Darlak

Dzatö   **Jyekundo**   Pema   Ngaba

Dzachukha   Sungchu

Denkhok   Sertha   Dzamthang

Nangchen   *KHAM*   Lingtsang   *GYALRONG*

Derge   Rongpatsa   Kandze   Choktse

Tengchen   Lhatho   Jomda   Drango   Tashiling

Riwoche   Pelyül   Nyarong   Tawu   Tsenha

Gonjo   Lingkashi   Rongdrak

Chakra   **CHAMDO**   **CHENGDU**
Pembar   Lho Dzong   Drakyab

Pakshö   Bathang   Lithang   **Dartsedo**

Pome   **Markham**   Druparong   *Minyak* △   Ya'an
         Gartok   *Gangkar*

Tsakhalho   Chatreng   Gyezil   Mianning

Dzayül   Dechen

Jöl   Mili

Gyalthang

Lijiang

Dali

CENTRAL LHASA (MARCH 1959)

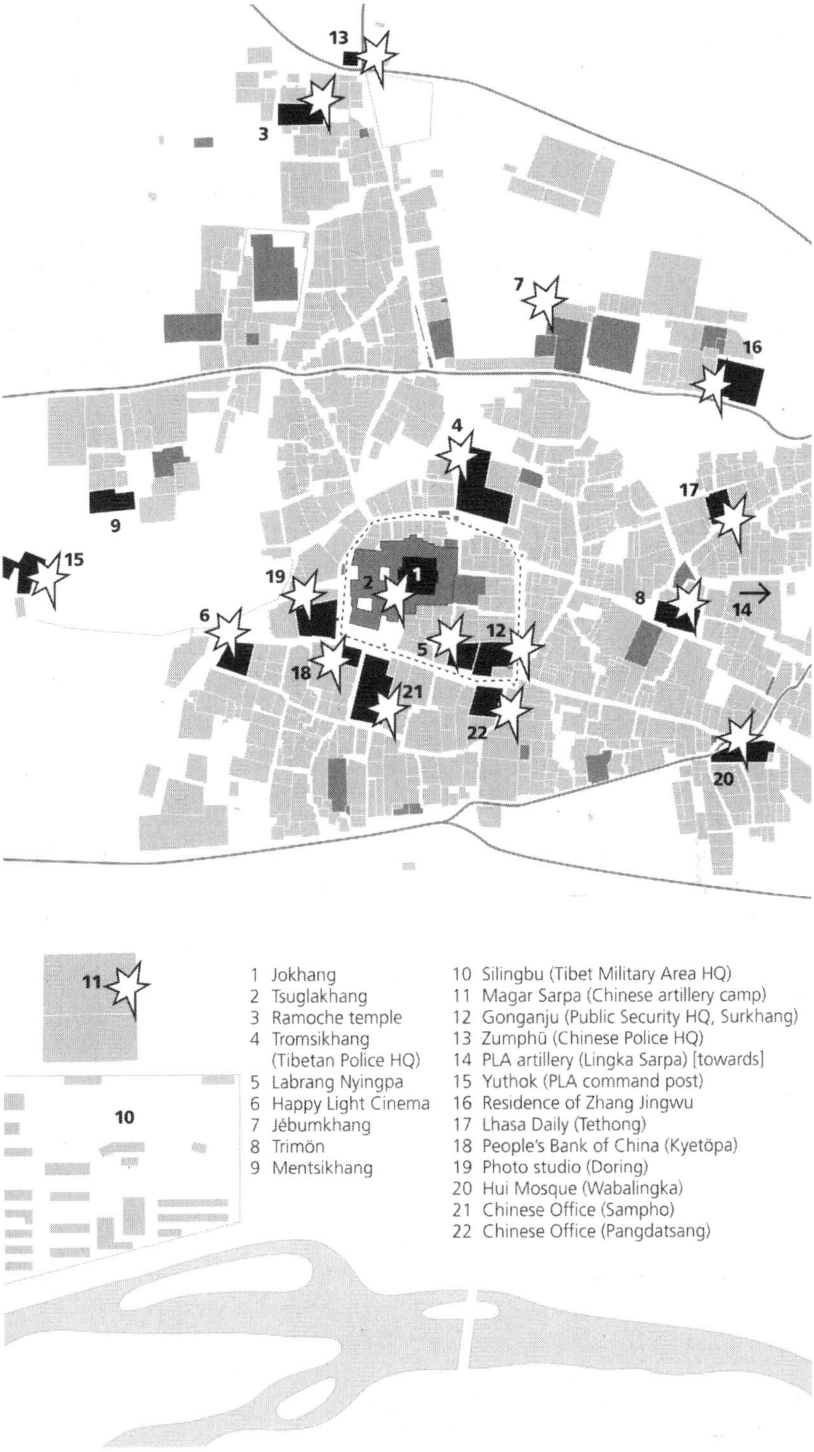

1 Jokhang
2 Tsuglakhang
3 Ramoche temple
4 Tromsikhang (Tibetan Police HQ)
5 Labrang Nyingpa
6 Happy Light Cinema
7 Jébumkhang
8 Trimön
9 Mentsikhang
10 Silingbu (Tibet Military Area HQ)
11 Magar Sarpa (Chinese artillery camp)
12 Gonganju (Public Security HQ, Surkhang)
13 Zumphü (Chinese Police HQ)
14 PLA artillery (Lingka Sarpa) [towards]
15 Yuthok (PLA command post)
16 Residence of Zhang Jingwu
17 Lhasa Daily (Tethong)
18 People's Bank of China (Kyetöpa)
19 Photo studio (Doring)
20 Hui Mosque (Wabalingka)
21 Chinese Office (Sampho)
22 Chinese Office (Pangdatsang)

MUSTANG GUERRILLA BASES

1

ORIGIN CHRONICLE: MATRILINEAL

There are mules and horses in the garden. I try and reach out to the animals, taking a few awkward steps towards them, but I am gently held back by firm hands. This is the earliest childhood memory I can safely claim to have, probably from when I was going on two and starting to walk. I would vaguely recall this sometimes in later years, but as with such things, I never really got around to figuring out the actual context of the event.

Some years ago, when talking to my mother about our life in Kalimpong, I mentioned this fuzzy but persistent memory. It took her just a minute to remember the incident. She had twenty-twenty-plus recall. She could remember the colour pattern (*tra*) on the apron of a certain lady at a Lhasa garden party from seventy years ago.

A senior retainer of the Tethong family, Thundup "*genba*" or "elder" Thundup (there was a younger Thundup in the family as well) had arrived in Kalimpong from Lhasa, after having concluded an important trading venture for the family. He was eager to report his success to my uncle Sonam Tomjor, the head of the Tethong household. However, instead of first settling his pack animals at the caravanserai by the 10th Mile* in Kalimpong, as he should have, Thundup had straightaway headed, with all his men and mules, to our house, a rambling British bungalow, "Fair Haven," at the Durpin Development Area. Thundup had a reputation for impetuosity, having once single-handedly confronted and shot two bandits at Penak, near the Pazel estate in Tsang province.

Mules in the garden of our bungalow were unusual, but mule-trains, invariably accompanied by rough-hewn Tibetan muleteers, were a common sight in Kalimpong and Darjeeling, the two adjacent towns of my childhood. These days, concrete high-rises, bumper-to-bumper Suzuki vans, and shoulder-to-shoulder crowds of tourists jam the narrow streets of those towns, leaving little space for even memories of the past. The only mules that can be seen in Darjeeling now are those in Satyajit Ray's lyrical film, *Kanchenjunga* (1962) where, incidental to the main story of a holidaying Bengali family, we get a glimpse of a mule-train hurrying along the Tungsung road, below the Belleview Hotel. The English film critic, Marie Seton (visiting the shooting site) tells us that Ray, in a fit of inspired spontaneity, recruited a passing column of "laughing" Tibetan muleteers and their animals, who, for the sum of twenty rupees ". . . became integrated as a background movement with the distinctive bell tones serving to italicize (the female lead) Monisha's emotions."[1]

They were tough working beasts, but I saw them as comely. They would be all prettied out with tassels of scarlet dyed yak-hair and bells of two kinds: small brass jingles (*lingshang*) and larger iron bells (*dom-dom*) that bonged like Swiss cowbells. Their foreheads were adorned with a diamond-shaped piece of brightly coloured rug material with a small mirror in the centre. Besides a crupper to prevent the wooden packsaddles from slipping forward on steep descents, a looser wood

---

*It was the practice in Kalimpong to name certain parts of the town by their distances (indicated in milestones) from the Teesta Bridge and along the principal road that led (eventually) to Tibet. The actual town of Kalimpong is reached at the "9th Mile" while the centre of the town, with its major stores and a bust of Queen Victoria, is at the 9½-milestone. The Tibetan enclave with its *tongba* (millet ale) houses and caravanserais was at the "10th Mile."

and leather restraint resting just below the beast's rump provided further insurance against vertiginous Himalayan slopes. A leather, or webbing, strap across the animal's chest prevented the saddle from slipping towards the back. Many of these beasts would have upset stomachs from the unfamiliar lush grazing of the lowlands. Bits of dry muck would be stuck to their flanks and cruppers, which I remember observing as a child, with mild horror.

Caravans to Tibet started at the Himalayan frontier town of Kalimpong. Manufactured goods, war surpluses and much else were hauled to Tibet from this crossroad town, while wool, Tibet's main export, came on muleback to Kalimpong's warehouses, was cleaned, re-baled, transported to Calcutta harbour and finally shipped abroad.* A major boost was given to this trade during World War II. With Australia cut off by Japanese submarines, demand for Tibetan wool in the U.S. created considerable prosperity, not only for the Tibetan merchants and Indian (Marwari) and Nepali (Newari) agencies involved, but also for the nomad suppliers and farmers leasing pack animals and selling fodder.

According to a report from the U.S. Consulate in Calcutta,[2] Tibet's wool export to America (in 1950) came to 1.7 million dollars, and to Britain, Italy and Japan around 116,000 dollars—roughly 25 million in today's dollars. Big money at the time. "The U.S. auto-industry discovered that the tough Tibetan wool made excellent automobile carpets, and it wasn't long before that industry provided the major part of Tibet's hard currency."[3]

The War also provided a crucial financial impetus to the opening up of Tibet to Western commercial products. Tibetan merchants bought consumer goods in Calcutta and Kalimpong and sold them,

---

*A Tibetan romance/adventure novel, *The Secret Tale of Tesur House* (1994), is set against the background of the forties' wool-trade. The Lhasa writer W. Tailing provides a wealth of information on the lives of muleteers, innkeepers and merchants, and also offers vivid descriptions of the various inns, taverns and postal stations from Lhasa to Kalimpong, including hand-drawn maps of the routes. The novel became popular in Tibet and won the *Lungta* literary award.

at considerable profit in south-west China where the Nationalist government, from its wartime capital Chunking, was holding out against the Japanese.* Everyone along the trade route: officials, herdsmen, farmers, muleteers and innkeepers profited from this trade. According to a White-Russian émigré, Peter Goullart, then living in Lijiang in northern Yunnan province, a main terminus on the trade route ". . . this caravan traffic was a unique and spectacular phenomenon." Consumer products of every description, even luxury items as Gordon's gin, Scotch, French brandies, liqueurs (*crème de menthe* being the choice of Lhasa ladies), Parker pens and Swiss watches (the three Tibetan favourites being Rolex, Omega and "Roamer of Switzerland") were efficiently transported from Kalimpong to Lhasa and Lijiang, thanks to the skill and resourcefulness of Tibetan packers and muleteers. Goullart dubbed this enterprise "Operation Caravan" and claimed that it would ". . . always live on in my mind as one of the great adventures of mankind."[4]

According to the Newari proprietor of a watch agency in Kalimpong (and vice-president of the Nepalese Chamber of Commerce in Lhasa), a representative of the Rolex Company came to Kalimpong in the forties to investigate the unexpected demand for his watches in this corner of the world '. . . and was astonished to discover that it was but a little village town'.[5] Tibetan farmers, nomads and artisans favoured the cheaper but dependable West End watch of Switzerland. Even in the 1980s and 1990s, this Swiss company regularly advertised its product in the exile journal, *Tibetan Review*.

This tremendous trans-Himalayan trade was conducted essentially on the back of small, sturdy Tibetan mules. The full load that a beast carried was called the *gyap*, which consisted of two side-loads about ninety pounds each—each called a *dhobo*. A dhobo was usually a bale of wool, a large leather-bound box of tea and, in later years, even jerry

---

*A British Pathé wartime documentary *Aid To China Via Tibet 1943* has actual footage of Tibet-bound mule convoys from Kalimpong hauling medical and other supplies for China, and also mule trains from Tibet bringing wool to India for the "war industries".

cans of petrol, all skilfully balanced and lashed securely to a wooden packsaddle on the mule's back.

The muleteers were hardy men with lined weather-beaten faces, clad in Tibetan boots and homespun *chuba* robes belted at the waist. Their long unkempt plaits were sometimes tied around their grimy felt hats or fur caps to tether them against the fierce winds of the Tibetan highlands. They all sported long daggers, some with ornamental silver hafts and scabbards. These were worn low at the back and swung provocatively to and fro as the men swaggered through the town. Some carried swords hitched across their waists. The caravan leader or outriders might carry a rifle or pistol, but firearms being strictly regulated in India, had to be left behind on the Tibetan side of the border, probably entrusted to an innkeeper at the border town of Dromo. After their long journey across the mountains, the muleteers, the caravan leaders, and the big merchants would want to let off steam.

Consequently, there was an element of Dodge City in Kalimpong's makeup. The Novelty Bioscope Theatre* a large corrugated-tin warehouse just below the football field employed hard-faced Tibetan ushers, who wielded knives with as much proficiency as flashlights. An Austrian ethnologist in Kalimpong noted: "Wild West films are particularly popular with the Tibetan muleteers."[6]

An English Buddhist resident added, somewhat disapprovingly, that ". . . Tibetans were great cinema-goers, and few were the sturdy exiles from the Land of Snows who did not see every film that was screened at the town's one and only '*bioscope*'. Thus, it was not surprising that their favourite genre should have been the Western, in which there was a clearly defined conflict, in which plenty of blows and shots were exchanged, which ended with dead bodies lying on the ground. If they had had the patience to wait for the last act, the Tibetans would probably have enjoyed *Hamlet*."[7]

---

*In the mid-fifties, Novelty proprietor, Leela Bose & Co., relocated the cinema to a proper theatre building at 9th Mile. A second cinema hall "Kanchan" (for Kanchenjunga) was opened around the time by a Marwari-Tibetan (Kaluram–Pangdatsang and Shakabpa) consortium.

The passage to Tibetan-inhabited areas from the surrounding low-lands of India, Nepal and China is not only unmistakable and dramatic but in every way a transition to a special world. Kalimpong and Darjeeling share with other such frontier towns as Gangtok in Sikkim, Dartsedo (Kangding) in Sichuan province, and Satham (Lijiang) in Yunnan province, certain unique features that give it this "gateway to Tibet" ambience. First of all, these towns are all located in the more precipitous and temperate (sometimes semi-tropical) regions of the Himalayas. Interestingly mixed populations also inhabit these areas—the core group usually being some indigenous tribal people, invariably of Tibeto-Burman stock. For instance, Kalimpong, Gangtok and Darjeeling had a population of Sikkimese, Bhutanese, Tibetan (including Sherpa and Bhutia), Nepalese (including Newar, Tamang, Rai and Limbu), Indians (Bengalis, Marwaris, Jains, Biharis, Punjabis, Sindhis, Kashmiris, Parsees, Anglo-Indians and a few Indian Jews), some Chinese and the original tribal inhabitants, the Rong Lepchas.

Lijiang and Dartsedo on the Sino-Tibetan frontier had Tibetans, Chinese, *Gyatsa* (mixed race) and such aboriginal people as the Jang (Naxi), Lolo (Yi), Qiang, Miao, Bai, Lisu and Moso. In most of these places, you also had a European and American presence, largely missionary, but in the case of Darjeeling, tea planters and some retired British officials as well. Trade with Tibet was important for these places. For some, it was vital. These were also thriving market towns. I have a sepia photograph (by Joseph Rock) of the crowded marketplace at Lijiang in Yunnan province, and it is surprising how much it looks—people, buildings, surrounding hills and all—like the old *hart* bazaar at Kalimpong.

The town of Kalimpong lies along a ridge at a mean elevation of 4,000 feet. The market or *hart* is located in the seat of the saddle with the two sentinel points of Deolo (5,590 feet) in the east and Rinkingpong (4,500 feet) to the west. The old Lepcha name, Rinkingpong, has given way to the newer Durpin Dara, which, in Nepali, means Telescope Ridge. The latter name is not inappropriate as this is the best point to survey the scene beyond Kalimpong. From here and from Deolo one gets an unobstructed view of the three kingdoms of Nepal, Sikkim and Bhutan, and directly north the Kanchenjunga range and most of its neighbouring peaks: Kabru I & II, Pandim, Siniolchhu and Lama Wangden, or the Mighty Lama. From Kalimpong town, the view of the mountain is not as spectacular as the one from Darjeeling—which the celebrated travel writer Jan Morris has rightfully extolled. "It is enough to say that to see Kanchenjunga and its peers from Darjeeling, in the cool of the morning, is one of the noblest experiences of travel. It is a kind of vision. It has moved generations of pilgrims to mysticism, and even more to overwriting."[8]

The town of Kalimpong is approached south from the railhead at Siliguri, or west from Darjeeling, both routes converging through a sweltering gorge at the Teesta Bazaar. This crossroad settlement is clustered on either side of the Teesta River around the site where the old Anderson Bridge once spanned the river before it was swept away in the great flood of 1968. The Teesta has its source high in the Zemu and Gangtse glaciers of northern Sikkim. According to Sir Charles Bell, the name of this powerful and turbulent river means "the Cleft of the Winds." Another expert claims that the name derives from a female Lepcha deity, who married the male deity of the Rangeet River so that the two rivers could join and flow south to the sea. One of the oldest folk dances of the Lepcha people symbolize the legendary marriage of the two rivers and is recounted in courtship and wedding songs:

I am a daughter of the Lepcha people,
I have been waiting
For you to climb down
From the glaciers

You a boy like the River Rangeet
And I who am like the waters of the Teesta
That we should meet,
This was the will of the Creator

Now that we two are united,
We will hasten together

To seek the turquoises and pearls
In the deep ocean[9]

The road to Kalimpong running beside the foaming Teesta River in the steep, tree-lined gorge, climbs up the mountain face for nine miles, Burma Road fashion, in a series of sweeping hairpin bends, even coiling over itself once by way of a bridge/underpass. It is a beautiful and breathtakingly dramatic drive, even when you are taking it in a ramshackle Land Rover or an over-crowded Jeep of WWII vintage— the standard conveyances at the time. Quite a few visitors to Kalimpong have, in their accounts, described this trip, so a selective blend from some of these may best do the route justice.

A few miles up from the Teesta River, the dark jungle foliage thins out, and the lighter green of terraced maize fields takes over. After the seventh milestone, the sides of the road become crowded with scarlet and purple bougainvillea and flaming rhododendron; the reds of Kalimpong's dominant flora giving way, here and there, to pink cherry blossoms, the delicate blue flowers of the jacaranda, white velvet-petal gardenias and the small white buds of the night-blooming jasmine, known locally as Raat-Ki-Rani or 'queen of the night,' that only open in the warm evenings to release their exotic scent.

I was born in neighbouring Darjeeling but spent my early years in Kalimpong. Another childhood memory of that frontier town, from when I was around six, derives from a visit to the Charteris hospital (named after Rev. A.H. Charteris, the founder of the Church of Scotland Guilds) when my sister Rigzin Dolkar came down with pneumonia. I have this fleeting memory of a European woman in a loose flowery dress, waving a red rose and bounding across the veranda of a ward. I clearly recall the creaking of the floorboards. Years later, I discovered that this somewhat extravagant personality was Princess Nina M'dvani, a White-Russian spiritualist. She had come to Kalimpong in the company of her brother-in-law, Adrian Conan-Doyle, to commune with the shades of his late father, Sir Arthur. The medium for this unique communication was allegedly the Princess's pet parrot, so I was told by a missionary and old

Kalimpong hand George Patterson—who claimed to have witnessed the séance.*

Kalimpong was a town that attracted unusual people. It was the gateway to Tibet, after all. The fact that the gate was firmly closed to outsiders meant that for most of them, this obscure frontier town was the closest they would get to their dream destination. So, theosophists and self-styled mystics rubbed shoulders in the town's bazaar with serious Tibetologists, Buddhist scholars and missionaries representing around half a dozen denominations. The largest of these was the Scottish Universal Mission (Presbyterian) headed by Rev. J.A. Graham from Edinburgh, who everyone held in high esteem for his major philanthropic and public-spirited projects, the best known being the extensive Barnardo style "Homes" and school for Eurasian or "Anglo-Indian" orphans that he set up on a five-hundred-acre campus at Deolo Hill.

The Tibetan Christian Church of Kalimpong was unique in having a pastor and moderator with strong cultural and ethnic links to Tibet. The Reverend Gergen Dorje Tharchin hailed from the Indian border district of Kinnaur. He was also the founder, publisher, editor, and, at times, the sole writer and reporter for the Tibetan newspaper, the *Tibet Mirror*.

The remoteness of the town made it a desirable place from the point of view of the authorities to park certain flotsam and jetsam of British Imperial legacy. So, you had the descendants of some long-forgotten Afghan ruler, the Akbars,† surviving on an official cheeseparing pension

---

*I received this tidbit at the Hotel Tibet (Dharamshala) in 1987 at a dinner hosted by Iain Smith, producer of the film *Seven Years in Tibet*, to which my scholar friend Tashi Tsering and I had been invited. We were joined by George Patterson, who was Iain's Tibet expert and David Hwang, screenwriter and playwright.

†Possibly the descendants of Mohammed Akbar Khan, who had led a successful uprising against the British in the First Afghan War and massacred General Elphinstone's army on its retreat from Kabul. Akbar Khan became Emir of Afghanistan in 1842 but died a few years later. Many believe he was poisoned by his father, Dost Mohammed, who was in exile at Mussoorie but returned to Kabul to become Emir in 1845. Akbar Khan's family may have sought sanctuary in British India and eventually ended up in Kalimpong.

at their bungalow "Niharika" at Durpin. The princesses did their shopping at the *hart* on Saturdays, but always managed to look proud and regal as they made their way through the crush of hill people. An Akbar son was at my school, St Josephs, for a few years. I don't recall his first name but remember getting into a schoolyard fight with him.

Then there was Prince K.M. Latthakin, who claimed to be the nephew of Thibaw, the last king of Burma. Whatever the validity of his claim, there was no dispute that his wife really was the second princess, Ashin Hteik Su Myat Phya Lat, daughter of Thibaw and his queen the notorious Supalayat, or "soup-plate" to the British Tommy. The couple resided at the red-roofed bungalow "Panorama" on the Upper Cart Road. Prince Latthakin was a grand personality ". . . sporting a pair of fierce handlebar moustaches of truly regal dimensions"[10] and living well in the past. Like the duelist, Silvio, in Pushkin's short story, "The Pistol Shot," he was ready to take offence at the slightest hint of a presumption. Town gossip had it that merely disagreeing with him was reason enough for the "Burma Rajah" to signal his valet, who would leave the room to return with a set of foils and pistols. The choice was yours. His large collection of weapons caused an actual stir on one occasion when Indian officialdom attempted to confiscate them and the Raja barricaded himself in his bungalow and threatened to shoot any policeman who approached the bungalow.[11]

Another exile was the white-Russian orientalist George (Yuri) Roerich who, at the time, was wrapping up his translation of the monumental Tibetan history, *The Blue Annals*, by Gö Lotsawa Zhonupal (1392–1481). The pioneering Tibetan scholar and artist Gedün Chöphel had collaborated with Roerich on this project. A regular guest at George's house was his brother Svetoslav, a painter, whose wife was the charming and vivacious Indian film star, Devika Rani, "the queen of the Indian silent screen"[12] and niece of Rabindranath Tagore. She was friendly with a number of Tibetan ladies, including my mother, and I was once taken along on a visit to the Roerich's house, "Crookety" (the former residence of Major George Sheriff, head of the 1945 British Mission to Lhasa), which was only a few minutes' walk above the Tethong bungalow, "Fair Haven."

For me, the main fascination of the Roerich establishment was the mother—a very grand old Russian lady, dressed in the most elegant of fin de siècle style and attended to by a couple of Russian maids, Ludmilla and Iraeda. Helena Ivanovna Roerich was the great-grand niece of Field-Marshal Kutuzov who brought about Napoleon's debacle in Russia and was immortalized by Tolstoy in *War and Peace*. In Kalimpong, she was known to a select few as a spiritualist and a medium who had produced ". . . a whole series of books that constituted the Bible, so to speak, of a small occult group within the wider Theosophical movement."[13] She died in Kalimpong in 1955 after repeated but unsuccessful efforts to obtain a visa to return to Russia.

Her husband, Nicolas Roerich, had died in 1947 at their main residence at Naggar in Kulu, a small hill town in the Western Himalayas. An influential artist of pre-revolutionary Russia, he had designed the sets and the costumes and contributed to the libretto of Diaghilev's first production of Stravinsky's, *Le Sacre du Printemps*. He "explored" Central Asia in a quest for the fabled Buddhist world of Shambhala, and later started a cult around himself. Among his devoted followers was Henry A. Wallace, secretary for agriculture in Roosevelt's New Deal government and later vice-president from 1941 to 1945.

The ethnologist, Prince Peter of Greece and Denmark, leader of the Third Royal Danish Expedition to Central Asia, lived with his wife Princess Irene (*née* Irina Aleksandrovna Ovtchinnikova) at "Tashiding," a Himalayan Mock Tudor house on Rinkingpong road. A fellow ethnologist, the young Austrian (of Czech ethnicity) René von Nebesky-Wojkowitz, besides conducting his research on the *Oracles and Demons of Tibet*, served as the Prince and Princess's unofficial social secretary. My mother would recall that Dr Nebesky's one-party piece at Tibetan gatherings was to sing, in a high-pitched quavering voice, the popular Lhasa song *"Marepela"* or "Isn't It So?"

Other fairly long-term fixtures in Kalimpong were the Buddhist scholars Anagarika Govinda (Ernst Lothar Hoffman) of Austria and the Theravadin *bhikshu,* Sangharakshita (Dennis Philip Edward Lingwood) from Tooting, London.

Europeans were not the only "unusual" residents of Kalimpong town. A Chinese Buddhist scholar, poet and mystic Yogi C.M. Chen occupied the "Five Leguminous Tree Hermitage," a tiny bungalow at the edge of the lower bazaar. He had studied in Tibet under several Tantric gurus but had left the country before its invasion by Red China, or "Slave China" , as he called it. Another Chinese Buddhist scholar in Kalimpong who had also studied in Tibet was Garma C.C. Chang (Zhang Chenji), known in the Buddhist world for his masterful English translation of the *One Hundred Thousand Songs of Milarepa*. A rare copy of the Tibetan original (*Mila Gurbum*) had been presented to him in 1950 by Lady Yuthok, the wife of a Tibetan cabinet minister, with the request that he translate this great Tibetan spiritual and literary classic " . . . so the people of the world could read and profit from it."

There was also an interesting political fugitive from China, Dr Carsun Chang (Zhang Junmai), who had opposed Mao's Communists but also took issue with the undemocratic policies of the Guomindang. A well-known public intellectual, neo-Confucian philosopher and former chairman of the China Democratic Socialist Party, Dr Chang stayed in Kalimpong for nearly a year before moving to the United States.[*]

Kalimpong's most celebrated resident was Rabindranath Tagore, poet, playwright, artist, philosopher and the first non-European to be awarded the Nobel Prize for Literature (1913). Throughout the thirties and forties, Tagore spent his summers at "Gauripur House" on Rinkingpong Road where he wrote many of his stories and poems.[†]

---

[*] Darjeeling in the early 1900s provided safe haven to another Confucian philosopher, Kang Youwei, who in 1898 led a reform movement to modernize Manchu China, under the aegis of the young Guangxu Emperor. Unfortunately, the Empress Dowager Cixi initiated a coup that ended the "Hundred Days' Reform". The emperor was placed under house arrest, but Kang managed to flee China, eventually ending up in Darjeeling where he wrote *The Book of Great Unity* (*Datong Shu*) in which he outlined a utopian future world free of political boundaries and democratically ruled by one government.

[†]The poet's son Rutindranath built another house, Chitrabhanu, on Atisha Road. George Patterson rented an apartment there after his flight from Tibet in 1950.

Kalimpong's astonishing and easygoing diversity of races, classes, faiths and backgrounds might have consoled the great philosopher and idealist somewhat for his unsuccessful attempts before the War to persuade Japan, China and the West to set aside their narrow barriers of ideology and nationalism.

> The night has ended.
> Put out the light of the lamp
> Of thine own narrow corner
> Smudged with smoke.

> The great morning which is for all
> Appears in the East.
> Let its light reveal us to each other
> Who walk on the same path of pilgrimage.

More transient pilgrims to Kalimpong were the English climber and Buddhist "pilgrim" Marco Pallis (Thupden Tendzin), the "white lama" Theos Barnard from New York, the American geographer and ethnologist Joseph Rock, the English Buddhist writer John Blofeld, the Swedish Buddhist scholar and leading authority on Mahayana iconography, Toni Schimd, and the French Tibetologues, R.A. Stein and Arienne and Alexander McDonald. The McDonalds did an ethnological study of the Tethong family.

An occasional visitor to Fair Haven was Dr Herbert V. (Vighnāntaka) Günther, a German Buddhist philosopher and leading Western scholar on Tantric Buddhism. He had somehow survived the War and from 1943 to 1950 taught at the University of Vienna. He told my uncle Sonam Tomjor that during the Soviet occupation of Vienna, a couple of very drunk Russian soldiers had banged on his door one evening demanding Schnapps. One soldier stuck a cocked pistol at Günther's head and playfully squeezed the trigger. The soldier, fortunately, collapsed before he could complete his action. That disturbing experience and his own misgivings about serving under a rehabilitated ex-Nazi, Erich Frauwallner (whose academic chair in the philosophy department had been restored to him), encouraged Günther to leave Europe and travel to India where he taught at Lucknow University and the Sanskrit University at Varanasi. He later moved to Kalimpong to study Tibetan Buddhism.

Other survivors of the War passed through Kalimpong, searching for mental peace, a spiritual haven, or at least a *laissez-passer* to enter Tibet. Once in a while, they got lucky. The French scholar and historian, Amaury de Riencourt, received an official *lamyik* (passport) in 1947 to visit Lhasa. Just five years earlier he was a starving, ragged, lice-covered prisoner in a Fascist concentration camp in Old Castile. A fellow inmate, a "Hindu", dying of disease and starvation, had told him stories of pilgrimages to Tibet, Mount Kailash and the holy Lake Mansarovar. "After a time . . . my mind gradually slithered into a dream world in which I pictured myself riding up to Tibet on a cloud, escaping altogether from this modern inferno of wars and concentration camps, searching for this forbidden land of mystery, the only place on earth where wisdom and happiness seemed to be a reality."

Another former prisoner-of-war who made it to Tibet via Kalimpong was the Italian photographer and anthropologist, Fosco Maraini, interned in wartime Japan for refusing to pledge allegiance to Mussolini's fascist state. He travelled in 1950 to Lhasa in the company of Professor Guiseppi Tucci and produced one of the more discerning travel books to Tibet, containing some of the most evocative and romantic black-and-white photographs of the land and the people, especially the women.

The last Western visitor to old Tibet was probably Richard Keith Sprig, who made it to Gyantsé and stayed there for three weeks before beating a quick retreat to Kalimpong when the Communist invasion took place. Sprig, a classics scholar from Cambridge and a linguist, was working on his PhD (for SOAS) on Tibetan and related languages. In Kalimpong, he married Ray Williams, the granddaughter of David MacDonald, proprietor of the Himalayan Hotel and former British trade agent at Dromo and Gyantsé. Sprig became a lecturer at SOAS and later retired with his wife at Kalimpong, where his occasional bagpipe playing was commented on in a *Times* travel article. "High on a hotel terrace in Kalimpong, an alarming noise pierced the Himalayan mists . . . etc."

Kalimpong then had a small population of Tibetan scholars. Dardo Rinpoche, a Gelugpa incarnate lama from Dartsedo in Eastern Tibet, had set up the Indo-Tibetan Buddhist Cultural Institute School for poorer Tibetan children in Kalimpong. Rinpoche also helped non-Tibetan Buddhists and academics with their doctrinal and spiritual inquiries. Many Western scholars took classes in Tibetan language and literature from the official Lobsang P. Lhalungpa whom the Lhasa government has appointed to teach Tibetan language and literature to Tibetan children studying at English schools in Darjeeling and Kalimpong. Another Tibetan scholar who aided Prince Peter, Nebesky, Marco Pallis and others with their studies was Rinzin Wangpo, the nephew of Rev. Tharchin's Lhasa-born wife, and a research assistant at SOAS in London from 1948 to 1949.

My uncle, Sonam Tomjor, a Chinese classics scholar and an extraordinary polymath, never turned away visitors who came up to Fair Haven to seek guidance on Tibetan history and Buddhism. My other uncle Rakra Rinpoche (who had a *geshe lharampa* degree from Drepung and a *ngagrampa* degree from the Lower Tantric College in Lhasa) taught at Tagore's University in Shantiniketan but was helpful to George Roerich and others when he was in Kalimpong during his holidays. Only from the late 1950s did such revered Buddhist masters as Jamyang Khentse Rinpoche, Chatral Sangye Dorje, Dudjom Rinpoche and Dhingo Khyentse Rinpoche begin to arrive in Kalimpong and Darjeeling from Tibet.

One prized rarity in old Kalimpong was the nomad bard, Jampa Sangdag, (aka Reting Labrang Gyaula) who, in addition to being a skilled narrator/singer of the Gesar Epic was a remarkable *ache lhamo* (opera) singer. He had been an artiste at the court of the Reting regent, but when his patron was arrested for treason in 1947, Jampa had sought exile in India.

A decade or so earlier, there had been other interesting political exiles in Kalimpong who had been of some consequence back in Tibet, and whom Western scholars and "seekers" probably approached for information or instruction. There was the Changlochen *gung*, or the "duke" of Changlochen who had been exiled for his role in an attempted coup in 1934. There was also Thupten Kunphel la, once the most powerful man in Tibet and the favourite of the Thirteenth Dalai Lama, who, after his master passed away, had been manoeuvred out of office by his political rival and banished from Tibet. Such "émigrés" managed to scrape a living working for the Tibetan newspaper and giving Tibetan lessons to the children of Sikkimese and Bhutanese aristocracy and European expatriates.

They also started a "revolutionary" party, the "West Tibet Improvement Association". If they hoped to avoid official attention through the innocuousness of the party name, they were badly mistaken, for the British CID developed a strong interest in this group. This was possibly since their rather elaborate party emblem happened to feature, among other tokens of the party's aspiration, a large sickle, presumably of Soviet inspiration.

The third member and true founder of the Tibet Improvement Association was a Khampa intellectual from the Pangdatsang family of Eastern Tibet. Rabga Pangdatsang was married to my father's aunt (the daughter of my great-grandfather Raja Tenduk Pulger), whom we addressed by her Sikkimese title, Jhomo-la, but whose name was Dechen Choden.[14] Rabga lived in Kalimpong in semi-exile, after his brother's unsuccessful rebellion in Eastern Tibet against the Tibetan government. Though Rabga's revolutionary ideas might have lacked originality (they were a somewhat laboured synthesis of nationalism and socialism, drawn from official Guomindang or Nationalist Chinese ideology), his political ambitions did not lack imagination and clarity. He lived with his wife and adopted son, Sonam, at "Reli View", a charming bungalow his wife had inherited from Raja Tenduk, which looked down on the Reli River, a tributary of the Teesta. In the living room of the bungalow hung a painting commissioned from a local Nepali artist. This interesting example of revolutionary/visionary art depicted Rabga addressing a crowd of assorted Asian proletariat, in the dramatic socialist-realist manner of Aleksandr Gerasimov's *Lenin on the Tribune* (1930).

My mother's family, the Tethongs, could, in a sense, be said to have been living in self-imposed exile at Kalimpong, away from their manorial estate, Kharag, in the Shigatsé district of Tsang province, and their much-loved town house in Lhasa. The head of the family, my mother's younger brother Sonam Tomjor, had been a close friend, student and drinking companion of the great Amdo scholar, artist and poet, Gedün Chöphel, whose controversial views and unconventional lifestyle had elicited the disapproval of some high officials in the Tibetan government and conservatives in the all-powerful Gelugpa church.

Returning to Lhasa from a journey to India, Gedün Chöphel had, somewhat guilelessly, accepted a few letters from Rabga Pangdatsang for delivery to certain Chinese merchants in the Tibetan capital and the Guomindang mission at Kyetöpa House. Rabga was, in fact, a paid agent of the Nationalist Chinese government, as a recent academic publication has convincingly revealed.[15] I remember that when I visited Reli View bungalow in the summer of 2012, I saw a small, framed photograph of Rabga wearing a full Guomindang officer's uniform. The Indian CID, which had kept a sharp eye on the doings of the Tibet Improvement Association, relayed their full report on Rabga and Gedün Chöphel to the British representative in Lhasa, who forwarded it to the Tibetan cabinet.

The Lhasa magistrates arrested Gedün Chöphel for being an agent of the Guomindang, but only made public a bogus charge of counterfeiting currency, possibly to forestall Chinese government protests. My uncle was not implicated but became disturbed by the suspicions that at least one minister in the cabinet appeared to harbour about him. The wife of this minister pointedly told my mother, "His young lordship (*sekusho*) should be careful with the company he keeps, or it may come to pass like the saying: 'the father a noble sandal wood tree, the son a feeble marsh reed (*pha tsenden dongpo la bhu chushing yunbu soro jay yong*)'."

Some years later, Sonam Tomjor managed to secure a transfer to the office of the Tibetan Trade Agency in Kalimpong, and discretely arranged for his family to leave Lhasa and settle in Kalimpong with him.

* * *

The ancestors of the Tethongs were originally from the district of Kharag, on the border of the Indian state of Himachal Pradesh. This area had once been a part of the ancient Tibetan kingdom of Gugé in Upper Western Tibet, founded by Kyidé Nimagon, the grandson of the last Tibetan emperor, Tri-darma Udumtsan (aka Lang Darma) that had then encompassed Purang, Ruthok, the Kailash region and such present-day areas of India as Lahaul, Zanskar and Spiti and parts of northern Ladakh. Five hundred years ago, when the First Dalai Lama was struggling to ensure the paramountcy of his "reformed school," the Gelugpa, in Central Tibet, his efforts were frustrated by an acute shortage of monks belonging to this new order. Most of the people in Central Tibet and Tsang at the time were followers of the older Buddhist schools such as the Nyingma and the Kagyü. So, the First Dalai Lama cast his eyes further afield, as far west as the old kingdom of Gugé, where the reformed school was flourishing. He not only managed to persuade monks from those places, but also certain local feudal lords and princes, patrons of those Gugé monks, to resettle in Central Tibet.

Thus, the first Tethongs left their ancestral home around the 1440s. In course of time, they were enfeoffed, and received an estate at Shigatsé in Tsang province. The Tethongs may possibly be descendants of a cadet branch of the Gugé dynasty. The revered Kinnauri saint and scholar, Khunu Lama Tenzin Gyaltsen (1894–1977) refers to the Tethong's royal Gugé ancestry in the colophon to his commentary on Atiśa's foundational manual on Buddhist practice, *A Lamp for the Path to Enlightenment*.

Since then, the sons of the Tethong family have served the Dalai Lamas, right up to the present day. At some point the family bloodline crossed that of the Menthangwa family whose founder Menla Thundup had, three hundred years earlier, established the dominant Mendri

School of *thangka* painting in Tibet. So nearly all my uncles, cousins, my mother, myself and now my two daughters can draw and paint competently, such being the staying power of the Menthangwa DNA in the Tethong genetic pool.

The Tethong family distinguished itself during the reign of the Fifth Dalai Lama. The family still has a personal letter from this great sovereign commending the loyalty of one Tethong patriarch to the state during the civil war between Ü (central Tibet) and Tsang (west-central Tibet). The Seventh Dalai Lama awarded another Tethong son a beautiful silk banner enscribed with an account of his exemplary service to the state when serving under the minister Pholanas in a military campaign against the Dzungar Mongols. Then for the next two centuries the Tethong men don't appear to have done very much, aside from living quietly at their country estate at Kharag near Shigatsé—till 1910.

At the age of eighteen, my mother's father, Gyurme Gyatso (Immutable Ocean), with four other hot-blooded young Tibetan officials, stood before the Prime Minister, Lönchen Shatra, at the make-shift court of the exiled Thirteenth Dalai Lama in Darjeeling, in British India, and volunteered, somewhat recklessly, to return to Tibet to raise an insurrection against the occupying Imperial Chinese army. If they were captured it would have meant their heads, quite literally, for the Manchu occupation army in Tibet was given to beheading people with the broad-bladed, *dadao*, or executioner's sword, on little, or sometimes no provocation.

Tibet's initial encounter with the Qing (Manchu) Empire began agreeably enough in 1651 with the third Emperor Shunzhi, a devout Buddhist, inviting the Fifth Dalai Lama to Beijing and receiving him as an "independent sovereign" according to most historical accounts.[16] A deeply spiritual person, the Emperor wanted to travel beyond the Great Wall to welcome the Dalai Lama. The Chinese ministers in the court opposed the Emperor's decision as being submissive and unseemly, and recruited the help of the Jesuit astronomer Johann Adam Schall von Bell (head of the Imperial Board of Astronomy) who submitted a memorial indicating that though ". . . the Sun is the symbol of the

Monarch, yet Venus dares to challenge its brilliance"[17] and so on—thus making it unsafe for the Emperor to undertake a long journey outside the Great Wall.

The Manchus gained a toehold in Tibet in 1720, helping the Tibetans expel a ravaging Dzungar Mongol army and escorting the twelve-year-old Seventh Dalai Lama to Lhasa. Actual Qing protectorate rule in Tibet was established some years later and done so with a memorably terrifying introduction. Exploiting a civil war in Tibet, a Manchu expeditionary army marched into Lhasa in 1728. On 1 November that year, in a meadow by the banks of the Bamari canal, a few miles south-west of the Potala, seventeen Tibetans (on the losing side of the civil war) were put to death by professional executioners of the Manchu army. The principal prisoners, two ministers of the Kashag (cabinet) Ngabö and Lumpa, were put to death by the uniquely Chinese form of execution known as *lingchi*, sometimes translated as the "lingering death" or "death of a thousand cuts," whereby the condemned person had small portions of his body methodically sliced off with a knife over an extended period of time—perhaps even a week or so—till he finally died.

Thirteen others were decapitated while two high lamas were slowly garroted to death. Concluding his description of this event the Italian historian, Luciano Petech, noted: "The work of Chinese justice was completed by the traditional execution of all the nearer relations of the culprits, small children not excepted."[18]

But by the beginning of the twentieth century, the power of the Manchu Imperial representatives in Lhasa, the Ambans, had waned considerably. A national consciousness had begun to assert itself in a new generation of Tibetan officials who came together around the young Thirteenth Dalai Lama forming a "National Party" according to L.A. Waddell, a contemporary British ethnologist based in Darjeeling, ". . . that saved the young Dalai from the tragic fate of his predecessors, and rescuing him and the Tibetan government out of Chinese leading-strings by a dramatic coup d'état."[19]

Acts of defiance against the Chinese increased. Even a somewhat rash military action was undertaken against the British, who, in addition to its annexation of Sikkim, Tibetans regarded as colluding with the Chinese to undermine Tibetan sovereignty. In fact, by recognizing China's claims of suzerain authority over Tibet, Britain had secured, in addition to favourable trade-agreements, China's formal recognition of Britain's military annexation of Burma in 1885.*

But, in 1905, in a last burst of imperial power play the energetic and ruthless Qing official Zhao Erfeng (later viceroy of Sichuan province) invaded and captured large areas of Eastern Tibet, burned down monasteries, butchered thousands of monks and deposed a number of ancient independent and semi-independent Tibetan kings and rulers on the Sino-Tibetan frontier. Tibetans were ordered to shave the front of their heads and adopt Chinese-style pigtails as a symbol of their allegiance to the Qing Emperor. Both sexes were enjoined to discard their traditional *chuba* robes and wear cotton trousers "in the interests of morality." The first large-scale population transfer of Chinese peasants, ex-soldiers and *lumpen* elements from such cities as Chengdu, Ya'an and others, to Tibet was, with European and American missionary collusion, set in motion. Zhao in a memorial to the throne proudly described his grand enterprise in Eastern Tibet ". . . as a colonial one, comparable to that of the British, French, Japanese and Americans in Asia and Africa."[20]

Finally on 12 February 1910, the troops of "Butcher" Zhao, as his Sichuanese subjects called him, approached Lhasa. The Tibetan cabinet sent a monk official, Khenchung Jampa Chosang, to parley with the Chinese, but he and his entourage of eight were all beheaded. When the Chinese force reached Lhasa, it fired on some Tibetan policemen and also on officials and citizens near the Jokhang Temple. The Thirteenth Dalai Lama had just returned to his own capital city a little more than a month earlier, from a previous exile forced on him by the British invasion of his country—the innocuously named Younghusband Expedition—ordered by Lord Curzon, Viceroy of India.

---

* "Convention Relating to Burmah and Thibet" signed on 24 July 1886. H.E. Richardson, *A Short History of Tibet* (New York: Dutton, 1962) p. 250.

His Holiness, accompanied by a few ministers, some officials and a small escort of soldiers, once again fled the capital city. The Dalai Lama took with him his brand-new seal of office, which the National Assembly, in a gesture of defiance to Imperial China, had presented him some day earlier. This time the Dalai Lama and his entourage headed south-west towards British India, the territory of their erstwhile enemy and invader. They were immediately pursued by a strong detachment of Chinese cavalrymen. The Chinese force was only just held back at the ferry crossing of Chaksam (at the confluence of the Tsangpo and the Kyichu River) by a hastily organized defense commanded by the Dalai Lama's attendant, Chensel Namgang—later known as Tsarong Dasang Damdul. His Holiness escaped to British India. The Dalai Lama and his ministers set up their exile court at the hill station of Darjeeling.

My grandfather, then a young man of eighteen, was at the family estate of Kharag in Shigatsé district with his parents. He was sent to Darjeeling a year later by his father to join the Dalai Lama's service and to carry out a mission. I heard an account of this journey at Dharamshala in 1990 from Jhola Chime Gompo-la, an old official of the Thirteenth Dalai Lama. Chime Gompo-la told me that he had heard the story in 1948, at the northern trade mart of Nakchukha, from my grandfather's companion and servitor, Palden Dhakpa, who claimed to have accompanied him on the trip to Darjeeling.

Palden Dhakpa was a poor cousin, an "inner servant" (*ngomayok*) in the phraseology of Tibetan extended families. He was a well-known gambler in Lhasa city and notorious for the fatal betrayal of a friend and gambling partner, the legendary nomad chief, Gagya Dramnak, or Gagya 'Black Cheek' (he had a large black birthmark on one cheek) to the governor of Northern Tibet, the *jhang-chi*. But Palden was a loyal retainer to Gyurme Gyatso and served him faithfully till the latter's death in 1938. They had played together as children, Palden being a couple of years younger. My mother thought his story somewhat dramatic to be credible, but this is Palden Dhakpa's own account of what happened in the Tethong household at the end of that ill-omened year.

About six months after the Thirteenth Dalai Lama had left for India, a mendicant priest, a *Chöd-pa* (a member of a mystic order established by the female saint Machik Labdron that practised the *Chöd* or "cutting" spiritual practice) appeared before the Tethong manor at their estate playing a large *damaru* drum and singing *chöd* songs and the *gurma* songs of the great yogi Milarepa. The priest wore the high pointed cap of his order and was dressed in a wine-red woollen *chuba*. The old robe had black and white patches all over it, stitched on with heavy thread. Despite the humbleness of his attire the priest was tall, imposing and of fair complexion. This happened in the last months of the Tibetan year, which would be somewhere around December of 1910 or January of 1911.

At that time, the head of the Tethong household was the old lord, Phuntsok, whom everyone called Tethong *yapchen* or "great father". He consulted with his wife the *lhayum* or "goddess mother", telling her that the *kungo lama-la* or the "Lord Lama" had come, and quickly whisked the priest inside to a private chamber. He then ordered all the children, including Palden, to go outside and not come near the chamber. He summoned servants to bring hot tea and to prepare a meal, and then also dismissed them and shut the chamber door. Palden was a curious and sharp-witted lad and realized that there was something more about this visitor than met the eye.

He went out and climbed up on the roof, from where he peeped down the ventilation hole (*namcha-tre*) on the roof. Looking down Palden saw the priest take off his old, patched robe, and put on a purple brocade robe lined with "*ee-pa*" or badger fur, that was offered to him. The old lord personally draped a brocade cloak (*dagam*) over his back and seated him in a *shugdrom*, which is a box-like seat with a thick cushion and low panels that cuts off drafts. The lady served the priest butter-tea in a fine porcelain cup with an ornamented silver and gold stand and cover.

Palden realized that this priest was an important person. He was, in fact, a secret agent of the Great Thirteenth, travelling across the country disguised as a mendicant priest to avoid the attention of Imperial Chinese officials and soldiers now occupying major towns and population centres, who stopped and searched all merchants and travellers on the trade routes and frontier crossings. James Fenmore Cooper in his early novel *The Spy,* describes a similar character, the patriot and peddler Harvey Birch, who travels back and forth across British lines to spy for George Washington.

Palden looked on as the priest spread his old robe on the floor and, carefully pulling out the stitches, removed the patches on it. Hidden under the patches were documents, special orders and dispatches from the Dalai Lama, known as, "inner seal proclamations (*buktam kayik*)." He gave one letter to the old Lord. The priest stayed and rested for three days. No servants were allowed into his chamber. On the third day he changed into his old, patched robe and left in the direction of Ü or Central Tibet.

It was getting to be around New Year's Day, about the 28th or the 29th day of the last moon when the old lord summoned my grandfather, Gyurme Gyatso and told him he had to go to India to meet the Dalai Lama. Palden Dhakpa was instructed to accompany Gyurme Gyatso as his retainer. The old lord also mentioned that the two of them could not stay home for the New Year celebrations but should depart immediately. The old lord gave Gyurme Gyatso two heavy bags of Indian rupee coins (they were silver in those days) and instructed him that on arriving in Darjeeling, he should present one bag to His Holiness, half of the other bag to the Prime Minister, Lonchen Shatra, and use the other half of the contents for his own expenses. He also told them that on the way, when they got to Dromo in the Chumbi valley, they should not try to cross the heavily guarded frontier on their own but go to the village of Dromo Jemae Pungyal. Someone from the village would escort them around the mountain by an unguarded route.

Mounted on two sturdy riding mules loaded with saddle-bags and some baggage, the two young men departed from Shigatsé, posing as petty traders. They reached Darjeeling after two weeks, without any incidents on the way. On arrival at Darjeeling, Gyurme Gyatso met the Prime Minister and gave him half the bag of silver rupees as instructed. He then requested an audience with the Dalai Lama, where he presented His Holiness with the bag of coins and told him he had come as summoned.

Gyurme Gyatso was then just a *tsetruk*, a student at the civil service school at the Tsuglakhang temple complex from where lay government officials were recruited (monk officials were trained at the *Tse Laptra* or "Peak School" at the Potala). But the Dalai Lama said it was good that he had come, and he should now report to the chief-secretary as a junior official. The Prime Minister added that he would have to attend the assembly-tea the next morning where he would be inducted into government service. He said that Gyurme Gyatso would need the special hair amulet for his *pachok*, the "warrior's topknot" (similar to the Japanese samurai's *chomage*) and his long *sogchil earring* set. He asked him if he had his official costume with him. Gyurme Gyatso replied that he had not brought his costume or the hair amulet with him. The Prime Minister said that something could be arranged and that the young man would just have to report his arrival at the morning tea assembly, where all the government officials gathered for duty. In this somewhat informal and unusual way, Gyurme Gyatso was inducted into the service of the Tibetan government.

The young men at the exile court found it hard to sit back and bide their time, as the Dalai Lama and his ministers were obliged to do because of British indifference and antipathy. As I mentioned earlier, Gyurme Gyatso and four other junior officials[21] Thangpon, Menpal, Khyungram and Gachang Tenpa volunteered to return to Tibet to raise an insurrection against the occupying Imperial Chinese army. Their offer was greeted with derision by senior Tibetan officials—one of whom is said to have employed the dismissive aphorism "children's handiwork smells of fart (*pugue layga thugri drima kha*)" to emphasize his scepticism. But return, the five young officials did. Mustering retainers and peasants from their family estates, they attacked Chinese garrisons at the towns of Shigatsé and Gyantsé and suffered severe losses. After one or two more futile attempts, the five men were forced to flee Tibet precipitously. Somewhat chastened, they returned to Darjeeling.

They expected the worst sort of ridicule from their seniors, but dreaded even more the censure of the Prime Minister, Lonchen Shatra.

After a few anxious days they were summoned to his presence. To their surprise ". . . he declared them to be heroes, saying that he was sure they would be more successful in their next venture." So, the historian Tsepon Shakabpa has recorded.[22] Inspired by the Prime Minister's confidence in them, the young officials returned to Tibet before long, and learning from their previous mistakes, organized and mounted an effective guerrilla campaign, eventually defeating the Chinese garrisons at Shigatsé and Gyantsé.

In October 1911, revolution broke out in China. It spread rapidly throughout the country resulting four months later in the overthrow of the Qing, China's last imperial dynasty. The Chinese garrison in Lhasa revolted and began looting, pillaging, and terrorizing the civilian population. Fortuitously, the Tibetans had managed to set up a secret War Office in the city under the officials Jampa Tendar and Trimon. Lhasa was turned into a battleground. The Thirteenth Dalai Lama quickly sent his personal attendant, Namgang, who had earlier saved his life at the Chaksam river crossing, to command this mixed bag of soldiery: Sera monks, Banakshöl Khampas, and assorted country levies. After about eight months of hard fighting, which Tibetans call the "Water Mouse Chinese War" (*Chuchi Gyamak*), and enormous destruction to the city (one-third of all buildings reduced to ruins according to Shakabpa), the Chinese were defeated.

In January 1913 the Thirteenth Dalai Lama returned triumphantly to Lhasa. That same month he issued an edict that is regarded as Tibet's Declaration of Independence. He followed it up by concluding a "Treaty of Friendship" with Mongolia where both nations declared their rejection of Qing rule, their separation from China and their establishment of self-governing independent nations. The Dalai Lama then appointed Namgang commander-in-chief of the Tibetan army, renaming him Dasang Damdul (Straight Arrow Foe Destroyer) and giving him the aristocratic patronymic and estates of a former cabinet minister Tsarong, who was senselessly killed as a traitor in the chaos of the uprising. Of the two officials who headed the clandestine War Office, the junior, Trimon, was appointed deputy commander. The senior official, Jampa Tendar was promoted to the rank of a cabinet minister and subsequently appointed governor-general of Eastern Tibet. The five young officials who were the first to volunteer to fight the Chinese, received commendations and promotions. My grandfather was given the rank of *dapön** or general.

I have this old photograph above my desk of Gyurme Gyatso at around twenty-six years of age, looking very dashing—very much the *beau sabreur*—a long Tibetan broadsword stuck in the belt of his fur-lined robe, and a smart fox-skin cap casting a dramatic shadow just above his intense eyes. He is holding a Mauser automatic pistol in his right hand in a business-like fashion and has one foot planted, in studied nonchalance, on the breech of the larger of the two mountain guns he and his men had captured from the Chinese at Riwoché in Eastern Tibet. His men, of the Shigatsé regiment, look a motley, battle-hardened lot with thick tussore-silk turbans wrapped around their heads to protect them from sword slashes, and each hung about with enough assorted weaponry and bandoliers as any caricature brigand.

The photograph was taken in February 1918 when the Tibetan army was desperately attempting to halt another Chinese invasion. Gyurme Gyatso was one of eight generals (three were killed in action) serving under the command of the governor-general of Eastern Tibet, Jampa Tendar, a native of Gyantsé district and a monk. The Tibetan commander's spiritual vocation did not, fortunately, get in the way of his military skills, which were considerable. Jampa Tendar was a big man, over six feet tall, and sported a handsome beard, which was much admired, for Tibetans are, on the whole, a not very hirsute race. It is said that when the Thirteenth Dalai Lama was in exile in Darjeeling, he had a dream in which he received a sign about this unusual monk. He summoned Jampa Tendar to his presence and forthwith had him give up his monk vows. He then dispatched him to Lhasa, where Jampa Tendar successfully put together and organized the Tibetan army that

---

* *Dapön* (literally "arrow chief") has been variously translated as "general" or "colonel." We will go with "general" as *dapön* was the highest rank in the army after that of *makchi* or commander-in-chief.

the commander Dasang Damdul used to defeat the Manchu occupation force in the city.

Now as commander of the Tibetan army in Eastern Tibet, Jampa Tendar found himself, on New Year's Day, under fierce attack from the Sichuan Frontier Force, when his troops were perhaps not as combat-ready on that festive day, as they should have been, and when he was himself bedridden with fever and flu. Recovering quickly from the initial Chinese attack, Jampa Tendar not only managed to halt the Chinese advance but within a couple of months converted this temporary advantage into a general rout of Chinese forces throughout Eastern Tibet. The victorious Tibetans intended to push all the way through Kham to the town of Dartsedo on the old frontier, and it is generally accepted that they could have at the time. Khampas regarded the 1918 victory as a turning point in their history, for they speak of it grandiloquently as *kalpa sa-ta lo*, or the 'The New Epoch of the Earth Horse.' It was not just a war but also a national liberation.

The Chinese government appealed to the British minister in Peking, and Eric Teichman of His Britannic Majesty's Consular Service was dispatched from the Chinese capital to negotiate a truce between the two forces. Teichman writes of his meeting the victorious Tibetan leader: "The majestic presence of the Kalön Lama, Governor and Commander-in-Chief in Eastern Tibet, overshadowed all other figures in the drama of the Sino-Tibetan borderland, and will not readily be forgotten by the three or four foreigners who were privileged to make his acquaintance." He also observed how the captured Chinese were cared for. "The Tibetans have undoubtedly behaved very well at Chamdo, treating their Chinese military prisoners with humanity and kindness . . . the civilian Chinese are at present moving freely about the town carrying on their usual business, each with a ticket on his arm, showing that he has been registered at the Tibetan headquarters."[23]

When Jampa Tendar was awarded the cabinet rank of kalön lama and appointed governor-general of Eastern Tibet, he had a new seal engraved for his administration. He incorporated his name Jampa meaning "love", and Tendar, meaning "Spread of the Dharma", into the message of the new seal, which read in Tibetan: *gyal-khab jam-pae kyang, diki ki tempa dhar-pae thamga.* The wordplay makes an exact translation difficult but could roughly be rendered as: "Rule the nation with love—the doctrine of happiness will flourish." General P'eng Jih-sheng, the Chinese commander at Chamdo, requested he not be returned to China. He was given a pension and settled in Dowa Dzong in southern Tibet with a Tibetan wife. He had, in fact, started the war and declared his intention in writing of invading Tibet and advancing to Lhasa. When Jampa Tendar had written to him seeking an explanation for his violating the ceasefire, General P'eng had returned his letters filled with excrement. General P'eng was notorious for his intolerance and cruelty to the Tibetans and was responsible for the destruction of the great monasteries of Chamdo, Drayab, Chatreng and Yendum in previous campaigns.

The historian Shakabpa provides some substance to the Tethong family legend of the two captured cannons on which my grandfather had struck his martial pose all those many years ago. Shakabpa writes that General Phulungwa and General Tethong commanded the force that pushed back the Chinese advance from Riwoché and Chakzamkha. "Within several months, Dapön Phulungwa and Dapön Tethong had expelled the Chinese. Two senior Chinese commanders and about six hundred ordinary soldiers escaped to Chamdo. Many of the remainder died, and many were captured. Among the weapons that the Tibetans seized were two German-made cannons." When this force finally arrived at Chamdo ". . . the famous Phulungwa was lost to the enemy."[24]

Teichman mentions that the final defeat (in late April 1918) of the principal Chinese garrison at the fortified town of Chamdo came about only after long and savage fighting, and the effective use by the Tibetans ". . . of a mountain gun which they had captured from the Chinese."[25]

Teichman met Gyurme Gyatso and describes him as ". . . a well-educated Tibetan of an aristocratic family from the Shigatsé neighbourhood, who had visited India and was well acquainted with foreign customs and ideas." An American officer from the consulate at Peking who visited Eastern Tibet some years later recorded in his diary that Tethong and his colleague Khyungram, who were then co-governors of Dergé, had brought back many "foreign ideas" from India, including "Eastman Kodaks that were better than ours . . . They were very intelligent and talked interestingly about the future of Tibet, saying that Tibet would soon have relations with foreign countries."[26]

In 1923 Tethong was recalled to Lhasa where, under the new commander-in-chief Tsarong, he became intimately involved in the modernization program of the Tibetan army and police. However, in the subsequent year the volatile situation in Eastern Tibet demanded Tethong's return to Dergé. The turbulent history of the semi-independent kingdom of Dergé, under intermittent Lhasa and Chinese administrations, had not been improved by the intrigue and rivalry between local factions supporting one or the other of two princely claimants to the throne. The Tibetan victory of 1918 restored the throne (under Lhasa administration) to the older brother Dorje Senge, but he passed away in Lhasa in 1926. The coronation of his young son Tsewang Dundul to the throne of Dergé that same year, presided over by the two governors and witnessed by all the nobles and chieftains of the land, provided a measure of peace and stability to Dergé for some years. The prince was ten years old at the time. His sister Yudon was fourteen.

My mother had fond memories of sleepovers at the Dergé Palace. Princess Yudon-la was a warm, affectionate girl and like an older sister to my mother. The prince was around my mother's age and a good playmate but a sensitive and proud boy. My mother had to be careful not to show too much interest in any of his toys or other belongings, as he would insist she keep it and would not take no for an answer. The two girls would sleep side-by-side, and my mother recalled Yudon-la whispering to her in the dark that the prince, who slept on a high ottoman, would sneak out of his bed and go over to sleep with his old nanny, when he thought everyone was asleep. She remembered how lonely it was for those two children in the enormous, old and empty Dergé palace. This princess later became the Queen of Nangchen. She had two older sisters who had already left Dergé to become queens of Lingtsang and Yabtsang.

In 1927 when she was around nine, my mother remembered being taken by her father on a diplomatic trip to Dzachukha, the north-eastern limit of our frontier with Chinese-occupied Eastern Tibet, where two important Golok chiefs were to be awarded Tibetan government ranks and honours. The occasion was a welcome break from her daily routine at Dergé of copying Tibetan letters on her wooden writing-board (*jangshing*).

When my mother passed away on 9 January 2005, at my home in Monteagle, Tennessee, I published an account of her trip as a memorial. I did not fail to mention her treasured recollection of galloping wildly on her small Tibetan pony (*yul-ta*) across the Dzachukha grassland, dressed as a Khampa boy, complete with ". . . a *ghawu* (amulet-box) and a small *sakchukha* pistol (.22 Berreta, JN) in a leather holster with the belt tied securely around my waist."[27]

After serving as governor of Dergé, Gyurme Gyatso transferred to Lhasa in 1928 and extended home leave. He had spent most of his official life in Kham where four of his eleven children were born.

But in 1932, the Sichuan warlord, Liu Wenhui, inflicted a serious defeat on the Tibetan army in Eastern Tibet. Gyurme Gyatso's leave was cut short. He was hurriedly appointed governor-general of Eastern Tibet, and he and his Shigatsé regiment made ready to depart for Chamdo. I deal with this next and final stage of his life in Chapter Seven.

Gyurme Gyatso was intelligent, well read (in Tibetan)[*] and a devoutly religious man. A few tours of British India had widened his horizon so that he was knowledgeable about nations and events in the world at large. He was a camera buff, a "Kodak enthusiast," and taught my mother, his eldest child, to be his darkroom assistant, at which she was quite adept, using the underneath of the family dining table— draped with blankets—as a darkroom. He enjoyed a whisky and soda

---

[*] In the early 1920s, Gyurme Gyatso sponsored and supervised the publication of the first print edition (woodblock) of *The Secret Biography of the Sixth Dalai Lama*, at Dergé Printing Press. Another title in the Tethong "Family Edition" is Gedün Chöphel's Tibetan translation (circa 1940) of the Pali *Dhammapada*, also in woodblock.

at the end of the day and it was one of my mother's great joys to be allowed to squirt the soda into his tumbler from the heavy glass siphon, encased in wire-mesh. The "gasogene" of Sherlock Holmes stories.

He was an able administrator and apparently a humane and enlightened one. Some years ago, a short local history of the district of Drayab in Eastern Tibet was published under Communist Chinese auspices. The work is, to a large extent, a litany of the administrative abuses of various Tibetan governors, magistrates, and tax collectors in "the bad old days" and it was probably for that reason allowed publication by the Communist authorities.[28] Yet the writer has refrained from criticizing Gyurme Gyatso when he was governor of Eastern Tibet. In fact, he mentions how the people of Drayab remembered him with gratitude for his honest administration and the reductions in taxes he granted them. Under similar circumstances, a former Tethong servitor Pemba Jamyang (now a Communist official) recently published a glowing biographical account of Gyurme Gyatso and his son Sonam Tomjor, in an official Chinese Communist journal.[29]

Gyurme Gyatso joined the *Kashag,* the Tibetan cabinet, in Lhasa in 1936, but died a couple of years later at the age of forty-two. A tribute filled obituary was published in the *Tibet Mirror* in Kalimpong. The Tethong family also received a gracious letter of condolence from Gyurme Gyatso's old adversary, the warlord of Sichuan, Marshal Liu Wenhui, who also served as the Guomindang-appointed governor of the province.

2

ORIGIN CHRONICLE: PATRILINEAL

My father's family, the Pulgers (anglicized from the Tibetan "Paljor" to sound like the Irish "Bulger"—perhaps?), has a lineage that goes back to the middle of the thirteenth century. This ancestor, Ngawang Thundup, a man of Denkhok (aka Denma or Ahden) in Eastern Tibet, entered the service of the great Sakya hierarch, Drogön Chögyal Phagpa, ruler of Tibet and the spiritual preceptor of the Emperor Kublai Khan.

Phagpa was not only a considerable Buddhist scholar but an extraordinarily skilled linguist, who in 1269, created a "universal" script for the Mongol Empire, an adaptation of which has survived till this day, according to some scholars, in the Korean alphabet, *hangul*.[1] Phagpa was a mystic as well. It could probably have been him who levitated the Emperor's cup to his lips, as the prosaic Marco Polo has recorded, though a Tibetan historian friend has suggested that it was more likely another priest in Phagpa's entourage—the principal exponent of the Sakya Mahakala tradition and renowned thaumaturge, Ga Anyen Dhampa. Phagpa, in his own memoirs, mentions that in 1271 Kublai Khan was friendly with a stranger from a faraway land. The date falls within the time of Polo's visit to the Mongol court.

I imagine this scene unfolding somewhere in an exquisite garden courtyard in Khanbalik (Beijing) or more likely Xanadu (Shangdu) where Coleridge tells us "Kubla" Khan did:

> A stately pleasure-dome decree:
> Where Alph, the sacred river, ran
> Through caverns measureless to man
> Down to a sunless sea.

The Lama Phagpa holds his right hand in a *mudra*, a tantric gesture, telepathically guiding a delicate Sung *kuan*-ware cup—floating unsteadily some feet above the floor—across the courtyard. A few drops of perfumed rice wine spill on the malachite parquets before the cup hovers to a rest, inches from the lips of the amazed Emperor, who claps his hands in delight. The mouths of the courtiers, including the young Venetian merchant, are wide open in astonishment. Two bearded Nestorian priests observe this demonstration with dismay and hurriedly cross themselves for protection against such heathen necromancy. I have, with considerable historical licence, inserted my ancestor into this scene. He stands discreetly behind his master, awed by the magnificence of the Mongol court but quietly pleased at the sensation his master is causing.

Phagpa was greatly revered by the Emperor. According to Henry H. Howarth's monumental four-volume history of the Mongols,[2] Kublai Khan took a lower seat when receiving teachings from Phagpa and an equal seat when discussing affairs of government and state. Kublai Khan was so enthusiastic a disciple that he proposed enacting ". . . a law compelling all the people of Tibet to give up the other traditions and follow only the tradition of the Sakya School. Such was Kublai Khan's enthusiasm. But Phagpa did not agree. Such a law, he said, would not be in accordance with the Dharma and that the other Buddhists of Tibet should be free to follow whatever school they wished. There must be no compulsion, no coercion."[3]

Phagpa and other Buddhist teachers of the Mongol Khans were unquestionably a civilizing influence on the ferocious Mongols who had initially planned to exterminate the Chinese and use China as grazing land for their horses and herds. No doubt, Chinese culture did its share in taming the Mongols, and we have the famous Khitan prince, Yelu Ch'u-ts'ai, who convinced the Mongols that it was more profitable to tax the Chinese than to exterminate them. But the Tibetans taught the Mongols of the sanctity of life—even Chinese lives. The biography of the Sakya lamas mentions the problems they faced in dissuading the Mongols from their annual practice of driving hundreds of thousands of Chinese into rivers, lakes and other large bodies of water.

After the Mongol conquest of China, the life of the last surviving prince, Gongdi, of the preceding Sung dynasty, and a possible claimant to the throne, was saved by the intervention of Phagpa. The Mongols were unwilling to let such a potential focus of insurrection remain alive, but on Phagpa's repeated requests, they were reluctantly persuaded not to kill the boy. To reassure the Mongols, Phagpa took the prince back with him to Tibet and made him a monk, according to Gö Lotsawa in his *The Blue Annals*,[4] a fact that has been later corroborated and expanded on by a Chinese scholar in the People's Republic of China (PRC).[5] But the young man probably found monastic life tedious. The minor aristocratic family of Meru Gyalpo, of Shang district, in south-western Tibet, still claims descent from the last of the Sung dynasty.

Getting back to my ancestor's story—according to the British ethnohistorian H.H. Risley[6]—Ngawang Thundup, on returning with the Phagpa Lama to Tibet, was advised by his master to seek his fortune south in the region of Sikkim. After the establishment of the kingdom of Sikkim in 1642, Ngawang Thundup's descendants served the Chögyals or 'religious kings' who were themselves originally exiles. The Sikkim royal house claims its origins from the principality of Minyak in Eastern Tibet. But there is another more likely theory that the Sikkimese kings are descended from a Tangut prince who survived Genghis Khan's destruction of the Tangut Empire in Central Asia in 1227, and the obliteration of its black-walled capital, Kharakhoto. The Tibetan name for the Tangut Empire is Ga-Minyak, which may account for the confusion. There is a further theory that even the principality of Minyak in Eastern Tibet was so called because it was settled by Tangut exiles fleeing Genghis Khan's invading army.

British intrusion into Sikkim began in the early nineteenth century. In 1829, Lt Col G.W.A. Lloyd first reported the excellent prospect that Darjeeling, mentioned by its original Tibetan name of Dorje Ling,[*] held out as a sanatorium for heat-exhausted servants of the East India Company. The British obtained a lease for the Darjeeling tract from the Sikkimese ruler in 1835, exclusively for this purpose. But step-by-step, in the usual manner of colonial acquisitions: through bluster, bribery, bullying, leading up, inevitably, to "punitive" expeditions (1850 and 1861), Darjeeling was detached from Sikkim.

My great-grandfather, Tenduk Pulger (Thundup Paljor), was then serving under the seventh Chögyal, Tsugphud Namgyal (1785–1863) as a *dzongpön*, or district administrator of Karmi, immediate north of Darjeeling. Following the first British punitive expedition into Sikkim in 1850, the Darjeeling area and Morang were annexed to British India in 1853, including adjacent Sikkimese territories such as the district of Karmi, where the Pulgers had their ancestral estate. So, it is possible that my great-grandfather saw the writing on the wall and, setting aside his allegiance to his erstwhile sovereign, threw in his lot with the Company *Bahadur*, the Honourable East India Company.

They made him a 'Rajah' for his troubles—not a hereditary kingship, but rather an official title with an accompanying estate, revenue and a resplendent uniform. He was honoured with that title after the Anglo-Tibetan War of 1888, in recognition of his long and faithful service as "Adviser on Frontier Matters". He had earlier served in a variety of official positions, including Darjeeling *Tehsildar* (Land Revenue Officer), Manager of *Khasmahals* (government buildings and property) and Municipal Commissioner of Darjeeling, during which period he built the Nepal Frontier Road with accompanying

---

[*]The official History of Sikkim (*Bras ljongs rgyal rabs*) of 1908 refers to Darjeeling as "Wangdu Dorje Ling" or "realm of the conquering adamantine sceptre." A possible earlier Lepcha name, Darjulyang (*dár jú lyáng*), meaning the abode of the gods, has been put forward in K.P. Tamsang's *The Lepcha-English Encyclopedic Dictionary* of 1980.

Dak Bungalows (rest houses). He encouraged the local peasantry to adopt modern farming methods and joined the Rev. J.A. Graham in organizing the first agricultural fairs in the district.

The British Raj turned out to be just the element for this energetic and forward-looking personality, and he thrived in it. He was rewarded with additional land grants, and his family estate of Karmi was expanded to around 25,000 acres.* He also acquired many houses and much property in and around Kalimpong and Darjeeling townships, becoming the richest man in that area. The locals said that he could dam the Teesta River if he threw all his money off the Anderson Bridge. He was also disliked by many in Sikkim who were loyal to the old monarch and hated the British Resident in Sikkim, John Claude White, described by a notable Himalayan scholar Alex McKay as ". . . a little god . . . the worst type of Imperial officer, arrogant, intolerant, petty . . . self-seeking . . . who ran the state as his own personal fiefdom."[7]

Claude White's arrogance and high-handedness became more pronounced in the reign of the next Chögyal, the weak Thutop Namgyal. The crown prince, Tsodak Namgyal, fled to Tibet and settled there as a Tibetan aristocrat under the name of Doptra Taring. The Chögyal himself and the queen, Yeshi Dolma, also attempted to escape to Tibet but were captured by Nepalese soldiers at the Tibetan border and handed over to the British authorities. They were detained under strict and humiliating circumstances, first at the small decrepit monastery of Ging near Darjeeling, and later at Kurseong, a small railway colony on the road to Siliguri.

The authorities wanted to make sure that the remaining prince, Sikyong Namgyal, was brought up as an English gentleman, so as J.A.H. Lewis, who travelled through the area in 1893, tells us, the prince ". . . is now being educated with the family of Rajah Tenduk Pulger in Darjeeling and is allowed to make occasional visits into Sikkhim."[8] The Rev. Graham also mentions that the prince was under

---

*All this property was expropriated after India's independence and the introduction of land reforms. In Karmi, the few acres allowed under the Land Ceiling Act has now become an ecotourism resort run by Andrew Pulger-Frame, the (half Scottish) maternal great-grandson of Rajah Tenduk Pulger.

Rajah Tenduk's care.[9] Rajah Tenduk is also reputed to have provided local help in organizing the logistics of the British military intrusion into Tibet in 1888 and the bloody battle at the fort of Lungthur on the Sikkim–Tibet frontier. The later decline of the Pulger family fortune was attributed by the locals to the displeasure of the gods of Sikkim and Tibet at Rajah Tenduk's perfidy.

A Sikkim historian of my acquaintance told me that I was perhaps over-censorious of my forebear. There are several references to Rajah Tenduk Pulger in the official *History of Sikkim*** and none of them are noticeably hostile. It comes through fairly clearly that he was someone with strong connections to the British authorities in Darjeeling, but one also gets the impression that the royal family might have benefited from his intercession. There is also mention of the king and queen visiting Rajah Tenduk at his house in Darjeeling, and the matter of the prince, Sikyong Namgyal, having to live with Rajah Tenduk for his education is noted in a matter-of-fact way without any apparent rancour. In fact, the remarkable thing about this traditional work of history is its attempt at balance, and the absence of any diatribe or tone of resentment, considering the circumstances under which it was written.

The *History of Sikkim*[10] was published as a nationalist or nativist response to the official British *Gazetteer of Sikhim*. The authorship of this history is jointly attributed to both the king Thutop Namgyal and his queen Yeshi Dolma but appears to be largely the work of the queen, who was a driving force in the opposition to British expansion into Sikkim and Tibet. She was Lhasa aristocracy, the daughter of the Lheding family. Her uncle, a dapön, "the Lhasa General" in British accounts of the Younghusband invasion of 1904, was killed at the battle of Guru.

Claude White noted she was a petite yet striking figure.

---

*A critical study on this important but obscure history is Tashi Tsering's "A Short Communication about the 1908 bras ljong rgyal rabs", in *The Bulletin of Tibetology*, vol. 48 no.1, 2012, Namgyal Institute of Tibetology, Sikkim.

She is extremely bright and intelligent and has been well educated . . .
she talks well on many subjects, which one would hardly have credited
her with a knowledge of, and can write well. On the occasion of
Queen Victoria's diamond jubilee, she personally composed and
engrossed in beautiful Tibetan characters the address presented by
the Sikhim Raj.

Her disposition is a masterful one and her bearing always
dignified. She has a great opinion of her own importance, and is the
possessor of a sweet musical voice, into which she can, when angry,
introduce a very sharp intonation. She is always interesting, whether
to look at or listen to, and had she been born within the sphere of
European politics she would most certainly have made her mark, for
there is no doubt she is a born intriguer and diplomat.[11]

In spite of the trials and humiliations inflicted on her and the Maharaja
by the British, Maharani Yeshi Dolma somehow kept up a civilized
front in her dealings with the Resident.* White concludes: "Her
common sense and clear-sightedness were on many occasions of the
greatest assistance to me in my task of administering and developing
Sikhim." White's plans for administering Sikkim involved the gradual
submergence of the Tibetan/Lepcha population by a large-scale transfer
of the more numerous and obliging immigrants from Nepal. *The
Gazetteer of Sikhim* explains: "The influx of these hereditary enemies of
Tibet is our surest guarantee against a revival of Tibetan influence."[12]

Raja Tenduk had two wives, five sons and two daughters. He sent
his sons to English schools (St. Pauls and St. Josephs) and acquired a
few medals before he died in 1902. He was important enough to have
his biography published in a "dictionary" of notables in the Indian
Empire—on the same page as William Makepeace Thackeray.[13] His
fourth son, my grandfather Kumar (Prince) Dawa Lhundup, appears
to have inherited much of the family estate at Karmi and property
in Darjeeling and Kalimpong. He was a tall, handsome man and the
star track-and-field athlete at St. Joseph's College. I remember when

---

*The Chögyal, on the other hand, absolutely refused to speak to Claude
White or acknowledge him in any way.

he was on his deathbed in May 1964. My mother took me to the Planter's Hospital to see him. He was so tall the nurses had to extend the bed by placing a bench at the end of it, otherwise his feet would have stuck out.

He bought the first motorcar in the district and, otherwise with horses, country mansions and liveried servants, contrived to live the life of a prosperous English gentleman. He spent much of his young life riding, going to dances and fancy-dress balls with the vivacious daughters of Dr Graham of Kalimpong. Yet, it must be said to their credit that the Pulgers never converted and always got their wives from the old country. Dawa Lhundup married Samdup Bhuti, "Rose-la," the pretty daughter of Wangchuk Tsering of Amdo and Tsezin Dolma of Chakra Pembar in Kham (from the family of Gyanyok Wangchutsang, chief secretary of the district governor). The fruit of this union was my father Thundup Lhawang or "Larry", as he was known in Darjeeling society.

Wangchuk Tsering, whose father Amdo Lama Sangpo hailed from the north-eastern region of Tibet known as Amdo (then ruled by the Chinese Muslim warlord of Sining), had received a Chinese education. He was employed as a junior official at the Manchu customs office at Chorten Karpo (White Stupa) at Dromo, on the Nathu la road in the Chumbi valley, and later promoted to a full (one of two) commissioner for customs at Dromo. He was a competent man, as his British counterpart, David MacDonald mentions.[14] It is also a part of family lore that he secretly assisted MacDonald in smuggling Chensel Namgang to India, disguised as a postal runner, after the latter held up Chinese troops at Chaksam for two days, thus allowing the Thirteenth Dalai Lama time to escape to India. There could be some substance to this claim as Wangchuk Tsering had a letter from the Thirteenth Dalai Lama thanking him for his service and offering him the governorship of Markham in Eastern Tibet. The appointment was respectfully declined. Wangchuk Tsering had by then re-settled in Darjeeling.

Another reason for the Dalai Lama's favour might have had to do with events in the years following His Holiness's return to Tibet. In 1913 Sir Henry McMahon, the foreign secretary of India, convened a major conference at Shimla to work out the status of Tibet and the frontier between Tibet and India. Representatives of the newly formed Republic of China, the British government and the Tibetan government met at Shimla, the summer capital of British India. Following the violent revolution of 1911, Manchu officials had been almost entirely removed from office and many killed.* The Chinese delegation at Shimla had no one with any knowledge or experience of Tibetan frontier affairs. It is, possibly, for this reason, that Wangchuk Tsering (though now retired and living in Darjeeling) was inducted into the Chinese delegation and even accorded a senior role, as the line-up in the official photograph of the Shimla Conference seems to indicate. Did he make a small (perhaps even clandestine) contribution to the partial victory that the Tibetan diplomats scored at that meeting when finally, the frustrated Chinese delegation withdrew in a huff? China was denied any privileges from the proceedings of the subsequent bilateral accord between Tibet and Britain.

And so, in the manner of his forbears, my father Thundup Lhawang Pulger married my mother Lodi (Lobsang Deki) Tethong, the oldest child of Tethong Gyurme Gyatso, who was probably regarded as a considerable catch. She was Lhasa aristocracy, the daughter of a cabinet minister and former governor-general of Eastern Tibet. For, despite the Pulgers' wealth and standing in Sikkim and Darjeeling they were, in the somewhat condescending Lhasa view of things, provincials. The two met in Darjeeling when she came there in 1948 to take her younger siblings home from English boarding schools for their winter holidays.

---

*The mass killing of Manchus was noted by W.H. Auden and Christopher Isherwood in their *Journey to a War* (1939). "Sian smells of murder . . . in 1911 the Chinese population fell upon the Manchus and massacred twenty-five thousand of them in the course of a single night."

3

MY JOURNEY TO LHASA

I was born on 14 April 1949. Four months later, wrapped warmly in soft woollen blankets and strapped to the back of a sturdy manservant, I crossed the Nathu-la (*la* being the Tibetan word for pass) from Sikkim to Tibet. My old nanny, Pema Tsewang (who later died of starvation during the Chinese occupation), rode beside us on a pony, while my mother and father rode ahead.

My mother's family, the Tethongs, had yet to make their decisive move to leave Tibet (which they would the next year), and my mother had to return to Lhasa to make arrangements for the marriage of her younger sister, Tashi Chödon, to the son of Changöpa (aka Ringang) one of the four young Tibetans sent by the Thirteenth Dalai Lama to study at Rugby. He had graduated in electrical engineering from what is now the Imperial College of the University of London, and ". . . single-handedly took on a plan to build a hydroelectric plant at Dodé, three miles from Lhasa behind Sera Monastery . . . providing all of Lhasa City with electricity for the first time."[1]

Of course, my mother had to show her new husband and baby around to her relatives and friends, but she had mixed feelings about that. She had been a nun since childhood and had not quite gotten over the discomfort of having given up her spiritual vocation.

42

The journey from Kalimpong to Shigatsé took us around twenty-one days, in easy stages of about twenty miles a day. Tibetans like to start early, preferably at the crack of dawn and ride briskly till noon. Then they looked around for lodgings, in a village or nomad encampment, or lacking that selected a good campsite and settled down for the rest of the day and for the night. The only memento I have of the journey is a photograph of my nanny Pema Tsewang at Gawu or Gautsa that McDonald translates as the "Meadow of Joy".[2] She is holding me on her lap while her nephew Tsering Phuntsok is sitting beside her. Our ponies graze peacefully in the background, before a distant waterfall.

Gawu is a fifteen-mile trip from the trade mart and customs post of Dromo or Yatung, a Chinese name meaning "eastern trade mart." You ride up a valley of "extraordinary steepness" on a stone-covered track that follows the eastern tributary of the Amo River, ". . . a rushing mountain stream overhung with thickets of wild rose, Daphne, and jasmine," till hours later you come upon a broad level tract of a meadow surrounded by fir-clad hills with snowy peaks beyond. The stream now meanders peacefully, ". . . through the verdant pasture which in most parts is carpeted with the cowslip-like blooms of *Primula Sikkimensis* and other flowers."[3] Phari, our next stop, was twenty-three miles away.

We arrived at Shigatsé just when the barley fields were being harvested. We stayed for a couple of months at the family estate of Kharag, about ten miles from Shigatsé town with my uncle Sonam Tomjor, the head of the Tethong family, after which, everyone departed for Lhasa, a week's journey from Shigatsé. We also attended the *Sigmo Chenmo*, or the "Great Spectacle" at Tashi Lhunpo, the famous monastery of the Panchen Lamas.

We stayed at the family mansion at Banakshöl, the eastern suburb of Lhasa. I was made much of by relatives and taken by my nanny to the many places of worship in and around Lhasa. Tibetans are diligent subscribers to auguries and omens, so my mother and nanny were pleased when some of my visits to these holy sites, as Tashi Lhunpo Monastery and Sera Monastery, coincided most auspiciously with occasions of sacred food being distributed after special services, and also encountering congregations of monks carrying bowls heaped with rich rice and raisin pudding; nothing extraordinary enough to warrant an investigation of my possibly being an incarnate lama, but sufficient to reassure my nanny and my mother that I was a blessed child.

I am told that I also attended the *Shotön* opera festival the next year at the Norbulingka, the Jewel Park, the Dalai Lama's summer palace. Tibetan operas are relaxed affairs lasting the entire day, from which babies, pet *apsos*, food, drink and intermittent conversation (during the boring bits) are not prohibited. The plays are performed on a large stone-flagged stage in the open air under an ornately decorated canopy, the "Innermost Sky" (*jhayab namkha ding*) in August or September when the flowers at the Jewel Park and the Lhasa weather are both at their delightful best.

But dark storm clouds were already gathering at the far horizon of the arcadian Tibetan world. Though most people carried on their regular lives in the same blissful ignorance as my burbling self, more astute individuals were beginning to hear disturbing accounts of the *Ulang Marpo*, or "the Red Ulan" (an inadvertent tautology, "*ulan*" being the Mongol word for red). The Communists were winning the civil war in China and were making clear their intentions of "liberating" Tibet.

In 1949 the Tibetan Foreign Bureau responded by sending a letter (with a typed English translation) to "The Honourable Mr. Mautsetung" [*sic*], pointing out that "Tibet has from the earliest times up to now, been an Independent Country . . . (that) also defended her own territories from Foreign invations [*sic*] . . . and we would like to have an assurance that no Chinese troops would cross the Tibetan frontier." The Foreign Bureau did not forget the Chinese occupied regions in eastern Tibet, "As regards those Tibetan territories annexed as part of Chinese territories some years back, the Government of Tibet would desire to open negotiations after the settlement of the Chinese Civil War."[4]

Earlier, in 1947, the creaky Tibetan government had, to drum up some international support, sent a trade (and political) mission to India, Britain and the United States, which a Washington journalist dubbed "The Yak-Tail Mission". This being one of the items of

Tibetan export, and used in the manufacture of Santa Claus beards, and also as ceremonial whisks in Hindu and Sikh temples. In spite of the facetiousness of the Washington journalist, America did regularly import a substantial quantity of Tibetan wool, as I mentioned in an earlier chapter.

Breaking further with its isolationist tradition, the Tibetan government also invited the famous journalist and radio commentator Lowell Thomas and his son for a visit. We encountered the Thomas's on our way to Lhasa from Shigatsé. Thomas Senior had fractured his hip falling off his horse, and was being carried by Tibetan porters on a makeshift stretcher on a long and somewhat painful journey back to India. They later made a documentary film* (in the brilliant technicolour of yesteryear) which is now chiefly memorable for some achingly haunting scenes of old Tibet on the eve of its disappearance. The commentary has a very "fifties" flavour with lines about "godless Communists" and the like. My favourite is the effusive description by Thomas Junior of the Potala Palace as "the penthouse of the gods."

Around eight in the evening of 15 August 1950, a year after the Thomases had left Lhasa, my nanny, Pema Tsewang, began crying out in her sleep that she was dying. I woke up and started howling as well. My mother rushed into the room and tried to reassure Pema Tsewang that she was all right, and that we were only experiencing an earthquake. My mother picked me up from my cot and ran out on the terrace where her younger brother, Rakra Rinpoche, an incarnate lama, joined us. From the east of the city came loud detonations. My mother counted fourteen. A huge red glow became visible in the cloudless dark sky from the hills to the east of the city. The cooks and other servants had come out into the courtyard below and were all staring in the direction of the explosions. The earthquake had been entirely unexpected and violent, without any premonitory tremors. Everyone was terrified. People began to whisper about "*Lha-mak,*" a Tibetan *Götterdämmerung* or *Ragnarok*. The gods of Tibet were doing battle

---

* *Out of This World—A Journey to Lhasa,* in the CBS series *High Adventure with Lowell Thomas* (1955–1958).

with the *Gyadré* demons of China, and the frightened Lhasa folk dared not presume as to the outcome.

Tibetan fears were magnified by the fact that no one had really seen a Communist before, and the more unsophisticated speculated whether such creatures would have fangs or horns. Simple Tibetans have never wavered in their belief that fabulous beings existed beyond the frontiers of their land, like those grotesques and monsters reported by Herodotus and the Greek traveller Cteseas, which also appear in the *Liber Chronicarium* and the *Collectanea Rerum Memorabilium* of Solinus. One such race with enormous ears, illustrated in these treatises, is familiar to Tibetans. It turns up as well in the Chinese *Shan Hai Ching* (*Classics of the Mountains and Rivers*), possibly the earliest travel book in the world (circa 500 BCE). In the Tibetan description of this unique race, their ears, besides performing their usual auditory function, served their owners in other useful ways. One ear could be used as a sleeping mat, the other as a blanket.

The titanic scale and destructiveness of the earthquake certainly had an apocalyptic feel to it, though, in Lhasa city itself there was little damage done, with only an old public toilet collapsing in the Barkhor Circle. The epicentre was in southern Tibet, on the outskirts of the village of Rima, where mountains and valleys were displaced. Large rivers had their courses changed. Many villages and monasteries disappeared altogether. The historian Shakabpa has recorded that "the earthquake struck the districts of Dhakpo/Kongpo, Powo, Ba, Lithang, Dzayül, Chatreng, Mili Gyalthang and so forth, killing many thousands of people and cattle."[5] The plant hunter Frank Kingdon-Ward was in the Rima area when the earthquake struck. In a *National Geographic Magazine* article, he wrote that the earthquake started exactly at 8 p.m. and also mentioned the succession of detonations, which he thought ". . . sounded like ack-ack shells bursting." The magnitude was 8.6 on the Richter scale. "No stronger earth shock has been recorded since the use of seismographs for measuring them became general about the turn of the century."[6]

Evil portents were seen everywhere. An old family retainer on a trip to Phari claimed to have encountered a long caravan of silent, spectral people and animals leaving the country. Such stories became common. In one account, a person even saw a recently deceased relative in one of these phantom caravans. People gradually began to interpret such ghostly phenomena as a sign that the gods of Tibet had lost the great battle, and that our entire multi-dimensional world of men, gods, animals, phantoms and wraiths was now at the mercy of the evil from China. Ghosts being the most pathetic creatures in the realm of existence, were, like rats from a sinking ship, deserting the country first.

Many people began to have strange dreams and unusual experiences, and fortune tellers and mediums were in great demand. Before a nation or a community undergoes a devastating catastrophe, they sometimes seem to receive a premonition of their common fate. This experience does not necessarily seem to be exclusive to primitive or ancient societies and individuals. A decade before Hitler came to power, Franz Kafka recorded a dream in which he and others were dragging and pushing a giant naked man into a red-hot oven with an ". . . extraordinarily large cast iron door . . . I awoke not only in cold sweat but with my teeth actually chattering." A follow-up entry from Kafka's diary: "a faint greyish-smoke was lightly and continuously wafted from the chimney."[7]

The "smokey long-tail star" (as Tibetans call a comet) of 1949, a year before the earthquake, was the first sign for Tibetans that their future was becoming uncertain. It made its appearance at the time we arrived in Tibet and could be seen around dawn in the direction of the Mindruzari Mountain south of Lhasa. Like ancient Romans, Tibetan's believed that the advent of a "long-haired star" (as Suetonius describes the comet that presaged the death of Emperor Claudius) augured a national calamity. The fact that the earlier Chinese invasion of 1910 had been immediately preceded by the appearance of Halley's Comet did not help matters. Besides, there were so many other omens—a glut of them, to drive home the point, as it were—that fear and uncertainty crept into the stoutest of hearts.

The well-known incident of a gargoyle on the roof of the Jokhang, the main temple in Lhasa, dripping water on a blazing hot day, also occurred around the time of the appearance of the comet. My uncle

Sonam Tomjor, the head of the Tethong family, was a member of the commission sent by the Kashag, or cabinet, to investigate this phenomenon.

Setting up ladders and scaffolding (used for the annual butter-sculpture displays), the commission checked the roof and the guttering around the particular gargoyle—more properly a *chusing* or *makara* (Sanskrit) a fabulous sea monster—and discovered everything to be bone dry. The head of the beast, fashioned of gilded copper, had not the least bit of condensation around it, and the drops of water appeared only at one point directly under the chin. The hollow inside of the head was also bone dry. The commission dried the head a number of times with towels, only to observe the phenomenon occurring again. They collected three full buckets of water before the monster finally let up. My uncle was convinced that there was no rational explanation for this *lusus naturae*.

Soon after fulfilling this official duty, my uncle, with his entire family, departed for India. My father also left with them. He had to travel to England that year to study for an engineering degree at Leeds. My mother stayed behind with her younger brother Rakra Rinpoche to wrap up the family business. The following year, a little more than a month after the great earthquake, my mother received telegrams from my father in England and my uncle in Kalimpong, urging her to leave Lhasa as quickly as possible. A year earlier, Communist China had begun to announce its mission to "liberate" Tibet from British and American imperialism. Then a Chinese radio broadcast in May 1950 made it clear that the Communists would use military force to achieve their goal. My mother, my uncle Rakra Rinpoche and I left Lhasa on 10 September 1950.

A month later, on 7 October, Communist China's Eighteenth Army crossed the Drichu, the Upper Yangtse River, and attacked Tibetan military headquarters at Chamdo and other defence outposts along the ceasefire line (*mentsam shagsa*)—negotiated on 15 June 1933, a month before my grandfather took over as governor-general of Eastern Tibet.

4

THE GHOSTS OF CHAMDO

The evening breeze at Chamdo, coming up the valley of the Dzachu or the upper Mekong River, carries with it a chill, an air of loneliness and melancholia. As the sun sets behind the bare and somewhat dreary-looking mountains, and the townspeople scurry home through the alleys and streets between rows of rammed earth and wood houses, the haunting sound of a woman singing in a sad beautiful voice could, it is said, be heard coming over from the "Yunnan" bridge on the West River.

One informant told me that it was always a *Pomé* song, the kind of high long-drawn song peculiar to the Powo region of southern Tibet. The townsfolk would look furtively over their shoulders as they hurried home, for it was common knowledge that at least one man had died after meeting the singer, his "life-force" sucked dry (*la-kampa*) or just scared to death as we might put it more prosaically. People would try and get indoors before the song concluded, for the peculiarly distressing quality of the tune came at the end when it would seem to slow down, like one of those old hand-cranked Victrolas winding down, and would finish with animal-like grunts, snorts and wheezing. One other account mentions that it ended with a long whistle.

Chamdo, the third-largest town in Tibet after Lhasa and Shigatsé, is located 10,640 feet above sea level on a triangular peninsula formed by the Ngomchu, the tributary on the west and the main Dzachu on the east, which joins to form the Mekong River to the south of the town.

> Chamdo was not made, Chamdo came into being
> At the confluence of two rivers.

> *Chamdo machag, Chamdo chag*
> *Chamdo chu nyi bar la chag*

Thus runs the description of this town in an old folk song, and also in the "Origin Chronicles of Tibet" (*bhod sipa chagpae chag-rap*) recited by the wandering "Drekar" vagabonds.

The Ngomchu is spanned by the "Yunnan" bridge near the confluence, while the Dzachu is spanned further up north by the "Sichuan" bridge. They had been so named, unofficially, since they connected Chamdo town to the trade routes that led (eventually) to these two major Chinese provinces. Both these massive wooden cantilever bridges are remarkable works of traditional Khampa engineering. Alan Winnington, the left-wing English journalist, and first foreign reporter allowed into Tibet after the Communist invasion, was clearly impressed by these structures. He writes, ". . . they are said to be the largest in the world built of timber on this principle".[1] General George Pereira, who in 1921 passed through Chamdo, offered this praise ". . . it is a wonderful engineering feat considering the fierce current which dashes against the piers".[2]

Dr André Migot, who travelled in these parts before the invasion, even derives a little observation of national character from these bridges: "It is instructive to compare these cantilever bridges—built entirely by hand without the help of a machine of any kind—with the modern bridges built in China by trained engineers, with modern machinery and an army of workmen to help them. Whereas the primitive Tibetan bridges stand up to every stress almost indefinitely, the Chinese bridge—as I learnt, all too often, at first hand—quickly collapse or are swept away. In the contrast between their bridges, one may, I think, discern the contrast between the characters of these two very different peoples."[3]

The two valleys are so narrow as to allow scarcely any cultivation. All around are brown, denuded mountains. Years of successive Chinese and Tibetan armies occupying or marching through this area had taken its toll on whatever forest cover it once might have had. To the north of the town rose the hill on which the monastery of Galden Jampa Ling ("Abode of Love") stood. It was the earliest and one of the most important Gelugpa institutions in Eastern Tibet, but according to a visitor ". . . certainly not the most beautiful: a brown and white red-fringed building, or rather collection of buildings, with a few gilded ornaments glinting on the roofs."[4] In 1912 it had been razed to the ground by the Chinese Republican General P'eng Jih-sheng, and what had been rebuilt after 1918 barely began to resemble the magnificent monastic complex it had been before when Chinese sources described it as "the finest in all Tibet."[5] What you had in 1950 was a significantly smaller and modest collection of buildings (destroyed again sixteen years later during the Cultural Revolution). The monastery formerly had three thousand monks attached to it, but there were only four hundred after its destruction.

Many of the houses in the town had also been damaged, some demolished in the siege of 1918. Most had been rebuilt, but you could still see ruins—blackened remains of a wall or the side of a collapsed roof—every so often between the rows of houses on either side of the dusty streets.

It was in this town, so the story goes, that a beautiful girl from a prominent Chamdo family was betrothed to the son of a wealthy merchant. She was a pathologically shy girl and, on her wedding day, refused the refreshments offered her and kept her head low and eyes averted. Late that evening, after everyone had gone to bed, she tiptoed to the kitchen for a drink of water. There, in the half-darkness she found what looked like a water barrel and gulped down a full ladle from it. Unfortunately, this barrel contained the blood of a pig slaughtered the day before. In her confusion, the girl knocked over a pile of dishes, waking up the household. Everyone hurried to the kitchen. Pine-flares were lit, revealing the unfortunate bride crouching by the corner of the hearth, her face covered with blood. The people around her stepped back in horror. The bride collapsed on the floor unconscious and died a few days later.

Forty-nine days after her death, when all the funeral prayers and rituals had been concluded, the first instance of the ghostly singing was heard in the town. Then one day, someone encountered a well-dressed young woman by the West Bridge. He tried to speak to her, but she turned her face away, covering it with her sleeve. He may have attempted a bit of banter with her, for she looked at him and lowered her hand. Where there should have been a pretty nose and mouth was instead the black hairy snout of a pig. So now the story of Chamdo *Phakjoma*, or the pig-spirit of Chamdo spread throughout Eastern Tibet and beyond.

A stock of stories grew up around her, and her singing cast a depressing pall over the town. Finally, when it seemed that the spirit was possessing actual people, even a monk from the monastery, the townspeople approached the lama, the Tenth Phagpala Rinpoche, the traditional ruler of the old principality of Chamdo, the emanation of Aryadeva, the chief disciple of the great second-century Indian philosopher Nagarjuna. Phagpala had been the most important lama in Chamdo, and one of the highest-ranking Gelugpa lamas in Eastern Tibet. He held the Mongol title of Hutoktu, which put him in the rank of those few lamas just below the Dalai and Panchen Lamas. After the destruction of Chamdo Monastery in 1912, Phagpala had been relieved of his title and office. This dismissal by the Chinese may have contributed to the next phase of his spiritual journey.

It is said that a vision or a mystical experience had made Phagpala Rinpoche adopt the life of a wandering Nyingma priest of the old school, specifically a *tertön* or "treasure seeker," a class of mystics who uncovered sacred texts hidden by Guru Rinpoche. Known as Tertön Phagchen Pema Lingpa, Phagpala wandered throughout Tibet, meditating at such sacred places as Mount Kailash and the holy mountain of Tsari. When he returned to Chamdo, he was not allowed to stay at his *labrang*, his residential palace (*Galden Thekchen Phodrang*) within the monastery walls, because he now lived with two women, or respectfully put, with two spiritual consorts (*sang-yum*), in the manner of Guru Rinpoche, the Indian tantric saint who introduced Buddhism to Tibet in the eighth century.

Phagpala and his consorts lived in a small house to the north of the town. In spite of his lifestyle, the old lama was much loved in Chamdo for his ministrations to the people. He was a humble man, and sometimes you could see him in the streets, following an old woman to her home, probably to perform the last rites for her dying husband, accompanied by a novice carrying his *damaru* drum, bell and other ritual objects.

It is said that Phagpala performed the pacification rituals successfully, laying to rest the troubled spirit of the young girl. The pig demon did not trouble the people of Chamdo anymore. But people being what they are, even in a devout Buddhist town, not everyone was satisfied, and there were those who insisted that they had heard singing in the evening, even after the pacification ritual. But as someone else pointed out, that could have been a real woman singing.

Phagpala Rinpoche's own story also has a conventional happy ending. The governor-general of Eastern Tibet (my grandfather Gyurme Gyatso Tethong at the time), much impressed with the saintliness of the old lama, petitioned the Dalai Lama that Phagpala's titles and privileges be restored to him. The Thirteenth Dalai Lama was known to be very strict on matters of monastic discipline, and on Gelugpa monks and lamas upholding the *vinaya* (Sanskrit) that Tibetans call the *dulwa,* or the rules of conduct that Buddha had laid down for monks. It is possible that the governor-general's petition was persuasive. His Holiness had also received a collection of prophetic verses composed by Phagpala, which may have convinced him of the old lama's authenticity as a mystic.

The whole of Chamdo joined in the joyful re-enthronement ceremony of Phagpala at the monastery.

It is also possible that there was some political consideration in the Dalai Lama's decision since Phagpala was very popular with the people of Chamdo, and it was important that the populace of this most important town, vital commercial crossroad, and headquarters of the civil and military administration of Eastern Tibet be happy under, or at least reconciled to, Lhasa rule.

Political considerations of a similar kind had certainly played an essential part in the decision of the Tibetan government in 1950 to make Chamdo the heart of its defence against the coming Communist invasion, even though the town, because of its exposed situation, could not be effectively defended. This was clearly demonstrated in 1918, when the roles had been reversed, and the Chinese had tried to hold Chamdo. The Tibetans had effectively winkled them out, sniping at them from the surrounding mountainsides, and blasting them with a couple of captured cannons from the high grounds behind the monastery.

But in 1950, the decision was made to fight at Chamdo. Communist China invaded. The Tibetan army was routed—or so standard accounts go. Every other event in Tibet's recent history followed in "inevitable" succession: the signing of the Seventeen Point Treaty, the Occupation Years, the Khampa Uprising, the Dalai Lama's Flight, the Lhasa Uprising, Escape and Exile, the Great Famine and the Cultural Revolution. It all began with the fall of Chamdo.

Over the years, one of the enduring pastimes in Dharamshala and other exile centres: around restaurant tables, in dorm-rooms filled with cigarette smoke, across office desks, in chang taverns and at the Hotel Tibet bar—has been speculating, or more often arguing, about why we were defeated at Chamdo. Could better leadership have made a difference at Chamdo? What might have happened had the army been reformed in time? What if the Kashag had sent a proven military leader like Tsarong to Chamdo? What if the UN had intervened before Chamdo fell? What if we had more machine guns? What if we had resorted to guerrilla warfare at Chamdo? Well, what about it? And so on. Chamdo, as a topic of conversation, was flogged to death.

"What if" speculations on events in history have generally been dismissed as frivolous by older established historians. E.H. Carr, the left-leaning Cambridge historian, dismissed "counterfactual" or "virtual" history as a mere "parlour game", a "red herring". But in recent years, this parlour game has become something of a new discipline with the fascinating yet rigorous writings of scholars such as Robert Fogel, Geoffrey Hawthorn and in particular, Niall Ferguson.

One reason for the development of this aspect of historical inquiry appears to be the growing awareness among historians of how anti-deterministic and non-linear a great many recent developments and discoveries in science have been. When quantum physics and chaos theory have introduced an unavoidable element of unpredictability or randomness in science at the most fundamental level, and when the possibilities of multiple dimensions and universes are integral in any discussion on String Theory, it does appear wilfully obtuse for a historian to insist that the Russian Revolution happened because it had to happen, and discussing alternate possibilities is an exercise in fantasy.

The mere fact that there is considerable entertainment value in exploring the might-have-beens of history, of which we were gratefully aware of in Dharamshala, should in no way detract from the higher functions of counterfactual history. Its proponents claim that it can lead us to question long-held assumptions, define true turning points and show that tiny occurrences may have major repercussions. One historian claims that counterfactual studies also help historians eliminate what he called "hindsight bias". After an event has taken place, people readjust their estimates of the probability of that happening. That makes history appear more pre-ordained than it really is. The economic historian, Niall Ferguson, argues that the real purpose of counterfactual history is "to recapture the chaotic nature of experience and see that there are no certain outcomes." This approach Ferguson says, ". . . is anti-determinist and anti-Marxist."[6]

In any case, one atypical Marxist, my late friend K. Dhondup, a historian and a founder of the Tibetan Communist party-in-exile, could not resist positing and publishing his own "what if" speculations on Chamdo. In an article in the *Tibetan Review* in 1980, he wrote: "Like all 'ifs' in history, 'if an organized Tibetan Communist Party had been active as late as 1940 . . . subsequent Tibetan situation and history would have been far different from what it is now. Above all, Maoist China would not have had a classic excuse to attack Chamdo and 'liberate' Tibet and subject it to one of the worst forms of Asian colonialism in Communist mask in our time."[7]

But Dhondup-la died much too young before he could fully develop his theory and include it in the final volume of his three-part history of Tibet, only two of which have been published. In the main though, the Tibetan defeat at Chamdo has for long been viewed through the distorting lens of "historical inevitability", not only by academics and intellectuals with a left bias but even by some Tibetan intellectuals from Indian universities, where in the late sixties and seventies the political fashion was dominantly radical left.

This "historical inevitability" about the fall of Chamdo does not appear to come from only a Marxist doctrinal viewpoint, but also from a more traditionally passive, even fatalistic, mindset as well, since the Tibetan official line has been that there was nothing we could have done to save the situation. The Dalai Lama himself, with his oft declared belief in a synthesis of Marxism and Buddhism, probably goes along with this view.

Then there is the general non-ideological view of most outside observers that the whole thing was hopeless to start with; that Tibet's army, variously described as a "musical comedy" army, a "comic opera" army, an "*opéra bouffe*" army, a "Gilbert and Sullivan" army, or a "Drury Lane" army, did not have a chance against the Chinese. This view is virtually caricatured in the Hollywood film, *Seven Years in Tibet*, where Tibetan soldiers dressed in a variety of ragged robes and cast-off British uniforms, topped with the occasional "Dad's Army" style tin helmet, are shown using bows and arrows against the Communist Chinese invasion force. This scene was probably not meant to be deliberately insulting; after all, the production had the blessing and cooperation of the Dalai Lama and the exile government, but it was perhaps included to underscore the pacifistic nature of the Tibetan people.

With such powerful biases and misconceptions colouring this important segment of Tibetan history, it might be useful to attempt a reassessment of what actually happened at Chamdo and see if the course of events there could possibly have taken another direction. There is more information on the subject now than there was before.

Many who wrote a book or two on the Tibetan tragedy, Lowell Thomas Jr, George Patterson, Noel Barber, Dawa Norbu, Isabelle Van Geem, Michel Piessel, John Avedon, Mary Craig and others, have discussed the fall of Chamdo, sometimes unearthing some fresh bits of information.

Those scholars attempting major histories of modern Tibet as Tsepon Shakabpa, Hugh Richardson, Melvyn Goldstein, Warren Smith, Tsering Shakya and Sam Van Schaik, have provided fairly detailed accounts of the invasion, though Goldstein has come up with a more comprehensive narrative than most. The only military historian who has written on the Chinese invasion of Tibet is Edgar O'Ballance, who provides a very different but interesting and valuable perspective. Then, of course, there are the Tibetan eyewitnesses and informants inside Tibet, including such key players as the two successive governors-general at Chamdo, Lhalu and Ngabö, who have had their accounts published in the official *Sources on Culture and History of Tibet* (in twenty-five volumes) that also includes a few Chinese eyewitnesses to the events.

I interviewed many Tibetan military and civil officers who served at Chamdo and other military and resistance personnel, who were peripherally involved. A Lhasa official, Maja Tsewang Gyurme,[8] who was on the staff of both governors-general, as quartermaster, but who, at the time, was also entrusted with several special missions, spoke to me at length, as did Major Sonam Tashi of the Guards regiment who served at Chamdo and wrote his own account in exile.[9] A two-volume *Military History of Tibet* (*Military History* from here on) was published in Dharamshala in 2003.[10] The writer, Namgyal Wangdu, had been a corporal in the Fourth (Gyantsé) regiment at the time of the invasion. Later in exile, he became first a *dapön* and then "Political Leader" of India's Special Frontier Force. Volume two of the *Military History* has extensive first-hand eyewitness accounts of the Chamdo fighting and also of the Lhasa Uprising of 1959. I interviewed Namgyal Wangdu at length in 2016, shortly before his death. I have also come across several minor Tibetan accounts dealing with the invasion and a remarkable one by a European missionary eyewitness that has not been cited in any published account to date.

There must, of course, be many shelves of official Chinese Communists documents on the subject, but only a select few are available. A useful resource in this respect is the website "War on Tibet" created by a Chinese academic Jianglin Li and an English scholar Matthew Akester that provides a limited selection of Chinese documents on the history of the Communist occupation of Tibet (in English translation) and the Battle of Chamdo.[11]

Official Chinese documents provide some information on troop disposition, planning and the like but deliberately downplay, sometimes completely pass over the actual fighting and casualties that resulted from the invasion; most probably to uphold the fundamental official line about "The Peaceful Liberation" of Tibet. Generally, even those Western academics and journalists supportive of China's invasion of Tibet, find it difficult to go along entirely with the pretence that the invasion was a peaceful one. Instead, they try to insinuate that there were very few casualties as the Chinese grand strategy was brilliantly conceived and executed, causing Tibetans to panic and flee. Mao's military genius is invariably brought up.

So far, the most incisive formal study I have come across on the subject has been "October 1950: the Battle of Chamdo" presented by French scholar Alex Raymond at an International Association of Tibet Studies conference in 2019. This paper was developed from his PhD dissertation that is possibly the most detailed study of the Chinese invasion of Tibet we have to date.[12]

Raymond dismisses traditional histories of the Chamdo invasion that have ". . . systematically presented this battle as a quick and easy campaign." He cites recent Chinese documents revealing that the progress of the PLA was extremely difficult due to reasons of terrain, altitude, cold, hunger, exhaustion, disease, desertion, local hostility and also the resistance of the Tibetan army. Raymond maintains that " . . . there were many victims on both sides. The final (but, in fact, not complete) victory of the PLA was obtained *in extremis*, and the Eighteenth Army's top staff and PRC leaders had real doubts about the outcome until the end."

The most accessible eyewitness account of the invasion is by Robert Ford, the young British radio operator, who the Tibetan government had employed in 1948 to man the few radio sets it had in Eastern Tibet and train native radio operators. He was attached to the staff of the governor-general of Eastern Tibet at Chamdo and essentially witnessed and experienced everything that happened there. He was captured along with his Tibetan co-officials, and then imprisoned in China. His book, *Captured in Tibet*, is an honest, straightforward account of his years in Tibet and China and is unexpectedly moving because of his genuine fondness for Tibet and its people, but also because he was not just an observer, but someone who made the decision to stand by his colleagues and friends in their fight to defend their country.

> I stayed because it would have been cowardly to run away; because
> I thought the Tibetans needed help and were worth helping . . ..
> I stayed because I liked Tibet and because I enjoyed life in Tibet
> and wanted it to go on. I did not stay because I was unaware of
> the risks.[13]

But Ford is honest in his description of the drawbacks of Tibetan society and is justifiably critical of the Tibetan government's weaknesses and failings. He is especially bitter about Lhasa not letting the world know that the army in Chamdo ". . . had put up a genuine fight against the Chinese." Yet he is proud of having been "the first European to receive the Dalai Lama's blessing as a Tibetan government official" and, from what I understand, has kept his appointment letter and talisman cord given to him by the Dalai Lama.

So, there is, on the whole, enough diverse sources of information to put together a reasonably full, if not a complete picture, of the events of October 1950. Interpretation has been the problem all along, especially when, before even starting on the process, certain overriding assumptions have tended to paralyse any kind of meaningful investigation or analysis—assumptions not just about the invincible nature of the Red Army, but about the hopelessness of the Tibetan army and the Tibetan cause.

One assumption can be dispelled right away—that the Tibetans did not have a strategy other than putting up a static defence of

Chamdo. The Tibetan high command in Lhasa was well aware of the inherent problems of defending the entire length of the Sino–Tibetan frontier, almost as long as the Western Front in World War One. In 1936, Brigadier Philip Neame, V.C., D.S.O., who visited Lhasa with the British Mission under Basil Gould, specifically to provide military advice to the Tibetans, had cautioned the Tibetans against stringing the few troops they had in penny-packets along the frontier with China. "From consideration of sound strategy, it is unwise to have all the available troops extended along a wide stretch of the frontier with no reserves behind to reinforce any threatened point."[14] He counselled that only small outposts be maintained at crucial points along the frontier and that a large reserve force be maintained well back west of the frontier that could be deployed with more effect when the intentions of a Chinese advance could be ascertained.

Neame's report and advice were presented to the Tibetan cabinet on 13 September 1936, in a three-hour long meeting. Tethong Gyurme Gyatso was one of the four ministers in that cabinet and the only one with military experience. According to his son (my uncle) Sonam Tomjor, Gyurme Gyatso was impressed with Neame's military acumen and considered his advice as valuable.

The governor-general of Eastern Tibet in 1949 Lhalu Tsewang Dorje, was aware of the problem of defending Chamdo[*] but, as he explained to Robert Ford, the political considerations could not be entirely ignored. "We cannot leave Chamdo yet," said Lhalu. "If we did, we should lose the support of all the Khampas, in both Tibet and Sikang (Chinese occupied Kham). We should be leaving their largest monastery to the mercy of the godless Chinese, and they would feel they had been betrayed. You must remember," Lhalu went on, "that until the Chinese captured it forty years ago, Chamdo was the capital of a semi-independent state. Lhasa troops helped to drive the Chinese out ten years later, and the people wanted us to stay to protect them

---

[*]Lhalu, though not intending a full-scale defence of Chamdo had set up fortified positions on the crucial high points surrounding the town as a precaution against any surprise Chinese attack.

from the Chinese. That's all we have to offer them in return for the taxes they pay. If we run away without a fight, they will never want us back."

"The plan, therefore," Ford tells us, " . . . was to hold Chamdo until the track to Lhasa was almost within reach of the Chinese. Then we would evacuate and, if necessary, fight our way out. As the first Chinese troops to reach the road would probably be only an advance party, it should thus be possible to escape military defeat without the sacrifice of political expedience. It was risky, but it could be done. Its success depended primarily on keeping the track open as long as possible and on obtaining quick and accurate information about the movement of the Chinese."

The overall strategy of the Tibetan army in Eastern Tibet appears to have been to maintain only small outposts along the actual frontier line, essentially to monitor Chinese military activities. The main regiments would be headquartered about a day's march to the rear. In the instance of a Chinese attack, the outposts would, in theory, immediately pull back to their main regimental unit, which would then conduct a fighting retreat, back towards Chamdo and then to Lho Dzong*, or wherever convenient, directly to Lho Dzong. The Tibetan historian Shakabpa also noted ". . . he (the governor-general) and his staff planned to go to Lho Dzong."[15] Of course, not everyone was privy to the plan, but it appears that the commanders in the field were. The subsequent operations of the Tibetan regiments once under attack, reveals this underlying strategy, whether the operations themselves were conducted successfully or not.

The choice of Lho Dzong as an operational base was in keeping with the first of ten suggestions made by Brigadier Neame. "The Tibetan government collect a body of troops at some central place where they would be available to reinforce any part of the frontier that was threatened." Ford tells us ". . . the obvious place for Eastern HQ was Lho Dzong, several day's march to the west, which guarded the

---

* *Dzong:* A castle or fort; the headquarters of a Tibetan district. In it resides the *Dzong-pon*, the district magistrate or administrator, with his staff.

only bridge* across the wide, swift-flowing river Salween. It could not be outflanked, and from Lho Dzong to Lhasa, the country was wild and rugged, with an average elevation of 12,000 feet and passes of up to 17,100 feet, snow-bound for most of the year."

The assessment of Lho Dzong being eminently defendable was confirmed to me by the official Maja, who had been posted there in 1946. Maja further mentioned that Lho Dzong had large stores of food, arms, ammunition and a permanent garrison of four to five hundred soldiers. The old Lho Dzong castle was located high on a steep mountainside, beside the Hok Shidram Gön Monastery, and gave every appearance of being unassailable. The only way to take it would have been to level the structure with heavy artillery. A former governor-general, Jampa Tendar, had, in 1916, built a new fort, the massive Khar Gungthang, on an adjacent mountainside.

When Lhalu's three-year term as governor-general ended in the summer of 1950 and was succeeded by Ngabö, Lhalu did not return to Lhasa as was customary but following orders ".. set up headquarters at Lho Dzong".[16] To shore up this vital defence position, fresh troops were sent from Lhasa.

The largest unit in the Tibetan army was the regiment or *magar*, commanded by a dapön or general. The regiment was sometimes split into two battalions of five hundred men, each commanded by a dapön. Tibetan regiments were named in various ways, most commonly by their regional origins, Shigatsé, Gyantsé, Dingri, etc. or by their duties: as in the Guards regiment (*kusung magar*), the police regiment (*polisi magar*), or sometimes by their regimental home-base, the Drapchi regiment being based near the village of Drapchi just north of Lhasa. A more systematic way of identifying regiments was introduced around 1914 using the letters of the Tibetan alphabet, *ka, kha, gha, nga* . . . and so on. Since many of these letters are often tonally difficult for a non-Tibetan to distinguish, there has been some confusion in accounts

---

*Shabyé Zampa was the only bridge on the upper Salween (*Gyalmo ngülchu* or "the queen's silver river") for hundreds of miles, upstream or downstream. Incidentally, the Chinese call the river Nu Jiang or "angry river".

where this system has been used. I have numbered the regiments according to the numerical succession of letters in the alphabet. For instance, *ka* being first, *kha* second and so on.

The disposition of Tibetan forces in Eastern Tibet was as follows: the central zone of the Tibetan frontier defence at Dergé Jomda, with outposts at Rangsum and Kamdo Drukha, the crucial ferry point on the Drichu river, was held by five hundred soldiers of the Third (Shigatsé) Regiment commanded by General Karchung Tsering Thundup and supported by two or three hundred Khampa militiamen. The second battalion of five hundred men of the Third Regiment under general Muja Tsewang Norbu, was posted at Khyungpo Tengchen near the frontier with Amdo (referred to as Qinghai or Xining in other accounts). Four hundred troops of the Seventh (Jhadang) Regiment under general Phulungwa Drakpa Tseten was garrisoned at Riwoché, the village north of the road between Chamdo and Lho Dzong. This force was entrusted with the task of holding back any Chinese attack from the north that could cut off the line of retreat of the main force from Chamdo to Lho Dzong. A batallion of the Seventh (Jhadang) Regiment, under general Shakjang Zurpa, were garrisoned at Lho Dzong.

Five hundred soldiers of the Fourth (Gyantsé) Regiment under Tsögo Ngodup Dorje were stationed at Khyungpo Tengchen, with Muja's regiment. One company from the Fourth, around a hundred soldiers, probably mortar and artillerymen, were stationed at Chamdo. This unit was commanded by Captain (*gyapön*) Dongra. Two hundred troops of the Eighth (Nyadang) Regiment constituted the Chamdo garrison under General Dimon. Ford thought that "He might not be an efficient officer, but there was no doubting his courage."

The Second (Drapchi) Regiment had one company of a hundred men serving as the Governor-general Lhalu's escort at Chamdo. Another company of the Second regiment, under Captain Kalsang Damdul (aka Kaldam) was serving as the escort to the Governor of Northern Tibet (*jangchi*) at Nagchukha. The Fifth (Dingri) Regiment also garrisoned at Nagchukha, had five hundred troops under general Ragashar Sonam Topgyal, son of the commander-in-chief, Ragashar Phuntsok Rabgyal. This was to check any Chinese invasion attempt coming due south from Amdo. As the area north of Nagchukha was largely unpopulated, troops of the Chinese Muslim warlord of Xining, Ma Bufang had, in 1942, invaded the Nangchen/Jyekundo area and advanced as far as Nagchukha without Lhasa receiving any news of their presence.

The Ninth (Tadang) Regiment had five hundred soldiers under Dergé-sey, the governor of Markham. They were the only regular Tibetan army unit in charge of the defence of this southern sector of Eastern Tibet, and were opposed by, at least, one division of the Chinese army. All in all, it appears that the Tibetans had 3,500 regular troops on the frontline in Eastern Tibet with a reserve of about 6,500 or 7,000 troops further west and around Lhasa. The Tibetan government was also hurriedly raising new units.

Most accounts of the defence of Chamdo mention that local levies were raised or that Khampas were conscripted, leaving one with the impression of a hurried eleventh-hour operation. Actually, a proper militia system (*yulmak*) had been instituted in the various districts of Kham decades earlier and were suitably organized and led. The two most important militia organizations were the Sho-ta-lho-sum *ghodom*, or the muster of the districts of Shopado, Pembar and Lhorong, and the Mar-dra-gon-sum ghodom, or the muster of Markham, Drayab and Gonjo districts. Each of these militias ostensibly had around a thousand militiamen in their roster or *mak-shung*. Some larger districts such as Markham had raised five hundred men and preparing to raise five hundred more. Following the 1932 defeat in Eastern Tibet and the loss of lower Dergé, another militia unit, the Po-mak militia had been created. Its recruits came from the three districts of the southern region of Powo.

Most of these militia units were commanded by Lhasa officials, local leaders filling all secondary positions. In the war of 1918, the Sho-ta-lho-sum militia distinguished itself under the command of a Khampa monk official, Khenchung Dawa-la of Chamdo, who was later awarded the title of Khenchen or "Great Abbot". The militiamen were provided training by regular instructors from the Tibetan army, and though they did not wear uniforms, the units did have their own distinct battle standards, buglers and the like. More significantly, by 1950, all militiamen were armed with British Lee Enfield rifles, the same standard weapon of the regular troops, and had been trained to use them.

Robert Ford arrived at Chamdo in October 1949 with radio sets and generators, and hundreds of gallons of petrol. He brought, with him, four trainee operators, ethnic Tibetan youths who had Indian high school education: Sonam Phuntsok from Gangtok, Dronyer from Kalimpong and Sonam Dorje and Wangda from Darjeeling. Ford had, in total, just three radio sets, one old large one and two portable sets he had purchased at Calcutta. Ford also had two Tibetan language clerks, Lobsang and Tashi, who had earlier been given some basic training as radio operators by Reginald Fox, the principal radio operator in Lhasa.

Lhalu was desperate for more arms, particularly machine guns, and had repeatedly sent urgent messages to Lhasa requesting more weapons. The entire Tibetan defence force in Kham had just four antiquated Lewis guns (light machine guns of World War I vintage) and three old mountain guns with so few shells that they were only fired for practice once a year. As I was writing this, some lines from a Noël Coward song, "The Home Guard's Lament" came to mind:

Could you please oblige us with a Bren gun?
Or failing that a hand grenade would do,
We've got some ammunition
In a rather damp condition . . .

Eventually, in March 1950, a consignment of Bren light machine guns, and Sten guns arrived at Chamdo. Accompanying the arms was a unit of instructors under the command of Major (*rupön*) Sonam Tashi, of the First regiment, the Dalai Lama's bodyguards. More artillery in the form of 2.75 "pack" howitzers and shells were also prepared for transport to Chamdo. A company of artillerymen from the Sixth (later the police) regiment, commanded by Major (rupön) Rinzin Paljor accompanied this shipment, but only made contact with the main Chamdo force when it was retreating.

With the civil war coming to a close in China by the end of 1949 and early 1950, Communist troops had begun moving into Amdo (Qinghai), East Turkestan (Xinjiang), Yunnan province in the south, and the eastern part of Kham, out of which the Chinese had created Xikang province.

According to an official Communist Party document: "On January 10, 1950, Mao Zedong approved the Eighteenth Army led by Zhang Guohua to shoulder the task of advancing into Tibet. A Communist Party Tibet Work Committee was formed. It was composed of seven members, including Zhang Guohua (army commander), Tan Guansan (political commissar), Wang Qimei (deputy political commissar), Chang Binggui (deputy army commander), Chen Mingyi (chief of staff) Liu Zhenguo (director of the political department), and Tian Bao (an ethnic Tibetan and representative of the local people's political consultative conference). Zhang Guohua served as the Party secretary and Tan Guansan, deputy Party secretary."[17]

A recent biography of Mao Zedong mentions that "When Mao met Stalin on January 22, 1950, he asked if the Soviet air force could transport supplies to Chinese troops 'currently preparing for an attack on Tibet.' Stalin's reply was: 'It is good that you are preparing for an attack on Tibet. The Tibetans need to be subdued.'" Stalin also advised flooding Tibet and other border regions with Han Chinese. 'In fact, all the border regions should be populated by Chinese.'"[18]

According to General Zhang Guohua the plan for the invasion was drawn up by three top Communist officials in the south-west military region: Liu Bocheng, Deng Xiaoping and He Long, who "personally planned and made preparations for the expedition" into Tibet.[19]

Interestingly enough, Edgar O'Ballance, the military historian, notes that "the Reds planned that their invasion and the military occupation should take place in the summer of 1950, but although the troops set off in the early spring, they were held up owing to the extremely difficult terrains, which they had underestimated, and were not able to work to their proposed timetable. In the western parts of the provinces of Xikang and Sichuan they had to construct roads through the mountains and build bridges over the many ravines."[20]

The Eighteenth Army was part of the Second Field Army, of the five enormous field armies of China. O'Ballance tells us that the Chinese "armies" were really what might in Western military terms be called "corps," but we will go with the Chinese designation. Each army consisted of three divisions, each division of about 13,000 to 15,000 men.

The composition and disposition the 18th Army's Tibet Invasion Force was as follows: the Fifty-fourth Division was tasked with taking the central zone across Dergé starting at the ferry crossing of Kamdo Druga. The 154th regiment of the Fifty-Second Division was assigned with attacking the Tibetan force at Denkhok to the north, while the 155th and 156th regiments from this same division, was tasked with capturing Riwoche from Jyekundo. The 157th regiment of the Fifty-Third Division was given the mission of attacking Markham in the southern zone. In addition, the 125th and 126th regiments of the Forty-Second Division from Yunnan, was tasked with capturing Tsakhalo in the southern tip of Markham.

On 23 March 1950, the Red Army moved into Dartsedo on the ethnic frontier with Tibet. In the middle of April an advance unit of the Eighteenth Army entered Kham from Dartsedo, reaching Kandzé on the 28th.[21] One regiment of the Eighteenth Army, about 5,000 troops marched through Lithang around the end of May 1950, on their way to Bathang and the Markham front.

South-west Military Command managed to get advance units in place on the frontier by May. Although patrols crossed the Drichu River in late May at a number of points in the central zone and also far south in Markham, they were apparently intent only on testing Tibetan defences or attempting some limited reconnaissance missions. Soon the logistical situation for the Chinese invasion force began to improve. Sonam Wangdu Chugatsang of Kandzé remembers as a child, Russian transport planes (possibly those promised by Stalin) dropping supplies in the area, many of which were smashed when their parachutes did not open. Ford mentions that parachutes were not used and that bags of rice were sewn in tough yak-hide and dropped by Russian transport planes flying low.

In Dartsedo, the PLA soon began a build-up of troops and supplies, including bridge-building equipment and girders. A motorable road was completed from Dartsedo to Kandzé in August 1950. Red army units that had entered Qinghai, now established a base at the Tibetan trade centre of Jyekundo (Chinese, *Yushu*) on the border of territory administered by the Tibetan government and began constructing a road to the south towards Chamdo. They also integrated the Hui Muslim cavalry of the Warlord Ma Bufang into their units.

It was to monitor Chinese troop movements at Jyekundo, that, a month or so after his arrival at Chamdo, Ford was instructed to set up a radio outpost at Denkhok which was a vital point on the frontier. This settlement was about the closest the Tibetan Army could position itself on the northern frontier to effectively monitor Chinese troops movements and activities in Jyekundo. It was vital that Tibetans kept an eye on this sector since a Chinese attack from Jyekundo could cut off the retreat of Tibetan troops falling back from the Lhochu River to Chamdo, or worse still, drive further south-west and cut the Chamdo–Lhasa road.

As soon as the Denkhok radio outpost began operating, Chamdo headquarters began to get hard news of Chinese activities on the frontier, which was relayed to Lhasa. But as radio traffic from Denkhok increased, the Chinese became aware of this vital Tibetan observation post. One day in July, Ford in Chamdo received this urgent message from Denkhok, from the youngest of his operators, his star pupil, Sonam Phuntsok. "He began to tap it out, but he did not finish. Suddenly he broke off and telegraphed in clear: 'The Chinese are here.' Then there was silence." Denkhok radio had closed down for good.

Lhalu immediately sent scouts from the Chamdo garrison with orders to ride hard, night and day to Denkhok to check out the situation there. He also sent a mounted courier for General Muja Tsewang Norbu who commanded five hundred men of the Third regiment at Khyungpo Tengchen, on the frontier of Amdo. Muja was a tough professional soldier. He was about forty-five at the time, and "energetic, confident, although very much alive to the dangers of the situation." His second-in-command Major (*rupön*) Bögangwa was a well-known veteran fighter, who had distinguished himself in the war of 1918.

Muja came to Chamdo with his men and picked up two hundred militiamen from the Sho-ta-lho-sum muster, commanded by Tsedrung Ludrup Namgyal, a monk official, and rapidly departed for Denkhok. My mother, who had been in that area once, described to me the landscape leading from Chamdo to Denkhok ". . . high mountains, dark forests, plunging gorges and swift rivers—many rivers." The valley widens near the Gelukpa monastery of Chökhor Gön, (where my paternal forbears had come from) and the adjoining village, on the West bank of the Lhochu River. On the east bank is the celebrated Langthang Dolma Lhakang, the Temple of Tara, which had been built by the Emperor Songtsen Gampo in the seventh century, as one of the twelve major geomantic temples located throughout Tibet to subdue the negative forces destabilizing the Tibetan land, usually represented as a supine demoness (*srinmu*).

Before arriving at Denkhok, Muja was met by the Derma Zöbpa, the excise officer of the district. He informed Muja that the Chinese attacking force had not yet retreated across the river but advised vigilance as the local people had observed movement and strange lights in the surrounding forests during the previous nights. The Tibetans advanced cautiously but came under fierce attack just before the river. The Chinese also opened up with mortars. One account mentions a mortar shell exploding against a rock face and the flying fragments of stone and shrapnel fatally wounded Major Bögangwa. The Tibetan force set up their one light mortar, manned by Captain Dongra, and commenced firing. General Muja then mounted a vigorous counteroffensive and overran the Chinese positions. Many of the fleeing Chinese soldiers drowned in the river while attempting to escape.[*]

---

[*] The French scholar Alex Raymond noted that this battle had ". . . a significant impact on Chinese leaders. On August 18, Mao sent a telegram to the South West Bureau, expressing his fears about the attack, suggesting an increase in the number of soldiers because 'the Tibetan army seems to have significant combat capacity, you must prepare for difficult battles, it is a point that you did not estimate sufficiently well.'"

Although the Chinese force was wiped out that day, Tibetan losses were considerable. Besides Major Bögangwa himself, his son, a sergeant, was also killed, as was Captain Dongra, the mortar man. The militiamen, who had fought fiercely, also took some casualties. One of the best-known Khampa warriors, Margo Phuyul (from the village of Phuyul in Tar Dzong) was killed that day. Like Bögangwa, Margo was a veteran of the 1918 war. Although the Tibetans managed to push the Chinese out of Denkhok, it was an expensive victory. Not only in terms of good men lost, but also as one of the irreplaceable radio sets and two operators, Sonam Phuntsok and Sonam Dorje, were now in Chinese hands. Muja and his men were ordered to remain at Denkhok.

Lhalu had earlier sent letters and messengers to high lamas and local leaders at Jyekundo, and other important centres in Amdo, alerting them to the Communist threat, and warning them not to be taken in by the blandishments of Communist officials and representatives. Where it was possible, he also urged them to resist the Chinese advance. The Dalai Lama's older brother Taktser Rinpoche, then Abbot of Kumbum Monastery, recalled receiving such a letter from the governor-general. It seems that Lhalu had also corresponded with some other Khampa chieftains and leaders. Maja remembers that when he was in charge of the *Po-mak* militia and posted near Trengo-la just south of Nangchen, Lhalu instructed him to forward messages to the King of Nangchen, one of the six kingdoms of Kham, but then under Chinese rule from Xining. Lhalu also appears to have contacted the abbot of the Dargye-gön Monastery in Kandzé, Tsedrung Thutop and other loyal chieftains, and the Queen of Dergé* (Jamyang Palmo) who proposed a joint action with Tibetan government forces to attack the Communist units entering Eastern Tibet.[22] But Lhasa immediately put a stop to this plan, considering it highly provocative.

Then in September 1950 Lhalu was replaced by Ngabö Ngawang Jigme. Lhalu had served his three-year term in Chamdo but remained to

---

*Her husband, the king Tsewang Dundul, enthroned as a child in 1926, had died in 1942. At the time of the invasion, the queen was acting as regent for her ten-year-old son.

assist the new governor-general. Some considered the new appointment ill omened, as an earlier governor-general from the Ngabö family had been defeated in 1932 at Kham. But others thought well of Ngawang Jigme. He had had served as a major (rupön) in the crack Drongdrak Regiment and had done his tour of duty in Eastern Tibet from 1936 to 1940 in the Chamdo administration. He also had a reputation as an intelligent and able administrator, but, as subsequent events were to prove, his virtues did not—despite his military resumé—extend to effective generalship. Initially Lhalu stayed at Chamdo to advise the new governor-general but was then ordered by the Kashag to ". . . set up headquarters at Lho Dzong."[23] Army HQ assured Lhalu that the Drongdrak Regiment had been sent from Lhasa to shore up the defence of this fortress.

Ngabö had brought the two radio sets from Lhasa that Lhalu and Ford had earlier urgently requested. But instead of allocating these two sets to advance forces defending vital points on the frontier, Ngabö decided to keep one radio set as a spare at Chamdo but allowed Lhalu to take the other to Lho Dzong. Ford urged Ngabö to send a radio set to Riwoché, so that advance information on a Chinese attack from the north—to cut off the route from Chamdo to Lho Dzong—could be received early enough. But Ngabö considered his own communication line with Lhasa so vital that it required a back-up radio unit.

A day or two before Ngabö's arrival, Rabga Pangdatsang,* by a curious coincidence, also arrived at Chamdo ". . . to deliver a proposal from the Communist Chinese for the peaceful liberation of Tibet."[24] Lhalu, in an interview with Goldstein, denied discussing any proposal with Rabga, but Ngabö appears not only to have done so but even made the decision to open communications with the Chinese. He sent Rabga and one of his officials Yeshi Thargye to Dhartsedo but the two only arrived there after the invasion started.

Perhaps to demonstrate his desire for peaceful communications with the Chinese, Ngabö ordered the dismantling of the fortified

----

*Rapga had been deported from Kalimpong in 1946 for his clandestine pro-Chinese activities.

positions on the crucial high points surrounding Chamdo that Lhalu had earlier ordered built.

In late September, it began to get colder and there was hope that an early winter would set in. The first few days of October were bitterly cold at night, below freezing, and the first snows had started to fall on the higher passes. Even some of the more cautious Tibetans were now allowing themselves to say that the Chinese could not attack before spring next year. "No," Ford agreed confidently with them. "It's too late for the Chinese to attack now."

The Chinese invasion came at dawn on Saturday, 7 October.[*] An overwhelming force, around ten thousand soldiers, (of the Fifty-fourth Division) crossed the Drichu River at the ferry crossing of Kamdo Drukha, on coracles, boats, and makeshift rafts. Chinese mortar and artillery fire rained down on the west bank of the river where the Tibetan defenders waited behind stone and driftwood *dzingra* or breastworks. This advance Tibetan unit was a mixed force of about 150 regulars from General Karchung's Third regiment, supported by fifty or more Khampa militia.

The Chinese enveloped the position, flanking it from both sides. The two hundred Tibetan defenders fought fiercely and ". . . initially inflicted heavy losses on the Chinese" (Goldstein). But eventually the Chinese closed in, and it became a desperate and vicious struggle at close quarters—with rifle butts, bayonets, swords and daggers. Most of the Tibetans died at their post[†] according to a survivor, a Khampa

---

[*] Despite the problematic early winter, China may have been compelled to invade Tibet because of American intervention in the Korean War, according to historian Warren Smith. By 1 October 1950, UN troops had crossed the 38 parallel into North Korea making armed conflict with Communist China almost inevitable. The Chinese may have feared that if Tibet's occupation was not a fait accompli before China's direct participation in the Korean War (October 25), America could then possibly become involved on Tibet's side.

[†] The *Military History* has a somewhat different take on this battle: ". . . many Chinese boats were sunk and the battle was intense and lasted for several days and nights. Many Chinese were killed or wounded and forced to retreat. A few days later a larger Chinese force attacked. The Tibetans put up a strong defense but were outnumbered and forced to pull back." Chinese sources cited

militiaman, who was captured by the Chinese and who later described the battle to Robert Ford.

"They had more men than us, but it was a good fight."
"Where are the rest of the Tibetan troops?" Ford asked.
"Dead, mostly."

As soon as the Chinese launched their attack across the ferry crossing, a courier had been sent to zonal headquarters with the news.

The headquarters for the central zone was at Dergé Jomda about thirty miles west of the river. But the courier probably delivered his message before that at Rangsum (present-day Tangpu) about twenty miles from the main river. General Karchung had prepared a secure and well-concealed defensive position along a rugged defile (on either side of the Dzinchu tributary) that opened out at Rangsum. The Tibetan ambush came as a surprise to the Chinese who suffered considerable casualties. Ford mentions seeing fresh Chinese graves in the area when he passed by it on his way to China. The strategic topographical advantage of the Tibetan defence at Rangsum made it difficult for the Chinese to execute their usual flanking movements, and their advance instead got funnelled into the defile and exposed to concentrated Tibetan fire.

But as the Chinese numbers built up at Rangsum and they pressed on their attack, Karchung began his planned retreat. He managed a fairly organized fighting withdrawal back to his headquarters at Dergé Jomda. Picking up his remaining force there (including camp followers) he continued his retreat west, till he reached Kyorshung in Lhatog, the smallest of the six kingdoms of Kham, wedged between Dergé, Nangchen and Chamdo. This place is "open grass country where not a tree or shrub is to be seen."[25]

Approaching the Lashi-la pass (14,600 ft) on the frontier of Lhatog and Chamdo, Karchung was met by a platoon of soldiers under Captain

---

by Alex Raymond concede that many more Chinese were killed at Kamdo Drukha than Tibetans, the majority of whom managed to withdraw.

Lishiba, holding a small outpost (*sa-sung*) there. By now Karchung probably had around three hundred soldiers left with him, perhaps even less, and he and his men had been moving continuously and fighting for full two days. It was getting difficult for his men to move any further without some rest. There were women and children in the force, and the general himself had his wife accompanying him. Out on the high grassland Karchung perhaps thought he had outdistanced the Chinese. Karchung, his wife and some others rested in the small sod barrack-house of the outpost (perhaps the "ruined Chinese rest house" mentioned by Teichman) while his dog-tired soldiers tried to find some protection against the wind and get a few hours of sleep, with perhaps Captain Lishiba and his men on guard.

Accounts of subsequent events are not clear, though all agree that the Chinese attack was sudden and unexpected. Most probably the advancing Chinese troops had managed to avoid Captain Lishiba's patrols by making a wide flanking movement and coming at the Tibetan force from the north. There was more space on the open plain to carry out such a manoeuver that the Chinese could not do so earlier in the defiles of Rangsum. But no one is sure. The attack was overwhelming.

A PLA veteran recounts how his unit began firing with "heavy machine guns on the sleeping Tibetan soldiers."[26] Another Chinese source[27] mentions that heavy artillery fire was directed at the Tibetans, but considering the circumstances perhaps the fast-moving Chinese units had only small howitzers and mortars with them. But these portable infantry weapons are capable of delivering, to lethal effect, a variety of fragmentation, high explosive and illumination projectiles. It is also possible that the use of illumination rounds to light up the battlefield might have given rise to the widespread fiction that the Red Army used fireworks to scare the Tibetans into surrendering[28]—a convenient propaganda myth suggesting that no actual violence had been committed and justifying the official Communist designation of the military invasion as "The Peaceful Liberation of Tibet."

When Robert Ford was eventually released and returned to London he came across Western press reports of the invasion. "I was ... depressed to read how the Tibetan resistance was belittled. The favourite story was that the Chinese let off some fireworks and the Tibetan troops ran away. Of course, the Lhasa government was to blame for not letting the world know that Tibet was putting up a genuine fight."

General Karchung's force was wiped out. He was captured in the morning. Later, when Robert Ford was being taken down to China, he saw on the plains of Kyorshung the frozen corpses of Tibetans soldiers "terribly lifelike" . . . and the "grave of Chinese soldiers that showed that the Tibetans had fought."

Further north at Denkhok, the Chinese mounted another major offensive across the river. This attack was carried out by at least one regiment from the Fifty-Second Division, which was over five thousand men strong. General Muja and his five hundred men from the Third regiment repulsed the initial assault. For three days, the Tibetans managed to check all Chinese attempts to cross the river, inflicting considerable casualties on the attacking force. But finally, a Chinese detachment managed to make a crossing upriver and attacked Muja's left flank. Muja managed to contain the initial attack but had to begin his retreat south-west towards Chamdo. General Muja's force had women, children and baggage trains, according to Ford, and had to fight all the way through very difficult country. Incredibly, the entire regiment, including Khampa militiamen and camp followers, held together. Muja made sure he had put enough distance between him and the Chinese, and then divided his force. The main unit, with the women and children, headed for the village of Ngamda, west of Chamdo on the road to Lho Dzong. General Muja himself and seventy mounted troopers rode swiftly as possible to Chamdo to take stock of the situation.

Tsedrung Ludrup Namgyal, commander of the Sho-ta-lho-sum militia, who was posted on the southern flank of Muja's main force at Denkhok, also managed to hold back the initial Chinese attack on his sector. The historian Shakabpa writes that he ". . . made excellent headway against the enemy."

From further north, possibly from Jyekundo, the 154th Regiment of the Fifty-Second Division, about five thousand men, began its advance. It made its way directly south-west toward Riwoché, with the clear intention of cutting of the retreat of the main Tibetan force from Chamdo.

Far south, on the Markham front, the Fifty-Third Division began its attack on 7 October.

The Chinese had also sent a force from East Turkestan (Xinjiang) through Khotan across the Kunlun Mountains to Western Tibet under regimental commander Li Disan. As it crossed the desert and highest points of the region, nearly half of the members of the detachment died of hunger, cold or disease. According to Chen Qingying's *Tibetan History*, commander Li Disan "laid down his life"[29] on arriving in Ngari in Western Tibet.

A few years ago, a fuller account of this military expedition was discovered in the biography of a PLA officer who was in the advance guard.[30] When the surviving remnants of the Chinese force reached the district of Gertsé in Western Tibet, it was brought to a standstill by a nomad militia force. The advance unit initially came across a single nomad scout armed with a musket that he aimed at the lead Chinese soldier. The Chinese soldier managed to back away from the encounter.

The problem the Chinese faced was the tenuousness of their supply line and the unimaginably desolate and hostile terrain of the Jhangtang, the Great Northern Highlands of Tibet. They faced the same logistical problem that Sven Hedin, the Swedish explorer did in 1906–07 when he attempted to cross this area without the cooperation of the local Tibetans, and when most of his pack animals died on him.

The Tibetan nomadic militia opposing the Chinese force refused to cooperate, surrender or even withdraw. What developed might be called a standoff. The Chinese troops hunkered down, and the Tibetans set up their position some way across, facing the Chinese. Occasionally a few nomad horsemen galloped before the Chinese line to display their courage and riding skills. Only after the signing of the Seventeen Point Treaty and the receipt of written instructions from Lhasa, did the nomad militia of Gertsé eventually allow Li Disan's regiment to proceed to Lhasa.

* * *

None of the Tibetan frontline units in Eastern Tibet had radios, so the first news of the long-feared Chinese invasion arrived at Chamdo military headquarters five days after the initial attack at the Kamdo Drukha ferry crossing. The exhausted messenger from General Karchung arrived at the governor-general's residency just before midnight on Wednesday, 11 October. Ngabö immediately informed the Kashag in Lhasa. On the evening when Radio Lhasa went on air at 5 p.m. with the news in English, Tibetan and Chinese, there was no mention of the invasion. Ford and some other Tibetan officials at Chamdo, who were listening, were stunned and dismayed. The next day, and the day after that, there was nothing from Lhasa. Ford found it difficult to comprehend the Tibetan government's bizarre silence.

Goldstein's and subsequent accounts in English recount the popular gossip of the Kashag being preoccupied with its annual three-day picnic (like Nero fiddling while Rome burned) concluding with the irresistible rebuke by Ngabö's "top" aide in Chamdo supposedly shouting *en clair* over the radio at the cabinet secretary in Lhasa about the Kashag's "shit of a picnic". The only problem with this account is that Robert Ford who oversaw all radio communications at Chamdo headquarters makes no mention of the picnic story.* Nonetheless Ford provides a nearly as damning, though politically more insightful, explanation for the Kashag's dithering:

"The actions of the Lhasa government would have been easier to understand if it had intended to offer only a token resistance to the Chinese and then sue for peace, but it was not doing anything of the kind. *The resistance was real . . . there was never any question of surrender.* I could only think it was a matter of habit. The Lhasa government was so used to the policy of saying nothing that might offend or provoke

---

* Historian Tsering Shakya makes no mention of a "picnic" but writes ". . . the Kashag did not give any publicity to the Chinese invasion because it would cause panic in Lhasa." He adds that the Kashag was having urgent meetings but the ministers ". . . could not agree among themselves on how to respond." The picnic story is likely as not an invention by Ngabö's "top" aide Tsogö Thundup Tsering to gloss over his master's subsequent surrender and betrayal.

the Chinese that it kept it up after provocation had become irrelevant. It was still trying to avert a war that had already broken out."

* * *

Late on 16 October, news came to Chamdo that Chinese units were approaching Riwoché. Goldstein writes that Ngabö urgently contacted Lhasa for orders "to surrender or *flee*." Sam Van Schaik writes that the Kashag's reply was "*flee*." It is inconceivable that the word "flee" (*dros*) was used in an official communication, either by Ngabö or the Kashag and misrepresents what actually took place. It is almost certain that the Kashag ordered Ngabö to "*retreat*" (*chir-ten*), as Goldstein corrects himself in his next sentence—evidently to the Lho Dzong fortress that Lhalu was holding.*

In retrospect it appears that Ngabö did not want to retreat to Lho Dzong but rather to surrender to the Chinese at Chamdo. Ford writes "I did not learn it until five years later—that one of the messages I had transmitted to Lhasa the day before (the retreat) had been a request from Ngabö for permission to surrender to the Chinese, and that permission had been refused."[31] Had Rapga Pangdatsang conveyed more than a proposal of "peaceful liberation" from the Chinese to the governor-general? Ngabö may have wanted to remain in Chamdo and surrender but could not do so without directly disobeying the Kashag's clear-cut orders not to surrender but to retreat.

So Ngabö commenced a last minute and disorganized retreat to Lho Dzong. The first action he took in this regard was ill advised. He ordered the government armoury at Chamdo to be set on fire. This alarmed the populace, causing chaos in the streets and even the looting of weapons from the armoury, which had not been properly destroyed.

---

* Even before the Kashag's order to retreat, a number of officials had pleaded with Ngabö to relocate his headquarters to Lho Dzong as Chamdo was exposed and indefensible. Ngabö replied that he would not leave Chamdo but the officials could, if they wished (Maja interview). Goldstein also cites this exchange.

The burning of the armoury was not a military necessity. The Chinese had no need for Tibetan weapons.

Ngabö's retreat was, according to Ford, not well organized, but the troops though ". . . tired and dispirited maintained order and the N.C.O.s kept them together as far as possible." Not enough transport had been requisitioned early enough from the various villages outside the town, where the pack animals were usually set out to graze. There was anger within the ranks of the Khampa militia because the regular soldiers received priority on transport. But there was not enough transport even for all the regular soldiers and Ford later noticed that some of Ngabö's own bodyguards were on foot.

The immediate objective for Ngabö, his staff, escort and the Chamdo garrison under General Dimon (whose wife was in labour) was to reach the crossroad settlement of Ngamda before the Chinese got there. The Chinese forces were now closing in on Riwoché from where it was just fifty miles due south to the crossroad. The major problem for the retreating Tibetan force from Chamdo was that it had to cross a rugged fifteen-thousand-foot pass to get to Ngamda on the other side. The Chinese drive south to Riwoché and Ngamda, by comparison, came through less difficult terrain.

Ford describes Riwoché as ". . . the prettiest little town I saw in Kham. Situated on a tributary of the Upper Salween, it was well wooded and wonderfully green—as perhaps, Chamdo had been before deforestation and soil erosion ruined it. It had a population of about five hundred, and three monasteries full of monks. There was a caravan track northward to Jyekundo, and it would need skilful defence." But as Ford pointed out ". . . it was not likely to get it."

The general who commanded the Riwoché garrison, Phulungwa Drakpa Tseten was ". . . one of the poorest types of officer produced by the Tibetan social system . . . a playboy out of his element in Kham." It is perhaps indicative of the demoralization of the military and aristocracy under two corrupt priestly regencies and monastic control of the administration and parliament. Phulungwa's great-grandfather had fought and defeated the great Khampa warrior chief, Nyarong Gompo Namgyal in 1865. Phulungwa's father, Wangchen Damdul, had fought beside my grandfather Gyurme Gyatso Tethong in 1918 and had been killed leading a charge against the Chinese at Chamdo.

The rapid Chinese advance south to Riwoché encountered initial Tibetan resistance at the Chagzamkha, a bridge or a ferry point about thirty miles north of Riwoché. According to Ford the garrison at Riwoché was outflanked and the general "taken by surprise." Goldstein states that after the first Chinese attack Phulungwa panicked and attempted to flee but his officers stopped him. Whatever the actual details of the incident, it is evident that Phulungwa's poor leadership prevented Riwoché from being defended in a vigorous and forceful manner, as might have been otherwise possible. An eyewitness, a young monk of Riwoché Monastery, stated in an interview that the Tibetans did put up a fight but that it was ineffectual. "We were so surprised. They were just suddenly there. There was some resistance for an hour or two. There were so few Tibetan soldiers supplied by the Central Government stationed in Riwoché. What could they have done against the thousands of PLA."[32]

Ngabö received news that Riwoché had fallen just when starting on the climb up the pass. Some way up, Ford turned around and looked back at the long line of soldiers. Most of them were on foot and appeared tired. But the officers "still maintained discipline, and all was not lost yet." Halfway down the pass they met reinforcements from Lhasa—a company of soldiers from the Sixth (artillery) regiment under Major Rinzin Paljor with mountain artillery, cases of machine guns and ammunition. Ford notes that "Ngabö ordered them to throw the loads of arms and ammunition over the side of the mountain" and join the retreating army.

Just as Ngabö and his men made it over the pass and down to the other side, his scouts informed him that the Chinese were already at the Ngamda crossroad. In fact, only a small advance unit of about a hundred PLA troops, exhausted by forced marches, had just made it to the crossroad, while the main 154th Regiment was still at Riwoché. Ngabö had nearly 2,000 soldiers with him but made the inexplicable decision to retire to the nearby Drugu Monastery. If he had just taken the trouble to verify the strength of the Chinese advance force, he could have then easily attacked it and, brushing it aside, continued on to Lho Dzong. Ford was told by Ngabö's staff that the reason for the governor-general's change of plan was that the Ngamda crossroad had been taken by Khampas and not by the Chinese.

This was, of course, not only false but ridiculous as well. It was common knowledge that no Khampa tribe had sided with the Chinese in the invasion or demonstrated any intention of doing so. Only Jhagö Topden, a freebooter from Dergé and Phüntso Wangye of Bathang had provided some guides and muleteers to the PLA. The only angry Khampas were the local militiamen at Chamdo who had not been provided transport by Ngabö. Even if a few of Jhagö Topden's men were at Ngamda they were probably there as guides to the advance PLA unit—as it later turned out to be the case. But Ngabö's last words to Ford seemed to imply that an overwhelming Khampa force was waiting to attack him at the crossroads.

"I am going to seek refuge," he said. "There is a monastery near here. The Khampas will not shed blood there."

Once at the monastery a depressed Ford was heartened by the unexpected sight of General Muja riding up with seventy mounted soldiers—confident and ready to fight. He also had the rest of his men, over four hundred men (with women, children and transport train), following close by. He was confident that the Chinese at the crossroad at Ngamda were only an advance guard and that they could be defeated, and the Tibetans could push on. He reassured a worried Ford. "Of course, we can reach Lho Dzong. The Chinese are not unbeatable. We have held them off without many casualties, and unless we are greatly outnumbered, we can beat them in a fight. Ah, here come the rest of our troops."

Before going inside the monastery to see Ngabö, Muja once again spoke to reassure Ford. "The Chinese cannot have reached the road in strength, and my troops can easily easily break through to Lho Dzong." When Muja finally came out of the monastery, he was angry and grim-faced. He told Ford that Ngabö had ordered him to surrender. He apologized to Ford for delaying him and ordered his men to make camp. Then Muja, Ford and the 2,500 soldiers of the Tibetan army of Chamdo waited haplessly before the walls of Drugu Monastery till eventually ". . . one hundred exhausted PLA troops" from the Ngamda crossroad arrived, and Ngabö was finally able to surrender.

* * *

The *People's Daily* in Beijing published a photograph of the captured British imperialist spy "Foo-te" wearing a Tibetan *chuba* with a bomber jacket over it. He is lined up with other Tibetan prisoners, and they all look uniformly miserable.

After a few days Ford was taken to Chinese military headquarters at Kandzé with his radio operators and other Tibetan prisoners. When on the march they came to the high plains where General Karchung and his men had fought their last battle. "I could imagine the night battle with all the women and children encamped on the plain."

In the evenings the prisoners would huddle around a campfire and Ford managed to laugh with them when they traded risqué stories. Ford liked the stories of Uncle Tompa,* who he describes as "the hero of Tibet's Decameron." He explains that that most of the tales are very ancient but so bawdy that they "are unprintable", though he admits that they "have a certain charm." His Communist captor Hsu did not think so. He asked Ford what he and the Tibetans prisoners were all laughing at. Ford told him the story of how Uncle Tompa disguised himself as a nun and sneaking into a nunnery impregnated a large number of nuns, much to the bewilderment of the abbess. "Such crimes are inevitable in a corrupt reactionary society" was Hsu's starchy response.

From Kandzé the Tibetan soldiers were sent back to Tibet, while Ford and his radio-operators were taken down to China. Ford was charged with the murder of Geda "the Red Lama" who the Chinese had sent as an envoy to convince the former Governor-general Lhalu to surrender. The Lama had died at Chamdo headquarters under mysterious circumstances. Ford was subjected to non-stop interrogation to admit to this crime and also subjected to intensive thought-reform or "brain-washing" (Chinese, *xinao*).

---

* See *Tales of Uncle Tompa, The Legendary Rascal of Tibet* by Rinjing Dorjee.

He spent nearly five years in prison, in constant fear of being executed. He was released and expelled from China in 1955.

He became an active supporter of the Tibetan cause till his death at the age of ninety. In early 2012 I started corresponding with Ford. I could not interview him at length, but he answered some crucial questions on the Chamdo defeat. I even persuaded him to fact-check the three chapters of this book dealing with Chamdo, which I mailed to his home in the London suburb of Barnet. He wrote back saying how much he had enjoyed going through them. "I found them most interesting with much that was new to me, particularly the personalities and background to events." He added that he ". . . frankly had no corrections or criticism" and looked forward to reading the finished book. The Dalai Lama's representative in London, Thupten Samdup, who introduced me to Ford, organized a celebration on his ninetieth birthday where he handed the former radio operator, and defender of Chamdo, the last of his Tibetan government salary, a 100 Tam Srang note worth 65 pounds. Robert Webster Ford died on 20 September 2013.

* * *

When Ngabö surrendered his command, the former Governor-general Lhalu was holding the fortress at Lho Dzong with his own personal escort of two hundred men from the Second (Drapchi) regiment, and one battalion of the Seventh (Jhadang) regiment under General Shakjang Zurpa. Lhasa had radioed Lhalu that the Drongdrak* regiment was being sent to Lho Dzong to support him.

---

*In 1932 the 13th Dalai Lama's favoured official, Kunphel-la, created the Drongdrak regiment with troops recruited from the lesser nobility and freeholders. F.W. Williamson, the British political officer, inspected the regiment in 1933 and was impressed. "Outside the regular units of the British and Indian armies, I have never seen such smartness and precision," he wrote in a report. But after the death of the Thirteenth the monk led opposition to Tibet's modernization manoeuvered Kunphel-la out of office and disbanded the regiment. In 1949 the regiment was hurriedly re-established under the command of Dapön Kharnak and Datsab Gokarwa.

Lhalu then set about reorganizing the other surviving Tibetan units west of Chamdo. The one other regiment left intact in Kham was the Fourth (Gyantsé) then stationed at Khyungpo Tengchen, on the northern road from Chamdo to Lhasa. Goldstein mentions that General Tsögo Ngodup Dorje commanded this regiment and that it managed to successfully retreat "intact" to Lho Dzong.

With his limited force, Lhalu had to rethink the earlier broad strategy of forming a defensive line at Lho Dzong. So, he began organizing a retreat further west to the important headquarter of Tar Dzong (in Pembar district) that administered the three districts of Pembar, Lhorong and Shopado (generally known by the acronym of Sho-ta-lho-sum) on the important *Gya-Lam* or "China Road", the trade route from China to Lhasa. He also managed to move a large supply of arms and ammunition and other stores from Lho Dzong to the west. It is important to note that Lhalu had a working radio set and kept up communications with Lhasa.

The following information was obtained from the previously mentioned *Military History* by Namgyal Wangdu.[33] Lhalu ordered the Fourth Gyantsé regiment at Tengchen to withdraw to Shopado. In case of another Chinese advance from the north he sent a small force to screen Tengchen, but Lhalu knew that the main thrust of the Chinese advance would be through Shopado.

Shopado was the seat of the Martsang Kagyü School, and the main monastery was extensive, with twelve temples and over 200 monks. The monastic heads and local leaders met with the Tibetan officers and appealed to them not to fight the Chinese at Shopado as it would surely cause great destruction to the monastery and the township. They advised a stand further west at Bari. Two companies of the Gyantsé regiment led by Major Phuntsok Yugyal and Major Kala Migmar prepared their position in the forests covering Bari Mountain overlooking the main path from Shopado. The Chinese took Lho Dzong on 22 October. The small Tibetan contingent there retreated in good order to Shopado and Bari where it joined the waiting Gyantsé regiment. The Chinese marched unopposed to Shopado on 27 October.

A PLA battalion advanced the few miles further west towards Bari, unaware of the Tibetan force waiting for them. The Tibetans suffered an initial setback when a scouting party was captured and two men killed. But this mishap was somewhat providential, as it appeared to confirm Chinese assumptions that only a few scattered Tibetan units remained in the area. So the Chinese continued their advance and were caught in an ambush. They attempted a counterattack up the mountain, but the Tibetan crossfire was murderous. Many PLA soldiers were killed, trapped or wounded in the forest. The fighting went on for a full day. In the evening the Chinese retreated leaving behind over fifty dead but managing to take their wounded with them. Aside from the two men killed earlier, only a few Tibetans were wounded. Even the captured Tibetans managed to escape.

This engagement may not have been an overwhelming Tibetan victory, but it slowed the PLA advance and perhaps alerted its leaders to the capacity of the Tibetan army to spring a last-minute surprise. A Chinese account of the battle makes no mention of the defeat. "Overtaking the troops of the Ngadang (Gyantsé) Regiment at Bari village, we severely assaulted them. Then we headed for Pembar where we crushed the remaining troops of the enemy."[34]

Lhalu continued his unhurried retreat from Tar Dzong, not leaving behind any units or detachments in the Sho-ta-lho-sum area, even taking the local militia with him. The Chinese only captured Tar Dzong on 31 October. But the Tibetan forces had by then retreated further west in good order. Around the beginning of November Lhalu's force finally arrived at the small town and postal station of Kongpo Gyamda, 175 miles east of Lhasa and established a defensive line along the Nyangchu River with the Fourth (Gyantsé), the Seventh (Jhadang), the Fourteenth (Phadang) and the Thirteenth (Drongdrak) regiment just sent from Lhasa. A number of Khampa militia contingents and also other surviving units, and individual soldiers that had managed to escape from Chamdo, shored up the defence. Considering the disgraceful capitulation of Ngabö at Drugu Monastery, Lhalu's subsequent performance comes across as surprisingly coolheaded—demonstrating considerable generalship.

Melvyn Goldstein is convinced that the Chinese stopped their advance at Kongpo Gyamda though they could have ". . . easily taken Gyamda", because ". . . they had wanted to liberate Tibet 'peacefully' Now, having demonstrated the military might of the People's Republic of China, they sat back to see whether this lesson would convince the Tibetans to open negotiations and accept their terms for liberation and reunification."*

Tsering Shakya is also certain that "The Chinese could have marched straight on to Lhasa" but desired to negotiate, as "they were still willing to seek 'peaceful liberation'."[35]

To date no other speculations have been put forward for the PLA's unexpected decision to halt its advance at Kongpo Gyamda. One crucial military reality comes across though. The Chinese invasion force was over-extended, perhaps even dangerously so, and also perhaps too close to Lhasa and Tibetan reserves. The Tibetan army retained more than half its original strength. Eight to possibly ten regiments were still largely intact: the First Guards, Second Drapchi, Fourth Gyantsé, Fifth Dingri, Sixth Artillery (later Police), a battalion of the Seventh Jhadang, Tenth Thadang, Eleventh Dhadang, Thirteenth Drongdrak, and Fourteenth Phadang. The Chinese had only destroyed or captured two battalions of the Third Shigatsé regiment at Chamdo under Muja and Karchung, one battalion of Seventh Jhadang at Riwoché, and the Ninth Tadang regiment at Markham. The Tibetans still retained, at Lhasa, most of their store of rifles, ammunition, Bren guns, and crucially, their Vickers heavy machine guns and howitzers.

A painful lesson Mao and Red Army generals had learned twenty years earlier during the Long March was not to get caught in the wilds of Eastern Tibet with tenuous and exposed supply lines. Now, deep inside Tibet, the Eighteenth Army could possibly not sustain more than a setback or two before the (thus far) placid Khampa tribesmen fell back on their traditional ways: attacking PLA transport, stealing weapons

---

* Some revisionist historians in Britain have speculated that Hitler halted his panzers outside Dunkirk for three days to allow the British army trapped there to escape and provide Britain a face-saving opportunity to seek a peace settlement with Germany.

and supplies, and then working themselves up to bigger things—all of which they did, just a few years later in 1956. In Mao's collected papers (in China's National Archives) there are two telegrams sent by the Chairman to the South-west Military Command that perhaps indicate his concerns. I have earlier mentioned his telegram of August 18 expressing his fears about the PLA defeat at Denkhok by General Muja. In another cable of 23 August 1950, Mao cautions that even if the PLA was successful in attacking Chamdo, the Eighteenth Army should withdraw east across the river and leave only 3,000 soldiers in Chamdo for the winter.[36]

Confidential Chinese army reports obtained by Alex Raymond mentions "that the totality of the PLA units had arrived at the end of the Chamdo battle, exhausted and lacking food" and there were "problems with the troop, such as desertions or suicides." One report notes ". . . the troops had lost confidence in the continuation of the offensive."

Another factor that might have influenced the PLA halt was China's entry into the Korean War on 25 October, and its commitment of over a million troops to that conflict. But the Tibetan government was unfortunately not aware of these critical predicaments that the PLA high command now faced.

* * *

At Lhasa the old Tagtra Regent resigned, and the decision was reached (with the help of the State Oracle) for the fifteen-year-old Dalai Lama to take up the reins of power. The Tibetan government also made a desperate appeal to the United Nations. But a further decision, the withdrawal of the Dalai Lama and the Kashag to Dromo on the Indian border, alarmed the Lhasa public. It would perhaps not be unfair to say that irresolution, impotence and confusion ruled the counsels of the Tibetan government at this juncture, but one last-ditch decision it took was undoubtedly effective, it might perhaps even be called inspired.

Two older officials, the white-bearded Lukhangwa and the cleric *khenchen* Lobsang Tashi were appointed prime ministers. They were instructed to remain in Lhasa and run the administration. The Dalai Lama mentions that they were given "full authority to decide all civil and military matters." Both were mid-level officials, nearing retirement, who had been overlooked for high office in the climate of corruption and sycophancy of the two preceding lama regencies. But these two officials were known to be competent, upright and courageous men, with considerable administrative and political experience between them. Hugh Richardson who knew Lukhangwa said this of him. "He had a reputation for being un-self-seeking and public spirited and was much respected as a speaker in the National Assembly (*tshogs-'du*) for plain speaking combined with a modest manner."[37] The two prime ministers immediately contacted Lhalu. They sent him instructions to hold the Kongpo Gyamda defence line and assured him of immediate reinforcements.

Martial law was imposed on the city to curb the spread of rumours, and alleviate the fear and uncertainty generated by the Chamdo defeat and the flight of the Dalai Lama and his cabinet. The prime ministers ordered the Lhasa magistrates and constables to organize regular night patrols of the streets and alleys and took steps to prevent hoarding of food and fuel. They appointed the feared monk disciplinarian of Drepung Monastery (*tsokchen-shalngo*) and gave him the authority to administer severe punishments on offenders. The Lhasa populace was greatly reassured by these clear-cut decisions and forceful action and felt that the ". . . prime-ministers ought to be praised for setting people's minds at rest."[38]

With a degree of order and calm restored over the capital and the front line at Kongpo Gyamda holding firm, the Kashag (at Dromo) gained breathing space enough to push forward its initiative to seek international support. The Dalai Lama wrote to the Chinese government calling on it ". . . to return the Tibetans who had been captured by their army, and to withdraw from the part of Tibet which they had occupied by force."[39] Repeated missives from Beijing calling on the Tibetan government to open negotiations were ignored.

"In point of fact, the Tibetan government was trying to stall real negotiations with China," according to Goldstein.[40] Lhasa was desperately hoping that its appeal to the United Nations would somehow find support from the global community, in particular from Britain, India and the United States. It managed to hold out from negotiating with China for more than five months after the invasion, before Lhasa eventually realized that Tibet had been "sold down the river" as Britain's last representative to Tibet, Hugh Richardson, later put it scathingly.

5

SEVENTEEN POINT SWINDLE

One history lesson that schoolchildren in both Nationalist and Communist China had drilled into them was the *bainian guochi,* or "century of humiliation." During this period, from roughly 1839 to 1949, a weak China was forced to sign a series of "unequal treaties" when faced with military defeat or threat of military action by foreign imperialist powers—namely Britain, France, Germany, Japan and the United States.

But as coerced and unequal as these treaties undoubtedly were, they nowhere involved the kind of flagrant deception—essentially an insidious confidence trick—that the Chinese government pulled off on the Tibetans through their "Seventeen Point Treaty". The term "agreement" and not "treaty" is insisted on by the Chinese (and their supporters) as they claim Tibet was not an independent nation. But we will use the latter term as under international law the two are considered the same: "A treaty may also be known as an (international) agreement, protocol, covenant, convention, pact, or exchange of letters, among other terms. Regardless of terminology, all of these forms of agreements are, under international law, equally considered treaties, and the rules are the same."[1]

The Dalai Lama and the Tibetan government have always insisted that the Seventeen Point Treaty was signed "through deception" (and also "under duress"), citing the fact that the seals used on the treaty were forged. But the Tibetans were never fully able to grasp the sophistication of the overall conspiracy, in particular the Communist techniques of psychological coercion, otherwise described as "thought control", "political indoctrination", "re-education" and even "brainwashing" (Chinese, *xinao*) or literally "wash brain"—a term Maoist ideologues coined when they first formulated the system during the Yan'an* years (1936 to 1948). Some sources mention that Ngabö Ngawang Jigme and his staff received "re-education" at Chamdo but go no further.

Though evidence of such duplicity on Beijing's part has never been adequately investigated by the Tibetan government, it does appear incidentally, in a couple of Goldstein's books where he discusses the events of Chamdo. Goldstein lets us know, inadvertently, how Ngabö was subjected to some sort of psychological manipulation immediately after his surrender at Drugu Monastery—perhaps to elicit a sort of Stockholm syndrome response from this defeated, confused, and insecure Tibetan leader.

> On the first day after the surrender he (Ngabö) was asked by the Chinese to speak at a meeting. After Ngabö made his speech, the Chinese took all the Tibetan officials back to Chamdo. There they were met by General Wang Qimei, who welcomed Ngabö with the gift of a scarf and said, 'The People's Liberation Army has no desire other than to render service to the people of Tibet. However, due to the negative propaganda of foreign reactionaries and imperialists, you have mistaken our intent and have run away from us, thus inflicting unnecessary hardship upon yourself. We are very sorry about this,' and *then he burst into tears* [emphasis added]. This impressed Ngabö, who thought that since it was not easy to shed tears without reason, Wang was probably sincere.[2]

---

*Yinhong Cheng, a Delaware State academic in his *Creating the 'New Man': From Enlightenment Ideals to Socialist Realities* (University of Hawaii Press, 2009) has noted: "In large part, the Yan'an Rectification Campaign began with the 'systematic remolding of human minds'."

Goldstein further details, perhaps unwittingly, subsequent manipulation of Ngabö in his (Goldstein's) biography of the collaborator, Bapa Phüntso Wangye, who told Goldstein,

"After arriving (at Chamdo) I took a ceremonial scarf, a new radio, and some fine brocade and went to see Ngabö." Wangye also made sure that Ngabö's former official quarters in Chamdo were returned to him, and that he was served his meals with Wangye and General Wang Qimei. "Mainly what I did was try to educate them about the new Chinese government. I *spent days and nights talking with Ngabö* [emphasis added] and Tsögo (Ngabö's aide) about the Soviet Union, Communism, the current situation in China, and, most importantly, the Chinese Communist Party's policies on nationality, equality, and religious freedom We sometimes *talked late—till two or three in the morning* [emphasis added]."[3]

"In addition to spending a lot of time explaining the positive aspects of Chinese policies, I also did everything I could to emphasize how futile it would be for Tibet to try and resist China militarily. I remember being very blunt."

Wangye's bluntness perhaps reveals concerns in the Chinese High Command that except for the troops immediately under Ngabö's command, the rest of the Tibetan army had not yet surrendered. China's leaders were almost certainly worried about Governor-General Lhalu's stubborn refusal to yield his now reinforced defense line at Kongpo Gyamda, and also the frustrating impasse at Gertsé in north-west Jhangthang, where a nomad militia army continued to successfully block the advance of the PLA Xinjiang force.

Furthermore, the Tibetan government's refusal to come to the negotiation table added to Beijing's anxieties, so much so, that ideological concerns were set aside, and a former high official of the despised Guomindang regime then living in Hong Kong was contacted. This official, Zhu Shigui, was the father of Zhu Dan (aka Nancy), the wife of the Dalai Lama's older brother, Gyalo Thondup. Beijing called on Zhu Shigui to set aside his enmity towards the Communist government and, for the sake of China's national unity, communicate with the Tibetan government and urge it to open negotiations with

China. My informant told me that this former Guomindang official did contact Gyalo Thondup with Beijing's proposal but was not sure if anything had come of it in the end.[4] Phüntso Wangye tells us that Chinese officials at Chamdo began to work on other ways to induce the Tibetans to the negotiating table.

> As the efforts to improve relations with Ngabö and the other Lhasa officials began to bear fruit, we discussed an idea that we thought might persuade Lhasa to negotiate. Ngabö should write a letter to his colleagues on the Council of Ministers explaining what had happened to them and the realities and opportunities—and urge that they agree to send representatives. Ngabö agreed, and we considered the contents of the letter with great care. After Ngabö's aide wrote the first draft, he, Ngabö, and I discussed and revised it several times. Then I took it to Wang Qimei, and he and Ngabö went over it carefully and revised it several more times. Finally, Ngabö and all the other Tibetan officials signed it, and it was sent on its way to Lhasa.[5]
>
> Several months went by, however, and *we got no reply* [emphasis added]. Since we had no communication with Lhasa, we had no idea what was going on. The tension began to build.

In 1949 "the National Assembly and the Kashag had adopted a two-pronged approach. First, the Kashag sought admission to the United Nations",[6] but this effort was unsuccessful. Following the invasion, the Tibetan official Tsepon Shakabpa* was instructed to forward Tibet's formal appeal for help to the United Nations, which he did on 7 November 1950. "On November 13, the Tibetan cabinet and National Assembly again appealed to the United Nations assuring the Secretary General that 'Tibet will not go down without a fight,

---

*Shakabpa was the finance secretary (*tsepön*) who between 1947 and 1949 headed the Tibetan Trade Mission to a number of countries in the West. Just prior to the invasion he was appointed (with a monk co-official) to negotiate with China. This mission was aborted after Ngabö's surrender but Shakabpa remained in Kalimpong from where he acted as the Kashag's representative to India, Britain the U.S. and the United Nations.

though there is little hope of a nation dedicated to peace resisting the brutal effort of men trained to war.'"[7] But Britain and independent India, the two nations that had the closest economic, historical, diplomatic and treaty relationships with Tibet, spinelessly avoided supporting Tibet's appeal.

The Nationalist (Guomindang) government in Taiwan was avowedly anti-Communist, and Taiwan was itself under imminent threat of a PLA invasion. Yet, fearing that support for Tibet in the UN might weaken Nationalist China's claims of sovereignty over Tibet, the Guomindang worked to undermine Tibet's appeal to the United Nations. Nationalist diplomats in Washington led by their ambassador Wellington Koo, did what they could to confuse, delay and water down U.S. State Department initiatives on behalf of Tibet.

Surprisingly, El Salvador's delegation at the United Nations responded to Tibet's appeal. The leader of the delegation, the distinguished diplomat Héctor David Castro, not only called for the condemnation of China's invasion but also proposed a discussion on Tibet in the UN General Assembly.

On Friday, 24 November 1950, the issue of whether to include "'the invasion of Tibet by foreign forces' as an additional item in the United Nations General Assembly was discussed by the General Committee at the request of El Salvador." The British representative led the way in calling for "no action to be taken"' and for shelving any proposed debate on Tibet in the General Assembly. India followed suit

---

*Hong Kong was overwhelmed with refugees from the mainland following the Communist takeover of China. There was real fear in Britain that Hong Kong would be "liberated" along with Tibet and Taiwan, and parliament debated whether its crown colony "would have to be handed back." Emergency plans were made for the evacuation of HK's administration and infrastructure to Australia (See Trea Wiltshire, *Old Hong Kong*, Vol. 3, 1987). Many Tibetan officials believed that Whitehall had secretly arrived at a *quid pro quo* with Beijing involving Hong Kong's future and Britain's non-support for Tibet in the UN. Agreements between Britain and China (secret or otherwise) at the expense of Tibet, is a recurring feature in Tibetan history, especially in the late nineteenth and early twentieth century.

and, finally, ". . . it was unanimously decided to adjourn consideration of El Salvador's proposal".[8]

Hugh Richardson, Britain's last representative in Tibet, wrote that "The British government, the only government among Western countries to have had treaty relations with Tibet, sold the Tibetans down the river, and since then have constantly cold-shouldered the Tibetans so that in 1959 they could not even support a resolution in the UN condemning the violation of human rights in Tibet by the Chinese."[9] Richardson further confessed that he was ". . . profoundly ashamed" not only at the British government's refusal to recognize that Tibet had a right to self-determination, but also at the government's treatment of the Fourteenth Dalai Lama. Later, when the Irish Republic raised the issue of Tibet in the UN, Richardson did everything he could to assist in this effort. In the words of an informed commentator in the UN, "he acted valiantly as a man of honour in a cause which has been largely lost because of the notions of political expediency."

Because of his efforts to promote the Tibetan issue in the UN and his "staunch support for the independence of Tibet" which ". . . set him openly at variance with the stance of the British Government . . ." his friend and colleague David Snellgrove has suggested, in the obituary[10] he wrote in 2001, that Richardson was denied any subsequent honours or recognition from the British government, in spite of his outstanding career as a member of the Indian Civil Service and his international reputation as the foremost scholar on Tibet of his time.[*]

Even after the shock and disappointment of the UN's rejection of its appeal, the Tibetan government did not give in to China's demands for negotiations, and holding firm, sent its second appeal on 8 December 1950. "The Tibetan government responded to the UN's rejection with a strong note emphasizing the United Nations'

---

[*] I corresponded with Hugh Richardson and also met him when I lived in Scotland. He was then living alone at a retirement apartment in St Andrews and was glad to see me and reminisce about Tibet. He contributed articles to two publications I edited and made a generous financial donation to TIPA when I was director. He also let me have some rare documents on the Drepuling musical tradition he had obtained from the Potala secretariat.

moral duty to uphold the rights of small powers against more powerful neighbour and inviting the United Nations to send a fact-finding mission to Tibet. They also indicated that they would send their own delegation to Lake Success",[11] the temporary headquarters of the UN. Tibet also sent appeals to Britain, USA and Canada, informing them of their plans to go to the UN headquarters at Lake Success (New York) and requested their support for this action. But the British Foreign Office and the Government of India were firmly against any support for the Tibetan issue in the UN.

However, the United States, according to Goldstein, was "moving towards more active support of Tibet" but was caught up in discussions with the British Foreign Office and the Indian government and had not communicated its possible intentions to the Tibetans.

So, Tibet's last diplomatic initiative fell through. Finally, in late March (more than five months after the invasion), the Dalai Lama and the Tibetan government at Dromo decided it had to abandon its UN initiative and accept China's demand to send a negotiating team to Beijing. The Tibetan government had earlier received Ngabö's letter reassuring the Kashag that not only were fruitful negotiations with the Chinese indeed possible but that Chinese leaders were prepared to accommodate Tibetan demands to a welcome degree.

The Kashag had no idea that the letter had been skilfully composed "with great care" and rewritten a number of times by the collaborator Phüntso Wangye, the Chinese General Wang Qimei and Ngabö. The Tibetan government assumed the letter had been written by Ngabö alone. "Ngabö, in the letter to Lhasa, proposed himself as a negotiator."[12] The Kashag at Dromo injudiciously took Ngabö at his word and appointed him to head the negotiation team. The Chinese though enormously gratified at how successfully Ngabö had responded to his "re-education", were careful not to take his conversion to their cause for granted. To ensure his ideological commitment, they appointed him a senior (but secret) Communist Party official with a high rank and salary. He was now vice-chairman of the Chamdo Liberation Committee, the official Chinese organ that administered the newly conquered Tibetan territories. General Wang Qimei was chairman.

The Tibetan government had no idea that their chief negotiator was now a communist official and sent him strict instructions not to give up Tibetan sovereignty and not agree to Chinese troops being stationed in Tibet. He was expressly informed that he was not authorized to sign any agreement in Beijing without first receiving approval from the Tibetan government. Tsering Shakya writes, "The delegation (as a whole) was given instructions that it should on no account accept Chinese sovereignty over Tibet. The delegation should refer all important points back to Dromo for consultation, and for that purpose, a direct wireless communication was to be established between Beijing and Dromo."[13]

Ngabö now travelled to Beijing via Chengdu and Chongqing. It is probably around this time that he started wearing a Chinese style jacket and trousers and not his official Tibetan robes. He also cut his long hair and *pachok* topknot that denoted his status as a Tibetan government official. This would have been an extreme, even traumatic, action for a Tibetan official to take, as untying much less cutting off the topknot was a prelude to dismissal (in disgrace) from government service. We have an official Chinese photograph of Ngabö in this un-Tibetan *déshabillé* alongside an applauding Deng Xiaoping in Chongqing. An enormous reception has been organized for the Tibetan negotiator with large crowds of people on either side of the road to receive him. Thousands of schoolgirls dressed in their best, are holding bouquets. There is at least one big brass band in the background, with four sousaphones, the oversized flaring bells, clearly visible above the crowd.

According to Phüntso Wangye, the trip was not exactly a direct one, and there were "change of plans" to prepare for big welcoming ceremonies in other cities. Finally, from Xian ". . . we boarded a train, and on the following day we arrived at Beijing, where we were greeted grandly.

Premier Zhou Enlai himself was at the station, along with other top officials and about three hundred people of different nationalities, all of them there to welcome the Tibetan delegation." In the sixties and seventies, Beijing successfully used such elaborately planned welcome ceremonies and parades to dazzle and overawe a succession of international politicians like Richard Nixon, Pierre Trudeau and Henry Kissinger.

In April, two additional Tibetan delegates arrived in Beijing. They brought with them further written instructions from the Kashag, the most important one being that the delegation *must make a claim for Tibetan independence*. According to the senior official, Khemey Sonam Wangdu, "the Tibetan negotiators were lodged in Beijing Hotel and isolated from any contact with the outside world."[14] The practice of taking hostages as security for the carrying out of a treaty between civilized states, is of course, now obsolete (the last occasion being at the Treaty of Aix-la-Chapelle in 1748), but the Tibetan delegates were unsure and fearful of what their situation was exactly. According to the assistant official Takla (who was serving as a Chinese language translator), the chief negotiator Ngabö was far from reassuring when he solemnly informed his Tibetan colleagues, "Now, we are in Chinese hands; they can beat or kill us."[15]

But the Tibetan officials had, at least, the reassurance that they would be able to communicate directly with the Tibetan government at Dromo through radio. This was a pre-condition to the negotiations that the Chinese had accepted. Goldstein mentions that the Tibetan negotiators had received instruction on this. "They were instructed to establish a wireless link between Peking and Yatung [Dromo] so that other important issues could be discussed. They were, clearly, not authorized to make major decisions on their own."[16]

But Ngabö, most likely on instructions from his Chinese handlers, now worked on persuading the other Tibetan negotiators to forgo radio communications with Dromo, and not trouble the Dalai Lama and the Tibetan government with complicated details of the deliberations that might jeopardize the entire negotiation and cause the PLA to launch a massive attack on Lhasa.

Goldstein also mentions Ngabö's proposal not to consult the Tibetan government. "Ngabö believed that they should not refer important issues back to Yatung but should take the responsibility upon themselves. He argued persuasively that the abbots and other conservatives in the assembly had no idea of the modern world and

Communist China and would refuse to accept the wording and terms the Chinese were going to present . . . He also pointed out that if the Dalai Lama and the government found this agreement unacceptable, they could later repudiate it on the grounds that the delegation did not have complete authority. As the leader of the delegation, Ngabö said, he would take full responsibility for this action and would accept any later punishment."[17]

It is possible that around this time, Ngabö managed to persuade the other lay officials and assistants to cut their long hair and official top-knots in order to demonstrate that they were progressive and aware of modern ways. Some observers have argued that the negotiators cut their hair to demonstrate they were no longer government officials, and hence whatever actions they were forced to take would have no official validation. This is not an improbable rationalization as Tibetan government regulations did not recognize the legitimacy of a secular official who did not have the long *pachok* hair. In fact, when Ngabö got back to Tibet, "he was told that he would not be allowed to enter Lhasa and had to wait outside the city until a wig could be made for him."[18]

The discussions in Beijing were long and, so heated that at one point, the Tibetans were told by the Chinese to "pack up your beddings go home"[19]—the implication being that the invasion would resume. Eventually, the Tibetans were worn down by a combination of relentless hectoring, bullying and threats from the Chinese team and the continual defeatist wheedling from the leader of their own team.

It is possible that the Tibetan negotiators were finally convinced about accepting the Chinese conditions as Ngabö had told them that the Tibetan government "could later repudiate it on the grounds that the delegation did not have complete authority." Tibetan negotiators were not only *not* authorized by Lhasa to sign any agreement but had been instructed not to take their official seals or even their personal seals to China. It is possible that the Tibetans regarded the fact of having no seals as an ace up their collective sleeves in the final phase of the negotiations.

Ngabö alone had bought his official seal with him but realized that it put him in an awkward situation if he alone among the delegation used an official seal when the others did not. So, he pretended that he had left it at Chamdo. According to Shakya, Ngabö later told the Dalai Lama's Lord Chamberlain Phala, in Lhasa ". . . that he refused to use the original seal because he wanted to show that he did not approve of the Agreement."[20]

The lack of official seals momentarily halted the flow of events in Beijing. But the Chinese quickly recovered from this unexpected setback and got a Beijing seal maker to carve five Chinese style seals or "chops" (Chinese, *yinzhang*) with the name of the five Tibetan negotiators on them. These ivory seals were identical in size and style to the name-seals used by the Chinese signatories, except that the Tibetan names are in the Tibetan *u-chen* print script—and not in the required *horyig* or seal script. None of the Tibetan delegation members, except perhaps for Ngabö, had asked for or given permission for such personal seals to be made in their names.

Goldstein attempts to explain the Chinese point of view on this issue. "The Chinese did make new seals for the Tibetans, but these were just personal seals with each delegate's name carved on them. Other than this, there were no forged government seals."

Goldstein's explanation would hold water if the Chinese had just made "personal seals" for the Tibetans to take home as souvenirs. But these seals were subsequently used to provide legal validation to the Seventeen Point Treaty; hence the seals were used as official government seals hence they were manufactured under false pretences; hence they were forged.

The illegality of these seals not only extended to the fact that the Tibetans had not authorized the making of these seals but also as none of these seals were officially registered (at the Department of Seals), as was traditionally required in China. Even these days in China, personal seals and seals of companies have to be registered with the Public Security Bureau. To use unregistered seals on any official document is an illegal and criminal act in China.

Besides the absence of authentic seals, the Seventeen Point Treaty also has no signatures and no mention of the ranks or official designations of the Tibetan negotiators. The names of the negotiators are all written uniformly in the mid-cursive *drutsa* script (a variant of the *umê*) and are not signatures. Tibet has a rich tradition of individualized signatures (*tsen-tak* or *sa-yik*), always written in the flowing *khyuk* cursive and very distinctive and stylized, as signatures are in most cultures. The present Dalai Lama's signature and the signature of the Tibetan plenipotentiary, Shatra Lonchen, on the Simla Convention of 1914 are dynamic examples of this particular kind of personal inscription.

The Tibetan officials in Beijing may have been out of their depth in negotiating with an implacable and cynical adversary. Nonetheless, in their own social and cultural milieu, they were literate and urbane people who would, in the normal course of events, not have hesitated to apply their signatures to official documents they were required to sign. Not signing the Seventeen Point Treaty was perhaps their ineffective compromise in expressing their opposition to the proceedings.

On 23 May, the "Agreement for the Peaceful Liberation of Tibet" was concluded and the news was broadcast over Beijing Radio. All the seventeen points of the Treaty were read out. According to Tsering Shakya, "The Tibetan government was shocked and alarmed." Clearly, the Tibetan government had no knowledge of what had been going on. The Dalai Lama was equally in the dark. "Neither I nor my government were told that an agreement had been signed. We first came to know of it from a broadcast that Ngabö made on Peking Radio. It was a terrible shock when we came to hear the terms of it."[21]

After the conclusion of the Treaty proceedings at Zhongnanhai and the official banquet presided over by Mao Zedong on the 24th, the Tibetan delegation made preparations to return to Tibet. They decided to sail to Calcutta from Shanghai as they could then travel quickly to Sikkim and make their personal report to the Dalai Lama and the cabinet at Dromo, just across the Sikkim border. But the chief negotiator was unable to travel with the delegation. Ngabö, in a statement in Lhasa in 1989, explained why, at the same time confessing to his colleagues his hitherto undisclosed status as a Chinese official. "I request the Chinese government to see to the safe return of the four other delegates to Tibet. As for me, I am a subject of Chamdo Liberation Committee . . . I am obligated to do whatever they tell me."[22]

According to Shakya, "The Chinese told Ngabö he must return via Chamdo because they feared for his life, but in reality, the Chinese were suspicious that Ngabö might remain in India."[23] The more likely reason for not allowing Ngabö to return with the other Tibetans and instead of sending him to Lhasa in the company of Phüntso Wangye and General Wang Qimei could have been a psychological one. Communist cadres were aware that ideological indoctrination or "thought control" required sustained monitoring and reinforcement.* Even in Lhasa, right up to 1959, Ngabö was escorted, round the clock, by PLA bodyguards, a Chinese chauffeur, a Chinese aide, and regularly accompanied by various Chinese officials.

In Lhasa, the Tibetan Prime Ministers Lukhangwa and Lobsang Tashi refused to recognize the Treaty. The National Assembly while declaring that the delegates had signed the "agreement" under "extenuating circumstances" (aka under duress) called on the Kashag to accept the "agreement", which the Kashag appears to have done so, in a radio message but not in a formal written document.

The strangest thing about the Seventeen Point Treaty as it stands today is that it still lacks proper signatures and does not contain a single *official or personal* Tibetan seal, which renders the document without any legal foundation in Tibetan or any other legal tradition. On the matter of the lack of signatures, one might perhaps grant that the written names could have sufficed as temporary expediency. Legally speaking, a representative may sign a treaty *ad referendum*, i.e., under the condition that the signature is subsequently confirmed by his state. In this case, the signature becomes definitive once confirmed by the responsible organ. But in the case of the Seventeen Point Treaty, there were no signatures at the time nor subsequently and no formal

---

*The American psychiatrist Robert Lifton interviewed many American servicemen who were brainwashed when they had been POWs during the Korean War. Lifton discovered that when the POWs returned to the United States their thinking soon returned to normal, contrary to the popular image of 'brainwashing' being a permanent or long-term condition. See *Thought Reform and the Psychology of Totalism: A Study of 'Brainwashing' in China*, Robert J. Lifton, 1961.

confirmation of the names of the officials later by Tibetan authorities in Lhasa.

This brings us to the fundamental reality that the Seventeen Point Treaty was never ratified. After they marched their troops into Lhasa, the Chinese had every opportunity to insist on a formal ratification ceremony at the Potala palace, where the great seal of the Dalai Lama, the seal of the Kashag, the seal of the National Assembly (*tsongdu*), and the seals of the three great monasteries Drepung, Sera, and Ganden would be affixed on the document (as was done on the Anglo–Tibet Treaty of 1904), and proper signatures obtained from all individual representatives.

If there were a scrap of legitimacy to the Seventeen Point Treaty, I have no doubt Chinese leaders would have insisted on such formal ratification of the document at Lhasa. Perhaps Beijing was wary about subjecting this document to any further and needless discussion or scrutiny that might, even inadvertently, bring about the unravelling of this intricate conspiracy—and the exposure of the big swindle to the Tibetan leadership and people. Better to let sleeping victims lie, no matter how restless or fitful their slumber.

So, all you have to this day is the barebones document cobbled together in Beijing in 1951. You can view the original Treaty at the Tibet Museum in Lhasa on 19 Luobulinka Road, alongside a tableau of life-sized terracotta statues of the Tibetan negotiators seated at a long table, diligently participating in this most wretched, heart-breaking and tragic of farces in Tibet's long history.

6

REQUIEM

"O Stranger, go tell the Lacedaemonians that here we lie at rest, obedient to their commands."

—Simonides of Ceos

In Lhasa city, news of the disaster at Chamdo came as a devastating shock. There was fear, alarm, and grief among the people and also deep anger. Public bitterness was directed not only at the Kashag and the governor-general of Kham, but also understandably (though perhaps not in all fairness) at the defeated generals. The anger and resentment of the Lhasa populace was expressed through the traditional medium of satirical songs that mocked the follies of the rich and powerful.

These songs were sung by young women of the city who gathered at the city's wells and springs in the evening to collect water. Such songs proliferated around the period of the Tibetan New Year and the Mönlam or "Great Prayer" Festival when thousands of monks from the "Three Seats" or the three major monasteries Ganden, Drepung and Sera would assemble in the city for special services and ceremonies. Since vast quantities of tea and meals would have to be prepared for this great assemblage, many young women of Lhasa would volunteer to carry water to the Jokhang Temple kitchens as an act of devotion.

The girls, dressed in their best, carrying terracotta flagons (secured to their backs with *tussore* silk scarves), sang these satirical and sometimes prophetic songs that were, as a genre, called "*mönlam chumae shay*" or "songs of the water carriers of the Great Prayer." These songs were said to be divinely transmitted to the girls by the goddess Pé Lhamo (Sanskrit, Śrīdēvī), but educated people were aware that more mundane (and politically motivated) agencies were often responsible for these verses. The first song heard in Lhasa after the fall of Chamdo:

Ngabö departed wrathfully
Lhalu remained leisurely
Older brother Ragashar
Just built a dam of sand

Ngabö ngar nas thay song
Lhalu lhod nas shug song
Jhola Ragashar gyis
Chemay rag chig kyon song

The verse plays on the homophonic syllables in the name Ngabö and the Tibetan word for wrath or anger, "*ngar*"; also for the "*lh*" consonant in Lhalu and the Tibetan word for leisure, "*lhoe*." Ragashar Phuntsog Rabgay was then commander-in-chief of the Tibetan army, and it is difficult to fault the people's perception that his defence plan was just a dam of sand. The Tibetan word for dam being incidentally "*ra*", the first syllable in the commander-in-chief's name. However, one can wholeheartedly agree with the sentiments expressed in the next song.

At the centre of a hundred good men
Is the able General Muja.
Just a worthless pack of foxes
Are the governor-general and his staff.

Mi zang gya kyi kyil na
Go chod Muja dapön

Jabchung wa moe khyu tsog
Dochi ngo las nam pa

General Muja received more than a song of praise. After the surviving officers and soldiers of the Tibetan army were finally released by the Chinese and allowed to return to Lhasa, the Tibetan government distributed awards and appointments to him and others who had conscientiously performed their duties in Eastern Tibet. Muja received a promotion to *rimshi* fourth rank and was appointed the administrator (*dro-che*) of Dromo, the principal trade centre on the Sikkim frontier. The appointment appears to have been made not only as a reward but also to make it convenient for Muja to leave Tibet in case the PLA wanted to exact revenge for the many Chinese soldiers he had killed.

Unfortunately, in order to not offend Ngabö and the Chinese military leadership that had been frustrated and antagonized by Lhalu's refusal to surrender and his stubborn defense of Kongpo Gyamda, the Tibetan government was obliged to gloss over the truth of Lhalu's remarkable accomplishment and deny it any public recognition. Since Lhalu was already a minister, he had to be reinstated in the Kashag. He was soon dismissed in 1952 on a trumped-up charge of maladministration during his tenure as governor-general.[1]

The families of those who died in the line of duty received cash, tax relief and awards. Major Bögangwa's family, headed by his wife Lhanzom, was granted, in perpetuity, an estate at Tö Dzelung in Western Tibet.[2] Even non-military officials who had performed their duties faithfully were rewarded. The official Maja Tsewang Gyurme told me he was awarded the magistracy of Duchung Dzong for his work in organizing military supplies and transport under desperate circum-stances.

But as natural and understandable as the anger and frustration of the Lhasa populace was, the two objects-of-scorn in the next song do perhaps require a reappraisal in terms of their perceived failings, since in the case of the former, I have been able to glean a few fresh insights from an old account, and in the case of the latter, there has been, because of the pain and bitterness of our own defeat, an inability to view the event in its true military context.

> Above all, the two-headed prince of Dergé
> Then the useless general Karchung
> Have filled Kham Military Headquarters
> With the awful smell of diarrhoea[3]

> *De-sey daru tsos chay*
> *Jaab chung karchung dapön*
> *Khams shung magar nang la*
> *Nyang mae dri mae gyang song*

The treachery of the Prince of Dergé is a given in any discussion on Chamdo. Everyone agrees that he capitulated without a fight when the Chinese attacked Markham. Goldstein maintains that "Dergé-sey must have had no will to fight: on 12 October he surrendered his entire force.[4] With such unanimity of condemnation, it will require more than a few lines or a paragraph to discuss this case to everyone's satisfaction, so perhaps it should receive a more thorough and exclusive examination in the next chapter.

As for General Karchung, I am persuaded that the lyricist for this particular song may have damned our general as much for his defeat as for the fact that his name rhymes perfectly with the Tibetan word "*japchung*" meaning silly or useless. Another, perhaps unconscious reason for this jeering dismissal of Karchung could have stemmed from his "landed gentry" (*gerpa*) status and his not belonging to the higher peerage (*dipön-midrag*). The aristocrat Phulungwa's flagrant cowardice was somehow overlooked in these songs.

Karchung Tsering Thondup was born in 1913 into a gerpa family in the Yarlung district.[5] He started his official career as a junior lay-official (*shol-drung*). In 1930, he received his military training at the Drapchi military camp most probably serving in the Drongdrak regiment based at Drapchi. In late 1932, he served as the ceremonial ADC (*gagpa*) to Tethong Gyurme Gyatso at his enthronement ceremony when he was appointed a cabinet minister. It must be borne in mind that

Karchung rose to become a general in the Tibetan army on his own merit, in a system that did not actually encourage such a thing. He was considered a capable and courageous officer by his peers and because of his record Lhalu had entrusted him with the defence of the most vital and dangerous sector on the Tibetan frontier. Khenchen Dawa-la, who knew most of the Lhasa officers in Kham from the war of 1918 to the present, assured Robert Ford about Karchung saying that "He is a very good officer."

Let us consider the facts of Karchung's predicament at the front. With a force of five hundred regulars and about two hundred militiamen, he was expected to defend the central zone in the path of the Chinese invasion. Since this was the crucial point of their attack, the Chinese would have certainly committed one, perhaps even two regiments, around ten thousand soldiers, to overpower this vital point in the Tibetan defence.

As a rule of thumb in war, an attacking force should be at least four times as strong as the defending force in order to overcome it, all other things being equal. The Chinese were about twenty times stronger than the Tibetans at the central zone. At Kamdo Drukha, the actual ferry-crossing itself, the PLA was about forty or fifty times stronger if we assume the Tibetans had a hundred and fifty or two hundred men there.

The small Tibetan force had the advantage of the river. Still, they had no artillery, mortars, mines, grenades, heavy machine guns and barbed wire emplacements to create an effective defensive position. The Chinese had most of these things. The Tibetans could not call in air strikes or artillery cover as American troops could in Korea and Vietnam or even expect medical care or evacuation for the wounded. They were also aware that they would not be relieved and could not expect reinforcements anytime in the foreseeable future.

The Tibetans also knew that even if they wiped out every Chinese soldier in the first attack, the Chinese could draw on a vast standing army to mount another attack. In the autumn of 1950, China had some five million, I repeat *five million*, men under arms. The bare fact that the Tibetan forward defence at Kamdo Drukha on the western bank of the Drichu River, a hundred and fifty regulars and fifty or so militiamen, stood their ground and fought almost to the last man is a memorable achievement, to be celebrated in epic verse, not ridiculed or forgotten.

Then the fact that General Karchung had prepared a secondary line of defence at Rangsum, where he surprised the advancing Chinese army, inflicting heavy casualties on them is astonishing; as is the orderly withdrawal he undertook towards Chamdo, but in the performance of which a lapse of judgement caused his force to be ambushed and wiped out.

One of the most challenging manoeuvres in war is conducting a fighting retreat. Napoleon said, ". . . a retreat, however skilful the manoeuvres may be, will always produce an injurious moral effect on the army." So, in order to maintain not just an orderly withdrawal but to keep up the vigilance and fighting spirit of your force requires leadership of the highest order. Karchung was perhaps unable to summon up such qualities in himself and his officers during the latter half of his retreat, but we must bear in mind that the Tibetan force was encumbered with baggage trains and the wives and children of the soldiers, while the pursuing Chinese were stripped for action, *in extremis*. They carried their own mixture, "*dai shih fen*" a mixture of flour, nuts, salt, eggs, in a canvas tube like a sausage curled around his body or over his shoulder. Officers brought up the rear, driving, pushing and bullying their men to the point of exhaustion—where they would "be coughing up blood." The fact that the Chinese caught up with Karchung was not inevitable, considering the fact that the Tibetans had horses (the Chinese also had some mounted units) but the Tibetans had only to pause but momentarily or stumble but once, for it to become so.

We have the other epic account of General Muja stopping a Chinese attack dead for three days and then conducting an orderly retreat, in incredibly difficult territory, for about a week, under constant attack. He was, certainly, not fighting a Chinese division as Karchung was, but he had, at the very least, to contend with five thousand Chinese troops against his five hundred regulars and a few hundred militiamen. It was, without doubt, a tremendous achievement. Ford certainly thought so:

Then I realized how remarkable Muja's orderly withdrawal had
been, for the soldier's wives and children had come too. The Tibetan
army was not designed for retreat. When troops went to the front
line, they took their families with them. With Muja's men now
came as many women and children, with all their household goods
and personal belongings piled up on yaks and mules. There were
tents, pots and pans, carpets, butter churns, bundles of clothes,
and babies in bundles on their mother's backs. It was a fantastic
sight. What made it more remarkable was the absence of panic or
even anxiety. The women began to unpack at once, pitched tents,
lit fires, and brewed tea. They would pack up again when their
husbands moved on.

The organization of the Tibetan army was indeed archaic. The
individual Tibetan soldier was not as well trained, certainly not as well
equipped as his European, American or Chinese counterpart. But he
had native toughness, courage and *amor patriae*. No Tibetan soldier
threw down his weapon and fled at the first sign of the enemy. Even
when defeated he gave a good account of himself. We might recall
the swift and catastrophic defeat of the French in WWII, when the
poilus threw away their rifles at the front and ran away shouting the
now infamous phrase "*sauve qui peut*" or save yourself. The overall size
and strength of the two opposing forces in that war were about the
same. The French and the British had about three million men, the
attacking Germans and Italians three point three million. The allies
had more armour.

Then there is the British surrender of Singapore. The defenders, in
point of fact, outnumbered the attacking Japanese 25th Army, four to
one, and they had more aircraft and some of the greatest fighting ships
in the world. Then there were Singapore's famous 'monster' guns,
which should have settled the matter, but as the face-saving myth goes,
they could not fire on the Japanese because they were facing south,
in the wrong direction. We now know they could have been turned
around without too much trouble. The main Japanese advance came
down from the north, on bicycles!

There is also the notable case in point, far more immediate and relevant to the conflict in Tibet, which took place a little more than a week after the Tibetan defeat at Chamdo. On 25 October 1950, China attacked the UN Coalition Forces in Korea. In terms of overall strength, the UN Command was nearly a million strong, the Communists just over a million. The Chinese also had no air power to speak of and lacked the overwhelming air and artillery cover that the American ground troops could summon, almost at will. The Americans also had many tanks and transport vehicles, which the Chinese did not. But the precipitous flight of the Americans and their allies from North Korea is regarded as one of the most humiliating of retreats in American military history—the big "bug out" as it has been referred to since.

Colonel Paul Freeman of the Twenty-Third Infantry put it bitterly to his executive officer. "This is a sight that hasn't been seen for hundreds of years—the men of the whole United States Army fleeing from a battlefield, abandoning their wounded, running for their lives . . . looting what they could carry from the vast supply dumps in Pyongyang—alcohol, tobacco, sugar, and acre upon acre of equipment was put to the torch."[6] A British officer from the Eight Royal Irish Hussars was struck by the apathy on the UN side. "Nothing appeared to have been attempted, let alone achieved. Millions of dollars' worth of equipment had been destroyed without a shot being fired, or any attempt made to consider its possible evacuation."[7]

Even in defeat, many of the Tibetan officers at Chamdo were unexpectedly defiant. Ford mentions that after being captured, the tired, dejected and denture-less General Karchung did not look afraid. In fact, when a "bandit chief" Jagoe Topden, who had provided the Chinese with transport and guides, swaggered past them in the company of Chinese officers, Karchung's eyes "flashed" as he ran past the guards to attack the traitor. Muja and the others had to struggle to hold the furious soldier back "spluttering toothless threats." Ford also mentions that even in captivity, Muja and Karchung fought over their battles again and explained to each other why the Tibetans ought to have won.

"'If we had one of your radios, and there had been another at Gangto Druga (Kamdo Drukha), they could not have caught us like that,' said Khatang. (Karchung).

'If there had been a radio at Riwoché, I should not be here now,' I said."

Inconsequential as it may seem now, this brief exchange does, in an actual sense, provide a direction towards where a historical reappraisal of the fall of Chamdo ought to focus. Yes, there were many factors for the defeat of the Tibetan army, a number of which could have, at one point or another in modern Tibetan history, possibly been rectified, or at least partially reformed. That the size of the army needed to be radically increased and its training and weaponry modernized requires no discussion.

But it is intriguing to speculate that even without the much-needed military reforms, a single item of equipment might have made the crucial strategic difference to the outcome of the entire campaign, as General Karchung pointed out to Robert Ford. If Karchung had just one radio transceiver, then Chamdo headquarters and Lhasa would have learned about the attack five days before they actually did. And what a difference those five days would have made. There would have been time to organize adequate transport at Chamdo for the retreating troops and their families, time to empty the Chamdo armoury, and time to make an unhurried retreat to Lho Dzong.

And to set the bar a little higher, what if there had been more radio sets? Maybe four more, or let's say eight, while we're at it: two for Muja, two for Karchung, two for Phulungwa at Riwoché and two for the general at Markham in the south. It would certainly have been possible to buy these sets (along with batteries and generators) at Calcutta as Ford did, without any trouble. They were WWII surpluses and easily affordable. Calcutta was floating in the stuff.* A dozen or so ethnic Tibetan youths from Gangtok, Darjeeling and Kalimpong with basic Indian school degrees could have been recruited and trained for

---

* Calcutta was the principal supply depot for Allied forces fighting in Burma and China.

the job, as Ford had done quite successfully with four such young men. This would have just meant enlarging a pre-existing program without having to overcome significant political or financial hurdles.

Since it did not involve buying weapons or ammunition, it did not require the authorization of the Government of India or the overcoming of any other diplomatic hurdles. And what a difference those radios would have made. Definite orders and information coming from Chamdo would have reduced the uncertainty and confusion that commanders faced on the front lines and maybe goaded Karchung to speed up his retreat, perhaps even prevented Phulungwa from panicking. But even with just the one spare radio set at Karchung's headquarters, sending the signal of the first Chinese attack, what a difference that would have made to the defence of Chamdo and Tibetan history.

But would it? Some will ask. Sooner or later, the Chinese would have made it to Lho Dzong, and with their enormous superiority in numbers, they would have wiped out the Tibetan defences there. That is the general opinion, but it ignores certain crucial factors operating against the Chinese.

First, as Ford tells us, winter was fast approaching, and it was bitterly cold from Chamdo to Dergé. In just, possibly, a week or so, the many high passes in that region would have become snowbound. Already the countryside from Chamdo to the West, "was frozen hard now, and for water we had to melt snow or crack the ice over streams. It was bitterly cold at night." "General Winter" was as much an ally of the Tibetans as of the Russians defending their homeland against Napoleon or Hitler. European travellers have recorded temperatures lower than minus sixty-seven degrees Fahrenheit on some of the high passes from Chamdo to Dergé. Tibetans also had dependable allies in the altitude and terrain. Comparing his Tibetan friends with his captors, Ford observed, "It was harder for the Chinese troops. They were not used to high altitudes, and their clothing gave them less protection than ours."

With the passes snowed in, it would have been impossible for the Chinese to transport supplies from the rear. The motor road only extended to Kandzé. Beyond that, the Chinese would have had to force their pack animals and porters through the many snowbound passes to Chamdo, and that would unquestionably have led to a disaster. We must remember that the retreating Tibetan army had already requisitioned most pack animals in the Chamdo area.

Some American academic accounts of the Chamdo invasion note, with awe, the speed of the Chinese advance units apparently unencumbered by any conventional supply train or convoy. But that intensity of forward movement could only have been sustained for a couple of days at the most. The military writer Edgar O'Ballance cautions, "Much capital is made of the idea that the Red Chinese soldier, on only a bandolier of rice which he carries himself, can march and fight on almost indefinitely. The harsh fact is that he can only march for short distances on such a Spartan diet. It is a fallacy to assume that the Red Chinese army does not need a conventional line-of-communication or supply."

Then we have to consider the overall fitness of the Communist Eighteenth Army to exploit its initial success. The Chinese government published casualty figures for the Chamdo offensive in 2011, claiming fifty-four Tibetan soldiers and seventy-four PLA troops killed in the battle. "These figures, are of course, completely improbable,"[8] a leading expert on the Chamdo invasion wrote to me. Ford mentions that when he was being taken down to China, he saw many wounded Chinese soldiers at the monastery of Dergé, brought back from the Tibetan front. On the high end, we have Edgar O'Ballance's figures that seem very approximate. He writes, "It is thought that out of the original total of 35,000 men who invaded Tibet, the Reds suffered at least 10,000 casualties, of whom perhaps 2,000 froze to death, 2,000 were killed in action, 3,000 'disappeared' and 3,000 died of fever." About the Chinese soldiers who disappeared, this is what O'Ballance maintains: "One Red division was diverted into the mountains to cut off a large detachment of the Tibetan Army, which was retreating, and it ran into the Kham tribesmen, who had massed to bar its way. The whole division, over 3,000 Red soldiers disappeared and was not heard of again."

Every Tibetan I know who first witnessed Chinese soldiers coming to Tibet remembers that they were in terrible shape: lips cracked, faces blistered and peeling (because of the savage Tibetan winds), feet bleeding, uniforms in rags, freezing and shivering, sometimes coughing blood, unable to eat tsampa properly, and choking and gagging on the powdery stuff. They were definitely on their last legs. Their officers had driven them on, for weeks, most probably without sleep, across some of the highest and harshest terrains in the world. We will perhaps never know how many of them died on the march.

Could the otherwise exhausted Eighteenth Army have been able to force-march another week to Lho Dzong, attempt a crossing of the turbulent, swift-flowing Upper Salween and then make an assault up a steep mountainside against the well-prepared defences of a massive fortress? The Tibetans would also have had some artillery, this time around, and about 2,000 to 2,500 men to defend the Dzong.

The Chinese also wouldn't have been able to bypass Lho Dzong and continue to Lhasa without capturing intact the one bridge (over the Upper Salween) that the Tibetans would have almost certainly destroyed. Ford was right to insist "It (Lho Dzong) could not be outflanked; and from Lho Dzong to Lhasa, the country was wild and rugged, with an average elevation of 12,000 feet and passes of up to 17,100 feet, snowbound for most of the year."* But assuming Ford was wrong, would the Chinese have risked bypassing this vital fortification?

Even under the best of circumstance, there are limits to how much bypassing you can do in a given battle situation without risking being cut off altogether. If the advancing Chinese army had left the Lho Dzong fortress intact and advanced on to Lhasa, they would certainly have risked compromising their supply lines and communications. The Chinese couldn't have also risked staying in the vicinity of Lho Dzong for the winter. The risk of the army being cut off would

---

* Of these passes, the Shar Dhang-la and Nub Dhang-la (East and West Dhang-la passes) were so high, frozen, and snowbound that it gave rise to a saying that when crossing these passes ". . . the fox-fur cap on one's head is as precious as one's dear parents (*go washa drinchen phamo ray*)." Further east on the same trail was the infamous Dergé Tro-la pass, where many invading PLA troops and later over three thousand road-workers lost their lives. The Communist propaganda song "*Gechang Erlang Shan*" (Sing the Erlang Mountain) was written in commemoration.

have been too great. No responsible commander would have kept an army in such a hostile and exposed area for a whole winter with little expectation of supplies or reinforcements, if he did not want a disaster on his hands. We must also remember that after Lhalu's establishment of a defensive line at Kongpo Gyamda, the PLA did not advance further towards Lhasa.

Goldstein explains this halt in the invasion as stemming from the benign and confident nature of the Chinese Communist regime than from strategic necessity. But it appears that Chinese commanders in the field were in no way confident or assured about their security in Kham. Even after the conclusion of the Seventeen Point Treaty and Lhalu's withdrawal from Kongpo Gyamda, General Wang Qimei, who commanded the Fifty-Second Division, and who was regarded as a "skilful and brave soldier," was absolutely convinced that the Tibetan army (or what remained of it) was capable of springing a last-minute surprise and would ambush the advance force he was leading to Lhasa.[9] If the Tibetan army had held out at Lho Dzong, it is almost certain that the Fifty-Second Division and its cautious commander would not have attempted to cross the Upper Mekong and attack the fortress, but would have retreated to Chamdo, perhaps even further east, before winter set in.

This, of course, leads us to the next obvious question, and one can almost sense the naysayers holding their breath in anticipation of this one. *The Chinese would have come back again the following year, in even greater force. What could the Tibetans have done then?*

But that is the easiest question to answer. There was no way that a second invasion force could have been organized and sent to Tibet. We must bear in mind that the Chinese army entered the Korean War on 19 October 1950, a week after the fall of Chamdo. If the Tibetan army was even partially intact and Lhasa had not surrendered, the whole Tibetan struggle against Communist China would have taken on a far greater international dimension, which it had lacked a few weeks earlier. Whether the United Nations or America would have opened up another front in Tibet is debatable, but the Tibetans would have received an infusion of military aid and maybe even some advisors from the U.S. army. Perhaps a backup force as well. And quite possibly, that might have been enough.

Although the Americans would have faced unique problems of transport and terrain that they had not in Korea (or later in Vietnam), they definitely would not have faced a divided population or an unpopular ruler. And the logistical problems in Tibet would not have been any more taxing than those posed by the Ledo/Burma Road in World War II—which were eventually overcome. Finally, we must remember that the Chinese took enormous losses in Korea. Over half a million Chinese troops were killed, including Mao's son, and the Russians completely cut off all their support for the war after Stalin's death in 1953.

It has been consistently pointed out by pro-Chinese academics that before the invasion, when the Tibetan government had attempted to gain the support of the Western democracies and had even sent a mission to the U.S., Britain and India, it had received disappointingly innocuous and noncommittal responses. The Dalai Lama too mentions in his autobiography that the U.S. was not interested in Tibetan independence, only in Tibetan resistance to communism. The Dalai Lama was correct, in so far as Communist China had not entered the Korean War, but after that Rubicon moment, there was a paradigm shift in Western thinking about Communist China.

There has been a tendency of the Western public to view the Korean War as a distant sideshow, and it has not received the intellectual and even creative attention and discussion as the Second World War or even the Vietnam War. As the military historian, Max Hastings asks in the introduction to his 1987 classic on the Korean War, "How is it, then, that the other great mid-twentieth-century conflict with communism, Korea, remains so neglected? Popular awareness of the Korean war today centres upon the television comedy show M*A*S*H." There is, consequently, a mistaken assumption that the war had little or no impact on the way subsequent historical events in Asia and even Europe turned out.

Only recently, certain historians, one being the late Professor Tony Judt of the Remarque Institute, have made clear how fundamentally that distant conflict altered the entire scale and urgency of the Cold War. Judt maintains that "If the Korean War had not broken out just at this moment, the contours of recent European history might look very different indeed." The uneasiness and resistance of France and other European nations to the rearming of Germany, even their reluctance to spending precious resources on their national rearmament, was resolved for them by the Korean War.

This is why Judt considers that Stalin's support for the Korean War ". . . was his most serious miscalculation of all. The Americans and West Europeans immediately drew the (erroneous) conclusion that Korea was a diversion or prelude and that Germany would be next—an inference encouraged by East German party boss Walter Ulbricht's imprudent boast that the Federal Republic would be next to fall. The Soviet Union had successfully tested an atomic bomb just eight months earlier, leading American military experts to exaggerate Soviet preparedness for war . . . The scale of (subsequent) Western rearmament was dramatic indeed. The U.S. defence budget rose from 15.5 billion in August 1950 to $70 billion by December of the following year. American allies in NATO also increased defence spending dramatically."[10]

The Korean War also led to other long-lasting effects. Until the conflict in Korea, the U.S. had no plans to intervene in the Chinese Civil War and had largely abandoned the government of Chiang Kai-Shek, which had retreated to Taiwan. The start of the Korean War rendered untenable any policy that would have caused Taiwan to fall under Communist control.

In such a climate, especially in the disastrous winter of 1950 when UN troops were "bugging out" of North Korea when General Macarthur was threatening to use the atomic bomb on China, and even the cautious president Truman affirmed such a possibility at a press conference,* is it even possible to consider, under such circumstances, that the "Free World" would not have—even if dictated by the

---

*On 2 February 1953, the new U.S. president, Eisenhower, suggested in his State of the Union address that he might use the atomic bomb on China.

narrowest of self-interests—supported an independent Tibet that had not surrendered and still had a military force engaging the Chinese?

Though we can cautiously conclude that it was quite possible for a truncated Tibet, west of Lho Dzong or Kongpo Gyamda, to have survived and even likely flourished as an independent nation up to the present day—much in the way of South Korea or Taiwan—such speculations have not been the primary object of this prolonged exercise. It was rather to draw some attention to the memory of the valiant Tibetan soldiers and Khampa militiamen whose courage and steadfastness in standing up to an enemy many, many times larger and more powerful—instead of being honoured and celebrated in an annual rite or enshrined in a memorial of some kind—has been invariably ignored by the Tibetan leadership and largely forgotten by Tibetans, and consequently by the world.

It was also to point that the invasion of October 1950 was, by no stretch of the imagination, a "peaceful liberation" of Tibet as the Chinese and their friends insisted on calling it, whereby brilliant Chinese strategy basically panicked the Tibetans into surrendering. Casualty records from the Tibetan military headquarters in Lhasa are unavailable, but a Lhasa official who served at Chamdo in 1950 gave me an approximate estimation of over three thousand regulars and militiamen killed. Writing in 1962, General Zhang Guohua, commander of the PLA invasion force, later made this somewhat inexplicable claim that at Chamdo, " . . . 5,738 enemy troops were liquidated (killed?), over 5,700 destroyed (captured?) and that more than 3,000 peacefully surrendered."[11] Alex Raymond, in an email to me, disagreed with these figures and felt that the above statement might have been mistranslated. "We cannot, therefore, know the real number of deaths until the archives are opened to researchers if they are one day. Until that date, I think the number of about 1,100 Tibetans dead seems plausible."[12]

Bapa Phüntso Wangye, the Tibetan Communist who was involved in the planning and the execution of the Chinese attack in the southern sector, made the admission that " . . . many Tibetans had been killed and wounded in the Chamdo campaign." In perhaps an unconscious act of contrition, he added that "The Tibetan soldiers fought bravely, but that they were no match for the superior numbers and better training" of the Chinese forces.

Lastly, this reappraisal was to draw attention to the arrogance and fallacy of those who suggest, sometimes even aggressively contend, that the goal for which the Tibetan army fought was backward-looking and unattainable; that the Chinese triumph at Chamdo was a dialectically predetermined event; that it was "historically inevitable" that the "People's Liberation" Army would march victoriously into Lhasa, and anyone not accepting this inescapable conclusion was either a dyed-in-the-wool reactionary or a hopeless romantic—possibly both.

Forty-six years earlier, another great Imperialist power, similarly assured of its military superiority and "progressive" mission, invaded Tibet from across the Himalayas. More than a few thousand Tibetan country-levies wielding swords, spears and muskets were slaughtered by well-trained professional soldiers armed with repeating rifles, Maxim machine-guns and modern artillery. But an epitaph of sorts, penned by an ethnologist and reporter embedded with this British military expedition, might also serve to honour those Tibetans who died for their country in October 1950:

> Enemies as the Tibetans were, they nevertheless were entitled to the credit that belongs to brave men defending their homes against odds. And, it may be, they deemed it not a wholly unenviable fate to have died within the gateway of their country, this Tibetan Thermopylae where their beautiful hills, their protectors during life, can still keep guard around them in death.[13]

7

FALL OF THE SOUTH

The sun sets rapidly in Tibet. It was already dark when the servants began lighting the Petromax Lanterns in the residency of the governor-general of Eastern Tibet at Chamdo.

It was the evening of 3 March 1934. In the spacious dining room designed in the European fashion, with a large rectangular oak table at the centre, sat the governor-general, a glass of Scotch and soda in his right hand. He was talking to a trader, an informant who had returned from a trip to Chengdu, the capital of Sichuan province in China. He had some fresh information about the warlord Liu Wenhui, who was also the Guomindang-appointed governor of Sichuan province, and Wenhui's nephew General Liu Xiang, who had revolted against him.

A couple of years earlier, the Sichuan warlord Liu Wenhui had inflicted a severe defeat on the Tibetan army in Eastern Tibet, forcing the Tibetans to withdraw from the territory they had gained in 1918 and retreat to a position across the Drichu River. The loss was a major one for the Tibetans and a brief moment of panic gripped Lhasa. A rumour spread that the defeated governor-general, Ngabö Tenzin Phuntsok* had committed suicide by swallowing a diamond ring. In fact, it appears that the old gentleman had died of heart failure from

---

*Ngabö's widow later married Ngawang Jigme, who took the Ngabö name and became governor-general of Kham in 1950.

the stress of the conflict. The historian Tsepon Shakabpa mentions that
". . . his wind element became agitated."

My grandfather, Tethong Gyurme Gyatso, was on home leave at
his estate in Shigatsé district but was ordered to return immediately
to Eastern Tibet and take charge of the disastrous situation. He
was appointed governor-general of Kham, with the cabinet rank of
"additional" minister (*kalön las-phar*). The entire town of Shigatsé
turned out to see Tethong Gyurme Gyatso and the Third (Shigatsé)
regiment depart for Kham. A dress review was held at the *jiaochang*
(Chinese), the old parade ground of the Manchu garrison in that town
before 1911. As the soldiers lined up in their ceremonial uniforms
with their rifles ready to present arms, the eight snare drums of the
regimental band struck up a tremendous roll. Startled by the sudden
noise, the General's horse bucked and reared. Gyurme Gyatso was
thrown off, and his right shoulder blade was fractured. Subsequently,
his entire right arm became paralysed.

But there could be no refusing an order from the Great Thirteenth
Dalai Lama. On instructions from Lhasa, the two Shigatsé magistrates,
accompanied by a physician, came to the Tethong manor to check on
Gyurme Gyatso's condition. Though they reported his injury as genuine,
and the Dalai Lama himself was, in a subsequent audience, extremely
solicitous (the Thirteenth was hard on his officials but invariably
polite) Gyurme Gyatso had to leave immediately for Chamdo. By the
time he got there, much territory had been lost. An unsatisfactory peace
treaty had already been concluded on 15 June 1933, and a cease-fire
line (*mentsam-shagsa*) established along the Drichu River. Gyurme
Gyatso was not happy with the situation he had inherited. Judging by
subsequent events, it appears he had unstated intentions of reordering
this situation in Tibet's favour should the opportunity present itself.

My mother remembered she was with her father at Chamdo that
night in 1934, in the dining room of the residency. He liked to smoke
a *hookah* pipe with his evening whiskey, a habit he had picked up on
a trip to India, which was unusual with Tibetans. She remembered
that as she uncoiled the long satin-covered tube and handed her father
the stem of the pipe, she heard the faint tinkle of *lingshang* bells in the

distance. Then the mastiffs at the gate of the residency began to bark, and she heard hoof beats coming into the courtyard.

A tired dusty courier came in with an urgent message from Markham in the south. There had been a violent mutiny in the Markham garrison led by Topgyal Pangdatsang, a major or rupön in the Sixth (Chadang) Regiment of the Tibetan army and a local chieftain. A band of about a hundred men from his tribe had attacked the Tibetan military headquarters at Garthok, the capital of Markham. Topgyal had managed to sneak a number of his men inside the fort and then fired on the unsuspecting Tibetan soldiers. They captured a senior monk official, Thupten Sangpo Tsathora, but Nornang Sonam Dorje, the Markham *theiji* or the governor of Markham, had been on a tour of the various monasteries of the district, making funeral offerings on behalf of the Thirteenth Dalai Lama who had passed on to "the heavenly fields" a couple of months earlier.

Nornang and his family were returning to Garthok when a leading Markham chieftain, Tsultrim Gyaltsen Phupatsang, warned them of Topgyal's treachery. They immediately rode north to Chamdo. My mother remembers the Markham *theiji* and his family arriving tired and dishevelled at the residency. She was sent by her mother with some servants to deliver clean clothes, towels, quilts and sheets for the Nornang family at the guest quarters of the Residency.

Gyurme Gyatso immediately sent a strong relief force to Garthok commanded by General Salungwa.* When the force got there, Topgyal and his men had already fled, crossing the Drichu to Bathang in Chinese-held territory. The Chamdo relief force only encountered a rear-guard unit of Topgyal's force, which retreated after a brief skirmish. At the fort, the bodies of the defenders were recovered. The senior-most officer among them was a major of the Second (Drapchi) regiment, Topgyal's co-officer, who had died defending the fort against his erstwhile colleague. The body of Chenjang-la, a once-

---

*My uncle, Rakra Rinpoche, then a child of nine and the incarnate lama of the monastery of Pakshö near Markham, remembers the general coming to check on his safety, on his way to Garthok.

famous Lhasa prostitute, who had married an officer and become a respectable army wife, was also discovered. She was found, shot dead, her head against a window sill, still holding a pistol from which she had fired every bullet.[1]

Tethong Gyurme Gyatso submitted a proposal to the Kashag in Lhasa for a military force to cross into Bathang and capture Topgyal, but the cabinet turned down the plan. Perhaps it was this rejection that contributed to his taking the initiative in the following crisis.

In 1935, Communist troops on their Long March made a sudden appearance in Eastern Tibet, forcing the Sichuan Governor to re-deploy part of his army away from the Tibetan frontier. Gyurme Gyatso took advantage of the situation and crossed the Drichu with a strong force and occupied Dergé and the districts surrounding it. Chiang Kai-shek wired the Tibetan government protesting this violation of the 1933 ceasefire agreement. The British also expressed concern. "The Tibetan government replied that the governor-general in Kham, Te-thong, had no authorization for the action, and that they were making inquiries. By December, the Tibetan forces had withdrawn to their previous boundary on the west bank of the Drichu."[2]

Gyurme Gyatso was then recalled to Lhasa and instated as a full minister in the Kashag. One regret he had on leaving Kham was being unable to restore the frontier he and two fellow officers had negotiated with the Chinese at Rongbatsa in 1918—under the mediation of Eric Teichman. Another was in not closing the books on the Topgyal Pangdatsang affair.[*]

Topgyal Pangdatsang was the youngest of the three Pangdatsang brothers who were famous throughout Tibet for their wealth and influence. The oldest, Yamphel, was the official Tibetan Trade Agent, a monopoly position that made him the richest man in Tibet. The second Rabga was the intellectual and revolutionary, mentioned in an earlier chapter as the founder of the West Tibet Improvement Association in

---

[*] Though he had his share of disappointments, Gyurme Gyatso was reputed to have never lost a battle. The Dalai Lama told me (in 2018) he had heard '. . . that Tethong Dapön had special "enemy subduing" (Tib: dra-thö) powers'. See my blog post https://bit.ly/2NcnnFU

Kalimpong, and who married my great-aunt from Sikkim. Topgyal, the youngest brother, remained on their ancestral lands in Gyakeg, south of Garthok, the capital of Markham. The Pangdatsangs had earlier been the stewards of the Sakya Monastery at Gyakeg, but around the turn of the century, became one of the eighteen traditional chieftains of Markham, ruling around 400 families.

Pangdatsang Nyima Gyalpo was the founder of the Pangdatsang family fortune. He had provided the Thirteenth Dalai Lama invaluable aid when His Holiness and his ministers were exiled in Darjeeling. Nima Gyalpo was subsequently appointed the official trade agent for the Tibetan government as a reward for his service. He was an enormously successful businessman, a real merchant prince, with agencies in Japan, Shanghai, Peking and Calcutta. The family was so powerful and so much in favour with the Dalai Lama that it gave rise to a wry expression, "*Sa pangdatsang, nam pangdatsang*" or "the earth is Pangdatsang's, the sky is Pangdatsang's." Pangdatsang servants might sometimes drop the phrase when bullying someone or flouting authority, or the law—in essence saying, "I am a Pangdatsang man, and what can you do about it?"

There was a joke in Kalimpong that a muleteer (all of whom were viewed as incorrigible rogues) was seen taking a dump in the middle of a tarmac road somewhere near the 11th milestone. A passerby shouted at him, "Hey you can't do that here."

"Why can't I?" The muleteer shot back, "When the earth belongs to Pangdatsang and the sky belongs to Pangdatsang, where else is there for me to take a shit?"

With so much power and privilege throughout Tibet, Topgyal Pangdatsang's revolt against the Tibetan government comes across as something of a mystery. All sorts of explanations, a few deprecatory, some sympathetic (even lionizing at times), and one supernatural have been put forward to explain the event. Of course, in the Tibetan world, it was the principal subject of gossip and discussion for a considerable while and also attracted the attention of the British authorities in India at the time. In fact interest in the Pangdatsang family and the rebellion has still not died out entirely, and one comes across the occasional article or paper on this family in the small but widespread world of International Tibetan Studies.*

The principal publicist for the Pangdatsang brothers was the Scottish missionary, George Patterson who, in half a dozen books and assorted writings, attempts to put forward the case for Topgyal Pangdatsang as a nationalist hero, a Khampa William Wallace, and once described Topgyal Pangdatsang as "the charismatic one, the horseman, the Braveheart." He also describes him as ". . . the Bonnie Prince Charlie of the Khampas, a passionately admired and idealized leader of all the Khampa tribes." When George Orwell coined the phrase "transferred nationalism" he was referring to jaded European intellectuals unconsciously seeking a substitute for old-fashioned patriotism in fascism or Stalinism, and not Scottish missionaries dreaming of Jacobite-style risings in Eastern Tibet—but he might as well have. Patterson also insists, on the most dubious genealogical grounds (as do quite a few writers on Kham), that these tribesmen were the descendants of Genghis Khan or the progenies of the Mongol Hordes.

Patterson first met Topgyal at the frontier town of Dartsedo and then later visited him at his hideout in the Bomé valley in the Bathang area, which was under Chinese administration. He was immediately taken with Topgyal's considerable charm and the warmth and kind-heartedness of his Lhasa-born wife, Tseten-la. Throughout his writings, Patterson attempts to represent Topygal as a brave and selfless Khampa nationalist, struggling to liberate his homeland from the maws, not just of Chinese tyranny, but also from the rule of an effete and foppish Lhasa aristocracy.

On closer scrutiny, the Pangdatsang mutiny appears to have less to do with Khampa nationalism than intramural Lhasa politics. At the time of the Thirteenth Dalai Lama's death, the Pangdatsangs were very close to Thupten Kunphel-la, the Dalai Lama's favourite, and the

---

*A leading authority on the Pangdatsang family and a scholar on modern Khampa history is the anthropologist and historian Carole McGranahan of the University of Colorado, Boulder—known in some Tibetan circles as 'Pangda' Carole.

most powerful political figure in Tibet. The arch-intriguer Lungshar managed to get Kunphel-la arrested, and in the National Assembly where Lungshar controlled the monastic representatives, attempted to charge Kunphel-la with murdering the Dalai Lama. But wiser counsel prevailed, and Kunphel-la was charged with not informing the government promptly of the Dalai Lama's ill health and was exiled to Southern Tibet. He later escaped to Kalimpong in India, where he joined Rabga Pangdatsang to form the Tibet Improvement Association mentioned in chapter one.

It is quite possible that on learning of Kunphel-la's arrest, Topgyal Pangdatsang became incensed at his friend's fate and assumed that his brother Yamphel, in Lhasa, would be arrested after the National Assembly had made the decision to convict Kunphel-la. The explanation that Topgyal himself put forward for his rebellion appeared in the form of printed leaflets that were distributed in Kham and also Central Tibet.

Two somewhat incompatible points of view are expressed in Topgyal's statement. The primary thrust of the message is an expression of loyalty to the Thirteenth Dalai Lama and outrage at the fact of His Holiness's most loyal and able official, Kunphel-la, being punished for his selfless services to his sovereign and his nation. The second half of the message construes Kunphel-la's arrest as being proof of the injustice and treachery of the Tibetan government and its officials. The message goes on to describe how unjustly Tibetan officials behaved in Eastern Tibet and how they treated Khampas with contempt and disdain. Topgyal concludes his statement with the declaration that Khampas could no longer live under the Lhasa government and that they should form a separate nation. Rabga, the family intellectual and politician, staying with Topgyal at the time in Markham, possibly drafted the declaration. Even though the Pangdatsang brothers appeared to live separate lives, they were close to each other and, in the main, operated as one family.

The Tibetan government assumed that the oldest Pangdatsang brother in Lhasa, Yamphel, was involved in the rebellion and was going to place him under arrest. But Yamphel managed to get important lamas and even the abbots of the "three seats" (the three

great monasteries around Lhasa) to intercede on his behalf with the
cabinet. There was also a rumour, probably well-founded, that a great
deal of money had changed hands. Topgyal agreed to compensate
the Tibetan government for his brother's offence, so no action was
taken against Yamphel in Lhasa. The cabinet made a request to the
Chinese government for Topgyal's extradition, but it was turned
down. Quite possibly, the deciding factor in the Kashag's decision not
to arrest Yamphel was that substantial government funds were tied up
in Pangdatsang's enterprises outside Tibet. Perhaps the Kashag feared
that if Yamphel were incarcerated, these funds could either disappear
or become frozen in some foreign banks.

The Pangdatsang rebellion did not strike a chord with most Khampas.
In Markham itself, of the eighteen tribal chiefs, not even one went over to
Topgyal's side. None of the surviving rulers of the six kingdoms of Kham
or any other chieftain of note expressed support for the Pangdatsangs.
The only major ally Topgyal had was Jhagö Topden (that Robert Ford
described as a "bandit chief") from the family of a renegade minister of
the old kings of Dergé, who operated as a freebooter in that part of Tibet,
and was strongly pro-Chinese and later pro-Communist.

Patterson's insistence that "Topgyal Pangdatsang had emerged as
a charismatic leader of the Kham and Amdo tribes, and they looked
to him to lead them to revolution and victory against both their own
central and Chinese Governments" has no basis in fact. The importance
and power of the Pangdatsang family came almost entirely from their
tremendous economic power as the exclusive trade agent of the Tibetan
government and their proximity to the most powerful political figures
in Tibet (even being on terms of intimate friendship with the family of
the Fourteenth Dalai Lama); not out of being the chieftain of a small
Khampa tribe in Markham.

After Topgyal crossed over to Bathang, he became entangled in
the local politics there and had a nasty run-in with Fu Dequan, the
Chinese commander of the Bathang garrison. Topgyal's force came
off worst in the encounter, and he and his men retreated to the Bomé
valley, where he remained till 1950. When the Communists marched

into Bathang, he went over to their side. He attended a meeting in
Dartsedo, chaired by the Bathang Communist leader Phüntso Wangye,
to prepare for the invasion of Tibet. His brother Rabga was dispatched
to Chamdo to persuade Governor-general Lhalu and subsequently
Ngabö to surrender his troops, while Topgyal's partner Jhagö Topden
arranged guides and transport animals for the Communist Eighteenth
Army. As a reward, Topgyal and Jhagö Topden were made members
of the "Chamdo Liberation Committee", the Communist entity that
was to administer the part of Kham that had been under Lhasa before
the invasion.[3]

When the whole of Eastern Tibet rose violently against the
Chinese in 1956, including the tribesmen of Bathang and his own
phayul or "homeland" of Markham, Topgyal Pangdatsang remained
loyal to the Communists. Even when the Communists launched
their genocidal campaign of reprisals against the Khampas, and
turned Eastern Tibet into a killing ground, Topgyal's allegiance
did not falter. The Chinese promoted Topgyal to deputy chairman
of the "Chamdo Liberation Committee" and later made him the
representative of the Chamdo branch of the Preparatory Committee
of the Tibet Autonomous Region.

Topgyal's older brother, Yamphel, became the official Chinese
trade agent in Kalimpong and was later appointed head of the
Commerce and Industries Department of the Preparatory Committee
for the Tibet Autonomous Region. But he was shrewd enough to
secretly transfer most of his assets to India and the United States. When
the Lhasa Uprising of March 1959 took place, he made his escape to
India from Sakya with his family, personal staff and "nearly 35 loads
of goods, considered 'valuable'," according to a Calcutta *Statesman*
report of 1 April 1959. Unlike the other Tibetan refugees in India,
Yamphel lived in style in his two mansions in Kalimpong. He served
briefly as an assistant cabinet minister in the exile government but
drew the ire of Gyalo Thondup, the Dalai Lama's older brother. In the
early 1960s Yamphel received a "Quit India" notice from the Indian
police. An American academic has claimed that this action was taken

on Gyalo Thondup's advice.[4] Yamphel left for the UK, then Hong Kong, eventually ending up in the PRC.

He was welcomed in Beijing and much was made of his "patriotism" in returning to China. His brother Topgyal Pangdatsang was arrested in Lhasa at the start of the Cultural Revolution and, in the fashion of the day, "struggled", marched around in public wearing a dunce cap, his face smeared with ink and filth. A photograph of Topgyal being "struggled" appears in a book on the Cultural Revolution in Tibet[5] by the award-winning Tibetan poet and blogger Tsering Woeser. He was also beaten and possibly tortured. According to a specialist on Kham, "Yamphel was not 'struggled' but made to watch his brother being tortured. Both brothers died in Lhasa towards the end of the Cultural Revolution (roughly around 1972–73)."[6]

Most of Pangdatsang's assets in American banks, were frozen under one of those "Enemy Alien" Acts passed by Congress during the Cold War. The remaining brother, Rabga, who by then had relocated (again) to Kalimpong, survived an assassination attempt. The gunman missed and wounded the wife of a Chinese shoemaker N. Sun (& Sons), whose riding boots were the male fashion statement in Lhasa and Kham. Rabga Pangdatsang died, a bitter man, in 1976.

Various explanations have been put forward to explain the Pangdatsang brothers' spectacular and inexplicable acts of self-destruction. Though sometimes ingenious, they are generally unconvincing. Till a credible and rational account is unearthed, it may serve to point out that many Tibetans subscribe to a more supernatural explanation which, put in modern terms, would be that the dazzling wealth and success of the Pangdatsang's had come about because of a fearsome Faustian bargain they had struck long ago, and as with all such transactions, things usually turn out badly in the end.

The Sakya Lamas of Tibet, preceptors to the great Mongol Emperor, Kublai Khan, were the root lamas of the Pangdatsang family. Though the Sakya Lamas had long lost their political authority, they were still respected and revered throughout Tibet for their spiritual attainments and also for their great supernatural powers. They were said to be able to subdue malevolent spirits and to control a class of terrifying female entities that Tibetans call *dumo* or *bamo*, which might be translated as "witches."

Such women were not regarded as inherently evil, and there is no record of witch trials, torture and burning, as there was in mediaeval Europe or seventeenth century Massachusetts. In fact, some intriguing studies[7] of this phenomenon have appeared over the last decade in academic journals inside Tibet as well as in exile. In the Buddhist tradition, such women with unique psychic powers are sometimes regarded as beings that could aid one's spiritual practice. There were, of course, occasions when such entities used their powers to harm or torment humans—for as the saying goes, "gods, demons and humans behave in much the same way" (*lha dre me sum choepa chik*). When that happened, the services of the Sakya Lamas were called for.

These female spirits were constrained in masks and in small statuettes, like children's dolls, and even dressed in miniature costumes: with ornaments, headdresses and tiny boots, suitable to their places of origin or social classes when they were in human form. They were housed in the main *gonkhang* chapel in the Sakya Monastery, where monks conducted regular services on their behalf. If the Sakya Lama entrusted you with one of these protective spirits, it would virtually guarantee success in whatever enterprise you undertook. On your part, you had to be unfailing in carrying out the daily rituals and observations and not otherwise offend the lady in any way. There was always a possibility of doing that, even unintentionally, for, with such earthly deities, major and minor, it is well established in myth and folklore that they could be capricious in their affections and volatile and unreasoning in their disappointments and rages. The Pangdatsang's, it was said, had such a creature as their family protector. When Topgyal Pangdatsang was "struggled" during the Cultural Revolution, he was dressed as a *bamo* witch and paraded through the streets of Lhasa.

* * *

Khampas had genuine grievances against the Lhasa administration. Too many officials were rapacious and contemptuous of the

Khampas, though, on the other hand, many were able and considerate administrators. Many aristocrats had blood ties to Kham. Four Dalai Lamas were born in Kham, the Seventh and the Tenth in Lithang, the Ninth in Denkhok and the Eleventh in Garthar. The Lhasa administration was aware of Khampa grievances, and government proclamations were regularly sent to officials in Kham warning them against "*dapsi*" or "oppression." Ford regarded Lhalu as a lenient magistrate and a fair administrator, stating that his prestige among the Khampas was high. But perhaps the kind of strict vigilance maintained under the Thirteenth Dalai Lama was absent in the more corrupt administration of the two regencies.

Furthermore, with the weakening of the military officer cadre in Lhasa, discipline had slackened in the ranks, and cases of soldiers bullying and exploiting the Khampa populace were being reported. During the administration of Kalön Lama Jampa Tendar, discipline had been extremely tight. Though a religious man, the governor-general had not hesitated to execute a Tibetan soldier for looting a Chinese store in Chamdo and beating up the owner. Gyurme Gyatso Tethong, during his tenure as governor-general of Eastern Tibet, relieved the local people of a number of tax burdens, including the obligation to provide firewood for the army. Soldiers, when hauling logs or chopping wood at Chamdo, were often heard cursing their commander as the Tethong *lakyog* (crooked arm) because of his paralysed right shoulder. The overall prestige of the Lhasa government had declined considerably from the time of Kalön Lama Jampa Tendar and the 1918 victory over Chinese forces. But as Ford writes "Yet there was no general resentment. It had always been like this, and the people knew nothing else. Tibet was under-populated, and there was work for all and enough food for everyone. And most Khampas, for all their spirit of independence, were bound inseparably to the Lhasa government by their worship of the Dalai Lama."

There was also the fact that for most Khampas, the only viable alternative to being exploited and oppressed by the Chinese was Lhasa rule, even if that rule was by no means a consistently just or enlightened one.

In 1916 an American missionary, with experience in Chinese administered Eastern Tibet wrote: "There is no method of torture known that is not practised in here on these Tibetans, slicing, boiling, tearing asunder and all . . . To sum up what China is doing here in eastern Tibet, the main things are collecting taxes, robbing, oppressing, confiscating and allowing her representatives to burn and loot and steal." This observation is mentioned in *Travels of a Consular Officer in Eastern Tibet* by Eric Teichman of the British Consular Service in China, who at the request of the Chinese government, travelled extensively through Eastern Tibet in 1918 to conclude an armistice between warring Tibetan and Chinese forces. In his book, he observes that the areas of Eastern Tibet controlled by the Tibetan government were peaceful, orderly, well-administered and contrasted dramatically with the lawlessness, poverty and misrule in Chinese administered areas.

Teichman also cites similar observations by other European travellers who had travelled to both areas.

Although the Tibetan administration was certainly not a democratic or egalitarian one, what bound the Khampas to Lhasa and the Tibetan nation were ethnic, linguistic, cultural, historical and religious ties. This bond was not just to the Dalai Lama and the Gelugpa church as many Western observers tend to believe. Even if a Khampa belonged to one of the other schools of Tibetan Buddhism: Kagyü, Nyingma, Sakya or even the pre-Buddhist Bön, his spiritual and cultural vision was still directed towards Lhasa, since the essential institutions and centres, indeed even the origins of these belief systems were located in Central Tibet.

There was, furthermore, reciprocity in this relationship. All the great lamas of Eastern Tibet were, without exception, honoured and respected by the people of Central Tibet, including aristocrats and government officials. Many of the important lamas and scholars of Kham were graduates of the great monastic universities of Central Tibet. They might even have had their studies sponsored by some aristocrat or Lhasa merchant, or in the case of unknown scholars aspiring to a *geshe* doctorate or entry into one of the two tantric colleges in Lhasa, have their studies supported by pious, but not necessarily affluent or socially prominent, Lhasa families.

The most obvious difference between the Khampa and the Central Tibetan, and one unfailingly picked up on by even the first-time observer, is the fact of the Khampa's warlike and independent spirit, and the more orderly and submissive nature of the Central Tibetan. But much of this can be explained by the violent and unsettled history of Eastern Tibet in modern times, which we know created a culture of violence. Some aspects of this culture can be pinned down to definite periods in Kham history, for instance the Nyarong War of 1865, when even men's hairstyles changed to suit the needs of that violent period. Observers with closer dealings with Khampas are sometimes able to see beyond the more obvious but crude comparisons. For instance, Eric Teichman, who toured Kham extensively in 1917–18 and was on close terms with many Khampa leaders and Lhasa officials, has this to say:

> Probably the Khambawa owe their reputation for turbulence to their distance from Lhasa, the metropolis of Tibet, which renders their manners uncouth in the eyes of the latter." He adds, "Yet the people of De-ge, for instance, are widely known for their skill in metalworking and other handicrafts and for their literary attainments. The number of people in Dege who can read and write (all monastery taught, of course) is surprising.

My, mother who lived in Dergé as a child always insisted that, by and large, the population of that town was more literate than that of Lhasa. And some Khampas resent the stereotype of violent, lawless men that has been thrust on them by their various chroniclers and even perpetuated in Tibetan folk tales and the Ache Lhamo opera. Without dismissing, out of hand, the courage and heroic qualities of the Khampa, it can perhaps be said that like the cowboy and the gunfighter legends of the Wild West, stories of Khampa bandits and warriors should be relegated to their proper place in popular myth and not be insisted upon in discussions about real people and their all too real histories and tragedies.

Khampas themselves have never regarded the warrior spirit as something exclusive to themselves, and the names of some of the great war leaders from Lhasa, the Rupön Bögangwa killed in 1950, and especially the Kalön Lama Jampa Tendar, victor of 1918, are still remembered by the people of Kham. One of the heroes of the 1918 war, another major from Lhasa, is celebrated to this day in a Khampa song:

Major Anen Dawa is like a hero of the Ling Epic
His Mauser pistol strikes like lightning from the sky.

Rupön Anen Dawa Ling kyi patul drajung,
Menda si si lendu namkye thok thang drajung

Yet, the Khampa-Lhasa divide cannot be entirely dismissed or papered over. It has been pointed out, even by Khampas, that they do not call themselves *Bhöpa* or Tibetan, but rather Khampa. For the Khampa, the Bhöpa is someone from Lhasa or Central Tibet. True, but it does also seem that this designation is applicable only in the context of Tibetans themselves. For instance, if a Khampa was asked by another Tibetan if he was a Bhöpa, he would probably answer no, that he was Khampa. But if that same Khampa were asked by a Chinese who he was, he would most certainly declare that he was Bhöpa or Tibetan.

It is perhaps comparable to the North-South divide in the United States, though without the residual hostility and bitterness that I, as a resident of the American South have discovered, still exists in these parts. Lhasa had fought wars in Kham, but the relationship between Khampas and Central Tibetans had never been traumatized by such a bitter and destructive conflict as the American Civil War. To continue the analogy: for anyone from the south, the term "Yankee", or better still a "damn Yankee", is not applicable to himself, but only to someone north of the Mason-Dixon line, preferably a New York or a Massachusetts liberal. But if the same Southerner were abroad and a mob of foreigners started howling, "Yankee Go Home!" he would certainly take it personally.

Khampas have also needed to let foreigners, besides the Chinese, know that they were Tibetans, or at least belonged to the Tibetan civilization. Khampas authored the first two books by Tibetans in English. *A Tibetan on Tibet* by Paul Sherap, or Dorje Zodpa of Dartsedo, is an analysis of Tibetan religion, culture and customs by a Christian convert who, judging by the dry didactical tone of the book, was earlier in life a Buddhist monk, and well acquainted with the subject. The interesting thing about this book is that although the author came from the farthest edges of Tibetan civilization, from a town that had become the capital of the new Chinese province of Xikang, he writes not about Dartsedo culture, or Khampa culture, but of Tibetan culture, and regards himself as qualified to hold forth on the subject as anyone from Lhasa.

We Tibetans by Rinchen Lhamo is an artless and moving defence of Tibet and Tibetan ways. Rinchen Lhamo was a woman from a patrician Khampa family who married Luis Magrath King, the British consular officer posted at Dartsedo, who had to resign from the consular service for marrying a woman "insufficiently civilized for the position of a consul's wife."[8] When they sailed to England, "Rinchen's ethnicity apparently precluded passage on a Western steamer" and they sailed on the Japanese registered SS *Kitano Maru*.

Born in Minyak on the Chinese frontier, the only town of any size that Rinchen had known was Dartsedo. She visited cities in China with her husband, yet it is evident that she had never actually visited Lhasa or travelled to Central Tibet. Yet she feels no hesitation about speaking on Tibet and defending it, vigorously in true Khampa fashion, against its critics and detractors in the West. When a senior British official at a party in London said, in her presence, that the Tibetans were a simple people, this was her response:

His remark was so wide of the fact that I could not refrain from laughing. He was embarrassed and said he meant, by simple—honest, direct, unsophisticated, but that was not what he had meant; it did not fit in with the context. He meant we were primitive, childish. He knows we are not so, for he has spent many years matching his wits with Tibetan wits without much result. He was merely giving utterance to a conventional statement about us put into vogue by the travelers. There were people present who knew nothing about Tibet, and he had no doubt often made this remark before and found it readily acceptable by those ignorant of us. He had not the courage of his own knowledge. It is so much easier to say what is expected than what is true, but contrary to established views.

It is perhaps an observation that is still applicable to those present-day experts who regard themselves as qualified to speak on Tibet but are unable to relinquish the politically correct views insisted upon by Communist China and its admirers in the West.

The thing that will strike Tibetan readers of Rinchen Lhamo's book is that what she writes about, though based on her personal experience of having lived in a remote corner of Tibet, are universal to the Tibetan experience. Her accounts and observations, not just in weighty matters as religion, philosophy, monastic life (her brother was a *geshe*, a Doctor of Divinity), incarnate lamas, festivals and so on, but right down to items of furniture in the house, kitchen utensils, food and drink, children's games, riddles and folk tales, all of which she remembers in loving detail, will be largely familiar to Tibetans from other parts of Tibet. She appears to have had a devoted and supportive husband, but it is clear from going through her book that she found it difficult living in turn-of-the-century London (she died of tuberculosis at the age of twenty-eight) and that her heart yearned for her native land.

Flowers in great profusion; of many kinds and every shade of colour. Rhododendron and poppy, primula and anemone, barberry, gentian, clematis, moccasin, larkspur, saxifrage and hydrangea, honeysuckle and lilac, roses and lilies and orchids, and many others. In summer, the country is a blaze of colour. Flowers and green grass and trees in foliage and flowered shrubs right up to the snows where they never melt. Then our country is like a great garden swung from the mountain peaks in the vault of Heaven.

Yes, there is a divide between Lhasa and Kham, but many bridges: racial, linguistic, literary, cultural, historical and religious span this gap. Like the old cantilever bridges across the Dzachu and the Ngomchu at Chamdo, they may look crude, primitive, even obsolete—nothing modern and magnificent like the world's largest dam at the Three Gorges—but those old Tibetan structures are strong, and they endure.

* * *

All the Khampa militia units in the Tibetan army in 1950 performed their duties with courage and honour. Not a single unit deserted the field or mutinied. A number of these units attached to Tibetan regular forces fought against incredible odds, and some were wiped out. In Chamdo town, one unit appears to have looted the residency after the governor-general had left, but that according to Robert Ford, was caused by the Khampa's anger for not having been provided with transport as had some of the regular Tibetan units, and had rightly felt were being deserted by their leaders. But Ford tells us that when General Muja's retreating force subsequently passed through Chamdo, morale was raised in the town and order restored.

Yes, certain individual Khampas: Geda Trulku, Baba Phüntso Wangye and Jhagö Topden, went over to the Communists, but contrary to some Western accounts, not a single Khampa tribe attacked Tibetan forces or joined the Chinese to do so. The only Khampas with the invasion force were some guides and muleteers that Jhagö Topden and Phüntso Wangye had provided.

The Khampas themselves believed that they had put up a good fight at Chamdo in 1950. After his capture, Robert Ford met his Khampa friend, Khenchen Dawa-la, the seventy-year-old monk and warrior who had commanded the Sho-ta-lho-sum militia unit in the 1918 war and had been rewarded with the official title of Khenchen or "Great Abbot." Dawa-la had striven to create a strong Khampa militia force in Eastern Tibet, and his vital role was recognized officially. Ford notes, "After the governor-general, he took precedence over every Lhasa official." "The grand old man of Chamdo" as Ford describes him, did not seem disheartened by the defeat. "Tell the world the Khampas fought" he whispered fiercely ". . . and that we'll fight again."

Besides Khenchen Dawa-la, prominent Khampa officials in the Tibetan administration, though not common, were not unknown. It should be mentioned that many princes and chieftains in Eastern Tibet, even a couple of the chiefs of the Golok tribesmen living in the shadow of the Amnye Machen mountains in the north-east, had traditionally received Tibetan government ranks, with appropriate costumes and honours. Though these did not entail any actual serving position in the administration, such honorary officials would, when visiting Lhasa, receive suitable receptions and due consideration in seating and such at festivals and ceremonies.

Yamphel Pangdatsang had received a *rimshi* (fourth) rank and had become the commissioner for the Chumbi valley, the most important trade terminus in Tibet. Topgyal Pangdatsang, though only a major in the army, was, with his family influence, definitely in line for a generalship. Khampas were also becoming part of the aristocracy and being recruited into government service as with such Khampa families as Sadutsang of Kandzé, whose son Rinchen served as a junior official in the delegation that signed the Seventeen Point Treaty. Another Khampa from the Tsatrultsang family, Nima Gyaltsen, served the Tibetan government as a *tsendron* official and died fighting the Communists in 1959.

At the time of the invasion, the second-highest ranking Khampa official in the Tibetan administration (after Yamphel Pangdatsang) was Dergé-sey, Kalsang Wangdu, the prince of Dergé, who had been appointed as the Markham *theiji*, or governor of Markham, and had been entrusted with the defence of the southern sector of the Tibetan frontier. As mentioned in the previous chapter, there is a common belief that he surrendered his command without putting up a fight,[9] giving rise to this rude Lhasa street-song:

Above all, the two-headed prince of Dergé
Then the useless general Karchung
Have filled the Kham military headquarters
With the awful smell of diarrhoea.

The reference to "two heads" underscores the belief that there was treachery involved in the surrender. I subscribed to the general opinion in this matter, as had everyone, it seems, who has studied or written on the subject, but a recent and careful rereading of a minor book I skimmed through twenty years ago, made me see those events at Markham in an altogether different light, and allowed me to re-evaluate the motives and actions of the principals in a less condemnatory manner.

As with Robert Ford at Chamdo, the Chinese Communist offensive at Markham was, by a remarkable coincidence, witnessed by another Englishman, a missionary, Geoffrey Taylor Bull. Like Ford, he was subsequently captured by the Communists and underwent brain-washing for three years before being released. His book, *When Iron Gates Yield,* deals largely with his own travels in Eastern Tibetan and his trials in a Communist prison but provides an overall eyewitness account of the Chinese invasion of south-eastern Tibet. Missionary accounts of Tibet are, on the whole, unreliable as they invariably have an axe to grind against Tibetan Buddhism and its institutions. Sometimes the man of God might also have a political agenda, undermining Lhasa rule and promoting a friendly local leader who might possibly be able to carve out an independent (and hopefully Christian friendly) enclave in Tibet.

Bull comes through in his writings as genuinely without any such underhand motives. Though he is convinced that Tibetan Buddhism was the work of the devil, he is truthful about things he actually witnessed and heard. I decided to trust his account of the Chinese attack, after reading this sentence about a visit he made to the abbot of the Dorjedrak Monastery at Dartsedo. "The abbot himself bore every appearance of being a kindly old man. It was hard to believe that he ruled over such a sinister institution." As George Orwell pronounced on an American missionary he met in Burma: "A complete ass but quite a good fellow."

Government headquarters was located at the fort on the plain of Garthok, at an elevation of about 14,000 feet. The Lhasa appointed governor, generally referred to as the Markham theiji, administered thirteen districts or *dzong* in south-west Kham and two districts in the far south bordering India, Burma and Yunnan province. He was the commander of the military force there as well and, as such, had the rank of a dapön or general. Next in rank, to the Markham theiji was an official who Bull refers to as "*kungo dzong*", who took care of the civil administration.

Dergé-sey, or the prince of Dergé, was the son of Ngawang Jampel, the exiled younger brother of the late king, Dorje Singe. The prince had taken up service with the Tibetan government, starting as a *tsetruk*, a student at the civil service school from which lay government officials were recruited. He was a well-educated man and also spoke fluent English. He had been one of Frank Ludlow's pupils at the short-lived English school at Gyantsé. He corresponded regularly in English with Robert Ford, who sent him books and magazines from Chamdo. Though Ford never met Dergé-sey, he was impressed by him and regarded him as "undoubtedly the most educated man in Kham . . . and by all accounts, he was one of the most progressive officials in the country."

He took his *drungkor-tsal-gyu* test in Lhasa the same year as my uncle Sonam Tomjor. This is the final part of the civil service examination (the preceding examinations being for literary composition and accounting) for all lay officials and involves a display of horsemanship and archery. In a colourful public ceremony, like the *yabusama* of old Japan, the candidate dressed in gorgeous costumes had at full gallop to hit given targets with a bow and arrow, a lance and lastly, a musket. It was not all medieval spectacle and pageantry, and accidents were not uncommon. That year my uncle's horse stumbled. Dergé-sey's mount also misbehaved, and the saddle-girth broke, throwing the rider on the ground, not a very auspicious beginning for a future military leader.

Geoffrey Bull, who got to know the Markham governor well, noted, "the Dege Sey was a man with a thirst for learning." Bull also tells us that he was thirty-eight years old at the time and "a man of magnificent physique." He was also a widower.

"His wife had died tragically following the birth of his third child, now about five years old. His other two children, a boy of seven and a girl of nine, were his constant companions and adored their father.

His love towards them and, in fact to all the children around him, was very touching. He had started a school for his own and the soldier's children. For several hours a day, one could hear them chanting their lessons. Sometimes when we sat talking in his big living-room, with the wide lattice windows open to the garden, little figures would peep through the curtain serving as a door, and seeing the General there, tiptoe up to his table with their big wooden slates and half bowing, display their laboriously written Tibetan letters."[10]

Bull mentions a sharp theological exchange he had with a young lama that Dergé-sey overheard and took up with him the next day. "'Last night,' he said, 'I was listening to your debate with the lama. I was standing outside the window. You became angry, you know. The thing is you do not yet understand the ideas of Buddhist debate. The question he asked you was quite valid from the standpoint of Buddhism. Even if his question had not been reasonable, yet in the circumstances, it should have been taken up reasonably.' He was very sincere with me. It was humbling and I realized, afresh how much I had to learn."

Dergé-sey was kind and patient not only with Bull but also with other missionaries fleeing the advance of the Red Army in China, and seeking refuge in Tibet. Six months earlier, he had hosted Bull's colleague, George Patterson, at Garthok and obtained a permit from Lhasa for him to cross Tibet to India. A year earlier, two American missionary families escaping from Bathang had arrived at Markham, also asking for Tibetan government permission to travel to India. There was Edgar and Mabel Nichols with their two adopted sons and a Chinese convert, Philip Ho. Then there was the Reverend and Mrs Ellis R. Back with their two children, a little boy and a golden-haired girl, Karen, who remembered playing with Dergé-sey's daughter.[11]

The Ninth regiment (Tadang) that Dergé-sey commanded had only four or five hundred troops, divided into companies. He also had a couple of hundred Markham militiamen, but a larger number had earlier been sent north to support the defence of Chamdo. The Markham front wasn't regarded as an important sector.

The Tibetan military force at Markham had two principal tasks: to prevent Chinese incursions from Tsakhalo in the south, bordering Yunnan province, and stop the expected Chinese attack across the Drichu River (the upper Yangtse) from Bathang. Four or five hundred troops were expected to defend the frontier of a region with an area of over seven thousand square miles.

Opposing the Tibetans was the Fifty-Third Division of the Eighteenth Army of the PLA's South-Western Military Command—probably 25,000 troops in all. One Khampa account mentions that 30,000 Chinese soldiers took part in the invasion. About 2,000 PLA troops of the 125th and 126th regiments from Yunnan were poised to attack Tsakhalo in the south, while the 157th Regiment from Bathang faced the main Tibetan defense across the lower Drichu River at Druparong near Markham. This regiment had 5,000 combat troops and was supported by engineering and logistical units from the Fifty-Third Division. In June of that year, when the Chinese armies started massing across that shore, Tibetan headquarters at Markham began receiving a stream of messages from its scouts and outposts at the "big river". Sometimes a Chinese patrol boat would be launched out towards the Tibetan bank, or there would be a volley of fire. The Tibetan defenders would fire back. The skirmishes continued for weeks.

Bull, who had earlier used the crossing when he first came to Tibetan-controlled Markham, describes the ford as having two settlements facing each other across the Drichu River, which forms the upper reaches of the Yangtse. He calls the crossing point on the Bathang side, Jubalung, which is a corruption of Druparong or "Boatman's gorge." "Gorge" is a modest description of the landscape. Like the Grand Canyon in Colorado, Druparong is an incredible sight, a savage gash on the surface of the earth, with the mountainsides rising sheer out of the waters of the Drichu.

The descent to the river is a half-day's journey by steep zigzag tracks that sometimes become non-existent, especially when the gradient becomes sheer, often nothing but a vertical rock face with just a narrow ledge doubtfully supported by precarious walls of loose stone, barely wide enough for a man or an unloaded animal to cross on their own. At the bottom of the gorge are the rocky shores of the Drichu River. Even at an elevation of 10,000 feet, the air here is hot and oppressive. The river is crossed at this point on yak-hide coracles (*kowa*), exactly like those on the Kyichu or Tsangpo rivers in Central Tibet. For a set fee, the oarsmen take passengers, generally three or four, to a boat, while the ponies and mules are "towed" behind, generally with much difficulty.

The current is powerful, especially midstream, with dangerous swirling eddies closer to shore. Despite the oarsmen's best efforts, the coracles are always swept downstream a considerable distance. Bull observed that nearing the other shore, a few hundred yards below, the river entered a dangerously narrow ravine where no landing would have been possible. But his boatmen were more in command of their craft than he supposed and manoeuvred their boat successfully out of the main flow. Another missionary, George Patterson, who had earlier made the crossing writes of it: "The journey paved the way for several grey hairs."

Just above the shore on the Markham side of the river was a small village with a large three-storeyed building standing flush against the sheer face of the mountain. This structure was an agency for handling caravans crossing the river, a hostel for muleteers, and a customs house maintained by the Tibetan governor of Markham. Pangdatsang also had an agent and warehouse at this place. Patterson noted that the building appeared to be a busy, bustling place with "tough looking characters coming in and out" throughout the day.

The initial flurry of probes and reconnaissance missions the Chinese conducted that summer soon came to a halt. Bull tells us that things were unusually quiet after that. Unknown to Bull and the Tibetans, a PLA regiment of five thousand men had begun advancing from the far south, towards Tsakhalo.

A peculiar lull now set in. There was no news from the river. One day a messenger had come to the Dege Sey with a letter. It was, to the General's surprise, from the other side of the river. He opened it in my presence. In bewilderment, he began to read. It was from

Pu tso Wanje (Phüntso Wangye), head of the Bathang Communists, written and sent to him secretly. He turned page after page of rather poor Tibetan. The virulent words castigated Britain and America as devils, exposed the plots of the Imperialists and explained the policy of the Communist party towards racial minorities. He pleaded with the General, to stage an uprising and surrender to the People's Liberation Armies. The disgust of the General was difficult to describe.

Tsering Topgyal Phupatsang of Markham told me that the person who brought this message to Dergé-sey from Phüntso Wangye was Drongdetsang Kalsang Tashi, a resident of Bathang.

Then one sunny day, in early October, when Bull was speaking with the General and his colonel in the garden where . . . "nasturtiums, red and gold, blossomed in profusion . . . " a messenger galloped into the fort and handed a dispatch to the General. A pass had been lost in the salt-producing district of Tsakhalo (the "Southern Brine Wells") which the Chinese called Yanjing, in the country of Gongkar Lama.[*] Treachery was suspected. The lama was still a boy, and the territory was in the hands of an unscrupulous regent whose loyalty was open to question. Bull writes that the General "had sent many of his men to defend the three vital southern passes."

My informant Tsering Topgyal claimed that Dergé-sey had committed the Second and the Third companies of his regiment to the south. Tsakhalo was an important revenue-generating district and the Markham governor could ill afford to lose it. Then news came again from the south, some days later, that a Tibetan magistrate (*dzong-pön*) had been captured by the Chinese. This account is confirmed by Lowell Thomas Jr. (*The Silent War in Tibet*), who also writes that a Chinese force had captured Yakalo, a neighbouring village a mile above Tsakhalo on the mountainside. John Avedon (*In Exile from the Land*

---

[*] This attack was launched on October 5th by the 126th Regiment (and part of the 125th) and was later criticized by senior PLA leaders for being premature and lacking coordination with the 18th Army (Alex Raymond).

of Snows) writes that although Tsakhalo, the southernmost town, held out, its defenders lost one of the three passes to the north, permitting the Red Army to cut it off.

Dergé-sey had the First company, a hundred regular soldiers and about eighty to a hundred Markham militia defending the main river crossing at Druparong under the command of a captain. Bull had met this officer on his arrival at the nearby village of Lhadun ("*before the gods*") and had referred to him as the "Lhadun centurion", a designation we may as well retain, with a bit of modification, since we do not know the name of this brave soldier.* Captain or gyapön (leader of one hundred) Lhadun is described by Bull as a stout man in his forties, with a very young wife, probably a Khampa woman, and was a generous host to our missionary friend.

The General had held two companies in reserve. The Tibetans seemed to be aware that the Chinese would not only force a crossing at Druparong but might attempt a flanking operation, probably upriver. Downstream the river entered a dangerous defile with tremendous rapids, and there was no safe landing place on the Markham side. So, it was obvious that the flanking attack would come from up-river. The only question being, from exactly where?

Late next day, after the last message from Tsakhalo, another courier came riding from the north with a report that three hundred Chinese troops had crossed the river north of Druparong and were advancing inland. Bull noticed that the General was not entirely convinced of the exactness of the report, but that "as a military man, he knew he could not ignore it." He immediately ordered a company of mounted soldiers to proceed at dawn to engage the enemy. One of the precious Bren light-machine guns went with this detachment. As they left, a column of white smoke ascended from the peak of the mountain dominating the Garthok plain—a traditional *sang* offering of juniper and sage smoke to the Buddha, bodhisattvas and all the

---

*The *Military History* mentions that a Captain Kunga Tsenje commanded the unit defending the river crossing and that another officer Captain Bhagdro was killed in the fighting.

mountain and earth sprits of Tibet. Bull saw it as ". . . a pathetic plea to the gods for their favour."

Soon after this force had ridden out, another courier came to the headquarter with the report that 1800 enemy troops had forced a crossing of the river and had broken through the Tibetan defences.

Over weeks, the Chinese had massed at Druparong, where they had somehow managed to transport and prepare for action, a large number of big wooden boats. On the eve of the offensive, a Chinese force had been dispatched northwards from Druparong. They had travelled well up the east bank and then crossed the river at dead of night at a desolate point, unguarded by the Tibetan Army. The force arrived on the west bank undetected. The Chinese then travelled down through the night over rough country until just before dawn, they were able to strike at the flank and the rear of the Tibetan force holding the village opposite Druparong. As the fateful morning of 7 October 1950, dawned over the mountains, they opened fire on the Tibetan defence.

The Tibetans were stunned by the attack. Captain Lhadun almost certainly had to divert some of his already small force to meet it. At this juncture, the main units of the Chinese army crossed the river in their wooden boats. The Chinese later told Bull that one boat had capsized and seven men washed away and that they had made the crossing in a matter of minutes "straight across the river". But there is reason to doubt this account. Bull's own harrowing account of his river crossing, as well as other reports, makes it more than clear how difficult and dangerous the passage was, at the best of times. Even a small Tibetan force opposing the Chinese would have compounded the problems and dangers of such a crossing. It was also impossible to make the crossing "straight across the river", as the Chinese described it. The powerful currents would invariably have pulled the boats downstream. There is no record available of the casualties suffered on either side.

Tsering Topgyal heard that it took three days for the Chinese to put down the Tibetan resistance in the village and the high building. Bull mentions that when he was taken captive by the Chinese to Bathang and crossed the scene of the fighting, it appeared that the Tibetans had put up a desperate struggle, falling back from the river to the houses in the village, and finally, the large customs building. The Chinese had taken the houses with hand grenades and small arms. An old villager told Bull that the Chinese had thrown grenades up at the windows, even in houses with civilians who pleaded with the Chinese soldiers.[12] But the Tibetan soldiers and Khampa militiaman seemed to have kept on fighting, with many subsequently dying at their posts.

An eyewitness, a Tibetan civilian who had been shot in the leg and couldn't move, recounted Captain Lhadun's heroic stand to Bull. "He resisted to the end. At last, he was caught in a room. They sent one man in to get him to surrender, but the 'centurion' shot him dead. Then they sent in another man. We don't know what happened but the second Chinese got him."

The company sent by the General to intercept the Chinese force that had crossed the river upstream almost certainly clashed with the advancing Chinese force and was destroyed, only a handful of survivors managing to escape. Tsering Topgyal remembered that "Early one morning around three o'clock the major and about eleven soldiers, all that was left of his force, came to our house at Chungbum. I was about seven years old and remember seeing them. The major hugged my father and cried. My father did his best to console his friend and got together men and horses to take them onwards to Drayab."

Back at Tibetan headquarters at Garthok, the General, and what remained of his staff, attempted to work out a possible course of action. The second morning after the attack, a mounted courier galloped into the fort, with the message that the principal Tibetan force at the river had resisted till the end and had been wiped out. The General had earlier hoped "to stage a big battle on the plain of Garthok", but without troops, this was now a fantasy. All he had was his staff and an escort of about twenty soldiers. He could attempt a retreat north to Chamdo, ". . . but not a word or an order had been received from the Chamdo command." Bull was certain that Dergé-sey and his staff could have effectively escaped westward to Lhasa or even India. In fact, it appears that Dergé-sey's co-governor who ran the civil administration, Theiji Majawa,[13] escaped to Lhasa with his staff after the initial attack a day earlier.

But Dergé-sey decided he had to save whatever remained of his men ". . . from being cut up any further." He decided to ride out to the advancing Chinese force and negotiate an end to the fighting. Bull, who spoke Chinese, bravely volunteered to go with him and act as his interpreter. With the few soldiers he had left, the General rode out of Garthok fort to the battlefront. Soon they met some of the Tibetan soldiers who had managed to survive the Chinese onslaught and escape. "They cried like children to the General, who, I was amazed to see, comforted them like a father. Never did I hear one word of harshness."

Dergé-sey was certainly no George Patton, and he may not have been an effective military leader, but no one can deny that he had done all that he could. He was also no coward. He told Bull that he expected to be killed by the Communists—and that was not an unreasonable expectation at the time. In 1909 a Tibetan government envoy, Khenchung Jampa Chosang, sent to negotiate with an invading Chinese army, had been beheaded with eight members of his escort. But Bull mentions that Dergé-sey appeared calm and held his head up high as he rode towards the advancing Chinese army.

Bull was present at the initial interrogation of the General. There were a number of Chinese officers, including the commanding officer and one English speaking junior officer, who had already introduced himself to Bull as Lieutenant Chang.

"The cross-examination of the General began in Chinese, English and Tibetan. I really had to say very little, but I did my best to ensure that a fair interpretation of the General's words was conveyed to those present. Back and forth in the different languages, the officers tried to elucidate why the General had resisted, which to them seemed a most extraordinary thing, although to anyone else the most natural thing in the world. He was very calm. "I acted on the orders of my government," he maintained to the last. "I surrender because I consider that further bloodshed is now absolutely useless."

One of the last things Bull saw in Tibet was the body of the "centurian", Captain Lhadun, lying on the ground outside the village by the river crossing. He was writhing and groaning in the shade of a roughly made shelter of branches. Someone said he had been badly wounded. All they could do was to let him lie where he was. It had probably been a few days since he had been wounded, but it appears that the Chinese had not bothered to give this Tibetan military officer even minimal medical attention. Bull asked his captors permission to go over and see him.[14]

"On kneeling at his side, I saw the extent of his wounds. There were some four gaping sores. He had been shot, strangely enough, in both arms and legs. He was thus completely helpless but wholly conscious. The wounds were already festering terribly and the flies, sucking at the pus. He seemed to be in great pain. All he could whimper was: '*kachrug, kachrug*',* the Tibetan term of entreaty. I had no medicines, all my boxes being with the mule train. I tried then to speak to him of the Lord Jesus Christ. Poor man, he was so demented he could hardly listen. He kept moaning for his son. His son lived some days away. If he could only get a word to him. I seemed impotent in my present position to do anything and felt very upset. When I returned to Lieutenant Chang, he inquired sarcastically, 'How are you getting along with your work?'

"Crossing the river, I watched Tibet receding from me. My last impression was of that wounded soldier—a man who from the sole of the foot unto the head had no soundness in him, only wounds and bruises and putrefying sores. They had not been closed, neither bound up, neither mollified with ointment. There could be no more eloquent symbol of the spiritual and moral condition of the Tibetan people. Thousands of miles away from this tragic scene, many were sitting at ease in Zion, glad to know that they themselves are complete in Christ."

---

*Possibly 'kuche, kuche' or 'please, please', prefacing his request to Bull to find his son.

8

"NEST OF SPIES"

Early one morning, I was on my way to school. It was in the late autumn of 1958, a few months before the uprising in Lhasa. I attended St. Joseph's College at North Point in Darjeeling and was a "day-scholar", which, in this Raj equivalent of an English public school, was regarded as being somewhat less exalted than a "boarder". Boarders came from America, England, Canada, Thailand, Burma, South Africa, Hong Kong or at least from Lhasa, Kathmandu, Calcutta or Bombay. Day-scholars were just local kids.

Running down the road past Glenary's restaurant, bakery and confectioners, which made the best doughnuts and ginger biscuits in Darjeeling, I bumped into my granduncle, Tsarong *pola* (grandfather), walking slowly up towards the Mall—the promenade circling the top of the ridge—probably to take his morning constitutional. He was an old man then, around seventy-three, and his hair, done in the topknot of the Tibetan aristocracy, was grey and thinning. I think I recall a stout gentleman dressed in a traditional silk robe. He had a square, much-lined face, and small animated eyes that looked at you with interest and humour. But this memory has probably been reinforced, if not unconsciously reconstructed, by photographs and what I subsequently heard about him from my mother and relatives. I don't recall anything from the conversation we presumably had that day. One fact of the meeting though, is still clear in my mind's eye. The old boy tipped me twenty rupees, which was a huge sum of money for a child then.

Shortly after that meeting I heard that Tsarong pola had gone back to Lhasa.

Years later, my uncle, Sonam Tomjor told me he had met Tsarong pola at the Gymkhana club in Darjeeling before his departure for Tibet. Over a drink at the bar, the old man let him know of his intentions to return to Lhasa. My uncle tried to dissuade him and suggested that he could perhaps do more for Tibet by remaining in India. By now, the Chinese had completed the Sichuan-Tibet and Qinghai-Tibet highways and a number of secondary roads and had built up a formidable military presence in Tibet. They also virtually controlled the Tibetan government. The resistance movement, starting in Eastern Tibet in 1956, had spread to Central Tibet. Khampa guerrilla bands were ambushing Chinese convoys and attacking Chinese garrisons all over the region. The Holy City was crowded with refugees from the fighting in Kham, and the general populace was seething with resentment and anger against the Chinese. The young Dalai Lama was effectively a prisoner in a city ringed by Chinese artillery and troops. It did not require undue perspicacity to see that events were coming to a head—relentlessly.

But Tsarong could not be dissuaded. He told my uncle that he did not think that anything useful could be served by working with the expatriates in Kalimpong and Darjeeling. He said that he had to return to Tibet to save the "little lama". My uncle assumed that Tsarong was referring to his grandson, who had been chosen as the leading incarnate lama of the Drigung Kagyü school. Later, it occurred to my uncle that Tsarong pola could have been talking about someone else. What if he was referring to the young Fourteenth Dalai Lama? Tsarong had made his mark on Tibetan politics and even history by saving the life of the Thirteenth Dalai Lama. Perhaps the old man intended to try something of the kind again.

Dasang Damdul, or "Straight Arrow, Foe Vanquisher" of the house of Tsarong, was the national hero who had held back Chinese troops at the Chaksam ferry in 1910 when the Thirteenth Dalai Lama made his escape to India. Tsarong had been close to the Dalai Lama and, unlike other aristocrats, owed his meteoric rise to power exclusively to the patronage of the Thirteenth Dalai Lama. He was born in 1885 on the eve of the Tibetan New Year into a middling peasant family in the fertile valley of Phembo north-east of Lhasa. His father was a farmer and a skilled arrow-maker, being known to all in the district as Aku Daso, or uncle arrow-maker. As a boy, Dasang Damdul was known by the less prepossessing name of Namgang, which is the astrological term for the last day of the month. Peasants in Tibet tended to give their children simple but hopeful names, which often included the day they were born, like Thursday Long Life (Phurbu Tsering) or Monday Wish Fulfilled (Dawa Thundup).

Tsarong's son, my uncle Dundul Namgyal, or George as he was known at school (also St. Joseph's), published a biography of his father[1] some years ago. He tells us that as a boy Namgang became the pupil and servitor of a monk official, a family friend who took him to Lhasa. The official was a senior administrator at the Norbulingka, the Dalai Lama's summer palace, and a personal attendant to His Holiness. This proximity got Namgang noticed by the Dalai Lama himself, who was struck by the boy's intelligence and retained him in his personal service. He was in the Dalai Lama's entourage when His Holiness fled to Mongolia, escaping from the British expeditionary force that invaded Tibet in 1904.

It is possible that Namgang got his more heroic name around this time, probably from the Dalai Lama himself. The "Straight Arrow" part of the name was probably a tacit acknowledgement of his humble origins. On the Dalai Lama's second flight from Lhasa in 1910—this time from the advance guard of an invading Chinese force—Dasang Damdul, supported by Khampa volunteers from the Banakshöl suburb of Lhasa, conducted a desperate rearguard action at the Chaksam Ferry, holding back Chinese troops while his master escaped to British India. Years later, in recounting the event to a fellow official, he said that as he had not slept for several days, he fell into a deep sleep at the Tibetan defensive position but was suddenly awoken by a painful slap in the face. The source of this blow was a complete mystery, but

Tsarong regarded it as a divine warning. Carefully surveying the enemy positions across the river, he realized that part of the Chinese force had managed to cross the river upstream. He immediately sent a rider to Samding Monastery, where the Dalai Lama was resting, and got him and his entourage to leave immediately. He ordered his men to conceal their weapons and disperse into the countryside while he escaped to Darjeeling behind his master.[2]

Dasang Damdul was ennobled after the Dalai Lama's return to Lhasa in 1913, and he married into the Tsarong family and took their name. Unfortunately, the former lord of the Tsarong family, a cabinet minister and his son had been lynched as traitors in the chaotic aftermath of the Chinese defeat in Lhasa. The Tethongs were related to the Tsarong family by blood, so Dasang Damdul, now Lord Tsarong, became our honorary relative, as it were, and pola to my cousins and myself.

Tsarong Dasang Damdul was also appointed commander-in-chief of the new Tibetan army and the supervisor of the mint and armoury, becoming, in fact, the most powerful man in Tibet, next to the Dalai Lama. My grandfather Tethong Gyurme Gyatso was a good friend of his and one of his trusted generals. Those were halcyon days for the young military officers, who strutted around Lhasa in their new British-style dress uniforms, like the kind in Alexander Korda's 1939 film, *Four Feathers*. Instead of the British redcoat, Tibetan officers wore an amber yellow jacket with epaulettes and gold buttons imprinted with the Crossed Vajra thunderbolt. Their trousers were navy blue with gold stripes down the side and with straps that went under the boots. A ceremonial sword hung by their side, and they wore, or just carried under their arm, large pith helmets, topped with a small *tse-bum* or the Buddhist treasure-vase instead of the regulation spike. These officers attracted considerable female attention.

General Tethong had, in his young days, the reputation of being a ladies' man. My mother, who was devoted to him, has this childhood memory of committing an innocent faux pas on such a matter. The young general and father, astonished at the precocity of his firstborn, would regularly trot my mother out before guests and make her sing the latest Lhasa street song, which the servants might have taught her.

These verses were set to popular tunes and were amusing and often topical. Once, on such an occasion, my mother, who was about three, thought that she would please her father by singing a song where his name was mentioned. So, in front of the family and guests, she piped up:

Oh! In the Lhasa parks and gardens.
Stop! Behind the cover of a willow is,
The one whom girls share their heartfelt secrets,
The honourable General Tethong.

Heth! Lingkae nang la.
Bas! Changmae khukyok.
Bumoe nyingtam choesa,
Tethong dapön kusho.

The words '*heth*' and '*bas*' before the first two lines are Urdu in origin and reflect the role of and contribution to Lhasa music culture by the small Kashmiri Muslim community in the Tibetan capital.

The officers of the military constituted a new power block in Tibetan politics and one that was committed to modernization and the realization of Tibet's independence from China. The new army proved itself in 1918 when it halted another Chinese invasion and effectively drove the invading army out of much of Eastern Tibet, earlier held by the Sichuan provincial government. Such an overwhelming Tibetan victory against China had not taken place in a thousand years.

But the British were Tibet's sole supplier of arms and ammunition and they, at the behest of the Chinese government, dispatched a consular officer to Eastern Tibet who called on the Tibetans to halt their advance and negotiate a peace settlement.[3] One of the fundamental weaknesses in the army's role as a modernizing force was its dependence on the British. Tibet was unable to import weapons from other countries as Japan or Russia for fear of offending the British, who provided only a limited (and undependable) supply of light weapons and ammunition to Tibet. It was essentially a reflection of Britain's overall policy of encouraging Tibetans to keep the Chinese out of Tibet, enough to

ensure the integrity of the Indian Empire's northern frontier but not
to allow for a militarily capable and independent Tibet that might sour
Britain's business relations with China. That consideration was, at all
times, of paramount significance in Whitehall's scheme of things in
Asia. Sir Charles Bell, the "architect of Britain's Tibet policy", pointedly
observed (in his last book on Tibet) that Britain and America's refusal
to recognize Tibet's independence (but which they sometimes tacitly
acknowledged when it was to their advantage) was "a convenient
arrangement for them" and was dictated largely by their desire "to
increase their commercial profits in China."[4]

Britain's failure to provide meaningful political and military support
to Tibet did much to discredit the new army and the modernization
program in the eyes of most Tibetans. The great monasteries and other
forces of conservatism and reaction in Tibet opposed the army, as they
did any kind of modernization, as a dangerous threat to their long-
established power. The monk cadre in the Tibetan civil service, the
tsedrungs, were instinctively opposed to the military since its officers
were lay officials. Gradually, through insinuation, rumours and
intrigues, the conservative forces worked to undermine the role of
the new army in the eyes of the Dalai Lama. Though the Dalai Lama
himself was instrumental in the creation of the modern army and had
found it useful in checking the ambitions of the big monasteries, he
now began to have doubts about its loyalty to him.

The backward-looking and ultraconservatives in the Tibetan
church, government and society were led by the arch-reactionary,
dronyer-chenmo Tenpa Dhargye, the Dalai Lama's Lord Chamberlain,
who was nicknamed *dronyer-chenmo* "Apso" because he had the
same beady eyes and the white facial hair as the Tibetan terrier. He
found an effective ally in the secular camp in the person of the finance
secretary, Lungshar, who was consumed with jealousy at Tsarong's
power. He instigated the Dalai Lama's nephew, Drumba, a general in
the army to complain about Tsarong's unfairness and high-handedness
and promised to support his candidature as commander-in-chief. In
1924, when the National Assembly was having a session on national
defence, a group of officers petitioned that the military be represented

in these discussions, as it always had been, till that year. Lungshar reported to the Assembly that mutinous officers had attempted to enter the Assembly chambers by force. Earlier, rumours had been spread that the military was plotting to overthrow the government, and consequently, the Assembly became alarmed by the report. The Dalai Lama's chamberlain carried out an investigation, and though only two military officers were demoted, it represented the beginning of the downfall of military modernization.

Some years later, the accidental death of a soldier from a drastic punishment ordered by Tsarong gave the conservatives the opportunity to weaken him. They used this incident to claim that Tsarong had disregarded the Dalai Lama's law against capital punishment and that he was becoming arrogant and power-hungry. Eventually, Tsarong was relieved of his duties as commander-in-chief in 1924. With the dismissal of Tsarong and other British trained officers, the army declined. Tibet's modernization drive ground to a halt.

My grandfather, Tethong Gyurme Gyatso, though a military man, was not personally affected by these events as he was serving in Eastern Tibet, where he would remain for much of his career. But with the deterioration of the army, his task of defending the Tibetan frontier grew increasingly more difficult.

Tsarong did not play any further major role in Tibetan politics. The death of the Thirteenth Dalai Lama and the successive installation of two corrupt lama regencies by the conservative National Assembly bought about further deterioration in the military and in the very fabric of government as well. By the time of the Communist invasion, the administration not only lacked the experienced military leaders it had in 1918 but even the sort of young, vigorous and uncorrupted civil servants and military officers that the Thirteenth Dalai Lama had used to expel the Chinese from Tibet.

Tsarong's only remaining official responsibility was as the supervisor of the Drapchi mint, where he oversaw the printing of the first Tibetan paper currency. He still retained his seat in the Tibetan Parliament, and used it to offer suggestions for "improving the lives of the Tibetan people and bringing the country forward into the international arena."

On his own initiative, he undertook the construction of the first modern steel trestle bridge over the Trisam River in 1936, on the main trade route from Lhasa to India and Western Tibet. Though the steel girders and trestles were ordered from Burns & Co. in Calcutta, the actual construction work was undertaken by Tsarong himself, who camped at the site, initially in a tent, and involved himself with every aspect of the construction, even mastering the art of mixing and pouring concrete for the piers.

When he first started surveying the area to find a suitable site to build his bridge, he came across the remains of an old iron suspension bridge built in the fifteenth century by the great Tibetan saint, engineer and artist, Thangtong Gyalpo. On studying the massive links of iron chain that had survived, Tsarong is said to have remarked, in his usual down-to-earth way, "Not bad for a wandering hermit."

It was well known that Tsarong had no formal education, and there was a story, perhaps apocryphal, that when writing a letter to his steward to send some horses to Lhasa, he misspelt the Tibetan word for horse "ta" with a "sa" superscript instead of the correct "ra." When someone pointed out the mistake, Tsarong is supposed to have replied, somewhat irascibly, "whether I spell it with the 'r' superscript or the 'sa' superscript, or without any superscripts at all, my steward will send me the horses I need."

He had a wonderful sense of humour, and his parties ". . . were always completely riotous, especially when his three children came home from school" according to Spencer Chapman who, like all those guests, Tibetans, English, American, German and others who partook of Mr and Mrs Tsarong's hospitality, remembered the occasion with real pleasure. "The Tsarongs are the most perfectly natural host and hostess. Tsarong always drank (or pretended to have drunk) a little more *chang* than his guests; Mrs Tsarong made us feel completely at home . . ." Chapman adds.

Tsarong was a keen photographer and passed on his enthusiasm and skill to his son. He also maintained extensive correspondence with all sorts of people outside Tibet, especially in the United States, and was a member of the National Geographic Society. He undertook a project to build a new hydroelectric station for Lhasa to replace the old plant built in 1927 and also a steel bridge over the Kyichu River at Lhasa. The Chinese invasion put a stop to these two projects.

* * *

After the Red Army marched into the Tibetan capital in September 1951, Darjeeling and Kalimpong began to receive a larger flow of Tibetans, especially those who were in trouble with the Chinese occupation or simply did not want to live under Chinese rule. Several aristocrats and traders bought the bungalows and cottages that the departing British had left behind in Kalimpong. Tsarong bought Penwryn House, an Art Deco style bungalow in the Durpin Development Area. Business began to flourish in Kalimpong, not only with the old wool trade but also from the silver, which the Chinese were pouring into Tibet to buy the cooperation, services and even supplies from Tibetans before they established their complete control of the entire country. Until the Chinese managed to complete their motor road to Lhasa in 1958, most of their non-military supplies were purchased in India and transported from Kalimpong on muleback.

The resistance, of course, found Kalimpong a convenient conduit to the outside world, not only to purchase supplies—from Marwari middlemen who could supply anything for the right price—but also to seek help from countries that might not be friendly to China. Agents of these and other governments and intelligence services had set up shop in Kalimpong.

Guomindang agents and Chinese Communist agents operated somewhat openly in the town; their work made easier by the fact that Kalimpong and Darjeeling both had small Chinese communities composed largely of the descendants of Chinese soldiers expelled from Tibet in 1912 and POWs from the 1918 war in Kham who did not want to return to China. Prime Minister Nehru was also courting Communist China during those years, hoping to establish an Asian alliance against Western "neo-colonialism," and consciously turned a blind eye to China's activities in Tibet and in Kalimpong as well.

It was generally accepted that Communist agents in this town were run by a mysterious spymaster operating out of the PRC consulate in Calcutta. No proof can be offered, but a possible nominee for this role might be Dai Ping, senior consular personnel without a specific official designation.[5] On 10 July 1951, he "blew cover" to accompany General Zhang Jingwu to Kalimpong (on his way to Yatung) to provide China's new proconsul for Tibet the necessary security in this dangerous "nest of imperialist spies," as Beijing's propagandists had labelled our sleepy one-hotel hill station.

From 1954 onwards, the Communist Chinese operated more openly in Kalimpong, setting up a Trade Agency and hosting lavish parties and distributing gifts. They also took over the Guomindang elementary school on Durpin Road and attempted to enrol children from poorer Tibetan families in the town. Dardo Rinpoche successfully countered this with the inauguration of the Indo-Tibetan Buddhist Cultural School. Rinpoche, in a 1987 video interview, mentions that three other Tibetans: Lobsang Lhalungpa, Rakra Rinpoche and Rigzin Wangpo helped him set up the school.[6]

The Indians had a few outfits running in tandem, the old CID, inherited from the British, and other agencies as the SIB (State Intelligence Bureau) and the CIB (Central Intelligence Bureau) that later became the IB (Intelligence Bureau). The chief counter-intelligence officer in Kalimpong was the Sikkimese Inspector, Lha Tsering (deputy director of SIB), who had earlier worked for the British under Eric Lambart who had overseen intelligence for the north-east frontier region. Under Lha Tsering was Inspector Atuk Tsering, another Sikkimese. There was also the affable Major Vasu of Military Intelligence, who got himself invited to all the parties in Kalimpong.[7] Indian Army intelligence officers could apparently be charming and persuasive, for they even recruited, on the strength of the old regimental tie, Sydney Wignall, a former Indian army officer and a climber, to spy for them in Western Tibet on the disposition of the Chinese forces there and the progress of their Sinkiang-Lhasa highway. Wignall was caught and suffered a fairly horrible captivity. He was released and eventually wrote a book on his experiences, for which his friend the actor, Trevor Howard, threw in the title, *Spy on the Roof of the World*.

Once, at a cocktail party in New Delhi, I was introduced to a Mr Ratan Sehgal (of IB) who, my hostess informed me in a whispered aside, was Prime Minister Indira Gandhi's advisor on intelligence matters. Ratan mentioned, matter-of-factly, that as a young man, he had been stationed at Kalimpong and had known a number of Khampa traders and other Tibetans there and inquired about their whereabouts.

Kalimpong was probably too small and incestuous a town for agents to maintain their cover without exercising considerable discretion. And it was a Kalimpong parlour game to try and guess at their identities. The British resident agent in Kalimpong was, at least to many Tibetans who still swear by it to this day, the English *bhikshu* from Tooting, Sangharakshita, who was called *gelong serpo* or yellow monk, for the colour of his robe. No credible evidence has ever been offered to support this allegation. Sangharakshita claims that the Jain editor of the local *Himalayan Times* started a bazaar rumour of him being a "Communist spy" after a disagreement about the unauthorized publication of a speech given by our *bhikshu* at the Town Hall, on the occasion of the Buddha Purnima celebrations.

Sangharakshita, meaning "protected by the *Sangha*", fought the good fight in our town to protect the Dharma and counter Christian missionary efforts to convert local Buddhists. One "particularly odious" method that Sangharakshita exposed in a letter to the Calcutta English-language dailies was "conversion through pregnancy" whereby a Christian girl would be encouraged to associate with a non-Christian boy, and when she became pregnant, would have the Mission pressurize the boy to convert and marry her.

Sangharakshita also established the Young Men's Buddhist Association (ping-pong table and all) at the "Hermitage" between the 10th and 11th Miles and edited and published a monthly journal, *Stepping-Stones*, which according to Nebesky ". . . contains a wealth of interesting information concerning the religious life of the inhabitants of Tibet and the Himalayas" and had an impressive roster of contributors and subscribers worldwide. He also edited the *Journal of the Maha Bodhi Society*, the principal Buddhist organization in the subcontinent.

A more credible candidate for the role of resident British agent might have been the less colourful but more qualified David Llewellyn Snellgrove, a captain in the British Army's Intelligence Directorate at Delhi during the war years, who had earlier ". . . attended various intelligence courses and further training at the War Office in London."[8] He also had the right social and educational background for a British spy, being upper middle class and a Cambridge graduate. Sangharakshita was a working-class Londoner who had deserted from his army unit in India in 1946. In the fifties, Snellgrove lived in Darjeeling, Kalimpong and Sikkim, studying Tibetan religion and culture. In the mid-fifties, he was served with a "Quit India" notice under the Foreigners Act. He later became a professor of Tibetan Studies at the School of Oriental and African Studies in London.

The Americans operated out of their Consulate in Calcutta on Harrington Street (provocatively renamed Ho Chi-Minh Sarani at the height of the Vietnam War). Their first foray to Kalimpong appears to have been made in the summer of 1950 following the Chinese invasion and the Dalai Lama's departure for Dromo on the Sikkim frontier. The State Department urgently needed a way of contacting the Tibetan government, so Vice Consul Nicholas G. Thacher (with his wife, young child and nanny as cover) was instructed to take the long thirteen-hour drive up to Darjeeling "to escape the Calcutta heat." He pulled into Kalimpong on 15th June. Dropping his family off at the Himalayan Hotel, he drove to the Tibetan Mission. "Entering, he introduced himself in English to the ensemble of officials. Sizing up the lone youthful diplomat they reacted with collective disappointment."[9]

Thacher was supplanted by First Secretary Fraser Wilkins, who became the principal American liaison to the Tibetan Mission. Other Americans frequenting Kalimpong in those years were Robert Linn, who headed the CIA station in Calcutta, and then John M. Turner, who had received his early education in Darjeeling (his parents were missionaries) and spoke Hindi, making him well suited for the job.

One of his tasks was maintaining "discreet contact" with the glamorous Princess Kukula (Pema Tsedun Phunkhang) of Sikkim, who was an early and useful informant for the CIA. Turner was, in time, succeeded by John Hoskins and Clay Cathy in 1958.

Two Japanese agents had earlier operated out of Kalimpong, but they could not really be considered as players in this Cold War sideshow. Their situation was closer to that of those octogenarian Japanese soldiers one occasionally read about in the sixties and seventies, allegedly lurking in the jungles of the Philippines or Malaya, unaware (or unwilling to acknowledge) the end of World War II. Kimura Hisao (Dawa Sangpo) and Nishikawa Kazumi (Lobsang Sangpo) were both Japanese intelligence officers who had been sent from Mongolia to Tibet in 1940 to collect intelligence on possible Russian or Chinese military incursions in those areas. Both came to Tibet posing as Mongol monks and appeared to have travelled all over the country, even managing to be in Chamdo some years before the Chinese invasion. Kimura met Tsarong in Lhasa and spoke to him in Mongol, a language in which Tsarong had retained his fluency. He was impressed by Tsarong's intelligence and integrity and regarded him as being ". . . the most progressive of the nobles, and the best of the old generation of Tibetan nationalists."[10]

After unbelievable hardships and many adventures, Kimura and Nishikawa made their separate ways to Kalimpong, where a penniless Kimura managed to find employment at the *Tibet Mirror*. He initially worked at the press but was later promoted to the editorial office, where he even contributed a few political cartoons on the Chinese Civil war and the defeat of Japan. Kimura also set up Nishikawa with a job as a typesetter. Kimura was later recruited by an unsuspecting Eric Lambart to spy in Mongolia and, like Kim, even assigned a code number—ATS5. The two Japanese agents finally gave themselves up to the Indian police in 1950 and returned to Japan.

I met Kimura *san* in 1988 at a reception of the Tibet Cultural Center in Tokyo. He still had an eye for the ladies, as had been his reputation among Tibetans,[11] and he gave my wife Tamsin a quick once-over.

Since she was not Tibetan, he might have assumed she was a girlfriend or an escort, for he said to me in fluent, idiomatic Tibetan, "You've caught yourself a nice one this evening."

The *Tibet Mirror* where Kimura once worked was a unique Kalimpong institution that for the apparent modesty of its operation, had an admittedly restricted yet surprisingly profound influence on Tibetan thinking and politics. The newspaper was owned and published by the Reverend Gergen Dorje Tharchin, a native of Poo in Kinnaur district, a culturally Tibetan area on the Indian frontier and the ancestral homeland of the Tethong family. As an orphan, Tharchin had been raised and educated by Moravian missionaries and later became the first national pastor and moderator of the Tibetan Christian Church. He travelled to Tibet a number of times and made many friends there, even in high society and the Buddhist church. Though a steadfast Christian all his life, his travels imbued in him a love for and pride in his native culture and history. His Christian upbringing made him want to do something practical to help his people and country, and he eventually hit on the idea of a Tibetan newspaper.

The first issue of the *Tibet Mirror* appeared in October 1925 and carried on for thirty-eight years until 1963. Its circulation was small, but copies were passed on and reread. The Thirteenth Dalai Lama, a personal friend of Tharchin's who encouraged and supported him in his venture, received the paper regularly, as did some important lamas and aristocrats, including my grandfather Tethong Gyurme Gyatso. Other Tibetans in Lhasa also subscribed. Copies of the paper even reached Chamdo and Dergé. "The *Mirror* published articles on world events and reported what was taking place in India, Tibet and in the Himalayan region. It was a rich source of information on the world of High Asia at the time."[12]

The *Mirror* carried profiles of contemporary international newsmakers as Gandhi, Stalin and Hitler, as well as Tibetan, Sikkimese and Bhutanese notables. It also reported on the doings of the great military powers and the latest scientific discoveries and inventions—important international events as the Olympic Games were also reported. The *Mirror* ran classified ads and reported on the Kalimpong wool market as well as international gold and silver prices. An occasional feature was a science and technology section where new inventions and scientific and natural phenomena were explained.

Some of the advertisements in the *Mirror* reveal how the products of modern technological civilization had already made substantial inroads into Tibet. In the May 1927 issue, there is an advertisement for a folding bellows camera, Primo No. 12 and for alarm clocks in the June 1926 issue, specifying that these could be ordered by mail. Horn Victrolas and gramophone records of the light classical music of Lhasa and Ache Lhamo opera arias were also promoted in the paper. The *Mirror* also carried the occasional obituary. When my grandfather, Tethong Gyurme Gyatso, died on the evening of the twenty-seventh day of the seventh moon in 1938, Tharchin, who had met him in Lhasa, came out with a glowing tribute to the Tibetan minister. On the same page, incidentally, is a translation of the parable of the Good Samaritan with a woodcut illustration.

But by the late 1940s, the *Tibet Mirror* published fewer Bible stories. It had become a more nationalistic, even crusading paper, warning Tibetans of the dangers of Communist China and urging everyone to join ranks against this common foe. He published his own version of Benjamin Franklin's famous "Join, or Die" editorial cartoon, warning the American colonies against disunity. Instead of Franklin's dismembered snake, Tharchin illustrated his message of unity with animals from the well-known Buddhist *Jataka* story of the "Four Devoted Friends," the elephant, the monkey, the rabbit and the bird helping each other to reach the high branch of a tree to obtain the fruit.

He also attempted to make Tibetans realize their place in the world and in history. This is how he explained his political mission in an interview:

In my articles, I often used to refer to Tibetan history and in particular to the "Great Religious Kings" (the Tibetan emperors) which prove Tibet's independence. The Chinese used to say Tibet is "backward", and my endeavour was to demonstrate in my writings that Tibet was far from being a backward country; it was a great civilization. It had everything in it.[13]

But Tharchin was alert to the negative aspects of Tibetan society, and his articles also stressed the need for reform, modernization and democratization in Tibet. He warned the aristocrats and clergy that they should not be deceived by Chinese "sweets", and tirelessly pleaded for change and for opening up Tibet to the world:

> Wouldn't it be better to contact the world? Wouldn't it be better to prevent the public from being deceived? When the Chinese arrive in Lhasa, surely the first thing they will do is to establish a printing press because they know that the newspaper is more powerful than any military. What is more powerful than hundreds of thousands of troops? What is more powerful than an atom bomb? We must distribute (our own) newspaper to our public and then contact other nations through wire and wireless means to let them know that our country has a long history of being an independent nation.

The editorial office of the *Tibet Mirror* at Mackenzie Cottage (the press itself was housed in a large tin shed below, on the Main Road at the 10th Mile) was probably the most reliable clearinghouse for news on Tibet in the Tibetan-speaking world. He reported the Chinese invasion and the fall of Chamdo and was the first to report on the outbreak of fighting in Eastern Tibet. All Tibetans: traders, resistance fighters, officials, spies, progressive aristocrats and lamas who came to Kalimpong were welcomed to his office, and over cups of tea and biscuits, persuaded to share whatever fresh news they had. People trusted him.

Physically he wasn't impressive. Sangharakshita describes him as having "bristly grey eyebrows and bad teeth. He habitually wore a shabby, ill-fitting three-piece suit, and (under it) a rather grimy collarless shirt from which a scraggy neck emerged. There was nothing wrong with the head on the neck, nor with the cheerful and good-humoured expression of the rather foxy looking face."

Tharchin did not just sit back and wait for information to come to him. He converted an old warehouse across the street from the press into a kind of free lodgings (of a basic kind) for pilgrims and indigent travellers from Tibet, giving him the first opportunity to glean whatever information they might have. On one occasion, he sent two Tibetans to Eastern Tibet to check up on Chinese invasion plans. When the two failed, he paid Kimura to take up the mission, which the Japanese accomplished with more success.[14] It does appear that Tharchin may have had some kind of mutually beneficial connection with British and later Indian intelligence. Still, that sort of thing is, I suppose, the kind of compromise that hands-on journalism sometimes demands, but which editors and reporters do not like to acknowledge.

And Tharchin did conscientiously publish the many stories that people got out to him from Tibet. The *Mirror* reported the uprising in Drayab, Markham, Drango, Bathang, Chatreng and Lithang and the bombing of the monasteries in the last four districts. He even reproduced sketches drawn by a Tibetan of these bombings. Tharchin was the first to alert the world to the brutality of Chinese reprisals, prison camps, torture, "struggles", and suicides. But it is also evident in the articles and news reports that he became frustrated with international apathy and the effectiveness of Communist propaganda in playing down the extent of the uprisings in Eastern Tibet. "The Chinese plan to destroy Tibet without the world even knowing about it . . . They are covering the eyes of the world with the dust of their lies."

Tharchin published books on Tibetan literature and language, and also political pamphlets and manifestos issued by Tibetan nationalist leaders, one of which contained the prophetic last testament of the Thirteenth Dalai Lama warning Tibetans of the coming dangers of a Communist takeover of Tibet and urging people and officials to work together to defend their country. Tharchin was aware of the dangers that disunity and internal strife could pose to the future of Tibet and issued this personal appeal to the people of Eastern Tibet on 1 October 1952:

To the communities of Kham both under Tibet and under China:
You are aware of how much you have suffered under the Chinese
occupation for many years. Today's new China follows the religion-
less Russia. They might treat you well for a short while, but sooner or
later, they will treat you even worse than the other Chinese regimes
did before. They will surely destroy the Tibetan race and religion.
Therefore, it is important that you act for the sake of the Tibetan
people and act to defend the Tibetan nation and history. Those of
you under the Tibetan administration might have in the past been
exploited by some Tibetan government officials in the border areas,
but it is better to suffer a little at the hands of your own leaders than
to betray your people and religion by being misled by China. There
will come a time someday to resolve the mistreatment of your people
and settle internal problems by appealing to compassionate lamas
and leaders. Right now, these internal problems must be put behind,
and every effort made to work together and regain our independence.

We, the tsampa eaters, *chuba* wearers, dice players, raw and
dried meat eaters, followers of Tibetan Buddhism, Tibetan language
speakers, the people of the Three Circuits of Western Tibet (*Ngari
Korsum*), the Four Horns of Central and Southern Tibet (*Ü-Tsang
Rushi*), the Six Ranges of Eastern Tibet (*Dokham Gangdrug*), and
the Thirteen Myriarchies of Tibet (*Bod Trikor Chuksum*)—we must
unite all our hearts and minds and make an effort to end Chinese
occupation. After freeing ourselves of the oppression of this foreign
enemy, we can then deal with internal troublemakers, and have
leaders chosen from a united Tibet. To achieve this, everyone should
make the most determined effort they can. This request is made by
the publisher.[15]

The Reverend Tharchin was proud that an American newspaper had
referred to his self-appointed mission as a "One Man War with Mao,"
but there were times when he felt disheartened and inadequate to the
task. In one of his pieces, he makes such an acknowledgement: "This is
the desperate voice of the person who has published this newspaper for
nineteen years. I apologize if it bothers anyone."

But there were positive, even triumphal moments for this old patriot. After the Tibetan army was defeated in 1950, the new Chinese representative to Tibet, General Zhang Jingwu, travelled to Lhasa via Calcutta and Kalimpong. Indian Communists and some members of the local Chinese community prepared a public reception at Kalimpong for the Chinese VIP at the old Chinese school established by the Guomindang. Tharchin, as an important local dignitary, was asked to address the gathering. This is what he said:

In Tibetan, we have a proverb which says that everything changes. For example, there is happiness, which can easily change into sorrow. Everything turns like a wheel. This, it seems, is quite true even today. Just the other day (pointing to the wall behind him), there was a different kind of picture on the wall, but now Chiang Kai-shek's picture has disappeared, and Mao Tsetung's picture has taken its place.

Tibet for centuries has been an independent country. The Chinese claim it was under China. This state of affairs will not last permanently. It, too, will change. They (the Chinese) will have to give up their claim to Tibet. Tibet will once again enjoy its original freedom and independence, free of all Chinese control.[16]

Immediately after the speech, Tibetans in the audience rushed up to Tharchin and carried him on their shoulders.[17] The Chinese delegates were infuriated, and Zhang Jingwu refused to be interviewed by Tharchin. The old man kept publishing the *Tibet Mirror* for thirteen more years, only stopping in 1963, when the Tibetan community-in-exile had started their own newspapers and magazines.

I remember visiting his home on the Tirpai ridge and his office a few times with my father. On one occasion, I remember him enthusiastically showing us his new machine for casting Tibetan metal type and giving me a few shiny pieces of type as a souvenir. I last saw him on the Christmas Eve of 1965. He came to the Tibetan Refugee School in Kalimpong with the orphans of his Himalayan Children's Home. The children performed a nativity scene and sang a selection of hymns and carols. Tharchin distributed books he had printed at his press, including a hundred copies of the Tibetan translation of European fairy tales, compiled by an American missionary, Flora Beale Shelton, at Bathang. Tharchin gave a rousing speech to the entire school, exhorting everyone to remain loyal to the Dalai Lama and never forget they were Tibetans. Finally, as the children sang the Tibetan national anthem, the old man stood erect, head held high, tears streaming down his cheeks. He died on 6 February 1976.

Other Christian missionaries were no less active in the secret world of Kalimpong. One, George Patterson, mentioned earlier on, tried to set himself up as a kind of "Lawrence of Tibet" figure in that small town. In one of his books, he tells us that his friend, Molly McCabe, announced him to a women's gathering in Kalimpong in this manner: "Ladies, Patterson of Tibet."[18] Sangharakshita regarded him as "bumptious", and another English Buddhist in that town, Major Joseph E. Cann, gave him the nickname "Springheel Jack" for his tireless socializing and self-promotion.[19] Patterson has written about ten books, the last one being published in 2006, where he finally put aside any lingering inhibitions and went ahead and called it *Patterson of Tibet*.

Patterson's books suffer from a paucity of hard information on the actual fighting in Tibet, though, to be fair, his information was as good if not a little better (if he had just stuck to it) than what other writers had at the time. Chapters titled "I Was to be Liquidated" and "I Organize the Dalai Lama's Escape" reveal occasional lapses into paranoia and megalomania. But Patterson's overriding transgression is his propensity to assign the paramount leadership of the Tibetan resistance to his old friend Tobgyal Pangdatsang of Markham when in fact, the man was a high-level collaborator. If Patterson saw himself as Lawrence, then Topgyal Pangdatsang was certainly his putative Emir Faisal.

Patterson's most useful book on the resistance is *Fool at Forty*, when with a British television team, he actually accompanied a Tibetan guerrilla band in Northern Nepal on a raid into Tibet. The book invariably contains descriptions of nocturnal communications with the Almighty and a lengthy exposition of his *folie de grandeur*, his virtuoso solution to the Tibetan problem—"the Himalayan Confederation", the merger of Nepal, Bhutan, Sikkim and Tibet, into an independent union, which he was confident Communist China would consider favourably but, which short-sighted idiots in the Tibetan exile leadership, notably the Dalai Lama's brother Gyalo Thondup and the government of India were incapable of appreciating.[20]

A couple of Patterson's earlier books contain colourful stories of Kalimpong and its sundry characters from the forties and fifties. Some of the stories suffer from hyperbole and laboured comparisons with more Hollywood-inspired places of romance and intrigue. The 10th Mile area of Kalimpong with its illegal *tongba* (fermented millet ale) drinking places and mahjong parlours, patronized largely by Tibetan traders and muleteers, is described as " . . the notorious 10th-mile in Kalimpong, as famous in its way as the 'Casbah' in Algiers." Patterson also could not resist the analogy of choice for Kalimpong, "the Casablanca of the Tibetan Revolt," as most other journalists who set foot on the beer-bottle-cap-mosaic floor of the Himalayan Hotel bar—invariably could not.

Patterson also mentions other exiles in the town besides Tibetans. In March 1957, ". . . a small thin Mongolian in Western-style suit, Mingwang, Prince of Mongolia, a scion of the Torguts, a 'Tsagor Yasse', 'white bone' noble of the first class, a descendant of Genghiz Khan" appeared. He spoke fluent Russian, French and English and had conducted a fighting retreat before advancing Russians and then Chinese troops, all the way from the Gobi, through Sinkiang and Tibet, ending up in Kalimpong accompanied by only twenty-three survivors." But even here, Russian agents—yes, Kalimpong had them too—were trying to intimidate him. Patterson continues in this breathless vein, writing of 'Madame X, a *femme fatale* . . . she managed to cloak her arrival and subsequent movements in Kalimpong with an air of mystery, and Kalimpong having already an international reputation for intrigue, welcomed her with open arms."

I did not meet Madame X, but the second wife of my granduncle Kazi Lhendup Dorje Khangsarpa of Chakung, a European woman, came close to fitting the bill. Actually, Kazi *sahib* was not related to the Pulgers by blood, but the Sikkimese lady he first married (and subsequently divorced) was my great-aunt Jhomo Dechen Choden, who later married Rabga Pangdatsang, as I mentioned in Chapter One.

Kazi Lhendup Dorje's second wife was a two-time divorcee, Elisa Maria (or Marie Elise) Langford-Rae, *née* Ethel Maud Shirran of Perthshire and daughter of a British army sergeant. I recall this old European woman who had on so much make-up that she looked like a character out of a Chinese opera. She claimed to be a Belgian aristocrat and the niece of Field Marshall Mannerheim of Finland, but her granddaughter has noted that she was "a fabulist" and invented stories about herself.[21] One dubious story doing the rounds in Kalimpong was that Elisa Maria had been a British "stay-behind" agent operating in Singapore after the Japanese occupation. She had run a nightclub where Japanese officers came to drink and unwind.[22]

Earlier in her life, she had married an English police officer in Burma, Bertram Langford Denis Rae. It was said of her that she had had an affair with the young George Orwell when he was the assistant-superintendent at Insein, north of Rangoon.[23]

One guest at Chakung House mentions an "accidental" peek he got inside Elisa Maria's locket, which contained a small photograph of another (improbable) former lover, the young Zhou Enlai. On a sideboard in the foyer of Chakung House, another visitor noticed ". . . the Dalai Lama's card on a silver salver, implying that His Holiness had called, but of course he had done no such thing."[24]

This "bizarre European women" as Sunanda K. Dutta-Ray (former editor of the *Statesman* and author of *Smash and Grab: The Annexation of Sikkim*) describes her, plotted for over two decades with her husband at Chakung House in Kalimpong to overthrow the Chogyal of Sikkim, finally succeeding in 1975 with the help of local Nepali politicians and their mobs, the armed Indian Central Reserve Police Force (CRPF) and the benediction of Prime Minister Indira Gandhi[25] and her thankfully short-lived dictatorship.

But "Pat-la", as his Tibetan friends knew Patterson, does seem to have performed an important service for the Tibetan cause by making what was possibly the first representation to the CIA about the Communist threat to Tibet. In early 1950, he travelled from Bathang, via Markham, to India through the jungles of Dzayül (in south-eastern Tibet) and, arriving in Calcutta, approached the American Consulate and the British Deputy High Commission there. He briefed them on the desperate situation in Tibet and requested material support for his friend Topgyal Pangdatsang. The Foreign Office in London, probably after digging into old reports on the Pangdatsang family, dismissed ". . . any idea that the Pangdatsangs are likely to form a bastion against Communism, or indeed to act from any other motive than immediate self-interest."[26]

Patterson was able to be of more help in another related matter. The Dalai Lama's eldest brother, Taktser Rinpoche, abbot of Kumbum Monastery, had managed to escape from Tibet in 1951. He had been taken prisoner in the early stages of the Communist advance in 1949. In August 1950, just ahead of the invading Red Army, he had been ordered, along with another high lama, Alak Shalupatsang of Serkhog, to Lhasa with a five-man Chinese diplomatic team, to persuade the Dalai Lama to accept Communist rule, and failing that to eliminate him.[27] Taktser Rinpoche used the occasion to warn his brother against the Communists and to make his own escape to Kalimpong.

Patterson got an American missionary friend he had known in China, Colonel Robert Ekvall, who spoke Chinese and Tibetan fluently, to help. Ekvall had served in the OSS during the war, and through his connections, Taktser Rinpoche was invited to travel to America by the Committee for Free Asia, purportedly an anti-Communist association of businessmen. Soon with Taktser Rinpoche serving as intermediary and interpreter, the first CIA Tibet operations began to take shape.

Patterson annoyed the Indian intelligence and security people no end, as the other clandestine residents of Kalimpong probably did as well. Those were the years when India was riding the moral high horse in international diplomacy, denouncing Western imperialism in Suez and Cyprus (but ignoring Communist aggression in Hungary and Tibet) and calling for the post-colonial solidarity of Asian and African nations. It must have been embarrassing for Indian leaders to be constantly subjected to crude and abusive Chinese denunciations about one of their frontier towns being "a nest of imperialist spies" and the centre of the Tibetan revolt.

In the Indian Parliament, Prime Minister Nehru hotly denied that Kalimpong was the centre of the Tibetan revolt, though he was forced to a lesser admission ". . . but I have said it was a center of trouble." He tried, somewhat unsuccessfully, to make light of the whole situation. "It has been described as a 'nest of spies', of innumerable nationalities—spies from Asia, spies from America, Communist spies, white spies, red spies, blue spies and pink spies. There is no doubt that so far as Kalimpong is concerned, there has been a good deal of espionage, counter-espionage, a complicated game of chess by various nationalities, by various numbers of spies and counter-spies there."

My father, as the leading ethnic Tibetan citizen of both Kalimpong and Darjeeling, issued his own statement to the press, loyally supporting the Prime Minister.

RED AGENTS IN KALIMPONG

Mr T. Lhawang Pulger, President of the Association of Indian Tibetans, told reporters that the deputation of Tibetans from Kalimpong (in New Delhi) "wholeheartedly welcomes the statement made by Prime Minister Nehru to-day in Parliament repudiating the Red China charge that Kalimpong is the center of the Tibetan rebellion."

Mr. Lhawang said, "The fact is otherwise. There are some active agents of Red China at Kalimpong. It is these people who spread all sorts of rumours to give a bad name to Kalimpong."

—PTI, 2 April 1950, New Delhi

Neither Nehru's (nor my father's) denial that Kalimpong was the centre of the Tibetan rebellion was entirely true. Many prominent anti-Chinese leaders and activists were living in Kalimpong. The most outstanding was the tall, white-bearded Lukhangwa, the former prime minister of Tibet. When in office, he had stood up so unyieldingly to Chinese enticements, pressure and threats that he and his monk colleague, the incorruptible Lobsang Tashi, had managed, for a considerable while, to effectively frustrate Chinese plans to influence the young Dalai Lama and take over the Tibetan administration and what remained of the Tibetan army.

There was the story that the Chinese occupation authorities had demanded that the Chinese flag be hoisted over the Potala, but that Lukhangwa had refused, declaring that as long as he lived, only the Tibetan national flag would be flown over the Potala. Rumours of this dispute spread among the Lhasa public, and as with such things, became more dramatized in the telling. Both prime ministers became folk heroes to the masses over this incident.

Finally, the Dalai Lama, under pressure from the Chinese occupation authorities, had called for his resignation. Fearing his arrest or assassination, Lukhangwa's family and friends finally persuaded the old Prime Minister to leave Tibet. He escaped to Kalimpong in 1955, where he kept up his opposition to the Chinese occupation. Still, because of age, lack of experience and familiarity with the outside world, he was less effective than he had been in Tibet. He nevertheless maintained his lonely struggle and tried to persuade the disparate Tibetan groups in Kalimpong to come together in a kind of united front.

Gyalo Thondup, the Dalai Lama's older brother, was a more formidable power in the exile resistance world. His cover organization was the "Tibet Welfare Society" (*bhod dedon tsokpa*), which had been set up in 1954 to provide aid to the survivors of the unprecedented Gyantsé flood that year, which killed hundreds of the town-folk and destroyed much property. Tibetans informally called the organization "*Chen-khen-tse-sum*," taking one syllable from the titles of the three (*sum*) founding members: Kue-*chen*-mo (honourable older brother) Gyalo Thondup, *Khen*-chung (junior abbot), Lobsang Gyaltsen, the Tibetan trade agent at Kalimpong and *Tse*-pon (Finance Secretary) Shakabpa, the nationalist historian.

But Gyalo Thondup was the effective leader of the organization. His old schoolmate from China, now his secretary, Tsongkha Lhamo Tsering, served as his chief of operations. A major catch for Gyalo was the minister Yuthok ". . . who had found life in Lhasa unbearable under the Chinese"[28] and had resettled in Kalimpong. The Tibetan scholar Lobsang Lhalungpa and Dardo Rinpoche were also active members of the Welfare Society.* Princess Kukula, the politics-enamored sister of the Chogyal of Sikkim, contributed her services to this conspiracy. The Tibet Welfare Society eventually became the channel for all CIA aid and operations in Tibet.[29]

In the spring of 1953, B.N. Mullick, the director of India's Intelligence Bureau (IB), visited Darjeeling and met with Gyalo Thondup. Nehru, it now seemed, wanted to hedge his bets, and furthermore keep an eye on Tibetan political activities in India. A clandestine working relationship between the Tibet Welfare Society and the IB liaison Mukul Bose now commenced, that, over time, furnished Tibetans with a valuable range of support, including funds, radio equipment, training and even communication access to the Indian Consulate in Lhasa.[30]

The constant squabbling among these Tibetan groups, between lay officials and monk officials, between the Dalai Lama's brother and senior aristocrats, and between Khampas and other Tibetans limited what the exiles could effectively do from Kalimpong. My father helped Gyalo Thondup, Lukhangwa and other Tibetan leaders in drafting their memorandums and appeals in English, dealing on their behalf with local officialdom, and otherwise doing what he could, but became frustrated by the endless disagreements within the exile Tibetan community.

One gadfly in this political agglomeration was the underground activist from Lhasa, Alo Chonzé (Tsering Dorje), a former monk and trader, originally from Lithang. He and four others had organized the Mimang, or "People's Organization" in Lhasa in 1955 and circulated anti-Chinese leaflets and stuck up patriotic posters. Three of them were arrested, but Alo Chonzé managed to escape to Kalimpong from where

---

* The Dalai Lama's Lord Chamberlain, Phala (the Welfare Society's main ally in Lhasa), sent three trusted junior officials, Thupten Nyinje, Jampa Tsundru and Jampa Wangdu, to Kalimpong in 1956 to assist the Tibet Welfare Society.

he continued his activities. He also added to the confusion and disunity by quarrelling with nearly every other faction. Another irrepressible anti-Chinese activist in Kalimpong was Lobsang Dorje, the manager of the White Crystal Monastery (Shelkar Chanzö).

But Lukhangwa's unmistakable sincerity, his great standing in the public eye, and his soft-spoken but constant urgings finally managed to get the Khampas, Amdowas, Central Tibetans, aristocrats, lamas, merchants, monastic administrators, and the various welfare associations and organizations to put aside their differences and hold a number of meetings in the summer of 1958. Finally, on 5 August, they issued a joint appeal to the government of India, the United Nations and the world, declaring Tibet's independence, condemning China's military occupation of Tibet and appealing for help and support. Seven people signed the appeal: Lukhangwa, and two representatives each from Kham, Amdo and Central Tibet, the three traditional regions of "Greater" Tibet. A declaration of loyalty was also issued and delegations sent to Gangtok, Darjeeling and elsewhere to collect signatures. Patterson tells us that, "From the members of the Dalai Lama's family through Cabinet Ministers, local union officials to the lowliest Tibetan coolie in the bazaar, all Tibetans rushed to sign." Only two Tibetans of note did not sign, Patterson recalls, with real disappointment, one of them being his old friend, Rapga Pangdatsang.

The exile aristocrats in Kalimpong were anti-Chinese and, on the whole, charming people, but they lacked the toughness and the military virtues of the previous generation of officials who had served the Thirteenth Dalai Lama. The rule of two corrupt lama regencies and the overwhelming and stifling dominance of the conservative monastic faction in the Tibetan political world had not only demoralized the bureaucracy but had effectively discouraged people of intelligence and integrity from joining government service.

Rock-like characters as Lukhangwa and Tsarong were rare among the nobles in exile who, besides their one act of protest in leaving Tibet, seemed incapable of any further effort. This lack of resolution and energy filtered down to the younger set, the sons and daughters of aristocrats and prosperous Khampa merchants, who studied at such schools as St. Josephs, St Paul's, Loreto Convent and Mount Hermon in Darjeeling; Goethals, Victoria and Dow Hill in Kurseong; and St. Josephs Convent and St. Augustines in Kalimpong. Though many distinguished themselves in their studies and sports, quite a few became notorious for spending their parents' money on parties, dances and the summer pony races in Darjeeling. The young prince of Lingtsang (a principality in Eastern Tibet) took first prize as the best Cha-Cha dancer at a Gymkhana Club sponsored dance event.

Tsewang Pemba, a Tibetan doctor and a Fellow of the Royal College of Surgeons, wrote an unusual novel describing the life and times of such people, then in Kalimpong, Darjeeling and Tibet. *Idols on the Path* is in part autobiographical, the author's own life hewing fairly close to that of his young protagonist, Rinzing, who grows up on the outskirts of Lhasa and enjoys life in the Holy City till his father, a minor official, sends him to St. George's school in Darjeeling to acquire a modern education. He studies medicine in Calcutta and on returning to Tibet becomes restless and dissatisfied with the backwardness and poverty of his country. Then the Chinese invade. Escaping from Tibet with a band of Khampa fighters, he attends to those wounded in the fighting. Finally, he gets to Darjeeling and finds peace nursing Tibetan refugees there.

Rinzing's fairly straightforward story becomes a complex and intriguing saga with the many characters he encounters on his life's journey: the degenerate magistrate of Pipithang who, among other things, arranges farting competitions among his subjects, Sawang Rangdhon the cabinet minister and traitor, Kunga, the saintly monk meditating for three years alone in a cave and gaining enlightenment, Drakpa the fanatical convert to Marxism, and the haughty aristocrat Saring, who fights the Chinese and dies after fourteen days of torture with his body broken but his pride intact.

The members of the "fast set" that Rinzing meets in Darjeeling and Kalimpong are entertaining but not the most convincing of the book's many characters. Their decadence appears a little too calculated to highlighting Rinzing's virtues. "The party ended, and the guests left. Rinzing surveyed the half-empty glasses, cigarette butts, the radiogram with the records spilt in disorder around it. Rinzing selected one record and put it on. It was a tune that had sent Tibetans bobbysoxers into a frenzy. These Tibetans were the sons and daughters of cabinet ministers, relatives of monks and hermits, children of Shangri-La, inhabitants of the Roof of the World. He shook his head and wondered."

Those Tibetans in Kalimpong who could afford it moved to Darjeeling in spring and early summer when the weather was perfect and the racing season started. The highest racecourse in the world had one unique rule—that only hill ponies could be entered. The other rules were perhaps not consistently observed, for besides being the smallest and the highest racecourse, it had the reputation of being the most crooked. A memorable if not entirely respectable character from the Darjeeling turf was a Tibetan, "Lhakpa Bookie," who in his grimy twill jacket, muffler and flat wool cap, resembled his English counterpart (or the cartoon-strip character Andy Capp) to a startling degree. One of the greatest ponies to race in the miniature racecourse and "winning the Governors Cup a dozen times" was "Gyatso" from the stable of Sardar Bahadur Laden la, the superintendent of the Darjeeling police, who had been given the pony by Tsarong in 1921.[31]

My father maintained a stable. His champion pony, Let-Me-Fly, a full-blooded Xining stallion from North-Eastern Tibet that he purchased in the Lhasa horse market at Hongtö Shingka in 1949, won the Governor's Cup twice. My dad's trainer, Bertie Holland, a former champion jockey, was of mixed German, Chinese and Nepali descent. At Bertie's home, I remember seeing a framed portrait of his grandfather, Von Scotch Holland, in the Kaiser's army, complete with jackboot and a spiked *pickelhaube*.

My father returned from England when I was three. My mother, sister and I, who had lived at our uncle's house in Kalimpong, now moved with my father to Darjeeling. Our new house was on Auckland Road, which was renamed Gandhi Road after the British left. The house was mock Tudor with cross beams but had a red corrugated-iron roof as most houses in Darjeeling did. Earlier, the playwright Tom Stoppard had lived in this house as a boy. His family had left their native Czechoslovakia for Singapore to escape the Nazi invasion and had then been evacuated to India. Our house was named Minto Villa after the viceroy, though Stoppard, in an article in the *Independent*, mentions that, as a boy, he wondered about the reason for a house being named after a sweet.[32]

The large house to our right, "Kopje", was a guest house run by two elderly English widows from South Africa, a Mrs Cootze and Mrs Adams. They had a beautiful garden that I remember being chased out of on several occasions. Havelock Villa, to our left, was the home of the eminent Bengali scientist, Sir Jagadis Chandra Bose, who, a year before Marconi, had demonstrated, that electric signals could be transmitted through space without wires. Later, in a series of elegant experiments before scientists at the Royal Society, Bose demonstrated the sentient nature of plants. When we moved into Minto Villa, Bose's old widow and his son Dilip, a correspondent for the Calcutta *Statesman*, and a specialist on Tibetan affairs, was living in Havelock Villa. As a child, I would wander around the grounds of Bose's deserted Research Institute on the Jalapahar Road and peer through the grimy glass panes at rheostats, galvanometers, glass beakers, flasks and other laboratory equipment covered with dust and cobwebs.

Tom Stoppard went to Mount Hermon School, founded by American Episcopal Methodists, a couple of miles below St. Joseph's College. But my school could also lay some claim to literary glory with Laurence Durrell, who studied there from 1919 to 1924, and his brother Gerald (*My Family and other Animals*) some years later. Laurence's biography mentions that "the Jesuits of North Point were not the martinets under whom James Joyce suffered. They were tolerant men, mostly Belgians, who accepted children of many faiths." Durrell recalled there being Hindus, Buddhists, Taoists, Sufis and Protestants like himself, as well as Catholics at the College, ". . . which was set among tea plantations on the Himalayan slopes, with Everest on the distant horizon."[33] Father J. de Gheldere, the college rector whom he once heard reading poetry, inspired in Durrell the wish to be a poet.

Father Thomas Edward McGuire, S. J., or "Magoo" as we called him, attempted, to instil in us an appreciation of Shakespeare, Dickens, Wordsworth and Tennyson. He also tolerated my infatuation with

Ernest Hemingway, and gently nudged me to come around to a more nuanced appreciation of my favourite author and role model. Coming from the more egalitarian world of rural Canada he also tried to knock the colonial stuffiness out of us. The first thing he did when he took over our class was to forbid us from addressing each other by our surnames. "You're kids, for crying out loud. Call each other by your first names."

He left the school some years after I graduated to start the Gandhi Ashram at Kalimpong, to provide meals and basic education to the poorest children in the district, especially those from the lower castes. Before his death in 2005, PBS aired a television documentary on him and his school.

Thomas Merton, the Trappist monk and writer, was not impressed with St Joseph's. In one of his books, he recounts his impression: "Noise, kids, tea, wide grassless playgrounds, gardens, hyper-Gothic buildings, a big Victorian courtyard, crests, blazers, scarves, and all sorts of exhortations (*sursum corda*) to the boys. Some were neat wide-eyed little kids, including a shy one from Bhutan, the only one I spoke to, and others with mod hairdos and perfect swaggers. Some of them looked like little bastards. Very much the Jesuit School! We got out as fast as possible."[34]

I was in the fifth standard when the Lhasa Uprising took place. I remember hearing the news that the Dalai Lama had escaped from Lhasa and recall how everyone was afraid and worried whether India would grant political asylum to him and the other fleeing Tibetans. There was a real cause for apprehension. A few years earlier, Prime Minister Zhou Enlai had come to India and had laid on his famous charm. Many in the Indian leadership were besotted with Communist China. "*Hindi Chini Bhai Bhai*" or "Indians and Chinese are brothers" was the watchword of the day.

I remember one night my mother in tears arguing with my father, pushing him to go to Delhi and, as an Indian citizen, insist that the Dalai Lama be allowed to enter India. My father had, by then, become absolutely fed up with the Tibetan factions and their squabbles, but my mother finally got him to go. A large delegation led by the former Prime

Minister Lukhangwa left for Delhi, but Nehru was initially reluctant to meet the Tibetans. Eventually, he agreed to speak to Lukhangwa. My father, representing all ethnic Tibetans of Indian nationality, was also received by the Indian prime minister and assured that the Dalai Lama would be allowed to enter India. CIA sources have revealed that two American-trained Tibetans accompanying the Dalai Lama on his flight had radioed the official request for sanctuary to Washington, which had forwarded the message to New Delhi. Nehru gave his consent to the Americans and also allowed the Tibetans in Delhi to let the world know of his decision. Lukhangwa and my father made the important announcement at a press conference in Delhi[35] on 31 March, with princess Kukula of Sikkim interpreting for Lukhangwa.

Tibetan refugees started to pour into Kalimpong and Darjeeling. Everyone had frightening stories of fighting, killing, torture, imprisonment, destruction, denunciations and public executions. Someone told us that Tsarong pola had taken part in the uprising and had been arrested by the Chinese and locked up in the central prison of the Tibet Military Area Headquarters (Chinese, *Junqu Silingbu*). Ngodup, the steward of the Tsarong family, was accused of assisting the "reactionaries" and taken to the nearby village of Nedrak Jüg, where the local people were forced to stone him to death. [36]

Now, instead of those wonderfully generous aunts and uncles, polas and *molas* from Tibet who on their earlier visits to India (especially, in 1956 during the 2,500th celebration of the Buddha's birth and enlightenment) had given you wonderful Tibetan goodies: yak-jerky, hard, chewy cheese (*chugom*), sweet cheese pretzels (*chungar*), dried sweet chang mash (*zenchang*), molasses candy (*bhurom garma*), sweet noodle bricks (*tsethang kozé*), and dried fruits, including lychees dried in their skin (*bhendé*) from Kham, and nonchalantly dispensed munificent tips, you now had desperately poor and traumatized people looking for aid and shelter.

Among the refugees were important lamas and religious figures. One day we heard that Jamyang Khyentse Rinpoche of Dzongsar had just arrived in Darjeeling, and we invited him to bless our house. This was the previous incarnation of Khyentse Norbu, the present-day celebrity lama and film-maker, director of the 1999 comedy, *The Cup* (*Phörpa*). My mother told me that she had taken religious teachings from Khyentse Rinpoche when she was a young girl in Kham, and that at one of his sermons, golden-hued snowflakes had drifted out of a clear blue sky. I was going through a difficult period where I had recurrent nightmares of dying. The old lama listened to me patiently and explained how I could seek refuge in the Buddha and the Dharma. Somewhat unexpectedly, he gave me a new name, Jamyang Norbu.

In Kalimpong, a performing troupe was set up to promote awareness of the Tibetan issue in the Indian public and raise funds for the growing flood of refugees. The members of this troupe came from a diverse background: officials, professional Lhasa musicians, opera performers and the children of aristocrats and Khampa merchants, one of the musicians even being a scion of the Lhagyari, one of the only two families in Tibet that carried the direct bloodline of the Tibetan emperors. This performing group became the core of what later was to be the Tibetan Institute of Performing Arts in Dharamshala.

A Tibetan Refugee Self-Help Center was set up with a committee headed by Nancy, or Zhu Dan, the wife of the Dalai Lama's older brother, Gyalo Thondup. The committee included such celebrities as Tenzing Norgay, the Everest hero, also Monseigneur Eric Benjamin bishop of the Darjeeling diocese, Palden Gyaltsen Tesur, my maternal uncle and former governor of Gyantsé, Colonel Thapa, the commander of the Gurkha regiment in the district, my father, my mother and others. With the active voluntary participation of local Tibetans and friends, various fundraising activities were organized. The stewards of the Darjeeling Race Course pitched in and held a big raffle for the refugees. Eric Avari, the Parsee owner of the two cinema halls in Darjeeling, arranged special screenings to raise funds.

One day my class at school was interrupted by a visit from the principal, Father Stanford, who announced that the Dalai Lama's young brother would join our class. He introduced the boy beside him to us as Tenzin Chögyal. He was actually an incarnate lama and respectfully called Ngari Rinpoche by Tibetans, but T. C., as he was quickly tagged, fitted right in with the other boys. There were many

Tibetans at St. Joseph's, sons of aristocrats and merchants. One small boy from our school left immediately after 1959. His parents had been caught in the Lhasa Uprising and were said to be missing. All he now had was his nanny, but she looked after him as her own child. At St. Augustine's School in Kalimpong, run by Catholic priests from Switzerland, four boys from Lhasa were completely cut off from their families by the uprising. Eventually, the priests took them to Valais in southern Switzerland and raised them there. Such stories became fairly frequent at that time.

Tibet was now cut off in a way that it had never ever been before. The borders were hermetically sealed, and no one could send a letter to, or receive one from Tibet. There was no Checkpoint Charlie on this section of the "Bamboo Curtain", not even some minimal human communication with the other side, an exchange of spies, for example, which the West had had with the Soviets at the height of the Cold War. Even during the worst days of World War II, Red Cross representatives moved back and forth between the warring nations, and allied POWs received mail and packages from home. There was nothing from Tibet. It was a black hole.

Trade with Tibet came to a complete dead stop. And the big wool warehouses in Kalimpong became shelters for refugees and schools for their children. I helped to teach refugee children during my school holidays and later organized and coached the football (soccer) team of the Tibetan Refugee School at Kalimpong.

In my last couple of years at school, I had, somewhat abruptly, put on a few inches and begun to mature. Earlier my interests had been limited to football, science and the guitar. The last band I played in was "Doc Ock and His Tentacles"—Marvel Comics and the Amazing Spiderman, having hit the Indian magazine stands a couple of years earlier. But then I began to take notice of what was happening around me.

Darjeeling in the early sixties had become the headquarters of the Resistance. The Dalai Lama's older brother, Gyalo Thondup, with his assistant, Lhamo Tsering, who was generally known as "The Honorable Secretary" (*kusho drunyik-la*), had by now dominated all the other organizations and become the sole liaison with the resistance groups in Tibet, with the CIA and with the Indian Intelligence Bureau (IB). Orders emanated from Gyalo Thondup's residence, Shiva Bhavan, on Gandhi Road, a stone's throw from our house, Minto Villa. The organization also acquired a large manor house, Caernarvon, below St. Paul's School, once the summer residence of an Indian *nawab*, which was used as a safe house and basic training school for agents, resistance-leaders and fighters till they were whisked away for training to the United States, or smuggled across the border into Tibet.

Much of this wasn't a big secret in the Tibetan community, but it had yet to make an impression on me. When it did, it was sudden and overwhelming—like the result of the simple chemistry experiment I helped my daughter Namtso for her science project one year, and which she still remembers as "awesome". You dissolve Epsom salt into a container of warm water and keep adding the salt and stir till it becomes supersaturated, and no more salt can be dissolved. When the solution cools, you drop a "seed", a grain of the chemical on the surface of this clear solution. Like magic, the area around the seed begins to solidify, and this ice cap spreads rapidly across the surface, then throughout the entire solution. The transition from clear liquid to solid crystal is so dramatic that it seems like magic.

Sometimes the only "seed" it takes to transform a callow intellect on the brink of formative change is a book. I had read Hemingway's short stories and a play about the Spanish Civil War, but it was his great novel *For Whom the Bell Tolls*, which helped put the confusing and tragic events taking place around me in a frame of reference, a story, which I could relate to the direction of my own life. The PLA was obviously Franco's trained fascist army, the Khampa fighters were the ragtag band of anti-fascist partisans in the Sierra de Guadarrama mountains, and I was, of course, Robert Jordan, as portrayed by Gary Cooper in the 1943 film, a rerun of which I saw at the Capitol Cinema the year before I finished school. My construal was admittedly crude, but I was just fifteen at the time and found it compelling.* That same year the *Reader's Digest* published a dramatic excerpt of George Patterson's account of a Tibetan guerrilla raid on a Chinese military convoy. Although I still knew very little about the Tibetan struggle and even less about the politics and people involved, I now wanted to be part of it. I had a mission in life, or so I thought.

Just after I finished school the following year, I had a nasty falling out with my father. He had always been a bit of a bully and was not happy when I stood up to him one day. He pulled out a handgun and pointed it at me. Looking back, I am sure he would not have used it, but I couldn't have known it then, and it took all the "grace under pressure" I could muster to tell him exactly what I thought of him. My great-grandmother, Tsezin Dolma, a Khampa, and quite a piece of work in her own right, intervened, scolding him fiercely. That same evening, despite the pleas of my grandmother, uncles and aunts, I left Darjeeling. I first went to Kalimpong, where my mother and sister were, at the time, bade them goodbye, and left home forever.

I think it was the year before when a rumour came out of Tibet that Tsarong pola had committed suicide in prison. Most Tibetans claimed he had swallowed a diamond ring, but I was a science guy and knew better than to subscribe to old wives' tales about diamonds or ground glass being lethal if ingested. Someone else suggested that he could have used poison, maybe a cyanide capsule that could have been given to him by a member of the SS scientific expedition to Tibet in 1938.† After all, Tsarong had had the Germans over at his house in Lhasa for dinner. Hitler and Goebbels had committed suicide with poison pills, but it was a stretch to believe that German travellers before the war went around with cyanide pills in their pockets and

---

*In later years, Orwell's *Homage to Catalonia* helped wean me away from this romantic viewpoint and develop a more substantial and politically grounded understanding of this most divisive of civil wars in modern history.

†Hugh Richardson, the British representative in Lhasa, had objected to the "Schaefer Expedition", but on the insistence of the British Foreign Office, an uneasy Kashag had been obliged to issue a formal invitation and passport to the Germans.

gave them away like aspirin. The whole thing remained a mystery for a long time. When I heard the news of his death, all I recalled was a stout old man who had given me a much-needed supplement to my inadequate pocket money.

By then, the Indian Intelligence Bureau (IB) was working openly with the CIA on the Tibet operations, and Gyalo Thondup had moved his headquarters to New Delhi. I travelled down to the Indian capital and went to his house in the posh neighbourhood of Golf Links. I told him I wanted to join the Resistance Force at Mustang. But he laughed at my naïveté and told me to go home. I didn't know what to do, and I was running out of money. I heard that large agricultural resettlement camps were being started in South India for Tibetan refugees, so I took the train to Mundgod in Karnataka State, where my uncle Tsewang Chogyal (T.C.) Tethong was director and began working for the Swiss Technical Cooperation.

Our job was to clear the jungles, drill for water, and prepare farmland. For the first time in my life, I worked with my hands on bulldozers and tractors, in the heat, mud, rain and (often) darkness, and enjoyed myself tremendously. I knew something about engines, so they made me the foreman of the tractor section. The jungles had leopards, pythons (one night I drove over one) and wild boars that the tribal people sometimes hunted and sold us the meat, which our mess-in-charge transformed into juicy chops. Other young Tibetan officials were working there in the settlement office and hospital, and I shared a tent with one.

The Tibetan refugees resettled in Mundgod had a difficult time adjusting to the very different conditions from their native homeland. Many of the new settlers had been nomads and had lived in some of the highest and coldest areas in the world and had never eaten rice or vegetables, much less cultivated such things. Now they were expected to be farmers in South India. Often a Tibetan managed to survive the tropical heat and diseases only to be trampled to death by wild elephants when protecting his crops. But gradually, he learned to cope with the climate, the new way of life, and even with beasts that back in Tibet had existed only in myths and stories.

I stayed over a year and a half at Mundgo, when a friend of mine assured me that he had an inside track with Gyalo Thondup and could get him to accept my service in the resistance. But that effort failed even more humiliatingly than the previous one. I decided to try my luck at the hill station of Dharamshala in Northern India, where the Dalai Lama had, a few years earlier, set up his government-in-exile.

I have this last memory of Mundgod: I'm looking out east over bare, dry fields, in the direction of the Arabian Sea, which is about fifty miles away as the crow flies. The sky is overcast, but then I notice a peculiar change in the light, which becomes noticeably more orange as if it were dawn. Then far into the horizon, I see a wall of dark, nearly black clouds that seem to stretch up and sideways forever, like an enormous tsunami, but a slow-moving one. I feel a slight breeze across my face and, looking down, see bits of grass and leaves stirring in the dust. The gust picks up, becoming a strong driving wind, and the immense rampart of dark clouds, suddenly seems much closer. Before I know it, I am in the middle of a terrific rainstorm, and am struggling with the others to hold down our flapping tents, ineffectually hammering loose pegs into the growing mud and yelling instructions at each other. The monsoon had finally hit Western India.

9

MARCH WINDS

March is stormy in Dharamshala, the small North Indian hill station that is the headquarters-in-exile of the Dalai Lama and the Tibetan government. March is also the month when Tibetan refugees in this town and elsewhere commemorate their national struggle against China's military occupation of Tibet—a violent struggle culminated in the desperate Uprising of 1959 and the flight of the Dalai Lama to India.

It had begun to rain on that morning of March 10, 1968—my first experience of this annual rite of remembrance—and the fife and drum band of the Tibetan Dance and Drama Society was losing snap in inverse proportion to the rain that the drum-heads (and the musicians) were steadily absorbing. School children in thin cotton uniforms shivered in the rain, while the adults, dressed in drab cotton versions of their national dress or odd combinations of ill-fitting gift clothes, waited patiently, clutching paper flags or holding placards and banners that proclaimed, "FREE TIBET" or "CHINA OUT OF TIBET". The only pleasant touch to this gloomy scene was provided by a row of marigolds in CARE milk powder cans arrayed before the Dalai Lama's small tent. His Holiness spoke briefly and precisely. This was the first time I had heard him speak, and though I don't recollect what he said exactly, I remember being moved and impressed. The same could not be said for the speeches that followed. The cabinet's statement was read in a mumble that buzzed irritatingly over the defective P. A. system. A monk, I think the deputy-speaker of the exile Tibetan parliament, came next, chanting a singsong litany couched in ornate classical Tibetan. He was incomprehensible.

Every year, Tibetan communities throughout India and elsewhere enact a variation of this ritual, which generally concludes with a procession through the closest town or city, where fierce slogans condemning Communist Chinese leaders from Mao to Xi Jinping have, through the years, been shouted, generally to the bemusement of Indian shopkeepers and passers-by.

My contact at Dharamshala was my cousin Tenzin Gyeche-la, the oldest son of my uncle Sonam Tomjor, and now the assistant private secretary to the Dalai Lama. He had become a monk since I had last seen him when he was in his senior year at Mount Hermon School. To my admiring young eyes, he had looked very cool then, wearing a pair of tight "drainpipes", a brilliant purple silk jacket with a bold logo at the back (like out of *West Side Story*) and his hair in a not-quite-Elvis quiff. Now neatly shorn and in a simple maroon robe, he conveyed quiet efficiency and dedication. Besides his official duties, he had, with his younger brother Tenzin Namgyal, set up a popular news magazine, *Sheja* or "Knowledge", to inform and educate the refugee population. He had written to me earlier that they needed editorial help at *Sheja*, but when I got to Dharamshala, he asked me if I would like to work at the Dance and Drama Society.

This Society had its origins in the performing group at Kalimpong, which raised funds for Tibetan refugees in 1958 and 1959, and promoted awareness of Tibetan culture to Indians and others. Now, the Lhasa musicians, opera singers, and various performers of the group were requested by the new exile government to come to Dharamshala and become a national institute. The Society was quite successful in the beginning, but the year before I came to Dharamshala, it had nearly been shut down because of fractious differences among senior staff and performers, many of whom had been dismissed or transferred from the Society. In a bid to save it, Tenzin Gyeche-la had taken over the administration, and he needed someone to run the Society's office and do whatever paperwork was required.

Followed by a burly Kashmiri porter (Ali) carrying my suitcase on his back, I walked up the hill from the small town of McLeod Ganj, the Tibetan section of Dharamshala, to the Dance and Drama Society. It might be mentioned here that the town was named after the Lt Governor of Punjab (1865–70), Sir Donald Friell McLeod. "Ganj" being the Urdu for neighborhood or enclave. The first mile of the walk on the rough unpaved road took me through a steep mountainside forest of towering deodar pines, where packs of chattering rhesus monkeys groomed each other in the sun and scolded passers-by. In the winter, the rhesuses would move further down the valley, and the *deodar* forest would echo with the hoots of the black-faced, silver-haired Himalayan *langurs*. They would jump from tree to tree, sometimes bounding off the roof of refugee dwellings before disappearing like fleeting apparitions into the winter mist. In between the trees were tents, shacks, and the kind of jury-rigged shelters you find in slum neighbourhoods throughout the world. But many of these humble makeshift dwellings had bright flowers (planted in a variety of tin cans) on windowsills and minuscule front porches.

The town was essentially a refugee camp, or what they called a Displaced Person or DP camp during the War. There was even an official Camp Commandant, an Indian bureaucrat, whose main job was to distribute food rations to all Tibetan DPs: the refugees living in the tent shelters, officials of the exile government, the Tibetan nursery, the Transit School, the Dance and Drama Society, and even the Dalai Lama and his entourage. The rations were not exciting: dal, rice, onions, chili peppers, sugar and tea leaves, but adequate when you fleshed it out with the occasional consignment of CARE milk powder, Bulgur Wheat, Wisconsin Cheese and Spam. The Camp Commandant even provided the sweepers to keep the town clean, a real doctor and a clinic to provide free treatment and free medicine, and language teachers (respectfully addressed as *guru-ji*) who, with the serendipitous influence of the local cinema hall (Himalaya Talkies) soon got Tibetans speaking Hindi, in a fashion of their own.

The Government of India (GOI) also set up large boarding schools at all major hill stations: Darjeeling, Kalimpong, Shimla, Mussoorie, Dalhousie, Mount Abu and Dharamshala. These provided an English medium based modern education to many thousands of refugee children. Though public education in India was run along strictly secular lines, the GOI recognized that Tibetan identity was closely bound to its unique Buddhist culture. So, these schools employed *geshes* and lamas to provide formal religious education to Tibetan children. Every *paisa* for this exemplary project came from the Indian taxpayer. Nehru's government may have failed dismally to support the Tibet issue in the United Nations, but there can be no question of the more than generous treatment of Tibetan refugees by the government and people of India.

Further up the track from McLeod Ganj to the Dance and Drama Society, the houses ended. The trees now became smaller, just chil pines and rhododendron trees. Some of the latter had already begun to bloom. In a matter of weeks, the whole mountainside would be covered with their brilliant red flowers. Following a bend in the road, a stirring Himalayan view opened up. Nestling in the saddle of the adjacent Triund ridge to the north-east, was a high snow-capped peak (of the Dauladhar range) that looked impressively like the Matterhorn but without as much of a bend at the top. The local Gaddi hill folk called the peak Natrar Jodh, after the Dancing Shiva, but officially it was called Moon Peak, after Captain (Willoughby?) Moon, who first climbed it in 1906, assisted by seven riflemen of the Fourth Gurkha Rifles (Prince of Wales' own Gurkha Rifles) from the nearby military cantonment at Forsyth Ganj.

Another half-mile further and you finally got to the Tibetan Dance and Drama Society, billeted in an old broken-down British bungalow, called Conium House. The central section of the rear pitch of the bungalow roof had been cut and raised to a near horizontal, and a stage had been built under it. The audience was seated before it in the veranda and open space. This was later covered with a wooden frame structure to form a makeshift auditorium. The rest of the bungalow was converted into dormitories (which also doubled as dressing-rooms) for the actors and dancers. As a staff member, I had a room to myself. Though it was only one of the four converted bathrooms of the bungalow (which were the designated staff quarters), it was a definite and welcome privilege.

Families lived in the stalls of the stables above the bungalow. Nearly all the windows at Conium House were missing or broken, and since there was very little money to replace them, people had to manage with bits of cardboard or plastic sheeting to keep out the wind and rain. It got very cold in winter, and the young actors suffered consequently. Many fell prey to tuberculosis. (About eighty per cent of the refugee population would contract TB at one point in their lives). Their diet lacked sufficient protein and was largely rice with lentils, or steamed bread with a watery stew of *kaddu* squash and potatoes, and a few bits of mutton gristle and fat floating (twice a week) on the stew. No milk, eggs or fruits.

It was still an improvement on conditions earlier when many of the refugees just died, not only because of malnutrition and exhaustion, but because they lacked the resistance to the many unfamiliar diseases that thrived in the humid tropical climate. As I mentioned earlier, the worst hit were those Tibetans resettled in farming colonies in the hot Indian plains. But even in the cooler hill stations of Darjeeling, Dalhousie, Mussoorie, Shimla and Dharamshala, conditions had not been easy, especially for the very young. In the early sixties, children, exhausted by their long journey and traumatized by war and separation, often died, soon after reaching the Tibetan Nursery at Dharamshala. When the matrons or the few nurses would do their morning rounds of the barrack-like dormitories lined with iron bunks, they would discover, almost every day, one or two cold little bodies. The cremations took place by a small mountain stream a mile and a half before McLeod Ganj, below the motor road. When you looked down at the spot through the grimy window of the morning bus, there always seemed to be a thin column of smoke rising from above the stream.

But it would be false to paint a picture of unrelieved suffering and deprivation. Whatever else the Tibetans had to leave behind in Tibet, it was not their cheerfulness and sense of humour. There was fun and happiness in the refugee community and, however seemingly unwarranted by actual circumstances, a firm belief that Tibet would be free someday, and everyone could then go home. This faith provided a sense of mission to many living and working in the exile community. They believed that they were laying the foundations for a free and modern Tibet and that their period of exile was an opportunity to learn from the outside world.

Many of the young actors and dancers were about my age and the girls were uniformly beautiful. So, there were dances, especially on Saturday evenings, where we were joined by young staff members of the exile government, many educated in Christian schools and colleges, Tibetan Muslim boys from the liberal Aligarh Muslim University and young nurses and mechanics returned from training in Sweden and Norway, and waiting to be sent out to one settlement or the other. They were still doing the "twist" and the "shake" in Dharamshala at the time, so having just come from a trendier place like Darjeeling, I introduced them to the "boogaloo" and the "frug."

The Indian beer, Golden Eagle, being generally unaffordable at five rupees a bottle, these gatherings were fuelled by the locally-brewed chang or barley ale which cost a quarter of a rupee per bottle and was eminently drinkable. The only record player and the latest records were owned by "T.T.-la", the junior steward of Ling Rinpoche, the Dalai Lama's senior tutor, but not always available to us. There were nights where one or two of us would sit by a small transistor radio and fiddle with the dials till we nailed Radio Ceylon, the only commercial station on the subcontinent that played the latest pop, rock and country. Then the dancing started.

There were other forms of entertainment at Dharamshala. The Tibetan public loved the programs of colourful folk dances that were put on by the Dance and Drama Society. There were also performances of "historical plays", which were rather wooden dramatizations of major events in Imperial Tibetan history, interspersed with song and dance routines that seemed jointly inspired by Chinese opera and the musical routines of Indian cinema. Unlike traditional Tibetan opera performed outdoors in the round, the historical plays were performed on a proscenium stage before crudely painted sets. But it must be said that the Tibetan public hugely enjoyed these colourful shows, which also served as an effective morale booster to the refugee population and as elementary history lessons on Tibet's glorious past.

Modern plays about the Uprising and the Resistance were also staged at the Dance and Drama Society, especially on the evening of 10 March. Most of these productions were crude and no doubt derived in structure and style from early Red Army propaganda skits that had been extensively performed throughout Tibet and were the forerunners of Madame Mao's revolutionary operas. But they served to inflame the patriotic passions of the Dharamshala refugees and ensure that the 10 March ceremonies ended on a satisfactorily upbeat and patriotic note.

Besides doing whatever office work there was, I was also required to teach English to the young performers. But I pitched in on the other tasks, helping to teach them new tunes for their fife and drum band and transcribed "Colonel Boogie", "Dixie" and some Sousa marches for the fife. I also played a passable *dranyen*, the Tibetan lute, in their orchestra. But most of all, I enjoyed helping in the production of patriotic plays: making spotlights out of (the everversatile) CARE milk powder cans, carving wooden burp-guns and potato-masher grenades for the actors playing Chinese soldiers, and painting sets on sewn-together canvas sacking that once contained CARE bulgur wheat. The public enjoyed the plays hugely. The *amalas* would have a good cry during the scenes of Tibetans being tortured or executed, but when the evil Chinese commander finally got his comeuppance at the hand of the resistance-hero the whole audience would break out in this incredible cheer, making the thin plywood proscenium of the jerry-built stage tremble in a discernable manner.

Stories were performed in their entirety with no effort made to focus on events that had theatrical merit or to leave out inappropriate or unimportant material. The final battle was always enacted on-stage in the most unrestrained pantomime fashion that invariably diminished the gravity and drama of the concluding scene. Being a cocksure young man, I, of course, had to voice my aesthetic reservations about these productions. I was challenged to produce a better play.

I got my chance on the occasion of the first Tibetan Youth Conference* in 1970. I was asked by the convening committee if I could write and produce a play especially for the occasion. Earlier, I had knocked out a couple of comic skits that the actors at the Drama Society had enjoyed performing, so I was not a complete novice at the business. But this was the real deal, a full-length tragedy, so I invested in a ream of foolscap, and sitting down before the old Imperial typewriter in the office, came up with a complete script for a three-act play in about a month. I called it *The Chinese Horse* (*gya nakpoe ta*), taking the title from a verse of a well-known *lu* or Khampa folk song:

> Do not ride a Chinese horse.
> For horses from Black China
> Cannot be held back by bit or bridle.

> *Ta shona gyata mashon shi*
> *Gya nakpoe ta la kha-lo me*

The play tells the story of a Lhasa merchant, his two sons and a little daughter. When the Communists march into the Holy City, the younger son is attracted to the novelty of the Communist modernization programs, while his older brother despises the Chinese and distrusts their pseudo-idealistic rhetoric. The inevitable conflict in their home results in the younger brother leaving to join the Communists. The violent Uprising of March 1959 brings this family quarrel full circle, with tragic consequences for everyone in this middle-class Tibetan home.

---

*This conference, from which the Tibetan Youth Congress (TYC) was born, was one of the most critical events in exile history. The TYC came into being in the wake of a crippling power struggle within the exile government. As such, the emergence of a democratic and free-thinking organization of young Tibetans at this dark moment in Tibetan history was an enormously exciting and important event. The founders of TYC were Tenzin Gyeche Tethong, the late Sonam Topgyal Zechutsang, the late Lodi Gyari and Tenzin Namgyal Tethong. I was a conference convener and subsequently elected member of the TYC Central Executive Committee.

I was pleased that I had managed to contain the story in just two interior sets, the living room of the merchant's home, and the office of the Chinese Secret Police in Lhasa. I also kept the triumphal march of the Red Army into Lhasa and the 1959 street fighting off-stage, and yet, managed to convey the dramatic impact of these important events in the performance. The dialogue was reworked extensively during rehearsals, but it should be mentioned that it was all written down and spoken as it was intended. In earlier plays at the Drama Society, only key dialogue lines were written down and memorized. The rest were improvised. My dialogue lines were, admittedly, florid, but they were written at a point in my life when I was reading, with considerable admiration, the early plays of Sean O'Casey (*The Shadow of a Gunman, The Plough and the Stars*), and I had yet to come across Orwell's cautionary words about romantic nationalism of the Irish variety.

The play was a big success at the Youth Conference. The Dalai Lama received a command performance three weeks later, and he gave every appearance of having enjoyed the show. After the final curtain, he insisted on climbing up on the stage and joining the actors. He asked for a photograph to be taken, but no one had a camera. Finally, someone ran down to McLeod Ganj to fetch one. While His Holiness waited, he talked to me and joked about the fake blood on my shirt, for I was playing the role of the older brother in the play. Finally, the group picture was taken with His Holiness holding my hand in a proprietorial fashion. But the photographer had gotten the exposure wrong, and the picture came out a nice solid grey.

As much as I was pleased with the modest success of my first play, I became dissatisfied with the fictional aspect of the story. I also began to have doubts about the main element of the story, the clash between the two brothers of conflicting personalities, which now seemed somewhat contrived and, worse still, unoriginal and clichéd. Whatever had been wrong with the old propaganda plays performed at the Dance and Drama Society, they had the supreme merit of being the tales of real people and actual events. I wanted to write something that was a straightforward story of resistance and heroism, and I wanted it to be based on bedrock reality.

In one of the propaganda plays about the uprising in Eastern Tibet, I was drawn to a sub-plot of the fighting in the Lithang region led by a young chieftain, Yunru Pön, who became the leader of his tribe when he was just fifteen years old. The story was straightforward. The chieftain and his warriors take an oath to defend Lithang Monastery to the last man and hold out against numerous Chinese attacks. Finally, the monastery is bombed to rubble, and Yunru Pön announces to the Chinese that he is prepared to surrender. The Chinese commander is reassured when Yunru throws out his rifle to the Chinese. But our hero has a pistol hidden in the sleeve of his robe, which he whips out and shoots the Chinese commander. The other Chinese soldiers gun down Yunru Pön.

The people who had put together the early patriotic plays had taken their material from refugee statements (*tsik-tho*) compiled by the government-in-exile in the early sixties, which were generally truthful and accurate but lacked the dramatic details I required. I wanted to expand a ten-minute scene into a full ninety-minute, or more, play. So, I began to look around for more information.

The government-in-exile was located a few miles below the town of McLeod Ganj at Amarnath Koti near Gamru Village (now renamed Gangchen Kyishong or the Happy Vale of the Great Snows), where a few houses and a couple of large bungalows were scattered. At the center of the estate was an old tennis court where the 10 March ceremonies were held. The largest bungalow below it housed the four departments of the government: Education, Religious, Home and Security. Each department office was located in one of the four large bedrooms, while the adjoining bathrooms became the offices of the respective ministers. I was directed to the Home department that had earlier undertaken the task of interviewing refugees and archiving the reports. The people there were helpful but could not find any more information on the fighting in Lithang than what the Dance and Drama Society already had. A secretary there told me that the leading resistance organization, the Four Rivers Six Ranges, had a hotel at McLeod Ganj, managed by someone from Lithang, who could give me more information.

I walked back up the steep mountain road to the town. At the time, McLeod Ganj was very small, really no larger than a modest village, with a branch post office, a couple of tiny restaurants, just eateries, that served some noodles and tea, and a few shops. One of the first things the refugees did was erect a large Buddhist stupa in the centre of the town, between the two narrow parallel streets that led to the bus-stand, where about twice a day a bus would arrive from the railhead at Pathankot in Punjab. At the corner where the motor road turned into the bus-stand stood an enormous, hexagonal, red letterbox that would have done any English town proud.

Facing the bus-stand was the establishment of "Nowrojee and Son, Wine and General Merchants, Estd. 1860" as the late-Victorian advertisement sign, a blue and white enamel job, proclaimed. Nauzer Nowrojee, the proprietor, was a Parsi gentleman. His grandfather had founded the general store which sold sweets, groceries, canned goods, medicine, toiletry, newspaper, magazines, stationery, household goods, kitchen supplies, beer and spirits to the British (of yore), the Indians, local Gaddi folk—and now to Tibetan refugees. Nowrojee even made his own brand of soft drinks, and it was Nauzer's boast that he once outsold Coca-Cola in the district. He had this Rube Goldberg bottling machine at the basement of his house that looked as though it could have been designed by a crazy anarchist bomber. To reinforce this impression, Nauzer would put on a thick leather apron, thick leather gloves, and a protective wire-grille mask (à la Hannibal Lecter) when he was operating the contraption that hissed, bubbled and occasionally exploded (or at least a bottle did) in a suitably alarming manner. But he produced an eminently drinkable apple-fizz, and his ginger beer was excellent.

Nowrojee's was practically catering to a ghost town when the Tibetans first came to the place. The early hope that McLeod Ganj would become a major hill station and administrative centre, was destroyed by the Great Kangra Valley earthquake of 1905. By the time of India's independence and partition in 1947, the last British resident had left, and seasonal Indian visitors from Lahore, capital of the Punjab—now in Pakistan—stopped visiting altogether. In late

1959, Nowrojee came across a news report in the *Times of India*, which mentioned that the government of India was looking for a suitable hill town to settle the Dalai Lama and his staff. Nauzer immediately wrote to the Home Ministry in Delhi, pointing out the suitability of Dharamshala's climate for the Tibetans, and also the availability of empty bungalows and cottages in the area for affordable rent or purchase, which was not always the case in the more popular and busier hill stations. Nowrojee was also the sole real estate agent in the area.

Rohinton Mistry, the Canadian/Indian writer, in his neorealist novel, *A Fine Balance*, provides a description of a place very much like McLeod Ganj and Nowrojee's general store, which should come as no surprise as Mistry happened to be the nephew of Nauzer's wife, Mani. In an article Mistry wrote for a *Granta* travel anthology, he provides an amusing account of his first visit to McLeod Ganj. He tells us that as a child in Bombay, he was fascinated by photographs of his uncle's store in the Himalayas and his cousins playing in the snow. One of the principal characters in his novel is a naive college student, Maneck Kohlah, who unwillingly leaves his small town in the mountain to study in the big city of Bombay. His parents run a general store back home, but their primary source of income, a small soft-drink business, is failing due to pressure and unfair competition from big-city corporations. In Bombay, he befriends a student activist Avinash, who is fascinated by Maneck's ". . . account of the hill-station, the settlements, the mountains, the *langurs*, the snow . . . " Maneck also describes a unique architectural feature of Nowrojee's general store: how it was lashed to a rock face with steel cables and tells us when and why it was done. "There was an earthquake and the foundation shifted downhill. That's why the cables were connected."

In later years whenever I returned to Dharamshala from a trip abroad, I would try not to forget to bring Nauzer some duty-free scotch—generally unobtainable in India then. He would fetch a couple of soda-waters (bottled at his machine), and we would go out on the high, somewhat precarious, verandah behind his store, which had a sweeping panoramic view of the entire Kangra valley, including Lower Dharamshala and Forsyth Ganj. Over a drink, he would talk about the old days and the great and notorious—Colonel Younghusband (who invaded Tibet), Lord Elgin (who pillaged and burned down the Old Summer Palace complex in Beijing) and others who had lived in the area or were buried at the Church of St. John in the Wilderness, just a mile from McLeod Ganj.

The Kailash Hotel was a stone's throw from Nowrojee's. At the time, it was the most popular gathering place in McLeod Ganj. It was, in fact, the only hotel in town and boasted eight tiny rooms, a common toilet and a bathroom. What gave the place its distinction was a large restaurant that had sofa-type seats covered with bilious green rexine. Seated on these relatively comfortable things, you could lean back and look up at the mountain or down on the main street of McLeod Ganj and "check out the action," as was the accepted phrase. The Kailash Hotel was operated by the "Four Rivers Six Ranges", the main Khampa resistance organization, which had its office at the hotel. A big man with what might be described as rugged good looks beckoned me into the office. Ratuk Ngawang of Lithang, had been a top lieutenant of Gonpo Tashi Andrugtsang, the paramount resistance chief, and he listened to what I had to say about my project.

He told me that he had been in Lhasa when the Lithang uprising had taken place and did not have first-hand knowledge of the events. But he suggested I talk to the manager of the hotel, another Lithangwa, Tamdin Tashi, or Aku Tamta (Uncle Tam-ta), who had been a monk at the Lithang Monastery at the time of the fighting. Uncle Tam-ta hadn't ridden with Yunru Pön or been by his side when he was killed, but he had at least been there in the fighting at the monastery and knew what he was talking about.

So, I sat down to write the play. In order to give the story the feel of an actual event, of history, I used a framing device, in this case, a narrator, Uncle Tam-ta himself, who recounts the epic of Yunru Pön and the tragedy of Lithang. The curtain opens on a darkened stage. A single baby spotlight—right downstage—slowly reveals an old man sitting on a small mound, telling his beads, the narrow beam half lights Uncle Tam-ta's aged features. He raises his head, and speaks to the audience: "My name is Tamdin Tashi. Some of you may have seen me sitting by the window of the Kailash Hotel here in Dharamshala. I am an old man now but I was once young and strong, and I fought the Chinese invaders at the side of the great warrior chief, Yunru Pön".

As he finishes his introductory lines, the spotlight dims, and Tam-ta disappears into the darkness. Dawn slowly breaks over the high plains of Lithang.

Ratuk Ngawang let me borrow a couple of old photographs of Lithang and the monastery, so I had a reasonably good idea of the geography of the place. Replicated on stage as low distant silhouettes against a cyclorama sky, this background mountain scene was satisfyingly more realistic than painted sets. With minimal lighting and effective use of shadows, we tried to keep the visuals simple and realistic. The bombing of Lithang Monastery was put together like a *son-et-lumière* and was surprisingly effective. The Society had earlier been presented with a tape recorder, one of those massive old machines with variable speed recording, so after a week or so of experimenting, recording banging drums, tea chests and tin cans at high speed and playing them back at low, and mixing them with long droning notes from an accordion (for the engine sounds), we managed to put together an impressive arrangement of bombing sounds. The Society did not have the big speakers necessary to reproduce the sounds effectively, so we strapped loudspeaker horns tightly against the rafters of the corrugated tin roof of the auditorium, which acted as an effective giant speaker, and vibrated alarmingly when we cranked up the volume.

The Society had one old amplifier that just about managed to do what had to be done, but there were no earphones to monitor the amplified sounds in the auditorium from our tiny control room at the side of the stage. I remembered a project from an old *Popular Science* magazine, so I put together a simple earphone with some insulated wire (from an old fan motor), two soft-iron bolts and a couple of chewing tobacco tins (*Babu* Brand), and sand-papered its lids thin for the diaphragms. A length of stiff wire shaped into an over-the-head band completed the headset. It looked like a joke, and everyone thought it was, until I plugged it into one of the speaker outlets on the amplifier and let them all have a turn listening to the tinny sounds.

The Society could not afford a control system for the stage lights. The lights were either switched on or off with nothing in between. We made do with a ceiling-fan regulator, and used it, in sequence, on the different lights we needed to fade up or down. To get through the lighting sequences in time, with just that one dimmer, we were obliged to leave a lot of terminals exposed, for quick connection to the dimmer. I remember to this day the harried stage electrician, Acho Nyendak, testing for a live wire by daintily touching the exposed end with the tip of a wetted finger.

But it all worked out without a hitch on opening night. After the dramatic death of Yunru Pön, the stage lights gradually went down on a *tableau vivant* of three armed Chinese soldiers poised dramatically over the supine figure of the dead resistance leader. The stage becomes dark and silent. Then a single baby spot slowly comes up—right downstage again—to reveal the seated figure of our narrator Uncle Tamta. He describes the torture and executions of lamas and chieftains in the aftermath of the fighting. Fleeting shadowy depictions of these atrocities flicker across the cyclorama screen. In conclusion, Uncle Tamta tells the audience of the final destruction of Lithang Monastery. The burning ruins of the great monastery can then be seen in the far distance, the flames flickering and rising over the dark silhouette of the distant mountain range.

There was none of the usual cheering, and whistling at the end of the show. People left the auditorium silently, many wiping away tears. I was enormously gratified.

The official exile government journal, *Tibetan Bulletin*, came out with a review discussing the "roaring success" of the play, and analyzed the strong points of the production ". . . what made it a rare performance was the various effects and excellent acoustics. The acting by the Society members, which was realistic and robust, was a far cry from the stylized performance which the Drama society previously used to present."[1]

Some years later, I came across an article in the *Far Eastern Economic Review* written by a left-leaning English journalist (later Labour MP for Sunderland South) that attempted to depict events in Lithang as the last-ditch rebellion of a corrupt and reactionary priesthood, and not a people's uprising. Chris Mullin describes Lithang's clergy as "not monks in the Western sense . . . many are involved in private trade; some carried guns and spent much of their time violently feuding with rival monasteries, one former citizen describes Lithang as 'like the Wild West'."[2]

Some years later, Mullin developed his Lithang article into a full-length spy thriller, *The Year of the Fire Monkey*.[3] A young Tibetan lama, Ari, who had fought in the Lithang Uprising and escaped to Kalimpong, is recruited by the CIA and trained by a dissolute senior agent Harvey Crocker to become a deep penetration "sleeper" with the mission to assassinate Chairman Mao. Isolated behind the Himalayas and unaware of the 180-degree turn in America's China policy, Ari sets out to execute his mission exactly at the time of Nixon's historic China visit. Fortunately for everyone, Virtuoso British agent and "assassin" Timothy Ogilvy is seconded by the "Directorate" to resolve "with extreme prejudice" this annoying and unexpected threat to the hoped-for Sino-Western friendship.

The leftist press in Britain gave this potboiler uniformly positive reviews, Graham Greene leading the way with: "A story, I think, every reader will enjoy—except perhaps a member of the CIA."

All this provoked in me an impulse to put together a more substantial account of the Lithang uprising—to straighten the record, as it were. Over the years, I managed to obtain bits of information, a little here and a little there, mostly in conversations with such Khampas as Alo Chonzé (who discusses Yunru Pön in his memoirs)[4], Kalsang Gyadotsang, Gyari Dorji Yudon, Gyari Nyima and others; and in lengthier interviews with Ratuk Ngawang, Athar Norbu and, as I mentioned earlier, Tamdin Tashi. Besides Alo Chonzé's self-published memoir, I later came across written accounts of the Lithang Uprising in Lotse Gatsetsang memoir/history (2001),[5] in Baritsang Dawa Tsering's chronicles (2007),[6] and Vol. II of Ratu Ngawang's autobiography.

I met a young Khampa in New York City in 2005, recently arrived from Lithang. He provided invaluable information on Yunru Pön, and told me that after Deng Xiaoping's liberalization, a monk from Lithang Monastery had gone around interviewing all those who had survived the 1956 uprising and had put together an eight-volume history of the conflict. He took his manuscript down to Chengdu and tried to get it printed at a Chinese press. During that period of "liberalization", Tibetans were re-printing a lot of religious texts and literary works without the official restrictions of earlier years, and our monk assumed that the Chinese would not be able to read his Tibetan text. Somehow the Public Security Bureau got wind of this and confiscated the manuscript. Whether our monk historian had kept a copy of his work is not unknown, but he was interrogated and released after signing a confession.

The informant with the most detailed information about the last battle at Lithang was a former monk of Lithang Monastery, Besa Chökyong.[*] My friend Lithang Athar Norbu arranged for me to speak with him when he came to Dharamshala[7] from the Tibetan settlement at Orissa, where he lived as a small farmer and petty trader. He had been an attendant of Tromthok Lama, one of the abbots of Lithang Monastery. Besa Chökyong was also a bodyguard to the abbot and belonged to the *dob-dob* fraternity of fighting monks. He had been with Yunru Pön through much of the fighting in the monastery.

His last sighting of Yunru Pön had been in the early evening, some hours before Yunru was killed. Besa was also separated from his own charge, the abbot, who was captured by the Chinese. Late that night, in the chaos and confusion of the fighting within the burning monastery, Besa Chökyong managed to escape, climbing over the rear of the monastery wall and making his way up the mountainside. After a few days of hiding in the mountains, he left Lithang forever.

---

[*] Besa Chökyong, interview with the author. Dharamshala: December 1981.

10

A CRANE FROM LITHANG

It is not far that I shall roam,
Lend me your wings white crane.
I go no farther than Lithang
And thence return again

The sixth Dalai Lama, Tsangyang Gyatso, Ocean of Melodious Purity, is affectionately remembered to this day for his romantic verses, some of which have been incorporated into popular songs. One verse in particular, in the epigraph above (translated by Sir Charles Bell), is sung in the light classical Nangma style and, under the somewhat cryptic title of "Amaleho", has long been a sentimental favourite in Lhasa and Central Tibet.

This Dalai Lama, to the despair of his tutors and his loyal prime minister, refused to be ordained a monk, kept his hair long, and with the other young bucks of Lhasa city, practised archery at the small island on the Lukhang or Naiad Temple Lake behind the Potala Palace. Unlike his predecessors and successors, young Melodious Purity also delighted in drinking barley ale ". . . playing games and diverting himself with Tibetan ladies" according to the Italian Jesuit, Ippolito Desideri, who was in Lhasa from 1716 to 1721 and ". . . almost an eyewitness to the events."[1] Till the imposition of absolute Chinese rule

in 1959, those houses and taverns* in Lhasa where Melodious Purity
caroused or even spent a night with a lover, were reverentially painted
yellow. All other buildings in the city were given a coat of whitewash
before the New Year.

The Qoshot Mongol chief, Lhazang Khan, the true power behind
the Tibetan throne, decided that Melodious Purity could not be the
rightful Dalai Lama and exiled him to China. The young Dalai Lama
died on the way and left the prophetic verse (in the epigraph of this
chapter) that indicated where his next incarnation, the seventh Dalai
Lama, would be born.

* * *

The high plain of Lithang lies nearly 14,000 feet above sea level
and is essentially rugged pastureland where only hardy grass and
wildflowers—edelweiss and gentian—grow. This flatland is about
eleven miles long and five miles wide and is bounded on the south
by a range of picturesque mountains, the Puborgang range, with
three peaks that are snow-capped part of the year, the highest of
which, is just around 17,000 feet.† The air on the high plain is so
rarefied and pellucid clear that judging distances become tricky.

---

*One such building has survived at the intersection of Barkhor South Street
and Barkhor East Street and still sports a distinctive mustard yellow exterior.
It has now become a popular restaurant, Makye Ama. The name is taken from
a verse by Melodious Purity where he recalls the face of a beautiful maiden, his
esoteric consort or "primordial mother", Makye Ama.

†The highest peak in the Lithang region is the holy mountain, Genyen,
(20,354 feet), hidden in a mountain valley complex in the south-west. It
cannot be seen from the Lithang plain. This beautiful mountain presides over
a broad alluvial vale awash with primula, oleander and the *tsi-tog* plant (an
indigenous light magenta flower). Nine hundred years ago, the first Karmapa
lama, Düsum Khyenpa, built a hermitage and monastery, Neygo Gompa,
below the mountain, in a beautiful green tract known as Shambala valley.
The monastery has managed to survive to this day, probably because of the
extreme isolation of the place. The Karmapa Lama's small meditation cave
overlooks the sacred lake Jampa Lha-tso.

Looking at the faraway mountains, you get this peculiar notion that you could just reach out and touch one of the snowy peaks with your finger.

The Great Monastery of Lithang (or Lithang *Gonchen*) lies high in a fold of a smaller mountain range to the north-west of the plain. The small town lies on the ridge forming the other side of the fold. The staple Tibetan crop, the highland barley, will not ripen in the plains of Lithang because of the altitude, and the grain supply of the town and the monastery must be imported from the Bathang valley to the West, which is low-lying and has good farming land. Other parts of Lithang sustain some agriculture, though herding is the chief occupation of the people of this high plain. Lithang farmers grow barley, buckwheat, potatoes, peas, turnips and radish, but they largely consume their own produce. Rhubarbs, whose roots are dug up in October, are plentiful in the valleys.

In the forests of Lithang are found *bhemu*, the small white bulbs of the *Coelogyne henryi Rolfe*, which are exported to China. They are used in medicine, as well as being a delicacy. Also exported is the caterpillar-fungus *yartsa gembu*, literally "summer-worm winter-grass" or in Latin, *Cordyceps sinensis*. It is the dried parasitical fungus that grows on the larva of a caterpillar and is highly regarded by the Chinese as a tonic. It is, these days, even used in Chinese sports medicine. Deer horn (old and in velvet) is also exported for Chinese medicine, in addition to gold dust, musk, sheep's wool, sheepskins and yak hide for packing tea-bricks at Dartsedo.

Lithang town has a population of about four or five hundred families. The chief industry of the town is the manufacture of silver jewellery and ritual objects for the Tibetan market.

Just west of the plain is the Lithang River or the Lichu, about fifty yards wide spanned by a wooden cantilever bridge with four arches resting on stout stone piers. East of the Lithang plain over the high Segi-la or Segi pass and down into the next valley is the Hochu or the Milk River. Travellers coming to Lithang from China via the frontier town of Dartsedo had to cross this river at the ford of Hochukha, spanned by an old wooden bridge.

Lithang is bounded on the east by the kingdoms of Minyak and Chagla (Dartsedo being the capital of the latter) and on the west by the state of Bathang. North of Lithang is Nyarong, to its south Chatreng and its south-west Gyalthang. These are all important states of Eastern Tibet, which Tibetans variously call Domed, Dokham or simply Kham. The scriptural definition of the word Kham is "realm", as in "Buddha realm", but it also carries the connotations of expanse and pristine wilderness, which provides a clue as to why this region was so named.

The artist-scholar Gedün Chöphel, when working on his (unfinished) history of Tibet, *The White Annals*, shared with my uncle Sonam Tomjor Tethong his theory that before the period of the Tibetan empire, Kham was largely uninhabited (by Tibetans) and uncharted. Then during the age of expansion and conquest by the Tibetan emperors, from the seventh century onwards, garrisons from Central Tibet were settled in these areas to guard the imperial frontiers. These Tibetan soldiers probably intermarried with the aboriginal people and, with the later collapse of the Tibetan empire, gradually settled in these areas to become farmers and herdsmen.

There are families in Kham with unusual surnames that point to these origins. A family of my acquaintance in Nyarong is called Miloktsang or "Do not return family." Another is Kamalok, or "Do not return till ordered." Families with such names claim they are descendants of Imperial garrisons posted to guard the Tibetan frontier. As far away as northern Nepal, some scholars from the Tamang tribe claim that their tribal name is derived from the Tibetan word *tamak*, as they are the descendants of Tibetan cavalry forces garrisoned in Nepal in the ninth century. In Lithang itself, the leading nomad chieftain was called Yunru, meaning "left horn" or left formation, one of the main units of the standard Tibetan military organization of the Imperial period.

When the Tibetan empire fragmented after the assassination, in the ninth century, of the Emperor Tri-darma Udum-tsan or Lhasé Darma,* described by some Western scholars as a Tibet's "Julian the

_____

*Lhasé Darma has been demonized by the Tibetan priesthood as Lang Darma "the ox." The scholar, Samten Karmay has made a convincing

Apostate," such far-flung regions on the imperial frontiers as Lithang and Chagla found themselves—like the Roman provinces of Britannia and Gallia during the failing reign of Emperor Honorius—ignored from the centre and left to fend for themselves.

Lithang became an independent kingdom and played a central role in this part of Kham, for a time allying itself with the Kagyüpa rulers of the Kingdom of Lijiang. But when the reunification of Tibet began under the Fifth Dalai Lama, Lithang was gradually absorbed in the irresistible political and religious expansion east of Gelugpa and Mongol power.

The great monastery of Lithang, Ganden Thubchen Chökhorling, to give it its full name, is a magnificent collection of buildings lying on the mountainside facing south, looking down on the Lithang plain. The roofs of the two main temple halls and subsidiary temples are adorned with a number of pinnacles or spires, all covered with gold. The monastery had a resident population of some 4,000 monks, but that number swelled twice a year to some 5,000 when the smaller monasteries throughout the district sent in their representatives. A twelve-foot wall around the complex protected the monastery.

Lithang Monastery was founded in 1580 by the Third Dalai Lama, Sonam Gyatso (Ocean of Merit), who converted Altan Khan, chief of the Tumed Mongols, the dominant power in Eastern Mongolia. Sonam Gyatso received the title of Talai or Dalai which in Mongol meant ocean, and started the relationship with Mongol military power that later made the Fifth Dalai Lama the ruler of Tibet, and which ended tragically in the death of Melodious Purity, the Sixth Dalai Lama.

It was in the reign of the Great Fifth Dalai Lama that all the regions of Tibet, from Ngari in the far west all the way to Dartsedo in the south-east and Kokonor to the north-east, were reunited for the first time since the collapse of the Tibetan Empire in the ninth century.

---

case that contrary to monastic propaganda, the emperor did not persecute Buddhists but was rather attempting to rein in the extraordinary privileges and political power accrued by the Buddhist clergy, which had gotten out of hand during the reign of his older brother Ralpachan, and undermined Tibetan military power.

This reunification came about through the Fifth Dalai Lama's political genius and the fresh reforming energy of the new Gelugpa church, allied with the military power of the Dalai Lama's Mongol patrons, the Qoshot Khanate.

The conflicts of this period could, in a sense, be regarded as religious wars, with the Gelugpa church defeating and displacing the dominant Kagyüpa and also Nyingma schools from power. It should be emphasized however, that these were not wars to exterminate rival schools and eliminate opposing doctrines but rather to dominate them politically. Several Kagyüpa and Jonangpa monastic structures were turned into Gelugpa ones, as were a number of pre-Buddhist Bon strongholds, but it appears that this was done more for political than doctrinal reasons since many of these monasteries were also important military and political strongholds.

The Fifth Dalai Lama, though imperious and even ruthless when required was, on the whole, an open-minded and practical man. In 1674, he received the leading Kagyüpa lama, Karmapa Chöying Dorje, at the Potala Palace, showing him all the respect due his rank. A welcome reconciliation took place between these two main rival schools. In that sense, the violence and destruction of this conflict never sunk to the level of the religious wars in Europe, and nowhere involved the kind of genocidal violence (eight million fatalities), mindless fanaticism and sheer devastation of the Thirty Year's War between Protestants and Catholics in the first half of the seventeenth century—around the same period as the Gelugpa reunification of Tibet.

In 1648, the Fifth Dalai Lama sent two senior officials Lhakhangpa and Bagdro, to Eastern Tibet. They undertook a thorough investigative tour of Lithang, Bathang, Chagla, Gyalthang, Gyalrong, Jün, Mili, Denkhok, Gakhok, Lingtsang, Lhatok, and Nangchen. They conducted a major census of the population and also established local administrative and judicial structures and a system for the collection of taxes from the landowners and herdsmen of Kham. Fifty-six registers on the census and collection of revenue in these districts were compiled. These same volumes were produced by Tibetan diplomats in 1914 at the Shimla Conference to refute China's claims to Eastern Tibet. Sir

Henry McMahon, the chief British mediator, signed each of these volumes in the verification of their contents.

Lithang was also the birthplace of the Tenth Dalai Lama, Tsultrim Gyatso. My mother's family, the Tethongs, were related to this Dalai Lama's family, the Yuthoks, which meant that occasionally we would receive a visitor or two from Lithang, a pilgrim or a merchant, at Tethong House in Lhasa, claiming to be a long lost fifth cousin or such, and in the matter-of-fact Khampa way, expecting hospitality.

Lhasa city also had many *tsongpöns*, literally "merchant chiefs" from Lithang: Andrugtsang, Jangtsatsang, Jhamatsang, Dewatsang and others, and from other parts of Eastern Tibet as well. A few of them, in their wealth, splendour and conspicuous patronage of lamas and monasteries, might be compared with the merchant princes of medieval Europe. Many monks and scholars from Lithang also studied at the great monasteries in and around Lhasa. So even though it was far removed from the capital and then controlled by the Chinese, Lithang was very important in the Tibetan scheme of things.

But after the Great Fifth, the power of the Dalai Lama's went into a decline, with, in fact, four incarnations passing away at tender ages. Manchu influence in Central Tibet gained ascendancy, and Qing Imperial power began to be reasserted, in fits and starts, throughout Eastern Tibet. Of course, the process was never smooth, was, for the most part, challenged (locally and from Lhasa) and, once in a while, reversed.

But from the early twentieth century onwards, the Qing began to pursue a more aggressive and strategic plan of action in subduing and occupying Eastern Tibet. The imposition of direct Manchu rule in this region in 1905, and the new strategy to make Eastern Tibet a province of China, Xikang, initiated a period of near continual rebellion by Tibetans and retaliatory massacres and razing of monasteries by the Chinese.[2] The great monasteries of Chamdo, Chatreng Sampheling, Drayab Jamdün, Yendum, Bathang and Sershül Monastery in Dzachukha were destroyed and the monk residents killed or executed.[3] To terrorize the population of Drayab the Chinese commander there boiled a number of the local monks in the giant iron cauldron used to make tea for the monastery. A visiting American missionary published a photograph of this utensil in the National Geographic Magazine with this caption "A cauldron which has been used by the Chinese for Cooking Tibetans."[4]

Bathang, to the west of Lithang, was, in the old days, ruled by two chiefs called the Ba *depa*, who were descendants of the two Lhasa governors who formerly administered Bathang (from the mid 17th century) from two castles in Bathang town. Following the rebellion by the Bathang Monastery in 1904, the Chinese took over completely, beheading the two chiefs and razing the great monastery of Bathang to the ground. One of the castles was occupied by the Chinese magistrate and his officers, and the other was given to the Catholic mission. The Tibetans managed to re-build a smaller monastery, which was later bombed by the Communists in 1956, and razed to the ground during the Cultural Revolution.

Though the Bathang valley was fertile farming land, the people here were much poorer than those in neighbouring states and also more demoralized, as an English traveller noted. This condition was probably exacerbated by the Chinese policy of using Bathang ". . . as a dumping ground for all the disabled, sick, and destitute Chinese in Eastern Tibet, who drift in here and somehow or other manage to get their names placed on the official rolls as entitled to public rations."[5] Such public rations were, in fact, incentives to encourage Chinese peasants, indigents and ex-soldiers to settle in Tibet.

In this period of political turmoil, violence and lawlessness prevailed, and feuding and banditry were almost becoming customary activities of Khampa men. The area around Chatreng, Bathang and Lithang was a particularly troubled one.

Bathang and Lithang are the land of robbers.
But you shouldn't say that, for they are
The sacred birthplaces of the Dalai Lamas.

Ba Lithang kumae saja ray,
Shay menye, gyalwae trungsa ray

This old saying is sometimes used in polite conversation whenever one wants to allude to a mistake of the Dalai Lama (or members of his family) but do not wish to make a direct criticism.

The many tribes of Lithang: Gaba, Shagpa Gyangpa, Yunru, Deshung, Othog, Molashipa, Tso-sumpo, Raba, Thilpa and others, were ruled by their traditional chiefs or *pön*. But five chieftains were traditionally accorded a special status. Three of the five were known as *Ra pönkhag*, or chiefs of three nomadic tribes—*ra* or *rakhue* meaning nomad in the local dialect and *pön* meaning leader or chief. Of these three *ra* chiefs, the most powerful one was Yunru Pön. The second, Othog Pön and the third was Deshung Pön.

The other two of the five special chieftains were not regarded as tribal leaders and were referred to as *depa* in reference to the *depa shung* or the central government of Lhasa, this being a throwback to the days when Lithang was ruled from Lhasa. As was the custom of the Tibetan government, dual governors had been appointed to Lithang, the *drung depa* being the *drungkor* or lay official, and the *tsashag depa*, being the *tsedrung* or the priestly official. These two officials were granted one nomad tribe each as their personal fiefs.

When the power of the central government receded in Eastern Tibet, the families of the two officials lost touch with Lhasa and gradually became integrated into their respective tribes, essentially becoming Lithangwa families. These two relics of Lhasa rule in Lithang were respected as the leading families of Lithang. In fact, the two Depa chiefs were regarded as the nominal rulers of Lithang but following the unsuccessful Khampa uprising against Imperial China in 1904, they were executed by Zhao Erfeng, the governor of Sichuan province along with the Bathang Depa and many other Khampa princes and rulers. In 1906 the institution of the Depa was abolished, and a commissariat officer (Chinese, *liangtai*) appointed to Lithang to represent Sichuan provincial authority. One Depa family appears to have survived the violent events and though much reduced in circumstances, continued to reside in a rambling old mansion on the plain below Lithang town.

After the fall of the Qing dynasty in 1912 and the defeat of the Sichuan provincial force in 1918 by the new Tibetan army, Chinese power was considerably reduced in Kham, and the traditional leadership of the region, secular and monastic, reasserted some of their former power and standing. The three Ra *pönkhag* or chiefs operated virtually as independent rulers.

One of the most respected of these nomad chieftainships was the family of Yunru Pön. The legendary resistance leader Sonam Wangyal was born to this family in 1931, in the year of the iron-sheep. Sonam Wangyal's grandfather, Chime Dorji, was reputedly a *tertön* or "treasure discoverer", a category of Tibetan mystics who have the power to discover lost tantric texts. These texts or "mind treasures" were said to have been hidden away by Guru Padmasambhava, who judged them too advanced for contemporary humanity, and only to be revealed to a future generation by the incarnations of his leading disciples.

The son of this "treasure discoverer" and father of young Sonam Wangyal was Sogyal, a deeply spiritual person who chafed at his responsibilities as a chief. He wanted to abandon his home and his wealth and seek spiritual release in the classic Buddhist tradition of the "great renunciation". When his son was fifteen years of age, he summoned a tribal gathering, and formally transferred all his wealth and responsibilities to his son. Then, carrying some food and a few scriptural texts tied up in a light wicker pack frame, he left Lithang in 1951 (or '52?) as a mendicant pilgrim. He travelled on foot to Lhasa, where the merchant chief, Andrugtsang Gonpo Tashi, is said to have spotted him in the Barkhor market and insisted on hosting him at his house. It is not clear where he traveled from thereon, but he must have visited the important pilgrimage sites of Central Tibet and then made his way to the bleak plains of Western Tibet and the sacred mountain of Kailash, or Gang Rinpoche. He is also said to have traveled to Sikkim and then to Bodh Gaya and other sacred places in India—but we cannot be certain.

In the early sixties, following the refugee diaspora to India, he was seen in Darjeeling, meditating in a small cave just above Gandhi Road, past Mount Everest Hotel, on the way to the house of Darjeeling's most famous citizen, Tenzing Norgay, the conqueror of Everest. Lithangwas and other Khampa refugees in Darjeeling are said to have prostrated before the cave and presented him with food and other offerings. I might have caught a glimpse of this holy man, for as a schoolboy I remember a couple of such caves and rock-overhangs where poor Tibetan refugees sought shelter. Then, once again, Sogyal disappeared from Darjeeling, and there is a lacuna concerning his whereabouts. I later learnt that he died sometime in 1975 or 1976 at Rewalsar or Tso Pema, the holy Lotus Lake, sacred to Padmasambhava, high in the mountains of Himachal Pradesh.

Young Sonam Wangyal initially found it difficult to be chief of the Yunru tribe of Lithang. He was not only young but shared his family predisposition towards a spiritual life. In the only photograph that we have of him, he is holding a long rosary in his right hand. He looks very young, almost a boy, and his sheepskin-lined robe large for his small figure. The photograph was possibly taken a year or so before he became chief. Judging by the painted backdrop of a Chinese garden scene, the picture was probably taken by a Chinese photographer at a studio in the frontier town of Dartsedo.

Though Yunru was a small person, in a land where men were usually muscular and tall, he could hold his own among the other warriors of Lithang. He was an excellent rider and a crack shot with a rifle. Unlike most young Khampa men of his age, he was without show or ostentation, and at tribal gatherings and festivals where young Lithangwa men gathered with the women to sing and dance, Yunru would not be found in their company. Instead, he would be by himself in his tent or alone by a stream or on grassy hillock clicking his rosary beads, his lips moving in silent prayer. He had his family's intense seriousness in the pursuit of a spiritual life.

Before Yunru Pön's father left on his religious quest, he had requested his nephew, Dago Trepo, to help Sonam Wangyal rule the tribe. Trepo or "the young lord" came from the surviving Depa family, descendants of the old Lhasa governors of Lithang. Dago Trepo was six years older than Sonam Wangyal and a wise counsellor. He helped the young chief sort through and arbitrate the many disputes involving pasturage rights, water rights and blood feuds that his people brought before him. The two cousins became fast friends. The Dago family owned the old manor on the Lithang plain, below the monastery. It was a huge broken-down shell of a building and quite uninhabitable, a nesting place for ravens, according to a Lithangwa man who remembered playing in the ruins as a child. Dago Trepo and his family lived in a newer house closer to the town.

Yunru Pön Sonam Wangyal was, of course, a full-blooded nomad and lived with his tribe principally in the high pasturelands' north-east of Lithang town, called Bumnyathang. This area was a particularly scenic and bountiful area with rolling meadows carpeted with wildflowers, where the large herds of the tribe's sheep and yaks had ample grazing. A prosperous nomad family might claim to have a "*kar-tri nak-tong*" herd, or ten thousand white (sheep) and a thousand black (yaks).

All nomads throughout Tibet live, winter and summer, in their black yak-hair tents that Tibetans call *ba*. Cotton tents lavishly decorated with auspicious designs were used in summer for picnics and formal ceremonies. Important chiefs and lamas might have their tents trimmed with tiger and leopard skin.

Yunru Pön being a prominent chief, owned an exceptionally large *banak* or black tent that was used for tribal gatherings. It was so big that it had to be carried in sections, and fifty yaks were required to transport it. It was famous throughout Lithang as "Yunru *banak*." Under this giant canopy, the Yunru family had its own temple, or rather a large chapel with its various images and *thangkas* (painted scrolls) and a library of over one hundred volumes of carved woodblock print of the Kangyur, the Buddhist scriptures that contain the entire teachings of the Buddha. The library also had the entire Tengyur collection of over 3,626 texts in 224 volumes containing a variety of later commentaries on the Kangyur and include a wide range of texts on other subjects as poetry, grammar, science, architecture, painting, and medicine. Under this giant tent, Yunru Pön, his ministers (*lönpo*) and lieutenants (*aptruk*) would convene tribal assemblies and hold trials and hearings. Even when there was not a big gathering, there would always be a small congregation of monks at the chapel, conducting prayer services and rituals for the welfare of the tribe and the well-being of the animals and the land. The young chief could often be found there himself, deep in prayer and meditation.

Yunru Pön was not a particularly wealthy man compared to the other tribal leaders and even monastic administrators in Eastern Tibet, who maintained their own mercantile organizations and added to their customary sources of revenue by trading extensively between Lhasa, Dartsedo, Lijiang in Yunnan Province and Kalimpong in India. Yunru Pön was reputedly not someone who showed a great desire for trade or wealth, nor finery and display. He dressed simply and affected none of the gold, turquoise, coral and *zi* ornaments that the men of Kham love to flaunt; and in a land where men swagger, as a matter of course, he conducted himself in a modest self-effacing manner. But his people gave him the respect due not only to a great chief but also the love and devotion they would otherwise give to their own root lama.

* * *

The 157th regiment of the Fifty-Third Division of the Eighteenth Army of the PLA's South West Military Command marched through Lithang around the end of May and the beginning of June 1950, on their way to Bathang to prepare for the invasion of Tibet. The Guomindang official at Lithang town and his small military escort had left in a hurry for Bathang at the first report of the Communist advance force. Earlier, in the Guomindang headquarters at Bathang, Chiang the magistrate and his garrison of two hundred soldiers had maintained an uneasy truce with the local Communist faction led by the Bathang Tibetan, Phüntso Wangye. Now with the advance of the Red Army, Magistrate Chiang and the Bathang garrison retreated south, joining a larger Guomindang force attempting to escape through Yunnan province to Burma.

A Lithangwa warrior, Tendar,* whom I befriended at Mustang in 1971, had as a boy witnessed the first Communist soldiers entering

---

*Tendar led the guerrilla raid on the Chinese truck convoy in 1964, filmed in the TV documentary *Raid into Tibet* and described in George Patterson's book *Fool at Forty* (1970). He died on 22 December 2019.

Lithang. He remembered the exact day the soldiers came. As a fifteen-year-old boy in 1950, he had been invited by his uncle, Sangpo, a monk, to watch a performance of the Tibetan opera (*ache lhamo*) at Lithang Monastery. The opera tradition had been imported from Lhasa by Shogdru Kyamgon, the previous Grand Lama of the monastery. Tendar remembered that the opera master was a Lhasa man called Bhötuk Dawa who trained a group of the younger monks of Lithang Monastery. For the convenience of the Lithang audience unfamiliar with the Ache Lhamo opera, an old monk narrated the story from a script during the performance.

Tendar also remembered that the performance took place on the twelfth day of the sixth moon, to commemorate the birthday of Kalsang Gyatso, the Seventh Dalai Lama, who was born in Lithang. This commemoration was called *Dhrukpa Kalsang Rigya* and started in the morning with everyone walking up the mountain behind the monastery and participating in a *sangsöl* ceremony where they burned large piles of green juniper sprigs, sage and incense, offering the clouds of sweet smoke to the Buddha, bodhisattvas and the gods of Tibet. Then the people came down from the mountain and sang songs, danced, picnicked and watched an opera performance in front of the monastery. It was then, Tendar remembered, that the first Communist soldiers came marching towards the monastery from the east.

"At first, I didn't see them. I was watching the show, but then people started talking loudly, standing up and pointing. I saw the Communist soldiers coming, carrying weapons and large bundles on their backs. When they got near, to where we were, they dropped their bundles on the ground and sat on them and smoked cigarettes. We looked at them. Then we looked at the opera performance. They looked at us and probably looked at the opera also. They came in small units, about nine or ten soldiers, to a unit. One group had two mules. They didn't seem to have many pack animals. Hundreds of such groups came marching into Lithang town. The formation stretched way back. One group had a *chikang*, a light machine gun [Russian DP-28] like a Bren gun or a BAR. There were other such automatic weapons.

"The soldier all looked poor and sickly. Their lips were cracked. There were sores on their head. They must have suffered terrible hardships. We all stared at them. The soldiers put down their guns with the barrels pointed in our direction and then rested. Everyone was saying that there would be a big fight between the Communist soldiers and the Guomindang soldiers of the Lithang garrison. Someone said that they would fight because they had already put on their badges [*lem-bar*], which was a sign they would fight. But there was no fighting.

"As the soldiers arrived before the monastery, they put up tents. We were not allowed to go inside the tents. The soldiers were probably exhausted because most of them lay down and slept. Some of them read newspapers. More and more soldiers came in that manner every day."

Once the Communists had firm control of the various districts, a large meeting was convened at Dartsedo to secure the cooperation of Khampa chiefs and lamas for the upcoming invasion of Tibet and the attack on Chamdo and Markham, specifically in the matter of pack animals and guides. The convener of the meeting was the Bathang Communist, Phüntso Wangye. Yunru Pön was asked to attend this meeting. He did not.

In Lithang, the civil authority in the Communist administration rested with a senior cadre, who all my Khampa informants called Lo Thepön, possibly the Tibetan rendering of "Luo *diabiao*". I will refer to him as Political Commissar Luo. According to Athar Norbu, he was a small man, thin and with weak eyes. He wore thick bottle glass spectacles. But he was a smooth talker and could get very articulate and impassioned when holding forth on the policies and accomplishments of the Communist Party.

The military side of the Communist administration in Lithang was run by Hu Guojun, CO of the Southern Kandzé command.* Tibetans

---

*The Kandzé military command was divided into the Southern military command (*gan-nan*) covering Lithang, Bathang, Chatreng, Nyagchukha and Gyalthang. The Northern Kandzé command (*gan-bei*) covered Dartsedo, Nyarong, Dergé, Peyul, the Hor States, Tawu, Serthar and Sershul. Kandzé Autonomous Prefecture was created in 1955 from the old Xikang province, called him *tuan-zhang bartsa* or "colonel pockmark". In some reports, he is also called *tuan-zhang jhalag*, or the "bird-hand" colonel, since the fingers of his hand were webbed like a duck's. One informant told me that the defect was only in one hand and seemed more the result of an accident than a birth defect. It could be that his fingers had burned or fused together, maybe in a battle somewhere. Communist troops had been fighting for a long time, and battle scars were not uncommon.

About a mile and a half away from the monastery, down on the plain, was an old fort that Guomindang officials and the military garrison had used. Now the Communists took it over for their headquarters. Close to this fort was the dilapidated manor house of Dago Trepo. The Communists requisitioned the building and the surrounding land and, after demolishing the ruins, began construction of a large military fort.

The Communists also started to hold meetings and political rallies, which they expected all the leaders, tribal and monastic, to attend. Nearly everyone did, for after the meetings, the Communists would distribute largesse of silver coins (Chinese, *dayuan*), the amount depending upon the person's rank and standing in society. But Yunru Pön never came to a single meeting. Nor did he accept a single coin from the Communists. Three separate informants, none of them from Yunru's tribe, confirmed this. He only sent a representative who reported back to him what had transpired at the meetings. This was inconvenient for the Communist administration as Yunru was one of the most important chiefs in Lithang and the most influential and respected. Yunru not only declined to attend the Communist meetings but also did not consider himself bound by any of the decisions taken or decrees announced at these meetings.

A crisis arose on the question of taxes. The Communists announced that all taxes, those previously collected by the Guomindang officials and those collected by tribal leaders, would now be collected by the Communist administration. This would include the traditional *tau-ulag* transport tax. Yunru Pön, for example, would annually change the

---

which in turn had been cobbled together by the Guomindang in 1939 from the various districts of Eastern Tibet then under Chinese rule.

location of his encampment to fresh pasturage, and it was his right as chief to call on his people to send their yaks to carry his tents, baggage, chapel and scriptures to his new camp.

In 1855, Yunru Pön was at Zomra, where the nomads of Lithang gathered for their annual festival, competed in horsemanship, met friends and relatives or simply had a good time. Men and women would be dressed in their finest robes (lined with sheepskin and trimmed with ermine, otter or leopard skin) and traditional ornaments, and would participate in "circle" dancing and singing. But the main event of this festival was the riding competition. Large tents and awnings worked with traditional designs were pitched all around the side of the festival ground, with the tents belonging to each team of riders, closest to the riding area. One of the easiest tricks was galloping your horse down the course and picking up *khatas* or white greeting scarves from the ground. Riders would do this to warm up, competing to see who could pick up the most scarves.

For the main competition, the rider was required to perform a series of acrobatic moves on his horse while it was moving at full gallop. In the style called the *gagyur*, the rider firmly grips the front and rear of his saddle and jumps off to one side. As soon as his feet touch the ground, he jumps right back over the horse to the other side and repeats the manoeuvre. The horse is galloping at full speed the whole time. The *chaba* style is like the *gagyur*, the only difference being that the rider must land on one foot, which though appearing the same, is more dangerous since he is liable to break his feet. The *goser* technique demands nerve. With the horse galloping at full speed, the rider throws his body back to one side of the horse. He leans back till his head is very close to the pounding rear hooves, and both his hands are nearly trailing on the ground. In this position, he proceeds to pick up *khata* scarves from the ground.

Other events involve the rider shooting at a target from the back of a racing steed. Rifles, as well as the Mongol recurve bow, are used. The riders also shoot their rifles with one hand from under the running horse. In between events, the riders swagger around the side of the field, feigning indifference to the admiring glances of the women.

At the end of the festival, all the riders were presented with *khata* scarves. These days, something like the old festival seems to have been revived in Lithang and permitted by the local Communist administration as a tourist attraction. It takes place in August every year for about a week and is billed as "The Lithang Horse Festival" by a number of international travel agencies. You can even buy Lithang Horse Festival T-shirts, postcards and other festival souvenirs (Made in China). At the opening ceremony, po-faced Communist party officials in shiny business suits and senior military officers in olive green uniforms and dark glasses are seated on folding chairs on a high platform before the festival ground. They clap their hands patronizingly when school children march by with massed red flags and battered tractors decked with the latest party slogans (in Chinese) and yet more red flags, rattle past the review stand. The Lithang women, dressed in their traditional costumes and jewellery still manage to look stunningly beautiful. There are fewer horsemen competing than in the old days, and their outfits and saddle gear lack the magnificence of the past, but the riding itself appears to be every bit as spectacular and dangerous as it used to be.

A half-century ago, at the festival at Zomra, a senior Communist administrative official, *xianzhang* Ata, who was a Tibetan collaborator from Bathang, rode to the festival with an escort of three hundred soldiers. He demanded to meet Yunru Pön and finally forced his way into the chief's tent. He said that he had a special message from the Central Government concerning a new policy. Henceforth all taxes were to be collected by Communist Party officials, and tribal chieftains, monastic officials and others were not permitted to collect any more taxes from the people. Yunru Pön replied that the service his tribesmen provided him in transporting his tents and baggage once a year was his traditional prerogative. It was not an undue burden on the people, and that they performed the service out of loyalty to him. He told the official the Chinese should not interfere in these matters. *Xianzhang* Ata responded with a mocking Tibetan proverb:

In the time of horses, grass can be eaten
In the time of donkeys, barley husk must be swallowed

Taye thaso tsa sa,
Bhungu thaso phuma gam go ray

This was an insulting way of implying that, though Yunru had once
enjoyed many privileges, now with the Communists in power, he
would have to settle for much less.

One of Yunru's lieutenants protested, "Our chief can do as he
wishes. He is the master of the grasslands."

Another shouted, "Successive Yunru Pöns have owned the 'golden
plains and the silver plains' (*serthang nguthang* i.e., the best pasture
lands). No one can take it away."

Someone hit or pushed *xianzhang* Ata, and a fight nearly broke out,
but Yunru Pön ordered his men to hold their peace. The atmosphere at
the festival became tense. A rumour began to circulate that the Chinese
were intending to arrest Yunru Pön and take him away. All the nomads
gathered there, including those not from Yunru's tribe, started to swear
and curse at the Chinese and touch their weapons. The Chinese quickly
returned to Lithang town.

Two days later, a few hundred of Yunru's warriors rode down
to Lithang town. They all carried the British Enfield rifles from the
Chamdo arsenal of the old Tibetan army in Kham. The men rode
into town and tore down posters of Mao and Stalin on the walls
of the houses and the large banners bearing Communist slogans.
The horsemen galloped past the Chinese garrison, firing shots in
the air and shouting insults and challenges. They were eager for a
fight. Lamas and administrators from Lithang Monastery quickly
intervened. After much discussion, they persuaded the men to return
to their tribal lands. The monastery and the townsfolk were relieved
that a fight had been avoided.

But a far greater conflict, the ultimate war, a conflagration that
would sweep all of Kham, was on the verge of igniting. Its cause was

spelled out in the slogans on the posters and banners that Yunru Pön's men had torn down:

CHAIRMAN MAO DECLARES
HIGH TIDE OF SOCIALIST TRANSFORMATION.
DILIGENTLY IMPLEMENT DEMOCRATIC
REFORMS NOW.

"Democratic Reforms" was the official propaganda term for the crucial first step in creating a Communist state. It involved class struggle and the violent suppression of all landlords and feudal "elements". It was essentially the Communist Party's program to eradicate monastic and tribal leadership and end the traditional social system.

11

THE CONFLUENCE

"Democratic reforms" in Eastern Tibet were first carried out in the frontier town of Dartsedo, known to Christian missionaries and European travellers coming up from China, as the "Gateway to Tibet". A Tibetan historical source refers to the area as "The Key to China and Tibet" (*gya-bod kyi dimi*).[1] High mountains enclose the town on all sides, forming a narrow depression through which·the Darchu River thunders down from the west, cutting right through the town (where it is spanned by five bridges) and meeting the onrushing waters of the Tsechu from the north, at the lower end of the valley. "Chu" means water in Tibetan but has the secondary meaning of river. Hence the name of the town "Dar-tse-do" or the "confluence" (*do*) of the Dar and Tse rivers. The Tibetan language lends itself well to precise and pithy descriptions.

In spite of being over 8,000 feet above sea level, Dartsedo is a fairly claustrophobic place. It is hemmed in by the surrounding heights that reduce the amount of daylight the town receives and limits any kind of view beyond them. But if you clambered high enough up the grassy slope to the north and turned around and looked back south (south-south-west to be precise), you might get a glimpse of one of the northernmost peaks of the Minyak Rabgang range—the ice sheathed Mt. Grosvenor, named by Joseph Rock in honour of the president of the National Geographic Society that had funded his expedition to locate this "stupendous range".[2] Rock claimed that this smaller peak "had been mistaken by the missionaries of Tatsienliu for the Minya Konka" or Minyak Gangkar, the highest mountain in Kham (24,900 feet). Rock himself had initially miscalculated the height of the Minyak Gangkar at 30,250 feet and had cabled the Society to announce his discovery of the highest mountain in the world. These miscalculations and mistakes aside, there is no disputing that the "stupendous" Minyak Rabgang range and its twenty mighty peaks (including Grosvenor) are unquestionably without peer in the Tibet–China borderland.

The town had seven monasteries: two Gelugpa, two Kagyüpa and three small Nyingmapa monasteries. One of the Nyingma monasteries, Dorjedrak, or Adamantine Rock—just outside the town on the road to Central Tibet—is often mentioned in travellers' accounts. The largest, Ngamchö Gompa, was a Gelugpa monastery. The Chinese called it the South Bridge Monastery from its location. This monastery had a distinctive pagoda-style roof, a cultural concession to the proximity of China. The chief incarnate lama of the monastery, Dardo Rinpoche had, in 1947, been appointed by the Tagtra regent of Tibet to head the newly founded Tibetan monastery and pilgrim hostel at Bodh Gaya in India. Dardo Rinpoche's duties only required him to stay at Gaya during the winter months when Tibetan pilgrims visited this holiest Buddhist site. The rest of the year Rinpoche lived with his mother in the cooler climate of Kalimpong, where, as mentioned in Chapter 1, he served as a teacher and informant to the Western scholars and travellers visiting this frontier town.

The great physical distance between the two towns could not obviate from the fact that they were both "gateways" to Tibet and shared a number of qualities: their location on the steeper and semi-tropical side of the Himalayas, though Kalimpong was situated on a saddle, just above the Dartsedo-like valley of the Teesta River. Both were important because of their favourable location on the trade routes with Tibet, and both had a significant Christian missionary presence. In the case of Dartsedo, this was represented by three organizations, the China Inland Mission, which was British, Société des Missions Etrangères, which was French, and the American Seventh Day Adventist Mission. The Chinese community worshipped at Taoist establishments and temples dedicated to the War God (Chinese, *Guandi*), the Goddess of Fertility (Chinese, *Niangniang*) and the legendary Emperor Yu.

The Chinese called the city Tachienlu "a transliteration of the Tibetan name *Dartsedo*" according to Eric Teichman and meaningless in Chinese. In 1905 after carving out the new province of Xikang from Eastern Tibet, the Chinese renamed the city Kangding, using the characters for "well-being" and "calm down", and made it the provincial capital. The French physician and scholar André Migot who travelled through this city in 1947 noted "Chinese governments have always had a mania for altering place names."[3]

Dartsedo was, earlier in its history, the capital of Chagla, one of the six semi-independent Tibetan kingdoms of Kham.[4] The importance of Dartsedo lay in the fact that it was the principal terminus for the tea trade, on what the Chinese called "Ancient Tea-Horse Road" (Chinese, *chama gudao*), between Tibet and China. Because of the importance of this trade for Lhasa ". . . the Fifth Dalai Lama had officials from Lhasa posted there to oversee trade and levy taxes", and eventually a Tibetan garrison was stationed at Dartsedo. Tibet's long control of Dartsedo may have been aided by the near anarchy in China after the fall of the Ming dynasty, but things began to change with the rise of Manchu power in China and Central Asia. The Qing Emperor Kangxi, in a missive to the Tibetan regent, Desi Sangye Gyatso, disputed Tibet's claim of sovereignty over Dartsedo and demanded its surrender.

The Tibetans refused. The Manchus attacked the town on 28 January 1701, in what a Chinese scholar has called "The Battle of Dartsedo", striking at the town from three different directions. The Tibetan garrison was overwhelmed, and the Qing army eventually took control of the town. "After the battle the Qing army inflicted massive slaughter on the town. Consequently, almost all male Tibetans were killed."[5]

Throughout these turbulent times, the traditional rulers of the kingdom had somehow managed to hold on to their titular status and their palace in Dartsedo, if not their actual sovereign power. The last native king, Gyaltsen Chöphel, who succeeded at the age of thirty-two on the death of his elder brother Gyaltsen Chöwang in 1901, was deposed by the Chinese in 1911, and since then, according to Eric Teichman, a British consular officer in China who had known him, "passed a somewhat precarious existence in his old palace in the town, hankering vainly after his lost Kingdom, sometimes in and sometimes out of favour with the Chinese authorities."[6]

In 1912, the new Republican government of China sent a military expedition under General Yin Changheng, which attacked Dartsedo and, after looting the town, burned down the king's palace and decapitated his younger brother. The king narrowly managed to escape, into the inaccessible mountain regions in the interior of the region. In 1922, he again fell out of favour with the Chinese authorities. He was first put in prison and then induced to escape only to be shot down and thrown into the raging torrents of the Darchu. In another account, the king's men managed to break into the prison, but the king drowned in the river during the escape. The king's son, a small, squat figure, who had been studying Tibetan medicine at Dergé, was stripped of his father's largely ceremonial rank by the Sichuan authorities. However, his Tibetan subjects still regarded him with respect and doffed their caps and bowed to him when they passed him in the streets.

A missionary passing through the town noticed the somewhat strained and antagonistic manner in which the two races interacted and attempted to explain why this was probably so.

The Chinese were generally dressed in rather prim blue gowns which reached to their feet, but alongside them, in the shops, you might suddenly see a wild-looking nomad from the grasslands. There he would stand, his shock of long, unkempt hair; unwieldy sheepskin gown; and naïve uncouth manner, drawing uneasy glances from more sedate customers. A huge bare shoulder, bristling with muscular strength and tanned a chocolate brown, would remind them not to make too many adverse comments. The wry grimaces of the townsfolk meant little to the nomad. Chinese officialdom and the wealthy merchants of the community might look contemptuously upon these "barbarians" from the hills, but when a big Tibetan trader came riding through the town, dressed to perfection in coloured silk, high-collared shirt and figured boots, they would think again. Sitting astride a well-groomed horse with his servants and well-laden beasts behind him, he would take possession of the road. With such, there was no question of inferiority, only a proud return of the Chinese disdain.[7]

The Tibetan side of the all-important tea-trade was controlled by major mercantile houses called *Ajakhapa** by the Khampas, or *Khochang* (Chinese, *guozhuang*) in the Sichuanese dialect. These remarkable establishments combined the functions of inns, general stores, taverns, warehouses and informal banks and were run mainly by women, according to the white-Russian émigré traveller Peter Goullart, who lived in this area in the early forties. The most "splendid" of these trading houses called the Welsakyap was the one owned and managed by Wangmo, the niece of the last Chagla king.[8] The husbands of these enterprising women generally handled other more peripatetic and physically arduous aspects of the business, organizing and leading caravans to Lhasa, Lijiang or even Kalimpong.[†]

The houses of the *Ajakhapas* were of massive construction, Khampa style, with wide foundations and thick walls made of undressed stone. These spacious buildings were constructed around an ample courtyard with stores and stalls opening off it. "The Tibetan houses are infinitely more handsome, more comfortable, cleaner, and more like our own— while retaining an individual style—than are those of the Chinese,"

---

*[*] '*Aja*' means older sister and is a respectful term used when addressing women. '*khapa*' means articulate. *The New Tibetan English Dictionary of Modern Tibetan* provides the additional meaning of 'go between' and 'negotiator between two traders/merchants' for the word *Khapa*.

[†] An important and fascinating study of the *Ajakhapa* was published by Dr. Yudru Tsomu of Sichuan University in 2016: '*Guozhuang* Trading Houses and Tibetan Middlemen in Dartsedo, the "Shanghai of Tibet"'. *Cross-Currents: East Asian History and Culture Review*. E-Journal No. 19 (June 2016) • (cross-currents.berkeley.edu/e-journal/issue-19)

the Vicomte D'Ollone noted when passing through the town at the beginning of the last century.[9]

The tea was imported by Sichuanese merchants, and the tax paid on it formed the largest slice of the official revenue of the city. It came into Dartsedo from Ya'an (or Yazhou-fu) on the back of Chinese coolies. They were opium smokers but unbelievably tough (though short-lived), each coolie carrying around 200-pound stacks of brick tea packed in cane mats. They covered six miles daily on the narrow, precipitous trail through the mountains to Dartsedo. Once purchased by the *Ajakhapa*, these bales had to be repacked in rawhide for transport on yaks to Tibet. A special guild of Tibetan packers handled this business. But, since yaks were not allowed into the city, the repacked tea had to be hauled out of the city on the road to Tibet, where the yak herds grazed.

Two roads led from Dartsedo to Lhasa: the *Shung lam* or "official (or main) route" through Lithang (about 175 miles away) and Bathang, and the *Jhang lam* or "Northern Route," via Kandzé and Jyekundo which was also called the "Tea Road" (*Jha lam*).

This job of getting the repacked tea to the two yak terminuses outside the city was the monopoly of the poorer Tibetan women of Dartsedo, mostly tough country girls, who had formed a union to protect this lucrative occupation. Peter Goullart tells us that when these women were paid, they would celebrate in the wine shops in the town drinking fiery *paku* liquor. After a few bowls of the stuff, "a leading woman would rise up shouting 'Girls, let us get men!' and out they would spill into the street grabbing passing Tibetans and drawing them back into the wine shops with them." They would then laugh, sing and dance through the evening. The men probably did not need much persuasion to join in the revelries. These girls were not only "cheerful" and "immensely strong" as Dr Migot, the French scholar, observes, but "many of them are quite pretty (and well aware of the fact); they look very gay and rather brazen as, giggling and chattering among themselves, they carry their heavy burdens."

Other visitors to Dartsedo had somewhat less indulgent opinions of these girls. The missionary Geoffrey Bull who was there in 1948, considered the city to be "blighted by an inward canker" and the girls "promiscuous" and "immoral".[10] George Patterson, in his usual sweeping way, deemed Dartsedo ". . . a notorious center of vice, with a reputation reaching all the way to, and even superseding, Shanghai."[11]

That is probably what the Communist cadres thought so, too, when the Red Army marched into Dartsedo in 1949, for they shared with some of the Christian missionaries the sour puritanism that viewed human pleasure, especially sex, with deep disapproval. They also shared the absolute conviction of moral and "spiritual" superiority over the Tibetans. The fundamental thing, though, that Dartsedo had going against it from the Communist point of view, was almost certainly its economic standing as the most important mercantile centre in Eastern Tibet and the freebooting capitalist spirit of its residents. According to a present-day Chinese historian of Kham, nine out of ten residents of Dartsedo were traders.[12]

The Communist occupation of Dartsedo had not been a straightforward affair. Opportunistic surrenders and intrigues on the provincial level had seen Communist troops march into the town in December 1949 only to have Nationalist troops invade the town the following month. But finally, the demoralized Nationalist forces surrendered wherever they could.* The garrison at Dartsedo escaped to Burma via Yunnan and most likely joined the "lost army" of the Guomindang in the Golden Triangle of Northern Thailand, Burma and Laos, which controlled much of the world's opium trade at that time.

There was no resistance when the Communists finally arrived at Dartsedo, and the single, heavily loop-holed concrete pillbox on the outskirts of the town on the Ya'an road was deserted. The Communists administration set up its headquarters at the "hideous municipal buildings" (Migot) on the tongue of land formed by the confluence of the two rivers, where stood a school and other offices

---

*The warlord Liu Wenhui who was then governor of Xikang "province", adroitly switched sides and joined the Communists on 9 December 1949. He was rewarded with a bureaucratic post in the new Communist government in Beijing.

of the provincial government. The cinema hall was closed and requisitioned for political meetings.

The first task of the Communists was rounding up "bandits" and "spies"—soldiers and officials of the old Guomindang regime. There were public trials and some executions, but these were, to everyone's way of viewing these things, fairly routine events, given the nature of political conflicts in China. Two monks from Lithang, business administrators (*chiso*) of Lithang Monastery, were in Dartsedo at the time the Communists marched in. One of them, Ratuk Ngawang, (later to become a leader of the Four Rivers Six Ranges resistance force), recalled the executions of Guomindang officials and soldiers at the small *feijichang* (Chinese) or airfield outside the city. He told me that the Communists exhorted everyone in the town to attend the executions. About a hundred people were shot over a period of three days.[13] Ngawang remembered being disturbed by the scene and later in the evening walked by the side of the river, saying his prayers. He came across a couple of bodies that had drifted ashore into the rocks and boulders. They were women, probably the wives of executed Guomindang soldiers or officials who had committed suicide by jumping into the river.

Then the executions stopped. Everyone hoped that, after the initial rush of revolutionary enthusiasm, the authorities would ease up, and business could go on as usual. For a while, it did seem like that would be the case. The large scale and savage land "reform" campaigns taking place in China bypassed the town either because the campaign was intended for rural rather than metropolitan targets or, more possibly, the Communists did not want any kind of disruption in this key terminus on their advance route to Tibet. The tea trade went on, and in fact, business increased with the Chinese troops marching into Tibet. Furthermore, the construction of a major motor road to Lhasa was started and provided everyone with many ways of making lucrative profits.

In the old days, although Dartsedo was under Chinese administration, the preferred currency of exchange for the Tibetans had been the old Indian Rupee, with the profiles of Queen Victoria and King George or King Edward on the obverse, especially the ones with the monarch in question wearing a crown. The Khampas called the coins "Lama Tomden", after itinerant priests whose distinctive headdresses were probably where the resemblance was observed.

The Communists now set up a mint at Ya'an to produce the old *dayuan* silver dollars that the Manchu's had first minted from Spanish-Mexican silver, imported to prop up the imperial currency. The silver for the new mint was now supplied from the various temples and shrines all over China that were being torn down or put to uses that the Communist authorities deemed more appropriate for a socialist nation. But the Dartsedo folk were not aware of that. There was so much business and so much money floating around the town that even the oldest resident could not remember when things had been so good.

In spite of all the capitalist ventures they tolerated, and sometimes even financed and supported, the Communist authorities had, all along, not been diverted from their primary ideological task. The political cadres and their agents maintained a file on every person in the city, even those of the least importance. Especially noted were the social and economic standing of each person from which his or her class label (Chinese, *chengfen*) was derived. Everyone in any way connected to that person was questioned, especially someone who might have a grievance, for whatever reason, against that person. Even children were interviewed about their parents at school or special gatherings, and given sweets, coloured ribbons, red scarves and certificates. Communist cadres paid visits to the homes and business places of people under investigation and took down detailed information of all their household items, jewellery, valuables, heirlooms and weapons. To allay suspicions, the cadres would maintain that these were social visits and offered gifts to the householders, especially silver coins.

The purpose of these surveys was to establish the correct socio-economic background of each individual within the class structure or "strata" in Tibetan society as established by Chinese Communist doctrine. The three main strata were the "Three Big Feudal Land-Owning Classes" (*ngadak chey sum*): the Government (the Lhasa government), the Aristocracy (including tribal chieftains and local rulers), and Monasteries (including lamas, priests and monastic officials). The two other strata were Serfs (peasants and nomads) and the Urban Proletariat. Within the five principal strata, there were numerous sub-strata—a sampling:

Representatives of the Feudal Land Owning Class (*ngatsab*): stewards, managers, tax collectors, senior servants and storekeepers.

Urban sub-strata: big merchants (*tsongchen*), intermediate merchants (*tsongdring*), small shopkeepers (*tsongchung*), urban residents (*drongmi*) and destitute urban residents (*drongmi ulphong*), what Marx called the *lumpenproletariat*. Then there were "Capital Investors" (*tsonglas matsa-chen*), who were just people who had liquid assets or cash over 5000 yuan.

Rural sub-strata: rich peasants (*shingba chukpo*), intermediate peasants (*shingdring*), lower intermediate peasants (*shingdring hogma*), destitute peasants (*shingba ulphong*).

Nomadic sub-strata: rich nomad (*drogdak*), intermediate nomads (*drogdring*), destitute nomads (*drogpa ulphong*).

It should be noted that the various class "strata" designations were sometimes altered or modified depending on the political climate and the particular "campaign" that was being carried out. During the Cultural Revolution, entirely new classes and political designations were created, and individuals and groups "labelled" as such.

The transformation of China to a full Communist state was to be implemented in two stages: "Democratic Reforms" and "Socialist Transformation." Democratic Reforms consisted of wide-scale land redistribution, the violent suppression of landlords and "counter-revolutionaries," and the initiation of class struggle. This program lasted from 1950 to 1953 in most of China and had resulted, according to Mao's calculation, in the public executions of some 700,000 landlords.[14] According to the acclaimed China scholar Simon Leys, the number of political executions in China between 1950 and 1952—based entirely on extrapolations by "the greatest specialists" from documents belonging to the Chinese Communist Party—was five million.[15] An official pamphlet circulated internally thirty years later in 1980 stated that the number of landlords and *kulaks* had fallen by 10.5 million after the campaign.[16] The Communists considered "Democratic Reforms" a pre-socialist stage to socialist transformation.

"Socialist Transformation" consisted of taking back all the farmland earlier redistributed to the peasants in the "Democratic Reform" stage, then organizing them into collectives, where the farmer was required to give up partial ownership of the land, and later into full-fledged communes where even the concept of ownership was to be completely done away with. The land that had earlier been distributed to poor farmers with much fanfare and publicity would now be fully resumed by the state. The Party giveth, and the Party taketh away. The farmer became, in practice, an unpaid labourer on state land, or a kind of a serf or a slave of the totalitarian state as the Austrian-born economist and philosopher F.A. Hayek had foreseen in his ground-breaking study, *The Road to Serfdom.* In Tibet, the deception was of a particularly cynical kind. Photographs and film footage of peasants happily burning old land documents in giant bonfires and gratefully receiving new land titles from benevolent Communist officials feature prominently in official Chinese propaganda, *even to the present day.*

In 1955–56 Chairman Mao initiated a rapid acceleration of the socialist transition process, known as the "High Tide of Socialist Transformation." He felt confident that Communist control was now secure in all minority nationality areas, and he called for these areas to also be included in the "High Tide". Now the first step, "Democratic Reforms", was to be carried out throughout the minority nationality areas of Kham, Amdo, Inner Mongolia and Xinjiang, with the exception of the Tibet Autonomous Region, where the Dalai Lama's government, though virtually powerless, still had nominal standing. That same year the motor-road to Lhasa was completed, which was marked by an exceptionally grand celebration at Dartsedo. Troops could now be moved quickly throughout Eastern Tibet.

The Communists began to organize and train groups of local agitators and denunciators they called *jijifenzi*, that in Stalinist Russia were known as *stakhanovites*. Tibetans called them "*hur-tsunpa*", literally zealots or activists. There were many poor and desperate people in Dartsedo, opium smokers, gold panners, tea coolies, and the usual scamps and town bullies, and it was not too difficult to find recruits to denounce and "struggle" those who had wealth and position. But generally, it was difficult to find peasants to denounce their landlords even in China itself, where farmers had been squeezed for generations on end. A report presented to the Military-Political Committee of Central-South described the difficulty of "arousing the masses." Many peasants were reluctant to act; in some places, they sympathized with the persecuted landowners.[17] Hence the need for trained agitators and denunciators.

In Dartsedo, mass meetings were called for "the mobilization of the masses." Gangs of trained denunciators marched around the streets of the town, waving red flags and banners, beating gongs, drums and cymbals, shouting slogans and calling on people to attend the meetings. At the meetings, the accused would be dragged before the crowd, generally on a platform or a stage. They would be forced to bow low, have their crimes against the people read out aloud, and then be "struggled". This could be anything from a collective verbal browbeating, physical humiliation by having ink or filth smeared on his or her face, beatings and even public torture and execution. It all depended on what the authorities wanted of that particular victim. The whole production was finely tuned. The denunciators would work the crowd, and soon howls for blood would resonate in the town square. The accused would have ". . . the shit squeezed out of them," according to one informant.

The first people to be dragged before the "People's Courts" were the Sichuanese merchants and the Tibetan *ajakhapa* of Dartsedo. Many of them took to committing suicide before they could be "struggled". It became a common sight in Dartsedo to see a body being washed away in the foaming torrents of the Darchu, and cries would go up on either bank asking who it was—Chinese or Tibetan? The difference could be made out by the person's attire. Many of the older innkeepers and merchants jumped into the river. One informant remembered hearing that Gyaltsen, the son of the last Chagla king, had also jumped into the river, but he could not be sure.

Large-scale suicides had taken place earlier in Shanghai in 1952 when the double-barrel "three-anti" (*san-fan*) and "five-anti" (*wu-fan*) corruption campaigns were launched. The "three-anti" was directed at party members, the "five-anti" at private businessmen. So many people had jumped from the tall buildings of the city that the phenomenon was called "parachutes".[18]

With Dartsedo cleared of feudal elements, capitalist-roaders and counter-revolutionaries, the campaign began to be pushed another step further into Eastern Tibet, in neighbouring Minyak to the west. But before "Democratic Reforms" could be initiated in these Khampa areas, a special preparatory stage preceded the main campaign—"collection of arms". The first mass meetings in Minyak regarding "Democratic Reforms" were primarily devoted to exhorting local Khampas to give up their weapons. Construction of a large prison was also started at Minyak Ra'ngakhar and a major prison and *Laogai* slave-labour camp north of Dartsedo at Yakraphuk, in the land of the baron of Gothom.

There was nothing random or unplanned about the way "Democratic Reforms" were implemented in Eastern Tibet. It was done methodically, as my friend, Athar Norbu, then a small trader passing through Minyak, remembered. "I came up to Minyak from Dartsedo when the 'Democratic Reforms' were starting there. The campaign was strictly localized. The Communists didn't bother travellers like me. There was this person I knew, Wangdra, from an important family in Minyak Ra'ngakhar—I can't remember the family name now—who came to see me at my lodgings one night to sell me a *pamaling*, a Czech rifle, and one hundred rounds of ammunition. I gave him two *dayuan* boxes for the lot. Wangdra was one of the richest men in Minyak, but the Chinese were collecting all weapons in the area, and he was afraid to hang on to his own rifle. He was terrified. That was how the 'Democratic Reforms' were carried out, first Dartsedo, then Minyak and then, of course, Lithang and the rest of Kham. That's how it was done—'step by step'", Athar concluded, using the English phrase.

12

LITHANG UPRISING

Lithang Monastery was one of the largest in Kham. It was also famous for the erudition of its *geshé* scholars and the saintliness of many of its lamas. The most important incarnate lama of Lithang was the Shogdru Kyamgon, who had the Mongol title of *Huthoktu* and was one of the highest lamas of Tibet.

According to Peter Goullart, who met the previous Lithang incarnation at Dartsedo in 1940, he was "a huge figure, tall and athletic, clad in a rusty red toga with one arm bare. His eyes, large and magnetic, bored into mine . . . looking into his forceful compelling eyes I felt a strong, warm tide of affinity, and understanding . . . this spontaneous and warm friendship continued until I left Xikang and I always looked forward, while in Tachienlu, to visiting the Great Lama and having the comfort of his warm goodwill and affection. I was to meet later many grand lamas, but none could compare with the royal bearing and friendly attitude of the Lithang Lama." The lama was in Dartsedo then to confer with the Governor of Xikang, and Goullart heard rumours that the Chinese were holding him hostage.

In 1943, Shogdru Kyamgon visited Lhasa. Although my grandfather, Tethong Gyurme Gyatso, had died a few years earlier, Shogdru Kyamgon paid a courtesy visit to our house. My uncle, my mother and most of the family were in India at the time, on a pilgrimage to make offerings at the Buddhist holy places in their father's memory, but Gyurme Gyatso's younger brother, Khenchung Lobsang Namgyal, a monk official, received him at our Lhasa house. The great lama talked about meeting Gyurme Gyatso in Chamdo and discussed the Tethong family's connection to Lithang. He gave a couple of important public teachings in Lhasa: one at Drepung Monastery and the other at the Sungchöra square beside the Jokhang. Both places were filled to capacity. Much as the Lhasa populace genuinely revered him, there was also the novelty factor that drew the city people to this big, pleasant and famous lama.

When Shogdru Kyamgon returned to Lithang, he took with him skilled artisans—*thangka* painters, metal workers, sculptors and woodcarvers to improve the artistic and cultural life in Lithang, which had suffered considerably from the violence and uncertainty of the previous decades. He even managed to persuade an *Ache Lhamo* or opera master from Lhasa to go with him and introduce this new performing tradition to the people of Lithang.

There are the usual stories of miraculous acts and displays of spiritual power from his disciples and followers. Shogdru Kyamgon died or "departed to the heavenly fields" in 1947, in his mid-forties, just a couple of years before the Communists came. Shortly before his death, he had been giving a Lamrim or "Graduated Path" teaching to the monks of Lithang Monastery, a *Summa Theologica* written by the Gelukpa founder Tsongkhapa, a summary of the whole of Mahayana Buddhism and a guide to the conquest of suffering and delusion. A disciple of the Lithang Lama recalls that after his teaching, the Lama made this prophetic statement: "I feel that a great calamity will befall the Land of Snows. Before that happens a great lama each from the three regions, Kham, Amdo and Central Tibet, will depart for the Heavenly Fields."[1] No one at the time knew what he meant, but later people remembered his words when Shogdru Kyamgon himself in Kham, Jamyang Shepa in Amdo, and Reting Rinpoche (the former regent of Tibet) all passed away within a month of each other.

But there were other precious lamas in Lithang Monastery. One was Nor-ri Khensur Rinpoche. This old lama was revered as a genuinely enlightened being. People claimed that they were suffused with a wonderful aroma when they came close to him. Tibetans believe that if a religious practitioner lived a pure life, observing the monastic code (Sanskrit, *vinaya*) the Buddha had laid down, he would acquire the scent of morality or virtue (*tsultrim kyi drima*). Similar beliefs seem to exist in other cultures about such special people or "those whom the gods look upon with favour." Plutarch tells us that after the death of Alexander the Great, while his commanders quarrelled among themselves for many days, his body remained fresh, pure and sweet-smelling for many days, even without receiving any special care.

Pilgrims from all over Eastern Tibet would visit Lithang Monastery. Quite a few beggars outside the wall of the monastery lived on the charity of the visitors and the monastery itself. Commissar Luo attempted to organize political education for the masses, especially the poor and needy. He held meetings where he gathered all the beggars and instructed them on how they should "speak bitterness" (Chinese, *suku*) against the feudal governing classes and capitalist roaders. But in contrast to Dartsedo, not many of the beggars in Lithang took up the offer with any enthusiasm. Piety and traditional loyalties were stronger in these areas. People did, of course, have problems and complaints to report, but no one was quite prepared to denounce each other in the way the Communist cadres wanted them to. These "mass mobilization" meetings were not successful. But the Chinese gave every beggar a brick of tea each and a little money for attending.

The implementation of "Democratic Reforms" in Lithang presented problems that the Communist administration had not faced earlier at Dartsedo. One was physical. The high altitude and cold of Lithang affected the health of many cadres and soldiers. This made it particularly difficult to send educational teams and delegations to the higher nomadic areas. Administrative staff in Lithang town constantly complained of headaches. So, with incapacitated officials, a disobliging urban public and an unfriendly if not hostile nomadic population, organizing mass meetings and rallies became a difficult and trying task for Political Commissar Luo.

He once arranged for a troupe of dancers and musicians from the PLA Theatrical and Cultural Training School in Chengdu to entice the Tibetan public to attend a special political meeting. That particular meeting was an important one, and was presided over by the Governor of Sichuan province. With him was a delegation of important Tibetans, Sakya Yeshi of Gyalrong and Khenpo Ngawang Gyatso, former abbot of the Jhey College of the Sera Monastery in Lhasa, who became a Chinese puppet after being expelled from Lhasa by the old Tibetan government in 1945.[2] They all took turns haranguing the Lithang public but were not able to generate much enthusiasm, even after the special entertainment. That night someone fired a rifle at the governor but missed. The next day the delegation continued on its tour of the region.

In July 1954, the nineteen-year-old Dalai Lama was invited by Mao Zedong to visit China. On his return journey, the following year, he was forced to make a long stop at Dartsedo as an earthquake in the region had damaged the new Chinese road. A delegation of high lamas from Lithang approached the Dalai Lama with the request to visit Lithang. Yunru Pön had personally gone to Chengdu to accompany His Holiness up to Dartsedo. There was a tremendous expectation among the people of Lithang that the Dalai Lama would visit their region. Two previous Dalai Lamas had been born there, and the great monastery had been founded by the Third Dalai Lama, making Lithang a significant place for the Dalai Lama and the Gelugpa church.

Many Lithangwas claim that the Chinese stopped the Dalai Lama from visiting Lithang, but in his biography, His Holiness writes that he could not visit all the different places in Eastern Tibet that wanted him to come, and so he sent three high lamas from his entourage in his stead. Karmapa Rinpoche was sent to Dergé and Nangchen, Menling Chung Rinpoche to Nyarong, and the Dalai Lama's tutor, Trijang Rinpoche visited Chatreng, Bathang and Lithang.

In Lithang, Trijang Rinpoche listened to the fear and concerns of the tribal chiefs, monastic leaders and the ordinary people. The most pressing question they had was how they should respond to the implementation of "Democratic Reforms". Trijang Rinpoche was a compassionate lama, but his answer was forthright and unvarnished. He told the people that if "Democratic Reforms" were implemented, it would mean the end of the monasteries, the tribal system and the traditional way of life of the people of Lithang. In 1956 when Lithang, Bathang and Chatreng became the first places in Eastern Tibet to stage uprisings, Trijang Rinpoche's statement was used by the Chinese authorities in their denunciation of this lama.

But the people of Lithang received the good news that the Dalai Lama would be giving teachings at the neighbouring district of Minyak, up to which point there was a motorable road. So, all the important lamas, tribal chiefs and the common folk of Lithang, and people from other parts of Kham, travelled to the crossroad settlement of Minyak Ra'ngakhar to receive his Holiness's teachings and his personal blessings. So many Lithangwas went to Minyak it seemed that Lithang itself was emptied out.

Just above Minyak Ra'ngakhar, there is a small plateau called Namdzongo, where an airstrip had been built by the Guomindang during World War II. A reception area was prepared there, and a magnificent tent-awning with three sides called the *tasugma*, decorated with traditional auspicious symbols done in appliqué, erected for the event. The side of the tent was lined with *thangka* paintings, and the floor, covered with plush rugs and leopard skins. A high throne stood in the center. His Holiness gave the "Great Avaloketesvara Empowerment" (*chenrezig wangchen*) teaching and initiation, and at the conclusion, blessed everyone there individually, one by one. His Holiness also received the high lamas and abbots of Lithang and other monasteries, the various tribal chiefs, including Yunru Pön, in personal audiences. It is said that His Holiness gave Yunru Pön a precious bronze image of the Sakyamuni Buddha. For all the Tibetans gathered there at Minyak Ra'ngakhar on that occasion, it was a tremendously happy and fulfilling moment in their lives, and for a brief while, the fear and uncertainty on their immediate horizon seemed to recede.

The crucial pre-condition that the Communist administration had to persuade Tibetans to accept, before even the first phase of "Democratic Reforms" could be carried out, was the surrender of weapons, particularly rifles. The Chinese organized rallies and gatherings where they announced that all weapons had to be surrendered to the authorities. Delegations went out to the grasslands to meet with tribal chiefs and their councils and persuade the tribesmen to give up their weapons.

Nearly everyone in Lithang was by now aware of what was going on in Dartsedo: the denunciations, "struggles", killings and suicides. A couple of years earlier, they had also heard of the fighting in Gyalthang to the south, where the Khampa population led by a popular chief, Wangchuk Tempa, who was also known as Aku Lemar or "Uncle Baldy", had revolted against the Chinese.* The Communists had stamped out the insurrection with great savagery, executing local leaders and lamas, and ravaging the countryside. Although the Communist authorities had been careful not to carry out "Democratic Reforms" in all Khampa areas in Sichuan province until 1956, Gyalthang, which was in Yunnan province, was somehow overlooked and had undergone "Democratic Reforms" in 1953, with all its brutal ramifications: denunciations, people's courts, struggles, beatings, torture and executions.

The resistance leader, Gonpo Tashi Andrugtsang, describes the event in his autobiography, "In the area of Gyalthang . . . the local population was divided into five strata and a terror campaign of selective arrests launched by the Chinese. Scores of Tibetans were arrested, and many of them were shot mercilessly at mass gatherings." Gyalthangwas fleeing the Communist terror in their homeland travelled north to Lithang. Everyone was troubled by these events. Lithang had a special relationship with Gyalthang as well as Bathang, whereby they would come to each other's aid in times of need or conflict. This alliance was known by the acronym "Ba-li-gyal-sum" or the Ba (thang)-Li (thang)-

*The Library of Tibetan Works & Archives in Dharamsala has a fairly detailed but unpublished account of Wangchuk Tenpa and the Gyalthang uprising: *Rgyal thang dpa' bo dbang phyug steng pa'i dpa' ba'i gtam rgyud rdo rje'i srog ldan*, by Blo bzang rgya mtsho and Ngag dbang chos 'pel. An English translation can be accessed at treasuryoflives.org under the entry "Pawo Wangchuk Tengpa Lobsang Nima".

Gyal (thang) triad of the lands that lay within the shadow of the Poborgang range, of the six ranges of Eastern Tibet.

The Communist officials in Lithang were well aware that the populace was by now deeply suspicious of them. They knew the monastery had great influence over the people, and so the cadres met with the monastic heads a number of times to convince them to cooperate on the crucial issue of weapons surrender. Commissar Luo even arranged a meeting with the full monastic council: the four *chagbuk* administrators, the *dronyer chenmo* or the representative of the abbot (the spiritual and academic head), the eighteen representatives of the nine *khamtsen* or colleges of Lithang Monastery and the two *gekoe* or disciplinarians. But the monastery insisted they could do little in this matter.

Finally, the Chinese managed to convene the biggest ever meeting of the Lithang monastic and lay community, traditionally called "Lidé-Nari-Shingkham", where the monastic representatives, the chiefs and representatives of all the *me-ser*, the subject people of Lithang, would be present. In addition, the *Ra* chieftains and the representatives of the *tongde-nga*, or the five divisions of thousands, representatives from other overlapping administrative systems that derived from Lithang's archaic past, that still retained token representation in such gatherings would also attend. Probably the closest thing we have in present times to such a broad gathering of chieftains, tribal elders and religious leaders would be the Afghan "grand assembly" or *Loya Jirga*.

Heading the Chinese side were Li Chunfang, the deputy party secretary of Kandzé Prefecture, Hu Guojun, the PLA commander of the Southern Command and Political Commissar Luo. The Chinese called this mass gathering in October 1955. It did not bode well for the Chinese that Yunru Pön did not attend even this biggest of meetings— but he had, at least, sent a representative. Commissar Luo tried to start the meeting off on a positive note speaking at length about the tremendous benefits "Democratic Reforms" would bring to the people of the region and the great motherland. He then attempted to explain why to achieve this objective, everyone had to first surrender their rifles, as well as other dangerous weapons. Almost immediately, there were angry murmuring and protests from the gathering. Someone shouted that the Chinese government was making impossible demands of them. Someone else declared that asking a Khampa to give up his rifle was the same as asking him to cut off his arm. People began to put their hands inside their robes. Although no one was supposed to bring weapons at such an assembly, quite a few had taken the precaution of carrying a handgun in their *amba*, or the fold of the robe above the belt where it becomes a pouch.

Most of my informants were agreed that it was Li Chunfang who spelled out clearly the extent to which the Communist Party was prepared to go to enforce its policy. He held out his hands to silence the crowd: "I am not saying that you do not have a choice in the matter. I am like your father and mother. I am only showing you the way. Each one of you has to choose which way you want to go. There is a white path, and there is a black path. If you choose the white path, then the Communist government will implement 'Democratic Reforms' in a peaceful and beneficial way. If you choose the black path, then 'Democratic Reforms' will be carried out by force. Over the years, I have educated you politically. I have told you how Chairman Mao has called for mass mobilization throughout the motherland to implement the High Tide of 'Democratic Reforms' and 'Socialist Transformation'. The minority peoples had been granted a special five-year reprieve in this matter, but that period is now finished. Let us now discuss the establishment of preparatory committees for the implementation of the first stages of 'Democratic Reforms'. We must also discuss the surrender of weapons to the state. The People's Liberation Army has now established peace and security throughout the Motherland, and there is no need for individuals to keep weapons to defend themselves as in the lawless old feudal days."

But he was interrupted by an old monk, Aku Yama, from the district of Lingkashi, just north of the Bathang River. He was representing the Shewa Khamtsen, his college at Lithang Monastery. The old man spoke scornfully: "I have heard that after you die, you have to choose between two roads, but I have not heard of such roads in this world. I know nothing of this. You order us to give up our guns. You tell us that

'Democratic Reforms' must be implemented. I cannot make any such decision for Lithang Monastery or this great assembly, or my college or even my own *drasha* (monk sleeping quarters). Every man will make decisions for himself. Everyone here in this assembly—and we have all manner of people here, high, low, rich and poor—everyone will make his own decision as he pleases. All who are here and possess weapons, have purchased them with their own wealth, received them as gifts, or inherited them from their father. No one has received such weapons as gifts from the Communist government or the previous government, or the Chinese nation. Show us the white or black path now as you please. I will not walk on either of them. I will not accept any of your demands."

Seru Jampa, who had formerly been a bandit, but was now a respectable citizen, spoke up in support of Aku Yama, saying that he was of the same mind as the previous speaker and refused to accept such orders from the Communist administration. He turned around to the rest of the delegates at the meeting and told them, "This is *our* decision. We have nothing more to say." Everyone shouted in agreement with the speakers, and although Political Commissar Luo had some soldiers escorting him, there was nothing he could do to continue the meeting. Every Khampa man seemed to have his right hand in the *amba* pouch of his robe, as if holding a pistol or a revolver.

Then Khagya Ngawang Phelgyel, *dronyer* (manager) of Lithang Monastery, spoke. He stood up at the meeting and declared that he personally refused to accept "Democratic Reforms". He also stated that Lithang Monastery would in no way support "Democratic Reforms". His parting statement was a pointed ideological insult "You Communists are worse than the Guomindang".[3] He then left the meeting.

All the people at the meeting rode back to the monastery or their respective tribes and communities and reported what had happened at the big meeting. Many smaller gatherings were now held, and representatives and messengers rode back and forth from the monastery to the different tribal areas. Yunru Pön brought his fighting men and set up an encampment at Tsachukha, about fifteen miles from the monastery, which he made his temporary headquarters. He held a number of meetings here with the leaders of other tribes and monastery officials. There were still cautious individuals who did not want to defy the Chinese and those who were not sure what to do, but gradually everyone came to realize that if "Democratic Reforms" were accepted, that would be the end of their old way of life—the end of everything. After much discussion, a decision was reached to fight.

Yunru Pön and the other Lithang chieftains now sent letters to monasteries and tribal leaders in Bathang, Markham, Chatreng, Lingkashi and Nyarong informing them of what had happened in Lithang calling on the Khampas there to rise up against the Chinese. It is said, letters were also sent to other areas though we cannot be certain. Contributing to the general sense of urgency was the official Chinese summons to all tribal chiefs, important lamas and monastic officials to attend an important conference at Dartsedo. Many were hesitant, fearing arrest, or at least being held hostage. But many of the chieftains and lamas were being paid regular stipends by the Chinese and were persuaded that it was in their best interest to attend the conference, according to one informant of mine, Kalsang Gyadotsang of Lithang. He told me that at least twenty-two incarnate lamas attended the conference, one of them being a senior abbot of Lithang Monastery, and another abbot, the Jhatsa Khempo, who was appointed a chairman (Chinese, *zhuxi*) of some kind at Dartsedo, and who was said to have declared at the conference that Mao Zedong was the true emanation of the Bodhisattva of Wisdom, Manjusri.[4]

From Lithang, letters were sent to the government in Lhasa appealing for help. Letters were also sent to high lamas in the Tibetan capital, such as Trijang Rinpoche, and administrators of the great monasteries. Other districts and principalities of Kham as Dergé, Gyalrong, Tawu, Tsawarong, Nyarong and the Five Hor states were also sent missives, calling on them to revolt. There appears to have been a flurry of correspondence back and forth, the new Chinese road, in this one instance, helping the Khampas by enabling their secret couriers to travel more quickly across Kham than in the old days. An approximate date for launching the uprising appears to have been agreed upon, the eighteenth day of the first month of the Fire Monkey Year, which would be Tuesday, 28 February 1956.

Yunru Pön had brought about one thousand men with him to Tsachukha. Back on his own tribal lands, more fighters were being called up and further preparations were being made. Other tribes were equally busy with their preparations. Every big family was required to produce at least five rifles, and three fighters to go with it. Even the poorest were required to contribute at least a clip of rifle ammunition to the common pool. The chiefs of the other Lithang tribes, Gyangba Pön, Othog Pön, Deshung Pön and Diu Atrin of the Molashipa nomads, rode to Lithang Monastery with their warriors.

* * *

Towards the end of the nineteenth century, an extensive variety of foreign weapons, especially rifles, had managed to make their way to Eastern Tibet. For a Khampa man, a gun was the most prized of possessions. Even a destitute Khampa had to own at least an old musket, and ride his own horse, even if the latter was just a bony nag. The most common rifle in Eastern Tibet at the beginning of the twentieth century was one of Chinese manufacture, from the Qing Hanyang Arsenal, apparently copied from an ancient Mauser (Type 88) design. Khampas called it the *gya-gubo*. It took a five-round clip and had a thick barrel. Its soft lead bullet, the size of a finger, caused fearful wounds, but it wasn't very accurate. These had come with the Sichuan invasion force of 1905, which the Tibetans called *Dothal*. Hence the weapon was sometimes called the *Dothal* rifle.

A more popular weapon was the early Japanese Arisaka rifle called the *Ripin chakshup* or "Japan metal cover", because of its distinctive sliding bolt cover. One of the most admired and prized weapons in Kham (and elsewhere in Tibet) was a light and accurate rifle from Brno, Czechoslovakia, that Tibetans called *"pamaling"*, This was almost certainly the Mannlicher M1895 bolt-action rifle of Czech, but also German/Austrian, manufacture. Some of these weapons had a lion crest stamped on the shank of the barrel, hence the additional Tibetan name *"Senge Lemba"* (lion brand). The *Pamaling* could also have been the Czech Puška vz. 33, bolt-action rifle with the name

"Československá zbrojovka in Brno" stamped on the breach and the Czech lion crest on the shank of the barrel.

Also, much appreciated was the Russian Moisin-Nagant 1891 rifle that Tibetans called *urusu bura*, as well as the German Mauser Gewehr 98, which Tibetans just called "*mosa*", The long-barrel British Lee Metford rifles, that the Tibetans called *Tashi Ta-ring* or *Tashi Tra ring* (Lucky-Long-Slim) had been purchased by the Lhasa government in 1915 for the modern Tibetan army and later even distributed to local militias in Kham, especially in the war of 1918. This was later replaced by the shorter-barrel Lee Enfield rifles that Tibetans called *Inji kha-dum* or the "short mouth Englishman." At the time of the uprising, the Enfield was probably the most ubiquitous rifle in Eastern Tibet and its .303 cartridge the most widely available ammunition.

George Orwell made this insightful observation in a newspaper column: "The great age of democracy and of national self-determination was the age of the musket and the rifle . . . the musket was a fairly efficient weapon, and at the same time so simple that it could be produced almost anywhere. Its combination of qualities made possible the success of the American and French revolutions. After the musket came the breech-loading rifle. This was a comparatively complex thing, but it was cheap, easily smuggled and economical of ammunition. Even the most backward nation could always get hold of rifles from one source or another, so that Boers, Bulgars, Abyssinians, Moroccans—even Tibetans—could put up a fight for their independence, sometimes with success. But thereafter every development in military technique has favoured the State as against the individual, and the industrialized country as against the backward one."[5]

A few American Springfield rifles circulated in Eastern Tibet, but after World War II, the compact, lightweight U.S. M1 carbine, known to Khampas as "*khabingchang*" became a much-coveted personal weapon throughout Tibet. Everybody who could afford it, had to have one. When my family travelled to Lhasa in 1949, our caravan leader Thundup *Genba* carried my father's carbine on his back.

The U.S. army Colt automatic pistol also became a popular sidearm in Kham. It was known by the pidgin Chinese-Tibetan term, *chisi popli* or by the more fitting contraction "*pop*". Another handgun that had earlier been in high demand throughout Tibet was the Mauser "broom-handle" automatic pistol called the *sisi lendu*. Khampas treasured their weapons, and it was not unusual to find rifles, especially muskets, with gold and silver decorative inlay work and even set with bits of turquoise and coral. I once saw an old Czech rifle that had little gold spots on the side of the stock, each spot for a man killed, like the notches on the handle of a gunfighter's revolver in the old West.

A more functional addition to the rifle was a pair of long antelope horns mounted on the front of the rifle, that could be folded down to serve as a bipod to hold the weapon steady when you were firing it. In the open plains and mountains of Tibet, with the air so clear, you could see your enemy from a long way off. So, range and accuracy were qualities one was looking for in a weapon, not high rate-of-fire or automatic features. Since ammunition was scarce and expensive at best of times, every bullet had to count. Probably the most anyone had were a couple of hundred rounds. Generally, people might have fifty to a hundred rounds, while it was not uncommon for someone to just have ten or twenty cartridges for the rifle he had inherited from his father.

* * *

Around the second or the third day of Losar, the New Year, the chiefs and leaders were summoned to a secret meeting at the monastery. The Chinese found out about this meeting and prepared an ambush for Yunru Pön. Yunru rode with fifteen of his men to the monastery. The ambush took place at Saser la or Yellow Earth Pass between Lithang town and Tsachukha, though another informant claimed that it happened at a place called Chakta Tangra, and yet another at Tromchen Chukor. Everyone agreed that the ambush did take place though they differ on details. One Tibetan historian has mistakenly written that Yunru was killed at this ambush, which was the immediate cause of the uprising.[6]

It seems that about thirty or forty Chinese soldiers were waiting in ambush, hiding behind a low ridge by the pass. Their first volley killed Yunru Pön's secretary, Ga Sogyaltsang, and another fighter next to him.

But Yunru was quickly able to rally his men and counterattack. One informant claimed that eighteen Chinese were killed in that encounter. The surviving Chinese soldiers withdrew. What saved Yunru Pön that day was probably his commonplace appearance and simple way of dressing. Since he had not attended any Chinese meetings or banquets, the Chinese soldiers and officers were also not sure what he really looked like. Ga Sogyaltsang, the scion of an important Lithang family, was a tall, good-looking young man reportedly wearing a rich brocade robe with fur trimming. The Chinese soldiers probably thought that he was the leader—that he was Yunru Pön. Ga Sogyaltsang was shot in the head and fell off his horse. His body was recovered and taken to the monastery.

This was the first battle or skirmish of the Lithang uprising. Everyone knew that after this, there was no turning back.

The Chinese military camp was only a couple of miles away from the monastery. The old Guomindang fort had by now been expanded and heavily fortified. The Chinese had also requisitioned the derelict mansion of Dago Trepo nearby, which they had demolished and built a new fort there. A few years earlier, the Chinese had a garrison of about five hundred soldiers at Lithang, but due to the unrest caused by the announcement of the "Democratic Reforms", more troops were sent to Lithang from Chengdu. After the attack on Yunru Pön at Saser la, the Chinese retreated inside their fort and waited for reinforcements. When they saw bands of Lithangwa warriors riding into the plain from all directions, Colonel Pockmark (Hu Guojun, CO of the Southern Kandzé command) ordered that all gates and weak points be reinforced and barricaded.

Though most accounts of the fighting are sketchy, it appears that initially, the Lithangwas attempted a straightforward frontal assault. While others provided cover fire, a dozen young volunteers galloped their horses straight at the wooden gate of the main fort, dragging large bundles of burning twigs and branches behind on ropes. It appears that this was a tactic that Khampas had used successfully in earlier conflicts, and there was a method to it. Ideally, I was told, you had two riders dragging the flaming bundle between them. When they got close to the gate, they would turn their horses away, fanning out as it were, and release the ropes. The blazing bundle would roll up to the gate and set it on fire. But more often than not, the bundles wouldn't come up just right against the target, and the effort had to be repeated. Sometimes riders would have to dismount and manhandle the burning bundle into position, all of which made the whole business very uncertain and dangerous. That day, three or four Khampas were killed, but they managed to set the wooden door ablaze. When the flames died down, it became apparent that the loss of lives had been for nothing. The Chinese had put up a solid stone and earth barrier behind the door.

The one weak point in the Chinese defences was its water supply. Normally the garrison got its water from a stream that flowed by the forts from the hills above the town. Now the Lithangwas dammed the stream and diverted it away from the forts. One evening, around sunset, a contingent of Chinese soldiers sneaked out from one fort and started to tear down the stone and earth barrier across the stream. The Lithangwas attacked the soldiers at the dam, who fought back. The Chinese also got covering fire from the fort. They had one machine gun there that made it difficult for the Lithang was to close in with the Chinese.

But as dusk fell, more Khampa fighters crawled up to the Chinese position by the stream, and some got close enough to use their swords and daggers. The Chinese soldiers fought back, lobbing hand grenades at the approaching Khampas. One group of Khampa fighters was pinned down and in a desperate situation for a time. But the Tibetans had the tactical advantage of this position and by nightfall had killed some of the Chinese there and forced the rest to retreat to the fort. Then the Tibetans built the damn up again and blocked the Chinese water supply. Some days later, the Chinese tried again, and although they did get a flow of water going for a while, the Tibetans attacked and stopped the stream. Over the days, more and more Chinese bodies could be seen piled around the banks of the stream.

The siege of the Chinese fort was not, militarily speaking, a very organized affair. Some contingents from the different tribes had thrown up stone and earth barricades, *zingra*, or dug shallow trenches to protect their positions. A few groups had just camped a little way off, waiting for the big fight they could join in. It is not clear how well these different groups worked together, but they were not disciplined units in a trained military force that could be coordinated in an exact or orderly fashion. It also appears that they did not operate under a single unified command and that the chiefs and their lieutenants would meet, discuss and argue about whatever course of action each group felt should be undertaken.

Yunru Pön was the paramount chief, *primus inter pares*, and everyone respected him and deferred to him, but he was not an overall military leader in the sense of a general giving out orders and expecting everyone to obey them unquestioningly. Much time and many lives were wasted in uncoordinated attacks on the Chinese forts by one tribal contingent or the other, with little consultation or coordination with other groups.

I was told this strange story of one such attack by Athar Norbu, who claimed to have heard it from someone who was there at Lithang at the time. After repeated attacks on the Chinese fort and repeated failures, one large group of Khampa fighters sat down to deliberate on a fresh course of action. During the meeting, one of their number, went into a spontaneous trance, what Tibetans call *thogbe*, and announced that he was the local protective deity and would personally lead the charge to wipe out the 'Red Chinese Enemies of the Dharma' (*tendra-gyamar*).

Everyone was excited, and morale, which had dropped in the last few days, soared again. The next day at dawn, the fighters got ready for the attack. The medium, now in full godly regalia (borrowed from the monastery) and armed with a sword—trembled and shook as monks performed the *chendre* or invocatory rites. As soon as the deity took possession of the medium, he rose, snarling and hissing, from his seat and climbed up on the rampart and brandished his sword in the air.

"A single shot rang out—tak-ka!" Athar told me, " . . . and the oracle fell over backwards on the ground. Right on his forehead, dead centre, was a hole. And that was that. No, he wasn't a fake. No one there had any doubts about the genuineness of the possession of the oracle. Perhaps it's just that their days were over, and it was another sort of world now."

Then the news came that Chinese reinforcements were marching to Lithang. Chinese troops were transported by truck from Chengdu and Dartsedo to Minyak Ra'ngakhar. The motor road then turned north-west to Kandzé, Chamdo and Lhasa. To get to Lithang, you still had to use horses and pack animals or walk, and it was about an eight-day march to Lithang from Minyak Ra'ngakhar. The Lithang chieftains and their lieutenants now gathered at the monastery to discuss this new situation. Some leaders suggested that they ride out and ambush the Chinese relief force, but the messenger was certain that this force was a powerful one, about twenty thousand men.

Diu Atrin, chief of the nomads from the Molashi grasslands, was for retreating deeper into the mountains, and fighting a guerrilla style war against the Chinese. He spoke about the futility of confronting the Chinese head-on. The abbot of Lithang Monastery, and the four administrative heads appealed to the fighters to stay and defend the monastery. After more discussion, Yunru Pön volunteered to stay and defend the monastery, as did Othog Pön and Deshung Pön. Diu Atrin said he and his men would also stay and fight at the monastery for the time being, but he was not convinced that it was the best way to fight the Chinese. Everyone was aware that Diu Atrin had reserved the right to leave the monastery when he saw fit, but no one raised any objection. Diu Atrin, although not one of the leading *Ra* chiefs, was an old warrior, someone who had fought the Chinese before and had a reputation for courage and cunning.

Now with news of the Chinese advance spreading throughout Lithang, the townspeople, farmers and nomads—men, women and children—began crowding into the monastery for protection. All available food supplies in the surrounding countryside were brought into the monastery, including whatever weapons and ammunition there were remaining in the town and countryside. Even the old muskets, swords and spears which were normally votive offerings in the monastery *gonkhang*, the temple of fierce protective deities, were now taken down and distributed among the monks and those who might not have weapons of their own. The blacksmiths and other metal-workers of the town were now kept busy repairing old weapons, making black powder for the muskets, and also resizing the more available .303 Lee Enfield cartridges to fit the breach of other rifles.

A stout twelve-foot wall surrounded the monastery on all sides. The wall and all the buildings and temples within it were constructed solidly of stone and rammed earth. Since the monastery was located against the mountainside, most of the buildings were sited *en échelon*, the building behind being somewhat higher than the one before it, so that nearly every rooftop provided a clear field of fire down on the plain. Now everyone worked on putting up barricades on the rooftops and cutting embrasures on the top of the monastery wall to shoot through. In about a week, when most of the preparations had been made, the Chinese army finally arrived at Lithang. Colonel Pockmark's soldiers at the fort gave a huge cheer when the advance guard marched in from the West.

Dorje Sherap, a young monk of Lithang Monastery, mentions his first impression of this force.

> The next day, the PLA moved across the plain. From the monastery, you could see for over fifty miles. I don't know how many thousands came, but they set up camp in a way that stretched out very far— probably to show off their numbers. The soldiers went to work digging trenches to let everybody know that they weren't going anywhere. They brought all kinds of automatic weapons and big artillery that was pointed at the monastery. The resistance had nothing like that— just different kinds of rifles, many of them antiques—and our stock of ammunition was not very good. But we had enough food to last for a long time. If the Chinese wanted a siege, that was fine with us. The siege lasted for one month and twenty-seven days.[7]

Another source mentions that the siege lasted for only twenty-seven days. The Chinese did not attempt a major offensive for a week or so, and just kept up a steady artillery barrage that caused a lot of damage and casualties inside the monastery. Most of the Khampas had never encountered artillery before, and initially, there was some panic among the defenders. But Yunru Pön and other leaders went around the defences and talked to their men, reassuring them and raising their morale. Soon people learned to take cover when they heard an incoming round, so although there were still casualties, the defenders gradually accommodated themselves to the artillery fire as best as they could. A few men attempted to flee from the monastery but were gunned down by the Chinese.

I was told that most of the artillery pieces used were small mountain-guns, and mortars that the Chinese had transported in sections on mule-back and not as destructive as bigger guns that could have been used if the motor road had extended to Lithang at that time.

Under the cover of their artillery fire, the Chinese moved their troops closer to the monastery, digging trenches and then rushing forward and putting up barricades and then digging trenches behind it. The defenders now got a chance to shoot at the attackers effectively, and many of the Khampas were crack shots. If a Chinese in the front trenches got careless, the top of his head would be blown off by a Khampa bullet. It also became apparent to the defenders that the Chinese were positioning themselves for a major assault.

Two separate accounts mention attempts by the Chinese to dig a tunnel (or tunnels?) under the monastery and launch a surprise attack. In one account by Baritsang Dawa Tsering, the Tibetans became aware of the digging "simply by kneeling down and putting our ears close to the ground."[8] Finally, the enemy broke through to the surface and started to come out from the tunnel one by one. The defenders were ready. As soon as one Chinese emerged from the tunnel, he was grabbed by several Tibetans who threw him to one side—while others stabbed him to death. As there was no gunfire, the unsuspecting Chinese kept on sending soldiers. Only after thirty or so Chinese soldiers had been killed silently, the defending Tibetans were forced to shoot a soldier who made a grab for his machine gun as he came out. The Chinese were now alerted to this danger and stopped sending any more troops through the tunnel.

Then one day, the Chinese signalled with a white flag and said they would send someone into the monastery to talk. Sogri Khetsun, one of the few Tibetans who had an official rank in the Communist Chinese administration, walked up to the monastery and was allowed in. It took a little while for him to get inside the monastery as the defenders had to remove all the stone and wood piled in front of the gate to reinforce it. Once inside, Sogri Khetsun looked around at the destruction caused by the artillery and said: 'I am sorry to see all this death and destruction here. But I have come to tell you that it will get worse. A decision has been made to send aeroplanes to bomb the monastery. Everyone here, women, children, men and monks, will be killed, and the monastery completely destroyed if you do not surrender. Believe me, this will happen.'[9]

Many of the Khampa leaders in the monastery knew Sogri Khetsun well, so they talked to him freely and asked him about the aeroplanes and about the Chinese strength and plans. From a few accounts, it appears that Sogri Khetsun, although a Communist official, did his best to mediate honestly between the Tibetans and the Chinese, and would help out his fellow Khampa with sound advice and information. The Lithangwas knew he was telling the truth when he warned them about the aeroplane attack, but they finally sent him back to the Chinese with the message that no one would surrender.[*]

The next day one aeroplane flew over Lithang Monastery and began to drop bombs.

The first bomb hit the large rock face opposite the stream just west of the monastery and made an impressive noise. The other bombs fell inside the monastery, though they did not do much damage. In fact, it was less damage than the artillery had caused, but this was the first time that many of the people in the monastery had ever seen an aeroplane, much less one that dropped bombs on them. It made many of them nervous. That evening a meeting was called with all the leaders. No one wanted to surrender, but it was suggested that the women, children and older lamas escape.

Diu Atrin now spoke up. "Right now, the mountains to the rear of the monastery are free of Chinese soldiers. So, this is probably the

---

[*] A year later Sogri Khetsun escaped from Dartsedo and joined the resistance at Rakha. He became well known as a fierce fighter.

last chance for me and my men to leave the monastery. If the Chinese manage to move their positions any closer now, they will be able to completely surround the monastery. I want to get my men out tonight and continue this fight from the interior, from a place where we will have a better chance at winning."

Yunru Pön was clear about his decision. "I will never leave this monastery. I will remain here and defend it till I die. I agree that the women and children should leave, and so perhaps should the old lamas and others if they wish. All fighting men who want to leave the monastery should join Diu Atrin and the Molashipa tribesmen and continue the fight."

That night all those who wanted to escape left from the rear of the monastery and climbed up the mountain. Diu Atrin and his men, along with some other groups of fighters, left for the interior of the country. Yunru Pön, his companion Dago Trepo, and all his men stayed, as did some of the other chiefs and their men. It seems that, about less than half the defending force at the monastery managed to escape. Those remaining prepared to meet the Chinese attack.

It came the following morning, preceded by an artillery barrage, the longest that the defenders had endured till now. Howitzer shells slammed into the monastery walls, and mortar shells fell on the buildings inside and in the alleys and byways, killing many people. Finally, the Chinese guns breached the monastery walls in a few places.

There was a pause in the fighting, a moment of silence. Then the strident blaring of bugles and trumpets reverberated from the Chinese positions, followed by massed shouts of "*sha, sha*. Kill! Kill!" Immediately after, thousands of soldiers scrambled out from their trenches and barricades and charged. The rifle fire from the monastery cut down the first wave of attackers. But the Chinese charged again and again. When they got to the breach at the wall, they lobbed grenades inside before rushing in. For about an hour, the defenders managed to prevent the Chinese from flooding through. There was desperate fighting at close quarters, with Khampas using their broad-swords and the Chinese their bayonets. More Chinese poured in through the breaches in the front wall. The Tibetans retreated from the front courtyard just behind the

wall and the gate, and to the temples and buildings. There was a pause
in the Chinese attack as the front courtyard was open ground and there
was little cover. Chinese soldiers who tried to cross it were shot down.

Now the Chinese broke through the eastern and western walls
and the defenders were forced to retreat further into the monastery.
House by house, building by building, the Chinese began to push the
Khampas back and the fighting in the side streets and alleys became
savage. The Chinese had the advantage of fighting with submachine
guns, the Type 50 burp guns. They also had American Thompson
submachine guns and hand grenades. The Chinese used the Type
67 stick grenades or "potato mashers", which were effective in such
combat. The Type 67 has a five-second-fuse and the Tibetans learned
that the delay sometimes gave them time to toss it back to the Chinese,
with satisfying effect. One advantage for the defenders in this sort of
close fighting was that the Tibetans were now able to pick up weapons
and ammunition from dead Chinese soldiers. It was desperately needed
as the Khampas had begun to run out of ammunition.

Yunru had been fighting fiercely, moving from position to position
and rallying the defenders to stand firm. But he was forced to retreat
as the Chinese poured into the monastery courtyard. He and his
men backed into the main Assembly Hall, the Jangchub Chökorling,
where the monks met for prayers and services, and where the thrones
of the Third Dalai Lama and the Shogdru Kyamgon were installed.
Dago Trepo and some other fighters had also retreated to this hall.
When Yunru and Dago Trepo met, they embraced. They had a brief
conversation, which my informant did not overhear, but he saw them
both walk over to the adjoining temple, the Shakya Thubpa Phodrang,
the Palace of the Buddha Sakyamuni. There, both took off their *ghawu*,
their amulet cases and placed them on the lap of the giant Buddha
statue there.

Yunru Pön and Dago Trepo believed that their protective amulets
had prevented them from being struck by bullets or shrapnel (and
so far, both had suffered no injury) but they now wanted to give up
their amulets since the Chinese were swarming into the monastery.
Both men wanted to die fighting than be captured. There were many

monks and fighters who had fallen back on this main building of the monastery and at least a few of them witnessed this last meeting of Yunru and Dago Trepo.

It was now also obvious to most defenders that they were losing the fight. The front courtyard was entirely in the hand of the Chinese, and they herded all their captured prisoners, mostly monks, there. The Chinese began to attack the main Assembly Hall and the fighters there, including Yunru Pön and the others, slowly retreated to the other temples and monks' quarters (*drasha*) behind the Assembly Hall.

All the older monks and scholars and those who were not fighting had earlier gathered at one of the main colleges at the rear of the monastery, the Shiwa Khamtsen. One of the geshe there saw thick smoke rising from the adjoining building and he shouted a warning to the others. Everyone feared that the Chinese were going to burn down the entire monastery to force the defenders out.

An hour or so after midnight, Yunru Pön, accompanied by just two of his men, came to the quarters of Nor-ri Khensur Rinpoche. It appears that Yunru had now completely run out of ammunition. He sat down and talked to the old lama. No one overheard his exact words. The Lama held Yunru's hand and leaned forward and touched his forehead to Yunru's in blessing and affection, as is the custom. Then Yunru got up, and as he was leaving the room, he was overheard saying, "*Dha lo de.* (Now my heart is at peace)".

Yunru sent a message to the Chinese calling for a *thungsi* or an official translator. A Bathang Tibetan in Chinese uniform came up to Yunru's position, which was now in the apartment of the monk official of the Dhongetsang family. Yunru declared that he would now surrender as he had no more ammunition. He then added, "I am chieftain of Lithang and will not surrender to any Chinese soldier. I will only give up my weapon to your leader, Colonel Pockmark."

When the translator got back to the Chinese position and delivered the message, the Colonel became very excited at this good news. Other reports make no mention of the Colonel specifically, and just speaks of two Chinese commanders. But we may assume that Colonel Pockmark was there at the monastery. He and another senior officer came up to the building where Yunru Pön was waiting and announced their presence. Through the translator, they also instructed Yunru Pön and others with him, to give up their weapons.

Yunru Pön tossed out two rifles, one by one, from the window of the apartment. Then he stepped out of the doorway and walked down the alleyway to the intersection where the Chinese officers and a large contingent of soldiers were waiting. He walked up to Colonel Pockmark and is said to have asked where he was going to be taken. The translator replied that he would be taken to the Chinese headquarters and could rest there. The term the translator used was the generic term *gya-khang* or just Chinese house. Yunru replied that he had never been inside a Chinese house and did not intend to step in one now. He pulled out a 45. Colt automatic pistol (*chisi-popli*) that he had hidden inside the long sleeve (*tsara phutung*) of his sheepskin robe and shot Colonel Pockmark in the head. He may have also shot the other officer. The Chinese soldiers opened fire on Yunru. Some of the Khampa fighters, probably Yunru's men, fought back and there was a chaotic firefight before these fighters were either killed or pushed back. The Chinese were now in force inside the monastery.

One of the earliest eyewitness informants on the Lithang Uprising had his testimony included in the report of the International Commission of Jurists (ICJ), Geneva, in 1959. "Yunru Pön Sonam Wangyal, 25 years old, was killed by 500 soldiers firing on him. I saw him being killed."[10] Another eyewitness, a steward of Lithang Monastery, testified in a subsequent ICJ report (1960) that "One Lama, Ga-Nori (Nor-ri Khensur Rinpoche) an ex-abbot in his seventies (who Yunru Pön had met earlier) was shot in the eye and killed by Chinese soldiers whilst he was sitting in meditation in his quarters."[11]

Yunru's body was riddled with bullets. He had been shot so many times that his face was unrecognizable. His pistol was found with the entire magazine discharged. Colonel Pockmark and the Chinese officer accompanying him were both killed. After the fighting, the Chinese dragged what was left of Yunru's body down to the main courtyard in the front of the monastery. Some captured fighters and lamas were bought before the body to try and identify it. Yunru's torn body was tied to the large stone edict pillar in the centre of the square. For a few days, many Chinese soldiers came out of curiosity to view the body of the fallen chieftain.

That night, after Yunru Pön's death, his cousin, Dago Trepo, kept on fighting in another part of the monastery. Finally, he was also struck down. A grenade blast is said to have wounded him mortally. It is not clear what exactly happened. One account says that he picked up a hand-grenade that a Chinese soldier had thrown, and was throwing it back when it exploded. Another said that he might have used a grenade to kill himself. Most probably, the former is correct, for the grenade did not kill him immediately. With the help of one of his men, he dragged himself to the chamber of Gyen Lushang, a geshe.

He asked the geshe to perform the *phowa* ritual, which is the practice of consciousness transfer at death. If done correctly by a lama, or by yourself in the prescribed manner, it is believed that the passage to your next birth can be achieved without trauma or disorientation. Dago Trepo told the geshe that it was difficult for him to die as he had his father's small *liku* (bell-metal image of the Buddha) with him. He overlooked it when he had earlier placed his own amulet case on the large statue of the Buddha at the Shakya Thubpa Phodrang temple. He took the small image from under his bloody shirt and told Gyen Lushang that he should have it as the *pho-ten*, the offering that is made to the lama who performs the phowa ritual. He also asked the geshe to pray for him. He looked around at his men and asked if anyone knew what had happened to Yunru Pön. One of the men told him about the shooting of the two Chinese officers and the death of Yunru Pön. Dago Trepo said that the right and proper thing had happened.

An old couple bought a kettle of water and offered him a drink. He thanked them and drank a little. He then transferred his phowa, his consciousness. It was around the time of the first cockcrow.

13

WIND AND WILDFIRE

NYARONG

I wasn't expecting a woman to be the leader of a major Khampa resistance force. Hemingway's description of Pilar, the *mujer* of Pablo, the tough, foul-mouthed, part-gypsy peasant woman and *de facto* commander of the anti-fascist guerrilla band in *For Whom the Bell Tolls*, hadn't faded entirely from my memory. But this Tibetan woman before me was so small, no more than five feet tall, and slight in build. Although age and adversity had taken its inevitable toll on her, it wasn't difficult to make out that she had been good looking once, perhaps even beautiful. She spoke softly, and it was hard to catch everything she said.

I also had some problem with her Nyarong accent. She pronounced the name of Yunru as "Yende", and instead of calling him *Pön* or "chieftain", she referred to him as Yende *sey* or "honourable son" of the Yunru family. So, for all these reasons, when she told me, quite casually, that she had personally received a letter from Yunru Pön, the leader of the Lithang Uprising, at the beginning of 1956, calling on all Khampas to rise up against the Chinese, it didn't immediately register with me.

Her name was Dorje Yudon, and she was born in the Water-Bird year (1932). She and her older sister Norzin Lhamo were from the

Miloktsang family, descendants of the warriors sent by the Tibetan Emperor Trisong Deutscn (755–97 CE) to guard the eastern frontiers of the Tibetan empire, and "never return" (*milok*) to Central Tibet. The two sisters had jointly married the paramount chief of Upper Nyarong, Nima Gyaritsang. I knew the Gyaritsang family well and was a good friend of their oldest son, Lodi Gyaltsen. I was then researching my first book, *Horseman in the Snow* (1979), the story of Aten, a freedom fighter from Nyarong, and talked to the Gyaritsang family about the history of the region. It was during one of the conversations that Dorje Yudon's personal saga gradually unfolded.

Towards the end of 1955, the Chinese were becoming uneasy with the stubborn Khampa opposition to "Democratic Reforms," and announced a major conference of Khampa chiefs and lamas at Dartsedo. Nima Gyaritsang, who had been appointed the Chief Administrator of Nyarong, was ordered to attend. When most of the Khampa leaders arrived at Dartsedo, it became clear that they were to be held as hostages. Back at Nyarong, Dorje Yudon had received the letter from Yunru Pön to her husband calling on the Nyarong people to revolt against the Chinese on the eighteenth day of the first Tibetan month.

She, at once, called a meeting of tribal leaders at the Gyaritsang stronghold of Ralung in Upper Nyarong, and an agreement was reached to raise a resistance army. Solemn pledges were made and weapons and horses collected from every family. Dorje Yudon sent a written message to Yunru Pön committing Nyarong to the uprising. She then received another message from Lithang stating that twenty-three chieftains of Kham had agreed to stage uprisings on the 18th. Her older sister Norzin Lhamo travelled to Dartsedo to inform Nima of what was happening and urge him to return home. But he and the other Khampa leaders there were now virtually prisoners. When Norzin Lhamo was returning home, she was also held at the Chinese garrison at Renuk in Nyarong.

The Chinese started a campaign of assassinations against Khampa leaders who they suspected of being counter-revolutionaries. Six members of the Gyarachipa family (of Lower Nyarong) were shot dead at their home by Chinese troops and *hur-tsunpa* collaborators. The head of the family, Gyurme, was away in Dartsedo for the conference.[1] But the Chinese found it difficult to ambush Dorje Yudon, as she had a contingent of eighteen fully armed and trusted men guarding the Gyaritsang home. These young men were called *taktru* or tiger cubs.

One day a Tibetan collaborator, Tsering Phuntsok, managed to sneak into the house and pull out a hand grenade.[2] Dorje Yudon's maid, a strong country girl named Lashi, saw him, and grabbing him from behind, wrestled him against the wall. Dorje managed to reach for the pistol beside her and shot the assassin dead. Dorje now realized that though she had not completed her preparations, there was little time left for her to act. That same day the Chinese attempted to arrest Dorje's uncle and Nima's grandmother at a public meeting, but the two managed to get away before the soldiers closed in on them. Four days before the agreed-upon date for the Khampa Uprising, Dorje Yudon launched her own uprising on the fourteenth day of the first month of the Fire Monkey year, on 25 February 1956. She attacked the small Chinese outposts and offices in Upper Nyarong and killed most of the Chinese in the area, including some collaborators. These collaborators were Khampas who had official positions (usually as interpreters) in the Chinese administration and were known as *shoshi gambu*, probably a corruption of the Chinese *shuming ganbu* or translation cadre.

This problematic subject of the execution of collaborators came up much later in exile, during a family conversation. Dorje insisted that the incident had resulted from a misunderstanding. She claimed she was on the eastern bank of the Nyakchu River while her men, on the other side of the river, rounded up a number of Tibetans working for the Chinese. One of her men shouted across to her, asking if they should throw the prisoners into the river. The Nyakchu is a powerful river, and its roaring and hissing can be deafening. Dorje Yudon claims that she could not hear the man clearly and thought that he had asked her if they should bring the prisoners across. So, she shouted at them to do that, and rode back to her house. During that family conversation, Atring, a tall, strapping Khampa with a magnificent moustache, who had been with Dorje that day, said he recalled her giving orders for the prisoners to be thrown in the river.[3] Dorje Yudon, in her characteristically soft-spoken but stubborn way, insisted that all of them had misunderstood her orders, and would not be budged from her standpoint.

Once she had settled affairs in Upper Nyarong, she headed south, gathering more weapons and fighters along the way. Dressed in a man's fur-lined robe, with a pistol strapped to her side, she rode before her warriors. Most of the remaining Chinese soldiers and officials scattered around Nyarong fled to Drugmo Dzong (The Castle of the Female Dragon) the traditional headquarters of the old Lhasa governor (*nyarong chikyap*) now the center of the Chinese administration. The castle was stormed, with Dorje Yudon herself leading the many charges, but the thick walls of that old castle were built to withstand such attacks. According to Atring, Dorje Yudon declared that she would personally shoot any man who fell back or retreated during the attack.[4] Many fighters were killed before the castle wall. Dorje Yudon now laid siege to the castle, but her task proved to be more difficult than she had anticipated. The Chinese garrison was well stocked with food and ammunition, and they also had a spring of clean water within the walls.

After a month, six hundred troops from the Eighteenth Division were rushed from Kandzé to relieve the beleaguered garrison at the Castle of the Female Dragon. Dorje Yudon got wind of this and took her men north to Upper Nyarong and successfully ambushed the relief force. Many Chinese soldiers were killed, but a small contingent broke through the Khampa lines and managed to get into the castle. Then a considerably larger Chinese military force poured in from Drango and Tawu in the east. Chinese troops managed to take over Lumora Monastery, where her sister's young son, Lodi Gyaltsen, was the incarnate lama, and held him hostage.

Nearly all Eastern Tibet was now up in arms. The Chinese responded by announcing a "peaceful suppression of rebels policy" whereby everyone who had taken up arms would not be punished or have criminal charges brought against them and would be allowed to retain their land and possessions, only having to surrender their weapons. Military headquarters in Chengdu now determined that the "political education" the Khampa chiefs and lamas had received during the conference at Dartsedo, had sufficiently persuaded them of the correctness of "Democratic Reforms" and the "Collection of Weapons" policies. All these leaders were now released and sent back, with Chinese military escorts, to their various localities, where they would begin negotiations with the "rebel bandits" and persuade them to give up their arms.

Khampa leaders sent back home under this new directive, that I know of, were Gyari Nyima of Nyarong, Gyarachipa Gyurme of Nyarong, Chigotsang Tenzin Dhakpa of Nyarong, Chago Tobden of Dergé, Khangsar Yedo of Kandzé, Chanzo Yeshi Dorje of Drango, Mawo Chanzo of Tawu, Gyakpontsang Chime Dorje of Lingkashi, Gya Yonten of Bathang, Labka Rinpoche, Pön Nyenang Dawa of Chatreng, Lobsang Gendun of Chatreng, and Sori Khetsun and a senior abbot from Lithang. This is a sketchy and incomplete list. My informant from Chatreng told me that Chatreng had sent twenty representatives to the Dartsedo conference, though he could only remember three names. It also appears that prior to their release, the chieftains and lamas had been taken on a tour of major Chinese cities and industrial centres to impress them with China's size, industrial power and modern advancement.

When Gyari Nyima crossed over into Nyarong territory, he took this opportunity to shake off his Chinese escort and return to his home and family. The Chinese now sent in large-scale reinforcements to Nyarong, bringing troop strength there to about 30,000, according to an American scholar.[5] The Nyarong resistance began to crumble. This force of about 1,000 fighters now split into two groups and retreated into the mountains. One contingent was led by Gyari

Nyima's uncle and brother and the other by Dorje Yudon and Gyari Nyima himself. Dorje and her husband's group travelled for months in the high mountains, constantly skirmishing with Chinese patrols, sometimes falling into ambushes and taking increasing casualties till only about a hundred or so fighters were left. The Gyari family had four children with them, and Dorje Yudon gave birth to another child during that time. As advancing Chinese units attempted to encircle the band, they fought their way further and further west till they were eventually headed for Lhasa.

* * *

Before concluding this account of the Nyarong resistance, it should be mentioned that Dorje Yudon was not the first female warrior in Nyarong history. Another woman from the Gyaritsang family, Chime Dolma (the mother of Gyari Nyima), rose against the Sichuan warlord governor Liu Wenhui in 1936. She and her warriors attacked the Castle of the Female Dragon and drove out the Chinese garrison there. The Chinese came back in greater numbers, forcing her to retreat, but she recaptured the castle in 1939. Finally, the Sichuan warlord army, reinforced with regular Guomindang troops, attacked Chime Dolma and forced her to retreat to her tribal land in Upper Nyarong. They laid siege to the family castle (Gyari *phodrang*) and burnt it to the ground. Chime Dolma came out of the burning building with a sword in her hand, apparently not prepared to surrender, and received several gunshot wounds. Finally, she was disabled by a bullet to her leg and captured.

She was taken in chains to the Castle of the Female Dragon and executed by firing squad. Before she fell, she was said to have cried out these words: "Never will I submit to the Chinese. I die for the freedom of my people and my land. People of Nyarong, do not forget me." My informant Nyarong Aten became angry with me when I inadvertently offended him by saying that people only made such patriotic statements in stories. He insisted I write it all down; her exact declaration, word for word. Chime Dolma's courage and defiance does seem to have resonated throughout Eastern Tibet.

Phüntso Wangye, the Tibetan Communist leader from Bathang, had highlighted Chime Dolma's uprising and execution in a "revolutionary" song he wrote in 1944 (that Tharchin published in the *Tibet Mirror*) calling on Tibetans to rise and take revenge against the "uncivilized" Chinese who treated Tibetans "as animals" and stole their wealth.[6] Phüntso Wangye later claimed he was merely referring to Chinese warlords and the Guomindang regime and not Communist China. But that explanation and his slavish devotion to Mao and Communist China did not save him from eighteen years of solitary confinement in China's top political prison, Quincheng No.1—Q1, also called China's Bastille.

BATHANG

One fact that comes through is that the resistance organizations in Lithang, Bathang, Chatreng, Lingkashi and Nyarong had all communicated with each other and attempted to coordinate their efforts, starting their uprising roughly around the same date.

In Bathang, the uprising started nine days before Lithang. The Chinese administrator and the garrison, when attacked by the Bathang insurgents, barricaded themselves behind the walls of the old castle that had originally been the headquarters of the Ba Depa, the traditional chief of Bathang, who was a descendent of the Lhasa governors who administered Bathang in the past. As with Lithang, the Khampas in Bathang cut off the water supply of the castle and attacked it day and night. But the Chinese garrison managed to hold out, and radioed headquarters for help. Some days later, two Chinese bombers from Chengdu flew over Bathang and commenced bombing the area. Their primary target was the monastery, generally referred to as Ba Chödé Gon, or Ba Chödé Gaden Phendeling, to give it its full and formal name.

This monastery was not the original Chödé Gon, which was looted of its great art treasures, demolished and burned to the ground in 1905 by the Chinese administrator of Sichuan province, Zhao Erfeng. According to American missionary sources, "Chao's (Zhao) efficient executioners beheaded Bathang's chief lama, and scores of Khampas. The Chinese buried some Khampas alive and boiled others to death in the monastery's enormous brass tea cauldrons."[7] Over the years, the Tibetans of Bathang managed to rebuild the monastery on a smaller and less resplendent scale. But the seventy-three bombs that Chinese planes dropped for twelve days straight, according to Lobsang Gyaltsen, an eyewitness chronicler of these events,[8] destroyed the monastery and many houses as well, and killed scores of monks and civilians. Aware that Chinese reinforcement were marching to Bathang, survivors now took to the mountains and commenced guerrilla operations against the Chinese. What was left of the monastery was completely flattened and razed during the Cultural Revolution.

LINGKASHI

Besides the main town of Bathang, the Chinese planes also dropped bombs on a northern enclave of the Bathang region known as Lingkashi, and destroyed the principal monastery there, the Chaba Gonpa. Lingkashi is the name of the valley of the upper Bathang river, which makes a near-complete bend on itself, creating a circular gorge-like valley that makes the place impregnable to outside attacks and inaccessible to outsiders.

This topographical advantage and the added convenience of only having to cross a single pass, from the Lingkashi valley, to descend on the main Lithang–Bathang trail, had given the Lingkashiba, as the inhabitants of this area are known, a reputation for occasional banditry and lawlessness. In early 1950, just before he set out on his journey to India from Bathang, George Patterson met the Lingkashi chief, Gyakpontsang Chime Dorje, whom he refers to as the "bandit chief", and claims he challenged him to a horse race which he, Patterson, won. Patterson calls Chime Dorje a "charming rogue" and describes him as the "burly, laughing young chieftain of the wildest crowd of bandits amongst all the warlike Khampas."

At the time of the bombing of Chaba Monastery, Chime Dorje was at Dartsedo with other Khampa leaders and lamas at the notorious "conference" mentioned earlier. Upon his release, he was sent back to Lingkashi to spread the policy of "peaceful suppression of rebels" and to persuade his people to give up their arms. Instead, he led the Lingkashiba people on a long war against Communist China, which ended for him and his remaining fighters, in a quite literal disappearance into what might be called the mists of legend—which I will elaborate on in a future chapter.

CHATRENG

Across the Lithang–Bathang section of the Dartsedo–Lhasa road which Tibetans called the Shung Lam or the "official" or "main route," all the way south to the border of the Chinese province of Yunnan, is the district of Chatreng. It is a comparatively low-lying region of agricultural valleys, drained by streams flowing south into the Yangtse. Agriculture, plus animal husbandry in the higher elevations of the region, provided the Chatrengwas, a relatively comfortable standard of living. The people of Chatreng are industrious and skilled metalworkers, famous throughout Kham, indeed all the way to Lhasa and Central Tibet, for the manufacture of kitchen utensils, but principally for their brass ladles, which every self-respecting Tibetan housewife must have at least half a dozen, of varying sizes, hanging in a neat, shiny row on her kitchen wall.

There is a degree of specialization in such industries in Eastern Tibet. As I mentioned before, Lithang is well known for the manufacture of silver jewellery. Dergé is, of course, the most famous centre for high quality metalwork in all of Tibet and is famous for its religious objects: principally silver and bronze Buddhist images, and the extensive range of ritual objects: prayers wheels, bells, *dorje, ting* bowls, *ghawu* amulet boxes, but also for swords, daggers and muskets. Nyarong was known for its beautifully turned wooden bowls and wooden plates, which in the past, they sent annually to Lhasa as a tax. Nyarong Aten told me these dishes even graced the tables of the Potala and Norbulingka palaces.

But, in spite of the relative prosperity and cultural attainment of these places in Eastern Tibet, China's colonial ambitions in Kham (inspired by European and American expansion into Asia and Africa and described as such by the Viceroy of Sichuan in a memorial to the throne) went into high gear at the beginning of the twentieth century, bringing devastation to the region. "An American missionary, a gentleman of long experience of life on the frontier wrote, in the foreign press of Shanghai, of Chinese rule on the frontier in the following terms: 'There is no method of torture known that is not practiced in here on these Tibetans, slicing, skinning, boiling, tearing asunder, and all . . . . To sum up what China is doing here in Eastern Tibet, the main things are collecting taxes, robbing, oppressing, confiscating, and allowing her representatives to burn and loot and steal.'"[9]

And Chatreng, according to Eric Teichman, the British diplomat who negotiated the treaty of Rongbatsa between the Tibetans and Chinese in 1918, was "The principal thorn in the side of the Chinese administration in Eastern Tibet, and their chief obstacle in the subjugation of the border states."[10]

Chatreng revolted against the Chinese administration in 1905. Zhao Erfeng's army laid siege to Sampheling, Chatreng's principal monastery, with " . . . two thousand seasoned soldiers trained in Western-style military methods. Zhao's army was equipped with German-made rifles and four Krupps field guns."[11] Even with artillery, the Chinese could not breach the massive twenty-foot high, four-foot-thick walls of the monastery and only succeeded in capturing it through a ruse. "After fierce fighting between the monks and Chinese troops, Sampheling fell on June 19, 1906. Zhao ordered the surviving rebels be put to the sword. The slaughter of the monks became legendary among the Khampas." The monastery was burned to the ground.

In 1910, the Chinese garrison in Chatreng mutinied, and the local Khampas took advantage of this to overthrow Chinese rule. "Zhao Erfeng suppressed the uprising with his usual severity, leaving the natives of this turbulent district more than ever irreconcilable to Chinese rule."

In 1914 "a serious revolt in Drayab" encouraged Chatreng to again rise against Chinese authority, this time the new "republic" under president/dictator Yuan Shih-k'ai. "Both risings were duly suppressed", with the monastery of Yemdo in Drayab being burned to the ground and all monks and rebels being "exterminated".

In the war of 1918, the Chatreng was once again revolted and prepared to attack the Chinese headquarters at Bathang, but the Tibetan Central government forces were by then preparing to negotiate with the Chinese, and the Markham *teiji*, the Tibetan governor of Markham, sent emissaries to Chatreng who persuaded the Chatreng was to abandon their projected attack, much to the relief of the Chinese officials, businessmen, and Western missionaries in Bathang.

The subsequent years of internal conflict in China and the war with Japan provided the people of Eastern Tibet some respite from Chinese violence and depredation. In Chatreng itself, Sampheling Monastery was gradually rebuilt, and the lives of the people resumed its traditional cycle of agriculture, trade, industry and religious observances and festivals—spiced with the occasional blood feud and banditry.

My principal informant on Chatreng, Jhadötsang Tenzin Tsultrim, told me that he was born in the Fire-Mouse year (1936) when a rearguard unit of the second Red Army (under General He Long) crossed through this area on its way north to join the main Red Army at Shaanxi. A number of Red Army units were pushed so far west during the Long March by more powerful Guomindang forces that they ended up clashing with discernibly foreign Tibetans rather than with Nationalist troops or soldiers of the Sichuan warlord, Liu Wenhui.

Gyari Chime Dolma is said to have taken on the Red Army at Tawu and killed many Communist soldiers there. Mao Zedong, when recounting the "Long March" to American Communist propagandist, Edgar Snow, told him that one particular ". . . Mantzu Queen (possibly Chime Dolma) had an implacable hatred for Chinese of any variety." Her mountaineers sniped at the Reds and rolled huge boulders down to crush them and their pack animals. "This is our only foreign debt", Mao told Snow "humorously . . . and some day we must pay the Tibetans for the provisions we were obliged to take from them."[12]

When news came to Chatreng of the approach of the Red Army detachment, the women, children and elders left their homes and retreated to the inaccessible higher reaches of the mountains, while the men prepared to fight. Tenzin's mother, Dolma Chonzom, was pregnant with him at the time and gave birth to him on a remote mountainside. She named him Dre-sang or "cleansed of demons," the demons being, of course, the Chinese who Tibetans generally referred to as *Gya-dre* (Chinese demons) or *Gya-pang* (Chinese beggars). He was later given the name of Tenzin Tsultrim when he became a monk at the Sampheling Monastery.

There was a close relationship between Sampheling and the Great Monastery of Lithang, Sampheling even maintaining a college (*khamtsen*) within Lithang Monastery. So, there is no question that Chatreng was fully involved with Lithang (and Bathang) in planning of the 1956 Uprising. A region-wide muster or mobilization, traditionally called the "Eighteen-Sixty", meaning all men from the age of eighteen to the age of sixty, was declared. Tenzin claims that the Chinese garrison at Chatreng was only about 300-strong and could have been overwhelmed if the initial attack had been made swiftly and with the full collaboration of everyone concerned, but the usual discussions and arguments got in the way. The managers and stewards of the monastery insisted that all the boxes of silver kept at the Chinese headquarters should be handed over to the monastery. The Chinese got wind of what the Khampas were planning and barricaded themselves securely behind the walls of their encampment, which they shored up and reinforced. The Chatreng was diverted the stream, the only water supply, going into the Chinese fort, and commenced their attacks. Before long, the situation inside the Chinese camp became desperate. It became clear to the Khampas that the garrison would fall before any substantial Chinese reinforcement could get to the area.

Then one day, a single Chinese plane flew over and dropped a few bombs. It hit some houses below the monastery but didn't do any substantial damage. The next day a plane flew over the monastery again and dropped yellow and red leaflets printed in Tibetan, calling on the rebels to surrender. Then on the fourth day, at around one o'clock, three planes flew over and began a systematic bombing of the monastery. Tenzin said that when the planes came, the monks rushed inside the monastery to hide. An older monk shouted at Tenzin to go inside and take cover. But Tenzin was curious and stayed outside to see what the planes would do. No one had ever seen an aeroplane in Chatreng. Many monks gathered inside the main assembly hall (*tsogchen*) and started to perform religious services, beating drums and burning incense—to ward off the evil. That day the Chinese dropped at least a hundred bombs on the monastery— one hundred and sixty-seven, according to another eyewitness. Many of the buildings in the monastery were destroyed, and over a hundred monks killed, and many wounded. Tenzin recalls that even a number of the pet animals of the monks, *apso* dogs and cats, were killed. Some of the monks rushed out to the hillside behind the monastery and started to fire their rifles at the planes. But they were strafed by machine gun fire.

The Chinese most likely concentrated their bombing efforts on Chatreng rather than Lithang, as they could not send troop reinforcements from Chengdu and Dartsedo quickly to Chatreng like they could to Lithang—and the Chinese garrison at Chatreng was in real danger of being wiped out. But soon, reinforcements were being sent not only from Dartsedo but also from Yunnan. The Chinese also released the Chatreng leaders Labka Rinpoche and Pön Nyenang Dawa from the "conference" at Dartsedo and sent them home to convince the Chatrengwas to put down their arms and accept "Democratic Reforms." But as it happened in Nyarong and elsewhere, the "Peaceful Suppression of Rebels" policy fell apart very soon. A large Chinese force of five thousand troops from Yunnan now approached Chatreng. Pön Nyenang Dawa and his fighters retreated to the mountains and commenced guerrilla operations. The one-month peace broke down entirely.

Chinese reprisals were brutal. People were made to denounce each other. "Sons were forced to beat their fathers, daughters forced to beat their mothers." Many people, especially women, committed suicide. Many jumped in the swift-flowing waters of the Shorchu River that flows through the middle of Chatreng.[13]

Quietly and unhurriedly, Tenzin Tsultrim and his relatives collected food and provisions and got their horses and pack animals ready. Tenzin even managed to recover a few boxes of silver owed to him by a Gyalthangwa trader, before leaving his homeland forever. They headed for Lhasa.

* * *

The world heard nothing of the Great Khampa Uprising of 1956, nor the bombings of Lithang, Chatreng, Bathang, Drango and Chaba monasteries. That year the Hungarian Revolution dominated international news, especially after Soviet tanks rolled into Budapest and violently crushed the popular uprising, prompting even an ardent Marxist intellectual as Jean-Paul Sartre to write his first and probably only criticism of the Soviet Union, "Le Fantôme de Staline."

Darjeeling's relative proximity to Tibet did not make us any more aware of events in Kham than the rest of the world. The Indian press at the time, still took its cue from Fleet Street and Times Square, and *LIFE* and *Time* magazines were cheap and dominated the Indian newsstands. I was around eight then, but I remember *Time*'s 1957 "Man of the Year" cover illustration, an artist's depiction of three Hungarian Freedom Fighters. Another image from that period, probably from *LIFE*, is virtually imprinted in my memory: that of the military leader of this revolution, Pál Maléter, almost certainly because of his extraordinary lankiness and bizarre headgear, a leather Russian tank helmet with block padding in the front and sausage ribbings on the side.

There were no photographs in *LIFE* of events in Kham, but the following year in Kalimpong, the Reverend Tharchin, published in his newspaper, the *Tibet Mirror* (July 1, 1957) a series of pencil drawings, with accompanying accounts, of the bombings of Lithang, Chatreng, Bathang and Drango monasteries. These were drawn by Kargyal Thondup, a native of Chatreng who had managed to flee from his homeland after the bombing and escape to Lhasa. From the Tibetan capital, he made his way to Kalimpong where he met the Reverend Tharchin, who published his account of the destruction of the monasteries and the uprisings in Eastern Tibet. Tharchin realized how important such an eyewitness testimony was, and he attempted to get Indian and Western journalists and organizations interested in Kargyal Thondup's accounts. Thondup was interviewed by the BBC, with Tharchin translating for him. But only a few scattered press reports appeared in 1957 of the uprisings in Eastern Tibet and the bombings of the monasteries. The *Times* (of London) correspondent in Kathmandu filed a story that "The Khambs [*sic*] are reported to be restless"[14], with no explanation of what a "Khamb" was.

Kargyal Thondup remained in India, where he worked for the resistance and later the exile government. He also began work on putting together a comprehensive account of his native region and the war and destruction he had witnessed. It took him seventeen years to finish the book, which was published in 1992 under a traditional style title with its obligatory nature reference, *The Golden Grain of the History of Do-Kham Chatreng*.[15]

All the uprisings in Kham in 1956 started at two different time periods. The first uprisings took place following the Tibetan New Year, around late February 1956, when the tribes and districts of Eastern Kham, discussed in this and the previous chapter, began their insurrection. The second period was in the autumn of 1956 when the more westerly areas of Kham: Markham, Drayab, Gonjo, Sho-ta-lho-sum, Dergé, Khyungpo Tengchen, Dzachukha, Ga Jyekundo, and Kandzé launched their uprisings. Kandzé, the heart and centre of the five Hor states (*hor-se-dhara-kha-nga*), is actually in the eastern part of Kham, but it was the vital mid-terminus on the newly built Chinese motor road from Dartsedo to Lhasa. The considerable concentration of Chinese troops at this site, made it difficult for the Khampas there to stage an uprising at the beginning of the year. Only one of the Hor states, Drango, seems to have joined the first uprising, and had its monastery bombed along with Lithang and Bathang.

There is another factor that may have caused the uprisings to start in the eastern areas of Kham. Chinese garrisons in these areas were, at the beginning of 1956, reportedly small. Most of the PLA forces in Kham had been shifted west, first for the invasion of Tibet (under Lhasa rule) in 1950, and later to reinforce the PLA occupation force in Lhasa. Hence in Lithang, the permanent Chinese garrison was only five hundred men strong. Chatreng had three hundred Chinese soldiers, while Bathang and Nyarong had even smaller Chinese garrisons. Of course, when the uprisings started in the east, then thousands of Chinese troops from the west (and also from Kandzé) had to be moved back east, giving the Khampas in the west the breathing space to organize their own uprisings.

Another possible reason for the difference in the starting points of the uprisings might be that the implementation of "Democratic Reforms"—which triggered the uprisings—were not carried out all at once throughout Kham, but in phases. As I mentioned before, Athar Norbu told me that it was done "step by step", starting from the east at Dartsedo.

The accounts I have given of the uprising in eastern Kham are far from comprehensive. I have provided a partial account of what took place in Lithang, Bathang, Chatreng and Lingkashi, but many other areas as Tawu, Drango and the Kandzé area have not been covered.

GYALTHANG
AND THE LOLO UPRISING

Earlier, I noted in passing the uprising in Gyalthang, south of Lithang, under the leadership of Wangchuk Tempa (aka "Aku Lemar" or Uncle Baldy). The Gyalthangwas staged their uprising a year before Lithang and I have heard (but with no confirmation) that they had the cooperation of a non-Tibetan tribal people of the region, the Lolo, also known as the Yi or Nuosu. They were led by their aristocracy, "the princes of the black bone," the name that Peter Goullart, used as a title for his book on ". . . the independent Lolos, those fierce tribesmen who for centuries defied the might of the Chinese empire and were immortalized in Chinese literature as the most ferocious and ruthless warriors in the world."[16]

I came to know about the Lolo uprising against the Communists through Nyarong Aten when I was writing his biography, *Horseman in the Snow*. The Chinese administration at Nyarong had sent Aten to study at the South-West School for National Minorities in Chengdu, where he made friends with Lolo students who told him their story.

> The Lolos were a tribal people living in the southern borders of China and Tibet. They were proud people and tough fighters, fond of weapons and strong drink. The men wore big turbans on their heads and bedecked themselves with ornaments made of coral, conch shells and cowries. The Lolo admired a man only for his strength and courage. Racially they were completely different from the Chinese, whom they despised.
>
> They revolted against the Chinese around 1955. It was a revolt of great magnitude and ferocity. The Lolos were reasonably well armed and operated in a terrain that was all jungle and craggy mountains. Their hatred of the Chinese was traditionally implacable, and it demonstrated itself very cruelly and savagely during the revolt. The Lolos never surrendered and never took prisoners. Many Chinese divisions were rushed to the area, and thousands of soldiers died in the subsequent fighting. Finally, through the sheer weight of numbers and superior arms, the revolt was crushed. The reprisals were savage. Lolo men, women and children were bayoneted or shot in mass executions. The extent of these massacres will probably never be known.[17]

GYALRONG

The extreme north-east of Kham, which spills over into Amdo and is now absorbed into Sichuan province, was traditionally one of the largest regions of the Kham/Amdo divide called Gyalrong, with a unique history and culture of its own. The great Tibetan scholar Samten Karmay, who hails from this area, notes that the name of this region is related to the name of the river Gyalmo Ngülchu (The Queen's Silver Stream) which is the main river of the region. Samten-la tells us that "In Tibetan geographical vocabulary, the region is described as a *rong* or 'gorge'. It is one of the four great gorges, *rong-chen bzhi*, of Tibet."[18]

My interest in this region first came about because one small district, Wolung, (literally "land below" in Tibetan) is the unique habitat of the giant panda. Khampas call the animal *bhila-dhomchen* (*chila-dhomchen* in Central Tibet), meaning "big cat bear". We know that in 1956 there was a major uprising in Gyalrong. This was the only uprising that received airdropped weapons and instructors from the Nationalist Government in Taiwan, according to Tibetan intelligence chief, Lhamo Tsering. When this Taiwan connection became known to the Communists, all available PLA forces were immediately rushed to Gyalrong and the uprising was ruthlessly crushed. The Taiwan agents were all killed or captured.

The traditional ruler of Gyalrong, Trochu Gyalpo Dorje Palsang, who led the uprising, was forced to flee his homeland and resettle in Taiwan. Very few survivors managed to make it out of this distant region, and I have not come across a single written account of the Gyalrong uprising. But the people here definitely retain memories of their resistance to Communist China. It should be mentioned that the history of Gyalrong's defiance of Chinese imperialism goes back well beyond the last century.

In the eighteenth century, when Manchu power was at its ascendancy in Asia, the Qing Imperial army fought two long wars in the Gyalrong region, which overshadowed all other campaigns undertaken during the reign of the Emperor Qianlong. Though these wars were fought against the two relatively small Tibetan kingdoms of Rabden and Tsanlha, they far exceeded, in expense alone to the Imperial treasury, the costs of the campaign against Burma in the late 1760s and the two campaigns against the Gurkhas from 1788 to 1792. Even the conquest of Ili and Dzungaria, a war that lasted five years (1755–60) and took place in a territory almost ten times as large as Gyalrong, involved only about one-third the cost of the two Gyalrong wars.[19]

Though ultimately Gyalrong was subdued, the effort and the colossal expense drastically weakened the power of the Manchu dynasty, which never again approached the height of its previous imperial power. The foremost historian on medieval Tibet, the late Professor Elliot Sperling, considered the Qing invasion of Gyalrong as being analogous to America's costly involvement in Vietnam that brought about the substantial and far-reaching diminution of its post-World War II prosperity.[20]

Besides the tenacity, military skill and the fighting spirit of the Tibetans of Gyalrong, the formidable stone towers and forts of the region played a vital role in its effective defense. Even in a photograph of the ruins of these imposing towers one is struck by the sense of power, skill and science that the Gyalrongwas brought to bear in their long struggle against Chinese hegemony. The towers come in different shapes: squares, octagons, hexagons and star-shapes. It is claimed that these unique configurations give the structures their strength to even withstand earthquakes.

According to the scholars J. Dehergne, Luo Shufu and A.W. Hummel, ". . . the stone forts would perhaps have been impregnable had A-kui, the Manchu General not made use of cannons constructed under the directions of the Portuguese, Felix da Rocha."[21] A Portuguese Jesuit missionary, da Rocha (1713–1781) was in the permanent employ of the Imperial court. "He not only directed the construction of the cannons to be used (perhaps designed for ease of transport in this rugged terrain) but he served as "surveyor" as well, when the cannons were actually in use, arriving at the front late in 1774 in time for the main assault on the Great Gold Stream," *Da Jinchuan*, the Chinese name for Rabden.

In 1775, the principal castle of the king of Rabden fell to Jesuit cannons. The same year the imperial army destroyed the Yundrung Lhateng, the great Bön monastery of the Rabden Royal House. A new Gelugpa monastery was built at the site. Gyalrong being one of the last strongholds of the pre-Buddhist Bön faith, the chief Gelugpa lama in Beijing, Changkya Hutoktu Rolpae Dorje, the religious advisor to the Manchu Emperor, had earlier performed a Buddhist "magico-religious" rite for the defeat and destruction of the Bönpos of Gyalrong, and for the victory of the Buddhist Manchu emperor.

14

NEVER RETURN

Amdo, one of the three traditional regions of Tibet, has now been largely incorporated into China's Qinghai province and parts of Gansu and Sichuan provinces. About halfway on the main motor road from Xining (the capital of Qinghai) and Lanzhou (the capital of Gansu) is the Tibetan autonomous county of Kamalok. The name in Tibetan means: "Never Return without Orders."

According to Dragön Konchog's monumental history of Amdo, *The Ocean Annals (Depter Gyamtso)*, nine great warrior generals were sent from Lhasa, during the reign of the Emperor Trisong Detsen, to defend the northern borders of the empire. Because of their courage, skill and accomplishments, they were called *guthup* or the "Accomplished Nine." After many years of defending the imperial frontier, the "nine" requested the Emperor's permission to return to Central Tibet. The Emperor replied that they were not to return until they received his orders. Thus, they settled in the region, and the descendants of these warriors were called "Never Return Without Orders."

In his autobiography *My Land and My People,* the Fourteenth Dalai Lama writes, ". . . my forefathers came from Central Tibet. How they came to settle in Eastern Tibet is a simple story. Hundreds of years ago, in the reign of King Mangsong Mangtsen, a Tibetan army was stationed in the northeastern part of Tibet to protect the frontiers.

In our part of Dokham (Amdo), a garrison from Phempo in Central Tibet was stationed, and family tradition said that my forefathers came with that garrison. In our family dialect, we still used many words from the Phempo district, rather than Amdo: words like *cheney* for bowl and *khenbu* for spoon."

According to *The White Annals* (*Dhepter Karpo*) of Gedün Chöphel, " . . . most of the wars between Tibet and Tang dynasty China were fought on Amdo soil." The sites of two great battlefields are known to this day: *Gyatrag Thang* (Field of Chinese Blood) and *Gyadur Thang* (Field of Chinese Graves). Before Communist rule, local guides would take visitors and travellers around these sites and tell of the great battles of bygone days.

It was probably one such major military defeat that unsettled the normally light-hearted Li Po (or Li Bai), Tang China's greatest poet, who alludes to such a battle in his poem "The Moon over Frontier Mountains." An excerpt:[1]

> Bright white moon over Mount Tianshan
> When looking at the endless sea of clouds,
> The fierce wind howling ten thousand *li*
> Spreads them everywhere up to the Yumen Pass.
> The Chinese forces are stuck at Baiding Mountain,
> Tibet's army forms a wall at Kokonor.
> Thus, till now, of old, it is
> A battlefield, among whose fighting masses
> Survivors are like daytime stars.
>
> No one has seen a soldier come
> Home from these ancient fields of war
> Where the exile men gaze across
> The frontier with homesick eyes,
> While women beneath this moon back home,
> Gaze overland, and sigh uncontrollably.

These stories underscore the strategic and commercial importance of this vast region, as its northern marches bordered the Silk Road and the route to the Tang capital of Changan. After the Tibetan conquest of the Tarim Basin, the Silk Road (*dhar-lam*) was regarded as being within the boundary of Amdo. This and its expansive grasslands made Amdo a natural passageway in later years for the movement of various nomadic tribes: Tanguts, Uyghurs, Mongols, including the armies of Ghengis Khan. In 1633 a powerful Mongol kingdom was established around Kokonor by the Qoshot ruler Gushri Khan. Gushri Khan became the Fifth Dalai Lama's patron and the military arm of the Dalai Lama's great undertaking for the reunification of Tibet.

The appointment by the Manchu emperor of an *amban* (imperial commissioner) at Xining in 1725 over the Mongol banners and Tibetan tribes of Amdo is often cited as the end of Tibetan influence in the region. But in reality, the Xining commissioner had little actual power, and in the case of the Golok tribesmen, apparently no influence at all.[2] Furthermore, according to the Italian scholar Luciano Petech, Lhasa maintained a parallel organization in Amdo ". . . till about the middle of the 19th century, a commissioner called the *garpön*, whose functions above all concerned trade and the control of local monasteries."[3] The garpön, like the Manchu *amban*, appears to have had little actual control over regional politics.

But from the late nineteenth century, much of Amdo was subjugated by the Hui Muslim warlords of the Ma clan, and from 1928 to 1949, Amdo was assimilated into Qinghai province and Gansu province. The Muslim cavalrymen of Ma Bufang, the last warlord and Guomindang governor of Qinghai, were well armed, well trained and regarded as the most powerful military force in the region. The Tibetan government in Lhasa had had an uneven relationship with Ma Bufang. His cavalry had defeated Tibetan troops at Denkhok in 1932, and in 1938 he held the child (who would be recognized as the Fourteenth Dalai Lama) hostage for a substantial ransom.

But in 1949, the Tibetan government was optimistic that the fierce Hui Muslim military force would serve as a dependable northern bulwark against the impending Communist advance. It was rumoured in Lhasa, that a senior Tibetan official had been sent to Xining, and some kind of agreement had been reached between Lhasa and Xining on a common defence. But when the Communists under General Peng

Dehuai defeated the Muslim and Guomindang force at Gansu, Ma Bufang flew out of Xining (with his wives and treasure trove) on two DC-3s and escaped, eventually making it to Cairo.

Most of the Muslim troops surrendered to the Communists. A number of Hui cavalry units were integrated into the PLA and later used against Tibetans, especially in the high grasslands of Dzachukha and Jyekundo. According to Taktser Rinpoche, the abbot of Kumbum Monastery and brother of the Fourteenth Dalai Lama, the Muslim community of Lusar (a day's ride from Kumbum) attempted an uprising. They were wiped out. Some Hui joined the Tibetans and Mongols and attempted to fight the Communists.

There are very few accounts of these uprisings in Amdo. Because of the distances involved, not many refugees from Amdo managed to make it all the way to Lhasa, and even fewer eventually managed to escape to India. A small number of these refugees were traders and agents from the great monastic city of Labrang. A few others were Amdowa pilgrims who had come to Lhasa to study at the monasteries of Drepung, Sera and Ganden, where there were special colleges for monks from that region. Not many Amdowas in Lhasa, or the handful who later escaped to India, had firsthand accounts of the fighting in their homeland.

The French Tibétologue Francoise Robin (aka Chönyi Wangmo) remarks on this unfortunate lacuna in her groundbreaking study, "La révolte en Amdo en 1958".[4] However, she manages to provide an extensive list of sources that have come to light in recent years. She cites substantial individual testimonies (unpublished) from such survivors as Thakpa Gyamtso and also discusses recently published (1994) accounts as Alak Tsayi Tenzin Palbar's *The Tragedy of My Homeland*"[5] where he details ". . . events in Amdo between the beginning of the years 1950 and also 1976, from his own experience, oral testimonies of others and even Chinese sources he has translated into Tibetan. One Chinese report lists 996 clashes between the PLA and local Tibetans in the first eight months of 1958, just in Choné and Labrang (in Gansu province)."

Professor Robin also mentions the 2007 memoir of Naktsang Nulo, where in the latter half of his book, ". . . he details the formation of a local resistance militia in his home region, Chukhama, in Machu in 1958. The author details the unequal clashes and rapid defeat of Tibetans, the numerous human losses and imprisonment. When this memoir appeared in Amdo, it was an immediate bestseller, and many clandestine editions appeared. But Communist authorities got wind of it, and it is now proscribed."

Francoise Robin also writes of two volumes of interviews with survivors of the uprisings in Amdo published locally around 2008 and banned by Chinese officialdom. "These interviews were conducted by Jamdo Rinzang, a young monk who has since been arrested."[6]

Another such valuable collated oral history (in Tibetan) *The Wounds of Three Generations*,[7] was published in Dharamshala in 2010. It is the story of Ngawa, the easternmost area of Amdo, whose people resisted the first known instance of Communist Chinese intrusion into Tibet when the Red Army on its Long March (1935–36) "left a trail of pillage, desecration and famine in these regions." The book recounts, in detail, the long and violent opposition by the local people, which they paid for in massacres, starvation and destruction of their monasteries and homes. At present, the grandchildren of these local people are, in their own grim fashion, still opposing Chinese rule, making Ngawa the "undisputed world capital of self-immolations", according to the American journalist Barbara Demick whose recent book[8] explores the tragedy of this Tibetan frontier-land.

The most recent and in-depth study of the insurrections in Amdo is by historian Benno Weiner. The core of his book (2020) has been culled largely from local Party archives in Qinghai and deals, principally with the "1958 Amdo Rebellion" that broke out in April of that year in such counties as Tsekhok, Chentsa, Rebkong, Machu, Luchu, Kachu (Linxia), Labrang, Bayen and Yülgennyin, and in such prefectures as Tsolho, Kanlho, Jyekundo, Malho and Golok.

"By the end of June, twenty-two thousand people across Qinghai in twenty-four counties, including representatives of 101 Tibetan Buddhist monasteries, reportedly had risen in revolt. As the rebellion spread to majority Muslim areas, including Hualong County in Qinghai and Lingxia, where there was a midsummer insurrection, mosques were also singled out." The rebellion, which sustained itself for over five years, was eventually put down with devastating violence and enormous loss of life. Weiner concludes, "The 1958 Amdo Rebellion and its violent aftermath were events unprecedented in Amdo's history."[9]

NANGRA AND HORMUKHA

Quite by chance, I came across a comprehensive account of the earliest uprising in Amdo when digging through the fairly extensive archives of refugee statements put together by the exile government in the sixties. An actual eyewitness and participant of the 1949 uprising in Chentsa Dzong district in Amdo had somehow made his way to Dharamshala in the mid-sixties, where he presented a lengthy and thorough account of his experiences to the exile Information Office.[10] In fact, the account was so atypically thorough, the informant providing exact place-names, dates and even times for all battles and skirmishes that for some time, I was not too sure how credible it all was. The statement was made by Dorje Tsering, who to evade Chinese security in Lhasa, had adopted the alias Rinzin, and later in exile was known as Amdo Rinzin. He had been a prosperous middle-class farmer from the sub-district of Nangra in East-Central Amdo, a part of Chentsa Dzong. Nangra, then had an approximate population of 17,000, including the monks of seven monasteries. The smaller neighbouring district of Hormukha had three monasteries and a population of about 15,000 people.

On 25 September 1949, the Red Army reached Nangra and Hormukha. "In December 1949, all the people of Nangra and Hormukha decided to fight under the leadership of Pön Wangchen of Nangra and Pön Chöje of Hormukha. Soon the two leaders had 60 assistants, about 6,000 voluntary soldiers and a sizable number of arms and ammunition collected."

In their first encounter with Chinese troops, twenty-five Tibetans, including Pön Wangchen's son Tashi Rabten were killed. But many Chinese were also killed. PLA reinforcements were rushed in from Rebkong, south of Nangra, and fighting continued in the following months, with many casualties on both sides.

In February 1951, a major battle was fought in Hormukha, and many Tibetans, including a relative of Rinzin's, were killed, and Hormukha was lost to the Tibetans. The chief of Hormukha, Pön Chöje, was badly wounded in his right arm but lay down on the battlefield, among the bodies of other Tibetans, and pretended to be dead. Late in the night, he managed to escape, helped by some of his men, including Rinzin, who came back to the battlefield to look for him. When they tried to hide in the nearby villages ". . . all the women whose husbands had died in the battle gathered and blamed us for the death of their husbands. They told us that if we did not surrender, the Chinese would attack again, and the whole population would be wiped out. As it was unthinkable for us to surrender, we left the village and headed for the rocky hills of Lhowa."

After more encounters with Chinese troops Pön Chöje and the remainder of his men finally reached Pön Wangchen's home at Khyampa in Nangra. There they received sanctuary. The Chinese had called on the "rebels" of Nangra, to surrender but the fighters there had jeered at this demand and continued their resistance. The Chinese now began a more systematic takeover of the region, working their way from the periphery, village by village, taking surveys of the population, of every family, of its wealth and social standing.

Rinzin took pride in mentioning that because of its fierce and unyielding opposition to the Communists for over three years, Nangra was called "Little Taiwan" by Chinese officials. When I first came across this claim in Rinzin's refugee statement, I, in my (then) left-intellectual knee-jerk fashion, assumed that he was probably exaggerating or boasting. But in 2012, I came across an article on a Chinese website that corroborated the claim. Titled "Xiang Qian's (Wangchen's) counterrevolutionary fight for Nganglha Tribe (Nangra)", the article gave a general account of the conflict in Nangra but was specific as to the Taiwan reference. "May 1, 1952, the PLA began to march to Angla (Nangra). May 2nd, the PLA conducted a comprehensive cleaning up, and in ten days' time, the 'Taiwan' painstakingly built up by Xiang Qian (Wangchen) and remnants of Ma Bu Fang's troops began to collapse."[11]

Chinese publications generally avoid discussing the violent uprisings in Kham, Amdo or the resistance in Central Tibet. But this account of the Nangra Uprising received considerable publicity throughout China in 2013 when Xi Jinping became president of the PRC. In their background stories, the Chinese media noted that the father of China's new president was the Communist veteran Xi Zhongxun. He had been the political commissar in charge of the pacification campaign for Nangra and Hormukha. Xi Zhongxun's official title then was director for the North-West Political and Military Affairs Bureau. An article in the CPC Hebei Provincial Committee Party History Research Center website mentions that after the surrender of Pön Wangchen, Xi Zhongxun met Mao Zedong, who praised him for his victory and compared Xi to the legendary military strategist Zhuge Liang, a historical personality and a leading character in the great Chinese historical novel *The Romance of the Three Kingdoms.*[12]

This article also mentions that seventeen specific attempts were made by Xi Zhongxun to negotiate with the Tibetans and get them to surrender. Rinzin, in his account, mentions eighteen negotiation efforts, some of them led by such important religious figures as Geshe Sherab Gyatso, vice-president of the Buddhist Association of China, who called on the rebels to surrender as the Chinese were far superior in numbers and arms. "We replied that although the Chinese were doubtless powerful compared to us few Tibetans, it would be out of the question for us to bow our heads to them. It would be an insulting and embarrassing course of action unprecedented in the history of our land. So, we will continue to fight till the end."

On 5 April 1952, four divisions of the PLA, one from the north-east through Khargang, one from the south through Rebkong, one from the north through Gyaltsa and one from the west through Chuma ". . . surrounded Nangra in five circles, and fighting started at about 5 a.m." After midnight the fighting was hand-to-hand and savage. Many hundreds were killed including, Rinzin's older brother.

About five hundred of the Amdo fighters tried to break out of the encirclement but were attacked by a large Chinese force. They managed to find safety at the Gyalthang Monastery in Dingtsar, where they took cover and resumed fighting. They tried to break out again and reach a nearby forest, but the Chinese opened up machine-gun fire from a hilltop and hit some fighters. Pön Wangchen's son Tsepel had his horse shot from under him, and his father stopped to help him. About thirty of the men who had gone forward now rushed back to the aid of their leader. They fought with the Chinese for two hours. Finally, the Chinese turned back.

When it became dark at around 7 p.m., the fighters continued their retreat through the forest, reaching a high nomadic area called Daka Tithung. They stopped to rest for a little while. Pön Wangchen told his men he was determined to go on fighting, but those who felt they had to surrender could do so. But the five hundred or so fighters remaining ". . . all vowed unanimously to fight and die alongside him."

They continued their withdrawal in the dark, but a large Chinese force was pursuing them. It caught up with them at around 11 p.m., and a skirmish broke out. The Amdowas fought bravely and did not hesitate to attack the much larger Chinese force. Because of the darkness, the Amdowas only lost three lives and managed to escape from their Chinese pursuers.

The escape in the dark and the near-continuous fighting scattered the force, and many fighters became lost. Rinzin found himself alone with two boys whose father had been killed in action. He explained to them that they would have to go with him wherever he went. He also advised them to die fighting or commit suicide rather than be captured by the Chinese. "They asked me how to commit suicide with rifles since we did not have pistols. I showed them how and then we continued our journey through the snow-covered forest." They caught three horses that had belonged to the Chinese but had to let them go and hide when they encountered a large PLA unit.

The next day they, fortunately, came across twenty-two fighters from their group riding Chinese horses and joined them. As they rode on, they caught sight of a large Chinese encampment but managed to pass to one side without arousing suspicion. They had earlier found some Chinese uniforms and caps in the saddlebags of the captured horses, which they used to disguise themselves.

But soon afterwards, they were stopped by another large force of PLA soldiers and had to fight, losing many of their horses. They carried on in this manner for a whole day and night, trying to avoid Chinese patrols and units, but fighting them when they had to. At about seven o'clock the following morning, they realized they had finally managed to break through the five military encirclements and were safe for the moment. They realized that seven members of their band were lost and that the remaining fifteen of them had become weak because of lack of food and sleep. But they kept on moving to put some distance between them and the Chinese.

On 11 April, they arrived at the high plain of Chensik Thang and towards evening came across sixty-five of their own men. To their great relief, their leader Pön Wangchen was with this group. From a nomad encampment nearby, they managed to steal a couple of yaks that they slaughtered and cooked. But once again, the Chinese got wind of their presence in the area and sent five thousand soldiers after them. "We skirmished with them and then gradually retreated up the higher reaches of the Gangze Mazer Mountains. When we got to the heights of this mountain, the Chinese did not follow us there."

They remained in this harsh and inhospitable area for a month, always hungry, weak and frozen with the constant cold ". . . like hopelessly sick patients waiting for death. There was no wood to make a fire, and it was so cold that we could not speak properly." They got some relief from cutting the throats of the few horses they had left and drinking the warm blood, but it was difficult to eat the raw meat as it quickly became frozen and kept slipping from their hands. They huddled together and covered themselves with saddle blankets. Their only consolation was that the Chinese could not come up the mountain as they would quickly die due to the cold and altitude.

About a month later, the Chinese sent Lama Shabdung Karpo and Serti Rinpoche of Dechen Monastery to persuade Pön Wangchen to surrender. The Chinese had declared a general amnesty to all rebels and stated that everyone was free to return home. So finally, after three years of fighting Pön Wangchen and his men agreed to surrender.

Rinzin says that Mao's representative came to Nangra Khyampa to meet them. This was probably Xi Zhongxun. Some days later, Pön Wangchen was taken to the provincial capital of Xining, where he attended a big banquet and a ceremony at Lanzhou, the capital of Gansu province, according to a Chinese account. Rinzin says that Wangchen was also taken on a plane to Beijing, where he met Mao. On his return, Pön Wangchen was appointed the district head of Chentsa Dzong. For about a year " . . . people led happy lives, and there was opportunity for both children and the old to play and laugh."

Then in 1953, "Democratic Reforms" and "Socialist Transformation" policies were implemented throughout Amdo. Now "denunciations", "criticism" and class struggle became the daily routine. Meetings were held every day in every village and town, and everyone was expected to criticize each other and make their own confessions. Innocent people were accused of various crimes and taken away to prison and labour camps. Executions by firing squad were a daily occurrence.[13] Every Tibetan settlement, no matter how small, had a contingent of Chinese troops close to it. There was little the men could do now as their rifles, swords and spears had been taken away. All those who had earlier received amnesty for rebelling against the Chinese government were once again accused of being counterrevolutionaries and "rebel bandits" and were arrested.[14] "Many people committed suicide in those desperate times . . . ." Rinzin recalled " . . . among them were my brother and six other people from Nangra, eight people from Ruche and five from Yulche." Most of the non-disabled were taken away to prison and labour camps. Many tried to resist and were killed. Only a few managed to get away.

Rinzin escaped from Nangra on 4 September 1954. He avoided suspicion by buying a ride on a Chinese truck going to Lanzhou city, the capital of Gansu province. From there, he travelled by train to Chengdu, in Sichuan province, and then, avoiding Chinese checkpoints, spies and informers, made his way to Dartsedo and then through Kham to Lhasa, where he arrived on 20 October 1954. That same year he heard that Pön Wangchen and Pön Chöje had been placed under house arrest. No one has heard of them since. Geshe

Sherab Gyatso, the lama collaborator who led one of the eighteen delegations to persuade the Amdo freedom fighters to surrender, was promoted from vice-chairman to chairman of the Buddhist Association of China. In 1968 he was struggled and beaten by Red Guards and died of his injuries.

Back at Nangra, as Rinzin put it bluntly, "Only a few blind people, cripples, fools and some children were left."

GOLOK

Though there is an unfortunate dearth of information on the conflict in Amdo, nearly every book or article that has discussed the "Revolt in Tibet" unfailingly makes mention of uprisings by Golok tribesmen—but invariably in vague generalizations. One of the first news reports in the international press of the fighting in Eastern Tibet stated with breathtaking inaccuracy, "General Mabofang a Golok leader, led an attack on a Chinese garrison in which about 900 Chinese troops were massacred."[15] Later, a bulletin with a "Ladakh" dateline reported, "Mabo Fano, Ladakh leader of the Golok tribe, has spearheaded an organized rebellion against the Peking government in Tibet, according to reports trickling across the No-Man's-Land touching the borders of Ladakh."

One reason for the general awareness in the international press of at least the name "Golok" might stem from the fact that the Amnye Machen mountain, in whose shadow these tribesmen roamed, was, from the beginning to the mid-twentieth century, rumoured to be higher than Mount Everest, and hence remained in the attention span of some in the West. A number of expeditions were undertaken to verify this rumour—which was only disproved by a U.S. expedition in 1981.

The other reason must surely come from the legendary, widespread and thoroughly deserved reputation of Golok warriors for ferocity in battle and general lawlessness—not only throughout Tibet but China as well. Victor Leotard was killed by Golok tribesmen on the second Guibaut-Liotard Expedition of 1940. Earlier, another French explorer,

Dutreuil de Rhins, was killed in this region. Christian missionaries attempting to pass through the Golok region have, in their accounts, never failed to make references to murders and massacres. In 1889 Petrus Rijnhart was killed by Golok bandits.

The reverend A.J. Fesmire, in a report, reveled in the "annihilation" of one tribe of Goloks, "a most haughty people", by the "up-to-date firearms" of the Chinese Muslim army. "Golok men, women, and children were ruthlessly put to the sword, and thousands were driven into the Yellow River to perish in its muddy water. Thus, is made safe for travel and missionary work a vast piece of country inhabited by thousands of nomads . . . we are praising God for the advance step He has enabled us to take."[16] The independent, outlaw life of the Golok nomads came at a heavy price. "The Muslim warlord Ma Qi launched a genocidal war against the Golok in 1928 inflicting a defeat upon them and seizing the great monastic centre of Labrang Tashikhyil."[17]

Perhaps that is why the American ethnologist Joseph Rock mentions that when he travelled across Golok territory in 1926, he was told that "the chief of the largest and most important Golok tribes, the Rimang, was absent from his encampment and said to have gone . . . to make his submission to the Tibetan government."

I heard this story of the submission by the Golok chief from my mother, who witnessed the event when she was a girl of nine, at the nomad centre of Dzachukha, the north-eastern limit of Tibet's frontier with Chinese-occupied Eastern Tibet. She travelled there from Dergé in the military entourage of her father, Gyurme Gyatso, who, at the time, was governor of Dergé. Gyurme Gyatso had been approached by the renowned Golok lama, Jampel Rolpae Lodrö, who told him that he had long tried to persuade his people to give up their lawless ways, as that would surely lead them to some future disaster. He finally managed to convince the principal Golok leader, Trulku Tendrak of Golok Arkhyong Gongmatsang, chief of the Ri-mang tribe, to make his submission to the Tibetan government and become part of their ancient nation with which the Goloks shared their religion, customs and heritage.

Neither Lhasa nor Beijing had earlier been able to subdue the Goloks, so this was a diplomatic coup for the Tibetans. Another important chief, Rinchen Wang-ghi Gyalpo of the Sershul nomads, also offered his submission. The Thirteenth Dalai Lama and the Kashag, when informed of this, sent the appropriate decrees, ceremonial costumes and gifts from Lhasa. At the "awarding of titles" ceremony at Dzachukha, my mother recalled that one of the chiefs was nearly thrown off his horse, as the animal did not recognize his master in his new ceremonial outfit. Probably the only chief or ruler who still wears such a costume these days, at least officially, is the King of Mustang. I saw him in full regalia at the gateway town of Dzong-Sarpa, in Mustang, in 1971, when I was serving with the Resistance. But I am getting ahead of myself.

As mentioned in Chapter 1, when my mother passed away in 2005, I published an account of her trip to Dzachukha and the submission of the Golok chiefs, as a memorial.

The actual Golok resistance to the Communist advance, which probably started in late 1949 or early 1950, has received little or no attention or documentation. In exile archives, practically nothing exists. In early 1950, some vague accounts of Golok resistance to the Communist advance appear to have reached Lhasa. I was told by a senior government official that during a meeting of the Tsongdu, the Tibetan Parliament, that year, Lukhangwa, who was then a *tsepön* (one of the four finance secretaries), urged the government to aid the Golok tribesmen and send them rifles and ammunition.

I understand that some scholars from the region have attempted to put together a comprehensive account of the conflicts these days. Since Chinese authorities are sensitive about such studies, I am not sure that such surveys might be suppressed, as were the eight-volume history of the Lithang uprising or the two books of interviews mentioned by Francoise Robin.

So far, we have only incidental information. Professor Melvyn Goldstein of Case Western Reserve University appears to have gained access to official Chinese records concerning the Goloks. In an online report, Goldstein made a passing reference to the uprisings:

Historically, the Goulou (Golok) tribes were politically autonomous. Consequently, when the People's Liberation Army (PLA) moved to liberate Goulou after it liberated Xining in late 1949, the Goulou herders opposed them militarily. Serious confrontations ensued with many casualties, and the area was pacified and liberated only in 1952. Because of this, 1952 is likely to represent an artificially low base year due to the livestock losses one would expect to accompany such fighting and disruptions. Similarly, the chaos and disruptions of collectivization and the Great Leap Forward are likely to have negatively, not positively, affected herd growth. And, in addition to these events, in Goulou there is said to have been a second substantial outbreak of fighting in the 1957–58 period.[18]

On this "second outbreak of fighting in 1957–58", Goldstein added, "It is interesting to note that the figure of Goulou population growth in the Socio-Economic Baseline Survey . . . reveals a sharp decline in population between 1957–58."

When I quoted Goldstein's report in a blog[19] on the uprisings in Eastern Tibet, he wrote a comment explaining that his facts and figures were only provided to show variations in "livestock" growth or losses among the "Goulou" herders—essentially chiding me for misusing his research statistics to point out the occurrence of a human tragedy. Joseph Stalin might have agreed with him. He is said to have remarked, "The death of one man is a tragedy; the death of millions is a statistic."

The late Tenth Panchen Lama was more outspoken about what happened to the Golok tribesmen. On 28 March 1987, in a speech at a meeting of the Tibetan Autonomous Region Sub-Committee (of the National People's Congress) in Beijing he said, "In Amdo and Kham, people were subjected to unspeakable atrocities. People were shot in groups of ten or twenty . . . Such actions have left deep wounds in the minds of the people." On the Goloks specifically, he said:

If there was a film made on all the atrocities perpetrated in Qinghai Province, it would shock the viewers. In the Golok area, many people were killed, and their dead bodies rolled down the hill into a big ditch. The soldiers told the family members and relatives of the dead people that they should celebrate since the rebels have been wiped out. They were forced to dance on the dead bodies. Soon after, they were also massacred with machine guns. They were all buried there.

A Chinese scholar, who in the eighties gained access to local records in the Golok area, more than confirmed the Panchen Lama's contention that a massacre had been perpetrated on the Golok people. In this scholar's estimation, an act of genocide had taken place. His figures published in the pro-democracy magazine *China Spring* (June 1986) estimated that the area of Golok had its population reduced from about 1,30,000 in 1956 to nearly 60,000 in 1963.

Francoise Robin remarks that though the source of the above statistic (often cited in exile publications) might not be entirely "clear", more recent figures cited about a specific Golok community " . . . in a local chronicle published in China and based on official statistics" provide supporting information. "The (Golok) community of Khisin (in Malho, Qinghai) of 11,000 people in 1958, had fallen to 5,749 in one year. Fifty-two per cent of the total population had thus disappeared. Death, famine, imprisonment were the reasons given for this demographic decline."[20]

According to these sources, more than half the Golok population had just disappeared in the span of seven years. And these surveys did not include the equally violent 1950–53 period when the first uprising had taken place and had been put down with great savagery by the PLA. Clearly, something akin to genocide or "an act of genocide" had taken place in the Golok region.[21]

What is evident is that in Kham and Amdo, "total war" had been waged by the world's largest military force against a pre-industrial people, lightly armed with bolt-action rifles, muskets, swords and spears. If we just considered the scale of the conflict and massacres it would seem that the uprisings and the subsequent reprisals in Amdo and Kham were comparable in magnitude to the events in Afghanistan following the Soviet invasion—possibly even larger. Though the uprisings throughout Tibet did not receive the same international attention, it was significant enough to be considered "the gravest episode of internal disorder (in the PRC) prior to the Cultural Revolution"[22] by Harvard's doyen of China studies, Roderick MacFarquhar.

We also cannot ignore the fact of intentionality in the actions of the Chinese leadership. In an article about the "Lhasa rebellion" of 1959, the author Chen Jian concludes from recently published official Chinese texts that "Mao and his colleagues believed that it was impossible to resolve the Tibetan question without using military force." He also explains that, for Mao and the CCP, the obstacles encountered in the Tibetan "liberation" were seen not so much as "threats" or "crises" as "opportunities" to overcome, once and for all, the thorny Tibetan question.[23]

Another Chinese academic, Jianglin Li, describing the scale of the total war ". . . waged on Tibetans in Kham, Amdo and Central Tibet from 1956 to 1962" tells us that ". . . Chinese official sources indicate that seven of the twelve PLA military commands were directly involved, and another two provided logistical support. The cumulative total of combat forces reached over 200,000, not including logistics personnel, local militia and civilians drafted for transportation, road building, etc.* The Central Military Commission sent nearly all PLA military branches to fight in Tibet, even the newly-formed chemical warfare unit."[24]

One barometer revealing the scale of this conflict is China's 1982 census, whose figures and extrapolations all appeared in the *Population Atlas of China.*[25] One map in this publication, showing the ratio of men to women throughout China, is illuminating as it registers (even twenty years after the events) a much larger proportion of women to men in Eastern and North-Eastern Tibet. Such disparate sex-ratio figures do not appear in other parts of Tibet or even China, although a

---

*If we use the minimal "tooth-to-tail" ratio of one combatant to two support personnel, we get the figure of 600,000—well over half-a-million PLA troops in Tibet.

large number of people died in these places too, for different reasons, as the 1960 to 1963 famine, which probably affected both sexes equally.

At the same time, it should be made clear that the unusually large number of men who died in Kham and Amdo were not just those who were killed in battle. Many were captured and shipped to *Laogai* slave-labour camps, where most perished of starvation, overwork, disease or execution.

Mass graves are being discovered with some regularity all over the Tibetan Plateau, especially in recent years as mining, building, and road construction have increased dramatically with China's push for "development" in Tibet. A recent article[26] by an American academic reported on the discovery in May 2012 of a mass grave at Nangchen country in Yushu Tibetan Autonomous Prefecture, which was discovered when excavation work for a building project started. The article also reported the discovery of three mass burial pits in the grasslands near Palthang in Yushu, filled with partially decomposed human bodies, some still having long hair. Remnants of lay clothing and monastic robes were also discovered in the pits. A few unsettlingly sharp photographs accompanied the article. "The images are clear, the local explanations were whispered: it was where monks and laypeople had been massacred in 1958, a bloody, terrible year in Eastern Tibet."

Though mostly Tibetan men were killed in the actual fighting, the reprisal killing and massacres that followed included women and children. And the latter deaths did not just occur as "collateral damage." Often there was clear intent in the decision to murder them. The Communists viewed the crime of being a counter-revolutionary, a rebel bandit or an imperialist lackey etc., not merely as a political or criminal offence committed by a specific person, but as an inheritable condition that was transferred, as if genetically, to subsequent generations. The child of a former landlord inherited his parent's class background and whatever disadvantages, even penalties, that went along with it.

One of my principal informants on the Nyarong uprising, Aten Dogyaltsang, who had been a minor official in the Chinese administration at the Castle of the Female Dragon and had even participated in a "Peaceful Suppression of Rebels" campaign or two, remembered coming across a nomad encampment at Thangkya where the Chinese had massacred everybody, including women and children, about five hundred people in all. Even babies had been killed, and he saw dogs tearing at their little bodies. He might have revealed his distress in his expression, for he remembered his commander, Captain Len, lecturing him on why it was the duty of the PLA to exterminate all counter-revolutionaries, even the women and children, concluding with a little homily on preventive hygiene, "If you squash the nits, there will be no more lice."[27] I heard this analogy of Tibetan children to "nits" in many more interviews and discussions with Tibetans who had had dealings with Chinese Communist officials.

Colonel (Reverend) John Millington Chivington of the Third Regiment of Colorado Volunteers defended his slaughter of Indian children by declaring: "Nits make lice." General Sheridan would remind the raw recruits signing up for Indian fighting with this exhortation for total war: "Always remember that nits grow into lice."

There is an intellectual back and forth on whether Native Americans were the victims of a clear-cut genocide, like the Jews in Nazi Germany. During the Vietnam War period, the sweeping charge of genocide by white America against Indians was popular with liberal academia and young people. In the following decades, the argument has shifted somewhat to the other side. Still, there is definitely no argument that large-scale massacres as Wounded Knee and Sand Creek or the Trail of Tears forced relocation did happen and could be described at least as "acts of genocide".

The International Commission of Jurists in Geneva (ICJ), in their report on Tibet of 24 June 1959, stated that there was *prima facie* evidence that the Communist Chinese had committed acts of genocide in Tibet, with the intention of destroying the Tibetan nation and the Buddhist religion in Tibet. This was the main document that the exile government for many years used to make its case, especially in the United Nations. But impressive as the ICJ's report was, it was patchy regarding sources, and since it was published in 1959, did not include the deaths that had occurred subsequently, in slave-labour camps and the "Great Famine".

For years, the Tibetan exile government in Dharamshala attempted to put together a comprehensive figure for Tibetans who had died under Chinese rule. A commission was set up under a senior official, Kungo Dhakden, who sent out junior officials to the Tibetans settlements in India, Nepal and Bhutan to examine the claims of refugees, especially those who had come out of Tibet after Mao's death and Deng's "liberalization". According to the English writer Patrick French "At the end of the process, it was concluded that precisely 1,207,387 Tibetans had died between 1950 and 1979 from starvation, fighting, torture, execution, suicide and struggle sessions." In his book *Tibet, Tibet: A Personal History of a Lost Land*, French devotes six full pages to describing the work of the commission and largely discrediting it.

French was not that far wrong about the accuracy of the report and the methodology employed in its formulation, which had not exactly been scientific. Kungo Dhakden had been an official of the old Tibetan government and spoke no English and had no idea of modern statistical methods, computing or analysis. Nor did any one of his tiny staff, or for that matter anyone in the exile government. They most probably used abacuses to tally their figures. Even those of us working in Dharamshala who spoke or read English were far from experts in any field. Most of us (including myself) had just managed to finish high school.

Twenty-five years earlier, I wrote about my frustration with left-leaning Western journalists as Chris Mullins and Felix Greene unfairly dismissing Tibetan refugee statements for some inadequacy in their presentation, overlooking the fundamental fact that there had been no intent to deceive when these statements were collected and compiled by a ". . . hole-in-the-wall office in Dharamshala that lacked the necessary trained personnel, money and know-how to do an adequate job."[28] No human rights organization or UN agency ever came to Dharamshala to provide expertise or funds for Tibetans to do the necessary research, archiving and evaluation of such information.

French, when discrediting the Tibetan report, also makes no allowance for the conditions under which they had been compiled and for the fact that, however lacking in methodology, there had been an

honest if inadequate attempt to get at the facts. French was allowed
the run of the exile information office and its staff, who answered all
his questions. He was even given a Tibetan translator to help him, and
who agreed with him about the limitations of the report. On the other
hand, French did not have access to official Chinese records on the
mass killing in Tibet, and he did not even bother to put in a request to
Beijing, probably knowing he would not get it. Yet, the fundamental
thesis of French's book is that Tibetans should give up their struggle
and stop condemning China on these matters, and that people in the
West should not encourage them.

Even when Tibetans have obtained and produced actual Chinese
records to back up their case, it has always been an uphill task to
convince Western academia of its contents. Dharamshala managed to
obtain official Chinese documents to base its figures, for those killed in
the Lhasa Uprising and its aftermath. A booklet marked "secret" and
published in Lhasa on 1 October 1960, by the political department
of the Tibetan Military District, says of the aftermath of the Lhasa
Uprising: "From last March up to now we have already wiped out
(*xiaomie*) over 87,000 of the enemy."[29]

At a conference I attended at Harvard in 2002, on "Tibet and the
Cold War," some American Sinologists there insisted on explaining
that the term *xiaomie*, though literally "wipe out", could be interpreted
to mean "imprisoned" or "removed" and so on. Of course, many
words in different languages have alternative or synonymous meanings.
At a famous libel trial in London in 1994, the notorious holocaust
denier, David Irving, made a similar comment about the German term
"*Ausrottung*" (extirpation) used by Hitler, which Irving argued did not
mean mass-murder but rather "uproot" or "enforced immigration".[30]
He also took issue with the word "*Vernichtung*," which historians
generally considered a euphemism for annihilation. Irving argued that
the term was used by the Nazis only in a rhetorical sense.

Samantha Power, founding director of the Harvard Carr Center
for Human Rights Policy and former United States Ambassador to the
United Nations offers us a useful rule-of-thumb for evaluating such
tragic though invariably complex events. "The stories that emerge from

genocidal societies are by definition incredible. That was the lesson the Holocaust should have taught us. In case after case of genocide, accounts that sounded far-fetched and that could not be independently verified repeatedly proved true. With so much wishful thinking debunked, we should have long ago shifted the burden of proof away from the refugees and to the sceptics, who should be required to offer a persuasive reason for disputing eyewitness claims. A bias towards belief would do less harm than a bias toward disbelief."[31]

One explanation of why this "bias towards disbelief", still persists is provided by the Pulitzer Prize-winning journalist and author Anne Applebaum, who tells us how ". . . the UN Convention [on Genocide of 1948] was shaped in large part by Soviet delegates who were eager to limit the definition of genocide to acts committed by proponents of fascists and racist ideologies."[32]

Raphael Lemkin, the Polish-Jewish lawyer who first coined the term "genocide" and whose many years of tireless campaigning initiated the UN Genocide Convention, had a broader view of the crime of genocide than what the Soviets managed to establish in the UN convention. "Genocide does not necessarily mean the immediate destruction of a nation . . . It is intended rather, to signify a coordinated plan of different actions aiming at the destruction of essential foundations of the life of national groups, with the eventual aim of annihilating the groups themselves."[33]

If we accept the expertise of the man who coined the term "genocide" and who initiated the UN Genocide Convention in 1948, then genocide had most certainly taken place in Tibet.

15

THE MAN WHOSE LUCK DRIED UP

The Rangzen (independence) Gym at McLeod Ganj is below the ramshackle wooden "Community Center" on Bhagsu Road. The place is not well lit. A couple of 75-watt bulbs just about push back the shadows on the discoloured patchy walls so you can see where most of the plaster has fallen off. Many of the glass panes on the windows are missing and have been replaced with bits of cardboard and packing wood.

The whole place has a musty odour of sweat and monsoon damp. There's nothing fancy about the equipment either. There are no treadmills, stair-masters or nautilus machines, just a chinning bar, a parallel bar, a punching bag and a few benches. A box full of scrap iron tied to a cable and looped over a pulley lashed to a roof beam serves as a counterweight for a makeshift "lat" pull-down machine. Scattered about the room are old free-weights, a row of mismatched dumbbells lined up neatly in a corner and a few barbells. Some of the plates are cracked and have been repaired with crude welds. On the back wall is a small picture of the Dalai Lama and a larger framed photograph of Thupten Ngodup, the former paratrooper who set himself on fire in 1998 to protest the UN's indifference to the Tibetan issue.

Two skinny bare-chested kids pose self-consciously in front of a mirror. The regulars are absorbed in their routines. They are fairly well built but lack the bulk of real bodybuilders. One tall young man with close-cropped hair, probably a monk, does overhead presses, and the muscles of his shoulders and back wriggle impressively. The preferred gym-wear, especially in the choice of trousers, seems to be military in inspiration: camouflage, olive-green or khaki fatigues with big side pockets.

There is a pause in the clanking of the weights and the grunt of lifters when an old man walks in. He appears to have a bad knee, which makes him drag his right leg slightly. He holds a rosary in his right hand and has probably been walking around the *Lingkor*, the *via sacra*, the narrow path encircling the Temple and the Dalai Lama's residence. Nearly all the older Tibetans in McLeod Ganj diligently perform this *kora* walk, this circumambulation, as a religious practice and for the exercise. The bodybuilders in the gym greet the old man in a friendly way and trade a little banter. The old man responds with a weak joke. "Okay boys, back to your training. We have to represent Tibet in the Olympic Games." He then goes to a corner and warms up with some stretching exercises. After that, he picks up a set of light dumbbells and slowly and somewhat painfully goes through his daily exercise routine.

No one seemed to know much about him. For the guys at the gym, he was just an unusual old man because most senior Tibetans never came to the gym or exercised, apart from their *kora* walks and prostrations at the Temple which were fairly effective workouts in themselves. One day, someone told me that the old man had been involved in the Lhasa Uprising of 1959 and had been one of the defenders of the Jokhang temple at the heart of the Holy City.

The first proper play I ever wrote, *The Chinese Horse*, had been the story of a merchant family of Lhasa torn apart by this conflict, and I had done a little research on this period and the specific event. Somehow, I hadn't really managed to get a clear picture of the whole insurrection. The people I had talked to were either fleeing civilians or volunteer fighters manning a barricade on a street corner, and their recollections were partial, often fragmentary. I didn't expect more than that from the old man, but I thought it would be interesting to get another personal account to add to those I already had. I got quite a bit more.

"I was born ill-omened—they told me that when I was a boy. Our family horse dropped dead the year I was born. The year after that, one of our best *dzo* [a cow/yak hybrid] died. People said I was someone whose "luck had dried up" [*sothey kambo*] as the phrase is. Well, I can believe that now . . . looking back at all that has happened to me."

He ran his hand through his thick spiky grey hair, cut *en brosse*, and scratched. He had contracted a skin infection in Chinese prison and was always scratching himself: his neck, his arms and his legs, sometimes reaching under his shirt to have a go at his chest or back. It made me itch just to watch. He seemed to have a defective ear, and his eyesight wasn't good either. He wore spectacles with thick lenses in a National Health type of frame. In spite of these shortcomings, he managed to maintain a soldierly appearance. He was neatly turned out and had a white handkerchief tied around his neck to protect his shirt collar. His rather ugly lined face retained some of the pugnacity that had caught my attention in an old photograph I had seen in the files of the Tibetan Security Office, where I had earlier asked for some background information on him.

He was one of the few still living who had been at the centre of the fighting in Lhasa in March 1959 and also one of the very few who had survived being parachuted into Chinese occupied Tibet on a secret mission. I heard stories of bloody battles and murderous firefights culminating in the death of his comrades and his own desperate capture after an attempt to bite a cyanide capsule. Somehow, he survived the poison and eighteen hellish years in Chinese prisons and *Laogai* labour camps. He was a hero, without a doubt, but not a lucky man, as he himself pointed out.

After all his appalling misadventures and suffering, he finally managed to make it to Dharamshala in 1980, a free but now an old and forgotten man. His bad luck still dogged him. For no apparent reason, he had been set upon by a gang of drunken Amdowa politicians in the exile capital who had beaten him senseless.

It had all taken its toll. In spite of his efforts to maintain a smart turnout, he looked far older than his sixty years; and he slowed down, now and then, like a wind-up toy at the end of its spring and became tongue-tied and confused.

But he was not reluctant to tell me his story. He invited me to his small one-room apartment. It had just enough space in it for two beds, covered with hand-woven rugs and placed at right angles to each other like an uppercase "L", the most common sleeping and sitting arrangement of poorer Tibetans and known as the "horse-head corner" (ta-summa). A square wooden table between the beds completed the furnishing. He had curtained off a corner of the room with a length of grey cambric for a tiny kitchen space. He at once set about making tea. He churned a large thermos flask of Tibetan tea for himself and made a flask of sweet tea for me. He poured me the first of many cups that I was to drink for over the next two weeks. He also placed a small Bhutanese basket of hard Tibetan biscuits on the table. He spoke very softly. He often mumbled and became inaudible. Sometimes he would start to say something and then, losing himself in thought, would let his words trail away. But he wanted to tell his story.[1]

He was called Bhusang or "Good Boy". It was the kind of simple and hopeful name favoured by peasants in Tibet. He was born in the Iron-Sheep year (1931) at the village of Bhartang in Nyemo district. His family name was Bhonshöd. It was a *drong-chima* family, which meant that it was the only family of that village and farmed most of the land around it. Since their farm was large, they sublet some of the land to other peasants and sharecroppers. They sowed forty to fifty *khels* of seed at one planting. (The khel is about 14 kilograms, and each khel can be subdivided into 28 *gyama*.) This was taking into account the land they had to leave fallow every year for it to recover its "earth-nutrition" (sa-chue). They also kept sheep, cows, a horse (the one that died) and *dzos* for ploughing.

"Were you a *gerpa* (free-holder) or a *me-ser* (the subject of an aristocrat or a monastery)?" I asked, for in spite of sometimes being described as a feudal country, about fifty per cent of agriculturalists in Tibet were free-holders with land leased to them directly by the central government. Even according to Chinese Communist statistics, the monasteries held only thirty per cent of the land and the aristocracy about twenty. The standard tax for cultivators was traditionally one-sixth (16.6 per cent) of the gross produce.

"An aristocrat," Bhusang replied, "The House of Thönpa. You know they are descendants of the great Minister Thönmi Sambhota."

Sambhota was a minister of the Emperor of Tibet, Songtsen Gampo, who first unified the various tribes and kingdoms on the Tibetan plateau and created the Tibetan Empire. With remarkable foresight and self-assurance, the Tibetan Emperor looked beyond the brilliant cultural attainments, the unprecedented grandeur and might of Tang dynasty China, then the world's most sophisticated and powerful country, and did not allow himself to be overwhelmed into adopting ". . . the most cumbersome of writing systems" (according to Edwin O. Reischauer) as did some of China's other neighbouring countries as Japan, Korea and Vietnam. Instead, the Emperor sent Thönmi Sambhota to India where, after a period of study, the minister came up with an uncomplicated alphabetic system, based on a Gupta Brahmi script, admirably suited to reproducing the sounds of spoken Tibetan.

"How did they treat their *me-ser* farmers?"

"They were hard," he replied without hesitation. "Very hard. My father, Tawang Norbu, was a good carpenter. He had learnt the craft from his father. But my father resented working for Thönpa. At the manor, they didn't serve him proper meals, tea and barley-ale, as was the custom. He, of course, received no wages, his service being part of his tax obligations. It was much more profitable being a craftsman in Lhasa than a farmer in Nyemo. It's a back-breaking, unrewarding business—farming. So, my dad abandoned us and went to Lhasa, where he joined the stonemason and carpenter's guild (*do-shing chiba*). There was nothing Thönpa could do to get my father back. The guild had influence in the government, and it wasn't easy to intimidate it. It even had representation in the National Assembly, the old parliament. So Thönpa became angry and spiteful. He resumed our land which, in a narrow legal sense he was entitled to do and sublet it to two other *me-ser* farmers."

"But didn't you have any other men in the family to clear your tax obligations—uncles and cousins?"

"My dad had three brothers, but none were any use to us then. One was a soldier with the Drapchi regiment. We were liable for the military tax (*mak-tre*) because of the size of our land. I don't remember his name. Another uncle, Kunchok, was sent as a bridegroom to a nomad family in Drigung [a hundred miles north-east of Lhasa]. I never met him. The oldest brother in the family was my uncle Gyatso who was a carpenter in Lhasa. I met him much later in life, during the 1959 Uprising and later in a Chinese prison camp. He died in 1987. My father died in 1946.

"My mother tried desperately to keep things together, but it was impossible. Her name was Sonam Yudon. She came from the neighbouring village of Tashiling, across the river, the very village where the great minister Thönmi Sambhota was born. So, in the end, we lost our land. My older sister Pemba Dolma was already married and had left home. She was a sensible, kind-hearted and strong girl—very hard-working. Like everyone else, she suffered under Chinese oppression. Her husband joined the Nyemo uprising in 1969. He was arrested and 'struggled' to death. My sister still lives there, in Nyemo. I write to her, now and then. I got a letter from her recently. She wanted to send her son—smuggle him across to India—to Dharamshala to study at the Tibetan Children's Village.

"Now, when the family broke up, my mother had to parcel out her other kids here and there. My younger sister was sent as a maid to the home of a tantric priest (*ngakpa*) who was a family friend and a good sort. She died of starvation in the sixties. I had a younger brother who was called Gyephur as he was born on the eighth (*gye*) day of the month on a Thursday (*phurbu*). A distant relative of ours, a monk,

Chönze Ngawang Lungtok, wanted to adopt the boy, as Chönze himself had no immediate family. So Gyephur went to live with him. Gyephur was also 'struggled' in 1969. He committed suicide by jumping into the river in front of our home.

"So Thönpa broke up our family, scattered us like a handful of seed grain. *Kunchok sum!*[*] When I think of all that I went through . . . my service, my loyalty to the government and my country . . . and the way Thönpa broke up my family . . . I sometimes ask myself why I did it, why I fought and suffered all these years, why I 'put my life on the target (*sok benla tsuk*)'—so many times. In prison, my Communist interrogators and other cadres would say I was stupid for being loyal to the old regime that had mistreated me and my family, especially when the Communist Party was 'giving land to the landless, and power to the people'."

"So why *did* you remain loyal?"

"Well, the Communists were lying. I knew that. I wasn't that stupid. They weren't giving anything away. Just taking—taking everything from our country: gold, silver, jewels, all our precious statues and ritual objects, and now our trees and minerals—everything, even our food. And hard as he was, Thönpa didn't murder anyone. The Communists killed my brother, my brother-in-law, and starved my sister and my children to death. To be fair to the aristocrats, not all of them were like Thönpa. The old Lord, Thönpa Jampa Khedrup, himself was not a particularly bad person. His mother was the hard one. To look at him, the Lord Thönpa was impressive, a big stout man, with large bright eyes. But he was a moody and ill-tempered sort of person and not well educated. His son wasn't too bright either. The son and I were in the same prison later on.

"The old lord died in 1959. Whatever his faults, he gave a good account of himself during the Uprising. The moment the fighting started in the city, he distributed the rifles and pistols in the house among his servants, and personally commenced shooting at the Chinese from his living-room window. Just next to the Thönpa Mansion is Surkhang house, which had become the headquarters of the Chinese Public Security Bureau, the *Gong'anju*, so the old lord didn't have to leave his home to join the fighting. He really fought well. In the end, of

---

[*] The Buddhist Trinity: the Buddha, the Dharma, and the Sangha—the most common of Tibetan oaths.

course, Chinese soldiers broke into the Thönpa Mansion and gunned him down. Shot him full of holes like a tea strainer. He distinguished himself and upheld the honour of his family and the Thönpa name, but he was not kind to his servants and *me-ser* farmers.

"I had a lot of time in prison to think over these things, and I feel it's no use blaming individuals for the wrongs of our old society. The whole thing is a historical process. Democracy and egalitarianism can only be realized gradually in stages. Society only changes when the cultural level of individuals in society increases. All societies have gone through a period of feudalism, like in Tibet. And we Tibetans could not have avoided that transition. In order to move further, we have to acquire knowledge and culture. If we don't, we will be forced by others to change. I formulated these ideas gradually over a period of years."

Marxist theories of history, derived in part from the Social Darwinism of the late nineteenth century, do not really square with Buddhist concepts of human evolution, which is progressive only in the sense that it postulates an ultimate theoretical future when all living creatures will have obtained nirvana. But many Tibetans (including the Dalai Lama) who have studied, or been made to study, the somewhat crude Chinese version of Marxist social and historical theories, seem to experience no internal contradiction in subscribing to these conflicting views at the same time.

There was, admittedly, a Candide-like naïveté in the way Bhusang tried to justify his loyalty to his old world, although he had been a far from a privileged member of it. The philosophy he had developed to explain his ideas and beliefs may have been derivative in large part and somewhat simplistic, but it was certainly more level-headed than the childish optimism of Voltaire's hero, also wandering from one disaster to another throughout his life, unshaken in his faith in Dr Pangloss, his tutor, whose philosophy of life was encapsulated in this assertion: "All is for the best in this best of all possible worlds." Bhusang's philosophy was not so starry-eyed, but being a Tibetan, it did not lack for a touch of the supernatural.

"I have also been told, and I am personally convinced that I am ill-omened. I think I told you about our horse and best *dzo* dying after

I was born." His eyes looked distant. "In summer, we would take the *dzo* and other animals up the mountains to graze, and in autumn, when they were nice and fat they would be brought down back to the farm. That was, of course, when we had our own farm. It was a wonderful time. A time of great happiness." He sighed. "It was such a beautiful place. I know everyone says that about their *phayul* (homeland). But Nyemo was very special."

Bhusang's childhood memories are borne out in the account of a young resistance fighter who rode through the Nyemo district with Andrugtsang Gonpo Tashi and the Four Rivers Six Ranges in 1958:

> We came to Nyemo from the south, after crossing the Tsangpo [Bhramputra] River. Initially, from the outside, it seemed barren and desolate. The mountains before it were rocky and bare. But when you entered the Nyemo valley, the landscape was transformed in an amazing way. It became surprisingly beautiful, like a dream. The surrounding hills were lush meadows and, in the distance, were three snow-covered mountains.*
>
> The fields in the broad valley were green and fertile, with trees growing everywhere. There were even peach trees in full bloom. The farmhouses and barns of the peasants were well constructed and delightful. Running through the length of the valley was this big river, the Nyemo Machu, with its tributaries and streams. All of it looked so whole, pure and sacred (*phusum tsokpa*)—a world in itself.
>
> As we rode by, the late afternoon sun cast a golden glow over the fields and mountains and made the place look like one of those hidden lands, *beyul*,† that Guru Rinpoche spoke about.[2]
>
> So, we had to leave Nyemo. My mother took my baby sister and me to Lhasa, where she worked as a maid in the Thönpa Mansion

---

*Kumalungpa Gangri and Jhomo Gangtse to the north and Gangri Pelkyi to the east.

†*Beyul* (literally "hidden land") are secret valleys inside Tibet revealed by Padmasambhava in the eighth century, whose locations were concealed in secret scrolls. They are idyllic, sacred places of refuge for the faithful during times of war and calamity.

there. Her main duty was to sweep the first floor of the large three-storeyed building. She also did much of the laundry and helped in the kitchen. I worked in the kitchen, too, carrying dried pats of yak-dung, which you know was the main fuel source in most of Tibet. I also helped to look after the horses and mules.

In the spring and autumn, I had to help with the farming at the Thönpa estate called Gutsa, which was about four or five kilometres from the city. Gutsa is now the site of a big Chinese prison camp—from what I've heard, the worst. Actually, the land didn't belong to Thönpa, but had been leased to him by the Namgyal Dratsang (the Dalai Lama's personal monastery at the Potala). Therefore Thönpa did not have any of his own *me-ser* farmers there and had to use whatever servants and men were available at his Lhasa mansion, you know, for sowing, harvesting and such things.

All of Thönpa's dung fuel came from this estate, and I had to go and fetch it on donkeys. I also carried messages to the estate, to the estate manager, and would ride a mule for that. From Gutsa, I would also haul hay in summer and straw in winter to feed Thönpa's horses and mules at his stables in Lhasa. I enjoyed working with the animals and riding them. Being a country boy, I was used to working with animals and liked being with them. When you are a kid, you don't think very much. I was quite happy riding the donkeys and mules—from Lhasa to Gutsa and back.

One day, on returning to the city, I found my mother tied to a pillar in the courtyard of the mansion. She seemed to be in a bad way and was crying. I let go of the mule I was leading and rushed to her. I hugged her, shouting "Ama! Ama!" I was a young boy, about eleven, and the scene frightened and upset me. The other servants tried to console me, giving me tea and tsampa and saying that my mother would soon be released.

Earlier that day, when my mother had been doing the household laundry, she had somehow lost a sleeveless dress belong to another servant. She was not sure whether she had left it behind at the river or lost it somewhere else. The head-steward of the Thönpa household accused her of stealing the dress and had her tied up to force a confession out of her, and prevent her from running away.

I should mention that she had not been beaten or anything, just tied up. She was locked up in an empty storeroom for two days. The steward searched our small room but, of course, found nothing. We had just come to Lhasa from our village and were completely artless. Anyhow, we had no place to hide anything in our small room. After being locked up in an empty storeroom for two days, my mother was released but had to pay compensation for the dress she had lost from her wages. It came to about a month's wages. She received about thirty-five *dre* of tsampa a month and a little butter. The *dre* is about half a kilo and is the standard for the measuring box. Twenty *dres* make up a *bo* which would be about fourteen kilograms. I received one *dre* of tsampa a day. The rations were inadequate.

The Thönpa family was exceptionally miserly and did not serve common meals to the servants. Even the tea the servants got was not the real thing, but the bark of a certain tree, *Popo-richa*, which gives a red liquid when boiled. Some people drink this infusion instead of tea for their health, but not us. We got it as it was cheap. The other servants were treated in much the same way. Many of them bought their own tea bricks in the market and brewed their own. Most of the time, everyone was just eating tsampa, without any soup or vegetables or meat stew to help it down. After a meal like that, you didn't have much washing up to do. It was all very convenient.

The Thönpa family was, quite possibly, the worst among the aristocracy in the way it treated its own people. It was typically my luck to have been born in its service. Even the minister Kapshöpa *daru-go* (two-faced) treated his servants and tenant farmers kindly. Soon afterwards, my mother ran away, taking my baby sister with her. I never saw her again till I came out of Chinese prison thirty-five years later.

The Thönpa Mansion in Lhasa is in the Barkhor [the Inner Sacred Circuit] and close to the Jokhang, the Central Temple. I don't know why, but the mansion was called Labrang Nyingpa or "the Old Lama's Abode". Maybe it was a part of a monastery before.

This mansion, on the northern side of Barkhor South, is one of the oldest and most imposing residential buildings in the Barkhor circuit and has a long and rich history. Tsongkhapa, the founder of the Gelukpa School of Tibetan Buddhism, lived here whenever he visited Lhasa. The Great Fifth Dalai Lama used this mansion as his town residence until he moved into a set of apartments in the Jokhang Temple complex. The construction of the Potala Palace was only completed after the death of the Great Fifth. This description of the Thönpa Mansion appeared in an architectural study of Lhasa city:

> The three-story stone building has a simple layout with a very pleasant and well-lit central courtyard. Labrang Nyingba is solidly built, with high quality craftsmanship and decorations visible throughout the building. The street façade is well proportioned and has an interesting rhythm of windows. The main gate has a small roof or overhang with cantilevered brackets . . . Handsome stone steps in the corner of the courtyard provide access to the gallery that surrounds the courtyard on three sides. Shops on the ground floor open towards Barkhor Square. A common feature of these buildings is the incense burner on the roof; at Labrang Nyingba, it is designed and built with particular care. Also of note is the roof shrine.[3]

"The Thönpa Mansion was huge and very old," Bhusang continued. "There were many rooms. Some of them were dark and rather scary. Whenever I had some free time, I would go upstairs and climb up on the low wall that encircled the flat roof space. The roof of the building had these enormous incense burners and a shrine room, where a couple of resident monks would be reading aloud from *pecha* texts or conducting a service. I would sit on the curved top of the wall called the *hapcha*, which was waterproofed to prevent rain from soaking into the rammed earth wall. I would look down from over the wall and watch all the various people of the city walking about in the street below, buying and selling things, talking to one another, going to the temple, fetching water from the well, or just hanging around. The ground floor of the mansion facing the street was lined with shops and stalls. This was the busiest part of Lhasa city, so it was always interesting and fun to watch."

For a boy from the countryside, there was much to marvel at. The Japanese spy, Hisao Kimura, mentioned in an earlier chapter, was amazed when after his long trek from Kokonor, he first set eyes on Lhasa. "After the past year and a half in the wilds, I was overwhelmed to find myself surrounded by such a wealth of merchandise. There were hardware stores, milliners, the shops of gold and silversmiths, others selling household needs, and not a few specializing in religious items. The street merchants offered mostly a dazzling array of goods imported from India: cotton and woollen textiles, blankets, shoes, hats, soaps (this a real novelty), matches, dyes, cups, mirrors, sunglasses, cigarettes, white and brown sugar and ivory bracelets. It was difficult for one accustomed to the simplicity of nomadic and caravan life to believe that such a variety of commodities could all have their uses. But most surprising was the quantity of American, British, and even Japanese military equipment openly for sale. I saw pistols, machine guns, grenades, and ammunition; all sorts of light weapons."[4]

A merchant from Nepal has written that when newcomers from Kathmandu saw street vendors selling rifles, pistols and ammunition on the streets of Lhasa, their "jaws dropped". He explains why. "In Nepal, in the oppressive political climate of the era, even talking about guns was treated like sedition."[5] Weapons sales were tightly regulated in British India also.[6] The government of Tibet, however slow, complacent and anachronistic, was not afraid of its people. Only in 1949, when Lhasa was awash with WWII surplus weapons and gun accidents had become alarmingly frequent, did the authorities realize that it was becoming too much of a good thing. Orders were issued for all firearms in the city to be registered. I still have the permit issued to my father for his carbine and pistol.

President Roosevelt's envoys to Tibet noticed Helena Rubenstein cosmetics and "Evening in Paris" perfumes being sold in the Lhasa marketplace. Heinrich Harrer mentions that "one might even find the Elizabeth Arden specialities . . ." and added that ". . . there is a keen demand for them." As might be expected, there was some monkish condemnation of this new foreign fad. But a witty Lhasa lady settled the matter in a popular verse that also underscored the financial independence of many Tibetan women.

I've put on the white (face powder) myself,
I've put on the red (lipstick, rouge)myself.
Don't be upset, you honourable fault-finders.
I've paid for it all, myself

Karpo nga-ras jhug-yöd,
marpo nga-ras jhug-yöd,
lhan-gai gong-pa ma-tsum,
nga-ras ba-kug trog-yöd

The basic essentials and relative luxuries obtainable in the marketplace of old Lhasa were sorely missed by Tibetans in the later years of the Chinese Communist occupation. Tashi Tsering, a Lhasa resident and admirer of Communist China, having escaped to the United States in 1957, decided to return home (via Havana and Beijing) in 1966. His first impression of the new worker's paradise of Lhasa:

> There was nothing for sale on the streets anymore. Gone were the cramped booths heaped full of wares, the voice of salespeople and customers laughing and haggling, and the many tea and beer shops I used to frequent. In their place were a few poorly stocked government stores. It soon became clear that the people weren't very well fed. Food was rationed, and there was almost no meat or butter or potatoes. I had lived in the old Lhasa for many years and was under no illusions about its shortcomings. However, there had always been a lot of food, and if you had any money to spend at all, you had quite a bit of freedom and choice. Now the food was rationed at low levels.[7]

The old medieval Lhasa of the 1940s that young Bhusang marvelled at from the roof of the Thönpa Mansion was a relatively prosperous town and a carefree haven compared to, not just the "socialist paradise" it was fated to become, but many other cities of Europe and East Asia then, bombed to rubble and consumed by war and misery.

"One day, I was leaning over the wall, in my usual way, when I saw this woman walking down the street in the direction of Thönpa house. I'm not sure why, but I instinctively felt that she might have something to do with me. Sure enough, she stopped at the front of our building, and after looking this way and that, walked through the main gate. Some moments later, I was summoned by one of the servants. She turned out to be my father's new wife. She had heard I was living alone at the Thönpa Mansion and had come to see if I needed anything. I went to stay with her and my father for a week. She was a kind woman and fed me well. My father was not unkind but somewhat indifferent. I had hoped for some show of affection from him, but there was not much of that. His wife was a kind and decent woman and insisted I stay with them. But I didn't know them, and they had two kids of their own, anyway. So, I went back to my master's house. I would visit my father, or rather his wife, now and then. She would always feed me a wonderful meal, but she never let me take home any. I had to eat it all there. I don't know why she did that. She probably didn't want me to get into any trouble back at the Thönpa household.

"You know, when you're a kid, you see things very differently. After a while, I didn't miss my mother all that much. I was okay with living at the Thönpa Mansion. The other servants were kind to me, and aside from work, I could do as I pleased. Besides, I had donkeys and mules to ride, which not every kid in Lhasa had. I really thought no end of myself when I rode into Lhasa on a mule, while the other urchins ran about the dusty streets.

"When I was around twelve, my master enlisted me in the Guards regiment. He had a skilled tailor called Topgyal, serving in that regiment, and Lord Thönpa wanted him out and working for him at the mansion. I was to be his replacement. Actually, the minimum age for getting into the army is sixteen, but the Thönpa steward lied and said that I was short for my age. So, I was taken to Army Headquarters at the Shöl administrative complex below the Potala, and there had the military identification band attached to my left wrist. It is our equivalent of the American dog tag, I guess, the kind the CIA gave me when I got to Colorado. Our Tibetan identification band is called the *lak-tey*. It is made of wool and has a round bit, like a watch face, on which the seal of the Army Headquarters (*makchi-khang*) is impressed. On the seal are the words 'The Central Military Headquarters of the Heavenly

Army of the Tibetan Nation.' You also had to answer questions about your background and sign a contract, which had to be countersigned by another person who was standing surety for you. Then they tied the I.D. band on your wrist, and you officially became a soldier of the government.

"From Headquarters, another boy, Thundup Gyalpo, and myself were sent to the Guards barracks at the Norbulingka, the Dalai Lama's summer palace. We only stayed there for about a week and were then sent to the Signals Training Section, where we would be taught to signal with flags and later with the heliograph. We would also be taught to play the various bugle calls. The soldiers made up funny lines to go with the tunes. I remember this one: 'Corporal Tashi eat my shit, ta-ta-ra-ra-ta-taaaa!'

"But I didn't have to stay with Signals very long. One day that summer, I was summoned by a young officer from the regiment and asked if I wanted to go to school or whether I wanted to stay at the military camp. I replied that I would like to go to school. He said that I would have to work hard at school and be a credit to the regiment. I was sent along with the other boy, Thundup Gyalpo—who became my best friend—to the Lhasa Mentsikhang School in the heart of the city to begin my education to become an army medical personnel."

The Lhasa Mentsikhang, or the Lhasa Medical and Astrological Center, was founded by the Thirteenth Dalai Lama and his physician Khenrab Norbu in 1916, in a major effort to improve the health and medical condition of all Tibetans, especially children. There was an older medical college on the Iron Hill, Chakpori, next to the Potala, but it was a smaller and largely ecclesiastical institution. It had been established during the reign of the Fifth Dalai Lama, and there are references in various Tibetan records and texts to other health and medical projects undertaken at that time by the Fifth Dalai Lama and his prime minister, Desi Sangye Gyatso, who authored a major treatise on Tibetan medicine, the *Mirror of Beryl*.

But the origins of medical science in Tibet go back much further. The historian Pawo Tsuglag-trengwa (1504–1555) in his *History of Tibetan Medicine* (sman-gyi chos-'byung dang'bam bcos) tells us that

the Tibetan emperor Songtsen Gampo invited the physician Bharad-
raja from India, the physician Han-wang Hang from China and, rather
intriguingly, a Greek physician Galenos* from Drom of Tagzik (The
Eastern Roman Empire) to Lhasa, for what might perhaps be described
as one of the first international medical conferences ever held.

The proceedings of the many discussions between these physicians
were compiled into a medical work, *The Weapon of the Fearless One* (mi-
'jigs-pa'i mtshon-cha). Galenos stayed behind in Lhasa to become the
emperor's personal physician and initiated the training and education
of Tibetan medical students, which his son Joros carried on after him.

The Lhasa Medical and Astrological Centre of the Thirteenth
Dalai Lama had two principal goals. One was to train a large number
of doctors in traditional Tibetan medicine. The students were selected
from every regiment in the Tibetan army, the major monasteries, and
from various district headquarters. The Lhasa Medical Centre had
no fewer than one hundred and fifty students in its roll, at any given
time. After a nine-year course of study and a rigorous examination, the
qualified doctor would be sent back to the organization or district he
had come from to set up his medical practice. An outpatient unit and
a small public welfare centre were also set up near the Mentsikhang to
distribute food and free medicine to the poor and disabled.

The other mission of the Lhasa Medical Centre was to combat
throughout Tibet the serious problem of infant mortality. For this,
the "Routine Child Care and Welfare" (*chipa nyerchö*) project was
initiated. Every district magistrate in Tibet was instructed to register
the birth of all children in the district. The names of the children,
along with their date and time of birth, were to be sent immediately to
the Medical Centre in Lhasa. At the centre the astrological department
would prepare individual horoscopes for the children, and the doctors
and pharmacists would prepare prescriptions for each child in keeping
with their respective astrological charts. This, according to the late state

---

*This was, of course, not Claudius Galenos, aka Galen of Pergamon
(CE 129–c. 216), the great physician and medical-researcher of antiquity,
but probably another doctor from the Graeco-Roman world who might
have adopted the name out of admiration for his illustrious predecessor.

astrologer, Drakthon Jampa Gyaltsen, was the chief reason why medical and astrological studies were brought together at the Lhasa Medical Centre. In pediatrics the theoretical symbiosis between medicine and astrology received greater emphasis than it did in general medicine.

The medicines for the Child Care Program would be bagged in individual cloth bags and sent back to the district headquarters, where the parents of the children would be summoned, and the horoscopes and medicines distributed. The names of the children were also added to the prayer rolls of the Namgyal Monastery at the Potala palace and special services conducted for their health and welfare. A small pamphlet titled *Routine Child Care and Welfare* was printed and distributed by the Medical Centre. It appears that the district magistrate, or more probably one of his clerical staff, would read the instructions on childcare to the assembled parents. This publication is still in print.

The late state astrologer, Drakton Jampa Gyaltsen was a good friend of mine and contributed a popular astrological column for a Tibetan newspaper I edited from 1993 to 1996. He told me that when his father was posted as the magistrate of Kyirong district in the 1950s, even after the Communist Chinese occupation, he remembered the district headquarters there receiving horoscopes and medicine from Lhasa for distribution to the newborn children of Kyirong. Though the science of this childcare service was wholly traditional, and its scope restricted because of the limited resources of the Tibetan government, it might be mentioned that it was provided free to all children.[*]

"All of us students had to get up early, before dawn, and gather in the assembly hall for the reading and memorization of texts. There were, of course, different texts for those studying medicine and for those studying astrology. The students from the army studied medicine. When the entire class started to read the pages of the text for that day, students had to go, one at a time, before our teacher and

---

[*] Mrs Dorje Yudon Yuthok, in her memoirs *House of the Turquoise Roof* (1990), writes about the *Chipa Nyerchö* program and mentions that these children's medicines were made twice a year and distributed to the ninety-six districts of Tibet. In Lhasa, they were available for the asking. Mrs Yuthok obtained them after the birth of her first child.

recite what we had studied the day before. The smaller boys would just be chanting their alphabets. We kept up our reading and recitations for two hours. At sunrise, there was a one-hour break for breakfast, which we ate at our own quarters. Ten to fifteen students shared each of these dormitories. My own dormitory housed students from the various military regiments.

"Every regiment in the army had two boys studying at the Lhasa Medical Centre. But the Center also had monk students, two from every major monastery. The monk students were not permitted to wear their clerical robes but had to wear laymen's *chubas*, though these were maroon as a concession to their chosen vocation. We army students received our allowance from our regiments, which was on an instructor's pay level, and not bad at all, considering we were only students. The Center also took private students. The prime minister Lukhangwa's two sons studied at the Medical Centre along with Apel, nephew of Gonpo Tashi Andrugtsang, one of the largest merchant chiefs from Eastern Tibet in Lhasa [who later organized and led the resistance against the Chinese in Central Tibet]. Years later, I met Apel in America.

"After breakfast, we had to assemble again, this time for specific classes where we received instructions and lectures. We were allowed a toilet-break after two hours, and then we had calligraphy lessons up to twelve-noon. Each of us was expected to write a certain number of lines every day. At the end of the class, you got a stroke of the rod for every line you hadn't finished. Beginners wrote on wooden boards (*jang-shing*) with caramel ink that could be wiped off with a damp cloth. Senior students were allowed to write on Tibetan paper—which was expensive and could not be wasted. We got an hour's break for lunch, which we had in our own rooms. Our dormitory was an improvident one, and we constantly ran out of supplies, often having to borrow tsampa from other dormitories and begging for hot water to make tea. For fuel, we got peat (*laama*) from the Kyangthang Nakha suburb. We spent most of our allowance on *chang* or barley-ale.

"The afternoon routine was much the same as the morning. We spent an hour before dinnertime doing our homework, generally memorizing texts. After dinner, we all assembled on the open roof of the Medical Centre building for a minimum of three hours, reciting texts. Sometimes, the recitations went on till after midnight, as the principal, Khyenrap Norbu, had his own religious practices to complete, only after which we were allowed to go to bed. Students, especially the younger kids, would constantly nod off and were beaten by the supervising teacher. In winter, it got awfully cold on that exposed rooftop.

"We had examinations twice a month: one on the fourteenth day of every month for calligraphy and another on the twenty-ninth for memorization of texts. The student who came first was called before the teacher, where he had to present an inflated cheek. The teacher pulled a springy length of bamboo back in a curve and then released it with a flick and let him have a good stinging whack. The teacher then handed the switch to his victim, who was privileged to do the same to everyone else in the class. After that came the turn of the student who had come second, and then the third—each one with one less victim—till it came to the turn of the unfortunate fellow at the bottom of the class, who was whacked on the cheek by everyone in the class. Since there was no one left, he was obliged to whack a hollow yak-skin container—like a hairy black football and used for packing butter—to the jeers of the rest of the class. The day after the examinations was a holiday. Students were beaten a lot, not only at the Medical Centre but also every other school in Lhasa. It did us no good, really, just made us incorrigible."

This Dickensian method of instruction was quite common throughout Tibet. In some schools, children who were regularly at the bottom of the class developed near-permanent sores on their cheeks from being constantly switched there. I was told of one particularly intractable young fellow who had even developed a small hole in his cheek and would amuse his classmates by squirting water through it.

"I'm afraid that book learning and discipline were not in my nature. Soon I picked up bad habits and became something of a problem for everybody. My friend Thundup Gyalpo was equally wild. In those days, the only sort of guidance or advice that kids like us got were those administered with a stick or a lash, and that just had the effect of making us even wilder. We carried small clubs and knives in the pouch of our robes and used them in our many fights with boys from other schools, the Nyarongshar School, the Gorkha School, the Jabakhangsar School, and even *dob-dobs* [fighting monks]. Of course, encounters with *dob-dobs* were very rare. We were just kids, and they were really scary and dangerous characters."

Bhusang's stories of his school days, with their peculiar medieval tenor, brought to mind an account in Procopius's *History of the Wars* of the great Byzantine general, Belisarius, who as a boy led his schoolmates in the famous snowball battle against the oblates of a monastic school in Adrianopole.

"There were about a hundred and fifty students at the Lhasa Medical Centre, and many of them were older kids, who were a bad influence on smaller boys like me. My friend Thundup Gyalpo ran away from the school a few times but was brought back and soundly thrashed. I ran away too with similar consequences. Later, in my teens, I learned to drink and gamble and, I'm sorry to say, indulged in both excessively. Thundup Gyalpo, to his credit, did not drink. But he was a wild one otherwise."

Nearly everyone I know who has ever been a young man in Lhasa likes to portray himself then as a devil-of-a-fellow. So, I asked around about Bhusang. My friend Drakton, the state astrologer at Dharamshala, had begun his education at Nyarongshar School in Lhasa, whose students had often clashed with the students of the Medical Centre. In a somewhat admiring tone of voice, he told me that Bhusang had been "incredibly" wild. I now looked across the table at the white-haired old man scratching himself under his shirt.

"Did you manage to find time to learn anything at the Medical Centre?" I laughed.

"Well, I did get quite a bit of education beaten into me. I stayed at the Mentsikhang for nine years, in spite of my wild ways. We had teachers without peer. The principal Khyenrab Norbu was the most skilled physician in Tibet. His assistant Chönze-la and other senior physicians as Amchi Jampa la, the Dalai Lama's personal physician, were great teachers. You know, my classmates at the Medical Centre became skilled doctors later on. Doctor Tenzin Choedrak, who is now the Dalai Lama's personal physician was with me, as was Doctor Wangyal-la, who is now the senior physician at the Medical Centre here in Dharamshala. Also with me was Doctor Tenzin Namgyal, who died some years ago. He was a great doctor. There were many other good and accomplished physicians in my school. Even Doctor Yeshi Dhonden in McLeod Ganj, another former physician of the Dalai Lama's, gave his medical examinations at the Lhasa Medical Centre when I was there. He didn't study with us though but got his training at his monastery in Lhoka. To become a qualified physician, you had to undergo a rigorous and detailed examination in at least three of the four medical tantras."

The Four Tantras (rgyud-bzhi) is the abridged title of the fundamental texts of Tibetan medicine, The Tantra of Secret Instructions on the Eight Branches, the Essences of the Elixir of Immortality. Its origins and history are fairly obscure and was (and is) the subject of debate among Tibetan scholars but is traditionally regarded as the authentic word of the Medicine Buddha, Bhaisajyaguru, Master of Remedies. The first tantra, The Root Manual, is an overview of all elements of medical teaching. The second, The Manual of Explanation, presents the general theoretical teaching on anatomy, physiology, physiopathology and treatment. The third, The Manual of Precepts provides practical advice regarding the treatment of various kinds of illnesses. Finally, the fourth The Appendix (phyi ma'i rgyud) discusses different advanced methods of diagnosis, preparations of medicine, as well as methods of bloodletting, moxibustion and so on.

A set of about eighty large thangka paintings in full colour, each finely detailed, provides an invaluable teaching tool for the medical student and a useful aide mémoire for the practising physician. These thangkas were commissioned by Desi Sangye Gyatso, the Fifth Dalai Lama's prime minister, but a few copies (one in the Republic of Buryatia) are known to exist. Certain paintings in the series, notably the anatomical charts, the topography of points of intervention and surgical instruments, had widespread diffusion in old Tibet and were available in black-and-white woodblock reproductions—in separate sheets or as pamphlets. In 1992, these thangkas were reproduced in a beautiful two-volume edition by Serindia Publications of London. When presenting me a review copy of the boxed set of this large and substantial tome, the publisher (and friend) the late Anthony Aris proudly assured me that no other traditional medical culture in the world had developed as comprehensive and complex a visual aid system.

"The examinations were tough. Candidates were first examined privately by the principal and then subsequently before the full congregation of students and staff. When one cleared the first examinations for fundamental medical knowledge, the student was obliged to have tea served to the entire body of students and staff, as did a new student when he first joined the school. On completing the final exams and graduating as a qualified physician, the student also had to have a meal served to the entire student and staff body. It was like the medical equivalent of undergoing a doctoral *geshe* examination in the 'Three Seats' (Drepung, Sera and Ganden). The highest degree awarded by the Medical Centre was the *menrampa* degree, a doctorate in medicine. I did not, of course, get that degree. I did not do well in my final *viva voce* on the fourth medical tantra. But I passed the earlier examinations on three of the four tantras and was awarded a certificate for that. That was more than enough to qualify me to become an army doctor."

16

MEMORY SONGS OF LHASA

When the Thirteenth Dalai Lama was in exile at Darjeeling from 1910 to 1912, his senior secretary, the poet and scholar Shelkar Lingpa wrote the celebrated long poem, *Songs in Remembrance of Lhasa* (lha-sa dran-glu), which is read and admired to this day—even appearing in a Tibetan Language and Literature textbook.

> Not hectic nor hurrying nervously about like here,
> Just relaxed folks, calm, improving with time and acquaintance,
> Doing honest work then leisurely enjoying their meals.
> In a place dependable and constant, thus . . .
> . . . Remembering Lhasa
>
> Amidst the many shops and stalls in the busy market square
> The thousand delightful movements of soft supple bodies All
> gathered there, the beauties, none missing,
> Showing off their sweet smiling faces . . .
> . . . Remembering Lhasa.

Other stanzas describe the landscape surrounding the Holy City, the temples, monasteries, famous buildings and ". . . the sounds and images of the daily and annual cycle of activity in this centre of

Tibetan life."[1] The poem has forty-six stanzas, each ending with the phrase "Remembering Lhasa" (*lhasa dran*). The repetition of the phrase "Remembering Lhasa" may have been inspired by Sanskrit poetic tradition (Sanskrit, *kaviya*) that educated Tibetans like Shelkar Lingpa had appreciable acquaintance with.

The great Sanskrit love poem, *Chaurapanchashika*, by the twelfth-century Kashmiri poet Bilhana, has fifty stanzas, each one starting with the word "*adyapi*", which has been variously translated as "even now"; "to this day"; or "even now I remember". Sir Edwin Arnold, who translated this poem (*An Indian Love-Lament*), felt that the repeated Sanskrit word gave the poem "a melodious and ingenious monotony of fanciful passion." Edward Powys Mather, who later produced a "second-hand translation" *Black Marigolds* (from which John Steinbeck reproduced some verses in *Cannery Row,* his elegiac novel of depression-era Monterey), thought that the word provided "a recurring monotone of retrospection."

Another Tibetan scholar, the historian Shakabpa, living in exile in India after the last Chinese invasion, wrote down the memories of his native city in the first chapter of his *Political History of Tibet.* Here the "monotone of retrospection" comes through not in a poetic device but his description of the ordinary, everyday quality of life in Lhasa.

> Throughout the year, there are many different and magnificent religious festivals in the city. All the residents of Lhasa, rich and poor, high and low, are peaceful. In the evenings, many people walk about the Barkhor singing and playing musical instruments. Even the beggars of Lhasa have only to ply their trade for some time in the morning to get enough food for the day. In the evenings, they are all nicely drunk. The people of Lhasa are physically relaxed, mentally contented and happy. The food of the city is tasty and nutritious. No one has to strive unduly hard to make a living. Life takes care of itself, as a matter of course. Everything is splendid.[2]

The absence of any alcohol tax in the Holy City might have contributed to Lhasa beggars getting "nicely drunk" in the evenings, as Shakabpa remembers. All *chang-khang* taverns and most private families in Lhasa brewed their own barley ale. Large families even had their own in-house brewer, usually an older woman respectfully called *Ama chang-ma*. Whenever a batch was ready, the initial "offering" (*chang-phud*) was poured into a clean pitcher and the daughter of the house or a maid, always dressed in her best, would take the pitcher to the *Pela-chog*, the chapel of the goddess Palden Lhamo (Sanskrit, *Sridevi*) at the south-eastern corner of the Jokhang roof. The sacristan at the temple would pour it out into a giant vat by the side. In the evening, the beggars of Lhasa would line up by a side door, and the monk caretaker would let each one have a whole jug of this pure and consecrated ale for the token payment of a *chek-ke* coin, the equivalent of a penny.

Walter Benjamin wrote that in observing a city, outsiders concentrate mostly on the exotic and picturesque, while the natives always see the place through layers of memory. My memories of the Holy City are, of course, those that have been passed on to me, over the years, by friends and relatives, especially my mother. It has given me a perspective of Lhasa that though not first-hand, is fairly intimate, and at times satisfyingly vivid.

Orhan Pamuk in *Istanbul: Memories and the City*, writes of his mother's stories of his own childhood in the Turkish capital and how listening to her was ". . . a sensation as sweet as seeing ourselves in our dreams." But he warns, ". . . we pay a heavy price for it. Once imprinted in our minds, other people's reports of what we've done end up mattering more than what we ourselves remember." That shouldn't matter to me since I was only a year and a half when I left Lhasa and have no actual recollection of the place. My mother's memories of the city have been by now thoroughly incorporated into my personal mental landscape of the city derived from photographs, books, stories, film clips and Peter Aufschnaiter's marvellous map of the old city. And the totality of this remembrance is now as "sweet" as a vision in a dream, becoming particularly vivid when recalling our home in Lhasa.

Tethong House was in the Banakshöl neighbourhood to the east of the city. A few hundred years earlier, when Lhasa was a smaller place, this suburb had been just empty pasturage and farmland where Khampa merchants, with their tea-caravans, would pitch their black yak-hair tents (*ba-nak*)—hence the name Banakshöl. Similarly, west of the Jokhang Temple is the built-up neighbourhood of Chinggurnang, where in earlier times, Mongol pilgrims and merchants would raise their felt-covered yurts (*chinggur*). Further west between the city and Drepung Monastery, is the area of Kyangthang Nakha (Wild Ass Meadow) that served as the caravanserai for the annual trains of Bactrian camels arriving from Khotan, Kashgar and other oasis towns of Central Asia.

Adjoining the Tethong residence, to the east, was the house belonging to the minor aristocratic family of Gonshampa. Adjacent to this was the house of the mercantile family of Gyanaktsang. Further east were the houses of other Khampa merchants: Dhoyontsang, Lagatsang, Gyamitsang and then the large Phulung Khangsar estate, after which the suburb ended at the Lingkor or the "Outer Circular Road," surrounding the city. At this point on the Lingkor road was the small Mondrong bridge that spanned an irrigation canal and the intersection where the road to Eastern Tibet started. Hence, the street in front of Tethong House was a busy one, as caravans from Kham passed through here to the centre of the city. In the evening, strings of horses would be led by their grooms on this street to be watered at that stretch of the canal under the Mondrong Bridge where the water was clean. The canal flowed through the city, but the water got dirtier after the bridge.

To the south-east of the suburb was the chapel of the Banakshöl Gyalpo, the protector spirit of the neighbourhood. The one storey temple was managed by a *khatsara* family of Tibetan-Newari descent and had a resident oracle, to whom a *khata* scarf and a cash offering could be made, and questions regarding health issues, family problems, and business ventures could be posed. Instead of a statue, the main shrine in the temple displayed a ritual mask of the deity—a coal-black wrathful face, sticking out a large crimson tongue. This temple was largely frequented by residents of the neighbourhood. Banakshöl also had a high concentration of other oracle chapels, dedicated to lesser spirits of the *tsan, dregpa, gyalpo* and *lu* classes, who were regarded as *jigten ki lha* or "deities bound to the six spheres of existence."

Once a year, at the festival of "Universal Incense Offering" (*zamling chisang*), all the various minor oracles of the city gathered for a banquet at the large outdoor park of the Karmashar Oracle, the protector and patron deity of Lhasa city. The Karmashar Oracle would be seated on the highest and grandest throne while the other oracles would be lined up on either side on respectively lower thrones. The oracles would all go into a collective trance, drink copious draughts of *chang,* and be entertained by their attendants and other merrymakers who sang, danced and played the Tibetan lute (*dranyen*). My uncle, Sonam Tomjor, remembered as a child going with his friends to the park to laugh and jeer at this improbable *bacchanalia*, provoking the Oracle to hurl his ritual throwing-knives (*yuk-dri*) at them and being chased away by irate attendants.

Because of the Karmashar Oracle's status as Lhasa's protector deity, the city magistrates from the Nangtseshag court and the old-style constables and bailiffs (*korchakpa*) would make offerings at the Karmashar Tsenkhang (temple) at the south-eastern end of the Hongtö Shingka horse market. Strangely enough, the oracle's authority and patronage extended even over the city's modest underworld of burglars,* professional gamblers, prostitutes, forgers, lock-pickers, pickpockets, scavengers, undertakers and beggars. Once a year, at the Shoton Opera Festival, the Karmashar Oracle would present a program of Tantric dances at the Norbulingka Palace for the Dalai Lama. The performers were the various criminals, vagrants and assorted minions of the oracle, including the city's constables.

Immediately west of Tethong House was the house belonging to Jhangtsatsang, a merchant from Lithang. This old building was painted yellow because it was one of those houses where the Sixth Dalai Lama, "Melodious Purity", went to drink or had a romantic assignation three hundred years ago. The lady of the house, a big handsome woman, would always have on full make-up and be impeccably dressed in Khampa

---

*This profession featured such improbable specialists as "ladder placers" (*ken-tsug*), "penetrators" (*beeg-gyabkhen*) and so on. See my post "The Lhasa Ripper" at bit.ly/1Ig4TKi.

style, the top of her brocade robe slipped off and the sleeves wrapped around the waist. My mother recalled seeing her every morning on the roof of her house burning incense. Jhangtsatsang himself became a minister in the exile government at Dharamshala. I remember his wife who, even in old age and relative poverty, was always elegantly dressed and never without make-up. She lived in a small hut on the road from McLeod Ganj to the Tibetan Dance and Drama Society.

Just behind Jhangtsatsang House and adjoining the Tethong residence was the garden and *trokhang* or "pleasure house", an expansive one-story pavilion covered with glass panes that served as a greenhouse and informal living room. At the west end of the garden were three small apartments which were rented to Shakya Dana-la, a Newari merchant, Laose-la, an old Manchu official who taught classical Chinese, and Babu Gombo-la of Sikkim, the English language secretary of the Pangdatsang mercantile house, who was the captain of the Lhasa United football team that played against the British Mission of 1936.

Directly across the road from Tethong House was the house of Tawutsang, a mercantile family from Tawu, in Eastern Tibet, who had one of its members studying at Drepung Monastery to be a *geshe*. To the left of the Tawutsang building was the house of Ghongkar Gyatso, a well-to-do family from the Ghonkar district south-west of Lhasa. My uncle Tsewang Chogyal (TC) remembered that squeezed between these buildings, was the humble lodgings of a down-at-heel alcoholic and musician called Tingsha, someone from the gentry, most likely, fallen on hard times.

Tethong House was large and spacious. The original building had been purchased by Gyurme Gyatso in 1913 and completely enlarged and rebuilt in 1937, after the conclusion of his long service in Eastern Tibet and his appointment as a minister in the Kashag at Lhasa. The new house was three stories high and had thirty rooms, of which the six largest served as living rooms, a formal dining room, and a *tsomchen* or assembly hall for the congregations of monks who were often invited to perform various prayer services. There were other smaller chapels, including a *gonkhang* for the wrathful deities of Tibetan Buddhism. Next to it was the gun room, always securely padlocked. The main living room, airy and sunlit, was named "*Zimchung Dewachen*" after the abode of the Amitabha Buddha, "The Land of Bliss". To avoid the standard requirement of pillars in rooms over a certain size, Gyurme Gyatso had used steel beams, imported from India, a novelty in Tibetan architecture.

The American traveller, Theos Bernard visited Lhasa in 1937 with his guide and interpreter the Reverend Tharchin of Kalimpong. Bernard wrote a book on his experience, which included a detailed description of the Tethong home:

> It is the custom that each year a different Shapé (cabinet minister) should have his turn at entertaining, and this year the honour fell to Tethong Shapé, who had just finished building his new house in the city. It was generally agreed that this house was the best in Lhasa, but my chief envy was its shrines and the gorgeous array of *thangkas*[*] that adorned the sitting room.
>
> The house is three stories high, with the best places at the top, where one can have a view and fresh sunlight. There at the top was an exquisite sitting room with large bay windows with beautiful awnings over them to keep out the mid-day glare. You climbed up to it through the usual dark passageways and Tibetan ladders. And there was a feeling of cleanliness about the whole place.
>
> I found the house full of guests. Every room through which I passed had a small party going on. Both high and low participated, it being the custom to entertain the servants as well as the honoured guests. My host said that he was able to accommodate only sixty guests at any one time, with any comfort, so he had to take on

---

[*] Many of these thangkas and all the murals in the various rooms of the house were painted by the artist Tsering Thundup, a Tethong *me-ser* or tenant farmer from the small Tethong estate of Lhonga Gyaba, at Dodé, near Sera Monastery. Tsering became the "favoured" artist of the Thirteenth Dalai Lama and was awarded an official rank. Another American visitor to the Holy City, Suydam Cutting, immortalized him with a wonderful photograph and this accolade, "Tsering, that sensitive young Michelangelo of Lhasa."

different groups each day. On the day of my visit, this entertaining had already gone on for ten days.

What principally held my attention in the beautiful private shrines was a set of nine *thangkas* portraying the life of Lord Buddha, all hand-embroidered. My host had another set just like this one, but which was painted; he sent it to China, where they made a duplicate set of hand embroidery. It was, by far, the finest thing of the kind that I have ever seen. The room itself was of a typical Tibetan design, with the pillars carved and painted blue and gold on a red background and the main part wrapped in beautiful silk, where the average shrine has only bare red poles upholding this cornice of lovely carvings.

On arrival, I was promptly served with several cups of tea with cookies and figs. I dare not branch out into the harder spirits there at your disposal; like all who have had experience, I knew it was the better part of valour not to want anything until it was forced on you. Indeed, food soon began to pour in, following the regular course already described in an earlier chapter. All I need to say is that nothing was omitted on this occasion. It was the most delicious cooking I had yet tasted in Tibet.

I was congratulating myself on having gotten through with it all with a minimum of discomfort when the *chang* girls came in, and everyone began to shout "*Tashi deli!*" which is equivalent to saying "Bottoms up!" So I had to drain cup after cup of their *chang* . . . there seemed to be no way of saying no to them; they simply didn't understand the word. Politeness in this country is entirely different from ours, and you must learn how to take it. Indeed, they go so far as to stick you with needles if you refuse . . . I finally fled to the roof to have a look at the scenery of Lhasa.

The rhythm of the music I had heard all that day persisted in my mind, and with it the picture of the three lady dancers who danced to it, making movements very much like those of the geisha girls of Japan. The orchestra consisted of a long wooden fife or flute, a fiddle and a banjo . . . After watching the children at play in the tent provided for them in the garden below, I rejoined the party.[3]

From the roof of the three-storey Tethong house, you got a clear view of the city, all the way north-west to the Potala Palace. My mother enjoyed spending time on the roof, looking down on the street life and the activities of our neighbours and tenants. I have a photograph of her on the roof holding me as a baby, with my father by her side, looking snappy with his dark glasses, fedora and "N. Son"* riding boots. This photograph, with the Potala floating in the distance, is all I have to reassure myself that I possess an actual connection, no matter how tenuous or far distant, to the city of my dreams.

From the flat roofs of the Lhasa houses, children flew kites in late summer. The season started exactly on the first day of the eighth month. It was, as other observers have noted, not just a "children's game" but a competitive sport where adults including monks and officials participated. Heinrich Harrer noted that "Children and grown-ups stand for hours on the roofs flying their kites with the intense concentration of chess or tennis champions. The kites are flown on lines of stout twine treated with glue and powdered glass. The chief object of the game is to cross your opponents' line and cut through it. When that happens, there are screams of joy from the roofs. The severed kite flutters slowly down, and the children pounce on it."

You also had to make sure that your kite didn't run into a high-flying lammergeyer vulture (*ghowa-lekar*). The Tibetan species is distinguished by a thick covering of leg feathers, which undoubtedly provided the inspiration for this nursery rhyme:

Lammergeyer,
Stealing your mother's trousers
Shame! Shame!

Ghowa-lekar,
Amae ghutung kuma gyap-ngen
Halay, Halay

---

*A Chinese firm in Kalimpong that produced quality riding boots prized throughout Tibet.

The markets are full of brightly coloured kites, but the enthusiast must have his specially designed for himself. The monk minister (*kalön lama*) Rampa, who loved kite flying and who sported a distinctive beard, had the lower edges of his kite-shaped and coloured recognizably like his white beard. When he flew it up into the deep blue Lhasa sky, children would shout, "Get the bearded minister."

Incidentally, Harrer and his companion Peter Aufschnaiter borrowed the Tethong garden *trokhang* to host a grand Christmas party in 1946, complete with Christmas tree, Santa Claus (their friend Wangdü-la in a white sheepskin *chuba* turned inside-out) and a singing of "*Stille Nacht, Heilige Nacht.*"

Immediately behind Tethong House was the Yükhang School and a little further on, about hundred yards away, the marshy pond of Adichangsip that froze over in winter. Children would skate on the pond using homemade ice skates of an inspired design. If you were a kid in Lhasa, it was important to start collecting peach stones in autumn. You split the stones in halves and took out the nut (and ate it if you liked) but saved as many intact half-shells as you could. You then filled the hollow shells with mud and warm spit and attached them to the soles of your boots, where they would freeze and stick tight. About six or seven evenly spaced half-shells on each boot would do the trick. You could then run, arms stretched out for balance, and glide across the surface of the ice, screaming, laughing and bumping into each other.

Other than my mother and my uncle Rakra Rinpoche, who was an incarnate lama, the five other Tethong children and three young servants were educated at the Yükhang School located conveniently behind our house. The school area was probably once a barn and a threshing floor (*yülkha-khang*) when Banakshöl was still agricultural land—hence the name. The old teacher Yükhang Gyenla, had once been a clerical official at the La-chag or the Labrang Chanzoe, the main government treasury located at the Tsuglakhang Temple complex, and had been dismissed because of a mix up at the festival of "The Offering of the Fifteenth," when butter sculptures were displayed. My uncle Sonam Tomjor remembered him as an unworldly, spiritual person but an excellent teacher. It was a small school with about fifty students.

There were a number of other private schools in Lhasa: the Kyirey School, the Jabakhangsar School and the Tarkhang School, educating around a hundred students each. There were smaller schools like the Dharpoling School run by the medium of the Rakyap Tsenkhang Oracle and the Pelgong School run by a former secretary of the Phala family. Another school near the Muru Monastery was run by a former secretary of the Kashag.

The largest private school was the Nyarongshar School, whose headmaster was a well-known physician and whose name, Lhundup Paljor, was respectfully prefaced in the schoolbooks with the title "Master of the Healing Sciences." This school had about two hundred students divided into four classes. A former student, Thupten Khetsun, in an account of his life in Lhasa,[4] writes affectionately of his school as an institution that ". . . suited the needs of the society at that time, and drew its students from all social strata . . . There was no set fee to be paid as a condition of attending the school, and students paid different rates according to their means . . . So it was that if a child from a noble family was studying in the same class as a child of his family's servant, and the servant child got better marks on the twice-monthly tests, school tradition required the servant child to give the son of his master a rap on the knuckles with a cane."

Most of these were elementary schools though the larger Tarkhang and Nyarongshar schools appear to have provided education up to what might be called a secondary level. After graduating, some students went on to study at Drepung, Ganden, and Sera to become geshes or to the Mentsikhang, the Medical Centre, to get a medical education. These schools also prepared boys for official careers at the two civil service academies, the Tse-labtra (Peak School) at the Potala for monk officials and the Tsitrukpa School of the Finance Department at the Tsuglakhang Temple complex, for lay officials.

After my uncle Sonam Tomjor joined government service, he and my mother decided that their three youngest siblings should receive a modern Western education at Darjeeling. My uncle TC was enrolled at St. Joseph's College, while his sisters Tashi and Sopal went to the co-ed Mount Hermon School run by the Methodist Episcopal Church of America.

The Tibetan government's efforts at modernizing Tibetan education by setting up an English school at Gyantsé under the naturalist Frank Ludlow, and later one in Lhasa under Colonel Parker were short-lived, thanks largely to the opposition of the ultra-conservative clergy. But more enlightened Tibetans, realizing a western education as vital to their own and their country's future, sent their children to Christian schools in Darjeeling and Kalimpong. I have drawn up a (still incomplete) list of one hundred and sixty students who studied in about eight English medium schools in the greater Darjeeling area. About thirty-six students on my list are girls. The interesting thing is that although a majority of the students were from the aristocracy, many were from business and non-aristocratic backgrounds. The legendary professional gambler, Dre Kusho (literally "Mister Phantom") of Lhasa, sent his adopted son, Sonam Ngudup, to study at St Augustine's school in Kalimpong. The cost of such a Western education was a considerable financial burden on the families, but they obviously saw it is as worthwhile. By the mid-forties, even the monasteries were beginning to realize that they needed Western-educated personnel. Reting Monastery, well known for its trading activities, sponsored ten students at the Kumudini Homes School in Kalimpong.

Contemporary historians on Tibet have invariably regarded the closure of the two official English schools in Tibet as representing the failure of the Thirteenth Dalai Lama's modernization program and do not seem to have noticed the circumvention of conservative opposition by such individual initiatives. The French *annales* school of historians taught us a hundred years ago that in the study of history, movements in society at large and development of social trends—all the ordinary but rich details of human history, matter as much if not more than the achievements (or failures) of governments or rulers.

To supplement the cost of the education of her brother and sisters, my mother decided to rent out one apartment unit on the ground floor of Tethong house to a wealthy merchant, Legyatsang from Lijiang city in Yunnan, and another to Gyen Lamé-la a simple monk from Drayab, but also a multi-millionaire, who is said to have lent money to the Tibetan government on more than one occasion.

My mother would travel to Darjeeling when her sibling's winter holidays started and bring them back to Lhasa. She would sometimes take her young lama brother, Rakra Rinpoche, with her. My uncle Rakra told me that on one journey home when they camped for the night, he was intrigued by his two little sisters making a small campfire of their own and sitting around it singing an "English" song which had the refrain "O my Darling, O my Darling" (Clementine?). It always puzzled him why it was necessary to sit around a campfire to sing that particular song.

The Kashmiri Muslim community had a small *madrassah* attached to their mosque (the *chota masjid*) but sent their children for further education to India, especially to the liberal Aligarh Muslim University. The Nepalese community had a larger school, the Gor-yik school, which also accepted children of mixed marriage between Tibetans and Nepalese. The Chinese legation at Kyetöpa, on South Barkhor road, had its own school attended by the children of Chinese officials, businesspeople and the Chinese Muslim community. Dressed in blue military uniforms, the fifty or so students could often be seen marching in formation and singing patriotic songs. The Guomindang were keen on military display. Tibetans who wanted to study Chinese usually took private lessons from such old Manchu officials as Lao-se la, the Tethong tenant, or attended the small school of Aja Yeshi Dolma-la, the daughter of the last Manchu *amban* in Lhasa, who spoke the most fluent Beijing *hua*.

There were probably no more than three to four hundred Chinese residents in Lhasa then and eight hundred[5] Chinese Muslims (Hui) in the Wabaling neighbourhood who served the capital as butchers and market gardeners. Right now, the Chinese population of the city outnumber the Tibetan, the new Chinese railway line to Lhasa inaugurated in 2006 having sped up the rate of Chinese migration to the Holy City enormously. The Chinese live in the newly developed areas of outer Lhasa, while Tibetans largely reside in the old city around the Jokhang Temple, which has to all purposes become a ghetto and a tourist attraction—overwhelmingly Chinese tourists these days, who take photographs of the natives and each other dressed in caricature versions of Tibetan costumes. Till a few years ago, this downtown area was packed with pilgrims from all over Tibet who circumambulated the temple on the Barkhor circle and prostrated and prayed before the Jokhang temple. But after the large-scale uprisings in 2008 and the ongoing self-immolation of Tibetan patriots, this has all changed.

Inner Lhasa today is quite possibly the most policed urban locale in the world. Numerous surveillance cameras in protective wire cages, and lately disguised (for Chinese tourists) as prayer wheels, command a view of every street and intersection. Snipers on the rooftops cover every point of the Barkhor area, and in the alleys and streets, constant patrols of Peoples Armed Police or *Wujing* in olive green uniform and carrying assault rifles and submachine guns intersect with patrols of the *Gong'an-ju* (Public Security Bureau) personnel in blue uniforms with side-arms and riot shields. Recently a new unit called the Special Police Unit, SPU or *Tejing (meksel nyentoepa)* in black uniform and advanced QBZ-95 assault rifles, has been added to the security regimen in Lhasa.

The latest advance in security has been the requirement for all Tibetan residents of Lhasa to carry a special ID card containing a biometric chip which must be produced at all police checkpoints in the city. Besides scanning the ID cards, security personnel also routinely download the "sim" cards in peoples' cell phones on police laptops.[6] Tibetans have been arrested for having photographs of the Dalai Lama on their cell phone.

Blue and white police cars constantly crisscross the main streets, while the occasional armoured troop carrier, sometimes even an armoured car, rolls by with deliberate slowness. When a demonstration threatens to get out of hand, as it did in 1989, then the T59 battle tanks are rolled out. The entire city is surrounded by military camps (PLA troops in olive-green camouflage uniforms) and tank and artillery battalions. After the 2008 uprising in the city, many more military encampments have been seen on the road to Lhasa from Dechen in the East. A report was sent to me by a troubled American woman who visited the city during the winter of 2012: "The majority of Tibetans live in an area which is now almost entirely enclosed by military compounds with walls between ten to sixteen feet high; some with barbed wire. This isolation gives the impression of what the Warsaw Ghetto might have been like."[7]

But a more fundamental and organic security system is maintained within Tibetan society through such true-and-tried methods as compulsory political education, confessions and denunciations that are still prevalent throughout Tibet, especially in Lhasa city. Everyone is exhorted to inform the authorities on friends or neighbours expressing "splittist" (separatist) opinions. Even school children are expected to betray their parents.

Then there are the professional informants that, like cockroaches, infest the dark spaces, the nooks and crannies of the Tibetan ghetto. Every courtyard in the old town has a resident informant who keeps tabs on the comings and goings of everyone living there or visiting. Every floor of an apartment building generally seems to have one informer lurking about at the end of the corridor. He is easy to spot. He usually wears a shabby, ill-fitting suit and sometimes dark glasses. He will invariably be smoking and always managing to look furtive and arrogant at the same time.

They also frequent the dark corners of restaurants, teashops, bars and especially nightclubs. If you were in a bar and your Lhasa friend touched her ear or pulled yours playfully, or just whispered one word, "*amcho*" or "ear," it would mean she had spotted one. The label is cleverer than the direct English translation might suggest. The Chinese term for "security" is *anquan*, reasonably close in pronunciation to *amcho*, especially when one is whispering it under one's breath to an indiscreet friend in a Lhasa bar. The Tibetan poet and blogger Tsering Woeser,* who writes in Chinese, points out this droll quality of the city's patois in her long poem *Secrets of Tibet*:

---

*Woeser lives and works in Beijing in a state of perpetual uncertainty. Her writings have been widely recognized, and she has received many awards, including the 2013 International Women of Courage Award presented to her in absentia by First Lady Michelle Obama and Secretary of State John Kerry.

These *amchos*, 'ears', are invisible informers.
A telling nickname—courtesy of Lhasa wit, Lhasa humor . . .
. . . Once, in the street,
Suddenly, strangely, I had to cover my ears,
Afraid someone might take control of them
And they'd turn into *amchos* reaching out everywhere,
Evermore pointy, as in the fairy tale,
Where the little fellow's nose grew longer every time he lied.
How many *amchos* in our midst can be detected?
How many unjustly shunned who are not *amcho*?
Thinking thus, sadly and reluctantly, I discovered
There is another Lhasa, hidden behind the Lhasa we live in.

If one had to assign an exact date to when the quantum fabric of this hidden, parallel Lhasa was torn open and its dystopian darkness began seeping into the Holy City of Tibetan memories, it would have to be 27 October 1951. Bhusang remembered that day very clearly when the "Peoples Liberation" Army marched into his city. He poured me another cup of tea and told me about it.

17

"THE MEN ESPECIALLY SENT BY CHAIRMAN MAO"

"I was, in my sixth or seventh year at the Lhasa Medical Centre when the Communists defeated our army at Chamdo and later marched into Lhasa. You know that His Holiness left Lhasa then and went to Dromo, near the Sikkim border. The principal of Mentsikhang, who was also the personal physician of the Dalai Lama, accompanied him on this journey.

"Before the Chinese invaded, there was a lot of fearful talk and wild rumours all over Lhasa. Some of us at the Medical Centre were better informed on what was happening as our assistant principal, Chönze-la, used to listen to the radio and pass on the news to us. He was a progressive sort of person. In addition to his great knowledge of Tibetan medicine, he studied some Western medicine and even learned to give injections from the British Mission infirmary at Dekyi Lingka. He had a radio set where he picked up Radio Lhasa, and perhaps All India Radio and Radio Beijing broadcasts.

"The first Chinese troops marched into Lhasa in the morning of . . . let me see . . . I can't recall exactly* . . . They marched from the ferry

---

* The ceremonial entry of the PLA to Lhasa took place on 27 October 1951. Earlier, on 9 September, General Wang Qimei with 600 troops escorted Ngabö to Lhasa. Goldstein say this was an "advance guard".

344

crossing, south-east of the city at Shanga, where the soldiers had been ferried across the Kyichu River in wooden ferry boats and coracles. At that place, the Chinese later built a temporary wooden bridge and finally the steel and concrete Kuru Bridge. From the ferry point, the troops marched in formation, right through the city, through the Barkhor, to the New Park (*Linga Sarpa*), which was formerly the barracks of the Shigatsé Regiment.

"Before the arrival of the troops, some Chinese leaders had travelled from China via India [General Zhang Jingwu and staff. They stayed at Kyetöpa house, the old Guomindang legation and school] in the Barkhor, where the Tibetan government had made arrangements for them. Some years later, the Communists made this into the Lhasa branch of the People's Bank, which was burned down by Tibetans in the 1959 uprising. The Tibetan government also made arrangements at Trimon house for other Chinese leaders.

"Nearly all of Lhasa turned out to watch the PLA march in. I guess the Chinese could lie and say that the crowd was there to welcome them. The parade was led by a large brass band with soldiers blowing these enormous horns. The clashing of a huge pair of cymbals is still very clear in my memory. This was followed by row after row of soldiers waving huge red flags. The troops were all armed with modern weapons: machine guns and assault rifles. The soldiers themselves looked poor and wretched. Their lips, faces and hands were cracked from exposure and covered with sores. They all wore shabby yellow cotton-padded uniforms and thin canvas sneakers. Physically they were not impressive. On their caps, they had red enamelled stars with Chinese characters on them [the Chinese numerals 'eight' and 'one,' for the first of August, the founding day of the Red Army]. Their skins were dry and cracked. They were all thin and emaciated, as if they were starving. But it didn't take them long before they looked like pigs on our food.

"The Chinese also stuck up a lot of posters on all the walls of Lhasa. But most of them were in Chinese, and none of us could read them.

"I was in the Barkhor, somewhere between Kapshöpa and Thönpa, my old master's mansion. There were quite a lot of young people around there that day, but I was with my usual gang: Chodru from

Gyantsé, a young monk from Pengö Chodé, Ngutup Tsering, now a schoolteacher at Rajpur, and my best friend, Thondup Gyalpo.

"Nobody made fun of the Chinese soldiers or did anything provocative. Usually, if it had been our own soldiers parading, young men like us would have jeered at them, or the kids on the street would have marched behind them—but not today. Everybody looked somewhat lost—really. No one knew what to do. No one was wailing or crying out, but no one was looking happy either. Some old people in the crowd were saying how bad it was, how wicked, you know like, old people always do. Some were weeping quietly. As for myself, I was young and only thought of having a good time. I was selfish, but I suppose I was at a selfish age. I had no political awareness at all.

"The first contingent of Chinese soldiers that marched into Lhasa was about six hundred strong. Some days later, more troops arrived in different groups. Another force arrived after a couple of weeks from the north-west [Commander Li Disan's regiment] with hundreds of camels."

Shaggy Bactrian camels with their two humps were not unusual in Lhasa. Merchants from Kashgar and Yarkand would bring their exotic wares into Lhasa on camel caravans, which would rest at the caravanserai of Kyangthang Nakha west of the city. If ever a Lhasa child saw a camel on the street, they would greet the beast with an old nursery rhyme:

Camel! O long-necked Camel!
Pay for the grass you ate on your way up
Pay for the water you drank on your way down.

Amo Gamo kye ringbu
Ya dothue tsa zaybae tsaring khisho
Ma yongthu chu thungbae churing khisho

"Some miles west of Lhasa, just south of Drepung Monastery was a wide empty plain, Nortölingka, which quickly filled up with rows and rows of army tents. I can only recollect two groups coming. After that so many more Chinese soldiers marched in, day and night, that it just got confusing. [In all 30,000 troops under General Wang Qimei, General Zhang Guohua and General Tan Guansan marched into Lhasa in 1951.] The Chinese would publicize the coming of each contingent, for they wanted the Tibetans to turn out to welcome them. But the novelty soon wore off."

A painting by the Chinese "art-worker" Han Shuli titled "The Men Especially Sent by Chairman Mao"[1] depicts the official "peaceful liberation" version of the PLA's victory march into Lhasa. It is not dated but was probably painted quite a few years after the actual event, for it is representative of the later development of Socialist Realist Art in China prevalent during the Cultural Revolution, when the earlier Soviet academic style (mostly executed in oils) had been rejected for a brighter comic-book-like style.

Han's canvas is crowded with welcoming Tibetans figures, so much so that the seven unarmed figures of Mao's special envoys, including a token female with a severe Jiang Qing hairstyle, are hardly discernable because of the multitude of smiling Tibetans crowding around them, shaking their hands, offering them *khata* scarves or otherwise applauding them in the new fashion—by clapping their hands; formerly a gesture for expelling bad fortune and evil. All segments of society are represented—the clergy as well as the aristocracy, though, in the interest of realism, peasants and nomads dominate. Everyone appears to be delighted at the turn of events. A few "progressive" aristocrats and monks welcome the PLA with smiles and applause. Only a couple of loutish monks in the background appear not too happy with Mao's envoys and are glowering at them in an exaggerated stage-villain manner.

In the right corner of the painting, a sinister-looking aristocrat views the scene disdainfully through his dark spectacles, all the while stroking his wispy white oriental beard. By the conventions of such propaganda art, he is almost certainly contemplating some fiendish counterrevolutionary plot to be carried out for his British or American imperialist masters. It is likely the artist meant to represent Lukhangwa Tsewang Rabten, one of the two prime-ministers (the other being the monk official Lobsang Tashi) who, following the Chamdo surrender and the flight of the Dalai Lama and his government to the Sikkim border, had been appointed at the eleventh-hour to run the administration in Lhasa. Both ministers were inflexibly anti-Chinese.

Like most propaganda art, the depiction was fairly remote from reality. The burden of maintaining "The Men Specially Sent by Mao"—all 30,000 of them, in a city of no more than 25,000 inhabitants—was soon felt by the populace, especially the poor. The Chinese had absolutely no means of supplying their troops from China and were completely dependent on local supplies. Gasoline and building materials as cement, steel and corrugated iron sheets for PLA barracks were imported from India. It would be some years before the motor road from Dartsedo would reach Lhasa.

"All they had when they came from China . . ." an old tailor from Lhasa put it to me acidly ". . . were their chopsticks, and chipped enamel bowls." Tibet's traditional economy was simply incapable of meeting the needs of its new masters. Very soon, food became scarce in Lhasa. Of course, it hit the poor worst of all, and there was a great deal of resentment against the Chinese. Prices of vegetables were the first to soar. "You know the Chinese have this compulsive need to eat greens and vegetables all the time," Bhusang explained to me, "We Tibetans like our vegetables, but we can manage with some tsampa, a bit of meat, butter and cheese, but not the Chinese. They'd die without their greens. So, prices of vegetables tripled in a matter of weeks. There was a lot of grumbling in the streets. Then the price of grain shot up. It became really hard for the poor."

It was around this time that a new "street song" began to make the rounds:

> The Liberation Army has arrived
> A horde of beggars has arrived
> Now all have become liberated
> Now all have become beggars

> *Chingtrol makmi lepsong,*
> *Pango khyu chik lepsong,*
> *Tsangma chingtrol tangsong*
> *Tsangma pango chagsong*

But not the rich. They got richer. The aristocrats and merchants soon discovered that the Chinese needed to rent or buy houses and land in and around Lhasa. They also needed all sorts of manufactured products, from steel, cement, canvas, gasoline, etc., which could only be practicably imported from India, all on the back of pack animals. They paid in the silver *dayuan* coins with which the Tibetans were familiar. The Chinese also paid whatever was demanded. Everybody, except the poor, made a killing. For the poor, the situation got worse. This massive influx of Chinese silver undermined the old Tibetan currency. The price of grain, meat and vegetables skyrocketed, and Tibet, for the first time in its history, was hit with inflation.

A verse satirizing the cravenness of the profiteers became popular all over Tibet:

The Chinese Communists are truly loving-parents
Silver coins are pouring down like rain.

Gya ghundren drenchen phama ray
Ngul dayang charpa bhab-bhab ray

The same versifier could well have penned the lines that circulated in Lhasa in 1904 after the invading British force entered the Holy City, and a number of citizens began to profit from their stay.

At first "Enemies of the Faith" they were;
And next "foreigners" we called them;
But when we beheld English silver,
"Honorable *sahibs*" they became.

"Did the price rises and food shortages affect you personally at the time?" I asked Bhusang.

"Oh yes, definitely. I received my rations and pay from the regiment though I was studying at the Medical Centre. But because of Chinese demands, the drain on government grain reserves made it impossible to pay our own soldiers with grain. We had to go without our grain rations for six months and were instead given cash by the government. This was really a bad arrangement for us because by then, the value of the Tibetan currency had fallen considerably, and grain prices had soared. There was a huge public outcry, as you would expect."

Posters went up on the streets of Lhasa, protesting the price rises and the presence of Chinese troops. On 5 March 1952, petitions were submitted to the Tibetan government and the Chinese commander by an organization that was initially called the Mimang or "The People", but later seemed to have been re-named as the Water Dragon Lhasa People's Association (*Chudruk Lhasa Mimang Tsokpa*), after the year in which it made its appearance, possibly to distinguish it from other people's organizations that sprung up in later years. Essentially, the petitions protested the large number of Chinese troops in Lhasa and the consequent suffering caused to the people. The Chinese authorities were furious with the Tibetan government and particularly incensed at the two Prime Ministers who they claimed were behind the protests. There is very little information, even now, on the "Mimang Movement", but a monk from the Lower College of Sera Monastery, Dhamchoe Sonam, appears to have been the leader.*

Whether the two Prime Ministers, the aristocrat Lukhangwa and the monk, Lobsang Tashi, were behind the Mimang, is not known; what is certain is that their unflagging and rock-like opposition to Chinese policies certainly became a major obstacle to Beijing's plans for Tibet. Both of them were strong-minded but soft-spoken gentlemen of the old school.

My mother remembered that whenever Lukhangwa was invited to a party at Tethong house he would have to be served Tibetan barley ale, chang, and not Scotch, which since the World War had become the fashionable tipple of upper-crust Lhasa. Arrangements also had to be made to find a good conversationalist to sit with him, for he frowned on the constant gambling, especially the interminable *Mahjong* games,

---

*This name is in the accounts of Gonpo Tashi Andrugtsang and Lhamo Tsering.

then endemic at Lhasa parties. Both the prime ministers regarded the Chinese, especially their leaders General Zhang Jingwu and General Tan Guansan, as boors and bullies. Their opinions were probably strengthened by the fact that the monk Prime Minister, Lobsang Tashi, unbeknown to the Chinese, spoke fluent Mandarin.

The Chinese authorities were careful to avoid any direct confrontation with the populace and made sure their soldiers stayed in their camps and did not come out to the city. Over and above the usual "Three Big Rules and the Eight Points for Attention" (Chinese, *Sanda jilu baxiang zhuyi*) that earlier Red Army troops were supposed to observe in their relationship to the people, additional rules were drawn up about respecting Tibetan religious customs, and these were enforced, at least till the vital Sichuan–Tibet and Qinghai–Tibet Highways were completed, and the occupation army in Tibet brought up to full strength.

Goldstein has repeatedly cited this initial conduct of the PLA as evidence that China's military presence in Tibet was essentially well-meaning if not benign. In Marcel Ophüls' epic documentary film of France under Nazi occupation, *The Sorrow and the Pity* (*Le Chagrin et la Pitié*), a French resident of the small industrial city of Clermont-Ferrand comments on how well-mannered the German soldiers were at the outset. "They were almost too nice, yes too nice, because they knew we didn't like them, so they tried hard. They'd almost always give their seat in a tram to an elderly passenger."

"The Chinese even distributed offerings of silver coins to all the monks of the Three Great Seats and other monasteries in and around Lhasa," Bhusang said.

"Did the monks take the cash?"

"Since when have they ever refused?" Bhusang replied, laughing.[2] "Oh, the Chinese were really cunning. They put on theatrical and cultural shows . . . and *beskop* (bioscope)."

Nepalese and South Africans are probably the only other people in the world who still use this somewhat archaic term for the cinema. Before the invasion, Lhasa had one small commercial cinema hall (owned by a Ladakhi Muslim family, the Tsakhurs) that screened

Hollywood classics as Tarzan, Jungle Jim and the Marx Brothers. Hindi films were popular; the most talked about in Lhasa being *Anarkali*, the great Moghul romance. The tragic story of a beautiful slave girl buried alive as punishment for her love of the prince Salim (son of Emperor Akbar), this film holds a place in the hearts of many older citizens of Lhasa, the same way as *Gone with the Wind* does with some senior Americans.*

The British mission in Lhasa appears to have used cinema as "a little mild propaganda" and a means of creating a friendly and informal atmosphere in their dealings with the Tibetans. They succeeded with Charlie Chaplin, Fritz the Cat, Rin Tin Tin and documentaries of the War. Another commercial cinema hall was built in 1957 by a senior monk-official and a Muslim merchant. It was auspiciously named the Happy Light Cinema (*Diki Wolnang*) and centrally located, just west of the Jokhang at Lubuk. Unfortunately, its location made it a focus of the street fighting in the Uprising two years later.

The Chinese occupation force in Lhasa initially screened their propaganda films in the evenings at the horse-market square of Hongtö Shingka. A large white cotton sheet was hung on the back wall of the Trimon house on the east side of the square. The films were the usual documentaries and newsreels about tractor plants, dams, farming communes, factory openings, the Korean War, and the life of Joseph Stalin. The one feature film that all Tibetans seemed to have enjoyed was *Bai Mao Nu* (1950) or *The White Haired Girl*, directed by Wang Bin and Shui Hua. The film tells the story of a courageous peasant girl who hides from a despotic landlord and his henchmen in the mountain wilderness of Hebei, where her hair becomes white from her trials. Her sweetheart, a Communist soldier in the Eighth Route Army, fighting the Japanese, eventually returns to save her. The film was re-made as a revolutionary ballet during the Cultural Revolution, under the "artistic" guidance of Madam Mao.

---

*For a historical overview of cinema in Tibet, check out my two-part essay "The Happy Light Bioscope Theatre & Other Stories" (2010): *https://bit.ly/3DBAqZP* and *https://bit.ly/3x96gKU*.

Then there were the "cultural shows", performed by the Liberation Army Drama Troupe, which were mainly programs of souped-up "folk" dances intended to demonstrate how thrilled the ethnic minorities (Uyghurs, Mongols, Hui, Miao, Yi and others) were to be part of Communist China, and how the Party respected their quaint, colourful ways. It didn't matter how ersatz the content, how hammy the acting, they were a big success, especially with younger people. There was colour, there was action, in the way of Cossack style dancing—that was before the Sino-Soviet split. There was music of an exciting new kind: violins, piano-accordions, cellos, trombones and "that fellow in the front waving that chopstick thing." For the first time in Tibet, there was a proscenium stage with electric floodlights and spotlights.

It was obvious what it was all for. One of Red China's warmest admirers, Edgar Snow, has explained it clearly: "There was no more powerful weapon of propaganda in the Communist movement than the Red's dramatic troupes, and none more subtly manipulated when the Reds occupied new areas, it was the Red Theatre that calmed the fears of the people, gave them rudimentary ideas of the Red program, and dispensed great quantities of revolutionary thoughts, to win the people's confidence."

Tibetans in Lhasa were not exactly deprived of entertainment before the arrival of the Red Army. The last British representative in Tibet, Hugh Richardson, put together a beautiful and evocative book of black-and-white photographs supported by detailed scholarly notes on the many *Ceremonies of the Lhasa Year*. The Lhasa social and ceremonial calendar for the common folk, monks, pilgrims, but especially the nobility and clergy appears to have been a crowded and enjoyable one. Besides the opera season, the picnic season, the kite flying season, the monastic dance festivals, the grand New Year pageants and the two state processions for the Dalai Lama's relocation from his winter palace to his summer palace (and back), provided an annual program of colour and entertainment for all Lhasa residents, rich and poor, while street performers, musicians and singers helped them while away the evenings in between, at humble taverns or aristocratic banquets. Yet the old pageants and religious dances, however colourful, grand and historical, were definitely sedate and slow-moving. Ache Lhamo operas were more fun, with the singing and the comic bits—especially the topical satires. But one had seen them many times before and probably knew the stories backwards and forwards. The Chinese shows were new.

This carnival atmosphere was soon enhanced with Chinese merchants, peddlers, traders and artisans arriving in the wake of the Red Army to scratch a living in the Holy City. Most of them set up shop at Lubuk, a patch of wasteland west of the Jokhang, where earlier in history the *yamen* or residence of the Manchu Amban, the barracks for his military escort and even a theatre for Chinese opera (*Jingju*) had been located. The Happy Light Cinema Hall was also conveniently adjacent to the new Chinese market fair. There were air-gun galleries, hoopla stalls, wheel-of-fortune stands, barbers, masseurs and every kind of street entertainer imaginable: musicians, conjurers, acrobats, and beggars with monkeys that performed tricks. And of course, there were restaurants; not just pushcart vendors selling noodles and dumplings, but tented spaces with chairs, tables and fancier menus.

In China, the "Five-Anti" (Chinese, *wufan*) campaign had been launched in January 1952. It was designed to target the capitalist class but soon became an all-out war against the bourgeoisie and the petty-bourgeoisie in China. The victims were beaten, terrorized and humiliated, and many were executed. Most were sent to *Laogai* labour camps around China. Many committed suicide. When announcing the campaign, Mao declared "We must probably execute 10,000 to several tens of thousands of embezzlers nationwide before we can solve the problem."[3] The "petty capitalists" (Chinese, *xiao zibenjia*) were not overlooked. Street vendors, peddlers and the like were also ensnared in this campaign. But itinerancy and avoidance of the law, being the traditional name-of-the-game for such petty capitalists, quite a few of them managed to stay on the road, just ahead of this or that campaign, and eventually ended up in Tibet, where the Communists had yet to implement any major campaign that would alert Tibetans to their pre-ordained fate.

All over Tibet, Communist cadres were patiently telling Tibetans that they had only come to Tibet to develop the country socially and economically. Once that was done, the Chinese would leave. Even if Tibetans insisted they stay, the Chinese would all leave. Absolutely! My friend Nyarong Aten told me he had believed them at the time and that to this day felt ashamed at his gullibility. The Dalai Lama himself recalled in his memoirs that General Zhang Guohua had told him and his ministers that "When you can stand on your own feet we will not stay here even if you ask us to."[4]

Even the Communist propaganda from that period about Tibet was glowing and positive. Enlightened feudal lords and ladies in full ceremonial regalia were depicted participating in the socialist reconstruction of their ancient nation alongside grinning peasants, yak-herders, monks and Chinese Communist cadres. The first Western journalist to be allowed into Tibet after the invasion was Alan Winnington, a British Communist Party member and correspondent for the British *Daily Worker*. He makes no mention of the exploitation of the masses by the feudal land-owning class but writes instead that the Chinese economic reform of Tibetan society included even the "wealthy" aristocrats because by the living standards of the West, they could not be regarded as wealthy, and might even prefer a well-paying job in the proposed Chinese hydro-electric project. Winnington visited the Lhasa courts and interviewed the chief magistrate and mayor, Gorkar Mebon. He mentions a sentence of flogging in a manslaughter case, but of the "barbaric feudal tortures" that is standard fare in post-1959 Communist propaganda, there is not a single reference. In fact, Winnington notes that the chief magistrate told him, "No death sentences have been imposed in Tibet for some years." Winnington also inquired about other ancient punishments as amputation of limbs "'. . . but such things have not been done in my memory,' The Mebon insisted."

In fact, capital punishment had been officially abolished in Tibet since 1896, making it one of the first nations in the world to do so. The Russian explorer, G.Ts. Tsybikoff who, visited Lhasa in 1900, wrote that "The Dalai Lama (the Thirteenth) assumed the head rule of Tibet, and one of his conspicuous acts is the abolition of capital punishment."[5] At least seven other visitors to old Tibet have noted this unexpected but enlightened judicial reform in their writings.[6] The government of Nepal sent a letter to Lhasa protesting this new policy, as it emboldened Tibetan bandits operating on the Nepal border.

At the unofficial Chinese market fair at Lubuk, there were even bicycle and motorcycle repairmen. Around this early period of the Chinese occupation, motorcycles became the rage in the Holy City. Anyone who was someone owned a bike, and the flow of silver from Chinese coffers contributed to this. Earlier, the only motorbike in Lhasa had belonged to the monk official, Mondrong, one of the four students sent by the Thirteenth Dalai Lama to study at Rugby. One day a high official had been thrown from his steed, the animal frightened by the roar of the machine. Mondrong was forbidden to use his motorcycle again. He made a present of it to the Dalai Lama, and that was the end of biking in Lhasa—till the Communists came. Once again motorbikes, mostly British BSAs, Triumphs and Nortons (and a few U.S. army-surplus Harleys and Red Indians) were taken apart and transported on mule-back across the high Himalayas from Kalimpong. Gasoline was also brought in from India—on mules.

Matters became farcical, with government officials in their brilliant brocade robes roaring to the *drung-jha* (the morning tea and rollcall at the Norbulingka) on motorcycles, with their servants pedalling furiously behind them on bicycles, trying to keep up. The conversation of the Lhasa smart-set switched from the usual trivia of gambling and assignations to matters more technical and *au courant*—like horse-power, mileage and so forth. Even people who couldn't ride a bike to save their lives were not to be deterred. My mother's uncle (Gyurme Gyatso's younger brother) Tethong Lobsang Namgyal, a monk official (*khenchung*) and the only family member who collaborated with the Chinese, had absolutely no sense of balance. He grimly kept on practising on a bicycle—falling off every time—till the uprising of 1959 took care of that problem. Another ardent but ineffectual motorcyclist, the aristocrat Numa, overcame his handicap by letting his manservant handle the machine while he rode pillion, with as much dignity as he could muster, as the street urchins of Lhasa ran after him jeering.

The most sensational biker in the city was the younger Lady Lhalu, Sonam Dekyi, a celebrated Lhasa beauty and the wife of the former governor-general of Eastern Tibet, Lhalu Tsewang Dorje. An uncle of mine, Ngudup Tesur, then a bike-obsessed pre-teen, lovingly recalled the black BSA on which she roared around the Holy City.

The big merchants and senior aristocrats went in for American jeeps. The first jeep in Lhasa was brought by the Khampa merchant Tsatrultsang, followed by such aristocrats as Yutok and Ragashar. Even the monastery of Kundeling got their own jeep. Tsarong *pola* imported a Land Rover.

"The Chinese asked other young men and me to join the Communist Youth Organization," Bhusang continued. "They recruited a large number of young people from all walks of life. Most young Tibetans joined for the novelty of the thing and also for the amenities provided. If you joined, you were paid a certain amount of silver dollars a month and provided free and comfortable accommodation and first-class food. Then there was also the entertainment: folk dance programs, theatre and movies—also dances, with girls—*tiaowu*."

Bhusang used the Chinese word for ballroom dancing, *tiaowu*. The Reds were fond of dancing since their Yan'an cave days, as Edgar Snow has described, invariably waltzes of a solemn and cheerless kind where severe-looking females in shapeless Mao-suits, held stiffly at arms-length by equally drab looking male partners, shuffled about to Khachaturian like music. Ballroom dancing of this sort disappeared soon after the split with Russia. By 1962 it was considered decadent and bourgeois. But in the fifties, ordinary Tibetans had never seen anything like this before. Only some modern aristocratic families in the old days danced the waltz or the foxtrot—in the privacy of their homes.

The Chinese started a primary school at the old Sayshim house, distributing candy, cookies and toys to the students and even providing them free lunch. Lhasa wits dubbed it the "Glutton's School" (*toglay laptra*). Another more advanced academy, the Society School (*chizo laptra*) was set up at Drungchi Lingka (the park for Lay Officials) that enrolled older children and even adults for political education. It was derisively labelled the "Parent's School" (*phamey laptra*) or the "Silver

Coin School" (*dayang laptra*) since the Chinese paid a stipend of silver coins to all who attended.

"Many of my friends tried to get me to join the Communist Youth Organization (officially called the Patriotic Youth League). But I didn't join. I was a stubborn young man—a bit stupid too. But they kept working on me. 'Look.' they said, 'When the whole country is flooded, you alone cannot keep dry.' But I didn't join.

"After completing nine years of studies at the Medical Centre, I had to return to the Guards Regiment. That was when I decided to desert. Not to run away altogether . . ." Bhusang assured me when he saw my quizzical expression, ". . . but to join another regiment. My main reason was that the government pay for the ordinary soldier was really not enough to live on. In the old days, it was laughable, just two *khels* of barley and one *sang* and five *sho* in cash. No one had ever bothered to revise this pay scale till 1949, when the soldier's pay was raised to forty-two *sangs* a month. But with the Chinese induced inflation a couple of years later, it went back to being a pittance. Still, I must admit that the quality of barley was of the best. It came from the same government granary that supplied officials and the monasteries."

"I was told that the court-dancers (*ghartrukpa*) got really bad quality tsampa" I interjected, ". . . mixed with chaff. I'm surprised that the government commissariat supplied you good stuff."

"No, no. The army tsampa was really good, sweet stuff, not the rubbish the court dancers got. To put it in terms of kilograms, we got about twenty-six . . . no, it would be about twenty-eight kilos of tsampa a month. Just about enough. No butter or meat. You were supposed to buy that with the cash part of your pay, which was a joke.

"Well, I decided to change regiments. Well-to-do families would pay you to be a substitute recruit for their sons—if they were liable for the army tax. A family from Lhoka called Sharlo, offered me twelve *khels* of barley a year—about half my army pay—if I joined the Police Regiment in place of their son.[7] So, I left the Guards and joined the Police Regiment. I knew the Guards would not come to look for me. The system was such that they would consider my old master Thönpa liable. But since Thönpa had no hold over me now, I was free.

"I joined the Police Regiment at the end of 1954. In the old days, it was called the 'Inner Chamber Regiment' as it was the old Guards Regiment of the Dalai Lama. But when the Thirteenth Dalai Lama returned from India, a modern Guards Regiment was created, and our regiment was converted to an artillery regiment. In that capacity, it saw action against the Chinese-Muslim Hui troops. But when the Communist Chinese invasion took place, the regiment was stationed at Shigatsé. I think it was to keep a check on the Panchen Lama's followers there, some of whom were suspected of being pro-Chinese. After the fall of Chamdo, our regiment was transferred to Lhasa for regular police duties. The former Lhasa police force, a rag-tag bunch of Western Tibetan peasants, were disbanded and sent home. Probably the Tibetan government wanted a police force that could be used for military purposes if required. You know, earlier, after the Thirteenth Dalai Lama returned from India, he established a trained modern police force,[8] with the latest weapons and smart uniforms. It was probably better than the police force in Nepal or India these days. Lhasa policemen then were as good as policemen in America and England. But the monks closed it all down.

"Unlike soldiers in the other regiments, we in the police were always busy, patrolling the streets and guarding the police boxes in various parts of the city. The strength of the regiment when I joined was about four hundred men. It had been about five hundred before the fall of Chamdo. The soldiers were issued a uniform of khaki-coloured woollen *chuba* robe, one broad-brimmed felt hat for summer and one fur cap with lappets for the winter. We were also issued black leather riding boots though formerly; the soldiers wore the traditional woollen boot called the *zompa*. The standard weapon was the Enfield .303 rifle.

"Discipline was not very tight in the Tibetan police and army. Soldiering was a relaxed sort of business, and the soldier's wife and children lived with him and accompanied him on campaigns. So, the barracks were somewhat untidy and disorganized. Only the guards, with their modern barracks at the Norbulingka, believed in spit and polish. They also had their hair cut short. The soldiers of the other regiments kept their hair long in the traditional style. We men of the

Police Regiment were billeted in rooms at the large Tromsikhang market building, close to the Jokhang temple and the centre of Lhasa.

"I was made to feel welcome at the Police Regiment. The regiment had few educated people in the ranks. For many years they had been on active duty in Shigatsé and elsewhere and had not been posted back to Lhasa for a long time. So although I had not completed the advanced doctorate course at the Astro-Medical Centre, I was a qualified medical personnel, and I could read, write letters, keep accounts—and stuff like that. So, I proved to be useful to my new regiment.

"I became a doctor to the policemen and their families, and a rather successful one at that. There was no official provision for buying medicine for sick soldiers, but I bought medicine from the Lhasa Medical Centre with my own money and dispensed it to whoever needed it. Most men paid back what they owed me. I was not very business-like, but I didn't lose money. All the soldiers appreciated my service. Well, even if I wasn't the highest qualified doctor, I didn't cause any harm—I'm glad to say, and I helped a lot of sick people. The commander of our regiment Dapön Jumpa greatly appreciated my work and told me so. He always insisted on calling me 'Amchi-la' or honourable physician, though everyone else in the regiment just called me by my name. He was a kind and courteous aristocrat, though not the soldierly type. The men liked him. He died in India later on.

"Serving immediately under him was the *rupön* [major], the famous Rupön Gura ['hunchback' major], whose real name was Rinzin Paljor. When I first met him, he was a *gyapön* [captain]. His back troubled him considerably, so I had to treat him often. When I initially examined him, I noticed that one of his vertebrae had been badly damaged and had formed a small lump on his lower back. I followed up my examination with a complete pulse diagnosis and discovered that a few of his vital nerves (*tsa-chen*) were also damaged, which was the main cause of his crooked posture. He always walked with his left hand pressing down on his left thigh. He was not born a hunchback, as people mistakenly assume these days. In fact, except for his back, he was a manly and impressive looking person. He had a moustache just like yours. He came from the area called Chantang near Chaksam Chuwori, in Ghongkar Dzong."

Rinzin Paljor had injured his back in 1933 when fighting the troops of the Chinese Muslim warlord Ma Bufang, military governor of Qinghai province. Rinzin Paljor had been captured by the Hui cavalry along with some other officers and twenty-two soldiers across the Drichu river at Denkhok (where Communist troops also first attacked in 1950). The Hui had beaten and tortured the captive Tibetans. Rinzin Penjor's back was permanently damaged from being clubbed repeatedly with rifle butts.

"My treatment seemed to help his condition. The Tibetan medicine I prescribed for him was Arkhyung, a compound of Agar-18 and Khyunga, which was also good for the kidneys. I also gave him injections when he had severe and painful attacks, which happened sometimes. There was a craze for injections at the time in Lhasa. I learnt the art from two students of the Medical Centre who had studied it at the British Mission infirmary. I injected the major with that pain killing medicine (*zukchag men*); you know the light tea cultured liquid [morphine] that came in small phials. They were sold by Newari traders from Kalimpong. [Penicillin injections were also available and very popular in Lhasa.] The morphine helped the major to attend long parades and ceremonies when he had to stand for a long time—which aggravated his back problem.

"He was about fifty-two then and sexually quite active. But the sex act would throw his back off and worsen his condition, and I would be required to go to his quarters in the morning and treat him. When I got to know the Major better, I would tease him about this, and he would laugh and admit that he had not been able to resist the charms of his wife the night before. He had five children: three girls and two boys. His wife, Tseten Dolkar la, was a kind-hearted and caring woman.

"Besides my doctoring, there were other tasks I had to perform for the regiment: clerical work, accounting and so on. I even took in a bit of sewing to supplement my income. I was a veritable Lama Methon Phangbo,* as the saying goes.

---

*A legendary trickster like Till Eulenspiegel of German folklore.

"I also got around a bit—to a lot of different places. I even travelled as far south as the sacred mountains of Tsari, where savage aboriginals live in the jungles there. Those people wear nothing more than a small basket-like thing to cover their sexual organs. That was in, let me see . . . yes . . . in 1956. I managed to get a berth in a government delegation that supervised the pilgrimage event to the sacred Crystal Mountain of Tsari. I was with the Major, accompanying the monk official Chikyab Dongtoepa Kalsang la, as a medical officer. But that's a long story. I'll tell you some other time. I went to Tsari in the 11th month of 1956 and returned to Lhasa four or five months later, the following year.

"My financial situation improved markedly with the trading and business I carried out on the Tsari trip. So, I decided to get married. I had set my eyes on the good-looking and sweet-natured daughter of our regimental sergeant, Pema Gyalpo. I was really lucky that Tashi Wangmo—that was her name—agreed to be my wife. But perhaps it wasn't such a great deal for her.

"Even after being married, I carried on with my wild ways, and worst of all, drank excessively.[9] Finally, the major took me to task. He told me to cut down on my drinking as it was getting in the way of my work. He said that I need not give up altogether but that I should only have a couple of drinks a day, and that too at home and not in taverns. I told him that it was impossible for me to cut down, as the moment my lips touched chang I could not stop. But I was personally not happy with my drinking and decided to give it up altogether. Everyone was sceptical about my resolution. But it wasn't too hard. It was in 1958 when I gave up drinking, and it was rather timely too.

"My wife was very happy with my newfound temperance, and so was her father, the sergeant, who became a good friend of mine. Sergeant Pema Gyalpo was an astute trader. One of his official responsibilities was purchasing woollen material (*nambu*) from various villages for soldier's uniforms, which gave him the opportunity to do some business of his own on the side. Speaking of uniforms, a privilege I enjoyed because of my special status as a doctor was that I did not have to wear the khaki uniform chuba. Instead, I wore a smart black Italian wool chuba and black N. Son riding-boots. I cut quite a dash in the city, I'll admit. I also did not have to attend parades and drills."

18

OCCUPATION YEARS

"On the subject of uniforms," I interrupted Bhusang, ". . . didn't your regiment have to wear Chinese uniforms by that time?"

"No, we didn't. Only the soldiers of the Guards Regiment changed to Chinese uniforms. It caused some problems, I can tell you."

One of the initial efforts by the Communist occupation authority to integrate the old Tibetan army into the People's Liberation Army (PLA) was to make Tibetans wear the PLA uniform. Tibetan officers wore the old-style British army uniforms from the time when the Thirteenth Dalai Lama created the modern Tibetan army, and the ceremonial swords, insignias, medals and epaulettes (which the drab Communist uniform did not have) appealed to the Tibetan officers' sense of style, and they cherished it. The uniform of the rank and file had initially been of British design but had been changed from 1929 onwards to a more practical Tibetan design which the enlisted men preferred: khaki woollen chuba with a colourful trim (each regiment having its own particular design), leather riding boots, a fur cap for winter and a broad-brimmed "Terai" hat for summer. Both officers and enlisted men stubbornly opposed Chinese demands for the change in uniforms. Only the Guards Regiment accepted the change.

But a change of uniform was not the only problem facing the Tibetan army. Since its defeat at Chamdo in 1950, it had shrunk considerably, and it had not been large, to begin with. A former officer of the Drapchi Regiment, Captain Kalsang Damdul[1] or Kaldam for short, told me about the efforts of Tibetan military officers to resist integration into the PLA.

"After His Holiness's visit to China in 1955, the government had a meeting for four days at the park for monk officials [Tsetrung Lingka]. Nearly all government officials, senior and junior, attended. On the agenda was a report on His Holiness's visit to China and the current state of discussions between the Chinese and Tibetan governments. It was also announced that in accordance with the Seventeen Point Treaty, the Tibetan army would be gradually wound down and disbanded. The Tibetan army was no longer needed as the PLA would guard Tibet's frontiers. Only a minimal force of five hundred soldiers from the Guards Regiment would be maintained to protect the person of the Dalai Lama and five hundred from the Police Regiment to enforce law and order in Lhasa. All other regiments would be disbanded, and the soldiers sent back to their villages. Those with nowhere to go to would be formed into a construction brigade to work on public construction projects. Officers would be accommodated in other government departments, depending on their ability.

"All the military representatives at the meeting were angered and distressed at this announcement. A petition was drafted, signed by all the regimental representatives, and submitted to the Kashag. In it, we stated that the Tibetan army had served the Dalai Lama and the Tibetan nation since time immemorial and that it was unacceptable it should be disbanded.

"In desperation, the regimental representatives decided to petition the Dalai Lama directly, which was normally a difficult thing to do. But we heard the news that His Holiness was going to visit Tsurphu, the monastery of Gyalwa Karmapa, so an opportunity was presented to us. Three men were selected: Drapchi Sergeant Tashi Wangdu, Gyantsé Sergeant Pema Gyalpo and Police Sergeant Sonam Wangdu. They managed to get to Tsurphu Monastery without arousing any suspicion, and when His Holiness and his retinue were circumambulating the main temple of Tsurphu's Monastery, the three sergeants prostrated before the Dalai Lama and halted the procession. One of them held the petition and a special *khata* scarf, a *nangdzö*, high in his hands."

It was customary that all petitions submitted in this manner be taken by an attendant and handed directly over to the Dalai Lama. It was also customary that such presumptuous petitioners be jailed, sometimes even lashed, till the matter was settled. Fortunately, the Lord Chamberlain, Phala, was in the retinue. He secretly sympathized with the military and made sure the petition was handed over to the Dalai Lama. He also saw to it that the three sergeants did not have to go to jail. Two months later, the government made an announcement that the army would not be disbanded. There was a further announcement that changes demanded by the Chinese, like the wearing of Chinese uniforms by Tibetan soldiers, would not be carried out immediately.

"But the Guards changed from their British uniforms to Chinese uniforms making many of us suspect their loyalty, which I suppose wasn't fair. In the 1959 uprising, all the Guards at the Norbulingka palace changed back into their old British uniforms before the big battle. There was also a change at Army Headquarters, and an assistant to the commander-in-chief was appointed who was much less accommodating to the Chinese and more in tune with his men. So, morale and discipline improved."

Another demand by the Chinese occupation authority was that all Tibetan regiments should cease carrying the Tibetan national flag and only fly the Chinese flag. Bhusang explained to me how the soldiers had resolved the problem in their own way.

"The Chinese ordered the regiments to carry only the Chinese flag on parades. We refused. Finally, we were ordered by our own Army HQ to carry the Chinese flag on parades in the place of our flag. So, we carried the Chinese flag as ordered, but we also flew two bigger Tibetan flags, on either side of the Chinese flag. Sort of masking it, in a way, I suppose. We also trimmed the Chinese flagpole so that it was shorter than the flagpoles for our flags. On Tibetan holidays, like the Shoton Opera Festival or the Dalai Lama's birthday, we absolutely refused to fly the Chinese flag on parades and only did so on Chinese ceremonies like the first of October, which is the anniversary of the establishment of the Communist government in Beijing, or the first of August which is the day when the Red Army was founded. The Chinese complained about the short flagpole to Tibetan Military HQ, which in turn reprimanded us."

Earlier the Chinese occupation authorities had taken up the issue of national flags with the two prime ministers. As a first step to incorporating the Tibetan army into the People's Liberation Army, under the terms of the Seventeen Point Treaty, the Chinese demanded that all Tibetan regiments fly the Chinese flag. Lukhangwa said he would never permit such a thing to happen as long as he was alive. Zhang Jingwu is reported to have thrown a temper tantrum and screamed threats and abuses but finally backed down in the face of the prime ministers' quiet but inflexible resolve. The story quickly spread through the city and became embellished and dramatized in the telling. All Tibetans now firmly believe that the Chinese had demanded that the Red flag be raised over the Potala Palace, and Lukhangwa had replied with a Tibetan equivalent of "over my dead body." Both old gentlemen became heroes with the public.

According to Lukhangwa's daughter-in-law,[2] confrontational meetings with Chinese officials were a regular state of affairs and created enormous tension and anxiety in the Prime Minister's household. Meetings of the Kashag, the cabinet, at the Tsuglakhang complex, would often run very late, and there would be much argument and shouting, especially between Lukhangwa and Ngabö. Earlier the two men had been good friends and colleagues, especially when serving together as *Tsepöns* or finance secretaries. According to Lukhangwa's daughter-in-law, they were distantly related. After Ngabö was appointed governor-general of Eastern Tibet and moved to Chamdo, she was sometimes sent to deliver cookies and candies to Ngabö's children in Lhasa.

All that changed after Ngabö surrendered his command and later headed the delegation to negotiate the Seventeen Point Treaty in Beijing. When Ngabö returned to Lhasa, Lukhangwa angrily told him: "You have brought the darkness of night on your own country and given the brightness of morning to theirs (*rang yul 'di sa rub pa 'dra bo bzos / mi yul 'di nam lang pa 'dra po bzos*)."

In subsequent cabinet meetings, discussions between the two became so heated that it seemed they were "fighting each other." Customarily the cabinet meeting room (*kashag lhenkhang*) at the Tsuglakhang complex was not guarded, nor were cabinet ministers accompanied by bodyguards. They would just have a personal servant or two, who waited for them in the waiting room (*kashag gag*) or the staircase (*kashag phepke*) from the entrance (*kashag gyal-go*) on the south. But Ngabö had been provided with an armed PLA escort by the Chinese. Once when the fist banging and shouting had gotten so loud, the Chinese soldiers rushed into the cabinet room with their submachine guns at the ready. Lukhangwa is supposed to have said, "It's alright, there's no need for your guns. I'm an old white-haired man. All you have to do is just blow, and I'll fall down."

Lukhangwa's family lived in constant fear of what might happen to him. Cabinet meetings regularly ran late in those troubled times, well past midnight, to two or three in the morning. But no one in the Lukhangwa household, young or old, could bring themselves to go to bed. Lady Lukhang would wait by the front gate of their house accompanied by her daughter-in-law, and the servants would wait with them. They would have flashlights and Petromax lanterns at the ready, in case they had to leave in a rush for the Tsuglakhang. Everyone prayed that nothing would happen to the old Lord. "At around one o'clock, we would see his tall, familiar figure riding towards us on a horse, a servant or two with lamps preceding him. A great sense of relief would overcome everyone."

The Chinese leadership sometimes visited Lukhangwa and tried to cultivate him. But the old man though courteous, was never accommodating. The very first time when Zhang Jingwu, Zhang Guohua, and Tan Guansan paid a courtesy visit, Lady Lukhang and her son wanted to borrow chairs for the Chinese to sit on, but the old Lord said there was no need and the Chinese would have to learn to sit on traditional *bol-dan* cushions, and if they couldn't, then it was too bad. "We don't have to change our customs for them."

The public was also aware of Lukhangwa's incorruptibility. He steadfastly refused the "presents" of silver (Chinese, *dayuan*) coins that the Chinese doled out to everyone—individual coins to school children and boxes of one thousand coins (*tong-gam*) to high officials and lamas. Even when the Chinese insisted, Lukhangwa politely maintained that the remuneration he received from the Tibetan government was sufficient for his needs. This was the income from his small estate* of Dekar Nangso in the Phenyul valley, north of Lhasa. The family was listed in the official rolls as Dekarwa, after their estate. A Lukhangwa son (Thinlay Namgyal) has written that the name Lukhangwa might have come from the fact that at one point in its history a family member had served as the caretaker of the Lukhang (Greek, *naiad*; Sanskrit, *naga*) Temple behind the Potala Palace.[3] According to Luciano Petech, the historian and authority on the Tibetan aristocracy, ". . . this family was not quite reckoned as belonging to the nobility."

On one occasion, Chinese officials even paid a visit to Lukhangwa's house in Lhasa when he was away at work and attempted to leave thirty or so boxes of silver with his wife, the lady Thupten Wangmo. She refused to accept them. But the officials would not leave and kept up their attempts to persuade her. They declared that they were aware the prime minister did not want any silver for himself, but that made him, in their eyes, ideally suited to take charge of distributing the people's wealth. They further claimed that the Chinese authorities did not have the connections and the knowledge to understand the needs of the Tibetan public, as the prime minister did. Surely, he could help the Communist authorities see that the silver was distributed where it was most needed and do the most good. With this and other persuasive arguments, they finally succeeded in leaving a number of *dayuan* boxes at Lukhangwa's house.

When the prime minister came home after work and learned what had happened, he ordered the silver be immediately returned to Chinese headquarters. Lady Lukhang told the servants to take

---

* ". . . one of the smallest" according to Shakabpa in his *Advanced Political History of Tibet* (p. 1036).

the boxes back, but her husband insisted that she accompany the servants. He explained to her that as she had accepted the silver from the Chinese, it was essential that she return it in person and obtain a proper receipt, otherwise doubts would linger in people's minds about what had transpired.[4]

The monk prime minister Lobsang Tashi was as incorruptible and dedicated as Lukhangwa, and they supported each other unfailingly. As I mentioned earlier, the Chinese did not know that Lobsang Tashi spoke fluent Mandarin (which he had learned when serving at the Tibetan legation at Nanjing), giving the two old gentlemen a definite edge in their dealings with the Communist authorities. The two prime ministers also made sure they were present whenever the Dalai Lama met any Chinese official. And they were always ready to intervene if the Chinese attempted to cajole or browbeat the young sovereign. The Chinese desperately wanted the two old men out. They put pressure on the Dalai Lama and the rest of the cabinet to dismiss them.

The Dalai Lama, in his autobiography, explains why he finally gave in to Chinese pressure. "There were two considerations: Lukhangwa's personal safety, and the future of our country as a whole . . . . Our only hope was to persuade the Chinese peaceably to fulfil the promises they had made in their agreement."

It was, of course, a fatal mistake. The two prime ministers' courageous defiance of Chinese authority had effectively impeded the full implementation of Chinese policies in Tibet. It had allowed Tibetans to retain a degree of self-government. The Indian chargé d'affaires in Lhasa, Sumul Sinha, in a report to Delhi, explained the resignation of these two Tibetan high officials: "The irony of the fact is that the very reasons for which they were being accused endeared the Prime Ministers all the more to their people. The Tibetans know them for their integrity of character and devotion to duty and will remember them long after they have departed from the political scene for the noble and courageous efforts they made to rescue the Tibetan administration from becoming a subsidiary bureau . . . [of the Chinese occupation administration]."[5]

The Dalai Lama's fears about "Lukhangwa's personal safety" were largely unfounded. The Dalai Lama mentions that at one meeting, "General Fan Ming lost his temper and accused Lukhangwa of having clandestine relations with foreign imperialist powers, and shouted that he would request me to dismiss Lukhangwa from his office." Lukhangwa replied that, of course, if the Dalai Lama were convinced that he had done any wrong, he would not only give up his office but also his life.

But in the early years of the occupation, the Chinese were in no position to arrest or punish any senior Tibetan official, especially someone as universally respected and admired as Lukhangwa. It was all bluff and bluster. The collaborator Baba Phüntso Wangye makes it clear in his biography that the Chinese leadership lived in constant fear of public riots or uprisings. Only after the Sichuan–Tibet Highway was completed in 1954, and reinforcements, supplies and heavy artillery were trucked into Lhasa did the Chinese feel more confident about their ability to control the situation in Tibet.

The Dalai Lama's underlying reason for dismissing the two prime ministers reflects his sincere but naïve conviction that if Tibetans did nothing to provoke or upset the occupation authorities, he could ". . . persuade the Chinese to peaceably fulfil the promises they had made in their agreement." In his autobiography, the Dalai Lama mentions that on his first interview with Mao in Beijing, the Chairman told him that the Chinese generals and officials in Lhasa were only there to help the Dalai Lama and ". . . not exercise any kind of authority over the Tibetan government or people. And he asked me point-blank whether these Chinese representatives had done anything against my wishes." The Dalai Lama replied tactfully that in discussions with the Chinese representatives in Lhasa there had been differences but ". . . we had expressed our opinions frankly." He made no mention of the screaming, the insults, the harassment and the threats that Generals Zhang Guohua, Zhang Jingwu and Fan Ming had directed at him and his ministers. "I told him that the people of Tibet had great hope for their future under his leadership."

Lukhangwa and Lobsang Tashi were dismissed on 29 April 1952. Even in retirement, Lukhangwa was tremendously popular with the public and hence a constant source of suspicion and apprehension for the Chinese. Finally, in 1956, he was persuaded by well-wishers to leave with his family for India, ostensibly on a pilgrimage. Prime Minister Lobsang Tashi went into retirement and devoted himself to spiritual pursuits. He was arrested in March 1959. According to Shakabpa, he was bound in shackles and chains and transported to a prison in Xining for two years. After that, he was transferred to the *Laogai* camp at Nachendrak, near Lhasa, where the new dam and hydroelectric plant were being built. He was released after five years but ". . . died before long."

That same year (1952), the Chinese also managed to get the former governor-general of Eastern Tibet, Lhalu, dismissed from the Kashag. Lhalu's refusal to surrender what remained of the Tibetan army, even after Ngabö's capitulation at Chamdo, and his creation of a viable defence line at Kongpo Gyamda, halting the Chinese advance, had unsettled the PLA leadership. Lhalu was accused of maladministration and reduced in rank.

With the two prime ministers and Lhalu out of the way, Chinese access to the Dalai Lama became less problematic. An even better opportunity to influence the young Dalai Lama presented itself in 1955 on his formal visit to China—which I will elaborate on in a later chapter. But the continuing rise in food prices and grain shortages created tremendous hardship for the ordinary Tibetans, and the public resentment of the Chinese occupation began to express itself in fresh anti-Chinese posters, songs and even the formation of new organizations as the Mimang Thun-tsog (organization of People's Representatives) the Lhasa Mangtsog Ruchen (Lhasa Public Formation) and other groups, most of which were short-lived. One managed to organize a large public demonstration and surrounded the residence of General Zhang Guohua with a few thousand angry Tibetans shouting anti-Chinese slogans. Chinese security was thrown into a panic.

The biography of General Zhang Jingwu claims that his official residence at Sandutsang House was "encircled by armed elements of the so-called People's Conference" on 31 March 1952, who "forced Zhang Jingwu to meet with the illegal People's Conference"[6] But the book was written in 2009 and the authors probably confused dates and events.

The Chinese were well aware of the increasing resentment of the populace to their presence and were making furtive military preparations to crush any insurrection that might take place in the city. One of the first indicators of Chinese military preparedness came in 1954 when a groom from the Norbulingka Palace was shot by a Chinese soldier. This groom was leading a few donkey carts of *arka* clay, collected from across the Kyichu River for the construction of the new Tagten Mingyur Palace at the Norbulingka. A Chinese guard at the new Kuru Bridge stopped the groom and his carts. It appears that there was an argument, and when the guard got aggressive, the Tibetan took out his whip and went to hit the Chinese, who shot him with his automatic rifle. The city was immediately abuzz with the news, and angry talk of revenge and throwing out the Chinese began to circulate in the teahouses and chang taverns. Armed Tibetan soldiers of the Drapchi Regiment went to the bridge and threatened the guards there. Chinese soldiers rushed out of their barracks at the *Silingbu* headquarters, and an incident was only avoided when Tibetan officials rushed there to defuse the situation. The Chinese administration offered its apologies and paid monetary compensation to the dead groom's family.

The following night the people of Lhasa began to hear trucks moving on the outskirts of the city and unusual activity in the various military camps that by now surrounded the city. In seemingly calculated sequence, units of the Red Army posted in districts outside Lhasa now began to appear in the various suburbs of the city. Lingka Sarpa ("New Park"), normally a peaceful, bucolic garden full of willow trees was, one morning, suddenly crowded with orderly rows of army tents rather than its seasonal complement of geraniums and chrysanthemums. An artillery regiment from Powo Tramo east of Lhasa had been rushed to the city. Colonel Jiang Heting, who later played an important but unexpected role in the events of 1958 and 1959, commanded this regiment.

The shooting death of the Norbulingka groom was not the only incident that caused suspicion and concern among the Lhasa populace. Phüntso Wangye, the Bathang collaborator, mentions a ". . . strange event that further heightened the general tension." A PLA soldier decided, prior to being transferred back to China, to pay a visit to the Potala Palace. The Tibetan guards there told him he needed a permit from Tibetan Military Headquarters. The Chinese tried to push his way in, and when the Tibetan guards held him back, they discovered he was carrying two hand grenades under his clothes. "The guards suspected that he might have been planning to kill the Dalai Lama, so they detained him and ultimately gave him a whipping. This, in turn, caused an uproar in the ranks of the PLA and the Tibet Work Committee because the Tibetan government did not have the authority to apprehend or punish PLA soldiers."

But the Tibetan public's concern for the safety and welfare of the Dalai Lama became most pronounced when it was announced that the Dalai Lama would travel to China to participate in the National People's Congress, of which he had been appointed vice-chairman. A major organization, the "Mimang Tsongdu" or "People's Conference," was created to try and stop the Dalai Lama's China visit. It was led by Alo Chonzé Tsering Dorje, a former monk and successful trader, Lhapchug Dhakpa Thinlay of Shigatsé, Bumthang Drunyik Gyaltsen Lobsang, secretary of the Bumthang Monastery in Lhoka, Kamikang Chönze, a minor monk official, and Amchi Anen-la, a paramedic who had worked at the Christian mission infirmary at the 11th Mile in Kalimpong.

They submitted petitions to the Tibetan government and the Chinese occupation authority, pointing out the suffering of the common people due to the excessive demands of the Chinese military. They also managed to extend their activities outside Lhasa and created branches in Gyantsé, Shigatsé and Tsethang. They received the support of senior officials as the Lord Chamberlain Phala and the senior cabinet minister Surkhang, who, according to the historian Tsering Shakya, even arranged for financial assistance to be given to the group, believing that their activities "would enable the Tibetan government to put pressure on the Chinese." But their provocative activities—sticking up incendiary posters all over Lhasa and distributing leaflets during the Mönlam Festival (of 1956) demanding that all Red Chinese "enemies of Buddhism" (*ten-dra gya-mar*) return to China—spurred the Chinese into action. The Kashag was forced to arrest three Mimang leaders, but when one died in prison, the other two were released. Alo Chonzé, the leader, escaped to Kalimpong with the help of the merchant Gonpo Tashi Andrugtsang who provided him ". . . two riding horses and one .45 calibre pistol with its magazine full of bullets."

Around the time the "People Conference" was putting up posters in Lhasa, the "Great Uprising" had started in Lithang, Bathang, Chatreng, Gyalrong and Nyarong, and was rapidly spreading throughout Eastern Tibet. The news of the conflict first came through on Chinese radio—in propaganda denunciations of what Beijing officially called the "Kangding revolt", since the insurrection had first taken place in the eastern part of Kham, which, forty years earlier, the Manchu viceroy of Sichuan had incorporated into his new province of Xikang with its capital at Kangding, the renamed Tibetan frontier town of Dartsedo. Very soon, the real and terrifying reports of the bloody fighting and the brutal Chinese reprisals were brought to Lhasa by merchants and pilgrims who had managed to buy rides on Chinese trucks—now ceaselessly plying the new military road from Dartsedo to Lhasa.

The opening of the Sichuan–Tibet and Qinghai–Tibet highways had been celebrated in Lhasa on 25 December 1954, with grand festivities and parades. A colour documentary film was made by two Czech film-makers on the creation of this unique mountain highway, and a special propaganda song "Singing the Erlang-Shan Mountain" composed to honour the valiant and indomitable road-builders— largely prisoners and former captured Guomindang soldiers, over 3,000 of whom perished in this great socialist enterprise.

Chinese forces could now be rushed from Xining or Chengdu in case of unrest, and also be supplied directly from China, and not be dependent on local provisions as they were earlier. The Chinese now trucked in heavy artillery and did not fail to roll them out, in impressive columns, the following year at the "Eight-One" Military Day parade. China's strategic hold over Tibet had now tightened considerably.

The first military airport was completed on 26 May 1956, at Damshung, north of Lhasa. The first two aircrafts to make the ceremonial landing were an Ilyushin Il-12 arriving from the north and a Convair CV-240-401 from the south.

Then refugees from the fighting in Kham began to trickle into Lhasa. The trickle soon became a flood, and long ragged caravans of women, children, monks and fighting men on horseback crowded the Holy City. They came from Lithang, Bathang, Chatreng, Dergé, Nyarong, Tawu and other districts of Kham. Some had relatives, friends and business associates in the city. Many had connections with specific colleges of the three great monastic universities. Some had even studied there for periods in their lives, in such institutions as Loseling College in Drepung, Jhey College in Sera and Shartse in Ganden, which traditionally admitted students from Kham but also maintained connections with monasteries and lamas in Eastern Tibet. The refugees mostly camped around the Banakshöl suburbs and the nearby parks, which were soon filled with ragged tents, grazing horses and pack animals.

During the initial period of the Chinese military occupation, the common people in Lhasa and Central Tibet had suffered because of hyperinflation and grain shortages created by the demands of the Red Army. The Dalai Lama, in his autobiography, states that these two conditions brought the country to the "edge of famine". Though the people had not experienced, thus far, direct Chinese aggression or violence, they found the behaviour and customs of the Chinese soldiers objectionable. The Dalai Lama writes that people complained about the burning of animal hides, bone, and garbage at the Chinese camps as Tibetans believed that such foul smoke polluted the air and disturbed the *lu* spirits and local gods, causing disease and misfortune.

The Tibetan government had to supply the PLA with grain and meat in the form of sheep and yak (on-the-hoof) that was distributed to the various units. Cases were reported of Chinese soldiers skinning live sheep and screaming with laughter when the animal ran around and rolled in the dirt in pain. Decades of devastating wars and cruel and inhumane governments had brutalized the soldiers. The climber Sidney Wignall, who was kept a prisoner at Taklakot in Western Tibet, was horrified at his PLA captors who gouged out the eyeballs of a live sheep and tussled with each other for this great delicacy, while the "still living animal bleated in pain."[7]

Now Tibetans in Lhasa began to hear stories of cruelty and violence inflicted on people in Eastern Tibet: on lamas, chieftains, farmers, nomads, women and even children. The stories affected everyone profoundly.

The Great Monastery of Lithang had been founded by the Third Dalai Lama, and the Fourteenth received presents and tributes from it annually. The "Great Monastery" was now a pile of smoking rubble, and its few thousand monks dead or scattered in the mountains. The Dalai Lama's junior tutor Trijang Rinpoche was the "root" (*tsawae*) lama of the Khampas of Chatreng. Now the Trijang Labrang (residence) in Lhasa was the first place that Chatrengwa refugees came to pour out their woes and seek comfort and support.

In his biography, the collaborator Phüntso Wangye mentions that Jhanju-la, the niece of the cabinet minister Surkhang, married to a Bathang notable, had somehow escaped from that embattled town on a Chinese truck and made it to Lhasa. She told her uncle of the confiscation of property, beatings at public "struggle" meetings, the suicides of her in-laws, the rebellion and the bombing of Ba Chödé Monastery.

"How could someone like Surkhang believe our promises when his niece was telling him her real experiences?"[8]

As the fighting in Kham extended westwards, more refugees poured into Lhasa. The Dalai Lama, in his biography, mentioned that there were at least ten thousand refugees in the city. That was about a third the size of the city's normal population.[*] One of the last big

---

[*] Richardson, in his *Tibet and its History,* notes that the population of Lhasa before the Chinese occupation was "some 25,000–30,000—about 45,000–50,000 if the population of the great monasteries on its outskirts be included."

caravans of fleeing fighters and civilians that made it to the Holy City came from the north, from Ga Jyekundo, the trade centre and main terminus on the Northern Tea Road. The Gaba nomads in the grasslands around Jyekundo were unable to stage a rebellion in early 1956 as the Chinese military had a strong presence in the area, which even boasted an airfield built in Guomindang times by the Hui Muslim warlord, Ma Bu-fang. But eventually, the whole of Ga Jyekundo exploded in a violent uprising, which the Chinese put down with great savagery, executing many of the traditional chiefs and lamas and wiping out entire nomad tribes and their herds.

The English journalist and author Noel Barber interviewed Radha Chime, son of the foremost patron family of Benchen Monastery, who led an exodus of over a thousand refugees and fighters from the Jyekundo area to Lhasa. "As they traversed a narrow, twisting ravine the long line of Khampas, horses and yaks were attacked by two Chinese planes that strafed them with machine-gun fire." A dramatic artist's impression of this attack appeared in a *Reader's Digest* (February 1970) "condensed" version of Barber's book.* Radha Chime and his people eventually reached Lhasa on the second day of the Tibetan New Year, 13 February 1959.[9]

Phüntso Wangye adds: "As more and more armed Khampas poured into Lhasa, rumours arose that they and the Tibetan government were planning to attack the PLA militarily." So, the Chinese secret police and intelligence were kept very busy. They tried to infiltrate the refugee camps with their spies and informers, but the Khampas were armed and angry enough to beat up, shoot or cut the throats of the Chinese Muslims or Bathang Khampas that the Communists employed as translators and informers.

"Didn't the Chinese try and use the Lhasa police force to arrest some of the Khampa refugees, or to spy on them?" I asked Bhusang.

---

* *From the Land of Lost Content* (1969) was the first book written on the Lhasa Uprising. Barber interviewed the Dalai Lama and high officials like Surkhang, Phala, Khemey, Taring and many of the other participants of the fighting. The book provides an accurate overview of the Uprising but is somewhat misinformed about the defence of the Tsuglakhang and Central Lhasa.

"No. Never. They didn't trust us. Every regiment in the Tibetan army, including the police, had served in Eastern Tibet at one time or the other, and many soldiers had Khampa wives and relatives. Some of the men had Khampa mothers too. You know that Captain Kaldam's mother was from Markham. But one day, my commanding officer, General Jumpa, gave me a spying job that I didn't mind at all. I was instructed to visit the various teahouses, restaurants and chang taverns around the Barkhor and report back on the activities of Chinese agents hanging out in those places. The Chinese had a lot of their youth activists and *hur-tsunpas* working the young clientele in these joints and spreading their Communist propaganda.

"One of their standard arguments to demoralize Tibetans was to point out how much larger the Chinese army was compared to the Tibetan army. The *hur-tsunpas* also never failed to point out that Tibetan soldiers had little ammunition for their Lee Enfields and also had few other weapons besides these WWII rifles. Another point the Communists would stress was that our soldiers were mostly uneducated while the PLA troops were politically educated. Somewhere in his long harangue, the agitprop would invariably come up with the analogy of 'the egg and the rock.'*

"'Tibet is like an egg and China like a rock', the agitprop would declare, holding out his hands, as if he actually had a rock in one and an egg in the other. 'If you hit the egg with the rock, the egg will certainly break. But if you hit the rock with the egg, does the rock get broken? Of course not—it is the egg that breaks. There is no getting away from this truth. Those who refuse to follow the socialist path to liberation and betray the motherland will be smashed.' Of course, the Tibetans there would argue and even shout insults and curses at the Chinese 'Shit on your egg. Shit on your motherland.' Fights would break out. I didn't join in the arguments or get involved. My job was to keep an eye on things. But one day I couldn't take it anymore. This really annoying 'diligent' *Wabalinga* (Chinese Muslim) started on his 'egg and rock' argument. I went out, picked up a rock and, going back in, let him have it on his face. 'Take this rock back to your shit motherland.' I yelled at him.

I managed to get away that time, but the next year I landed in trouble with the Chinese.

"Traffic control in Lhasa was the joint responsibility of the Tibetan and Chinese police. The policemen worked in pairs, one Tibetan and one Chinese. The Tibetans carried rifles but were not issued ammunition. The Chinese policemen had pistols, which were, of course, loaded. One day, for some reason or the other, a Tibetan policeman and a Chinese policeman quarrelled in the middle of the marketplace. So both were hauled away by other policemen to our HQ, to sort things out. But the Chinese policeman kept behaving aggressively and showing off—waving his pistol about and shouting abuses at all the Tibetan policemen around.

I got rather annoyed, so I stepped up to him, took away his pistol and hit him on the jaw. I didn't hit him very hard, but the Chinese police made a big deal out of it, and even had him taken to the People's Hospital for a checkup. Later a group of his comrades came to the Tromsikhang area to beat me up, but I managed to avoid them [Laughs]. The Chinese police chief insisted that I be thrown out of the police force, but my own superiors and mates stuck by me and refused. Finally, I was made to apologize, which I did. You know the Chinese are as mean as scorpions. They never forget even a trivial incident like this. Years later, during my interrogation in prison they brought that up, in every detail, to prove what a counterrevolutionary I had been all along.

"There was a lot of public display of resentment against the Chinese that showed up in various ways when ordinary Tibetans interacted with them. In the marketplace Chinese soldiers often had their fountain pens, watches and wallets stolen. We, policemen, knew all the Lhasa pickpockets [theptre], but we looked the other way and sometimes even encouraged them to 'liberate' stuff from the Chinese."

A former Dob-dob, or fighting monk of Sera Monastery, Tashi Khedrup, describes in his biography the reaction of his fraternity to the Chinese efforts at proselytizing. "Children who went there [to Chinese schools] were fitted out with free clothes—shorts, shirts, Chinese caps and so on—and they were given a red scarf to wear round their necks.

That annoyed the monks very much because a red scarf (*jandu*) used to be given to them by the Dalai Lama as a sign of his blessing. Whenever they saw a boy or girl wearing one, they made them take it off; one Dob-dob even strangled a boy by twisting the scarf tightly around his neck . . . The huge posters of Mao and Stalin which the Chinese put up were regularly plastered with filth."[10]

According to Bhusang, the pent-up hostility of the Tibetan population of Lhasa found a common focus of expression in sports. "Our regiments had races, and tug-of-war matches with the PLA, and the competition became so fierce that to lose against the Chinese was unacceptable. On the Chinese Army Day festivities, they had a big sports meet. Our regiment and a Chinese regiment, I don't remember which, were placed in the finals in the tug-of-war event. We practised a great deal but also had a secret weapon to ensure victory. In those days, large copper coins were still in circulation—and they were heavy. We got a whole lot of them and tied them around our waists in tubular bags, under our clothes, to give us extra weight. Weight is the crucial thing in tug-of-war. We beat them."

A friend of mine, Ngawang Dhakpa-la, from the old Jhidiling neighbourhood of Central Lhasa, was a player for the Potala FC, the best Tibetan football team in Lhasa then. He told me of his experience during those tense times, and why he thought that it had been a mistake to give his team such an august name. When, on an occasion or two, the Potala lost a match to a Chinese team, every Tibetan spectator would consider it an inauspicious omen. The monk football fans would invade the pitch, to beat up the Chinese players and the Tibetan footballers who had not striven hard enough to defend the honour and name of the great palace. The goalposts in the Chinese football fields were being constantly sawed off in the night and stolen by pranksters.

Ngawang Dhakpa-la had a fund of stories of life in Lhasa in those troubled times, but one story, in particular, managed to capture not only the tension and chaos of that period but the international "Cold War" dimension of the conflict as well:

"My friends and I liked the war movies the Chinese showed at Hongtö Shingka. They didn't have a proper screen but showed it against the back wall of Trimon house that they covered with a large white cotton sheet. Some of the houses around the square had step-like raised abutments, where you could sit, if you got there early enough. It could get quite cold there in winter, and we would invite the girls in the audience to sit on our laps. We went to every movie they screened, even the ones about factories and dams, but war movies were everyone's favourite, even the monks—although the Communists invariably won in every one of them.

"One night they screened a feature film on the Red Army fighting in Korea. The story was about a company of Chinese soldiers who had to capture this hill, heavily defended by American troops. Each time the Chinese soldiers charged up the hill they were cut down by machine-gun and rifle-fire from the Americans. Adding insult to injury, the G.I.'s would snarl and hurl racist insults at the Chinese while gunning them down. The Americans were played by Chinese actors wearing large rubber noses or something like that, which didn't fool anyone. But it didn't matter how phoney these 'American imperialists' looked; each time they beat back a Chinese attack, all the Tibetans cheered and whistled. Things looked bad for the PLA.

"The low point for the Chinese came when their cook, who was also the company joker, became so crazed by the cruelty and arrogance of the Americans that grabbing his soup ladle, he charged up the hill all by himself, only to be riddled by American bullets. But then the wise Communist Party commissar, using cookie's sacrifice as the theme for his pep talk, convinced the remaining troops to undertake one last charge. Red flags flying, bugles blaring, the Communist soldiers grimly fought their way up the hill. We knew this time they would make it. The Tibetans in the audience shouted all sorts of encouragement to the Americans, but the Yanks were showing signs of weakening. The audience was now in near chaos, screaming at the Americans to stand firm and stop the Chinese, but it looked like once again the Red Army would triumph, at least on screen.

"Then someone in the audience started shooting at the screen. The sound was very different from the muffled, tinny gunfire coming from the old loudspeakers. This was distinct, sharp and real—Tak! tak! tak!

He must have gotten off about three rounds before he paused. It was then that I saw the shooter, or rather his dark outline standing at the edge of the crowd. I couldn't see much in the darkness, but he looked like a Khampa, big build and long hair coiled around his head. After his initial outburst, he must have wised up, for he turned away from the screen and pointed his pistol at the projector and started shooting again. Whether he hit it or someone pushed it over I don't know, but there was a crash, a flash of light and then complete darkness. Everyone started shouting and pushing, trying to get away.

"Well, the next day, we found out that an old lady had been hit in the thigh by a stray bullet and one of the Chinese agitprop men showing the film had been stabbed by someone. After that, the Chinese had soldiers with submachine guns to guard these open-air film shows."

19

THE GOLDEN THRONE

It was a typical Darjeeling day, overcast, misty and miserable, even though it was the second day of October, and the monsoon should have let up by then. The funeral procession was a long one, with seemingly the entire Tibetan population of the town turning out for the occasion. It took over an hour for the procession to pass by our house on Gandhi Road. Six hundred or so students and staff of the Tibetan Refugee School walked in two files before the open jeep that carried the body. Many of the students held incense sticks and chanted prayers. The procession was led by a man carrying a wheel-of-life (*srid-pai khor-lo*) *thangka* on a pole. He was followed by a formation of maroon clad monks, from the two monasteries of Yiga Chöling and Samten Chöling, wearing their *tsesha*, those high yellow caps that look like Greek helmets of antiquity, and carrying banners, censors and other ritual objects. Occasionally they would blow their large *dungchen* horns and *gyaling* oboes and beat their handled drums and cymbals. My father walked beside the open jeep with the leaders of the Four Rivers Six Ranges and other Tibetan organizations. The rest of the public followed solemnly behind.

Just before the house of Tenzing Norgay (the Everest hero), the funeral procession descended to the lower Hill Cart Road, which winds by the side of the ultra-narrow (24 inch) gauge tracks of the slow Darjeeling Himalayan Railway (DHR) or "don't hurry railway" to local schoolboys.

The Hill Cart Road continues for five miles to Ghoom, the highest railway station in the world (for steam trains). Ghoom also has one of the oldest Buddhist monasteries in Darjeeling, which was where the funeral procession was headed, and where the body would be cremated.

The body on the jeep was wrapped in a cotton shroud and bound in a fetal position as tradition required. It was placed upright, and with all the *khata* scarves offered by people covering it, the whole thing looked like a white mound. On the top, where the head was, a five-panel *rik-nga* crown, the kind worn by tantric practitioners, had been placed, as was customary. The young editor of the English language fortnightly *Voice of Tibet*, in a stab at a more political and modern sort of statement, had placed the national flag over the body.* Tibetans don't usually go for overt displays of nationalist symbols on such occasions, and it was evident that the effort was somewhat improvised. Since the flag couldn't be draped in the Western military fashion, as over a supine body or a coffin, the problem had been overcome by wrapping the flag around the back of the upright mound, like the cape of a comic book superhero.

In life, Gonpo Tashi Andrugtsang did not look like a hero. It probably worked to his advantage in Chinese occupied Lhasa. Many of the Khampa merchants in the city were conspicuous men, sharp dressers, always elegantly turned out in silk robes, furs and black riding boots from Kalimpong, but Gonpo Tashi, by most accounts, had a lived-in, couch potato sort of appearance. Someone told me that he had once bumped into him in the main Barkhor circle in Lhasa one morning, wandering around in what looked like his pyjama pants.

His officers once dressed him up in full Khampa regalia: silk robe, boots, fox-skin cap, sword, dagger, etc., for a studio portrait at Kalimpong. The photograph somehow doesn't work. Gonpo Tashi looks just like a nice old man (with spectacles) wearing an oversize

---

*This editor, Lodi Gyaltsen Gyari, became the especial envoy of the Dalai Lama at Washington, DC in later years.

fancy dress costume. He also gave the impression of being a bit slow. His lifelong private secretary Loten-la told me that he was no orator. He spoke somewhat slowly and deliberately and was given to repeating a few stock proverbs and quotations in most of his conversations.

People of Lhasa and Central Tibet are ready to concede that Khampas are brave and straightforward, but regard them, somewhat condescendingly, as political naïfs. Hence Gonpo Tashi's creation of the Four Rivers Six Ranges (*chu-shi-gang-druk*), the paramount resistance force in Tibet, though acknowledged as courageous and patriotic, has often been dismissed as the futile last-act of Khampa defiance— or bloody-mindedness, if you prefer. What has nearly always been overlooked is the subtle, even sophisticated political thinking that went into the creation of this pan-Tibetan national resistance, which in fact even now largely defines contemporary Tibetan nationalist identity.

Gonpo Tashi was born in the Fire Horse Year (1905) in the Mola Khashar district of Lithang, to Pön Nyendak (the youngest of three brothers heading the extended Andrugtsang family) and his wife, Dichok Lhamo. Gonpo Tashi provides us, some affectionate and playful accounts of his mother, but says little about his father except that he died when Gonpo Tashi was eight. One reason for the diffidence could have resulted from the unusual marital and household tradition observed by the Andrugtsang clan, with many of the women staying home in Lithang at their tribal land of Mola Khashar, taking care of the children and their fields and herds, while the men travelled and traded throughout Tibet, operating mainly out of their base in Lhasa city.

Gonpo Tashi's early years were spent in Lithang. "In the middle of the forest, which was near my home, there was a rocky peak. This peak was over 10,000 feet high, and on top of it, there was the Tibetan letter 'Ah' which had been formed naturally. This mountain range extended from the north, south-west to the Lithang River, and it looked as if a dragon (*drug*) had come to drink water from the river." That was how the family acquired the name A-drug-tsang, according to Gonpo Tashi who described this legend in a lengthy weeklong debriefing interview with the CIA officer Roger McCarthy at Darjeeling in the early fall of 1959. It appears that the interview was taken down both in Tibetan and in a simultaneous English translation. I obtained the typewritten transcript (in the form of a photocopy of a smudged carbon copy) some years ago.[1]

The English translation is surprisingly faithful and retains all the flavour of the speaker's personality and cultural background. It starts, as all proper Tibetan narratives should, with an invocation to the "Triple Gem", the Buddha, the Dharma and the Sangha, an offering of reverence to the Dalai Lama and a brief karmic overview of Gonpo Tashi's own life and achievements that he concludes with the requisite but somewhat off-hand expression of humility. "I, Gonpo Tashi, had enough wealth because of my fortune or karma, accumulated as a result of my deeds in my past life. I have offered my life and wealth in order to serve the cause of Buddhism, our government and our great people, with a pure heart and mind. By doing this, I was able to leave a result which was 'not too bad'."

As a boy, he helped look after the horses and the family herds of yak and sheep. He also seemed to have received an education and some religious instructions, and he provides us with a list of religious texts such as Sakya Pandita's *Kunrig* (*All Knowing*) and *Mitak Drenkul* (*Reminder of Impermanence*) and others that he was probably required to commit to memory. At the age of fifteen, Gonpo Tashi was admitted to the Lithang Monastery and seems to have stayed there for two years studying other Buddhist texts, of which he provides us another list.

At the end of his second year at Lithang Gonchen, a band of outlaws attacked and robbed several families in the Mola Khashar and neighbouring areas. Local and monastic leaders called for the formation of a militia or rather a "posse" to deal with the bandits, and each family had to contribute some manpower to the project. Since most of the Andrugtsang men were away from home on business, Gonpo Tashi was instructed by his family to join the posse, which now totalled four hundred and thirty men. He saddled a good horse and took a German (Mauser Gewehr 98) rifle his brothers had purchased in Lhasa.

When the armed company finally caught up with the bandits, Gonpo Tashi and a few of the youngest members of the group were told to look after the horses, while the rest of the men went to ambush the outlaws. But Gonpo Tashi refused to accept this order, and managed to persuade the posse leaders to let him take part in the fighting. The ambush was successful and ended with the defeat and surrender of the bandits. Gonpo Tashi tells us that all the older fighting men " . . . were surprised at my skill with a weapon and praised me for it." He also realized that he had an innate ability to plan and strategize, and that he liked shooting. He admits that he was also fond of hunting, and "didn't bother about the sinful nature" of his pastime. His mother scolded him and told him that his conduct was sinful especially since he had received Buddhist teachings. "Sometimes she even beat me because of my fondness for hunting." Gonpo Tashi recalled, possibly with a smile, since he was a full-grown man by then.

His mother passed away when he was twenty-one, and he took over the responsibility for their immediate family. He commenced trading ventures of his own to Lijiang, Mili and Dartsedo. Some years later he made his first trip to Lhasa with a large consignment of tea from Dartsedo. He was welcomed by the main Andrugtsang household in Lhasa, and later given the responsibility of running the branch trading-house at Shigatsé.

The Andrugtsang House had come into prominence in Lhasa in 1875 when, headed by Andrug Gendun, the family became very successful in its mercantile ventures, and for the first time offered tea and money to the many thousands of monks of the Three Great "Seats" (Sera, Drepung and Ganden) that assembled in Lhasa for the annual Great Prayer (*Mönlam*) Festival. This offering constituted an enormous outlay of money for one family, but it brought spiritual merit and social prestige to the Andrugtsang name.

The Andrugtsang house in Lhasa was in the northern part of the city just a few houses east of the Tsomonling temple and monastery complex. The old Lhasa municipal map[2] notes two adjoining buildings. No. 44 (Cha) is designated Old Andrugtsang House while the larger No. 55, to its immediate south, is designated Andrugtsang House, and in addition carries the survey number 500. I was told by Gonpo Tashi's secretary Loten-la that the latter building was the old Trimon Mansion and had been bought, probably in the late thirties, from the former minister in the Tibetan government, Norbu Wangyal Trimon. According to Spencer Chapman, who visited Lhasa in 1936, the minister Trimon had "just married a new and attractive wife, in whose Lhasa house he now lives" (in the Hongtö Shingka Horse Market area). The old mansion was big, with large courtyards both in the front and back of the house. The building was three storeys high, and some of the rooms inside were a bit dark, because the house was so old. But it was well maintained.

In 1942, the year of the Water Horse, the head of the household and Gonpo Tashi's uncle, Jamyang Norbu, died after drinking a large quantity of arak and taking a dip in a hot spring. The secretary Loten-la told me that a year later, Jamyang Norbu's younger brother also died of alcohol-related causes. The two brothers had between them three children, a daughter, Chuki, and two sons Tamdin Tsepel (a school boy at the Astro-Medical Centre) and Lotö Phuntsok, the oldest, a pleasant, easy-going young man, clearly not up to the task of running the extensive Andrugtsang businesses. Members of the Andrugtsang family from Lhasa, Lithang and elsewhere, including the womenfolk, senior retainers and employees, gathered for a family council at their mansion in Lhasa to select a new head for the Andrugtsang household and business consortium. There was a sense of urgency in the discussions at the council, as the family business had gone into decline for a number of years.

Only the Andrugtsang branch trading-house at Shigatsé was functioning efficiently and profitably under Gonpo Tashi's stewardship. It did not take long for most family members at the council to agree that Gonpo Tashi should head the Andrugtsang household. But this choice was not unopposed. Jamyang Norbu's wife, Kesang Lhamo, an unquestioned virago, did not accept the decision of the family council and refused to give up the family holdings she controlled. She also quarrelled with everyone in the family and harassed them constantly. Her bullying even drove one cousin's wife to hang herself, which of course, made it a criminal matter that had to be reported to the Lhasa magistrates at the central Nangtseshag City Court, and also to the Lhasa Municipal Office (*lhasa nyertsang*) at the Tsuglakhang.[3]

Kesang Lhamo refused to accept any mediation or resolution regarding control of the Andrugtsang wealth, and when one decided against her, she would present the case to another government department. Finally, she even petitioned the Tibetan Army Headquarters at the Shöl office complex below the Potala, where the dispute went on unceasingly. At the interview in Darjeeling in 1959, Gonpo Tashi admitted wryly, "It is still not settled."

But Gonpo Tashi took up the responsibility the rest of the family had placed on him and worked patiently and humbly "like a calf carrying the load of an elephant," as he put it modestly. Within the space of a year, he increased the family fortune considerably, and even made the prestigious donations to the monks at the Mönlam Festival. In subsequent years he also created a recurring fund that would allow each monk to receive five "sho" of Tibetan currency every year. For this, he became known to most as Andrug Jindak or Andrug the "great patron".

Gonpo Tashi loved travelling. In the interview, or "debriefing", he provides an exhaustive list of all the pilgrimage sites, monasteries, temples, sacred mountains and lakes he had visited throughout Central and Western Tibet, as far west as Mustang, but even places in India, Nepal and China. The knowledge he gained of these places served him well in later years when he was leading the resistance force across many of these areas and in south-central Tibet in the Lhoka region, then the Jhangthang or the Great Northern Highlands.

Of course, these pilgrimages combined other less spiritual purposes such as trade and even sightseeing. Hugh Richardson has pointed out that like pilgrims in medieval England in Chaucer's days, Tibetan pilgrims ". . . manage to combine a sincere intention of acquiring merit at the end of the journey with a determination not to miss the pleasures of some attractive holy place" and also perhaps not miss a business opportunity that might present itself on the way.

Gonpo Tashi could be light-hearted and was a bit of a ladies man. He shared a wife, a Lhasa woman called Phuntsok, with his brother Lotö Phuntsok, jointly fathering five offsprings.

Gonpo Tashi was fond of alcohol but never allowed himself to get drunk. Loten-la told me he had a system that served him well. He would start the evening drinking barley ale, chang. When he felt a little full, he would call for a bowl of arak. But when the raw alcohol made him feel tipsy, he would stop and drink a pot of hot black tea to clear his head. He was an early riser and would get up around four in the morning to walk the Lingkor circuit around the city. He was observant in his other religious practices as well, and regularly consulted the Gyalchen Shugden Oracle at the Panglung Hermitage (*ritrö*) near Sera Monastery, in whose visions and predictions he had great faith.

Following the Communist occupation of Tibet and the triumphal march of the PLA into Lhasa, Gonpo Tashi kept a low profile and tried to have as little direct contact with the Chinese as possible. In 1952 the Communist occupation authority ordered the thirteen leading merchant families of Lhasa to send their senior-most personnel on a tour of China. Gonpo Tashi was somehow able to persuade the Chinese that his cousin, Lotö Phuntsok, was the real head of the Andrugtsang family, and had him go on the tour.

Gonpo Tashi kept out of the public eye, and instead discreetly began collecting information on Communist Chinese programs, personnel and activities, using his own extensive network of traders and muleteers and those of fellow merchants. Gonpo Tashi also began buying weapons. He had a stroke of luck when his cousin Lotö Phuntsok, on his way to China, met a local merchant at Dartsedo, who secretly offered to sell him a consignment of British Enfield rifles (and ammunition) at bargain prices (100 to 150 Chinese silver dollars apiece). These were almost certainly Tibetan army weapons issued to regular troops and Khampa militia before the invasion. Gonpo Tashi sent instructions to his cousin to buy every single one.

In March 1956, the year of the Fire Monkey, Gonpo Tashi made the trip to Tsari, in southern Tibet, to perform the holy circuit of the sacred Crystal Mountain there. That was the same year Bhusang made the Tsari trip with the Tibetan government delegation whose task it was to open the pilgrim route or gate (*ney-go*) to this normally inaccessible area. The delegation offered gifts of food, trinkets and fabrics to the aboriginal tribes (some of who were headhunters) inhabiting the jungles of that region, and in return, received their pledge not to harm Buddhist pilgrims. In the twelve years of the Tibetan calendar cycle, the Monkey year was considered to be an especially auspicious year to perform this difficult pilgrimage to the realm of the great tantric deity Demchok (Sanskrit, *Chakrasamvara*).

On his return journey, when he arrived at the district of Lhoka, Gonpo Tashi received news of the uprisings in Lithang and Kham. When he got back to Lhasa city, a delegation of about fifty angry and troubled men: traders and pilgrims, mostly Lithangwas, came to the Andrugtsang Mansion and approached Gonpo Tashi for advice on what to do about the crisis in Kham.

In the delegation was the young trader Athar Norbu of Lithang, whom I have mentioned and quoted before. He had heard about the uprisings in Lithang when he was in Chamdo and had just managed to leave for Lhasa on a supply truck, before the Chinese authorities had imposed a complete halt on civilian travel on the Sichuan–Lhasa highway. Once in Lhasa city, he had contacted other Khampas there and had met to discuss what they could do to help their countrymen back in Kham and avenge the destruction of the great monastery of Lithang. But as Athar admitted in an interview, they were all very young and inexperienced and didn't know where to start. Finally they agreed to seek the advice of Andrug Jindak, since, as Athar mentioned, in a lengthy interview he gave me, "Gonpo Tashi was a man of great standing and a patron of the three great monasteries."[4]

The delegation of young Khampas asked Gonpo Tashi if he would approach the Tibetan government and request its support for the Khampas. Gonpo Tashi confided to them that he was already in contact with the Tibetan government. He then advised the young men not to return to Kham and become preoccupied with trade and business but to start collecting arms and ammunition.

He also suggested that the first thing they could do to help their beleaguered countrymen back in Kham would be to arrange themselves into two groups. One group would stay behind in Lhasa and organize support for those fighting in Kham and, under Gonpo

Tashi's guidance, contact the Tibetan government and seeks its help. The other group "would travel out of Tibet and seek the support and aid of such countries as Taiwan, America and India."

A leading member of the group that remained in Lhasa was Ratuk Ngawang, a *chiso*, or business manager of Lithang Monastery, and who later became one of Gonpo Tashi's best fighters and commanders of the resistance force. He was also the first Khampa to provide me with information and even a photograph of Lithang Monastery when I was researching my play *Yunru* in Dharamshala. Ratuk Ngawang's four-volume autobiography was published by the Amnye Machen Institute in 2010.[5]

Among the twenty-three people selected to leave Tibet, nineteen were Lithangwa, among them being two brothers from the Gyadotsang family, Kalsang and Wangdü. One Lithangwa, Lobsang Palden, was entrusted with a sealed tin of snuff tobacco, in which was a letter from Gonpo Tashi to Gyalo Thondup's secret organization in Kalimpong, innocuously known as The Tibet Welfare Society. My informant, Athar Norbu, was also in this group. Three members of the group, Legshé, Changra Tashi and Ating were from Bathang. The last person, Kargyal Thundup was from Chatreng, and has been mentioned earlier as providing information to the Tibetan newspaper in Kalimpong on the destruction of the Lithang, Bathang and Drango monasteries. A few in this group, including Thundup, had been involved in the recent uprisings in Kham and had witnessed the Chinese bombings and reprisals.

That December, Gonpo Tashi sent three emissaries to various parts of Kham with a message of encouragement and support to the resistance leaders and fighters in Lithang, Bathang and Gyalthang and also to Gonjo, Gongkar, Dergé and Markham. His chief emissary Akhu Tsultrim headed straight to Lithang.

In Lithang, following the death of Yunru Pön and the destruction of the great monastery, the Chinese had undertaken a large-scale crackdown throughout the region. People in Lithang were demoralized but also angry. Diu Atrin of Meba Jelung, the leader of the Molashi nomads, now started to recruit fighters. He had earlier made the difficult and contentious decision not to stay behind and defend Lithang Monastery with Yunru Pön and the other *Ra* chieftains. Some of the chiefs and the monastic leaders had strongly opposed Atrin's decision, but Yunru Pön had not.

Diu Atrin had clashed with the Chinese earlier in Guomindang times and was a brave and experienced fighter. He was opposed to any head-on confrontation with the Chinese army. He had retreated from Lithang Monastery, and heading south-east, had set up several encampments (*makhar*) in the high inhospitable region of Rakhak or Rawa, with his headquarters at a place called Kapre Tsatok. From there, he sent out messengers all over Lithang, urging people not to surrender their weapons to the Chinese but to join the resistance. Other surviving Lithangwa chieftains Tayang Phuntsok Thundup and the Gyadotsang brothers, Bhugan and Thundup came to Rakhak, with their fighters.

When the news arrived that Andrugtsang Gonpo Tashi's representative from Lhasa was coming to Rakhak, a big meeting was called of Diu Atrin's fighters and resistance groups from other areas. The emissary Akhu Tsultrim read Gonpo Tashi's letter of support and encouragement to all the assembled fighters. The message that the assembly sent back to Lhasa emphasized their desperate lack of weapons and ammunition to fight the Chinese effectively and requested Gonpo Tashi to seek, without delay, the support of the Tibetan government and also the support and aid of foreign nations opposed to Communist China.

A number of younger Lithangwa chiefs and fighters were chosen to go to Lhasa to ensure that the resistance in Lithang and Kham would receive outside help. Gonpo Tashi's emissary, Akhu Tsultrim, stayed behind in Lithang and became one of the principal leaders of the resistance group. According to one source, the young chief Gyadotsang Wangdü was present at the Rakhak meeting and was selected to go to Lhasa. Another source mentioned that he was already at Lhasa and had approached Gonpo Tashi earlier that year for advice. In any case, he was later selected to be in the group sent from Lhasa to seek the support of foreign nations.

Wangdü did manage to return to Lithang the next year with the hoped-for "foreign" military training, but how all that turned out is another story. I might add here that I first met Wangdü in 1971, when he commanded the resistance force at Mustang, which I had just joined that June, as a very raw recruit.

After Gonpo Tashi had sent Wangdü, Athar Norbu and the twenty-three other young Khampas to Kalimpong, he focused his efforts on developing and extending the contacts he had in the ranks of the Tibetan government officialdom, including the army, and among the powerful abbots and incarnate lamas of the great monasteries. He was surprisingly successful in this. One old friend and trusted confidante was the prime minister, Lukhangwa. The prime minister's daughter-in-law mentioned in her interview[6] that the two men appeared to have been friends "from a long time ago", possibly from when Lukhangwa had been a finance secretary. Lukhangwa was out of office at the time of the Khampa Uprising. She said that even after she came to the Lukhangwa household as a bride, Gonpo Tashi would regularly come to visit. The Lukhangwa servants would say that a Gonpo Tashi visit was like a holiday for them as the two men would be so preoccupied, for hours-on-end, with their conversation that the servants had little to do but serve them tea occasionally. The senior finance secretary Namseling Paljor Jigme was also a trusted supporter, and Gonpo Tashi had a number of secret meetings with him at the Namseling manor in central Lhasa.

Another important friend and powerful (though secret) political ally was the Dalai Lama's Lord Chamberlain, Phala Thupten Wöden, as was the Dalai Lama's junior tutor Trijang Rinpoche. It was probably through Phala that Gonpo Tashi managed to gain access to senior officers of the old Tibetan army, a leading one being Tashi Palrab, the commander of the Drapchi Regiment. I spoke at length to an officer of this regiment, Captain Kalsang Damdul (henceforth Captain Kaldam) who was specifically tasked by commander Tashi Palrab to liaise with Gonpo Tashi.[7]

"My first contact with Andrug Jindak came about the time of the making of the Golden Throne. I didn't know it then, but Lord

Chamberlain Phala was the main person behind all this. The new commander-in-chief Lokéy-la (Lhotö Kalsang), was involved, but not directly. Major Wangden Tashi of Dranang, was entrusted with this task along with myself. Later, the Major and I were instructed by Tashi Palrab to introduce other trustworthy army officers to Andrug Jindak. We introduced about six officers: Major Phuntsok Yügyal of the Gyantsé Regiment, Captain Tsering Lhagyal of the Police, Captain Kharsham Gyalpo of Gyantsé and others. Our general did not want anyone from the Guards Regiment to get involved. Ever since the Guards had changed from their British style uniforms to PLA uniforms, people began to suspect their loyalty. The suspicions later proved unfounded.

Major Wangden and I were told that only the two of us should routinely contact Andrug Jindak.

"I had many discussions with Andrug Jindak and passed many messages to him and his associates. I am not well educated but, I was asked to write letters for Andrug Jindak. I don't know why, since he also had his own secretary, Loten-la. Letters were sent to Kalimpong and also to Diu Atrin, Sori Khetsun and other resistance leaders in Lithang. I also wrote letters to Phupa Pön of Markham and Karu Pön of Khyungbo. I had to write a lot of letters. They had made up code words to use in their letters. For instance, 'sheep' meant Chinese, 'tea' weapons, 'horses' trucks—something like that. I don't remember them all now—but you get the idea. Letters to Kalimpong were not coded. There was a lot of communication. Sometimes I was even woken up in the middle of the night to write letters for Andrug Jindak. There were times when it got so late with all the writing that I slept over at Andrugtsang house."

Andrugtsang's secretary Loten la confirmed that Captain Kaldam wrote letters for Gonpo Tashi. He thought that it might have had to do with security—not allowing one secretary to be privy to the contents of all the letters sent from the Andrugtsang house. Another secretary Gonpo Tashi used was Kunchok Dorje of Chamdo, who I got to know personally in Dharamshala around 1975 when we worked together at TORA, the Tibetan Office of Research and Analysis.

Quite understandably, many Khampa leaders and refugees in Lhasa were outspokenly critical and bitter about the Tibetan government's lack of support for the uprisings in Kham. But Gonpo Tashi appears to have remained silent on the issue. In nearly every account we have of the fighting in Eastern Tibet, Khampas have never failed to point out that the Tibetan government did not support them when they most needed it. Even Western writers on this subject as Michel Peissel, George Patterson and others have invariably raised the issue of the Lhasa government not supporting the Khampas, sometimes even accusing it of betrayal.[8] But nowhere in Gonpo Tashi's entire debriefing are any such accusations made. Instead, he points out that when fighting broke out in Kham in 1956 ". . . the government of Tibet made a lot of religious offerings that year and requested the three great monasteries (Sera, Ganden and Drepung) and Gyü Töpa and Gyü Mepa, and many other monasteries to pray and read religious texts for the spiritual benefit of those who had been killed. The government also requested all incarnate lamas, including His Holiness the Dalai Lama, to conduct prayers on behalf of the fallen."

This is perhaps Gonpo Tashi being diplomatic, but it is also a reflection of his down-to-earth realism. He saw that the political situation in Lhasa had deteriorated beyond the point where overt support for the Khampas could not be expected from the Tibetan government. With the forced resignations of the two strong-willed prime ministers and the minister Lhalu, the Chinese authorities were now pressuring the Lhasa government to send Tibetan military units to Kham to help the PLA put down the uprisings. In a surprising and somewhat Machiavellian move, the Kashag agreed on the condition that the Chinese supported the expansion of the Tibetan army and also supplied it with modern weapons. The Chinese, of course, refused. In the end, the cabinet only had to send a small unit of soldiers to Markham to act as interpreters. Many of these soldiers deserted to join the resistance.

The Chinese also called on the Kashag to expel all Khampa traders and refugees in Lhasa. The cabinet, to its credit, refused to do so. The Tibetan government was timid, powerless, faction-ridden and hobbled by a number of pro-Chinese officials within its ranks, but it never sunk to the level of the Vichy government that conducted mass arrests of its own Jewish citizens for the Nazis; or the Afghan government that used the Afghan national army to wage genocidal war on its own people in support of the Soviet invasion of its own country. The senior cabinet minister Surkhang was said to have been very firm on not deporting Khampa refugees back to Eastern Tibet. His niece had escaped from Bathang and had told her uncle of the confiscation of property, the public "struggles", the beatings, the suicides of her in-laws and the bombing of Bathang Monastery.

Gonpo Tashi saw that there was a wellspring of sympathy, and a genuine if fitful support, of a kind, for the Khampas in Lhasa, as demonstrated by the extensive religious services—a considerable expense for the treasury—that the Tibetan government conducted for the benefit of the people of Kham. And Gonpo Tashi realized that this empathy, kinship, and common culture could somehow be made to serve his greater purpose, so long as he was patient and did not alienate Central Tibetans with recriminations and angry talk. How exactly he was going to do it, he was not sure yet.

Gonpo Tashi had, all along, been planning to set up a resistance organization and seems to have established a few networks of agents. But he was unable to do anything more because of the omnipresence of the Chinese security apparatus, and its swarm of spies, informers and *hur-tsunpas* throughout the city. What he needed was a good plausible cover operation. He got the germ of an idea for one when the Dalai Lama concluded his pilgrimage to India, during the 2,500th celebration of the birth of the Buddha. On his return trip, the Dalai Lama passed through Shigatsé, the second-largest city in Tibet, where the public and the great monastery of Tashi Lhunpo offered him a "*tenshuk*" or a Long Life Prayer Offering, which expressed the people's loyalty and faith in the Dalai Lama.

Gonpo Tashi realized that the Long Life Prayer Offering to the Dalai Lama had an underlying political significance that could serve a greater national purpose, and he began planning to hold one in Lhasa. In his debriefing report, he mentions that such an offering should have, ideally, been made by the people of Amdo, Kham and Central Tibet (*bhöd cholkha sum*) together, but in the prevailing state of affairs, it would have been conspicuous and provocative, like "a thorn in the eyes of the Chinese." So, he decided to start small, and build up the project as the opportunity arose.

Still keeping himself in the background, Gonpo Tashi managed to persuade the business manager (*chiso*) of the Phara college of Drepung Monastery, to head a committee of Khampa merchants and leaders to approach the Lord Chamberlain Phala, and request that the Dalai Lama accept a *Tenshuk* offering from the people of Eastern Tibet. Gonpo Tashi also somehow managed to convince the Drepung *chiso* that once Phala had agreed to the *Tenshuk* offering, he should ask Phala to request the Dalai Lama to grant them a Kalachakra initiation, and if possible, also a teaching of the *Lamrim Kati*. This "upping" of the *Tenshuk* "ante" veered on the presumptuous, but for Gonpo Tashi, it was a necessary move as the Tenshuk offering, though symbolically significant, was a brief ceremony, while the other religious initiations and teachings were spiritually more important and would attract greater public attention and participation. It is possible that Gonpo Tashi had secretly contacted Phala on this issue, earlier. The delegation, much to its surprise, was told by Phala that he approved of their request and would forward it to the Dalai Lama.

When the public learnt that the Dalai Lama would not only accept the *Tenshuk* ceremony from the people of Eastern Tibet, but also give a three-day Kalachakra initiation and even a *Lamrim* (*Graduated Path to Enlightenment*) teaching, which is a lengthy and detailed teaching on the many stages in the path to enlightenment as taught by the Buddha—the whole program of events took on universal significance for all Tibetans. These forthcoming events were discussed endlessly in all the towns, villages and nomad encampments throughout Tibet. In Lhasa city, everyone wanted to participate and contribute to the events.

This conferring of the Kalachakra initiation by the Dalai Lama took on a compelling significance for all Tibetans at the time because of the desperate fear and uncertainty everyone felt about the future of their world and even the survival of their own families and themselves.

For a Buddhist *tantra*, the Kalachakra has an unusual and un-Buddhist "end of days" quality to it. Some scholars have discerned the possible influence of Manichaeism in this teaching, especially in its dualistic view of the conflict between good and evil. The Kalachakra was one of the last *tantras* imported from India, in the wake of the Muslim invasions and the destruction of Buddhist civilization in the subcontinent. The Kalachakra contains prophecies of an apocalyptic war where the utopian Buddhist kingdom of Shambhala defeats (with futuristic weapons) the forces of darkness and ushers in a universal Golden Age. Those who received the Kalachakra initiation were ensured a rebirth in this happy period.

With public support and enthusiasm for the religious events reaching a fever pitch in Lhasa, everyone in the organizing committee (which had swollen considerably) decided that something very special had to be done for the Dalai Lama to thank him for this precious spiritual boon.

At one point in the committee discussions, an idea was proposed that no one later quite recalled who had put forward. It was so tailor-made for Gonpo Tashi's purpose, that one cannot but suspect that he had a hand in its creation. The proposal was to offer the Dalai Lama a golden throne. Of course, the Dalai Lama already had thrones at the Norbulingka and the Potala palaces, but this one would be special. This would not only be the most magnificent and precious throne ever built for a Tibetan sovereign but would be wholly paid for and offered to His Holiness by his subjects—his people from the three traditional regions of Tibet.

What seemed to have escaped the notice of the Chinese occupation authorities and even the Tibetan government and the Dalai Lama himself, at the time, was that a revolutionary political statement was being made with this offering of the golden throne. Of course, the statement was symbolic and wrapped in arcane Buddhist ritual and imagery, but it was supremely nationalistic in that it clearly asserted, not only that Tibet was an independent sovereign state under the sovereign leadership of the Dalai Lama, but that all the people of Tibet were absolutely loyal to him. Furthermore, the statement was being made that this loyalty was not confined to Tibetans under the jurisdiction of the Lhasa government but furthermore by Tibetans from the regions of Kham and Amdo, now within the Chinese provinces of Qinghai, Gansu, Sichuan and Yunnan.

In earlier anti-Chinese posters, pamphlets and protest-slogans in Lhasa, the denotation of Tibet had generally been confined to the area under the Lhasa administration. Now the concept of a "Greater Tibet", of a Tibet harking back to the period of the old empire was being invoked, and the public was eagerly though largely unconsciously subscribing to the whole enterprise. Gonpo Tashi had raised the political stakes, and the absolutely inspired part of it was that the Chinese were completely unaware of what was really going on.

As befitting the importance of this venture Gonpo Tashi gives us a detailed list of those involved in the organization of the golden throne, and he provides us with their full names and titles, and even their places of origin. Four managers (including Gonpo Tashi himself) were appointed from forty-six groups to collect contributions from Kham and Amdo. Six managers were appointed to collect contributions from various districts and estates in Central and Western Tibet. In this list, he even gives the name of one of the persons who was replaced for some reason. Another four were appointed to supervise the contributions from the monasteries, incarnate lamas, government officials and aristocrats. Six overseers were appointed to sort and assess the precious jewels: diamonds, onyx, coral turquoise, pearls and so on, which were received as contributions. Four trusted volunteers were entrusted with maintaining an inventory of the gold and silver collected, and for its distribution to the artisans whenever needed. Five people, including a head chef, were appointed to prepare meals and other refreshments for the workers. Two water carriers are also mentioned.

Three men were appointed to make the rounds of monasteries and temples throughout Lhasa and neighbouring areas to request special prayers, rituals, and readings of the *sutras* to ward off any negative influences that could hinder the project. Another two were appointed to raise prayer flags periodically in auspicious places and make smoke offerings (*sangsöl*) of juniper, sage and incense, to propitiate the gods and spirits and obtain their support for the project. Three important people were selected to keep in regular touch with government officials and important personalities in Lhasa, in case of unforeseen problems that might arise.

The organization of the golden throne project takes on a special significance when we see that many of those taking part in it later became the military commanders and administrative heads of the resistance organization. Gonpo Tashi was creating the structural framework of his resistance army with the organization of the golden throne project.

Gonpo Tashi also used the task of collecting contributions to meet as many people as possible. His secretary Loten-la told me Gonpo Tashi set up a small table and a chair by the front entrance of the Jokhang temple and personally collected donations from all those who came to pray and worship at the temple. He also issued handwritten receipts to the donors. This task might seem innocuous enough, though perhaps not a suitable one for the commander-in-chief of the future resistance army, but the Jokhang is the most sacred shrine in the whole of Tibet and a central meeting point for all Tibetans in Lhasa, especially those coming from Kham and Amdo.

Every Tibetan, from the furthest reaches of the Tibetan plateau, had, since childhood, heard miraculous stories of the Jowo or Jowo Rinpoche, the principal image of the Buddha Shakyamuni (as a young prince prior to his great renunciation) in the Jokhang Temple, and did not regard it merely as a sacred image but as an actual living teacher and protector. In stories of magic and miracles in Tibet, there is a whole subgenre of tales relating to the Lhasa Jowo and how devout, unsophisticated pilgrims would speak to him as if he were a long-lost friend or a relative and, lo and behold, he would sometimes respond. In one well-known story, a simple guileless peasant, Kongpo Ben, from south-eastern Tibet, is said to have asked the Jowo to look after his pack and heavy boots, while he went around the Barkhor for a bite. This caused a hue and cry with the sacristans who were going to throw out Ben's gear but were told to stop, by the Jowo himself.

The last British representative in Tibet, Hugh Richardson, was a frequent visitor to the Jokhang. "I went unaccompanied except for a Sikkimese member of my staff. Going through the entrance passage, I would sometimes reach up to tap the bell inscribed *Te Deum Laudamus*, a relic of the Capuchin Mission from the eighteenth century. I wonder if it has survived. There was always a feeling of sanctity there, but to enter the Jokhang during the month of the Great Prayer (Mönlam Chenmo) was to be struck almost physically by a wave of faith. The passageways were solid with pilgrims—men, women and children—many from remote regions. One was met by a reek of greasy clothes, nomad sheepskins and rancid butter carried in pots to be ladled into the offering lamps at each shrine. But to join that hushed, patient crowd breathing deeply in awed devotion and gently murmuring the *Om Mani* prayer, was suddenly deeply moving."

A standing tradition with all Khampas and Amdowas who made the long, difficult journey to Lhasa was, on arriving, not to seek lodgings or pause for rest, not even freshen up or drink a cup of tea, but straightaway head to the Jokhang and offer their prayers to the Jowo Rinpoche.

Gonpo Tashi at his little table in front of the Jokhang made sure that he would be the first person in the city to meet and talk to these Khampas and Amdowas, many of them refugees from war-torn homelands, and get their names and stories before they could be intimidated by Chinese security or influenced by well-meaning but wary souls. When he could not be there, he made sure that a trusted subordinate would man the table, keep collecting the information, and let them know that there was one name in the city they could trust—Andrugtsang.

The contributions that came in exceeded every one's expectations. Housewives and aristocratic ladies contributed ornaments, jeweled headdresses (*patruk*) and their silver and gold amulet boxes. Even the city beggars could not be denied contributing their mite, or in a few cases, considerably more. Gonpo Tashi's business-like memory recalls a surprising gift of 50 *tamdo* or 2,500 *sangs* from the city's beggars. In fact, so many generous contributions poured in that he describes it as "just like drawing water from the ocean."

Work on the throne started under the supervision of the *Serdung Chenmo* or the Master Goldsmith, who had a government rank and wore the long turquoise *sogchil* earring of officialdom. Under him were forty-nine goldsmiths, nineteen engravers, five silversmiths, six painters, eight tailors, six carpenters, three blacksmiths and three specialists to do the soldering and brazing.

Gonpo Tashi provides a detailed inventory of the gold and silver (in the Asian "tola" unit of weight for precious metals) and various jewels that went into the making of the "fabulous golden throne" and all its accessories including a gold table, a gold "Wheel of the Dharma" and also a number of gold lamps, sets of gold water bowls, and pitchers, and silver lamps, bowls and pitchers for the Jokhang and other temples and monasteries in and around Lhasa. In total, 55.7 kilograms of gold was expended on this project, not counting the silver, gems and precious stones used, and the money spent on payment and expenses. Aside from the financial, political and even spiritual considerations of this project, the throne is a magnificent, unabashedly spectacular work of traditional craftsmanship and artistry. The Swiss art historian Michael Henns recently published a finely detailed photograph of it in his magnum opus, *The Cultural Monuments of Tibet*. He considered the golden throne ". . . a unique masterpiece of Tibetan gilt *repoussé* work."[9]

On July 4, 1957 (on the seventh day of the fifth Tibetan month of the Fire-Bird year), which Gonpo Tashi notes was a "good astrological day," the Golden Throne was placed in the Northern Audience Hall (*'Og min dga' ldan chos ling*) of the Norbulingka palace, and the people of Tibet were granted a special audience on that occasion, when the Dalai Lama first sat on the throne. He conducted a special ritual and blessed the gathering. It was also then that he was offered the *Tenshuk* or "Long Life Ceremony," which was accompanied by many valuable gifts. Gonpo Tashi reflects on why the people of Tibet were able to construct and offer such a "fabulous and unobtainable" throne to the Dalai Lama, and offers this verse from the sutras:

For those who have crossed the rosary of life,
For those who are fortunate and exalted,
There is no obstacle to the road of success
Even in deeds of great wonder and glory.

20

DROP ZONE TIBET

I was sitting with a couple of school friends in the Capitol Theatre at Darjeeling, waiting for the one movie I was allowed a week, when the obligatory *Pathé* style "newsreel" of the Indian News Review came up. This was in early December of 1956.

We were treated to a news report on the Dalai Lama and Panchen Lama's arrival at Willingdon Airport in New Delhi and their reception by Vice President Dr Radhakrishnan and Prime Minister Nehru. "The Vice President and Prime Minister welcomes our honoured guests from Tibet," the newscaster announced in the plummy BBC accent of Indian newscasters then, as the young Dalai Lama stepped out of the plane and waved. In the seats before me in the darkened movie theatre were a few senior girls from the Loreto Convent School, one of who piped up, "My, the Dalai Lama's so handsome, isn't he?

I kicked the back of her seat to register my disapproval. Tibetans dislike having their Dalai Lama criticized and also prefer praise to be of a specifically decorous kind. Tibetan conservatism can be very dyed-in-the-wool in matters relating to the Dalai Lama, as Sir Charles Bell had noted. When the Thirteenth was returning to Tibet from India in 1913, Bell was told by some Tibetans in Kalimpong that the Dalai Lama's "sanctity has been tarnished" by living in a non-Buddhist country "and by mixing with all sorts of people including white men."

But this time around, the Fourteenth Dalai Lama's trip to India from Chinese-occupied Tibet was greeted with relief by most Tibetans. Many even hoped he would seek asylum in India and be free of Chinese control. As the Tibetan saying goes, "when one has seen the scorpion the frog appears divine (*dikpa thongna balba lha la ngon*)." Many merchants and officials in Tibet also saw this as an opportunity to obtain Chinese permits to leave Tibet, even if only temporarily—as at least one family member had to stay back as a hostage of sorts.[1] During the last couple of years the Chinese had tightened travel regulations and regulations concerning transfer of assets abroad. They also raised objections to Tibetan children being educated in English and American schools and colleges in India and demanded they instead be sent to Communist Minorities Institutes (Chinese, *Zhongyang Minzu Daxue*) in Chengdu and Beijing.

The Chinese occupation authorities in Tibet were not happy about letting the Dalai Lama visit India in 1956 to participate in the "Buddha Jayanti"—the 2,500th anniversary celebrations of the Buddha's birth and enlightenment. They became especially nervous after the Hungarian Revolution broke out later that year. But nearly all Asian nations were to be represented at this momentous religious occasion, and the absence of the leading Buddhist cleric—the Buddhist "pope" as some in the international press conveniently labelled him—would have raised awkward questions for the Chinese prime minister (and foreign minister) Zhou Enlai, who had, just a year earlier concluded the *Panchsheel* (Five Principles of Peaceful Coexistence)* agreement with India, and was trying hard to refurbish China's international image following the end of the Korean War. Finally, the Dalai Lama, after being subjected to intense political and ideological briefings and

---

*In his editorials and cartoons in the *Tibet Mirror*, Rev. Tharchin castigated Nehru for the spineless Panchsheel agreement that gave up Tibet's sovereignty (and India's treaty rights and privileges in Tibet) in return not even receiving token acknowledgement of India's legitimate rights to its frontier territories in Ladakh, Sikkim and Arunachal Pradesh which China aggressively disputes to this day.

re-briefings, all the way up to the Sikkim border (as he notes in his memoirs) was allowed to leave.

A flood of Tibetans poured into Kalimpong and Darjeeling in 1956. Many of them were my mother's relatives who, as I mentioned earlier, brought those wonderful treats unique to Tibet. One visiting senior relative I remember was the old monk-minister Rampa (who flew the famous "bearded" kites in the Lhasa sky). He visited my school in his brilliant yellow silk robes and magnificent beard, and was shown around the campus by our principal, Father Stanford.

Among the Tibetans visiting India that year were the twenty-three young Khampas sent by Gonpo Tashi Andrugtsang. The rush of Tibetan pilgrims to India had been a perfect cover for them, and they had no problems getting to Kalimpong. The first thing they did on arrival at the frontier town was to meet the former Prime Minister Lukhangwa and the leaders of the Tibet Welfare Society, the cover name for Gyalo Thondup and Tsepon Shakabpa's clandestine organization. They delivered the letters sent by Andrugtsang from Lhasa. Still, aside from invitations to work together for the cause, the young men did not receive the offer of "military training, and arms and ammunition" they were seeking.

Exile Tibetan leaders were caught up in the Dalai Lama's visit, and it is possible that the young Khampas did not get the attention they might have in less hectic times. But someone had the good idea to send the men to New Delhi to give the international press and Indian officialdom a first-hand account of the Khampa Uprising and its tragic aftermath. A local Tibetan from Darjeeling, Bhagdo-la, was appointed as their translator and guide, and they were sent with another delegation of monastic leaders to the Indian capital.

The twenty-three Khampas met the Dalai Lama at Hyderabad House, the official Government of India guesthouse, designed by Sir Edwin Lutyens. The men received their sovereign's blessings. Athar told me that "During that meeting one of the elders in our group told him about the situation in Kham and how the Chinese were killing and torturing Tibetans there. His Holiness the Dalai Lama didn't say much but consoled us and told us not to worry. He said that things would improve slowly."

Top: my three-month-old self, with my nanny Pema Tsewang and her nephew Tsering Phuntsok at Gautsa the "Meadow of Joy", June 1949. [High Asia]

The caravan to Lhasa takes a tea break. [High Asia]

Bottom left: me with my father and mother on the roof of Tethong House, Lhasa, circa 1949. [High Asia]

Bottom right: caravan outrider.

Top: General Gyurme Gyatso Tethong (foot on captured Chinese cannon) with soldiers of the Shigatsé regiment, Riwoche, Kham, 1918. [High Asia]

Left: Kalon Lama Jampa Tendar, governor-general of Eastern Tibet, Chamdo, 1918.

Right: commander-in-chief of the Tibetan Army, Tsarong Dasang Dadul, Lhasa, 1920.

From left: Diki Lhalungpa, Lodey Lhawang (my mother), Devika Rani Roerich "first lady of Indian cinema", artist Svetoslav Roerich, and my aunts Sopal Terhong and Peldon Tethong (née Sampho) at the Roerich bungalow "Crookety", Kalimpong, 1955. [High Asia]

Top left: Raja Tenduk Pulger, my great-grandfather, Darjeeling, 1893. [High Asia]

Top right: Her Highness Yeshi Dolma, queen of Sikkim, daughter of the noble Lhasa family of Lheding, 1885.

Bottom left: Kumar Dawa Lhundup Pulger, my grandfather, Darjeeling, 1910. [High Asia]

Bottom right: my grandmother, Samdup Bhuti (*seated left*), and my great-grandmother, Tsenze Dolma (*seated right*). Wangchuk Tsering (my great-grandfather) holding my father Thundup Lhawang, Darjeeling, circa 1928. [High Asia]

From left: my father T. Lhawang Pulger, Everest hero Tenzing Norgay and District Commissioner Choki Talukdar welcoming His Holiness the Dalai Lama to Darjeeling in 1956. [High Asia]

Top: Kalimpong's celebrated resident, Rabindranath Tagore, reading his poem "Janmodin" over All India Radio at Gauripur House on his 78th birthday, 25 April 1938. [High Asia]

Left: Reverend Gergen Dorje Tharchin, editor at the *Tibet Mirror Press*, Kalimpong 1959. [Transhimalayan Heritage Art]

SCHOLARS AND SAGES: (*from left*) Herbert Guenther, Buddhist scholar; Gedun Chophel, savant extraordinaire; George Roerich, Tibetologist; Lama Govinda, mystic; Jamyang Khentse, spiritual master; Amoury de Riencourt, historian; Garma Chang, scholar and translator; Lobsang P. Lhalungpa, scholar; Rinzin Wangpo, cartoonist and scholar; Dhardo Rinpoché, educator; Tethong Tomjor, polymath; Sangharakshita, bikshu; Prince Peter of Greece and Denmark, anthropologist; and René de Nebesky-Wojkowitz, ethnologist.

NEST OF SPIES: (*from left*) Hisao Kimura, Japanese agent; David Snellgrove, British intelligence officer; George Patterson, missionary, wheeler-dealer; B.N. Mullick, director of Intelligence Bureau (IB); Ratan Sehgal, IB agent; Jayangki Khenchung, Tibet Welfare Society; Fraser Wilkins, US liaison to Tibet Mission; Clay Cathey, CIA agent in Kalimpong, 1958; Princess Kukula of Sikkim, early CIA informant; Alo Chonzé, underground activist from Lhasa; Calcutta-based PRC spymaster, Dai Ping in Kalimpong with General Zhang Jingwu, 10 July 1951; Inspector Lha Tsering, SIB counter-intelligence [Transhimalayan Heritage Art]; David Dorje McDonald, ex-diplomat and hotelier to spies; and Sarat Chandra Das, father of Himalayan spying.

Tibet Welfare Society gathering at Kalimpong. *From left*: Sonam Tomjor Tethong, Tsepon W.D. Shakabpa, Surkhang Rimshi and Gyalo Thondup, the Dalai Lama's older brother, circa 1956. [High Asia]

Former PM of Tibet, Lukhangwa (*seated left*), addresses newsmen in Delhi after meeting with Indian PM Nehru. With him are T. Lhawang leader of Indian Tibetans (*centre*), and Princess Kukula of Sikkim (*right*), 31 March 1959.

Communist China's 18th Army marches into Dhartsedo, 1949.

From left: Governor-General Lhalu Tsewang Dorje, 1937 [Chapman]; Governor-General Ngabo Ngawang Jigme, 1946 [Harrer]; General Muja Tsewang Norbu, 1955; possible photo of General Karchung Tsering Thundup as a trainee officer, 1930s; Robert Ford, captured by PLA.

Left: Geoffrey Bull and General Dergé Sey after capture by the Chinese, Markham, 1950.

Botttom left: first point of attack in the 1950 invasion—Kamdo Drukha ferry crossing on the Dri-chu River. 18th Army bridge-building unit at work after attack.

CHINA'S OCCUPATION LEADERSHIP IN TIBET: (*from left*) collaborator Phüntso Wangye, General Zhang Jingwu, General Zhang Guohua, General Tan Guansan and General Wang Qimei, Lhasa, September 1952.

From left: Lithang Yunru Pon [Alo Chonzé], Markham Phupa Pon [R. Pangdatsang] and the legendary seven-foot warrior of Jöl, Reting Zimgak [Spencer Chapman].

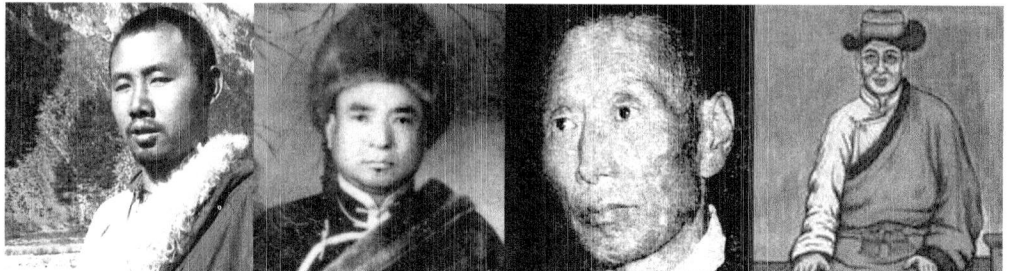

From left: Gyakpontsang Chemé Dorje of Lengkashi [Patterson], Trochupon Dorje Palsang of Gyalrong [AMI], Dochö Kunchok Tendar of Drayab (Berlin, May 2000) and Gyalthang Wangchuk Tenpa (aka Akhu Lemar), biographer's sketch [LTWA].

From left: Gyari Dorje Yudon of Nyarong [Gyaritsang], Ani Pachen Lemdatsang of Gonjo [Timothy Allen], Amdo Nangra Rigzin [AMI] and Pon Wangchen Dhundup [Gerald Roche].

Andrugtsang Gonpo Tashi reviews his resistance army at Drigu-thang base, 16 June 1958. [Thinlay Samdup]

From left: Gyalthang Karchen Chanzö, one of Gonpo Tashi's principal commanders on the "Long Ride North", Lithang Ratu Ngawang, another commander on the "Long Ride" and Cha-tring Tenzin Tsultrim Chadötsang, the youngest fighter on the Long Ride North. [High Asia]

COMMANDERS (MAKCHI): (*from left*) Lithang Alo Dawa, Amdo Jinpa Gyatso, Chatring Yangphel Tsultrim, Chatring Kalsang Chözin, Chamdo Shangri Lhagyal, Lithang Dewatsang Kunga Samten, Gaba Drahu-pon Rinchen Tsering, Lingtsang Phuntsok Gelek Rabten, Chatring Dawa, Trehor Sandu Lo Nyendrak, Chamdo Dotse, Chamdo Kunchok Dorje, Drayab Loten Chiso, Baba Yeshi Kalsang, Dhargon Pedor Gyau, Ganden Nyakri Khentrul, Derge Jhago Namgyal Dorje and Chatring Kowa Tenpa Gyaltsen. [High Asia]

HQ administrator Lithang Jhamatsang Samphel (*left*) and PLA colonel, Jiang Heting, aka Gya Lobsang Tashi (*right*), 1982. [High Asia]

Resistance fighters on the Long Ride North. [High Asia]

  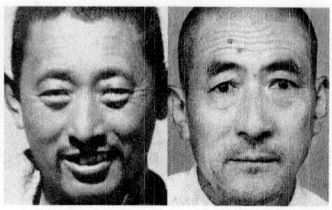

AIR TEAM ONE: Athar Norbu "Tom" (*left*) and Lotse Gatsetsang "Lou" (*right*). [Lhamo Tsering Archives (LTA)]

AIR TEAM TWO: Wangdü Gyadotsang "Walt" (*left*) and Tsewang Dorje Gyalthuptsang "Sam" (*right*) [LTA]. The team comprised two other members: Changra Tashi "Dick" and Thundup "Dan".

AIR TEAM THREE: Markham Tenpa Thinlay and Baba Lekshey [LTA]. This team included seven other members later inducted into Team Seven (see Team Seven below).

AIR TEAM FOUR: (*from left*) Dergé Sey Dhonyö "Bruce", Karze Loga, Dergé Rarutsang Yeshi Phuntsok and Markham Rishotsang Yeshi Gyatso [LTA]. The team included three other members: Markham Sherab Gyatso, Tsakhalo Tsegyal and Rishotsang Yeshi Gyaltsen. A single agent, Kalden, was also dropped in a supply flight.

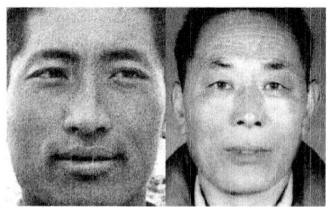   

AIR TEAM FIVE: Dergé Buche Utsatsang (*left*) and Lithang Lobsang Wöser (*right*) [LTA]. Other members included Lithang Aphel, Lithang Ganden, Gyalthang Lobsang Gyaltsen and Lithang Wangchen.

AIR TEAM SIX: (*from left*) Alak Sangsang Tulku, Lhasa Karchen and Amdo Tenzin Trinlay [LTA]. Two members, Drayab Tsering and Nangra Tashi Tsekho, not pictured here.

 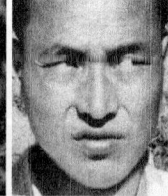    

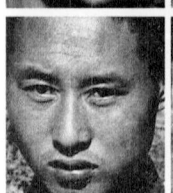  

AIR TEAM SEVEN: (*from left*) Ngawang Phulchung Adrugtsang "Nathan", Lobsang Gelek Draduktsang, Drapchi Nethang Chonze, Lithang Droli Phulchung, Kyalotsang Atsok, Gehogtsang Doma Thundup, Lhoka Choenyi Yeshi, Gyangtse Taythi Tashi Thundup and Gaba Rigzin Tsewang. [LTA]

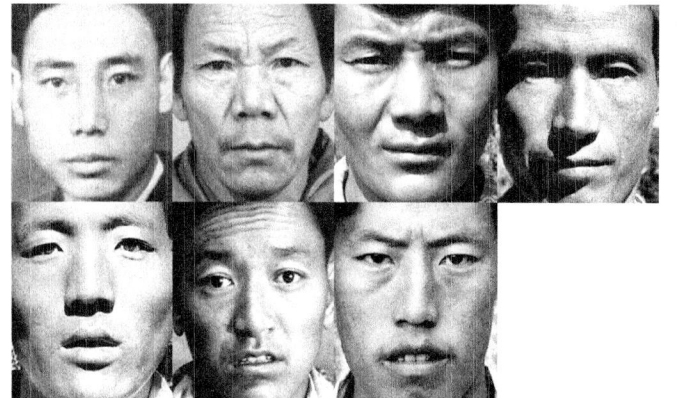

AIR TEAM EIGHT: (*from left*) Markham Phupatsang Yeshi Wangyal "Tim", Nyemo Bhonshod Bhusang "Ken", Gyangtse Damdul "Philip", Lithang Nasang Tashi Gyaltsen "Aaron", Tsawarong Ugyen Dorje "Duke", Drapchi Dorje Phuntsok "Colin" and Lithang Golo Lobsang "Luke". [LTA]

OVERLAND TEAMS: (*from left*) some of the agents who set up intelligence networks and bases inside Tibet: Lithang Jamyang Tsultrim, Amdo Tenzin, Lhasa Phurbu Tsering, Chatreng Tenzin Tsultrim "Clyde", Dergé Rinchen Dhargay, Trehor Pema Namgyal, Nyetang Yeshi and Phadrug Nyima Gyalpo. [LTA]

Above: Gyalo Thondup, exile Tibetan minister of foreign affairs (also security & war). Taktser Rinpoché (*centre*) Tibet's first contact with the CIA. He and Mongol Geshé Wangyal (*right*) helped develop Tibetan language training manuals for guerilla warfare, sabotage, etc., and devised a tele-code system in Tibetan.

Left: Lhamo Tsering "Larry" operations chief (Darjeeling HQ) on first trip to Lhasa, 1952. [LTA]

SOME UNDERGROUND ACTIVISTS: (*from left*) Tsesum, blind beggar and spy; Amchi Anen-la of old Mimang cell; Yungon Yeshi Dhargay of Tsedrung cell; Chone Alak Jampel, Gurten Kunsang and Maja Tsewang Gyurme of United cell; Lhanga Tseten Namgyal, Phuntsok Wangdu Jhangdré, Narkyid Ngawang Thondup of Freedom Alliance cell and Seynang Lobsang Yeshey, key organizer.

(*From left*) **DALAI LAMA'S ESCAPE ORGANIZERS:** Lord Chamberlain Phala (1974), Kundeling Dzasa, Seynang Lobsang Yeshi, Kalon Surkhang, General Tashi Palrab, Khenchung Tara, Tsendron Bharshi, Tsendron Yeshi Lhundup, Trijang Rinpoche, Captain Kaldam and Major Wangden.
RAMAGANG ESCORT LEADERS: Dewatsang Kunga Samten, Kanze Tenpa Dhargay, Dapon Ragashar Sonam Topgyal and Gyangtse Namgyal Wangdu.

WOMEN LEADERS AND DEMONSTRATORS: (*from left*) Galingshar Ani-la, Gurten Kunsang-la, Dolma Chönzom, Sampho Ngudup Wangmo, Lobsang Dekyong and Lhalu Sonam Deki, who fired a Bren gun at PLA troops from the roof of Lhalu mansion.

PEOPLE'S CONFERENCE REPRESENTATIVES: (*from left*) Tsarong, former PM Lobsang Tashi, Manang Abo, Phala steward Loyon, former commander-in-chief Lokay-la, coracle-overseer Wangchuk, Chamdo Jampa Kalden, master-carpenter Nyemo Gyatso, Amchi Anen, former commander-in-chief Kusangtse, Maja Tsewang Gyurme, former commander-in-chief Mönkiling, Ta-Lama Chokteng Thupten Norsang and Tsedrung Drakpa Tendar.

SOME FIGHTERS: (*from left*) Nyemo Bhusang, Dzasak Jigme Taring, Choedak Dawa, Amdo Samdup, Amdo Lekshe, Kunchok, Gyapontsang Gonpo Chimé, Juchen Thupten Namgyal, Sandutsang Wandor, Dhoyontsang Tsewang Norbu, Chamdo Yaptsang Lobsang Kunchok and Trehor Pema Namgyal.

Above: Artist's impression of the fighting around the Jokhang Temple. Artist unknown.

Above: Police major Rinzin Paljor (*left*), aka Rupon Gura, defender of the Jokhang and Sandutsang Lo Gendun (*right*), killed at Ramagang Ferry. [High Asia]

CAPTURED FIGHTERS: (*from left*) General Muja, Lhalu Tsewang Dorje, Tsepon Shugupa, Seynang Yeshi Dhargay, Shakabpa Khenchung, Lhagyari Trichen, Thupten Khetsun, Tsedrung Tenpa Soepa, Rimshi Sumdowa, Thunsur Lobsang Tenzin, Palden Gyatso, Dapon Sampho, Rimshi Rasa Gyagen, Major Sekshing and "rebel leader" Langthong Pema Dorje released at official ceremony in Lhasa, November 1978.

Tibet's highest female incarnate lama, the 12th Samding Dorje Phagmo being struggled. The jewels on her sacred black hat have been torn off. Her parents (*beside her*) were beaten and imprisoned. Lhasa, 1966. [Tsering Woeser]

Above: Senior monks and lamas being struggled at Sera. Monasteries in Tibet were closed in 1966 and monks were sent to the fields for slave labour. [High Asia]

Left: Ani Trinlay Chödön, the nun leader of the Nyemo Uprising before her execution, Dodé, 1970. [AMI]

Nyemo Bhusang released after serving nineteen years in Chinese prisons.

Nyemo prisoners prepared for execution, Dodé, 1970. [AMI]

SENIOR LEADERS: (*from left*) CO Wangdü Gyadotsang, former CO Yeshi Kalsang, Dhargon Ngatruk, Rakra Gyadhar, Chatreng Dawa, Trehor Pachen, Nyarong Kalsang Dorje, Gyen Ah Trinlay, Chamdo Tsering Dorje and Dergé Buché Utsatsang. [LTA]

OFFICERS: (*from left*) Tashi Thundup "Sandy", Kanze Sonam Wangyal, Derge Khaley Jhampa, Tsawarong Pema Rigzin, Lithang Lobsang Jhampa, Gyalthang Ngawang Sangpo, Dhargon Pema Dorje, Dergé Tsewang, Chatreng Gyaltsen. [LTA]

RADIO TEAM 'K': (*from left*) Jedung Jampel Legmon, Gyangtse Namgyal and Lithang Trinlay. Other comms staff: Dhargon Norbu Dorje, Amdo Ngawang Samdup and Baba Gedun Thargay.

Gyen Tendar and his men preparing for a raid, 1964. [George Patterson]

Subsequently, a press conference was arranged with the national and international press corps in the Indian capital. This was probably when Kargyal Thondup of Chatreng gave his account of the bombing of Chatreng Monastery to the BBC, as he mentioned in a later interview.[2]

After that, they went on a pilgrimage to Bodh Gaya, where the Dalai Lama gave the Ganden Lhagya teachings, which they received. But so far they had made no contacts with anyone who could help them with their principal mission—and they were losing hope. Their group began to break up. Then one day, the Dalai Lama's oldest brother, Taktser Rinpoche, the former abbot of Kumbum Monastery, came over to the guest house where they were staying and asked about them. They did not expect the Dalai Lama's brother to be any more helpful, especially since he was a religious leader himself, but they politely went through their story again and expressed their hope of acquiring training and arms so they could return to their homeland and fight the Chinese. To their surprise, Rinpoche told them that he could help them do that.

Taktser Rinpoche, who was thirteen years older than his brother Gyalo Thondup, was convinced, from personal experience, that Communist China's intentions regarding Tibet were unequivocally malevolent. Rinpoche had witnessed how the Communists dealt with opposition when they wiped out the Muslim Hui of Lusar, close to his monastery at Kumbum. He was also in Amdo when the Red Army slaughtered the Amdowas of Nangra and Hormukha and started their genocidal campaign against the Goloks.

Rinpoche was not without some guile himself, and he managed to give the impression to his captors that he was receptive to their overtures.

They decided to send him to Lhasa to win over the Dalai Lama. In his biography, Rinpoche describes the unbelievably crude way the Communist leaders approached him, promising to appoint him "governor-general" (*chikyap*) of Tibet if he convinced the Dalai Lama and the Tibetan government not to resist the Chinese advance into Tibet. They even went so far as to hint that "should the young Dalai Lama resist the march of progress, ways and means would have to be found to get rid of him. They even let me see quite clearly that if necessary, they would regard fratricide as justifiable in the circumstances if there remained no other way of advancing the cause of Communism."[3] After his escape from Kumbum and Lhasa, which I described in chapter eight, he managed to get to the United States and make the initial contact with the CIA.

But after Tibet signed the Seventeen Point Treaty in 1951 and the Dalai Lama returned to Lhasa from the Sikkim border, the CIA lost interest in the Tibetan issue. Taktser Rinpoche had considerable difficulty getting his visa renewed to stay in the USA. He earned a modest income giving Tibetan language classes to a handful of American students as a part of a non-credited course at Columbia University, while his loyal servitor Gyaltsen worked in an aircraft factory in New Jersey. I got the impression from his autobiography that Rinpoche spent his evenings in his small New York apartment making *thenthuk* (pulled-dough dumpling soup) for himself and Gyaltsen ". . . according to a typical Tibetan recipe."

But in early 1956, when uprisings broke out in Eastern Tibet, the CIA and the State Department renewed its relationship with Taktser Rinpoche. Discussions also started on initiating covert operations inside Tibet, and Rinpoche contacted his brother Gyalo Thondup and his organization in Kalimpong, about these developments. As plans began to take shape, Rinpoche made arrangements to visit India that summer, when he received the news that the Dalai Lama would also be in India in November. He immediately flew to Delhi and met Gyalo Thondup and Tsepon Shakabpa.

When Taktser Rinpoche and Gyalo Thondup met the Dalai Lama later that year they tried to persuade him to seek asylum in India. Other Tibetan leaders-in-exile, such as the former Prime Minister Lukhangwa, pleaded with the Dalai Lama not to return to Tibet. But in the end, the Dalai Lama consulted the state oracle. The Dalai Lama mentions in his *Compassion in Exile* that Lukhangwa refused to leave the room even when the oracle became angry with him. The old aristocrat warned the Dalai Lama, "When men become desperate, they consult the gods. And when gods become desperate, they tell lies." But his Holiness chose to heed the oracle rather than his old prime minister or his two brothers.

Taktser Rinpoche was luckier in finding the resistance fighters that the CIA could train and arm for operations inside Tibet. According to Athar, Taktser Rinpoche took photographs of him and his friends and noted their personal information. He told them that he would personally contact Gyalo Thondup in Kalimpong and let him know about them. A couple of weeks later, they received a message to go to Kalimpong, and very soon, they met Gyalo Thondup. He came to their lodgings and selected six of them for an important mission and told them ". . . they were not to disclose anything to family or friends." The six selected were: Athar Norbu, Lotse Gatsetsang, Wangdü Gyadotsang, Tsewang Dorje Gyalthuptsang, Baba Changra Tashi and Thundup Chöbulu.

On 20 March 1957, shortly after dark, Gyalo Thondup drove the six Khampas in his jeep down to the railhead town of Siliguri. From the town they drove further south towards the border of East Pakistan (now Bangladesh). Gyalo Thondup then left the men with a guide, his cook Gelong, who led them on foot in the dark. They had to cross the Teesta River, which was a difficult task though the river was at its lowest point, being winter. Finally, after about a four-hour trek, they saw half a dozen armed soldiers signalling with flashlights. Their guide signalled back with his flashlight and walked towards them. They were Pakistani soldiers, and accompanying them was Taktser Rinpoche's servitor, Gyaltsen, who now acted as an interpreter for the six men.

They walked some distance to a house where they were greeted by an American who offered them tea and biscuits. They were then driven in a jeep until the next morning, when they reached a town with a railway station. Pakistani soldiers put them in a private carriage. They travelled for twenty-four hours, after which they were put aboard a covered truck and driven for some hours to Dacca airport. The truck drove right up to the steps of a military plane. The six men quickly boarded the plane, which then took off for Thailand. From Bangkok they flew to the American military base at Okinawa, where Taktser Rinpoche met them. The men were all given medical examinations and pronounced fit. From Okinawa they were again flown, this time to Saipan, where they stayed in two Quonset huts on an old military base.

Athar refers to Saipan as "Dursa" or "land of the dead" and this is how he describes the island in an interview: "It was full of destroyed planes and ships. In the forests, there were still dead bodies of Japanese soldiers. The flesh of the corpses had decayed, but their skeletons, still with their arms and ammunition and grenades, were to be seen everywhere. We landed at the head of the island that was forested in several places. At some distance, along the shores, there were a few villages."

The CIA officer in charge of the training program at Saipan, Roger McCarthy,* later wrote the first book on the CIA and the Tibetan Resistance. Roger kindly sent me a copy of his *Tears of the Lotus* (1997) as he had quoted some passages from my 1979 book on the Nyarong uprising. A number of books have since been published on the Agency's involvement with Tibet, of which Conboy and Morrison's *The CIA's Secret War in Tibet* (2002) is the most comprehensive on operational details. Mikel Dunham's *Buddha's Warriors* (2004) is also very thorough and an engrossing read, while Carole McGranahan's *Arrested Histories* (2010) provides the human element, describing the lives of the many Tibetan participants and their personal views of the operations. John Kenneth Knaus' *Orphans of the Cold War* (2000) is excellent on the history of the program and the political aspects of American involvement in Tibet. Lhamo Tsering's eight-volume *Resistance*, published by Amnye Machen Institute (AMI), contains the most detailed information, especially on the individual Tibetans involved.

There is no substantial disagreement in these books on the broad course of events, but there are discrepancies in the minutiae. I sifted through all these sources and obtained much valuable information, but ultimately fell back largely on Lhamo Tsering's *opus* and my own lengthy interviews with him and Tibetan officials, tribal leaders,

---

*Roger McCarthy ('Mac' to his Tibetan trainees) is considered by many to be the godfather of the Tibet Task Force. He co-created the operation with Frank Holober early in 1957 and began training the first team in Saipan by March, later taking the reins as Project Manager in 1958. McCarthy left the Tibetan operation in 1961, but his personal passion for the Tibetan fight for freedom kept him active in their cause until his death in October 2007.

resistance fighters, military personnel, secret agents and others for the
bulk of my narrative. I did so in order that I could focus on telling
the Tibetan side of the story and not because the accounts by these
Americans experts and academics were in any way flawed. In fact, I
would strongly recommend that readers go through these excellent
works to gain a better understanding of this forgotten but significant
episode of the Cold War.

Taktser Rinpoche assisted in the training of the first group of
Tibetan agents acting as an interpreter for the instructors. In one of the
Quonset huts a private bedroom and bath was set aside for Rinpoche
". . . as befitted the older brother of the Dalai Lama. Taktser Rinpoche
became, in essence, McCarthy's crash-course in all things Tibetan."[4]

Rinpoche and the Mongolian (Kalmuk) Geshe Wangyal worked
with a CIA communications team to devise a tele-code system to
describe items that were not in the Tibetan vocabulary and created
a system of writing precise, intelligible messages concerning modern
warfare and intelligence, within an archaic traditional language.
Rinpoche and Geshe Wangyal were also involved in putting together
the training manuals for guerrilla warfare, sabotage and so on.

The first order of business for the Khampas was remembering
their American training names, devised for security reasons and the
convenience of the half-dozen American instructors. So, Athar became
Tom, Lotse—Lou, Wangdü—Walt, Tsewang Dorje—Sam, Changra
Tashi—Dick and Thundup—Dan. In his book McCarthy provides
a detailed description of their training program, and tells us that they
managed to cover it in a four-and-a-half-month period—which is
impressive, even astonishing:

"Training included Morse code, cut numbers, radio signal plans,
the U.S.-made RS-1 crystal operated radio transmitter and receiver
(powered by a hand-cranked generator), encoding and decoding
using one-time pads, map and compass reading, small arms up to and
including 60 mm mortar and 57 mm recoilless rifles, fragmentation
and incendiary grenades and movement tactics . . . offensive and
defensive ambushes, an array of simple sabotage techniques, use of
demolitions, Molotov cocktails, booby traps, unarmed and hand to

hand combat, cross country and night movement, observation, casing, authentication, elicitation, information collection, reports writing, tradecraft techniques, resistance organizations, sketching, preparation of drop zones, parachute ground training, simple psychological warfare techniques, first aid, simple disguise techniques, etc."[5]

In an interview, McCarthy recalled the trainees being open, fun loving and gregarious, with no physical challenge being too great for them, and demolition training being like "happy hour" for them. "The bigger the bang and the more damage that the explosives achieved the better!"

"And in spite of their antics, they were very disciplined. They understood the value of intelligence nets—what would work, what couldn't work. Their attention to detail during observation exercises was superior. In fact, I don't know of any subject in which they ever failed . . . To my surprise, they quickly learned how to read and use maps, a skill few can claim. (From simple coordinates concepts to eight-digit accurate grid coordinates and transposing the resultant coordinates into accurate insertions in the one-time pad system to be used . . . all six did very well."

Where the trainees didn't manage equally well was mastering the "dot-dash" Morse signals, which they had to recognize by ear and write down, and also tap out on a key. Athar Norbu told me, with no false modesty, that he was the best at this and could recognize and take down forty groups a minute, easily. Athar explained: "Each group consists of four numerals, e.g., 1, 2, 3 and 4, and each group forms one word of the message which we could later decode. Changra Tashi could do thirty-two groups a minute, Lotse thirty and Tsewang Dorje twenty-four. Wangdü had a hard time recognizing the radio signals. He used to say that all he could hear was the same sound, "chiu chiu chiu" like a bird chirping. Actually, it does sound a bit like that, at the beginning. Thundup or Dan, who was Wangdü's servant, was hopeless. 'Like master like servant' as the saying goes."[6]

But Wangdü was a natural leader and an experienced fighter, so he was assigned to lead the team to be dropped into Lithang and meet up with the resistance groups there. Wangdü and Thundup would train the fighters in guerrilla warfare, weapons, demolitions and so on. Changra Tashi and Tsewang Dorje would be in charge of the vital radio-sets with which they would communicate with the CIA and through which the Lithang Resistance would eventually receive their crucial arms drops.

Athar Norbu and Lotse were to be dropped near Lhasa. They were to make contact with Gonpo Tashi and also explore ways to connect with prominent Tibetan government officials who were opposed to the Chinese. If possible, they were to try and meet the Dalai Lama himself and obtain his approval for the undertaking and for American support.

In October, the six were taken to an airfield where they made their first parachute jumps. Athar remembers making seven practice jumps in all, sometimes landing in the fields of Okinawan farmers who would come running to see them. But the men were quickly hustled into covered trucks and driven away.

Everything was going without a hitch when during weapons training, Tsewang Dorje accidentally shot himself in the foot. Fortunately, the wound was not a serious one, but it meant that he would not be able to accompany the Lithang team.

DROP ZONE SAMYE

On 20 October, the five men boarded an unmarked B17 bomber, painted dull black, and took off from an old WWII airstrip at Kurmitola in East Pakistan. The plane wound its way north to the Sikkim corridor across the Himalayas, avoiding Indian radar at Calcutta. Before the plane flew over the Tibetan frontier, Athar mentions that he saw points of lights on the ground that he thought might be Darjeeling or Kalimpong. A couple of hours later, just before they were dropped, he checked his watch. It was exactly 11 p.m. He took his position by the "joe hole" the circular trap door on the aircraft floor, through which he would jump. It was a clear moonlit night, and when he looked down on the ground, he could see the silvery Tsangpo, the Brahmaputra River and just beyond it the shining golden canopies of Samye, the first Buddhist monastery built in Tibet (circa 775–779 CE).

Immediately after flying over the river, the green jump light started flashing. Pushing their bundles out first, Athar and Lotse jumped. They landed a couple of miles east of the monastery on a stretch of sand dunes, which is the distinctive geographical feature of this area. Their landing was soft, but it set off the dogs in the area barking, so the men quickly got their parachutes and bundles together and laid low.

The B17 circled once and continued east, but there was a solid cloud cover over Eastern Tibet, so the second team could not be dropped, and the plane had to return to Kurmitola.

Athar and Lotse had with them two RS-1 HF Transceiver sets, and one GN-58 hand-crank generator, to charge the 6-volt batteries. They also had two Tibetan codebooks, twelve maps printed on thin nylon fabric, compasses, cameras, binoculars, signalling mirrors, wrist watches, Tibetan *chuba* robes, cooking pots, 600 *dotse* in Tibetan currency, 100 Chinese silver dollars, grenades and handguns. When they jumped, they each had a British Sten gun strapped to their chests for quick use. The same basic submachine gun the British supplied the French Resistance in WWII.

They dug seven holes in the dunes. They buried one radio set, other equipment and the parachutes and things they did not need immediately. It took them a few hours to do that and it was only at dawn, around five, when they finished. They were thirsty and hungry, but they knew it was not safe to stay in this exposed area. Carrying one radio set, and their weapons they set off for the nearby mountain of Hepori, the heights of which they reached at around nine. They found a small spring and some large rocks, which provided shelter. They ate the bread they had brought with them and rested for a while.

Then they surveyed the area below them with their binoculars. They had a broad unobstructed view of Samye Monastery. In fact, it is from this mountain that most panoramic photographs we have of this famous monastery have been taken. They did not see any Chinese troops in the area but saw Tibetan traders and travellers on the road. Reassured, Athar decided to go down to the village close to the monastery and buy provisions at the small market there. Lotse was to stay back just in case anything happened to Athar, in which event he would try to make it to Lhasa by himself. Athar and Lotse both changed into Tibetan *chubas*, boots and hats. Before departing, Athar stashed a pistol and a couple of hand grenades in the capacious pouch of his *chuba* robe.

He stopped at a small inn and eatery (*netsang*) where he overheard a couple of young women, probably the maids, talking excitedly to each other. One of the girls asked, "Do you think that roaring sound last night was a *nam-dru* (sky-ship)?" Strangely enough, in 1943 an American C87 (a modified version of the B-24 bomber) flying over "The Hump" had been blown far off its intended course by a storm and had crashed at Samye, fairly close to the monastery.* The five American airmen had managed to bail out and survive. They were taken to Lhasa, where the Tibetan government provided them shelter and hospitality, which included warm sheepskin and fur robes, as it was winter. After the requisite round of mandatory banquets, the airmen were escorted out to India. One young Lhasa man remembered that some of the Americans looked very uncomfortable on their small but tough Tibetan ponies, their feet hanging fairly low to the ground.

Athar went around the market and bought meat, butter, tea leaves, wooden bowls (*phorba*), a horse and a saddle. After dark, he got back to the mountain and used his flashlight to send a pre-arranged signal to his comrade. Lotse came down with the rest of their equipment, and they loaded up the horse. After having a hearty meal and feeding the horse lumps of tsampa dough, they walked south towards the Tsangpo River. After a few hours' walk and finding a secure hiding

---

*That afternoon in 1943, just before the crash, Tseumara, the guardian deity and principal oracle of Samye, manifested spontaneously in his human medium. He charged out of his temple in full trance and shot an arrow in the sky. A report was sent to Lhasa, where it was later concluded that the oracle had somehow saved the monastery from the falling plane. Tseumara, the ruler of all Tsan demons, is an important guardian deity of Tibet. There is a popular belief that when a Tibetan dies, his life-force or consciousness (*namshé*) makes its way to Samye, to the chapel known as the "*Oo-khang*" (breath-house), where it is placed on a chopping block and severed from this existence with a large cleaver. The block and cleaver have to be replaced every year.

place on a small hill, they unpacked their radio set and attempted to send a signal back to headquarters. To their dismay, they found that the set had been damaged in the drop. "The light on the transmitter was very faint," recalled Athar, "I tapped a few words but had no way of knowing if the message was actually sent." They rested there for the night.

The next morning they joined other travellers and walked towards the river. Just south of the Tsangpo River is the town of Tsethang, the principal commercial centre for the whole region and the gateway to the Yarlung valley and the districts all the way to the Indian border. Because of its strategic location, the Chinese had already set up two garrisons around Tsethang and had started digging tunnels and underground fortifications inside the mountain, Gonpori, overlooking the town. But even on the northern bank of the river Athar and Lotse noticed an encampment of around five hundred Chinese soldiers armed with automatic weapons. Athar surreptitiously took some photographs of the soldiers.

The two men decided not to cross the river, but instead headed east towards the Wölga valley, which is a pastoral nomadic area, and less populated. Wölga also has many hot springs and caves and was a place of pilgrimage, especially the two hermitages of Chölung and Chusang, where Tsongkhapa, the founder of the Geluk school of Tibetan Buddhism, is said to have meditated. They stayed in this idyllic place for some days, where they providently came across a band of seven Khampa horsemen. To their surprise and delight, they discovered that the seven were old acquaintances, in fact, members of the group of twenty-three who had travelled from Lhasa to India on Gonpo Tashi's instructions. The seven (which included Athar's old friend, Bhulu Chodak) had, after returning to Tibet from India, decided to go on a pilgrimage of the sacred places around Samye and the Yarlung valley. After this they were planning to go to Lhasa as they had heard that Gonpo Tashi was building a golden throne for the Dalai Lama. The seven were also very curious about the sudden disappearance of Athar, Lotse and the four others at Kalimpong. They had heard rumours about them being sent to America for training and now demanded to know the full story.

Athar swore them to secrecy and gave them a general account of their experience and their mission and concluded by telling them that now was not the time for pilgrimage, and that they had to work together to fight the Chinese. The seven were thrilled with the information and agreed wholeheartedly. Together they headed back to Samye and recovered the spare RS-1 trans-receiver and the rest of their equipment and weapons buried in the sand. They then headed north. The following night at the foot of the Gökar pass, Athar and Lotse successfully sent their first signal from the spare RS-1 set, briefly outlining their activities over the past ten days. But they were unable to receive an answer. They then dispatched one man, Gowa Chodak, to Lhasa to inform Gonpo Tashi of their arrival, and request a meeting at Phembo, north of Lhasa.

When they arrived at Phembo, at the village of Dodé-phug, they found safe lodgings, and sent another radio message back to headquarters. This time the signal was much clearer, and Athar and Lotse managed to receive a message from the Americans congratulating them. They waited at Phembo for five days. Finally, two messengers came from Lhasa with instructions from Gonpo Tashi for Athar and Lotse to come quickly to Lhasa.

DROP ZONE LITHANG

On 13 November 1957, the second team of Wangdü Gyadotsang (Walt), Thundup (Dan), Tsewang Dorje (Sam) and Changra Tashi (Dick), climbed aboard the black B17 at Kurmitola and made a moonlit departure for Lithang. Tsewang Dorje had recovered sufficiently from his shooting accident to rejoin the team. When the Lithang River, the Lichu, was sighted, the men prepared to jump. But as the first jumper Changra Tashi approached the "joe hole", he hyperventilated and fell unconscious. He was quickly pulled to one side, and the other three dropped their supply bundles and jumped into the night. The plane returned to Kurmitola with the unconscious Changra Tashi.

They had planned on dropping in the Gangthang area of Mola-Tö (Upper Mola) in Lithang but had overshot their destination by about six miles and landed in a wooded mountainside. On the other side of the mountain was the village of Pongo Gyelong of about forty households. A few hundred Chinese soldiers were stationed in this village. When they heard the sound of the plane in the night, the soldiers seemed to have taken cover and not sent out any patrols to the mountains to investigate.

The three fighters landed in the forest without any problem, and a as luck would have it, immediately came across a large guerrilla band of about three hundred fighters under Lithang Akhu Tsultrim. This was Gonpo Tashi's emissary from Lhasa who had decided to stay back in Lithang and join the resistance. They had arrived the previous evening in the forest above the village and were planning a dawn attack on the Chinese garrison there. These guerrillas had heard the roar of the plane in the night but didn't expect their countrymen to drop down on them using "umbrellas" (duk). Akhu Tsultrim realized the importance of this new development and aborted his attack plan. They quickly got together all the parachutes and equipment and headed out of the area. Tsultrim sent a courier ahead with a message for the Lithang resistance leaders, especially Diu Atrin of Mewa Jelung, to meet as soon as possible.

As I mentioned before, Diu Atrin was an experienced fighter who had clashed with the Chinese army earlier, in Guomindang times. Immediately after the destruction of Lithang Monastery, he retreated from that area and headed south-east, had set up a number of encampments (makhar) in the high inhospitable region of Rakhak or Rawa, with his headquarters at a place called Kapre Tsatok. He had used this place as his secret base, years before, when he had fought against the Guomindang, and defeated them. So he considered this base to be an auspicious one.

Since Rakhak was situated on the border of Bathang and Chatreng, Diu Atrin's force also got many recruits from those areas, and also from Lingkashi, where the Chinese had completely crushed the uprising there. He sent out messengers all over Lithang, urging people not to surrender their weapons to the Chinese but to come and join the resistance. He set up a number of resistance camps throughout the area. Diu Atrin drew up a twenty-five-point set of regulations (*tsatrim*) and initiated the traditional *chopgay-drukchu* (eighteen-sixty) muster, whereby men from the age of eighteen to sixty were required to join the local militia to defend their homeland. Diu Atrin gathered about twenty thousand fighters under him.

He was against any head-on confrontation with the Chinese army and preferred a more guerrilla-style approach with surprise attacks and ambushes. Initially, the resistance was successful, and managed to wipe out many Chinese outposts and even push back the Chinese to their base at Lithang town.

All the stories I heard about Diu Atrin made it clear that he was very cunning, and always had his wits about him. One rather unusual story I heard about Atrin was from a former fighter, who, like George Orwell's famous fascist soldier taking a toilet break in the trenches at Catalonia, had his pants down when the unexpected happened. Atrin and his men were camping in a forest, some eating a meal, others resting. Atrin was sitting under a lean-to, reading a *sutra* and telling his beads. My informant was some way off from the encampment with his pants down. He heard some pattering sounds and also occasional thuds but didn't pay them any particular attention. He then noticed in the distance Atrin standing up with his rifle in his hand. Suddenly Atrin fired, and a firefight broke out. The Chinese had attempted to attack the camp. They even fired a signal flare. My informant quickly pulled up his pants and joined the fight.

They survived this ambush thanks to Atrin's great experience and well-honed instincts. He had heard soft pattering through the forest and had suspected they were footsteps of Chinese soldiers running towards them. The Chinese wore cloth shoes and sneakers with soft soles. The thuds were their bodies dropping on the ground for cover. That was how the Chinese advanced for an attack. One squad ran a given distance and then dropped for cover. Another squad behind them did the same. There was an audible rhythm to this procedure. From these sounds alone, Atrin had figured out what was happening, and had started shooting before the Chinese could effectively coordinate their final assault.

The foremost problem that the Lithang resistance faced was insufficient rifles and a dire shortage of ammunition. They had captured some Chinese weapons, and once even a major cache of ammunition, but of a different calibre to the rifles the Khampas were using. They were desperate, when news came of the return of Wangdü Gyadotsang from America.

A couple of days' ride from the drop-zone, Wangdü and his team were able to contact the key resistance leaders in the region, including the principal leader Diu Atrin, and Tayang Phuntsok Thundup and Topden, the oldest sons of the Gyadotsang family who were Wangdü's cousins. Wangdü's immediate older brother Bhugen was the leader of the Molashipa tribesmen and the trusted lieutenant of Diu Atrin. They met at Pang Tsethang, in the grasslands near Dhapa Dzara, and established a temporary base. Tsewang Dorje (Sam) transmitted a radio message to the Americans and informed them about their safe arrival at Dhapa Dzara.

The resistance leaders met for seven days. Wangdü told them about the training he had received, and informed them that the Americans had agreed to provide arms and support, and do what was necessary to help the resistance continue its struggle against the Communist Chinese. After the meeting, Wangdü and Sam sent a message to the Americans and to Gyalo Thondup in India, asking for an immediate arms drop. Both the radio sets that Wangdü and his team had bought with them were undamaged and working perfectly.

They received a reply instructing them to send information on the number of Tibetan fighters in the area, the kind of weapons they were using—make and quantity—and how much ammunition they had. They were also instructed to send the size and locations of the guerrilla forces and the names of their leaders.

Though both their radio sets were working perfectly, the messages they sent were, unfortunately, not always understood by the Americans. The team also had problems figuring out the instructions they received.

The problem lay in the fact that their best radioman, Changra Tashi (Dick), was not with them. Athar recalled that Dick was nearly as good as he was and could manage thirty-two groups a minute to Athar's forty. The substitute Tsewang Dorje (Sam) wasn't very good, though better than Dan and Wangdü. Still, the team kept on desperately trying for days but were unable to establish satisfactory communications with the base. And this was a major problem, since there was no way the Americans could arrange any arms drops or even understand what exactly the resistance needed without clear communications. To add to the bottleneck, the Americans also wanted to know the make and model of the weapons the Khampas possessed in order to provide them with similar weapons and matching ammunition. During this early period, the CIA wanted to keep American involvement ultra-secret, and dropping American made weapons and equipment in Tibet would have given the game away.

The absent radioman Changra Tashi was rushed to Kalimpong and instructed to make his way by land to Lithang. It took him a couple of months, but finally, when he reached his hometown of Bathang, bordering Lithang, he was recognized and betrayed. He was cornered at a water-mill by Chinese troops (some say bandits) and killed when he tried to shoot his way out.

In spite of attempts at secrecy, the news of Wangdü's return to Lithang with the additional news that he and his team had been trained in America and that they had parachuted into Lithang from an American aeroplane was just too irresistible for any Lithangwa to keep to himself. Soon Chinese intelligence at Dartsedo got wind of this development and was troubled by the renewed hope and boldness that the news was instilling into the people of Lithang.

They sent an open message to Wangdü in both Chinese and Tibetan. It read: "You, Gyadotsang Wangdü may have come from the sky. If you can return from where you came, there is nothing more to say. Otherwise, the only choice you have is to surrender or die. There is no other alternative. If you surrender, not only will your life be spared, but you will have a bright future ahead of you."

But the news of possible arms support from America encouraged many Lithangwas to join the resistance and very quickly the movement grew. Lhamo Tsering says that the strength of the Lithang force was around 40,000 to 50,000 fighters at this time. Wangdü became tremendously buoyed and radioed headquarters about the many new volunteers. He stressed the urgent need for arms drops, as many of these new recruits did not have their own weapons. The Americans thought that Wangdü might have made a mistake with the numbers and asked for clarification. All this took time, compounded by the fact that both Tsewang Dorje and Wangdü were not skilful radio operators.

But the Chinese now managed to bring in a couple of divisions into Lithang and commenced a broad advance towards Dhapa Dzara. Soon their advanced units were clashing with resistance outposts. The fighting intensified daily, and word got out that the Chinese wanted to capture Wangdü or any other team member—and wanted them alive.

The fighting at Dhapa Dzara raged for about twenty days and nights. Wangdü radioed several urgent appeals for arms-drops. The Resistance was now getting dangerously low on ammunition and supplies. They had to move away from this area before they were completely surrounded by the Chinese and trapped. Then Wangdü received a signal that an arms drop was now nearly ready and that they should remain close to the pre-arranged drop zone.

But the Chinese intensified their attack and, in the fight, Topden Gyadotsang, a principal resistance leader and Wangdü's cousin was killed. During another firefight the next night, Tsewang Dorje (Sam) was separated from the others and never seen again. Lhamo Tsering in his history of the Resistance thinks that he may have become lost in the mountains and ". . . died of starvation, after his food supply ran out."

Now Wangdü and the other resistance leaders gave up all hope of receiving the arms drops in time. One account notes that before the Khampas retreated from Dhapa Dzara, Wangdü and Dan buried their radio equipment. Another account mentions radio messages that Wangdü sent out later, so it is possible that he kept one radio set with him during his retreat.

The fighters moved west towards the Langdhar Pass, but Chinese troops with fresh reinforcements kept up their pursuit of the Khampas. By the time they got to the pass, most of the resistance forces managed to disperse. Wangdü and his older brother Bhugen, with about a hundred and thirty men, crossed the pass and headed west. Another band of fighters under Tayang Phuntsok Thundup followed them. For the next few months, the two bands managed to survive in the high mountains of Dokha and Ghara in north-west Lithang, and beat back a number of Chinese attacks. It is not certain, but Wangdü is said to have made one more attempt to radio the Americans for an arms drop. But nothing came of it.[7]

Wangdü felt deeply betrayed by the Americans. He was especially bitter as his return had encouraged so many of his people to join the resistance, and he had been unable to provide them the weapons he had promised. He blamed himself, and he blamed the Americans for all those Lithangwas who died in the subsequent fighting. To make matters worse Wangdü's loyal servitor and sidekick Thundup (Dan) was killed in an ambush, just the day after they decided to leave Lithang.

In April 1958, Wangdü, his brother Bhugen, Akhu Tsultrim, and other surviving fighters, about a hundred men, left Lithang for good. They headed north towards Kandzé, and passed by the famous Dargyé Gompa Monastery, then travelled west to Jyekundo, Dzachukha and finally arcing south reached Wökha Dzong in Central Tibet.

The resistance in Lithang is said to have survived till 1959. The great guerrilla leader Diu Atrin disappeared completely with a small band of his men in the mountains. Athar heard rumours that Diu Atrin was finally lured into a trap and captured by the Chinese. He was said to have been taken in chains to Chengdu, the capital of Sichuan province, and the military headquarters for Western China. But Athar didn't give much credence to this account. "He was a very intelligent and careful person. I just don't see him being taken in by any Chinese trick. No way."

21

FOUR RIVERS SIX RANGES

thar and Lotse rode into Lhasa city late at night, some distance
behind their two escorts. As a security measure, the two agents
were disguised as monks. Accommodations had been arranged for
them at the home of a monastic official on the eastern outskirts
of the city. The next day Gonpo Tashi met the agents at another
secret location. The two gave Gonpo Tashi a detailed report of their
training with the Americans. It had been a long shot for Gonpo
Tashi to send the twenty-three young Khampas to India to seek
foreign support, and he was overjoyed with Athar and Lotse's
report and with the American assurance of support for the Tibetan
resistance. He wasn't happy, though, with the proviso that came
with the message.

The agents told Gonpo Tashi that the Americans had instructed
them to contact high officials in the Tibetan government, if possible,
the Dalai Lama himself, and get official approval for American support.
Gonpo Tashi had already received such a message from Shakabpa in
Kalimpong. He told Athar and Lotse he would arrange for them to
meet the Dalai Lama's Lord Chamberlain, Phala, but it would take a
few days to set up the meeting.

He also suggested that it would be safer in the meantime for Athar
and Lotse to stay outside Lhasa as the city was teeming with Chinese

spies and informers. Gonpo Tashi made arrangements for the two agents; first at the Gangtö estate of the aristocrat Chaktra, and then further north at the hot springs of Sangyip in the Sera Valley, from where they were able to transmit a radio message back to HQ confirming their meeting with Gonpo Tashi.

Gonpo Tashi rented a secluded hut for them on the top of Mount Gembé-utsé, eight kilometers west of Lhasa, at the foot of which is Drepung Monastery. From this high isolated place the two agents could securely transmit and receive radio messages. It was close enough to Lhasa so they could conveniently visit the city when they had to, for meetings with Gonpo Tashi or for gathering intelligence. They had been instructed to study the strength and disposition of Chinese military units, the activities of different Communist Party organizations, administrative offices, and other agencies; and also conduct a survey of the roads and bridges in and around the city.

Finally, Gonpo Tashi was able to arrange a meeting for Athar and Lotse with the Dalai Lama's Chamberlain, Phala. Their liaison was the young official Seynang Lobsang Yeshi, whom Phala trusted and used when dealing with such covert matters. This official led the two men surreptitiously through a small gate at the rear of the Norbulingka garden wall, and to Phala's suite. Athar and Lotse gave Phala a detailed account of their training, and the message from the Americans. Phala was clearly pleased to see them. He told them that the Dalai Lama had been informed about them and the Americans, but he also made it clear that the Dalai Lama would not commit himself to any open expression of support for them or the venture.

Gonpo Tashi knew the impossibility of getting the Tibetan government or any of its high officials (even those opposed to the Chinese) to make a decision to request American support formally. Many officials of courage and conviction like Lukhangwa, Lobsang Tashi and Lhalu had been dismissed from office years ago. Now the long shadow of the minister Ngabö ensured a nervous state of evasion and irresolution within the Kashag.

Phala told Athar and Lotse that they should concentrate on persuading the Americans to send arms and ammunition. Athar and

Lotse's principal mission was to get the Dalai Lama and the Tibetan government to approve American support and involvement formally. They wanted a second meeting with Phala to make their case again. Gonpo Tashi told them that he would see what he could do, and that they should be patient. He had problems of his own.

In spite of the resounding success of the Golden Throne ceremony, Gonpo Tashi found it difficult to get the various Khampa groups and factions to commit themselves to form a single resistance organization. Numerous meetings had been held at the houses of trusted merchant friends, and a few other secure locations in and around Lhasa, but a clear-cut agreement had been hard to reach. The initial meetings had ended in fierce arguments, with Khampas of one tribe accusing the others of not coming to their aid when they fought the Chinese, and of just "standing by and watching the show" (*tenmo tené desong*). Khampas from the other tribes let the "accusers" have it right back. Innuendoes and counter-innuendoes of accepting Chinese silver and official titles were also freely exchanged. It is surprising that it didn't all end in blows, and that, somehow, when the next meeting was called, everyone managed to be there. The recent experience they all shared of suffering and violence under the Chinese undoubtedly helped them overcome their immediate passions, as did, almost certainly, the quiet and understated leadership of Gonpo Tashi.

A young Lithangwa[1] whose father had served in the resistance as a storekeeper, remembered hearing a story about a meeting where his father was present as one of Gonpo Tashi's attendants. "Everyone was shouting and screaming at each other far more than usual. But the Master (*jindag*) remained silent and calm and let everyone have their say till they were exhausted. When they were good and finished, he turned around to us and said '*Dha dro* (now let us go)' and got up and left. Everyone in the room was stunned. On the way back home, someone asked the Master why he hadn't stopped the quarrelling. He explained. 'Khampa men are like erect penises. There's nothing you can do or tell them when they're like that. You have to give them time to poke around and get it over with. They'll listen next time around.' Sure enough, at the next meeting everyone kept a respectful silence and let the Master explain his plans to them. But it was never easy."

In the meantime, Gonpo Tashi put together his own personal contingent of forty-six men. In his interview with Roger McCarthy, he mentions that he "armed them to the teeth" with rifles, pistols, horses and amulet boxes. He also purchased another hundred horses and mules, and in addition, began buying every weapon he could lay his hands on in the market, even a few light machine guns—British Brens. He arranged for Captain Kaldam and other soldiers of the Drapchi Regiment to start a training program for some of his men to handle, strip and clean this weapon: ". . . we (Kaldam) instructed Ratuk Ngawang, Gyadotsang Thundup and Nagung Dorge (now in the exile parliament) on handling the Bren gun. All this happened at Andrug's home in Lhasa."

Now with a personal line of communication with the Americans established and the possibility of receiving weapons becoming a reality, Gonpo Tashi took the important first step of getting together all the tribal chiefs, monastery representatives and big merchants he could, to commit themselves to take an oath, to begin the task of creating the Resistance Force.

On the evening of 18 February 1958, he got all these leaders to gather at Andrugtsang house. In order not to arouse the suspicion of Chinese spies and informers or the undue curiosity of neighbours, the Khampa leaders were instructed to arrive separately in twos and threes. Gonpo Tashi had also requested the presence of the two Drapchi regiment officers, Major Wangden Tashi and Captain Kaldam, to witness the proceedings as official representatives of the Tibetan army. He had earlier asked Captain Kaldam to draft the covenant that everyone would sign.

The initial name they chose for the organization had been "The Volunteer Army to Defend the Dharma" (*tensung dhanglang makhar*), which had been used in one form or the other by earlier resistance groups in Kham. One of Gonpo Tashi's principal deputies, Ratuk Ngawang, told me that he and "the Master" had paid a visit to the Dalai Lama's junior tutor Trijang Rinpoche, and informed him of their plans to create a Resistance Force in Central Tibet, and had requested a name for the Force. "A few days later, he sent for us and told us he had selected the name Four Rivers Six Ranges (*chushi gangdruk*). He said he had discovered it in old historical accounts, and that he had also performed a divination (*mo*) to see if the name would be auspicious." Notwithstanding it being such a marvellously descriptive and all-encompassing term for the whole of Kham and Amdo, the name *chushi-gangdruk* is four syllables, easy to remember and just rolls off the tongue. Soon the name would be echoing all over the Tibetan plateau.

The ceremony started with a serving of butter tea and the auspicious *dresil* dish (rice flavoured with butter, sugar and the sweet *droma* root). Then Gonpo Tashi gave a brief speech where he outlined the reasons for setting up the Force. He made it clear that there would be no going back, no surrender and no deal-making with the Chinese. He called on everyone to commit themselves fully to the struggle, liquidate their businesses and assets and use whatever wealth they had to fight the Chinese. He said the Chinese would take it all, anyway, if the Tibetans lost this war. He also emphasized that everyone should remain true to the Four Rivers Six Ranges and support each other like brothers. He concluded with a nomadic proverb: "In happiness eating the grass of the high pastures together/ in sorrow drinking the water of the blue lake together (*skyid la kha'i rtsa la nyam za dang/ sdug sn gon mo'i chu la mnyam 'thung*)"— meaning to remain united through good times and bad.

Gonpo Tashi then introduced the two official representatives of the Tibetan army and asked them to speak. Major Wangden praised the commitment of all those gathered there at the chapel and stressed the need for unity in their undertaking. He also declared that the Tibetan army gave its full support to the Four Rivers Six Ranges. The two officers then left.

The forty-three representatives then entered the Andrugtsang *kangyur* chapel, which housed a complete set of the Buddhist canons, besides other texts, and a life-size statue of the goddess Tara. When everyone had assembled there, the Chamdo secretary, Kunchok Dorje read out the full covenant, item by item. Following this, everyone took turns approaching the altar and, after prostrating three times and touching his head against the sacred canon, signed his name on the document. Many applied their personal seals and some even their thumbprints. Below are the names of the forty-three signatories taken from the autobiography of Ratuk Ngawang.[2] The person's area of origin or monastery, precedes the name:

Lithang Andrugtsang Gonpo Tashi, *Chatreng* Sengelong, *Chatreng* Chöphel, *Chatreng* Dawa, *Chatreng* Kalsang Chönze, *Amdo* Ngawang, *Amdo* Tselo, *Amdo* Trangmo, *Julpa* Lobsang Phuntsok (manager of Samdong Labrang), *Lithang* Gyadotsang Thundup, *Lithang* Ratuk Ngawang, *Lithang* Dewatsang Kunga Samten, *Nyarong* Yeshi, *Nyarong* Abong, *Tsawarong* Apag, *Tsawarong* Dhampa Lotoe, *Gyalthang* Thupten Gelek (manager of Karchen Labrang), *Gyalthang* Aben Tsultrim, *Kandzé* Pema Yeshi (manager of Lamdrak Labrang), *Kandzé* Tsultrim (manager of Kyapgon Labrang), *Dargyé Monastery* Jhama Ngatruk, *Dargyé Monastery* Pedor Gyau, *Tawu* Norbu, *Tawu* Khedrup, *Gonjo* Dhondup Phuntsok, *Tehor-Bhere* Sheser Wanga, *Drango* Lobsang Tashi, *Chamdo* Dortse, *Chamdo* Kunchok Dorje, *Chamdo* Tsega, *Derg*é Jhagotsang Namgyal Dorje, *Derg*é Phurba Trinlay, *Drayab* Andrug Lama, *Gyalrong* Yarphel, *Gaba* Drahu-pon Rinchen Tsering, *Gaba* Wangchen Lhagon, *Markham* Lobsang Rabgyal, *Markham* Lotse, *Minyak* Yonten Gyamtso, *Trehor* Sandutsang Tenzin Phuntsok, *Dergé-Shenyen* Tsering Ngodup, *Amdo* Hönko, *Drayab* Loten Chéso (Andrugtsang secretary).

A delegation chosen from the leadership, including Chamdo Dortse and Kalsang Chönze, was sent to the Panglung Hermitage near Sera Monastery to consult the protector deity and oracle, Gyalchen Shugden.

Gonpo Tashi had spent much time thinking about a secure and suitable place to set up the base for his new resistance army. He had travelled extensively throughout Tibet and had a good idea of the physical features, population and resources of the various nomadic areas and agricultural districts. He narrowed his selection to the Lhoka region of Southern Tibet, across the Yarlung River, due south of Lhasa, and sent small teams of men to the various districts there to conduct detailed surveys.

This region is sometimes called the cradle of Tibetan civilization. Legend has it that the first Tibetans were born there, in a cave above Tsethang, the gateway town to the region. Eight miles south of the town is Yambu-lhakar, Tibet's first castle and the palace of the first Yarlung ruler, Nyatri Tsenpo. Further south and west, you enter the "Valley of the Kings" at Chongye, where the giant tombs of the emperors still stand. Tradition has it that all the rulers from Drigum Tsenpo onwards are buried there. As the site now presents itself, there are two groups of identifiable tumuli, one group is of the major tombs of all the kings from Songtsen Gampo to Trisong Detsen and others, and just to the north another group of sixteen tombs not completely identified.

Although Tsethang town and neighbouring Nedong village were garrisoned by Chinese troops, there was no Chinese military presence throughout the rest of Lhoka. In fact, south of Tsethang, all the way to the Indian border in northern Assam, the region was free of Chinese troops. Furthermore, being in the watershed of several tributaries of the Yarlung River, the Lhoka region of twenty-five districts sustained much productive farmland and many villages and estates of freeholders, aristocrats and monasteries that could support the Resistance Force.

Gonpo Tashi narrowed his search to the locale of Driguthang or Drigu "Plain", about forty miles south of Tsethang. His secretary Loten liked the area very much and appears to have headed the team that first surveyed it. He told me he found the area pleasant and agreeable and that ". . . it was verdant grassland, meadows, with a large lake, Drigu-Tso in the centre. The western and northern side of the plain was bounded by a mountain range. At the foot of the mountain on the north-west shore of the lake was a hamlet, Chaktsa Drigu, of about a hundred households." A unit of the administrative wing of the Resistance force started its work at Drigu, organizing transport and storage of food and other supplies, especially tents and shelter for the volunteers who would gather there. It was not a moment too soon.

Back in Lhasa, on 1 April 1958, many hundreds of armed PLA troops surrounded the whole Lubuk area, west of the Jokhang. All the Chinese peddlers, street entertainers, repairmen, artisans, small businessmen and their families were rounded up at gunpoint and loaded into lines of waiting trucks. Other soldiers tore down the shacks, tents and stalls and, piling the wreckage in large heaps, set them ablaze. It was a big operation. There were at least two or three thousand Chinese civilians to round up. Many of the Chinese in the trucks, clutching their bundles, boxes and baskets, began to weep and cry as the convoy of trucks rolled past the Jokhang temple and took them all back to China—almost certainly to one or another of the many slave labour camps, in China's *Laogai* "archipelago."[3]

Tibetan bystanders noted the precision of the operation, and how it took the Chinese just three days to complete the roundup without any interruptions. They also observed how Chinese officers already had the names of every civilian on their registers, and how they methodically ticked off the name of each civilian, as they were loaded, one by one, on the trucks.

A groundswell of fear spread through the Khampa and Amdo community in Lhasa. There was no doubt who would be next. Groups of refugees began to leave the city. Everyone was aware that a number of PLA regiments guarded the traditional route to India via Nathu-la in Sikkim. So most of the refugees headed due south to the unguarded Lhoka region. The Four Rivers Six Ranges began to receive more volunteers.

On 12 April, the Chinese convened a meeting of the abbots of the three great monasteries, senior officers of the Tibetan army and police, ministers of the cabinet, and announced that they had irrefutable evidence that Khampas and Amdowas in Lhasa had plotted to create an illegal organization to oppose the PLA and the Chinese Occupation Authority. They declared that no monk or soldier must be allowed to join this organization. It was clear that the Chinese now knew about the formation of the Four Rivers Six Ranges, and would soon uncover who its leaders were, if they hadn't done so already.

On 25 May, a Chinese Muslim interpreter (*thungsi*), riding a bicycle around the Barkhor Square repeatedly shouted the announcement that all people from Kham and Amdo must apply for resident permits at the Public Security HQ in the Barkhor. Only individuals with such permits would be allowed to stay in Lhasa. Everyone else would be expelled.

Gonpo Tashi realized there was nothing more he could do in Lhasa, and that if he did not leave for Driguthang immediately, there was the real possibility of being detained by the Chinese. But just as Gonpo Tashi was preparing to leave Lhasa, something unexpected happened.

* * *

Colonel Jiang Heting was born in 1914 in Laiyang County, in the province of Shandong in north-east China. His father was a small farmer and the headman of their village. When the war with Japan started in 1937, his small secondary school received a direct hit from a Japanese bomb, and he and other teenagers were organized as an auxiliary unit to support the Communist guerrilla force fighting in the area. Soon he became a soldier in the Red Army. He trained as a radio operator and joined an artillery regiment, later training at an artillery school in Shandong Province. It was at this school that his uncle managed to contact him and tell him of his father's death.

During the Civil War, when the Communists retreated from Shandong, they had instructed the local peasants to hide their stocks of grain and not give any to the advancing Guomindang troops. But some villagers told the Guomindang about the hidden store of grain in their village, and the headman was compelled to bring it out and let them have it. When the Communists returned, Jiang's father was struggled as a Guomindang agent and beaten to death publicly.[4] Jiang Heting only learned of his father's fate three years later. But this knowledge embittered him against the Communist Party and disillusioned him about his country, for which he had fought since his youth.

At the graduation ceremony at the artillery school, the commandant spoke of how Tibet had to be liberated from American and British imperialists and the feudal aristocracy and called for volunteers. Everyone was aware of the forbidding cold and altitude of Tibet and had heard the fearsome (and racist) stories of Tibetan savagery: their custom of using Chinese skulls for drinking cups and Chinese skins for drumheads. Jiang had heard these tales and didn't put much stock in them, but he knew that Tibet bordered India. He was the only graduate to volunteer. He received high praise and was promoted from captain to major. He was then transferred to the Fifty-Second Division for the attack on Chamdo. After the invasion, his unit was transferred to the Powo Tramo district east of Lhasa. In 1954, when a PLA soldier shot a groom from the Norbulingka stables, and an anti-Chinese riot nearly broke out in the city, Jiang's regiment was quickly rushed to Lhasa and posted at the Lingka Sarpa (New Park), just east of the Lingkor circuit.

He soon got to know the groundskeeper of the park, an old man, Jampa Kalden, who supplemented his income selling home-made barley ale. The old man made it clear that he did not like the Chinese, but Jiang enjoyed chatting with him and tried to learn some Tibetan. The groundskeeper had a beautiful daughter, and Jiang would bring her *Jinhua* ham, candied fruits, Baichu spirits, and other delicacies from the camp commissariat. He also met a Tibetan military officer Major Wangden Tashi of the Drapchi Regiment, at the park-keeper's home, and they sometimes had a drink together.

In late 1956 the "Hundred Flowers" campaign was launched through out China. All PLA officers in Lhasa were ordered to express their opinions and feelings freely on issues of national importance and also on the Communist Party. Initially, everyone was reticent, but when they realized that Mao himself had called for this campaign in his famous speech, *On the Correct Handling of Contradictions Among the People,* officers began to speak out. There were complaints of injustice and unfairness. Some officers declared that the government had lied about Tibet's "Liberation"; that there were no imperialists in Tibet; that the Tibetan people were peaceful and just wanted to be left alone. They complained that the military occupation was a great economic burden on China and a great hardship on the soldiers who missed their wives and family. The meetings went on for over a month. Jiang also made some mild criticism but was careful not to overly expose himself.

Then in February of the following year, Mao declared that he had "enticed the snakes out of their caves" and launched the Anti-Rightist Movement. In Tibet, the most outspoken critics were denounced, struggled, arrested and taken to China. The authorities then worked their way down their list. Jiang was warned by an officer from his own province that he was under suspicion, and that they knew about his dalliance with the park-keeper's daughter.

He made his escape in mid-May 1958. He took two horses and two automatic rifles with him. One night when his men were engaged in a night training exercise, he made his way to the Tibetan military camp at Drapchi. He gave himself up to Major Wangden and told him he wanted to defect.[5] By this time, the Chinese officers at the artillery regiment realized Jiang had defected and gave chase. Major Wangden consulted with his superior, General Tashi Palrab, who decided to hide him at the nearby Drapchi Monastery. The Tibetan officers consulted the oracle goddess, Drapchi Lhamo, there. The oracle told them that the Chinese officer had a previous karmic relationship with Tibetans and would benefit them. General Tashi Palrab sent word to Gonpo Tashi at Lhasa about this Chinese officer who could prove useful to the Resistance. Gonpo Tashi consulted the Shugden Oracle at Panglung, who told him that the Chinese officer would be of great service to him. His deputy Ratuk Ngawang and a contingent of men were leaving for Driguthang, and he arranged for them to take the Chinese officer there.

Captain Kaldam escorted Jiang from Drapchi Monastery with a few of his soldiers in civvies providing a secret escort. He mentions that it was on the eighth day of the Saga Dawa festival (commemorating the enlightenment of the Buddha), and many Lhasa folk and pilgrims were circumambulating the outer Lingkor circuit. They mingled with these worshippers and, walking past the Bamari and Bhanjori hills, made their way to the ferry crossing at Ramagang. They were met by Ratuk Ngawang, who had a spare horse and Tibetan clothes for the Chinese officer. The last Kaldam saw of his charge was when the ferry left the shore and moved some way off. The Chinese Colonel was now wearing a Khampa fox-skin cap (*wa-sha*) and had his face covered with a woollen muffler.

* * *

Before Gonpo Tashi left Lhasa, he also arranged for the two agents Athar Norbu and Lotse, to leave for Driguthang. The two men had been unable to obtain a formal expression of support from the Dalai Lama or the Kashag. They asked Gonpo Tashi to arrange another meeting with Chamberlain Phala. But they had to be satisfied meeting Phala's representative, the official Seynang Lobsang Yeshi, who told them that the situation was now so dangerous in Lhasa, and the government so compromised, that no senior official would risk seeing them.

Gonpo Tashi left Lhasa on 1 June 1958. A day earlier, he had sent some of his men with his baggage and horses to the Tsechokling Monastery at Drip, across the Kyichu River. Gonpo Tashi himself crossed the river at the new Chinese built Kuru Bridge. He rode his motorcycle and tried to blend with the crowd of pilgrims and holidaymakers who were all heading to the Tsechokling Monastery to see its annual Tantric dance performance. Gonpo Tashi's men and horses were waiting there, and also ten of his commanders. They rode over the Drip-la Pass and rested for the night at the village of Trango. The next morning they continued over the Trango-la pass and headed south for the ferry at Dorjedra, where they crossed the Yarlung River. South of the river at Chideshöl township they were met by the Gyalthang commander, Thupten Gelek (aka Karchen Chanzö) who had with him ten of his own men and a hundred other volunteers that had gathered there.

Instead of heading directly south to Driguthang, they took a longer circuitous route around the celebrated ring lake of Yamdrok Yümtso (literally "Turquoise Lake") that is considered the "life-force lake" or (*la-tso*) of the Tibetan nation. Athar Norbu, who was riding with Gonpo Tashi, tells us that they rested their horses and pack animals for two days at the broad pasture-land of Karmoling on the eastern shore of the lake, where herds of Tibetan government ponies are customarily grazed. The villagers of Karmoling fled in terror at the sight of so many armed riders, but in the evening returned and offered the Khampas tsampa and butter. From Karmoling, they rode south to Lhodrak district, bordering Bhutan.

Andrug's secretary Loten-la told me that all groups heading to Drigu deliberately took roundabout routes to throw off Chinese attention or possible surveillance and keep the location of their base a secret for as long as possible. Loten himself set out from Lhasa in the company of seventeen riders, north across the Phembo-gola Pass to Phembo (birthplace of Tsarong Dasang Damdul) and then headed east to the Hön valley, and then finally south to Drigu. Ratuk Ngawang made his final departure from Lhasa via the Drigung Valley north-east of Lhasa.

Lhodrak district is celebrated as the home of Marpa the Translator, the spiritual master of the saint and poet Milarepa (1052–1135). To atone for the great crimes he had committed earlier in life, his master made Milarepa perform numerous back-breaking tasks, one being the construction of a nine-story temple tower (*Sekar Guthog*) that still stands to this day at Se village in Lhodrak. Gonpo Tashi and his fighters headed to the district headquarters at Dowa Dzong. There they explained to the local officials their purpose in setting up the Resistance Force and asked for local support. They received a few thousand *khels* of barley grain from the district, which included a large contribution from the Taklung (Kagyü) Monastery. Then they headed for Driguthang.

The beautiful lake and the surrounding meadows of Driguthang had been consecrated by Guru Rinpoche over a thousand years ago and were regarded as sacred. The place was also a bird sanctuary* (*jhasa*). Flocks of migrating birds from India would rest at Drigu Lake on

---

*There are a number of monasteries and sites in Tibet on migration routes across the Himalayas, where annual festivals are held and where birds are fed and protected. The government and certain religious institutions implemented a traditional system of nature conservancy through moral codes, festivals and legislation, one being the Mountain Valley Edict (*ri-lung tsatsik*) issued every year from Lhasa to districts throughout Tibet instructing the public that '. . . the fish and otter in the water, animals in the hills and forests, the birds in the

their way north to the great inland sea of Jhang Namtso, seventy miles
north of Lhasa. According to one account Drigu Lake ". . . is located
in a pristine nomadic area of internal drainage. There are hot springs
near its north-west corner; and yak pastures all around. The motion
and subtle color tones of its waters are said to portend good and bad
auspices; and like neighbouring Lake Yamdrok Yümtso, it is said to
have a talismanic connection with the wellbeing of the Tibetan nation.
Prosperity is considered directly proportionate to the rise in its water
level."[6] Another source mentions that before the invasion of Tibet ". . .
the birds disappeared, the lake's color deepened, and the surroundings
took on a haunting eeriness. According to the villagers, these omens
foretold an impending disaster."[7]

All the volunteers had been instructed to leave the local people
alone and not seek billets in their homes. Bales of canvas had been
imported from Kalimpong and hundreds of tents stitched by Lhasa
tentmakers. Now the resistance fighters were accommodated in neat
rows of canvas tents.

Gonpo Tashi, in his debriefing interview, mentions that on the
morning of 16 June 1958, at 9 o'clock, the formal founding ceremony
of the Force was held at the "Drigu Castle for the Invocation of Good
Fortune and Prosperity" (*drigu tashi thogmon dzong*). It is not clear if
this was just a grandiose name he had conferred on his new base, or the
actual name of the old district headquarters of Drigu.

The founding of the Force was celebrated with a grand parade of
the cavalry force, led by the Lithang commander, Alo Dawa, and a
review of all the fighters by Gonpo Tashi himself. There are a few black
and white photos of the event, but these are unfortunately of poor
quality. Still, the momentous historicity of the event somehow comes
through. In one photograph, we see a long line of riders parading past
a flagpole. In another, we see Gonpo Tashi in traditional chuba robe,
riding boots and a fedora, striding briskly past a formation of volunteers
standing at attention. The flag they had designed for the force had

---

air, all animals endowed with the gift of life, whether great or small should be
protected and saved'. See 'High Sanctuary', https://bit.ly/3T7mQnS

two swords, crossed, on a field of gold; one sword a traditional *padam* broadsword, the other the flaming *radri* two-edged blade of Manjushri the bodhisattva of wisdom ". . . which cuts through the chains of ignorance, apathy and fear, liberating all beings."

District officials, village elders and monastic leaders from the surrounding districts and from Drigu hamlet were invited to the ceremony. At the conclusion, a framed photograph of the Dalai Lama was solemnly carried over to a large tent and placed on a high throne. Piles of incense, juniper and sage were burnt. Everyone gathered before the photograph, offered white *khata* scarves and prostrated before it. A prayer service was conducted, after which a representative of the force made an announcement describing the bombings, violence and atrocities of the Chinese Communist invaders in eastern Tibet, and how the Chinese intended to completely wipe out the traditional Tibetan government, religion and way of life. The gathering was also informed that the volunteers of the Four Rivers Six Ranges had given up their homes, families and even their lives to fight for the survival of the Tibetan people. Hence it was necessary for all Tibetan people everywhere to support the resistance in every way they could. What the resistance needed most urgently was barley grain, meat, and butter. All such requisitioned supplies would be regarded as loans, and proper receipts would be issued for them. Repayment would be made by the Tibetan government when the Chinese were defeated.

Gonpo Tashi, in his statement, mentions that the representatives patriotically agreed to collect food grain from the monasteries, estates, and villages of the twenty-five districts of Lhoka and also agreed to call for volunteers from their communities to join the Resistance Force. These representatives were perhaps not all so uniformly enthusiastic and acquiescent as Gonpo Tashi tactfully mentions. Still, from most accounts, it does appear that the Resistance was supplied on a fairly regular basis by the people of Lhoka. Secretary Loten mentions that veiled threats were successfully used on certain aristocratic families in the area who were reputed to be Chinese sympathizers.[8] The representatives of Lhoka also requested the Four Rivers Six Ranges not to permit its fighters to rob or harm any of the people of the region and also requested to protect them from bandits and Chinese reprisals.

One of the first tasks Gonpo Tashi undertook at Lhoka was setting up a committee to draft a twenty-seven-point code of conduct and military justice. The original, penned on a single sheet of Tibetan paper, the size of a large table cloth, still exists, a bit faded and frayed, but still remarkably legible, at the Four Rivers Six Ranges Welfare organization in New York City. The Khampas mounted the document, like a *thangka*, on a sheet of backing fabric with a muslin screen in the front and a wooden roller at the bottom, around which it was rolled up and carried when they were on the move. It hung in the office tent of the administrators Jhamatsang Samphel and Jhangtsatsang Chönze at Drigu headquarters.

Enforcing discipline within the Force was vital in order not to alienate the local population. Some Khampa refugees who had left Lhasa were now operating as bandits in the region. The Chinese taking advantage of this situation launched a fear campaign to drive a wedge between the local public and the Khampas. They dressed up some of their soldiers as Khampa fighters and sent them around in small bands to rob and even kill Tibetan farmers and traders. The resistance put up posters, even in Lhasa city, warning the populace of "fake Khampas", (*kham-dzün*), and sent out patrols to search for the bandits and the Chinese posing as Khampas. A number of them were caught and punished. The captured Khampa bandits were severely whipped. The Chinese soldiers posing as bandits were executed.

Besides the military tribunal that took care of the bandits and "fake Khampas" the Four Rivers Six Ranges administration in Drigu had a finance section, a secretariat, an armoury, a liaison office (to communicate and cooperate with the populace at large) and a supply section with five quartermasters. Ratuk Ngawang in his book mentions "leaders" (*tsonzin*) who were senior figures who ran the administration and gives us some names: Jhangtsatsang Chönze Tsering Gonpo, Amdo Jinpa Gyatso, Tsawarong Dhampa Lhotoe, Chatreng Thupten, Bathang Chanzö Tashi, Dergé Jhago Namgyal Dorje, Chamdo Dorje

Tsering, Chamdo Lobsang Nyima, Lingtsang Phuntsok Gelek Rapten, Jhamatsang Samphel and others.

The force was sub-divided into units called *makhar* or commands, based on the tribe or area of origin of the fighters. Each of these commands was designated with a letter from the Tibetan alphabet. The first letter of the alphabet, "ka" was reserved for the administrative section of the force. Lots were drawn for the other commands. Bathang got the 2nd letter, Kongzeralpa 3rd, Chatreng 4th, Amdo 5th, Jul 6th, Lithang 7th, Nyarong 8th, Gyalthang 9th, Tsawarong 10th, Kandzé 11th, Shota-lhosum 12th, Dargyé Monastery 13th, Tawu 14th, Gonjo 15th, She-ser 16th, Drango 17th, Chamdo 18th, Dergé 19th, Drayab 20th, Gyalrong 21st, Gaba 22nd, Markham 23rd, and Minyak 24th. Later, two more units were formed at Lhagyari estate, Trehor-Sandu 25th, and Ganden Monastery 26th. Smaller units were created for a volunteer contingent from Gyantsé in south-central Tibet, and also for deserters from the Tibetan army who were beginning to join the Resistance in increasing numbers.

Commanders (*makchi*) were appointed for each *makhar* command, which varied from 100 to 300 fighters in strength. Ratuk Ngawang gives us a list of nineteen of these commanders: Lithang Alo Dawa, Lithang Ratuk Ngawang, Lithang Gyado Thundup, Chatreng Yangphel Tsultrum, Chatreng Kalsang Chözin, Gyalthang Karchen Chanzö, Julpa Lobsang Phuntsok, Tsawarong Apag, Markham Lotse, Drayab Atruk Lama, Gonjo Atsang, Chamdo Tsering Dorje, Tawu Khedrup, Dargön Pedor Gyau, Kandzé Pema Yeshi, Dergé Phuba Thinlay, Gaba Gelek Phuntsok, Amdo Trangmo and Gyalrong Sherap. The other units were not appointed commanders as they were in the process of getting their fighters to Drigu and did not have enough men to constitute a proper *makhar*.

Gonpo Tashi had his army. What he needed now, and needed desperately, were weapons.

22

CALCUTTA INTERLUDE

The assorted rifles, pistols, few submachine guns, and the two Bren guns that Gonpo Tashi and the Resistance had collected over the years were only enough to arm about a third of the fighters who had gathered at Driguthang. Volunteers were arriving every day, and more were expected. An additional problem was the bewildering variety of makes, models, calibres and vintage of most of these firearms, compounding the problem of ammunition supply, of which, before the first shot in this war had been fired, there already was a crippling shortage.

Athar had radioed the Americans about the urgent need for weapons, but the CIA told Gyalo Thondup and the Welfare Society in Kalimpong that they did not want to undertake any major arms drop without a full understanding of Gonpo Tashi's plans. Athar's brief radio reports had not been able to convey the size and scope of the Four Rivers and Six Ranges. So, Athar was instructed to confer with Gonpo Tashi, obtain a detailed and written strategic plan and then personally report back to India with it. Gonpo Tashi was not happy with the American demands, but he and his secretary Loten drafted a detailed account of the formation of the Four Rivers Six Ranges and the plans they had to fight the Chinese.

Athar left for Dromo, on the Sikkim border a few days after the inauguration ceremony, probably around 20 June. He was disguised as a beggar and accompanied by a young lad. The Chinese had set up several check-posts on the border and required everyone to show Chinese-issued permits. But Athar had an old friend at Dromo Rinchengang, who helped disguise him and his companion as local yak-herders grazing their animals on the high mountains, and they managed to cross over to Sikkim. On the Sikkim side of the border, Athar bribed a local policeman fifty rupees and obtained a travel document that allowed him to enter the capital, Gangtok. From there, it was a three-hour bus ride to Darjeeling.

He quickly made his way to Darjeeling and met Gyalo Thondup and his chief of operations, Lhamo Tsering. It took them a full day to go through Gonpo Tashi's report. The following day the three of them flew to Calcutta from Siliguri, where at a safe house, they were met by Frank Holober, head of the CIA's Tibet Task Force, as this project was now called. Holober spoke fluent Chinese, as did Lhamo Tsering. So with Holober posing the questions and Lhamo Tsering translating into Tibetan, a detailed debriefing of Athar was undertaken for a full week. What became clear was that Gonpo Tashi had already created his resistance army and started his war, and that Gyalo Thondup and the Tibet Welfare Society might have overstated to the CIA their influence and authority over the resistance movement inside Tibet. Holober recalled that ". . . Gyalo did a lot of nodding."[1] In another interview, Holober added: "My recollection is that Gyalo hemmed and hawed a lot. It wasn't my intention to pin him down, really. I think I already knew what the situation was, and the limitations therein."[2] Holober concluded that the Tibetan people had already started their revolution. "It was very extensive, and the numbers amassed in Lhoka were alarming."

The CIA had not been prepared to support a full-blown resistance force inside Tibet and instead wanted Tibetans to split up into many autonomous bands and carry out small-scale operations. But Athar's report on the formation of the resistance army at Drigu, eventually forced the Agency's hand. Holober concluded, "With or without the

CIA, the resistance was going to continue. So ultimately, we decided to proceed with limited material support, and to train a second group of Tibetans." These men would be coached as guerrilla instructors to help the resistance put up a more effective and sustainable fight against the PLA.

But the immediate task of getting even the "limited material support" into Tibet took far more organization and time than had been anticipated. First of all, in the interest of deniability, it had been decided at Langley that no American weapons or equipment were to be dropped, and it took a while to gather the necessary quantity and acceptable vintage of British and European weapons and ammunition. Furthermore, the CIA air team used for the first two Tibet flights had suffered fatalities during a subsequent CIA operation in Indonesia, and a new aircrew (of smoke-jumpers) had to be assembled. All this took time. Meteorological considerations also had to be taken into account, which meant that there could be no flights over the Himalayas during the hazardous monsoon season. The decision was finally made for the supply drop to be made in mid-October when a full moon and likely clear skies could be expected.

Athar was now instructed to return to Tibet along with three companions, one a trained photographer.* When they arrived at Sharsima (Yatung) in Dromo they were stopped at the Chinese check-post, and somewhat unexpectedly, ordered to unpack their loads. Chinese troops surrounded the four men. Athar immediately pulled out his pistol and shot one of the Chinese. One of his companions, Phuntsok Topden, stabbed another Chinese soldier with a dagger, but was shot and died right there.

The three remaining men got on their horses and tried to escape, but Athar's horse bolted and threw him off. He managed to drag himself behind a boulder and started shooting at the advancing Chinese soldiers, killing one and making another beat a quick retreat. But more Chinese soldiers came running towards them from the distance,

---

*Possibly Tsongkha Jhanjup Jinpa (Lhamo Tsering's nephew), who had earlier received some basic training in photography at the Das Studio in Darjeeling.

firing automatic rifles and submachine guns. Athar's companions were able to grab Athar's horse and shouted at him to run. From behind the boulder, Athar rapidly fired off a full magazine at the advancing Chinese, who all took cover. Athar then quickly got on his horse, and the three of them managed to escape. They made it up the mountain and hid out on the frozen heights till the Chinese search patrols were withdrawn a few days later. After a week of hiding and surviving in the ice and snow, the three men eventually managed to cross the border to Sikkim again and made it back to Kalimpong.

A month later, Lhamo Tsering managed to arrange travel permits for Athar and his comrades to enter Bhutan. At Thimpu, the capital of Bhutan, they fortunately met a group of Khampa merchants who were travelling to Tibet and were able to join them. From Bhutan, they crossed over into Lhodrak, and then made their way without further incident to Driguthang. But Gonpo Tashi had already left the base by then.

Gonpo Tashi was not happy with the American request to send Athar to Calcutta for a meeting before an arms drop could be made, nor the request for a written report of the resistance's organization and strategy. According to secretary Loten, Gonpo Tashi regarded all these requests as a sign of American indecision and procrastination and began to doubt America's commitment to support the resistance. Gonpo Tashi had also perhaps not been made sufficiently aware of the Agency's strong desire to maintain deniability of its Tibet operations, with the implicit codicil that the Agency would not send him American-made weapons, and that collecting weapons of non-American make would take time.

So the radio message that Gonpo Tashi received after Athar's Calcutta meeting, that an arms drop would only come after four or five months, was a major disappointment to him, though not entirely an unexpected one. Gonpo Tashi came to the conclusion that he could not wait. He did not have the leeway in time or strength to wait for the promised CIA arms drop, even if it did eventually arrive. So far, he had been lucky, but the Chinese were, by now, aware of the existence of the resistance force in Lhoka, and he could expect the PLA to start operations against them any day. Just waiting for American arms would be to court disaster.

Gonpo Tashi decided to fall back on another plan to obtain weapons. He had earlier received information that a large but secret cache of Tibetan government weapons and ammunition was stored at the monastery of Ganden Chökor, in Shang district, north of Shigatsé. Another secret government weapons cache was located further west at Shelkar Dzong, just thirty miles north-west of Mount Everest, and close to Nepal. Gonpo Tashi may have received this information from the Dalai Lama's Chamberlain, Phala, though Secretary Loten thought it probably came from Kalimpong, from the Welfare Society.

These secret weapon depots appear to have been set up in 1950, around the time the Dalai Lama and the Tibetan government left Lhasa in October 1950 for Dromo on the Sikkim frontier, following the Chinese invasion and capture of Chamdo. These weapons caches were probably intended to be used by Tibetan troops, or local militia if the invading Chinese force advanced on Dromo and attempted to cut off the Dalai Lama's escape route to India, in which case another escape route via Nepal would have to be taken and a well-armed rearguard established to slow down the Chinese advance.

23

THE LONG RIDE NORTH

Gonpo Tashi himself led the expedition to the monastery of Shang Ganden Chökor to secure weapons. Under him were twelve commanders and six hundred and seventy fighters, all on horseback. One of these commanders was Gyalthang Karchen Chanzö (aka Thupten Gelek) a senior leader and trusted comrade of Gonpo Tashi's. Secretary Loten-la was also in this force, as was commander Ratuk Ngawang, both of whom gave me their accounts of the journey. A very young Tenzin Tsultrim Jhadötsang of Chatreng rode with them and remembered it all. He was so animated when recounting the journey. It was, as if, in his mind, the events had taken place only the day before. Gonpo Tashi decided to take the Chinese Colonel Jiang Heting, now renamed Gya Lobsang Tashi, with him. Jiang's biographer generously provided me with the Colonel's personal account of the "long ride" before the publication of the biography.[1]

Jhangtsatsang Chönze, Jhamatsang Sampel and the other senior administrative leaders were entrusted with taking care of headquarters, while Lithang Alo Dawa was left to command the remaining 1,000 men at the base. The expedition left Driguthang on 12 August 1958.

To reach Shang district they rode north-west and crossed the Tsangpo (the Brahmaputra River) in the Chushül area. The river was wide and the currents swift and powerful with the summer snowmelt.

It was only with great difficulty that all the horses and men managed to cross without any major mishap. This noisy and conspicuous river crossing might have alerted the Chinese to the presence of the Resistance in the area. Some of the Khampas I interviewed blamed a Chinese sergeant (*bhaitang*) for revealing their plans. This soldier had earlier deserted from the PLA and joined the Khampas, but at Chushül had left the force and presumably rejoined his unit. But it is conjecture.

From the northern banks of the Tsangpo, the expedition now entered the valley of the tributary, Nyemo Machu River, in the watershed formed by the snow mountains of Kumalungpa Gangri and Jho-mo Gangtse, which could be seen to the north of the Nyemo valley (a description of the idyllic Nyemo countryside by Tenzin Tsultrim Jhadötsang is in Chapter 14). About twenty miles further north, the Dzochu River joins the Nyemo-Machu River at Dokar Sumdo (White Rock confluence), where the river is spanned by a bridge. In present day maps, the place is called Dardrong.

Gonpo Tashi sent an advance unit of one hundred and fifty riders to scout the area ahead. Chatreng Yamphel Tsultrim commanded this unit. They crossed the bridge and rode ahead through low-lying fields but soon came across two local women, who warned them that there were Chinese troops ahead digging trenches and preparing defensive positions. The unit stopped for a council of war. The commander Yamphel Tsultrim said they should not advance directly but move higher along the mountainside and get a better view of the ground ahead. All the men agreed to the plan except one fighter Zinang Akhar of Zachukha (who had been a monk of Dargyé Monastery in Trehor). Zinang, well known as a fierce warrior, declared, "We all made a decision to fight the Chinese. Now when we learn there are Chinese waiting for us, how can we talk of avoiding them? We must fight them." A heated argument took place. Finally, Yamphel Tsultrim, who was short-tempered, got on his horse and rode ahead, followed by Zinang Akhar and others. Another version says that Zinang galloped ahead, followed by Tsultrim and the other men. The Chinese had prepared their positions in the barley fields and the high grass and were well concealed. When the Khampas got to this place and realized how ideal it was for an ambush, they slowed down. They spread out, and even sent a few men on foot to scout the area ahead. After riding past some sheep pens and animal shelters, one teenage fighter from Lithang, Sholu, spotted a field telephone line. He pulled out a knife and cut it. Precisely at that moment, the Chinese opened up with everything they had. They even had mortars and light machine guns. What probably saved the Khampas was their instinctive reaction to the ambush, which was not to freeze or seek cover, but to charge at the Chinese positions from where the fire was coming. The Khampas fought fiercely, constantly moving and charging the Chinese positions, keeping the Chinese off-balance. Some of the Chinese defenders even panicked and fired on their own positions. The Khampas lost fifteen men in the initial encounter, including their leader Yamphel Tsultrim. But once they located the Chinese positions, they managed to return effective fire against the Chinese soldiers, killing many of them.

Another unit commanded by Ratuk Ngawang (accompanied by the Chinese Colonel) was following the advance guard when they too came under fire. The Khampas fought back effectively. The Colonel, Gya Lobsang Tashi, made a name for himself that day when he took out the Chinese officer commanding that ambush.

Gonpo Tashi and his unit were on the other side of the river. When he realized that the Chinese had set up a number of ambush points, he quickly divided his force into small platoons, dispersed them around the surrounding hillsides and ordered them to attack the Chinese positions from the flank and rear.

The battle started from around ten in the morning and went on till evening. Under cover of darkness, the Khampas managed to pull back. Gonpo Tashi mentions that they lost forty men. Three leaders, the Chatreng commander, Yamphel Tsultrim, the Gonjo commander Takhang Tsempel, the Gaba commander Gelek Phuntsok and three captains (gyapöns) were killed. It was later learned that about two hundred Chinese had been killed. But it was an expensive encounter for the Khampas.

Gonpo Tashi ordered a withdrawal, and they rode out by another route to Tsang across the Marjang-la pass (Shogu-la according to

Ratuk Ngawang), where they skirmished with another detachment of Chinese, but managed to get through without any casualties. Earlier, during the withdrawal in the night, everyone was exhausted. One of Ratuk Ngawang's immediate retinue, a young man Nalo, fell asleep and fell off his horse. He was captured by the Chinese.

They travelled by Tsang Tanak, and finally, the advance unit led by Ratuk Ngawang entered the Shang valley, whose main river, the Shang-chu drains into the Tsangpo River to its south. The monastery of Ganden Chökorling (aka Namling Chöde), the biggest monastery in the district, was located on the mountainside above the village of Namling. The river to the east of the village was spanned by an old chain-link iron suspension bridge, one of many believed to have been built by the great engineer, artist, physician, explorer and mystic, Thangtong Gyalpo.* The seventeenth century castle and district headquarters of Namling Dzong is located on a nearby hill. Ratuk Ngawang and his men rode up to the gates of the Dzong and asked to meet the governor.

They met with two senior officials of the district and the monastery and explained to them about the Four Rivers Six Ranges, and its mission to fight Chinese oppression. Ratuk Ngawang also told them about the Golden Throne they had presented the Dalai Lama, which made the officials friendlier to them. They were served tea, tsampa, meat and butter and told that they would have to stay in the village till they had confirmed their stories.

That night, the rest of the Force rode into the village and forced their way into the District Headquarters. Their entry was dramatic, with bugles playing and flags fluttering. This contingent also had some soldiers from the old Tibetan army and two officers, Gyapön Tenpa and Meja Jhapo, both from the Drapchi Regiment. It was hoped that these ex-army officers would provide sufficient official legitimacy to persuade the local functionaries to surrender their secret weapon supply. But the Dzong and monastery officials were initially unwilling to admit they

---

*Wolf Kahlen, a Berlin art professor and consultant to the Royal Government of Bhutan on art and architecture, has dubbed Thangtong Gyalpo "the Leonardo Da Vinci of Tibet" for his amazing artistic and technological achievements.

even had a cache of weapons, much less give it up. Gonpo Tashi talked patiently to the officials and explained the mission of the Four Rivers Six Ranges to save the government and people of Tibet and to protect the Dharma. Eventually, through persuasion and implied threats, the walled-up door of the secret storeroom in the monastery was broken open and the weapons removed.[2]

There were 385 Enfield rifles. These were brand new in factory casing, with bayonets and with over 10,000 rounds of ammunition. There were also ten Bren light machine guns, with 13,300 rounds, eighteen Sten submachine guns, four 51 mm (2 in) medium mortars with 288 shells and two 154 mm (6 in) mortars with 108 shells. Everything was nicely boxed and in pristine condition. All the men were tremendously pleased with the haul. It took about a hundred pack mules, that the Resistance "borrowed" from the nearby estates of two officials of Tashi Lhunpo Monastery, to carry the whole stockpile of arms and ammunition.

The Chinese Colonel took charge of the six mortars. He was assisted by Amdo Kalsang Gya, who had been a gunner in the army of the Xining warlord Ma Pufang. They immediately set about providing rudimentary training to some of the fighters and organized a test firing, for which the whole village turned out. The target was a patch of rocks across the river. The first shell was a dud, but the next two shells landed on the rocks and exploded with satisfyingly loud explosions. Everyone was enormously pleased and excited.

Gonpo Tashi knew the Chinese would be alerted to their presence and that the PLA had a large military base at Shigatsé just forty miles south-west of Namling. He decided to send some of the weapons and ammunition back to Driguthang, as the main force there had been stripped of the best weapons to arm Gonpo Tashi's expedition to Shang. A strong escort was provided to the mule train, and Gonpo Tashi himself instructed them on a circuitous but safe route back to Driguthang.

Then Gonpo Tashi and his commanders discussed their next move. Someone suggested riding to Shelkar Dzong (White Crystal Castle), close to the Mount Everest area, and grabbing the stash of Tibetan government weapons they had been told was stored there. But that would have meant travelling over a hundred miles further south-west, cutting through the Shigatsé area where the PLA was in force.* They decided on returning to their base at Driguthang, but they did not have much choice in the matter of safe routes.

According to Loten, the leaders then went to the temple of the goddess Palden Lhamo (Sanskrit, *Sridevi*) at the monastery and requested the priest there to perform a dough-ball (*singri*) divination. They wrote the names of the few routes they had discussed on slips of paper that they rolled into small balls of dough. Accompanied by invocations to the goddesses, the priest slowly rolled the balls on the inside surface of a large silver bowl, till finally, one of the balls fell out. Opening the dough-ball they read the name—Nyemo.

Initially, things went well. One advance unit crossing the motor road from Shigatsé at Uyug Zomthang, managed to ambush a convoy of three trucks. One truck had a propaganda team of eight or ten Chinese with a movie projector, and some armed soldiers. The other two trucks had horses. They killed everyone, burnt the trucks and took the horses. Another unit advancing further south at Bhakchang destroyed another convoy of six trucks. Five were Chinese supply trucks, but one was from the Dhunkar Monastery of Dromo Geshé Rinpoche. The men felt bad about this as the child incarnation of this famous lama had given many of the Khampa fighters his special amulet pills that were universally regarded as infallible talismans.†

---

*The Chinese occupation force had conducted the young incarnation of the Panchen Lama from Amdo and installed him in 1952 at his monastery of Tashi Lhunpo in Shigatsé district. The Chinese played skilfully on the old rift between the Dalai Lama's government and the Panchen Lama's administration. They even designated the Panchen Lama's estates in Shigatsé and the Tsang region under the Tashi Lhunpo "local government"—separate from Lhasa.

†This boy lama was imprisoned by the Chinese in March 1959. His disciples in Sikkim and the Darjeeling area appealed to the Indian government. Since he was born in Sikkim, hence an Indian national, Prime Minister Nehru personally intervened on his behalf. Geshé Rinpoché was released in 1961.

Gonpo Tashi recalls sixteen trucks being destroyed in all. After those ambushes, trucks owned by Tibetans began to fly colourful prayer flags on the front and sides, to distinguish them from Chinese trucks. Following the successful ambushes, the main force came upon the mule train and escort that Gonpo Tashi had earlier sent back to Drigu base with a part of the weapons cache. The escort commander reported that they had encountered some Chinese units on the way and had been unable to advance any further.

The Resistance Force finally arrived at Nyemo, west of the Nyemochu River, where the first ambush by the Chinese had taken place. The local people there told the Khampas that they had been ordered to collect the bodies of Chinese soldiers from the battlefield, and had lost count after a hundred. Scouts were sent ahead. They reported back that the Chinese were in force on the eastern side of the river, by the bridge. The Chinese garrison at Nyemo had been reinforced with fresh troops from Shigatsé, Lhasa and Yangpachen in the north.

One contingent of Khampas immediately engaged the Chinese by the bridge at Dokar Sumdo, while the main force rode north into the valley, and crossed upstream at an unguarded ferry-point. As they rode towards the village of Nyemo Thil, they encountered a strong Chinese defensive position. Gonpo Tashi decided ". . . our best course of action was to hack our way through the Chinese." He led the charge. The Khampas galloped full speed ahead, screaming their *kisha* battle-cry[*] "*ke he-hee*", and stormed the Chinese positions. "The Chinese were unable to resist the onslaught . . ." and began to fall back on the village. But the Khampas, their confidence raised with new weapons, now attacked the Chinese fiercely, pushing them out of the houses and animal pens, till finally, the Chinese troops retreated into two large buildings at the foot of the monastery (Nyemo Shöl) where they had set up their headquarters and their radio communications—and which was heavily fortified.

---

[*]The Khampa *kisha* resembles the American Indian war cry and the Confederate rebel yell.

Gya Lobsang Tashi, the Chinese Colonel, now took charge of the fighting at this place and impressed everyone with his coolness and courage. He had a captured Chinese light machine gun and used it very effectively against the Chinese defenders. He also strongly advised Gonpo Tashi not to lead the charges against Chinese positions but to stay in the rear and direct the fighting. He told Andrug that he was too important to lose. Secretary Loten remembers the Colonel telling Gonpo Tashi, "Even if you kill a few hundred Chinese by yourself, it doesn't matter, but if you get killed, then it will all be over."

The Chinese resisted fiercely, but the Khampas managed to set fire to the buildings. Many Chinese were killed in the fire and were also shot when they ran out of the burning houses. Gonpo Tashi mentions remorsefully that some local Tibetans were also killed in the fire. Twelve Khampas were killed and twenty wounded. A few hundred Chinese were killed. The Khampas also managed to capture many rifles, some machine guns, grenades and ammunition. But the main Chinese weapons store caught fire, and large explosions lit up the night.

My source Tenzin Tsultrim was in a separate unit of a hundred men sent south-east to hold the vital crossing at Chushül on the main Yarlung Tsangpo River. But the Chinese had prepared an ambush there. "It was lucky that we got there after dark, otherwise we might not have escaped. The Chinese fired illumination flares, which lit up the sky and then their machine guns opened up. Miraculously, only two of our fighters were killed. One rider in front of me got hit. I could hear the bullets whistling around me but we could not see any Chinese in that dark, and could not return fire. We managed to retreat safely and rejoined the main force at Nyemo."

The next afternoon, Gonpo Tashi rode up a hilltop and saw through his field glasses that Chinese reinforcement was arriving at Nyemo. Another source mentioned that reinforcements were being sent from Shigatsé in the south-west and from Lhasa in the east. After a brief council with his commanders, Gonpo Tashi decided to retreat north to the nomad grassland of Jhang Yangpachen. The Khampas retreated in good order, sending out an advance guard and also a screen of riders as rear-guard to ensure that the advancing Chinese did not catch up. They all crossed the Nyemo-la, or pass, and came to Nyemo Junpa close to the Kargang, a local administrative office of the Tibetan government.

Gonpo Tashi decided to rest here as the men were all exhausted after the fighting in lower Nyemo. But scouts now reported strong Chinese troop presence around the area. The Khampas rode on. A couple of mortar shells landed near them, but no one was injured.

Gonpo Tashi made the decision that the main force would continue to ride north to Yangpachen and avoid engaging the Chinese. He rode towards Kargang, taking with him a hundred of the men who were not too spent. They encountered a Chinese force defending the place and quickly attacked, flanking it on two sides. A three-hour battle took place with many Chinese soldiers dead at the end of it. On the Khampa side, they lost a commander, Lithang Zimgak, a giant of a man, who had been a monk bodyguard of the Dalai Lama. Two men were wounded. They captured many weapons and ammunition. Then they rode north and rejoined the main force at Yangpachen, where everyone took a well-deserved but short rest.

The upland valley of Yangpachen, just south of the Nyenchentangla range, is lush and green, with clear streams meandering through the meadows and many hot springs bubbling in the lower mountainsides. The area is generally regarded, in song and stories all over Tibet, as a nomad idyll. The valley and the hillsides are dotted with hundreds of grazing sheep and yaks, and the occasional black tents of nomads. An old Karma Kagyü monastery founded by the first Shamar Rinpoche nestles in the foothills on the north-western side of the valley. The men purchased yaks and sheep from the nomads, exchanging them for the extra rifles and ammunition they had captured from the Chinese, which the nomads prized. The fighters were allowed only half a day's rest, but they got all the mutton and yak meat they could eat.

A scouting contingent had been sent ahead, led by commander Pedor of Dargyé Monastery and Gaba Jinpa. They met some nomad families further north who told them that a huge Chinese force had dug trenches, built barricades and made other preparations for an attack further up the valley. Another scouting team rode in to report that a long convoy of Chinese trucks full of soldiers were moving on the new Tibet-Qinghai highway and headed north towards this area.

Gonpo Tashi and his commanders were not expecting this concentration of Chinese troops in the area, which scouts had earlier not reported. According to the biographer of the Chinese Colonel, the Chinese Military Area Headquarters in Lhasa were convinced that the Khampas were planning an attack on the new Chinese airfield at Damshung, just 45 miles (73 km) north-east of Yangpachen and had radioed for reinforcements.

Gonpo Tashi decided to attack the Chinese forward position with his entire force, as quickly as he could, and gain the element of surprise. He claims that the fury and weight of the attack, and ". . . our unearthly battle cries, created utter confusion among the Chinese ranks." The Chinese fell back in disorder and returned fire erratically. The PLA defence position did not seem like a strong one, but the Chinese Colonel advised Gonpo Tashi not to advance further as this unit could just be a bait and that a stronger force could be waiting at the rear. He suggested that they instead attack the advancing convoy.

Soon a part of the force rode back quickly towards the Tibet-Qinghai highway where it traversed the Yangpachen valley. Tenzin Tsultrim remembers that they had sufficient time to prepare an effective ambush. He recalled the line of headlights advancing in the darkness and Gonpo Tashi opening fire on the lead truck with a Bren gun. They managed to destroy most of the trucks though a few managed to escape back to Shigatsé, where they had come from. Seven senior PLA officers were killed. The convoy also had a medical unit with medical officers and nurses, all of whom were caught in the ambush and killed. Tenzin Tsultrim remembers the Chinese Colonel studying the captured documents and telling Gonpo Tashi that one of the officers from Shigatsé was a colonel. So far, this was the most senior PLA officer they had killed. Loten-la said to me that Lobsang Tashi showed no regret at killing Chinese soldiers, and, in fact, seemed quite elated. A few boxes of apples, probably imported from Sikkim, were discovered in one of the trucks. Lobsang Tashi happily munched on one as he went about inspecting the documents, weapons and bodies recovered from the trucks. Finally, the Khampas burnt the twenty odd trucks and everything they could not carry away.

They rode away from the highway, and headed north-west, crossing the Nyenchentangla range toward Jhang Namtso, the Great Sky Lake. This second largest lake on the Tibetan plateau is home to countless birds, resident as well as migratory, which fly there from India in the spring and summer and lay their eggs on the shores of the lake. The wildlife in this area was once exceptionally varied and abundant but has been greatly depleted due to hunting and commercial fishing by the Chinese. This entire area is said to be under the protection of one of Tibet's oldest mountain deities, Nyenchentangla, ruler of the "Trans-Himalayas", as Sven Hedin has described this range. The goddess of the lake, Namtso Chugmo, was considered the mountain deity's consort. There were many caves and hermitages around the lake where meditators undertook their spiritual practices in peace and solitude.

The largest monastery in the area, at the north shore of the lake, was the Jha-do Gompa, or "Bird Confluence Monastery", which was shut down by the Chinese in late 1959 after its monks rose against the Chinese. Fourteen monks were summarily executed. An American archeologist and explorer, who visited the area fifty years later wrote ". . . a band of Khampas who were veterans of ongoing battles with Chinese troops . . . sought refuge at Jha-do Monastery.'[3] It is likely that the Resistance Force or a contingent of it circled the Namtso Lake and came to Jha-do Gompa on the north shore. "The monastery was razed to the ground during the Cultural Revolution." Efforts to rebuild it have been blocked by Chinese officialdom till the present day.

This monastery is possibly the site where an annual festival to welcome and feed migrating birds took place. Charles Bell writes: "It is believed that every year the birds hold their parliament at a large lake north of Lhasa, where justice is administered by their king, the cuckoo. The saying runs that law and justice will prevail among men and women for so long as there is law and justice among birds . . . so he (the Dalai Lama) sends a yearly deputation to this parliament of birds. A lama addresses them on the importance of law and order, and at the same time gives them a present of food."[4]

The Force managed to get a few days rest and put their weapons, gear, horses and mules in order. They also managed to buy some yak and sheep from the nomads around the lake. They had left Commander Phurba Thinlay of Dergé and five trusted men behind at Yangpachen to spy on the movement of the Chinese forces concentrating there. Now, this scouting team caught up with the main force and reported that a large Chinese force of about a thousand men was headed towards Namtso and that more Chinese troops were closing in from other directions. The scouts had also seen a few Chinese aircraft, almost certainly searching for the Khampas.

The Force now moved north-east but spread out in companies of about a hundred men, riding five to ten miles apart but keeping in touch through scouts and couriers. One company skirting Damshung attacked a large supply depot, close to the airfield, killing many Chinese soldiers there. They took all the rice and food there and burnt everything else, including the buildings. Another company attacked a convoy of trucks headed towards Lhasa. They were now moving north-east towards Nagchukha, the leading nomad trade and administrative centre.

Tenzin Tsultrim says they were following the motor road, when at the Kyokche-La pass, they encountered a Chinese survey team and its military escort in three trucks. The Khampas killed all of them and burned the trucks. But PLA troop presence became more discernable the closer they got to Nagchukha, so the decision was made to swing south to the district of Drigung and the famous Drigung Thil Monastery (overlooking the Shorong valley), the seat of the Drigung Kagyü order. When they arrived at Drigung Khago Sumdo, the Khampas sent out foraging teams as they were running low on food. Gonpo Tashi states somewhat bitterly that a steward of the Drigung Monastery sold them a bagful of tsampa for the exorbitant rate of forty-nine *do-tsey*.

But suddenly, far more serious problems than overpriced tsampa came up. One company on the left flank was attacked by a large PLA contingent and forced to withdraw north. On receiving news of this, the rest of the resistance force swung north-east towards the interior of Drigung Phug and managed to attack the PLA contingent successfully. On proceeding further they clashed with a number of other Chinese detachments in the next few days. But these units were not large enough to surround and trap the Khampas, who managed to stay together, and fight the Chinese off. With strong PLA forces in the north and reportedly in the south too, the Khampas now had to make the difficult decision of where to proceed next.

Ratuk Ngawang claims that the Force finally consulted the oracle. Ratuk himself was not happy with this decision as the oracle's earlier prophecies had been vague to the point of being useless. He did not trust the oracle. Secretary Loten had no reservations about accusing this medium of being a fake. Loten-la mentioned that the old man constantly demanded special privileges, a servant or a better horse, and was simply a nuisance. Finally, after much trembling, moaning and panting, the old medium directed the force north-east towards Jhang Mamshung.

After a couple of days, they arrived at the broad pastoral valley of Mamshung. Scouts were sent out ahead. Tenzin Tsultrim mentions that their scouts had spotted some Chinese patrols on the heights, on either side of the valley, but nothing large enough to worry them. He was feeling elated as the new Chatreng commander, Dawa,* had ordered him to take charge of their unit Bren gun, and the mule which carried its ammunition. Dawa had been appointed the commander of the Chatreng *makhar*, after the tragic death of commander Yamphel Tsultrim at Nyemo Dokar-sumdo. After they had ridden about a couple of miles into the valley, a shower of mortar shells began to fall around them, and the ground beneath the riders began to explode.

Tenzin Tsultrim was some distance behind Gonpo Tashi, who was riding with a group of about twenty men along a slightly higher ground on the side of the valley—by a cluster of large boulders. Some of the falling mortar shells exploded on the rocks, killing a number of the riders and wounding nearly everyone else. Tenzin Tsultrim was shocked by the power of the explosions. "It was amazing. A couple of

---

* I met Dawa at Mustang in 1971. He was a big (six foot five or thereabouts) genial person, and he welcomed me to his camp (No. 2) with a meal of tsampa, butter tea and boiled yak meat.

the mules were literally picked up and thrown in the air. People were torn to pieces."

But he also saw why he and others riding lower in the valley were less vulnerable. "What saved most of us that day, I think, was that the ground of the valley was a bit soft, covered with *naga-podo,* which is the layers of sod and grass growing over each other like a carpet. The mortar shells needed hard ground to explode, so some shells just sank into the sod. But quite a few exploded, killing several pack animals and horses and scattering the rest. But I couldn't see the Chinese who were firing the mortars."

Ratuk Ngawang was overwhelmed by the effect of the exploding mortar shells.

The Chinese probably had a couple of hundred mortar positions on either side of the valley, up on the heights. We could not see any of the Chinese and could not fire on them. I saw Gonpo Tashi being hit, and saw a plume of dust rising from that place where he was riding. I immediately rode in that direction and dismounted by the dust plume. Commander Rakra came out of the dust, wounded and bloody. He said "The Master is wounded. We must fight here and die." I told him to look after his own wounds and that I would check on the Master and make sure he was all right.

A number of the men riding with Gonpo Tashi had been hit by shell fragments and were wounded. Few were dead. Even those not badly injured were all bloody. The Master was wounded but managed to sit up. He seemed to have been hit in a number of places. There was a lot of blood on his face. I took off his balaclava cap and used it to wipe off the blood. He was injured on the side of his head. I turned to his retainer, Tamdin Wangyal, and told him to get some water. There was a small stream running in the valley close by. Tamdin was a good man. He immediately ran towards the stream shouting *"Drakchen Dorje Shugden khen!"* again and again, imploring the deity to protect them.

There was no point returning fire. You couldn't see any Chinese at all, and mortar shells were whistling down everywhere. Tamdin came back holding his felt hat half-full of water. The Master gulped it all down. I asked him if he could ride out of this place. He said he could and that it was no problem. I took off the woollen scarf I was wearing and tied it around his head to staunch the bleeding. Then I held him by his elbow and tried to help him up, but he said a bit testily, "Don't hold me. I don't need anybody's help." He was a tough old rogue.

I looked around for the Master's horse. His white stallion was a couple of hundred feet away and apparently not hurt. As I hurried towards it I came across this old Markhampa whose arms were nearly torn off his body. He was dying. He pushed his Enfield rifle over to me and said "Take the gun. I am no use to anyone now." I took the rifle and grabbing the reins of the white horse, headed back to Gonpo Tashi.

I helped the Master climb on his horse. All of us then moved quickly by the side of the valley. A little way ahead, there was a small rift in the hillside that did not seem too exposed. We stopped there. Five or six of the commanders and some of their men gathered around the Master to protect him.

But the mortar shells were still raining down across most of the valley. About a hundred of our men had been killed along with many horses and pack animals. It was all mortar fire. Most of the other fighters had done the sensible thing and galloped straight through the explosions and up the valley. I noticed they had managed to get to the head of the valley up a rise, a pass of sorts, and crossed it without being stopped. I told the Master of this, and he replied that we could not afford to lose this escape route. He added that the Chinese would have seen this gap in their encirclement and would try to close it as soon as they could, and we would then be trapped here. He told me to ride quickly with some men to that pass and hold it.

With the Master, there were six of our commanders Kalsang Chönze, Gyalthang Karchen Chanzö, Baba Thundup, Gyen Namgyal, Kandzé Pema Yeshi, Chamdowa Tsering Topgyal and some other fighters, so I knew he would be safe. I told them what I was going to do and told them to protect the Master and bring him up the valley when there was a break in the mortar fire.

I yelled for some of the men to follow me, but everyone was now fighting his own battle or trying to make his own way out. But Lithang Bhu Tsempel came behind me, as did Kyarutsang Chönze. Both of them had good horses. My own horse served me well that day. I galloped ahead of the others, through the falling mortar shells and explosions, and finally reached the top of the pass.

As soon as I got there, I dismounted, cocked my submachine gun, and ran forward. I could see Chinese soldiers coming up on the other side of the pass. I started shooting down at them. Tsempel came to my side and began firing his rifle also. There were nearly a hundred Chinese soldiers, but we were on higher ground and had some rock cover. The Chinese were on an exposed slope and scrabbling uphill. We quickly killed a number of them. The rest retreated towards a patch of rocks below on the right. I knew that if they found cover they would probably try to circle us. I quickly rammed a fresh magazine in my Sten gun and charged down the hillside, shooting and screaming my *kisha* battle cry, "*Ke He Hee!*" Bhu Tsempel followed screaming and firing. We didn't give the Chinese any opportunity to regroup but forced them to retreat.

I, then, looked around me and noticed that many of our fighters had managed to cross the pass and reached the other side without any problems. I thought I recognized some of the men, one being Jhama Ngatruk's brother, but I couldn't be sure. I saw quite a few riders in the distance and hoped that the Master and the others had managed to make it out. We were far to the right, shooting and pushing back the Chinese troops who would otherwise have followed our escaping fighters, none of whom saw Tsempel and me. I later found out that they thought we had both been killed. Kyarutsang Chönze and another fighter who had followed me were shot and fell off their horses. But the Chinese now managed to regroup and were slipping past us towards the main trail below the pass. There was no way for Tsempel and me to stop them or follow the Master and the other fighters. Both of us were without any horses. So we circled the area on foot in the opposite direction from where the

Chinese soldiers were advancing and eventually came down to the Mamshung valley where the mortar fire had stopped.

In the fighting and chaos that day, many of the fighters, besides Ratuk Ngawang and Tsempel, got separated from the main force. The Chinese Colonel, along with two fighters, a Lithangwa and a Chatrengwa, became separated from the main force and ended up taking cover in a patch of rocks far from away from the others.

Despite the exploding shells and the destruction, young Tenzin Tsultrim managed to round up some stray horses and mules and led them over to the side of the valley where Gonpo Tashi was sheltering. "I remember seeing a wounded Rakra with the Master who was also wounded. The valley was filled with dead and wounded animals and our scattered supplies. After Gonpo Tashi got on his horse we tied some branches to his body and to the saddle to make sure he didn't fall off. When we all rode out of the valley, the explosions had let up a bit. No Chinese soldiers followed us and we managed to get away."

Gonpo Tashi tells us shell fragments hit him at twelve places on his body, ". . . but that by the grace of the Three Precious Jewels" his life was not in immediate danger. He and the others now began to ride up the pass. One of the fighters, Sonam Gyatso, made Gonpo Tashi change his horse with him in case the Chinese recognized Gonpo Tashi's distinctive white stallion. They got safely across the pass and moved east, riding the whole night. A few companies of Chinese soldiers followed them at one point in the night and used parachute flares to try and locate the Khampas. The Chinese also fired their rifles and machine guns in their direction. But no one was hit.

Gonpo Tashi and his contingent rode for two days and nights, meeting up with other scattered fighters. They rode together again till they got to the tri-junction area of Kongtse la, where they set up camp, rested and cared for the wounded. According to secretary Loten, they used captured Chinese medical kits to treat Gonpo Tashi and others who were injured. They also made Gonpo Tashi drink melted *dri* butter as a tonic to make up for the blood he had lost. Loten was amazed and impressed at how tough the old man was. "He didn't show any pain, but just carried on as usual. He even laughed when someone who had been shot on one side of his butt and riding on the edge of his saddle, slipped off his horse." Tenzin Tsultrim mentions a red pill, a folk medicine called *gyaltsen chonga*, normally used to treat sores on horses and mules. They now applied it to the injured fighters, and it worked surprisingly well. He claims that in about ten days, everyone, including the horses and mules, were reasonably well again.

But the next day, Chinese advance units were sighted, and there were a number of skirmishes with the patrols and perimeter guards the Khampas had established. The resistance was running low on ammunition, and a couple of Khampa patrols were captured when they ran out of bullets. Gonpo Tashi realized he could not outrun the Chinese and prepared an ambush, but the Chinese got wind of that and tried to outflank the Khampas. There was a back and forth for a day or two, both sides trying to gain an advantage over the other, the Khampas slowly retreating north all the while.

After a few days, the resistance outran the Chinese and reached high pastureland called Jhapo-Jhakay at the confluence of two rivers, the Jhapo (male bird) and the Jhakay (bird call). They camped there and sent a foraging team of fifty men to find food around the Atsar-Tso or lake, to the east, where nomads and their herds were reportedly grazing. The main force moved up the valley of the Jhakay River and camped there for two days.

Scouts soon reported a large force of Chinese approaching the area, so immediately a detachment led by Gyalthang Karchen Chanzö, Chatreng Kalsang Chözin and Amdo Trangmo, rode out and attacked the Chinese. They managed to wipe out the Chinese advance guard, but other Chinese units got through. As the fighting progressed, the Khampas began to suffer from a shortage of ammunition. But another outlying Khampa force provided support, and they all managed to escape from that area.

Gonpo Tashi had hoped to ride east toward the Lharigo settlement in Lhari district, but scouts reported that a PLA force of over a thousand men was based at that settlement and was preparing to defend it. So the Khampas moved north-east to Jhang Mithika. They captured a Chinese scout and, taking his rifle and pistol, killed him.

They kept moving north. They were riding in the interior of the Jhangthang, where the elevation is around 16,000 feet and extremely windy and cold. Gonpo Tashi mentions the snow being knee-deep at places. They pushed on slowly till they reached Mithika, where they encountered some herdsmen of the Chungyu Woma grassland. They managed to obtain ample supplies from them in exchange for "two rifles, 300 bullets, two mules and 160 *do-tsey* in currency. We promised to repay them fully when a free Tibetan government was reestablished. We left behind a written bond that I signed."

One of the commanders, Ahzin, who had earlier been captured by the Chinese had somehow managed to escape from his captors, and now rejoined the force. He could speak some Chinese and had heard PLA officers sending out radio messages calling for reinforcements from such outlying administrative areas as Chamdo and Nagchukha. He heard them repeatedly saying that the Khampas had to be completely wiped out. That even if one or two Khampas were allowed to roam freely, they would cause tremendous harm. All Khampas had to be exterminated."

Around this time eighty of the men with three leaders decided to break away from the force and go their own way. Gonpo Tashi remarked, ". . . sadly for them, life was more precious than the cause and the goal." Immediately after this desertion, the warrior Zinang Akhar, whose rash provocation had caused the unnecessary loss of many fighters at Nyemo, along with Repa Bhulchung and forty other men, also deserted. They rode east toward Sho-ta-lho-sum and became bandits.[5]

After Mithika, the Chinese gave up their pursuit of the Khampas. It was a most fortunate reprieve as all that was now left of the Resistance Force were fifty men. Tenzin Tsultrim claims that this was the lowest point in his experience. To make matters worse ". . . the oracle came in a trance, a spontaneous manifestation (*thonbê*). Taso Chönze appealed to the deity to show us the way. I laughed out loud." But over the days, many of the fighters who had been scattered or left behind now began to gather at Mithika. Finally, we had about one hundred and fifty men. On 27 October 1958, what remained of the force rode into the settlement of Bhenkar, on the old northern caravan route (Gya-Lam) from Lhasa to Kham.

* * *

Coincidentally, 27 October was the date when the first CIA arms drop was made at Driguthang. Athar was still on his way back to Tibet, but Lotse was at Drigu Headquarters and received the radio message. In nearly all accounts, there is some confusion about this date. Lhamo Tsering gives us 15 July, which is clearly wrong as Gonpo Tashi was still in Driguthang in July and would have mentioned the arms drop in his debriefing report. Perhaps Lhamo Tsering meant the fifteenth (a full moon) of the seventh Tibetan month and not the seventh Gregorian month. So post-monsoon October is the likely month with the full moon date of 27th (or perhaps a day before or after) being the likely day. Lhamo Tsering gives the time of the drop as 2200 hours.

Athar's partner Lotse had received the radio message and immediately passed it onto Jhamatsang Sampel, the administrator at Drigu headquarters. Lotse was instructed to take charge of the preparations for the drop. The first thing he did was select a level stretch of grassland west of the lake. He radioed the coordinates back to the Americans. Because of the lack of trees or firewood in the area, Lotse's men collected dried yak dung and piled it at the centre of the drop zone and covered it with a sheet of tarpaulin. On the night of the drop, just before sunset, Lotse marked out the ground of the zone with a large cross, and had the men cover the cross evenly with yak dung fuel. Then he and his contingent of fighters waited.

According to Conboy and Morrison, the CIA had decided to use a larger plane, the C-118 (the military version of the Douglas DC-6), which had more cargo capability, and also had an oversized rear door which allowed for a much larger bundle than could be squeezed through the "joe hole" of a B-17 (used in the two earlier drops). The floor of the cargo space in the C-118 had also been retrofitted with a set of rollers to speed up the operation. "But because the rear door had not been designed to open inward during flight, it had to be taken off and left behind. The plane, as a result, would be flying unpressurized for the duration of the mission. Not only did this mean an uncomfortably cold cockpit and cabin, but the crew would need to use oxygen masks to keep from passing out in the thin air over the Tibetan plateau. Worse still, the C-118's four engines had barely enough power to clear the Himalayas; if one engine shut down en route, they had little hope of getting back home."[6]

In spite of these and other difficulties such as World War II-era maps that showed big blank sections north of the Himalayas, and the navigator nearly passing out because of a kink in the tube of his oxygen bottle, the plane eventually made it to the drop zone on time.

One of the resistance fighters waiting on the ground, Lagyen Hora, who I met in Mustang in 1971, told me that he could somehow not bring himself to believe that a "sky-ship" (*namdru*) would fly all the way from America and drop weapons on them. He became even more sceptical and annoyed when Lotse ordered them around and instructed them to stay out of the direct area of the drops, or they might be hit by falling cargo.

Lagyen Hora waited quietly in the dark, telling his beads, when eventually he heard a faint droning sound coming from the south. He felt a prickling sensation, and the hair on the nape of his neck began to rise. When the sound got louder, Lotse gave orders for two men to pour bottles of kerosene on the dry yak dung cross. He tossed a lighted twist of grass on the cross, and as the flames rose in the night sky, the men all cheered. The noise of the plane now became deafening, and soon the first parachute or "umbrella" (*nyi-dug*) was spotted swaying down from the sky. Nine parachutes were dropped on the ground. As the plane roared away, the men quickly ran towards the drop zone and began collecting the cargo. They opened up the nine large loads and divided the boxes and packages so that they could be carried by the forty horses and mules that Lotse had waiting.

Lhamo Tsering gives us a detailed list of what the Tibetans received in this first arms drop: 100 British Lee Metford (.303) rifles,

100 British Lee Enfield (.303) rifles, twenty submachine guns, sixty hand grenades, sixty packets of C4 explosives, tens boxes of primer cord and 90 detonators, thirty medical kits, two Rolex watches, three large binoculars, spare parts and accessories for the radio sets and 1,00,000 Indian rupees. 20,000 rounds of ammo were also dropped for the Czech Brno rifle (*pamaling*) and Russian Moisin-Nagant (*bura*) rifles that many fighters were using. Lhamo Tsering mentions that a sniper rifle with scope was also dropped, but this is not certain.

As excited as everyone was with the novelty of the arms drop, the size of the consignment, just 200 rifles, was a big letdown. Headquarters immediately had Lotse send a message to the Americans, asking for more weapons. The reply he received was that it would take four months before they could arrange another arms drop.

The second drop took place on 22 February and was pretty much the same except for more ammunition. This time two mortars with fifteen boxes of shells were also dropped along with fifteen pistols, four crimping pliers for the detonators and 2,00,000 Indian rupees.

* * *

A wounded and exhausted Gonpo Tashi and his small force of about a hundred and fifty fighters, rode into Bhenkar on 27 October 1958. But his reputation and that of the Resistance Force had preceded them and Gonpo Tashi tells us, "We were given a very warm welcome both by the monastery and by the local people." They got all the tsampa, butter and yak meat they needed, and also hay and firewood. The abbot of the monastery was a doctor of divinity, Geshé Rinpoche, who was a good man, as Tenzin Tsultrim remembered. The monastery, a Gelugpa one, was a subsidiary monastery (*gon-lhag*) of the great monastery at Chamdo and called Pekar Gon Namgyal Ling (White Lotus Monastery realm of the Sky Victor). They rested at Bhenkar for four days and then rode east to Dramthang. On the way, they heard stories about Khampa bandits who were robbing the local people. On questioning the victims, they realized that the bandits were Zinang Akhar, Repa Bhulchung and their men.[7]

From Bhenkar, they were travelling within the marches of Eastern Tibet. They learned that at Chamdo, the Shiwalha Rinpoche and the abbot of Chamdo Monastery had been thrown in Chinese prison, and that people all over the region were suffering tremendously under Chinese rule. The force began to receive new recruits. Many of the old fighters who had been scattered now caught up with them. According to Tenzin Tsultrim, the force was then reorganized. Four new military commanders were appointed: Chatreng Dawa, Lithang Gyado Thundup, Dergé Phurba Thinlay and Chamdo Tsering Dorje. At Sarteng, the fighters took possession of a large Chinese granary with over 10,000 *khel* of barley, so they were well set for the near future. Gonpo Tashi also received a message from headquarters in Driguthang about the first American arms drop, and one from the Markham resistance leader, Phupa Pön.

They also heard more stories of their own men who had turned bandits and were preying on the people of Sho-ta-lho-sum, who could not defend themselves as the Chinese had earlier taken away their weapons. The locals eagerly provided information on the activities and movement of these bandits. Gonpo Tashi sent out a large force that quickly captured all of them. A court-martial was held. Zinang Akhar, Repa Bhulchung and their men were charged with ". . . bringing disgrace and shame to the Resistance Force." The two leaders were found guilty and shot. Their men were all given fifty lashes of the whip and their weapons and horses taken away.[8] All their loot and possessions were gathered and distributed to the locals whom they had robbed.

On 6 December 1958, the Four Rivers Six Ranges rode into Chakra Pembar. There was a small Chinese garrison holding the Tar Dzong castle, but the Chinese troops quickly retreated to Chamdo before the Force arrived. There were no large Chinese forces in the Sho-ta-lho-sum area, which consisted of the three districts of Shopado, Tar Dzong and Lho Dzong. Tar Dzong was the district headquarters of Chakra Pembar, and the Tibetan government officer in charge was Dundul Chöying. Tenzin Tsultrim remembered that the official hosted Gonpo Tashi at his own home near the monastery.

"The Master knew him from before and were friends. He was the principal official in the district and much respected by everyone. He was known as Pembar Drunyik, or the secretary of Pembar. He was a tall imposing man." They had a weeklong meeting with leaders of Khampas from Sho-ta-lho-sum and other places as Rongbo Rabten Gön, Khyungpo Tengchen in the north-east, whose chieftain Karu Pön came to Tar Dzong, and further east from Riwoché and Dergé, to try and work out a plan of action. The main concentration of Chinese troops was in the new settlement of Powo Tramo, south of Pembar. It was vital that this settlement be captured or destroyed because PLA troops there could move north to Sho-ta-lho-sum or east to Lhasa and Lhoka, with little to no problem.

Gonpo Tashi prepared a force of two hundred fighters supported by another two hundred local volunteers. He also sent a messenger to Lhoka and instructed the headquarters there to send five hundred horsemen immediately to Powo Tramo and attack it on 25 December. His officers and men insisted that Gonpo Tashi stay behind at Chakra Pembar and recuperate. Though he had gradually recovered, he still had about twelve pieces of shrapnel inside him, and his men were worried how long he could keep up his strength. But from most accounts, Gonpo Tashi appears to have led this operation.

On the given day Gonpo Tashi's men attacked Powo Tramo. The Khampas burnt down hundreds of Chinese houses and killed many soldiers and settlers there. But the hoped for contingent from Drigu headquarters could not make it in time, and Chinese reinforcements poured in from Lhasa, Chamdo and Kongpo. Gonpo Tashi mentions that the Chinese newspaper published from Chamdo reported that over five hundred PLA soldiers were killed at Powo Tramo. The Khampas had to retreat but did so carefully, only suffering a few casualties. They also destroyed many trucks and set ablaze Chinese settlements and road worker camps on the way.

On 29 December 1958, several scouting teams were sent out to enroll volunteers and also scout the areas of Nagshoe Tsogu, Wakho Maring, Shabyé Zampa (the principal bridge on the upper Salween River) and Lho Dzong.

On 24 January, Gonpo Tashi's main force also attacked Khyungpo Tengchen in the north-east, supported by fighters from that area led by their chief Karu Pön. Gonpo Tashi did not take part in this operation, but Tenzin Tsultrim was there. According to him, they managed to surprise the Chinese soldiers defending the district headquarters, Tengchen Dzong, and quickly captured the headquarters. Some of the Chinese soldiers fled to the nearby Chinese fort, which was held by a larger force. But many thousands of local volunteers now joined the fighters at Tengchen. They surrounded the Chinese fortress and laid siege to it. The water supply was cut, and the Khampas came close to destroying the entire garrison, but on 23 February, Chinese planes came and bombed and machine-gunned the fighters. Twenty-one Khampas were killed and many wounded. But they had managed to kill many Chinese at Tengchen, and so they withdrew. According to Tenzin Tsultrim, this same force had attacked the Chinese garrison at Rongbo Rabten Gön and wiped them out.

On 22 January, Gonpo Tashi rode out from Pembar to Tsawa Pakshö, with one hundred and fifty men to obtain weapons. Gonpo Tashi knew that the Tibetan district magistrate of Pakshö had managed to hold on to his stock of arms. He also knew the man well. He was a family friend from Lhasa. When he got to Pakshö he appealed to the official to let him have the store of weapons and ammunition, and allow Gonpo Tashi to recruit local volunteers. The official let Gonpo Tashi have a hundred rifles and most of his ammunition. He kept six rifles to defend the local people against bandits. He also let them have food-grain and meat, and also 200 loads of "Chinese supplies": rice, candles, soap, medicine and also a small printing (cyclostyling?) equipment. However, he did not allow Gonpo Tashi to recruit volunteers.

Gonpo Tashi then proceeded to Lho Dzong, a major administrative centre of the Tibetan government in Kham, which, in 1950 the Tibetan army had prepared as its strategic fallback base and headquarters. Gonpo Tashi and his men reached Lho Dzong on the Tibetan New Year's (Earth Hog) Day, which they observed with much celebration, not only slaughtering ten yaks, but having earlier had their men prepare New Year cookies (*khabsay*) and barley ale (*chang*). At the old and extensive monastery, Hok Shidram Gön, they set up a throne at the *Lama Phodrang* literally "Lama Palace" on the eastern wing of the monastic complex that Gonpo Tashi explains was where the Fifth Dalai Lama had once stayed. Setting up a portrait of the Fourteenth Dalai Lama on the throne, the fighters had a ceremonial parade, followed by horse racing, archery competition, singing and circle dancing (*dhro*).

Now people from all over Eastern Tibet began to gather at the Sho-ta-lho-sum area. Secretary Dundul Chöying went through the militia roster (*mak-dhep*) of the districts in Sho-ta-lho-sum and used that to call up fighting men and as many volunteers as possible to create a new resistance army. Tenzin Tsultrim said that tens of thousands of men gathered in the area.

Commanders and junior officers were appointed. A flag of the Four Rivers Six Ranges was presented to this new army and white *khata* scarves to the newly appointed commanders. But there were not enough weapons to equip the new army. Unlike the period before the uprising of 1956, the Chinese had effectively disarmed most of the Khampas in Eastern Tibet. Gonpo Tashi mentions, somewhat resignedly, that the leaders of the different contingents were each presented with whatever rifles the Four Rivers Six Ranges could spare. Pön Phuntsok Wangyal of Rongpo Gyalrub received "four rifles and 300 bullets", Pön Ngodup Dorje "5 rifles and 250 bullets", and Pön Ahde "eight rifles and 400 bullets", while Karu Pön of Tingchen who was leading 4,000 men got "10 rifles and 1,000 bullets."

But Gonpo Tashi promised these Khampa leaders that more weapons and ammunition would arrive soon. He had received a written report from Driguthang HQ that the Americans had made two successful arms drops and that more drops had been promised. Lhamo Tsering reproduces part of the reply sent by Gonpo Tashi to Drigu HQ.

I am very happy to hear the news about receiving arms support through airdrops after your radio contact with superiors. Right now is the best time to establish a new military organization in the Sho-ta-lho-sum area. If anyone of you could come here, it will immensely help the organizing work here.

But Drigu headquarters replied that they could not spare fighters as the Chinese had reinforced their garrison at the crossroad town of Tsethang, and fighting had escalated throughout the Lhoka region. Also mentioned was the disagreement within the leadership at Driguthang about the distribution of the weapons that had been air dropped. An urgent appeal was made for the immediate return of Gonpo Tashi to headquarters.

Gonpo Tashi realized he had to get back to his headquarters and his radio operators as soon as possible to effectively arm this potential new army he had created in Western Kham.

After the last meeting on 21 February 1959, Gonpo Tashi and remnants of his old force left Chakra Pembar. He also had 200 men from Sho-ta-lho-sum and another 150 volunteers from Tengchen and 100 other volunteers from other areas—about 700 men in all, according to secretary Loten. They rode from Chakra Pembar to Lhari in the west and then south-west to Kongpo Gyamda, being careful to avoid any clashes with Chinese forces. After crossing the Wölga River, the force finally arrived at Tsethang, where a large contingent of the Resistance was now engaged in a desperate struggle with two Chinese garrisons they had under siege at Tsethang and Nedong.

* * *

What had Gonpo Tashi's long ride achieved? A historian friend of mine argued that the initial goal of recovering the weapons from the Ganden Chökor Monastery was really not worth the enormous effort and casualties that the Resistance Force suffered throughout this long ordeal. Instead, if they had waited at Driguthang for the CIA arms drops it would have served them better. One writer on the CIA and Tibet says that despite "a string of tactical wins"[9] against Chinese forces, Gonpo Tashi's overall tactics did not work because he was deploying his fighters by the hundreds, nearly all of them on horseback. And instead of frontal charges, they should have resorted to small hit-and-run guerrilla-style attacks.

All these criticisms are legitimate, but it might be pointed out Gonpo Tashi was desperate for arms, and the CIA's support was far from a sure thing. In fact, the demand that Athar (of the first radio team) return to India for debriefing before any arms drops could be considered, made Gonpo Tashi realize (quite correctly) that the Americans were procrastinating and not fully committed then to helping the Resistance.

Tactically Gonpo Tashi and his men did make mistakes in their advance north, but it might be pointed out that Gonpo Tashi and his fighters were all merchants, ex-monks and common folk, not experienced military experts. But they did manage to learn on the job, and through sheer ferocity and reckless courage, overpowered larger Chinese forces and inflicted many more casualties on the enemy than they suffered themselves.

But what is important to note is that the string of attacks, encounters and many victories they achieved, resounded all over Tibet, Lhasa in particular, where it certainly contributed to the atmosphere of defiance and rebellion that brought about the March Uprising the following year. Gonpo Tashi's long ride was also instrumental in creating a second uprising in Eastern Tibet, and in many nomadic areas in northern Tibet that I will enlarge on in Chapter 29.

I have called this epic journey Gonpo Tashi's "Long Ride North" although it was strictly speaking more of a looping arc north-east with many detours here and there. "When I rode north with the Master (*jindak nyenpo jhang la drothoe*)" is a phrase used with pride by fighters who accompanied him. The north, in this case, being a reference to the Jhangthang* or the Great Northern Highlands that Gonpo Tashi traversed, in his incredible and epic odyssey, across "one of the most

---

*This high-altitude plateau (average elevation 16,500 feet) of giant lakes, vast stretches of grassland and frozen desert stretches 1,400 miles from Ladakh in the west across northern Tibet to Amdo in the east. The Jhangthang makes up two-thirds of the landmass of the Tibetan plateau, covering an area almost as large as Spain and France combined.

forbidding terrain known to man." Variations on the last phrase have been used in the memoirs of such European explorers as Sven Hedin, Nikolai Przhevalsky, Prince Henri of Orléans, Gabriel Bonvalot and escaped POWs Peter Aufschnaiter and Heinrich Harrer, who travelled across different parts of this region.

I think the term "epic" is not inappropriate to describe the seven-month ride on horseback for 3,100 miles (5,000 km)—about the distance from Paris to Baghdad, as the crow flies. This is, of course, not counting the many detours, backtracking, and so forth that would easily add many hundred miles more to the total distance. Gonpo Tashi, a fifty-four-year-old, which by Tibetan reckoning made him an old man, covered about half the distance with over a dozen pieces of shrapnel inside his body. A cartographer friend of mine (who also made the maps for this book) calculated the above distance of the "Long Ride"* starting from resistance headquarter at Driguthang and ending at the refugee camp at Missamari, in northern India, when the fighters surrendered their weapons to Indian authorities on 29 April 1959, and Gonpo Tashi presented the District Commissioner with a white *khata* scarf and "a horse complete with a fine Tibetan saddle."

Gonpo Tashi's legendary ride is about twice the distance covered in the great march of 431 BCE by the Athenian general, Xenophon, and his 10,000 men. In his book, *Anabasis*, (literally "Going Up"), Xenophon, a pupil and friend of Socrates, tells us how, stranded deep in hostile Persia, he led his men from the interior of Babylon across barren deserts and snow-covered mountains to the coast of the Black Sea and safety. The American historian and philosopher, Will Durant has described it as "one of the great adventures in human history."

---

*Mao's biographer Edgar Snow wrote that the Red Army's famous "Long March" of 1934–35 was 25,000 li or about 8,000 miles. In 2003, two British researchers, Ed Jocelyn and Andrew McEwen, retraced the route. In their 2006 book *The Long March: The True Story Behind the Legendary Journey That Made Mao's China* estimated that the march actually covered only about 6,000 km (3,700 miles). The book concludes that the Long March was exaggerated and mythologized to demonstrate that Mao "had single-handedly saved the Red Army and defeated Chiang Kai-shek."

24

PRIMORDIAL PLAYGROUND

By the middle of October, the administrative leaders at Drigu Headquarters were beginning to realize that the Drigu base, though idyllic in summer, was much too cold the rest of the year because of its elevation (15,000 ft). It would be difficult for everyone to hold out the winter in thin cotton tents. Volunteers with accompanying families were billeted in low-lying villages and towns throughout the Lhoka region where food was plentiful. Now the entire force had to be moved, with the exception of about a hundred of the youngest men who would remain at Driguthang.

The new headquarters selected was in the district of É-Yul, at the estate of Lhagyari, one of two aristocratic families (the other being Ragashar) whose heirs were recognized as being descendants from an unbroken male line of the Tibetan emperors going back to Songtsen Gampo. Owing to their historical ancestry, the head of the family receives both civil and religious honors on state occasions including the installation of the Dalai Lamas. Peasants of the estate always greeted the head of the family with the obeisance accorded only to high religious dignitaries and lamas.

The oldest male son of this family receives the title of Trichen, or "great throne" (holder), and is not obliged to enter government service, as sons of aristocratic families are required to do. The throne holder at the time, Lhagyari Namgyal Gyatso was patriotic and civic-minded and had entered government service as a regular official. When approached by the Resistance administrator, Jhangtsatsang Chönze, he agreed to supply them with food grain and allowed them to use his estate.[1] The new headquarters of the Four Rivers Six Ranges was established in a spacious outlying building of the Lhagyari palace complex. About 370 fighters were garrisoned here.

There is a panoramic colour photograph of the great Lhagyari palace, built on a hill like the Potala, with a column of Resistance fighters riding below it, most probably taken by Jhanjup Jinpa in late 1958 or early 1959. After the Lhasa Uprising, Lhagyari Namgyal Gyatso was arrested and publicly "struggled", and made to serve over twenty years at a Laogai slave labour camp. The old palace of the Lhagyari "Throne Holders" was razed to the ground.

The estate of the aristocrat (and former commander-in-chief of the Tibetan army) Khemey at Yartö district in the Lhoka valley district, forty kilometres south-west of É-Yul, was also requisitioned by the Resistance. Tsewang Thundup, the brother-in-law of Khemey, may have allowed the Khampas to use the Khemey estate as a base. There is a reference to him being ". . . involved in the resistance."[2]

A company of fighters was posted further south in the Chongye valley, the ancient capital of the Tibetan kings, until Songtsen Gampo moved it to Lhasa. Within the Chongye valley are the giant burial mounds of the early Tibetan rulers. A hundred fighters were billeted at the large Gelugpa monastery of Riwo Dechen in Chongye, founded in the fifteenth century. Incidentally, just above the monastery is Chingwa Taktse castle, the stronghold of the early kings who preceded Songtsen Gampo.

The force was dispersed not only for the convenience of getting the men sheltered and supplied locally, but with a broader strategic goal in mind. Garrisons had been established beyond the Lhoka region at such important points as Dranang by the shore of the Tsangpo River on the main trade route from Lhasa to Tsethang. A garrison of over 200 fighters was established at Nakartsé on the western shore of the "ring lake" of Yamdrok so that it could patrol the vital Ghampa-la pass separating Ü (Central Tibet) and Tsang (South-Central Tibet). But other strategically vital areas, such as the crossroad town of Tsethang, could not be adequately garrisoned due to internal dissension within the force, following the departure of Gonpo Tashi.

After the first CIA weapons drop, there had been some wrangling among the leadership of the different contingents about the distribution of the weapons. A detachment of around five hundred fighters under Jhago Namgyal Dorje of Dergé had managed to obtain some of the weapons, and without the approval of Headquarters had decided to establish their own base at Dhakpo, east of Lhoka. The district is low-lying, temperate, and renowned for walnuts and peaches. The people of the district sent petitions to É-Yul Headquarters complaining about having to feed and house this contingent. Headquarters dispatched orders to Namgyal Dorje to return to Lhoka with his men, but received evasive answers.

* * *

It was around this time that the resistance commander Ratuk Ngawang, returned to Lhoka. I last mentioned him being with Gonpo Tashi at the deadly Chinese ambush at Mamshung, where Gonpo Tashi was wounded and many others killed. Ratuk Ngawang and another fighter Bhu Tsempel had ridden through the mortar fire, towards a distant ridge to secure an escape route for Gonpo Tashi and other survivors. Ratuk and Tsempel managed to reach the ridge just before Chinese soldiers climbing up from the other side could get to it. The two managed to fight back the Chinese advance but were separated from the main force.

In his autobiography, Ratuk writes that he and his comrade Tsempel, eventually managed to circle the ridge and get back to the valley where the main attack had taken place.[3] They eventually found a horse and a mule that was slightly wounded. Using reins cut from lengths of rope, they rode in the direction where they last saw the main force heading. At nightfall, they clashed with a contingent of Chinese soldiers who used flares to light up the night sky. Ratuk's horse was shot from under him, and he fell to the ground. Fortunately, he rolled close to a dead Chinese soldier clutching a *chikhang* light machine gun (Russian DP-28 with circular pan magazine). He grabbed the weapon and fired it in the direction of the Chinese gunfire. Tsempel joined him with his pistol. After a while, the flares died down, and the Chinese stopped firing altogether.

They remained hidden behind a rocky outcrop. Early next morning, Ratuk used his binoculars to check out the mountains and did not see any Chinese troops. They drank some water from a nearby stream and started walking out of the valley. They spotted a Chinese aeroplane circling in the distance but managed to move away from it. A couple of days later, they came across a small nomad encampment. They had nothing to eat for the past three days and were very hungry. The nomads gave them tsampa, butter and milk. Ratuk and Tsempel gradually recovered from their ordeal.

Another fighter, Kongtserepa Chaknam, rode into the nomad camp. The three of them decided to ride south to one of the most important monasteries of the Drigung Kagyü School. The nomads could only lend them one horse to ride for part of their journey. Taking turns riding, the three of them eventually arrived at the Drigung Yangri-gar Monastery, in a beautiful valley surrounded by many barley fields. There they had the unexpected privilege of meeting and receiving the blessings of the twelve-year-old Drigung Kyamgon Rinpoche* (the grandson of Tsarong Dasang Damdul). At the request of Ratuk Ngawang the young lama performed a dice divination, and the monastery conducted a prayer service to help Gonpo Tashi and his men survive their dangerous ordeal. The three fighters then decided to travel through the extensive Phempo valley system, directly north of Lhasa. On arriving at the district headquarters of Lhundup Dzong, they came across some Khampa travellers, who, on hearing their story, volunteered to join the Four Rivers Six Ranges. Ratuk Ngawang now decided to head for Lhasa.

---

* In Drigung Rinpoche's biography (*From the Heart of Tibet*, 2010) by Elmar R. Gruber, three resistance scouts are mentioned as coming to the monastery and the child lama spotting them through his field glasses.

That evening, they crossed the Phempo Gola pass and rode south the whole night, arriving at Sera Monastery around first light. From friends and relatives at the monastery, they managed to obtain monk's robes. Thus disguised, they finally arrived at Lhasa, and rode to the Kyalutsang (Tsempel's) home, near the Ramoche temple in North Lhasa. One of their first tasks was to offer butter lamps at the Jokhang and have the monks conduct services for the safety and wellbeing of Gonpo Tashi and his men. They also freed over one hundred sheep and goats and carried out other instructions given to them by Drigung Rinpoche. Ratuk also visited the oracle of the deity Dorje Shugden at the Panglung retreat near Sera and sought his aid.

Ratuk and Tsempel also went to the cantonment of the Drapchi Regiment, where Ratuk met his old army friends Major Wangden and Captain Kaldam, who were overjoyed to see him. Kaldam told me that he also went to see Ratuk at the Kyalutsang house and mentioned that Ratuk was slightly wounded in one hand. Captain Kaldam gave Ratuk a Sten gun and ammunition for the Enfield he also carried. Ratuk told them about everything that had happened to the Resistance after its founding at Driguthang, and obtained Captain Kaldam's help in sending a message to headquarters at Lhoka.

Someone then came up with the idea of writing down a full account of the battles and victories of the Four Rivers Six Ranges and using it to inform the Tibetan public of these important and gratifying events. Captain Kaldam, who, a year earlier, had drafted the covenant signed by the Khampa leaders at the Andrugtsang chapel, was entrusted with this task.

Ratuk Ngawang then secretly met the Drapchi general, Tashi Palrab and also the Lord Chamberlain, Phala. After recounting his adventures and the accomplishments of the Resistance, he requested Phala to obtain Tibetan government weapons for the Force.

Captain Kaldam put together a detailed account of the Resistance's exploits, highlighting its victories and its dramatic destruction of Chinese military convoys and PLA troops. As many copies as possible were drafted and stuck in conspicuous places in the Outer Lingkor Circuit, the Inner Barkhor Circuit, (including the side of the famous

Kani Goshi "four-entrance" stupa) and also the circuit around the Ramoche temple. One copy was pasted directly across the entrance of the Jokhang, on the walled enclosure housing the sacred willow tree. Copies were also sent to the monasteries of Sera, Drepung and Ganden. One copy was stuck on a wall in the Shöl hamlet below the Potala, and another even pasted on the Great Edict Pillar (Doring Chima) in front of the Potala Palace. The inscription on this pillar describes a major Tibetan military victory and the capture of the Tang Imperial capital of Changan in 763 CE.

Captain Kaldam mentions that he and some Drapchi soldiers made copies of the posters, and Lhasa policemen were given the task of pasting them across the city. These posters created a tremendous stir in Lhasa and beyond. The Chinese police and security attempted to tear down the posters but not before they were seen and read by many people, some of whom even copied down as much of the information as possible, and further spread the message. The dramatic account of the fierce battles and daring raids of the Four Rivers Six Ranges, told and retold in peasant homes and nomad tents all over Tibet, stirred people's imagination and patriotic sensibilities.

Ratuk Ngawang recruited twenty-two volunteers in Lhasa, and then rode out with them back to Phembo. He recruited more men there, putting together, in total, a company of sixty-two fighters. On the eighth day of the eleventh Tibetan month (18 December) they rode south to Gongkar Dzong, on their way to Lhoka. Gongkar is on the motor road from Lhasa to Tsethang, and there, Ratuk Ngawang and his volunteers, ambushed a convoy of Chinese trucks and captured enough weapons to arm the entire company fully.

From Gongkar, Ratuk's contingent left for Chongye Riwo Dechen and finally arrived at the new resistance headquarters at É-Yul Lhagyari, on the fifteenth day of the eleventh month (25 December 1958). He was welcomed by the administrative commander Jhangtsatsang Chönze who immediately dispatched couriers to all commanders to assemble at É-Yul. The meeting took place on 29 December in the great hall (tsomchen) of the Lhagyari Palace. Besides Ratuk and Jhangtsatsang Chönze, the other leaders who attended the meeting were Amdo Jinpa Gyatso, Tsawarong Dhampa Lodoe, Jhamatsang Samphel, Baba Gyen Yeshi, Sandutsang Lo Nyendrag and others. Jhago Namgyal Dorje had been sent a message but remained in Dhakpo. Since Gonpo Tashi's departure, other new commanders had been appointed, and they also attended the meeting. An incarnate lama of the Shartse College of Ganden Monastery, Nyakri Khentrul Rinpoche, had joined the resistance with a large band of volunteer monks. Some other new commanders were Tsang Pesur Jhola, Minyak Abo Yoten and Amdo Lekshey.

Ratuk gave the assembled commanders a full report of all that had happened to the Force after it left Driguthang the last summer, including the deadly mortar attack at Mamshung. He recounted his own escape with Tsempel, and his activities in Phembo and Lhasa, recruiting new volunteers and publicizing the deeds of the Force.

He also discussed his meeting with the general and officers of the Drapchi Regiment in Lhasa and the intelligence he had received from them about a major offensive the Chinese Military Headquarters was organizing against the Resistance. To that end, the Chinese were planning to reinforce the garrison at Tsethang as the first step to creating a large force to control the entire Lhoka region. Over a few hundred trucks of PLA soldiers, arms and supplies were being prepared at Lhasa for this operation.

* * *

Tsethang was the largest and most important town in the Lhoka region. Situated at the mouth of the Yalsa Shambo-chu tributary flowing to the Brahmaputra, it was the gateway to the Yarlung Valley and the south, all the way to the Indian border. The British "pundit" or spy, Kishen Singh (alias A.K.) reported in 1870, "Tsethang is an ancient *entrepot* and a flourishing town with over 1,000 houses, a prosperous market and monasteries and a fort." Samye, Tibet's first monastery, was only twenty miles from Tsethang.

Tsethang means "playground" and according to the "origin chronicles" it was where the six children of Tibet's primordial ancestor wrestled, ran around and chased each other.* Sir Charles Bell first noted that Tibetans had anticipated Darwin in claiming descent from a monkey. But Tibet's primal ancestor, the "Bodhisattva Father Monkey" (*pha tiu jhanjup-sempa*) appears to have gone one further, mating with the female of a less advanced species of proto-humans, the *drak-sinmu*, usually translated as "rock-ogress", to produce modern Tibetans. The discovery at the Max Planck Institute of Evolutionary Anthropology in 2010, of Neanderthal genes in the DNA of living humans has shown that mankind's out-of-Africa forebears mated with Neanderthal troglodytes, somewhat in the manner of Tibet's primate ancestor.

In July 2014, in a paper in the journal *Nature*, we learn that a cousin of the Neanderthals, a Paleolithic-era species of the genus Homo, the Denisovans, mated with early Tibetans, and even conferred on the Tibetan DNA make-up a special gene variant, EPAS1, which gives people of Tibetan ethnicity their unique ability to survive at extremely high altitudes.[4] By happy coincidence, a Tibetan researcher, Dr Tsewang Tashi, was one of the authors of another study led by University of Utah scientists, which found a further gene variant, EGLN1 (changed by a single DNA base pair) inherited from Denisovans, which also helped in the high altitude adaptation of the first Tibetan people.[5] Earlier, the only fossil remains we had of this ancient-hominem group came from a female pinkie tip, discovered inside a cave in Denisova, Siberia. However, in 2019 scientists uncovered the most complete remains yet, half an entire jaw of a Denisovan adult, at a sacred cave by the Kangya Drakar Monastery, under the Gongri Khandroma mountain, just north of Labrang on the Tibetan Plateau.[6]

In Tibetan legends, this inter-species mating even has a specific place, a high cave near the summit of Mount Zodang Gongpo-ri (or

---

*Scientists previously thought that humans first set foot on the Tibetan Plateau 15,000 years ago. New genomic and archaeological studies now push this as far back as 62,000 years, in the middle of the last Ice Age. The studies also reveal a startling genetic continuity since the plateau was first colonized, suggesting "that Tibet has always been populated—even during the toughest times as far as climate was concerned." *Scientific American*, 1 March 2017.

Gangpo-ri) that still features a naturally produced rock image of the monkey ancestor. The triangular-peaked mountain is just south-east of the town and is considered one of the four sacred mountains of Central Tibet. Nesting below it is the town of Tsethang. The mountain rises above the town, its spurs protecting it from the elements and creating a defensible nexus at the valley's mouth.

* * *

In 1958, the Chinese army held the mountain, on the lower slopes of which they had built their principal garrison, the buildings of which were protected by high walls, and barbed wire fences. The entire defence perimeter and strategic points on the mountainside were fortified by a series of bunkers and pillboxes linked through a network of tunnels.

About ten miles south of Tsethang is Nedong, once the seat of the Phagmodrupa kings.* The royal castle, Nedong Dzong, a derelict but imposing structure, stood on the eastern spur of a low mountain. Lower, on the western slope, approaching the Yarlung River, is the Sakya monastery of Tse Tsokpa. The Chinese had taken over and fortified the area around the monastery.

When the resistance had earlier been based further south at Driguthang, they had not given much thought to the strategic importance of Tsethang, but after their move to Lhagyari, closer to Tsethang, they realized that Tsethang was not only important as the "capital" of Yarlung but that it was a vital crossroad straddling not only the important route south all the way to Bhutan and India, but also the route west to Chushül and Shigatsé, the route east to Kongpo Gyamda and Kham and the route northwards to the Kyichu valley, and Lhasa. The resistance leaders realized that the Chinese garrison at Tsethang had to be destroyed, or neutralized. A month before Ratuk's arrival at Lhoka, the resistance had made two attempts to attack the Chinese HQ

---

*The Phagmodrupa dynasty founded by Jhanjup Gyaltsen of the Lang clan, overthrew the Sakya kings who ruled Tibet under Imperial Mongol (Yuan) patronage. Jhanjup Gyaltsen created a stable, prosperous, culturally dynamic and independent Tibetan state from around 1354 to the early 1600s.

and garrison, just below the mountainside facing Tsethang town. The first problem they faced was getting close enough to the mountain to launch an effective charge.

In early November, Lithang commander Jhamatsang Samphel, gathered two hundred fighters in a large house in Tsethang town. Most of his men were in and around the courtyard of this house, while he and some of his officers were in the main room planning the attack. The Chinese lookouts on the mountainside may have noticed this concentration of Tibetan fighters or been given this information by a local spy. The next day, with no warning, artillery and mortar fire began to rain down on the house the Khampas were occupying. They managed to get out and disperse to safety.

A week later, under cover of darkness, Drayab commander Adruk Lama and Lithang Alo Dawa led around four hundred fighters into the town and positioned them at three crucial points on the suburb of the town, just before the Chinese defence works. The men were instructed to remain concealed inside the houses till they received instructions to attack. But once again. The Chinese directed intense mortar and artillery fire at exactly the places where the fighters were gathered. The Khampas returned Bren gun and rifle fire at the Chinese and managed to make a safe retreat, only suffering a few casualties. It now became clear that the Chinese were somehow receiving information of the Resistance's plans, or about the movement of Khampa fighters in Tsethang town.

In early January, Ratuk Ngawang and other commanders: Dargön Sese, Bapa Gyen Aleg, Drayab Ngawang Yonten, Chatreng Pharo Sherab, Dargön Pachen and five hundred men moved into Tsethang town. This time they were careful not to move too far forward and instead first occupied Tsethang Monastery, located in the centre of the town and a number of houses in the surrounding neighborhood. Tsethang Gompa, also called Ganden Chokorling, was initially founded by Phagmodrupa Jhanjup Gyaltsen in 1351 as a Kagyüpa monastery, but rebuilt at the time of the Seventh Dalai Lama as a Gelugpa center. The Khampas received some Chinese mortar fire a day after their arrival at the town. They quickly convened a meeting of the monks and townspeople. Ratuk Ngawang explained to the gathering the national and spiritual cause for which the Four Rivers and Six Ranges was fighting, and why everyone in Tsethang should support them and not assist the Chinese in any way. They also took down the names of everyone living in the town, and checked on them every morning at a roll call. After that, Chinese mortar fire lessened considerably.

The Khampas now settled down and began to study the Chinese defenses. Most of the commanders had binoculars. The Chinese headquarters building, barracks and storehouses were located at the foot of the mountain. Bunkers, pillboxes and trenches surrounded these structures. On the side of the mountain, they also built concealed bunkers and machine gun emplacements, connected to each other by tunnels. Surrounding the whole fortification and the bunkers were a series of nasty looking barbed wire fences. The Khampas soon realized how impregnable the Chinese fortress was and that it would take time to work out an effective plan of attack.

It was decided that a separate force should, in the meantime, attack the other Chinese garrison at the Tse Tsokpa Monastery, below Nedong Dzong, south of Tsethang town. Scouts had told them that the defences there were not so formidable and, in fact, still in the process of being completed. Leaving behind a detachment to hold Tsethang Monastery, the rest of the force moved out of the town and rode south to Nedong.

After studying the defences at Tse Tsokpa, it was decided that before tackling the main garrison, they should get as close as possible to the forward trenches and bunkers (*sokhung*) and use them as staging areas to mount an attack on the main garrison. The Chinese had only managed to put up one barbed wire fence, and everyone was confident they could cut through it.

Ratuk Ngawang and four other commanders, Dargön Sese, Pachen, Nyarong Kalsang Dorje and Tawu Gonpo, in two detachments of forty men each, crawled under cover of darkness as close to the Chinese forward line as possible and waited. At dawn, the Khampas fired their four mortars at the main Chinese defences and others provided covering fire to the advance detachment that attacked the Chinese bunkers and trenches.

The advance fighters managed to cut through the barbed wire and got close to the Chinese bunkers but were pinned down by machine-gun fire. However, the Khampas had grenades and managed to clear most of the advance trenches and bunkers, killing many of the Chinese within them. But they could not silence the two machine-gun emplacements, which were on higher ground. They continued the attack for about an hour more, but two Khampas were killed and six wounded including two commanders. When they ran out of grenades, the Khampas withdrew.

That same night another attack was initiated on the south-western side of the Tse Tsokpa fortifications close to the Yarlung River. This time around, two hundred Khampas sneaked towards this area and attacked a large farmhouse on the edge of the Chinese defences. A PLA company defended the old farmhouse called Chukor wog (Under the Water Mill). Around 1 p.m. the Khampas attacked. They were able to surprise the Chinese defenders and killed about twenty of them. The rest of the Chinese retreated to the main fortress.

The next night the Chinese tried to retake the farmhouse, but the Khampas beat them back. The Chinese tried a few more times, unsuccessfully. The Khampas also took over the monastery of Tse Tsokpa and, from the roof of the building, were able to establish a clear field of fire against Chinese defences. By taking these two strategic positions, the Khampas were able to immobilize the Chinese garrison.

However, by then, the Khampas realized that it was not possible to destroy the Chinese fortifications and the garrison by frontal assaults. Instead, because the soil in the area was fairly soft and sandy, they decided to dig under the Chinese fortress. Fortunately for the Khampas, two volunteers from Nedong Dzong came forward to help. Phuntsok Namgyal Dumkhang, the son of a former cabinet secretary in Lhasa, and Nangra Shakya recruited thirty peasants from nearby Chongye, who came with pickaxes, shovels and crowbars. From the courtyard of the Chukor-wog farmyard, they started digging a tunnel. They dug successfully for about twenty days and managed to get close to the main defences . But then they came up against a large rock face that stopped them dead. They tried digging around the obstacle but realized that the rock was very big—enormous, in fact. Ratuk Ngawang describes it as like a "hill in itself." So the idea had to be dropped. Though everyone was disappointed at the failure and wasted effort, the resistance leaders quickly realized that perhaps the defences of the principal Chinese garrison at Tsethang might be more vulnerable to this form of subversive attack.

The decision was made to leave a strong force at Tse Tsokpa, with instructions to keep the Chinese there pinned down. On 8 February 1959, Commander Ratuk and Dargön Sese and other commanders and their fighters left in the night and rode to Tsethang town. Other detachments had been sent messages to gather at Tsethang. The commanders, Baba Aleg, Sandhu Sonam Wangyal, Drayab Ngawang Yonten, Ganden Nyara Khentrul and their men gathered at the town.

There were no Chinese in Tsethang town itself or at the monastery. The Khampas gathered at the large house where they had earlier set up headquarters. They billeted the fighters in other houses and also at the Ganden Chokorling Monastery in the town. Since this was *Losar*, the first day of the Tibetan New Year, the townspeople offered them a festive meal with lots of chang and arak to drink.

The next day, a meeting was held, and it was decided to let the men have a good time for two days, it being Losar, after all. É-Yul Headquarters had sent meat, butter, tsampa and flour, according to the ration allotment for each fighter. All this got to the men in time. The New Year festivities ended on the evening of the third day when the Chinese fired hundreds of artillery and mortar rounds at the Khampas. Some of the houses were damaged, but no one was hurt.

Another meeting was held with the town headmen and monastic officials. They were warned that spies in the town were informing the Chinese where the Resistance fighters were located, and that this had to stop. The local leadership was given the task of organizing a morning roll call of everyone in the town and make sure no one was missing. Ratuk Ngawang addressed the meeting and declared that all the Four Rivers Six Ranges volunteers were giving up their lives to protect the religion and polity (*chos-si-nyi*) of the Tibetan nation, and that putting the lives of these volunteers in danger was a serious crime.[7] When studying the Chinese defences the resistance commanders noticed a large manor house at the edge of Tsethang town, close to the Chinese lines, that offered an opening. The house had earlier belonged to a prominent citizen, Tsethang Dorje, but the Chinese had taken over the place and garrisoned it with a company of soldiers. Using the alleyways and the nearby ruins for cover, the Khampas managed to get close to the manor house and surreptitiously place explosives against the western wall. A month earlier, they had captured thirty cases of dynamite in a successful raid on a Chinese truck convoy.

Early in the morning they pulled the cord on the jury-rigged hand grenade detonator and blew up one side of the house. The explosion immediately killed twenty Chinese soliders. The survivors were shot dead when they tried to run back to their own lines. Now the Khampa fighters were close to the main Chinese defence line, yet effectively protected by the thick rammed-earth walls of the ruined manor house.

The main Chinese garrison building and bunkers were surrounded by a series of barbed wire fences. The barbed wire was strung with hundreds of empty tin cans of ration pork (with pebbles inside them) that clanged and clattered loudly when anyone touched the wire, making it tricky to cut, even under cover of darkness. One night they hooked a section of the wire and tried to pull it from a distance with long ropes, but the moment the clanging started, the Chinese machine guns opened up, and the Khampas had to retreat. Another time an old donkey somehow wandered into the lines and got entangled in the barbed wire, making a racket. The machine guns cut the beast to shreds.

Despite the barbed wire, the fighters in the ruins of the manor house were now close enough to limit Chinese freedom of movement at the garrison itself. Khampa snipers at the manor itself further back on the roof on the Tsethang Monastery were able to kill unwary Chinese soldiers moving around the garrison.

The Chinese had dug a network of tunnels to connect their various buildings, and positions and many of the bunkers were partially underground, so it was difficult to always get a clear shot at them. The Resistance did not have telescopic sights, but those old bolt action rifles, in particular, the long barrel Czech *pamaling* and Russian *bura,* were accurate at great distances, and the young Khampas and nomads had twenty-twenty eyesight.

The standard Chinese rifle was the semi-automatic Russian SKS, which did not have much range. But the Chinese deployed heavy machine guns and the Russian DP-28 light machine guns, which were deadly. So Khampa snipers had to change their positions constantly in order not to be spotted. When the Chinese pinpointed their location, they would immediately fire an illumination flare above them and open up with machine gun and mortar fire.

But the constant and accurate sniper fire from the Khampas prevented the Chinese from getting to their main water supply, which was the "Chuyuk" irrigation canal, as the locals called it. It ran just by the barbed wire fence to the south. When surveying the area around the canal, the Khampas discovered a weakness in the Chinese defenses where it intersected with the canal. In order for Chinese soldiers to fetch water from the canal they had been obliged to leave a gap in the barbed wire fencing. It was a small gap and you couldn't see it right away as the path leading to it was at an angle to the wire fence, but a sharp-eyed fighter saw it and reported it to his commander.

So, a night attack was planned to exploit this opportunity. Around midnight, twenty volunteers crawled towards the canal, dragging four ladders behind them. They managed to place two of these across the canal, but the other two were not long enough. Half the fighters managed to make it across the canal, but the Chinese guards must have heard or seen something. They opened up with their machine guns. The Chinese fire was intense. A couple of the fighters who were on the ladders couldn't move forward or backwards, and the dozen or so who had already crossed were stuck on the Chinese side. The Khampas poured covering fire on the machine gun emplacements, and eventually most of the fighters managed to make it back across the canal. Four men didn't. After some days, the Chinese stopped trying to get water from the canal. Most probably, they had managed to dig a well within their own compound.

Every night the resistance fighters probed the Chinese defences. Many were killed and wounded. In two months, the resistance lost forty men. The wounded were taken for treatment and recovery at the hospital that was set up at the estate of the aristocrat Khemey. The resistance would have taken many more casualties if not for the fact that many of the hundreds of mortar and artillery shells the Chinese fired at the Tibetan lines were duds. The unexploded ordinance was carefully collected and brought to the *sungma* (protector deity) temple of the Tsethang Monastery and stacked against the walls, for use in future "mining" operations for which the resistance men were already digging a number of tunnels.

The ancient military art of "mining", or tunnel warfare as we would call it these days, is a method of destroying an enemy stronghold like a castle or fortress wall by digging a tunnel and placing barrels of gunpowder directly under it, and when the structure collapsed in the explosion, launching a mass infantry attack on the position. During the American Civil War, Colonel Henry Pleasants managed to dig a long tunnel under the Confederate lines along Elliot's Salient at the Siege of Petersburg and successfully detonated an enormous mine there. But the Union generals were not able to) exploit the initial success, resulting in indecisive and bloody infantry engagement.

Tibetans had made extensive use of "mining" in the "Water-Mouse Chinese War" (*chuchi gyamak)* of 1912 when attacking the fortified Chinese defences in Lhasa city. Of course, such underground operations could often go wrong. An old Lhasa resident told me that instead of exploding under the Chinese garrison, a Tibetan mine went off directly under a Chinese outhouse, spraying the defenders with their own waste-matter.

Many of the street fighters in Lhasa were Khampas from the Banakshöl suburb of Lhasa, so it is possible that such old Banakshöl residents as the administrative leaders Jhamatsang and Jhangtsatsang may have recalled past exploits to aid them in their present enterprise. Among the fighters were volunteers from the old Tibetan army, some of whom may have taken part in mining operations in the Water-Bird War.

Several tunnels were started from the Tibetan lines, using the courtyard of houses on the frontline for cover. Enthusiasm for digging tunnels became contagious and many of the different *makhar* commands at Tsethang: Ganden makhar, Chatreng makhar, Lithang makhar, Sandhu makhar and Nyarong makhar each started digging tunnels on their own. There was friendly competition among the commands to see who could get to the Chinese defences first.

The actual digging didn't pose many problems. The distance from the Tibetan frontline to the Chinese defences wasn't far and the ground wasn't too hard.

The first thing you had to do was dig straight down about ten feet, then clear out enough space for a kind of antechamber. Then you dug horizontally towards the Chinese lines. Sometimes when the soil was not compact, you had to shore up the walls and the ceiling with planks and pieces of wood. It wasn't difficult to obtain waste wood as many of the houses in Tsethang had been destroyed by Chinese mortar and artillery fire and abandoned by the owners. Most people from Tsethang and Nedong who had fled the fighting were taken to a sort of "displaced person's" camp at the Khemey estate where some of them helped at the hospital.

The problem with the tunnels came up when they got close to the Chinese lines. Somehow the Chinese seemed to know where the tunnels were and took countermeasures. The PLA had acquired a reputation for tunnel warfare during the Korean War. I also read somewhere that the Chinese used makeshift ear trumpets to hear the faint sounds of underground digging by their opponents. The Vietcong, at the Cuchi tunnels, placed bowls of water on the ground. Vibrations from American patrols overhead or movement by American "tunnel-rats" caused tiny but visible ripples on the surface of the water.

One tunnel opened up under a Chinese bunker. The Chinese soldiers realized what was happening and started shooting and throwing hand grenades down at the diggers. The fighters quickly retreated but not before hurriedly setting off the explosive charge they had brought with them. But the blast did not do much damage. The next time around, the Tibetans were more careful, making as little noise as possible when digging. They were able to dig all the way undetected under a Chinese bunker and place their explosives effectively for maximum destruction. That bunker completely disappeared in an enormous explosion. The Chinese countered by digging their own tunnels towards where they thought the Tibetans were approaching. Sometimes when they met, they would open fire at each other with handguns and Sten guns. On one occasion, a Chinese rammed a crowbar down through the roof of a Tibetan tunnel and impaled the digger underneath.

On the surface, the fighting continued with marksmen shooting at each other's positions, whenever anyone was exposed, even briefly. The Chinese also started a propaganda campaign using loudspeakers pointed in the direction of the Resistance lines. Tibetan-speaking announcers would shout that the Khampas were merely reactionary rebel bandits and the People's Liberation Army would crush them, and so on. They called on the fighters to surrender and acknowledge their crimes and that the Chinese Central Government would forgive them. The fighters were also assured that they could return to their wives and families, who must surely be waiting for them.

Orwell, in his personal and incisive account of the Spanish Civil War, *Homage to Catalonia*, mentions that at the frontline trenches in Spain, the propaganda announcements from ". . . the government side, in the party militias, had been developed to a regular technique." One such propagandist with his megaphone ". . . was an artist at the job. Sometimes, instead of shouting revolutionary slogans, he told the Fascists how much better we were fed than they were. 'Buttered toast!'—you could hear his voice echoing across the lonely valley— 'We're just sitting down to buttered toast over here! Lovely slices of buttered toast!'"

The Chinese had captured two Andrugtsang muleteers and made them talk over their loudspeakers. The muleteers repeated the lines the Chinese taught them: that Tibetans should not listen to the words of a few bandit leaders who were just criminals and exploiters. Those who surrendered would be forgiven. They would also be well fed on rice and pork. The last line was probably inserted by one of the muleteers, rice being something of a treat for barley-eating Tibetans.

The Chinese also used the former General Karchung of the Tibetan army and his wife to speak over the loudspeakers. Karchung called on the Khampas to surrender. He said it was no use fighting the Chinese, who were the benefactors of the Tibetan people, and that the Khampas were being forced to fight by their own chieftains, who were actually their oppressors. At the same time, Karchung and his wife warned the people of Tsethang not to trust the Khampas and told them that the Four Rivers Six Ranges were a band of beggars and bandits, with no home of their own to return to.[8]

This was the same General Karchung who in October 1950 had courageously defended the Tibetan frontline at Chamdo against a division of the PLA, until his small force of five hundred men and a couple of hundred Khampa militia, were wiped out and he himself captured. As I mentioned in an earlier chapter, he was publicly and unfairly humiliated by his own countrymen (in a satirical song) for being defeated after three days of fierce and heroic resistance. Governor-general Ngabö, who had surrendered the Chamdo command without firing a shot was made a senior member of the Tibetan cabinet.

It is possible that this experience may have caused Karchung to go over to the Chinese side. He was then living at his estate in Chongye.

The resistance did not have amplifiers and loudspeakers, but they fashioned their own bullhorns with sheet metal and placed them on the frontline. Fighters who were good talkers and possessed loud voices were recruited to broadcast a litany of atrocities committed by the Chinese in Eastern Tibet, including the torture and murder of lamas and monks, and the destruction and looting of monasteries and temples.

Athar Norbu told me that one contingent of resistance fighters posted at the Tsethang Monastery had taken the huge *dhungchen* horns there and used them to shout insults at the Chinese: "Chinese beggars (*gyapang*), Chinese corpses (*gyaro*)", and also the usual "eat shit! (*kyakpa za*)" and so on. A few of the fighters spoke some basic Chinese that they used to shout insults at the defenders. But according to Athar, the Chinese-language skills of these Khampas were fairly basic, and they were probably not understood too well, if at all, by the enemy. Orwell mentions a well-understood and stock insult shouted from his side across the trenches, "*Fascistas—maricones!*"

One day the Chinese Colonel Lobsang Tashi, who had also been separated from the main force at Mamshung, made his way back to the resistance HQ and Tsethang. Now with his cooperation, a more sophisticated propaganda broadcast was aimed at the Chinese.

After being separated from the force at the Mamshung ambush, Lobsang Tashi had wandered into a small Tibetan village where they fed him but took away his rifle and pistol. They also took his robe and gave him a tattered old chuba and torn boots, which later served as a good disguise. After a day at that village, he made his way to the battle-field where he found his horse. He rode south-east and eventually came to the Sichuan Lhasa highway—the stretch from Kongpo Gyamda to Meldro Gungkar. He travelled mostly by night. Chinese trucks with soldiers passed by him but ignored him as he looked like a ragged Tibetan beggar leading a broken-down nag. This was fortunate as he only had a bayonet to defend himself. When he eventually reached Kyichu River at Lhasa, both he and his horse were too weak and tired to ford the river. The new Kuru Bridge was well guarded, so he rested for the night some distance from it. Early next morning, a train of donkeys carrying dung-fuel passed by. Lobsang Tashi walked casually beside the donkey-driver and made it across the bridge and to Lhasa. He went over to Lingka Sarpa to the home of the old park-keeper, who let him stay for a few days. The old man then found a monk who was travelling to Lhoka and arranged with him to take Lobsang Tashi south, back to resistance territory.

Lobsang Tashi's many adventures are documented in a fascinating biography by Lamotsang Tsering Wangchuk of Lhasa, who concludes his chronicle with this sentence: "Like the old treaty pillars that Imperial Tibet and the Tang Dynasty erected as symbols of peace and friendship between these two great nations, the memory of Gya Lobsang Tashi will endure."[9]

Lobsang Tashi was welcomed back at Tsethang, where they used him to shout at the Chinese defenders to surrender, and used his technical skills to improve their tunneling and mining efforts. Lobsang Tashi's biographer claims that due to his efforts two more Chinese posts were destroyed.

Ratuk Ngawang mentions that Lobsang Tashi was involved in the planning and execution of their most ambitious "mining" undertaking. This came about at a meeting of the resistance leaders where there was a reluctant but unanimous admission by all commanders that their separate tunnelling projects were not bringing about the desired destruction of the Tsethang fortress.

Finally, everyone agreed that all resources and energy should be concentrated on one large tunnel, and that it should be dug as deep as possible so that it could not be detected by the Chinese and should end directly under the main fortress. Then, all the explosives that the Resistance possessed, including the dud artillery shells they had stored at the *sungma* temple, would be detonated in one big blast that would surely destroy much of the fortress. This explosion would immediately be followed by a combined assault by all fighters at Tsethang.

They dug the entry shaft twenty feet straight down. The tunnel itself was cut wide enough so that diggers could move back and forth comfortably. At places it was even wide enough for two people to cross. They also shored up the walls and roof with planks and beams, throughout the tunnel. After they dug for about fifteen days, a number of the men, especially the diggers, figured they had come close under the Chinese lines, and began to get uneasy. They voiced their concern that the Chinese would detect the tunnel and explode a "counter-mine" above them, as they had done once before, killing some fighters. They insisted that it was time to detonate the big mine under the tunnel and destroy whatever Chinese position they were under.

The diggers had measured the distance they had tunnelled with a rope, but on the surface, they found it difficult to gauge the distance to the main Chinese fortress they wanted to destroy. Lobsang Tashi being an artilleryman tried to make a rough estimation, but without a rangefinder or similar equipment found it difficult to arrive at an accurate figure.

Ratuk Ngawang and Lobsang Tashi went out at night and, getting as close as safely possible to the front line, threw a long rope with a stone tied to the end, across no-man's land. Chinese machine guns opened up immediately and made it impossible to carry out that task effectively. They tried again from behind the cover of the wall of the ruined manor house, but the rope was not long enough. Nonetheless, their efforts at the front made Ratuk and Lobsang Tashi realize that the tunnel was not close enough yet.

Ratuk Ngawang mentions that it was difficult to tell the men who had worked so hard that they had to dig for some more days. To encourage them, he offered to stay underground with them and take his turn at the tunnel face. But the fighters told him they could do their job, and he need not stay in the tunnel.

Finally, after another six days of digging, there was a general consensus that they were probably now under the Chinese fortress, and it was time for the big mine to explode. They placed all the unexploded mortar and artillery shells they had collected against the end of the tunnel, and also packed it with the captured dynamite they had left and most of the C4 from the CIA airdrop. Even a couple of barrels of old-fashioned gunpowder, recovered from the town, was crammed in. The night before the big mine was to explode, all resistance fighters in Tsethang were positioned as close as possible to the frontlines so that when the big explosion took place, they could immediately attack and overwhelm the remaining Chinese defenders.

Ratuk Ngawang on the final day: "Early in the morning, around dawn, Lobsang Tashi lit the long fuse he had laid at the mouth of the tunnel. All the fighters waited anxiously behind houses, broken walls and parapets, hoping and praying that this time the mine would explode successfully, and they could attack the Chinese fortress. For a long while, it seemed that nothing would happen, but then the ground shook, and there was a dull booming sound. Smoke came out from under the Chinese bunkers but there was no big, spectacular explosion as everyone had hoped. The surface of the ground cracked in many places. A couple of the Chinese pillboxes collapsed, and one of the walls of an empty house on our side fell. But that was all.

"There was tremendous disappointment among the fighters, and a lot of cursing and swearing. That was the end of our hopes for destroying the Chinese defences and storming the fortress. We later learned that though the mine had not exploded in a spectacular fashion as hoped, the explosion had destroyed a network of Chinese tunnels leading to the bunkers and killed many of the Chinese soldiers inside. Perhaps if we had all charged at that moment, we might have caught them off guard and overwhelmed them. But we will never know."

None of the fighters could understand why the big mine had failed. Perhaps the tunnel had not been the right length. Perhaps the explosives had not been packed enough or placed correctly. But the most likely answer was that the Khampas did not have enough bombs and C4 to cause the devastating explosion they desperately needed. As one of the fighters explained, using a common saying, "the arm was too long for the sleeve" or that expectations had exceeded resources.

In spite of the disappointment everyone felt, it became apparent in the next few days that the limited explosion had somehow done appreciable damage and caused enough concern among the Chinese that they abandoned all their forward defenses and retreated to the main fortress. This was, in retrospect, a significant victory and a timely one.

It was around this period, just after the failed assault, that resistance headquarters received information from several sources in Lhasa about a major crisis brewing there, and even the likelihood of an uprising in the Holy City. Orders were sent out to all outposts and contingents to closely observe Chinese troop movement, and where possible, attack truck convoys or units heading south to Lhoka.

Finally, in early March, Resistance Headquarters received a high-priority dispatch from Dewatsang Kunga Samten,* the commander of a detachment guarding the Tsadzong Drukha ferry crossing on the

_____

*His biography *Flight at the Cuckoo's Behest: The Life and Times of a Tibetan Freedom Fighter* was published in 2002 by Paljor Publications.

Tsangpo River. He had been contacted by an important Lhasa official who claimed to be a representative of the Lord Chamberlain Phala. He had asked if the Resistance could have a strong force ready, in case the Dalai Lama would have to leave Lhasa and needed an escort. This official had also inquired as to the whereabouts of the two radio operators, Athar and Lotse, and requested that they be on standby in the immediate future.

The fighters in Tsethang were now issued urgent instructions from Resistance headquarters to hold their position at all costs and under no circumstances allow any Chinese troops to break out of the beleaguered Tsethang fortress.

The crisis in Lhasa was coming to a head.

25

LHASA TWILIGHT

There is probably no better way of inserting yourself permanently in a child's memory than with a memorable gift. The recollection of myself as a schoolboy in Darjeeling running into my great-uncle Tsarong Dasang Damdul outside Glenary's Restaurant (mentioned in Chapter 7) has never quite faded. I'm sure Tsarong pola's generous tip of twenty rupees had much to do with that. Shortly after, just a few months before the Uprising of 1959, he returned to Lhasa.

At the beginning of 1959, especially around the Tibetan New Year, Lhasa was seething with unrest and tension. The city was more crowded than ever with pilgrims and visitors, especially as the Dalai Lama was to take his geshe (doctoral) examination during the Mönlam Festival, immediately after the New Year celebration. Strange, troubling rumours floated around the city, a particularly nagging one being that, following his examinations, the Dalai Lama would be invited to China and, once there, would be held hostage to pressure the Khampa Resistance to surrender.

The clandestine posters that had earlier appeared all over the city, describing the daring attacks by the Four Rivers Six Ranges on Chinese convoys and fierce battles with PLA forces, had electrified the Lhasa citizenry. Even after the posters had been taken down, fragments of the information had been passed around by word of mouth and spread throughout Tibet, becoming, in the retelling, exciting episodes of a new Tibetan epic. We heard these stories even as far away as Darjeeling and Kalimpong.

With the opening of the two major highways from China, Chinese truck convoys were pouring into Lhasa daily with PLA troops, workers, building materials and of course, weapons and ammunition, including heavy artillery. The military airport at Damshung, north of Lhasa, was now fully operational. The Chinese had also built a network of secondary roads linking the major towns and districts in Central and Eastern Tibet.

It was on the road from Shigatsé to the town of Dromo Rinchengang on the Sikkim border that Tsarong's daughter Tsering Yangzom (aka Betty-la) and nephew, Tseten Namgyal, had driven in the family Land Rover to receive the old gentleman at the border town. They had brought provisions and warm clothes as winter had begun to set in, and it was getting cold. Tsetan Namgyal told me that Tsarong stayed a week at Rinchengang, saying he wanted to study the situation and see if it was still possible to cross secretly from Dromo to India, as he had done some forty-five years ago. He said that it was no longer safe for the Dalai Lama to remain in Tibet.

Before he left Kalimpong, Tsarong had been approached by Shakabpa and others who requested him to lead the exile movement as he had the experience of fighting a Chinese occupation army— even defeating one in 1912. Tsarong replied, "I am not going to stay here and lead you. I am going back to Tibet to serve the Dalai Lama, because the Dalai Lama is there."[1] Tsarong saw that safeguarding the Dalai Lama and getting him to safety took priority over everything else.

Tsetan Namgyal confirmed the old man's worst fears by telling him everything that had been taking place in Lhasa. Tsetan Namgyal was well informed as he was a member of an underground group in Lhasa.

The Kashag had shut down the few clandestine organizations that had sprung up in the fifties under pressure from the Chinese occupation authorities. The old Mimang organization, whose leader Alo Chonzé had escaped to India, had just two members left, Amchi Anen-la and the secretary of the Tsatultsang mercantile family, who tried their best to carry on. A blind beggar, Tsesum, has left an account[2] of being recruited by this organization to spy on a heavily guarded Chinese hydroelectric construction project at Nachendrak, north-east of Lhasa. Lhasa residents feared that the Chinese would use the large dam being built there to flood the city, if the need arose.

But Tsetan Namgyal belonged to a relatively larger secret society, the Tibet Freedom Alliance (*Bhod Rawang Langdren Tsokpa*), whose aim was ". . . to drive out Chinese imperialists from Tibet and establish a democratic government in the country." He remembered there being about seven members in his cell, "One was Jhangdré-la (Phuntsok Wangdu), you know, the secretary of the exile Parliament. Our leader was the young official, Seynang Lobsang Yeshi."[3]

Maja Tsewang Gyurme,[4] who had served under Governor-general Lhalu and Ngabö in Chamdo in 1950, told me he had been a member of another underground organization, the United Tibetan Society (*Bhörig Chigdril Tsokpa*). This organization had around nine senior members: officials, monks, Khampa merchants and army officers, who recruited other members in separate cells. In its early years, its self-appointed task was to keep Tibetans united and prevent them from joining Communist organizations. It only took on a more radical and covert role in the late 1950s, recruiting storekeepers, tea shop owners and even street beggars to spy on Chinese informants and police. It was a loose-knit, cell-based organization. Maja told me that the other principal members were Seynang Lobsang Yeshi, Bharshi *Tsendron* Ngawang Tenkyong, Manang Abo, Captain Kaldam, Tsawa Mani Trulku, Jhepa Alak of Choné (who calligraphed posters and letters), Kendrong Sey (later called Tsedrung Jampa Yonten) and one woman, Gurteng Kunsang, who was the niece of Tsarong Dasang Damdul. Maja said that they didn't exactly have a single leader but that the senior and most active member was the official Lobsang Yeshi.

The monk official, Bharshi *Tsendron* Ngawang Tenkyong, told me in a telephone interview that he had also organized a secret cell of monk officials (*tsedrung*). He mentioned that Seynang Lobsang Yeshi, though a lay official, had been included as a member, since he had formerly been a monk official.

I began to ask around about this enigmatic Lobsang Yeshi, who, in one way or another, had been involved in a surprising number of anti-Chinese organizations and activities, but remains a mysterious and relatively unknown figure. He was from the Dhampa Zinga family of Shigatsé, and his career as a junior monk official had advanced rapidly in the administration of the Taktra Regency. He had travelled to Kalimpong in the mid-1950s and had attempted to contact patriotic Tibetan exiles there but had been unable to convince the members of the Tibet Welfare Society of his *bona fides*, perhaps as he had spent a year studying in China. George Patterson, who got to know Lobsang Yeshi well in Kalimpong, was impressed with him and considered him to be one of the "foremost patriotic officials"[5] he had met.

In 1952, when the Chinese occupation authorities called on the Kashag to send young Tibetans to study at the Central Institute for Nationalities at Beijing, most families were fearful of complying. Lobsang Yeshi was one of the first to volunteer. He told a friend that studying in Beijing was the only way to understand China's true intentions regarding Tibet. Tibetans who were at the Institute remembered him for his generosity, and the guidance he had given them to see through the self-serving propaganda that permeated the lessons on 'history' and 'politics' the students received. There was also mention of an underground society at the Nationalities Institute.

The autobiography of a Nationalities Institute student from Phari[6] mentions that many Tibetans at the Institute belonged to one of two secret anti-Chinese organizations, the "Nose Society" and the "Ear Society", that kept apart from each other. Lobsang Yeshi was said to have had a hand in setting up the latter.

It then struck me what Lobsang Yeshi might have actually done in Beijing and later replicated in Lhasa. It appears he set up these organizations in the classic cell system, with no lateral communication among the cells except through himself or another leader. He might have come across the idea perhaps from reading the history of the Russian Communist Party that in its early underground years had taken the clandestine cell structure as its basic organizational unit, to withstand penetration by the Ochrana, the Tsarist secret police.

On the other hand, these organizations in Lhasa might have formed on their own and that somehow, more out of a natural sense of self-preservation than a grasp of conspiratorial tradecraft, had kept themselves small, inconspicuous and separate from each other to minimize infiltration by the many spies and informers deployed by the Chinese security agencies in Lhasa. It is also possible that Lobsang Yeshi came across these secret organizations as he was a trusted aide to Phala Thupten Wönden, the *dronyerchenmo* or Lord Chamberlain of the Dalai Lama. Phala was a well-connected political player and appears to have used Lobsang Yeshi as his principal go-between or "cut-out" for crucial but problematic meetings. The CIA agent Athar Norbu mentions Lobsang Yeshi as the liaison official that he and Lotse met in Lhasa, and arranged their meeting with Phala.

Lobsang Yeshi's various aliases added to my frustration in researching his story. His name as a monk official was Lobsang Yeshi. His family name was Dhampa Zinga, but he took up the name Seynang when he gave up his monk vows and became a lay official (*drungkor*). He was also known as Ngawang Singe. Was all this identity switching an indication of a conspiratorial bent? Perhaps not, but it might have confused people and subsequently made them overlook the magnitude of his contribution to the coming events. The Dalai Lama refers to him as a "brave boy" in his memoirs and mentions his resisting Chinese indoctrination in Beijing and being killed in the Uprising. Lobsang Yeshi provided the first contingent of armed escorts to the Dalai Lama and his entourage after they crossed the Kyichu River.

One of the organizations that we know for sure Lobsang Yeshi started was a small but secret private militia. He had used the resources of the Taktra administration to arm and mount thirty or forty volunteers: Lhasa city toughs, fighting monks and, in particular, Amdowa monks and refugees.* He kept them at the ready, but hidden away at the village of Nyetang, twenty miles south-west of Lhasa.

---

*In 1937, as a very junior official, Lobsang Yeshi had been a member of the north-east search team to find the incarnation of the Thirteenth Dalai Lama. As all Tibetans know, the Hui Muslim warlord of Qinghai (Amdo) demanded an exorbitant ransom that the search-team officials could only make part

The somewhat elaborate security precautions that Lobsang Yeshi took might have helped the main underground organization from being infiltrated by informers. One of the smaller cells had a member that some people suspected of being a Chinese informant. This cell was later exposed by Chinese Public Security. Lobsang Yeshi himself had told another source[7] of his doubts regarding this particular person, who had also studied in Beijing. This alleged informant escaped to India in 1959 and worked in the exile government.

When Tsarong arrived in Lhasa, he immediately requested the Dalai Lama's Lord Chamberlain for a private audience. On meeting the Dalai Lama, Tsarong requested that he seriously consider leaving Tibet and seeking asylum in India or another friendly country. The Dalai Lama mentions this meeting in a recorded interview[8] with Tsarong's grandson.

Tsarong reported the alarming buildup of Chinese military strength in Lhasa and the Chinese had completed the construction of the major highways and secondary roads. He described to the Dalai Lama the recent completion of the road from Shigatsé to Dromo on the Sikkim border, on which he had travelled from the border to Lhasa. Tsarong was convinced that within a year, the Chinese would be able to seal off the entire Tibetan frontier with India with a chain of military bases. He told the Dalai Lama that there was still a small window of opportunity for him to escape from Tibet but was shrinking every passing day.

The Dalai Lama thanked Tsarong for his concern and service to the nation but explained that despite the present misunderstandings and disagreements with the Chinese occupation authority, the best way forward for Tibet was sincere cooperation with China in implementing the provisions of the Seventeen Point Treaty. The Dalai Lama had by now become more than convinced that China and Communism were forces for good.[9]

* * *

---

payment. Leaving behind Lobsang Yeshi as a hostage, the child-incarnate was taken to Lhasa. Lobsang Yeshi eventually escaped from Amdo, but not before making many friends there.

The Dalai Lama's conversion to Marxism, which His Holiness openly espouses to the present day,[10] appears to have been set in motion with the young pontiff's formal visit to China in 1954. As the Chinese controlled the travel arrangement for this trip, they managed, for the first time, to pry the Dalai Lama away from his usual ultra-protective entourage, especially his two spiritual tutors and his Lord Chamberlain, Phala. As mentioned earlier, the collaborator Phüntso Wangye and another senior Communist ideologue, Liu Geping, accompanied the Dalai Lama throughout the visit. Liu instructed the Dalai Lama on the history of the Chinese Communist Party while Phüntso Wangye gave him an abbreviated course on Marxism-Leninism and the Soviet Union's nationality policy. Phüntso Wangye claimed that "The Dalai Lama was very eager to learn about all aspects of Communism, and I think we had an effect on his thinking."[11]

Besides the Dalai Lama's meeting with Chairman Mao and his participation in the National People's Congress and other official functions, he was taken on an extensive tour of China's major industrial cities: Tianjin, Shanghai, Hangzhou, Harbin and Shenyang. The Chinese sought to use this opportunity to impress the Dalai Lama and the high lamas and officials accompanying him, with China's modernization and industrial development. The Tibetans were taken to shipyards, steel mills and factories (even department stores) where, as one young official (a graduate of my school, St. Josephs College) noted in his autobiography, they were told that ". . . all the machinery in the plants had been manufactured by the Chinese themselves, and since most of the Tibetans present could not read English, they didn't doubt it. However, I could read the words 'made in the UK' and 'made in USA' on most machinery."

In fact, most plants and mills in China in 1955 dated back to the Nationalist era, even the Qing period, when following a series of military defeats and concessions to foreign powers, institutional reform was undertaken under the "Self-Strengthening Movement" (1861–1895), and modern shipyards, arsenals, factories and railroads were first established. The new industries in Communist China around the time of the Dalai Lama's visit were largely the product of

Soviet economic and technological aid, on which Communist China was then heavily dependent.

The Tibetan official Rinchen Sadutsang also mentions a tour of an idyllic senior citizens' home with the residents "... enjoying themselves, playing mahjong, cards and other games in a prettily decorated hall. After our visit there, one of our colleagues had to go back to retrieve something he'd left behind and was amazed to find the entire hall empty and deserted. The whole thing had been staged for us!"[12]

This "Potemkin" tour of China's cities that the Dalai Lama and his officials had been taken on, was in fact, a standard visitor indoctrination technique of Communist regimes. Stalin had earlier used it with great success to impress, even astonish, George Bernard Shaw, Nancy (Viscountess) Astor, Theodore Dreiser, H.G. Wells, Lion Feuchtwanger, W.E.B. Du Bois, Pablo Neruda and other unwary travellers to the Soviet Union.

Communist China, in turn, applied the same technique in later decades to great effect, successfully dazzling and befuddling such literary and intellectual luminaries as Jean-Paul Sartre, Simone de Beauvoir, Alberto Moravia, Roland Barthes, Susan Sontag, Edward Friedman, Barbara Tuchman, John King Fairbank and even savvy political figures as Pierre Trudeau, Edward Heath, David Rockefeller and of course Richard Nixon and Henry Kissinger. America's leading liberal economist, diplomat and Kennedy advisor, John Kenneth Galbraith, was "lavish in his praise"[13] of Chairman Mao and the "exquisite" banquets he was served, while touring a country bled white by the Great Famine and the Cultural Revolution.*

The inexperienced nineteen-year-old Dalai Lama, who had never been outside Tibet, was understandably overwhelmed by it all. Mao was particularly attentive and friendly to the Dalai Lama,

---

*To understand why such intellectuals and respected leaders of Western liberal democracies embraced the vision of these 'revolutionary' societies, often in their most repressive historical periods, the reader will be well served by a reading of Simon Leys' brilliant, stiletto-thin pamphlet, *Chinese Shadows*, and also the more academic but no less enlightening *Political Pilgrims* by Professor Paul Hollander.

so much so that His Holiness later told an Indian journalist "Mao was like a father to me."[14] Whenever the Dalai Lama went to visit Chinese cities, all leading officials—the governor, mayor, party chief *et al*, backed by enormous cheering crowds with costumed representatives of minority nationalities in the front, and brass bands and lines of beribboned schoolgirls waving paper flowers and jumping up and down shouting: "Warm Welcome! Warm Welcome! (Chinese, *relie huanying!*)"—would turn out to greet him at the railway station or airport.

One day in a conversation with his two ideological mentors, the Dalai Lama expressed an earnest desire to become a member of the Communist Party.[15] Phüntso Wangye and his colleague Liu Geping realized they had been a little too successful in their indoctrination and, that if it became known to the Tibetan public, there would be a major outcry. With considerable difficulty they persuaded the Dalai Lama to put off his decision and not discuss it with anyone else.

But the Dalai Lama's senior ministers, his two spiritual tutors and the Chamberlain Phala were aware of what was happening to their charge and were deeply troubled. It is possible that the senior minister Surkhang also knew of this problem, as he was close to the junior tutor Trijang Rinpoche, but there was little they could do. The Dalai Lama was no longer in his minority but an enthroned sovereign and doing exceptionally well in his religious studies to a point where he would be ready to take his geshé exams within the next couple of years. Furthermore, the Dalai Lama was strong-willed.

On his return to Lhasa, the Dalai Lama kept up his warm relationship with Mao, corresponding regularly, sending a variety of exotic presents to the Chairman and even penning a lengthy paean "The Timely Rain" (in the somewhat formulaic style of classical *nyenga* poetry) praising Mao's revolutionary accomplishments. This poem was, in later years, used by China's propagandists in the West, one even bringing out a book under that title, with all the verses in English translation.[16] An excerpt:

O! Chairman Mao
Our vast land was burdened with pain, with shackles and darkness.
You liberated all with your brilliance . . .
Your will is like the gathering of clouds, your call like thunder,
From these comes timely rain to nourish selflessly the earth!

But following the Khampa Uprising of 1956, and the brutal Chinese attempts to suppress it, the Dalai Lama's enthusiasm for China and Communism began to waver, and he, once again, began to have doubts about China's actual intentions in Tibet. Then the flood of Khampa refugees to Lhasa, and his own meetings with some of these refugee leaders added to his growing disquiet with his Communist patrons. When he visited India in 1956 and heard the warnings of his former prime minister, Lukhangwa and his two older brothers, he began to hedge his bets. The Dalai Lama appears to have then given some tacit support to the efforts of his Lord Chamberlain, Phala, to contact the resistance and other anti-Chinese groups and establish some covert working relationship with them.

But the fact of his support for Tibetans who opposed China being tacit and secret, and his endorsement of China's policies being open and vocal, only sowed indecision and confusion on the Tibetan side and gave the Chinese time and opportunity to strengthen their hold over the country. The Dalai Lama's balancing act, his policy of not antagonizing China *at all costs,* was essentially one of refusing to face reality. And this reality was becoming ever more irreversible, each passing day.

One refugee leader from the grasslands of Ga Jyekundo, Rada Chemé Yungdung who gained an audience with the Dalai Lama in 1958, described to him in detail the bloody and ferocious conflict that had engulfed his land and the terrible suffering endured by his people at the hand of the Chinese. But the Dalai Lama only remarked, "I am strongly opposed to the force of arms."

Chemé replied, "But your Holiness—you cannot expect my people to do nothing while the Chinese kill our women and children and plunder our monasteries."

Finally, the Dalai Lama said very simply, "There is nothing I can do. I think your people should show a little more tolerance and try to abide by the Seventeen Point Agreement."[17]

In December 1958, the Dalai Lama received an invitation from the Central Committee of the Communist Party to visit Beijing and participate in the Second National People's Congress in the coming spring. "The Dalai Lama readily accepted the invitation."[18] It appears that he may have done this spontaneously without consulting the Kashag or his Lord Chamberlain.

A secret meeting of junior and mid-level Tibetan officials and army officers took place the same month to discuss this disturbing situation. A decision was reached to oppose the visit to China, and an oath was taken to that effect by everyone at the meeting. News of the Dalai Lama's trip to China quickly spread to the public. In addition, an alarming rumour began to circulate that once in Beijing, the Dalai Lama would be held hostage to pressure the Four Rivers Six Ranges, and other resistance forces in Eastern Tibet to surrender. Whether this conclusion was arrived at independently by the public or whether it was part of a strategy formulated by participants of the secret meeting of officials, is not clear.

A day before the Tibetan New Year's Eve, a grand program of Tantric dances and rituals was held at the eastern courtyard (*Deyang Shar*) of the Potala Palace. Of the whole cycle of ceremonies of the Lhasa year, the *Tse Gutor*, is the most deeply charged with mystic—almost sacramental—significance and is intended to purge the accumulated negative influences and misfortune of the past and clear the way for the year to come.

This ceremony was attended by the Dalai Lama, government officials, lamas and everyone of importance in the Holy City. The guests also included the representatives of Nepal, Bhutan, India, and in the past, Britain. This year Guo Xilan, administrative director of the CCP work committee, and General Deng Shaodong, the deputy commander of the Tibet Military Command, attended the ceremony. During a break in the ceremony, the Dalai Lama met the two Chinese leaders and chatted politely with them. General Deng mentioned that a PLA theatrical troupe had just returned from a training course in Beijing and brought a fresh repertoire of performances with it. The Dalai Lama replied that he would like to see this. The newly built auditorium at the Tibet Military Area Headquarters (Chinese, *Junqu Silingbu*) was agreed upon as the venue, though the date for the performance was not decided.

There is considerable disagreement between Tibetan and Chinese accounts of this conversation and its aftermath. PLA Headquarters subsequently made repeated requests to the Dalai Lama to finalize a date for the performance. On 7 March, the Dalai Lama told his senior aide Gadrang to inform the Chinese he would attend the performance three days later on 10 March. Only on the morning of 9 March was the Dalai Lama's visit to the Military Area Headquarters announced to officials gathered at the Norbulingka for the *drung-jha* or the morning tea and roll call.

In their accounts, the minister Ngabö and the commander of the Dalai Lama's personal Guards Regiment, his brother-in-law Phuntsok Tashi Takla, claim that they also heard this news only on the morning of the 9th. A more disturbing coda to this news was that the Chinese military had requested the Dalai Lama not be accompanied by his usual retinue of bodyguards. Another account mentions that the bodyguards were asked to remain at the old stone bridge (*Lubuk Dozam*) a couple of hundred yards north of the outer gate of the Military Area Headquarters.

One of the officials at the morning roll call was the monk official, Bharshi *Tsendron*. Six days earlier, Bharshi and another monk official had consulted the Nechung Oracle and asked what could be done to protect the Dalai Lama and the religion and polity of Tibet. The oracle had made vague rambling pronouncements of prayers-rituals (*shabten*) to be conducted and offerings to be made to the monks of the "Three Seats" (*sendrel sum*). But Bharshi and his friend badgered the oracle for a more assertive and helpful answer till he began "to show signs of irritation." Finally, he came out and said "It is time for the all-knowing Guru *not to venture outside*."[19] This being the prophecy the two officials had wanted, they immediately copied it on

Tibetan paper and had the seal of the Nechung Oracle affixed to it. Bharshi submitted the prophecy to Phala but also made copies and shared them with other officials.

Bharshi's description of these and the subsequent actions he undertook, suggest they were spontaneous and personal. But there are difficulties with accepting his account at face value. First of all, it would be almost impossible for a junior official to obtain a private consultation with the State Oracle, unless someone quite senior had arranged it for him. Secondly, badgering the State Oracle to change or adjust his prophecy is not something that Tibetans are temperamentally capable of doing, unless they have very powerful political or spiritual forces behind them. We also have to ask if the Nechung administrators would have, without high official sanction, put their seal on such an incendiary document that would have gotten them into serious trouble, not only with the *Kashag* (especially the minister Ngabö) but almost certainly with the Chinese Occupation Authority.

A more satisfactory explanation is that Bharshi was the empowered agent of a larger conspiracy of Tibetan political figures using their influence and power to prevent the Dalai Lama from attending the cultural show at the Chinese Military HQ, but also seeking to curtail, possibly even sever, China's growing influence over the young sovereign. Of course, they were not acting to "kidnap the Dalai Lama" as the Chinese premier Zhou Enlai later accused this "reactionary clique of the upper social strata" of doing. But it does appear that this "clique" was somehow able to arrange subsequent events in such a way that— as much as the Dalai Lama desired to continue cooperating with the Chinese authorities—he was, in the following days and weeks, skilfully persuaded, perhaps even coerced, into leaving Lhasa and breaking free of Communist China's psycho-ideological grip over him.

The American academics Ginsburg and Mathos, who published the first study of Tibet under Communist Chinese rule (1950 to 1962) have suggested that Tibetans may have started the March Uprising not only because of their fear that the Dalai Lama was about to be kidnapped, but because of the fear that he would make more concessions to Chinese demands.[20]

This "reactionary clique" was almost certainly led by the Lord Chamberlain Phala, and steadfastly supported by the senior monk official of the Kundeling Monastery, Dzasak Wöser Gyaltsen (Kundeling Dzasak from here on), the commander of the Drapchi Regiment Tashi Palrab, and his officers Captain Kaldam and Major Wangden. This "clique" also involved such officials as Seynang Lobsang Yeshi, Bharshi *Tsendron*, *Khenchung* Tara (Tenzin Chönyi), *Tsedrung* Yeshi Lhundup, *Tseja* Gyaltsen and others. The Dalai Lama's junior tutor Trijang Rinpoche was almost certainly involved, but perhaps in a peripheral and supportive role. Although subsequently the minister Surkhang was denounced by Zhou Enlai as the leading "traitor and reactionary" responsible for the "rebellion" and the "kidnapping" of the Dalai Lama,[21] he may not have been overtly involved in this conspiracy in its early stages. Captain Kaldam told me that the former army commander Lokay-la (Lotö Kalsang) and the finance secretary Tsepön Namseling were active members of the group.

Goldstein is convinced that Namseling (Paljor Jigme) was, after Phala, the principal anti-Chinese conspirator in Lhasa. In volume two of his *History of Modern Tibet*, in a subchapter titled "The Namseling Clique,"[22] Goldstein claims that Namseling, the powerful finance secretary, had organized his "clique" as early as "November 12, 1951, just seventeen days after the first contingent of the PLA Eighteenth Army arrived in Lhasa" and was involved in creating and "instigating" from 1952 onwards, most of the anti-Chinese organizations in Lhasa. He also arranged secret meetings with Gonpo Tashi Andrugtsang and Phala at his own home, where his wife would personally serve tea and refreshments and not allow any servants to enter the room.

Tsering Shakya writes, "It was common knowledge that Namseling was sympathetic to the Khampa cause and had been present during the first meeting held at Gonpo Tashi's house in Lhasa to discuss the formation of the Four Rivers Six Ranges."[23] While the latter claim is uncertain, the "common knowledge" about Namseling's sympathy for Khampas, may have led to him being appointed by the Kashag (with the support of the Chinese) to head a delegation to Lhoka on 4 August 1958, to persuade the Khampas to surrender as ". . . the Chinese felt the

Khampas would listen to someone they trusted." Gonpo Tashi flatly turned down the Kashag's demands. Namseling and the delegation, instead of returning to Lhasa, joined the Resistance.* So Namseling played no further role in planning the Dalai Lama's escape or the March Uprising, though he had, without doubt, been a prime mover of events that led up to this crucial moment in Tibetan history.

In 2017, when I was working on a memorial website[24] and Facebook page[25] for the forgotten heroes of the 10 March uprising, and putting together all the photographic and textual materials, and constructing timelines, drawing maps, etc., it struck me how, in spite of the overwhelming superiority of the Chinese military and their pervasive security apparatus in Lhasa, the events of March 1959 had so "spontaneously" worked out for the Tibetans. The "unplanned" demonstration by the Lhasa public and the subsequent "spur-of-the-moment" efforts by Tibetan officials to spirit the Dalai Lama out of Tibet—which has been the accepted official mythos for so long—requires serious re-evaluation.

Getting back to the events of 9 March. Although the Dalai Lama's senior officials were now gravely concerned about the conditions imposed by the Chinese, the Dalai Lama himself did not take their warnings seriously and insisted he would attend the performance. Bharshi's next move confirms my suspicion that the seemingly independent actions of this junior official were actually sanctioned, if not ordered, by higher authority. In the anteroom of Lord Chamberlain Phala's apartment at the Norbulingka, Bharshi drafted, without any apparent authorization, an official letter addressed to the monastic leaders of Drepung and Sera monasteries calling on them to send their monks to the Norbulingka Palace next morning to pay their respects to the Dalai Lama, as he would be visiting the Chinese Military HQ that day. Bharshi also

---

*Namseling served in the resistance leadership at Lhoka and worked to regularize delivery of supplies to the Force from district officials and started to recruit local Tibetan militias in Lhoka and neighbouring areas. He arranged for Khampa leaders Jhangtsatsang Chonzé, Sandu Lo Nyendrag, and Jhago Namgyal Dorje to travel to Kalimpong to solicit arms and support. This mission was unsuccessful.

surreptitiously took the official seal of the Yiktsang Secretariat (one of the two main departments of the Tibetan government) and used it to authenticate his letter although he had, it would appear, no authority to do so.[26]

Then Bharshi rode out of the Norbulingka gate on a bicycle and headed to the Potala where he met with Captain Kaldam of the Drapchi Regiment, which had a company of soldiers stationed there at the Shöl administration complex below the palace. Captain Kaldam told me of this meeting in a personal interview. "Bharshi *Tsendron* came to the Potala where we were posted and told us that His Holiness was definitely going to the Chinese show the next day. He told me that it had now become a very serious matter, and I should immediately report this to my regimental commander and then inform the leaders of Sera Monastery. He also told me that I should bring as many soldiers as I could to the Norbulingka the next morning but they should be in civilian clothes and not carry weapons. I reported this to my commander General Tashi Palrab. I then went to Sera Monastery and met the abbot Ngawang Legden and also the Sera *Lachi* or monk assembly leader, who agreed to send their monks in the morning."[27]

In the meantime, Bharshi's fellow official Yeshi Lhundup and others had gone around Lhasa city spreading the word that the public should gather before the Norbulingka gate the next morning and petition the Dalai Lama not to attend the show at the Chinese Military HQ. Another official had gone to Drepung Monastery with a copy of Bharshi's letter. The various underground organizations also seem to have been contacted, and their members had diligently propagated the rumour that the Chinese were going to kidnap the Dalai Lama and that a special aircraft, fuelled and ready at Damshung, would fly him away to Beijing.

Early next morning around five o'clock, Captain Kaldam rode on a bicycle from Shöl to the Norbulingka. "Nobody had arrived, and I was worried. But when I rode back to the city and came towards Bhargokaling (*Drago Kani*), the Gateway Stupas, I saw the people from the Shöl neighborhood walking down the road towards the Norbulingka. There were many of them. I quickly went to the Potala and reported this to General Tashi Palrab. We arranged for a contingent of our soldiers to change from their uniforms to civvies, and then we all walked out on the road towards the Norbulingka. It was now crowded with people from the city."

By early morning an enormous crowd had gathered before the main gate of the Norbulingka Palace. Figures vary from the low 2,000 in Chinese reports to a high 30,000 in one Tibetan account. The few photographs we have reveal a huge gathering of perhaps no less than 20,000 people. It was also an angry crowd shouting anti-Chinese slogans. When Tibetan officials began arriving for the morning-tea roll call, the crowd also began shouting insults at them, demanding that they do not sell out the Dalai Lama for Chinese silver. Many in the crowd were brandishing daggers and broadswords.

The Dalai Lama in his first autobiography[28] mentions that at around 9 a.m. two cabinet ministers: assistant minister (*kalön chagrok*) Shengka Gyurme Topgyal and surrogate minister (*katsab*) Liushar Thupten Tharpa, managed to get through the crowd and enter the main Norbulingka gate. These ministers had unthinkingly driven up in their "Chinese army jeeps allotted to all senior officials" and though not seriously manhandled , may have been shoved around a bit by the people. According to Captain Kaldam, Shengka was sweating and breathing hard when he finally got through the Palace gate.

The new minister Sampho arrived next in a car driven by a Chinese chauffeur, which provoked the angry gathering. Sampho had been nominally appointed the deputy commander of the Tibet Area Military Command by the Chinese and had been given a staff car—a swanky Russian Volga (and not a jeep as some accounts have it). People began pelting the car with stones.* The minister got out of the car and was hit on the head with a stone. The crowd then surged forward and overturned the car. Palace guards and bystanders, including Captain Kaldam, managed to rescue the wounded minister and took him to the infirmary at the Indian consulate nearby. The Chinese later moved him to the PLA hospital.

---

*Some footage of the damaged car and also the minister Sampho lying on a Chinese hospital bed with head bandaged, appears in the CPC propaganda film *Putting Down the Rebellion in Tibet* (August 1959).

Another account maintains that the crowd mistook the new minister for the collaborator Ngabö. The Chinese had given Ngabö the first Volga staff car they imported to Lhasa. Soon, that black Volga with its Chinese chauffeur and the jeep escort of armed PLA men became a recognized and despised sight in the city.

On this day, Ngabö had driven up the willow-lined Lhasa-Norbulingka road, but seeing the enormous crowd in front of the main Eastern Gate, had stopped his Volga at the Chango bridge a quarter of a mile before the palace and returned with his escort to the PLA Military Area Headquarters.

When the minister Surkhang saw the crowd from a distance, Noel Barber writes that ". . . he had the intelligence to leave his jeep (near the bridge) and walk to the palace."[29] According to Captain Kaldam, Surkhang did not get flustered and walked slowly through the angry mob with his head bowed and hands held together in supplication, apologizing "*la gondha, la gondha*" At the same time, the press of people around him shouted menacingly, "Do not sell our Dalai Lama for Chinese silver". Surkhang managed to make his way safely into the Norbulingka.

Around 11 o'clock (according to the Dalai Lama), a monk official Phakpala Khenchung, riding a bicycle and wearing goggles and face-mask, and carrying a pistol, was stoned by the crowd and killed. Captain Kaldam maintains that Phakpala panicked when he was surrounded by the crowd and pulled out his pistol. The crowd immediately turned on him with stone, sticks and knives. There is a disturbing photograph of his mutilated body partially hidden by a pair of snow lion statues before the main gate, surrounded by people brandishing daggers and even a hatchet. Some of the people are looking up at the photographer* who evidently took his picture

---

*This photographer was most likely Jigme Taring, who, by his own admission, took many of the photographs of the demonstration and the fighting at the Norbulingka. The public knew him as the Dalai Lama's official photographer. He had earlier shot the colour film of the Dalai Lama's geshe examinations and the New Year and Mönlam Festival. See my post 'The Mystery of the March 10 Photographer' at www.jamyangnorbu.com/ blog/2017/03/08/the-mystery-of-the-march-10-photographer/

from one of the two trapezoid turrets on either side of the main gate, most likely the one on the right. The enraged crowd now started a new chant, demanding to see the Dalai Lama.

Finally, the minister Surkhang appeared and spoke to the public. He most likely stood on the same turret above the statue of the snow-lion, where an hour earlier, the photograph of the battered corpse of Phakpala Khenchung had been taken.

Using a megaphone, Surkhang addressed the crowd. He attempted to reassure everyone gathered there that the Dalai Lama had decided not to attend the Chinese show. He, Surkhang and the other cabinet ministers would immediately proceed to the Military Area Headquarters and let the Chinese leaders know this. But the crowd demanded to see the Dalai Lama in person. Surkhang replied that it was impossible for everyone in the crowd to meet the Dalai Lama, but that the Tibetan government would give its solemn assurance that the Dalai Lama would never set foot in the Chinese Military Headquarters. But the people continued their clamour to see the Dalai Lama, and repeated threats against officials who would sell him to the Chinese.

Whether it was a desperate ploy by the minister to defuse the mob's anger, or an inspired strategy to channel its passion to a useful end will never be known, but Surkhang had a reputation for quick thinking. Liushar recalled Surkhang requesting the crowd to select their own trusted representatives who would be allowed to enter the Norbulingka and present their demands to the government, even to the Dalai Lama himself.[30] The crowd was mollified by Surkhang's concession and quickly went about choosing their representatives. In this interim, Surkhang and the two other ministers drove out of the Norbulingka to the Military Area Headquarters to parlay with the Chinese. The crowd first searched the interior of the car to make sure the Dalai Lama was not being smuggled out.

The people gathered outside the Norbulingka walls soon picked sixty men to represent them. Bharshi, Khenchung Tara and one other official were given the task of vetting the sixty representatives and escorting them through the gates. I obtained some background information and names of eleven of these "People's Representatives" from half-a-dozen sources[31], with some names appearing in multiple accounts. But few as they are, the eleven names reveal an interesting mix of city folk, activists, conspirators, minor functionaries and popular leaders.

Bharshi remembered that the first person to come up to the gate was Manang Abo* (aka Pema Tsewang) son of the chieftain of one of the eighteen tribes of Markham, but now a Lhasa resident and a dapper, well-known man-about-town. He was also a member of an underground organization. Bharshi also remembered another representative, the medic, Amchi Anen-la, a member of the "Mimang", an early underground organization. The most forceful personality and outspoken speaker among the representatives was an old government stable-in-charge (*shöl tatongpa*) Tseten Phuntsok, described as "a man in his forties with light yellow speckled hair (*tra ser-tsup-tsup*) like a caucasian."[32] Following him was a white-haired coracle-supervisor (*kopon nyerpa*) Wangchuk. Then there was Ganden Abra-la, a monk of Ganden Monastery known by his nickname "Abra" or "pika mouse-hare", a monk Tamdrin; another monk and minor official, Ngawang Chöphel, a storeroom clerk from the Potala Palace, and Lhakyap, the steward of a Dalai Lama family (*yabshi dzopa*), who later died of starvation in a *Laogai* camp in China. This same source cited Loyon la (aka Phala Pelgong Chanzoe), a teacher who ran one of the small primary schools in Lhasa, as one of the sixty chosen. He also died in a Chinese *Laogai* camp. People from Chamdo who had gathered at the Norbulingka, chose their own representative, Aukatsang Jampa Kalden.[33] Another Khampa representative was Chime Gyaltsen of the Ledrungtsang family from Markham.

---

* Manang Abo had travelled widely in Asia. During WWII, he was recruited by Japanese intelligence. The sinologist Paul Hyer writes that Abo thought ". . . the Japanese were the best to work with, in view of . . . Tibet's survival in the new world that was emerging." After the war, Abo returned to Lhasa. Subsequently, in exile he fell out with the Dalai Lama's older brother, Gyalo Thondup. He was denounced as a Chinese spy and arrested by the Indian police. He died in 1965 in Calcutta, under distressing circumstances.

In a report by Lhasa carpenter Langdun Gyatso,[34] five representatives were chosen from various craftsmen's guilds for the conference. Bhusang claims that his uncle Nyemo Gyatso was a guild-master of the important Carpenters and Stonemason's guild (*doshing chiba*), and not only attended the conference, but took part in the defence of the Jokhang.

These sixty representatives were allowed to use the ritual prayer hall (*shabten lhakhang*) at the west end of the Norbulingka for their deliberations. From most accounts, it appears that around ten officials—Khenchung Tara, Kundeling Dzasak and others joined the meeting. They advised everyone there not to provoke the Chinese and to speak and act prudently, but the momentousness of that day had stirred the blood of the People's Representatives. They were outspoken in their denunciation of China's military occupation of Tibet and defiantly called for Tibetan independence.

The Dalai Lama, in his biography, mentions that he decided to speak directly to the "people's leaders" and summoned "all seventy of them." He told them that the Chinese had not compelled him to accept the invitation to the show and that he was "not in any fear of personal danger from the Chinese."[35] He also urged them to stop holding these meetings at the Norbulingka, which would only provoke the Chinese further. "They quietly left the meeting and held a conference among themselves by the outer gate of the Palace. They agreed that it was impossible for them to disobey my orders . . . in the end they carried out my wishes to the extent of holding no more meetings within the Norbulingka."

Instead, the People's Representatives relocated to the Shöl hamlet below the Potala. Before leaving, they arranged for armed volunteers from the crowd to defend the Norbulingka in case of any attack by the Chinese. These volunteers dug trenches and erected barricades outside the walls.

The Representatives met at the Shöl hamlet in the Yamantaka Temple (*jig je lhakang*) but were soon joined by more people. The next day they moved to the new Sutra Printing House that had just been built and was large and spacious. The sixty representatives were now joined by some retired senior government officials, monastic officials, regimental commanders, Khampa and Amdowa residents of Lhasa, and even the masters of the professional guilds of masons, wood-workers, metal smiths and artists. It could be said that nearly the whole Tibetan parliament "the National Assembly" (*tsongdu gyenzom*) was now reconstituted here.

One might, in a sense, call this gathering the first democratic parliament of Tibet, a section of it, being popularly elected, albeit in a rough and ready fashion. This gathering called itself the Great Conference of People's Representatives (*Mimang Thunmi Tsokchen*), but the Chinese, in all their subsequent propaganda, referred to it scornfully as the "so-called national conference." Yet in a real sense a revolutionary drama was being played out at this gathering that had a point or two of congruity with the more famous but similarly extempore meeting of the French "third estate" (the non-privileged deputies) at an indoor tennis court at Versailles where the famous oath was taken which launched the French Revolution.

Among the aristocrats and senior government officials now present and some of whom took up leadership roles were former commanders-in-chief (C-in-C) Tsarong Dasang Damdul, Dzasak Lobsang Tsewang Mönkiling, Lotö Kalsang (aka Lokay-la), Dzasak Khemey Sonam Wangdu, and also the retired prime minister Lobsang Tashi and Lhalu the former governor-general of Eastern Tibet. Unfortunately, most of the people's representatives objected to Lhalu's participation in the conference, according to *Military History*.[36] As the government had never released a complete account of the events of October 1950, the public mistakenly regarded Lhalu as culpable as Ngabö for the Chamdo surrender. Lhalu did not raise any objection at the conference and left the hall, but according to the historian Petech ". . . he was prominent among the Tibetan officials who advised resistance against the Chinese."[37] Leaving the conference, Lhalu returned to his mansion from where he "took active part in the Uprising."*

---

* Lhalu's unswerving patriotism is remarkable considering he was the younger son of Tsepon Lungshar, who had been imprisoned and blinded by the Kashag

Tsarong, as the senior-most official, appears to have been acknowledged as the de facto chairman of the conference, but publicly elected leaders as Manang Abo and the old stable-in-charge, Tseten Phuntsok, participated vigorously in the discussions, according to reports. "Speaker after speaker denounced the Chinese and demanded the restoration of Tibet's independence"[38] and the withdrawal of all Chinese troops from Tibet. For good measure, the Seventeen Point Treaty was condemned and repudiated.

A junior official at the meeting remembered that Tseten Phuntsok made this declaration "From today onwards, Tibetans should draw a clear line between themselves and the Chinese." He called on everyone to sign a pledge establishing that they were "tsampa" eaters and that their allegiance was to Tibet, not China. People who signed would have no trouble, he assured the gathering, even if they had worked with the Chinese before. Everyone signed.[39]

With the cooperation of the People's Conference, a historic demonstration by Tibetan women took place on 12 March. Many thousands of Lhasa women first gathered at the open ground just before the Potala called the *Dribu Yukhai Thang* (where government barley was dried and threshed). Many speeches were given, and the gathering prayed for the long life of the Dalai Lama. A resolution was passed declaring that Tibetans were the rightful owners of Tibet (*bhö kyi dakpo bhödme ray*) that the Chinese must leave Tibet (*gyamar bhö ney cheten jhegö*) and that Tibet was a fully independent nation (*bhö rangzen tsangma yin*). The gathering ended with a prayer for the long life of the Dalai Lama.

The women performed a Sacred Smoke Offering (*sangsöl*) ceremony and raised prayer flags. They then marched in a procession all over the city, chanting the three demands of the resolution. One report mentions that ". . . they burnt the Chinese flag and an effigy of Mao." Another added that there were ". . . many anti-Chinese posters" stuck

---

for a failed conspiracy. The young Lungshar Tsewang Dorje was adopted by the senior Lady Lhalu (Tsepon Lungshar's paramour) and made the head of the illustrious Lhalu house, as it had no male heir to carry on the family line.

on the walls of the Barkhor. The same source writes, "It was frightening to walk through the Barkhor, where the Chinese soldiers with machine guns were watching us from the roofs." The Chinese also threatened the demonstrators "through microphones saying that if all Tibetans did not surrender, Lhasa would be shelled."[40] The demonstrators stopped before the Indian[*41] and Nepalese Consulates and the residence of the Bhutanese representative and submitted written petitions calling on these friendly neighbouring states to support the Tibetan cause and publicize the plight of the Tibetan people to the world. Another report mentions that demonstrations were also held on subsequent days.

One leader of the gathering was a senior nun of the Galingshar nunnery in North Lhasa, whose actual name is not known but who was respectfully addressed as Galingshar Chöla. She was arrested after the Uprising. A joint statement by two eyewitnesses in 1961, describes her fate. "On October 21, 1959, a 60-year-old nun named Gyanisha (Galingshar) Anila was taken around the Barkhor in Lhasa. The Chinese ordered the people to beat her, but no one would do so. Then the Chinese gathered some thieves and beggars, gave them some money and had them beat her at her house in Tsoksya Khangsar. They pulled her ears and nose and kicked her in the face. She died on the 31st of the same month [October]."[42]

We have more information on the other leader, popularly known as "*Pamo*" (heroine) Kunsang, who was a niece of Tsarong Dasang

---

[*]India's Consul General J.N.Chibber, "one of the few 'neutral' eyewitnesses" in Lhasa, sent a stream of radio reports to Delhi on the course of the Uprising. He is clear that the revolt was a popular one with the support of " . . . almost 99% of the Tibetans who do not want Chinese rule, though many were leading hard lives under the feudal system." He reported intense artillery shelling (and automatic weapons fire) for four days, "starting on March 20 at 1:50 am that continued till March 23", damaging the Potala, Shöl, Norbulingka, Jokhang and many other structures. His conclusion: "Unless something extraordinary happens . . . the Chinese will go forward with their policy of annihilating the Tibetan race." Chibber's reports appear to have been overlooked at Delhi, and none of his information ever made public. See Claude Arpi, *The End of An Era, India Exits Tibet – India Tibet Relations 1947-1962*, Part 4, (New Delhi: Vij Book India, 2020).

Damdul and married to Gurteng Lobsang Tashi, a senior steward (*dechang*) of the Kundeling monastery. I have a damp-damaged photograph of a handsome woman in her forties. She had one daughter, Tseten Yangkyi, who I interviewed in 1984. Tseten was six when she was arrested with her mother after the Uprising and locked up in the central prison at the headquarters of the Tibet Military District (*Junqu Silingbu*). After her arrest, Kunsang-la kept up her defiance in jail and refused to make a confession or collaborate with her Chinese captors in any way. She was transferred to Drapchi prison in December 1964 and in November 1970 executed by firing squad with fifteen (or twenty) other prisoners at the Dodé execution ground near Sera Monastery. Her body was buried in a shallow unmarked grave.[43]

Of the many women who took part in the great demonstration, I managed to unearth only eighteen names.[44] As few as they are, they are enough to give one a sense of the solid plebeian background of these women: housewives, shopkeepers, stallholders, perhaps a *chang* brewer and seller (*ama changma*) and almost certainly one nanny (*meme-la*). Some of their names: Lhoka Tamdrin Tsomo (imprisoned and executed), Pekong Penpa Dolma-la (leader, executed), Tawutsang Dolkar-la, Demo Chime, Tsokhang Meme-la, Kukarshar Kalsang-la, Rizur Yangchen-la, Tsokhang Tsam-la and Lhamotsang Dolma Choezom, whose biography[45] was published in 2001. This biography provides us with four more names: two ladies, Sholshar Chamkushog and Shidroghang Cham, and two housekeepers, Liushar *khangnyer* Tsering Dolma and Rampa *khangnyer* Tseten. Noel Barber was told of a tall, good-looking Lhasa woman Tsering Dolma, twenty-one years of age, who took a leading role in the event. Sampho Ngodup Wangmo, the wife of an aristocrat, told me that she had been at the gathering below the Potala and remembered another nun, obviously a leader, who addressed the crowd, but could not recall her name. The Norwegian academic Hanna Havnevik mentions a nun, Tsangkhung Ani Yonten, as one of those heading the demonstration.[46]

Back at the Norbulingka Palace, the Dalai Lama was still hopeful of convincing the Chinese of his desire to cooperate. He wrote three letters[47] to General Tan Guansan that the Dalai Lama admits the

Chinese later published ". . . to prove that I wanted to seek shelter in the Chinese headquarters, but was kept under duress in the Norbulingka by what they called a 'reactionary clique' and finally abducted out of the country to India against my will."

The tone and phrasing of the letters did perhaps convince the Chinese that the Dalai Lama was being held at the Norbulingka against his will. In his first letter (11 March), the Dalai Lama describes his ". . . indescribable shame" at the behavior of his people, instigated by ". . . reactionary evil elements carrying out activities endangering me under the pretext of my safety." In his next letter (12 March) he writes that he ordered the "immediate dissolution of the illegal people's conference" and the ". . . immediate withdrawal of the reactionaries who arrogantly moved into the Norbulingka under the pretext of protecting me." He concludes his third letter (16 March) with a sentence that is somewhat uncomfortable to read, even if one might not disagree with the Dalai Lama's covert purpose. "A few days from now when there are enough forces I can trust, I shall make my way in secret to the Military Area Headquarters."

The Dalai Lama says he wrote these letters "to gain time." Barber agrees. ". . . the whole of this curious correspondence was in fact a ruse to hoodwink the Chinese."[48] The ruse worked because the Chinese were convinced that the Dalai Lama genuinely wanted to cooperate with them in implementing "Democratic Reforms" and "Socialist Transformation" in Tibet, and had no intention of leaving, much less fleeing Tibet.

This was the impossible situation the Lord Chamberlain Phala had to deal with in his surreptitious but so far unsuccessful manoeuvring to limit if not prevent Chinese influence from completely captivating the Dalai Lama. Now the physical blockade of the Norbulingka by the Lhasa public provided him much-needed respite. It also gave him an opportunity to obtain official cabinet approval for his plans. Earlier, Phala had been unable to even open a discussion with the Kashag on this matter, because of Ngabö's baleful presence in that executive body. Ngabö effectively controlled the Kashag's deliberations, playing on the fears of the new inexperienced minister, Sampho, and the accommodating minister Shengka, who Goldstein maintains was "closely associated with Ngabö."[49] But now, with Ngabö incommunicado at the Chinese Military Area Headquarters and a working majority of the Kashag members "trapped" within the walls of the Norbulingka, Phala finally had the upper hand.

The Lord Chamberlain had earlier only confided his plans to Surkhang, but now he laid it out before the other Kashag ministers and requested their support. According to the Chinese academic, Jianglin Li, who has published the most recent work[*] on the Lhasa Uprising ". . . the cabinet ministers adopted a contingency plan: to take the Dalai Lama across the Tsangpo River into the zone controlled by Chushi Gangdruk Defenders of the Faith (Four Rivers Six Ranges) and then try and negotiate with the Chinese government from there. The cabinet authorized Phala to take care of the details, *but the arrangements were kept secret from the Dalai Lama for days.*"[50]

On the whole, it is surprising how Phala managed to maintain the secrecy that he did about his plans. Following the lead of the Dalai Lama, some within Tibetan officialdom believed that China's "reform" policies in Tibet were genuine and had begun to cooperate with the occupation authorities. For Phala, one of the more problematic of such officials was Gyamtsoling, an incarnate lama and the Dalai Lama's debating partner, who General Tan Guansan and Ngabö were using as a courier to communicate with the Dalai Lama. Eventually, Phala found a way to neutralize him. Returning from his last trip to Chinese Headquarters, he was manhandled and threatened by the crowd outside the Norbulingka. Phala sent his men to rescue the lama and then had him thoroughly searched. Hidden within the recess of his *chablu*, the decorative bag (to carry a water filter and bottle) customarily worn by high lamas, Tan Guansan's reply to the Dalai Lama was discovered. Phala advised Gyamtsoling to lie low in a room at the Palace till the

---

[*] *Tibet in Agony: Lhasa 1959* (2016). This book is useful for the Chinese reports and accounts that previous works lacked. Li has also interviewed a number of Tibetan participants in the Uprising, mostly junior officials.

furore abated and placed a guard at the door. Gyamtsoling later told the Chinese he was held as a virtual prisoner and "repeatedly threatened."[51]

But Phala's security precautions extended beyond the obvious. Some officials who could in no way be considered Chinese collaborators, but who had spouses or relatives with work-related or social connections to the Chinese, were tactfully excluded from any deliberations. For instance, the Dalai Lama's photographer Dzasak Jigme Taring, inside the Norbulingka, was kept ignorant of the planning and arrangements for the escape. He was trustworthy and would have been invaluable on the flight to India as he was the only official at the Norbulingka who spoke fluent English. He was also a senior military officer trained by the British at Quetta and an amateur cartographer. He was furthermore a prince of Sikkim and had valuable connections in India. But he was married to Rinchen Dolma Taring (née Tsarong), who was friendly with many Chinese officials and was herself a vice-chairman of the Patriotic Women's Association, a Chinese Communist organization.

The actual Chairperson of the Patriotic Women's Association was the Dalai Lama's older sister, Tsering Dolma. She was close to the Chinese authorities and openly opposed to her brother Taktser Rinpoche and Gyalo Thondup, for their hostility to Chinese rule in Tibet and their efforts to seek American aid for the resistance. Gyalo Thondup in his memoir[52] mentions, somewhat contemptuously, that she and her husband, Phuntsok Tashi Takla, were both on the Chinese payroll and paid "seven hundred silver dollars a month each."

Unfortunately for Phala, Phuntsok Tashi Takla was the commander of the Guards Regiment at the Norbulingka. He was popular with Chinese officials because he spoke Chinese (his Chinese name was Huang Guozhen) and, at least on one occasion, took their side in a dispute with Tibetan officialdom. When the Chinese wanted all Tibetan soldiers to wear the PLA uniform, and the Tibetan soldiers and officers refused, Takla ordered the Guards Regiment to change from their British style uniforms to the PLA one. A photograph of Takla in full PLA (then Soviet-style) senior officer's uniform with shoulder boards, collar insignia and visor-peaked hat with the Communist star, appears in his memoirs of 1995.[53]

The Dalai Lama was fond of his brother-in-law, Takla, and trusted him, so it was out of the question for him to be completely sidelined from the deliberations. But Phala only let Takla into the planning in its last stage and arranged matters in such a way that Takla and his Guards Regiment were only charged with the security arrangements within the walls of the Norbulingka palace but excluded from the actual planning and execution of the escape itself. Only one company of Guardsmen under an officer (personally trusted by Phala), Major Sonam Tashi, was used as a rear guard for the escape, and orders were only given to the Major at 8 p.m. on the night of the escape itself.[54] The other Guards officer, Major Sekshing Lobsang Thondup, was left behind to command the remaining soldiers defending the Norbulingka. The military component of Phala's escape plan was entrusted primarily to the Drapchi Regiment, based just north of Lhasa. The Drapchi commander Tashi Palrab and two of his officers, Captain Kaldam and Major Wangden, had earlier been charged by Phala to maintain communications with Andrugstang Gonpo Tashi and the Resistance Force, and also with the CIA agents Athar and Lotse. The Drapchi Regiment was openly hostile to the Chinese and had been involved in a near-violent confrontation with the PLA in 1954, over the shooting of a Norbulingka groom.

Phala also made sure that most discussions and planning took place at the nearby Kundeling Monastery, east of the Norbulingka.

The senior manager of the Monastery, Dzasak Wöser Gyaltsen (aka Kundeling Dzasak), was a staunch patriot and a steadfast Phala man. He was entrusted with making the physical arrangements: horses, mules, bedding and supplies for the escape. Phala made sure that no unusual activity of any kind took place within the Norbulingka compound that might pique the curiosity of any possible Chinese informer inside, or even the armed Tibetan defenders now patrolling the walls. There was also the Qinghai–Tibet Highway Depot* (and

---

*The depot occupied the area of Kyangthang Nakha (Wild Ass Meadow) that in the pre-invasion years served as the caravanserai for the trains of Bactrian camels from Khotan and Kashgar.

Administration Bureau) a stone's throw away, north of the Norbulingka. This depot was guarded and fortified, and from its rooftop, you could check on the coming and goings at the Norbulingka with a pair of binoculars.

Kundeling Dzasak took the additional precaution of making his preparations for the Dalai Lama's travel not at the Kundeling Monastery itself, which was close to the city and visited by pilgrims and sightseers. Instead, he set up his base for this undertaking at Tsagur, an isolated country farm the monastery owned, south of the Kyichu River and away from curious eyes. Horses and pack animals were slowly and secretly collected at the country estate. Fresh tsampa was milled, and butter, dry cheese, yak jerky and other supplies were bagged for the journey. Even provisions for the Dalai Lama himself were prepared at the country estate, and nothing was taken from the Norbulingka storerooms or kitchens.

Another meeting was held at the Kundeling Monastery to organize armed escorts, and work out the escape route and contacts with the Resistance. Captain Kaldam described it to me in his interview. "Kundeling Dzasak, our commander Tashi Palrab, some officers of the Drapchi Regiment including myself met at the Kundeling Monastery at the Dzasak's apartment. We were all sworn to secrecy, and we were told that His Holiness would leave the Norbulingka very soon. I was ordered to go to Nyetang* and find the official Seynang Lobsang Yeshi and his militiamen and deliver a message to him.

"I rode out with Major Wangden who had been instructed to make a secret survey of the first stage of the escape route, from Norbulingka to the Ramagang ferry, across the Kyichu River and then about forty-five miles south-east to the Namgyal Gang (or Segang) village that we wanted to use as the first staging point. A recent report had mentioned

---

* Atiśa Dipankara of Bengal, one of the greatest figures in the history of Tibetan Buddhism, died at Nyetang in 1054. His tomb at the village was desecrated during the Cultural Revolution. Beijing presented some remains from the mausoleum to Bangladesh in 1978 as a belated gesture of friendship. China, supporting Pakistan, had vehemently opposed the creation of Bangladesh and its membership in the UN.

that around a hundred Chinese soldiers were posted there. The major was to offer tea to the monks at a cloister in the village, make inquiries and carefully study the situation. When we got to Namgyal Gang, we were told that the Chinese soldiers had returned to their main encampment at Nortölingka [between Norbulingka and Drepung Monastery] the previous night. This was good news, as otherwise, we would have had to use a longer alternate route across the mountains. The dharma protectors (*chökyong*) were doing their work. I was light-hearted when I re-crossed the river a little further south and rode on to Nyetang.

"When I got to Nyetang, I met the official Lobsang Yeshi and gave him the message from Chamberlain Phala, which instructed Lobsang Yeshi to make contact with the Resistance and arrange for an armed escort to be ready in a few days. Lobsang Yeshi told me that he had already contacted a resistance unit at the Tsadzong Drukha ferry point in Gongkar district. They had a hundred and fifty fighters there, under the command of Dewatsang Kunga Samten of Lithang. Lobsang Yeshi said that he had good relations with Dewatsang and could arrange for him to provide a substantial escort in addition to the forty fighters Lobsang Yeshi had with him at Nyetang. I also gave him a sealed message he was to forward to Resistance Headquarters. This message contained instructions for the two radio operators, Athar and Lotse, to rendezvous with the Dalai Lama's escape party at Lhoka.

"I noticed some of Lobsang Yeshi's men gambling* outside the room. They were not regular soldiers but Lhasa toughs, and I suppose I was unfair, but I felt it was regrettable that at such a moment of terrible upheaval in our country, they should be playing cards and fooling around. I mentioned this to Lobsang Yeshi and asked him to have his

---

*One of the militiamen, Samdup, was a Drepung *dob-dob* originally from Amdo. In exile he ran a three-table eatery at McLeod Ganj. Hippies dubbed it "Crazy Horse's Noodle Palace" as he yelled and gesticulated wildly at them when they lounged overlong in his tiny restaurant, drinking tea and smoking *ganja*. On the other hand, he never failed to serve his customers heaped bowls of steaming hot delicious *bhöthuk*, or Tibetan ramen, and extended generous credit to those of us working on a tiny salary for the exile government.

men patrol the motor road from Nyetang to Chushül and check on Chinese troop movements. He laughed and assured me it would be done. "They don't have the discipline and drill of your Drapchi soldiers, but they are brave men and will not hesitate to do as I tell them. We will be there at the ferry crossing (*dru-kha*) when we get your message."

26

CROSSING THE RIVER OF HAPPINESS

As tension mounted in the following days, the discussions at the Conference of People's Representatives (*Mimang Thunmi Tsokchen*) shifted from political declarations to somber deliberations on what actually should be done if the Chinese attacked the Norbulingka, or fighting broke out in the city. Former commanders-in-chief Tsarong and Lokay-la appear to have been closely involved in the military planning, while the other former commanders-in-chief Khemey (who had no actual military experience) and Mönkiling served as liaisons between the conference and the Norbulingka Palace. Fortunately for the conference, the Tibetan Army headquarters and its principal weapons depot were located within the Shöl administrative complex—which simplified matters.

The conference issued orders that all Tibetan soldiers and policemen in the city, armed with only the standard issue Lee Enfield rifle each and fifty rounds of ammunition, should be issued new rifles, more ammunition, and more powerful weapons. Bhusang told me that his commander General Jumpa and Major Gura attended many secret meetings of army officers and officials, and received instructions to collect weapons and ammunition from the Shöl armoury.

"We were instructed to keep this operation secret. We went to the Army headquarters late at night. My company of one hundred policemen were issued eight Bren light machine-guns, about sixteen Sten submachine guns, also eight 2-inch mortars, two 3-inch mortars and one artillery piece—a howitzer.* We got about fifty boxes of shells for the 3-inch mortar, some more for the 2-inch mortars, and many boxes of hand grenades. We were also issued brand-new Enfield rifles and replacements for the damaged rifles we had. There was an amazing amount of ordnance stored in the Shöl Army HQ. I had never seen anything like it in my life. We had three horse-drawn carts to carry the stuff from Shöl to Police headquarters at Tromsikhang. It took us four trips. We covered the carts with old tents so nobody could see the stuff we were hauling away."

All the other regiments received their share of Enfield rifles, Bren guns, mortars and even howitzers. Rifles were also distributed to the civilian volunteers defending the Norbulingka, and also to the populace of the Shöl hamlet where the People's Conference was meeting. Unfortunately, these weapons were not distributed early enough to the population at large of the city, or the Sera, Drepung and Ganden monasteries. Only after the actual fighting started was some effort made to do this, but it was much too late. In fact, many civilians were killed trying to get to Shöl from the city to obtain weapons. Perhaps there was confusion within officialdom, and orders from the People's Conference did not carry the same authority with some of the storekeepers and functionaries that it should have. Bhusang remembers the reluctance of one storeroom clerk to let the soldiers and volunteers have weapons.

"Back at our own barracks, secret training was immediately started for operating the mortars and the howitzers. We had very good

---

*These were all British BL (breech-loading) 2.75-inch mountain guns. Tibetans probably had fifteen or twenty of these howitzers. The Chinese claim that the Tibetans had thirty mountain guns.

instructors. As I told you earlier, the Lhasa police force had been an artillery regiment before it was converted to police duty in 1948. The principal instructors were Sergeant Sonam Wangdu and Sergeant Tsegya Bhagtro. Our major Rinzin Paljor [aka Rupön Gura] was also a skilled gunner, as he proved to everyone in Lhasa when the fighting started. We also had other instructors for the Bren guns—in all, about twenty instructors. Training took place at night. We couldn't fire live rounds, of course—just dry firing. Our instructors also had to go to other regiments to train them to use the howitzers and mortars, but mostly it was refresher training as all regiments already had some training with these weapons."

The Guards Regiment was assigned to be the principal defenders of the Norbulingka and defend the palace from within the outer walls. The volunteers from the Lhasa public occupied the trenches and barricades immediately outside the walls. Some of them were Khampa residents of the city, merchants and the like, and a few refugees from Eastern Tibet. There were no resistance fighters from the Four Rivers Six Ranges in the Lhasa uprising, as a some accounts have concluded.

The Norbulingka defences were also reinforced by a few hundred Gyantsé Regiment troops. One company was posted at the Gyatso Tö compound (the summer home of the Dalai Lama's family) close to the fortified Qinghai–Tibet Highway Depot, directly north of the Norbulingka, which posed an immediate threat to the Summer Palace. The other Gyantsé Company was posted at Zaralingka Park just north-east of Norbulingka, and covered the road to Lhasa. A third Gyantsé Company was posted at the Shöl hamlet.

The Drapchi Regiment was given the task of defending the Potala Palace, the Shöl hamlet below it and the Chakpori or Iron Mountain, where the Old Medical College was located. This was an important position as the hill overlooked the Norbulingka and the Chinese military camp at Shugtri Lingka Park immediately south of the Shöl, and the Autonomous Region Compound.

Four, perhaps five howitzers* had been dragged up to the Chakpori and set up there. These mountain guns could be disassembled and carried in pieces on mules. On the south-east slope of the Iron Hill just above the Gateway Stupa, was the Ghomzö Dorjeling (or Zeykhang Dorjeling), the main ordnance depot of the Tibetan army—guarded by fifty Drapchi soldiers. A contingent of Drapchi soldiers was left to guard its own base at the Drapchi district, which was directly across from a Chinese military camp separated by the road running due north from Lhasa to Sera Monastery. This small force was later reinforced with monks from Sera Monastery. They also had one howitzer.

Since it was their regular beat, the Police Regiment was entrusted to defend central Lhasa, especially the Jokhang temple and the Tsuglakhang complex enclosing it, which housed government offices and storehouses. Police headquarters and barracks were located at the old Tromsikhang Mansion directly across the north Barkhor road from the Nangtseshag City Court. In previous centuries this historic building had been the residence of the Sixth Dalai Lama, and later the Mongol ruler Lhazang Khan.

A police company under Captain Tsering Lhagyal was charged with defending the Ramoche temple in northern Lhasa, the second most sacred temple in Lhasa after the Jokhang. This temple was first built in the sixth century by Princess Wencheng, the Chinese consort of Emperor Songtsen Gampo. The statue of the Buddha Akshobhya Vajra (*Jowo Mikyö Dorje*), part of the dowry of Bhrikuti, the Nepalese Queen, was subsequently placed there. This temple was used in later times as the main assembly hall of the Upper Tantric College (Gyutö). In south-eastern Lhasa, at the Thaypungkhang police station, a force of sixty policemen was posted as well as a small contingent at Kongpo Drukhang further south.

The following is a breakdown of Chinese military camps and garrisons in and around Lhasa city based primarily on the information provided by the Chinese Colonel Gya Lobsang Tashi to Captain

---

*Noel Barber was told there were five guns on Chakpori. His informant had a record of the engagement and described it to the author.

Kaldam and the Drapchi commander. The Chinese Colonel had been careful to note the locations and strength of the PLA artillery batteries. The regimental identification numbers have been taken from other Chinese sources. The commonly used names for these places have been given first, followed by the official designations and brief descriptions.

SILINGBU or Tibet Military Area Headquarters (*Junqu Silingbu*). This large fortress complex was surrounded by high walls and towers occupied by guards with machine guns and garrisoned by a full PLA regiment. Within the outer walls was the main central prison surrounded by its own high walls and guard towers. This fortress was just outside the city limits and due south of the Jokhang Temple. To get to its main northern gate, one had to cross an irrigation canal over which stood an old stone bridge (*Lubuk Dozam*) where the Chinese had insisted that the Dalai Lama's guards would have to remain when His Holiness was to attend the show at Silingbu. This fortress was just north of the Kyichu River. The area was formerly a park, Gyawu Lingka or "bearded park", perhaps as it had been covered with thick groves of willow trees then.

MAGAR SARPA New Military Camp was just north of and adjacent to the Silingbu HQ. This cantonment was created in the late forties by the Tibetan government when new regiments were being raised in response to the Chinese invasion threat. Reginald Fox trained his radio operators here, and Radio Lhasa broadcasted from this camp. The camp was requisitioned by the Chinese occupation authority in 1953, and in 1959 appears to have at least one PLA regiment stationed there with heavy artillery and mortar batteries. The camp was tasked with shelling Chakpori Mountain and the Potala.

NORTÖLINGKA,* the stretch of grassland below Drepung Monastery extending as far west as the village of Shing Dongkar was a large encampment of PLA infantry, transport units, and the PLA August First Farm. The PLA Artillery Regiment 155 was also based

---

*The first international soccer match in Tibet took place in 1936 at Nortölingka between the visiting British Political Mission team and the Lhasa United team of Nepali, Sikkimese, Kashmiri (Muslim) and Tibetan players.

here. Nortölingka was renamed "Heroes National Park" sometime after the uprising and had its own Revolutionary Heroes Cemetery where most of the Chinese soldiers killed in the uprising were buried. Much of the shelling of Norbulingka came from artillery batteries in this camp, and perhaps also from Dongkar.

DONGKAR OR SHING-DONGKAR was a village just west of Nortölingka. It was the last village before Lhasa on the main western road to the city. North of this village, on the mountainside contiguous to Drepung Monastery, were the ruins of the old Dongkar castle. A couple of informants told me that the Chinese had a large artillery regiment garrisoned at Dongkar, that fired on the Norbulingka.

KYANGTHANG NAKHA (Wild Ass Meadow): this area was just north of the Norbulingka palace. The Qinghai–Tibet Highway Depot (and Administration Bureau) was located here. The whole compound was fortified and guarded by a garrison of battalion strength, with a mortar battery. According to Chinese accounts, it was first attacked on the night of 19 March. Tibetan mortar shells heavily damaged the building in the subsequent fighting. The initial mortar rounds landing in the Norbulingka pond appear to have been fired from this compound.

RANGKYONGJONG, the Tibet Autonomous Region Compound was just north of the Kyichu River. Inside its walls were offices, living quarters and the People's Cultural Palace (*mimang tsokhang*). The compound was walled and was securely defended by a battalion of infantry and mortar batteries—perhaps even some artillery. To its immediate west was Shugtri Lingka.

SHUGTRI LINGKA or Throne Park was a large wooded park with a stone platform or "throne" from which the Seventh Dalai Lama had given teachings. A small herd of deer survived in this park till the turn of the last century. It appears that around the end of 1958, the PLA had gone about quietly setting up a large military camp in this bucolic park. Many in the Lhasa public were unaware of this since no high walls and buildings had been erected, and the soldiers were living in tents spread out through the forest. Nonetheless, from later accounts, it appears that the PLA regiment #159, based here, had mortar batteries and even heavy artillery pieces hidden under camouflage netting, according to Noel Barber.[1]

LINGKA SARPA, or "New Park", was to the east of Lhasa outside the Lingkor circuit. A PLA artillery regiment was based here. It was earlier commanded by the Chinese Colonel, Jiang Heting. Before the invasion, it was the base camp of the Third Shigatsé (*ghadang*) Regiment that had been defeated at Chamdo in 1950 and disbanded. The first Chinese regiment to arrive in Lhasa was quartered at Lingka Sarpa. Chinese Artillery fire from this camp appears to have been largely directed at positions within the city itself, especially at the Tromsikhang police barracks and the Ramoche Temple and surroundings.

JIAOCHANG (Drapchi area): this was the old barracks and parade ground of the Manchu garrison in Lhasa before 1911. It was located north of Lhasa on the road to Sera Monastery and Phembo. In 1959 this camp was occupied by a PLA infantry battalion and an artillery battery. The PLA camp was located east of the Lhasa–Sera Road. West of the road was the regimental base camp of the Second or Drapchi Regiment, named after the area where it was based. During the uprising, most of the Tibetan soldiers from Drapchi left to defend the Potala and the Chakpori, and only a company of soldiers were left to fight the PLA battalion across the road. The Chinese artillery battery here not only fired on the Drapchi military camp but also on Sera Monastery.

DRIP, a major Chinese military base south of the Kyichu River across the main Kuru Bridge, next to the Drip Tsecholing Monastery. The PLA artillery regiment #308 was based here and was responsible for shelling the Potala Palace, Chakpori Mountain and other areas in the city.

PEDING was formerly a village fifteen kilometres east from Lhasa across Kuru Bridge on the Sichuan–Tibet Highway. This was the principal PLA supply and storage depot for all military supplies being hauled from China, and a base for troop reinforcements, artillery, transport, etc.

YUTHOK: the fighting within the city, especially around the Barkhor circuit, appears to have been directed from the command post at Yuthok house to the west of the Jokhang Temple. Earlier this was the residence of the junior Kashag minister Yuthok, who in 1956 protested Chinese interference in Tibetan government affairs and remained in India. Yuthok house was rebuilt and named "Representative Building". It was the office of the CCP Tibet Work Committee.

The Chinese also began fortifying the buildings in central Lhasa where they had their various administrative offices, and were most vulnerable to attacks. Within the Barkhor was the People's Bank of China at Kyetöpa house, the Public Security Bureau HQ at Surkhang House and trade and administrative offices at Pangdatsang House and Sampho House. The Second Battalion of PLA Regiment #159 was posted to protect the Chinese Muslim community and its school and mosque at the Wabaling suburb east of the city, close to the Tibetan police station at Thaypungkhang. The large Chinese Hospital between the city and the Potala palace was also fortified and heavily guarded by armed troops. Tethong House at Banakshöl was now the office of the *Tibet Daily*, while Zumphü Mansion in Northern Lhasa was the main Chinese Police HQ. The roofs of these buildings were lined with sandbags and protected by machine-gun emplacements.

All these buildings were guarded not only by regular PLA troops but also the Chinese Lhasa Militia. The PLA Tibet Military Command established a Lhasa militia on 8 November 1958, ". . . some of them PLA veterans recruited from Chinese-run shops, post offices, banks and the newspaper offices."[2] These were organized into fighting units and equipped with rifles, submachine guns, hand grenades and even mortars and machine guns.

Tension mounted as warlike preparations on both sides increased, and random gunfire could be heard throughout the city, especially at night. Chinese troop movement increased, and their signals personnel were kept busy repairing and stringing new telephone wires that Tibetans cut down during the night.

A Chinese journalist in Lhasa, Shan Chao, wrote that the "rebels" were taking up positions on Yaowang Hill (Chakpori) and hauling artillery and ammunition. He added somewhat lyrically "The windowsills of the innumerable windows of the Potala, usually a favourite playground of doves, now had rifle barrels glinting from them."[3] Shan Chao accompanied Chinese officers in a convoy of three armoured cars on Monday the 16th to survey the trenches and fortifications the "rebels" were building at the northern end of the Norbulingka. He mentions that a cameraman from the propaganda department recorded the scene on film, from a distance. The Chinese also drove around the city, making on-site measurements of Tibetan buildings and positions. On the pretext of repairing their vehicles, they stopped before these sites and ". . . obtained precise measurements of every spot in Lhasa within our firing range."[4]

A Lhasa resident wrote: "By night, the noise and electric lights of the soldiers and military transport vehicles could be heard and seen in the streets and from the army bases, terrifying the people of Lhasa."[5] The minister Ngabö in a message to the Kashag, mentioned that from his mansion near the Drungchi Lingka (the lay officials park) and close to main Kuru Bridge, he could hear the rumbling of transport vehicles day and night. These trucks were almost certainly coming from Peding, the main PLA supply depot and base for reinforcements. Ngabö warned the Kashag not to contemplate any resistance ". . . as the outcome was predetermined." The Kashag had already sent a message to Ngabö informing him that the Dalai Lama had instructed the People's Representatives not to meet at the Norbulingka and that the ministers were doing everything they could to stabilize the situation. Ngabö sent a brief reply of approval and said he would send a detailed response in a day or two.

On the afternoon of Tuesday, 17 March, the Dalai Lama was discussing Ngabö's reply with his cabinet ministers when around 4 p.m. ". . . we heard the boom of two heavy mortar shells fired from a nearby Chinese camp. And we also heard the splash of the shells in a marsh outside the northern gate."

This claim by the Dalai Lama, which he made in his first international press conference after his arrival in India, was disputed by China's Xinhua News agency as ". . . a brazen outright fabrication." But in 1991 an official Chinese account (*Xizang gemingshi*) ". . . while alleging that the Tibetans had initiated the conflict, acknowledged for the first time that two shells had indeed been fired: it also revealed that they were fired by Chinese militiamen who did so without permission."[6] Subsequent Chinese accounts (1993 and 1995) support this with some variations.

The minister Surkhang in an interview, said he realized that the mortar shell explosions would provoke the Tibetan crowd outside the walls ". . . and anything could happen. Running into the garden (and puffing slightly), he reached the main gates—just in time. Several Tibetan soldiers armed with submachine guns wanted to lead the crowd in an attack on the Chinese. He ordered the troops to return to their barracks, and not until he was convinced that they had abandoned their plan, did he return to the palace."[7]

Alarming as it may have been for the Tibetan officials, the two mortar shells enabled Phala and Surkhang to convince the Dalai Lama that he had to leave the Norbulingka. The People's Conference liaisons also added their voices. The Dalai Lama writes in his memoirs that he consulted "the popular leaders" and "begged them not to open fire unless they were attacked." He hoped that as soon as he was gone, the situation would be defused. "Phala may have helped the Dalai Lama make his decision less agonizing by pointing out that if he insisted on remaining, the crowds would also remain, and would be massacred, whereas when they learned of his escape, they would certainly disperse, and many lives would be saved."[8]

There appears to be an element of what we might call supernatural revisionism in later accounts[9] where the Nechung Oracle tells the Dalai Lama to flee Lhasa. There is no mention of this in the Dalai Lama's first autobiography, *My Land and My People* (1962) or other contemporary accounts. But in his second biography *Freedom in Exile* (1991), His Holiness writes that on Tuesday the 17th he consulted the Nechung Oracle.*

---

*It is not clear if the Nechung medium was at the Norbulingka on 17 March. John Avedon (*In Exile from the Land of Snows*, 1997), who interviewed the medium, makes no mention of any consultation with the Dalai Lama on the 17th and says the medium was stricken at that period with a painful illness.

"To my astonishment he shouted 'Go! Go! Tonight.' The medium, still in his trance, then staggered forward and, snatching up some paper and a pen, wrote down, quite clearly and explicitly, the route that I should take out of the Norbulingka, down to the last Tibetan town on the India border." Then the medium collapsed in a faint, and immediately afterwards the two mortar shells exploded outside ". . . as if to reinforce the oracle's instructions."

Proponents of the Shugden deity claim that a prophetic warning was also given by Shugden, and cite a passage from the autobiography of Trijang Rinpoche, the Dalai Lama's tutor, to support their story.[10] Trijang Rinpoche writes that he sent Ratö Rimpoche to the Shugden Oracle's temple at Paglung, which is confirmed in Ratö Rimpoche's own memoir.

With due respect to both oracles we have to consider the likelier possibility that Phala had already made the decision for the Dalai Lama to leave on the 17th and that the mortar attack was happenstance and incidental, though helpful to Phala's plans. Following the incident, the Kashag entrusted Phala with the task of moving the Dalai Lama to southern Tibet.[11]

Phala himself, in a lengthy interview in 1970, made it clear who was in charge. "Only one person was entrusted with the sole responsibility for the arrangement and organization of the escape. The Kashag entrusted this task to me." Phala makes no mention of the oracle or the mortar incident and simply states, "We decided to leave on the 8th day of the second Tibetan month of the Earth-Pig year, corresponding to March 17, 1959."

If the decision to escape had been made hurriedly after the mortar attack at 4 p.m. on the 17th, there would have been only a few hours, four at most, to carry out all the necessary preparations for the escape, which, logistically speaking, would have been impossible. At a bare minimum, a messenger had to be dispatched from Norbulingka to Nyetang to summon Lobsang Yeshi's militia and the Resistance escort, and these forces would have had to get their horses, weapons and supplies ready, and then ride to the Ramagang Ferry Crossing—all in the space of three or four hours. Also, in this short space of time, all the supplies for the journey, the hundred or so horses and pack-animals at the Kundeling country estate would have to be readied, and brought to the ferry. As we shall see, Phala's plan had too many moving parts for it to be hurriedly carried out in a short space of time.

In the interview, Phala mentions that *the day before* the appointed date of the Dalai Lama's flight, he summoned all the palace guards and gatekeepers for a meeting. He instructed them that, from that night on, they were to stop shining their flashlights on the faces of officials going on security rounds, or ask them who they were, as there were many Chinese spies around, and it would put them all in danger. He also told them that the *next day* he would send a truck to fetch weapons from the Shöl armoury, and they should let it pass without opening the tarpaulin flaps or checking inside the truck.

The next afternoon, Phala loaded this truck with all the ministers of the Kashag (with immediate family members and attendants) and the Dalai Lama's two tutors and their servitors. Using the truck also ". . . gave Phala the opportunity to smuggle out a few official State papers in the palace, some personal baggage for the Dalai Lama, and the gold Seal of Office, and the Seal of the cabinet." according to another source.[12] They were driven to the residence of Kundeling Dzasak at the Dekyi Lingka Park (near the Indian Mission), which was fairly close to the ferry and where they waited till nightfall.*

At around 9:30 p.m., the second group consisting of the Dalai Lama's mother, his sister Tsering Dolma, his youngest brother Ngari Rinpoche, a couple of other relatives and a few servants were taken to the Guards barracks at the south-eastern end of the Norbulingka. They had earlier changed their clothes and were now dressed as Khampa men. A prearranged squad of soldiers led by an officer screened this small group and, claiming to be conducting a patrol of the riverbank, walked past the guards at the gates and made their way to the north ferry point.

---

*This sequence of events was confirmed to me by the senior tutor's young attendant, Lingtsang Thupten Tsering, who was one of the passengers in the truck.

The Dalai Lama's maternal grandmother, Doma Yangzom, had been left behind at the Yabshi manor in Changsebshar Park, with the Dalai Lama's aunt and some servants. She was too old and frail to ride a horse and could not have made the trip to India. The Dalai Lama's mother, who had arthritis, had some problems walking in the dark and had to be supported by her daughter and maid. Despite their improbable disguise, they soon made it to the Ramagang Ferry point where a platoon of Drapchi soldiers helped them into the waiting coracles* that silently transported them across the river. The large flat-bottomed wooden ferry (with its distinctive horsehead prow) was not used as it was slower, noisier and furthermore, no horses and pack animals had to be ferried across the Kyichu.

Word got back to Phala around 10 p.m. that the first group had successfully made the crossing. Now the Dalai Lama, his Guards commander, Takla, Chief Ecclesiastical Official (*Chikyap Khenpo*) Gadang, Phala himself and some retainers walked out of the Norbulingka south gate. We know the Dalai Lama was disguised as a soldier and carried a rifle. Half a mile from the palace, Captain Kaldam and an escort of Drapchi soldiers met the party. Captain Kaldam also had a horse ready for the Dalai Lama, which His Holiness rode to the ferry crossing. Half an hour later, the cabinet ministers, the Dalai Lama's two tutors and their attendants, left the Dekyi Lingka Park and, making their way to the ferry, managed the crossing without any problems. They were escorted by a contingent of Gyantsé Regiment troops led by Dapön Ragashar Sonam Topgyal.[13]

When the Dalai Lama's coracle got to the other side of the river, the oarsman threw a rope, and two soldiers pulled the coracle ashore. The Dalai Lama was greeted by the official Seynang Lobsang Yeshi who introduced him to the resistance commander Dewatsang Kunga Samten and some of his officers, one being the tall, striking Tenpa

---

*These lightweight crafts are made of half-a-dozen or more yak hides stretched over a willow frame, and about 8'x5' in size. A single oarsman rowed the coracle with two long oars. The craft could hold five to six people in the water but was light enough to be carried by the boatman when he walked back upstream—a pet sheep trotting by his side carrying his provisions.

Thargay or "Triumph of the Dharma", whose name the Dalai Lama found auspicious and assuring. Of course, no matter how fraught the moment, white *khata* scarves had to be presented to the Dalai Lama and blessings received—albeit hurriedly, likely as not.

Also, as prearranged, Kundeling Dzasak and his servants had arrived at the south ferry point with horses, pack animals and supplies from the Kundeling estate farm at Tsagur. There were horses for everyone, including attendants and escorts, about seventy people in all. Within the hour, everyone was mounted, and the escape journey began, in surprisingly good order.

Their first stop was the village of Namgyal Gang, which had earlier been chosen as a staging point. Saddlebags, bedding and supplies were rearranged, girths tightened, stirrups adjusted and so on. The Dalai Lama rested briefly in the altar room of a farmhouse. Then the party rode along through the night, and the next morning made the ascent of the difficult Che-la or "Sandy Pass". In the late afternoon, they crossed the Tsangpo or the Brahmaputra River at a ferry crossing held by the resistance, to Kyeshong Village on the southern bank. They continued east to Rawame Monastery and the town of Chideshöl, and then proceeded south, skirting Tsethang where the siege and fighting were still going on, finally arriving on the 22nd at the Riwo Dechen Monastery at Chongye in "the valley of the kings". There they were met by the two radio-operators Athar and Lotse, who sent the first message to the outside world that the Dalai Lama had escaped from a beleaguered Lhasa, and was safe.

The rest of the Dalai Lama's journey requires no retelling, having been extensively covered in many books and magazine articles, through the decades.

In a bit of face-saving emendation, Beijing later claimed it had allowed the Dalai Lama to leave Tibet. Melvyn Goldstein (in the final volume of his history) cites a telegram Mao Zedong is said to have sent to General Tan Guansan:"Let him leave. Don't stop him." But in his next chapter, Goldstein mentions that ". . . the Chinese (in Lhasa) felt vulnerable, because they believed they were badly outnumbered."[14] No Chinese troops could be spared to hunt down the Dalai Lama even if General Tan had wanted to. The only PLA regiments on the Dalai Lama's escape route were at Tsethang and Nedong Dzong, but both garrisons were effectively under siege by the Resistance. Only in mid-April were troops from Lhasa sent to relieve Tsethang.

One last observation should be made about the escape before we move on to the story of the actual fighting in Lhasa. In retrospect, it is astonishing that Phala's complex plan worked out as well as it did. Many Tibetans these days attribute this to the supernatural powers of the Nechung Oracle or the Shugden Oracle (depending on your deity of choice) and quote vague, mysterious prophecies* much in the way ancient Roman writers embellished their accounts of another historic river crossing—that of Julius Caesar's across the Rubicon, with ". . . dramatic appearances of the gods, uncanny omens and prophetic dreams" according to the celebrated Cambridge classicist, Mary Beard. Be that as it may, my objection to the claims of supernatural intervention in the crossing of the "River of Happiness" is that they obscure, sometimes even deny, the actual contribution and sacrifices made by real people in planning and carrying out this incredible story-book escape of the Dalai Lama, his family members and principal government officials, from a beleaguered city ringed by over 30,000 Chinese troops, artillery, tanks and armoured cars, and infiltrated with spies and informers.

I met Kungo or "Lord" Phala, as I respectfully addressed him, in early 1973 when I visited Switzerland, on what might be called a "clandestine" mission for the exile government (see Chapter 37). Kungo Phala was then the Dalai Lama's representative in Europe. He was tall and stately, a sharp dresser and still handsome at sixty-one.

---

*A rough translation of two Nechung prophecies: "Our inner treasure of great bliss / I adjure you leave without delay" (*ngoe kyi nang nor dewa chenmo di/ cheshoe maypae kunma deb reng rer*) and "On your journey be not distracted / I will set up a wooden ferry."(*khyo rangme khayang la /de ngaeki dhru shing tsuktap yod*). The Shugden prophecy given to Ratö Rimpoche: "Leave immediately! If you go by the south-western route no harm will come to the Dalai Lama or anyone in his entourage. I guarantee it! Raise this sword in my name at the head of the Dalai Lama's column."

He looked the part of an elder European diplomat in his dark grey suit and matching homburg. He came to see me at my uncle Rakra Rinpoche's home at the Pestalozzi Children Village, with a bottle of the local Dôle. He did not drink himself but ate endless little tubs of flavoured yoghurt, staying up late into the night talking to me. I was a very junior official then and quite flattered by the attention.

Kungo Phala appeared to enjoy the information and gossip I shared with him about the goings-on at the exile capital. I was outspoken and dreadfully opinionated, but he seemed not to mind, and listened patiently to what I had to say. This capacity to pay attention to the frustrated outpourings of such young men as Lobsang Yeshi, Captain Kaldam, the monk official Barshi and perhaps even the CIA agent, Athar Norbu, might have helped bend them to his will, and got them to play the crucial roles they did in his great scheme. I don't know. Phala loved to tell stories about his life in old Tibet and gave me much information about the Dalai Lama's escape, but he never once claimed to have masterminded it. "A complicated headache of an operation" was as far as he would go, but he said that with a satisfied smile. I suppose he wanted it to remain the Dalai Lama's story.*

The Phala family claims its origins from Western Bhutan. Kungo.

Phala had two younger brothers, Dorje Wangdu, a senior officer in the army, and Wangchuk, who managed the family estate and manor near Gyantsé where they had started a school for the children of their estate and the district. Other than the three Rs, the Phala School provided physical training, folk dance lessons and organized games. A Tibetan official visiting the estate (a graduate of St. Joseph's College) was impressed by the "high quality" of the education.[15]

A single unpleasant blemish tarnishes Phala's otherwise distinguished career. In 1941, as a rising monk official, Phala was appointed governor

---

*In the 1970s the Library of Tibetan Works and Archives collected "oral history" interviews from Chamberlain Phala and other organizers of the escape as Kundeling Dzasa and Barshi, but did not release or publish them for decades because the exile government " . . . felt that some of these accounts compromised the official version of history." (Tsering Shakya, *Dragon in the Land of Snows*, p. xxvii) of Northern Tibet (*jhang-chi*) and drew up plans to capture the nomad chief Gagya Dramnak who had just attacked a Tibetan garrison in the district. Using the Tethong servitor Palden Dhakpa, a friend and gambling partner of the nomad chief, Phala invited Gagya Dramnak to Bachen Dzong for a parlay and a Mahjong evening. When Gagya Dramnak became intoxicated, he was overpowered by Phala's soldiers. One report has the nomad chief being stabbed to death in the scuffle. Another version claims he was captured but suffered an "in-custody" death that same night.[16] Many in Lhasa were scandalized. When the roof of the Phala Mansion (*Zimshag Bhangeshar*) in east Lhasa collapsed that same year, the role of *karma*, in general, and the terrible power, in particular, of the *Tsan* demon who had reputedly sired the murdered nomad chief, were frequently mentioned in speculations and gossip about the incident.

Whenever I visited Switzerland, Kungo Phala would come to see me. On a couple of occasions, I stayed at his apartment, at the village of Rämismühle-Zell, where he was a generous and entertaining host. He came to Dharamshala in 1984 when I was the director of the Tibetan Institute of Performing Arts. Kungo Phala was a huge Ache Lhamo opera aficionado. Even now, it warms me to recall that I was able to host him and other retired officials to an all-day performance of the historical play *Gyasa Bhelsa*,* with drinks, refreshments and a Lhasa-picnic style banquet lunch. He died in 1985.

---

* *The Chinese Princess and the Nepalese Princess* tells the story of the wily minister Gar Tongtsen sent by the Emperor Songtsen Gampo to China to seek the hand of the princess Wencheng. Gar competes with the ministers of India, Nepal, Persia and Rome in contests of wisdom and skill and defeating them, returns to Tibet with the princess and her dowry, the image of the Buddha Shakyamuni that still resides at the Jokhang Temple in Lhasa.

27

THE LHASA UPRISING

When the Dalai Lama's escape was announced at the People's Conference, the *Military History* mentions that ". . . Tsarong, Manang Abo-la and others who had some military experience suggested that since the Dalai Lama and the Kashag had already left Lhasa, those remaining should establish contact with the Chinese and try to defuse the situation. They said the public should return to their homes, and only a small force be kept in Lhasa. The rest of the troops and volunteers should be secretly deployed along the major mountain passes, cross-roads and river crossings where effective guerrilla operations could be carried out against Chinese troops, if the PLA attempted to follow the Dalai Lama."

Someone who was at the meeting confirms that Tsarong spelt out the case for guerrilla warfare and explained, "Our southern land is blessed with natural forests, and we could easily fight the Chinese for a longer period, during which we shall have time to plan our next move."[1]

But the other representatives, especially the old stable-in-charge Tseten Phuntsok, the monk Ganden Abra-la, and a couple of others argued that if Tibetan troops and volunteers left the city, ". . . it would be tantamount to surrendering Lhasa to the Chinese."[2] The *Military*

History adds, "They boastfully voiced they should go ahead with their preparations to fight, whether it brought victory or defeat."

Though these unsophisticated volunteers might have failed to grasp the strategic necessity of dispersing their forces and conducting a guerrilla-style campaign, their defiant call for a final showdown, for one last dramatic battle in Lhasa—which as destructive, tragic and even hopeless, as it turned out to be—did, arguably, succeed in turning a humiliating defeat into an enduring symbol of national defiance, in a "Dunkirk Spirit" sort of way. Even now, sixty years later, new generations of Tibetans world-over turn out on 10 March to carry on the legacy of that sacred day, much to the displeasure of the PRC leader and *fenqing** students in the West. Oddly enough even the Dalai Lama and his administration-in-exile, hoping to convince Beijing that Tibetans have given up their struggle for freedom and independence, have tried to put a damper on the 10 March demonstrations.

Though the majority of the People's Conference may not have agreed with Tsarong's strategy, I was told by Maja that the old commander-in-chief was asked to assume command of the military operations, probably as he was the senior-most leader in the conference who had actual military experience. Tsarong commanded the irregular Tibetan forces in the 1912 street fighting in Lhasa and had defeated the Manchu garrison there. But the Communist occupation army in Lhasa was a vastly different matter, and Tsarong was aware of that. The former commander-in-chief almost certainly had a copy of the report from the Chinese Colonel, Lobsang Tashi, that gave a detailed breakdown of the PLA forces in and around Lhasa city, including names of commanders, troop strength and artillery emplacements.

Maja told me that Tsarong set up his headquarters at the eastern end (*Shöl Shar*) of the complex near the Army headquarters (*Mak chikhang*). Maja recalled Tsarong sitting on an ottoman before a low table on which he had spread out a map of the city—almost certainly

---

* *Fenqing*—"angry youth" or "shitty youth"—the term first used in Hong Kong to describe young Chinese of self-righteous and aggressive nationalist tendency.

a copy of the municipal map of Lhasa, surveyed and drawn by Peter Aufschnaiter in 1948.

Several officers had gathered around Tsarong, one of them being the former general, Muja Tsewang Norbu, the hero of Chamdo. Messengers were rushing in and out of this room. Before the actual outbreak of the fighting, written missives were sent through couriers, sometimes disguised as monks or beggars. It became more difficult to use messengers once the actual fighting started. The telephone system was controlled by the Chinese, and the Tibetans did not have radio communication, so they went back to using the old British army system of signalling with semaphore flags they had used some decades earlier.

A heliograph* system was also set up between Tromsikhang, the Potala and the Norbulingka.

In spite of sporadic rifle fire around Lhasa for the next two days (18 and 19 March), no actual fighting took place.

Bhusang recalled: "The Chinese intensified their propaganda all over the city—over loudspeakers in street corners and through collaborators, spies and *hur-tsunpa* activists in tea shops and restaurants. They kept repeating that it was futile for Tibetans to fight, that we had no weapons and only ten or so bullets each, anyway. It was no use, they said, dreaming and hoping that the Khampa 'rebel bandits' would show up in Lhasa, as they were all being driven out of Lhoka by the PLA and would soon be destroyed to a man. It would be best for everyone to surrender their weapons right now and go home, and so on. One *hur-tsunpa* from Bathang, probably a herdsman earlier in life, kept insisting that we stupid Tibetans were pushing ourselves further and further inside the horn of a yak, i.e., getting ourselves into a progressively tighter and ultimately impossible situation."

One of the Dalai Lama's principal reasons for leaving was to defuse the armed standoff in the city. He hoped that when the public learned of his escape, all the volunteers would put down their weapons and

---

*The heliograph was a portable signalling device that used reflected sunlight of a mirror mounted on a tripod. It was a standard issue in the British army till WWII. General Miles used it during the Geronimo campaign in south-west USA.

return to their homes. But in the haste and hustle of the escape, the Dalai Lama's public message to that effect was almost forgotten. The 2008 autobiography of the official Tenpa Soepa clears up this mystery.[3] Tenpa had accompanied the Dalai Lama's escape party, but when it arrived at Neu Dzong at one in the morning, he was summoned by Kundeling Dzasak and ordered to deliver a letter (the Dalai Lama's message to Khenchung Tara, the senior-most official who was in charge of the Norbulingka). Tenpa rode back to Lhasa and delivered the message.* After a brief discussion, Khenchung Tara and his colleagues decided to hold back the announcement for two days, till the morning of the 20th, to allow the Dalai Lama time to get as far away as possible from Lhasa. Unfortunately, events overtook this decision.

"The fighting started in the early hours of the 20th, a Friday, with an intense artillery barrage at 2 a.m." Bhusang told me. He was on the roof of the Tromsikhang building in the Barkhor with other policemen. "That night, we only had a contingent of twenty-five men guarding the Tsuglakhang Temple. Most of us were at the Tromsikhang, including Major Gura. From the roof, we could clearly see the shells bursting, near continuously, and lighting up the whole Norbulingka area. The barrage was intense."

Jigme Taring, who was in the Norbulingka, remembers that the artillery barrage started at 2 a.m.[4] which is also confirmed in the *Military History*: "At around 2 a.m. on March 20, 1959, the Chinese at first fired artillery . . . "[5] Tenpa Soepa writes that "in the early hours of March 20, 1959, the Chinese fired the first shell at the residence of the Dalai Lama"[6] while another junior official at the Norbulingka, Thupten Khetsun writes that the artillery fire started at 4 a.m. The Chinese journalist Shan Chao insists that the fighting started at 3.40 a.m. One explanation for this difference in the reports might have to do with time zones. Tibetans had traditionally set their watches and

---

*Tenpa had another message for Tara from the official Lobsang Yeshi, who desperately wanted more weapons for his militia. Lobsang wrote he would return to Norbulingka to collect them after escorting the Dalai Lama into resistance territory.

clocks by Indian time, while the Chinese were probably using China Standard Time—which is about a couple of hours ahead.

Tenpa Soepa claims that one of the first shells struck the Dalai Lama's "New Palace" (*Phodrang Sarpa*), destroying the top floor and damaging the rear of the bedchamber. Khetsun writes, ". . . inside the palace ground shells were falling fast and pounding the area." The Chinese artillery fire on the Norbulingka shredded the willows and other trees in the gardens killing off not only many of the defenders but the horses as well, including those in the Dalai Lama's personal stable. Confusion and panic initially overwhelmed everyone within the walls, especially those officials only armed with pistols and revolvers and who could not see any Chinese soldiers to shoot at. Khetsun admits, "We had absolutely no experience of warfare, and since we also had no experienced commanders . . . instead of staying in our shelters, we began running here and there trying to avoid the falling shells, making our casualties even heavier."[7]

Major Sekshing Lobsang Thondup of the Guards Regiment had been assigned the task of defending the Palace grounds. According to Jianglin Li who refers to his memoirs published in "an official Chinese Communist compilation"[8] he does not come across as an effective military leader. But it is possible that since his account was intended for an official Chinese publication, he downplayed his role in the events.

Sekshing set up his howitzer and machine guns on the south side of the Norbulingka. Chinese artillery shells soon rained down on their position destroying the howitzers and killing and scattering his men. Khetsun writes that the Tibetan soldiers from the Guards Regiment fired their howitzer and mortars at the Chinese camp at Nortölingka (where the PLA Artillery Regiment #155 was based) and from where most of the shelling of the Norbulingka was coming, but the Chinese artillery strikes destroyed the Tibetan howitzers and killed many of the soldiers.

The small Tibetan howitzers were no match for Chinese heavy artillery, and the Tibetans were devastated by the attack, especially by the scale and intensity of the shelling. No Tibetan had ever faced the concentrated fire of multiple field batteries, and could not possibly have imagined how destructive it could be.

The Chinese Colonel Lobsang Tashi had warned of the enormous destructive power of PLA artillery. He had stressed to the Drapchi commander and his officers that when fighting broke out in the city, the artillery emplacements had to be taken out first—whatever the cost in Tibetans lives. Captain Kaldam repeated the Colonel's warnings to me but admitted that neither he nor anyone else had then fully grasped the scale of the danger.

Kaldam had seen the big guns, as had everyone else in the city. They were not a secret. On every Chinese National Day on 1 October the PLA would hold a big military parade and review at the "Great Field of the People" (*Mimang Thangten Chenmo*), the highlight of which would be the rolling-out of hundreds of different artillery pieces behind trucks and carriers. Everyone was, of course, duly impressed, but unable to grasp the devastating capability of these modern weapons. In pre-invasion Lhasa, cannon-fire had, for the public, been just one exciting ritual spectacle (among many) during the annual Mönlam Festival, when three ancient cannons, dubbed the "Idiot Cannons" (*meykyo kukpa*) were fired at the White Bird-Poop Mountain (*Jhakya Karpori*) across the Kyichu, to ward off evil.

I tried to get Captain Kaldam to identify the PLA artillery pieces for me from photographs. He pointed out some WWII Russian artillery pieces he thought he recognized: the 76 mm regimental M1943 (OB-25), the 122 mm howitzer M1938 (M-30), and the 152 mm howitzer M1943 (D-1). The first two have been mentioned in Chinese accounts of the Lhasa Uprising. Captain Kaldam said that at the Drip camp they had twenty or so "*otomoto*" (automatic) guns that could fire a number of rounds without reloading. I showed him a picture of a Russian 37 mm anti-aircraft gun M1939 (61-K), which was magazine-fed, but Kaldam was uncertain. Flipping through my *Illustrated Weapons of WWII,* he tapped his finger on the photo of the self-propelled Katushya multiple rocket launcher, the fearsome "Stalin Organs" of WWII, which delivered twenty-four high explosive warheads in a single salvo.

Captain Kaldam explained to me why Chinese artillery fire was so accurate, and Tibetan mountain guns were not. The Chinese had a special scientific instrument, the "earth-sky viewing-glass" (*sashey-nam-*

shey), which allowed Chinese gunners to see through mountains and tall buildings and hence direct their fire exactly where they wanted. This bit of popular misinformation most likely stemmed from the optical range-finders people saw PLA gunners use.

Now Major Sekshing approached Khenchung Tara and asked what he should do. Sekshing was clearly out of his depth. Khenchung Tara took over and attempted to organize the defence.[9] Khetsun mentions Tara's effort to rally the defenders and how he succeeded to some extent. The Amdo volunteer unit facing Nortölingka to the west commenced firing at the Chinese camp. The defenders (including Tenpa Soepa) along the northern wall began firing on the heavily fortified Qinghai-Tibet Highway Depot. A photograph shows a fighter using an up turned cart to fire from the top of the high wall.

Many of the volunteer fighters manning the trenches and barricades outside the Norbulingka walls, who were exposed to Chinese artillery fire, were brought inside the palace where they manned the high walls and began firing at the Depot. The Highway Depot was also fired upon by a company of Gyantsé Regiment soldiers, who were defending the Gyatso Tö compound (the summer home of the Dalai Lama's family) just outside the north wall of the Norbulingka. Thupten Khetsun remembers, "the Tibetan army and volunteers at the Chakpori and Bongwari had a clear view of the Chinese and engaged with them in exchanges of fire for some time." Many of the buildings in the Depot were destroyed or damaged, and many Chinese soldiers there killed and wounded.

"At dawn the barrage on the Norbulingka lifted and the bombardment of the Potala Palace began. It lasted for over two hours, perhaps three. I can't be sure." Bhusang described it to me: "It was a rolling barrage and moved from the Shöl village up towards the Potala, the shells falling in advance of those that had just landed before. There were about fifteen or twenty shells exploding closely in every single barrage. After one particularly intense barrage, the entire Potala was covered with smoke and dust, and you couldn't see anything. I felt that the Great Palace was destroyed. Everyone was upset, and many people began to cry. I had tears in my eyes. But when the dust and smoke cleared, there was the Potala looking untouched. It was a miracle. We all smiled again and cheered. But then the shelling started again."

When artillery shells began to fall inside the Shöl complex, the defenders there were not entirely unprepared. Tsarong had earlier overseen the digging of trenches within the Shöl walls.[10] According to Maja, Tsarong had taken charge of the fighters there and was shouting instructions at everyone to hide in the trenches with their rifles and not come out till the Chinese soldiers attacked. The main gate of the Shöl was closed and reinforced with large stones piled one on top of the other. Maja was nervous and approached Tsarong. "I asked him what I should do. He said 'Find a trench and hide in it. Wait until the Chinese come and then fight them at close quarters.' What I hoped he would say was that we should find a way out and try to reach the mountains, and maybe join the Khampas. But Tsarong seemed set on defending the Shöl and the Potala."

"I followed him and his officers when he went inside his chambers, which was now the command post. The place was filled with cigarette smoke. A grey cloud seemed to be hanging from the ceiling. Everyone was smoking and so was Tsarong, who had a few cartons of State Express 555 on his table with his maps and other things. He was wearing a dove grey (hangu-dok) woollen tsaychima robe and had a pistol[*] strapped to his side. When I left that room, I saw Tsarong's Land Rover parked outside, between two houses."

Following the lifting of the artillery barrage on the Norbulingka, Tibetan accounts mention a PLA infantry offensive on the Norbulingka palace. But the defenders rallied and managed to push it back. Barber writes that when the first assault was launched from the Shugtri Lingka camp at Norbulingka, the Chinese soldiers ". . . were totally unprepared for the reception that awaited them."[11] The Chinese journalist Shan Chao wrote, "When the rebel bandits in the Norbulingka were

---

[*] According to his nephew Tseten Namgyal, when leaving home Tsarong took with him a pair of engraved pistols that had been presented to the 13th Dalai Lama by the U.S. minister to China, W.W. Rockhill, at Mount Wutaishan in China in 1908. His Holiness subsequently gave the pistols to Tsarong.

cornered, they put up a desperate fight, knocked out corners of houses, broke down walls, dug holes and put their rifles through."

The Chinese advance from Shugtri Lingka was also checked by rifle fire from the company of Gyantsé soldiers at Gyatso Tö and also the other Gyantsé Company at Zaralingka Park close by. This Chinese attack was most probably a probing one. The attack may have also been hampered by Tibetan artillery and mortar fire from the heights of Chakpori Mountain.

Chakpori was defended by a hundred and seventy Drapchi soldiers and fifty or more volunteer fighters. One source told me that there were only seventy or eighty Drapchi soldiers supported by monks of the Medical College. Both sources however agreed that the force was commanded by Lieutenant (*dingpön*) Tashi Tsewang. Captain Kaldam further informed me that this officer was the son of Rupön Anen Dawa, the heroic major of the 1918 war in Kham who, in a popular song, had been compared to a warrior from the Ling epic.

The Chakpori defenders had four howitzers and some mortars. Noel Barber was told that there were five howitzers on the hill,[12] and it is possible that the decision was made to concentrate many of the precious guns on Chakpori because of its elevation and strategic location. From the heights of Chakpori, the defenders could provide effective supporting fire to the defenders at Norbulingka, Shöl, Potala, and target Chinese positions below at Shugtri Lingka, the Autonomous Region Compound, the Highway Depot at Kyangthangnaga, PLA Military HQ, and Makar Sarpa.

Once the howitzers and mortars on Chakpori began dropping shells on Chinese positions, the PLA regiment based at Shugtri Lingka at the foot of the mountain launched an attack up the hill, preceded by a mass barrage of artillery fire from Shugtri Lingka and Drip. Chakpori defenders were well-armed with rifles and Bren guns and put up a spirited defence. This first Chinese assault, which took place early in the morning, was beaten back. The howitzers and mortars on Chakpori now increased their shelling of Chinese positions.

According to a number of sources, the Chakpori defenders were given supporting fire by the defenders of the Shöl and the Potala. At

Shöl, there was a full company of Gyantsé soldiers. After the initial
artillery shelling, Tsarong and General Muja positioned these soldiers
along the high walls and battlements surrounding the large compound.
They also ordered the civilian volunteers out of their trenches and
shelters to provide support to the defenders. A company of Drapchi
soldiers defended the Potala. At first, an effective volume of rifle and
light machine-gun fire was directed at the PLA camp at Shugtri Lingka
nearby, and the troops attacking Chakpori Mountain.

Tsarong tried to communicate with the other commanders but
could no longer use runners, as it was too dangerous. He waited till
mid-morning to try the semaphore, but his signalmen had to expose
themselves and were shot at by PLA soldiers from the Shugtri Lingka.[13]
Bhusang said that from the roof of the Tromsikhang building, he saw
glints of reflected sunlight from the Shöl battlement, but the dust and
smoke around the Potala made it impossible to send any complete and
meaningful heliograph signal. It now became obvious to Tsarong and
other commanders that Central Lhasa, Norbulingka and the Potala
commands were completely cut off from each other.

Only between the Norbulingka and Chakpori was there some kind
of safe passage. The mountainside provided cover from Chinese artillery
fire from the east, and the two Gyantsé companies holding Gyatso Tö
and Zaralingka Park prevented any Chinese infantry incursion from
Shugtri Lingka.

Volunteer fighters from Norbulingka were now sent to the assistance
of the Chakpori defenders. A number of Norbulingka survivors have
written that their leader Khenchung Tara recognized that Chakpori
was vital to the defence of Norbulingka because of its strategic vantage
point and elevation. According to Khetsun, Khenchung Tara had
been up at Chakpori before the first PLA assault and had returned to
Norbulingka to collect more volunteers. He organized a meeting of
officials and soldiers where he exhorted them to join him. Tenpa Soepa
was one of these volunteers but was subsequently separated when he
went to collect ammunition. Another person who joined Khenchung
Tara was a junior official, Seychung Yeshi Dhargye. Seychung later
recalled firing down from the Chakpori mountainside with an Enfield

rifle at the Chinese, killing at least three PLA soldiers.[14] But he ran out of ammunition and was wounded and captured.

* * *

In the Barkhor in Central Lhasa, preparations were made at the police headquarters (and barracks) at Tromsikhang to defend the Tsuglakhang Temple, which was just across the street. Major Gura deployed his main force of around two hundred policemen in and around the Tsuglakhang. Then the Major took a team of twenty men under Sergeant Pema Gyalpo (Bhusang's father-in-law) and two howitzers out on the street. They were joined by a large group of cheering Lhasa citizenry, who helped pull the guns through the streets and carry the shells.

They dragged the guns north to the Ramoche Temple, where adjacent to it was the North Lhasa police station defended by a company of policemen under Captain Tsering Lhagyal. They were supported by monks of the Upper Tantric College (Gyutö). Directly across the Temple was Zumphü Mansion, the headquarters of the Chinese police force in Lhasa, and heavily fortified.

Major Gura was an experienced gunner. Helping him lay the mountain guns was a private from Shigatsé, who had the reputation of being an incorrigible rogue and troublemaker, even having been whipped on a couple of occasions. But he was a trained gunner and a good shot. They blasted away at the walls of the Zumphü house, weakening the outer defences enough for Captain Tsering Lhagyal's men to use their two Bren guns and rifles. At least thirty-five Chinese defenders, including "a very important PLA officer", were killed, according to a monk eyewitness, Tashi Palden, who with other monk survivors at Ramoche, was subsequently charged by the Chinese with this "crime".[15]

Leaving the captain and his men at Ramoche, Major Gura, his guns and crew of policemen and enthusiastic volunteers, moved south and fired on Chinese administrative buildings within the Barkhor: Kyetöpa, Surkhang, Sampho, Pangdatsang and also further west, Yuthok House, the office of the CCP Tibet Work Committee but which was now serving as the command post for the fighting in Central Lhasa. These buildings were barricaded and heavily defended with sandbags lined on the rooftops. Tibetan gunners had to be careful to avoid the machine gun and small arms fire from these places. But Major Gura had appointed twenty police men armed with Bren guns, Sten guns and Enfields to provide security for the gunners.

Bhusang was at the Tromsikhang building providing security for a mortar team with two three-inch mortars, commanded by Sergeant Sonam Wangdu and mortar instructor Tsegya Bhagtro, who had, in the forties, received gunnery training at the British (later Indian) military garrison at Gyantsé. Bhusang claims that one of their shells hit the big loudspeaker at Public Security Bureau HQ at Surkhang House. "It was a lucky shot, I'll admit. One moment it was blaring out propaganda: 'Give up your weapons. Don't be stupid and listen to the lies of the *lokchoepa* (counter-revolutionaries) and *tsengyal-ringluk* (foreign imperialists). Remember what happens if the egg tries to smash the rock . . . and so on.' The next moment there was a welcome silence, except for the sound of artillery and rifle fire. They had really cranked up the volume that day which irritated all of us. So, the Barkhor folks celebrated, bringing us hot tea and *khapsay* cookies.

"People began burning *sang* incense, sage and juniper sprigs from the rooftops. Major Gura's team was also being feted by the Barkhor populace with tea, *khapsay* and *khata* scarves. It sounds a bit improbable, but many of the civilians not only followed the howitzer team, hauling the guns and the ammunition, but also carrying Bhutanese snack baskets (*loma*) of *khapsay*, yak jerkey and pots of teas with which they kept refilling the cups of the policemen whenever there was a lull in the fighting."

The Chinese were probably not able to return artillery fire on the Tibetan positions as there were many Chinese administrative offices in the Barkhor—cheek by jowl with the Tibetan fighters. But the police howitzer and mortar teams used up their ammunition supply in a few hours and then fell back on the Tsuglakhang and prepared to defend it.

* * *

The Chinese artillery batteries at Drip, Makar Sarpa and Shugtri Lingka were concentrating their fire at Chakpori Mountain, from where an unending stream of artillery and mortar shells rained down on Chinese troops at Shugtri Lingka and even further west at Nortölingka. The Chakpori defenders were able to keep up this volume of fire as the hill was conveniently close to the main ammunition depot of the Tibetan army, officially called Ghomzö Dorjeling[16] (Vajra arsenal) or to the general public simply "zeykhang" or gunpowder storehouse. It was located just fifty yards or so down the north-western slope of the Iron Hill above the Gateway Stupa (*Drago Kani*), which linked the Iron Hill to the mountain on which the Potala stood. This Arsenal was guarded by fifty or so Drapchi soldiers. With the help of the monks of the Medical College and other volunteers, the soldiers formed a human chain to pass the ammunition up to the Chakpori gunners. Barber writes that shells were hauled up the heights in "Jack and Jill fashion"[17] each man carrying two shells, but mistakenly states that this was being done from the Norbulingka.

A few hours into the fighting, a Chinese artillery shell, an unlucky fluke, landed directly on the ordnance depot, completely destroying it. The noise of the explosion was heard all over Lhasa, above the sound of the artillery and rifle fire. Many of the troops guarding the depot and volunteer monks and civilians hauling the shells were instantly killed. But the main force at the top of the mountain, though shaken, held on to their positions and prepared to face the next PLA assault.

Jianglin Li mentions that "At 10 a.m., on March 20 . . . General Tan Guansan issued orders to launch the first stage of the formal plan for the Battle of Lhasa, the shelling of Chakpori Hill (Chinese, *Yaowang Shan*). The soldiers of the Artillery Regiment #308, camped on the south side of the river (at Drip), had 76 mm cannons and 122 mm howitzers at the ready."[18]

Li also cites a report "Thunderbolt from Heaven Punishes the Fierce Outlaws" by Wang Guozhen, the commander of Company Three of #308 Regiment: "From our lookout post, I saw every volley land precisely on target. Chakpori Hill was ablaze, and debris swirled in the air. Our artillery fire increased in precision and intensity, shells flying faster and faster! I felt the earth shaking, and the sky itself seemed to be on fire. With nowhere to hide, the rebel bandits scattered in confusion. I relentlessly ordered our men to keep shelling the bandits as they fled. 'That'll teach you, you rebels,' our men whooped as they fired. What an outlet for our hatred!"

Li writes that Professor Xu Yan of the PLA National Defence University wrote that more than a thousand rounds of artillery fire landed on the hill, and destroyed all the pillboxes, trenches and buildings so that, according to another Chinese historian Ji Youquan "nine thousand Khampa rebel bandits" on Chakpori, were "obliterated". This grossly inflated figure of nine thousand fighters on Chakpori is as mistaken as the claim that Chinese troops charging up the hill at 10 o'clock "did not encounter any resistance."

The Chinese propaganda documentary film* released in late 1959 depicts the PLA assault of Yaowang hill coming up against fighting defenders. Intense as the Chinese artillery barrage on Chakpori may have been, we have two eyewitness accounts that enough Tibetan fighters survived the artillery barrage to put up a last-ditch defence of the mountain. A government clerk, Lobsang, who had managed to make it to the summit of the hill from the Norbulingka, reported " . . . a rain of shells so fierce that he could barely see the shell-lashed skeletons of wall enveloped in smoke. It was no longer a college, not even a building, and certainly not a fortified position. Barely a dozen out of the original fifty men were still alive. Lobsang almost vomited as '. . . I tried to avoid treading on the bodies of men,' slaughtered by heavy lumps of metal, mangled and torn, shattered into fragments so that no one could ever hope to recognize the human ruins."

"Four of the five cannons had been smashed by direct hits, but Lobsang mentions that the commander surrounded by dead and wounded, decided that—with or without his beloved gun—he was going to stay. 'If the Chinese want me,' Lobsang heard him say, 'they

---

Putting Down the Rebellion in Tibet (1959), a documentary produced by the Propaganda Department of the Communist Party of China (*Zhonggong Xuanchuanbu*). This film can be viewed at m10memorial.org/videos/ putting-down-the-rebellion-in-tibet/.

will have to climb the Iron Mountain.'" He then ordered Lobsang and the other volunteers to return to the Norbulingka, but to leave all their weapons and ammunition behind as "they were going to fight to the last bullet."[19]

Of the dozen-odd soldiers left defending Chakpori, only one survived to leave behind an oral report, eventually. Private Tasang (aka Tashi Sangpo) of the Drapchi Regiment remembered the final Chinese artillery barrage and the "overwhelming" assault of the Chinese army. He was fighting besides his comrades, corporal Dhonden Karpo, private Kathog Rigzin and private Pögey Wangdu, all of whom ". . . lost their lives right in front of my eyes." He also mentions the commander of their company Lieutenant (*dingpon*) Tashi Tsewang, and his son being killed.

Private Tasang, in a later conversation with Captain Kaldam in Dharamshala, provided more details of the fighting at Chakpori, and the fate of the soldiers and monks commanded by Lieutenant Tashi Tsewang, the son of Major Anan Dawa. Tasang recalled there were three Chinese assaults and that they managed to repel two.

He also remembered that at the end, they only had their rifles and a Bren gun left to fire down on the advancing Chinese troops. He recalled that Tibetan soldiers from the Potala fired on the Chinese attackers on the Chakpori hillside when the Chinese charged up. He also remembered Lieutenant Tashi Tsewang firing his Bren gun at the Chinese. "He kept on firing even with his face covered with blood. He would not let go of it. His son, Private Kalsang Wangdu, who was beside him firing his rifle, pleaded with his father when he saw he had been badly wounded. 'Pala, give me the Bren gun, please.' As he took the Bren gun from his father's hand, the lieutenant died, his head falling to one side. Then the son began firing at the Chinese. A minute or two later, the main Medical College building collapsed. The young man died under the wreckage. I somehow survived and managed to crawl out from under the rubble." Tasang escaped down the side of the mountain and made it to the rear staircase of the Potala, where he joined the soldiers defending the palace.

As soon as the Chinese captured Chakpori, they fired a red signal flare in the sky.

* * *

The artillery fire on the Norbulingka intensified after the destruction of Chakpori, according to most accounts. But no infantry attack appears to have been launched just then. Norbulingka had many more defenders, soldiers of the Guards and Gyantsé regiments, officials, Amdowa and Khampa volunteers, nearly a thousand strong, that though not effectively led, were nonetheless armed and willing to fight. The Chinese kept up the artillery barrage for another four or five hours.

The official Chinese claim was that Premier Zhou Enlai had given orders that the Norbulingka and the Potala Palace should be spared in the fighting, and that little or no damage had been done to these historic buildings. China supporters and left-wing writers and academics in the West took up this refrain to claim that exiled Tibetans had lied about the destruction.

A personal friend of Zhou Enlai, Stuart Gelder and his wife Roma, visited Tibet in late 1962 and later published a book, *The Timely Rain: Travels in New Tibet* (1964), that featured a glowing foreword by the famous American friend-of-Communist-China, Edgar Snow. The Gelders visited the Chensel Palace in the Norbulingka and observed, "If the Dalai Lama returned to his lovely home today he would find it as he left it five years ago." No mention is made of any artillery damage. They were told that some windows had been broken, and there were some bullet marks on the outer walls but otherwise "there were no signs of serious damage." The Gelders also rejected the explanation by exile Tibetans—even by eyewitnesses[20]—that major repair and rebuilding* had taken place after the fighting. "Was it rebuilt?" they asked a gardener. "You can see for yourself" he replied noncommittally.

---

*Lhasa-born master carpenter Langdun Gyatso reported that he and thousands of other prisoners were set to work by the Chinese to repair the damaged monuments and buildings, which took them eight months to complete.

The Norbulingka is a complex of gardens, temples and palaces, but the Gelders were only allowed to visit the Chensel Palace. Gelder says, "we found it intact with all its contents meticulously preserved." In a book packed with twenty-seven full colour plates and forty black and white photos, their only record of the Jewel Park is one black and white photo of the entrance of the Chensel Palace. Eyewitness Tenpa Soepa recalls that one of the first shells struck the Dalai Lama's Phodrang Sarpa (New Palace), destroying the top floor and damaging the rear of the bedchamber.

The Gelders devote a chapter of their book to ridiculing traditional Tibetan medicine and refer to the ". . . school of medicine on top of the Iron Hill, the highest building in the city, overlooking the Potala, which was established 500 years ago."[21] They conveniently fail to mention that there was no "highest building", nothing at all on the Iron Hill except for some blackened ruins, when they visited the Holy City.

Recent Chinese accounts of the Lhasa Uprising are less ambiguous about the shelling of the Summer Palace. Historian Ji Youquan writes: "The attack on the Norbulingka began at 2 p.m. The entire artillery force of Regiment #308 (south of the river) joined with the 60 mm cannons, 82 mm mortars, and recoilless guns of Regiment #155 at Heroes Memorial Park. This was an all-out artillery strike. They used a rolling barrage strategy, steadily inching the line of fire forward in fifteen-yard increments from east to west and driving the fleeing rebel bandits on the advancing line of exploding shells."[22]

Wang Guozhen, commander of the Artillery Regiment #308, Third Company reported, "After we took Chakpori Hill . . . we turned our regiment's whole firepower onto the Norbulingka almost immediately."[23] According to Jianglin Li, the final Chinese onslaught on the Norbulingka took place after nightfall. There was nothing tentative about this attack. "Under cover of fierce artillery fire, Regiment #155, Transport Regiment #16, and a portion of Regiment #159 stormed the Norbulingka from all sides. Crowds of people surged out of the smoking palace to the north, but Vice-Commander Deng Shaodong ordered Regiment #308 to drive them back in and pound them to death with heavy artillery.

"At 7.30 p.m., PLA soldier charged into the unguarded main gate . . . other troops blew up the palace walls with dynamite and marched in."[24]

The Chinese troops encountered "sporadic resistance", but most of the defenders were either dead or wounded. Many committed suicide, according to Tenpa Soepa. The case of two monk officials Tsechak Khenchung Gyaltsen and Tsedrung Lobsang Nyendrak is often cited. When the PLA broke through the Norbulingka walls, "these two old friends shot each other with their pistols."[25] Another possible case of two Norbulingka defenders shooting each other in a suicide pact is cited by Tsarong's grandson in a *Tibetan Review* article.[26]

Dzasak Taring made a pact with a soldier Pasang Thondup that if either of them became wounded, "the injured one should be shot dead by the other."

Although PLA soldiers were kicking the bodies on the ground and stabbing them with bayonets to see if they were dead, quite a few survivors managed to hide in the rubble and slip away and escape towards the river.

Earlier in the afternoon, people from the city and from Norbulingka had attempted to cross the Kyichu River at the Ramagang ferry crossing. The operators of the wooden ferry and coracles had all fled with their crafts. A more pressing problem now was the substantial PLA presence on Jhakya Karpoe Ri (White Bird-Poop Mountain) overlooking Ramagang Ferry. On the night of the Dalai Lama's escape, Drapchi soldiers had patrolled the side of that mountain but, on not discovering any Chinese presence, had left. Now Chinese troops occupied the rocky mountainside and had set up machine guns on the escarpments just above the southern bank of the Kyichu, across the ferry point.

A unit of volunteers under the command of Juchen Thupten Namgyal of Dergé was stationed by the ferry crossing. Li writes that the Tibetans were asleep when the Chinese attack started but immediately responded and "charged towards the hilltop." Many were killed and wounded in the hail of Chinese gunfire. "Juchen Thupten and two others took a circuitous route, dodging Chinese fire" and finally made it further up the mountain and away from Chinese fire.[27]

This Chinese machine gun fire also pinned down Seynang Lobsang Yeshi and his personal militia at the crossing. This young official had escorted the Dalai Lama to resistance territory and then returned to collect weapons from the Norbulingka. His fighters were lightly armed with pistols and a few rifles he had purchased himself, and he desperately needed better weapons: Bren guns, Sten guns, Enfields and grenades—whatever he could get from the government arsenal. Tenpa Soepa and other Norbulingka staff had collected a substantial cache of weapons and ammunition, and on the 19th evening, helped Lobsang Yeshi's men load the thirty pack animals they had brought with them.[28] Lobsang Yeshi himself was at the ferry-crossing making arrangements to get his pack animals and weapons across the Kyichu when they appear to have been attacked. There is no first-hand account of what happened, but it is generally believed that Lobsang Yeshi led a charge against the machine-gun emplacements, and he and his men were mowed down.

At dusk, after the final Chinese assault on the Norbulingka, many of the Tibetan survivors poured out of the battered palace towards the river and were met with machine-gun fire. Li writes that "thousands . . . waves of people surged out of the Norbulingka towards the riverbank." They tried to escape across the river, and they were killed, not only by machine-gun fire but also by artillery shells.

Many of the escapees who made it to the river tried to ford across, holding each other's hands and making a human chain. Unfortunately, in the clear moonlight (waxing gibbous) they were visible to the Chinese and were cut down. A twelve-year-old boy, Thupten Anyetsang, trying to escape with his older brother, Kalsang, described the scene to me when I interviewed him twenty years later.* He clearly remembered the bodies from the broken human chain floating away downstream.

---

*I used Thupten's account in a short story, 'Flight', that appeared in *The Illustrated Weekly of India* in 1979.

Other escapees were more careful. Khenchung Tara and his companions, after a few unsuccessful attempts, lay flat on the river bank—others crawled into ditches. Finally, when a cloud appeared and darkened the sky "Everyone rose and hurried west to a shallow crossing. A hundred more people appeared just as they were about to strip and wade in, and they all forded the river together holding hands."[29]

* * *

The thunderous roar of the artillery strikes on the Norbulingka could easily be heard from Sera (Wild Rose Fence) Monastery a few miles north of Lhasa. The monks could also see the "explosions of dust and clouds of smoke from the direction of Lhasa." Many of the monks had earlier joined the demonstration on 10 March but were now "forbidden by the abbots to leave the monastery", according to Tashi Khedrup,* a monk who belonged to the *dob-dob* fraternity at Sera. Members of this organization served the monastery as heavy workers, security guards, athletes and sometimes musicians (blowing the giant *dungchen* horns) but were notorious in Lhasa city as street brawlers.

On 20th morning, three artillery shells hit the hillside behind Sera. Some monks in the monastery claimed the shells were a warning from the Chinese and that everyone should stay in the monastery and not join the fighting. But most monks wanted to do something. According to Tashi Khedrup, "A powerfully built young monk stood out as the leader. He was not a *dob-dob* but a man of learning and authority; in fact, he was a *geshe*, a teacher, of the Pompora Khamtsen (college). He proposed that we should go to the Potala and get weapons from the arms store there. About five hundred monks and all the *dob-dobs*, volunteered to follow him."[30]

"From Sera, you can see the Potala a couple of miles away. Between it and the monastery is a stream running inside a high sand embankment

---

*Tashi Khedrup eventually ended up in England, where he met Hugh Richardson, the last British representative in Tibet, who recorded and published his life story as *The Adventures of a Tibetan Fighting Monk*.

(*cherag*). Our party made as fast as we could for the shelter of that embankment while the Chinese in the Drapchi barracks, to our south, opened fire on us. No one was hit; as soon as we were under cover we could hurry along quite safely until we came in sight of another Chinese camp on the north side of the Potala. The Chinese soldiers opened up on us with machine guns, but the embankment gave us good cover. However, we could not move further.

"Tibetan soldiers high up in the Potala fired at the Chinese to distract them. After a while, three armoured cars rushed towards the Potala from Drapchi, possibly to cut us off. I suppose the Chinese in the other camp had called them up. By a great stroke of luck, the Tibetans in the Potala hit one of the armoured cars, probably with a mortar. It burst into flames, and the other two turned and hurried back."

This incident is confirmed by the author of *Military History,* who was at the Potala with Drapchi Captain Phuntsok Dorje and other soldiers. They provided cover fire from the Talam Gormo, north-west of the Potala, which allowed the Sera monks to move forward and eventually get to the north gate on the Potala hill.[31] The soldiers directed the Sera monks to the lower storehouse of the Potala, where they could obtain rifles. The monks had to run down the front of the Potala stairs facing Chinese mortar and machine-gun fire from Shugtri Lingka. But their leader, the Pompora geshe, said there was nothing for it but to take the risk. The Tibetan soldiers gave them covering fire, but some of the monks were killed. They obtained about a thousand rifles and ammunition from the armoury at Sharchenjok. Then the Drapchi soldiers gave the monks a quick lesson "on how to use and clean the guns."

Inside the Potala, Tashi Khedrup found parties of women and children, most probably from the Shöl hamlet below, which was being pounded by artillery. Many fighters and civilians had been killed and their bodies were lying all around. Many were wounded. The monks and soldiers tried firing at the Chinese from the Potala windows, but they were out of range.

About midday, the Chinese turned their heavy fire on the temple, on the western end of the Potala, "which had a solid round tower and more or less blew it to bits. Kundeling Monastery, not far from it, suddenly went up in flames and we could see the monks running in terror and being shot down as they ran." Tashi Khedrup mentions that ". . . the Shöl, at the foot of the Potala hill was flattened, the Namgyal Dratsang (the Dalai Lama's personal monastery) was in ruins, and there were gaping holes at several places along the front. At the Potala, the great mausoleum of the Fifth Dalai Lama (*Sidung Chenmo*) was pierced right through by an artillery shell, which, fortunately, did not explode.

Another informant reported that the Potala was heavily damaged by artillery fire at the Sharchenjok wing and the Deyang Shar courtyard (where the annual *cham* performances were staged). But the massive outer stonewalls held. One observer marvelled at the architectural genius of Desi Sangye Gyatso, the Fifth Dalai Lama's prime minister, who had designed and built the palace three hundred years ago.[32]

After dark, the Sera monks were able to take their weapons and make their way back to their monastery, suffering some casualties. But when they got there, the Chinese started shelling the monastery from the nearby Drapchi camp, causing much damage and many deaths. But the monks now had weapons and fired back at the Chinese.

* * *

Other attempts by members of the public to arm themselves were less successful. In one instance, it went disastrously wrong. After Bhusang and the policemen at the Tromsikhang headquarters had fired off all their mortar shells to the delight of the ordinary citizens of Lhasa, many of these people declared their eagerness to fight and demanded weapons.

"Most of these volunteers were brandishing knives, swords, choppers, axes and a few pistols, but they wanted real weapons, rifles and machine guns, and were disappointed when we said we had none to spare. We told them they had to get it from the Shöl armoury at the Potala. They declared they would march there, but that was easier said than done. The Chinese Military Hospital compound was smack in the way to Shöl, and it was surrounded by high walls and heavily defended by at least two companies of PLA soldiers.

"There were thirty of us policemen with three mortars, two Bren guns and rifles and around four hundred volunteers. But as word got around that we were going to get weapons from the Potala, others began to rush out of their houses to join us. In spite of the sound of exploding artillery shells from the Potala and the Norbulingka, the crowd was in high spirits. From the Barkhor we marched west by Shidé Dratsang and Tsomoling Monastery, after which it was largely wasteland. You could see the Military Hospital which consisted of a number of buildings surrounded by a long stone and adobe wall about eight feet high. They had sharpshooters and *chigang* machine guns, and even a couple of heavy machine guns on the roof of the houses, all well protected by sandbags. On the top of the walls, they had soldiers with rifles. Lower down, at eye level, they had also dug loopholes along the walls—but not all the way through. You couldn't see the holes from the front, but when an attacker came close, the Chinese soldier poked a stick through and fired his rifle from this fresh loophole.

"Many people in the crowd just charged the Chinese positions and were immediately gunned down. About fifteen were killed, just like that. It was not an auspicious start. We shouted at everyone to pull back, and explained to them that we policemen would give them covering fire with our mortars, Bren guns and rifles, and only then should they try and storm the hospital. Many of the volunteers, men and women—yes, there were some brave women also, had cans and bottles of kerosene and also paper twists and burning torches, even firewood.

They intended to burn the place down. The moment we started firing, the volunteers charged the hospital wall. The fire from the Chinese, especially the machine-gun fire was tremendous. It just churned up the ground. It was as if the ground before the wall was boiling. It was a massacre.

"Our return fire was ineffective. The Chinese were safe behind the thick walls and sand-bags, and we couldn't hit them. Only our mortar shells seemed to have some effect—slowed their firing a bit, but we soon ran out of ammunition. We had been firing our mortars the whole morning. Our old Bren guns were useless against Chinese heavy machine guns. The American Browning automatic rifles (BAR) I fired some years later were more powerful weapons. You could fire tracer bullets from a BAR—one tracer between every five regular rounds. If I only had a BAR then—Shit! I could have burnt those Chinese out from that hospital.

"The volunteers were so enthusiastic and so fired up that they charged the hospital wall a couple of times more, before realizing how hopeless and suicidal it was. At least a hundred or so were killed before we finally withdrew, helping carry away whatever wounded we could with us.

"All of us policemen returned to Tromsikhang. We barely got there when we were hit with a tremendous artillery barrage. We didn't even get time to drink a cup of tea. Shells began raining down, and the building took a number of direct hits. More civilians and policemen were killed. We retreated towards the Tsuglakhang as best as we could, carrying all our weapons and ammunition. It was around 7 p.m."

The Ramoche Temple and the adjoining police station also received an artillery attack around the same time as the one at Tromsikhang. The barrage there first destroyed the gilded roofs of Ramoche and then the rest of the building. In spite of the shelling, Captain Tsering Lhagyal and his men kept up their fire on the Chinese police headquarters at Zumphü Mansion. Eventually, the Captain and most of his men were killed. The surviving policemen, about thirty, all told, managed to retreat to the Jokhang and joined their comrades there.

* * *

I gave a brief account of the Jokhang in Chapter 19, but that basilica is only the inner sanctum of the Great Temple of Lhasa known to Tibetans as the Tsuglakhang. Like the Tower of London, the Tsuglakhang complex serves various ancillary purposes seemingly unconnected to its principal spiritual one. It was mystifying to me at first but, Zasak Jigme Taring, who had once been a senior official at the Tsuglakhang, patiently explained it all to me, using a set of ground plans he had drawn from memory and which he published in 1980.[33] At the heart of the Tsuglakhang is the Jokhang Temple which is surrounded by numerous chapels dedicated not only to the many saints and deities of the Buddhist pantheon but also such local deities as the five goddesses of the Everest range (*tseringchenga*) and others.

Historical personalities and events are no less honoured. We have chapels for the Emperor Songtsen Gampo, his Nepalese consort, his Chinese consort, the Wothang Lake (on which the temple and the city were built), the Sacred Goat (which carried the first load of soil for the temple construction), Songtsen Gampo's horse-head wine jar (*chögyal trungben ta-go-ma*), the minister Sambhota (who created the Tibetan script), a nook for "the first offering of the Tibetan script" (*yig-phue mani*) carved on stone and the vestibule for the Dalai Lama's Great Throne (*shugtri chenmo*).

To honour the pre-Buddhist religion of Tibet, there is a pile of juniper branches and prayer flags (*bönpoe-pasol*) on a veranda and the Bonpo Treasure chamber (*bönpoe yang-khang*). In one basement treasure chamber, there is a blood-stained suit of armour and a helmet offered "on behalf of the deceased as a dedication of merit" belonging to the warrior Nangu Yutak, son of Rongtsa Tragen, supreme commander under King Gesar, who had been killed in the great war between Ling and Hor.[34]

History also follows us up to the first floor and the Great Hall of the Three Realms (*Khamsum Tsomchen*), where in 1727 the Prime Minister Khangchenné was hacked and stabbed to death by his cabinet colleagues and other officials ("Like Julius Caesar" my uncle Sonam Tomjor told me) precipitating a civil war that ended in the consolidation of Qing protectorate rule over Tibet. On this floor to the east, you also had the hall (*kashag tsokhang*) for cabinet meetings with adjoining rooms for the Kashag secretariat, archives, a waiting room and so on. Other government departments in the Tsuglakhang were the Foreign Office (*chisee lekhung*), Agricultural Office (*sonam lekhung*), the High Court of Tibet (*sherkhang*), Treasury Office (*lachag*), Salt & Tea Tax Office (*jha-tsa lekhung*), Revenue Office (*babshi lekhung*), Paymaster's Office (*phokhang*), Lhasa Municipality Office (*lhaesa nyertsang*) and the Department of General Accounts and School for Lay Civil Servants (*tsikhang*).

The Dalai Lama had his own extensive apartment unit, with a toilet (*zim-chos*), but there are chambers for the regent and oddly enough for the emperors of old (*chogyal zimchung*) as well. There are many more treasuries, storerooms, kitchens and so on, too many to list here. But we should not forget the four toilets that I counted in Taring's *Index & Plan*, which, as few as they are, compare favourably with the Tower of London, which appears to have only one, and the great Château de Versailles, which has none.

Adjacent to the Tsuglakhang in the east is the large Sungchöra Square where the Dalai Lama and other major lamas gave public teachings, and where later during the Cultural Revolution, monster rallies and ferocious *thamzing* struggles were held. Before the front entrance of the Tsuglakhang to the west is an ancient willow tree called the hair of the Shakyamuni (*Jowo utra*) and next to it the Treaty Pillar of CE 821–822 concluded between the Tibetan and Chinese Empires, after a decisive Tibetan military victory.

Now at the Tsuglakhang, General Jumpa and Major Gura organized the defence of the complex. Their main force consisted of three hundred policemen armed with rifles, some Bren guns, Sten guns and hand grenades. They had used up most of their artillery ammunition and only had a few cases of mortar rockets left. The Official Guild of Carpenters and Masons (*do-shing chiba*) had been assigned to defend the Tsuglakhang and about a couple of hundred of their members gathered there, with whatever weapons they had, which was not very much—swords, daggers, axes and a few handguns, but no rifles or machine guns. Other volunteers from around the Barkhor had also gathered there to defend the Holy site, bringing the number of defenders up to around seven or eight hundred.

Major Gura set the volunteers to work, collecting food and water and shoring up the barricades at the entryways to west Barkhor and the front of the Tsuglakhang. Large bales of government tax-wool in the storehouses were piled against all the large windows, leaving only enough space to shoot from. Most of the defenders took up positions on the roof of the Tsuglakhang, some even under the golden canopies. Embrasures were cut into the *hapcha* walls on top of the temple roofs. The main doors of the Tsuglakhang complex were closed, and large boulders piled up against them. Only one small side entrance called the *Lugong-Sang-go*, or "Secret Door of the "Scapegoat"" was not closed off entirely, but securely guarded.

"All around the Tsuglakhang, we were closely surrounded by Chinese administrative offices. Many of the old aristocratic homes across the Tsuglakhang, especially on the south side of the Barkhor, were now occupied by the Chinese. Directly across the main Jokhang entrance in the west was the Paljor Rabten and Palrab Khangsar Mansions belonging to the Panchen Lama's estate, and the mansion of the Doring family. Clockwise, in the south were Ragashar, Kyetöpa (People's Bank of China), Sampho (China Trade Agency), then Kapshoba and two houses further east, Pangdatsang Mansion (Commerce and Industry Office). Directly across Pangdatsang on the eastern end of the Barkhor was Surkhang House, the headquarters of the Public Security Bureau.

"All of these offices had a company or two of PLA soldiers supported by the office staff and other Chinese civilians who had earlier been formed into militia units and had received arms and training. In most of these houses, the Chinese had dug trenches inside the courtyards and covered them with wooden beams and sand bags, so that they were well protected from our small-arms fire and whatever artillery we had left.

"We were still receiving some mortar fire at the Tsuglakhang, probably from Yuthok, but some men and I went up on the roof and tried to check out the buildings and streets around us. It was around twilight, but we could make out Chinese troops moving towards the

---

*The Lugong Gyalpo, or "scapegoat king", makes his appearance at the New Year Festival. Wearing a goatskin robe, face painted half black and half white, he plays a game of dice, wearing a goatskin robe with the Jhanjupling abbot and loses. Loaded with gifts and alms, he is driven out of Lhasa, symbolically bearing the city's misfortunes for the year. First made known to the West in Sir James Fraser's *The Golden Bough* (1890), one of the earliest comparative studies in mythology and religion.

Tsuglakhang from the west, through the Lubuk area. They were being careful and sticking close to the side of the alleyways—but we could see them. They appeared to be coming from the Yuthok compound [which the Chinese were using as a command base] moving through Lubuk and the cinema hall, sidling by the walls of the Jhidiling buildings and towards the Barkhor.

"We reported this to Major Gura, who told us to hold our positions, and he would get others to take care of this problem. He organized a contingent of volunteers led by a platoon of policemen to approach the Lubuk area from the north where they would not be expected and attack the advancing Chinese troops."

The historian Shakapba writes of the bravery of volunteer fighters ". . . stealthily assaulting the Chinese camp at Lubuk."[35] This might have been the same or a related operation that Barber mentions of seventy volunteers attacking unsuspecting Chinese troops inside the New Light Cinema Hall (at Lubuk) and overpowering them.[36] But these accounts are unfortunately unconfirmed and lacking in detail. A volunteer from the Tsuglakhang, Langdun Gyatso, said that he and other volunteers attempted to ". . . set Yuthok House on fire with tins of kerosene oil. But the Chinese spotted us and opened machine-gun fire on us."[37]

In any case, none of these attacks succeeded in slowing down the Chinese advance on the Tsuglakhang. Bhusang and his comrades could see the advancing Chinese from the roof of the Jokhang. The Chinese stuck close to the buildings on either side of the road and took care not to debouch out in the front of the Tsuglakhang from the Lubuk entryway where they could be picked off by fighters on the roof and windows of the temple.

Bhusang spoke of a Chinese photo studio on the ground floor of Doring House that Chinese troops managed to enter. The Tibetans shot some of them, but the rest entered Doring House and made their way to the roof where they set up a light machine gun. Concentrated fire from the Jokhang defenders eventually killed all the Chinese on the Doring rooftop. One Chinese soldier panicked and jumped off the roof. But more Chinese troops kept coming.

Chinese soldiers also used the alley parallel to the Lubuk road, just south of Doring House, where the Phodrang Sarpa (New Palace) and Ragashar Mansion joined the other houses (Kyetöpa, Sampho, Pangdatsang, etc.) on south Barkhor road. These buildings were separated from each other by narrow alleyways and tenement housing. My friend, the Lhasa musician Ngawang Dhakpa, whose family lived in the old Jhidiling neighbourhood (a warren of tenement houses) just behind Doring House, told me that many of the Chinese occupied buildings were connected by tunnels.

When the fighting started, he said that the Chinese troops burrowed through the walls of adjoining Tibetan-owned houses to create a continuous passage for their troops to encircle the Barkhor. They would first throw basins or buckets of water on the rammed-earth (*ghyang*) walls to soften it. They would then dig through the walls with spades and picks, and having made a large enough hole, toss a stick grenade through it. They would follow it up with a burst of submachine-gun fire. The soldiers would then enter this house and start the drill all over again.[38]

Pretty soon, the Chinese had occupied nearly all the buildings surrounding the Tsuglakhang. They began firing through the windows and from the rooftops at Bhusang and other policemen on the roof of the temple. Bhusang described what the defenders did. "The walls surrounding the roof were over a metre high, so we cut sections or made holes for embrasures for firing. We kept up a steady fire against the buildings occupied by the Chinese. We were very close to the enemy, just across the Barkhor road—a stone's throw away. At places, we were no more than twenty-five to thirty feet apart."

Other Tibetans around the Barkhor joined in the fighting. Bhusang's old master Lord Thönpa and members of his household began firing across the road the Chinese Security (PSB) headquarters at Surkhang House and at the Commerce Department at Pangdatsang House. Thönpa's personal battle against the Chinese became well known in exile, his story being included in T.Y. Pemba's novel, where, as the haughty Lord Saring, he fires on the attacking Chinese with a Mauser rifle equipped with telescopic sights. Unlike Thönpa, who

Bhusang claims was shot by PLA soldiers who broke into his house, the fictional Lord Saring's defiance was cut short by a hand grenade.

Ngawang Dhakpa told me that twenty or so young Lhasa bucks gathered at Mentöpa, south of the Barkhor. They didn't have much in the way of weapons except for a couple of handguns, some knives and swords, but they were determined to strike at the Chinese. Lugging jerry cans of petrol, and kerosene they made their way north towards the Barkhor. Being city lads, they were well acquainted with the alleys and by-ways (*trab-lam*) of Lhasa, and managed to gain access inside the courtyard of Kyetöpa House (People's Bank of China) from the rear. Since the Chinese defenders of the Bank were at the front of the building, firing at the Tsuglakhang, the young men went unnoticed. The near-continuous crackle and roar of rifle and machine-gun fire and the explosions of shells and grenades, also covered whatever noise they might have made. The Tibetans quickly poured the cans of gasoline through the windows and doors on the back of the main building and set the place alight. The conflagration was sudden and dramatic. The building was lit up from the rear and the fighters at the Tsuglakhang could clearly see the outlines of the Chinese soldiers on the rooftops and windows across the Barkhor.

Bhusang, describing the defenders of the Kyetöpa and adjacent buildings, ". . . you could almost see their shit-eating faces, we were so close. We were firing near continuously now. My Enfield became so hot the wooden butt started oozing this oily stuff. A rifle loses accuracy when it gets that hot. I changed it with someone else who had been shot in the arm and was being bandaged, and I kept on firing."

The People's Bank of China was completely burnt down by morning.

Another building damaged that night in the fighting was the school and mosque of the Chinese Muslim community at the Wabaling suburb, a mile and a half directly south-east from the Barkhor on the narrow Thaypungkhang road. According to Jianglin Li the Second Battalion of PLA Regiment #159 was occupying the schoolhouse. A stone's throw away to the north was the Tibetan police station charged with maintaining law and order in south Lhasa. They had about one hundred men there, and many volunteer fighters from adjoining Thaypungkhang—the metalworker's enclave. The fighting was particularly fierce as both sides were about evenly matched, and the Tibetan policemen had a couple of mortars they used to good effect. The metalworkers were well armed, not only with swords, but indigenous firearms as well. Tibetans in the past had produced their own muskets and smooth-bore weapons, but in the early 1900s, the Tibetan government secretly employed two "Mohammedan mechanics" from an arsenal in North India who trained Tibetan metalworkers to manufacture Martini pattern rifles that were "fairly modern and not to be despised."[39] Only after the Tibetan government signed the Simla Accord in 1914 and in a secret protocol ceded Tawang,[*] and two adjacent valleys on the Indian border, did Britain allow Tibet to import modern weapons—but never quite enough, and always to be fully paid for in silver.

The Wabaling Mosque was heavily damaged but not ". . . burned down in Lhasa because Muslims were accused of collaborating with the Chinese" as Ian Buruma mistakenly mentions in a *New York Review of Books* article.[40] The mosque was caught in the crossfire of a battle. Religion was incidental. Nothing happened to the smaller mosque (Urdu, *chota masjid*) of the Kashmiri Muslims in downtown Lhasa, south of the Barkhor.

Groups of Lhasa citizens, on their own initiative, attacked Chinese positions wherever they could. At Banakshöl, quite a few of the Khampa merchants had already left to join the resistance at Lhoka, but some of those remaining now organized themselves and attacked the office of the *Tibet Daily* newspaper and the *New China News Agency* office at Tethong House.[†] They somehow managed to enter the

---

[*] The PRC and many academics in the West labour under the impression that Tibetans had ceded the entire NEFA area (present-day state of Arunachal Pradesh) to the British. In fact, the three valleys (*la-og yul-sum*) under Lhasa rule were only 7 per cent of NEFA, the rest being tribal areas the British had subjugated and annexed themselves.

[†] Tethong House was sold to the Chinese in 1956 by Tethong Lobsang Namgyal, younger brother of Gyurme Gyatso. He insisted that my uncle

mansion, and kill most of the Chinese personnel inside. Many of the attackers were also killed and wounded, including their leader,[41] the nephew of Jhangtsatsang Chönze, a resistance commander at Lhoka. It is possible that as Jhangtsatsang House was adjacent to the Tethong summerhouse, it somehow made it convenient for the attackers to enter the *Tibet Daily* office. The *Military History* recounts other isolated incidents of Tibetans attacking Chinese at Trimon House and also at Gyabum Gang, with many Tibetans losing their lives.

The *Military History* also recounts the story of the former minister Lhalu who, when Chinese troops came close to his mansion, began firing at them from his rooftop. Lady Lhalu (the biker) also fired at the Chinese with a Bren gun. She is said to have learned to handle that particular weapon at Chamdo when her husband was the governor-general there. When they ran out of ammunition, Lhalu was captured and some months later subjected to a major public "struggle", the only one witnessed by a foreigner, the American journalist, Anna Louise Strong.[42]

When I published the above account on my March 10 Memorial website, I received a message from the daughter of Lhalu's youngest brother (in Switzerland) that the lady Lhalu had been heavily pregnant at the time. She was forced to stop shooting when she began to go into labour. Her maid and relatives managed to conceal her in a storeroom, but the delivery was problematic, and baby's health suffered as a consequence.[43]

Throughout the night and the next day, the fighting carried on, and the sound of rifle and machine-gun fire was near-continuous. The next afternoon, Bhusang remembered a strange lull in the small arms fire around the Tsuglakhang. "Just after 3 p.m. that day (the 21st), there was a mortar attack on the temple. I counted over fifty bombs, but most of them did not do much damage. We all lay low and casualties were few. The mortar barrage ended around 4 p.m. and then the Chinese tanks made their first appearance in the Barkhor Square in front of

---

Sonam Tomjor, the head of the family, return to Lhasa from Kalimpong to receive payment, which my uncle did not.

the Tsuglakhang. Actually, they were not really tanks, you know, with metal tracks and cannons, but vehicles with rubber tires like jeeps, but covered with sheet metal. They also had this dome thing on top.[*] You know, Tibetans call all tanks and vehicles of that sort *thang-gari* (tank-vehicle). So possibly that's where the mix-up came from. There were four of them, and they came right in front of the Jokhang and began to move around slowly, testing our defences. These armoured cars didn't have cannons on them, just light machine guns. But these could point straight up, so we had to be careful when we fired down on them, which we did but which was not of much use.

"Someone mentioned that if you threw bottles of arak, kerosene or petrol at them, they would burn and explode. So, we quickly sent some volunteers around to find whatever they could. Finally, we got a few bottles of kerosene that we threw at the armoured cars, followed by grenades to ignite them, but they didn't do anything. We threw more grenades, but the old British grenades, you know the pineapple type, didn't make any impression on the vehicles. Then, someone, I think it may have been Tsegya Bhagtro, who was quick-witted, picked up a mortar bomb and, taking off the safety cap on the impact fuze, threw it down on one of the armoured cars. These things have fins, so they fly straight down, fuze end first. It went off with a loud bang and tore off the front fender of one car. This cheered everyone up. Before we could lay our hands on any more mortar shells, the armoured cars drove out of the Sungchöra courtyard, followed by our rifle-fire and whoops and jeers.

"As I told you, I think the armoured cars had come to scout the area and test our defences. They probably reported back to their HQ that we didn't have much in the way of artillery or anything left. Chinese soldiers now began to pour into the Barkhor in ever-larger numbers, and from all directions. They were everywhere. They also set up barricades and machine-gun emplacements in the alleyways and main entranceways to the Barkhor circle. We began to take intense

---

[*]From eyewitness descriptions, possibly Russian BA-20 or BA-64 armoured cars of WWII vintage.

fire. It was dead certain that before long, there would be overwhelming numbers of Chinese troops assaulting our positions.

"I went down to the Jokhang Assembly Hall (*chöra*) where Major Gura was having a serious discussion with General Jumpa. I reported how desperate our situation had become and told them we could not defend the Tsuglakhang for much longer. Some of the officers joined us, and a suggestion was floated that we should try to break out—perhaps even escape south and join the Four Rivers Six Ranges at Lhoka. But the Major pointed out that we were surrounded by Chinese troops and would be cut down if we left the protection of the Jokhang walls. Others said we should take the risk, but it was pointed out that all the main exits were now sealed with rocks and beams and would take a lot of effort to clear them, which would also alert the Chinese. Finally, the Major came up with an escape plan that all of us had to agree was doable. It was not suicidal but still very dangerous.

"General Jumpa sent the officers and NCOs around to inform other policemen of the upcoming escape. He told them to let every policeman make his own choice, but not to tell the civilian volunteers as they would panic. About fifty policemen wanted to escape with us and join the Four Rivers Six Ranges at Lhoka. Those who chose to remain were instructed to surrender only when things got really bad, and not before. They hung in there for a full twenty-four hours before surrendering. So they did good.

"'Have some tea, Bhusang', the Major told me pointing to the ceramic teapot-brazier (*mephor-khoti*) by his side. 'Don't wander too far. We'll leave around seven tonight.' I had no plans of going anywhere. I had a leather bag of tsampa with me and some cheese and butter. So, I sat down and mixed myself a bowl of tsampa and had a meal while I waited.

"Some time after seven, we all gathered at the rear of the Temple on the easternmost end of the Tsuglakhang where normally there was a door, which was now closed and heavily barricaded. Next to it was a large kitchen. Abutting the kitchen on the outside was the Muru Nyingba Chapel, which was a separate building but adjoining the Tsuglakhang. The windows of the kitchen were very high and open, about the level of a two-storey house, probably for the smoke to get out. We found the tall ladders and scaffolding used during the Mönlam Festival to erect the giant butter sculptures, which were stored nearby. We set them up against the windows and climbed up. From the windows, we jumped out on the roof of the Muru Nyingba Chapel. The plan was to then climb down and exit by the alley that faced the famous Four-Door Stupa (*Kani Goshi*)* in Northern Barkhor. The moment our men started jumping down, the Chinese began firing at them from the roof of the Tromsikhang building that they had captured (but which we had not realized) and from around Phorongkha.

"I and another policeman Tsering and the bugler Kalsang were still up on the window. We fired back at the Chinese, giving some covering fire to our comrades. The three of us were the last to jump down on the Chapel roof so we got separated from the main body of men.

"The three of us then jumped down into the alley and ran past Nangtseshag jail and the Lhasa courts and came out into the Barkhor by the Kani Goshi Stupa. It was a killing ground there. The Chinese were firing at us from seemingly everywhere, and the confusion and noise were just terrifying. It was every man for himself. Somehow, I really don't know how, my two mates and I managed to get out of there and make it towards the Ganden Prayer Flag Pole† in East Barkhor,

---

*The Kani Goshi Stupa, especially venerated by the Newari business community in Lhasa, is said to contain a bone relic of the Buddha from his previous life as a merchant prince, Simhala (Sanskrit) or Tsongpon Norsang (Tibetan). These tales in the *Simhalasartabahu avadana*, preserved in the *Mahāvastu* text of early Buddhism, resemble Sinbad the Sailor stories. Some scholars, including the writer Salman Rushdie, have noted that many of the Arabian Nights stories can be traced back to Indian sources.

†The four giant Prayer Flag Poles (*dharchen*) were well-known city landmarks that celebrated certain events in Tibetan history: the arrival of a Seventh Dalai Lama to Lhasa in 1720 (Kalsang Dharchen), the subjugation of Kham by Gushri Khan in 1634 (Jhuyag Dharchen), the victory of commander Tsewang Pelsang over Ladakh in 1681 (Ganden Dharchen) and the establishment of the 'Great Prayer' Festival by Tsongkhapa in 1409 (Sharkyaring Dharchen). An English equivalent might be the famous Cornhill Maypole in London, destroyed by Oliver Cromwell.

where the firing was less intense. We then ran toward the Hongtö Shingka horse-market and after a while made it to Banakshöl.

"There, we came across a group of Khampas and soldiers—about a hundred of them. They had horses, mules and some rifles and pistols, so we decided to join forces and go on together. Beyond Banakshöl, when we were cutting across the northern side of the New Park (*Lingka Sarpa*), we were hit by Chinese rifle and machine gun fire. Some years ago, a Chinese artillery regiment had been based there but was said to have transferred to Kongpo. We assumed it was long gone. But now for whatever reason we were getting a lot of fire from that park. But we had to head east to make it out of Lhasa. We had to cut across the park. We had no choice.

"We tried three times to break through, but the Chinese fire was too intense, and we were driven back. So, we divided ourselves into two groups, one to give covering fire while the other charged forward. The charging group would stop after a bit and then provide covering fire to the other group when it ran forward. I was in the first covering group. We could see the muzzle flashes coming from the Chinese positions, and we trained our counter-fire at those points. I'm afraid we didn't carry out this plan very effectively. In the dark, we couldn't really see what we were doing or where we were heading, but in a confused, disorganized way, it worked as well as it could have.

"We managed to make it through the park and then crossed some fields. We may have skirted by Gonshampa House. But the Chinese shot many of us down. There was a lot of yelling and shouting in the dark. Men screaming with pain and pleading: "I'm dead! Don't leave me! Kill me! It hurts!" . . . and so on. Horses and mules were being gunned down also, their whinnying and screaming adding to the noise of gunfire and the wounded and dying men. The chaos and confusion were incredible. Close to me, Kalsang, our regimental bugler, was hit and fell down. I stopped by him. He was in pain and screamed for someone to shoot him. I couldn't do it.

"Finally, after what seemed like an endless nightmare we broke through. Tsering and I found ourselves far outside the city, but we kept on jogging and in a little while got to the bottom of those mountains just north of Lhasa that we called Gyab-Ri (Rear Mountains). Rigya Monastery should have been nearby, but I couldn't see it. I figured that if we followed the valley north-east we would get to Nachendrak and the Chinese hydroelectric plant—and Chinese soldiers. So, instead we began climbing directly up the steep slope of the mountain. After an hour or so, we came up on a level area, a shoulder, where some of the survivors of our escape-run across the New Park were resting.

"There weren't too many of them, and they were happy to see the two of us. Their pack animals had scattered or been shot, but the Khampas told us that they had horses at Drigung and that we should travel with them. But we refused the offer. I explained that our first task was to find the rest of our police contingent. So we split up. Tsering and I continued to trudge up the mountain in the dark. We reached the top of the ridge before dawn.

"Looking back at Lhasa in the far distance, we could hear the sound of gunfire and artillery, which was unending, and see the flashes of exploding shells. We rested there till first light. Before moving on, I took a last look at my city blanketed by a pall of smoke—like morning fog. Even at that distance, the smell of cordite was so strong it was choking. I thought of my wife and child in that smoke and hell.

"I had said goodbye to my wife the night before the fighting. It was a difficult and sad business. I told you I was 'a man whose luck had dried up' [sothey-kambo]. But for a little while in my life, with Tashi Wangmo, I was blessed. She was a wonderful wife, the jewel of our home [nangkyi norbu]—really. We had a small apartment at Tromsikhang and were very happy, but it wasn't safe there any longer. I took her to her aunt's house near Ganden Khangsar in northern Lhasa. I gave her most of the money I had on me, and my gold earring* [aalong]. The earring had at least four tolas of gold and a good quality

---

*All laymen in Tibet wore earrings. Spencer Chapman describing the attire of a muleteer, mentions ". . . a large single earring in the left ear and a plain piece of turquoise in the other. This earing took the form of a fluted gold ring about two inches in diameter, with a turquoise mounted in the front. As this ring is very heavy, it is supported by a loop of red cotton over the top of the ear."

turquoise. I told her that it would help her survive. That was all I could say. I had a baby son then who was at the stage where he was crawling all over the place. My wife also had another baby inside her.

"After the Uprising, they really suffered. She was made to do forced labour [*nyetsol*] and couldn't look after the kids. Food became so scarce that she had to look for grass and edible plants in the fields, when she had some spare time. Then the three-year famine came. My wife was sent to Chamdo to build the power plant there. She had to leave the children behind with her aunt. They died of starvation—one little boy and a baby girl. So many others died.* Whatever was wrong with the old society [*chizo-nyingpa*], we had enough then. We never imported barley or wheat. We imported rice from Nepal, but that was a kind of treat, and not a necessity. Under the Chinese, you got a ration of twenty-three *gyama* of barley a month. A *gyama* is around 250 grams. That was all. No meat, no butter. Not even oil. And you need a lot of fat to survive in Tibet. There was so much butter and mustard oil in Tibet before. Nomads used butter, and farmers used mustard oil for everything: cooking, lighting, offering lamps [*chömé*], massaging babies—everything. But now there was not enough to eat. It all went to feed the Chinese soldiers."

* * *

At the Tsuglakang, the remaining policemen and volunteer fighters held out for another day. Li writes, "Armored vehicles rolled into the Barkhor Street just before daybreak on March 22. Traversing the improvised barriers with ease they pulled right up to the Tsuglakhang Temple. Behind them came ranks of soldiers, who surrounded the temple, rifles cocked and awaiting the order to fire."[44]

The account of Langdun Gyatso, a volunteer defender, differs significantly: "On the fourth day [23 March] Chinese tanks arrived

---

*Yang Jisheng, in his book *Tombstone, the Great Chinese Famine 1958–1962*, the most comprehensive account of Mao's Great Famine cites 76 million deaths. The largest famine in human history.

from Nagchukha.* The tanks and armoured cars soon put an end to the pockets of resistance in North Lhasa".[45] The tanks also surrounded the city and blocked all the crossroads and major intersections.

"At 6 p.m. on the third day the loudspeakers proclaimed that Norbulingka, Potala and Chakpori were taken, that the Dalai Lama was safe in custody at the Military Headquarters and that further resistance was useless. That day for the first time the Red Chinese flag was flying on the top of the Potala.

"The firing was now only sporadic and sounded far away. The streets were littered with corpses, some of them heaped in piles. Already street dogs were tearing bits and pieces from the bodies. Women were rushing frantically from corpse to corpse, searching for their menfolk. Chinese soldiers were out on the street rounding up all who surrendered. On roofs and from windows, people were holding *khatas* (white scarves) tied to sticks as a token of surrender. Others were standing in front of their doors with raised hands holding *khatas*."[46]

From the Potala and Shöl, the volunteer fighters who had survived the fighting were marched out in a long column, with burp gun toting Chinese soldiers by their side. At the head of the column was Tsarong with his hands raised. By his side was General Muja Tsewang Norbu, holding a pole with a white *khata* tied on top. This was an important propaganda moment for Communist China, and there were reporters, photographers and cameramen documenting the event. Tsarong was taken to the Central Prison at the Tibet Military Area Headquarters. He refused to be cowed and laughed and joked with the other prisoners, to the great annoyance of his captors. He held his six-year-old grand-niece, Tseten Yangkyi† on his lap and told stories to those in his cell of the old days when he had accompanied the Thirteenth Dalai Lama to Mongolia and India. It took three months for the Communist

---

*Another report states that the tanks (Soviet T54) had come from Damshung where the principal Chinese military airbase was located and connected to Lhasa by a motor road.

†I interviewed Tseten Yangkyi in 1984. Her mother, Kundeling Kunsang, had led the women's demonstrations and was in the same prison as her uncle Tsarong.

authorities to prepare the public trial and *thamzing* struggle against this arch "reactionary rebel leader" who in their propaganda film they describe as "the biggest serf owner—Serong." Denunciators were tracked down and coached for that momentous propaganda event. The night before the big rally Tsarong Dasang Damdul, my Tsarong pola, died peacefully in his sleep.

When the column of prisoners were marched past the Chinese reporters and photographers, the journalist Shan Chao recognized General Muja, who he had earlier met in 1950. "When the PLA units marched to Chamdo, it was this man who personally directed a machine-gun ambush against our cavalrymen at Kingsha River (the Upper Yangtze at Denkhok) and caused us quite a few casualties. Later on, he put up a stubborn fight at Chamdo city, but we finally captured him. We gave him very lenient treatment . . . but he refused to mend his ways. Now for the second time, he has been taken prisoner."[47] An unintended one, perhaps, but a tribute nonetheless to Tibet's hero of the Chamdo invasion.

General Muja was taken with seventy-six other prisoners to China. They were incarcerated at the Jiabiangou *Laogai* camp at Jiuquan in Gansu province. During its operation, this slave labour camp ". . . held approximately 3,000 political prisoners, of whom about 2,500 died at Jiabianguo, mostly of starvation."[48] General Muja Tsewang Norbu starved to death. Fellow inmate Tenpa Soepa wrote that only seven of the seventy-six Tibetan prisoners there survived.[49]

28

SILENT STRUGGLE

He was the George Smiley of the Tibetan intelligence world. He was not "tubby" and "myopic" as his fictional English counterpart has been described, but a lean, good-looking man, who worked out every morning of his adult life until a few weeks before his death from cancer in 1999. Tsongkha Lhamo Tsering was an exceptionally organized and dedicated spymaster and genuinely solicitous of the welfare of his agents. Like Smiley, he was soft-spoken and mild-mannered. He was also not very adept at bureaucratic and political manoeuvrings.

Lhamo Tsering's modesty and concern for others were among the qualities that elicited the loyalty and dedication of his many agents and fighters. At the height of the Cultural Revolution, when intelligence from China was near non-existent, and—as an old hand informed me—"not a sparrow could move from one village to another without the dozen-odd necessary permits" Lhamo Tsering managed to place (and nurture for years) a high-level agent in Lhasa city itself.

He was born in 1924 in the village of Sina Nagatsang near Kumbum Monastery in Amdo, then under the Chinese Muslim (*Hui*) warlord, Ma Qi. Chinese immigration had, since Ming times, asserted itself in those parts of Amdo, and Nagatsang had over fifty Chinese families to two Tibetan. Till the age of eight, Lhamo Tsering was a monk at Kumbum Monastery, when he began attending the local Chinese school in the nearby village of Rusar. Following his schooling, he went to the Teacher's Training School in Xining city and graduated from there.

The end of his schooling in Xining coincided with the Sino-Japanese war, and was briefly conscripted into the Youth Volunteer Force of the Nationalist Chinese Army. Before he saw action, the war came to an end. He then went to the Institute for Frontier Minorities in Nanjing to pursue further studies.

That same year a Tibetan government mission arrived at Nanjing to offer congratulations to the Chinese government on its victory over Japan. Accompanying the mission was the Dalai Lama's elder brother Gyalo Thondup, who had come to Nanjing to study at the Central University of Political Studies. Lhamo Tsering told me about this first encounter with the man who he was to work with most of his life.

"He was around seventeen then, about four years younger than I was. His older sister, Tsering Dolma, asked me to help him because he was not fluent in Chinese and would be alone in Nanjing. So we lived together, sharing an apartment. I found it difficult to help Gyalo Thondup and also concentrate on my studies, but things became easier when I managed a transfer to Gyalo Thondup's school."

In 1949 when China's major cities were falling one-by-one to the Communists, Lhamo Tsering and Gyalo Thondup escaped from Nanjing to Shanghai. As the Communist Third Field Army approached Shanghai, Gyalo Thondup departed for Hong Kong and left Lhamo Tsering behind to collect a bank transfer. But the money didn't arrive on time, and Communist troops surrounded Shanghai. Lhamo Tsering's vivid description of the period stirred memories in me of old *Life Magazine* photographs (perhaps by Cartier Bresson) of Shanghai's last days: panic-stricken Chinese men in western suits or traditional gowns topped with fedoras, women in Anna May Wong *cheongsams* and cloche hats desperately shoving each other before the steel-shuttered entrance of a Shanghai bank; bedraggled Guomindang officers and their mountains of possessions alongside other desperate refugees at the railway station, waiting for a train that would probably never come. And of course, the inevitable abandoned baby by the tracks.

Lhamo Tsering escaped from Shanghai just before the city fell. He and another Tibetan from Labrang forced a local fisherman (at knifepoint) to row them out beyond the harbour to the open sea where a last ship bound for Hong Kong picked them up.[1]

Lhamo Tsering settled in Kalimpong, the Indian frontier town and centre for the wool trade with Tibet. In February 1952, he accompanied Gyalo Thondup to Lhasa. This was Lhamo Tsering's first trip to the Tibetan capital. Here he was able to observe and experience first-hand the implications of the Communist Chinese invasion of Tibet. After four months, Gyalo Thondup and Lhamo Tsering managed to leave Lhasa and return to India.

On 6 August 1954, Gyalo Thondup, along with two Tibetans officials, Tsepon Shakabpa and Jayangki Khenchung, founded the Tibet Welfare Society in Kalimpong. Lhamo Tsering was what might be called the executive secretary. The objectives of the Tibet Welfare Society were to oppose the Chinese occupation, publicize the situation inside Tibet to the world, and initiate underground movements inside Tibet.

As mentioned in Chapters 8 and 20, when the Dalai Lama's oldest brother Taktser Rinpoche escaped to Kalimpong in 1950, George Patterson introduced him to Colonel Robert Ekvall, a former missionary, anthropologist and former OSS officer, who spoke fluent Tibetan—helpfully enough, in the Amdo dialect. Through Ekvall's connections, Taktser Rinpoche was invited to travel to America by the Committee for Free Asia, purportedly an anti-Communist association of businessmen, and also establish relationships with the State Department and the CIA.

But following the signing of the Seventeen Point Treaty and the Dalai Lama's return to Lhasa from the Sikkim border, America lost interest in Tibet as a useful asset in its Cold War strategy, and also in their big-name Tibetan Lama. But when the Khampa Uprising flared up in 1956 and spread all over Eastern Tibet, America became interested in Tibet once again, and Rinpoche's contacts with the CIA and the State Department were restored. In an interview[2] with me he said that he later passed on all these contacts to his brother. He did not explicitly say so, but I assumed he must have realized that Gyalo Thondup had the more conspiratorial bent and political skills necessary to use these connections effectively to benefit the Tibetan cause. But as I also mentioned earlier, Rinpoche assisted in training the first team of Tibetan agents in Saipan, acting as an interpreter, and helped devise a Tibetan "tele-code" system.

With American support, Gyalo Thondup and Lhamo Tsering were now able to help the resistance effort inside Tibet directly. They shifted their base of operations to Darjeeling, to the large manor house, Caernarvon, mentioned in Chapter 8. With the training and parachuting of the two teams to Samye and Lithang, and with organizing the arms drops at Driguthang for the Four Rivers Six Ranges, Lhamo Tsering in particular, began to show a flair for the organizational side of his new profession, as the CIA agent Frank Holober recognized during the debriefing of Athar Norbu in Calcutta. Lhamo Tsering could also speak and read English passably well, and his Chinese was excellent, but he needed to learn the "tradecraft" of his new profession.

So in July 1958, when a team of ten Lithangwas under the leadership of Andrugtsang Ngawang Phulchung was sent for training to America, Lhamo Tsering signed on as interpreter and supervisor. They were taken to "The Farm", the CIA training base at Camp Peary near Williamsburg, Virginia. The Tibetans were not told where they were, but in an interview in 1991, Lhamo Tsering mentioned how he had figured out the location of their camp. "It was a somewhat mountainous area and thickly forested. I would often help out in the kitchen. Our supplies were purchased in the city and delivered to our cook every day, along with the bills and receipts. One day I took a quick peek at a receipt. Below the name of the store were the words, 'Richmond, VA.' We were in Virginia."

The team was then moved to the now completed training base at Camp Hale in Colorado, which in addition to its elevation and environment being as close to Tibet as you could get in the continental USA, was also conveniently isolated and secure. Lhamo Tsering received specialized training in Washington DC at the "Zebra" safe house (near the Zebra Room Restaurant at 3238 Wisconsin Ave) in more traditional intelligence tradecraft: setting up networks, intelligence gathering and analysis, debriefing agents, planning operations, etc.

Near the end of his training, Lhamo Tsering was urgently recalled to India. Caernarvon HQ in Darjeeling had been receiving information about large-scale uprisings breaking out in northern and eastern Tibet. The Dalai Lama had also escaped from Lhasa, and fighting had broken out in the city.

From the many reports and scraps of information received from refugees, messengers and radio signals from Lhoka, four possible operations inside Tibet were initially conceived and gradually began to take shape between the CIA Tibet Task Force and Darjeeling HQ. Lhamo Tsering described these to me in an interview in 1991.

29

AIR OPERATIONS

DROP ZONE SHENTSA

"The first operation was planned for Shentsa district, west of the great inland sea of Jhang Namtso. A nomad chieftain Naktsang Powo had gathered a few thousand fighting men in that district and had started an uprising against the Chinese. We felt that this was an ideal situation for us to provide help, and I approached Gyalo Thondup with a plan to provide arms and instructors to the nomad insurgents. But the CIA did not commit itself immediately to this operation and procrastinated.[1] Finally, after some months, the CIA changed its mind and agreed to provide support to the nomads. Gyalo Thondup told us that the operation was on. We argued that it was somewhat late, as the last information we received was that Naktsang Powo's army was facing tremendous pressure from the Chinese. The actual present situation was unknown. But Gyalo Thondup insisted.

"So, a nine-man team of combat instructors and radio operators, designated Team Three, was readied. They were: Tenpa Trinley of Markham (team leader), Yeshi Wangyal Phupatsang of Markham (senior radio operator), Baba Lekshey of Bathang, Ngawang Phuljung Andrugtsang of Lithang (deputy leader), Droli Phuljung of Lithang, Atsok of Lithang, Doma Dhondup of Lithang, Lobsang Gelek of Lithang and Chönyi Yeshi of Lhoka. On 19 September 1959, at around 3 a.m., the team was successfully dropped at Ra-tsogen, half a day's march west of Namtso."

Lhamo Tsering, in the second volume of *Resistance,* writes "When Team Three arrived . . . the Communist Chinese had already destroyed the armed organization and nomadic people in the region who resisted them. Besides, the Communist Chinese had now constructed a road link from Nagchu to Shentsa district."[2] Not only was all armed resistance completely wiped out in the area, but the remaining nomad population was thoroughly cowed. Unable to locate even a pocket of resistance Team Three left the area. They luckily managed to buy fifteen horses from the small Dargyé Monastery near Namtso, which was initially reluctant to have anything to do with them. Then they started on their long journey west through the Jhangthang, the Great Northern Highlands, and finally made it through Mustang to Nepal.

DROP ZONE CHAKRA PEMBAR

The next operation was planned around a report sent by Gonpo Tashi Andrugtsang from the Chakra Pembar district in the Sho-ta-lho-sum area of Kham. After his "Long Ride" from Drigu, across the Jhangthang and his arrival at Sho-ta-lho-sum at the end of 1958, Gonpo Tashi managed to gather together a new resistance army around the core of fighters he had with him. Volunteers not only came from the three districts of Sho-ta-lho-sum but also Tengchen and Tsawa Pakshö. One informant mentions 40,000 men, but it is possible that around 10,000 men actually gathered at Chakra Pembar. Gonpo Tashi's appeals to Resistance HQ at Lhoka had been radioed on to the CIA. So, a team of seven volunteers (Team Four) was put together for Chakra Pembar: Sey Dhonyö of Dergé (team leader), Yeshi Gyaltsen Ryishötsang of Markham (guerrilla warfare instructor), Yeshi Phuntsok Rarutsang of Dergé (chief radio-operator), Yeshi Gyatso Ryishötsang of Markham, Sherab Gyatso of Markham, Loga of Karze and Tsegyal of Tsakhalho.

Two messengers had also arrived at Darjeeling all the way from Dzayül in the unexplored jungles of south-eastern Tibet (bordering

Burma and the north-eastern tip of India). Akar Gyaltsen, a chieftain of Jöl (present day Dechen Autonomous Prefecture in Yunnan province) who had been fighting the Chinese from the mid-fifties, had gradually retreated west and was now based with his men at the Sangak Chödzong Monastery with other groups led by such a legendary fighter as Reting Zimgak (more on this "giant" of a man in Chapter 31). They claimed to have a force of some thousand men but desperately needed rifles and ammunition. Another team with radio operators and combat instructors was readied for the Dzayül operation. Designated Team Five, the members were: Bhuché Utsatsang of Dergé (team leader), Aphel of Lithang (senior radio operator), Ganden of Lithang (guerrilla warfare instructor), Lobsang Gyaltsen of Gyalthang, Wangchen of Lithang and Lobsang Wöser of Lithang.

Reports had also reached Darjeeling of major uprisings against the Chinese by nomad tribes in northern Tibet, specifically in the area of Sogdé overlapping southern Amdo. The area is sometimes called Amdo "Tömey" or "Upper Lower" Amdo, appropriately enough. This was welcome news to Lhamo Tsering as he had been unable, thus far, to establish any communication with insurgent groups in his homeland, Amdo. He also had three trained Amdowa operatives standing by, so a team was quickly put together. Designated Team Six, the members were: Alak Sangsang Tulku of Amdo (team leader), Karchen of Lhasa (senior radio operator), Tsering of Drayab, Nangra Tashi Tsekho of Amdo and Tenzin Trinley of Amdo.

The Tibet Task Force decided that all three teams would be dropped together at Chakra Pembar in the Sho-ta-lho-sum area, as the resistance force there had freed the three districts of Chinese troops. The Amdo and Dzayül teams would then travel onwards and separately to their final destinations on horseback. "To map out the exact routes to and from these (three) locations, a U-2 over-flight was sanctioned (by the White House) on 4 November to cover Tibet, China and Burma."[3]

A single C-130 dropped the eighteen men at midnight Sunday, 15 November, in the light of a full moon, near the village of Tingka west of Pembar Monastery. Team Three leader Sey Dhonyö (aka Bruce) later recounted in an interview that he was petrified at the plane door but ". . . as soon as he launched himself into the slipstream the fear vanished. Bruce was overwhelmed by the prospect of being home. Dangling from the risers, he could clearly see that he was heading for a valley with snow caps glistening on either side."[4]

The villagers, having turned out to investigate the noise of the air teams landing, helped the parachutists recover their supply pallets, "including one that had to be fished from a river."

The following day, Bruce radioed Tibet Task Force a report of their safe landing and their meeting with resistance leaders. The principal resistance leader was the same person Gonpo Tashi had met over a year ago, Dundul Chöying,[*] the forty-nine-year-old secretary of the district headquarters of Tar Dzong that administered the district of Chakra Pembar, and it now seems also commanded the fighting men of the entire Sho-ta-lho-sum area. The young incarnate lama Pembar Tulku was a co-leader.

Befitting a traditional social system, the three supreme commanders were the Prince of Dergé, Pembar Tulku and Shabdrung Rinpoche, though these might have been symbolic ranks. Lhamo Tsering appears to have obtained the record maintained by secretary Dundul of the exact number of fighting men in each unit, their leaders and places of origin[5] and reproduces it in the second volume of his opus. I reproduce part of it to give the reader an idea of the extent to which surviving fighters from all over eastern Tibet had been gathering at Chakra Pembar, first of all responding to Gonpo Tashi's call, and later the arrival of the air-dropped teams, in the hope of receiving American weapons.

"All those who enlisted in the resistance organization to fight the Communist Chinese, were clearly noted in the record book. According to it, there were a total of 7,857 men and their leaders from eighteen districts: 1,900 fighters from the three districts of Sho ta-lho-sum, 500 fighters from Potö, 50 fighters from Nagshö Driru, 500 fighters from Khyungpo Tengchen, 150 fighters from Rongbo Rabten Gön,

---

[*]He was from the same family (of Gyanyok Wangchuktsang) as my great-grandmother Tsizin Dolma in Darjeeling, and possibly her nephew or cousin.

1600 fighters from Dergé, 1500 from Nangchen Gaba, 150 from Gaba Alatoe, 50 fighters from Lithang, Gyalthang and Chatreng, 120 fighters from Markham, 60 fighters from Dergé Tsaphung, 400 fighters from Chamdo, 37 fighters from Tsawa Monastery and Pomé, 50 fighters from Drayab, 60 fighters from Chamdadhe Monastery, 60 from Dargyé Monastery, 30 fighters from Amdo, 100 fighters from Gonjo, sixty from Lhari Monastery, and 200 fighters from Sok Tsenden Monastery. Total 7,857."

Lamas led some of these fighting units. The Shiwala Tulku, the second highest lama of Chamdo, led the Chamdo fighters. The fighters from Gonjo were led by a woman, a "warrior" nun as her biography describes her.[6] Lemda Pachen, who I got to know in Dharamshala, decades later, and interviewed at length, became a good friend of mine. Her father, the chieftain Lemdatsang Gonpo Norbu, wanted his only child Pachen to marry so he could have a grandson to carry on his line. But she was determined to lead a spiritual life and was also a strong-willed girl. She ran away from home, and eventually, her father had to come around to her decision. When he died during the uprising, she took up the leadership of her father's fighting men. When the Chinese overwhelmed Gonjo, Drayab, Dergé and Markham, she retreated with her fighters, her old mother and other members of her family west towards Sho-ta-lho-sum.

The refugee population, at least three or four times the size of the fighting force, was another of the many problems that Team Four had to deal with, in addition to the growing number of fighters now making their way to Pembar and threatening to overwhelm the organizing capacity of Dhonyö and his teammates.

Finally, the decision was made at Task Force headquarters that the Dzayül operation was to be scrapped and Team Five would join Team Four and help organize the resistance at Chakra Pembar. In mid-December, a single Hercules C-130 dropped hundreds of bundles of Garand rifles, Enfield rifles, four M60 machine guns, medical packs, two radio sets, and a large consignment of varied ammunition for the Enfield, Mausers, Czech and Russian rifles that the guerrillas were carrying. It was a very gratifying experience for the resistance, and the weapons and ammunition were distributed widely to the satisfaction of everyone on the ground. Fifty Garand rifles were set aside for Team Six's journey north to Amdo.

In the next few months, at least five other C-130 flights over Pembar dropped hundreds of bundles of M1 Springfield and M2 Garand rifles, machine guns and submachine guns, explosives, medicines, spare radio sets, mortars, even a duplicating machine— and, of course, lots of ammunition.

Lhamo Tsering attempts to provide dates and details of each drop, but there are some inconsistencies with the dates in the CIA reports (Conboy and Morrison). Both sources are agreed that on one of these drops, a single agent Kalden was parachuted into Chakra Pembar with the supplies. Both also seem to agree that the fighters on the ground had received ample weapons, ammunition and supplies all-round.

Selected fighters were then given training on the handling of different weapons, their maintenance, and guerrilla warfare tactics. But it was next to impossible to get the fighters to disperse in the forests and countryside and not remain with their families and other refugees in their group. Large tent encampments had sprung up around Pembar Monastery, with different groups in their own demarcated spaces—the civilians and the fighters clustering together. For many of the fighters, protecting their own families and kinfolk was the priority. The Team leaders and instructors repeatedly told the tribal leaders that such a large gathering of fighters, refugees and herds would be not only visible to Chinese aerial reconnaissance but also difficult to protect. But the chieftains and local fighters felt that with their new American weapons and ammunition they were no longer vulnerable and began to discuss battle plans that owed their inspiration more to the Gesar Epic than to modern guerrilla strategy. All the protestations of the American trained instructors fell on deaf ears as the leader of Team Five, Buché Utsatsang, who I met in 1972 at Mustang, explained to me, shaking his head in sorrow.

On 11 January 1960, a fleet of four Communist Chinese planes flew over the monastery around 9 a.m. They dropped many bombs and also raked the area with machine-gun fire. At around noon, the planes left.

On 12 January, three planes dropped bombs on the forest surrounding the monastery where many tent encampments were located.

On 14 January 1960, following another large air strike, the PLA launched a massive infantry attack. The Tibetans succeeded in holding their positions for about a week and inflicted heavy casualties on the enemy. But the Chinese attacks only increased.

When first planning this operation, the choice of Chakra Pembar had appealed to the Tibet Task Force as "Pembar was within striking distance of the drivable road* the Chinese had constructed between Chamdo and Lhasa."[7] According to Lhamo Tsering, "the successful build-up of a large guerrilla force in the Pembar region had struck a severe blow to the main Communist Chinese supply route."[8]

But the very tactical appeal of this target was, in fact, its major strategic drawback. First, the Chinese could, in no way, allow the endangerment of their vital supply route to Lhasa and the rest of Tibet, risking their gains in Central Tibet following the March Uprising. Secondly, Pembar being within striking range of the Sichuan–Tibet Highway, made Pembar and Tengchen vulnerable to PLA reinforcements now being trucked in from Chamdo. The Chinese offensive was ferocious. Lhamo Tsering notes that the Tibetans fought for many weeks, holding out in the Lho Dzong area, Khyungpo Tengchen, Lharigo and Damla and inflicted significant casualties on the Chinese attackers. The Tibetans also killed a number of PLA officers, even a battalion commander, and captured machine guns, mortars and a radio set. But Chinese reinforcements poured in endlessly.

After two months of relentless fighting, the Tibetan front began to break. At Pembar Monastery, Dundul Chöying and Pembar Tulku continued to fight until all their men were killed or wounded, and both seriously injured and captured. Everywhere else, fighters and their families tried to escape into the high mountains. The warrior nun Lemda Pachen and her men had all their horses shot from under them. In the end, carrying her grandmother on her back, Pachen was surrounded by Chinese troops and captured.

---

*The present-day northern Sichuan–Tibet Highway.

Of the two teams and the one lone agent parachuted into Pembar, a total of fourteen men, only five survived: Sey Dhonyö, Lobsang Woeser, Loga, Wangchen and Utsatsang Buché. The survivors initially headed north, perhaps to join Team Six, who had been sending positive reports of their progress in northern Tibet. But their horses, underfed and weak, could not ford the now swollen Gyamo Ngochu, the upper reaches of the Salween River, which even at the best of times is wild and swift-flowing. They reversed course, and headed south past the Namcha Barwa (Burning Meteorite) Mountain where the Tsangpo River turns south, and finally crossed into Assam in India.

Team Six (with its five members) had earlier obtained horses and pack animals at Chakra Pembar and headed due north as planned, to Amdo Tomay. On the way, they had a couple of encounters with Chinese patrols but managed to keep moving and not lose any men, horses or weapons. Finally, when crossing the Thagla pass in northern Tibet, they discovered a large gathering of resistance fighters, nearly all nomads, at an area called Behu-Seldzong in the Jhangthang. This area was actually on the border between Qinghai province (Amdo) and the Sokdé district of Northern Tibet. Six thousand fighters had gathered there, from Sogdé under Pön Norbu Tsering, and from Kyitse, Golok (Adrak Zamar), Lholungchen and other areas. Unfortunately, there were large numbers of refugees and enormous herds of yak and sheep accompanying this nomad army.

Lhamo Tsering says that one of the main objectives of the Amdo operation was ". . . disrupting the enemy's key supply route on the Qinghai–Tibet Highway"[9] and it appears that the guerrilla forces there were quite successful in doing that, to the point where the Chinese now deployed tanks and armoured cars to patrol the areas.

DROP ZONE NIRATSOGEN

Team Six contacted Tibet Task Force HQ to ask for more support, and also reported that the Chinese were using armour in the area. Earlier, Team Three whose mission to Namtso was a washout, but who had managed to escape through Mustang, was now reorganized at Okinawa to assist Team Six. Two of the older team members Tenpa Trinley and Baba Lekshey were dropped because of age and bad health, and Yeshi Wangyal Phupatsang was kept back for a future mission to Markham.

The new Team Seven members were: Ngawang Phulchung Adrugtsang of Lithang (team leader), Droli Phulchung of Lithang, Atsok Kyalotsang of Lithang, Doma Dhondup Gehogtsang of Lithang, Chönyi Yeshi of Lhoka, and Lobsang Gelek Draduktsang of Lithang—all members of the previous Namtso mission. Three additional agents included in the team were: Taythi Tashi Thundup of Gyantsé, Nethang Chönze of Drapchi, and Gaba Rigzin Tsewang of Jyekundo.

Team Seven was also trained in anti-tank warfare. On a full moon night in March 1960, four C-130 planes flew over the Niratsogen Lake, where the resistance force had now moved. The planes successfully dropped all members of Team Seven, followed by hundreds of parachutes of weapons and equipment, including bazookas, anti-tank M8 (57 mm) recoilless guns and shells. Two medium machine guns (MMG) with anti-aircraft tripod mounts were also dropped.

Chinese planes now began to fly over the resistance encampment, initially dropping propaganda leaflets that read: "If you surrender, we will reward you and treat you well. If you collude with the American imperialist, we will send troops from the ground and war planes from the sky and annihilate you all."

Tibet Task Force had printed an attractive leaflet with the Dalai Lama's proclamation declaring Tibetan independence and calling for all Tibetans to resist Communist Chinese tyranny. The leaflet also had a photograph of the Dalai Lama with his signature and seal, which made this a very precious document for Tibetans. Thousands of these leaflets were dropped with the weapons. They were distributed to all the fighters and refugees, who kept them as talismans. I saw one of these leaflets in Dharamshala in 1991. Dechen, a survivor of the fighting at Niratsogen, showed it to my colleagues and I at the Amnye Machen Institute. He had folded the thing up many times into a tight little square packet that he had wrapped in cloth and stuck inside his amulet box. Along with the Dalai Lama's proclamation, Dechen also had a square of yellow cambric that had Tibetan letters printed (with woodblock) on it. It read *"tensung dhanglang makar"* or "the Volunteer Army to Defend the Dharma." It was an ID badge that fighters were supposed to sew on their clothes to distinguish them from the civilian refugees.

And this badge, in a sense, revealed what the resistance force at Niratsogen thought of itself—an army to fight and defeat the Chinese Communists in big battles, not as small guerrilla bands to frustrate and gradually nibble away at PLA strength. But as Lhamo Tsering writes ". . . talk of a large military camp being formed in the region was spreading across Tibet. With high hope and expectation, the number of refugees and guerrillas continued to trickle into the region on a daily basis from all parts of Tibet."

More and more fighters gathered at Niratsogen. Many survivors of the fighting at Chakra Pembar also managed to make it this far north. Unlike stretches of the Jhangthang in Western Tibet, the grassland around Niratsogen, all the way east to Jyekundo is incredibly rich and capable of supporting enormous herds of yaks and sheep as foreign travellers like the missionary Susie Rijnhart had noted (in 1897). The fighters did not have to worry about provisions and, with the continuing CIA supply drops, and with the thousands of tents now dotting the vast grassland, a false sense of strength and security was created in everyone's mind.

Chinese bombers and MIG jets began to attack in force by the end of April. According to Dechen, the attacks were fairly indiscriminate, and civilians and herds of animals were strafed and bombed.[10]

Chinese infantry began a wide encirclement advance supported by tanks and armoured cars. The anti-tank gunners of Team Seven were kept busy rushing around to whichever point on the frontline that Chinese armour threatened to break through. Tens of thousands of Chinese troops from Chengdu and also from Qinghai, supported by Hui cavalry, attacked the Tibetans, and more PLA reinforcements were said to be on the way.

But the Tibetan defenders managed to hold on to their positions for around two months. The leader of Team Seven, Ngawang Phulchung

Andrugtsang (Nathan), was diligent in his radio messages back to the Task Force and managed to receive some more supply drops, a total of nine air drops in all, according to Lhamo Tsering.

But on 1 May that year, a CIA ultra-high altitude spy plane flown by Francis Gary Powers, was shot down by a Russian surface to air missile over the Soviet Union.* It was then believed that the U-2 aircraft flying at 70,000 feet (21,300 m) was beyond the reach of Soviet fighters, missiles or even radar, and the loss of the spy plane came as a great shock to Washington, which ordered the immediate shut down of all CIA over-flights over Communist bloc air-space, including Tibet. Incidentally, the CIA issued Powers with a neurotoxin-coated pin to use if captured and not the "L-pill" of potassium cyanide given to Tibetan agents.

Conboy and Morrison notes: "With its hands tied by the senior policy-makers in the Eisenhower administration, the Tibet Task Force was powerless to help its Tibetan fighters in their greatest hour of need. The radio near Amdo soon fell silent. None of the twelve [fourteen according to Lhamo Tsering] agents ever reached India."[11]

The Tibetans managed to fight for another month and Nathan continued sending desperate radio messages requesting immediate supply drops, or whatever back-up was possible. Athar Norbu who, later reviewed the radio messages from Team Seven at Colorado, mentioned in a subsequent interview that "under withering fire, Nathan, the leader of the Amdo augmentation team, radioed frantic messages that tank-led columns were closing in on their position."

According to Lhamo Tsering, "There was fierce fighting for more than two months. Many thousands were killed and wounded on both sides." The Chinese were resorting to full-frontal charges, with officers and cadres in the rear threatening to shoot their own troops if they faltered or retreated. Many of the PLA reinforcements were raw recruits who were unable to function effectively at such high altitudes and were massacred by the Tibetans. Even when, eventually, the Tibetan

---

*The Steven Spielberg film *Bridge of Spies* (2015) gives a fairly detailed and accurate account of this Cold War incident.

positions broke and the different groups and fighting units began retreating, the Chinese leadership did not allow their men any rest or respite, insisting that every vestige of Tibetan resistance be wiped out.[12]

Dechen and his comrades kept up a fighting retreat into the interior of the Jhangthang. The weather got colder and the winds more savage, but the PLA troops kept following them. After about a week, Dechen could still see the Chinese soldiers in the distance behind him. At one point he and some of his comrades turned around to fight them. As the Tibetans closed in on the enemy, Dechen realized that the Chinese were, quite literally, on their last legs. They were down on their knees, shivering and shaking, lips cracked and bleeding, unable to do anything. Dechen did not bother to shoot them.

All but two of the fourteen team-members were either killed in the fighting or died using the cyanide capsules they carried. One was knocked out by a grenade blast and subsequently captured. He committed suicide in prison. Only one agent surrendered.

The Tibet Task Force in Colorado and the Darjeeling HQ were shocked by this disaster but did not have time to chew over this setback to the Tibet operations. Gonpo Tashi Andrugtsang and what was left of the Four Rivers Six Ranges finally crossed over into India on 29 April 1959.

RETREAT TO INDIA

As mentioned before, Gonpo Tashi had convened a last big meeting at Pembar on 21 February 1959, not only of the commanders but all the fighters as well, where the decision was made that Gonpo Tashi and his men, along with volunteers, a total of 700 men, would leave for Lhoka, to reorganize the failing resistance leadership there and also radio America to obtain weapons and ammunition for the larger force which would remain and hold the Sho-ta-lho-sum and Tengchen areas.

They rode out from Chakra Pembar to Lhari in the west and then south to Kongpo Gyamda, being careful to avoid encounters with Chinese forces. They crossed the Wölga River, finally arriving at Tsethang on 2 April, where the Khampa fighters were still laying siege to the Chinese fortress there. Gonpo Tashi then rode to resistance headquarters at Lhagyari. It was there he received information about Chinese reinforcements approaching Tsethang. The two radio-operators Athar Norbu and Lotse had returned to Lhoka after escorting the Dalai Lama to the Indian border. They met Gonpo Tashi and the other leaders at Lhagyari and discussed plans for future operations.

First, a new and secure base had to be found where the scattered resistance groups could fall back on, and reorganize, and where CIA arms-drops could be safely carried out. One proposal was the Nyal Valley, about sixty kilometres south of Lhagyari. Lhamo Tsering writes that this area was ideal for a new base as local monasteries (Drawo Labrang) and important local personages had offered to help the resistance with food supplies and fodder. It is possible that the Dalai Lama's recent stay at Lhüntsé Dzong in Nyal Mey (lower Nyal) and his proclamation of the provisional government of Tibet had inspired the population of the Nyalchu Valley. Lhamo Tsering also writes that ". . . the area was well suited for secret military training and the features of the place were ideal for arms support through air drops. Lastly, it was mentioned that from Nyal up to the Indian border, the area was clean" (of Chinese troop presence).[13]

On 9 April, news came that the Chinese had recaptured Tsethang. Orders were given for the Lhagyari headquarters to immediately relocate to Lhüntsé Dzong, where they were met by other resistance contingents and also a company of Drapchi soldiers, led by General Tashi Palrab. Then news came that the area of Lhodrak to the west, bordering Bhutan, was now occupied by Chinese troops. Many in the leadership became nervous as one more avenue of escape was denied to them, but Gonpo Tashi called on the remaining contingents in the Lhoka region to fall back on the new base at Nyal. Athar Norbu radioed the Tibet Task Force of this new plan.

Then on 14 April, a report arrived at Lhüntsé Dzong that the Chinese had attacked Tsona Dzong, ninety kilometres to the west, from where the easiest crossing, relatively speaking, could be made to India. Gonpo Tashi called for a counterattack on the Chinese at

Tsona, but none of his commanders showed any enthusiasm for the idea. Individual groups were now making their own way to the Indian frontier. The resistance was falling apart.

Gonpo Tashi, wounded, spent, and carrying half a pound of shrapnel inside him, could do little to rally whatever remained of his scattered resistance force. But around a hundred of his most loyal fighters joined him in his proposed counterattack on the Chinese force advancing on Tsona. At Khartak Monastery, he met the resistance commander Amdo Jinpa Gyatso and Commander Tramo, who told Gonpo Tashi that they had "a wish and order" from the Dalai Lama that he now retreat to India and not risk his life any further. Tsona had fallen to the Chinese, so they now had to make the crossing to India over the Mago-la Pass, not the easier (relatively speaking) Khenzimana Pass, which the Dalai Lama had used earlier.

Once Gonpo Tashi had crossed over into India, Gyalo Thondup and Lhamo Tsering had to deal with Indian bureaucratic red tape to rush the old man to Darjeeling, not only to get him to a proper hospital, but also discuss with him, future plans for reorganizing the resistance. Lhamo Tsering also made arrangements for a full debriefing of Gonpo Tashi to be conducted by CIA officer Roger McCarthy at Darjeeling. Lhamo Tsering's wife, Tashi Dolma, remembered the occasion as she was charged with the catering for the week-long event. The leaders also sat down to make plans for establishing a new resistance base and appointing new commanders.

Gonpo Tashi was now ailing and in constant pain. In 1963 he became completely paralyzed from the waist down. With the help of the CIA, he was flown to London and operated on by neurosurgeons at Maudsley Hospital. Ten shrapnel pieces were removed from his body. He slowly recovered in the following months and returned to India in July that year. The following year he passed away on 27 September. Before his death, he entrusted Lhamo Tsering with the old battle standard of the "Four Rivers Six Ranges", his Browning pistol and personal seal.

Lhamo Tsering began scouting around the various refugee camps all over northern India, for suitable young Tibetans to be trained for intelligence and guerrilla operations inside Tibet. One of these recruits was Bhusang.

After escaping from the embattled capital and making his way up the mountains behind Lhasa, Bhusang eventually met up with General Jumpa, Major Gura and twenty-five surviving police officers. They made it to Lhoka, where they contacted the Four Rivers Six Ranges and Tibetan army personnel who had escaped from Lhasa. They were asked to join the Resistance *makhar* under commander Alo Dawa and Amdo Lekshey and help them defend Samye. But before this force could be organized, the Chinese took Samye. Bhusang and the others were then ordered to retreat to Lhüntsé Dzong and join Gonpo Tashi and General Tashi Palrab there.

When they got there, everyone had left, except for a rear-guard under the Chatreng commander Kowa Tempa Gyaltsen. Bhusang had known him from Lhasa, and he told me how impressed he was at Kowa Tempa's calm demeanour when a scout breathlessly reported a Chinese advance from the north. Bhusang mentioned that Kowa Tempa also had a *trey-kyok*, an M18 recoilless gun and some boxes of shells strapped to the side of a mule, which was reassuring. Kowa Tempa calmly ordered his men to pack and load up their animals. Quite unhurriedly, he drank a cup of tea. When he finished, they all rode out of Lhüntsé, for the difficult journey to the Indian border.

Bhusang's description of the Mago-la Pass: "It was high, really high—just went on up forever. Made you shit with exhaustion. The narrow track leading to the top was icy, snow covered in parts and treacherous. Many Tibetans didn't make it. Looking down on the ravine floor, littered with dead horses, mules and the bodies of our less fortunate countrymen (*phayul-chikpa*) was a wretched experience."

After crossing into India, Bhusang was interned at the Indian DP camp at Missamari for a couple of months. When he was finally processed out, he made his way to northern Sikkim, where he joined other refugees at a road construction project for building the vital Nathu-la Road for the Indian Army.

30

CAMP HALE, COLORADO

The bus ride from Gangtok to Darjeeling (via the Teesta Bridge) is, to put it mildly, an uncomfortable experience. Passengers are packed together like cattle inside a rickety vehicle (a locally made wood/tin bus body mounted on a truck chassis) that races around the steep mountain curves with vomit-inducing alacrity while the daredevil conductor, or "cleaner" as he is called, hangs on outside with one hand, and bangs on the roof with the other to attract more hill-people to squeeze into his death trap. But Bhusang told me that on his bus-ride, he felt not only excited but also happy for the first time since his escape from Lhasa. "Finally I would get the necessary modern training to fight the Chinese. You know, I felt so helpless in Lhasa during the Uprising, not just at the power of the Chinese army, but that all us Tibetan fighters did not know what to do. We needed modern equipment and weapons, but more than anything, we needed knowledge and training.

"I was on the bus with twelve other Tibetan soldiers. We had all been working at this road camp with other refugees, building the Indian military road from Gangtok to Nathu-la on the Tibetan border. I was asked to act as the camp doctor as the camp had no medical facility. I did the best I could. I had earlier treated Major Gura at the Missamari refugee camp. He had never been a very healthy person and the fighting and travel affected him badly. He became very ill. The heat and humidity of Missamari made it worse. He died a year later at a hospital in Darjeeling.

"Then one day Captain Kaldam of the Drapchi Regiment came by the road-workers camp and announced that a group of twelve volunteers with a military background would be selected for special training. I put up my name. Captain Kaldam suggested I stay in Sikkim as I was useful there as a doctor. But I insisted that I wanted to be trained so I could fight more effectively in the future.

"Our escort to Darjeeling was sergeant Jhapok of the Drapchi Regiment. He had run away from Tibet when he was a boy and joined the Indian army for a while, so he could speak some Hindi. In Darjeeling, we were taken to a safe house where Gyalo Thondup's assistant, Lhamo Tsering, who was generally addressed as Drunyik-la, or "the honourable secretary", met us. We were given a basic literacy test. I came out on top. So Drunyik-la asked me to teach the other men to read and write Tibetan and gave me money to buy exercise books, pencils and pens. After about a month we were told that we had to move to another house. This was the former palace [Caernarvon] of an Indian aristocrat or prince and was a larger place. It was high on a ridge above Darjeeling city. Lhamo Tsering and his staff members, Yapshi Tenzin, Chungchung and others, also had their offices there.

"Lhamo Tsering told me that after my training, I would have to go back to Tibet to fight. I replied that I was ready to go anywhere and undertake any task, no matter how difficult. Lhamo Tsering said it was commendable I felt that way. So, from the twelve former soldiers, four of us were selected to be in the first training group. There was Namgyal Wangdu [author of the *Military History*] and Damdul both from the Gyantsé Regiment, Sonam from the Drapchi Regiment, and myself. With us were other Khampas and Amdowas, all young people. There were twenty of us in all. We were taken to a private hospital in Darjeeling to have medical check-ups and X-rays.

"Then on the night of 22 February 1960, just less than a year since the fighting in Lhasa, we left Darjeeling for the railhead town of Siliguri.

"We travelled in three jeeps with Lhamo Tsering and his nephew Jhanjup Jinpa* as escorts. We drove through the city, past the suburbs in the east, till we reached a deserted stretch of dirt road. Our Jeep headlights had been turned off a little while before. We got off the jeeps and walked for a couple of hours across dry paddy fields. We might have crossed the Teesta River at some point, but I don't remember. Probably the river was shallow and easy to cross, this being the dry season.

"Lhamo Tsering led us. He seemed to know the route well, even though it was almost pitch dark. Finally, after an hour or so, we heard dogs barking somewhere close to us. Lhamo Tsering told us to wait. He and Jhanjup Jinpa went on ahead, maybe to buy off the people around there, I don't know. They came back and we resumed our march. We walked between some peasant huts, through a lane, and after a while, we came across a group of Pakistani soldiers waiting for us. It had taken us three hours to walk here from our jeeps. Lhamo Tsering shook our hands and told us to work hard at our training. He and Jhanjup Jinpa then left us.

"The Pakistani soldiers took us to a small army camp nearby. We were loaded on a covered truck and driven to a small, deserted railway station. We were then put inside a large carriage and placed in the charge of two policemen, who took over from there on. Once we were seated on our hard wooden seats, we were served a meal: whole-wheat chapati bread and a rich spicy mutton-curry, and lots of it. This was the most delicious meal I had eaten for quite some time. Even now, the memory of it just pops up in my head sometimes, for no reason. Strange. Some of the others also had good memories of that meal.

"The windows of our carriage were covered with newspaper—glued on messily. There was no one else in the carriage besides the

---

* Jhanjup Jinpa is the first Tibetan war photographer on record. Most of the film footage and stills of the Dalai Lama's escape in 1959 were taken by him, as were the photographs of the Four Rivers Six Ranges fighters operating in Lhoka and the establishment of the Mustang base. Unfortunately, his work, though widely used, has never been properly credited to him. See 'Tibet's First War Photographer', *Shadow Tibet*, https://bit. ly/2EATyL5.b

twenty of us, and our police escort. We travelled the whole night. The next morning we arrived at a large station full of travellers, peddlers and hawkers—bustling with activity. Additional policemen came and pushing aside the crowd, escorted us out of the station quickly. We were put in cars and driven to a small military airfield, probably of World War II vintage. There were two or three military planes parked there. A couple of men, foreigners, white men, rode over to us on bicycles. This was my first time seeing white foreigners. Hold on, though. No, it wasn't. In Lhasa, I saw those American airmen whose plane crashed at Samye. I was a kid then and thought it the weirdest thing when they rode into the Barkhor on our small Tibetan ponies, their long legs dangling way below the stirrups. Lhasa folk commented on their pale blue eyes ('How can they see?') and their white (blonde) hair, which everyone thought had to do with them being old.

"We arrived at the airbase around noon and were given some tea. Some of the younger men fooled around riding the bicycles. I just sat inside the small terminal building and waited. After an hour or so we were served a meal, with lots of fruits, which didn't bother me. I had acquired a liking for bananas, which I had never seen in Lhasa. When it got dark, one of the white men came over and told us that our plane was arriving, and for us to stay inside the building and not come out on the field. To translate for us, we had Gyantse Sonam Wangchuk from Darjeeling, who spoke some English. How fluent he was I don't know. I suspect he was about adequate, but I am sure he improved with time. I stayed in as ordered. But the others were very excited and peered out of the windows and the open door as the sound of the plane got louder. After it landed, a number of people got off and came towards the building. One of them was a Tibetan, Trinlay Paljor, of the Shasok family of Shigatsé, who was to be our translator. With him were two of our American instructors.

"They were not in uniform, just regular trousers and shirts. They quickly escorted us out of the building to the waiting plane. We boarded the plane and strapped ourselves into the seats, which were two in a row, facing forward. With Trinlay Paljor interpreting, one of the instructors welcomed us and told us that we were with friends and need not worry about anything. He hoped we did not have a difficult time getting here.

"Finally, we took off. We flew over the ocean. I had never seen the ocean before, and of course, never from a plane. We just flew over endless water after that. We were served tea and coffee by one of the instructors with Trinlay helping. Lhamo Tsering had told me that it took fifty-six hours to get to America. I don't know. I couldn't keep track of the time. Anyway, we landed in the Philippines to refuel, and then again at another place, but I couldn't be sure. Before we landed, we were told to close the curtains on the windows and not look out. We took off again and finally landed in Japan, or so we were told by Trinlay Paljor. We were taken from the large airfield in a closed truck, through a town and then beyond to a village by the sea. Above the village were two houses on the side of a mountain, which was our first training base. In Japan, there was also Tamdin Tsepel Andrugtsang, or Apel, as he was commonly known, to help with the interpreting. I knew him from Lhasa. He had been my junior at the Medical Centre in Lhasa. Four of the instructors were there, and we started classes in map reading and using a compass.

"We trained in the morning and afternoon. In the evenings we watched Japanese TV. We liked the historical dramas though none of us could make head or tail of the story; they had lots of sword fighting, which didn't need explaining. The meals were very good, with lots of meat. We got coffee, tea, milk and juice to drink—nothing alcoholic of course. But they gave us American cigarettes to smoke. We had the brand with the red circle [Lucky Strike] in Lhasa before. We wore civilian clothes. In Darjeeling, we received cotton trousers, shirts and sneakers, and in Japan, we got a change of clothes. We stayed ten days in Japan. The two houses we stayed in were adjacent and had large gardens. There was nothing military about it, and no guards were posted. None of the Japanese from the village below ever came up.

"One day, we were driven to a big hospital nearby. All of us were stripped naked and given a complete check-up, with X-rays and so on. Those of us who had any serious illness would be sent back to India. But we need not have worried. No one in our group had any problems.

An X-ray revealed that a young Amdowa had broken his hand as a child, and the bone had not set properly. But it was not a serious thing. Some people in previous groups had been sent back to India, including Wangyal from the Drapchi Regiment, who had Tuberculosis.

"The staff of the hospital was entirely American. It was a wonderful hospital. I had never seen such a magnificent place before. Everything was white and shining and clean. The doctors, nurses and other staff members were such courteous and kind people. I was surprised and amazed by it all. In Tibet, we had nothing like this. The Lhasa Medical Centre was a great school and produced great doctors, but it was another thing altogether. Of course, the new Chinese hospital in Lhasa was modern and fancier than our Medical Centre, but it was still nothing compared to this American hospital.

"We finally left Japan and flew east to America. We stopped once at an island to refuel. There was a high mountain behind the airfield. In front was the ocean. There were a lot of warplanes there. The people were oriental looking. We arrived in the afternoon, and after getting off the plane, walked to a guesthouse in the airfield itself. The next morning, we flew out of this place. I later learnt that the island was called Hawaii.

"We landed in America that night. I think they had planned our landing in America to be at night and had made us stay overnight at that island. We had to pull the curtains on the plane windows shut. All the lights on the plane were turned off. Two covered trucks came right up to the plane door, and we boarded them. We could see nothing of the airport.* We were driven away. The interior of the truck was dark, and we could not look out as the tarpaulin covering the back was drawn closed and laced up. After an hour or so of driving the trucks stopped out in the dark countryside, and we were told to get off. A bus was waiting for us there. The windows of the bus were painted so we could not see outside. We stopped once to pee. We were out in the countryside, and you could see some lights in the distance. Some of the

---

*Peterson Military Airport doubled as the municipal airport for Colorado Springs.

men claimed to have seen a large animal lumbering about in the dark. It was probably an American yak.

"At dawn, we reached the training camp. We were served breakfast after which we all lined up before the storeroom and were issued our uniforms and kits. For winter wear, we were issued two pairs of wool trousers and two woollen shirts each; also underwear, T-shirts and socks. They gave us everything we needed: soap, toothbrush, toothpaste, Vaseline, boot polish, even a sewing kit. We also received a pair of boots, a pair of canvas running shoes and a forage cap. We also receive cloth labels with our training names on them. Mine was 'Ken'. We had to stitch the labels on all our articles of clothing. We were also issued one M1 Garand rifle, cleaning-kit, water bottle, sheath knife, compass and so on. No ammunition. To store all our stuff, we got an upright metal locker each and a wooden chest, both of which we had to lock. After getting our stuff and putting them away as we were shown, we were introduced to our instructors.

"A couple of the instructors were those who had taught us in Japan. The camp in-charge was Mr Mark. Mark only taught us occasionally as he was away from the camp quite often. Mr Tom was the head-instructor, and based permanently at the camp. I got to know him quite well. Tom left us after about eight months. He worked really hard at training and taking care of us. You could see he liked us Tibetans, and it got quite emotional when he left. He was a polite, soft-spoken and decent man. We shook hands with him and were quite sad. We did not have *khata* scarves to offer him, but managed with lengths of clean white cotton material that we ironed and folded nicely.

"Tony took his place as the instructor. Our other regular instructors were Bruce, Ray and Zeke. There was also Mr Bill, who was the explosives and weapons instructor. Mr Roy was the instructor in guerrilla warfare. He was young and drove fast in a flashy (*tok-tok*) car. I don't know if those were their real names. We didn't know very much about them or their lives, but I think all of us managed to get along with each other in a friendly, respectful way. It was quite surprising, because we had a lot of wild, strong-willed people among us. Once in a while, some of the trainees had to be brought into line. For instance, Mr Tony stopped some of our younger men from wasting cigarettes and food. He told us that America had to help the world, and that we should not waste anything.* The food we were given at camp was *inji* (English) food, meat, potatoes, vegetables, all good stuff—couldn't complain.

"The person who handled the political side of things was Mr Ken [John Kenneth Knaus]. He gave us some classes on national liberation struggles in other parts of the world, but he was away most of the time. He travelled to India to meet Gyalo Thondup and Lhamo Tsering to discuss operations and training. He also met the Dalai Lama. Before he made a trip to India, I asked Ken if he could get me some sacred relic pills (*chaatsa*) and sacred strings (*jandue*) from the Dalai Lama's office. That was just before my mission. I wrote a note in Tibetan, with a hundred rupees, and gave it to Ken. He contacted Gyalo Thondup, who got it all from Dharamshala. Ken could speak some Tibetan. He might have been about forty at the time.

"The Tibetan translators were Tashi Chödhar (Mark), Pema Wangdü (Pete), Tamdin Tsepel Andrugtsang (Bill), Trinlay Paljor Shasok (Rocky), Wangchuk Tsering (Arnold) and our Sonam Wangchuk (Lee).

"Our camp was located on a triangular-shaped piece of land at the foot of a low mountain. A broad valley with a river flowing through it in the distance was just before us. In the interior of the valley, a lot of gold and silver mining had taken place in the past, or so we were told. The mountains were very beautiful with forests and open areas in the distance, where people would ski in winter. We could see the tiny figures of skiers gliding down the slopes. A railway line ran through the far side of the valley, and every evening, we would hear the lonely whistle of the freight train in the distance.

"The camp itself was a collection of wooden structures—military huts. But they were well built and warm. The compound was surrounded by a wooden fence. The fence was old. The western side

---

*Another CIA agent who knew Tony described him as a "man with a mission in life".

of the camp, where the hill sloped up, was unfenced. Our sleeping quarters were at the northernmost part of the camp. Two huts were connected with toilets and showers at one end. Each hut housed forty men, who slept in two-tier bunks. South of the bunkhouse was the hut for the interpreters, and a little further away, a long hut for the American staff. Adjoining this was the office and a classroom. All these structures were built around the central parade ground. South of the office was another classroom. The radio hut was just behind the classroom. Behind this was the kitchen, and close to the wooden fence on the south was the armoury. Outside the fence and across the road that came in from the west was the storeroom where clothes, blankets and other stuff were kept.

"A month after we arrived at the camp, a group of important leaders and fighters from the Four Rivers Six Ranges came to the camp for training. There was Rakra (Ross), Kowa Tempa Gyaltsen of Chatreng, Baba Namgyal, Dargön Pachen, Chatreng Dawa, Chamdo Tsering Dorje and others—all well-known names. Thirty of them all told. They were put in a different hut. After them, a group of eleven Amdowas came. Accompanying them was another translator, Tashi Paljor (Noel). More construction activities took place in the camp to accommodate the increasing number of trainees.

"The training was for a whole year. Our main training was in guerrilla warfare. We learned to read maps, use a compass, prepare secret weapons caches, conceal them and mark the location on a map. We also learned to shoot, strip and clean various weapons, including mortars, bazookas and 57 mm anti-tank recoilless guns. We were also trained to lay ambushes, prepare explosive charges and set booby traps. I also learned how to operate a radio set, encrypt, send and receive messages. I received a complete course in first aid and rudimentary western medicine. We even had classes in the evenings after dinner, though most of the time, they showed us U.S.-army training-films. Whether it was cleaning a rifle, throwing a grenade, operating radios, first-aid or anything, they had an instructional movie. The men liked them very much. Many of them had never seen a movie in their lives, so it was a great novelty. They also showed movies with stories in them, like cowboy movies,* which everyone enjoyed.

"I knew a number of the Four Rivers Six Ranges fighters from Lhasa and later Darjeeling, and they wanted me to join them in setting up the Mustang force. They had known me as a doctor in Lhasa and respectfully called me *amchi-la*. Kowa Tempa and Baba Namgyal were very friendly with me. Juba Chanzö also knew me from Sikkim, where I had treated him when he came down with a bad fever. They had no doctor in the Mustang force, and they valued the medical skills I had. But I told them that I had decided I would go where I was ordered to go by our leaders.

"Around that time, Markham Tempa Thinlay and Yeshi Wangyal (Tim) told me that they wanted me for an operation in Markham, where the resistance was holding out successfully, but needed support and training.

"I was sent for by our head instructor Tom and asked where I wanted to go—to Mustang or the operation in Markham. I replied that I would go where I could contribute most. Tom said that he liked my attitude, and suggested I join the Markham operation. Tom was not very tall like the other Americans, but strong and heavyset. He was a very nice person and a good instructor. He was about forty-five then. "So, I was selected to go on this mission to Markham. The team leader was Tempa Thinlay, who had been a monk and the steward of a big lama in Markham. The deputy leader was Yeshi Wangyal (Tim)", who was the son of an important chieftain of Markham, Phupa Pön. The team also had Damdul (Philip), a soldier from the Fourth Gyantsé Regiment, Dorje Phuntsok (Colin) from the Second Drapchi Regiment and Ugen Dorje (Duke) from Tsawarong in north-eastern Kham. Then there were two very young fellows from Lithang, Tashi Gyalsten (Aaron) who was a big guy, and Golo Lobsang (Luke) who was small. Those two were very close.

---

* "The CIA procured reels of television westerns and showed them every night. A favourite was *Cheyenne*, with the hulking Clint Walker in the title role" (Conboy and Morrison). According to the instructor, Don Cesare, "The Tibetans even began imitating Walker's mannerisms around camp."

"To prepare for the mission, we had to learn how to jump from a plane, wearing parachutes. We were taken to another military base, some hours away from our camp. We practised a lot on the ground, jumping off a ramp and rolling in the proper way so you didn't break a leg or injure yourself. Finally, we all made three actual jumps from a plane, and were ready to go. We left Colorado and flew to Japan with our weapons and all our other equipment. But when we got to Japan, we were told that the mission was postponed because of bad weather conditions in Tibet.

"Only years later did I learn that we were held back because the previous operation to Chakra Pembar and Sogdé had been a disaster. The resistance force there, including a whole nomad army, had been wiped out, together with the support teams that had parachuted there. I didn't know anything about it at the time.[*]

"This was in December of 1960. We had to wait at a U.S. military base for a month, near a city where the Americans had previously dropped the Atomic bomb [probably Nagasaki]. They celebrated the Christian festival [Christmas] with a big party with lots of good food and drink. Then we were sent back to the United States to our camp in Colorado. They told us that the weather was not improving in Tibet. We discussed the situation among ourselves and agreed that you could not have bad weather at one place for a month or more, so that planes couldn't fly there. We began to suspect some other reason though we were not sure what it was. But it made us apprehensive.

"Our team leader Tempa Thinlay knew more than us, I think. One day when we were playing football he fell down and injured his back. So he was dropped from the team. He had been parachuted on a previous mission to northern Tibet at Jhang Namtso (the great inland sea). The mission had fallen through because the resistance army of nomads had been destroyed by the time the team got there. The team

---

[*] As mentioned earlier, CIA airdrops in Tibet were put on hold when an American U2 spy plane was shot down on 1 May 1960. The White House only gave permission for Tibet operations to resume on 4 February 1961.

had managed to survive and make its way west across the Jhangthang to Mustang, and escape to India.

"Yeshi Wangyal (Tim), who had also been on this mission to Jhang Namtso, was now appointed our team leader. He selected me as his deputy leader. I had first met Tim at Darjeeling and got to know him quite well. He was a very good comrade and a good leader. He was brave but also level-headed and dependable. He was very intelligent and was the only trainee who could speak directly to our instructors in English. I thought he was more fluent than one or two of our translators, but that's just my impression. I know he hadn't been to any school in Darjeeling, so it was surprising and impressive. Tim was good with his hands, and could draw, and colour maps better than everyone else. He and I always got along well.

"The second time we left America, our stuff was already in Japan. Another team was going to be dropped into Markham after us, but only when we had landed safely and had established contact with the local resistance there. Our departure was supposed to be secret, but everyone in the camp seemed to know about it. Once again, we flew to Japan where we picked up all our gear and then flew to a large military airfield in Thailand. It was warm there. We were driven in jeeps from the airfield to a large bungalow in a forest where we slept and waited. We also made last minute preparations. We had to leave most of our uniforms behind in Colorado and wore regular white shirts and cotton pants only. We were issued Tibetan chubas, and overalls, helmets and para-boots to wear when we jumped. After three nights we were driven out to the big airbase where there were many planes.

"Our plane (a Lockheed C-130) was in the corner of this huge air base. The plane was of metallic colour and had small round windows on the side. It had four enormous and noisy engines, and a crew of about five. Earlier at my suggestion, we had drawn up a covenant or a pledge where we all swore to support each other and never betray our country and our cause. We also agreed to act like blood brothers even though we were from different parts of Tibet and that we would carry out our mission together and we would never surrender. We would fight together and die together. I asked one of our instructors, Mark, to witness this document, which he did. He was quite affected by the nature of our pact and said we were doing the right thing and that it was something few people would do.

"Before we got on the plane Mark* and Tony shook hands with all of us and hugged us. They told us that what we were doing for our country was a good thing, a great sacrifice. They got quite emotional. I can't explain why, but I was feeling absolutely happy. We had just had a great meal back at our bungalow, and I felt I did not have a worry in the world. I was so happy to be going back to Tibet.

"In retrospect, this was probably a bad sign, but that's what I felt then. I will be back in Tibet, I repeated to myself. Everyone in our team felt this joy. When our mission had been cancelled before, and we had that Christmas party in Japan, and later the Losar celebration at Camp Hale, none of us seemed to enjoy it. We were served many good things to eat and drink there, but we just wanted to return to Tibet. We kept pestering our instructors about when we would leave. All we wanted was to fly into this unknown danger. What can I say? This is man's nature, 'kyi makyok, duk kyok, man cannot cope with happiness, but he can endure suffering.'

"Tim also seemed strangely happy to be going back home to Markham. He smiled a lot, which was not a usual thing with him. He was a very serious person, most of the time."

I came across the following interview on a website[1] for a proposed documentary film on the CIA and the Tibetan Resistance. A CIA instructor, Ray Starke, talks about Tim and mentions a conversation he had with Tim before he left on his mission to Markham:

> They were great guys, the Tibetans; they were easy to train. They were very bright. One of them was extremely intelligent, very serious, a tall guy. I could hardly teach him fast enough, amazing man. His English was pretty good as I remember, one of the chief's sons.

---

* One of the translators, Tashi Chödhar, remembered that Mark, who was the same age as Tim, had grown close to him during the training and was in tears at the tarmac. Tim, his voice choked, passed on a request for Lhamo Tsering to take care of his wife and children in Darjeeling.

I think his training name was Tim. Anyway, he was very intelligent. I had a serious conversation with him about the operation he was preparing for, about the fact that it really had a very slim chance of getting his country back. I asked him, 'Why are you doing this?' He said he'd rather die with a gun in his hand than live away from Tibet. At the time, I felt that, under the same circumstances, I'd hope that I would have the courage and honor to feel that way. A proud man. I suspect he died in that operation, but I don't feel sorry for him. I could see his reasons for going, and his reason for not feeling discouraged. I could see he had no fear about going, and I think he got the satisfaction of at least doing what he could for his country, even though he felt that in the end, it wouldn't be successful. I think he felt that. I certainly did.

31

THE GREAT FORESTS OF KHAM

Of the "Six Ranges" that define Eastern Tibet, the Markham range is probably the most heavily forested. Vast expanses of ancient—in part primaeval—forests of pine, silver fir, yew, juniper, birch and rhododendron covered the lower mountainsides of this land. The valleys were mostly open farmland. Above the forest line were open stretches of high pasturage where nomads raised yak and sheep. Higher still were rocky, desiccated wilderness, home to the blue sheep, the solitary argali and the *Sa* or *Sa-zig*, the snow leopard. Here only a few hardy shrubs and occasional dwarf pines braved the freezing winds.

One European traveller who rode through some of these great forests of Eastern Tibet recalled "immense avenues of silver fir"[1] with trunks of enormous girth, some over ten feet in diameter. The branches of these firs would have moss drooping in long light green streamers described as "fairy scarves". These were a lichen, *usnea barbeta*, related to Spanish moss. My mother told me that as a child, when she and her friend went riding, and it rained, they would take shelter under one of these great trees and would stay perfectly dry. The great silver fir forests would generally be on north-facing slopes. South-facing slopes would have prickly oak.

Much of the forest cover has been reduced due to extensive Chinese logging. The dusty mountainsides, dotted with tree-stumps and many gaping holes, are scarred with slashes of crumbling landslide-prone roads where seemingly endless columns of battered Chinese Jiefang and Mitsubishi trucks haul what remains of Tibet's forests down to China. Even the stumps have been dug up by Chinese road workers and burnt for fuel.

Sixty years ago, these forests gave cover and protection to the fighting men of Markham. It concealed their positions and movement from Chinese aircraft, and provided a barrier, a shock absorber, to the sheer mass impact of the Red Army, that in other more open nomadic areas like Naktsang and Sogdé, even Lithang, had invariably overwhelmed static Tibetan defences. It is probably one of the main reasons why in the whole of Eastern Tibet, the Markham Resistance lasted the longest and why the last CIA supported operation took place there.

The principal resistance leader in Markham was the chieftain, Tsultrim Gyaltsen of Chungbum Phupa, which is about a day's ride north of Garthok, the capital. He was commonly known as Phupa Pön or the chieftain of Phupa. The only photograph we have of this resistance leader was reproduced in the mid-1960s in the exile-weekly newspaper *Freedom*, published in Darjeeling. Even taking into account the poor quality of the original picture and the inferior halftone on low-grade newsprint, it is not a flattering reproduction. His gaze is frankly menacing. The photograph was said to have been taken by Rabga Pangdatsang at Draktsar Khar near Markham Dzong in 1953. Phupa Pön's long hair, braided with silk tassels and decorated with large turquoise-on-silver rings and ivory thumb rings, is coiled around his head in the traditional manner, serving not only the requirements of Khampa male fashion but also as a protection against sword cuts. Strands of yak hair and metal wire were sometimes woven into the braids for additional protection. This style, called the *tagtra*, came into fashion in the violent period of the Nyarong War in the mid-nineteenth century.

Though forbidding in appearance, Phupa Pön seems to have been a person of considerable forethought and compassion. His only surviving son, Tsering Topgyal, now working in Dharamshala as the manager of the printing press of the Tibetan Information Office, told me that early in the uprising, when the resistance had captured a number of Chinese soldiers, his father had insisted on their being treated humanely and had given them food and cigarettes and personally talked to them. These prisoners taught the Markham fighters how to handle captured Chinese equipment, especially mortars and machine guns. Tsering Topgyal, or Tsetop for short, accompanied his father in the war and was wounded and captured in early 1961. He was initially imprisoned in the Chinese military headquarters at Markham Garthok and then sentenced to a *Laogai*, "reform through labour" camp for eighteen years at Powo Tramo in southern Tibet. He was released in 1979 and managed to make his way to India.

Tsetop talked to me for four days[2] about the fighting in Markham, at his apartment below the Tibetan government offices in Gangchen Kyishong. He was living there with the widow of his older brother, Yeshi Wangyal. Tsetop was an animated speaker, and his recall was clear, but it was as definite and unsubtle as that of the teenager he had been then. He still stood in awe of his father and his older brother, and laughed in derision when describing Chinese bugle calls that sounded to him like the bleating of sheep. "Their signals did not have the grand rousing quality of our bugle calls." He told me. "Our force had buglers from the old Tibetan army." Tsetop has since written and published a detailed account of the uprising at Markham,[3] and a general history of the Khampa resistance.[4]

There were eighteen chieftains in Markham and Phupa Pön, though not the paramount leader, was acknowledged to be *primus inter pares* because of his solid qualities. Earlier, the Pangdatsang family had been influential in Markham, but that had ended with the failed rebellion by Topgyal Pangdatsang in 1934 and his flight to Chinese occupied Bathang. Phupa Pön had warned the Lhasa appointed governor of Topgyal's treachery and had helped him escape to Chamdo and alert the governor-general of Eastern Tibet.

Phupa Pön was one of the two chieftains of Markham who held Tibetan government rank and assisted the Lhasa governor, the

Markham *theiji*, at the great *dzong* or castle at Garthok. These two chiefs who served as representatives of the eighteen tribes generally had to be in residence at the small town (of about five hundred households) at the foot of the castle. East of the castle was a large military camp where five hundred Tibetan government soldiers were garrisoned. There were also several small villages and homesteads around the area. Close to the town was the large monastery of Garthok.

Tsetop was seven years old at the time of the Chinese invasion of October 1950. He remembers his father organizing the Markham militia units to support the regular Tibetan army. Markham was liable for a muster of five hundred militiamen, but that year, more were raised. Over half the force was sent to Chamdo. Tsetop was woken early one morning in October, an hour or so before dawn, by a commotion in the courtyard of their ancestral home at Chungbum Phupa. A rupön or major (of the third company) and eleven soldiers, had managed to survive the massive Chinese onslaught at the Druparong Gorge on the western bank of the Drichu River. They had fought their way through the encircling PLA units and eventually made it to Chungbum, where the major knew they would get help from Phupa Pön. Tsering Topgyal remembers the Tibetan officer weeping with rage and frustration, and his father doing his best to console and advise him. After being rested and fed, Phupa Pön arranged for the Major and his men to be escorted to Drayab to join the Tibetan regiment posted there, which had not yet been attacked.

Immediately after the invasion, a large number of Chinese troops marched through Garthok towards Lhasa. After the fall of Chamdo and the signing of the Seventeen Point Treaty, a garrison of five hundred PLA troops was stationed at Garthok. The Chinese administration in Markham was a military one, but they set up a local "Liberation Committee" in which Phupa Pön was appointed as one of the two chairmen.

As everywhere else, people grudgingly accepted Chinese rule. Then in 1954, "Democratic Reforms" were announced; the first indication that the Communists would not tolerate even a vestige of the traditional Khampa way of life. The same year when the Dalai Lama was passing through Eastern Tibet on his return journey from China, he could not come through Markham but sent his representatives, Trijang Rinpoche, his junior tutor, and Kalön Surkhang. Trijang Rinpoche gave some religious initiations and teachings at Garthok, and though he counselled prudence and patience at a meeting with Markham chiefs and elders, he told them that if they accepted "Democratic Reforms" then it was all over for their religion and their traditional way of life.

In November of 1955, the Chinese military administrator for Chamdo, Wang Qimei, summoned a meeting of all the chiefs and representatives of Eastern Tibet, falling under the Chamdo administration. A stocky man in his late forties Wang Qimei was deputy commander of all Chinese forces in Tibet. At the meeting, Phupa Pön spoke out against the imposition of "Democratic Reforms" and pointed out that this new policy went entirely against what had been decided when the Seventeen Point Treaty was signed. The two ministers of the king of Dergé, Raru Tenam and Khardo Chime Gonpo supported Phupa Pön. A chieftain from Lemda in Gonjo, Gonpo Norbu, also expressed his support of Phupa Pön. Topgyal Pangdatsang, who was chairman of the Chamdo Liberation Committee, remained silent. Only two minor chiefs and Phagpala, the young incarnate lama of Chamdo, expressed agreement with Wang Qimei.

After the meeting broke up, Phupa Pön met with a number of other Khampa leaders and arranged a secret conference at Chumik Sumdo between Gonjo and Dergé. This meeting was attended by Gonpo Norbu, the chieftain of Gonjo Lemda, Gowa Nyerpa of Drayab, Karu Pön of Khyungpo Tengchen, Tsetop of Pobo, Dundul Chöying of the three districts of Sho-ta-lho-sum, and Raru Tenam and Khardo Chime Gonpo, the two ministers of the kingdom of Dergé, and some other tribal chiefs. Phupa Pön and some of the other leaders had received the letter from Yunru Pön of Lithang calling for an uprising against the Chinese. All the chiefs gathered at Chumik Sumdo took an oath never to accept the imposition of "Democratic Reforms", and to revolt against the Chinese if this policy should be imposed by force. They also agreed that "If one rifle was fired by any group, all the others would not hesitate to join in the fight." To seal their agreement, everyone took part in a pre-Buddhist Bön oath-taking ceremony called the "Red Hide Blood Oath" (*komar trag bok*), whereby a yak was slaughtered, its freshly flayed skin spread on the ground, and a rifle hung over it. The oath-takers walked under the rifle and then drank a little of the warm heart-blood of the yak to seal the pact.

A few months later, the uprising in Lithang broke out, before the tribes in Markham and other tribes west of the Drichu River had even made adequate preparations. But the conflict spilled over into Markham when the Chinese plane, bombing Bathang Monastery, also dropped a couple of bombs on the monastery at Garthok. The damage to the monastery was minimal, as the bombs did not explode. The Chinese claimed it was a mistake and apologized to the monastic officials and the Markham chiefs. But many felt that the bombs were a warning, of an unsubtle kind, rather than an actual "mistake".[5]

The Chinese began to get tougher all around. Tsamchoe, a representative of the Markham people at the Chamdo Liberation Committee, was arrested for speaking out against "Democratic Reforms" at a meeting He was beaten in public, "struggled" and then given a long prison sentence. [6] Other arrests and "struggles" followed.

Phupa Pön initially put together a personal force of five hundred men, recruited from his own tribal area of Chungbum Phupa. All the men were tough, well-armed and mounted. He then met with the other eighteen chiefs to form a united Markham resistance army. Finally, after some months of discussions and the inevitable horse-trading, the resistance army was created.

Phupa Pön was chosen to be the overall commander. Dhakpa Lama, one of Markham's two most important lamas who had recruited a large contingent of monk fighters from the thirty-six monasteries of Markham, was selected to be deputy commander. The other deputy commander chosen was Mepa Pön, Kalsang Wangyal, the ruler of the tribal land of Chungbum Mepa, adjoining Chungbum Phupa. Other officers and administrative personnel were also selected. Every member of the force walked under a copy of the Buddhist *sutras* and swore a sacred oath to give up his life to defend his land and religion, and never accept even "a needle or a thread" (*khap-kupa*) from the Chinese.

Since the entire force could not gather together in one place, this same ceremony was organized in other parts of Markham, where different units were gathered.

The resistance force was named "The Great Snows Volunteer Army of the Defenders of the Dharma" (*gangchen tensung dhanglang magar*). A battle standard was created along with an official emblem: a snow lion prancing before three snowy peaks. Training commenced, and soldiers from the old Tibetan Army, who had stayed behind in Markham after 1950, became instructors. The resistance force also used bugles like the Tibetan army did, and the fighters had to learn to recognize the various calls. A set of rules and regulations was agreed upon and written down. Copies were made and distributed to all units.

Hostilities commenced on the 29th day of the ninth Tibetan month in 1956. The main resistance force, of around three thousand fighters, attacked the Chinese garrison at Garthok. The plan was to ambush the Chinese soldiers, when most of them were outside the walls of their fort going about their daily duties, foraging in the forest for firewood, fetching water and so on, but the Chinese had somehow gotten wind of the attack and had stayed securely holed up inside the fort. So, the Khampas had to change their plans and began a siege of the Chinese garrison.

Concurrent to the attack on the fort, a smaller operation was planned to neutralize the main Chinese transport and supply centre at a place called Sampa Drenkha, east of Garthok by the Drichu River on the Bathang-Markham Road. Phupa Pön and five hundred of his men successfully overcame the three hundred-odd Chinese defending this post. Nearly all the Chinese were killed. Nineteen were taken prisoner. When the Chinese command at Garthok fort received word of the attack on Sampa Drenkha, he made a desperate attempt to send a relief force from the fort to help the supply centre at Samba Drenka. But the relief force could not break through the siege lines and was wiped out to a man.

Because of the continuing conflict throughout Eastern Tibet, the Chinese were unable to send reinforcements to support or relieve the garrison at Garthok fort, and soon the situation got desperate for the Chinese there. Unlike most of the other districts in Eastern Tibet, Markham was still regarded as under the Dalai Lama's government, so the Tibet Military Area Headquarters (*Silingbu*) at Lhasa called on the cabinet and instructed it to do something about the matter. A couple of months after the initial attack at the fort, Topgyal Pangdatsang, chairman of the Chamdo Liberation Committee, accompanied by the young Karmapa Lama, came to Markham with a message from the Lhasa government ordering the resistance force to stop fighting, and surrender to the Chinese Military Command at Chamdo.

Most of the resistance leaders were not prepared to obey this order, but it demoralized them. A meeting was held between the Chinese and the leaders of the resistance, which the Chinese used to gain time. A group of monk fighters under Shiba Lama, a deputy commander, surrendered to the Chinese. Then in the following weeks, Chinese reinforcement began to pour into Markham from Chamdo and Bathang. The resistance fighters were forced to retreat to the mountains. The main force now split up into smaller units and began to conduct hit and run raids against Chinese transport, outposts and patrols all over Markham.

The Chinese attempted to parley with the resistance leaders. Even General Tan Guansan, commander of the Chinese army in Tibet, personally called on Phupa Pön and other leaders to surrender. But the guerrilla war continued. The Chinese had learnt their lesson well and were careful. The Chinese garrison at Garthok was now heavily defended with barbed wire emplacement and trenches and a whole system of underground tunnels to link the fort and outposts.

Around the beginning of 1958, General Tan Guansan managed to force the Kashag in Lhasa to send some Tibetan troops to support Chinese efforts to fight the Khampa "rebel bandits". About fifty Tibetan soldiers were sent from Lhasa. But the Chinese could not bring themselves to trust the Tibetans, and soon this small unit was split up, and individual soldiers were used as interpreters. Most of these soldiers eventually deserted and joined the resistance.

Dhakpa Lama sent two monks to Lhasa with a letter to Trijang Rinpoche, the Dalai Lama's tutor, requesting him to petition the Tibetan government not to oppose the resistance, even if it could not support it. One of these monks was Dhakpa Lama's steward, Tenpa Trinley, who later trained at Colorado. Trijang Rinpoche replied that though the Chinese had demanded that Tibetan troops be sent to Markham, the Kashag had only sent a small token force. He called on the resistance leaders not to lose heart and advised them to send representatives to India to contact Gyalo Thondup and former prime minister, Lukhangwa, who were organizing outside help for Tibet. Trijang Rinpoche ended his message with the assurance that though the Tibetan government could not help them at this moment, it had the best interests of the Markham people at heart.

A set of the Thirteenth Dalai Lama's ecclesiastical robes was sent to Markham by the Tibetan government, which was considered a great honour and blessing for the people. The messengers also brought with them other gifts from Lhasa, like the precious Yamantanka talisman (*jig je mahe*), which was distributed among the resistance leaders. Tsetop claims that he later managed to get one of these charms from his father.

The resistance leaders decided to send Phupa Pön's oldest son, Yeshi Wangyal, twenty-three, to India. Disguised as poor pilgrims, Yeshi Wangyal, his wife, baby daughter, a manservant and a maid departed for India. At Lhasa, they stayed with Andrugtsang Gonpo Tashi and gave him the latest news about the fighting in Markham. Gonpo Tashi was then preparing to leave Lhasa for the resistance base at Driguthang in the Lhoka area. Fearing he might be discovered by Chinese Security or inadvertently exposed by other Khampas in Lhasa, Yeshi Wangyal only stayed three days in the city, just long enough to visit the Jokhang, secretly, like a thief, and then headed for India.

The Sikkim–Tibet border was now heavily guarded by PLA troops, but with the help of a local Dromowa guide that Gonpo Tashi had arranged, they were able to cross the border at an unguarded section. Nonetheless, they came across one Chinese patrol and had to take cover and remain silent while it passed by. The maid nearly suffocated the girl to death when she covered the baby's mouth with her hand to prevent her from crying out.

Finally, they got to Kampong, where Yeshi Wangyal tried to meet Gyalo Thondup and Lukhangwa, but could not, as they were preoccupied. This was the period when mass meetings were being organized all over Kalimpong, Darjeeling and Sikkim, and a campaign was underway to have all Tibetans sign a joint declaration of independence and a declaration of loyalty to the Dalai Lama and the government of Tibet. On 5 August 1958, Tibetans in exile issued a joint appeal to the government of India, the United Nations and the free nations of the world declaring Tibetan independence, condemning China's military occupation of Tibet and appealing for help and support.

While he waited, Yeshi Wangyal used the time to learn English from two American missionaries in the 11th mile area, almost certainly Lillian Carlson and Dorothy Christianson of the World Mission Prayer League, who ran a small infirmary by the caravan road to Tibet. These two ladies, who spoke and read Tibetan, had earlier run a mission at Dartsedo, before the Communist takeover of China. Yeshi Wangyal studied English diligently for only a few months, but it appears that he became passably fluent. Finally, he managed to make contact with Gyalo Thondup's organization and was taken to Darjeeling to the safe house where recruits were accommodated. In Darjeeling, he met Dhakpa Lama's steward, Tenpa Trinley, and also had a private meeting with Gyalo Thondup, who asked Yeshi Wangyal if he could arrange for more young men from Markham to come to Darjeeling for training. Yeshi Wangyal sent his servant back to Markham with a letter for his father describing his meeting with the Dalai Lama's brother and also forwarding the request for recruits. Yeshi Wangyal was then selected for training at Colorado.

Around September of 1958, the Chinese took the initiative and began to attack the various resistance groups all across Markham. Over the last year, Chinese units from other areas of Eastern Tibet and even from Central Tibet had been transferred to Markham. Fresh troops from Yunnan and Sichuan were also sent to Markham. Nearly every resistance encampment now came under attack. The Chinese also used planes for reconnaissance, and bombing. Chengdu, the capital of Sichuan province, had many abandoned airfields built in 1944 for American B29 Superfortress bomber raids to Japan, which were now used for operations in Eastern Tibet. The effectiveness of aerial reconnaissance and bombing was limited by Markham's forest cover, but contributed to the added pressure the resistance was now feeling.

The new troops from China were better equipped with AK-47 assault rifles. Furthermore, the completion of the motor road from Bathang to Markham and Chamdo, allowed heavy mortar, artillery, and heavy machine guns (with plate-armour shields) to be trucked into Markham. In spite of their superiority in numbers and equipment, the Chinese had not become as proficient in moving and fighting in the forests and high mountains as the Khampa fighters and suffered greater casualties in most encounters. But its vastly superior manpower and equipment did give the Chinese a formidable advantage. Some resistance groups that had grown careless or impetuous were wiped out.

The Chinese now stepped up their pressure on the civilian population. Everyday Chinese soldiers arrested men and women in villages and nomad encampments, shooting those that tried to run away. People were beaten and tortured to make them reveal the identity and hideouts of the resistance fighters. The homes of those suspected of aiding the fighters were burnt, and the senior members of the household denounced and violently "struggled" in mass meetings and political rallies. They were invariably imprisoned, sentenced to slave-labour camps and sometimes publicly executed. Large-scale raids were conducted on monasteries, with Chinese soldiers storming congregation-halls and temples, weapons raised, and arresting the younger monks.[7] Some older lamas and monastic officials pleaded with resistance leaders to make peace with the Chinese—or at least win decisively.

Phupa Pön, Dhakpa Lama and Mepa Pön, who had been operating together, realized there was no way of keeping the entire resistance organization together. They decided to break up the force into small bands of twenty to thirty fighters that could hide out in the forests and mountains, not too distant from their homes, and be supported locally with food supplies and information. They instructed those fighters who had been wounded, or had lost their horses or weapons to return home and work discreetly to collect provisions and supplies for the force. Only one main force of a thousand men led by Phupa Pön, Mepa Pön and Dhakpa Lama, would leave Markham and head north for Drayab and, if necessary further north to Gonjo, where they hoped to find some respite from Chinese attacks.

The resistance got some breathing space in Drayab, where the Chinese did not have significant major military presence (most had been transferred to Markham). The local people were friendly and though they did not have much, they provided the resistance with tsampa, meat and butter. When the resistance arrived at the township of Jamdün in Drayab, the small Chinese garrison of about a hundred soldiers fled. Phupa Pön and the other resistance leaders now met with Gowa Nyerpa, Dochoe Kunchok Tendar* and other leaders of the Drayab resistance. Some chiefs of Gonjo also came to the meeting, including Gonpo Norbu Lemdatsang (the father of the warrior nun, Lemda Pachen). Phupa Pön called on them to honour the blood oath they had taken some years back at Chumik Sumdo, to fight the Chinese. The chief of Drayab and Gonjo all agreed but said they would need time to prepare.

Early one morning, a resistance outpost at Jamdün was attacked by a Chinese cavalry detachment that had followed them from Markham.

More Chinese reinforcements began to pour into Drayab. The resistance launched a quick strike on a detachment of advancing Chinese infantry. This attack turned into a fiasco when the detachment turned out to have considerable supporting units behind it. That day the resistance lost one of its best commanders and, at least, eighty fighters and four machine guns. Finally, when they discovered that Chinese reinforcements were making their way south from Dergé, Phupa Pön and the others headed back to Markham.

---

*In the Introduction, I mention this fighter showing the draft of his memoirs to my friend Tashi Tsering at the AMI office in Dharamshala.

When they got home, they discovered that the situation in Markham had seriously deteriorated. The Chinese had now instituted a system of collective punishment for all "crimes" committed by resistance fighters. If any ambush or attack against the Chinese happened close to some village or nomad encampment, the Chinese immediately took reprisals on those villages or homesteads nearby, burning houses and crops, killing livestock and imprisoning people.[8] The resistance now had to be very careful about where they planned their attacks and ambushes, and make sure that as few civilians as possible were implicated. The Chinese also initiated a drastic campaign to neutralize the one big defensive advantage the Khampa fighters had. In areas where fighters were suspected of hiding, entire forests were burnt to the ground before Chinese troops were sent to flush out the survivors.[9] The only feasible strategy for the Markham resistance was to split up into even smaller bands and limit operations to hit-and-run guerrilla style operations.

In 1958, when the Four Rivers Six Ranges under Gonpo Tashi undertook its now-famous "ride north" that ended at Chakra Pembar, it created considerable concern at Chinese Military HQ at Lhasa, Chamdo and Chengdu. When Gonpo Tashi's fighters attacked Po Tramo, wiping out supply convoys destroying bridges and transport units, PLA units were pulled out from other sectors and sent to Po Tramo. A whole division was withdrawn from the Markham sector. The remaining Chinese troops from the smaller outposts in Markham retreated to the fortress at Garthok and held out there.

This gave the Markham Resistance an opportunity to regroup their scattered bands of fighters and make more ambitious plans for the coming year. Things definitely began to look brighter. A courier had come to Phupa Pön from Kalimpong with the message that by the beginning of 1959, a radio operator would be sent to Markham, after which arms drops and instructors would be possible. Dhakpa Lama managed to convince Gongkar Lama and his men from Tsakhalo in the south to join the fighting. Drayab sent a fully equipped force of over fifteen hundred men to Markham. Gonjo also sent a contingent of fighters, as did Dergé, under the leadership of Raru Tenam and Khardo Nyerpa. Another contingent of fighters came from Lingkashi, east of the Drichu River.

Around this time, the remaining tribesmen in the south-eastern parts of Kham: Gyalthang, Jöl, Sathang and even Chatreng, were finally forced to leave their homelands and flee west to Markham. At the end of that year (1958) according to my informant Tsetop, it seemed that about twenty to thirty thousand fighters gathered at Markham. Most tribes-people in north-eastern Kham retreated towards Chakra Pembar in Sho-ta-lho-sum, where another large force began to assemble.

In Markham, the concentration of refugees and fighters caused tremendous food shortages, but the newfound strength of the resistance took its toll on the remaining Chinese outposts and garrisons, except for the fortress at Garthok, where they continued to hold out. The Chinese had strengthened their defences at Garthok with high walls and ramparts surrounded by barbed wire entanglements and minefields. They had also created a network of tunnels that connected the fort to the mountaintop behind and even to a couple of distant outposts. They also had artillery and heavy mortars. The resistance needed artillery, which they did not have, to take this Chinese stronghold. They were also running out of ammunition and weapons. But this they hoped would soon be remedied with the arrival of the American trained radio-operator and American arms drops.

But by the beginning of 1959, no radio operator had managed to make it to Markham. Two Markham fighters Jamyang Sherap and Apay Yonten, who had been sent to Kalimpong for aid, attempted to return to Markham through Kongpo Miling. They had disguised themselves as pilgrims and, according to one source, had a radio-set on the back of a donkey. But this is doubtful. The two unfortunately encountered a Chinese patrol and were killed in the ensuing firefight.

With the suppression of the Lhasa Uprising at the end of March 1959 and the retreat of the Four Rivers Six Ranges from the Lhoka area, the PLA now commenced large-scale transfer of troops to areas of Eastern Tibet where the resistance persisted. In Markham, the resistance once again began to feel mounting pressure from the Chinese. Desperate for help, the Markham Resistance sent two more messengers to Kalimpong asking for help. Since Lhasa had fallen, the messengers were sent through the unexplored jungle region of Dzayül, which lies between Markham and the north-eastern Indian state of Assam, but the two messengers did not return.

The resistance leaders were now at a loss on how to proceed, and intense discussions took place to find some workable strategy. One plan called for the Chatrengwa contingent, under the command of the warrior Reting Zimgak to leave Markham and hold Dzayül so that the resistance would, at least, secure its rear, and have a line of access and communications to India. This warrior was a giant of a man, in courage as well as physique. Earlier in life, his exceptional size and strength had gained him a job in Lhasa as a bodyguard to the regent of Tibet, the Reting Rinpoche, hence the name Reting Zimgak,* or "Reting body-guard." When the Tibetan government troops arrested the regent on charges of treason, this bodyguard unsuccessfully attempted to save his master. He attacked the troops with his broadsword killing a number of them and finally fought his way through the army cordon, and escaped, making his way back to his home in Jöl, at the foot of the spectacular Khawa Karpo (White Snow) mountains in Dechen district, now in Yunnan Province. In the uprising against the Chinese, Reting Zimgak added to his reputation by holding out alone against a whole company of Chinese soldiers for seven days, killing many of them, some with his sword, and then again miraculously escaping to fight again—like a hero from the Gesar Epic. His talisman was said never to fail him. Known by the sobriquet "Reting Zimgak" (childhood name Gonpo Lang-gyü), his fame was widespread throughout Kham. He led the contingent of two hundred Chatrengwa fighters to Dzayül. Now the resistance in Markham once again had to face increasing Chinese troops to a point where it seemed to one fighter that "the thousands of Chinese soldiers in their yellow (khaki) uniforms covered the Markham range like lice." The crackle of rifle fire and the rumble of artillery could now be heard constantly throughout Markham, especially during clear cloudless

---

*We have a wonderful photograph of him taken by Spencer Chapman, a member of the British Mission to Lhasa in 1936–37. Chapman noted, ". . . the giant lama was some seven feet high."

nights. In three months of fighting, about 3,000 Khampa fighters were killed and about 10,000 wounded or captured.

The Chinese also began arresting farmers, especially the heads of households and herded them in large stockades in Garthok.[10] These concentration camps were surrounded by high barbed wire fences, guard towers with machine guns, and constant patrols of armed guards. All families were expected to surrender their grain stores to the Chinese authorities. Those that did not comply were immediately arrested, and often shot, there and then.[11]

When Chakra Pembar finally fell, and all the resistance groups in that area were wiped out, more Chinese troops were freed up to be sent to Markham. The Chinese had also discovered that the resistance had their main base at Kinggo in the high mountains of northern Markham, and, subsequently, a large-scale offensive was directed there. The fighting at Kinggo went on for seven days and nights and was intense ". . . often at close quarters with swords, daggers and bayonets." The Chinese finally called off their attack and retreated from the Kinggo area, leaving behind hundreds of bodies. The Chinese always buried their soldiers near the site of the battle, but officer's bodies were taken to Garthok to be buried at the "Martyrs Memorial" cemetery (Chinese, *Lishimu*), which one informant claimed had well over a thousand graves by the end of the overall conflict.

The resistance also suffered terrible casualties, and lamas and monks walked about the dying and wounded at Kinggo, giving them holy water and praying to them. Now the resistance leaders met and decided that they had to disperse the force into small guerrilla bands as they had done before, to survive. Gongkar Lama returned with his men to Tsakhalo. The fighters from Drayab returned to their land. The men of Lingkashi, under their leader Gyakpontsang Chime Dorje, could not return to their tribal lands east of the river, which was now fully under Chinese control. They decided to risk a foray south to Dzayül and join Reting Zimgak's force there. Chime Dorje and a few hundred of his men are said to have managed to make the formidable jungle trip south.

In 2014, I met a young Khampa man at a bar in Jackson Heights, New York, who told me that Chime Dorje and his men had succeeded in meeting up with the warrior Reting Zimgak and his men, and another contingent of fighters from Jöl. This force held out in Dzayül for a couple of years with other fugitives, including women and children, gradually being pushed from the lowlands towards the snowy heights of the Ghangri Karpo range. Eventually, Chinese troops invaded Dzayül in force and wiped out the resistance. My informant (who was born in Dzayül), his parents and other survivors were shipped to *Laogai* camps, but eventually managed to return to Kham. He remembered his parents talking of Reting Zimgak and Chime Dorje leading the fighting in Dzayül but did not know of their eventual fate.

But this is where all accounts of George Patterson's "charming rogue" of a friend, veers into "the mists of legend" as I mentioned in a previous chapter. One account has him escaping through Dzayül to northern Burma. In the exile capital of Dharamshala, rumours persisted till well into the eighties, that Chime Dorje and his men were alive and settled in northern Burma in the Kachin hills.

All the wounded and sick fighters in the Markham Resistance force were now allowed to return to the relative safety of their homes, though everyone was given instructions on how to rejoin their units when the opportunity might arise to restart the uprising. The last encounter at Kinggo had also taken its toll on the Chinese army, which in addition to battle casualties had also suffered terribly from the freezing cold of the high mountains and a shortage of food supplies, especially rice and wheat. Many Chinese soldiers got caught in blizzards and snowdrifts and suffered from frostbite and snow-blindness. Many died of exposure.

The Chinese military command at Garthok announced a great victory over the "rebel bandits" and withdrew their troops from the front lines of the fight against the Khampa fighters. Some units were withdrawn from Markham and sent back to Chengdu. The unrelenting grinding pressure that the Chinese had been putting on the resistance for the last five months, now decreased considerably.

The resistance force left in Markham was now less than a thousand men strong, and they had to keep moving from one part of the country to the other in order to avoid being trapped by the Chinese. Though the overall military pressure had lessened, the Chinese were still very strong and vigilant.

In May or June of 1960, the main resistance force was camped at Lekhor, a high pastureland in Chungbum Phupa. A couple of fighters had returned to their native village to look for supplies and told their wives about being with Phupa Pön at Lekhor. Unfortunately, one of the women later repeated the conversation to her father, a prosperous farmer, who reported it to the Chinese.

A large Chinese force moving secretly at night, managed to surround Lekhor and pull off a surprise attack at dawn. The Khampa fighters were woken by machine-gun fire and exploding mortar shells. Though they took some casualties in the initial attack they quickly managed to establish a defense line and kept up an effective fire to prevent the Chinese from overwhelming them.

Phupa Pön's son, Tsetop was there that day. These were his impressions: "Smoke from the mortar rounds and dust covered the area like patches of cloud. Chinese fire was so intense that the usual sporadic whistling of bullets now had a more continuous quality to it—like the sound of falling rain. With bullets ploughing into the ground everywhere, some hares jumped out of their holes. One or two got hit. Nothing else but our amulets saved us that day. Through the noise and confusion of the battle, I heard Chinese bugle calls. They were manoeuvring their units to prevent us escaping."

In the confusion following the initial surprise attack, Phupa Pön and a small band of fighters got separated from the main force. When mounting his horse, a mortar shell struck a large rock near Phupa Pön. He was hit in the face with rock splinters and thrown off his horse. His men managed to get him back on his horse, and together, they tried to rush the advancing Chinese and break out of the encirclement. The fighting got desperate. Phupa Pön was hit again, this time by a bullet, and fell off his horse unconscious. The eleven men around him fought till they were all killed. By the end of the day the main resistance force managed to break out of the Chinese encirclement and escape, though suffering significant losses.

The Chinese took Phupa Pön's body to Garthok and hung it up on a stake before the fort for public display. Speeches were given by Chinese leaders, and insults were directed to the body of the dead chieftain by Chinese cadres and Tibetan collaborators. "Where are your American imperialist friends now . . . this is a fitting end for you, miserable rebel bandit" and so on. The body was also dragged around the town.[12] One night the body disappeared. It was probably stolen by someone loyal to the great chieftain who gave it a proper burial or cremation.

Dhakpa Lama and Mepa Pön now led what remained of the force. They decided to take the initiative before it was too late. A number of raids were conducted on Chinese outposts, and convoys and many soldiers were killed. But encouraged by the death of Phupa Pön, the Chinese began to intensify their efforts. At the southern tip of Markham at Tsakhalo in the district of salt wells, Gongkar Lama and his fighters were wiped out. By the end of the 1960s, the resistance was losing ground, losing fighters, and losing hope that help would arrive from outside. Yet somehow, the rumour that Phupa Pön's older son would return from America persisted. The Chinese now increased their strength in Markham to about 30,000 men. Among these were fresh troops from China, much better equipped with new Russian AKM assault rifles.

This new Chinese initiative also had a carrot aspect to persuade Tibetans to give up their fight. Posters were stuck all over Markham announcing a "Liberalization Policy", whereby all "rebel bandits" who surrendered would be forgiven by the government and the Communist Party, and not have their past investigated. Further announcements were made that Dhakpa Lama would be appointed chairman (Chinese, *zhuxi)* of the official Buddhist Association of Kham if he surrendered, and that Mepa Pön would be given the rank of chairman of the administration of Eastern Tibet. Other chieftains as Nyima Pön and Mashang Pön were promised official ranks and honours if they surrendered. Tsetop, the teenage son of Phupa Pön was also promised his late father's official rank if he submitted. The Chinese rounded up several women with their children and babies and sent them around to different villages and towns to loudly weep and wail and call on the men of Markham to surrender to the Chinese.

Around the beginning of 1961, young Tsetop was captured in a skirmish and taken to the Chinese military headquarters at Garthok. The main resistance force was now reduced to about four hundred men. Some scattered bands of fighters still survived in the most inaccessible heights of the Markham Range, but they were small, and were being gradually wiped out, one by one.

Sensing impending victory, the Chinese became impatient and even more ruthless. Khampas suspected of helping the resistance were now executed by firing squad, on a near daily basis at Garthok. Particularly defiant prisoners were even burnt alive at the stake to teach the Khampa public a lesson. Tens of thousands of people were herded together at close quarters in the open stockades at Garthok, living even worse than animals, with no protection from the cold and rain, with very little food, and with so little room to move that they had to urinate and defecate where they stood. In the villages, starving children and old grandmothers were eating grass.[13]

Yeshi Wangyal (training name "Tim"), the oldest son of the late Phupa Pön Tsultrim Gyaltsen, now returned from America to his ancestral homeland (*phayul*) of Markham.

32

MISSION TO MARKHAM

"It was 6 p.m. on 15 March 1961, when the plane took off," Bhusang finally declared decisively, after muttering various dates and months to himself for a while, trying to remember. "Tim was sitting opposite me. We sat on these seats of webbing. All of us were silent, and the engines filled the inside of the plane with this tremendous roar. You could not see anything outside as the curtains were drawn across the small circular windows. Once we were up in the air, the curtains were pulled aside. There was an aircrew of five Americans, who were strangers to us. None of our instructors accompanied us. When I first saw these young pilots and crew members in their flying outfits, each carrying his own parachute and packing a pistol in a shoulder holster, I couldn't help feeling that it was brave and selfless of them to risk this danger for us. Of course, I knew it was their profession to fly such dangerous missions, but this whole affair was not their quarrel, at least not in the direct way it was for us. On the plane, I mentioned this to the others in the team, and we talked about it.

"Tim (Yeshi Wangyal Phupatsang) was the team leader. Colin (Dorje Phuntsok), a Lhasa man like myself and a corporal in the Second (Drapchi) Regiment, was the radio operator, while Duke (Ugen Dorge) from Tsawarong was the back-up radio operator. Philip (Damdul) from Gyantsé was a private from the Fourth (Gyantsé) Regiment, while

Aaron (Nasang Tashi Gyaltsen) and Luke (Golo Lobsang) were both from Lithang and the youngest members of our team. We got used to calling each other by our American training names since that was how we were introduced to each other when we met at the training centre in Colorado. We were not allowed to call each other by our real names. I was the deputy leader and medic. My training name was 'Ken'. For the mission, we were given Tibetan cover names that we had to use when meeting other Tibetans. Mine was Phuntsok.

"Once the plane had settled on its course, we started dressing. We put on overalls over the plain cotton shirts and trousers we had been wearing in the warm climate of Thailand. I also wore a checked woollen jacket underneath, that I had bought in Kalimpong. Only after we landed in Markham would we change into Tibetan clothes. Tim and I had a sheepskin chuba each. The others had woollen chubas.

"We also helped one of the crew members to check our equipment and supplies, which were lashed down on wheeled pallets. These had earlier been loaded from the back of the plane that had a large hatch door that dropped down. But the supplies would be thrown out from a door on the left of the plane while the team jumped from a door on the right. We had twelve bundles of stuff, one each for every member of the team and five bundles of common equipment. The bundles on the wheeled pallets could be easily pushed out, one after the other, by the aircrew. The most important items of equipment were our two radio sets. They were the old heavy kind. We also had two hand-cranked generators.

"For weapons, we had eight M1 Garand rifles (one modified for sniper work with telescopic sights, cheek pad-rest and flash suppressor), two .30 calibre submachine guns, boxes of grenades and a great deal of ammunition. All of us had compasses and maps, besides one still camera, a movie camera and a small film supply. The heavy equipment like machine guns, mortars and explosives would be dropped later, once we had established contact with the resistance, and communicated back to headquarters. We also had a basic medical kit, for which I was responsible, and a blanket each. For food, we had packets of beef jerky.

"We had each been issued personal side-arms—Browning automatic pistols—in Japan. Two of them, Tim's and mine, had silencers. We had also been given a poison capsule each. I had heard that earlier the poison was issued in the form of round pills, but we got this transparent plastic phial, about an inch and a half long. You could see the poison, which was clear and watery-like, inside.

"After going through our equipment, we also rechecked our own parachutes.

"We didn't talk much throughout the trip . . . no . . . we didn't pray either. None of us was particularly religious. We were caught up in our own thoughts. After about three hours all the lights on the plane were turned off, and it became completely dark. One of the crew came out of the pilot's cabin and told us that the plane was flying over Chamdo. We looked out of the window and saw tiny dots of light twinkling below in one sector of the darkness. Once we left Chamdo behind, the plane turned rather sharply and flew in a new direction, which we didn't have to be told was south, in the direction of Markham.

"Just before 10 p.m. we were told to make preparations for the jump. The plane circled over the drop zone three times. The doors on either side of the plane were opened and two of the crew came out from the front cabin to prepare for the drop. Tim and one of the crew stood by the open door and peered down into the darkness. Tim was asked if he recognized the landscape. He was hesitant and replied in the negative a couple of times. I don't know how they expected him to recognize anything. It was dark outside, and he had been away from home for some years now. Finally, around 11 p.m., Tim may have thought he recognized something, for he said 'OK' in English.

"I quickly went over to the door, as it was the rule that the deputy leader jumped first. Tim, as the team leader, would only jump after he had made sure we were all out. I held on to the side of the open door. I was surprised to see how white it was below me. The mountains were all covered with snow or frost and seemed to move—to rise and fall like waves—as we flew over them. Even the dark sky seemed to sparkle in the moonlight. There was a sudden roar and this breath-stopping shock, and I was out in black empty space.

"There was no wind, and the dropping pattern was tight. All of us landed within sight of each other. The drop zone was on the top of a bare, treeless mountain, on fairly flat and even ground covered with a light surface of fresh snow. All of us made it to the ground without any problems, except for Aaron, who hurt his hand landing, but it was not very serious, and he recovered after a few days.

"We quickly collected all the parachutes and the bundles of equipment. None of the equipment was lost or damaged. We sorted out what we had to take with us, and searched for a place to cache the rest. Close to the drop zone, we found a large sheep-pen, quite deserted as it was winter, and surrounded by a low wall of stone and sod. We quickly dug up the layer of old sheep dropping and earth and buried the equipment. We covered the hole and smoothed it over till it looked just as it had been before. We were lucky to have found the sheep-pen as the ground was otherwise rock hard with the freezing cold, and it would have been difficult for us to dig a hole large enough to bury our stuff properly. We collected all the parachutes—there were about thirty-four in all—all the boxes, wrappers and wadding. We rechecked the ground to make sure we hadn't left anything for the Chinese to find.

"As day came, we saw that the area was completely deserted and, other than the sheep-pen, we found no sign that anyone had been here recently. We were on this high ridge that ran in a north-south direction. The ridge carried on level towards the north, but it became a kind of escarpment to the southern side where it climbed up steeply from where we were, for a considerable distance till it disappeared into some low clouds. We split up into three groups to scout the area thoroughly and get some bearings on our location. Tim and I climbed up the southern slope for a few hours till we got to a place with a clear view of the surrounding area. Tim carefully tracked the mountain ranges around us with his binoculars, occasionally checking the open map on the ground by his side.

"I asked if he had figured out where we were, but he replied that he wasn't sure. I don't know how he finally worked it out, but after some time, he told me that we had been dropped north of Markham, and were probably somewhere in Gonjo territory, and would have to walk south for some days before we got to his home district. He then told me how we would have to proceed. All I could do was agree with him. I had never been to Eastern Tibet before, much less Markham or Gonjo. We took some photographs of the surrounding area and also shot some length of movie film.

"We got back down to our drop zone in the late afternoon and talked to the rest of the team about our situation and what we planned to do. We had a meal of beef jerky and water, and then, after burning all the parachutes and packing our stuff, leaving no trace of our visit there, we started walking up the mountain that Tim and I had earlier ascended. We got to the top early the next morning. It was that high.

"After a brief rest in the early morning, Colin, who was our radio operator, unpacked the set to send out our first signal. The radio pack was very heavy, not like the small light ones they supplied the Mustang Resistance later. The generator was also a cumbersome piece of equipment that needed two people to operate it—to turn the crank handles. Philip and I took first turns on the generator. The thing really made you shit with exhaustion—even if you were tough. Following procedure, the rest of the team spread out around the area as lookouts. We reported back to headquarters that we had landed safely, though off-target, that Aaron had a slight injury but that we were now on our way to Markham. The signal we sent was in Morse and tapped out with a key. We had this codebook from which we encoded each word into four-digit 'groups'. So you sent a twenty-group or fifty-group message depending on the length of your report. All of us had been taught Morse code, but our competence with the key varied.

"We only travelled by night. At first light, we looked around for a secure place to hide and rest. We used this opportunity to send a report back to base and to also survey our surroundings and work out our route for the coming night's march. For the next four days and nights, we did not come across any Chinese patrols or any nomad encampments. For that matter, we did not meet a single human being. But just in case we bumped into any passing Tibetan, we had prepared a cover story—that we were an advance team of guides and porters for a Chinese road survey team and that we had taken a wrong turn somewhere and had gotten lost. It was a good story, for it gave us a credible reason to question people closely about routes and villages, nomad encampments and even Chinese military positions. Our cover story had a sneaky touch. Somewhere during the conversation, one of us would confess to being afraid of being attacked by 'rebel bandits'— the Chinese term for resistance fighters—and would ask whether there were any in that area so that we could avoid them. We would also ask for locations of nearby Chinese army camps or outposts that we could turn to for help in case of trouble.

"On the fifth day, we came across a Chinese patrol. It was, in a way, a blessing in disguise. Let me explain. It was not dark, but we were starting a little earlier as we had to cross a high pass. We had gone a little way up when one of us spotted some movement at the top of the pass. We stopped in our tracks, and Tim surveyed the heights with his binoculars. It appeared that there were Chinese soldiers moving on the ridge towards the pass. Tim could not tell whether they had seen us or not, but if we continued the way we were going, we would definitely bump into them. While the others lay low, Tim and I went up to the pass to check things out. The two of us moved very cautiously in a wide arc so the Chinese would not see us. After a long time, we got close enough to the top to discover the Chinese soldiers in secure positions behind rocks and boulders, ready to shoot at us when we got up there. Through the binoculars, we saw that there were ten soldiers and a local man, most probably a guide. So, Tim and I reversed course, very quietly. That night we backtracked for a couple of hours and then cut east to circle that mountain. We cursed a bit at the extra travelling, for we didn't know that our previous route was wrong, and only now, after our forced detour were we headed in the right direction. The next day we reached Markham, though we didn't realize it immediately.

"This was the sixth day since we were dropped. Early in the morning, we caught sight of three black nomad tents. Here finally was an opportunity to make some enquiries of our whereabouts. Tim, Duke and Philip went over to the tents. The rest of us hid out there on the side of the mountain and waited.

"After about an hour, the three of them emerged from the largest tent and returned hurriedly to where the rest of us were. I noticed at once that Tim was upset. I asked him how things had gone, but he only replied that we should move on immediately. I asked him again. He sat down and said that everything had gone wrong, and that our mission was finished. I asked how. Finally, he told us what had happened back there in the tent.

"When the three of them got to the tents, they discovered a nomad woman and her three children in one of them. The head of the household was away. On questioning the woman, Tim discovered that the nomad family was a member of his tribe, specifically from the group headed by the steward of the Phupatsang family. Tim had been away from his land for many years and was overjoyed to be with his people again. He told the woman that he was Yeshi Wangyal, the son of their chieftain, Phupa Pön. The woman refused to believe him and replied that Yeshi Wangyal had gone away to India many years ago.

"Tim tried to explain. He asked her if she had heard a strange sound on the night of the fifteenth. He explained to her that the sound had come from the aeroplane that had brought him back to his own country. The woman replied that she had heard roaring sounds that night that had frightened the animals in her herd. A couple of the horses had snapped their tether ropes and bolted. Tim then asked her if she had any food to sell. She said she had nothing to sell, as grain was now terribly hard to come by, but she gave them some thin gruel.

She then told Tim that his father, Phupa Pön, had been killed last year, fighting the Chinese. This was the first time Tim had heard of his father's death, and he was severely affected by the news. The nomad woman said that the fighting had taken place on the mountainside just across the valley from them. She also told them that the surviving leaders of the Markham resistance, Dhakpa Lama and Mepa Pön, were wandering around the mountains like wild animals, with the Chinese chasing them relentlessly. Their situation was so bad, she had heard, that they did not even have boots to wear on their feet.

"The nomad woman told Tim that he and his friends should leave or she would have to call the Chinese. A short distance away from the nomad encampment, a small Chinese military post was situated within a large horse corral that had previously belonged to the Phupatsang family. The walls of the corral were made of sod and high enough to give some protection from the wind to the Chinese soldiers. On coming down the mountain towards the nomad camp we had passed by this empty corral. We were lucky as there were no Chinese soldiers in the early morning. It seemed that they only guarded this post during the day and withdrew at dusk to their main camp further down the mountain.

"We were never sure if the nomad woman later informed the Chinese of our arrival. If she did, she probably did so out of fear. Tim had not been in his own country for many years now and imagined his people to be as kind, and stout-hearted as before. But years of war, devastation and famine had hardened their hearts, and the relentless cruelty, power and propaganda of the Chinese had filled them with fear and suspicion. Tim was distraught and angry with himself. He told me that he shouldn't have talked to the woman at all. He was fond of me and spoke to me freely. We were very close. I told him that what was done was done, and there was no point worrying about it anymore. We just had to think of what to do next. Anyhow, now that I reflect on all that happened in the subsequent days, I don't think it would have made any difference in the end whether the woman had reported us to the Chinese or not.

"By now, Tim had gotten the lay of the land. He told us about an isolated farmhouse that belonged to a close relative of his, a maternal uncle, about two days' walk from where we were. Tim figured that our best chance of meeting the resistance, or what was left of it, would be to first get to that farmhouse and contact his uncle. We travelled hard that whole night, only taking a few short rests. The next day we came to this great coniferous forest that seemed to go on forever, so we took a chance and continued to walk during the day.

"I had never seen a forest like this in my life. In Central Tibet, we have small forests in places like Reting but nothing like this. I had been through vast jungles in Tsari, but this marvellous forest was something out of an old story. The trees were enormous and rose straight up high into a gloom of heavy foliage, but occasional shafts of sunlight broke through the high cover and fell on the dark forest floor covered with layers of mouldering pine needles and cones. The seven of us moved so silently through the shadowy forest that for me, bringing up the rear, it didn't feel as though it was real—just a strange dream.

"At about four o'clock, in a clearing on the higher reaches of the mountains, we spotted a flock of sheep. On getting closer, Tim recognized the old shepherd who was from Tim's family. Tim talked to the old man, who told him that his uncle's farmhouse was safe and that there were no Chinese nearby. The old shepherd said that we should all go down to the house for a meal and a rest. We understood that Tim's relative was a prosperous man and still maintained a large and prosperous farm, despite the war and famine. But we decided to take precautions. Tim and Philip went down to the farmhouse, while the rest of us stayed up on the mountain. I went part way down the mountain with Tim till I could spot the farmhouse in the valley below. I checked it out with my binoculars. It was a large stone and log building with little black dots—*dzos* or cows, I guess—in a spacious open courtyard. I didn't see Tim and the others enter, but I was a considerable distance away, up in the mountain.

"When Tim and Philip returned the next morning, they had with them tsampa, butter, cheese and meat. While we ate, Tim told us that he had met his uncle, who was not only well informed about all developments in Markham but would make arrangements for us to meet the remaining resistance leaders, Dhakpa Lama and Mepa Pön. Tim's uncle had milled a quantity of barley for the resistance, which would be collected by some of their fighters that day. Through them, he would inform the resistance leaders of our presence and arrange a meeting.

"We waited in the mountain for two days. Finally, the old shepherd came up and told us that a meeting had been arranged. On the appointed day, we travelled to the prearranged rendezvous, half-a-day's march down the valley. That was on the night of March 25th. Only Tim and I went to the actual meeting place, which was at the edge of the forest, just by a couple of large boulders. The other five remained at a distance, as a precaution. We didn't know what to expect. If Tim and I were caught in an ambush, the rest of our team were to fight their way out and escape. By now, we realized that we couldn't be sure of anything, and to survive had to be very careful. There was no way of knowing that the resistance leaders we were trying to contact had not already been captured, and that, instead, Chinese soldiers would be waiting for us at the rendezvous. So, we took precautions. Tim and I waited in the dark, behind a tree, clutching our Garand rifles—safety catches off.

"They came around midnight. Someone whistled. I turned my rifle slowly toward the sound. We maintained our silence for a while. Then Tim whistled back. There was another whistle. This time it was closer. 'Who are you?' Tim asked. His voice seemed very loud in the darkness though it was probably not. The reply was one word 'Dhonyo'.

"Tim whispered excitedly to me that this was the voice of a close retainer of the Phupatsang family and the person who had accompanied him to India. Later, we learned that the resistance leaders had sent Dhonyo to make the contact since he knew Tim well and could make sure that it was not an impostor sent by the Chinese. The dark outline of a human form came out of the darkness and Tim got up to meet him. They clasped hands. Another figure appeared. Then we all met face to face. Dhonyo was accompanied by a captain of Phupatsang's tribal militia. Tim told Dhonyo that it was vital that he meet Dhakpa Lama and Mepa Pön as we had very important things to discuss with them. We then arranged with Dhonyo to meet with the leaders of the resistance in three days' time, at another rendezvous point. This time we would meet in daylight, at ten in the morning.

"Three days later, we met in the middle of a thick forest. Dhonyo returned with Dhakpa Lama and Mepa Pön along with six other men. Dhakpa Lama also had two monks escorting him, though none of them were wearing monastic robes any longer. The lama himself was wearing a dark maroon chuba and had a pistol strapped to his waist. He sat on a tree stump and watched us approach, a long-barrel Czech rifle, which we called *pamaling*, resting on his lap. He had taken off his hat and had this monk-head, you know, shaven. He belonged to the Gelugpa sect and was, in fact, a very high lama, of *hutoktu* rank. He seemed to be in his early forties and was of middling height and weight. His face was rather full, but it had great dignity. He had studied at the Lower Tantric College (*gyumey*) in Lhasa for many years and was well known for his learning, and his skill at bead divination. I never set much store in divinations and things, but I bowed before the lama with the rest of my comrades. He gave us his blessings.

"Mepa Pön was a stocky man in his fifties. He had long braided hair tied around his head in the Nyarong fashion and was armed with a Chinese made submachine gun.

"Tim had a letter for Dhakpa Lama from the Dalai Lama, and handed it over to him. After he had read the letter, Tim and I told them about all that was happening in India with the Dalai Lama, the government-in-exile, the refugees, and the tremendous support we were receiving from the Americans to train and supply the resistance. We told them that the Americans would provide them with as many arms and as much ammunition as they needed.

"The two leaders gave us a complete account of the Markham resistance and its decline in the last year. We had suspected that the resistance had weakened and the nomad woman had confirmed our fears, but it was a sickening shock to be told by Dhakpa Lama and Mepa Pön that they now had only sixty-odd fighters left—from an initial force of over 20,000 men. They told us that the very success of the resistance had in some ways contributed to its downfall. The concentration of fighters from many neighbouring areas, who came to join the efforts of Phupa Pön, Dhakpa Lama and Mepa Pön, had also drawn overwhelming Chinese response. The presence of so many fighting men in Markham, and the fact that there were very few men left on the land, had also caused a drastic food shortage and famine in the area.

"We sent a signal back to base that we had managed to contact the Markham resistance leaders and also transmitted a full report of the situation. Since our departure, there had always been one operator at the Tibet Task Force base waiting for our transmissions. As soon as the signal was received, preparations were made in America to send in another team of five men with more equipment in a bid to resuscitate the Markham resistance. Preparations were also made for an arms drop. One of the men in this forthcoming team, the radio operator, was Gyangtse Jedung, who now lives in Kathmandu. I learned about all this much later.

"That day, we also linked up with the main body of the surviving resistance force. For Tim, it was a tremendously happy moment, and also a bitterly sad one, for he met what was left of his family. His sister, Ashé, who was sixteen, and Thupten Dolkar who was twelve, were in tears as they hugged their brother. His youngest brother, aged fifteen, was also there. For some years now, he had been a fighter with the band and carried his father's rifle. They told Tim about the death of his father and the capture of Tim's younger brother, Tsering Topgyal. These were the children of a great Markham chieftain and they now looked like beggars, dressed in rags and torn boots with worn-out soles. Every one of us in the team felt really bad for Tim. There were other women and children in the group. Mepa Pön had a fourteen-year-old daughter there, who I got to know well later.

"In our next meeting with the resistance leaders, Tim and I told them that our first task was to recover the equipment we had cached after landing. In that cache, we had a great deal of ammunition; two submachine guns, the sniper rifle, grenades and other things. We asked for six of their men to help us carry the stuff. From our team, we had decided that four of us should go, including me. But the resistance fighters replied that we could not embark on such an expedition immediately since arrangements had to be made to collect the extra food for the journey. Barley was hard to come by. No one had any surplus but ate what they got from day to day. I pointed out that if we collected enough tsampa just to get to the place, we had sufficient American beef jerky cached there for the return journey. This bit of information reassured the fighters somewhat. Tim described the place to them and, fortunately, they knew where it was. In fact, they told us it was not as far away as we had thought.

"Yet a decision was not easily arrived at. The resistance fighters asked Dhakpa lama to perform a *mo*, a divination. He closed his eyes and rubbed his rosary vigorously with both hands. He then blew on it, and holding it up, moved some of the worn shiny beads back and forth on the string. Finally, the lama declared that we could leave the day after tomorrow. What do you call such a thing, belief, superstition. All the fighters seemed to have great faith in the lama. There were a few monks or rather ex-monks in that group, some even from Sera Monastery and the tantric colleges in Lhasa.

"Aaron, Philip and Duke, who was our back-up radio man, accompanied me. Tim, Colin and Luke stayed with the guerrilla band. Six fighters from the resistance force accompanied us. As I told you earlier, it took us six days to get here from the drop zone. This time we managed to make the trip back in two. On the previous occasion, not only had we been unsure of our route, but had been wary of exposure and had only travelled by night. This had limited our speed and made us lose our way frequently. But now, with our guides, we did not have to worry.

"When we got near the site of the cache, I first surveyed the surrounding area with my binoculars to make sure the Chinese had not set a trap for us. We had earlier placed stones in a seemingly random way around the cache area, but whose positions we had memorized. These would have been moved if the Chinese had searched the place or dug up anything. But everything seemed to be okay. We then entered the sheep pen and checked for booby traps. No one had come here after us. We dug up all our stuff and repacked them for the return journey. The resistance fighters with us were amazed and delighted with our sophisticated equipment. What surprised them most was our inflatable rubber dinghy.

"I don't think I mentioned that to you before. It could seat about ten people and came complete with four light paddles and a foot pump. The whole region from Markham through Dzayül to Assam in India was scoured with many gorges, rivers and streams. There were only a few bridges and ferries, and those would probably be guarded by Chinese troops by now. So, the dinghy would be invaluable if we were to travel that way. This was a contingency plan we had discussed back at base. But the dinghy was a heavy load for one man to carry. With the spare radio set, generator and all the other weapons, ammunition and grenades, the ten of us were really weighted down. But looking back now, it seems amazing how all that hiking up and down mountains with those enormous loads, never exhausted us. We were ready to do anything. Even when we got tired sometimes, why, a little rest, a bite to eat, and we were ready to carry on, just like that.

"The return journey was no problem. Just four days after we had left the main group, we finally arrived at a prearranged rendezvous point in the forest and waited for our comrades. We were very careful. Using every cover available, Duke and I advanced cautiously to the meeting place. The rest of our group was spread out behind us in a wide screen, ready to give us cover fire in case of a betrayal. But nobody was there. We waited for hours. We scouted the area and found evidence of a recent firefight there—empty cartridges, broken twigs and bullet scars on trees. All of us were troubled by these signs.

"I felt this lump in my stomach. I forced myself not to imagine the worst that could have happened to the others. I reminded myself that we had worked out other fallback rendezvous points and times, in case our group or the main resistance band could not make it the first time. In fact, we had three other contingency plans. So we tried again the next day at another previously selected site, but there too, our friends did not show up. The third rendezvous also proved to be a disappointment. We were now worried sick. All the signs indicated that the resistance band was being constantly attacked and chased by a large force of Chinese troops. The resistance fighters with us told us that the Chinese presence in the area had increased considerably of late. It was just luck that our small group had managed to avoid any encounter with them.

"Finally, eleven days after splitting up from the main band, we trudged wearily to the last rendezvous point. By then, my hopes of ever seeing my comrades again were not high, but I fervently prayed that nothing had happened to them and the other fighters. Around mid-morning, just on the perimeter of the last assigned rendezvous area, we encountered one fighter on lookout duty. It was as if the sun had come out through dark storm clouds. Suddenly I felt weak and tired. We had been walking the whole night with our heavy loads. The guard ran off to inform the others while we rested, tired but relieved.

"Then out of the trees, followed by a few Markham fighters, Luke and Colin came running towards us. Both of them hugged us all in turn and cried. We could not hold back our own tears. We were like family to each other. All we had in our lives was each other. They cried and hugged us again and again, not letting go of us.

"The fighters accompanying Tim and Colin carried our loads, and after a while, we picked up our rifles and went over to where the resistance force had set up camp. Tim came over to meet us, holding a couple of bowls of black tea. That was all they had left in the way of provisions—no tsampa, no meat. He was visibly moved and affected to see us, and he broke down. He and the others had thought that the ten of us had been wiped out. When he told us this, tears filled his eyes."

Bhusang's voice faltered. He turned away from me and began to cry. He lowered his grey head and turned away, but I could hear him sobbing. I fiddled with the controls of my cassette recorder. Finally, I asked him if he wanted to continue the interview some other time.

"No. It's all right. I just remembered how much we cared for each other. You know, it is so important to care. Caring (*tsewa*) is such a precious thing."

His voice broke again, but after a little while, he recovered. He took a thin Chinese towel from under his pillow and wiped his eyes with it, and also noisily blew his nose.

"I remember all of them so well . . . so clearly. I swear, *Kunchok sum* (by the Three Jewels). I can't remember my own family, my wife, children, and mother, but I see my comrades' faces all the time. I always remember them. We went through so much together. But I can't do anything for them now. They were such brave, loyal and patriotic men. I asked the Dalai Lama for a *thonmö*, a special prayer, for them. They were like no one else. They were all so young. I was the oldest at thirty-two. Tim was twenty-five. Colin, Philip, Luke, Aaron and Duke were no older than twenty."

Bhusang dabbed at his eyes with the towel and sniffed a bit. For a while, he was silent, but then he drank some tea and continued his story.

"Just a day after our group had left them, Tim and the main resistance band had been suddenly attacked by a large force of Chinese troops. Though the resistance had managed to hold back the attack and retreat in order, the soldiers followed them relentlessly. It seemed that the Chinese had mounted a special campaign to wipe out the last remaining resistance group in Markham. The arrival of our seven-man team from America, news of which had probably reached the Chinese from the nomad woman or someone else, had made the Chinese even more determined to finish off the Markham resistance before it could be resuscitated with American aid. Tim and the other fighters had undergone the most dangerous and arduous time in the last many days. About six men had been killed and many more wounded. Now they had no food, and nearly all their personal belongings had been lost in the continuous fighting and retreating. All they had were the clothes on their backs and their weapons.

"Since the resistance groups in Sog, Pembar, Central Tibet and other areas had been wiped out, and the Lhasa Uprising crushed, the Chinese could now concentrate many more troops here in Markham. From what I gathered later, troops had even been sent directly from the PLA headquarters at Chengdu, the capital of Sichuan province. In all, the Chinese now had a force of over 70,000 soldiers in Markham for one final campaign to wipe out what remained of the resistance.

"Every town, village and even isolated farmhouses had contingents of Chinese soldiers stationed there in order to deny the resistance any access to food or support from the people. Every main route in and out of the villages and towns and major crossroads was illuminated during the night with electric floodlights. You could hear the generators throbbing throughout the night. In other places, they kept bonfires going and truck headlights lighting up the roadside. Hundreds and hundreds of armed patrols scoured the mountains and valleys of Markham, day and night, searching for resistance fighters. Wherever the fighters went, they encountered Chinese troops. The land was crawling with them like lice on a beggar's sheepskin robe.

"The Chinese were also distributing leaflets warning the people of Markham not to provide help to the 'rebel bandits'—that's what they called us—and to report any sighting or information about us. The Chinese also promised cash rewards for anyone capturing a 'rebel bandit' or providing information leading to a capture. Posters were also stuck in the villages and towns. But there were very few people left in these hamlets. Most of them were deserted, their occupants having fled to the mountains or Lhasa, or been imprisoned in the concentration camp at Garthok, or executed or just killed in the fighting.

"That night, the seven of us sat down to discuss what options we had left. All of us realized that our mission was essentially over. Far from reviving the Markham resistance and providing it with American support, all we could do was just about manage not to be wiped out by the Chinese. Tim was very depressed and did not say much.

"'You are the team leader,' I said to Tim, trying to remind him of his responsibilities. 'We need to know what your ideas are on our situation. Yes, I know our instructions were to do everything possible to help the resistance, but we were also told that in case the resistance collapsed, we were to get out of Tibet and to bring out as many other resistance fighters as we could. We cannot do what is impossible. We have to think of the future. There will be other opportunities to fight the Chinese, and under less impossible conditions.' The others expressed pretty much the same views.

"'You are right,' Tim raised his head and looked across at us. 'I agree with you on everything. But it is hard for me to talk of leaving my land and my people once again. I also do not have the heart to tell Dhakpa Lama, Mepa Pön and my other friends that we have to leave.' I think it was Colin who suggested that perhaps someone else should talk to the Markham leaders. After some discussion, we agreed that Tim would not have to speak, and that it would be my job to speak to the resistance leaders. We arranged a meeting with them where I informed them of our outlook on the situation and our plan.

"'There is nothing we can do here in Markham,' I said to Dhakpa Lama and the other leaders. 'The Chinese here are just too many and too strong. Your force has lost so many men that it would be of no use even if we got help now. As it is, there is no way we could set up air-drops here since the Chinese control every bit of open space in

Markham. We should consider retreating to a safe place where we will be able to join other fighters, receive arms and training, and reorganize.'

"'Everything you have said is true,' Dhakpa Lama replied, 'and your advice is also good. But for five years, we have been fighting against the Chinese, and we cannot leave now. Once I, Dhakpa Lama alone, had an army of 10,000 men, fully armed. Now the combined army of Markham is what you see here before you. My monastery is a Chinese prison, as is the great fort of Garthok. Tens of thousands of our people are in those prisons—thousand more are dead. No, we cannot leave. But the seven of you are young and strong. You are men with special knowledge, and it would be a waste if you died here with us. I have discussed this with Mepa Pön and the others. They are all in agreement with me on this. We will try and provide whatever help you need to get out of Markham. You will have to wait for some time until Chinese pressure eases and you can collect some food for your journey.'

"I replied to Dhakpa Lama that he and the others had misunderstood us. The seven of us were not saying that we would leave the resistance force here and go on our own. All seven of us had come here voluntarily to fight. So if we were to die, we would die together with everyone in the resistance force. If we survived, we would survive together. We wanted what remained of the resistance to come with us. We would not leave them. I told him that we had two alternative escape routes. One was to proceed south west to Tsawarong and then via Dzayül into Assam in India. The longer route would be to go straight north and then travel west in a wide arc across the Jhangthang to Western Tibet, and then into Nepal.

"Dhakpa Lama said he was delighted to hear my words, but he would first discuss things with the men and then convey their decision to us.

"The resistance fighters were reasonably well armed with old Czech, Russian and English rifles. They also had captured Chinese weapons. Every man had a rifle, but they lacked ammunition. Many had less than twenty or thirty rounds left. Though all of us in our team had been trained in guerrilla warfare, the Markham fighters were better than us in the real thing. They had been fighting since 1956, and they knew every inch of the land like the back of their own hands, which is the most important thing in guerrilla warfare. They marched only in single file, keeping a good distance between each fighter. Scouts were sent ahead, and the person who brought up the rear had the duty of sweeping away any trace of footprints with a leafy branch. They were so experienced that they could tell whether a shoe print was Chinese or not, and roughly how much time had elapsed since it had been made. They could read Chinese tracks like a book. They were also very good at posting guards and sending out patrols, and taking precautions like that.

"Finally, Dhakpa Lama returned from his meeting with the group and informed us of their decision. Everyone had agreed to make the attempt to escape with us. He said that the first escape route would be quicker, but it involved many river crossings. Also, food would be difficult to find in those areas. If we travelled north, it would take longer, but the possibility of shooting game, or getting a yak or sheep was much greater. Since right then we were completely out of food and had no hope of getting any in Markham, it would be best if we left immediately, early next morning, for the north. All of us agreed. Once the decision had been made, the situation seemed more hopeful than before. We were calm and relaxed as we prepared to leave. Curiously enough, after his announcement, Dhakpa Lama took me aside and addressing me politely as "*amchi-la*" or "honourable doctor", asked me if I could give him a poison capsule, which he understood we all carried. I replied that I was really sorry that we did not have any extra pills, and that I could not give him my own since I had taken a vow with the others in my team to use it if captured.

"Early next morning, before leaving the area, we prepared to radio Headquarters about our new plans. This was on the 10th of April. Whenever we could, we had tried to send a message every couple of days at a fixed time, although in the last week that had been impossible. Colin had set up the radio and had a couple of the local fighters vigorously turning the crank handles of the generator. Tim and the others were spread across the mountainside. Barely had the message been sent when a scout came running, shouting that a large Chinese force was rapidly making its way up to where we were. I helped Colin pack away the radio. Just as I finished strapping the set on his back and picked up my rifle from the ground, we heard the sound of gunfire.

"In a matter of minutes, the Chinese were upon us. We retreated slowly, keeping up a covering fire on the approaching soldiers, while Colin and others encumbered with the radio-set, baggage and things, ran into the woods. We gradually had to increase the pace of our retreat as the Chinese made a number of attempts to flank us. Their firepower was tremendous. Bullets chopped the leaves and branches on the trees. A bit of flying tree bark hit me on the side of my face. I saw a couple of the Markham men falling around me, but I could not stop to help them. There was no time to do anything but keep up a rapid fire against the approaching Chinese. If you stopped shooting or stopped retreating, they would be all over you in minutes.

"I realized after a while that the Chinese were not just pushing us from one direction or trying to flank us here and there, but that they were all over the mountain. As soon as we managed to get a little distance from the initial attacking force, we bumped into another one a little way ahead. The fact that we kept moving all the time prevented the different Chinese forces from encircling us or pinning us down. The gunfire was tremendous. I even heard gunfire in the far distance and wondered who they were firing at. It was confusing and chaotic in that forest. In all we had nine separate encounters that day with the Chinese, from early morning till early evening when we finally managed to shake off our tormentors.

"We had started out with sixty-seven men that morning: sixty from the resistance and seven from our team. There were only thirty of us left as we rested in a rapidly darkening world. Our radioman Colin was also missing. One of Mepa Pön's men told us that he had seen Colin hit by a bullet on the forehead. Some of the others, not realizing that he was shot, but thinking he had stumbled, had tried to help him up. But he was stone cold dead. This had happened in the morning. I had not seen anything , as I was bringing up the rear and concentrating on just stopping the advancing Chinese. I felt really awful. In the morning, when Colin was sending his message, he had confided to me that he did not feel well. He also looked quite depressed, unlike the rest of us who were elated to be leaving Markham. Colin was not a very strong person physically, so I thought it could be that he was ill or something. I asked him if he wanted any medicine, but he said he was not sick but was just feeling bad. Thinking about it now, he must have had a premonition or something like that. Like me, Colin had been a soldier in the old Tibetan army—the Drapchi Regiment. He was also a fellow Lhasa man. I felt really terrible.

"The next day, we expected the Chinese to find us and renew their attack, but nothing happened. It was a small breathing space, so we pushed on. On the 12th, we got into a big shootout with the Chinese. This time we were luckier. We spotted their approach first and managed to prepare our positions in such a way that we locked them in a very effective and gratifying crossfire. None of us was wounded or killed that day, but we killed many Chinese; everyone in that platoon. We didn't even bother to count the bodies and just moved on quickly. The resistance fighters picked up the Chinese weapons and ammunition. We had considerable ammunition for our M1 rifles, which were semi-automatic so we could keep up a good rate of fire. We did not have too many grenades, and anyway, those grenades were the small pineapple, fragmentation grenades, like the British type the Tibetan army used, which were not very effective.

"On the thirteenth, we also managed to avoid any encounter with the Chinese and moved on quickly. But we were running short of food, and all of us were very hungry.

"What had protected us all along were the forests of Markham, which covered most of the mountainsides. Nearly all the farming took place in the valleys, where land was fertile and water plentiful. Further up the mountains, the forests gave way to grasslands where nomads roamed with their herds. Now we were coming out to terrain that did not conceal us or give us protection. But we had to take the chance to find some food.

"On the fourteenth, we came out of the forest somewhere in the high grasslands. We were all so exhausted and hungry by now that many of us were falling asleep even as we walked. Others collapsed as they walked and had to be forcibly woken up. Finally, we came across a nomad tent. An old nomad man greeted us. He seemed a bit nervous, but agreed to sell us a yak. We paid him sixty Chinese *yuan*, double what it cost normally. We slaughtered it there and then and everyone set about cutting the meat and preparing a meal. I am ashamed to say it now, but I was terribly impatient with hunger and took a mugful of the warm yak blood and quickly drank it down.

"Probably that hot blood, on top of the exhaustion and hunger, affected the *lung*, the wind humor, for I fell sound asleep right there. Try as they might my friends could not wake me up for some hours. That night we roasted the meat and had a wonderful meal. We all felt relaxed and rested.

"We moved on that night around two o'clock and did not come across any Chinese soldiers. Early next morning on the fifteenth, we found ourselves walking up a high and open valley that gradually closed in and ended in a mountain pass which we would probably reach in a few hours. There was a stream flowing through this dale. It wasn't very big. You could jump over it, but the water was clean and fresh. The stream flowed in an easterly direction. Our little band was walking on the mountainside to the right of the stream. At about 6 a.m., we spotted Chinese troops on the ridge of the opposite slope. Suddenly the whole length of the ridge seemed to be covered with thousands of Chinese soldiers, tiny dots of yellow in their khaki uniform. Some came running down the mountainside others ran further up the ridge in an arc to cut us off.

"We tried to jog as fast as we could up the valley, but the Chinese were rapidly closing in, and it was obvious that we would be cut off in the front before long. We came to a small patch of trees and shrubs just above the stream. It was not really a forest, but it afforded us a little cover. But more critically, just behind the trees, the mountain slope became a cliff, a steep rock face that curved inwards, in a way that sheltered this little grove. It was probably why the trees and bushes grew there, since they were partially protected from the wind. The advantage for us was that the rock cliff protected our rear. The Chinese could not attack us from that direction.

"We quickly prepared our positions. Since the six of us from the team had the M1 rifles and most of the ammunition, we spread ourselves in the three main directions the Chinese were coming from.

Philip and Aaron covered the east, downstream, Luke and Duke the west, upstream. Tim and I covered the centre. All of us were about ten or fifteen feet away from the next member of the team. The others filled in the gaps. The Chinese came charging from all directions except behind, where the cliff face protected us. They ran down the slope on the other side, splashed across the brook, and came up the slope on our side. We opened fire when they were about fifty feet away from us. I really cannot tell you how many soldiers there were that day. A thousand, more . . . there were so many—everywhere.

"But our position was a strong one, and the stream and the uphill climb on our side of the slope slowed down the Chinese enough to give us the opportunity to gun them down before they closed in on us. There were a lot of dead and dying Chinese out there after their initial charge. Blood ran in the stream, flowing through the tufts of reedy *churu* grass that grew there. Khampa farmers would collect this grass to feed to their animals, and kids would chew on it.

"The Chinese soldiers then tried to advance their position in small groups of four or five men. Under heavy covering fire, they dashed forward and then hit the dirt, taking cover behind rocks and mounds and even behind the bodies of their fallen comrades. Such dashes were taking place from all directions. It was crucial for us to stop these attacks dead, otherwise the soldiers would get close enough to rush us. As soon as we saw such an attempt, we would cut it down at once. I remember that I always seemed to fire off a whole clip, eight bullets, to stop every dash forward the Chinese made. Our fire seemed effective initially, and it appeared to us that we were stopping most of the small attacks. But gradually, they managed to close in. In spite of the many soldiers we shot down, some others managed to find cover, and advance a bit more forward.

"About four hours later, at around ten, during a brief lull in the fighting, I moved from my position and looked around me. Luke and Aaron were lying still on the ground. I crawled over to check. They were dead. They did not seem to be shot. They had probably bitten into their poison capsules. These two kids were close. They came from the same area of Lithang. I noticed that one of their rifles had been hit by a Chinese bullet and damaged. I crawled over to Tim and told him that Luke and Aaron were dead. Tim said that we were not to bite the poison capsules before we ran out of ammunition. Otherwise, it would be a waste of ammunition. Also, we needed to find time to hide all our radios and other equipment in order to maintain security. We must keep on fighting. He shouted to Philip and Duke to hold their ground and fight. Duke stuck up his thumb and gave us an okay sign.

"The Chinese began closing in. Some of them were yelling at us in Chinese, probably insults. Then someone called out in Tibetan for us to surrender. That was too much. We shouted back insults. 'Eat shit!' we said. 'Eat shit!' I yelled 'This is our land. Why should we surrender—you surrender!' Someone else shouted, 'Go back to China and eat shit!' The Tibetan speaker on the Chinese side was probably Baba Dawa or Dawa of Bathang, a well-known collaborator and Communist officer. We later learnt that he had been sent to Markham, especially to participate in the capture of our team.

"A lot of our men were now dead and some wounded. Tim's youngest brother had been shot in the stomach and was crying out in pain. The girls were upset and weeping. The gunfire we were receiving was incredible. Sometimes you couldn't distinguish the separate sounds, and the noise came together like a roar. All the leaves of the trees were chopped to ribbons by the Chinese gunfire and fell on our heads like green snowflakes.

"Now the Chinese were getting really close. Our ammunition supply was low. I clearly remember I had about twenty rounds for my pistol, and fifty for the rifle. And it was being used up fast. I figured I must have fired over eight hundred rounds. There was a little pause now between the charges. I was firing clip after clip, nearly continuously. Eight rounds then 'ping!' the spent clip ejecting and me jamming in another full clip into the breach before the expended clip hit the ground. Then firing again. I was fast. I didn't feel scared or anything.

It was all like a dream that day. All you thought about was stopping the Chinese. You had to stop them dead; otherwise it was over. They were that close. 'Eat shit!' I shouted, 'Eat shit!' They were really close. About ten, even eight meters away. But life is important, even for a Chinese person, and they didn't want to throw theirs away. So they hesitated to make the final charge. You could hear PLA officers yelling from the back, threatening them and screaming at them to charge.

"Then the covering fire would come. It was intense. The sound of bullets whizzing by you, the whine of ricochets, the 'fup fup' of leaves and twigs being cut, the rattle and roar of the gunfire, would momentarily stun you. But you immediately recovered and started shooting again. We were killing Chinese like bugs here. In fact, we killed so many PLA soldiers that day, I later learned that the local people sent to recover and bury the bodies lost count of them after a while.

"I got up and fired off one of my last clips. I felt a burning sensation against my skin. A bullet had passed through my chuba and grazed my side. But I ignored it and continued to fire till the clip was empty. Then I looked around and saw Tim, lying on the ground, dead. He was about thirty feet away. Philip was also dead, and so was Duke. All of them had probably bitten into their poison capsules. There were very few people left now on our side firing, just four or five men. In front of me was this pile of Chinese bodies. 'This is the end', I thought. I took out my poison capsule from my shirt pocket and put it in my mouth. Then I started firing rapidly at the Chinese squad just a few yards left of me—about seven or eight men. I didn't miss that day. I think I got all of them and used up my last clip. I then dropped the Garand and reached over to my shoulder holster for my pistol.

"Suddenly something struck me hard on the back of my neck and I lost consciousness."

33

CONFESSIONS OF AN
AMERICAN IMPERIALIST SPY

"I regained consciousness the next day, or so I thought. I was mistaken. Two full days and nights had passed. By the light of pine fire, I saw a Chinese soldier standing over me, pointing a submachine gun down at my face. I was lying on the floor of a small room that I later learnt was a meditation hut, probably once used by a hermit in these desolate mountains. It was dark when I woke up. The door of the hut was open, and there were more soldiers outside, hunkered under a canvas awning.

"Then Tim's sister, Ashé, came into the room. We had managed to send her away from the battlefield before the Chinese had completely encircled us, along with her twelve-year-old sister, Thupten Dolkar, and also Mepa Pön's daughter and Tim's youngest brother who had been badly wounded. Ashé carried a wooden bowl of *chamdur*, a soup of tsampa and butter tea. She fed me like a baby, as I could not move at all. She wept when she saw me but did not utter a word. The Chinese probably told her not to say anything to me. But it didn't matter as I was in a complete daze and could not talk at all.

"I later learnt that after I had been knocked out, the Chinese had overrun our position. By that time, there was no one really left to defend anything. Eleven of the Markham fighters were captured, barely alive, all badly wounded and unable to fight. No one from our team had survived. Tim's younger brother Tsering Topgyal who was in Garthok prison at that time, and who I later met in Dharamshala, told me that I was carried down from the battlefield on a crude stretcher made of branches and blankets, and that I was vomiting blood. I don't remember anything. Tsering Topgyal also told me that the bodies of the six men from our team were carried on yaks, requisitioned from the local nomads.

"The next day, two Chinese soldiers lifted me out of the hut and put me on a horse. I was then tied securely to the saddle and taken to the monastery of Dhakpa Lama. This monastery had been turned into a massive prison and had about four hundred prisoners. But more construction was taking place to hold additional prisoners. When we got there, I was laid on the ground in the courtyard of the monastery, alongside the dead bodies of my teammates. The other prisoners, wounded or not, were made to stand in a line behind us. The Chinese also made the local people gather in the courtyard and hold red flags and large banners emblazoned with Chinese characters. A speech was given by a Chinese officer about how the rebel bandits leaders: Phupa Pön, Dhakpa Lama and Mepa Pön were now finally crushed, and how their American imperialist spy accomplices were also completely destroyed. The speech was a long one. At the end of it, the local people were made to applaud and shout slogans. They were also exhorted to 'speak bitterness' (Chinese, *suku*) and demonstrate their anger. One old man came over and grabbed me by the hair and slapped me once. He shouted at me, 'American spy! Have you come here to eat shit?' The Chinese guards rushed over to stop the man. I remember this clearly. It was such a transparent piece of theatre.

"After the meeting, I was lifted up by the guards and taken to a cell in the monastery. It was formerly a monk's bedchamber. A Chinese doctor came into the room, and I was stripped naked. I was given a long and thorough check-up. I had earlier realized I was completely paralyzed, all over, and couldn't even talk. They took off all my clothes and personal stuff, ring and wristwatch, carefully noted down everything, and took them away for examination. I was dressed in scraps of discarded Chinese army uniform.

"An armed soldier was in my cell at all times, guarding me. This soldier was relieved every two hours. There were more armed guards outside the cell. Even at night, one soldier sat across me with a submachine gun across his chest. A small oil lamp provided a little light. I realized I was a very special prisoner. I was given an old cushion, and a felt cover to sleep on. For blankets, they gave me three chuba robes of hand-woven wool (*nambu*). I was securely handcuffed all the time. The food wasn't bad, considering people were dying of starvation all over Tibet and China at the time. For breakfast, I got some tsampa porridge or bread. For lunch, one of those big round Khampa bread, and Tibetan tea with butter in it—butter! Dinner was usually Chinese *kuomien* noodles with canned pork mixed in.

"Since I was paralyzed and couldn't move at all, I was spoon-fed, with a wooden spoon. This time another Khampa girl, the daughter of Sonam Topgyal [a member of the exile parliament in Dharamshala in the 1990s] fed me. I couldn't even hold a bowl in my hands. There was no feeling in them. When I tried holding something, I would always drop it. I could not even wipe my nose. This girl did it for me. At the time, I had a lot of mucus coming out of my nose because of my condition, and this girl cleaned it all with bits of cloth and her apron. She nursed me wonderfully, considering her own miserable state, and I owe her so much, maybe even my life. Later, when I got out to India, I sent her some sacred relic pills from the Dalai Lama. I'm afraid that I was a big problem for her. I could not even control my bladder, so my mattress and bedding were stinking wet most of the time. I would be taken in the morning to the toilet by other prisoners, who held me up. But there's only so much people can do for you under such circumstances.

"When I was taken to the toilet, I noticed that all the other cells and rooms were full of prisoners. But I have to say that I was treated so much better than the other prisoners. I was even given a cigarette occasionally. I could not hold it in my hand, but a guard would stick one in my mouth and light it. I would puff away as much as I could and when it got short, would spit it out on the floor. Prisoners who came in to clean the cell or perform some other chores would rush to grab the butt. My cell door was constantly open with one guard inside, and others outside, so I could see, to a small extent, what was taking place in the corridor. I saw prisoners lining up to go to work and also getting their rations—one small can of tsampa a day. They were all on the verge of starvation. I was given three full meals a day. I was the chief VIP guest in that establishment.

"I could not speak a word at the time. I don't know why but I was, sort of, struck dumb after my capture. The Chinese tried to ask me questions, but it was of no use. They discovered my cover name, "Phuntsok" that everyone in the resistance group called me by. One of those who questioned me was this Tibetan woman interpreter (*thongsé*) who I remember shouting at me, 'Phuntsok! Can you speak? Talk to me. Do you want a cigarette?' She had been sent from Lhasa especially to assist with my interrogation. But I remained dumb, much to her frustration. In spite of my frail condition, I was always handcuffed, always very tight. My wrists and hands were white because the blood could not circulate properly.

"After twelve or thirteen days, a more important officer, Baba Dawa, came to interrogate me. He was a Tibetan originally from Bathang, and a well-known traitor. Although I could not speak, he did not let it get in the way of his assignment. He asked me if I could hear him. I nodded. He then went into a long monologue about the policies of the Communist Party: how those who genuinely repented and confessed would be dealt with leniently by the people's government, but stubborn and unrelenting elements would be destroyed. Of course, it was much longer than I am telling you. He also told me that I was to make a full and frank confession of my counterrevolutionary crimes against the people and the nation. He put a cigarette in my mouth and lit it. He then went on outlining the various points in the Communist Party's policy towards those who sincerely confessed and reformed themselves. I must say this for him; he had persistence, and he had deviousness. Dawa was a colonel and had four stars on his shoulder boards.

"He was very devious. You know, with the Chinese, the more devious the person, the higher the rank he seems to hold. With us Tibetans, the higher the rank, the more stupid and pompous the person is. Dawa had some tricks. He tried a few times to catch me of my guard to make sure I was not pretending to be dumb.

"Then some sixteen or eighteen days later, I am not sure, Dawa came to my cell and once again gave me a long political lecture. At the end of it, he announced that I would be taken to Lhasa. He also said I would now be given special medical treatment to help me recover my voice. A Chinese acupuncturist came to my cell the next day. Every day after that, I received two therapy sessions daily and a white tablet to put under my tongue every evening.

"Then my old clothes were returned. I had a nice checked woollen jacket bought in Kalimpong, that I had worn under my sheepskin chuba. It had a hole at the armpit where a bullet had passed through during the final battle. My chuba was torn and also had some bullet holes. The strange thing is that I was not wounded at all, except for a graze and the rifle-butt whack on my neck. So I got my jacket back and my woollen trousers (U.S. army winter issue) and my U.S. Army para-boots. They returned nothing else. They kept my gold ring and my Swiss Westend wristwatch. I was also given an old Chinese army *dayi* overcoat. It was bitterly cold by then.

"I was taken first to Chamdo in a convoy of two army trucks and a jeep. I was handcuffed and had to sit on the floor of one of the trucks with armed soldiers around me on benches. Baba Dawa travelled in the lead jeep. The roads were very primitive and rough. The ride was a painfully uncomfortable one. The first night on the road, I had to sleep on the floor of the truck itself with no blankets or mats. It was incredibly cold. Since I was handcuffed and had leg-irons on, I could not move in any way to warm myself. I nearly froze to death that night.

"When we reached Chamdo the night after that, I was taken to a prison within the main army camp. There were thousands of Tibetan prisoners there doing construction work, and also working on the roads. I was taken straight to the military hospital, where I was given a check-up. Then I was locked up by myself in a cell. My food was delivered to me by a man called Thupten, who was a cook at the prison. His son Kunga now works at the Research Office here in Dharamshala. Thupten cut my hair and washed my feet in a tin basin. He also trimmed my nails and otherwise did everything he could to clean me up and make me comfortable. He was a good man. I was still paralyzed. I had to stay in Chamdo prison for ten days. The road to Lhasa was probably closed then.

"Finally, we continued our journey to Lhasa. I now got to ride in Baba Dawa's jeep at the back with four soldiers. It takes two days to get to Lhasa from Chamdo. Every evening we halted at Chinese army camps. At each of these stops, I would be stripped naked and searched very carefully. They had obviously been told that I was a spy who had come from America, so they were all extra careful and vigilant. They tied me in such a way that I couldn't move from side to side when I was sleeping. Since they kept my cell door open, I could see Chinese soldiers coming in to have a look at me and talking excitedly among themselves. At one stop, they made me sleep on a Ping-Pong table. That night the *bhaitang* (sergeant) put my handcuffs on very tightly. Whenever I moved the cuff bit deeper and deeper into my flesh, till I was howling in pain.

"The last stretch of my trip to Lhasa was on April 18, 1961. We drove past Medrogongkar for about an hour and then came to Dechen Dzong, which is only about twenty kilometers from Lhasa. From the back of the jeep, I received this unexpected but wonderful view of the Potala Palace, in the distance, almost like a sacred vision. When I saw the great palace my pain and despair were forgotten, for a moment, and my heart filled with joy. Of course, the Potala is in a way a paradise, the sacred realm of Chenrezig, the Bodhisattva of Compassion, so it is not strange that a vision of it should fill one with happiness. I don't know how it is for foreigners when they see the Potala. Do you think it affects them like that as well? After passing Dechen, we drove by Ganden Monastery, Tsal Gungthang and then finally came to Lhasa.

"We got to the city and the prison inside the Tibet Military Area Headquarters (Chinese, *Silingbu*) at around four p.m. I didn't have my wristwatch with me, but I managed to guess the time. Chinese soldiers took a regulation afternoon nap that ended at three. But the soldiers here were up and about carrying on with their duties, so I figured it was around four. Baba Dawa handed me over to a Chinese *tzu-tang* officer who had a harelip. Dawa gave a verbal report of my condition, my dumbness, paralysis and so on. My Chinese comprehension wasn't very good, but I could guess what the conversation was about. My handcuffs were taken off, and new ones from this Military Prison put on.

"I was carried into a small cell, about eight-by-eight feet square, one side of which, from wall to wall was a rough earthen platform, which served as a bed for up to three prisoners. Between the platform and the door were a couple of feet of space where the piss-bucket was kept. One small window behind the platform, about one-foot square, provided a view of the outside world, which was just the main prison wall. There were solid steel bars set vertically as well as horizontally in this window. There was only enough space between the bars to stick a couple of fingers out. I was given an old felt mat and a dirty, lumpy cotton quilt—a Chinese army issue. There were two Chinese prisoners in the cell with me.

"In the evening, they gave me a plate of tsampa and black tea. But I was still very sick and could not move. The supervisor ordered one of the Chinese prisoners to spoon-feed me. But eating dry tsampa is tricky business, even usually, and for me in my condition, it was impossible. The guard reported the problem to the supervisor, and the next morning I was switched from the diet for Tibetan prisoners to that of Chinese prisoners. So, I got things like rice gruel and steamed wheat buns which were easier for me to eat in my condition. A day later, Baba Dawa took me to the military hospital within the camp for a checkup. I was given acupuncture treatment every day after that and also received Western medicine, tablets and stuff. They added an egg to my daily diet. Gradually life returned to my paralyzed body. In about a week, I had improved to the point where I could move a bit and feed myself, but I could not bend my body.'

Bhusang suspected that his condition might have resulted from his cyanide capsule leaking a little of the poison in his mouth before the Chinese pulled it out. But I think it was probably the blow to the back of his neck that temporarily affected the spinal column causing his paralysis, incontinence and inability to speak.

"I was told, much later, by Wangyal, a cook in the prison but formerly a Tibetan government official (and son of Bumthang Drunyik Chenmo) that a rumour had gone around of a special mystery prisoner at the *Silingbu* prison, who was paralyzed, dumb and very sick, but so important that he had more security around him than any other prisoner in the camp. He and the other prisoners racked their brains trying to guess who this important person was. They got a good laugh when they later realized it was just me.

"But the more my condition improved, the more anxious I became. I now began to realize the predicament I was in. Earlier everything was blurry and confusing. Most of the time, it just felt like I was in a kind of dream. But when my health began to improve and my guards and others could see that happening, the interrogations became much more intense. Up to now, they had mostly given me long lectures, political discourses on Marxism-Leninism and so on, but now the questions came one after the other, endlessly, and the tone of the interrogations became sharp and threatening. I was really worried.

"One day, an official from the Tibet Autonomous Region (TAR) Security Department came to question me. He was a tough-looking Chinese, but to my surprise, spoke fluent Tibetan. He got straight to the point. He said they knew everything about me. They had all the information they needed. So he was not going to bother asking questions. I should make a full confession, or it would be the worse for me. He went on in this ominous manner for a couple of hours before he left. He did not ask me a single question, which was unusual and scary. He was setting me up for something big and nasty.

"I had recovered my voice a week before, but I kept pretending that I could not speak. I knew I couldn't keep that up for long. But once I started to talk, they would, of course, want me to tell them everything. I seriously tried to think of different ways I could commit suicide, but there was no way of doing that. They had even removed the laces on my boots. Furthermore, one of the Chinese prisoners was in the cell with me all the time. The other Chinese went out in the day with the general prison population for *Laogai* tasks. I thought about my situation very carefully and tried to figure out a realistic way of dealing with this. I finally decided that it would be best to tell them everything about my early life as a peasant boy and servant of the Thönpa family and my service in the Tibetan army and police, and my involvement in the Lhasa Uprising. I decided to tell them everything up till that point, but lie about everything else after that, especially my training in America and my mission. But I also decided to play it by ear and answer questions only when I absolutely had to—and then as briefly as possible. Stretch the whole thing out. That was my plan. I am, by nature, very stubborn, so I thought I could hold out somehow.

"I first began to answer their questions sometime in mid-July.

"The interrogation room was large and dark and had no windows. The walls were thick—stone and concrete construction. It was absolutely bare. In the middle of the room was a rough wooden table. The interrogators sat in wooden chairs behind the table. Across them, some distance from the table, was a wooden stool where the prisoner sat. Above the stool was a large naked light bulb hanging from the ceiling. Just that. No lampshade, nothing fancy.

"When my interrogation began in July, there were five officers sitting behind the table. But the main interrogators were Baba Dawa and the Chinese official from the TAR Security Bureau. They took turns asking questions about my background: parents, early life, education and so on. The Chinese interrogator was slow and painstaking. I later learned that he was well known for his skill in this field. He also asked me about my wife, and I answered him in detail. I told him everything, even my role in the uprising, and then, starting from my escape to India, I began to invent a whole new story.

"At once, the Chinese interrogator shouted at me and told me that I would be punished for attempting to deceive the Party. He told me that the People's government had shown me every way in which I could redeem myself. It was as if the government had taken me to a big store and patiently explained all the different articles I could choose, and which I couldn't. But I was taking advantage of the government's policy of leniency and attempting to deceive the People and the Party. I needed to be taught a harder lesson.

"He instructed the guard to put on my handcuffs behind my back. They then tied a rope to the handcuffs and slung the other end of the rope over a roof beam. They pulled the rope till my feet were dangling off the floor, and my arms were yanked up behind me painfully. Then they beat me with truncheons. When they finally let me down, they tied the rope tight around my neck so that I choked myself if I pulled my arms down for relief. I was then dragged back to my cell.[*]

"For a week, I had those cuffs on like that. All that time, I was either in terrible pain with my arms pulled up hard behind me or in panic and choking when I tried to pull it down. I just wanted to die. I tried a few times to pull down really hard on the rope and choke myself to death, but I would pass out, then wake up again because of the tremendous pain in my shoulder sockets. It is an impossible thing to kill yourself. Our instincts are to survive. I remember in my pain even trying to eat some food off the floor like a dog. By the end of the week, I was a mess.

"After a week, I was again taken to the interrogation room where I faced my tormentors once more. The Chinese interrogator asked me if I had thought over my stupid and deceitful behaviour, and if I had used the time in my cell for self-reflection and self-criticism (Chinese, *jiantao*). Would I now answer their questions honestly? I replied that I had told them everything, and that I had nothing more to add.

"Baba Dawa lashed out at me with a truncheon. I could not avoid the blow as my hands were still tightly cuffed behind me and my arms chained tightly to my body. I fell, but Dawa kept hitting me again and again with his club till I passed out. When I recovered, there was a doctor by my side. He was wearing a white coat. He said something in Chinese to the interrogators. Dawa was standing behind him, still holding the club and breathing hard from his exertion. Then the officer

---

[*]There is a Goya painting—brown wash on paper—of a Spanish inquisition torture called the "Strappado", which appears to be what Bhusang had to endure. The same torture is used by police in present-day China.

from the TAR Security Bureau said to me that what I had experienced was merely to jog my memory and help me remember everything I had done after 1959. Was my memory now revived? Would I answer their questions truthfully? Stupidly I said no, and was knocked down and beaten again till I was unconscious. Finally, I was dragged to my cell by the guards.

"Back in my cell, I tried desperately to think what I could do. I knew they would keep on beating me and torturing me with the handcuffs for as long as they wanted, and that sooner or later, they would break me, and I would have to talk. The interrogators had also let me know that they already had a great deal of information about my training, secret operations and our base in America. What troubled me was that the bits of information they revealed were accurate. They didn't tell me how they had come by the information, but I already had a good idea.

"Before I had fully recovered, I was always kept in my cell. I was taken to the toilet once a day and then escorted by guards and never saw the other prisoners. The one barred window in my cell had only a view of the main prison wall, but I discovered that if you looked at an angle from the left of the window, you got a partial view of the main courtyard. The prisoners would take an exercise walk around this courtyard in the evenings, shuffling along slowly in a long formation in their shackles. One day I caught sight of this person who appeared to be wearing U.S. Army issue para-boots. I had a limited view of the exercise line and didn't see that particular prisoner again, but it made me wonder if another America-trained agent was also in this prison.

"Some weeks later, I got confirmation on this score. One morning when I was being handed my food through the Judas hatch on my cell door, I saw this prisoner being led away down the corridor by some guards. I couldn't see if he had para-boots on, but he was close enough that I recognized him. His name was Chönyi Yeshi. I had met him in Darjeeling but didn't know him that well. He was a native of Lhoka and recruited by the Four Rivers Six Ranges when it was operating in that area in 1958–59. He had been sent to Colorado in the batch preceding mine. It didn't hit me at once, but it gradually became clear to me that he must have talked. There was no way the Chinese would otherwise have let him out with the general run of the prison population if he hadn't told them everything. He would be in solitary if they didn't trust him, or at least locked up with Chinese prisoners to watch over him, as I was.

"The next day after the beating, I was taken to the interrogation room again. To my surprise, the officers treated me very gently, and to top it all told me that not only was it the policy of the People's government to give lenient sentences to those who confessed their crimes freely, without reservation, but that the policy could be extended to the point where a criminal would be freed altogether and restored to normal society. They told me that *Kalön* Sampho of the old aristocratic family of Samdup Photang a leading feudal reactionary who had taken part in the Lhasa Uprising had been released. So had the famous Lama, Dromo Geshe Rinpoche, who had distributed amulets and sacred pills to resistance fighters. He was even sent back home to Sikkim in India. But I kept quiet.

"The beatings started again the day after that. They also handcuffed me tightly behind the back for days. They varied their technique every day. So, finally, I talked. Not all at once; I just couldn't. But little by little, I started talking. In the end, I told them how I had volunteered in India to join the special operations, and about my training in Colorado, and everything. There were many, many interrogation sessions. They checked, cross-checked and double-checked everything I said. They knew everything, often even before I opened my mouth. They always caught me out in a lie, and then they worked me over for hours about that, from every angle, till they got me not only to confess finally, but also give up more information than they had initially asked for. It took over a month of continuous interrogations, every day for eight or nine hours, before they were satisfied. There were many different interrogators, from various departments, not only from the Military Headquarters and TAR Security, but from the People's Court, Public Security (Chinese, *Gong'an*) and so on.

"I shared my cell with two Chinese prisoners. One went out the whole day to work in the prison laundry and only came in late at night to sleep. The other was locked in the cell the whole day, like me, although he didn't have to go through any interrogations. He probably had gone through all that before. But he had on leg-irons all the time, day and night. The first time I came into the cell, he looked at my jump boots and smiled. He made the noise of an aeroplane and began to chant in English: 'One thousand. Two thousand, Three thousand', the litany that every paratrooper knows like a mantra when he counts off the seconds till his parachute opens. I couldn't speak Chinese, but later, I learned that he was a Guomindang officer, a radio operator who had been captured in Tibet with a team of twenty-four other agents. He was a fairly old man, nearing fifty. They had initially been imprisoned in Kongpo in southern Tibet in a labour camp, but then he and his friends had tried to escape to India and had been recaptured and transferred to the high- security *Silingbu* prison in Lhasa. He helped me a lot, fetching me water, and helping to feed me when I was unable to do so. Finally, when I felt I could trust him I replied to his initial question by counting off: 'one thousand two thousand three thousand . . .' I got a big laugh out of him. He and his mates were later all sent back to China. They were probably executed.

"After my interrogation and confession, I fell into a deep depression. Even recovering my health somewhat, did nothing to make me look forward to life. I felt absolutely helpless. Then I remembered a story that an instructor, I think it was Mr Ken (Ken Knaus), told us in a political class. During the Algerian struggle for independence, when many of the freedom fighters had been thrown in French prison, they had gone on a mass hunger strike for nineteen or twenty-nine days—something like that, which had roused the Algerian public, when they heard about it. Ken explained that even a non-violent method like a hunger strike could be used as a weapon against the enemy.

"So, on October 1, which the Chinese call *Shi yi*, the day when the Communists took power and the founding day of the People's Republic, I went on my personal hunger strike. I refused my regular ration of food and even refused the special food we got on that holiday. That could be a small bit of pork, tofu, sometimes mutton or kiang*

---

*PLA units in open trucks with light machine guns mounted on the cabin roof slaughtered, to near extinction, the vast herds of kiang, the beautiful Tibetan wild ass (*Equus kiang*) that roamed the Jhangtang grasslands.

meat. This was at the Military Headquarter prison. Later, when I was transferred to the Sangyip Prison, we got no meat or anything on holidays, or any other day. When I refused my food, the guards asked me why I was being rebellious. I did not reply but stayed silent. They then called the chief prison commissar (Chinese, *shouxi ganbu*), but I refused to talk and remained without eating or drinking anything for seven days, when the prison authorities definitely realized I was on a hunger strike. But by then, I felt so thirsty that I finally had to give up. I was given a good beating for my troubles.

"I realized that I had not thought the whole thing through, and I should prepare myself mentally for my next attempt. In February of 1962, on Tibetan New Year's Day which, that year coincided with the Chinese New Year, I began my second hunger strike. Prisoners were given a little extra food on the Chinese New Year, but I refused to eat anything. This time the guards and prison cadres knew what I was doing, and they accused me of being unrepentant and stubborn, and they criticized and struggled me. But I was not struggled before the other prisoners, just by myself in my cell. One day one of the kitchen-workers who brought my food, spoke to me quickly when the guards were not listening. He had formerly been a cook at the Kundeling Monastery. His name was Khenrab Wöser. When I refused to accept the food, he quoted this old proverb to me. He was probably being sarcastic: '*Jhang tsakha laythue tiri migpa chuso* (when the *tiri* bird reached the Jhangthang salt-flats, its throat became constricted)'. Normally, the *tiri* bird is said to love eating salt, but when it sees a lot of salt, as at the northern salt-flats, it gets so excited that it finds it impossible to swallow any. Khenrab Wöser probably thought I was being silly and petulant. I can't blame him because he and the other prisoners were getting by on so little food, and here I was refusing not only my privileged diet but even the extra New Year treat. He was not a bad man and probably just trying to help, but he did not understand the political nature of my action.

"The next day, the guards marched into my cell and held me down while a hospital staff stuck me with a big injection. Just minutes later, I had a bad case of diarrhea, after which I had a raging thirst and felt very weak. The guards tried to pry open my mouth. They even used a stick, but I gritted my teeth hard. So, they forced a rubber tube inside through my nose, really pushed it down, and it hurt a lot. The tube was quite thick, and I could feel it tear the inside of my nose and throat. Then they poured some slop down inside me, quite a lot actually, a full meal, and it stayed in my stomach. So, my second hunger strike ended. For weeks afterwards, I was spitting out blood and bits of skin and cartilage. I felt completely shattered at not being able to carry out my resolve to die. I felt bitterly angry with myself at my impotence and uselessness.

"After my main interrogation, I was left pretty much to myself in my cell. I was not allowed to meet anybody. I did not have to go to work or attend political meetings, struggles and re-education classes like the other prisoners, but was locked up all alone. The two Chinese prisoners had also been transferred to China by then. Once in a while, an officer from the Public Security Bureau (Chinese, *Gong'anju*) would come to ask a question or two, mostly verifying some points I had made earlier during my confession.

"My cell was made of stone and cement and had a roof of corrugated iron. The door was three inches thick and made with wood reinforced with angle-iron strips. The cell was in a one-story building. It had two rows of eight cells facing each other with a passage in between. The building was surrounded by a barbed-wire fence and in the north of the main prison compound, where the general prison population was incarcerated. Those prisoners lived in two large dormitory buildings, one of which was to the west of the camp. The other dormitory building was to the south, as were the kitchens, administrative offices, interrogation rooms, guard's barracks and vegetable plots. There was an empty bit of waste ground to the east. A high stonewall topped with barbed wire surrounded the whole prison compound. I had a view of the north wall from my cell window. The four corners of the prison camp had high guard towers, each with two guards, one with a rifle and the other, a machine gun. There was also a high guard tower in the middle of the compound. This large prison camp was within the Military Headquarters Complex known as the

Jinqiu Siling Bu, which was itself surrounded by another vast wall, and guarded day and night.

"Alone in my cell, month after month—I was in solitary till November 1963—I lost all hope. But I was unable to commit suicide as even my belt and bootlaces had been taken away. It was terribly lonely being in that semi-dark cell all by myself. The only thing to break the solitude was going to the common toilet twice a day, once in the morning, when you also emptied your piss bucket, and once in the evening. They made sure no other prisoners were there in the toilet when I went. The other important event that helped break the monotony of my existence was getting my food twice a day.

"No matter how unbearable I found my solitary confinement, I could not really complain about the food. At the time, all over China and Tibet, many millions of ordinary people were dying of starvation in the Great Famine. Worst- hit were inmates of *Laogai* (Reform through Labor) camps and prisons in general. But I was getting Chinese army rations, a 45 *gyama* grain ration (about 30 kilos) a month. This was an absolute luxury for a prisoner, in fact, a luxury for any ordinary citizen of the PRC at that time. I could not eat everything I was given at a meal, and my leftovers were dumped in the pig-swill drum. I was also given vegetables about twice a week, which were grown by the prisoners: radishes, Chinese cabbage, bokchoy, turnips and greens. The prisoners grew them all. It was, of course, meant for the soldiers, not for the prisoners.

"What was keeping me alive was, of course, not the generosity of the Communist Party, or the People's Republic of China, but the fact that I was a trained American agent. So, I was a special VIP prisoner even in my ideological villainy and had to be kept alive, for a future purpose, whatever that could be. The general prison population at the *Silingbu* had a diet that barely kept breath and body together. It was essentially a method of starving them slowly to death over a period of a few years during which they could be made to work. But not me. America may have been many thousands of miles away, but American power was keeping me alive and well fed. I knew that. The Chinese were not giving me shit.

"But it was still terribly lonely in my cell. The general run of prisoners had to do forced labour the whole day and attend political meetings, but they at least had human company. The only people I could talk to, and even that only very occasionally, were the guards. And they only spoke Chinese. The kitchen staff who brought me my food, were not allowed to talk to me at all.

"When I was a young man in Lhasa, I had never lacked for interesting company. I had roamed about the city, from teahouse to chang taverns and restaurants, enjoying myself with my friends. I had never sat down alone and thought seriously about anything for any length of time. Now I was forced to think. And my mind turned to religion. Religion is good only if you can practice it. Otherwise, it is just a big swindle. But I knew very little about religion; I had never bothered to learn anything. I had memorized *sutra* passages when I was a student at the Lhasa Medical Centre, but I was shaky on the meaning. So, I concentrated on repeating the mantra of Chenrezig the Bodhisattva of Compassion, '*om mani padme hum*' and the "Three Refuges" (*kyamdo*) again and again, day after day, week after week, month after month. Of course, you couldn't chant it aloud or even move your lips, otherwise the guards would be on you in a flash, and you would be punished. For the Communists, religion, prayers and mantras were a manifestation of ignorance and superstition, a tool of the priestly class to deceive the people. You had to recite the mantras in your mind. I got pretty good at doing that, all the while looking quite normal and harmless. I can't say I achieved anything spiritual through my efforts, but when I concentrated on repeating the mantras, my mind would, at least for that period, be drawn away from thinking about my misfortunes.

"I had been locked up from 18 April 1961, and remained in my cell, in solitary confinement for over two and half years, till November of 1963, when I was finally released from my cell and allowed to join the general prison population. It was then I discovered that I was in a very exclusive penal institution, the most important prison in Tibet. The prisoners were largely aristocrats, high lamas and tribal chiefs. This was the prison where after the Lhasa Uprising they held Tsarong

Dzasak and other leaders, but that was a few years ago. Now among the prisoners were also the two other America trained agents, Chönyi Yeshi, who I mentioned earlier and Taythi Tashi Thundup, who I will tell you more about later. To my surprise, I also bumped into an uncle of mine, Gyatso, my father's older brother. He was a master carpenter for the Tibetan government and the guild-master of the important Carpenters and Stonemason's guild. He had taken part in the uprising and was actually with me when we were defending the Jokhang temple.

"I remember he had a pistol with him but he was low on ammunition. I gave him some Enfield bullets that our regimental blacksmith had resized for a .30 calibre pistols. But we got separated during the fighting. My uncle was happy to see me now, but he also accused me of not letting him know about my regiment leaving that night from the Jokhang. "You should have at least told me, your uncle." I replied that I had orders from General Jumpa and Major Gura not to let anyone know about our plans. My uncle told me that just two nights later, the Chinese soldiers managed to get on the roof of the Jokhang, and by morning had captured the whole place. All the remaining Tibetan defenders had to raise their hands and surrender. "Accompanying the Chinese troops was the traitor, the monk official, Sholkang Jedung Thupten Nima. He was acting as their translator. He took a sack of handcuffs from a Chinese soldier and personally shackled each one of us, all the while remarking sarcastically, 'You must be very tired from your exertions.'

"So with all the aristocrats and officials, the cultural and intellectual level of this prison was quite high. Almost everyone was eloquent, and argumentative. They could be quite troublesome, sometimes. The inmates were divided into workgroups, what the Chinese called *tzu*, a group of twenty to thirty people, with one work leader called the *tzu-tang*. There was a laundry *tzu*, a tailoring *tzu*, a cobbler's *tzu* and so on. All the work we did was for the upkeep of the soldiers of the Military HQ.

"My first work assignment at the prison was also one of the most difficult. We had to mill tsampa and other grain. The millstone was huge, about eight feet in diameter and four feet high. And it must have weighed a few tons. At four points in the stone were holes where long, thick wooden poles were inserted. Two men were assigned to each pole, and we had to push and turn the millstone. It was a tremendously laborious task. Since I had just been sitting in solitary confinement for two years, I was very weak, and found it impossible to push the stone like the others. But I gave it everything I had since otherwise I would be criticized or even struggled during the political meetings. So, I pushed that mountain of a millstone every day. We went around it slowly, around and around, hour after hour, the whole day. You were not only completely exhausted at the end but spinning with dizziness as well. To make matters worse for me, the rations for the general prisoners were nearly half of what I was issued earlier when I was in solitary. Earlier I had received the ration of a PLA soldier, 45 *gyama* (about 30 kilos), but now I only got 26 *gyama*, about 16 kilos of grain a month.

"Later, I was set to work on the manufacture of tofu for the soldiers. The Chinese love tofu. It was sold by the prison warders to the soldiers and other Chinese officials as well. Chinese from outside the HQ would come to buy it. Prisoners only got a bit in their meal on certain special days like October 1. The work was as hard as milling grain. You had to get up at three in the morning to be able to get the tofu ready for distribution by mid-morning. First, you had to mill the soaked soybean and get a kind of soy milk, which was separated from the sediment and dross. This soymilk was boiled, cooled and then curdled. The resultant cottage cheese-like substance was put in a wooden frame and pressed a number of times. Finally, you got the tofu that you cut into exact squares for distribution. The process was repetitious and tiring. After we had made our quota of tofu for the day, we had to go over to the giant millstone and grind corn.

"I worked at making tofu and milling barley till the 4th month of 1964. Then I was transferred to the laundry *tzu*. Our *tzu* had about ten men, and we had to wash the clothes and bedding of all the soldiers at HQ. We also had to wash the sheets, towels and quilts of the guest house attached to Army HQ. The water for the laundry was electrically heated in huge wooden vats. Washing soda was added to the water and the clothes were soaked in them. There was very little soap in Tibet at the time, since all imports from India had stopped. So borax soda (*bültok*) was used a lot, especially for dirty collars and so on, although it was more wearing on the clothes. After the war with India in 1962, the Chinese managed to capture many things, including trucks, cigarettes, clothes, and so on, including laundry soap. This was then issued to us for laundering clothes.

"Our *tzu-tang* was Lhalu, the former governor-general of Eastern Tibet, a cabinet minister, and one of the most famous aristocrats at the time.* The Chinese considered him a leading reactionary feudal counter-revolutionary, since after Ngabö had surrendered at Chamdo, Lhalu had kept on fighting with the troops under his command. I heard that he and his wife had also shot at Chinese troops from the roof of Lhalu Mansion during the Lhasa Uprising.'

[Lhalu's public struggle took place at the newly named Great Square of the People (*mimang thangchen*) in front of the Potala Palace, before a crowd of many thousands. It was the most publicized "struggle" of a Tibetan official and accounts and images appeared in propaganda films and journals.]

"There were many things wrong with the Tibetan aristocracy, but it had some good points too. You know, many of the nobles were sophisticated people, in the polite way they talked, always with honorifics (*shay-za*) and their administrative abilities. It demonstrated to the world that we were an old and civilized nation. Lhalu had some good qualities too. He was organized, and he did things to help all the other prisoners. Aristocrats could manage people without shouting, screaming and threatening everyone, like the Chinese always did.

"From Sunday noon, the prisoners were given a break till five p.m., to wash their own clothes and clean their cells, and so on. We also got

---

*Tseten Yangkyi, the daughter of Kundeling Kunsang, remembered that her mother worked with Lhalu and Bhusang-la at the prison laundry. "My mother's hands became cracked and sore after washing all the clothes of the army camp. But whenever my mother came across any Chinese money or articles in the pockets of the uniforms, she would pound them with a stone. Lhalu tried to stop her, to prevent her from getting into trouble, but she refused to listen to him."

only two meals on Sunday, one at ten and the other at five—no lunch. When all of us at the laundry *tzu* stopped work at noon, Lhalu would save the remaining hot water and put what was left of the soap and the borax into it, so that the prisoners would have an easier time washing their clothes in the afternoon instead of just using only cold water as was otherwise the case.

"But during a weekly political meeting, a couple of diligent *hurtsunpas* among the prisoners accused Lhalu of providing luxuries to prisoners who were enemies of the people and denounced him for wasting hot water and soap that belonged to the People's government. Lhalu quietly replied to this by saying that if he did not use up the people's soap and borax already mixed in hot water and threw it away, that would be a real waste. Letting the prisoners use what was otherwise going to waste was saving the people's wealth. The warden said that Lhalu was correct in his thinking. So that was that.

"Once I was out of solitary confinement and working, I also had to join in all the political indoctrination meetings, criticism sessions and struggles. Most of the political meetings were held in the evenings after work. And they were conducted within one's own *tzu*. On Sundays, there was a mass meeting that all prisoners had to attend. Here we had to confess to all the offences and crimes we had committed during the week. 'I went to piss during work without asking for permission', 'I committed sabotage by breaking my shovel handle', 'I talked when I should have been working.' and so on. You had to confess every insignificant and stupid thing. If you didn't confess freely, you would almost certainly be denounced and struggled, sometimes for many hours at a stretch.

"The most intense political meetings and indoctrination classes took place in winter, November and December, when there was less work to do in the fields and vegetable patches. At the end of the year, there was a complete review of all one's crimes, attitudes, confessions and criticisms for the whole year. This program would start at the bottom, at *tzu* level and then work up to the dormitory level, brigade level and then the whole prison. The big mass-meetings were intense, with all the prisoners chanting slogans and screaming for the blood of the accused. The struggles were always ferocious, and prisoners were often mobbed and beaten unconscious. Prisoners being struggled, often had their ears pulled so hard by their persecutors that they flopped like loose skin afterwards. Their hair would often be pulled out in clumps, by the handful. Once in a while, someone might even be beaten to death.

"The clothes we wore at this prison camp were all cast-off PLA uniforms. They were in tatters, to begin with and we had to patch them continuously. For bedding, we got old Tibetan army *chuba* robes, or old Chinese army quilts. Nothing new was issued to prisoners, just discards.

"On 30 December 1964, all the prisoners at the Military HQ Prison were now transferred to the civilian jurisdiction of the TAR Public Security Bureau. The prison population was divided and sent to two different prisons, one to Drapchi, the old regimental barracks of the Second Drapchi Regiment, north of Lhasa and the other to Sangyip, north-east of the city. Early that morning, many trucks came to the prison gate and we were loaded aboard with our few possessions and bedding rolls. The army issued enamel bowl and tin mug had to be returned. I was in the first batch taken out. We were driven out of the city for about four kilometres to an isolated valley called Sangyip. The name literally means "secret hideout." The story was that when Emperor Songtsen Gampo's clever minister Gar was bringing the Chinese bride of Emperor to Lhasa, he hid her for a while at a cave in the Sangyip valley because she was pregnant with his child.

"This place was one of the most miserable and cold places I have ever known. The entire stretch of the valley was just desert, sand and rock without a blade of vegetation. To the east was this high mountain, Mechuri, which was so close and so high that we only had sunrise around 11.30 in the morning in winter. It was so, so incredibly cold there. It makes me shiver just to think about it.

"When we got there, the construction hadn't been completed. We were put in a unit that had two adjoining cells. Taythi Tashi Thundup, a lama from Ganden and myself were assigned the rear cell. The front cell was occupied by three aristocrats, Changra Lobsang

Nima, who had been a regimental commander at Chamdo in 1950, Shuguba Tsepon Jamyang Khedrup and Sumdo Gyaltsen Yonden, both of whom had taken part in the 1959 Uprising. There were four such units of two cells each in every block, and a total of six such blocks in one compound. They had only built one compound at the time, but more were being added.

"When the first of us were locked in our cells we were issued a large empty tin can each that had once contained pork. But were given nothing to eat or drink for the whole day. Late that evening, when the other prisoners were driven up and put in their cells, the prison cook came by and gave us all some hot water with a little tea in it. He poured it through the bars of the Judas hatch into the tins we held up. Because there was no piss bucket in our cell some of us had earlier used the can to piss in. But we drank the hot tea/water anyway. We didn't get sick or anything. You get used to this sort of thing pretty quick. No beds, mattresses or groundsheets were issued to us. We used whatever bits of bedding we had brought from our former prison. Some weeks later, we were allowed to collect grass and straw to lie on. In the morning, we were given a little tsampa.

"We were locked up in our cell till July, with no work, but also very little grain to eat. Officially we were supposed to receive 26 *gyamas* of barley, which was very little, to begin with, but at Sangyip, all we got was a small can-measure (about 200 grams of tsampa in the morning, another at noon, and for supper a ladle of watery gruel).

"All of us who had been assigned to the individual cells were interviewed by the warden and security cadres for many days. We were asked questions about our attitudes and political developments. Then one by one, we were finally allowed to leave the special cells and were transferred to the working sections. Most of our work here was quarrying and cutting stones for building the prison. We also worked in the fields nearby, growing vegetables.

"It was in June the next year when some officials accompanied by soldiers came from the People's Court in Lhasa. I was to be interrogated again and also formally arraigned for my crimes. I was charged with a whole catalogue of crimes: espionage, sabotage, murder, rebellion, treason, and the stock-standard ones of being a counter-revolutionary and a stooge and lackey of imperialism and colonialism. I received the death sentence, which was suspended, because of the clemency of the Communist Party and the People's Republic of China. I really didn't give a shit about this clemency. I would have preferred being executed. But something unusual happened that day which made it memorable, and also lifted my spirit a bit.

"When I was led from my cell to the interrogation hall, I noticed a scrap of paper on the ground near the common toilets, which caught my attention. I thought I saw the Dalai Lama's picture on it. During the interrogation, I screwed up my face as if in great anguish. The interrogator asked me if I was ill. I said no, but that my bladder was so full, it was beginning to hurt. He told me to go immediately to the toilet. I left the hall and walked over to the toilet. When I got near the scrap of paper, I pretended to stumble and managed to pick it up without being noticed by anyone. I was tremendously elated. Later, when I was by myself, I smoothed it out and took a closer look. It was a square bit of newspaper or magazine, which somebody had probably intended to use as toilet paper. One side of it had a photograph of the Dalai Lama and the Panchen Lama when they were in China in 1954. Both had on those fancy brocade *chubas* and those ornamental helmets that they wore on that trip. They probably couldn't wear their usual monk robes in a Communist country. It wasn't in colour, but the quality of the picture was pretty good. I was really happy.

"I knew I had to be very careful, but I couldn't resist the temptation of showing it to Tenzin Choedrak, who had been a schoolmate of mine at the Medical Centre. He is now the Dalai Lama's personal physician. I asked him if he wanted an audience with the Dalai Lama. He looked at me as if I had gone mad. I told him with a straight face that I could arrange for him to get a personal audience. Then I took him to one side and showed him my picture. He was thrilled and amazed. I also placed it on his head for the blessing. He said that I was an incorrigible rogue, keeping a dangerous thing like that. I also gave a few other people audiences with the Dalai Lama. No one betrayed me.

"Then in 1965, on the first of June, four leading inmates of our prison were released. They were Lhalu, the governor-general of Kham and the *tzu-tang* of my laundry *tzu*, the old Prime Minister Lobsang Tashi, Sumdo Gyalsten Yonden and one other person I don't recall. Four people in all. Before their release, they had to attend intensive re-education classes for one month. But this did not signal any general amnesty for other prisoners. The four were released because they were well known to Tibetan society in Tibet as well as outside, so it was essentially a propaganda ploy to show that things were peaceful and settled in Tibet. The Sangyip Prison now had about five hundred inmates.

"There were not many escape attempts, and even those which prisoners managed to start, invariably failed. There was this kid Gelek, who now works at the Tibetan Institute of Performing Arts, his friend Sonam Tsering, one Amdowa and two Chinese prisoners. Their plan was to escape during work detail, killing the guard with a shovel and taking his AK47. They would fight their way out and escape to India. It was a rotten plan. Before they could execute it, one of the Chinese denounced them. All of them were rounded up and punished. The ringleader was the other Chinese prisoner, an old ex-party man, who hated the Communists and did not fear them at all. When they were struggled before the entire prison, and beaten and kicked, this old Chinese man refused to bow his head in the prescribed manner and was unyieldingly defiant. 'Kill me!' he shouted 'Kill me and use my flesh to make *momos* (meat dumplings) for the prisoners.' After that, we didn't see him at all. No one knew what happened to him.

"At Sangyip, I was in a workgroup, a *tzu*, with a number of aristocrats and also Chönyi Yeshi and Taythi Tashi Thundup. We lived together in one dormitory. I didn't get on with Yeshi, who was a real *hur-tsunpa*. He impressed the Chinese so much with his diligence that they appointed him our section *tzu-tang*. Much later, he was rehabilitated, and his class background improved on his official record to that of a 'worker.'" But some years later after he was released from prison, he just died. On the other hand, I got on very well with Tashi Thundup.

"Both Yeshi and Tashi had been trained in Colorado. They had been in the training batch preceding mine. They had been parachuted into Sogdé, in a team of sixteen men, near the Niratsogen Lake in the Jhangthang area, after the great nomad uprising got started there. The nomad resistance was wiped out by an overwhelming Chinese force supported by armoured cars, tanks and jet fighters. Chönyi Yeshi had surrendered. He was the only one among those of us air-dropped into Tibet to ever surrender to the Chinese. Tashi Thundup had been captured at Sogdé while fighting. He had not surrendered but had been knocked unconscious by a grenade blast and taken prisoner. Everyone else in that team was killed.

'Tashi Thundup was a little older than me, a year or two probably. He was from a village called Taythi near Gyantsé, in South-Central Tibet. He was a yeoman farmer of the house of Doring and had also served as a steward at the Doring estate. They were a respectable family of good background and reasonably prosperous. When the Four Rivers Six Ranges started in Lhoka, south of Lhasa, Tashi Thundup and a number of other men from the Gyantsé district volunteered to join and formed a Gyantsé contingent in the resistance force.

"Tashi Thundup was a well-mannered, courteous and amiable person, but when required, he could be absolutely tough and unyielding. He was physically smaller than I was and thinner, but much tougher inside. He was also probably the only prisoner who never participated in political education and meetings in prison. He just sat in the corner, in the dark, his head covered with a blanket. He was a follower of the Nyingma tradition (the oldest of the four major schools of Tibetan Buddhism), and he recited the mantra of Guru Rinpoche (Padmasambhava) silently but at every opportunity. In the beginning, the guards and cadres screamed at him and struggled and beat him for not taking part in the political meetings and criticisms. They even put him in solitary several times. In the end, the Chinese had to give up and leave him alone. He never came out in the sun but remained indoors reciting his mantras.

"He went on a hunger strike around 1965 or 1966, some months before the Cultural Revolution. Just as they did to me, the Chinese gave him medicine and injections, and he had a violent bout of diarrhea.

They also shoved the feeding tube through his nose and guts and forced slop inside him. But after a few weeks, he tried again. This time even when they gave him their injections and medicine, with the inevitable consequences, he persisted. He tore out the tube when they shoved it right inside his stomach, and he struggled with the guards and nurses so much, and his whole face was covered with blood and their slop that they had to give up. He lasted thirteen days and then died. He was very weak, to begin with. He didn't tell me the exact political statement he was making with his hunger strike. But he certainly carried it out to the bitter end. He was a very tough man. He never said a harsh word to anyone, not even to the Chinese guards. He was a good man, never talked very much, just prayed a lot. He counted his mantras on his fingers. I think I was the only one to notice that; otherwise his mouth never moved. The Chinese guards and officials said that it was his own fault he died, and that he had caused his own problems.

"He left behind a wife at Darjeeling. When I returned to that town many years later after my release, I met her there. She was taking care of their only child, a son, who was then a schoolboy. All those years, she had not remarried but waited for him to come back from his mission. She cared for him tremendously."

34

"SEA OF INHUMANITY"

"The Cultural Revolution came down on us like a crazy sickness (*nyo-nas*). One morning in 1966—I remember it being a warm day, in May, I think it was—all the prisoners were herded together in the main prison compound for a mass meeting. The chief cadre (Chinese, *shouxi ganbu*) reading from a document told us that Chairman Mao had called on the masses to 'Seize Power' and to 'Bombard the Headquarters'. I realized that something very strange was happening. Of course, none of us had any idea of what it was all about, or what was in store for us.

"In the following days, Communist officials read documents and newspapers calling on us to vigorously criticize and even attack those in power taking China down the wrong road to capitalism. The cadres, reading these exhortations down at us, looked hesitant and confused themselves. In the following months, this call for mass action was followed up by a succession of Party directives. There was one proclaiming a nationwide campaign to flush out and exterminate bad elements. Then we got the campaign to 'Destroy the Four Olds and Build the Four News.' Finally, we heard of the arrival of Red Guards (*marsung-mak*) to Lhasa from Beijing and their recruitment of Tibetan youths to attack and 'struggle' those in power. We got only occasional and fragmentary news of events in Lhasa. None of us prisoners were allowed any visitations, and conversation between prisoners, except for 'mutual criticisms' was strictly forbidden."

For a time, the Party leadership in Lhasa succeeded in controlling the Cultural Revolution by organizing parades and giving revolutionary Chinese names to prominent sites and streets: Chakpori was called Victory Peak (Chinese, *Shengli gaofeng*), Norbulingka became the People's Park (Chinese, *Renmin gongyuan*), the Naiad Lake Temple became the People's Palace (Chinese, *Renmín gongdian*), and the Tsuglakhang was converted to Guest House No. 5 (Chinese, *Wu suo*). The Dalai Lama's Family Home was Guest House No. 2 (Chinese, *Er suo*). The road before the Shöl and the Potala was called "The Great Leap Forward Street". The Yuthok Bridge – Lubuk road was renamed "People's Street" and the road south of the Barkhor was called "Liberation Street", while the Banakshol–Barkhor path was called "Forward Road". According to Tsering Woeser on 28 August 1966, the Barkhor circuit itself was renamed "Establish-the-New Avenue" (Chinese, *Linxin dajie*).

A Tibetan reporter from the *Tibet Daily* (who escaped to India in late 1969) wrote that " . . . the Red Guards ordered Tibetans to adopt revolutionary Chinese names, or names containing part of the Chairman's name, i.e. either Mao, Ze or Dong."[1] The reporter's co-worker Tenzin called himself *Mao Hong-Hu* or 'Mao's Red Thoughts', Jampa became *Mao Yung-Hen* or 'Dedicated to Mao's Class Struggle', Yeshi became *O-Dong* or 'Defender of (Mao Ze) Dong', while Wangmo was called *Da Yuejin* or 'Great Leap Forward'. In the old days, Tibetans would swear or take oaths in the name of the Jowo Shakyamuni of the Jokhang, e.g., "*Jowo Rimpo" (ché)*, or by the Triple Gem, "*Kunchok sum*" but that was now forbidden. Instead you declared "I Swear by Mao" (*mao tsey tsuk*) or simply raised your right hand and declared "Mao!"

Red Guards also began the destruction and demolition of Tibet's temples, monasteries and historic buildings, which at the end of the Cultural Revolution resulted in nearly ninety percent of the many thousands of such structures all over Tibet being levelled to rubble,[*] very much like the houses, churches and buildings in Dresden after the Allied bombing raids of February 1945.

The Jokhang in Lhasa was targeted by the Red Guards ". . . who dismantled the shrines and dragged the sacred statue with ropes through the filth of the streets."[2] The tens of thousands of Buddhist texts, historical and official documents and volumes were taken out before the edict pillar in front of the Temple and set ablaze in a giant bonfire. The enormous butter lamps were toppled over, and the floors of the Jokhang, covered with grease. Many in the mob slipped and tumbled all over the flagstones, to the merriment of street kids joining in the fun.

Then the Red Guards turned on lamas and aristocrats, particularly those who had gained favour with Communist authorities and held official jobs and positions. They were all generically designated "Ox Demons and Snake Spirits" (Chinese, *niugui-sheshen*), a term Mao had taken from classical literature and used in his many speeches during the Cultural Revolution to refer to "class enemies." This became the most popular term during this period to denounce and dehumanize any enemy, real or perceived. In Lhasa the "Ox Demons and Snake Spirits" were paraded around the Barkhor with dunce caps on their heads and dressed in bizarre grab bags of religious, official and opera costumes. Around their necks, they carried large placards, listing their crimes.[3] A book of black and white photographs of the Cultural Revolution in Tibet, *Forbidden Memory*,[4] compiled by the Beijing-based Tibetan writer Tsering Woeser, is a horrifying and pitiful visual and textual record, one of the only few we have, of that nightmare period in Tibetan history.

---

[*] The razing of the "Gateway to Lhasa" stupas (Drago Kaling) in the 1980s appears to have inspired the first "protest" song against China's destruction of Tibet's artworks and monuments. Sung by the Tibetan pop star Dadon, who had earlier won top awards at China's National Song Competition, "Gateway to Lhasa" became hugely popular across Tibet. The success of this and a couple of other songs expressing "local nationalism" gained Dadon the unwelcome attention of the Public Security Bureau. She escaped from Tibet in 1992. Hear the song at https://bit.ly/3zKE4Rj

Pangdatsang Topgyal is in the costume of a witch (from an Aché Lhamo opera) complete with sagging breasts. Tibet's highest female incarnate lama,* Samding Dorje Phagmo, is dressed in an expensive lady's silk dress but with a nun's *zhen* shawl over it—to demonstrate her hypocrisy and deceitfulness. She is also wearing the wool lining of her sacred black hat from which all the jewels and religious ornamentation have been ripped off. The well-known amateur photographer and high lama, Demo Tulku, is in full oracle regalia but with his Leica camera around his neck. The aristocrat Phunkhang Rimshi is in the imperial *gyaluchey* costume and holds, before him, a boxed Sheffield cutlery set, evidence of his being a "running-dog" (Chinese, *goutuizi*) of British imperialists. The former minister, Sampho, wearing a ceremonial Kalön costume, and with mucus streaming down his nose, contorts his face in pain. These and other victims, including less highborn victims, as the principal of the Nyarongshar School and his family, were paraded around the Barkhor and, of course, spat upon, kicked, beaten and tortured.

Other victims of the Red Guards were, ironically enough, such collaborators as Gyamtsoling the Dalai Lama's debating partner and Chinese informer within the Norbulingka in 1959, and Phakpala Gelek Namgyal (vice-chair of the Chamdo Liberation Committee), whose younger brother Phakpala Khenchung was beaten to death by an angry crowd in March 1959. Another collaborator was Tsögo Thundup Tsering, Ngabö's "top" aide at Chamdo whose devotion to Ngabö and the Communist Party did not save him from the wrath of

---

*Many Western travellers to old Tibet were fascinated by this exotic institution, in particular, it's reputedly frisky twelfth (and present) incarnation. She is the principal love interest in Lionel Hinton's novel *The Rose of Tibet* (much praised by Daphne Du Maurier and Graham Greene) and, strangely enough, in a real-life biography *The Adventures of a Manchurian* by Sylvian Mangiot. Resistance fighters escorted her to India in 1959, but she was persuaded to return to Tibet the following year and was rewarded with a high, albeit nominal, position in the TAR administration. In 1985 a Beijing writer Qin Wenyu published a best-selling romantic novel, *Nu huofo* (*Female Living Buddha*), about our indefatigable incarnatrix.

the Red Guards who "savagely denounced" him according to Woeser, first decking him out in a dunce cap, prayer beads, and, in recognition of his military role at Chamdo, a binocular, a saddle and fittingly enough an empty pistol holster.

When they had run out of "upper strata" victims the Red Guard factions in their competitive zeal to expose "class enemies" and "undercover spies" took to tormenting ordinary householders with accusations, beatings and "struggles", resulting in a rash of suicides throughout the city—even a couple and their three children jumping into the Kyichu River from the Kuru bridge.*

The Red Guards could not touch Ngabö Ngawang Jigme, who was the crown jewel in the PRC's propaganda narrative of their "peaceful liberation" of Tibet. The Panchen Lama was already in solitary confinement since 1964 for writing a petition detailing Communist China's abuse of power in Tibet. So, the Red Guards cast their stern revolutionary gaze on the blackest "running dogs" of Western imperialism—those Tibetans who had taken part in the 1959 Uprising. But these people were, unfortunately, all in prison or *Laogai* camps. Bhusang told me that the Red Guards came to Sangyip and demanded that all prisoners be handed over to them for revolutionary justice.

"Our prison held the 'blackest' counterrevolutionaries, 'man-eating' feudal lords, and the 'running-dogs' and spies of American imperialists. But still had potential political and propaganda value to the Chinese leadership, so the Red Guards were informed that as villainous as these prisoners were, they were all striving diligently to reform themselves. But our chief cadre warned us that if we showed any sign of relapsing, we would be handed over to the Red Guards. With the Cultural Revolution now in full swing, the political re-education in our prison became much more intense. Every bit of spare time was spent studying *Chairman Mao's Thoughts* and memorizing as many lines from it as we could. The *Little Red Book* was issued to every prisoner and we had to look after it very

---

*Excerpted from Thupten Khetsun's *Memories of Life in Lhasa Under Chinese Rule* (Columbia University Press, 2008), possibly the most chilling account of the factional fighting and atrocities in Lhasa during the Cultural Revolution.

carefully. We even hand-stitched cloth covers or little bags with shoulder straps for it from whatever scraps of fabric we could find.

"Then it became difficult to get cooking fuel at our prison. All the trucks that normally plied to Lhasa and back went missing as various Red Guard gangs began to hijack them. Firewood and animal dung was also not easily available locally, and soon it became absolutely unobtainable. It got to a point where we had nothing hot to drink or eat for weeks on end. Finally, the prison officials sent us prisoners out to forage for fuel in the surrounding countryside. We stole from the villages around. No one thought of escaping. The countryside was deserted and scary, but could become suddenly violent, just like that. The prison at least offered some security."

As the countryside descended into anarchy, the different Red Guard groups in Lhasa now battled each other for territory, power and recruits. Soon these groups sorted themselves out into two main factions: the "Revolutionary Alliance" (*sarje nyamdrel*) favoured by senior party functionaries and General Zhang Guohua, the most powerful figure in Tibet, and the "Red Rebels" (*marpo genlok*) about sixty groups that banded together in December of 1966, the core being Red Guards from China. The "Rebels" were supported by lower-ranking cadres and junior PLA officers and were said to have the ideological endorsement of Madame Mao. General Zhang Guohua and the "Alliance" received some support from the "moderate" Zhou Enlai in Beijing. But all these relationships were fluid and ever-shifting. Every faction claimed that it alone was the true representatives of Maoist thought.

The first-line weapon of all Red Guard factions in defining their particular revolutionary identity, announcing their campaigns and attacking their enemies were "big-character posters" (Chinese, *dazibao*), written or calligraphed on large sheets of paper and pasted on walls all over the city. Since factions churned out these propaganda posters every day there was a limit to premium wall space in the city. Very often ". . . the posters of one party were pasted over by those of the other party before the glue had even dried."[5] This led to encounters, brawls and gang fights that deteriorated into deadly street battles conducted with bricks, slingshots, knives, clubs, spears and even home-made bombs filled with gunpowder and pebbles and launched by crude ballistas or catapults.

The Rebels captured the Jokhang and used it as their headquarters, from where they "broadcasted" their propaganda using loudspeakers and amplifiers. The skirmishes and battles to capture and recapture such important locations from each other escalated, and the factions began to seek more lethal weapons. The Alliance, in particular, was supplied by the PLA with automatic rifles and grenades. But the Rebels also had some supporters within the PLA and acquired similar weapons, though not as many as the Alliance. Soon a real shooting war broke out in the streets and alleys of Lhasa for some months. Then, in June 1968, PLA troops stormed Rebel headquarters at the Jokhang, killing and wounding sixty-one defenders. This event was dubbed the "June 7th Massacre" by Rebel groups all over Tibet. According to the *Tibet Daily* journalist ". . . it turned the Tsuglakhang, that holy place of worship, into a gory, blood-spattered butcher's shop."[6] Following the massacre, a PLA company was garrisoned at the Tsuglakhang. The troops raised pigs in some of the rooms and courtyards to supplement their rations. The chapel of the goddess Pé Lhamo (Sanskrit, *Sridevi*), popular with women, was converted to a toilet. According to Thupten Khetsun, "The main temple was turned into a slaughterhouse where yaks, sheep, goats, pigs and chicken were butchered."

Such bloody and murderous conflicts between Rebel and Alliance factions were taking place throughout the villages and towns of Tibet. The most well known of these conflicts happened in Bhusang's home district of Nyemo. This uprising captured the imagination of the Tibetan people not only because the leader of the Nyemo Rebel faction was a young woman, and a nun at that, but as she transformed Mao's supreme political campaign into a patriotic religious war against Communist Chinese rule. Even Chinese officialdom admitted that the Nyemo Uprising was an ". . . armed counter-revolutionary revolt . . . paralleling the 1959 uprising."[7]

The nun of Nyemo or "*Nyemo Ani*" as Tibetans remember her, had since the age of twelve been a nun at a Kagyüpa nunnery at Phusum village in Nyemo, and apparently happy with her spiritual life. Her *dharma* name was Trinlay Chödön. Her life was disrupted traumatically when the monasteries and temples were closed and lamas were "struggled", executed, and even driven to suicide. She started having strange dreams and visions, and began going into trances, uttering prophecies and even healing people. She became well known throughout the district. She joined the Nyemo Rebels at a crucial moment in their struggle to wrest administrative power from the powerful local Alliance faction.

She had earlier been possessed by a couple of different spirits but now claimed to be possessed by Gongmen Gyalmo (aka Ma Ne-ne), the heavenly aunt and advisor of the epic hero, King Gesar. Inspired by her stirring prophecies and her reputed magic powers, some hundred Rebels and villagers attacked the sub-district headquarters at Phusum, capturing all the Alliance officials and beating and "struggling" them. Such successful attacks continued in the following months as the Rebels captured all major administrative centres in Nyemo. A number of Alliance officials were killed, and some had their hands and feet brutally cut off. Armed with swords, spears, muskets and homemade bombs, they also attacked PLA outposts and camps—initially with consider able success. They renamed themselves the "Rebel Army of the Gods" (*ghelnok lhamak*) and the nun's lieutenants were now called *pathül* or avatars of Gesar's warrior knights.

An English academic, Robbie Barnett, noted that "As a charismatic rural leader, she had been able to mobilize large numbers of armed male followers, who had swept across northern Tibet killing many officials and soldiers in isolated garrisons."[8] It might be noted that one of the nun's principal lieutenants was a peasant woman, Nyemo Rindron (aka Rinzin Dronkar). A Norwegian scholar Hanna Havnevik writes ". . . it is said that she (Nyemo Ani) had a network of contacts stretching from Mount Kailash to Kham,* and that she organized a guerrilla movement which killed many Chinese."[9]

---

*The contact in Kham may have been with the Rebel faction in Pembar district, where one of the most violent "rebellions" took place in 1968–69. I interviewed the incarnate lama of Pembar monastery in Dharamshala in 1992, and he told me that the primary reason for the success of this "rebellion" was the discovery by the Rebel faction of a large cache of arms in the ruins of the

Nyemo Ani's fame became so widespread that people in Lhasa were convinced that it was just a matter of time before the nun and her warriors would attack Lhasa and drive out the Chinese. The story also took on some fabulous trimmings. When the Rebel Army of the Gods arrived at the far shore of the Kyichu, Nyemo Ani would strike the water with the edge of her hand—and the river would cleave apart (like the Red Sea parted by Moses). Then she and her army would walk across to liberate the Holy City.

Some feminists in the exile Tibetan world appear to have embraced our revolutionary nun as well. A Tibetan student at Columbia University wrote in a blog post of a discussion on the Nyemo Revolt where her friends and classmates spoke of Nyemo Ani as ". . . the Joan of Arc of Tibet. Like Joan, Ani Trinley was young—around the age of twenty-eight and claimed that she was possessed by a divine entity as she led the 1969 revolt. Trinlay Chödön is important not only because she was a remarkable woman who led a resistance against incredible odds, she also matters because she is part of a battle against the revision of our history. The Chinese have attempted, in a million ways, to distort the true desires of the Tibetan people. Ani Trinlay, with her humble roots and her peasant following, shows how the Tibetan people fought against the Chinese occupation of Tibet. She is a precious example of our history, and history only survives if we remember."[10]

Finally, in the summer of 1969, a hundred or so trucks loaded with several thousand PLA troops armed with AK-47 assault rifles, machine guns and mortars invaded Nyemo. After three days of intense fighting and the death of hundreds of Rebel fighters, many of whom committed suicide by jumping in the Nyemo River—the nun and some of her followers escaped to the mountains. She was eventually captured and taken to Lhasa with twenty-nine other prisoners.

---

monastery destroyed by Chinese bombers in 1960. The CIA had dropped these weapons in late 1959 to support Air Team 3 and 4 (see Chapter 29) and the resistance army gathered at Pembar. Before this army was wiped out, some surviving fighters managed to hide a stock of weapons in the monastery ruins. A few locals who had served in the resistance now passed on their weapons training to the Rebels.

Bhusang's younger brother Gyephur had been a rebel fighter and had committed suicide by jumping in a river. Bhusang learned of it a decade later. But that year, in the autumn of 1969, thirty people from Nyemo were brought to his prison. "One of the most famous Red Guard Rebels from my own district of Nyemo, the nun Trinlay Chödön was brought to Sangyip under heavy guard. Also with her were those people who joined her uprising. I caught a glimpse of her when they were being pushed across the compound to their cells. They were all trussed up tightly with ropes. I never saw any of them again. Then one day, the next year, I think it was, I heard that the nun and her followers were put in trucks and taken to Lhasa to be executed."

An eyewitness to the execution of Nyemo Ani was a young Lhasa man, a Red Guard of the Rebel faction. He was actually a high incarnate lama, Drigung Chetsang Rinpoche, the grandson of Tsarong Dasang Damdul, and was, in fact, one of the two "little lamas", (the other being the Dalai Lama) that the old man had returned to Lhasa from Darjeeling to try and spirit away out of Tibet.* Although the Dalai Lama had disagreed with Tsarong about the need to leave Tibet, the old man had managed to make escape preparations for his thirteen-year-old grandson when, at the last moment, the Drigung Monastery manager procrastinated in getting the boy to Lhasa, till it was too late.[11] Rinpoche's 2010 biography[12] provides a detailed description of his subsequent life and execution of Nyemo Ani, which he witnessed in early 1970.

---

*Another young lama ensnared in Red Guard violence was Khato Tulku (Tenzin Norbu), the son of the finance secretary Namseling. When he was fourteen, two nomad leaders from around his former monastery in the Nagchu district visited him in Lhasa. They offered him meat and butter and requested his photograph, shirt and some hair. They subsequently distributed these to their Rebel followers as protective talismans in their fight against the Alliance faction and PLA troops. This bewildered, hapless boy was later accused of instigating the violence and incarcerated at Sangyip prison in strict solitary confinement. He tried to commit suicide many times but eventually, as he relates in a magazine interview (https://bit.ly/2XnjLX0), began watching birds from his cell window and listening to them and, over time, even understanding them.

"On that day, Rinpoche borrowed a bicycle and rode to the People's Stadium at Po Lingka (formerly the home and park of the Foreign Secretary Surkhang Dzasak) where an enormous public gathering of over 10,000 people had been assembled. Before the execution, the newest weapons of the PLA were paraded before the audience: brand new machine guns, enormous artillery pieces, on special transport with giant wheels which rolled slowly past the astonished crowd. No one had ever seen such weapons, and the display was clearly to impress and intimidate the Tibetans.

"Then the sixteen bound prisoners were driven into the stadium on open-bed trucks, and the convoy passed by where Rinpoche was sitting, so he had a good view of their faces. Trinlay Chödön was looking straight ahead, steadfast and fearless. She reminded him of the heroines portrayed on Chinese Communist propaganda posters, with their proudly resolute poses, utterly determined and seeming to glow from within. Three elderly Tibetan women near him spat at her and pelted her with refuse but Trinlay Chödön remained unmoved. Over the loud-speakers, the crimes of the nun Trinlay Chödön and her followers were described in gory detail.

"The prisoners were then driven out of the city to an open space below the Michungri Nunnery in the Dodé valley, immediately east of Sera Monastery. When Drigung Rinpoche arrived on his bicycle, his view was blocked by trucks full of spectators. But one of the trucks was equipped with a crane on which only one man was sitting. Rinpoche climbed up to join him, high above the huge crowd of civilians and the even greater number of PLA soldiers with heavy artillery. Anti-aircraft guns were pointed at the heavens, as if they were about to be attacked by air. The excessive display of threatening weaponry and the theatrical staging of troops seemed absurd to Rinpoche, like the backdrops and extras in a propaganda film. The prisoners were thrown from the trucks, kicked to make them stand up again, and ordered to run. The firing squad lined up, and a soldier gave the signal to fire. The crowd surged forward to see the victims, and the army almost lost control. Photographers pushed their way through the chaos and took pictures of the sixteen bodies which were then buried on the spot without ceremony. Rinpoche climbed down from the crane with shaking knees."[13]

Woeser, writing on this and other such executions, mentions that the bodies were dropped into shallow graves " . . . hastily dug beforehand. Sometimes their feet were left sticking out of the holes, and wild dogs would chew on them." She also notes that the relatives of the victims were not allowed to collect the bodies " . . . but had to pay for the rope and bullets used for the execution and were required to publicly thank the CCP for having eliminated the 'class enemies'."

Woeser cites a Chinese official in Lhasa, Tao Changsong, that 295 individuals were executed by court order between 1970 and 1971. But from her own extensive interviews, she concluded that the number of executions had been far greater. "In Pembar and Tengchen counties over a hundred people had been shot in one execution session alone." A member of a work team sent to Pembar told her that throughout the district " . . . there were nearly no men left, only women in their black clothes."

I saw a couple of blurry reproductions of the Lhasa execution photographs on a Chinese website in early 1991. Around that time at Dharamshala, four Tibetans: Tashi Tsering, Pema Bhum, Lhasang Tsering and myself had set up the Amnye Machen Institute (AMI), a research and educational project that we hoped would become a secular and liberal counterpoint to what we felt was the near-exclusive preoccupation of the Tibetan leadership with Tibetan Buddhism, including its propagation in the West.

One remit in our charter was the Occupied Tibet Studies, within which the Cultural Revolution was, of course, an important sub-section. A Dutch tourist had come to our office at McLeod Ganj and told us he had recently travelled to Nyemo. At county headquarters, he had come across an old photographic exhibition of the "crimes" of the Nyemo rebels and their trial and execution. He told us that the exhibition appeared to be a permanent, if neglected one, and probably maintained as a warning to the people of Nyemo. It was housed in a large shed with only an old caretaker in charge. After some discussion, the Dutch tourist, who also happened to be a professional photographer, agreed to travel to Nyemo once again, this time for AMI. Our Dutch friend had his tourist guide shepherd the old "curator" away from the exhibition shed, to drink tea and smoke a few cigarettes, giving him the opportunity to shoot excellent reproductions of all the photographs there.

We displayed these photographs in 1996 on the 30th anniversary of the Cultural Revolution. Our exhibition also featured copies of important Party Directives relating to the Cultural Revolution, rare posters, documents, *Tibet Daily* issues (in red ink) and related paraphernalia as decals, badges, souvenir plates, *Little Red Books* and so on.

Parallel with the exhibition, AMI organized a conference, *Sea of Inhumanity: Tibet in the Cultural Revolution*,[14] where for three days Tibetans from Lhasa, Gonjo, Khyungpo Tengchen, Pembar, Lhoka, Dzachukha, Golok, Amdo Labrang, Amdo Ngawa and elsewhere presented accounts and papers of their experiences. A former Red Guard from Lhasa gave a detailed eyewitness account of the destruction of the Jokhang, while one participant discussed Tibetan short stories and novels dealing with the Cultural Revolution.

An unexpected contribution came from the Tibetan spymaster, Lhamo Tsering, who was then Minister of Security in the exile government. He read out transcripts of telephone conversations between the Chinese military and political leaders during the Cultural Revolution, obtained through a CIA operation. Tibetan agents had managed to place state-of-the-art wiretap transmitting devices on the principal telephone line between Lhasa and Chengdu. The information transmitted revealed that the Rebel-Alliance fighting in Tibet had gotten completely out of hand and that military storehouses and armouries had been raided by Red Guards* who were promoting a dangerous and violent "local nationalism". Red Guards had raided military storehouses

---

*Tsering Woeser confirms that the PLA armoury of the Chamdo area was frequently broken into and looted by Red Guards, who outnumbered the few PLA guards at these locations. Thousands of Rebels looted the PLA armory at Po Tramo that had enough guns and ammunition to equip an entire army division. Many of the weapons were then rushed to other Rebel groups at

and armouries that were promoting a dangerous and violent "local nationalism". In the telephone conversations, another term regularly used was "Second Tibetan Rebellion", to refer to the conflict taking place in Tibet.

In recent years, there has been some disagreement among academics on how to define the Nyemo Uprising and similar events in Tibet during that period. Our *Tibet Daily* reporter depicted the Lhasa Rebels rather extravagantly as Tibetan patriots devoted to the Dalai Lama and Buddhism, while such scholars as Tsering Shakya and Warren Smith have been more nuanced, though acknowledging that ethnic or nationalistic motives were part of the reasons for the uprising. The Chinese intellectual Wang Lixiong claimed there was no nationalistic fervour in the Nyemo conflict and that the Dalai Lama was almost forgotten in Tibet by then. He explained that Tibetans were fighting for land and livestock earlier distributed to them, but now taken away by the People's Commune movement.

His Tibetan partner Tsering Woeser in her definitive work on the Cultural Revolution in Tibet, instead asks " . . . why years after Tibet had been 'liberated' such a large number of 'emancipated serfs' were so determined to slaughter PLA soldiers . . . Does this mean Tibetan nationalism was alive during the Cultural Revolution? Or if it had remained hidden there all along, since the very beginning, only waiting for the right moment to erupt?"[15]

Melvyn Goldstein, in the conclusion of his monograph on the Cultural Revolution in Tibet, states categorically, that "The Nyemo 'disturbance' was not a spontaneous Tibetan nationalistic uprising against the Chinese 'oppressor,' nor was it a revolt aimed at creating an independent Tibet." He is careful though to note that in interviews he conducted in Tibet he was told of Rebels shouting ". . . explicitly separatist political slogans as 'Tibet is independent,' and that they were even carrying the Tibetan national flag."[16]

Lhasa, Chamdo and other places. "From that point onward, armed fighting went out of control . . . and shocked the central government in Beijing."

Of course, it is beyond dispute that the Cultural Revolution in Tibet did not start out as a nationalist uprising, but there is also little doubt that it eventually morphed into something almost indistinguishable—a Tibetan underclass versus Chinese (plus collaborators) conflict that had definite nationalistic undertones. Nyemo Ani put it in succinct, colourful terms as "white against blue and yellow," i.e., Tibetan peasants (who wore white wool chubas) against Communist cadres (in blue uniforms) and PLA (in yellow khaki).

It also appears that a Rebel recruiting pitch promised villagers an end to the onerous "patriotic grain tax," but also restoration of "religious freedom"—a particularly appealing assurance to former monks and nuns. I even heard of a Rebel group in Chakra Pembar promising to bring the Dalai Lama back if they gained power. The Rebel leaders might not have been uniformly sincere about their pledges, and they certainly did not anticipate the unintended and fundamental changes that their commitments brought about to the structure of their faction and to the very nature of the conflict. Hence you have the strange phenomenon of radical Maoist groups consulting oracles and mountain deities, and in Nyemo, as mentioned earlier, their leader claiming to be Gesar's heavenly aunt. The phenomenon of Red Guards invoking Gesar or calling themselves Gesar's warrior knights (*pathül*) was surprisingly widespread during the Cultural Revolution, especially in nomadic areas such as Dzachukha, Sog, Naktsang and Reting.

In spite of the dominance of Buddhism, there continues to be among the lay people of Tibet, particularly in Kham, Amdo and the nomadic tribes of Northern Tibet, a need to see Gesar as a saviour figure during periods of war or national calamity. Professor R.A. Stein has noted "It was said that Gesar was to come back at the head of an army from the mythical land of Sambhala, in the north, when Buddhism and Tibet were faring badly."[17] When travelling across the Jhangthang, Alexandra David-Neel met a lama who told her: "Oh you know the Story of Gesar . . . he is coming back to lead a great army. He will be reborn among us. The power of our united thoughts will construct him. He will be the *tulku* of the minds of all of us whom the foreigners wish to make their slaves."[18]

There is an old legend among the Golok and other nomadic tribes living around the Amnye Machen range, that hidden deep within the heart of that mountain, surrounded by fabulous treasures, lies the great sword of Gesar. It is also believed that one day this sword will be found, and the people of Tibet will be freed from their oppressors. Many years ago, in Dharamshala, I wrote the first draft of a children's story about a Golok child surviving a PLA massacre. He hides in the mountains and discovers Gesar's sword deep within a cave. He then goes ahead and does what every Tibetan child wants to do, if they had a magic sword. I told the story to the kids at the Dance & Drama Society, who loved it. Perhaps when I'm done with this book, I'll try and finish that story.

The great Tibetan scholar, Samten Karmay, has written that inside Tibet these days the nationalist's overt consciousness of his own identity is now expressed through such secular traditions as the Gesar Epic. "The hero of the epic, King Gesar, is, in fact, a personification of the ideal Tibetan man. It is evident that the stories of his conquest of different countries and his other heroic exploits, however fictitious they may be, have contributed to the awakening of the national consciousness."[19]

In China itself, the Cultural Revolution moved into the realm of religious fundamentalism with the actual deification of Mao, not only in art, music, literature and education but even in bizarre rites and sacraments as the mass ritual chanting of Mao's quotations (started by Lin Biao), the consumption of Maoist sacred food,[20] the belief in Mao inspired miracles[21] and the obsessive memorizing of Mao's quotations and their ritual recitation (sometimes even backwards). Hand gestures and dance steps were choreographed for every one of the 267 quotations in the *Little Red Book* (Chinese, *Mao Zhuxi Yulu*), and this sacred dance, [was] sometimes performed in conjunction with the recitations. On a more sinister note, Maoist radicals in some provinces ritually consumed the warm liver of class enemies to demonstrate their immeasurable revolutionary devotion to the "Great Helmsman."[*]

---

[*] Zheng Yi, *Scarlet Memorial: Tales of Cannibalism in Modern China* (Westview Press, 1996).

Simon Leys, in his seminal study[22] of the Cultural Revolution, tells us bluntly, as no one else had done before him, what, at its core, this madness was all about. "The 'Cultural Revolution' had nothing revolutionary about it except the name, and nothing cultural about it except the initial tactical pretext. It was a power struggle waged at the top between a handful of men and behind the smokescreen of a fictitious mass movement. As things turned out, the disorder unleashed by this power struggle created a genuinely revolutionary mass current, which developed spontaneously at the grass roots in the form of army mutinies and worker strikes on a vast scale. These were crushed pitilessly." In this "genuinely revolutionary mass current" I think we could include the proto-nationalistic uprisings in Nyemo and other parts of Tibet.

For all its genocidal ferocity and arcane ideological justification, all that Mao Zedong's master plan achieved in the end was to bring everything in China: the administration, education, economy, even basic agriculture, to a staggering halt. The "Second Great Famine" (1968–1973) now hit China and Tibet.

"Then the grain ration was reduced in our prison from twenty-six *gyama* to twenty-three, and reduced again, shortly after. None of us ever had even a half-full stomach, after that. Prisoners began to complain of shooting pains and cramps in their stomach. Our prison didn't have a doctor. One "barefoot doctor" (Chinese, *chijiao yisheng*) visited once a week. He was not a real doctor, just some rustic with a red cross patch sewn on his shoulder bag, a week's training in first-aid and equipped with that listening thing [stethoscope] and some aspirin. He told us to eat a more varied diet!

"The guards ate well. They also kept pigs and fed them with their uneaten food. When we sometimes went out of our compound and passed by the large steel drums where they kept the pig-swill, we would quickly dip our hands in them and try to get a scrap of vegetable, a piece of steamed bun, anything, which we ate quickly or put in our pocket. The sleeves of our padded cotton jackets became solid like plastic from the constant dipping in the dirty swill. One of the young men in the camp invented a better system for fishing scraps from the swill. He got himself an empty pork can and punched the bottom full of holes with a nail. All he had to do was to dip the can in the bin, and trawl around once or twice and then lift the can out. The liquid would drain through the holes, and you could quickly shove the can with whatever solid you collected under your jacket.

"Every day, we went out into the fields with our slop buckets, which we had to empty in the toilets nearby, and which were later used for fertilizer. We would sometimes steal a vegetable or two from the fields and put it in the slop bucket. Since the bucket had a lid, the guards or *hur-tsunpas* wouldn't notice us taking a cabbage or a turnip back to our block, and which we ate in secret. None of us minded the taste of urine and other things, which stuck to the vegetables. We just ate it quickly and with relish. Eating all this disgusting stuff never did me any harm. I never got sick from the shit and muck. The only pain we had was that which came from the lack of food. You could also find a kind of white maggot out in the fields that we initially used to rub into our hands like face cream. Because of the lack of fat in our diet and the hard work we had to do, the palm and fingers of our hands would crack and regularly develop painful sores. When you rubbed the greasy little maggots in your hand, it helped a bit. Later we began to eat them. They were just like little slivers of lard.

"When our tsampa ration was cut again, people began to crack up. One old Chinese man began to augment his diet by mixing his own shit with his ration, and ate it cackling with glee. The famine was spreading everywhere. Doctor Wangyal who was with me at the Medical Centre before, was now transferred to Sangyip Prison. He told me some strange stories of his experiences at Samye Monastery. Before his transfer, he had been sent to a *Laogai* slave labour camp at Samye. Samye is semi-desert with a lot of sand all around. When the food shortage hit the prisoners there, the first thing they did was bring down the great prayer flag and strip of all the layers of old rawhide tied around it to reinforce the wood. Then they boiled the hide for a long time and ate it, and drank the liquid. In Samye Monastery, there is one temple called the '*Oo-khang*' or Breath House where it is believed that the dying breath of every person in Tibet is caught and put in a large painted leather sack called the *oo-kyel* or "breath-delivery bag." Every year a new sack is placed there. The prisoners ate all the sacks. There were also leather masks there, which the prisoners ate. Some prisoners had been careful and scraped off the paint. Others had been too hungry to bother and died of poisoning.

"Dr. Wangyal also told me that they ate every dog they could find in the district. But that was no big deal. At Sangyip, we had eaten every dog in the locality a long time ago. They tasted very good. At Drapchi prison, many if not most prisoners died. I was later told that all they got to eat were five beans counted out on their palms in the morning and five at noon. At night they got a ladle of hot water with a sprinkle of tsampa in it that they called *tsamthuk* or tsampa-gruel. At Sangyip, prisoners now began to weaken really fast, and started dying. Soon, so many prisoners were dying every day that the grave-digging details didn't bother to check each body, and some people were buried before their last breath had left their bodies.

"You should talk to this Khampa woman, Ama Adhe* from Kandzé. She now lives at the Reception Center at McLeod Ganj. She told me she was sent to this giant *Laogai* camp in the land of the Baron of Gothom, north of Dartsedo. There was a big lead mine there. Most of the prisoners were so starved they could not walk upright but crawled on their hands and knees: thousands of them, just crawling around. One day, the guards thought she had died, stripped her of her clothes and tossed her in an open pit full of corpses. But she somehow regained consciousness and though she could not move, tried to bite a human hand by her face. But the flesh was dry, and she lost a couple of her teeth. She sucked and gnawed at the dry flesh and somehow eventually got enough sustenance to survive. It sounds crazy, but that was the kind of story you heard from prisoners then.

"From around the summer of 1972, even the guards were going hungry. They did not bother us much now with criticism meetings or

---

*I interviewed her a month later. Ama Adhe subsequently met an American writer who published her story as *The Voice that Remembers: A Tibetan Woman's Inspiring Story of Survival*, by Adhe Tapontsang as told to Joy Blakeslee, (Boston: Wisdom Publications, 1999).

political campaigns. Sometimes some of them would leave their posts to search for something to shoot at and eat. But there was not much left in the countryside that had been bled white a long time ago. We prisoners did not have the energy or will to escape. We sat still all day staring at nothing, slowly breathing the few whispers of breath we had left. It was all coming to an end."

35

GUERRILLA TRAILS TO MUSTANG

It was dark and stiflingly hot. We sat on hard wooden seats, waiting silently for our third-class carriage to be joined to the incoming Howrah express. My travel companion had the side of his head pressed against the steel bars on the window, trying to catch whatever little movement of air there was outside. The harsh fluorescent lights of the shunting yard of Old Delhi railway station cast a glow around the outline of his sweat-beaded features. It was the sort of face that, in the severity of its lines, could well have been chiseled out of a block of hardwood. It reminded me in some ways of a photograph of an American Indian warrior, Young-Man-Afraid-of-his-Horses, that I had seen in a book somewhere.

My companion, on the other hand, was more prosaically named Bhuché, or "Beloved Son," probably a nickname or a pet name, but one he used by preference. He was generally addressed as "Gyen" Bhuché or "teacher" Bhuché because he was one of the instructors at the resistance base at Mustang. He had been trained at Camp Hale, Colorado and was the leader of Team Five that had been parachuted into Kham in 1959, for the Dzayül operation.

With a bump and a bang, our carriage was finally attached to the train. The lights came on. Fan blades clattered against the protective mesh cover. We got fresh chapati flatbread and curried potatoes and peas from a platform vendor and had dinner. Bhuché was from Dergé, one of the largest Tibetan principalities in Eastern Tibet. His family name was Utsatsang. His father had been a minister in the court of the king of Dergé. He had heard of my grandfather, Tethong Gyurme Gyatso, who had been governor of Dergé and presided over the coronation of the child king of Dergé in 1926. We discovered that both of us shared the same root lama, Jamyang Khyentse Rinpoche of Dzongsar, so Bhuché warmed to me. He told me that I had done the right thing in joining the Mustang Resistance Force.

I needed reassurance. I had tried to join the Force earlier when I finished school but had been told to go back home. I had made the mistake of approaching the Dalai Lama's older brother Gyalo Thondup, who was the very controversial *éminence grise* of the resistance movement, and a friend of my father's. They sometimes played tennis together at the Gymkhana Club at Darjeeling. I had been upset with Gyalo Thondup for turning me down, but unbeknown to me, disagreements had begun to surface in the Mustang Force that would eventually lead to a clash within the leadership. Gyalo Thondup had, possibly, no time to spare then for a boy and his dreams.

But that was four years ago. Now, in 1971, I was a leader of the Tibetan Youth Congress (TYC), the largest independent political organization in exile society, so I was taken more seriously this time around when I approached Gyalo Thondup's assistant, Lhamo Tsering, to join the Mustang force. He was a quiet, hardworking man, lacking the bluff heartiness of his boss. He seemed to be very busy, but listened patiently to what I had to say.

The dissension within the Mustang Force appears to have come about largely from the leadership style of Baba Yeshi Kalsang, the commander who, though a brave and skilful leader had, over the years, begun to view the Force as a traditional tribal organization, with himself as supreme chief. The Colorado trained officers and instructors wanted more input and accountability in the administration. Gyalo Thondup and Lhamo Tsering could be faulted for letting such a situation fester over seven years, allowing Commander Yeshi free rein even after being approached by a delegation of the Colorado officers in Darjeeling. They requested Gyalo Thondup to visit Mustang and sort out the mess. The inevitable break-up was messy and, unfortunately not without a few clashes and fatalities. Finally, the old commander, Baba Yeshi and about eighty of his followers split off from the main Force and submitted to the government of Nepal. Wangdü Gyadotsang and Lhamo Tsering took charge of the Mustang Force and the remaining two thousand fighters. But now, a new and more fundamental threat loomed on the horizon.

I did not let any of these problems dampen my excitement and enthusiasm. I was at long last off to join the Resistance. That was all that mattered. Maybe it was not quite the fighting force it had once been, but, hey, it was still—Mustang. Just the name conjured dreams of adventure and valorous deeds, and I was on my way there. I asked Bhuché many questions as the train roared through the hot Indian night. In the corner of the compartment, our minder from Indian Intelligence dozed fitfully, a grey blanket pulled over his head, like a shroud. His job was to see that Bhuché and I got safely over the border to Nepal. Otherwise, he kept his distance. The Indian "Research and Analysis Wing" (RAW) and the CIA shared the product gathered by the agents and networks that the Resistance Force maintained inside Tibet and all along the border.

At the ramshackle Indian border town of Nautanwa, the Force maintained an agent, a gaunt but wiry native of Lhasa, with shrewd beady eyes and a ready if low wit. Everyone called him "Skinny" Lobsang, but his real name was Lobsang Topgyal. He ran a small boarding house behind the railway station for cover, with his handsome Khampa wife, Tsundru. There Bhuché and I joined up with our commander, Wangdü Gyadotsang, and four of his men, who had come there from Darjeeling. The boarding house was next to some incredibly black and bubbly open sewers. The one night I spent at Nautanwa was a sleepless one, with swarms of mosquitoes, no doubt based in those pestilent sewers, keeping up near continuous sorties till sunrise.

The next day we crossed the border into Nepal. The Khampa woman went before us through the check-post. Under her dress, taped to the insides of her legs, were a couple of handguns that belonged to Wangdü and his men. From the Nepalese border town of Butwal, a day and a night's bus journey took us to Pokhara, from where we could see the towering peaks of the Central Himalayas. The Resistance Force ran a hotel in this small tourist town, where we hung around for a few days while Wangdü conducted some business with our people there. A week later, we started for Mustang.

There was a bit of subterfuge involved in our departure. It was necessary. Though the old commander, Baba Yeshi, had left Mustang with his men, he had not, unfortunately, considered the matter of his dismissal closed. A month earlier, three couriers of the Force carrying a large amount of money had been ambushed a couple of days' journey from Pokhara at a bridge near the village of Shekhar. The leader of the courier team, a young Colorado-trained instructor, Gyen Tenzin (of Chatreng), had been shot and fallen into the river. His two companions had managed to escape with the money.

We did not leave by the normal route from Pokhara to the Tibetan refugee settlement of Tashi Phalkhel and from there up along the ridge to the village of Naudanda. Instead, Wangdü, six of his men, Bhuché and myself, proceeded casually in twos and threes to a hotel by the Pokhara lake, the Fish Tail Lodge. Our packs had already been sent there in a jeep, so to any casual observer, it would seem that we were just going to the Fish Tail lodge for a walk, or maybe a game of *Mahjong*.

Fred Sharp, the manager of the Fish Tail Lodge, was an enthusiastic *Mahjong* player. He was American, of indeterminate age and unremarkable appearance. His outstanding feature was his thick beard, on which account the local Tibetans called him "*sab gyau*" or the bearded "*sahib*." He spoke fluent Tibetan and was a good friend of our commander, and some of the other Khampa officers as well. I could perhaps be maligning a perfectly innocent American hotelier, but the moment I saw him I said to myself "Aha! CIA." The setup was just too neat. Some of the others may have had their suspicions, but probably thought it best to pretend otherwise. I later decided that Fred could well have been an observer for the CIA, keeping an eye on the Agency's interests in that part of the world and providing an extra perspective on the doings of the Mustang Force.

Wangdü called for some beer, and one of Fred's Nepali waiters brought in a tray of ice-cold cans of Kirin, dripping with beads of condensation. It was a hot day. I gulped mine down with pleasure. We got our gear out of the jeep. Besides everyone's personal backpacks, there was a heavy-looking bundle rolled up in a sheet of tarpaulin. We carried it over to the shore of the lake, where two long dugout canoes gently bobbed up and down on the placid surface of the water. Close by, four Nepalese boatmen sat hunkered down together in a circle smoking crude hand-rolled cigarettes called *churut*. Somewhat uneasily, we got into the primitive crafts and pushed off. I was sitting just behind the paddler at the fore—close enough to smell the wood-smoke and coarse-leaf tobacco that clung to the bodies of most of these hill men. He had on a grimy singlet and faded khaki shorts. A black *topi*, the national cap, shiny with wear, was perched at a rakish angle on his bony head.

"*Thyo himal ko nam kay ho?*" What's the name of that mountain?" I asked in Nepali, pointing up to the shapely spire of ice and snow, a bit like the Matterhorn. On the still surface of the lake, just ahead of the boat, was a clear reflection of the great peak floating upside-down, serene in its looking glass world.

"*Machapuchare*. The Fish Tail," he replied, turning around finishing a paddle stroke, his broad Mongoloid face breaking into a grin.

The Fish Tail was the southernmost peak of the Annapurna massif, one of the highest in the world. Dividing it north to south from another great massif, the Dhaulagiri, is the Kali Gandaki river which we would encounter after a day's march, and which we would have to follow north, up-stream, to get to Mustang.

We paddled along the entire length of the lake, till we got to a marshy tract covered with reeds. We had to leave our boats there. Waist deep in tepid water, our packs held above our heads, we waded over to some paddy fields in the distance. We probably looked like a team of jungle-fighters in some Southeast Asian war. The paddy fields were at the base of a high mountain, the top of which was covered with dense

---

*I learned to speak Nepali as a boy in Darjeeling, where the population was then largely immigrants from Nepal and their descendants.

monsoon clouds, but on which, the friendly boatman had assured me, was the village of Naudanda. We walked for hours up a steep mountain path, past terraced fields overflowing with monsoon rain, and scores of silvery-white streams gushing out from the side of the hills.

We got to the tiny hamlet of Naudanda towards evening, but kept on marching to the next village of Chandracote, where we rested and had a meal at one of the inns there, a very basic kind of hostelry that Tibetans called *netsang*. After dark, we set out again. After about an hour, we stopped. The mysterious tarpaulin bundle was opened. Flashlight beams played on a motley collection of small arms: two Chinese Type 56 carbines, a couple of Swedish Carl Gustav submachine guns, two Chinese Type 43 submachine guns, and a few pistols.

"Have you ever handled any of these things before?" Buché asked me. "Only the pistol. I've fired my father's *chisi-popli* (U.S. Army Colt automatic) quite often."

"Well, then this *chanata* will suit you fine. It's nearly the same except it doesn't have the grip safety that the Colt has. The magazine holds more bullets too." He handed me a Browning HP-35, in a leather holster, and two full magazines in individual leather cases. I tried out the action of the Browning and then strapped the thing on.

We marched single file into the darkness. Walking near blind on the rough mountain tracks, especially when going downhill, was grueling. It began to rain heavily after an hour or so, which made things worse for me as I wore spectacles and couldn't see without them. I had also picked up some very spirited stomach bugs at Pokhara, which was notorious for its bad water and had to "go" every hour or so during the march. My pack was very heavy and the leather strap chaffed my skin, causing it to bleed. The pistol got heavier and heavier, and the belt bit viciously into my waist. Struggling through the jungle, dead tired, unable to see a foot ahead of me, I was separated from my companions. I sat down—in a small stream. I could feel the water flowing under me. But I didn't care. Even my cigarettes had congealed into a mess of tobacco particles and disintegrating paper in my shirt pocket. I felt very sorry for myself as I sat there in the stream, in the rain and darkness, chewing the tobacco and paper for a bit of nicotine rush to go on. This was definitely not the way I had imagined events would transpire. I had signed up for action in high Tibet, not bloody Vietnam. But somehow, I managed to get up and get going again, and, after what seemed like a million dark years, finally caught up with the rest of the group.

Things got better the next day. A dose of arak (Nepalese, *rakshi*) at the next *netsang* settled my stomach a bit. I soon found my mountain legs, and nothing really bothered me any further, not even the leeches that seemed to cling to every leaf and blade of grass along the way, one end of their wormy bodies sniffing the air for any indication of human blood. At Tatopani, a tiny hamlet deep at the bottom of a near vertical gorge, we came upon the Kali Gandaki River, which we had to follow to take us up to Mustang. That night we bathed in the hot springs nearby. 'Tatopani' in Nepalese means "hot water". Acting on traditional Tibetan medical wisdom and counteracting the debilitation of the "wind" humor by the otherwise healing properties of the sulphurous water, we drank chang, as we lolled about neck deep in the steaming, bubbling pool. Looking up into the night sky, I saw a couple of strange flickering stars, which I learnt, much to the amusement of my companions, were actually distant camp-fires, high up on the mountainside. The night had not only blotted out the towering forms but my daylight memory of them as well.

This entire route from Pokhara to Mustang is now a busy tourist trek, with small restaurants and "hotels" providing cold beer, coke, pizzas, pancakes and apple pies, practically every few hundred yards along the way. But things were very basic back then when tourism was just starting in these areas, and muleteers, couriers and other people from the Force, travelling up and down this trail, were the main source of business for the local inns and shops.

These were generally managed by pretty, vivacious young Thakali girls, belonging to an ethnically Tibetan/Nepalese tribe from the region of Thak Khola bordering Mustang. Earlier, the Thakali had a monopoly of the lucrative salt trade with Tibet but after the closure of the border in 1959, had to fall back on small-scale agriculture and running shops and inns. These businesses were patronized by our fighters from the Mustang Force and the Thakali girls who ran these inns would call the men "Agu" Khampa or "Uncle" Khampa, and flirt with them a bit. At main points along the trail, the Force also maintained checkpoints, with a resident agent or two keeping a wary eye out for any unusual traveller heading towards Mustang.

At Tukche, capital of the Thak Khola region, we left behind the steamy dense zone of bamboos, ferns, creepers and other tropical vegetation, and as the valley broadened, entered an enchanted realm of tall conifer forests and alpine pastures. Ponies were waiting for us there. Just a couple of hours ride up the trail, the character of the valley was transformed again to that of a dry semi-desert dotted with hardy shrubs, and occasional twisted, wind-racked, dwarf pines.

We bypassed the small town of Jomsom, the Nepalese district headquarters, and rode up the mountain trails towards the Nilgiri peaks, the westerly part of the Annapurna massif. Towards nightfall, the track levelled and we rode through a forest of pine into the interior of the mountains. The tough little ponies snorted, puffed, and occasionally farted as they struggled up the trail. In the darkness, sounds were all that gave form to one's world: hooves scrabbling and clomping up the track, and the creaking of saddle leather, and the jingle of harness. I switched on my flashlight to help my pony find the trail. The rider behind me, Tendar, laughed and said there was no need.

Finally, we arrived at headquarters.

The deep percussive bark of a Tibetan mastiff echoed in the night. Guards called out low greetings at the checkpoints. We dismounted and led our ponies through a large wooden gate into a wide courtyard. After handing over the reins of my pony to someone, I followed the others into a sizeable kitchen where we all sat down on yak-hide covered wooden divans. Everyone pulled out their mugs and bowls from their packs. Hot butter tea was served. We filled our bowls with tsampa from a leather bag of the stuff and, mixing it with some tea, kneaded our evening meal. Someone brought down a haunch of yak meat, hanging from a rafter, and dumped it with a bang on the thick wooden table. Another stirred a simple sauce of butter tea, salt and chilli powder in a tin plate. Others pulled out their sheath knives and sliced bits of raw meat off the haunch and, dipping it in the sauce, popped it into their mouths. It was my first experience of eating raw yak meat and I enjoyed the meal hugely.

The following morning, I got my first view of the headquarters of the Resistance Force. The camp was situated in a fastness dramatically close to the Nilgiri range and at the end of a high valley of one of the tributaries of the Kali Gandaki River. Its interior location shielded it from the constant desiccating wind that swept the main valley of the Gandaki from Jomsom onwards. The Khampas had named the place Kalsang Phug, Kalsang meaning "Fortunate Era" and *phug* being the geographical term for the high interior of a valley. It was surrounded on three sides by pine forests and grassy slopes. A sheer cliff at the front of the fastness, with only a single narrow track leading up to the camp, gave it all the protection it needed.

All the buildings in the area were solidly constructed of rammed earth with flat roofs, in typical Tibetan fashion. The Khampas were accomplished architects and built with a good eye for location and tradition. The main building complex was two stories high, with two courtyards, side by side, at the front. These were surrounded by thick walls and could be effectively defended—so long as the attackers did not have artillery. The smaller courtyard enclosed the main kitchen and stables, above which were the offices and living quarters of our commander, Wangdü Gyadotsang, and some of his staff. The larger courtyard was below the temple and the prayer hall located on the floor above the main commissariat and armory. There was also a small general store that sold cigarettes, toilet goods, tea leaves, Nescafé, Panda condensed milk, candy and Annapurna biscuits, which were manufactured at Pokhara from milled wheat husks, corn stalks and saccharin, or so it seemed—they were so tasteless.

The parade ground was located a short distance away, and beside it was the library building. All around the camp were laid a profusion of vegetable patches and flowerbeds, diligently tended by the men. Water for the plants as well as for the camp itself was brought a long way from up the mountain in a fairly elaborate system of canals and wooden pipes, regulated at points with diversionary gates and plugs to distribute water where required, and also to prevent the freezing and the splitting of wooden pipes in the cold winter months.

The living quarters for the men were built in clusters of houses slightly away from the main building and were uniformly single-storied. Every squad of about ten men occupied two or three houses and cooked for themselves. I shared a large room with Damdul, a young man from the border village of Tsum in Nepal (whose snub nose and spiky hair immediately recalled Cruikshank's illustration of the Artful Dodger) and Tashi or "Little" Tashi as everyone called him, for he was just over five feet tall. He was the shortest Khampa I had ever met, but also one of the toughest. He had a cheerful puckish face. We had come up together from Pokhara and had gotten to know each other well. He was a fine companion, friendly, always ready for a joke or a song. He had been trained at Colorado as a communications-man but his energy and intelligence kept him at headquarters for many other tasks.

In the next room was the chief weapons instructor of our camp, Khaleg Jhampa of Dergé, tough, wiry, and immensely self-contained and organized. His gear was always in meticulous condition. His pistol still had the blue factory sheen on it, though he had had it for over ten years. He was fastidiously clean and always wore a sparkling white baseball cap. When you went out on patrol with Jhampa, you got the feeling that you were walking with a Japanese trekker rather than a Khampa guerrilla. Across from us were the rooms of two clerical staff members, Dhakpa Dorje (of Sok) and Jhampa Chodrak, and our cook, an old nomad named Shenga. He was a pious, kind man but a terrible cook. Aside from a small sweet tuber called the *droma*, no-mads in their highlands probably never get to see, much less eat, common vegetables, so all that our cook knew what to do with the potatoes, cabbages, radishes, and greens we grew, was to boil them. The seven of us messed together, and on the whole, were resigned to what we got. But every now and then, someone would get desperate enough to drop some not very subtle hints about the insipidity of our menu. These were invariably ignored. But to be fair to the old man, he was an accomplished hand at getting the most out of a slaughtered yak. The taste of his blood-sausage and meat jelly still lingers in my memory like the refrain of an old tune.

In the beginning, I found the altitude and cold a bit trying, but that was soon fixed by drinking mugs of melted *dri* (female yak) butter, and also bowls of warm blood from the heart of a freshly slaughtered *dri*. Consumptives in Europe, in the nineteenth century, visited abattoirs to drink the hot blood of freshly slaughtered animals as a tonic. Lafcadio Hearn, in his essay, *Haceldama*, maintains that the best sources for such a drink were animals butchered at a Jewish slaughterhouse. Since the *Sochet*, the Jewish butcher, was skilled in his profession, the animals died without fear, and the blood was consequently "warm, creamy and sweet."

Every morning at five, we would be woken up by the shrill blast of a whistle. We would dress hurriedly and run over to the parade ground for an hour's vigorous physical training. We ended our morning routine with everyone having to complete an obstacle course of high bars, parallel bars, rope swings and a vaulting horse. The last was a wicked thing. Essentially a smooth log with the bark peeled off, it was fifteen inches in diameter and four feet in length and raised to about three and a half feet off the ground on four stout wooden legs. That was it. No padding; no frills. You were supposed to clear the thing in one neat vault. The problem was that the log was not only rock hard but also its surface slick with the passage of countless sweaty hands. This hazard was compounded by the patina of ice or frost that sometimes covered it early in the morning. Mishaps were common.

Following the PT and drill, we would line up in formation, stand to attention and holding a salute, sing the national anthem. We sang it badly. No one had really mastered the tune, and the obscurely literary, symbol-steeped lyrics were barked out in plain honest staccato nomadic and Khampa accents. The old man in front of me had his large prayer wheel, or rather its long handle, stuck down the back of his shirt collar, while he stood rigidly to attention belting out words he probably didn't understand. The whole thing was faintly ridiculous. But it touched something in me. In a safe civilized world patriotic demonstrations may seem silly, but when you know that your survival depended to a large part on the strength of the collective belief in what you were fighting for, then the symbols of that belief: the national flag, the national anthem (though badly sung) took on meaning and substance—and became quite moving.

In spite of our martial demonstrations, we (our company of about ninety men) were not an impressive lot. We varied in age from a white-haired ancient of sixty-odd years to two small boys (the product of a liaison of one of our men with a local Lopa woman). We also had no standard uniform, except for homemade forage caps and anoraks that we stitched ourselves out of cotton khaki fabric. Some men wore shirts made of camouflage parachute nylon and odds and ends of Chinese uniforms.

Footwear varied from traditional Tibetan boots to Chinese canvas sneakers. A few lucky soldiers had vibram-soled army boots bought at Pokhara or Butwal from British Gurkha soldiers on leave. But the informality of our attire didn't bother me. I felt about it much as Orwell did on the turnout of his comrades at the Lenin barracks in Barcelona during the Spanish Civil War: ". . . the mashed forage caps and ragtag, hand-me-down uniforms gave the men a grizzled courageous look you see in embattled legionnaires—a kind of sloppiness that seemed in-distinguishable from hard won experience."

After physical training the men would diligently perform their ablutions, brushing their teeth with "Oxygen" toothpaste, the more fastidious concluding their toilet with an application of another Chinese product, "Butterfly" facial cream. A quick breakfast of butter tea and tsampa, and we would be at work by six-thirty.

Most of the men worked in the administration or tended the fields and vegetable patches. In the beginning, I did not have much to do in the mornings, so I studied. I had brought a number of books from India and had arranged for their delivery from Pokhara to headquarters by mule. Here are some of the titles I recall:

1. Collins English Dictionary
2. Shakespeare's *Complete Works*
3. Bertrand Russell's *Wisdom of the West*
4. C.P. Fitzgerald's *China: A Cultural History*
5. Immanuel C.Y. Hsü: *The Rise of Modern China*

6. The three-volume Penguin *China Readings: Imperial China, Republican China* and *Communist China*
7. All of George Bernard Shaw's plays, the cheap college editions published by Orient Longman, Bombay, with excellent introductory essays by A. C. Ward.
8. J.C. Fuller's *Great Battles of the Western World* (in two volumes)
9. Che Guevera's *Reminiscences of the Cuban Revolutionary War*
10. Che Guevera's handbook, *Guerrilla Warfare.*
11. T.E. Lawrence's *Seven Pillars of Wisdom.*
12. Livy's *The War With Hannibal* (Book XXI-XXX) (Selincourt's translation)
13. Arrian, *The Campaigns of Alexander* (also Selincourt's translation)
14. Clauswitz, *On War*
15. Harold Lamb's *Hannibal*
16. Vo Nguyen Giap's *People's War People's Army*
17. J.G. Lockhart's *History of Napoleon Bonaparte*
18. Captain B.H. Liddel Hart's *Strategy: The Indirect Approach,*
19. Captain B.H. Liddel Hart's *History of the Second World War.*
20. E.W. Sheppard's *The Study of Military History.*

The last was a text for Staff College Entrance Examinations and had questions and answers on a range of battles and campaigns. With it, I could test my progress in my military studies. I had read somewhere that General Giap, when a village schoolmaster, enlivened his history lessons with detailed accounts of Napoleon's campaigns, all of which he had committed to memory. This fact impressed me no end, and I made a serious (but unsuccessful) effort to emulate it. The only immediate bit of military wisdom I gleaned from my studies that came into practical use at Mustang was from Che's handbook.

The great revolutionary leader advises prospective guerrillas to carry a pipe around with them in case of a cigarette shortage, when they could use the pipe to smoke shredded cigarette butts, coarse tobacco leaves or whatever substitute they might find. Up in Mustang, we had supply problems during the monsoons when a bridge or a track was washed away, and the mule trains couldn't get through. So, when

Bhuché left for Kathmandu on some official business, I asked him to buy me a pipe, which he obligingly did. Shenga, the cook, taught me to pick giant rhubarb (*cholo*) leaves that grew high in the mountains and could be mixed with tobacco after being dried in the sun. This not only stretched your tobacco supply, but also gave it a fragrant tang.

The only book in English that I managed to find at headquarters was an English translation of Sun Tzu's *Art of War*. It belonged to Lhamo Tsering. He had extensively annotated every page of the book in English and Chinese. It was reassuring to know that our chief of operations—for that, more or less, was his job—took his business seriously. Lhamo Tsering was also kind enough to send me copies of *Time* and *Newsweek* from Delhi, where he was based. These were usually about three weeks to a month out of date by the time they got to Mustang, but they were very welcome.

A couple of weeks later, I was given one-on-one weapons instructions in the morning by Khaleg Jhampa. Jhampa had, many years ago, been the *sölpön* or cupbearer or chamberlain to the king of Dergé, but after many battles and training at Colorado, he was now our best weapon's instructor. He taught me to strip and assemble the M1 Garand rifle, the Browning automatic rifle (BAR), Browning HP-35 pistol, and a variety of submachine guns. I was also issued an M1 Garand rifle and two hundred rounds, and a Browning pistol. My rifle had previously belonged to Tenzin, the instructor who had been shot at the Shekar Bridge ambush. It was a well-maintained weapon. Instead of the standard webbing sling, he had substituted a broad leather strap that glistened with dubbin. We had no weapons inspection, but none of the men needed to be told to take care of their weapons. Every one of them cleaned and oiled their weapons regularly. Before hanging up their rifles on the walls above their beds, they would carefully wrap the breech in a piece of silk and stop the barrel with a tuft of yak-hair dyed red, one end shaped into a plug.

The men had great respect for the M1 and had given it the roughly homophonous and somewhat inappropriate title of "Emaho", which according to Sarat Chandra Das's great *Tibetan English Dictionary* is ". . . a Buddhist salutation expressing compassion." The high velocity round which generated shock waves in its path caused massive exit wounds. With an M1, they always knew when they had hit a Chinese soldier as his cotton padded jacket exploded at the back, causing a visible cloud of white fluffy particles. Nearly all the weapons were of WWII vintage, which did not bother the men. What they had fought with before were of even earlier vintages, WWI, even the Russo-Japanese War. Moreover, since the men had to carry all their ammunition on their backs when going on raids, they had natural fire discipline, and preferred single action, and semi-automatic weapons.

We usually had lunch around ten, and then got back to work. I would go over to the school a little distance from the main camp to teach younger members of the Force. The schoolhouse was designed like a fort, but surrounded by small trees, well-tended flowerbeds and vegetable patches, which gave it a pleasing bucolic appearance. There were about fifty students, in their late teens and early twenties, mostly tough wild nomad kids with reputations for being unmanageable. But they had met their match in their headmaster, a tough sergeant from the Guards Regiment, Thundup Gyalpo, of the old Tibetan army. He had been Bhusang's best friend when the two of them had studied at the Lhasa Medical Centre.

When Thundup Gyalpo and I entered the classroom on my first day, the students stood to attention, ramrod straight, while he introduced me to them. Most of them had been illiterate, and Thundup Gyalpo had, in the span of a few years, given them a good grounding in written Tibetan. They had tremendous respect for him. I taught them arithmetic and simple accounting, for the main purpose of the school was to produce clerical and administrative personnel for the various companies and departments of the force. I also taught them English, Nepali and current events, focusing on the wars of national liberation that were then being fought around the world.

The resistance published a magazine, *Ghotok,* (Hear and Understand) from Kalsang Phug, which was distributed to the various companies in the Mustang and Nyeshang region. The editor was my roommate from Tsum, Damdul. My own contribution to the journal was picking up stories from the BBC World Service and sometimes doing a piece. The magazine was mimeographed or, as the Tibetans called it, "oil printed" (*num-par*). The Gestetner machine would sit out in the blazing sun for an hour or two, and when the rollers and works were nearly too hot to touch, we would crank out the voice of the Resistance. The heat made the ink flow nice, and we got perfect results every time.

In the afternoons, when I did not have classes, I would sometimes help the men out in the fields. Not that I was any good at it, but it was pleasant to be out shelling a pea pod and eating the fresh peas, in between picking them. Besides vegetables and flowers, we also planted potatoes and barley. Most of the fields we cultivated belonged to local Thakali and Lopa people, and we had to lease from them. Manure was the only fertilizer, and was very carefully composted and managed. The alkaline wood-ash from the kitchen fires was collected daily for the fields. Even our urine was saved, to be processed into fertilizer. We were careful not to piss everywhere, but only in our own squad piss-bucket, which was at the bottom of the garden.

Traditional Tibetan farming practice emphasizes careful composting of waste matter, and the Chinese practice of individually ladling raw night soil on growing plants was studiously avoided. Raw night soil collection and spreading, was one of the punishment tasks that the Communists forced Tibetan lamas, chieftains, aristocrats and other counterrevolutionaries and "bad elements" to perform in collectives and *Laogai* farms. Though we were over an altitude of 13,000 feet above sea level, and the summers were short, we managed to grow large, fine tasting vegetables. Our turnips were as sweet as apples. The altitude allowed for very strong sunlight during the day. The snow on the mountain range just behind us acted as a giant reflector and increased the sunshine we received.

The Nilgiri Mountains were very close. A few hours walk would take you right to the base. Lying down on the fields, chewing a blade of grass, you could look up high above you and sometimes see an avalanche—thousands of tons of ice and snow breaking away from the side of the mountain and falling down, in slow motion, finally hitting bottom in an explosion of whiteness. The sound, a thunderous boom, would reverberate over the icefalls, moraines and forests, finally arriving down at Kalsang Phug some moments later. Once, after an unusually powerful avalanche, a misty cloud of powder snow descended on our camp. Outside my window, I saw an old soldier dust the snow off his cap, look up at the clear blue sky and laugh.

One night, clear and moonlit, I woke up and, heavy with sleep, staggered out to the garden to relieve myself. Halfway through my business, I looked up, and my heart nearly stopped. The mountain, dazzlingly white, impossibly vast, towering miles above, seemed to be rearing directly over me. In the altered perception and mind-state of night, this scene appeared, momentarily, to be beyond the scale of a terrestrial phenomenon, but more an apocalyptic, William Blake-ish sort of vision. My impressions of that night found a faint echo many years later when I was living in Japan and saw copies of some unusual Hokusai paintings. A Japanese artist friend of mine had made a pilgrimage to the small town of Obusé in Nagano prefecture, which this peerless artist-sage had visited when he was eighty-five, and where he had lived for some years. The village maintained a collection of some of his work at a *kinenkan* or museum. A few of these were studies of waves. Not the more well-known waves from his "One Hundred Views of Fuji," reproduced on postcards and tourist kimonos, but something from another and perhaps more mystical vision. There were breakers and swells that seemed cosmic in their conception, with innumerable stars and galaxies growing from inside the curve of the waves. One, in particular, an immense column of water appeared to rise many hundreds of miles high, with the vast nebula-like crest poised to descend. The reproduction was just four by ten inches, but the vastness of scale and the awe-inspiring mystery of the universe that Hokusai had so skilfully suggested in that one small painting, made you hold your breath for a moment.

Most of the men went to bed early, but some of us contrived to stay up a bit after sunset, to drink black tea and talk by the light of a small Chinese kerosene lamp.

"My father took me with him once when he went north to trade. He was a merchant, you know," said Little Tashi, stirring in some Panda condensed milk into a mug of tea, and licking the spoon afterwards in his boyish way, though he was then thirty-five, if he was a day.

"Did he operate out of Lhasa or Kham?" asked Damdul, who was sitting cross-legged on his bed, picking the few hairs on his chin with a special tweezer.

"Oh, Lhasa, of course. He had left his home in Sho-ta-lho-sum a long time ago. I was born and raised in Lhasa. I was ten, no . . . I think I was more like twelve when my dad took me with him when he went to trade at the nomad centre of Nagchukha. The place was covered with hundreds and hundreds of *ba-nak*, black yak-hair tents, for the northern market fair. My dad traded brick tea from China and stuff from India, for butter, cheese, wool and other things from the nomads. There were a lot of nomad women around too, all dressed up and covered with ornaments. Some were very pretty and lively. One night, I was falling asleep when I heard the jingle of silver ornaments and giggles.

My dad was bringing a girl over to our tent. I got really mad, I tell you. I rushed out of the tent and kicked him in the shin.

"Well, it didn't take very long before I was getting into girl trouble myself in Lhasa. By that time the Chinese had come, and I had to attend the Chinese "Social" School (*chizo labtra*). You must have heard about it; it was quite famous at the time. One of the instructors was a girl from Bathang. The Chinese used a lot of Babas as interpreters and agents. The young men in our class, including myself, made life difficult for her. One day she broke down and cried. I felt rotten and after school told her I was sorry and talked to her. Well, we got to know each other. She told me the story of her life, which was quite sad. Her parents had died when she was little. She had no relatives, no one really, to look after her. When the Communists got to Bathang, they put her in one of their schools. That was all the family she had.

"She was pretty. We fell in love. The Communists didn't like it. Neither did my father. But I took her over to my mother and told her the story of this girl's life. My mother was a gentle and kind woman. She started to cry, out of compassion, you know. So, I married that girl in the end, made her a real Tibetan woman. My family bought her Tibetan clothes, and a complete set of ornaments: a *patruk* (headdress), a *ghawu* (women's star-shaped charm box made of gold and turquoises, and worn on the chest) and earrings. Everything, in fact. She didn't own anything of value, no jewellery, nothing. Not a cowrie shell. A year later, she gave birth to a baby girl, and we were all very happy, including my father. But 1958 came along, and when Gonpo Tashi Andrugtsang called for fighters to gather at Driguthang, my dad took the few rifles and pistols we had in the house and volunteered. I went with him."

"You never saw your wife again or your little girl?"

"Of course not," Tashi replied irritably. "It was just fighting all the way after that. After the Lhasa Uprising, I couldn't get any news, nothing at all about my family. And then we were finally forced to escape to India. I remember them a lot, my wife, my mother, my baby, especially at night, lying awake in bed. I guess my girl is about thirteen now, if nothing has happened to her."

But Tashi told other stories, less personal and tragic. He had, after all, been trained in the United States (his training name was Sandy) and had seen a bit of the world, unlike most of the other men at Mustang, some of whom had never seen an automobile or a movie in their life. So Little Tashi told stories from movies he had seen, Indian and Western. He was a talented man. He had taught himself three other languages, English, Hindi and Nepali. He spoke the last two with native fluency. He sang well, too, in these languages, and when he told a story from a Hindi film, he would sing all the songs—in a clear tenor—at the appropriate moments in the story. He had also seen a number of Westerns and took his cue from them in the way he wore his pistol—slung low, for a quick draw. He could also twirl his piece backwards and forwards like an accomplished gunfighter.

But the story that the men loved best was the Epic of Gesar, King of Ling. This was my first experience of having the saga actually sung in the manner of the bards in Tibet, who could sing the entire epic from memory, and who would often go into a kind of rapture during the recital, the spirit of the legendary characters inspiring the performance of these bardic mediums. Our singer, a young nomad, Ariyo, had a printed text to read from and came nowhere near a trance, but he had a fine voice and sang with vigour and expression. The others, except for myself, joined in when a well-known verse came by.

> "I sing the song 'Ala la la! Tala la la!'
> Oh! You three brothers, known as foxes!
> Have you any courage? If so, arise!
>
> Oh! Thou Sky-god of the White Tent tribe!
> If thou possess power, display miracles!
> If the army of one hundred thousand men
> Of Hor are brave, let them come forth.
> The swords of other men are made of iron;
> We do not need swords; our right hands are enough.
> We will split the body in the middle,
> And cut the side into pieces.
>
> Other men use clubs of wood; We require no wood;
> Our thumbs and forefingers are enough.
> We can destroy by rubbing thrice with our fingers.
>
> The blood of the liver will escape from the mouth.
> Though we do not injure the skin,
> We will take out all the entrails through the mouth.
> The man will still be alive,
> Though his heart will come to his mouth.
>
> The body with eyes and head Will be made into a hat for
> The king of the White Tent tribe.
> I offer the heart to the War God
> Of the White People of Ling.
> Oh! Yellow Hor, wait and listen to me.

Speaking thus, he rained blows upon the man and held his head down, so that he became unconscious, and the bones came out of his mouth. He threw the man's right hand with the thumb ring to Mirutse, the

Butcher. He threw the left leg with the boot to Topchen. He threw the lungs, liver and intestines to Shechen. He waved the skin and head over the white Tents of Hor three times. Then he tied them to one side of his body and slowly returned to Ling. When he arrived at the fort of the men of Ling, the heroes praised and comforted him."[1]

The violence and bloodthirstiness of the epic hark back to a time before Buddhism had made its impact on Tibet and when Tibetans took joy in hunting, raiding and making war. Stripping the story of the pious prologue of Padmasambhava making the necessary arrangements in his celestial realm to send the hero Gesar down to a Tibet afflicted by suffering and chaos—the introductory story essentially falls into two parts. The first is the saga of the boy Joru. He is an unlikely hero, ugly, offensive and despised by everybody. He undergoes many trials and humiliations, but he also has supernatural powers and often plays nasty practical jokes on his enemies. In this character, he resembles the "divine trickster" of American-Indian mythology, also present in certain Indo-European traditions, as Till Eulenspiegel of German folklore.

In the second part of the story, Joru, after winning a horse race, is transformed into a heroic character and is proclaimed Gesar, King of Ling. He then sets out to perform great deeds: he recovers magic weapons and fabulous treasures from the Amnye Machen mountain, destroys the Demon of the North, Lutsen, and makes war on the evil rulers of Hor who have attacked his kingdom and abducted his beautiful but unfaithful queen. In his many adventures, he is accompanied by his magic horse Kyanggo-yerpa, and protected and guided by his heavenly aunt Ma-nene, or Gungman Gyalmo "Queen Goddess of Heaven," much in the way that Odysseus was aided by the goddess Athena.

Gesar's valiant brothers and his eighty *pathül* or heroes stand by his side to fight the enemies of their king. The Homeric ambience and valor of these warriors are nicely offset by the self-serving duplicity of Gesar's uncle, Trothung, a fat, ambitious, ridiculous, cowardly but entertaining character, playing a treacherous Falstaff to Gesar's Prince Hal.

Gesar's adventures do not end with the destruction of Hor and its chiefs but move from sequel to sequel. An official Chinese publication calls the Gesar saga the world's longest epic poem—with over ten million words, a million lines and five times longer than the great Indian epic, the Mahabharata. This claim is not entirely accurate. Many of the sequels are not authentic segments of a single complete epic like the Iliad. They are closer in form, to the medieval French *Chansons de geste*, and the Spanish *Cantares de gesta*, where many stories were added in later times, written in imitation of the original epic. Unlike the European stories though, the Tibetan sequels always feature the original hero, Gesar.

A few Gesar stories have even been written in living memory by known authors. One example is the tale of Gesar's war with Germany, written by the Eight Khamtrul Rinpoche (1931–79) of the Tashijong Monastery near Dharamshala. Another Gesar tale written in exile (published in 1975) by a Tibetan monk scholar, Lama Kalu, is Gesar's victory over the Lord of Death. Still, another Gesar story takes our hero to the court of a Victoria-like queen-empress, whose ministers and marshals are addressed as "sahibs." The scholar Lhagé, a chieftain of Drongpa in Kham, who died in 1990, wrote seven volumes of Gesar stories.

Far more important than the need of the Ministry of Truth in Beijing to find a place for the Tibetan epic in the *Guinness Book of World Records*, is that it is still a living source of literary creation. In fact, from Dergé, Trepa Pegyal, has written an account of his people's heroic struggle against the military might of Communist China in the manner of the Gesar Epic. And I have mentioned in my introduction the Drayab resistance leader who wrote the first draft of his biography in the epic style.

Ever since the Chinese literati discovered Homer at the end of the nineteenth century, they have keenly felt the lack of a national epic poem, their own traditional fiction of "knight-errant" (*wuxia*) stories being considered too episodic and prosaic. Chinese poets have attempted to create Chinese epic poetry or *shi-shi*, literally historical poetry, though the results have been limited to story poems and ballads. So, in a sense, the Chinese arrogation of the Gesar epics as the "national cultural treasure" of China and their inflated claims for it can be viewed in this light.

It is not only the Chinese who have been captivated by the Gesar saga enough to stake their claim to it. The epic has been known in Sikkim, Bhutan, Ladakh and among the Naxi and Bai people in Sichuan and Yunnan. In Mongolia, the story of "Gesar Khan" has been known for many centuries and in many versions and dialects, especially Khalka, Kalmuk and Buriat. Shortened versions of the epic are popular in Baltistan, on the Pakistan frontier (written in Persian) and in Gilgit, in the Burushaski language.

The very name, Gesar, is revealing, of the extent of ancient Tibet's shadowy contact with the West. Besides the Tibetan Gesar of Ling, another Gesar, a non-Tibetan warrior king, is mentioned in certain Tibetan accounts as the ruler of Khrom, a fabulous martial nation far to the north of Tibet. It is now fairly certain that the name Gesar is a version of the Roman *Caesar* and its later variant, the Turkic *Kaiser*. Khrom is quite a close adaptation of the name Rome, though some scholars regard it as being derived from the Syrian and Persian "Frim" for Byzantium, or the Eastern Roman Empire. The Chinese took their old name for Rome, Fulin, from this source, with the difficult to pronounce "fr" sound undergoing a change to "fu," and the subsequent ". . . rim" being transformed to "lin."

Gesar also lives on in the belief system of Tibetans. Cults built around Gesar as a powerful protective deity still flourish, and so do divination techniques, one known as the "Gesar Arrow Divination" and another, said to have been introduced by the hero himself, called the "Six-Bird Divination." In a 2014 documentary film, Dawa, an illiterate nomad bard, channels Gesar's power, to heal sick and injured victims of the 2010 Kyigudo earthquake.[2]

But the epics are strongly condemned by the official Gelugpa Church as being a violent and disruptive distraction to those undertaking religious studies. There is another, more partisan reason for this objection. Tibetan historians (Tashi Tsering et al) place Gesar of Ling around the eleventh century[*] but his destruction of the Hor

---

[*]The historical Gesar, possibly an actual tribal ruler of Eastern Tibet, may have emerged as the heroic leader of his people following the breakup of the

tribes is still said to rankle with the deity, Pehar of Nechung Monastery, who was once the guardian genius of Hor, though he is now regarded as the principal protector of the Dalai Lama, and the foremost oracular deity consulted by the Tibetan government.

The young fighters around me sang the verses of the epic with fierce pleasure, and it wasn't too difficult to see why the official church disapproved of it. The violence in the stories was palpable, though Buddhist piety had succeeded in toning it down over the centuries. One of the disconcerting Buddhist expurgations in the epic is the way that after having a terrific fight with one of his demonic opponents, and cutting of his or her head, Gesar invariably uses his spiritual powers to direct the spirit of the deceased fiend to the Western Paradise. In the early pre-Buddhist cycle of legends, from which the Gesar Epic might have been derived, such fine gestures were perhaps not so frequent on the part of our hero.

But the men were also devout in their Buddhist belief, and practices. Quite a few of them had been monks earlier in their lives but had given up their vows to fight for their country and faith. Every evening before sunset, many of them would walk around the temple and spin the prayer wheels mounted in recesses in the walls. By the side of the paths winding throughout the camp and the school, cairns of stones had been piled to honour the Buddha and the gods of Tibet. When you passed by one, you recited a mantra and placed a stone on it as an offering. Prayer meetings were held regularly at the temple, which housed a complete set of the Kangyur and the Tengyur, the 108 volumes of the Buddhist scripture and the accompanying 224 volumes of commentary. The temple also had many sacred images and religious objects that had been brought out from Tibet by fleeing refugees.

Sometimes when the men talked about the Chinese they had killed, they would conclude their accounts with an invocation to the Bodhisattva of Compassion, in effect a prayer for the better rebirth

---

Tibetan Empire. Correspondingly, some English scholars have speculated that the Arthurian legend was based around a shadowy Romano-British figure, the commander of a Roman auxiliary force, who led the defence of Britain against Saxon invaders following Rome's withdrawal from the British Isles.

of their victim. "There were three of them in that trench, sticking their thumbs up in the air begging for mercy, crying out 'Dalai Lama, Dalai Lama.' But what could I do? I shot them all. *Om Mani Padme Hum.*" There was often an element of mock boasting involved in such piety. When someone talked about what a great sinner he had been, it was a roundabout way of letting you know that he had killed many Chinese soldiers.

We slaughtered yaks in late autumn for our winter meat supply. I remember an old officer from Chamdo, Lonye, rushing around with a large bottle of consecrated water, dispensing doses of the stuff to the dying animals, all the while muttering his mantras. One could accuse these people of hypocrisy, but Tibetans don't quite see things that way. For them having faith in the Buddha's teachings was essential. Whether one was able to live up to them fully was another thing altogether. It was a tough world, so one just did what one could and did not worry too much about what couldn't be helped. Buddhist hells were not forever, the Buddha and Bodhisattvas had limitless compassion, and after a few thousand or million lifetimes, one would eventually be liberated, one way or the other, out of the cycle of existence.

Whether one approved of this attitude or not, the subscription to high moral standards by people not consistently observing them is not necessarily a bad thing for society, as Orwell points out in his essay "The Decline of the English Murder." He felt that the pervasive hypocrisy of Victorian society did, at least, help to ensure that serious crimes like murder were not committed casually, but when they did occur, they had strong emotional motives behind them.

The ubiquity of Buddhist principles among the soldiers, even if sometimes honoured more in the breach than the observance, at least served to make these armed and essentially violent men reluctant to take any more life than was necessary. The hills and forests around our camp had a fair amount of game, mostly blue sheep and musk deer, and once in a rare while, a snow leopard. But there was little hunting. Although we were all armed with high powered rifles and needed all the meat we could get, I never saw anyone take a pot shot at the cranes, geese and lammergeiers that flew across the sky above

Mustang, or at the little pikas that came out of their holes in the day to bask in the sun.

Every man possessed some kind of religious text depending on the practice he was undertaking. He would also have a rosary or sometimes a prayer wheel. But the most valuable religious object a soldier owned was his *ghawu* amulet. It was generally the size of a cigar box and made of silver with gold filigree ornamentation. It was, in fact, a portable shrine and often had a picture of the Dalai Lama, a root lama, or a small Buddha image showing from the opening in the centre. Fighting men have probably carried amulets and charms ever since the resident of Cave A attacked the resident of Cave B, and with all the technological advances of modern warfare, will probably continue to do so, so long as you cannot kill your enemy without also exposing yourself to some degree of danger.

John Steinbeck, in one of his reports from the front during World War II, wrote that St. Christopher medals, lucky rabbit's feet, Indian Head Pennies, pictures of loved ones all served to help a man reach outside himself for help and comfort during times of great danger and great emotional tumult. Steinbeck adds, somewhat disapprovingly, that novelty companies in America had taken advantage of this almost universal urge of soldiers towards magic to turn out thousands of lucky rings and figures. He reserves particular condemnation for one company ". . . that has brought out a Testament bound in steel covers to be carried in the shirt pocket over the heart, a gruesome little piece of expediency which has faith in neither the metal nor the testament but hopes that the combination may work."

But the *Ghawu* amulets that Tibetans carried were in another class altogether than the steel covered testaments or lucky rabbit feet. Generally packed with numerous relics, ancient religious heirlooms, sacred images and objects, Tibetan charm-boxes had artistic, historical as well as spiritual associations to endow them, in the minds of their owners, with real power. In my charm box, I had a small clay image of the deity Yamantanka, a tiny scrap of the robe of Tsongkhapa, the fifteenth century founder of the Gelugpa sect and a small packet of the embalming salt, used on the body of the Fifth Dalai Lama. One of the most important items in my collection was a tiny but genuine granule of the Buddha's relic from the collection of the Dalai Lama's tutor, Trijang Rinpoche.

The men believed implicitly in the power of these amulets. Stories of men returning home from battle unharmed by the bullets that had shredded their clothes were fairly common. But it was accepted that amulets didn't work all the time, especially if a woman had handled it, or it had been defiled by blood. I was uniformly sceptical of all these claims. There was another qualification, one that bothered me a lot. No amulet in the world could save you, it was said, if your karma was weighed against you to a degree where it could not be altered. Amulets only worked in that grey area where various possibilities were still open in one's future. I was young and regarded myself as being of a rational turn of mind, so I argued that either an amulet worked or it didn't, and all such qualifications were merely evidence of the latter. The men tolerated my scepticism good-humouredly, but their faith was set in reinforced concrete.

But whatever its powers against bullets, knives or swords, amulets weren't regarded as any protection against disease or illness. So it was fortunate that nearly all the men enjoyed rude good health, for medical facilities were, for the most part, non-existent. Around the time I was there, the Force was building a small hospital at the settlement of Marpha, south of Jomsom, where retired veterans were being settled. But this hospital only had a single Tibetan doctor, practicing traditional medicine. Tibetan medicine has its uses but is not really suited for battlefield work.

The Force also sometimes purchased medical supplies from mountaineering expeditions that came to climb the peaks around the Annapurna and Dhaulagiri massifs. I was asked one day to sort out some large boxes of medicine acquired in this manner. To my dismay, all the bottles and packets were labelled in Japanese.

I am not sure of the reason for this, but at high altitudes, one of the besetting problems nearly everyone had was toothache. In his indispensable handbook, Che advises having a dentist at your guerrilla base, with basic equipment and a "campaign-type drill," probably one of those old foot-powered machines. We had nothing of the kind at Mustang. The men believed that tiny "worms" ate into your teeth, and the bits of dead nerves they found when they broke apart and extracted teeth seemed to confirm their theory. Extractions were not always possible, so many inventive, though somewhat drastic, methods had been worked out to take care of the "worms." One of these was to bend the end of a wire at a right angle and heat it till it glowed red-hot. You then poked it hard into the cavity and worked it about vigorously till the little beggars were done for.

Another method was to take, in a dropper, a tiny measure of sulphuric acid—meant for the batteries that powered our radio sets—and gently release a drop or two in the cavity. There would be a fizzing reaction in the hollow of the tooth and though a cure of sorts might be affected, the patient would have blisters and sores in his mouth for a week or two.

The most dramatic of these "cures" involved an element of danger for the patient. First, you dried the inside of the cavity with a bit of cotton wool. Then you broke apart a cartridge (the one time I saw this treatment being administered, they used a Lee Enfield round) and took the charge inside. The Lee Enfield charge is shaped like a thin pencil lead. You broke bits of the charge and tamped it into the cavity, around one unbroken length that would act as the fuse. You touched the fuse off with the lighted end of your cigarette. With a fizz and a whoosh, the miniature charge would go off. A small cloud of smoke would billow out from the mouth of the patient, who would roar with pain and fall backwards from his seat.

When one of my own teeth developed a cavity and began to hurt like hell, I firmly declined such ministrations when solicitous friends proposed them. I tried one of the gentler cures ; inserting a bit of musk in the cavity, but it only made the pain worse. At the time, Rakra Gyadhar (of Lithang), the commander of First *Detsen* (camp) and one of the legends of the Force, had arrived at headquarters for some official business. He came to pay me a visit and, seeing my predicament, took charge of the situation. I protested feebly, but he waved aside my objections.

"Just got to get it out. That's all. Yank it out, I say, and be done with it. That'll be the end of your problems."

He pulled out a bottle of arak from his saddlebag and made me drink about half of it. Strictly speaking, we were not allowed to have any alcohol inside the camp and this rule was scrupulously observed by everyone. But Rakra was Rakra. He summoned some volunteers to hold me down and, sitting on my chest, waved a large pair of pliers.

"Well, Jamyang Norbu, you better resign yourself to this. Even if you crap in your pants and stink out the room, I'm going to keep on pulling till I get that tooth out."

But somehow, he couldn't. It still makes me wince to recollect the experience. Rakra tugged and twisted the pair of pliers for what seemed an eternity. His forehead glistened with little beads of sweat, but the bicuspid sat there unmoved. Finally, Rakra gave up, exhausted.

"The beggar's rooted there like a boulder." he complained.

But strangely enough, the pain subsided a bit that night. When I met Rakra the next morning, I told him about it. "That's because of my *jhinlap*, my sacred healing touch," joked Rakra. The tooth only flared up again a year later when I was in India and I finally got it surgically removed by a dentist.

There was nothing sacred or spiritual about Rakra. He was a big man, in spirit as well as stature. He was over six feet tall and had rough-hewn features, a bit puffy with drink. His teeth were broken but his small eyes, though often bloodshot, were alive with intelligence and humour. He was from Lithang, where some of the most savage fighting had taken place in the mid and late fifties. Though that tragedy had probably taken its toll somewhere inside him, he had managed to retain his essential fearlessness, a largeness of heart and a sense of the absurd. Like a lot of the other resistance fighters, he was not young. Though he didn't own up to it, he must have been in his mid-forties. He dyed his hair as did some of the others. Even Little Tashi dyed his.

A brand of hair dye from India marketed under the brand name "Helene Curtis" sold well in Mustang. I thought the practice somewhat ridiculous, especially since all the men wore khaki forage caps practically all the time, outdoors and in.

Finally, I asked Rakra, "Why?"

"If I should be killed in an operation, I don't want the Chinese to see how old I have become," he said simply.

36

RAIDS INTO TIBET

Rakra need not have worried about dying old and forgotten, or a nameless casualty in a trivial raid or firefight. He is possibly the only guerrilla leader in military history who has had an operation he led commemorated in an oil painting—and that too, commissioned by the CIA.

On 26 October 2009, the CIA's Intelligence Art Gallery (there does appear to be such a place at Langley), in a ceremony that included the surviving members of the CIA's Tibet Task Force and their families, dedicated a large painting by British military artist Keith Woodcock. "Titled *The Secret PLA Pouch Heads to K Building,* the painting depicts Tibetan resistance fighters capturing the PLA commander's pouch in full battlefield detail: the army truck on fire, its driver and passengers shot dead, blood on the snow, rifles in the arms of the retreating Tibetan fighters, and the blue pouch being carried away"[1] . . . presumably by the leader, Rakra. Another recent acquisition of the CIA Art Gallery, a painting titled *ARGO—The Rescue of the Canadian Six,* also celebrates a success in the agency's operational history that had to be kept secret at the time.[2]

I heard the account of Rakra's operation not from him, but from a fighter who had been there with him, his second-in-command, Ah-Trinlay. He had come to headquarters for some business and stayed overnight at our squad quarters as we had a couple of spare bunks. After dinner, when we were drinking black tea around the kitchen fire, someone asked him about the raid, which had become the stuff of legend by then.

"This was way back in 1961, you know, before your time. That year we launched at least half-a-dozen operations into Tibet. Rakra took charge of one team, and I was glad to be going with him, as was everyone in our unit. We had thirty-two fighters in ours. Rakra was born under a warlike star. He had the reputation of attracting conflict and action. All of us wanted to fight and not just wander all over the Jhangthang and not encounter any Chinese. This could happen, you know. The Jhangthang is a big place. If you didn't have a good local guide, you could easily get lost. And that sometimes happened even with a guide. Do you remember that fellow they called 'the swanky nomad' (*dokpa tok-tok*)?"

"Yeah, he was from Tradün, wasn't he?"

"Yes, from somewhere around there. Anyway, he was our guide on another raid, and just kept getting lost. Finally, he said, 'I think this is the place.' 'Are you sure?' I asked him, 'you don't sound too confident.' 'I know this is the place', Dokpa Tok-tok declared indignantly, 'it's just that the last time I was here, that mountain wasn't there.'"

We all laughed.

"It's a good thing we weren't using him on this raid. But with Rakra, our luck held. He was good with maps.* We got to exactly the place we wanted on the Xinjiang–Tibet Highway, around the Lektse area, north-east of the Tsangpo River."

The Chinese built the Xinjiang–Tibet Highway (1957) as the final section of their greater all-season roadway from the railhead in Lanzhou in the north-east all the way to Kashgar in Xinjiang (East Turkestan) in the west, then looping south to Rutok and Gar in the far west of Tibet and finally running south-east to Shigatsé in Central Tibet, a distance of about 3,000 miles. The more direct Sichuan–

---

*Rakra Gyadhar, cover name "Ross", was trained in Colorado in the same period as Bhusang.

Tibet Highway (1954) from Chengdu to Lhasa, carved out of the high mountainsides of Eastern Tibet, was snowbound in winter and often washed away or damaged by landslides in summer. The incredibly cold and desolate Qinghai–Tibet Highway (1954), built largely on permafrost with road surfaces that constantly cracked, buckled, and shifted in unexpected directions, was a trucker's nightmare. The all-season roadway got around most of these problems, but its enormous length made its designated advantages questionable. It was said that, if two fuel-tankers loaded with petrol set out from Xining, one of them would be empty when they got to Shigatsé. The advantage of the Xinjiang–Tibet Highway for the Mustang fighters was that it came fairly close (relatively speaking) to Mustang on the Nepal border and was eminently attackable. In his eight-volume history of the resistance, Lhamo Tsering provides the date and time of Rakra's famous raid: 13.20 hours, 25 October 1961, and the coded map coordinates (1060:1496) of the site.

"It took us three days of riding from the Kora-la pass on the border to get to the ambush site. We didn't run into any Chinese patrols, and only passed some local nomads in the distance. No problems. Finally, we hit the highway just before evening and scouted around for a good site to set up our ambush. Most of the area was flat but we found a place where the road ran adjacent to a rocky hillside. We tied the horses together behind the hill, where they could not be seen from the road, and we all huddled there that night trying to get some sleep in the bone-chilling cold.

"Early next morning, Rakra deployed most of the men along the ridge and also behind some of the boulders below. At the highest point on the hill, he had posted a couple of men with binoculars to track the road at either end, so we would know early enough if any Chinese transport came our way. Around two in the afternoon, one of the lookouts shouted that he could see a truck approaching in the distance. There was a brief discussion on whether we should attack this single truck or let it go and wait for a bigger convoy. Rakra cut through the discussion, and said we should take this truck, and if it didn't work out, we could always wait for some more.

"So we concealed ourselves and waited. The truck came from the west, from the direction of Ngari, and was the usual six-wheel kind(Jiefang CA-30), its body with a full tarpaulin cover. I wondered why only a single truck was risking travel on this dangerous road. As the truck approached, you could see two Chinese soldiers in the front cabin. I think it was Rakra who took the first shot. He hit the driver, and the truck veered to one side and stopped dead. We all started shooting. The second soldier in the cabin was killed immediately, and we concentrated our fire on the tarp-covered cabin. There were people inside for sure; you could see the bulges on the tarp as they jumped around. But none of them managed to get out or fire a single shot. We got them all. The whole thing took less than fifteen minutes. Rakra signalled us to stop firing. The truck was still. The engine was running and from between the floorboards of the truck-body, blood began to drip down on the dusty road. Soon there was a large dark splotch on the road.

"Rakra rose from behind his rock cover on the ridge and stood up to survey the scene below. He looked quite grand and imposing. He had a camera with him, and he was preparing to take a photograph when suddenly machine-gun fire came from the truck—ta-ta-ta-ta-ta-ta—like that, continuously. Rakra stepped back instinctively and lost his footing. The entire slope of this ridge was just loose stone and gravel, very unstable. He fell on his butt and slid down the hillside, finally ending up at the bottom near the road. We all burst out laughing. But the machine gun was still firing. Rakra got up and shouted at us furiously, 'Fire your damn weapons, you beggars (*pango*)! What's there to laugh at?'

"But before we could do anything, the machine-gun fire stopped.

"Rakra pulled out his handgun and walked over to the truck. We ran down the slope to support him. One of us pulled back the cover from the rear of the truck, and we looked in. The machine-gun fire had come from a Chinese soldier who had been shot dead earlier, but in a kind of reflexive death-twitch or something had pulled the trigger of the submachine gun and kept on pulling till he had unloaded the entire magazine through the roof of the truck body.

"There were nine other bodies at the back. We pulled them all out on the road and searched them. We searched the two bodies in the driver's cabin. When we took off the Mao cap from the soldier sitting next to the driver, we discovered that she was a young woman with a short bob haircut. This was unusual. So we checked out the whole truck and everyone in it carefully—going through their pockets, even taking off their shoes. We discovered we had killed a very important officer, and the woman in the front-seat was his secretary. We captured quite a few weapons but most importantly, we got hold of bags of important documents. But you all know about that."

According to Lhamo Tsering, the officer was a PLA colonel, a regimental commander, Sheng Yuanshen, of the Fifth Regiment, Eleventh Division. He had most of his staff with him in the truck. It would seem that this senior officer was bringing a hoard of confidential documents: complete sets of Party directives, political manuals, secret bulletins and so on, from the Army High Command in Xinjiang to be delivered to the various TAR area commanders in Tibet. In total, there were three large canvas bags of documents and a canvas pouch full of correspondence. In an interview in 1991, Lhamo Tsering explained to me the value of these documents.

"They were of tremendous importance not only in a military sense, but also in areas of national policy, CPC ideology, and international relations. The documents revealed that Mao Zedong's much-vaunted Great Leap Forward had been a disaster and described in detail the tremendous suffering and loss the campaign had caused the Chinese people and nation. This was information that neither the CIA, the KGB, nor any other intelligence agency in the world was aware of. One of the bulletins even mentioned a discussion within the Politburo on whether China should begin negotiations with the United States. Other documents gave the disposition of every PLA unit in Tibet and Xinjiang and names of various commanders and their location. One document also described the entire system of information gathering on the Indo–Tibetan border by various networks, and how they were processed, reviewed and transmitted to Beijing."

"It does seem extremely careless of the Chinese to have had such documents being transported quite so casually." I remarked.

"Yes, it is surprising, isn't it? We never really found out why they weren't more careful that day. But you must remember that the raid was the first one we conducted from Mustang, which was totally unexpected. The successes of the other six raids that year were less spectacular but great victories all the same. Every year after that, we would send in raiding teams into Tibet around winter, from October onwards.

"Why winter?"

"Conditions were much more favourable for us then, especially since the Tsangpo River that was usually impassable in the summer, was at its lowest in winter."

Lhamo Tsering personally took the documents with him from Darjeeling to the CIA station chief at Calcutta. Ken Knaus, the head of the CIA Tibet program, in his book *Orphans of the Cold War*, refers to the haul of more than 1,600 different classified documents as a major "intelligence goldmine."

". . . they provided firsthand intelligence on the serious problems of governance that had grown out of the Great Leap Forward. They described famine conditions and their effect on the morale of troops who knew how their own families were suffering at home. The People's Militia, listed in Pentagon order of battle estimates as part of China's military forces, was revealed not only to be an empty asset but in some cases, to be participants in uprisings against the government they had been formed to protect. The documents also acknowledged the necessity to accept the fact that it would be 'temporarily' impossible for China to regain control of Taiwan, and also discussed the strained relationship with the Soviet Union, from whom Beijing could expect no help if attacked with nuclear weapons."

The dramatic intelligence haul arrived in Washington at a critical time in the policy debate over whether the U.S. should continue to support the resistance force at Mustang. John Kenneth Galbraith, the distinguished Harvard economist, author and Kennedy's ambassador to India deeply disapproved of this "particularly insane enterprise" to support ". . . the deeply unhygienic tribesmen who had once roamed over the neighbouring

Tibetan countryside and who now relieve their boredom with raids back into the territory from which they had been extruded."[3]

Though Galbraith had a long friendship with the president and his family, Kennedy did not yield to his articulate and persuasive ambassador. "The Tibetan guerrillas represented the kind of unconventional force that he had long advocated as an alternative to the Dulles-Eisenhower doctrine of massive nuclear retaliation."

Besides the unqualified success of the "document" raid, one particular evaluation report within the document haul probably served to reassure the CIA that their support of the Tibetan resistance was not misguided. A bulletin entitled "Work Report of Tibet Military Command"[4] revealed in surprisingly objective and positive details the courage, determination and fighting skills of the "rebel bandits". It noted their coolness and fire discipline, their skill at seeking cover and manoeuvring, and their courage and determination in always closing in during combat. It contrasted the security consciousness of the "rebel bandits" in not leaving equipment and documents behind when retreating and deplored the "disgraceful" action of a PLA unit in Tibet when it fled a battlefield and left behind maps, codebooks and radio equipment. It also mentioned the general tendency of Chinese soldiers to fire blindly from a distance, and not make each shot count as the "rebel bandits" did, and so on.

The secret documents were later released to the Library of Congress for use by the press and academia on 4 August 1963. The *New York Times* summarized much of the information in an article on 5 August 1963, "Ordeals in China Show in U.S. Data" the *New York Times*. I remember a *Time Magazine* cover story from that year. The illustration was of the sinking ship of the Chinese State, overfilled with millions of tiny people, the dragon prow chipped and broken, sailing through a stormy sea.

The disaster of the Great Leap and the subsequent "Great Famine" had not gone entirely unnoticed in the free world. A handful of experts working out of Hong Kong, Miriam and Ivan London, and the great Jesuit China watcher, László Ladány had written with remarkable insight into these events but had been largely ignored or belittled by experts in the West. The dean of China Studies in Harvard, John

King Fairbank, had pronounced Mao to be an "agrarian reformer," and nearly everyone commenting or writing on China tended to repeat what had become an article of faith in formal China Studies—that famines were a thing of the past in Mao's Brave New China.

But sending raiding parties into Tibet became progressively more difficult in the following years. The resistance had been a bit too effective for its own good. The Chinese stopped sending convoys to Tibet on the Xinjiang-Tibet Highway just across from Nepal, and instead fell back on using the older Qinghai–Tibet and Sichuan–Tibet Highways further east, in spite of their serious limitations. A couple of years later, the Chinese built an alternative route that went north from Saka Dzong to the Jhangthang and then west to Garthok, bypassing Mustang and the Kailash region. Sending raiding parties deep into Tibet was possible, but it was very dangerous, and the logistical problems were substantial. You had to have many horses and pack animals to carry the extra ammunition, food and equipment needed for the weeks of travel.

Lhamo Tsering told me, years later, that from the start, they had recognized the problems of using such a remote and desolate area as Mustang for a base and had worked on alternatives. "Just after we set up the Mustang base we started planning a base at Pemakö in south-eastern Tibet, which was a wild, isolated and jungle-covered area. Most important of all, the Chinese had yet to move there. Another advantage was that Pemakö was on the Indian border, just across the Indian town of Sadiya, so our rear was protected. We began to implement this plan around the July of 1960.

"Initially, we sent in a three person survey team. Their report was very positive so a ten-man team[*] of instructors and radio operators was

---

[*] I came to know two members of the team very well in later years. One, Trehor Pema Namgyal, was the manager of the Kailash Hotel at McLeod Ganj. Always dressed impeccably in full Khampa gear: black robe, riding boots, rosary and a dagger, he sported the grandest Zapata moustache in town. The other, Lithang Jamyang Tsultrim, was the leader of the Tibetan refugee camp at Delhi for many years and gave unstinting hospitality and support to all Tibetan activists. He was himself always front, and centre in every anti-Chinese demonstration in that city.

sent there. They set up their base near the old district headquarters of Metok Dzong (Castle of Flowers), and occupied the area below the knee of the Brahmaputra River (the Dihang Tributary), where it does a U turn and heads south-west towards Assam. The area could be accessed from the north from only one pass, the rugged Dashung-la, and so was very safe. We trained many local youths—about one thousand of them in all, and also built roads and bridges. All the bridges were the local kind, made of cane and bamboo and tubular in shape. Drop zones were also cleared for the expected American supplies. A number of Khampa refugees had moved to Pemakö from the fighting in their own lands, and so we distributed virgin land to them and organized farming ventures in cooperation with the local people. Since the area was greatly underpopulated, this was no problem.

"But it took time to convince the Americans that this project was feasible. This waiting period proved fatal. In 1962 China attacked India. Indian troops began to retreat from the border, blowing up bridges behind them. A five thousand-strong Chinese force advanced on Metok Dzong. We had not yet received a single arms drop and only had three or four rifles and one submachine gun and a pistol. So, we had to retreat. Many of the Pemaköba people had to leave their homes and escape with our team. But our instructors and officers organized this mass evacuation very efficiently. No one was killed, captured or left behind. The Pemaköbas now live in agricultural settlement camps at Miao and Tezu in Arunachal Pradesh.

"I am convinced this base had tremendous potential. First of all, we were operating from within Tibetan territory, unlike Mustang, which is in another country. So, it would make it that much easier, in the legal sense, for the Americans to support us there. Furthermore, the impenetrable jungles that covered this area gave us a better opportunity to conduct real guerrilla-style operations against the Chinese, unlike Mustang, where you could be seen from miles away. Because of the thick forest cover, we did not have to fear Chinese aerial reconnaissance or air attacks. The area was also warm and fertile. With proper organization, we could have supported a large number of fighting men. Mustang did not have any such advantages, but that was where we ended up."

He also told me about how the Mustang base was first set up, and heartbreaking but inspiring stories of the problems that the fighters had overcome in the early years.

* * *

"When Gonpo Tashi Andrugtsang and I first drew up the plan in early 1960 to establish a resistance base at Mustang, the CIA only agreed to support a small contingent of no more than three hundred men. Our office in Darjeeling began a selection process from among the many thousands of fighting men who had escaped to India and were now working at the road camps in Sikkim. These men had been eating their hearts out to get back to Tibet and resume the war with the Chinese, and the news of the secret Mustang base did not, unfortunately, stay secret very long. Indian officials and contractors began to discover that their Tibetan road-workers were suddenly disappearing. Even more embarrassing for us, reports began to appear in Indian newspapers. A headline from *The Statesman* of August 1, 1960: MYSTERIOUS EXODUS FROM SIKKIM, KHAMPAS LEAVING IN HUNDREDS.

"Gonpo Tashi Andrugtsang had personally selected Yeshi Kalsang of Bathang, one of his old commanders, to lead the Mustang operation, and one of his secretaries, Kunchok Dorje of Chamdo, as deputy commander. I sent my nephew Tsongkha Jhanjup Jinpa to assist them. With them, we sent a radio team 'K' manned by three operators: Jedrung Jampel Lekmon and Namgyal from Gyantsé, and Trinlay from Lithang. This team managed to get to Mustang and make the necessary preparations for the first group of three hundred men that arrived at Mustang at the end of July. But soon, many hundreds more began to turn up. They came from Sikkim and other areas like Dalhousie and Simla, till by the end of 1960 there were nearly three thousand men in Mustang. The Americans became very upset with this unexpected development, and also with the Indian newspaper reports. In spite of our pleas, they withdrew their support for the Mustang operation. But enthusiastic Tibetan volunteers kept on pouring into Mustang."

The passage of many hundreds of rough-looking Tibetans through the India-Nepal border at Raxaul and Gorakhpur caused the Prime Minister of Nepal, B.P. Koirala, to send a letter of protest to the Government of India. Prime Minister Nehru was questioned in Parliament on this new refugee exodus. In spite of some suffering and rough treatment at the hands of the Nepali police, everyone eventually managed to get through to Mustang. But their troubles were just beginning.

"The overwhelming problem we faced at Mustang was that of food supply. What was barely enough for three hundred could not be expected to cover the needs of three thousand volunteers. Men were sent out to the villages and towns of Mustang and adjacent districts to buy whatever food grain was available. Our Darjeeling office had little operating money and absolutely no contingency fund for this sort of emergency. We tried to borrow whatever we could from Tibetan business persons in Darjeeling and Kalimpong, and I am proud to say most of them responded quickly and generously. We rushed couriers with the cash to Nepal.

"But Mustang is an arid and sparsely populated area. Surplus food grain was not available from local farmers easily, who generally managed to survive just above subsistence level. Furthermore, because of the remoteness and poverty of the area, the local people had never seen currency bills, even the official Nepalese rupee notes, and insisted on being paid in the old *mohar* coins (*tranka*), for the little they had to sell. So, the currency notes had to be taken to banks in Pokhara and Kathmandu and converted to *tranka* coins, bags of which had to be hauled up to Mustang.

"Some hunting was attempted, but we had very few rifles as the Americans had not yet made any arms-drops. Soon the men were forced to cut up the leather from saddlebags, harnesses and even boots, and boil them for some minimal sustenance. Although everyone suffered tremendous hardships the first year, no one died of starvation. But they came pretty close to it. A few men froze to death in the winter snow, but the rest survived. The cold and the snow gave the men many problems, especially since they had no tents, and not enough warm clothes either. Fortunately, a couple of the wealthier residents of that region turned out to be Khampas who had settled in Mustang decades earlier. One of them, Garnag Yeshi Sangbo, provided the force with tents and supplies. He also arranged for nomads in the higher regions to bring their flocks of sheep down and sell them to the Force.

"Gradually, conditions got better as the leadership at Mustang came to grips with their logistical problems. We eventually managed to buy enough mules and pack horses to establish a working supply route from Pokhara to Mustang. In just more than a year, we managed to overcome our first crisis. Finally, the Americans relented and made their first arms drop. For the sake of deniability, the drop zone was established inside Tibet, about a day's march from the Kora-la pass, the border between Tibet and Mustang. On 15 March 1961, late at night, three transport planes dropped arms and ammunition, enough to equip four companies of soldiers. Three more arms drops were made in the following months."

* * *

Another reason for the lull in operations from the mid-sixties was, ironically enough, occasioned by the successful raid of 1964 led by my friend Tendar, where a truck convoy on the Xinjiang–Tibet Highway was destroyed and eight Chinese soldiers killed. This raid was filmed by George Patterson and Adrian Cowell and aired on British TV in 1966. The CIA became nervous about this unwanted publicity and insisted that all raids into Tibet be halted. They also insisted that the Mustang force should disperse in small units along the lengthy Tibet-Nepal border and concentrate on intelligence gathering.

But our commander Wangdü Gyadotsang wasn't ready to do that just yet. I approached him about letting me take part in a raid into Tibet. I had proven useful to him as a Nepali interpreter, and he took me on almost all his trips throughout the region. He trusted me enough to use me to negotiate with local Nepalese leaders. He confided to me that he and the other commanders were working on a major long-range, multiple-target raid inside Tibet, and that I would get my chance if I kept my mouth shut, and not talk about it with anyone.

Other than the major problem of Mustang's isolation and remoteness from suitable raiding targets, was the fact of its situation within a foreign country. Historically Mustang had been a Tibetan principality, and a Tibetan king still survived in his decrepit castle at Lo Manthang, but he was now a vassal of Nepal. The kingdom had been incorporated into Nepal as an autonomous region at the end of the eighteenth century, though, for a long time, the people of Mustang had considered their land to be part of Ngari or far-western Tibet.[5] Non-Tibetans primarily used the name Mustang while the people of the kingdom and Tibetan speakers, in general, have always known it as Lo or Lo Manthang. It appears in the earliest Tibetan chronicles (*The Tun Huang Annals*) as the name of a distinct territory and people in the western borderlands of the early Tibetan empire.

Geographically and culturally, the whole of the Mustang valley was a part of Tibet, but politically it was not, and that was where our problem lay. The government of Nepal was not happy with the presence of a large force of armed Tibetan guerrillas on its soil. In the early sixties, when the fear of a Chinese invasion across the Himalayas had been a real and unsettling one, the presence of an armed anti-Chinese force at a vital entry point on their border had not been unwelcome to the Nepalese. There was also a rumour in Kathmandu that the Americans had provided the king of Nepal with a stipend to make the *fait accompli* more palatable to him.[*]

But that was ten years ago. Nepal now had more disagreements with India than with China, with whom relations were becoming ever cozier—spoiled only by the presence of the Tibetan Resistance Force in Mustang. The Nepalese also resented the subtle but real control that the Force exerted over the Mustang and Thak valley. On China's insistence the Nepalese authorities were beginning to address the issue.[6]

---

[*] The U.S. also built Tribhuvan University (Nepal's then only institution of higher studies) and funded malaria eradication in the Terai, among many other programs vital to Nepal.

At the forefront of Nepal's efforts to deal with this problem was the governor of the districts of Mustang and Baglung, Raj Bhandari, who operated out of the district headquarters of Jomsom some ten miles away from our headquarters. The small town of Jomsom; the name being a Nepalese distortion of the Tibetan *dzong sarpa* or "new castle," was the point of separation between the territory of Thak and Mustang proper, or culturally between Nepal and Tibet. It was a small town of rough mud-brick houses on the eastern banks of the Kali Gandaki River. Just across the river the Resistance force had built a small hotel and a general store. Also on that side of the river were the office and quarters of the governor, a garrison of Nepalese troops commanded by Major Rana, and an airstrip.

The strip wasn't being used when I was there. A year earlier the one plane the Nepalese had flown between Pokhara and Jomsom had crashed. The craft was a battered old DC-3 (Dakota) flown by a daredevil Sikh who had a reputation for heavy drinking, and for being the only pilot with the nerve and skill to snake that war-surplus machine between those peaks and gorges and land it on the tiny strip at Jomsom. One day, his luck ran out, and overshooting the strip he crashed his plane on a patch of large boulders. Everyone in the craft was killed. The whole town turned out for souvenirs, and the wreckage was picked clean. Someone from the force managed to get one of the plane doors, which was later used as a signboard for our hotel. As the man with the modern education, I was assigned the task of painting the words "Matsang Hotel" in English, Devanagari and Tibetan on the door of that ill-fated aircraft. Matsang Tsangpo being the Tibetan name for the Brahmaputra River, before it got to Central Tibet from where it was called the Yarlung Tsangpo.

Jomsom was the windiest place in my experience. From mid-morning, the wind howled up the valley from the south till about one or two in the afternoon when it finally let up. Then at around 5 or 6 p.m. a wind from the north, from Tibet, would sweep down the valley and continue the whole night till the early hours of the morning. And this happened every day with unrelenting and wearisome regularity. There was a window of tranquility in the afternoon from about one to five, when everyone came out of their houses and socialized or fetched water from the river. The young men then managed a rather dusty game of volleyball in the schoolyard. Most of them yearned to get away to the bright lights of Kathmandu.

For the men of the Force, Jomsom was a nice change from their monastic existence in the camps. Nearly all the taverns and inns were run by Thakali girls who were admirably hardworking, hospitable, friendly and pretty. They spoke Tibetan and served clean wholesome arak. A few establishments were run by Lopa women (from Upper Mustang) who had come from even colder and windier places up north and upriver and were consequently a little grubbier. But the prettiest girl in Jomsom town was a Lopa. She was called Lhenjam. On occasions when she washed her face, she became strikingly beautiful. Her arak joint was always crowded.

Little Tashi was quite the ladies' man and was on very friendly terms with all the young women in town. I did the rounds with him of the various drinking places in Jomsom. Being a town mouse, with stories about the Indian cities of Delhi, Darjeeling and Calcutta, I daresay I managed to cut a bit of a dash in that remote place. I could also play the *dranyen*, the Tibetan lute, quite well then, and providentially found an old instrument up at headquarters, that I fixed, re-strung, and, in due course, played to good effect in the inns of Jomsom.

Since Tashi and I were the only Nepali speakers up at headquarters we had many opportunities to go down to Jomsom to interpret for our commander Gyato Wangdü, to carry messages, or negotiate with the Nepalese authorities at Jomsom. I often had to meet the governor, Raj Bhandari, a physically unimpressive but shrewd and patient man. He seemed to suffer considerably from the cold, and whenever I saw him, he would be ensconced in a bulky down jacket many sizes too big for him, which made him look like the Michelin Man. He also wore the *topi*, the national cap, on all occasions. On ceremonial functions, he would come out in full national costume with the baggy cotton trousers (Nepalese, *daura-sural*) that fitted tightly below the knee, like jodhpurs. Schoolboys in Darjeeling called them fart-traps.

One of the governor's main objectives was apparently to find out the quantity and make of weapons the Force had. For that, he would resort to a subterfuge that I thought rather pettifogging, but with which he persisted, in spite of the lack of cooperation from us. He insisted that we register all our arms with him and he would issue licenses for them—also for the machine-guns, mortars and even artillery pieces we might have. On the other hand, we would protest that the Force had very little in the way of arms, only possessing some captured Chinese weapons and old rifles, more family heirlooms than anything else, that we had brought along with us from Tibet. This exchange became something of a ritual whenever we met. The force had brought down about a dozen captured Chinese rifles, submachine guns and pistols, and had duly obtained licenses for them to oblige him partway. But nothing more was conceded.

I always wore my pistol when visiting the governor and dressed as smartly as I could. I polished my British Army combat boots and added a white silk cravat (cut out of a parachute) to the khaki anorak and forage cap I regularly wore, and which I thought gave me an added officer-like appearance. Major Rana's soldiers at the guard post would present arms smartly, and I would respond with a more casual American style salute.

I got on nicely with the governor. He was well read and had written a history of the Newari people of the Kathmandu Valley. When we discovered we had a mutual interest in poetry, especially Omar Khayyam's *Rubaiyat*, our relationship transcended such mundane issues as gun licenses and hovered, occasionally, on a more refined plane. I had committed most of the quatrains to memory and would recite them in a voice that I thought carried the appropriate *weltschmerz*:

Ah. Come with old Khayyam and leave the wise
To talk; one thing is certain, that life flies
One thing is certain, and the rest is lies
The flower that once has blown forever dies. Etc. etc.,

The governor would respond with expressions of appreciation: "*Wah!* *Wah!*"—in the approved manner of Urdu poetry readings—both of us holding up cheap glass tumblers of *rakshi* to suitably honour the memory of the great poet, mathematician, astronomer, mystic and oenophile. Outside the crude walls of the governor's mud hut, the wind howled like ten thousand demented djinns.

Besides his task of keeping an eye on the resistance force, the duties of the governor did not seem very burdensome. The town was too remote and small for any onerous official activities or ceremonies, though I remember, on the occasion of the King of Nepal's birthday, he presided over a function to present honours of some kind to the King of Mustang. The function was held in the walled courtyard of the local school. The town elders and guests were seated on wooden school benches while the snotty-nosed, ragged children stood, coughing and pushing each other, in uneven rows before the governor and the King of Mustang. These worthies sat on metal folding chairs behind a small table covered with a green-check bed sheet on which a few plastic flowers in a cheap Chinese vase served to lend a decorative touch to the occasion. The schoolmaster led his charges in a faltering rendition of the national anthem. The double triangle of the Nepalese national flag, tied to a not very straight bit of branch, kicked about in the ubiquitous wind. The Khampas called this unusual flag the "harelip" (*shopto*).

Gyen Wangdü and the other leaders at Kalsang Phug had asked me to represent the Force on this occasion and make a speech. I thought it best to address the gathering in Nepali, but Wangdü suggested English to impress the locals. I think Rakra who insisted that I deliver the speech in a succession of all the languages I knew not only to impress the listeners but also to confuse them. We finally settled on the main speech being in Nepali, with the formal introduction and conclusion in English, just to let it be inferred that we Khampas were an educated and cosmopolitan lot.

With all the speeches made, the moment came for the presentation of the honour. The governor opened a flat box and pulled out, on the end of a red ribbon, a large and incredibly vulgar looking medal replete with sunbursts, wreaths, a star, a mountain, a trident and a bit of Horace thrown in for good measure:

dulce et decorum est pro patria mori

Since the strongman of Nepal, Jang Bahadur Rana, visited England in 1850, the Nepalese court had consciously modeled itself, as best as it could, after Balmoral and Buckingham palace. Old photographs of Nepalese royalty show even the *ranees* dressed up in all the later frumpery of Victoria's court. The guiding aesthetic principles of the Prince Consort, Albert—responsible for some of the more hideous awards and decorations of that era (or so we are informed by Lytton Strachey)—was surely inspirational in the design of the medal that was draped around the neck of the Mustang Rajah that day. The monarch, Jigme Dorje Palbar (twenty-fifth in line from King Ame Pal, who founded the kingdom in 1380) received this national honour with impressive equanimity, but he did not make a speech. He was dressed in complete Lhasa ceremonial raiment: a silk *tsondra* robe, brocade cummerbund (*serkheb koerag*), rainbow boots (*lham jachen*), a brocade summer hat (*usha changda*) with a fringe of red silk thread and "precious jewel" crest, a long turquoise earring (*sogchil*) and the dagger and pen case accessory (*gyadri pushuk*) that a Tibetan prince of his rank was entitled and required to wear on such formal occasions.

In the evening, the Resistance Force hosted a dinner for the King at the largest hostelry in the town belonging to *neymo* Kanag, or "hostess" Kanag—nearly all these places being known by the name of the women who ran them. We kept a couple of rooms there on a permanent basis. His Majesty was probably in his early forties and was a soft-spoken and self-effacing person. He had a broad, pleasant and intelligent face, and sported a thin wispy moustache. He spoke Tibetan fluently but with a noticeable Western Tibetan accent. After a few glasses of arak, he sang some popular Lhasa songs of yesteryear. I accompanied him on the *dra-nyen*, and when the slow half of the song was concluded, he got up to perform the quick-stepping dance (*trukshay*) for the brisk finale.

He was married to the lady Sidol-la from the aristocratic family of Shalu Kushang in Tsang, South-Central Tibet. But she had not accompanied her husband on this occasion. It was customary in the past for daughters of the Lhasa and Tsang nobility to be sent as brides to the various rulers of distant principalities as Mustang, Sikkim, Dergé and elsewhere, though the remoteness and physical hardship of living in a bleak, barren area like Mustang had resulted in a queen (or two?) returning to Lhasa in desperation. One is even said to have composed this melancholy couplet of her immurement in the gloomy castle of the Mustang Rajahs:

The King of Mustang lives at the edge of the sky
The lonely sound of his court drums makes my heart ache (for home)

Lo Gyalpo namkae tha la yin
Do dama sem kyi chongdo ray

37

FRENCH CONNECTION

Does a life of political exile somehow predispose a person to be drawn into the secret world? In Joseph Conrad's *roman à clef*, *The Secret Agent*, his eponymous spy and anarchist comrades are presumably exiled Russians living in London in the 1880s. The non-British characters of John le Carré's classic Cold War novels—East European and Russian émigrés in London, Paris, Berlin and Hamburg—serve much the same function. The renegade Soviet General, the Estonian truck driver, the Hungarian art dealer, the Czech mechanic (and "baby-sitter"), the East German nightclub owner and the *babushka* toiling in a Paris sweatshop, all appear to have been co-opted into the world of espionage and intelligence, largely through the uncertainty of their lives as political exiles.

Many exile Tibetans worked for the CIA. But many more were employed in such Indian agencies as the Research and Analysis Wing (RAW), Intelligence Bureau (IB), the Indo-Tibetan Border Police (ITBP) and other services. Many thousands of exile-Tibetans served in the elite and hush-hush Special Frontier Force (SFF)* that ". . . was extremely successful against Pakistan during the Indo-Pakistan

---

*The SFF was set up on 14 November 1962 with CIA assistance. The project was jointly conceived by B. N. Mullick, head of India's Intelligence Bureau (IB) and Gyalo Thondup.

Military Conflict of 1971"[1] also known as the liberation of Bangladesh. They trained the Mukti Bahini, the Bangladesh underground, and conducted pre-emptive strikes along the Chittagong Hill Tracts in eastern Bangladesh, to support the Indian Army advance from the west. The SFF also served to block the escape route of the Pakistani army to Burma, which contributed substantially to the total surrender of the Pakistani forces on 16 December 1971. One hundred and ninety SFF paratroopers were wounded and fifty-six killed, including their commander, Dapön Thundup Gyadotsang, the younger brother of Wangdü Gyadotsang.

Incidentally, the SFF managed to save the lives of the Chakma Queen Mother, Binita Roy and her family from revenge-seeking Mukti Bahini fighters. The Chakmas were the principal tribe in the Chittagong Hill Tracts, and Buddhists, who, when the subcontinent was partitioned, had unsuccessfully petitioned to be part of India. Their ruler Raja Tridev Roy was a member of the Parliament in Pakistan and had not supported the creation of Bangladesh.

A team of SFF climbers from its "Spider Colony" training base, together with a CIA agent and a top Indian army climber, were tasked with installing an ELINT device on the top of Nanda Devi (25,643 ft.). This was a large nuclear-powered trans-receiver that could detect China's secret nuclear tests at Lop Nor in the Tarim Basin, and transmit the information to the CIA's listening station at Orissa. The project encountered some setbacks but was eventually successful in detecting China's first thermonuclear test in 1967.

Tibetans welcomed the opportunity to work for these intelligence and paramilitary services, not only as these jobs were relatively well paid, but furthermore provided specialized training and skills they hoped to use in the coming struggle to free Tibet. The trade-off for India at the time was not disadvantageous. The entire northern frontier of India favoured Tibetan troops, in terms of altitude and terrain, and as the local populace was, in terms of ethnicity, religion and lifestyle, closer to Tibetans than to lowland Indians.

In 1969 as American foreign policy objectives changed and Nixon sought a rapprochement with China, the White House decided that the training and support of Tibetan freedom fighters by the CIA would have to cease. The CIA provided an "alimony" payment (in three instalments) to the Mustang Force that was invested in several carpet-weaving centres, general stores, hotels, restaurants and other small businesses to create a source of funding for the Force. Being the odd-job man of the Force I was asked by Wangdü to fly to Kathmandu from Pokhara and take care of some bureaucratic paperwork for a taxicab service the Force had recently set up in the Nepalese capital. I finished this task and was preparing to return to Mustang when another order came from Gyen Wangdü. I was to immediately fly to India and report to the Private Secretariate of the Dalai Lama. I did not want to return to Dharamshala, but there was no way I could refuse a direct order from the Dalai Lama's office. It also sounded very mysterious and hush-hush. I was intrigued.

After the American departure, Tibetans began to reach out to any country in the world that might have some interest in the Tibetan issue. Taiwan had for some time held out an offer of financial help but it was contingent on the exile government acknowledging that Tibet was a part of China—which was unacceptable. Taiwan agents (of the Mongolian and Tibetan Affairs Commission) had also fuelled divisions and violent quarrels within the exile community.[2]

In a last-ditch effort, the Dalai Lama's representative in Delhi, Phuntsok Thonden, approached the Russians at their embassy. The Sino–Soviet split, which had begun in 1956 with Nikita Khrushchev's denunciation of Stalin's legacy, had, by the time of Nixon's visit to China, become a serious conflict with violent border clashes and the potential of becoming a major land war. Reports from Soviet sources had implied a ". . . possible first strike against the Lop Nor basin nuclear weapons testing site."[3] So the Tibetan approach was not as hopeless as it might appear at first glance. The Russian officials in Delhi were interested though noncommittal. But the defence attaché at the Soviet Embassy in Kathmandu, a Colonel Anatoli Logonov, showed more initiative, and met with Wangdü on three separate occasions. Logonov said that funding for Mustang was not feasible at that time, but ". . . he offered payment for specific items of information, such as the location of PLA border posts and the deployment of aircraft at Tibetan airfields."[4] The Tibetans offered a sampling of intelligence material, but the deal fell through.

Then something unexpected happened.

"The Parliamentary Group for Tibet" was an office set up in Delhi by the exile government to lobby Indian MPs (mostly in the opposition) to raise the Tibetan issue in the legislature whenever possible. The secretary of this office was a junior Tibetan official, Lodi Gyari, who at a cocktail party in the capital had a rewarding conversation with the French military attaché.

In the latter half of the Cultural Revolution, China had crawled into what might be described as a belligerent, paranoid carapace, of the kind that present-day North Korea manifests. All foreigners in China: visitors, students, journalists, diplomats, everyone, in fact, were so effectively restricted in their everyday movements that any meaningful contact with the Chinese population was out of the question. In such an environment collecting human and ground intelligence in China became a near-impossible task. Much of the CIA's intelligence breaks on China had come from Tibetan sources—and other spy agencies had become aware of this over time.

The French wanted intelligence on China and were willing to pay for it. They were not interested in the Tibetan cause but wanted a straightforward business relationship where they would get regular intelligence reports on Tibet and China and would pay an agreed-upon sum at regular intervals. They were given a couple of sample reports on the Cultural Revolution in Tibet (one of which I wrote) and were satisfied. A deal was set up.

And it was a big deal for the exile government, desperate for any international support, no matter how modest or clandestine.

I was briefed by the Dalai Lama's Private Secretary, Kungo Tara and Minister of Security, P.T. Takla, that I was to go to Paris for intelligence training and to establish a working relationship with France's External Intelligence Agency, the "Service de Documentation Extérieure et de Contre-Espionnage" (SDECE). I had a separate meeting with His Holiness where he displayed an unexpected but sagacious curiosity in this project.

I flew to Switzerland in early 1973. When I arrived at Zurich airport, I proceeded, as instructed, to the "Hall of Flags" and waited under the French flag with a folded *Time* Magazine (cover side out) under my arm. A middle-aged man in a brown suit approached me and asked me a prearranged question (which I don't recall), to which I gave a prearranged answer—like in the Bond films. Unlike Bond, I was not wearing a Savile Row suit—just jeans and a beat-up leather jacket. I also had long hair, a goatee and a moustache, and looked somewhat scruffy, as the photograph on my "Autorisation Provisoire de Séjour" card shows. But there were a fair bit of hippies and backpackers on the move those days so I wasn't entirely out of place. I was handed a ticket for the next flight to Paris.

It was rather late when "brown suit" checked me in at a Paris hotel. I rode the creaky cage elevator up to a small room in the attic. Early next morning, I opened the recessed window and gazed out over the Paris rooftops, like Jean Gabin in René Clair's *Sous les toits de Paris.* Then I saw the Eiffel Tower in the distance, and for a Francophile like me, it was a thrilling moment.

After a couple of days, I was set up in a sunny studio apartment at 100 Boulevard de Charonne in the 20th arrondissement, Metro stop—Nation. The apartment had a toilet with a *bidet* (yes, it puzzled me first) and another bathroom where a dark room and lab were set up. This was in the days before the Internet and the iPhone, so film photography was a vital component of the kind of intelligence tradecraft that I was to master, and I would be trained in a whole slew of photography related spy work. For starters, they kitted me out with two Nikon 35 mm cameras and some lenses and had me go around the city taking pictures of the monuments and sights, and developing and printing them back at the apartment. I mastered this fairly quickly as my boyhood friend Ratna was from the family that owned the famous Das Studios at Darjeeling, and I had picked up some basics of photography as a boy, playing in the large darkrooms of the studio.

We conducted "dead letter drop" exercises (chalk marks, drawing pins, hidey holes) at the nearby Bois de Vincennes, where Mata Hari was executed by firing squad, and where I occasionally went jogging. Foot surveillance exercises were carried out on the streets with me as the target—checking reflections in storefronts, doubling back and carrying out other evasive manoeuvres. I also practised as the surveillant or the shadow or tail—working solo, and in two- and three-man teams. It got trickier when you carried out moving surveillance on the Metro and in department stores. In one exercise, I slipped into the Printemps branch near my metro stop at the Place de la Nations, where after entering from the front at Cours de Vincennes, I took a couple of escalators up, wandered around a bit, finally doing a quick change with a soft hat and light mac that I had in a shopping bag, and left from the rear entrance undetected—*et voilà*. It may sound unconvincing, but it works in real life, better than the elaborate disguises and masks in spy movies. Keeping it simple was the watchword of my instructors.

In Peter Wright's *Spy Catcher*, his exposé of British Intelligence, he mentions the old but effective split-bamboo technique for getting a letter out of a closed envelope and also steaming kettles. But the French had raised the business of opening someone else's mail to an art form, with a wide variety of ingenious techniques. There was the "hot method" where you heated the back of an envelope with an infrared lamp, so that the glue dried to a point where it sometimes got brittle and didn't stick. They also used a "wet method," where you put the envelope in a "humid box" overnight, and the glue weakened, and you could gently pry the flap open. You could check if someone else were opening your mail by putting the suspect envelope in the "humid" box for some days, till the whole envelope fell apart at the seams and you could see if the glue on the flap had been tampered with in any way. Another, "the cold method" was to put the envelope in the freezer compartment of your refrigerator. Some glues lose their adhesive properties at low temperatures. Since different brands of envelopes used different glues, it was essential that you experimented with as many brands as possible and kept a list for future reference.

Then there was, of course, the classic steaming method. You didn't use your mother's teakettle, as the wet steam from it would make the envelope crinkle and even smudge the writing. The French had a special electric kettle with a long copper pipe spout with a heating element wrapped around it. The resultant "dry steam" would not wet or smudge the envelope. But you still had to be very careful and not over-do anything.

If, for one reason or another, none of the above techniques worked, then your last resort was the "cesarean" method, which required considerable skill and lots of practice. You cut a very fine sliver of one side of the envelope with a sharp X-Acto knife and a metal ruler and got the letter out. You always used tweezers and always wore surgical gloves. The tricky part was resealing the envelope. You slid a thin plastic triangle like a set square in the space you cut and then sliced off another tiny sliver of the back of the envelope. You then folded (this was difficult) the exposed section of the front and stuck it under the back with a minimum of transparent adhesive. You gently scuffed it down with a bit of well-used sandpaper when it dried. The whole operation was impossible without a lot of practice.

My instructor could even do a "double cesarean" on an airmail envelope with the extra lining inside. He had put together a specialized set of tools, all nicely laid out in a homemade leather case, and let me take a photograph of it. I didn't know his name, but I thought of him as Maigret. He was intelligent, meticulous and smoked a pipe. ORTF had a series running on the great Inspector's cases, which was eminently watchable and helped improve my *comme ci comme ça* spoken French.

The Tibetan Resistance and intelligence had been trained to use radio for all its communications. But by the mid-sixties, the Chinese had rolled up all our radio networks[*] inside Tibet, and we needed to find new ways to communicate with agents in the field. Furthermore,

---

[*]All radio messages from agents inside Tibet were picked up at the Charbatia Air Base near Cuttack in Orissa and relayed to the Tibet Task Force at Colorado and Langley. The CIA had set up the innocuous-sounding Aviation Research Centre (ARC) at Charbatia in 1961, specifically for this purpose, and also for conducting aerial reconnaissance flights into Tibet. Earlier,

the old codebooks we used were just too bulky and conspicuous for undercover agents in Chinese occupied towns and villages. Getting caught with one was a death warrant.

I explained our problems to the instructor from the cryptographic division of the SDECE. He told me we had to use cypher systems that could be memorized and gave me a sample range of these starting from the simple Playfair to more advanced systems we could use, depending on the skill and educational level of the agents using them. I peppered him with questions, so he let me have David Kahn's encyclopedic history of secret communications from the SDECE Library. Going through this "bible of cryptology", I was pleasantly surprised to learn that "Tibetans used a kind of cipher called '*rin-spuns*' for official correspondence; it is named for its inventor Rin-(chhen-) spuns(pa), who lived in the 1300s."[5] Sadly there was no mention of the Tibetan "poetry code" used in Imperial times. In *The Old Tibetan Chronicle* Songtsen Gampo's sister Semarkar is said to have inserted a secret message in verse she sent to her brother, which betrayed her husband, the powerful King Likmigya of Zhang-Zhung, to the Tibetan Emperor.

We moved on to another branch of communications, steganography. Whereas cryptography protects the contents of a message, steganography conceals the fact of there being a secret message at all. We started out with invisible inks. Not your lemon juice or urine of stories, that become visible under heat, but specific transparent chemicals that could be made visible only by another specific developer; also invisible fluorescent inks that could be revealed by ultraviolet or "black light."

My instructor stressed that there were differences in these chemical products from country to country, and experimentation was vital. He also gave me a list of qualities required of invisible inks, for instance, no obvious smell, easily obtainable, innocuous in appearance, not developing under heat, and so on.

Then we moved on to photographic steganography, where you could print invisible photographic messages on shirts and handkerchiefs,

---

radio messages from Tibet had been picked up by CIA listening posts in East Pakistan and Thailand.

and later develop them when they were received. All spy buffs know about the "microdot" used by the Abwehr in WWII, which was then the most effective form of steganography. My instructor explained to me that the Germans had developed a particularly sensitive kind of photographic emulsion, which resolved images on a molecular level and not on a granular level as all photographic emulsions do, so that a message on an A4 paper could be reduced to the size of a dot, less than a millimetre in diameter, and could only be read with a microscope. My instructor explained to me that the equipment and process for creating microdots were complicated and that a more convenient fallback was the "mikrat." Kodak manufactured a commercial, ultra high-resolution film called "Kodalith" for architects and graphic designers. Although it resolved images on a granular level, the grain was so fine you could reduce an A4 document to a 2 mm square, smaller than a match head. The East German Stasi used Mikrat cameras that were small and could take photos of A4 documents reduced to 1.5 to 2 mm.

The process was fairly simple. In a darkroom under a red light, you cut a piece of the film, large enough to cover the film gate on the inside of your 35 mm camera. You then closed the back and set up the camera on a tripod about six or seven feet away from the document, taped on a wall opposite. You had to experiment a bit with the distance to get the image size right. Once you exposed the film and developed and fixed it in the dark room, you got a tiny negative image of the document in the centre. You then cut and lifted this small bit of emulsion from the film base (with the trusty X-Acto knife) and transferred it to the back of a postage stamp, the flap of an envelope, or wherever you wanted.[*]

For convenient photographing of multiple documents, there was the Minox subminiature camera, made famous in many spy films. The Swiss Tessina miniature camera could also do that job, and in addition,

---

[*]The Kodalith stripping film could also be used to fix a new image over an existing passport photograph, using a chemical toning process to bleach out the original photo. The thinness of the Kodalith emulsion allowed the relief of the embossing seal on the original passport photograph to come through convincingly. Afterwards, this emulsion could be removed and the original image restored with a developing bath.

be concealed in a modified cigarette case so you could take photos of people close up without them catching on. These days the iPhone can do all that and even encrypt the images before forwarding them to your handler—in between your playing Pokémon Go, or whatever. But where is the romance in that?

The reader should not think I was overworked. I enjoyed the training and requested my instructors for more information and technical material than they initially provided me. They let me borrow a lot of books and pamphlets from the agency library. I loved the minutiae of the tradecraft though I realized, in retrospect, that I might not have had the temperament for clandestine intelligence work.

Every day we started around eight in the morning and generally finished by around one. I usually took my lunch break by the Seine with a baguette, paté or ham, pickles and a bottle of Alsace beer. My modest stipend allowed for two, three-course bistro meals a day, but I only did one, every other day. Just the range of breads at the *boulangerie* down the street ("*Bonjour Madame, une baguette s'il vous plaît*"), the cheeses, and the amazing variety of cold cuts you could pick up at the *charcuterie*, were more than a treat for me. I saved my money for shows, movies and books. I browsed the *bouquiniste* stalls by the banks of the Seine, picking up the occasional bargain. I still have my second-hand copy of Herodotus' *Histories* (Rawlinson's translation) that I bought at Shakespeare and Company for nine francs.

I walked everywhere, snapping away with my camera as my instructors wanted, always noting the streets, boulevards and landmarks, so that I could put together a dossier for a simple operation, say a document transfer, and be able to provide the agent in question with instructions on getting to the meeting point, with a detailed sketch map, with numbered visual references (photographs or sketches) of distinctive features, crossings and tricky turns *en route*. They called this the "British Patrol Method."

In those days, museums and monuments were not very crowded, and bags and cameras were not a problem. Museums were also free on most days. I only paid for the Rodin Museum and the Musée de l'Armée at the Invalides if I remember correctly. Around evening

I would wander around the Champs-Élysées, or the Left Bank, or Montparnasse, have a drink, catch a movie or head to North Paris for couscous or tagine. By the end of my stay, I could honestly say I knew the city inside out.

In Hemingway's *A Moveable Feast,* the posthumously published account of his years as a struggling writer in Paris, he declares, "If you are lucky enough to have lived in Paris as a young man, then wherever you go for the rest of your life it stays with you, for Paris is a moveable feast." He didn't exactly explain what he meant by a "moveable feast," but if he was saying that your sublime memories of this beautiful city would be with you always, wherever you were, he got it dead right.

Every morning at seven, I'd be at an outside table at the café in front of my building. I'd have a large cup of *café au lait*, with, now and then, a shot of Calvados on the side. I'd smoke my first *Royale* and work on the crossword puzzle in yesterday's *International Herald Tribune*, and sometimes re-read Art Buchwald's column if he had been particularly funny or incisive. There would be, of course, besides the Dubonnet ashtray, my notebook and pen, for those moments of inspiration that "*La Ville Lumière*" had granted so many expatriate writers.

The last four months of my training were spent at the village of La Valette near Toulouse with the fifty-two-year old Sinologue, Jean Golfin, who was an SDECE consultant on China. As a young man, he had served in the colonial service in Indochina and later taught Chinese history at the University of Toulouse. He had retired to carry out his own research and write his three books[6] on China. Jean was to give me a run down on the history of Communist China and educate me on all its various institutions.

He also worked with me to create a system for debriefing agents and refugees from Tibet. The SDECE had provided us with a specimen text, a NATO manual for debriefing escapees from behind the Iron Curtain. It offered a wide range of questions, many of which might never occur to one, off hand. These were all categorized into sections that covered industry, transport, communications, economy, education, culture, military, politics, and subsections within that, so that nothing was overlooked by the interrogator. We worked on such a manual for China and Tibet, with Jean filling in those specific areas where French intelligence particularly wanted more information.

Our workplace was his farmhouse kitchen, which had an enormous open fireplace with an iron swivel arm for holding pots. We sat around his old kitchen/dining table, where he unhurriedly worked on producing simple rural meals: *pot-au-feu, cassoulet, coq au vin* and so on, the recipes for which I jotted down in my notebook, along with the professor's musings on the on-going "*pi Lin pi* Kong"* campaign in China. We drank the local rouge, *Troubadour*, a magnificent plonk, three bottles of which I cycled over to the village tavern every day to collect. The only thing with Jean that I might have questioned, but which I never did, was his habit of tucking the baguette tightly under his armpit to carve off individual slices with the kitchen knife. I suppose it was a kind of country thing.

Back in Dharamshala, we worked out a two-pronged strategy to best put to use the new French support. TORA, or the Tibetan Office of Research and Analysis, was set up under the directorship of Lodi Gyari, with myself filling in as head of China desk. This required me to bring my personal library on China, which I had built up over the years, down to the new TORA office at Gangchen Kyishong. Our standard fare of agent reports and escapee briefs were supplemented by issues of the *Survey of China Mainland Press* (SCMP), and *Selections from China Mainland Magazines* (SCMM) regularly published by the U.S. Consulate General in Hong Kong, which also contained news reports and articles on Tibet and other minority nationalities. But going through all those arcane texts from the PRC (even in English translation) dense with Maoist rhetoric and Marxist ideological clichés, made my eyes glaze over. Simon Leys has noted that reading such literature from the mainland was ". . . akin to swallowing sawdust by the bucketful."

---

*'Criticize Lin Biao Criticize Confucius (*Kong Fuzi*)' campaign 1973–76. In Tibet, this had a secondary manifestation, the 'Criticize Dalai Criticize Panchen' campaign (Chinese, *pi da, pi pan*).

But Jean Golfin had made me study some issues of another newsletter, a weekly one, from Hong Kong. It was put together by the Hungarian Jesuit priest, László Ladány, whose analysis relied on Chinese sources, but which he used to shrewdly penetrate the surreal world of the People's Republic. In the 10 August 1962, issue of *China News Analysis*, Ladány noted the existence of the massive famine resulting from Mao's Great Leap Forward and offered a "realistic estimate" of fifty million deaths. This was based on letters sent from the Chinese mainland and on refugee reports. I had found my Rosetta Stone.

Though I enjoyed the research, I saw myself as a field man, and the French had wanted us to find new avenues of getting hard intelligence. I approached Lhamo Tsering, who was, at the time, working with the Indian Research and Analysis Wing (RAW) in Delhi, about training agents for an entirely new kind of network. He agreed with me that a fresh approach was needed. He mentioned that a number of camps at Mustang were being closed, and the old fighters were sent down to retirement homes at Marpha and Pokhara. One of those camps would be ideal for a secret training base.

I gave him a full rundown of my training in France. He enjoyed hearing about the techniques, methods and technology I had acquired, different in quite a few ways from the tradecraft he had learned from the Americans. He was particularly pleased when I told him about the alternative possibilities for agent communication that the French had trained me in. He was desperate for something to replace his radio networks that the Chinese had rolled up.

"We set up such networks from as far west as Ngari to the south-east in Kongpo in places like Dzongkha, Tsela Dzong, Tsethang, Shelkar, Rutok and other places.* We also had an agent in Lhasa in a very sensitive position. Each of these networks worked around a radio operator. But, one by one, these teams were blown, and the networks rolled up by Chinese counter-intelligence. They were extremely vigilant

---

*My informant from Chatreng, Tenzing Tsultim (and his associate Nima Gyalpo) had run few such networks in 1964 that covered Solokhumbu, Nangpala, Rutok, Dingri, Shelkar, Ngamring and Lhatse—around five districts.

and effective. The Communist Party controlled every little detail of people's daily life in Tibet—like in no other place on earth. We knew a network was blown when the signals stopped, or when the operator used a different call sign. All our operators had been given a secret call sign to use if captured and forced to contact us—to draw us into a 'double-cross' gambit. The Chinese counter-intelligence made one radio-operator in Kongpo signal us for over a year. We kept up the game on our end as it gave the agent time to survive. That our networks lasted as long as they did was, in a way, a testimony to the courage, determination and skill of our agents."

Wangdü had come to India to urge the exile government to seek funding for the Force. I approached him, and he was highly amused that we had managed to get the French to support us. He agreed to let us have a vacant camp at Mustang to train agents and promised us the rations, weapons and equipment we would need. Two young Tibetans, Lhasang Tsering and Gyalpo Tsering, came down from Mustang to help me put the whole project together. They were both graduates from Christian schools—Wynberg Allen School in Mussoorie and Dr Graham's Homes in Kalimpong, respectively, and had a year earlier, volunteered to serve at Mustang. We travelled around schools and colleges where young Tibetans were studying. We wanted recruits who had a grasp of mathematics, chemistry, and geography. We also purchased the necessary equipment, chemicals, books, and so on that would be needed for the training. The exile government was less than enthusiastic, but we were finally able to overcome most problems.

A week before our proposed departure date for Mustang, there was bad news. We were told that the Nepalese police had arrested Lhamo Tsering (19 April 1974) at the Annapurna Hotel. He had been traveling to inspect the new carpet-weaving centres, shops and animal husbandry farms at Pokhara. As these projects were part of the announced demobilization of the Mustang Force, to which the Nepalese Home Ministry had given its blessings, the arrest came as a complete surprise. The Nepalese now began amassing an infantry brigade at Pokhara of about five thousand men.

We all assumed that Chinese pressure was behind Nepal's move, especially as the king had made his first trip to China in December of 1973. Moreover, Nepal was now receiving some aid from China. But China experts, especially in America, took the view that China had long regarded the Mustang Force as inconsequential. Mao valued the new relationship with America and would not do anything to affect it adversely.

But a well-documented study by a Nepali journalist and Fulbright Scholar reveals that China had, in fact, pressured Nepal to act. Nepal had always chafed under the "special relationship" it had to accept with its giant southern neighbour. The situation worsened during Mrs Gandhi's premiership with her showing "displeasure" at the young king, Birendra, on his first visit to India in October 1973. He had voiced Nepal's desire to have an equal relationship with both India and China, a month earlier at a Non-Aligned Nations Conference in Algeria.

> In December, Birendra carried his new foreign policy outlook to Beijing where he held extensive talks with Chairman Mao Zedong. Sympathetic to the Royal message, Mao broached the potential of a Beijing-Lhasa train service that might ultimately be extended to the Nepalese border to link the two countries economically and physically. However, Mao told Birendra that the Khampa rebels were posing a major obstacle to better relations. Although American support to the Tibetan rebels had dried up, the Chinese leader had continuing reasons for concern. The Soviets had been in touch with Tibetan refugees in Nepal and in India and had stepped up their propaganda war against the Chinese occupation.[7]

The Nepalese now began moving their troops to Pokhara. According to Conboy and Morrison, "All their troops were green. The ranking officer at Jomsom, Brigadier Singha, had absolutely no combat experience. 'None of us did,' added company commander, Gyanu Babu Adhikari." Major Gyanu also admitted, "The Khampas had better weapons than we did . . . and better terrain."[8]

Gurkhas have the deserved reputation as fierce fighting men, but the fittest young recruits in Nepal were invariably enrolled in the British

Gurkhas, while the Indian Army recruited the bulk of able young men in Nepal. The Nepalese Army, where pay and conditions were poor, only received low-quality recruits from the non-martial tribes of Nepal. Lhamo Tsering confirmed this assessment in an interview.

"The Nepalese had five to six thousand soldiers in Jomsom, but the morale of the troops and officers was very low. Everyone in our Force had agreed not to surrender. Plans were prepared to destroy the Nepalese army base at Jomsom, and the airfield and the one small Russian transport plane they were using. The plane made about two trips daily to Pokhara and back. We had a few advantages. We were holding the high ground and all the critical points in that area. We had ample supplies of food grain at our supply depots at Kag Beni and Tsug—more than two years supply for the entire Force. Furthermore, every one of the sixteen camps (*detsen*), spread out over Mustang, had a year's supply of food grain in stock for their immediate needs. So, all things considered, we could hold out for three years, at the very least.

I am convinced that if we had attacked the Nepalese at the time, we would have succeeded without too much trouble. But I did worry somewhat about the death and casualties, and the suffering it would cause the local people.

"In my jail cell, I got a secret message informing me that our men were going to pull a surprise raid at Jomsom to rescue me. Plans had been made, and everyone was ready to go. Gyen Rakra would lead the raid, and I was to stay ready. I managed to get a message to them instructing them to cancel the operation. The chance of things going wrong and Nepalese troops being killed was high, which would definitely worsen the situation. I was in no immediate danger, and I was sure we could, in time, come to an agreement with the Nepalese government, where I would be released for some concession."

The Force had contacted the exile government in Dharamshala and requested a Kashag minister to travel to Mustang to negotiate with the Nepalese Government, and bring outside pressure to bear so that Tibetan refugees in Kathmandu and elsewhere in the country would not be persecuted by Nepali officialdom. Nepal relied heavily on Foreign Aid, especially from the West and the United Nations, far more than what they received from China. The Tibetans had good connections with the UNHCR, and it would have been possible to bring a UN official and even a journalist or two up to Mustang to monitor the negotiations.

Dharamshala sent the Minister for Security, P.T. Takla, the Dalai Lama's brother-in-law, with a taped message from His Holiness. He was accompanied by the Dalai Lama's representative in Nepal. When they arrived at the Kalsang Phug headquarters, a meeting was held at the prayer-hall where commander Wangdü and all the other officers and instructors were gathered. Before any discussions could begin, Takla switched on the tape recorder and played the Dalai Lama's message. In the message, the Dalai Lama thanked the Mustang commanders and soldiers for their patriotism and sacrifice, and then ordered them to surrender their weapons to the Nepalese government.

Everyone in the prayer-hall was stunned. For a moment, there was dead silence, then Gyen Rakra Gyadhar, the commander of the first *detsen*, stood up and said he would not be able to obey this order. Another commander, Chatreng Gyurme, stood up and made the same declaration. Commander Dargön Pachen, who was in charge of security, walked out of the hall and to the courtyard outside (another account says to his own room) and pulling out his knife, cut his own throat. All the other commanders were in tears but could not bring themselves to disobey the Dalai Lama.

In the next few days, Takla and his assistant travelled from one *detsen* to another and played the Dalai Lama's message, causing two more suicides. According to Lhamo Tsering, an officer of the Fifth *detsen* and Chatreng Gyurme's secretary, Tsewang, both committed suicide, drowning in the Kali Gandaki River. I heard reports of other suicides and some men going mad and leaping off cliffs.

With the Force now in complete disarray, Wangdü had no choice but to negotiate with the Nepalese. He offered to surrender half his weapons first and give up the remainder on the release of Lhamo Tsering. The Nepalese leaders in Jomsom agreed to the deal. "As promised, two days later, half the rebels surrendered their weapons in Jomsom. Wangdü waited for the news that Lhamo Tsering had been freed. The news never came. The Nepalese Army reneged on their deal"[9] according to an American observer in Nepal.

Lhamo Tsering told me he was taken to Marpha as the weather was bad at Jomsom, and then put on their helicopter and flown to Pokhara and prison. Accompanying him to Pokhara was the minister Takla, who, in spite of Wangdü's request to remain at Kalsang Phug and help see the negotiations through, claimed he had to attend an important religious conference in Japan, where he would be representing the Dalai Lama.

Now the Nepalese Army came after Gyen Wangdü. He and his men headed west from Mustang into the Dolpo region of Nepal. In *Resistance Vol. 8*, Lhamo Tsering gives us a list of the names of twenty-eight officers and twenty-six fighters who accompanied Wangdu. They were all mounted and well-armed and had in addition thirty-four mules to carry their supplies. The Nepalese had sent out radio alerts to their army and police units in a number of the crossings in that area. The Khampas made their way into Tibet and almost immediately clashed with a PLA patrol but survived the encounter unscathed. They rode on for some days, finally crossing back into Nepal in the Mugu district. Hopscotching back and forth a couple of times between Tibet and Nepal, they made their final entry into Nepal in the northern Humla district, and then made their final run west towards the Indian border. By the end of August (September, according to Conboy and Morrison), they finally came close to the border, where the frontiers of India, Nepal and Tibet converged around the high Tingkar-la or "White Cloud Pass" (17,697 ft). After the final ascent of this pass, it was only a brief distance downhill to the Indian side of the border.

The Tibetans did not know it, but the Nepalese had set up an ambush at the rocky heights of the pass. They already had a company of riflemen posted in the area, but according to a Nepalese informant, the army had, a few days earlier, airlifted more troops on their one Russian transport helicopter. These were all members of their elite unit trained by the Israelis and armed with Belgian FAL automatic rifles.

It was a bright sunny day, and Wangdü was in high spirits, clearly in anticipation of reaching India. This information was later given to Lhamo Tsering by Ashangma (aka Sonam Chogyal) a cook and dogsbody at Kalsang Phug. He narrowly survived the shoot-out and was jailed in Kathmandu Central with Lhamo Tsering and others.

Wangdü and his men took a break at the bottom of the pass and had a meal of tsampa and yak meat. The horses and mules were allowed to graze. When the main body of men finished packing their gear, Wangdü and six others, including Ashangma, rode ahead. When they got near the top of the pass, a deadly crossfire opened up. Ashangma remembered a bullet hitting his right arm and his horse being shot and sinking to the ground, all at the same time. He saw his comrades being struck by a hail of bullets and falling around him. Only Wangdü appeared not to have been hit by the initial fusillade. He had his Bura rifle in one hand and with the other urged his horse on up the pass, towards the Nepalese position. He did not get far. Concentrated rifle and machine-gun fire cut down his horse and hit Wangdü multiple times.

The rest of the twenty-odd men had by now made it up the rise where the fighting was taking place. They started firing at the Nepalese and engaged them for about an hour. But the Nepalese troops had the advantage of height and though the Khampas found some cover behind the surrounding rocks, took a few casualties. Finally, realizing that Wangdü and the other six had been killed (Ashangma was playing dead behind his horse), they made a staggered withdrawal. The Nepalese troops did not follow them. They took a more southern route across the mountains and made it safely to India.

Besides Wangdü, five other fighters Rapten Gyatso, Tamding Tsering, Tsering Rhithar, and Tsering Namgyal, were killed in the initial surprise attack. Only Ashangma survived. Some men were wounded in the subsequent firefight but managed to get away with the main body of fighters. Wangdü's body was taken to Kathmandu. His personal effects: wristwatch, Beretta pistol, dagger, rifle, binoculars and *ghawu* amulet were displayed at a tented exhibition at the Tundikhel field in the centre of the city. Also on display were the surrendered weapons of the Mustang Force: recoilless rifles, BAR's, mortars, radio-sets, machine guns, Garand rifles, etc.

* * *

I have never been able to understand why Wangdü just rode into that final, fatal trap. It was so unlike him to take a chance like that on open ground in broad daylight. I travelled with him several times, acting as his translator with the Nepalese, and it often struck me how careful he always was—to the point of being obsessive. Night marches were his thing, and to be honest, I cursed him under my breath whenever we chose to do that. He often varied his routine and used alternate routes that were invariably more difficult and punishing. My first march to Mustang from Pokhara became a nightmare because he insisted on travelling at night in a monsoon downpour—through a jungle. But that was how he survived for so long.

When on the move, even in *netsang* rooms, he never took off his clothes or his boots when going to bed. He would wash his feet, put on a clean pair of socks, put his boots back on and go to bed. His pistol was strapped to his waist all the time. He leaned his rifle by the head of his bed, so he could reach for it easily. He also kept a small tumbler of *arak* by his bedstead, as he had problems sleeping. He even wore his forage cap to bed.

He drank very little, did not smoke but bummed an occasional cigarette off me. He would let down his guard, now and then. He liked to talk and enjoyed a bit of gossip. He had an eye for the ladies and asked me many questions about Tibetan women in exile—e.g. Did I know the Dalai Lama's younger sister? "Yes." Was she fast? "No!" He also asked me about the girls at the Dance and Drama Society and made me promise to introduce them to him when he came down to Dharamshala. In those moments, he was intensely human. You could see he missed having a regular life, with a wife and a family, or at least a girlfriend. He had lived all his life fighting, and most of relatives, friends and sidekicks had been killed over the years, in one battle or another. He did have a short fuse, and his CIA handlers and some Khampa leaders had problems with him, but he and I got along fine, most of the time. The memory of Gyen Wangdü that remains with me is not that of my commander or the great resistance hero. I see him sitting happily on a deckchair in the sun at the Fish Tail Lodge at Pokhara, dark glasses perched on his nose and a Nepali *topi* at a rakish angle on his head. He raises a frosted can of Kirin beer to toast my signing up for Mustang. He was forty-four when he died.

38

MAO IS DEAD! LONG LIVE MAO!

Mao died on 9 September 1976. The formal announcement was made by the Central People's Broadcasting Station at 4 p.m. and transmitted across China. The radio message was relayed throughout cities, towns and villages—blaring and inescapable—over millions of loudspeakers: in classrooms, halls, dormitories, barracks and prisons, on bamboo poles high over rooftops, street corners, rice fields, grasslands and the vast, far-flung archipelago of *Laogai* labour camps—as effective, inexorable and soul-destroying as the ubiquitous telescreens in Orwell's totalitarian world of *1984*—minus the sci-fi-tech feature.

People living in Tibet at the time told me that even before fully absorbing the implications of the news, their overriding concern was not to reveal their feelings to those around them. Decades of practice had, of course, made them skilled at this. But now and then, someone would slip up. A friend of mine from Lhasa (who is still there in an official position of some consequence, so no names will be revealed) told me that his work unit had to stand to attention, out in the sun for a full day, as a mark of respect for the departed Chairman. They lined up in formation and took off their caps. Immediately in front of my friend was someone with a large bald patch on the crown of his head. As the fierce Tibetan sun got higher and stronger, the back of the bald man's head began to redden, and beads of sweat started to trickle down his neck. My informant was standing alongside a friend of his who on noticing the discomfort of the person before them, started to go into a fit of giggles. This affected my informant too, who desperately tried to control himself. His friend, unfortunately, lacked similar resolve. After a desperate struggle, he burst out in a loud fit of laughter. He got eight years of "Reform through Labour."

A former incarnate lama friend, Tenor-la, now living in Washington DC, told me this story. As an ex-prisoner, he was part of a probation labour unit (*layme-rukha*) in a village outside Lhasa. "Our team leader was an older woman, and although no better off than the other wretched ex-prisoners in our unit, she was a real *hur-tsunba* (Chinese, *jijifenzi*). This was in the period just after the Cultural Revolution when everyone had been reduced to a hungry ghost (*yidak*) like state, and we had barely recovered from the second famine. Our work unit heard the news of Mao's death over the loudspeakers when we were out in the fields. Everyone responded predictably, doffing their caps, lowering their heads, and keeping their thoughts to themselves. Except for the *hur-tsunba*.

"She started off predictably, weeping and wailing. Gradually she worked herself up to a hysterical frenzy, screaming and shrieking at the top of her voice, eventually climaxing in total collapse. She lay on the ground, foaming at the mouth, only an occasional convulsion or moan indicating she had not completely left this world. Her co-workers, including the Lama, carried her to her shack and laid her on her earthen pallet bed. One of them pointed out that her 'wind' condition had to be lowered. Tibetans believe an imbalance in the 'wind humor' or *loong* is the cause of hysteria. Someone else volunteered the traditional cure for 'wind imbalance'—massaging the temples (*yama*) of the head with butter. The supine *hur-tsunpa* paused a moment in her moaning. Raising her head, she wailed, 'There is no butter in this house'."

A universe away in Dharamshala, Mao's death also got me into trouble. With the end of the Mustang resistance, the exile government wanted nothing more to do with spy networks or working with French intelligence. One minister suggested I meet my French contact in Delhi and ask him to let us use their funding for refugee resettlement work.

I then decided to leave government service and work full-time for the Tibetan Youth Congress (TYC), which, against all odds, was doing everything it could to sustain the struggle for Tibetan independence. Since the exile parliament was as woefully tame as the Kashag, the TYC began to play the role of an unofficial but loyal opposition.

One of my tasks as a member of the TYC Executive Committee was to put together the English language edition of its news journal *Rangzen* (*Independence*). I had pretty much free rein except for the editorial, where I consulted with other executive members.

When Mao died, everyone in the Tibetan world was thrilled, literally adrenalized in an uncontrollable way. Tea shops and restaurants in the exile community buzzed with speculation about how this long-awaited moment would galvanize our national struggle. Everyone expected, at the very least, an emergency national conference. To our disbelief, the exile government, in particular the four-man cabinet, the Kashag, showed no sign of having heard about the passing of Tibet's greatest scourge. Weeks, even a month passed, and not a single Kashag meeting took place. I pestered the cabinet secretary for updates, but he just shrugged his shoulder in resignation.

The Kashag of the early exile government had been filled with ministers and officials from Tibet, who, despite their unfamiliarity with the modern world, were nonetheless relatively experienced politicians and administrators. But a vicious power struggle in the sixties involving Gyalo Thondup, the Dalai Lama's older brother, forced these senior officials out of office. For a while, Gyalo Thondup set himself up as the preeminent leader in the exile world, but an inevitable confrontation with the Dalai Lama, in the late sixties forced Thondup's retirement to Hong Kong.* The Kashag in Dharamshala was now occupied by inexperienced, insecure, second-tier personnel who, in spite of their

---

*For a detailed account of this crucial period in exile in Tibetan history, see my 2016 post "Untangling a Mess of Petrified Noodles II" in *Shadow Tibet*, https://bit.ly/2muxVpn.

sincerity and loyalty, were often overwhelmed by the larger political issues and, as might be expected, adopted a reflexive head-in-the-sand approach to such matters.

Something had to be done. I made my play in the editorial of the forthcoming *Rangzen*. Borrowing from Zola's celebrated polemic, "*J'accuse*" that appeared in the socialist newspaper *L'Aurore*, during the Dreyfus Affair, I started every paragraph of my piece, not with the finger-pointing "*J'accuse*" but with the declaration "Mao is Dead!" The accusations followed. Though the prose was somewhat excruciating, and the style, admittedly laboured, the charges against the Tibetan government of ignoring crucial developments in China and Tibet (even the death of Mao) while focusing on petty issues of exile politics, resettlements camps, religious rituals and the like, had substance—and it infuriated the cabinet.

The entire Central Committee of the TYC was hauled up before the Kashag. I've forgotten the details of the discussion but remember a sarcastic and repeated comment. "What can you youngsters do against Communist China when more experienced and courageous people have failed? Please, let us know?" Before we were allowed to leave, one minister made a not so veiled threat that the privilege TYC enjoyed in recruiting members from exile schools, and government offices might have to be reconsidered.

We held a special meeting of the full TYC leadership with presidents and secretaries from all the chapters throughout India and Nepal. We decided to take up the Kashag's challenge. An ambitious strategy of international campaigns and activism was worked out, which would be kicked off with a monster rally on 10 March before the Chinese Embassy in New Delhi. The TYC reached out to other organizations in the exile world and also Tibetan university students and the refugee community in Delhi that survived largely by selling sweaters, running small eateries and (illegal) chang shops. Some radical monk activists now joined the leadership. One was the Ladakhi monk politician and social worker, Lama Lobzang, another the most venerable Thupten Jungney, aka "Goser" Lama, from Ngö-Gyamtsoling in Kham, who, for his physical girth, threadbare robes and happy indomitable activism was dubbed the "Friar Tuck" of the Rangzen Movement. Our treasurer was a prosperous restaurateur and *thangka* painter, Amdo Phuntsok (of Rebkong), who paid all our bills out of his own pocket, and told us we could reimburse him eventually, when we could. A Coordination Committee (*zungdril-tsokchung*) was set up of leaders from various organizations and communities.

Our plan was to assemble some thousand demonstrators outside the Chinese Embassy and, charging through the police cordon, physically take over the place. This would, of course, make international news and definitely provoke a furious response from the Chinese Government. The response would, we hoped, arouse all Tibetans, especially those inside Tibet. It was a simple plan and a good one but had not taken into account the new political reality in India.

Prime Minister Indira Gandhi had, a year earlier, assumed extraordinary "Emergency" powers, conducting a draconian crackdown on civil liberties, the media and political opposition throughout India, particularly in Delhi—which film-maker Satyajit Ray said had become "a nightmare city at that point." The Tibetan community had not been directly affected by the Emergency, hence our oversight. Now we were to learn our lesson. Tens of thousands of Delhi police and the Central Reserve Police descended on the Tibetan refugee camp and before the Chinese Embassy. The demonstrators battled it out with the police but were overwhelmed and hauled off to Delhi Central Jail.

When the many hundreds of bruised and dispirited Tibetans entered the jail compound, they were confronted by a scary giant of a prisoner. Stepping out of his private cell (which boasted a color TV set), he demanded to know what was going on. He was the *dada*, the prison boss and formerly a bandit, and now serving life for multiple murders. The Tibetans explained their national struggle to him as best as they could, and why they had been arrested. The *dada* now proceeded to lecture them. "Why are you all looking so miserable? For me, this is a place of shame, a jail. For you all this is a royal palace, a palace! (*Hindi, terey leay mahal hai, mahal*)" he declared, perhaps alluding to India's founding fathers who had all served time in British jails. He then got them to sing the Tibetan national anthem every morning and shout their slogans. One peeved Tibetan asked, "Who's going to hear us inside these walls?" Our *dada* pointed to the sky and said simply "The one up there will hear you (Hindi, *oopar wala sunayga*)."

Those of us who escaped the police roundup now worked on hiring lawyers and contacting friendly Indian politicians to free our compatriots. We sent out urgent appeals to all Tibetan communities in exile, calling on them to send volunteers to Delhi so we could carry out the next phase of our campaign—a seven-person hunger strike "to death" before the office of the United Nations Information Center, with a successive batches of volunteers to replace them when they died or were taken to hospital. Our one demand for the United Nations was that it implement the three resolutions on Tibet (1959, 1961 and 1965), calling "for the cessation of practices which deprive the Tibetan people of their fundamental human rights and freedoms, including their right to self-determination."[1]

We managed to set up a large awning and platform directly across the UN office at the Lodi Estate, and installed our first batch of seven hunger strikers, all in white Gandhian *khadi kurtas* with large, framed portraits of the Mahatma and the Dalai Lama behind them. We knew the police would raid the place in force soon and there was nothing we could do to stop them, except gather as many Tibetans as we could to battle the cops. A suggestion was made to put a box of dynamite under the platform and threaten to blow ourselves up if the police attacked us. We immediately sent someone to Dharamshala to steal a box of the stuff from the local slate quarry or bribe some workers there. But that would take four or five days, and we probably didn't have the time. Nonetheless, we voted unanimously to hold out.

Then five days after the start of the hunger strike Prime Minister Indira Gandhi, in a completely unexpected turn of events, ordered the release of all political prisoners, called for fresh elections and on 23 March 1977, officially ended the Emergency. Policemen now vanished from the streets. Journalists, an almost extinct species, began to emerge in the clear light of post-emergency freedom. They dropped by the hunger-strike camp and began interviewing everyone they could. Foreign reporters and TV news teams began to appear. The American

Embassy warmly received a delegation from us. We were assured that President Carter would be fully briefed on the legitimacy of the Tibetan issue and the need for American support on the question of human rights in Tibet. Just a couple of months earlier, Carter had declared that human rights would be "the central concern" of U.S. Foreign Policy. When it rains, it pours. It was wonderful.

Then national elections were held, and Mrs. Gandhi and the Congress Party were wiped out. The spanking new Janata Party, loaded with opposition leaders, mostly all veteran Tibet supporters (and members of the Parliamentary Group for Tibet), now came to power. Freshly released from jail, many of them visited the hunger strike camp. I recall three of them: Atal Bihari Vajpayee (future foreign minister and prime minister), Raj Narain (future health minister), and George Fernandes (future defense minister).

Goser Lama, TYC president Lodi Gyari, and I, pushing our way through a horde of journalists, politicians and aides, got to meet Jayaprakash Narayan, Mrs. Gandhi's nemesis, and the leader of the Janata Party, when he came to Delhi to form the new government, and select the new prime minister. J.P. as he was reverentially known throughout India, was an old, unwavering and outspoken friend of Tibet.* He now promised us that the new government of India would do everything to support the cause of a free Tibet. The next day, Surendra Mohan, the general secretary of the Janata Party dashed off a cable to the UN secretariat in New York, calling for a General Assembly meeting to discuss the implementation of the three resolutions on Tibet.

The formal ending of the hunger strike was presided over by the Gandhian socialist leader, Acharya Kripalani, another outspoken

---

*'In view of the unquestioned right to self-determination for all nations, it is sad to find that, even outside the ranks of the apologists, the argument about Chinese suzerainty being trotted out to deny this birthright to Tibet. It is sadder still to find countries that only recently fought for and won their independence taking shelter behind a moth-eaten, imperialistic formula to deny Tibet what they had claimed for themselves.' *Jayaprakash Narayan—A Centenary Volume*, New Delhi, 2005.

champion* of Tibetan freedom. He was the president of the Indian National Congress when India became independent. I was tasked with escorting this veteran freedom fighter to the hunger strike camp, sitting by his side when he spoke and supporting him when he offered lime juice to our volunteers to break their strike. It was an important and memorable moment for me.

No other Tibetan action in India had received so much publicity since 1959. The strike was given extensive coverage, not just in Indian and international papers, but by various foreign radio and television networks as well. Every exile Tibetan was galvanized by this movement, and sympathy strikes took place, not only in India, but also abroad. The Coordination Committee, the leadership of this new Tibetan mass movement, went to Dharamshala, where we presented the exile government all the letters and documents of support we had received from senior Indian leaders and ministers. We urged the Kashag and the exile parliament to conduct immediate follow-up meetings with India's new leaders and lock them into the commitments they had made.

But, as I wrote subsequently, in a somewhat despairing article in the *Tibetan Review*, "However, Dharamshala condemned this mass movement, branded its leaders as 'spies and traitors', denigrated the pledge of the Janata Party as 'useless', and in the name of the Dalai Lama, forbade any patriotic movement of this sort."[2] Furthermore, all the members of the Central Executive Committee, including president Lodi Gyari and myself, were forced to resign to prevent the Dalai Lama

---

*In refuting Nehru's argument in Parliament for not recognizing Tibet's sovereignty, Kripalani said, "The plea is that China had the ancient right of suzerainty. This right was out of date, old and antiquated. It is not right in these days of democracy by which our Communists friends swear, by which the Chinese swear, to talk of this ancient suzerainty and exercise it in a new shape in a country that has and had nothing to do with China. I consider this as much a colonial aggression on the part of China as any indulged in by Western nations. In this age of democracy, when we hold that all people should be free and equal, I say that China's occupation of Tibet is a deliberate act of aggression."

from coming out and denouncing the Tibetan Youth Congress and ending its existence in the exile world.

For some time, my anger and bitterness led me to conclude that the exile government had acted out of its usual stupidity and pettiness, but later, on reflection, came to realize that there was another underlying reason why Dharamshala might not have wanted a revival of the freedom struggle, or even India's open support for Tibet's independence.

The first indication of this had already appeared in the Dalai Lama's 10 March address in 1973, though it did not register on most of us then. "The aim of the struggle of the Tibetans outside Tibet is the attainment of the happiness of the Tibetan people. If the Tibetans in Tibet are truly happy under Chinese rule then there is no reason for us here in exile to argue otherwise."[3]

In April, a secret meeting was held in Hong Kong between a Tibetan minister and a Chinese official, brokered by our old missionary friend and self-appointed international wheeler-dealer, George Patterson. In his memoirs, *Patterson of Tibet*, he writes: "The substance of the talks was not divulged to me by either party, but I was able to gather that the Chinese wanted to discuss the possibilities of the Dalai Lama's return to Tibet, and what conditions would be required."[4]

We do not know if this meeting led to further developments but following the death of Mao and the first stirrings of change inside China, a more hopeful period began for the Dalai Lama's policy to reconcile with China. In Tibet, it was signaled with considerable fanfare. Twenty-four (twenty-three according to Bhusang) important prisoners were released from Sangyip and Drapchi prison. These were according to *Beijing Review* ". . . officials of the former local government in Tibet, living Buddhas and former commanders of local rebel forces."[5] Bhusang was to be in the next group.

* * *

"All of us prisoners were eaten up with excitement, though we were careful not to show it, when on the occasion of the Chinese National Day, October 1st, twenty-three aristocrats were released from Sangyip.

Outside the prison walls was a block of huts where ex-prisoners in probation work teams (*layme-rukhag*) lived. These were carpenters, tailors, labourers and so on, legally free, but still having to report to the authorities at the end of every workday. Next to the probation work team block was a large hut, called the prison guesthouse but was more like a transit hut. It was here that the released aristocrats were housed. Most of these ex-prisoners were from our own prison, but some were brought here from Drapchi. Their release on October 1st was made much of officially and extensively publicized throughout Tibet and China.

"The rest of the prisoners now began to secretly hope that they might be next on the list. I didn't hold out much hope for myself as I knew that my record was poor, but the excitement even got to me. On the morning of October 5th, after we prisoners had drunk our black tea and eaten some tsampa, a cadre walked up before us carrying a sheet of paper and read out ten names. Mine was on it. We were told to go out to the *layme-rukhag* block and clean out the guest house, which was now empty as the first group of twenty-three aristocrats had left by then. That was all we were told. Nothing more. So, the ten of us went out with brooms and mops and cleaned out the guesthouse/transit hut. After we had finished and reported back to the cadre, he told us to take our bedding and stuff and move over to the hut. That was when we realized something unusual was going on.

"After we moved our things to the transit hut, the chief cadre (Chinese, *shouxi ganbu*) came over and told us that we had been released from prison. That was all. There were no formalities, nothing. No courts or magistrates. No legal documents—nothing at all—just the chief cadre's announcement. I couldn't believe him at all. There had to be some devious trick behind this announcement. The Chinese always lied. You could never trust them, never. A few of the silly and weak prisoners in our group, the usual *hur-tsunpa*s, became terribly excited. The rest of us remained silent, deadpan. Later, alone among ourselves, we talked a bit, but we were careful not to hope for anything. The Chinese were so devious that we Tibetans were no match for them when it came to this sort of shit trickery. Two days later we were issued new clothes—one cotton trouser, one shirt and a cotton cap. We were also issued new blankets and quilts. These were of the poorest quality, but at least they were new. For seventeen years now, I had been wearing the grimiest of rags, patched over and over again. You could not see anything of the original material. We were later issued a jacket and pants, also made of this inferior cotton. The Chinese called this cotton suit worn by the poorest labourers, *lao dong bu*.

"Then we were subjected to a course of political re-education. The chief cadre opened the discussion. "You are being released because most of you have accepted the Party's advice and direction and have successfully reformed. Of course, there are a few of you who are as unrelenting and stubborn as ever. But the decision to release all of you has been made as an exceptional policy of Party forgiveness, so this time even those bad elements will be given leniency by the Central Government.

"Another evening, a *kuotang*, a senior official, gave a talk where he said that the policies of the People's Government had been directed towards the reforming and transformation of criminals like us, even stubborn and unrelenting elements like myself. He mentioned me by name and wagged his finger in warning. 'Bhusang has three negative qualities that have not changed even with years of political education and the kindness of the government. Of all the prisoners in Sangyip he has the worst mental attitude, worst work-record and the worst record of reform. It is up to us to help him realize the errors of his ways, reform him and make this exceptional policy of Party forgiveness a success. Otherwise, even after his release, he will have to be brought back to prison. So, everyone must criticize him vigorously and force him to acknowledge his mistakes and crimes."

I am not making up what the cadre said. Lhagyari Trichen was with me at this meeting, so was Chamtsun la. He works at the Dalai Lama's private office these days. You can ask them. We were kept at the transit hut for over a month.

"Then the ten of us, along with the previous group of twenty-three aristocrats, were taken together on a sightseeing tour to show us the great changes that had been brought about in Tibet by Communism.

One aristocrat from the twenty-three couldn't come, so there were thirty-two of us in total. Travelling with us were important Chinese and Tibetan officials, cadres, journalists, photographers and documentary film-makers to record this momentous tour. We travelled in two buses and a jeep. We were first taken on a tour of Lhasa and then driven to Kongpo, where we were shown the vast apple and peach orchards and the settlements there. We knew all these trees had been planted by Tibetan prisoners and the houses for Chinese settlers there (retired PLA soldiers) were built by prisoners also. Every stick of construction and every grain of harvest, everything, came from the forced labour (*nyezö*) of prisoners. No one else.

"We also went to Kongpo Nyingtri where we were shown around the *Baiyi Tang* 'Patriotic' factory (aka Linzhi Woollen Mill) that made woollen products like blankets, yarn and fabric. In Kongpo we also toured a paper mill, a match factory, and sawmills for cutting lumber. We toured about ten different factories and commune farms. We were housed in different official guesthouses. Every factory and work group held receptions and hosted extravagant banquets for us, as if we were very important people. It was crazy. It made my head spin.

"We also travelled to Lhoka, south of Lhasa, where we toured the model agricultural commune at Nyelmé [Liemai]. This place had been modelled on the famous agricultural commune of Dazhai* in China that Mao had praised effusively. The peasants of this commune were formerly tenant farmers of the Yapshi, the Dalai Lama's family, and we had to listen to an old farmer on how cruelly they had been oppressed in the bad old days.

"The Chairman of the Revolutionary Committee of Nyelmé Commune was this fellow, Gyaltsen Wangyal, who was a real big shot in Tibet and even in China. He was a member of the administrative

---

*'In agriculture, learn from Dazhai', Mao had declared to the nation. Simon Leys, who visited this Maoist Disneyland, wrote that the lodging houses and banquets served at Dazhai had 'subtle rustic touches' for the international capitalist and tourist who wanted to commune with the hard task of building socialism but who were more '. . . like Marie Antoinette playing at being a shepherdess.'

committee (*oyon*) of the Tibet Autonomous Region, and even a
representative at the National People's Congress in Beijing. He always
appeared on television and in movies and spoke regularly on the radio,
where he called on Tibetans to diligently learn from the thoughts of
Chairman Mao—as workers of the Nyelmé Model Commune had so
successfully done. The Party had even given him a big, chauffeured
car. In public, especially when he was in Beijing, he made a show of
his peasant origins. He always wore a *chuba* robe of coarse white hand-
woven woollen material (*nambu*) and a felt hat, just like a farmer in the
old days. But of course, his *chuba* was crisp and new. Wangyal was a
hustler, but I heard he kept the people of his commune from starving."
[He also managed to secretly hide most of the sacred statuary and ritual
objects in Nyelmé before the Cultural Revolution, only bringing them
out and restoring them to the temples and monasteries of the district
when "liberalization" was well underway.]

"We were also taken to see the hydroelectric plant at Hön. It was not
fully complete. Workers from eighteen districts of Lhoka had worked
on the construction of this plant. The current of the Höga River was
swift and strong. They had five giant turbines, though only two were
operating at the time. I was told that there was something wrong with
the specifications for the other three, so they were useless. But just with
the two turbines, we were told that there was more electricity than was
needed in the region, so they put the surplus electricity back in the
river. We were told that the plant could easily provide all the electricity
for the whole of Lhasa. In Tsethang, we were taken to see a mustard
oil factory, a large shed with a few oil presses, where the mustard crop
from the surrounding areas was processed for mustard oil. Whatever
progress the Chinese claimed to have made in Tibet, the roads were still
the same. I had been in prison for eighteen years, but the roads were
just like when I went in, dusty and un-surfaced.

"In Chongye Dzong, we were taken to the village of Chö, belonging
to the estate of the aristocrat Tekhang. We were taken to the home
of a doddering old couple, formerly servants of the Tekhang family.
You could see that there was no love lost for their old master here.
The couple showed us the many sacks of barley lining the walls of

their house and proudly declared that they had money in the People's Bank. 'Listen, all you reactionaries and counter-revolutionaries! As serfs of the Tekhang family, we had nothing, but we were liberated by the Communist Party and have now become free and prosperous. Then you counterrevolutionaries and imperialist agents tried to bring back the man-eating feudal system that oppressed us so unmercifully in the past. But you all failed. Now, if you do not bow to the will of the Communist Party; if you do not reform your evil ways and still try to deceive the people again, we will destroy you. Do you understand? All counterrevolutionaries will be destroyed!'

"Those two creaking ancients insisted we shout their slogan with them. They were quite aggressive about it. We had to raise our fists in the air and shout. 'Destroy the counterrevolutionaries!' a few times. (Bhusang laughs.) Even when we were leaving their house, the two of them kept on shouting. 'Look at us now. Can you see our prosperity under socialism? Look at all these sacks of grain and our money in the People's Bank. We are now masters of our own destiny and masters of the nation.'"

"After the tour, in November 1978, there was a grand ceremony at the People's Cultural Palace in the Tibet Autonomous Region (TAR) Compound in Lhasa. Chairs were arranged in rows, and red flags and buntings hung in profusion over the walls. Representatives from the Communist Party, PLA, TAR, industrial and agricultural units, and all the offices and departments in Lhasa were present for this great occasion. There were at least around five hundred people. All of us former prisoners of Sangyip and Drapchi were seated in the front. We were dressed in clean, good quality traditional wool chubas, fur caps and leather boots, like actors in costume, while photographers and film-makers took our pictures. Speeches were made by many officials, which were recorded and written down by journalists. We were then issued certificates of release and given a hundred Yuan each to start our lives as free men.

"After the ceremony, a big banquet was hosted by the two most powerful officials in Tibet: Ren Rong, Communist Party chief of TAR and Tian Bao (Sangay Yeshi) chairman of the Regional People's

Government. There were two long rows of tables, with our hosts at the head. Individual prisoners were seated between officials and cadres. We not only had to make polite conversation with them, but were called upon to make speeches. The photographers and cameramen moved around taking pictures. In spite of many requests and coaxing, I declined to speak, saying I was not a good speaker. Finally, I got up and said I was glad to be released. That's all. Nothing more. Then I sat down. Everything we said was recorded and later broadcasted on radio. Some of the prisoners praised the Chinese government and the Communist Party again and again, in a way that was shameful and disgusting to watch.

"Ten people were seated at each table, and the food was incredibly good. There were also cigarettes, the best brand, *Mutan* (Peony), for us to smoke. In prison, we had no cigarettes. We sometimes picked up butts the guards and cadres threw away and lit them with spectacle lenses. The high point of the evening was when we were served *Baijiu* or Chinese spirits. Ren Rong got up from his chair and holding a large bottle of *Baijiu* in one hand and a small *bizi* (shot glass) in the other, began to go around from table to table, from prisoner to prisoner, toasting each one personally. He poured a shot in the prisoner's glass and one in his own. Then he shouted '*Gan bei!*' (Cheers or bottoms up) and clinking glasses with the prisoner knocked it back. All the while, he was smiling in the most animated fashion, showing all his teeth.

"Other leaders like Tian Bao and the commander of the Military Headquarters began to do the same, all grinning like madmen. My head nearly split in two, watching this performance. Did they think we would be taken in by all this smiling shit? Did they really care for Tibetans? Did they feel even a tiny scrap of empathy for us? Of course not! This unbelievable performance was to deceive us, all over again— to steal our minds. Isn't that so? *Kunchok sum!* I am not making it up. They were really doing it, even the female officials—toasting, showing all their teeth, grinning like lunatics.

"You or I, or any normal Tibetan, could never do such a thing. We would feel too embarrassed or ashamed. But those people have no shame at all. They just went around toasting and grinning. All of us prisoners were addressed as 'comrades' that night. *Kunchok sum*! All that the Chinese say and do are lies. Lies! They are so skilled at it. '*Gan bei*, comrade!' Shit on them! Most of us prisoners were stunned, absolutely dumbstruck that night. To add to the disorientation, none of us had drunk a drop of alcohol for over eighteen or nineteen years, and we were now being encouraged to knock it back. It was a dizzying experience. We were even shown a movie, somewhere during the banquet."

With this much-publicized release of all the important prisoners, the Chinese government now hoped to persuade the Dalai Lama to return to Tibet and permanently resolve the issue of the legitimacy of Chinese rule in Tibet. But, as an American scholar on Tibet has pointed out, "Beijing's ignorance of actual conditions in Tibet, cultivated by glowing reports and wildly exaggerated claims conveyed to Beijing by Chinese cadres in Tibet led to an overly optimistic view of the ease with which it would be possible to impress the Dalai Lama and other Tibetans in exile and to convince them to return. The Chinese believed much of their own propaganda about material progress, the achievement of 'people's democracy' under socialism, and their characterization of pre-liberation Tibet as a 'hell on earth'."[6]

So much so, that when in August 1979 the first delegation from Dharamshala, led by the Dalai Lama's brother Lobsang Samten, visited Tibet, the Chinese cadres in Tibet headed by Ren Rong, expressly issued instructions to the Tibetan public to ". . . suppress their animosity towards the hated serf-owners." But in Amdo large crowds of Tibetans "desperate for any contact with representatives of the Dalai Lama mobbed the delegation members, whom they greeted as potential deliverers from their Chinese tormentors."

When the delegation arrived at the capital, "The people of Lhasa could not be restrained in greeting them; thousands gathered at the Jokhang and broke through the gate of the high iron fence in front of the temple, to reach the delegation." Amidst the weeping and chaos, one wild-haired Lhasa woman, Tsering Lhamo, rose above the crowd and gave its anguish, excitement and hope the needed political direction. "She shouted again and again 'Tibet is independent. Long Live the Dalai Lama.' She was subsequently arrested and tortured."[*]

---

[*]Warren Smith in *Tibetan Nation* writes that she was thereafter popularly known as Rangzen Ama, "Mother of Independence".

39

BHUSANG GOES HOME

"All freed prisoners who were transferred to the probationary labour unit block at Sangyip Prison were visited by officers of the Gong'anju (Public Security Bureau). They gave us lectures on what we were to do once we were released and became members of free society—how we were to behave and how we were never to discuss our prison experiences with anyone. A few of the most important aristocrats and lamas released were appointed members of the People's Political Consultative Conference (*chapsi-droltsog*). It was a showpiece organization with no real power, but you received special privileges and a high rank. Others just went home.

"I got a job at the automobile repair shop at the prison itself, making seat covers for cars and trucks. When I joined the workshop, there was this Chinese ex-prisoner in charge who taught me the work. He was a good man, and we became friends. When I joined, I told him that I didn't know anything about stitching seat covers, but he said it didn't matter, that he would teach me everything. Chönyi Yeshi and another former agent, Lama Tsering, who had been 'model prisoners' for years, received the great honor of having their class backgrounds re-evaluated. They were now registered as 'working class'. There were many advantages to being working class. You were entitled to a pension and even received 6,000 Yuan to build a house, besides other things. But Yeshi, for one, did not live to enjoy these benefits. He died soon after. I was still registered as a member of the *layme-rukha* or probationary work unit, just a step above being a prisoner. I stayed in this unit for two years.

"I told you earlier about Chönyi Yeshi and also Taythi Tashi Thundup of Gyantsé. Both were trained in Colorado and had been air dropped in Sogdé in the Jhangthang in the team led by Andrugtsang Ngawang Phulchung, when the great nomad uprising took place at the end of 1959. When the nomad army was being wiped out, Yeshi surrendered to the Chinese. Among all those of us parachuted into Tibet, he was the only one to surrender. Tashi Thundup did not surrender but had been knocked unconscious by a grenade blast and captured. He successfully carried out a hunger strike in prison and killed himself.

"Let me tell you a little about the fighting at Sogdé. The centre of this vast nomadic area is Sog Dzong. The area is called Sog because many of the tribes there, especially the chiefs, are believed to be descendants of Mongols who had settled in the region a few hundred years earlier. The paramount chief of Sogdé was Pön Norbu Tsering. He held the Tibetan government rank of 'outside category fifth rank' (*chee rimba neyrim ngapa*). The outside ranks were not allowed certain privileges that other senior government officials were entitled to, like displaying a *dom-dom* tassel on one's horse during ceremonies, and other things. They were also not supposed to tie their hair in the *pachog*, the hero's knot like officials did. The chiefs of Nangchen, Dergé and Sogdé , held such outside ranks. But of course, in spite of his chieftaincy Norbu Tsering normally lived like other nomads, herding his animals and doing other chores.

"When he revolted against the Chinese, it was a tremendous thing. He had twenty to thirty thousand fighting men with him. Most of them were nomads from that area but many were Khampas who had retreated to Sogdé after the fall of Chakra Pembar, and also monks from the great Sog Tsenden Gön or the 'Sandalwood Monastery of Sog.' Many planeloads of American arms were dropped at Sogdé, also instructors and radiomen like Tashi Thundup and others.

"But in the end, the Chinese wiped them all out. The Chinese had jet planes, tanks and thousands and thousands of troops.

"Pön Norbu Tsering was badly wounded and unconscious when he was finally captured. He was with me at the *Silingbu* Military HQ Prison and later at Sangyip. We were released together. His people held him in the highest esteem. His " bones" (*rü*) or ancestry was considered to be very sacred. He was not an educated man but a natural leader. During the winter months, nomads came to Lhasa from all over the Jhangthang and also from Sogdé. Many of his people would come to visit him at the probationary unit block outside Sangyip, where we ex-prisoners lived. Even nomad children would sometimes come on their own, expressly to see him. I would tease these snotty-nosed kids in their thick sheepskin robes and wild hair.

"'Why do you want to see someone from the distant feudal past, someone you have never seen or known anything about? You kids were all born under Communist Party rule and only know Chairman Mao.' Of course, I was just teasing them. The children would reply that Pön Norbu Tsering was so famous and their parents and tribal elders talked about him so much that they wanted, more than anything else, to see what he was actually like. He did not look very special. He was rather short and stout. But he was a big man inside. After his release, he was allowed a brief visit home. Every member of his extended family had been killed except for an older sister. When he returned to Sangyip, he brought back with him a truck full of butter, meat and cheese for all his prison mates.

"At Sangyip we also had other captured Colorado trained agents who had not been parachuted into Tibet but had crossed overland. They were Baba Kalsang, Lama Tsering of Gonjo, Tawu Tseten Tashi, Kunchok Dhondup, Amdo Gyamtso and someone from Drigung whose name I don't remember. These agents had not been issued poison pills. There were also captured agents who had been trained in India. There was Tamding, a village headman from Porong, and Lhadruk, an ex-Drapchi soldier. There were also two agents from Taiwan, a Ganden monk Lobsang Dhakpa and a Mongol monk. Most were eventually released. Only one agent, Amdo Gyamtso, is still in prison. Of course, there were hundreds of others who died in combat, committed suicide, starved to death or were executed.

"On 12 October 1980, it was announced that certain ex-prisoners would be allowed to leave Tibet. The government would, furthermore, pay all their expenses. This was part of the policy to get exile Tibetans to return. Tseten Tashi at once applied to leave, as did Tamding. The two of them claimed that they had wives and children in India and were given official permission to leave Tibet. I also applied to leave for India but was refused permission, most likely as I could not claim family or relatives in India. I was told that since I had now been given a release certificate, I should participate in building a new socialist society in Tibet. Tseten Tashi had a wife at Forsyth Ganj (in Dharamshala) who baked and sold Tibetan bread. Tashi didn't know it, but she had re-married. Tashi was given a cash indemnity by Indian intelligence. He tried petty trade, or something like that, and spent it all. He later disappeared. He was not a good prison mate."

A high-level fact-finding mission to Tibet, led by Communist Party General Secretary Hu Yaobang, visited Tibet from 22 to 31 May 1980. "Hu was reportedly shocked by the poverty of Tibetans and is reported to have commented in a closed meeting with Chinese cadres that the apparent results of China's role in Tibet was reminiscent of colonialism." TAR Party Secretary Ren Rong was removed from office and sent back to China and, "Hu proposed a radical reform program for the TAR Han cadres in the TAR with the exception of the PLA, were to be reduced by 85 per cent . . . .. In addition, there would be a general liberalization of economic policies in Tibet aimed at a diversification of the Tibetan economy; Chinese subsidies to Tibet would be increased; Tibetan culture, including religion, would be revived, with the state financing the reconstruction of some religious monuments and monasteries."[1]

Everyone in the exile community, including the Dalai Lama, was tremendously encouraged and excited by these developments. Unfortunately, they began to read too much into these largely economic changes taking place in Tibet and China. Tibetan leaders were encouraged in this belief by naïve foreign supporters and certain Western leaders* who persuaded them that China was now definitely on the path to free-market capitalism and democracy and that Tibetans should give up their national cause and seek a constructive and rewarding role within the new democratic China.

I commenced on my self-appointed mission of pouring cold water on these pipe dreams and began contributing political essays (almost exclusively) to the *Tibetan Review*. Repeated readings and, it might be said, osmotic absorption of Orwell's *Collected Essays, Journalism and Letters* (in their four Penguin paperback volumes) had significantly improved my English prose and political acumen, since the early "*J'accuse*" days. Another four-volume set, this time a selection of the short, sharp, incisive essays (Chinese, *zawen*) of China's greatest modern writer Lu Xun, provided me with a harder-edged perspective on the many fuzzy discussions on "reformers" said to be emerging in post-Mao China. This is Lu Xun's pronouncement on the power shifts in Chinese politics:

"Whoever *is* in power favours the status quo. Whoever *was* in power wants a restoration. Whoever *is not* yet in power calls for reforms. The situation is generally such."

I began to receive critical and even condemnatory letters-to-the-editor from Tibetan and Western readers of the *Tibetan Review*, while the exile government attempted to suppress my writings. His Holiness summoned me and gave me a severe dressing-down.

The Chinese convinced me I was having an impact as a writer when the first exile visitor to Tibet reported in the *Tibetan Review*[2] that at an official meeting in Lhasa, he was told that the writings of Jamyang Norbu and the activism of the TYC were harming Sino-Tibetan relations.

A few years later, I received, through the Tibetan Security Office, a message from the Chinese authorities in Lhasa that my writings were "as futile as the wings of a fly beating against a rock" and as an educated Tibetan, I should return to join in the socialist reconstruction of Tibet.

---

*The Dalai Lama is on record that British PM Edward Heath and President Jimmy Carter advised him to accept China's rule over Tibet.

However unfounded the hope of the Dalai Lama for "genuine autonomy" within a democratic China, the economic "liberalization" that had begun under Hu and later expanded under Deng Xiaoping, did begin to change the lives of the common Tibetan from its previous bone-grinding misery to something a little more endurable. Bhusang explained it to me.

"Things got better when Hu Yaobang came to Tibet and declared his Six Point Policy for improving the Tibetan economy. The most important thing Hu said was that 85 per cent of Chinese cadres would return to China. He was later criticized by other Chinese leaders, but he did shake up the system in Tibet. The Reform Through Labor Department (Chinese, *Laogai chu*), to which I belonged as an ex-prisoner, even sent an official around to ask for the opinions of all ex-prisoners. I was employed at the auto workshop at the time. There were three main questions: 1. What is your opinion of the liberalization policy? 2. What do you think of 85% of Chinese cadres being sent back to China? (and) 3. What personal request do you have? My replies to the first two questions were heartfelt, even contentious, but they did not get me into trouble.

"As for the personal request, I told them that I had previously asked for permission to go to India, but was refused. TAR officials had earlier made the announcement that all ex-prisoners could leave the country, if they wanted to, and they would even be given travel expenses. But when I applied, I was told that I should work for the reconstruction of New Tibet. I said it was personally important for me to go to India. I thought I was being clever, but I made a serious mistake in my next statement. I claimed that Gyalo Thondup and Lhamo Tsering in India owed me, and I could not give up the money. I needed the money as I had to support many poor relatives. I said I would like to make a quick trip to India so I could return to Tibet before the summer heat in India. I told them I was now old and sickly. After eighteen years in Laogai, all I had left was this broken body. I had no education and no skills. I was now nearly blind, deaf and partially crippled. I could not do anything for myself anymore and had to depend on the Party. The money I was owed in India would help me to survive in Tibet. I requested the People's Government to consider my request which was denied, again.

"A year earlier in March 1979, after my initial request to leave Tibet had been refused, I went to Nyemo to meet whatever relatives I had left. It only took me three hours to get there from Lhasa. I got a ride on a truck. Just across the ferry point on the Nyemo River is our village of Bhartang. When I got there, I discovered that my sister, Pemba Dolma was still alive. She was three years older than me. Her husband had joined the Nyemo revolt in 1969 and had been captured, struggled and executed. My younger brother Gyephur had also joined the uprising. He had committed suicide by jumping in the river flowing past our home. My younger sister, Sonam Yanchen, who had gone to work as a maid for the family of the tantric priest, had married and lived in the village of Kharak in Nyemo. But her husband had also been involved in the Nyemo revolt and had subsequently been struggled and executed. She died of sorrow, or starvation, perhaps both. So, the only relatives I had left in Nyemo were my older sister and my brother Gyephur's wife.

"When we first met, all we could do was cry. Then we told each other stories of what had happened, and we cried again. We were crying most of the time. They also had so little food, and no chang to drink, something unthinkable in the old days. Fortunately, I had brought one month's barley rations with me from Lhasa, which at once made a marked improvement in their lives. Later in the evening, a few old family friends dropped by to see me. One of them brought with him a single egg as a gift. It was a big sacrifice for him. It sounds ridiculous but it's the truth. Those people in Nyemo were so poor that it was unbelievable. What had they done to deserve this? The Chinese could say that I was an American spy and a counter-revolutionary criminal and starve and torture me, but these people were not even minor wrongdoers, even by Chinese law, and they had been subjected to a far more horrendous life than those of us in prison.

"Gyephur had left behind him three children. My sister had five. A couple of them were old enough to work in the fields with her. One of her younger sons was a quiet, contemplative lad. He did not talk much but could read letters well and figure numbers. He went to the school at Rinpung Dzong. The rest of the family thought he was slow. They were all in rags and so dreadfully poor. Even an ex-prisoner like me was much better off. I stayed with them for thirteen days (I had only been given seven days leave) and then returned to my work unit. I left behind what remained of the barley I had brought. Later, I went a few more times to visit them, and helped them out with as much foodstuff as I could.

"I tried to locate my mother through my sister and other relatives and friends, but could not find her at all. I tried many times. Then I went to Lhasa city and asked around. I was finally able to establish that she was in the Tölung district, north-west of Lhasa, in a small village close to a hot spring. It was somewhere in the interior of the valley from Dechen Dzong. An acquaintance of mine who travelled there finally located her and sent me a message. I got a ride to the Dzong and walked to the small village. I had been told to find a certain farmhouse, which I did.

"Outside, sitting on a mat before the front entrance, I saw this old woman carding wool. She was wearing a dark *nambu*-wool chuba. A small child was playing beside her. I figured she might be my mother, but I couldn't be sure. She didn't recognize me at all. We had been separated for over thirty-five years. It was impossible for her to remember me.

"I greeted her 'Do you live here, Grandmother?' She nodded in assent. I asked her name. 'Sonam Yudon' she replied. That was my mother's name.

"I sat down beside her and started a casual conversation. I asked her where she had been born, how many children she had, and how she had gotten here to Tölung from her home in Nyemo. She didn't mind answering my questions and told me her story. She also said that she had a son born in the Sheep Year, and how she had lost him. People had told her that he was a student at the Medical Centre in Lhasa, but she could not make contact with him, and later, with the fighting and disaster in Lhasa, there was nothing she could do.

"So finally, I realized with absolute conviction that this old grey-haired woman, her face covered with wrinkles, was the young mother I lost at the age of twelve. But I didn't tell her right away that I was her son. I just said that she was not to worry, and I was sure that she would soon find all her children. She seemed to like talking to me. I asked her where she lived. She said that she lived with her daughter and son-in-law here at this farmhouse. It was beginning to get dark, so I said, 'Let's go inside your house.' I helped carry her wool inside. All the while, we were talking. She told me that someone passing by (possibly the friend who located my mother) had told her that she might be receiving a visitor soon. So, she had laid in a supply of chang mash. 'Would you like me to prepare you some chang?' she asked. 'Do you drink chang?'

"'Yes, I do.' I replied 'Many thanks.' As she poured warm water on the fermented mash and waited for the *chang* to infuse, I asked her, 'Mother, if I manage to arrange for you to meet your son, would it be alright with you?' She replied that it would be a very difficult thing to do now—perhaps even impossible. But still, if that were ever to happen, she would be very happy. The only desire she had left in life would be fulfilled. I told her it was not at all that impossible to find her son, and that she should not worry about it. I would take care of everything.

"After a while, I asked her if I looked like the son she had lost. She at once replied that I did not look like him at all. I then talked about our early life together. I told her about the place where we had lived in Lhasa, at the Thönpa Mansion, and also the bad things that had happened there, and why she had to leave. I asked her if she remembered all these things.

"'Yes, I remember. But you do not look like him at all.'

"I finally said straight up 'I am your son'. But she refused to believe me and became quite upset. She asked a neighbour to call her daughter, who was working in the fields. Soon a woman, my little sister, entered the house. She didn't recognize me. She was just a baby when we were separated. Now thirty-five years had passed, and she was the mother of four children. I asked my sister if she recognized me, even in a small way. She said no. I then told them about my meeting with my older sister, Pemba Dolma, and other surviving relatives at Nyemo. They knew a bit about them, and had heard about Gyephur's death, but had not been able to see them as the Chinese enforced strict travel restrictions, even from one village to the next, and you needed all sorts of permits and papers, including your grain ration coupons. It was a little better now.

"Then finally, I told them my whole story—everything. They were visibly moved by it, but my mother was still not entirely convinced. It was now getting towards evening, so I asked her if I could stay the night. She replied, addressing me as *gyenla* or teacher. 'I would be very happy if *gyenla* stayed with us.' So I knew it would be all right. My sister's husband came in from the fields. His name was Lhundup. He seemed like a decent, solid person, and was very good to me. I stayed with them that night. They were not too badly off, and the *thukpa* stew they offered me did have some meat, cheese and dumplings in it. Of course, we all talked for a long time about so many things, and then gradually, my mother realized that I was her son.

She first sat close to me, then held my hand in hers and stroked it. She hugged me a lot after that and also cried a lot. So did my sister. We were all crying. We would stop crying for a while and laugh with happiness at having found each other, and then we would start crying again. I found myself telling them, again and again, 'Don't cry, don't cry. It's all right now.' We were very happy. I stayed with them for seven days. Their economic condition was not too bad. They owned the house they lived in, and Lhundup was not only an intelligent and hard working person but was also very active and had good contacts. They owned five cows, four yaks and one horse. He was also very good to my sister and my mother.

My mother was worried that I might be sent to prison again, so I had to reassure her that that would not happen. I told her not to worry, and that everything I had done was for the good of our people and our nation and the safeguarding of our *Chös*, the Buddha *dharma*.

"I got to see them once again before I was finally allowed to leave for India. With the liberalization policies now taking effect, they needed people to go out to India, to convince Tibetans there to give up the fight for Independence, and for the Dalai Lama to return. They had allowed other prisoners to leave, but had refused me permission, till I had despaired of ever being allowed to leave the country. But as I suspected, I had made a mistake in my approach, which was set right in a strange way.

"One night, as I was in the workshop stitching car seats, a Chinese cadre, a young *kuo-tang*, slapped me on the back. 'Don't you recognize me, Bhusang, No?' He was smiling. I thought he was another official who wanted his car seat done before the others, or with special material (different departments always tried to jump the queue for automobile repairs and bribed us with cigarettes and drinks). 'No'. I replied sourly. He walked away.

"My workmate Tashi turned to me and said 'Bhusang-la, you better be careful with your attitude. That was *Gong'anju* and not just anybody either. He's a *pu kuo-tang*.'

"'Come on, a young fellow like that? You're having me on.'
"'*Kunchok sum*, I'm not.'

"I quickly went out of the workshop after him and found him a little way ahead. I told him I was sorry that I hadn't recognized him and hoped he hadn't taken offence. He replied that it was all right and it didn't matter. We chatted a bit. I told him about the answers I had given to the three questions regarding the liberalization policies and being denied permission to leave Tibet. I asked him if there really was any chance for me to go to India. He replied that it was certainly possible. All I had to do was to submit a fresh application. I should not mention anything about trying to get money from Gyalo Thondup, or anything like that. 'Just say you have relatives in India you want to meet. It doesn't matter if you don't. No one's going to check.'"

"It was simple as that. The Chinese were really something. Now that the policy had changed, even the attitude of the cadres had changed.

"So I applied, claiming an old Medical Centre schoolmate, Tsering Dorje, as my relative in India. He was a former soldier in the old Tibetan army, like me. Two months later, my application was accepted. I then had to apply to the Reform Through Labor Department for permission to leave my work unit, which I received. But then I came down with a nasty chest problem and had to stay for eighteen days at the infirmary at Sangyip. When I was there, I received a message saying that my travel permit had been issued.

"I visited my older sister at Nyemo and my mother again. My mother was very upset about my leaving Tibet and could not understand why I was going away. She was worried I would get myself in a situation where I would be arrested again. She said that I had put this heavy burden on her again. All she had in her heart was this great love for me. But she did not understand the political obligations that I had.

"I got a letter from her last year (December 1990) when I went to Varanasi, you know, when the Dalai Lama gave his Kalachakra initiation at Sarnath. She was all right then and wanted nothing from me except for some relics pills and blessing scarves (*jandü*) from His Holiness, which I managed to send her. My younger sister sent me a letter a month ago (August 1991), saying our mother had died just a few days earlier, peacefully, in her sleep.

Before I left Lhasa, I met my wife, Tashi Lhamo. After the uprising she had been sent to Chamdo to do forced labour (*nyezö*), building the big power plant there. She had married another prisoner and had only been allowed to return to Lhasa after the Cultural Revolution. She and her husband now belonged to a construction team and were doing quite well. They had five children. Her father, my old sergeant friend in the Lhasa police force, Pema Gyalpo, had died in prison. We did not talk about our little boy and girl that she had to leave behind in Lhasa, and who starved to death in the Great Famine. What would be the point? I knew she still carried the pain in her heart as I did.

"So finally on 12 November 1980, I climbed aboard this construction truck that was headed for Dram (Kodari) at the Nepal border. At the time, many people were going to Nepal and India, and it was not easy finding seats. There were no busses or taxis or anything like that at the time. The truck I was on belonged to the Lhasa Medical Department. I knew this Tibetan girl who was a doctor at Mentsikhang, and she went out of her way to help me. No one took any payment. They were just glad to help an old doctor from their school.

"In New Delhi, I met Lhamo Tsering. He had just been released from Nepalese prison, after serving seven years. It was a very sad meeting. The Indian intelligence had rented a nice apartment for him. I stayed with him for a month and helped out my old boss, cooking and cleaning his place. We talked a lot, and he advised me not to even think of returning to Tibet. Things might be improving now, but if anything went wrong, my old criminal record of being an American spy would definitely be dug up. I wrote my report, and then after a month I finally went to Dharamshala. At the Security Office at Gangchen Kyishong, I met Captain Kaldam-la, who I knew from Lhasa, and from working together before the Uprising. He was delighted to see me and took me to his quarters and insisted I eat a proper Tibetan meal with tsampa and meat stew.

"A few days later, I got my audience with the Dalai Lama. He had been briefed beforehand about me. When I prostrated before him, he said jokingly, "Ah, the secret agent of the counterrevolutionary clique, Bhusang, has come" (*logchoepae sang-nyu bhusang laysonga*). We talked for four hours. I told him everything that had happened to me. He held my hand and asked me many questions. I requested his personal *thonmö* prayers for my dead comrades. He said I was not to worry, that it would be done, and he had received my report and had all their names. He asked me if I was going to return to Tibet. I told him I would do anything he ordered. It was now quite late in the night.

None of his servants were around. He showed me to the back door. I awkwardly pushed the door when I should have pulled it. His Holiness laughed and said 'You stupid man' and opened the door for me.

"There were no guards in the corridor. When I got to the door leading outside, I had some difficulty with it. The official Gedar-la came and opened it for me. I finally got out but was lost for a while between the palace and the temple. My companion from Delhi had left by then, as it was very late, so I went on alone in the dark, and got lost again. I finally met a monk who gave me directions to Gangkyi, where I was staying with Kaldam-la. After walking down the road for a bit, I got lost."

40

HIGH MOUNTAIN ELEGY

I was waiting at Denver International Airport for my ride when I got a call from an excited young Tibetan friend in Queens, New York. "Jamyang-la, someone told me the CIA is calling for Tibetans to come to Colorado. Have they re-started the training program? Are they really going to support guerrilla operations inside Tibet? I called your home this morning, and Tenzing-la told me you were in Colorado. What's going on? Tell me. You got to let me know."

I explained to him that nothing of the sort was happening. I was on my way to Camp Hale in the Rockies where a U.S. senator and some retired CIA officers involved in the Tibet Task Force were going to dedicate a commemorative plaque to the memory of the three hundred odd Tibetan freedom fighters who were secretly trained there, many of whom lost their lives in subsequent operations. I had been invited to join the dedication ceremony and to say a few words.

It would take about three hours to get to Camp Hale from the airport, but the sunlight was glittering on the distant mountains, and the trip was a pleasant one. Tenzin Pasang-la of Boulder had offered to drive me and we were accompanied by two other friends. The SUV climbed steadily up past mountainsides covered with aspen, spruce and pine—the last, devastated in places by pine beetle infestation. But the aspen had begun to change colour and would, in a month, turn into their spectacular reds and yellows.

I had been living in the United States since 1996. After my resignation from the leadership of the Tibetan Youth Congress in 1977, I went back to my political writing and began contributing short stories to Indian magazines and Sunday supplements. But the Tibetan Dance and Drama Society at Dharamshala, where I had worked before (see Chapter 9) and which was run by an independent board of governors, asked me to take over as director. I renamed it the Tibetan Institute of Performing Arts (TIPA) and served for five happy and productive years, not just writing and producing new plays, but also bringing about the revival of the traditional Ache Lhamo opera tradition,[1] resurrecting old operas and even writing my libretto on Thangton Gyalpo, divine madman, bridge builder and founder of the Tibetan theatre.

I also kept up my political writing, which, of course, displeased the Tibetan leadership. One day a mob of around two hundred members of the United Association and the Tibetan Women's Association assaulted me at work and subjected me to a "struggle," complete with experienced denunciators and the rhetoric of the Cultural Revolution. The Tibetan Parliament piled on, setting up a kangaroo court that accused me of insulting the Dalai Lama, hurting the feelings of the Tibetan people and causing social unrest. My immediate ouster was demanded. My English wife Tamsin persuaded me to leave with her for Japan, where for a year or two I got by teaching English and writing the occasional book review for the English language *Japan Times.*

Then in 1990, my old comrade Lhasang Tsering, the scholar Tashi Tsering and a young littérateur, Pema Bhum, who had just arrived from Amdo, asked me to return to Dharamshala and work with them in creating a new liberal research and publishing organization to counteract what we all felt was the near-exclusive preoccupation of exile Tibetan leadership with religion and ritual. I mentioned in an earlier chapter the establishment of the Amnye Machen Institute (AMI) and a subset of the work we did on the Cultural Revolution. In the five hectic years that we held AMI together, we published *Jangzhon,* a literary journal, *Lungta,* an illustrated Journal on Tibetan History and Culture and *Yum-tso,* the Journal of Tibetan Women's Studies. We also published (for the first time in exile) translations in Tibetan of classic literary and intellectual works as Thomas Paine's *Common Sense,* Solzhenitsyn's *A Day in the Life of Ivan Denisovitch,* Orwell's *Animal Farm,* Gandhi's *Hind Swaraj* and even Heinrich Harrer's *Seven Years in Tibet,* which fascinated our older readers and became a minor best seller in the exile world. We also published many original works by Tibetan writers and scholars, including Lhamo Tsering's eight-volume history of the Tibetan Resistance, Ratuk Ngawang's four-volume biography, and landmark literary works from inside Tibet such as *The Waterfall of Youth* by Dhondup Gyal.

We organized the first film festivals in exile society, the first exhibitions of Contemporary Tibetan Art, as well as exhibitions on Tibetan photography, the Cultural Revolution and the history of Tibetan Newspapers. A feather* in AMI's cap was "Literature For Freedom: The First National Conference of Tibetan Writers" that we hosted from 15 to 17 March, 1995, which was enthusiastically welcomed by Tibetan intellectual, literary and spiritual figures from inside and outside Tibet. PEN International sent their warmest wishes and the poet, anti-Stalinist writer and Nobel laureate Czeslaw Milosz, this heartfelt message:

> Please receive my words of solidarity and sympathy. I lived a long time in exile, and I understand your problems and your hopes. You have friends in many countries of the world, and you should be convinced that what you write in solitude and isolation will one day be known and remembered with gratitude.

Much of everything that AMI achieved was with the contribution of our young staff, primarily new arrivals from Tibet, and also non-

---

*The conference symbol was a pair of courting black-neck cranes recalling the greatest of Tibetan poets, the Sixth Dalai Lama, and his prophetic verse of flying on the wings of a crane to be reborn in Lithang.

Tibetan volunteers, in particular a Swiss graphic artist and cartographer, Christophe Besuchet, who besides designing our book covers, posters, the layout of our magazines and newspaper, also created for AMI the first authentic modern maps of Tibet and Lhasa city.

But the religious-right in exile society started a nasty campaign to undermine AMI. Pema Bhum, speaking at a Tibetan Language Conference in Arcidosso, Italy, had mentioned in passing the problems that classical religious literature imposed on the development of colloquial and modern Tibetan writing. He was denounced for blasphemy and a reward of Rs. 100,000, essentially a *fatwa*, placed on his head by the leader of the United Association who brazenly made the denunciation and reward offer in a magazine interview.[2]

I was editing AMI's weekly paper, *Mangtso* (*Democracy*), which became the most widely read newspaper in the exile community, not only for its investigative journalism but also its cartoons, photographs and even its unique astrology column drawn up by the State Astrologer. Soon our vendors were being beaten up, and I received a number of death threats and an occult effigy on my doorstep. A mob tried to burn down Nalanda Cottage, my house at McLeod Ganj. The attempt was thwarted by two old but fierce women friends of mine—the warrior nun Lemda Pachen and Ama Adhe—who I had earlier interviewed for their roles in the Khampa Uprising.

We were also informed by well-wishers in the bureaucracy that the exile government was working to undercut the financial support AMI was receiving from some friends and organizations in the West. These donors were told that the Dalai Lama was fond of the four AMI directors who were well-meaning and capable young Tibetans. It was only their "nationalist" agenda that caused His Holiness distress as it undermined his greater international vision of bringing the Tibetan and Chinese people together, and shepherding China into the mainstream global community.

Eventually, Pema Bhum left for a teaching job at Indiana University, and Lhasang Tsering retired to run the Bookworm, the go-to place for travellers and book lovers in McLeod Ganj. Tashi Tsering, exile Tibet's premier scholar, stuck it out in Dharamshala with AMI, focusing on the academic side of our overall undertaking. In spite of enormous political and financial obstacles, Tashi Tsering and AMI have not only survived to date, but steadily released an impressive catalogue of works on Tibetan history and culture.

My first marriage did not survive the upheavals in my life. In 1994, I married Lhamo Tsering's daughter, Tenzing Chounzom. She was a gynecologist, who had served the exile community for many years, but eventually moved to the United States to practice at an "underserved" area in the mountains of Tennessee. That's how I ended up in America as well and was now driving out of Denver airport to Camp Hale.

We drove on Interstate 70 for a couple of hours and then took the exit to U.S. Highway 24, renamed Mountain Division Memorial Highway. Camp Hale was established during World War II as a home base for the Tenth Mountain Division, and to provide winter and mountain warfare training, including skiing, for other military units. After the war, the camp had been decommissioned and most of the buildings and facilities removed.

Camp Hale was selected for the secret program to train Tibetan fighters in the USA because of its isolation, altitude and Tibet-like terrain. A small section of the vast military camp had survived. This section was wired off, and some extra Quonset huts and a log-cabin recreation centre erected.

We finally got over the mountains and came to a broad windswept plain, 11,000 feet high, surrounded by low mountains and covered with scrub and purple sagebrush. Like Native Americans, Tibetans burn sagebrush (*sang ganden khampa*) as a purifying ritual and an offering to the Buddha and the old gods and spirits (*yul-lha ship-dag*) of Tibet. About two-thirds of the way across the plain, we came to a place by the side of the road where a large group of people had gathered. The main speaker, Colorado Senator Mark Udall hadn't arrived, but about a hundred guests were already seated. TV and film crews were setting up their equipment, and reporters from local Colorado newspapers, Radio Free Asia and Voice of America correspondents were already interviewing people. Academics specializing in the Tibetan Resistance and good friends Warren Smith and Carole McGranahan were also present.

Tibetans had set up an altar on a picnic table, with an image of the Lord Buddha, a Dalai Lama portrait, seven silver bowls of water and a couple of butter lamps. The Tibetan national flag and the American flag (along with the battle standard of the Four Rivers Six Ranges) were raised on either side of the brass commemorative plaque. We also strung up a length of prayer flags behind the plaque (about 20 x 15 inches) erected on a metal stand. The plaque read:

From 1958 to 1964, Camp Hale played an important role as a training site for Tibetan Freedom Fighters. Trained by the CIA, many of these brave men lost their lives in the struggle for freedom.

"They were the best and the bravest of their generation, and we wept together when they were killed fighting alongside their countrymen."
—*Orphans of the Cold War* by John Kenneth Knaus.

This plaque is dedicated to their memory.

The event opened with a speech by the young Colorado Senator Mark Udall, who thanked all those who had worked hard to make the event possible. The senator had become interested in the Tibetan Resistance thanks, in part, to his background as a mountaineer in the Himalayas. With the collaboration of retired CIA officer John Kenneth Knaus, he had managed to get Congressional approval for the commemorative plaque.

Ken Knaus, who had come to the event with his wife Lois Ann, spoke of the courage and dedication of the Tibetan trainees, and exhorted all of us gathered there: "This is not a funeral. This is the continuation of a fight that started fifty years ago."

Tashi Choedak (Mark), who had been Ken's translator at Camp Hale gave a historical outline of the program. He also mentioned that the Tibetan code name for Camp Hale, was "Dumra", or garden, because the place was beautiful and made the Tibetans feel they were back home, in Tibet.

Several former trainees, Ga Tridhu Pön Chime Namgyal (Conrad), Tashi Paljor (Noel), Sonam Wangchuk (Lee), Pema Wangdu (Pete) and instructors Ray Starke and Don Cesare also spoke of their experiences. It became clear from everyone's stories that the Tibetan trainees got on surprisingly well with their instructors, and, in turn, the CIA instructors developed a real friendship for their trainees and came to admire them. One of the instructors mentioned how diligent the trainees were and how some of them would, after dinner, go back to practice Morse code. "Really, we used to comment back and forth that we were grateful that we were working with the Tibetans instead of the Central American problem, which was the Bay of Pigs. We knew we were fortunate to be involved with a good program."

Quite a few of the younger guests spoke about their fathers and friends who had been at Camp Hale. Doma Norbu, the daughter of Athar Norbu, one of the first CIA trainees, recalled her father's American accent when he spoke English, which quite intrigued her as she and her sister, educated at Loreto Convent in Darjeeling, spoke English with a more Indian accent. She also introduced her friend, Sonam Yangzom, daughter of the great warrior Ratuk Ngawang, who though not a trainee at Camp Hale, was one of the leading Tibetan Resistance fighters who had fought beside Gonpo Tashi Andrugtsang in Tibet, and later commanded the CIA initiated Special Frontier Force in India.

Kevin McCarthy, the son of Roger McCarthy ("godfather" of the Tibet Task Force), came with his two sisters and spoke of how much the project had meant to his father. He also shared stories he had heard from his father of the escapades of the Tibetan trainees, one being the launching of a large homemade rocket, which went seriously off course and damaged the buildings of a distant molybdenum mine, east of Leadville. Julie Holober, the daughter of Frank Holober, co-creator of the Tibet Task Force and Lisa Cathy, daughter of the CIA resident at Calcutta, Clay Cathy, also spoke.

I said I had come to honour the memory of my late father-in-law, Tsongkha Lhamo Tsering (Larry). I added that I was not a Camp Hale trainee but knew many of them when I was in the Mustang Resistance. I mentioned the names of some who had passed away: Utsatsang Bhuché of Dergé, Tashi Thundup (Sandy) of Lhasa,

Tendar (Bill), who led the 1966 raid and Rakra Gyadhar (Ross), who led the famous 1961 raid.

In particular, I wanted everyone to know about Camp Hale trainee Bhusang (Ken) of Nyemo, who had been parachuted into Tibet in March 1961 but had, two years earlier, been in the heart of the fighting at the Jokhang, during the 1959 uprising.

Bhusang-la never doubted the righteousness of the cause for which he had fought and suffered. The last time I met him was in 2009, in Dharamshala, a week after the Dalai Lama's previous negotiation team to Beijing had been humiliated by Communist "United Front" *apparatchiks* before the international press. Bhusang-la was ill and bed-ridden, but he was furious enough to sit up and let me know how he felt about the debacle.

"The Tibetan government has no grasp of how the Chinese think. It doesn't matter if they threaten you or praise you; you must never forget their fundamental negotiation philosophy (*tawa*). "What is mine, is mine, and I want yours also." It sounded snappier in Tibetan "*ngae di ngarae yin, khyorae diyae go yoe*" and reflected, I suppose, the fact that he had lived most of his life in Lhasa—a city that prided itself on its wit and urbanity, and for which he had "put his life on the target" to defend, fifty-one years ago. Bhusang-la died on 25 March 2010 at the age of eighty.

I was glad to have had this occasion to let everyone there know something about this brave freedom-fighter and ever defiant *Laogai* survivor. Had he been alive, he would have thanked his American instructors for commemorating him and his comrades, but would have insisted that, as grateful as he was, he had not fought for America but Tibet, and it would have made him happier if the exile Tibetan government had organized such a commemoration, or at least sent an official representative to the Camp Hale event—which it shamefully had not.

One of the more wretched expedients of the exile government in its quest to ingratiate itself with Communist China has been to maintain a pervasive silence about about Andrugtsang Gonpo Tashi and the Four Rivers Six Ranges, Wangdü Gyadotsang and the

Mustang Resistance Force, and all the individual agents and fighters who parachuted into Chinese occupied Tibet in missions that were all but suicidal. Even the loyalty and patriotism of its own officials: Prime Minister Lukhangwa, Chamberlain Phala, Khenchung Tara, the historian Tsepon Shakabpa, Tsarong Dasang Damdul, General Muja Tsewang Norbu, Lhalu Tsewang Dorje, Tsepon Namseling, Seynang Lobsang Yeshi, Tsongkha Lhamo Tsering and many others, have been conspicuously ignored, while the deaths of such collaborators in Beijing as Ngabö Ngawang Jigme (2009) and Bapa Phüntso Wangye (2014) have seen the publication of effusive and shameful official eulogies from Dharamshala.[3]

Even the annual 10 March commemoration has been phased out, with the Dalai Lama no longer making his annual statement on the occasion. Instead, demonstrators have been instructed not to shout slogans offensive to the Chinese leadership like "Free Tibet" or "China out of Tibet."

This cravenness has, of course, not been lost on the Chinese leadership. It has put in place (as it explained to its cadres in the TAR) a "policy of prolonging" or "policy of time wasting" (Chinese, *tuo yan zheng ce*, Tibetan, *dhu gyang kyi sichue*). Simply put, this is to string the exile administration along with vague promises of possible future negotiations until the Dalai Lama died. Beijing would then, as it announced in 2015,[4] select the next incarnation of the Dalai Lama. In course of time, as the tame Panchen Lama had done before him, the young Fifteenth Dalai Lama would declare his undying loyalty to the PRC and president-for-life Xi Jinping. When you are playing the long game, as Beijing always is, waiting a few decades for things to work out your way is a minor inconvenience.

In Tibet, the Chinese have been systematically working towards eradicating Tibetan national and cultural identity. Some exiles have referred to this as ethnic cleansing and have been tut-tutted at by commentators and academics in the West as, strictly speaking, no massacre of Tibetans is taking place, right this moment. But I feel China's present strategy is something altogether more sinister, though gradual and measured, whose ultimate purpose is to bring about the functional extinction of the Tibetan people without destabilizing the Communist occupation administration on the plateau, without arousing international outcry and without negatively impacting China's global trade figures.

Ergo, China's grand strategy to deal with the Tibetan people can unquestionably be said to fit the supplemental definition of "genocide" as laid out by Raphael Lemkin, the man who coined the term and who initiated the UN Genocide Convention. I quoted him at the conclusion of Chapter 13, but his definition needs to be communicated as widely as possible. "Genocide does not necessarily mean the immediate destruction of a nation. It is intended, rather, to signify a coordinated plan of different actions aiming at the destruction of essential foundations of the life of national groups, with the *eventual* (my emphasis) aim of annihilating the groups themselves."

Many hundreds of thousands of previously self-sustaining Tibetan pastoral and nomadic families are being relocated to " urban settlements" that bear a troubling resemblance to old Stalinist labour camps. The architectural scheme is a standard one: row upon row of uniform cinder-block huts surrounded by high walls, without a temple, a school or even a "company store." Closer to major cities and motor roads, the lintels of the huts and the top of the walls are tarted up with pseudo-Tibetan designs so as not to scare away tourists. A little distance from the outside walls, police cars maintain constant surveillance, as an award-winning British television documentary *Undercover in Tibet* (2008)[5] revealed in chilling detail. Unable to speak or read Chinese, the Tibetan inmates of these settlements, particularly the men, are slowly sinking into unemployment, depression and alcoholism.

Chinese occupation authorities in Tibet have set up a regionwide network of boarding schools for over 800,000 Tibetan children (aged six to eighteen), separating them from their parents and homes to reduce their contact with their native language and culture. Classes in the schools are taught primarily in Chinese and feature intense political indoctrination, according to a report released in December 2021 by the Tibet Action Institute.[6]

In July 2021, the Pope apologized for the boarding school program run by the Catholic Church in Canada for indigenous children. The pontiff said that genocide had taken place at these schools.

Tibet's vast deposits of gold, copper, iron, lead, zinc, chromium and in particular lithium are being exploited by Chinese, Australian and Canadian mining companies, almost exclusively with imported Chinese labour. The impact of China's population transfer policy is most apparent in Lhasa, where Tibetans are now a minority in a sea of Chinese migrants and tourists. Tibetans in Lhasa are pressured to leave the capital because of stringent security measures that apply only to the native born.

Tibetans are constantly stopped at multiple checkpoints where they need to show their mandatory IDs, which contain a biometric chip with their personal information. They are also routinely required to produce their cellphones whose sim cards are removed and downloaded—a Dalai Lama image getting you arrested immediately. Surveillance cameras have been ubiquitous throughout Lhasa and major towns and cities in Tibet since the early 1980s, but now a facial recognition database has reportedly been incorporated into the system and is operational in Xinjiang and Tibet. In addition, a major Chinese company, iFlytek, now "provides voice-recognition services for police bureaus in Xinjiang, the region home to the heavily surveilled Uyghur ethnic minority."[7]

Recently a Human Rights Watch report (2017) has revealed that Chinese authorities are collecting DNA samples, fingerprints and other biometric data from *every resident* in Xinjiang.[8] In September 2022 Human Rights Watch released another report that mass DNA collection program was well underway in Tibet, primarily targeting children.[9] It is just a matter of time before all Tibetans are tagged and monitored in this ultimate genetic-based security system that till now existed only in futuristic films as *Gattaca*. A BBC report of 25 May 2021 fills us in on another such science-fiction surveillance tool ". . .a camera system that uses AI and facial recognition intended to reveal *states of emotion*. It has been tested on Uyghurs in Xinjiang. A software engineer claimed to have installed such systems in police stations in the province"

A decade earlier, Tibetans fled Chinese oppression by trekking across the high (19,000 ft) mountain pass of Nangpala into Nepal, braving sub-zero temperatures and PLA border guards eager to gun them down. "In recent years, the flow of refugees from Tibet has almost completely stopped. In 2007, about 3,000 Tibetans entered India; that number dwindled to only 80 by 2017. The reason is due to new technology that has allowed China to build a nearly impassable digital and securitized border wall along its southern and western borders in Tibet, and also in Xinjiang, the homeland of Uyghurs."[10]

China Daily reported on the deployment of a Chinese-made integrated frontier monitoring system with advanced radars, acoustic monitoring devices, and drones. A spokesperson said that anyone trying to cross the border would be detected by the system, which automatically notifies soldiers. "China has also deployed GGJ-2 Unmanned Aerial Vehicles that can operate at high altitude for up to 20 hours along both the Tibet and Xinjiang borders, in regions where troops cannot be stationed. A researcher at the Tibet Policy Institute based in India, believes that satellites are also part of the increasingly automated digital wall."

Lhasa, the Tibetan capital, does not have a single, I repeat, single, representative of the international media posted there, not even a stringer. There is no one from the United Nations (or its many related agencies), The Red Cross, Amnesty International, Human Rights Watch, Médecins Sans Frontières or Reporters Without Borders. You name it, not a sole representative from any of those various agencies, usually jostling for turf or a story in every other conflict or disaster zone in the world. Even beleaguered Gaza has half-a-dozen such UN agencies and NGOs stationed there. Reporters Without Borders describes North Korea as the world's most closed country, ranking it last in the Press Freedom Index. But half a dozen international agencies, including *Associated Press* and *Agence France-Presse* have bureaus of some kind in Pyongyang. Only Lhasa has *nothing* besides China's propaganda machine. It is a dead zone as far as journalistic access is concerned.

No region in China, not even Xinjiang, sees more per-capita spending on security than Tibet, where in 2017 China spent 3,137 yuan per person—more than the 2,417 for Xinjiang and well ahead of the national average of just 763 yuan. The inescapable ubiquity and omnipotence of China's giant internal security apparatus, on which it spends more than its defence budget ($110 billion in 2016, according to the *Economist*), did, for a time, put a crimp on Tibetan activism, especially after the last major uprising in 2008. But Tibetans have countered by radically altering their method of protest to one requiring no underground organizations, no secret meetings, not even the briefest of exchanges—anything that could be spied upon or overheard by the regime.

All it takes these days for an uprising in Tibet is a solitary committed Tibetan, fed up to the teeth with living under Chinese rule, and armed simply with a plastic jug of gasoline and a Bic lighter. To date, one hundred and sixty-four self-immolations have taken place all over the Tibetan plateau, some even within the exile community. A horrendous world record, no other country coming a distant, even a far distant, second. Most of the protagonists are very young, often monks or nuns, who, before carrying out their last brave act, nearly always call out for the return of the Dalai Lama to a free and independent Tibet.[*] Barbara Demick's recent and comprehensive study of self-immolations in Ngawa county notes that the immolators have perfected their technique, wrapping themselves in quilts and wire *to prevent rescue*, dousing themselves in gasoline and swallowing it, too, to ensure they will burn from the inside.[11]

Analysts in the West[12] now agree that the self-immolations by Tibetans protesting Chinese domination of Tibet have had a greater impact than earlier protests, where despite considerable loss of life,

---

[*]The nomad poet Zungshu Kyi from the Tsanak grasslands of Amdo gave voice to the aspirations and grim resolve of the young self-immolators in her 2012 poem "I Will Burn Myself Again and Again (*nga yang yang bardö*)." An excerpt: "Brothers and sisters, old and young, who will live forever in my heart/ Gods and goddesses illuminated by the conviction of my love and faith/ What I want is lasting peace and freedom/ What I am searching for is an existence of equality and caring/ Until I can accomplish this/ I will burn myself again and again." http://www.rangzen.net.

as in 2008, casualty figures were simply suppressed by the Chinese government. Self-immolations, on the other hand, result in dramatic images and videos easily transmitted by Internet and cell phones to news media and supporters outside and even to remote and far-flung areas on the Tibetan plateau.

Chinese authorities, mindful of the fact that the self-immolation of a Tunisian street vendor in 2010 sparked off the cataclysmic Arab Spring uprisings, even inspiring a series of "Jasmine" protests in China itself, have attempted to clamp down on the self-immolations in Tibet by punishing family members and friends of the immolators with fines and prison sentences. Even collective punishment has been meted out to some communities unwittingly involved. Adding to the leadership's unease is that most self-immolations have taken place not in the hinterlands of Tibet but populated areas closer to China as Ngawa, Kanlho and Choné.

The lack of results from such heavy-handed tactics and unremitting pressure from Beijing has motivated desperate local Communist authorities in Tibetan areas to seek alternative means of discouraging self-immolations. One is, I am informed, the unexpected but welcome official encouragement of young Tibetans to undertake educational and cultural projects, for which, apparently even a small measure of funding (siphoned off from China's precious infrastructure spending?) is being provided.

The self-immolations have not entirely ended, and there is no way of knowing what is really going on inside the Kafkaesque confines of occupied Tibet, but it appears (and that is all it is at the moment—just an appearance) that less drastic and more intellectual, artistic, spiritual and literary forms of indirect opposition to Chinese oppression are somehow beginning to make themselves felt—and even (it is whispered) ushering in a modest cultural renaissance throughout the plateau.

Individual Tibetans and institutions are now engaged in publishing ventures in traditional, religious texts and new writing and scholarship. One group of Tibetan *philosophes*, surely inspired by Denis Diderot and the Encyclopédistes, are collecting and publishing the writings and researches of hundreds of contributors on history, language, medicine, folklore, the Gesar Epic, music, art, architecture and much more within the "Great Cultural Treasury of the Himalayas" (*himalaya rig-zod chenmo*).[13]

Despite China having some of the world's most onerous Internet restrictions* the Net is nonetheless the only true medium of free expression in the PRC. The late Liu Xiaobo, the writer, political prisoner and Nobel Peace Prize Laureate, was in no way exaggerating when he gratefully acknowledged that " . . . the Internet is truly God's gift to the Chinese people." Inside Tibet, many websites, blogs and chat-rooms—most of which have been being closed down multiple times and restarted under different digital incarnations—have become the principal intellectual and political lifeline to the outside world. This Internet revolution in Tibet also gave my writing a new lease of life.

Earlier I had published my essays and stories only in print, reaching less than a thousand readers in India and perhaps a hundred or so in the West. Now in my mountain retreat in Tennessee, in between changing diapers, preparing my specialty baby food blend and organic fruit compotes for two successive daughters—Namkha Lhamo and Namtso Kyi, I started posting my opinions and essays on various exile web journals, including my own blog *Shadow Tibet*.

This increased my readership dramatically, and, of course, drew immediate fire from the exile-establishment and its henchmen. In a public talk exile, Prime Minister Samdong Rinpoche called me and other Tibetan independence advocates more dangerous than the Chinese Communists.[14] The Tibetan Service at Radio Free Asia (funded by the U.S. Congress) that had regularly carried interviews and feature programs of mine was directed by Samdhong Rinpoche to have nothing further to do with me—which it tamely did.

Then quite unexpectedly and to my enormous gratification, my writings began attracting readership inside Tibet, where some of my essays were translated into Tibetan and Chinese, re-posted on a variety

---

*China has been named "the world's worst abuser of internet freedom" for the third consecutive year. According to the new report released by Freedom House, Freedom of the Net 2017—*Manipulating Social Media to Undermine Democracy*, China leads in violating Internet freedom, followed by Syria and Ethiopia.

of websites and discussed.˙ One post analyzing my 'Black Annals' review essay even won the "blog of the year" award in 2008 and was included *sub rosa* in a couple of university history syllabi inside Tibet. My writings of course drew some official Chinese response, and once in the *People's Daily* I was labeled "the radical Tibetan separatist"[15] but was also gratifyingly quoted at length for having "pitilessly exposed" the "Dalai Lama's democracy myth" when in fact all I had done was discuss the fundamental flaws in the exile democratic system and suggested certain reforms. Readers inside Tibet seemed to enjoy my Orwell inspired writings on Tibetan popular culture: folktales, oracles, nature conservancy, superstitions, ghost stories, courtesans, criminals, even the "Lhasa Ripper", and also my culinary posts on Tibetan New Year cookies, momo dumplings, the millet chang of Sikkim and the origins and evolution of Tibetan restaurant culture.

I was rewarded with friendship and appreciation (of a limited clandestine sort) from inside Tibet, including an honoured placement in a sharp political cartoon[16] and in an extraordinary painting by Benchung of Lhasa. I also received a beautiful ceramic statuette of Lu Xun, the Orwell of China, whose writings I had long admired and attempted to emulate. Reviewing my writings in her *Scarlet Ruins: Essays on Tibet*,[17] the Beijing based Tibet writer Tsering Woeser paid me the supreme compliment of considering me ". . . the Lu Xun of Tibet." My pieces on the resistance were particularly valued by readers on the plateau, and a post on the Camp Hale commemoration (in *Shadow Tibet* and *Huffington Post*) pulled me into a couple of Skype and WeChat discussions.

Once the formal ceremony at the Camp Hale site had concluded late in the afternoon, we moved over to the remains of a structure, possibly the foundation of a Quonset hut, and held a *Sangsöl* ceremony there. Two monks had come from Boulder, and everyone joined in the prayers. We started a small fire and burned juniper, sage, incense and tsampa

---

˙To the most prolific John Lee and other Chinese and Tibetan translators I owe a profound debt of gratitude for their skilful "samizdat" transference of my words across the "Great Firewall", http://beyondhighwall.blogspot.com/2014/08/blog-post.html

and soon got a nice column of aromatic smoke rising into the clear but darkening sky. It was just before sunset when we all formed a circle and, tossing tsampa in the air, shouted, *"lha gyalo"* or "Victory to the Gods".

After the *Sangsöl* ceremony, most of us left for Leadville, a once roaring frontier mining town, to find the Cloud City Bar, where fifty years ago CIA instructors drove down from Camp Hale for a drink after putting their Tibetans trainees to bed. We didn't find Cloud City but eventually settled on Quincy's, a real old West establishment with great steaks, spare ribs and plenty of beer and whiskey. About thirty-five of us, Tibetans and Americans, crowded around the large tables and talked late into the night.

Early next morning, my friend Warren Smith and I took Highway 82 to Aspen. We drove high up the Rockies to Independence Pass (renamed Rangzen-La) that at 12,095 feet is about six hundred feet higher than Lhasa city. Unlike mountain passes in Tibet, there were no cairns on the top here—no large piles of stone topped with yak horns and ragged prayer flags flapping in the wind. But I tied a pristine white *khata* scarf to a guardrail at the scenic overlook, and closing my eyes, offered a supplication to whatever deity presided over these heights. The pass was deserted, so I did not feel like a complete idiot when I bellowed my victory cry *"lha gyalo—ki-hi-hi!"* as loudly as I could, and heard it echo over the distant mountains. Having got that off my chest, I walked back to the car, and we drove on.

> I will remember them always . . .
>
> I'd like to name them all by name,
> But the list, confiscated, is nowhere to be found.
>
> I have woven a wide mantle for them
> From their meager, overheard words.
>
> I will remember them always and everywhere,
> I will never forget them no matter what comes.
>
> —Anna Akhmatova "Second Epilogue" *Requiem.*

ACKNOWLEDGEMENTS

Boris Pasternak recalled the words of his friend Ekaterina Krashennikova upon reading *Doctor Zhivago*. She had said, "Don't forget yourself to the point of believing that it was you who wrote this work. It was the Russian people and their sufferings who created it. You should thank God for allowing you to express it through your pen."

Echoes from Forgotten Mountains has been created from the memories, stories and suffering of the Tibetan people. It would be remiss of me if I did not thank as many of them individually as I possibly could for the interviews, recollections, conversations and even casual throwaway lines that have breathed substance and life to the pages of this book.

For all members of the Resistance who gave me interviews, reminiscenses, information and banter: Tsongkha Lhamo Tsering, Athar Norbu, Ratruk Ngawang, Tenzin Tsultrim Jhadötsang, Taktser Trulku Thupten Jigme Norbu, Gyalo Thondup, Drunyik Loden Chiso, Chamdo Kunchok Dorje, Tsering Topgyal Phupatsang, Ani Pachen Lemdatsang, Nyrarong Aten Dogyaltsang, Dorji Yudon Gyari, Nyarong Atring, Nima Gyaritsang, Lodi Gyaltsen Gyari, Lithang Jamyang Tsultrim, Kalsang Gyadotsang, Alo Chonze Tsering Dorje, Besa Chökyong, Tamdin Tashi, Lotse Gatsetsang, Baba Gedun

Thargay, Lhamotsang Tsering Wangchuk, Tashi Dolma (Mrs Lhamo Tsering) and Adhi Tapontsang—THANK YOU.

For information on the Lhasa Uprising, the Dalai Lama's Escape and the Cultural Revolution I must thank: Nyemo Bhonshod Bhusang, Phala Thupten Wöden, Maja Tsewang Gyurme, Gyakpon Kalsang Damdul, Rupon Sonam Tashi, Bharshi Tsendron Ngawang Tenkyong, Zasak Jigme Taring, Lhenga Tseten Namgyal, Ngawang Dhakpa Chitiling, Taktra Rimpoche, Namgyal Wangdu Gyaltse, Amdo Samdup, Thunsur Lobsang Tenzin, Tseten Yangki (Kundeling), Thupten Anyetsang, Kalsang Dhargay Anyetsang, Thupten Tsering Lingtsang, Manang Sonam Topgyal, Kunsang Paljor, Tsering Woeser, Pembar Trulku and Khardo Tulku.

For comrades and informants from the Mustang force: Wangdü Gyadotsang, Tashi "Chungchung" Thundup, Thupten "Gyau", Drayab Lobsang "Kambo" Topgyal, Dhakpa Dorje, Damdul, Gyen Tendar, Bhutuk, Kalsang, Gyen Rakra Gyadhar, Ayo Dawa, Machen Shanga, Khalay Jhampa, Drunyik Jhampa, Chamdo Lonye, Chatreng Dawa, Ah-Trinlay, Gyakpon Tenpa, Dhargon Norbu Dorje, Lhasang Tsering, Gyalpo Tsering and others. Thank you for the support and the stories.

My own story that provides the "frame device" for the book, has been constructed in large part from the memories of my mother, grandaunt, uncles, aunts and cousins who need to be acknowledged and thanked: Lobsang Deki Lhawang, Tesur Yangchen Palmo, Tethong Sonam Tomjor, Rakra Rinpoche, Tsewang Chogyal Tethong, Tenzin Gyeche Tethong, Tenzin Namgyal Tethong, Sonam Gyaltsen, Tesur Ngutup, Dundul Namgyal Tsarong, Paljor Tsarong, Nornang Ganden, Rinchen Dolma Taring, Sampho Ngutup Wangmo and Jhola Chime Gompo la (Gelong Loden).

For scholarly guidance and generous help I must above all thank Tibet's great scholar Josayma Tashi Tsering former director Amnye Machen Institute. I must also thank Professor Drakton Jampa Gyaltsen, Hugh Richardson, the late Elliot Sperling, Dr Yudru Tsomo, Lisa Cathey and Alex Raymond for valuable information and advice. For reading the manuscript and providing necessary corrections and suggestions I must thank: Robert Webster Ford, Donald Lopez Jr, Peter Brown, Tenzing Sonam and my dear sister Rigzin Dolkar.

Christophe Besuchet needs special thanks for structuring my basic manuscript and creating the index and endnotes. Christophe especially needs to be thanked for the body of authoritative and outstanding maps he has produced for the book. Christophe has also put together the photo pages, retouching and enhancing the individual images where needed.

For photographs I must thank High Asia Archives, Amnye Machen Institute, Tenzing Sonam and Lhamo Tsering Archives, Claire Harris and Oxford Pitt Rivers Museum (for photos by Spencer Chapman), Trans-Himalayan Heritage Art and Tempa Bhutia (Lha Tsering family), Tsongkha Jhanjup Jinpa, Thinlay Samdup, Alo Chonze, Rabga Pangdatsang, Gerald Roche, Timothy Allen and Tsering Woeser la and George Patterson. I must also thank Stefan Daehler for sending me a collection of lost family (Pulger/Tethong) photographs he had recovered and restored.

I must thank Liz Calder who first commissioned this work for Bloomsbury Publications and Meru Gokhale who accepted my finished book for publication by Penguin Random House India—and also throwing in the neat Tolstoian subtitle. Thanks are due to Tenzing Sonam and Ritu Sarin for making the initial serendipitous introduction to Meru.

Lastly, I must thank my dearest wife Tenzing Chounzom la who gave me unflinching and unquestioning support and love during all those years it took for *Echoes from Forgotten Mountains* to get written and finally published, and also my wonderful daughters Namkha and Namtso, who never lost faith in their "Pala" and his never-ending book.

NOTES

INTRODUCTION

1. David Jackson, *The Mollas of Mustang: Historical, Religious, and Oratorical Traditions of the Nepalese–Tibetan Borderland* (Dharamshala: Library of Tibetan Works and Archives, 1984).

2. Aten Dogyaltsang, *An Historical Oration from Khams: The Ancient Recitations of Nyagrong* (Dharamshala: Amnye Machen Institute, 1993).

3. F.W. Thomas, *Documents of Eighth-Century Tibetan Military Occupation of Turkestan* (London: Royal Asiatic Society, 1951), p. 139.

4. Charles Bell, *The People of Tibet* (Oxford: Clarendon Press, 1928), frontispiece. My grand-aunt Yangchen Palmo Tesur is sitting front-centre on a carpet.

5. Hugh Richardson, *High Peaks, Pure Earth: Collected Writings on Tibetan History and Culture* (London: Serindia, 1998), p. 703.

6. Anthony Thomas (director), *The Tankman*, Frontline, 11 April 2006, www.pbs.org/wgbh/pages/frontline/tankman/

7. Simone Weil and Rachel Bespaloff, *War and the Iliad* (New York: New York Review Books, 2005).

8. Do-choe Kunchok Tendar, *Tears of Blood (Trag-ge mik-chu) The Life Experience of Do-choe Kunchok Tendar* (Dharamshala: self-published, 2002).

9. Janet Gyatso, 'Autobiography in Tibetan Religious Literature: Reflections on its Modes of Self-Presentation', in *Tibetan Studies, Proceedings of the 5th Seminar of the IATS*, ed. Shoren Ihara and Zuiho Yamaguchi (Narita: 1989).

    Janet Gyatso, 'Counting Crow's Teeth: Tibetans and Their Diary-Writing Practises', in *Les Habitants du Toit du Monde*, ed. Samten Karmay and P. Sagent (Paris: 1997).

    Charlene Makley, '"Speaking Bitterness" Autobiography, History and Mnemonic Politics on the Sino Tibetan Frontiers', *Comparitive Studies of Society and History*, 47, no.1 (January 2005).

10. Isabelle Henrion-Dourcy, *From Tibet to Exile, and Back to China: A Contemporary Autobiography Published on Both Sides of the Border* (work in progress).

11. Ratuk Ngawang, *Mi tshe'i lo rgyus zol med srong po'i gtam gyi rol mo, The Autobiography of Dasur Ratuk Ngawang of Lithang*, 4 volumes (Dharamshala: Amnye Machen Institute, 2008).

12. Tsongkha Lhamo Tsering, *Resistance* (Btsan rgol rgyal skyob) Occupied Tibet Series, ed. Tashi Tsering (Dharamshala: AMI Books, Amnye Machen Institute, 2017).

13. Jamyang Norbu, 'Buddha's "Theory of Everything"', *Tricycle*, 29 August 2019, tricycle.org/trikedaily/buddhism-universal-theory/

CHAPTER 1 ORIGIN CHRONICLE: MATRILINEAL

1. Marie Seton, *Portrait of a Director: Satyajit Ray* (Bloomington & London: Indiana University Press, 1971), p. 248.

2. US National Archives, 893B.24222/ 2–1651, American Consulate, Calcutta, to US State Department, 16 February 1951.

3. Douglas Veenhof, *White Lama: The Life of Tantric Yogi Theos Bernard, Tibet's Lost Emissary to the New World* (New York: Harmony Books, 2011).

4. Peter Goullart, *Forgotten Kingdom: Eight Years in Likiang* (London: John Murray, 1955).

5. D. S. Kansakar Hilker, *Syamukapu; the Lhasa Newars of Kalimpong and Kathamandu* (Kathamandu: Vajra Publications, 2005), p. 81.

6. René von Nebesky–Wojkowitz, *Where the Gods Are Mountains* (New York: Reynal and Company, 1957), pp. 69–70.

7. Sangharakshita, *In The Sign of The Golden Wheel: Indian Memoirs of an English Buddhist* (Glasgow: Windhorse Publications, 1996), p. 108.

8. Jan Morris, *A Writer's World Travels: 1950–2000* (London: Faber & Faber, 2004), p. 193.

9. Nebesky–Wojkowitz, *Where the Gods Are Mountains*, p. 58.

10. Sudha Shah, *The King in Exile: The Fall of the Royal Family of Burma* (Delhi: HarperCollins India, 2012), p. 262.

11. Sangharakshita, *Facing Mount Kanchenjunga: An English Buddhist in the Eastern Himalayas* (Glasgow: Windhorse Publications, 1991).

12. Alena Adamkova, *Devika Rani Roerich—Queen of the Silver Screen* (Naggar: International Roerich Memorial Trust, 2008).

13. Sangharakshita, pp. 344–45

14. Dr T. Pulger, *Family History of Raja Tenduk Pulger (Clan: Adenphu-so)* (unpublished manuscript), p. 37.

15. Hsiao-Ting Lin, *Tibet and Nationalist China's Frontier: Intrigues and Ethnopolitics 1928–49* (Vancouver: UBC Press, 2006), p. 145.

16. William Woodville Rockhill, 'The Dalai Lamas of Lhasa and their relations with The Manchu Emperors of China 1644–1908', *T'oung Pao* 通報, *Series III,* I, no 4. (1998), p. 15

17. Lo-Shu-Fu, comp. and trans., *A Documentary Chronicle of Sino-Western Relations (1644–1820)* (Tucson: University of Arizona Press, 1966), p. 10.

18. Luciano Petech, *China and Tibet in the Early XVIIth Century: History of the Establishment of Chinese Protectorate in Tibet* (Leiden: E. J. Brill, 1972), p. 149.

19. L. A. Waddell, *Lhasa and Its Mysteries: With a Record of the Expedition of 1903–1904* (London: Methuen, 1905), pp. 48–49.

20. Elliot Sperling, *The Tibet–China Conflict: History and Polemics, Policy Studies 7* (Washington: East-West Center, 2004),p.76

21. K. Dhondup, *The Water-Bird and Other Years: A History of the 13th Dalai Lama and After* (New Delhi: Rangwang Publishers, 1986), p. 42. [Dhondup mentions the names of four generals, including Tethong.]

22. Tsepon W. D. Shakabpa, *Tibet: A Political History* (New Haven & London: Yale University Press, 1960), p. 239.

23. Eric Teichman, *Travels of a Consular Officer in Eastern Tibet* (Cambridge: Cambridge University Press, 1922), p. 118.

24. Tsepon Wangchuk Deden Shakabpa, *One Hundred Thousand Moons: An Advanced Political History of Tibet, Vol 2* (Lieden/Boston: Brill, 1908), p. 790.

25. Teichman, *Travels*, p. 117.

26. Diary of Howard Bucknell Jr, American Legation, Peking, Yunnan, Szechuan and Tibet. 11 January 1921–1 July 1921, 31 May 1921, 8th Day, Dergé (Chung Ra). Courtesy of Lucy Needham.
[Howard Bucknell Jr was a Student Interpreter at the American Legation, Peking. He accompanied Major John Magruder, F. A., Assistant Military Attaché, Peking, China on the trip]

27. Jamyang Norbu, 'The Girl and the Golok Chief', Phayul.com, 25 January 2005, www.phayul.com/news/article.aspx?id=8887&t=1

28. *Account of Drayab Tribes and Monasteries*, official *neibu* (restricted circulation) publication from Tibet, photocopy, 23 pages. Kindly shown to me by Tashi Tsering, director of AMI.

29. Pempa Jamyang, 'Miscellaneous Account of the Tethong family head, Gyurme Gyatso, and son Sonam Topjor Wangchuk', in *Bod-kyi lo-rgyus rig-gnas dpyad- gzhi'i rgyu-cha bdams-bsgrigs* (*Research materials for Tibetan History and Culture*) (Shigatse: Shigatse Municipal Publication Committee, 2005).

CHAPTER 2 ORIGIN CHRONICLE: PATRILINEAL

1. Roy Andrew Miller, *Languages and History: Japanese, Korean, and Altaic* (Oslo: White Orchid Press, The Institute for Comparative Research in Human Culture, 1996).

2. Henry H. Howarth, *History of the Mongols: From the 9th to the 19th Century,* 4 volumes (London: Longman Green and Co, 1876–1927).

3. Sangharakshita, *Tibetan Buddhism: An Introduction* (Birmingham: Windhorse Publications, 1996), p. 41.

4. Gos lo-tsa-ba gZon-nu dpal, *Deb-t'er sngon-po*, trans. George N. Roerich, *The Blue Annals* (Calcutta: Royal Asiatic Society of Bengal, 1949), p. 56.

5. Wang Yao, 'Fragments From Historical Records About the Life of Emperor Gongdi of the Song Dynasty', *Tibet Studies (A Semi-Annual)* (June 1989).

6. H. H. Risley, *The Gazetteer of Sikhim* (Calcutta: Bengal Secretariat Press, 1894), p. 33.

7. Alex McKay, *Tibet and the British Raj: The Frontier Cadre 1904–1947* (London: Curzon Press, 1997), p. 99.

8. J. A. H. Louis, *The Gates of Thibet*, (Calcutta: Catholic Orphan Press, 1894. Reprint Delhi: Vivek Publishing House, 1972), p. 127.

9. J. A. Graham, *On the Threshold of Three Close Lands—The Guild Outpost in the Eastern Himalayas* (Edinburgh: R&R Clark, 1897).

10. Their Highnesses Chögyal Thutob Namgyal and Queen Yeshi Dolma of Sikkim, *'Bras ljongs rgyal rabs (The History of Sikkim)* (Gangtok: The Tsuklakhang Trust, 2003, compiled in 1908).

11. John Claude White, *Sikhim & Bhutan: Twenty-one Years on the North-East Frontier, 1887–1908* (New York: Longmans, 1909), p. 23.

12. Risley, *Gazetteer*, p. xxi.

13. C. E. Buckland C.I.E, *Dictionary of Indian Biography* (London: Swan Sonnenschein & Co., LIM., 1906), p. 419.

14. David Macdonald, *Twenty Years in Tibet* (London: Seeley Service & Co, 1932), p. 49.

CHAPTER 3 MY JOURNEY TO LHASA

1. Dundul Namgyal Tsarong, *In the Service of His Country: The Biography of Dasang Damdul Tsarong Commander General of Tibet* (Ithaca, NY: Snow Lion Publications, 2000), p. 62.

2. David Macdonald, *Touring in Sikkim and Tibet* (Siliguri: OBS Publishers, 1943), p. 84.

3. Spencer Chapman, *Lhasa: The Holy City* (London: Chatto & Windus, 1940), p. 29.

4. *Mangtso Newspaper*, Dharamshala, 31 October 1993. Facsimile of Foreign Bureau letter on the cover page of special supplementary edition. Image reproduced with kind permission of Public Records Office, London.

5. Shakabpa, *Advanced History*, p. 923.

6. Frank Kingdon–Ward, *National Geographic Magazine* CI, no. 3 (March 1952):

7. Joseph Kresh, trans., *The Diaries of Franz Kafka 1910–1923* (New York: Shlocken Books, 1948), p. 357, 360.

CHAPTER 4 GHOSTS OF CHAMDO

1. Alan Winnington, *Tibet: the Record of a Journey* (London: Lawrence & Wishart Ltd., 1957).
2. George Pereira and Francis Younghusband, *Peking to Lhasa* (Boston: Houghton Mifflin, 1926).
3. André Migot, *Tibetan Marches* (London: Rupert Hart-Davis, 1956).
4. Robert Ford, *Captured in Tibet* (London: George G. Harrap, 1957).
5. William Woodville Rockhill, 'Tibet. A Geographical, Ethnographical and Historical Sketch, derived from Chinese Sources', *Journal of the Royal Asiatic Society*, (1891).
6. Niall Ferguson, *Virtual History: Alternatives and Counterfactuals* (New York: Basic Books, 1999).
7. K. Dhondup, 'Controversy Over the Tibetan Communist Movement—A Personal View', *Tibetan Review*, 15, no. 7 (July, 1980): pp. 9–15.
8. Maja Tsewang Gyurme, interview, 14 March 1992, Dharamshala.
9. Sonam Tashi, *The Life of a Tibet Soldier: Biography of Kusung Rupon Sonam Tashi, (bhod dmag gchig ge me tsay).* (Dharamshala: self-published, 2004).
10. Namgyal Wangdu Gyaltse, *Political and Military History of Tibet*, Vol. 2, trans. Yeshi Dhondup (Dharamshala: Library of Tibetan Works and Archives, 2010) Tibetan language: *Bhod gyalkhap kyi chapsee dhang drelwae magdon logyus* (Dharamshala: Tibetan Veterans Association of Dharamshala, 2003).
11. Jianglin Li and Matthew Akester, *WAR ON TIBET: Chinese and Tibetan documents on the history of the Communist occupation* (website) Has a section on the Battle of Chamdo, historicaldocs.blogspot.com/p/chinese.html
12. Alex Raymond, *La politique tibétaine du gouvernement de la RPC de 1949 à 1951* (PhD diss., unpublished, 2017).
13. Ford, *Captured,* pp. 37 38
14. British Foreign Office Records, London, 371/20222, Neame's Recommendations.
15. Shakabpa, *Advanced History,* p. 937.
16. Melvyn C. Goldstein, *The Demise of the Lamaist State, A History of Modern Tibet 1913–1951: Vol. 1* (Berkeley: University of California Press, 1989), p. 688.

17. CPC Chronicles on Tibet 1949–1966, p. 2, www.tibet.cn/english/zt/ history/..%5Chistory/200402004525133727.htm

18. Jung Chang and Jon Halliday, *Mao: The Unknown Story* (London: Jonathan Cape, 2005).

19. Chang Kuohua (Zhang Guohua), 'Tibet Returns to the Bosom of the Motherland (Revolutionary Reminiscence)', *South China Morning Post*, November 6, 1962, no. 2854.

20. Edgar O' Balance, *The Red Army of China* (London: Faber & Faber, 1962).

21. Melvyn C. Goldstein, Dawei Sherap and William R. Siebenschuh, *A Tibetan Revolutionary: The Political Life and Times of Bapa Phuntso Wangye* (Berkeley: University of California Press, 2004).

22. Warren W. Smith Jr, *Tibetan Nation: A History of Tibetan Nationalism and Sino–Tibetan Relations* (Boulder: Westview Press, 1996).

23. Shakabpa, *Advanced History*, p. 935.

24. Goldstein, *History Vol. 1*, p. 688.

25. Teichman, *Travels*, p. 156.

26. Alex Raymond, 'October 1950: the battle of Chamdo' (unpublished paper read at the International Tibet Studies Conference, Paris, France, July 2019).

27. Khreng tse kre, 'Eyewitness Account of the Liberation of Chamdo', Chab-mdo sa-khul bcings-'grol btang-ba'i dmag 'thab. *Sources on the Culture and History of Tibet: bhod kyi lo-rgyus rig-gnas dpyad-gzhi'i rgyu-cha bdams-bsgrigs*, Vol. 1. (Lhasa: 1982).

28. René von Nebesky–Wojkowitz, *Where the Gods Are Mountains* (New York: Reynal and Company, 1957), p. 91.

29. Qingying Chen, *Tibetan History* (Beijing: China Intercontinental Press, 2003).

30. Kong Fei-tsi, *Tse srog gi bhul skyes* (Gift of Life), trans. Wanglag (Lhasa: Tibetan Peoples Publishing House, 2001).

31. Ford, *Captured*, pp. 127–28.

32. Mikel Dunham, *Buddha's Warriors: The Story of the CIA-Backed Tibetan Freedom Fighters, the Chinese Invasion and the Ultimate Fall of Tibet* (New York: Penguin, 2004), p. 73.

33. Namgyal Wangdu, *Military History*, pp. 135–37.

34. Ibid., p. 136. The author refers to an article 'One thousand Kilometer March by the PLA Advance Troops' by Chen Ziyi, in the first volume of the *Selected Materials on the History and Culture of Tibet.*

35. Tsering Shakya, *The Dragon in the Land of Snows: A History of Modern Tibet Since 1947* (New York: Columbia U Press, 1999). p. 45.

36. 建国以来毛泽东文稿 (Jianguo Yilai Mao Zedong Wengao), *Mao Zedong's Manuscript Since Establishment of the* PRC. Vol 1 (Beijing), pp. 470–76. Photocopies and translation of the pages kindly provided to the author by Tseten Wangchuk of VOA Tibetan section.

37. Luciano Petech, *Aristocracy and Government in Tibet 1728–1959* (Rome: Serie Orientalia Roma XLV, Is.M.E.O. 1973), p. 111.

38. Shakabpa, *Advanced History*, p. 957.

39. Dalai Lama, *My Land and My People,* pp. 84–85.

40. Goldstein, *History Vol. 1,* p. 746.

CHAPTER 5 SEVENTEEN POINT SWINDLE

1. www.degreesoflatitude.com/entity/treaty/
   www.nassakb.com/treaties-in-international-relations-and-internation- al-law/
   en.wikipedia.org/wiki/Treaty

2. Goldstein, *History Vol. 1,* p. 741.

3. Goldstein, *Tibetan Revolutionary*, p. 141.

4. Lhamo Tsering, interview, Dharamshala, 17–18 September 1991.

5. Goldstein, *Tibetan Revolutionary*, pp. 141–43.

6. Shakya, *Dragon,* p. 17.

7. John Kenneth Knaus, *Orphans of the Cold War: America and the Tibetan Struggle for Survival* (New York: Public Affairs, 1999), p. 73.

8. Goldstein, *History Vol. 1*, p. 736.

9 World Tibet Network News, *'Eyewitness to History',* 24 November 1994. www.tibet.ca/en/library/wtn/archive/old?y=1994&m=11&p=24-2_1

10. David Snellgrove, 'Hugh Richardson Obituary', in *Buddhist Studies Review* 18, no. I (2001).

11. Goldstein, *History Vol. 1,* p. 746.

12. Ibid., p. 743.

13. Shakya, *Dragon,* p. 64.

14. Khemey Sonam Wangdu, *Ge-poi Lo-gyud Bel-tam* (Dharamsala: Library of Tibetan Works and Archives, 1982), pp. 134–35.
15. Takla Phuntsok Tashi, *Mi-tsei Jungwa Jodpa* vol. 2 (Dharamsala: Library of Tibetan Works and Archives, 1995), p. 52.
16. Goldstein, *History Vol. 1*, p. 759.
17. Ibid., p. 760.
18. Sam Van Shaik, *Tibet: A History* (New Haven & London: Yale University Press, 2011), p. 219.
19. Goldstein, *Tibetan Revolutionary,* p. 150.
20. Shakya, *Dragon*, p. 70.
21. Dalai Lama, *My Land and My People* (New York: McGraw–Hill, 1962), p. 88.
22. Ngabö Ngawang Jigme, 'Statement at the second session of the fifth people Congress, Lhasa, July 31, 1989', in *Facts about the 17-Point "Agreement" between Tibet and China* (Dharamshala: Central Tibetan Administration), p. 10.
23. Shakya, *Dragon*, p. 71.

CHAPTER 6 REQUIEM

1. Lhalu Se Biography, Tibet Album, Pitt Rivers Museum, https://tibet.prm.ox.ac.uk › biography_118
2. Namgyal Wangdu, *Military History*, p. 114.
3. This song has been repeated in other Tibetan histories, notably Goldstein, *History of Modern Tibet*, vol. 1, p. 297.
4. Goldstein, *History*, vol. 1, p. 691.
5. Khedrup and Shingza Tenzin Chodrag, 'A Brief Account of The Great Patriot Karchung Tsering Thondup', in *Tibetan History & Cultural Research and Compilation,* Lhasa 2006. Any reference to Karchung's battle with the PLA is avoided and only the 'peaceful' nature of the invasion and Ngabö's surrender of '1,700' troops is mentioned.
6. Max Hasting, *The Korean War* (New York: Simon and Schuster, 1987).
7. Ibid.
8. Alex Raymond. Email correspondence with the author, 9 February 2020.

9. Goldstein, *Tibetan Revolutionary*, p. 156.

10. Tony Judt, *Postwar: A History of Europe Since 1945* (New York: Penguin Press, 2005).

11. 'Survey of China Mainland Press' (American Consulate General, Hong Kong) No. 2854, pp. 5–6.

12. Alex Raymond, private email correspondence with the author, 9 February 2020.

13. L. A. Waddell, *Lhasa and Its Mysteries: With a Record of the Expedition of 1903–1904* (London: Methuen, 1905), p. 160.

CHAPTER 7 FALL OF THE SOUTH

1. My uncle Sonam Tomjor Tethong told me this story at Dharamshala in October 1980.

2. Goldstein, *History*, vol. 1, p. 274.

3. Kalsang Gyadotsang, interview, 2 November 1989, New York City.

4. Carole McGranahan, 'Lobzang Yampel Pangdatsang', in *Treasury of Lives*, February 2016, www.treasuryoflives.org/biographies/view/Yampel-Pangdatsang/13523

5. Tsering Woeser, *Forbidden Memory: Tibet During the Cultural Revolution* (Taipei: Locus, 2006), pp. 132–33.

6. Carole McGranahan, 'On Social Death: The Spang Mda'Tsang Family and 20th Century Tibetan History', in *Trails of the Tibetan Tradition*, ed. Roberto Vitali (Dharamshala: Amnye Machen Institute, 2014).

7. Pema Wangdu, 'Origins and Accounts of so-called "Bamo" of Sakya', *Yum-Tsho: The Journal of Tibetan Women's Studies* 1, no. 3, (1995).

8. Tim Chamberlain, 'Edge of Empires', *British Museum Magazine* spring/summer (2010).

9. Goldstein, *History*, vol. 1, p. 691.

10. Geoffrey T. Bull, *When Iron Gates Yield* (London: Hodder & Stoughton, 1955), pp. 87–88.

11. Email correspondence with Karen Backman, April 2015.

12. Bull, *Iron Gates*, p. 130.

13. Namgyal Wangdu, *Military History*, p. 129.

14. Bull, *Iron Gates*, p. 131.

CHAPTER 8 "NEST OF SPIES"

1. Dundul Namgyal Tsarong, *In the Service of His Country: The Biography of Dasang Damdul Tsarong Commander General of Tibet* (Ithaca, NY: Snow Lion Publications, 2000).

2. Wangchen Gelek Surkhang, 'Tibet in the Early 20th Century', *Tibetan Studies Internet Newsletter* January (1999).

3. Eric Teichman, *Travels of a Consular Officer in Eastern Tibet* (Cambridge: Cambridge University Press, 1922), preface.

4. Charles Bell, *Portrait of a Dalai Lama: The Life and Times of the Great Thirteenth* (London: Collins, 1946), p. 352.

5. Che Minghuai/Zhang Huachuan, *Zhang Jingwu: The Representative of the Central People's Government in Tibet* (Beijing: China Tibetology Publishing House, 2009), pp. 32–34.

6. *Meetings With Dhardo Rinpoche* (UK: Clear Vision, 1987), https://bit. Ly/3opzEYV

7. Nebesky, *Mountains*, p. 117.

8. David Snellgrove, *Wikipedia*, en.wikipedia.org/wiki/David_Snellgrove

9. Kenneth Conboy and James Morrison, *The CIA's Secret War in Tibet* (Lawrence: University Press of Kansas, 2002), p. 13.

10. Hisao Kimura and Scott Berry, *Japanese Agent in Tibet: My Ten Years of Travel in Disguise* (London: Serindia Publications, 1990). pp. 195–97.

11. Ibid., p. 202–03.

12. Tashi Tsering, 'The Life of Rev. G. Tharchin: Missionary and Pioneer', *Christian Missionaries and Tibet Issue, Lungta* winter (1999).

13. Dawa Norbu, 'Pioneer and Patriot' (extract from an interview with Rev. G. Tharchin), *Christian Missionaries and Tibet Issue, Lungta* winter (1999).

14. Scott Berry, *Monks, Spies and a Soldier of Fortune: The Japanese in Tibet* (New York: St. Martin's Press, 1995).

15. *The Tibet Mirror*, October 1, 1952, vol. XX, no. 7, p. 8. Carole McGranahan, trans., 'Arrested Histories: Between Empire and Exile in 20th Century Tibet', (PhD diss., University of Michigan, 2001), pp. 247–48.

16. Shakya, *Dragon*, p. 80.

17. H. Louis Fader, *Called From Obscurity: The Life and Times of a True Son of Tibet Gergan Dorje Tharchin, Vol. 3* (Kalimpong: Tibet Mirror Press, 2009), p. 301.

18. George Patterson, *Up and Down Asia* (London: Faber & Faber, 1958).

19. Sangharakshita, *Facing Mount Kanchenjunga: An English Buddhist in the Eastern Himalayas* (Glasgow: Windhorse Publications, 1991), p. 386.

20. George Patterson, *A Fool At Forty* (Waco Texas: Word Books, 1970).

21. Claire Margaret Jordan (aka whitehound), members.madasafish. com/~cj_whitehound/family/Ethel_Maud_Shirran_b1904.htm

22. Conversation with George Patterson at the Hotel Tibet restaurant, Dharamshala, 1987.

23. Gordon Bowker, *George Orwell*, (London: Abacus, 2003), p. 88.

24. Sunanda K. Dutta–Ray, 'Solomon Calling', *The Asian Age*, June 28, 2011, archive.asianage.com/columnists/solomon-s-calling-926

25. Sunanda K. Dutta–Ray, *Smash and Grab: The Annexation of Sikkim* (Vikas, New Delhi, 1984).

26. John Kenneth Knaus, *Orphans of the Cold War: America and the Tibetan Struggle for Survival* (New York: Public Affairs, 1999), p. 60.

27. George Patterson, *Tibet In Revolt* (London: Faber & Faber, 1960).

28. Knaus, *Orphans*, p. 122.

29. Ibid.

30. Melvyn C. Goldstein, *The Storm Clouds Descend, 1955–1957, A History of Modern Tibet: Volume 3* (Berkeley: University of California Press, 2014), pp. 179–87.

31. Nicholas and Deki Rhodes, *A Man of the Frontier: S.W. Laden La (1876–1936), His Life and Times in Darjeeling and Tibet* (Kolkota: Library of Numismatic Studies, 2006).

32. Tom Stoppard, 'Going Back', *Independent Magazine*, 23 March (1991): 29.

33. Gordon Bowker, *Through the Dark Labyrinth; a Biography of Lawrence Durrell* (New York: St. Martin's Press, 1997).

34. Thomas Merton, *The Asian Journal of Thomas Merton* (New York: New Directions Pub. Corp., 1973), p. 101.

35. Associated Press, Reports on Nehru Meeting. New York: April 1, 1959.
    —AP Wirephoto via radio from New Delhi, (OB407 30HOA): 59.

36. 'Statement of Chomphel Sonam', *Tibet Under Chinese Communist Rule: A Compilation of Refugee Statements 1958–1975* (Dharamshala: Information and Publicity Office of His Holiness the Dalai Lama, 1976), p. 89.

CHAPTER 9 MARCH WINDS

1. Thupten Samphel, 'The Tibetan Music, Dance and Drama Society's New Drama', *Tibetan Bulletin* XIII, no. 2 (March–April 1981): p. 18.
2. Chris Mullin, 'Tibetan Conspiracy', *Far Eastern Economic Review*, Hong Kong (1975).
3. Chris Mullin, *The Year of the Fire Monkey* (London: Chatto & Windus, 1991).
4. Alo Chonzé, *Bod kyi gnas lugs bden 'dzin sgo phye ba'I lde mig zhes by aba alo chos mdzad kyi gdamz, spyi lo 1920 nas 1982 bar* (The Key that Opens the Door of Truth to the Tibetan Situation) (Sydney: self-published, 1983).
5. Lotse Gatsetang, *Bod cholkha gsum gyi ya gyal mdo khams sgang druglot shg tshan lithang spo 'bor raba sgang du she shing tsher long jon ye bstanlot shee nas so sos rgyal khab kyi don du shabs 'deg shus pa'i mi tshe'i lo rgyus tshans pa'i thig shing bzhugs so* (Darjeeling: Tibetan Refugee Self-Help Center Printing Department, 2001).
6. Baritsang, Dawa Tsering, *Zhungs khrag dron mo gangs can ljong su mchod* (An offering of warm blood as a sacrifice to the land of the snows), vol. 1 (Dharamshala: Central Tibetan Administration. 2007).
7. Besa Chökyong, interview with the author, December 1981, Dharamshala.

CHAPTER 10 A CRANE FROM LITHANG

1. Michael Henns, *The Cultural Monuments of Tibet* (Munich: Prestel, 2014), p. 144.
2. Eric Teichman. *Travels of a Consular Officer in Eastern Tibet* (Cambridge: Cambridge University Press, 1922), pp. 20-26.
3. Ibid., p. 43.

4. *A.L. Shelton*, 'Life Among the People of Eastern Tibet', *National Geographic Magazine XL*, no. 3 (September 1921).
5. Teichman, *Travels*, p. 137.

CHAPTER 11 THE CONFLUENCE

1. A gro Sgra rams pa Gyur med rnamrgyal, *Lha thog rgyal rabs* (A History of the Lords of the Lha thog principality of Khams) (Palampur: Sungrab Nyamso Gyunphel Parkhang, Tibetan Craft Community, 1971).
2. Joseph F. Rock, 'The Glories of the Minya Kongka', *National Geographic Magazine* LVIII, no. 4 (October 1930): 385.
3. André Migot, *Tibetan Marches* (London: Rupert Hart–Davis, 1956).
4. Yudru Tsomu, 'Survival in Sino-Tibetan Borderland: A Case Study of the Lcags La Kingdom in Sino-Tibetan Relations During the Qing Dynasty'. The author of this paper is related to the Chagla kings, and provided me with important information on the history of Kham.
5. Dai Yingcong, *The Sichuan Frontier and Tibet: Imperial Strategy in the Early Qing* (Seattle: University of Washington Press, 2009).
6. Eric Teichman, *Travels of a Consular Officer in Eastern Tibet* (Cambridge: Cambridge University Press, 1922).
7. Geoffrey T. Bull, *Tibetan Tales* (London: Hodder & Stoughton, 1966).
8. Peter Goullart, *Princes of the Black Bone* (London: John Murray, 1959).
9. Vicomte D'Ollone, *In Forbidden China* (London: T. Fisher Unwin, 1912).
10. Bull, *Iron Gates*,
11. George Patterson, *God's Fool* (London: Faber & Faber, 1956).
12. Ren Naiqiang, *Kangzang shidi dagang* (Synopsis of History and Geography of Khams) (Lhasa: Tibet Ancient Book and Classics Publishing House, 2000).
13. Ratu Ngawang, interview, 1 April 1993, Majnu-ka-tilla, Delhi.
14. Mao Tse–tung, 'Contradictions Among the People' (Speaking Notes), in *The Secret Speeches of Chairman Mao*, ed. Roderick MacFarquhar, Timothy Cheek and Eugene Wu (Cambridge: Harvard University Press, 1989), p. 142.

15. Philippe Paquet, *Simon Leys: Navigator Between Worlds* (Victoria: La Trobe University Press, 2016), p. 387.

16. Kan-pu hsueh-hsi ts'an-k'ao (Cadres Study Material), Beijing: People's Broadcasting House, no. 1 (1980) (for internal circulation only)

17. Laszlo Ladany, *The Communist Party of China and Marxism 1921–1985. A Self Portrait* (Stanford, CA: Hoover Institution Press, 1988).

18. Jung Chang and Jon Halliday, *Mao, The Unknown Story* (London: Jonathan Cape, 2005), p. 342.

CHAPTER 12 LITHANG UPRISING

1. Denma Locho Rinpoche, *My Life in the Land of Snow* www.jamyang.co.uk/teachers/ denma_ locho_rinpoche.html

2. Lithang Athar Norbu, interview with author, 18 March 1989, Majnu-ka-tilla, Delhi.

3. Kalsang Gyadotsang (Bhuga), interview, 20 June 1990, New York City.

4. Kalsang Gyadotsang, interview with author, 2 November 1989, New York City.

5. George Orwell, 'In Front of your Nose', *The Collected Essays, Journalism and Letters of George Orwell, Volume 4, 1945–1950* (London: Penguin Books, 1978), p. 24.

6. Shakya, *Dragon*, p. 141.

7. Mikel Dunham, *Buddha's Warriors: The Story of the CIA-Backed Tibetan Freedom Fighters, the Chinese Invasion and the Ultimate Fall of Tibet* (New York: Penguin, 2004), p. 162.

8. Baritsang Dawa Tsering, *Zhungs khrag dron mo gangs can ljong su mchod* (An offering of warm blood as a sacrifice to the land of the snows). Vol. 1 (Dharamshala, India; Central Tibetan Administration), p. 137. Also cited in Goldstein's *A History of Modern Tibet* Vol. 3. The other account is from Lotse Gatsetsang's *Li thang khul kyi lo rgyus* (an account of the Lithang region).

9. Lithang Athar Norbu, interview, 18 March 1989, Majnu-ka-tilla, Delhi.

10. International Commission of Jurists, *The Question of Tibet and the Rule of Law* (Geneva: 1959), p. 206.

11. International Commission of Jurists, *Tibet and the Chinese People's Republic* (Geneva: 1960), p. 248.

CHAPTER 13 WIND AND WILDFIRE

1. Jamyang Norbu, *Warriors of Tibet: The Story of Aten and the Khampas' Fight for the Freedom of their Country* (London: Wisdom Publications, 1986).
2. Carole McGranahan, *Arrested Histories: Tibet, the CIA, and Memories of a Forgotten War* (Durham and London: Duke University Press, 2010).
3. Nyarong Atring, interview with author, 30 May 1996, Bir, Himachal Pradesh.
4. Ibid.
5. Carole McGranahan, *Arrested Histories: Tibet, the CIA, and Memories of a Forgotten War* Durham and London: Duke University Press, 2010), p. 84.
6. Goldstein, *Tibetan Revolutionary*, pp. 251–53.
7. Douglas A. Wissing, *Pioneer in Tibet: The Life and Perils of Dr. Albert Shelton* (New York: Palgrave MacMillan, 2004), p. 84.
8. Lobsang Gyaltsen, *'Ba' kyi lo rgyus (History of Kham Ba-pa)* (Dehradun: Nyingmapa Lamah Press, 1971).
9. Teichman, *Consular Officer*, p. 228.
10. Ibid., p. 22.
11. Wissing, *Pioneer*, p. 86.
12. Edgar Snow, *Red Star Over China* (London: Penguin Books, 1972), p. 235.
13. Tenzin Tsultrim Jhadötsang, interview with author, 22 December 2006, Queens, New York City.
14. Raja Hutheesing, ed., *Tibet Fights For Freedom—A White Book, Indian Committee for Cultural Freedom* (Bombay: Orient Longmans, 1966), p. 4.
15. Kargyal Thondup, *Mdo Khams cha phreng kyi lo rgyus gser gyi snye ma* (The Golden Grain of Dokham Chatreng's History) (Dharamshala: Library of Tibetan Works and Archives, 1992).
16. Peter Goullart, *Princes of the Black Bone* (London: John Murray, 1959), p. 120.

17. Jamyang Norbu, *Warriors of Tibet: The Story of Aten and the Khampas' Fight for the Freedom of their Country* (London: Wisdom Publications, 1986), pp. 96–97.

18. Samten G. Karmay, *Feast of the Morning Light: The Eighteenth Century Wood-engravings of Shenrab's Life-stories and the Bon Canon from Gyalrong* (Osaka: Senri Ethnological Reports 57, National Museum of Ethnology, 2005).

19. Dan Martin, 'Bonpo Canons and Jesuit Cannons', *The Tibet Journal* XV, no. 2 (Summer 1990).

20. Elliot Sperling, 'Part 4: The Rise of Ganden Phodrang and the Sprouts of Modernity', in *The History of Tibetan Civilization: A Talk Series with Elliot Sperling* (New York: Latse Library, 2016).

21. Roger Greatrex, 'A Brief Introduction to the First Jinchuan War 1747–1749)', in *Tibetan Studies: Proceedings of the 6th Seminar of the International Association for Tibetan Studies, Fagernes 1992. Vol. I.* (Oslo: The Institute for Comparative Research in Human Culture, 1994), p. 1.

CHAPTER 14 NEVER RETURN

1. Drigung Kyapgon Chetsang, *A History of the Tibetan Empire* (Dehradun: Songtsen Library, 2011), p. 523.

2. Paul Kocot Nietupski, *Labrang Monastery: A Tibetan Buddhist Community on the Inner Asian Borderlands, 1709–1958* (UK: Lexington books, 2011), p. 117.

3. Luciano Petech, *Aristocracy and Government in Tibet 1728–1959* (Rome: Serie Orientalia Roma XLV, Is.M.E.O., 1973), p. 13.

4. Françoise Robin, 'La Révolte en Amdo en 1958', *L'histoire du Tibet du XVIIème au XXIème siècle,* Rapport de groupe interparlementaire d'amitié n° 104, 18 June 2012.

5. A lags Tsa yis Bstan 'dzin dpal 'bar, *Nga'i pha yul gyi ya nga ba'i lo rgyus* (Dharamsala: Narthang Publications, 1994).

6. Robin, 'La Révolte En Amdo'.

7. *Me-thog sum gyi rma-kha 1935–2009, 'Wounds of Three Generations':* a history of Ngaba under Chinese Communism (Dharmshala: Kirti monastery in exile, 2010).

8. Barbara Demick, *Eat the Buddha: Life and Death in a Tibetan Town* (New York: Random House, 2020).

9. Benno Weiner, *The Chinese Revolution on the Tibetan Frontier* (Ithaca: Cornell University Press, 2020), p. 203.

10. 'Statement of Rinzin (Alias Dorji Tsering)', in *Tibet Under Chinese Communist Rule: A Compilation of Refugee Statements 1958–1975* (Dharamshala: Information & Publicity Office of His Holiness the Dalai Lama, 1976), pp. 13–21.

11. www.hhwhjj.com/lishi/xiandai/2011/0909/13816.html.

12. history.huanqiu.com/people/2011-11/2177025.html

13. 'Statement of Rinzin', p. 20.

14. Ibid., p. 21.

15. Hutheesing, *Tibet Fights*, p. 25.

16. A. J. Fesmire, 'New Openings in Tibet', *The Alliance Weekly*, 5 August (1922).

17. Dinesh Lal, *Indo–Tibet–China Conflict* (New Delhi: Gyan Publishing House, 2008), p. 58.

18. Melvyn C. Goldstein, *Nomads of Golok: A Report* (PhD, Case Western Reserve University, 1996). www.case.edu/affil/tibet/booksAndPapers/RDPFinal%20Final%20 Mission%20ReportEU.htm%23_ftn9

19. Jamyang Norbu, 'March Winds', *Shadow Tibet Blog* 6 March 2009, www.jamyangnorbu.com/blog/2009/03/06/march-winds/

20. Tshe brtan rgya mtsho, n.d., *A rig bka' bcu ma'i lo rgyus gangs dkar bsil ma'i chab rgyan.*

21. Françoise Robin, 'La Révolte en Amdo en 1958', L'histoire du Tibet du XVIIème au XXIème siècle, Rapport de groupe interparlementaire d'amitié n° 104, 18 June 2012.

22. Roderick MacFarquhar, *The Origins of the Cultural Revolution* (New York: Columbia University Press, 1983).

23. Chen Jian, 'The Tibetan Rebellion of 1959 and China's Changing Relations with India and the Soviet Union', *Journal of Cold War Studies*, Summer 2006, www.fas.harvard.edu/~hpcws/jcws.2006.8.3.pdf.

24. Jianglin Li, '"Suppressing Rebellion in Tibet" and the China–India Border War', *War on Tibet: Chinese and Tibetan Documents on the History of the Chinese Occupation in English Translation*, December 5, 2017. historicaldocs.blogspot.com

25. Population Census Office of the State Council of the People's Republic of China and the Institute of Geography of the Chinese Academy of Sciences, *The Population Atlas of China* (USA: Oxford University Press, 1987), p. 40.

26. Elliot Sperling, 'The Body Count', *Rangzen Alliance*, 14 September 2012, www.rangzen.net/2012/09/14/the-body-count-2/

27. Jamyang Norbu, *Warriors*, p. 112.

28. Jamyang Norbu, 'Adding Insult to Injury', *Tibetan Review*, July (1978), p. 15.

29. *Xizang xingshi wenwu jiaoyu di jiben jiaocai* (Lhasa: Political Department of the Tibetan Military District, 1960).

30. Deborah E. Lipstadt, *History on Trial: My Day in Court with David Irving* (New York: Ecco Harper Collins, 2005), p. 225.

31. Samantha Power, *"A Problem From Hell": America and the Age of Genocide* (New York: Basic Books, 2002).

32. Serhii Plokhy, 'Killing by Hunger', *New York Review of Books* LXV, no. 13 (16 August 2018).

33. Ibid.

CHAPTER 15 THE MAN WHOSE LUCK DRIED UP

1. Nyemo Bhodshod Bhusang, interview with the author, 9–24 September 1991 and 8 February 1993, McLeod Ganj, Dharamshala.

2. Tenzin Tsultrim Jhadötsang, interview with author, 22 December 2006, Queens, New York City.

3. Knud Larsen and Amund Sinding–Larsen, *The Lhasa Atlas: Tradition- al Tibetan Architecture and Townscape* (Boston: Shambala, 2001), p. 121.

4. Kimura, *Japanese Agent,* pp. 118–19.

5. Kamal Ratna Tuladhar, *Caravans to Lhasa* (Kathmandu: Lijala & Tisa, 2011), p. 66.

6. In present-day China, citizens have even been imprisoned for possessing children's toy firearms according to this article: Chris Buckley and Raymond Zhong, 'A Game Designer in Beijing Bought Toy Guns. China Imprisoned Him', in the *New York Times*, available at https://nyti.ms/3Gc0lbn.

7. Melvyn Goldstein, William Siebenschuh and Tashi Tsering, *The Struggle for Modern Tibet: The Autobiography of Tashi Tsering* (New York: East Gate Book, M. E. Sharpe, 1997), p. 108.

CHAPTER 16 MEMORY SONGS OF LHASA

1. Janet L. Upton, 'Cascades of Change: Modern and contemporary Literature in the PRC's Junior–Secondary Tibetan Language and Literature Curriculum', *Contemporary Tibetan Literature* Summer (1999): pp. 19–21.
2. This translation (of mine) appeared in the introduction of *Map and Index of Lhasa City* (Dharamshala: Amnye Machen Institute, 1995), p. 14.
3. Theos Bernard, *Penthouse of the Gods* (New York: Scribner's Sons, 1938), pp. 216–18.
4. Thupten Khetsun, *Memories of Life in Lhasa Under Chinese Rule* (New York: Columbia University Press, 2008), pp. 9–10
5. Jin Zhou, ed., *Tibet No Longer Mediaeval* (Beijing: Foreign Language Press, 1981), p. 160.
6. Anonymous, 'Report From Lhasa', *Shadow Tibet*, www.jamyangnorbu. com/blog/2012/02/20/report-from-lhasa/
7. Ibid.

CHAPTER 17 THE MEN ESPECIALLY SENT BY MAO

1. *Tibetan Contemporary Art* (Lhasa/Beijing: 1991), p. 26.
2. Nyemo Bhodshod Bhusang, interview with the author, 9–24 September 1991 and 8 February 1993, McLeod Ganj, Dharamshala.
3. Changyu Li, 'Mao's "Killing Quotas"', *Human Rights in China (HRIC)* (Jinan: Shandong University, 26 September 2005).
4. Dalai Lama, *My Land and My People* (New York: McGraw–Hill, 1962), p. 93.
5. G. Ts. Tsybikoff, 'Lhasa and Central Tibet', *Izvestia of the Imperial Russian Geographical Society,* vol. XXXIX, part III (1903), pp. 187–218.
6. i. Charles Bell, *Tibet Past and Present* (Oxford: Oxford University Press, 1924), index: pp. 142–43, 236.

ii. Henrietta Sands Merrick, *Spoken in Tibetan* (New York: G.P. Putnam's Sons, 1933), p. 157.

iii. Robert Byron, *First Russia then Tibet* (London: Macmillan & Co., 1933), p. 204.

iv. William McGovern, *To Lhasa in Disguise* (New York: Century, 1924), pp. 388–89.

v. Frank Kingdon–Ward, *In the Land of The Blue Poppies* (New York: Modern Library, 2003), p. 22.

vi. Alan Winnington, *Tibet: The Record of a Journey* (London: Lawrence & Wishart, 1957), p. 99.

vii. Martin Brauen, *Peter Aufschnaiter's Eight Years in Tibet* (Bangkok: Orchid Press, 2002), p. 77.

7. Bhusang, interview, 9–24 September 1991 and 8 February 1993, McLeod Ganj, Dharamshala.

8. Jamyang Norbu, 'The Lhasa Ripper: A Preliminary Investigation into the "Dark Underbelly" of Social Life in the Holy City', *Shadow Tibet,* www.jamyangnorbu.com/blog/2015/03/22/the-lhasa-ripper/

9. Bhusang, interview, 9–24 September 1991 and 8 February 1993, McLeod Ganj, Dharamshala.

CHAPTER 18 OCCUPATION YEARS

1. Drapchi Captain Kalsang Dadul, *Zhidrag gi seeshu drup pae zay byang* (My Accomplishments in Peace and War) (Dharamshala: Library of Tibetan Works and Archives, 2001), p. 65.

2. Lukhang Jamjung [klu khang lcam chung], Tibetan Oral History Archive Project, interview H0024, September 1993, India. tibetoralhistoryarchive.org/resource.xqy?q=&uri=%2Flscoll%2Fto-hap%2Floc.natlib.tohap.H0024.xml&index=4&segment=seg01

3. Dekarwa Thinlay Namgyal, *Selon lukhangwae kutsae zayshas nyingdhus* (A Brief Account of the Life of Prime Minister Lukhangwa) (Dharamshala: Library of Tibetan Works and Archives, 1997), p. 99.

4. Drakton Jampa Gyaltsen, interview, 2 March 1992, Dharamshala.

5. Shakya, *Dragon*, p. 109.

6. Che Minghuai and Zhang Huachan, comp., *Zhang Jingwu: The Representative of the Central People's Government in Tibet* (Beijing: China Tibetology Publishing House, 2009). p. 59.
7. Sydney Wignall, *Spy on the Roof of the World* (London: The Lyons Press, 2000).
8. Goldstein, *Tibetan Revolutionary,* pp. 221–22.
9. Noel Barber, *From the Land of Lost Content* (London: Collins, 1969), p. 27.
10. Tashi Khedrup and Hugh Richardson, *Adventures of Tibetan Fighting Monk*, ed. Tadeusz Skorupski (Bangkok: Orchid Press, 1986), pp. 87–88.

CHAPTER 19 THE GOLDEN THRONE

1. *Autobiography of Gompo Tashi Andrutsang*, 35 photocopied pages of original typed document of the debriefing by Roger McCarthy. A copy was kindly given to the author by Lisa Cathey, daughter of CIA officer Clay Cathey, in 2008.
2. Peter Aufschnaiter, Map 1: *Area of Inner City Lhasa*, Map 2: *Lhasa & Norbulingka,* surveyed by Peter Aufschnaiter in 1948 (assisted by Heinrich Harrer) for the Lhasa Municipal Office (*lhasa nyertsang*).
3. Copies given to the author by Heinrich Harrer. Original maps are in the Ethnological Museum, University of Zurich.
4. *Autobiography of Gompo Tashi Andrutsang*, 35 photocopied pages of original typed document of the debriefing by Roger McCarthy.
5. Athar Norbu, interview, March 1989, Majnu-ka-tilla, Delhi. Athar Norbu, *Btensung dangblang dpawo lithang athar norbue mi tshe'i lo rgyus* (The life story of Lithang Athar Norbu, warrior and defender of the dharma) (Majnu-ka- tilla, Delhi: Phuntsok Chodon, 2004).
6. Ratuk Ngawang, *Mi tshe'i lo rgyus zol med srong po'i gtam gyi rol mo, The Autobiography of Dasur Ratuk Ngawang of Lithang* in four volumes (Dharamshala: Amnye Machen Institute, 2008), p. 227.
7. Lukhang Jamjung, interview, Tibetan Oral History Archive Project. tibetoralhistoryarchive.org/resource.xqy?q=&uri=%2Flscoll%2Fto-hap%2Floc.natlib.tohap.H0024.xml&index=4&segment=seg01
8. Kalsang Damdul, interview, 10 May 1994, Dharamshala.

9. Michel Peissel, *Cavaliers of Kham* (London: Heinemann, 1972); George Patterson, *Tibet in Revolt* (London: Faber & Faber, 1960).

10. Michael Henns, *The Cultural Monuments of Tibet* (Munich: Prestel, 2014), p. 162.

CHAPTER 20 DROP ZONE TIBET

1. Dalai Lama, *My Land and My People* (New York: McGraw–Hill, 1962).

2. Carole McGranahan, *Arrested Histories* (Durham: Duke University Press, 2010).

3. Thupten Jigme Norbu, *Tibet Is My Country* (London: Rupert Hart–Davis, 1961), p. 208.

4. Mikel Dunham, *Buddha's Warriors: The Story of the CIA-backed Tibetan Freedom Fighters* (Delhi: Penguin India, 2004), p. 203

5. Roger E. McCarthy, *Tears of the Lotus: Accounts of Tibetan Resistance to the Chinese Invasion, 1950–1962* (Jefferson, NC: McFarland, 1997).

6. Athar Norbu, interview, March 1989, Majnu-ka-tilla, Delhi.

7. Ibid.

CHAPTER 21 FOUR RIVERS SIX RANGES

1. Lobsang Sangay (former president of the exile Tibetan administration at Dharamshala), conversation, 1998, Boston.

2. This list of names is taken from *The Autobiography of Dasur Ratuk Ngawang of Lithang; Lithang Historical Records Vol. 3 (Part 1)* by Ratuk Ngawang, AMI Books, India, 2008. Besides Ngawang's information my interviews with Captain Kasang Damdul, secretary Loten la, and also information from Lhamo Tsering's *Resistance Vol. 2*, has contributed to this account of the oath-taking ceremony.

3. Drayab Loten Chiso (Adrugtsang Secretary), interview, 2 October 1993, Dharamshala.

4. Buzong Lamotsang Tsering Wangchuk, *Gya Lobsang Tashi dang Chu Gang* (The Chinese Lobsang Tashi and the Four Rivers and Six Ranges) (Dharamshala: Library of Tibetan Works and Archives, 2007).

5. Buzong Lamotsang Tsering Wangchuk, *Gya Lobsang Tashi dang Chu Gang*, p. 230.
6. Gyurme Dorje, *Tibet Handbook, with Bhutan* (Bristol: Footprint Handbooks, 1999), p. 206.
7. Victor Chan, *Tibet Handbook: A Pilgrimage Guide* (Chico, CA: Moon Publications, 1994), p. 683.
8. Drayab Loten Chiso (Adrugtsang Secretary) 2 October 1993, Dharamshala.

CHAPTER 22 CALCUTTA INTERLUDE

1. Kenneth Conboy and James Morrison, *The CIA's Secret War in Tibet* (Lawrence: University Press of Kansas, 2002), p. 73.
2. Mikel Dunham, *Buddha's Warriors: The Story of the CIA-Backed Tibetan Freedom Fighters, The Chinese invasion, and the Ultimate Fall of Tibet* (New York: Tarcher/Penguin, 2004), pp. 242–43.

CHAPTER 23 THE LONG RIDE NORTH

1. Lhamotsang Tsering Wangchuk, interview, 1998, Dharamshala.
2. Ratuk Ngawang, *The Autobiography of Dasur Ratuk Ngawang of Lithang* (Dharamshala: Amnye Machen Institute, 2008), p. 132.
3. John Vincent Bellezza, *Divine Dyads: Ancient Civilization in Tibet* (Dharamshala: Library of Tibetan Works and Archives, 1997), p. 254.
4. Charles Bell, *Portrait of a Dalai Lama* (London: Collins, 1946), p. 169.
5. Gompo Tashi Andrugtsang, *Four Rivers Six Ranges: A True Account of Khampa Resistance to Chinese in Tibet* (Dharamshala: Information and Publicity Office of H.H. The Dalai Lama, 1973), p. 88.
6. Conboy and Morrison, *Secret War*, p. 76.
7. Andrugtsang, *Four Rivers Six Ranges*, p. 89.
8. Ibid., p. 90.
9. Conboy and Morrison, *Secret War*, p. 77.

CHAPTER 24 PRIMORDIAL PLAYGROUND

1. Juchen Thupten Namgyal, *Hjuchan thup-stan gyi kutsehe log-ryus, Vol. 20* (Chauntra: self-published, 2013), p. 218.

2. Luciano Petech, *Aristocracy and Government in Tibet 1728–1959* (Rome: Serie Orientalia Roma XLV, Is.M.E.O., 1973), p. 94.

3. Ratuk Ngawang, *The Autobiography of Dasur Ratuk Ngawang of Lithang, Vol. 3* (Dharamshala: AMI Books, 2008), p. 127.

4. Rasmus Nielsen et al., 'Altitude adaptation in Tibetans caused by introgression of Denisovan-like DNA', Nature.com, 2 July 2014. www.nature.com/nature/journal/v512/n7513/full/nature13408.html

5. Kristen Moulton, '8,000-year-old genetic mystery in Tibet solved by Utah study', *Salt Lake Tribune*, August 19, 2014, www.sltrib.com/sltrib/news/58292738-78/prchal-research-tibet-ans-blood.html.csp

6. A. Witze, 'Biggest Denisovan fossil yet spills ancient human's secrets', *Nature*, 1 May (2019): 16–17, www.nature.com/articles/d41586-019-01395-0

7. Ratuk Ngawang, *The Autobiography of Dasur Ratuk Ngawang of Lithang* (Dharamshala: Amnye Machen Institute, 2008), p. 221.

8. 'A Brief Account of The Great Patriot Karchung Tsering Thondup', in *Tibetan History & Cultural Research and Compilation* (Lhasa: 2006).

9. Buzong Lamotsang Tsering Wangchuk, *Gya Lobsang Tashi dang Chu Gang* (The Chinese Lobsang Tashi and the Four Rivers and Six Ranges) (Dharamshala: Library of Tibetan Works and Archives, 2007).

CHAPTER 25 LHASA TWILIGHT

1. Melvyn C. Goldstein, *A History of Modern Tibet, Volume 4, In the Eye of the Storm, 1957–1959* (Berkeley: University of California Press, 2019), pp. 313–14.

2. 'Statement of Tsesum', in *Tibet Under Chinese Communist Rule* (Dharamshala: Information and Publicity Office of His Holiness the Dalai Lama, 1976), pp. 64–76.

3. Lhenga Tseten Namgyal, interview with the author, 15 April 1994, Dharamshala.

4. Maja Tsewang Gyurme, interview with the author, 20 July 1993, Dharamshala.

5. George Patterson, *Tibet in Revolt* (London: Faber & Faber, 1960), pp. 96–97.

6. Tsering Dorje Phariwa Gashi, *The Four Loves of Phari: An Autobiography and Other Writings* (Toronto: Pig Mountain Publications, 2013), p. 45.

7. Nornang Ganden, former student of the Beijing Minorities Institute, conversation in 2004, Bellville, Canada.

8. Paljor Tsarong, 'A Factual Account of the Tibetan Government's Gold and Silver', *The Tibetan Political Review*, 22 April (2015) webpage: sites.google.com/site/tibetanpoliticalreview/articles/afactualaccoun-tofthetibetangovernmentsgoldandsilver

9. Ibid.

10. Cheryl K. Chumley, 'Dalai Lama slams capitalism for world's ills: "I am Marxist"', *Washington Times*, January 16, 2015. www.washingtontimes.com/news/2015/jan/16/dalai-lama-slams-capitalism-for-worlds-ills-i-am-m/
    ---Joanna Rothkopf, 'Dalai Lama self-identifies as a Marxist', *Salon*, January 16, 2015,
    www.salon.com/2015/01/16/dalai_lama_self_identifies_as_a_marxist/
    ---Selwyn Duke, 'Dalai Lama: "I am a Marxist"', *American Thinker*, 10 June 2011, www.americanthinker.com/blog/2011/06/dalai_lama_i_am_a_marx- ist.html

11. Goldstein, *Tibetan Revolutionary*, p. 195.

12. Sadutsang Rinchen, *A Life Unforeseen: A Memoir of Service to Tibet* (Somerville, MA: Wisdom Publications, 2016), pp. 180–82.

13. Paul Hollander, *Political Pilgrims: Travels of Western Intellectuals to the Soviet Union, China, and Cuba* (New York: Harper Colophon, 1983), p. 367.

14. Hasan Suroor, 'Mao was like a father to me, says the Dalai Lama', *The Hindu*, June 24, 2012, www.thehindu.com/news/international/mao-was-like-a-father-to-me- says-the-dalai-lama/article3566341.ece

15. Melvyn Goldstein, *A History of Modern Tibet Vol 2: The Calm Before the Storm, 1951–55* (Berkeley: University of California Press, 2007), pp. 504–05.

16. Stuart and Roma Gelder, *The Timely Rain: Travels in a New Tibet* (London: Hutchinson, 1964).

17. Barber, *Lost Content*, p. 52.

18. Jianglin Li, *Tibet in Agony: Lhasa 1959* (Cambridge, MA: Harvard University Press, 2016), p. 75.

19. Shakya, *Dragon*, p. 187.
     ----Quoted from Bharshi Tsedrung Ngawang Tenkyong, *Mi tshe'i lo rgyus Ngos Jhung Denpae Rang sGra*, (The Natural Sound of My True Life Story) Oral History Series 20 (Dharamshala: Library of Tibetan Works and Archives, No date).

20. George Ginsburgs and Michael Mathos, *Communist China and Tibet: the First Dozen Years* (The Hague: Martinus Nijhoff, 1964), p. 122.

21. Anonymous, *Concerning the Question of Tibet* (Peking: Foreign Language Press, 1959) (All official statements and reports).

22. Melvyn Goldstein, *A History of Modern Tibet Vol 2: The Calm Before the Storm, 1951–55* (Berkeley: University of California Press, 2007), pp. 327–40.

23. Shakya, *Dragon*, p. 182.

24. M10 Memorial. www.m10memorial.org

25. M10 Memorial. www.facebook.com/m10memorial/

26. Shakya, Dragon, p. 187.
     ---Quoted from Bharshi Tsedrung Ngawang Tenkyong, The Natural Sound of My True Life, Dharamshala: Library of Tibetan Works and Archives.

27. Kalsang Damdul (Kaldam), interview, 10 May 1994, Dharamshala.

28. Dalai Lama, *My Land and My People* (New York: McGraw–Hill, 1962), pp. 170–71.

29. Barber, *Lost Content*, p. 82.

30. Shakya, *Dragon*, p. 195.

31. The names of the representatives appear in the following sources:
     1. Bharshi Ngawang Tenkyong, phone interview with the author, 7 March 1916.
     2. Namgyal Wangdu (Gyaltse), *Political and Military History of Tibet*, 2 volumes, trans. Yeshi Dhondup (Dharamshala: Library of Tibetan Works and Archives, 2010), pp. 176–97.
     3. Thupten Khetsun, *Memories of Life in Lhasa Under Chinese Rule* (New York: Columbia University Press, 2008), p. 77.
     4. Tenpa Soepa, *20 Years of My Life in China's Death Camp* (Bloomington, IN: Author House, 2008), p. 68.

5. Jampa Kalden Aukatsang, *My lifelong civil and military service to the Tibetan cause.* (*metsae ring bhod chi dhon ched zhi-drak gi las gan lang rem*), Oral History Series 38 (Dharamshala: Library of Tibetan Works and Archives, 1915).

32. Khetsun, *Memories,* p. 28.

33. Youdon Aukatsang, 'The Lion From Chamdo', *Phayul,* 7 March 2013, www.phayul.com/news/article.aspx?id=33135&t=1

34. Langdun Gyatso, 'Eye Witness Account 1', *Tibetan National Uprising: 20th Anniversary of 10th March, 1959* (Dharamshala: Information Office, Central Tibetan Secretariat, 1979), p. 26.

35. Dalai Lama, *My Land,* p. 189.

36. Namgyal Wangdu, *Military History,* p. 183.

37. Petech, *Aristocracy,* p. 49.

38. Shakya, *Dragon,* p. 197.

39. Thupten Khetsun, *Memories of Life in Lhasa Under Chinese Rule* (New York: Columbia University Press, 2008), p. 30.

40. Rinchen Dolma Taring, *Daughter of Tibet* (Boston: Wisdom Publications, 1970), p. 168.

41. Claude Arpi, *The End of An Era, India Exits Tibet–India Tibet Relations 1947–1962 Part 4* (New Delhi: Vij Book India, 2020), pp. 147–74.

42. 'Joint Statement of Lobsang Wangmo and Rinzin', *Tibet Under Chinese Communist Rule* (Dharamshala: Information and Publicity Office of His Holiness the Dalai Lama, 1976), p. 57.

43. Tseten Yangki, interview with the author, 1984, Dharamshala.

44. Tibetan Women's Association, 'The Genesis Of The Tibetan Women's Struggle For Independence', www.tibetanwomen.org/history/womens-uprising-day-tibet/

45. *Genmoe macos drang tam* (Truthful recollections of an old woman) Political Prisoner Statement No. 12 (Dharamshala: GuChuSum Political Prisoner's Movement of Tibet, 2001), p. 57.

46. Hanna Havnevik, 'The Role of Nuns in Contemporary Tibet', in *Resistance and Reform in Tibet,* ed. Bartnett and Aikiner (London: Hurst, 1994), p. 265.

47. Anonymous, *Concerning the Question of Tibet* (Peking: Foreign Language Press, 1959), pp. 36–40.

48. Barber, *Lost Content,* p. 101.

49. Goldstein, *History, Vol. 2,* p. 456.

50. Li, *Agony*, p. 175.

51. *Tibet Born Again* (Beijing: Foreign Language Press, 1960).

52. Gyalo Thondup, *The Noodle Maker of Kalimpong: The Untold Story of My Struggle for Tibet* (New York: Public Affairs, 2015), p. 133.

53. Takla Phuntsok Tashi, *Dmetse nyung-wa brtsod-pa (The Conflict of Life's Experience)*, vol. 2 (Dharamshala: Library of Tibetan Works and Archives, 1995),p. 129.

54. Li, *Agony*, p. 201.

CHAPTER 26 CROSSING THE RIVER OF HAPPINESS

1. Barber, *Lost Content,* p. 130.

2. Jianglin Li, *Tibet in Agony: Lhasa 1959.* Cambridge, MA: Harvard University Press, 2016.

3. Shan Chao, 'Sunshine After Rain: From a Lhasa Diary', *Peking Review* 18, 5 May (1959): 46.

4. Li, *Agony,* p. 188.

5. Khetsun, *Memories*, p. 31.

6. Li, *Agony,* p. 194.

7. Barber, *Lost Content,* p. 108.

8. Barber, *Lost Content,* p. 108–09.

9. Li. *Agony,* pp. 194–95.

10. 'Evidence of how Dorje Shugden was actually behind the Dalai Lama's escape out of Tibet to India in 1959', Dorjeshugden.com, September 2, 2013, www.dorjeshugden.com/all-articles/the-controversy/uncovered-truth- evidence-of-how-dorje-shugden-was-actually-behind-the-dalai-lamas- escape-out-of-tibet-to-india-in-1959/

11. Namgyal Wangdu, *Military History*, p. 186–87.

12. Barber, *Lost Content,* p. 114.

13. Shakabpa, *Advanced History,* p. 1018.

14. Goldstein, *History Vol. 4*, p. 688.

15. Rinchen Sadutshang, *A Life Unforeseen: A Memoir of Service to Tibet* (Boston: Wisdom Publications, 2016), p. 117.

16. Tsering Shakya, 'Ga rgya 'gram nag: A Bandit or a Proto Rebel? The Question of Banditry as Social Protest in Nagchu', in *Trails of the*

Tibetan Tradition, ed. Roberti Vitalli (Dharamshala: AMI books, 2014), p. 243.

CHAPTER 27 THE LHASA UPRISING

1. Tsarong, *Service*, p. 144.
2. Namgyal Wangdu, *Military History*, p. 200.
3. Tenpa Soepa, *20 Years of My Life in China's Death Camp*. (Bloomington, IN: Author House, 2008), pp. 25–27.
4. Noel Barber, *Lost Content*, p. 134.
5. Namgyal Wangdu, *Military History*, p. 201.
6. Soepa, *20 Years*, p. 29.
7. Khetsun, *Memories*, p. 35.
8. Li, *Agony*, p. 364.
9. Tarawa Tenzin Chonyi, *Rangnyed ngo sprod (Introduction to Myself)* (Dharamshala: Library of Tibetan Works and Archives, 2005),
10. Tsarong, *Service*, p. 145.
11. Barber, *Lost Content*, p. 163.
12. Barber, *Lost Content*, p. 164.
13. Maja Tsewang Gyurme, interview with the author, 20 July 1993, Dharamshala.
14. M10 Memorial https://www.facebook.com/m10memorial/
15. 'Statement of Tashi Palden', in *Tibet Under Chinese Communist Rule: A Compilation of Refugee Statements 1958–1975* (Dharamshala: Information and Publicity Office of His Holiness the Dalai Lama, 1976), p. 32.
16. Shakabpa, *Advanced History*, p. 1015.
17. Barber, *Lost Content*, p. 165.
18. Li, *Agony*, p. 254.
19. Barber, *Lost Content*, pp. 165–66.
20. Langdun Gyatso, *Eye Witness*, p. 28.
21. Stuart and Roma Gelder, *The Timely Rain: Travels in New Tibet* (London: Hutchinson, 1964), p. 87.
22. Li. *Agony*, p. 262.
23. Ibid., p. 263.
24. Ibid., p. 274.
25. Shakabpa, *Advanced History*, p. 1026.

26. Paljor Tsarong, 'Sixty Years Today: A Martyr Shot on the Banks of Lhasa's Kyichu River', *Tibetan Review* 26 August (2020).

27. Li, *Agony,* p. 248.

28. Soepa, *20 Years,* pp. 25–28

29. Li, *Agony,* pp. 274–75.

30. Tashi Khedrup and Hugh Richardson, *Adventures of Tibetan Fighting Monk,* ed. Tadeusz Skorupski (Bangkok: Orchid Press, 1986), pp. 92–95.

31. Namgyal Wangdu, *Military History,* pp. 204–05

32. Ibid., p. 204.

33. Zasak J. Taring, *Lhasa Tsug-Lag Khang Gi Sata and Karchag (The Index and Plan of Lhasa Cathedral in Tibet).* (Dehradun, UK: self-published, 1980), p. 123.

34. Tashi Tsering et al., *Jokhang: Tibet's Most Sacred Buddhist Temple* (London and Bangkok: Editions Hansjorg Meyer, 2010), p. 146.

35. Shakabpa, *Advanced History,* p. 1027.

36. Barber, *Lost Content,* p. 158.

37. Langdun, *Eye Witness,* p. 28.

38. Ngawang Dhakpa (aka Chitiling Bhula), interview, June 1975, Turbenthal, Switzerland.

39. L.A. Waddell, *Lhasa and Its Mysteries: With a Record of the Expedition of 1903–1904* (London: Methuen, 1905), p. 170, 427.

40. Jamyang Norbu, 'The Muslims of Tibet', in the *New York Review of Books,* 4 October (2001): www.nybooks.com/articles/2001/10/04/the-muslims-of-tibet/

41. Namgyal Wangdu, *Military History,* p. 206.

42. Anna Louise Strong, *When Serfs Stood Up* (Beijing: New World Press, 1960), Chapter VIII reports on the event and writes that 'Lhalu Tsewong-Dorje, (was the) commander-in-chief of the March rebellion in Lhasa.' She also repeats what the Chinese had told her about him. 'His plotting for Tibet's secession from China continued; it had a history of years.'

43. M10 Memorial Facebook Page, 13 March 2016, https://www.facebook.com/m10memorial/

44. Li, *Agony,* p. 289.

45. Langdun, *Eye Witness,* p. 28.

46. Ibid., p. 28.

47. Shan Chao, 'Sunshine After Rain, From A Lhasa Diary', *Peking Review* 18 5 May (1959), p. 36.

48. Wikipedia, 'Jiabiangou Labor Camp', https://en.wikipedia.org/wiki/ Jiabiangou

49. Soepa, *20 Years,* p. 96.

CHAPTER 28 SILENT STRUGGLE

1. Tsongkha Lhamo Tsering, interview with the author, 17–18 September 1991, Delek Guest House, Dharamshala.

2. Thupten Jigme Norbu, interview with the author, 23 May 1984, Kashmir Cottage, Dharamshala.

CHAPTER 29 AIR OPERATIONS

1. Tsongkha Lhamo Tsering, interview with the author, 17–18 September, 1991, Delek Guest House, Dharamshala.

2. Tsongkha Lhamo Tsering, *Resistance Volume 2, The Secret Operations Into Tibet (1957–1962)* (*Btsan rgol rgyal skyob, Deb gnyis pa, Bod nang du drag po'i 'than rtsod byas skor, 1957 nas 1962 bar*) Occupied Tibet Series, no 4, ed. Tashi Tsering (Dharamshala: AMI Books, Amnye Machen Institute, 1998), p. 107.

3. Conboy and Morrison. *Secret War,* p. 120.

4. Ibid., p. 122.

5. Lhamo Tsering, *Resistance Vol. 2,* pp. 135–37.

6. Ani Pachen and Adelaide Donnelley, *Sorrow Mountain: The Journey of a Tibetan Warrior Nun* (New York: Kodansha America Inc., 2000).

7. Conboy and Morrison, *Secret War,* p. 120.

8. Lhamo Tsering, *Resistance Vol. 2,* p. 150.

9. Ibid., p. 188.

10. Dechen, interview, April 1991, Amnye Machen Institute, Dharamshala.

11. Conboy and Morrison, *Secret War,* p. 133.

12. Tsongkha Lhamo Tsering, *Resistance Volume 2,* The Secret Operations into Tibet (Dharamshala: Amnye Machen Institute, 1957–1962), p. 57.

13. Lhamo Tsering, *Resistance Vol. 2,* p. 69.

CHAPTER 30 CAMP HALE, COLORADO

1. Lisa Cathey, Ray Starke, 'CIA in Tibet', interview, 31 August 2010, Washington DC: Kefiworks.

CHAPTER 31 THE GREAT FORESTS OF KHAM

1. A. Hosie, *Mr. Hosie's Journey to Tibet 1904 (A Report by Mr. A. Hosie, His Majesty's Consul at Chengtu, On a Journey from Chengtu to The Eastern Frontier of Tibet)* (London: the Stationary Office, 2001), pp. 119–20.
2. Phupa Tsering Topgyal, interview with the author, 21–24 October 1991, Gangchen Kyishong, Dharamshala.
3. Phupa Tsering Topgyal, *Great Snows Volunteer Army to Defend the Dharma: The Story of the Nationalist Fighters of the Markham Range. (Gangchen Tensung Dhanglang Mag: Markham gang gi gyalsrung magthap lorgyus)* (Dharamshala: Narthang Press, 1998).
4. Phupa Tsering Topgyal, *The Story of Dokham Four Rivers Six Ranges Volunteer Army to Defend the Dharma (do kham chushi gangdruk ten srung dangling mag gi lo gyus)* (Dharamshala: Central Dhoto Chushi Gangdruk, 2000).
5. Phupa Tsering Topgyal, interview with the author, 21–24 October 1991, Gangchen Kyishong, Dharamshala.
6. Ibid.
7. Ibid.
8. Ibid.
9. Ibid.
10. Ibid.
11. Ibid.
12. Ibid.
13. Ibid.

CHAPTER 34 SEA OF INHUMANITY

1. Kunsang Paljor, *Tibet The Undying Flame* (Dharamshala: Information & Publicity Office of the Dalai Lama, 1977), p. 57.
2. Ibid., p. 21.

3. Barbara Demick, 'Uncovering the Cultural Revolution's Awful Truths', *The Atlantic*, December 18 (2020).

4. Tsering Woser, *Forbidden Memory: Tibet During the Cultural Revolution* (Lincoln, NE: Potomac Books, University of Nebraska Press, 2020).

5. Elmar R. Gruber, *From the Heart of Tibet: The Biography of Drigung Chetsang Rinpoche* (Boston: Shambhala, 2010), p. 123.

6. Paljor, *Undying Flame*, p. 33.

7. Melvyn C. Goldstein, Ben Jiao and Tanzin Lhundrup, *On the Cultural Revolution in Tibet: The Nyemo Incident of 1969* (Berkeley: University of California Press, 2009), p. 4.

8. Robert Barnett, 'Women and Politics in Contemporary Tibet', in *Women in Tibet*, ed. Janet Gyatso and Hanna Havnevik (London: Hurst & Company, 2005), p. 349.

9. Hanna Havnevik, 'The Role of Nuns in Contemporary Tibet', in *Resistance and Reform in Tibet*, ed. Barnett and Aikiner (London: Hurst, 1994), p. 265.

10. Nycyak, 'Tibetan women: Trinley Chodon & the Nyemo Revolt', *Lhakar Diaries*, 4 April (2012): lhakardiaries.com/2012/04/04/ tibetan-women-trinley-cho-don-the-nyemo-revolt/

11. Elmar R. Gruber, *From the Heart of Tibet: The Biography of Drigung Chetsang Rinpoche* (Boston: Shambhala, 2010), front cover

12. Ibid., p. 187.

13. Ibid., pp. 143–44.

14. *Cairn: Newsletter of the Amnye Machen Institute*, no.3–4 (1996–97).

15. Tsering Woser, *Forbidden Memory: Tibet During the Cultural Revolution* (Lincoln, NE: Potomac Books, University of Nebraska Press, 2020), p. 219.

16. Goldstein et al., *Cultural Revolution,* p. 125.

17. R.A. Stein, *Tibetan Civilization* (Stanford: Stanford University Press, 1972), p. 88.

18. Alexandra David–Neel and Lama Yongden, *The Superhuman Life of Gesar of Ling* (Boston: Shambala, 1981), p. 269.

19. Samten G. Karmay, *The Arrow and the Spindle: Studies in History, Myths, Rituals and Beliefs in Tibet* (Kathmandu: Mandala Book Point, 1998), p. 425.

20. BBC, 'China's Curious Cult of the Mango', 11 February 2016, www.bbc.com/news/magazine-35461265

21. G. R. Urban, *Miracles of Chairman Mao* (London: Tom Stacey Ltd, 1971), p. 183.

22. Simon Leys, *The Chairman's New Clothes: Mao and the Cultural Revolution* (London: Allison & Busby, 1977), p. 13.

CHAPTER 35 GUERRILLA TRAILS TO MUSTANG

1. Charles Bell, *The Religion of Tibet* (Oxford: Clarendon Press, 1931), pp. 13–14.

2. Donagh Coleman and Lharigtso, *A Gesar Bard's Tale* (Kino Lorber, 2015), Geneva(video).

CHAPTER 36 RAID INTO TIBET

1. Carole McGranahan, *Arrested Histories: Tibet, the CIA, and Memories of a Forgotten War* (Durham and London: Duke University Press, 2010), p. 150.

2. CIA, 'Painting Commemorating ARGO Operation Joins Intelligence Art Gallery', 14 March 2013.
https://www.cia.gov/news-information/featured-story-ar-chive/2013-featured-story-archive/argo-painting-joins-intelligence-gal- lery.html

3. Evan Thomas, *The Very Best Men: The Daring Early Years of the CIA* (Simon & Schuster, 2006).

4. Tsongkha Lhamo Tsering, *Resistance Vol. 4: An Account of the Establishment of the Tibetan National Volunteer Defence Force in Mustang and Operations Against the Communist Chinese Inside Tibet, 1960–1974* (Dharamshala: AMI Books, 2003), pp. 73–74.

5. Michel Peissel, *Mustang, A Lost Tibetan Kingdom* (London: Collins and Harvill Press, 1968).

6. Sanjay Upadhya, *Nepal and the Geo-Strategic Rivalry between China and India* (London: Routledge, 2012), pp. 100–01.

CHAPTER 37 FRENCH CONNECTION

1. M.S. Kohli and Kenneth Conboy, *Spies in the Himalayas: Secret Missions and Perilous Climbs* (Kansas: University Press of Kansas, 2002), p. 49.

2. Tsering W. Dhompa, *On the Margins in Exile: Unity in the Tibetan exile Nation* (unpublished manuscript), P. 61–65

3. Harrison Salisbury, *The Coming War Between Russia and China* (London: Macmillan, 1969), p. 167.

4. Conboy and Morrison, *Secret War,* p. 241.

5. David Kahn, *The Codebreakers: The Story of Secret Writing* (New York: Macmillan Publishing Company, 1967), p. 84.

6. *La Pensée de Mao Tsé–Toung* (1971), *La Chine et ses populations* (1982), and *Saint François en Chine* (2012). www.editionsducerf.fr/html/fiche/ficheauteur.asp?n_aut=7277

7. Sanjay Upadhya, *Nepal and the Geo-Strategic Rivalry between China and India* (London: Routledge, 2012), pp. 100–01.

8. Conboy and Morrison, *Secret War,* pp. 250–51.

9. Mikel Dunham, *Buddha's Warriors,* p. 389.

CHAPTER 38 MAO IS DEAD! LONG LIVE MAO!

1. General Assembly Resolution 1723 (XVI).

2. Jamyang Norbu, 'Rogues Gallery', *Tibetan Review* May (1980): 24.

3. 'Statement of His Holiness the Dalai Lama on the Fourteenth Anniversary of the Tibetan National Uprising Day', Dharamshala: 10 March 1973.

4. George N. Patterson, *Patterson of Tibet: Death Throes of a Nation* (San Diego, CA: Pro-Motion Publishing, 1998), p. 436.

5. 'Major Criminals in Tibet Released', *Beijing Review* 24 November (1978): 3.

6. Warren Smith, *Tibetan Nation,* p. 565.

CHAPTER 39 BHUSANG GOES HOME

1. Warren Smith, *Tibetan Nation,* p. 569.

2. Tsultrim Chhonphel Tersey, 'One Month in Tibet', *Tibetan Review,* 14, no. 6 (June 1979): pp. 12–27.

CHAPTER 40 HIGH MOUNTAIN ELEGY

1. Jamyang Norbu, 'The Wandering Goddess: Reviving and Sustaining the Spirit of Ache Lhamo in Exile', *The Singing Mask, Echoes of Tibetan*

Opera, *Lungta* No. 15 (January 2001). Also posted on 3 April 2015 at www.jamyangnorbu.com/blog/2015/04/03/the-wandering-goddess/

2. Editor, *DA-SAR periodical*, (1992): 33.

3. Vijay Kranti, 'An Alternate Tribute to Bapa Phuntsog Wangyal: A SLAVE MINDSET', *Tibet Telegraph*, April 2, 2014, http://www.tibettelegraph.com/2014/04/an-alternate-tribute-to-bapa-phuntsok.html (Kranti also mentions the eulogy by Dharamshala of Ngabo).

4. Hannah Beech, 'China Says It Will Decide Who the Dalai Lama Shall Be Reincarnated As', *TIME*, 13 March (2015), time.com/3743742/dalai-lama-china-reincarnation-tibet-buddhism/

5. Jezza Neumann and interviewer Tash Despa, *Undercover in Tibet*, a documentary film. Britain's Channel 4 program *Dispatches*, 31 March 1980, www.youtube.com/watch?v=Wq07anmgFHc.

6. Tibet Action Institute, 'Separated From Their Families, Hidden From the World', December 2021, https://ipdefenseforum.com/2021/12/report-tibetan-children-taken-from-homes-sent-to-chinese-boarding-schools/#:~:text=Describing%20the%20boarding%20schools%20as,from%20their%20families%20and%20culture.

7. Echu Huang, 'After faces, China is moving quickly to identify people by their voices', *QUARTZ*, March 20, 2018, qz.com/1232988/after-faces-china-is-moving-quickly-to-identify-peo- ple-by-their-voices/

8. 'Chinese authorities collecting DNA from all residents of Xinjiang', *The Guardian*, December 12, 2017, https://www.theguardian.com/world/2017/dec/13/chinese-authorities-collecting-dna-residents-xinji-ang.
   ---Sui-Lee Wee, 'China Uses DNA to Track Its People, With the Help of American Expertise', the *New York Times*, February 21, 2019, www.nytimes.com/2019/02/21/business/china-xinjiang-ui-ghur-dna-thermo-fisher.html

9. 'China: New Evidence of Mass DNA Collection in Tibet', Human Rights Watch, September 5, 2022, https://www.hrw.org/news/2022/09/05/china-new-evidence-mass-dna-collection-tibet?fbclid=IwAR2sCVGmvABeKIUpHxUHKRkmryeKhKBlcjSuwIA-FhY9JYwFmf66mlHbHjs

10. Nithin Coca, 'China's Digital Wall Around Tibet', Coda Story, May 16, 2019, codastory.com/authoritarian-tech/china-digital-wall-tibet/

11. Barbara Demick, *Eat the Buddha: Life and Death in a Tibetan Town* (New York: Random House, 2020), p. 155.
12. Andrew Jacobs, 'Technology Reaches Remote Tibetan Corners —Fanning Unrest', *New York Times*, April 20, 2012, www.nytimes.com/2012/05/24/world/asia/technology-reaches-re-mote-tibetan-corners-fanning-unrest.html
13. *Himalayae Rigzod Dratsig*, www.himalayane.com.
14. YouTube, 'A Bit More Dangerous than the Chinese Communists', www.youtube.com/watch?v=c-_7sBcuyqA
15. 'Tibetan separatist exposes Dalai Lama's "democracy myth"', *China Tibet Online*, October 21, 2009. chinatibet.people.com.cn/6789022.html
16. Sangdor, 'Slave to Tradition and My Words', 13 December 2012, highpeakspureearth.com/2013/a-commentary-on-tibetan-society-slave-to-tradition-and-my-words/
17. Tsering Woeser, *Scarlet Ruins: Essays on Tibet* (Taipei: Locus Publishing, 2017), p. 111.

INDEX

A

"Adviser on Frontier Matters," 36

A Fine Balance, 200

"Agreement for the Peaceful
    Liberation of Tibet," 101

air operations
    drop zone chakra pembar,
        596–602
    drop zone niratsogen, 602–606
    drop zones hentsa, 595–596
    retreat to India, 606–609

Ajakhapa, 230

*A Lamp for the Path to
    Enlightenment*, 18

Aligarh Muslim University, 194

"Amaleho", 206

Amdo
    fighters, Chinese force attacked,
        290–292
    history of, 283
    tribes of, 285
    1949 uprising in, 288

uprisings in, 286

wars in, 284

"1958 Amdo Rebellion", 287–288

Amdo Rinzin, 288

American Episcopal Methodists,
    180

American imperialist spy,
    confessions of, 669–695

American Seventh Day Adventist
    Mission, 228

Amnye Machen Institute (AMI),
    393, 412, 707, xx

Anabasis, 476

"Ancient Tea-Horse Road", 228

Anderson Bridge, 7

Andrugtsang House, 388

Anglo-Tibetan War (1888), 36

Anti-Rightist Movement, 436

*ARGO—The Rescue of the
    Canadian Six,* 746

Arrested Histories, 412

Artillery Regiment, 566

A Tibetan on Tibet, 136

B

Ba Chödé Monastery, 377
Bahadur, 36
Bai Mao Nu, 352
bainian guochi, 90
Bamari canal, 20
"Bamboo Curtain", 184
"barbaric feudal tortures", 355
Bathang Monastery, 213
    bombing of, 398
Bathang, uprising in, 270–271
Battle of Chamdo, 58
Beijing
    discussions in, 99
Bell, Sir Charles, 7
Benchen Monastery, 378
Bespaloff, Rachel, xx
Bhötuk Dawa, 219
"Bird Confluence Monastery", 458
"bird-hand" colonel, 221
"bizarre European women", 172
The Blue Annals, 10, 35
"Bodhisattva Father Monkey", 484
Bren light machine guns, 65
British Enfield rifles, 224
British Lee Metford rifles, 250
Browning automatic rifle (BAR),
    573, 729
Buddha Akshobhya Vajra, 536
"Buddha Jayanti", 407
"Buddha realm", 209
Buddha's Warriors, 412
Bumnyathang, 217
"Burma Rajah", 10

Burns & Co., 158
"Butcher" Zhao, 21

C

Camp Hale (Colorado), 610–623
Capitol Cinema, 185
Captured in Tibet, 59
caravan leader, 5
    journey across the mountains, 5
CARE milk-powder, 189
CCP Tibet Work Committee,
    540, 561
1933 ceasefire agreement, 124
Central Intelligence Bureau (CIB),
    160
Central Military Commission, 299
Central Reserve Police Force
    (CRPF), 172
"century of humiliation," 90
"*Ceremonies of the Lhasa Year*", 353
Chaba Monastery, bombing of,
    271
Chamdo
    communist China invasion in,
        54
    disaster at, 104
    evening breeze at, 49
    fall of, 54
    location, 49–50
    Monastery, destruction of, 52
    Robert Ford at, 65
Chamdo battle, 87
Chamdo campaign
    Tibetans killed in, 119–120
Chamdo Liberation Committee,
    96, 101, 628

"Chamdo Liberation Committee," 129

Chamdo offensive, in 2011, 114

Chang, Garma C.C., 12

Changlochen *gung*, 16

Chatreng, attack Chinese headquarters, 274

Chatreng, Chinese soldiers in, 279

Chatreng, people of, 272

"*Chen-khen-tse-sum*", 175

Chen, Yogi C.M., 12

chikang, 219

China

    in 1958, 485

    attacked the UN Coalition Forces, 111

    civil war in, 44, 66

    international agreement, 90

    Laogai "archipelago", 433

    Mongol conquest of, 35

    "Potemkin" tour of, 508

    Seventeen Point Treaty, 506

    sign "un-equal treaties," 90

    Socialist Realist Art in, 347

China Democratic Socialist Party, 12

"CHINA OUT OF TIBET", 189

"China Road", 84

China Spring, 298

Chinese

    army enter the Korean War, 116

    arresting farmers in Garthok, 639

    artillery batteries, 562

    attacked Khampas, 491–492

    captured Andrugtsang muleteers, 494–495

    "Chuyuk" irrigation canal, 491

    defenses, Khampas study, 487–488

    fired at Khampas, 489

    fired at Tibetan lines, 492

    information of Resistance's plans, 486

    military administrator for Chamdo, 628

    National Day, 555

    plane bombing Bathang Monastery, 629

    in propaganda campaign of Resistance lines, 494

    propaganda documentary film, 563

    rifle, 491

    surrounded by barbed wire fences, 490

    Tibetan fighters and, 486

Chinese Army Day festivities, 381

Chinese civil war, 44, 163

Chinese Communist doctrine, 234

Chinese flag fly, on Communist government anniversary, 366–367

Chinese invasion, of 1910, 47

Chinese Public Security, 506

Chinese Public Security Bureau, 311

Chinese tyranny, 126

Chukor wog, 488

CIA's Intelligence Art Gallery, 746

Coelogyne henryi Rolfe, 208

Collectanea Rerum Memorabilium,
    46
"colonel pockmark", 221
45. Colt automatic pistol, 262
Communist China's Eighteenth
    Army, 48
Communist invasion, 157
"Communist spy," 161
Communists, task of, 233
Conium House, 192
Convair CV-240-401, 376
cradle of Tibetan civilization, 432
Cultural Revolution, 213
Cultural Revolution, in Tibet,
    130, 131
Czech Brno rifle, 469

D
Daily Worker, 355
Dance and Drama Society, 194
Darjeeling Himalayan Railway
    (DHR), 385
"death of a thousand cuts", 20
"Democratic Reforms", 235, 236,
    238
    Khampa opposition to, 265
'Destroy the Four Olds and Build
    the Four News', 696
Dhapa Dzara, fighting at, 424
Dharamshala
    Tibetan exile government in,
        302
    Tibetan Nursery at, 193
dhobo, 4
Dhrukpa Kalsang Rigya, 219
Displaced Person (DP) camp, 191
    Tibetan, 191

"Doc Ock and His Tentacles", 184
Dorjedrak Monastery, 140
Dothal, 249
Drapchi military camp, 107
Drapchi Regiment, 365, 373, 395,
    435, 535, 611
Drekar Samphe Thundup, xii
Drepung Monastery, 88, 240, 331,
    333, 538
Drigung Thil Monastery, 459
Drip Tsecholing Monastery, 539
Drongdrak regiment, 71, 83
drop zone
    chakra pembar, 596–602
    hentsa, 595–596
    niratsogen, 602–606
Drugu Monastery, 80, 91
drungkor-tsal-gyu test, 141
"Drury Lane" army, 56
dulwa, 53
Durpin Development Area, 2, 159
Dzayül operation, 716
Dzong, Lho
    assessment of, 62
    castle, 62

E
'egg and rock' argument, 379
"Eight-One" Military Day parade,
    376
Eight Royal Irish Hussars, 111
Eleventh Dhadang, 86
"Enemy Alien" Acts, 130

F
"Fair Haven", 10
Fair Haven, visitor to, 13

"fairy scarves", 624
Far Eastern Economic Review, 203
Fifth Dingri, 86
Fire-Mouse year, 274
First Guards, 86
"Five-Anti" campaign, 354
"Five Leguminous Tree
    Hermitage", 12
Fool At Forty, 170
Forsyth Ganj, 192
For Whom the Bell Tolls, 185, 264
"Four Devoted Friends", 165
Four Feathers, 154
Four Rivers Six Ranges, 426–442
    flag of, 473
    inaugurational ceremony, 430
    rode to Chakra Pembar, 470
    Tibetan army support to, 430
"Four Rivers Six Ranges", 201
Fourteenth Phadang, 86
Fourth Gurkha Rifles, 192
Fourth Gyantsé, 86
Freedom From Exile, 542
"FREE TIBET", 189
Frontline documentary, xvii

G
gagyur, 222
Galden Jampa Ling, monastery of,
    51
Ganden Chökorling monastery,
    451
Ganden Chökor Monastery, 474
Ganden Monastery, 520
Gangtok
    to Darjeeling, journey from,
        610
    to Nathu-la, 610
Gangtse glacier, 7
"Gateway to Tibet", 6, 226
"Gauripur House", 12
Gazetteer of Sikhim, 38
Gelugpa monastery, 227
Gelugpa monks, 53
Gelukpa monastery, of Chökhor
    Gön, 69
Ghomzö Dorjeling, 562
Golden Eagle, 194
Golden Triangle, of Northern
    Thailand, 232
Golok, 294–304
    Amnye Machen mountain in,
        294
    genocidal war against, 295
    tribesmen, 294
Golok population, 298
Gone with the Wind, 352
goser technique, 222
Goullart, Peter, 4
    in Lijiang, 4
Government of India (GOI)
    set up boarding schools,
        192
"Great Abbot", 64, 138
"Great Avaloketesvara
    Empowerment", 243
The Great Conference of People's
    Representatives, 522
"Greater Tibet", 401
Great Kangra Valley earthquake,
    199
Great Khampa Uprising, of 1956,
    277
"Great Spectacle", 43

Guibaut-Liotard Expedition (1940), 294
Guomindang fort, 252
Gyadur Thang, 284
Gyalrong, 280–282
    Qing invasion of, 281–282
    traditional ruler of, 281
Gyalthang and the lolo uprising, 279–280
Gyalthang Monastery, 290
gyaltsen chonga, 465
Gyantsé Regiment troops, 535
gyap, 4
Gyasa Bhelsa, 549
Gyatrag Thang, 284
Gyatso, Lhagyari Namgyal
    arrest, 478
    at Mamshung, 479
Gyurme Gyatso
    biographical account of, 32
    joined *Kashag*, 32

H
hangul, 33
Happy Light Cinema, 352
"Heroes National Park", 538
"High Tide of Socialist Transformation", 236
Himalayan Children's Home, 169
Himalayan Times, 161
"*Hindi Chini Bhai Bhai*", 181
"hindsight bias", 55
"historical inevitability", 56
History of Modern Tibet, 514
History of Sikkim, 38
History of the Wars, 325
History of Tibetan Medicine, 320

Hok Shidram Gön Monastery, 62
Homage to Catalonia, 494
Honourable East India Company, 36
Hormukha, 288–294
    battle (February 1951) fought in, 289
    Red Army in, 288
Horpa, xi
Horseman in the Snow, 265, 280
"Hundred Flowers" campaign, 435
Hungarian Revolution, 277
"*hur-tsunpa*", 236

I
Idols on the Path, 178
Illustrated Weapons of WWII, 555
Ilyushin Il-12, 376
Imperial Chinese army, 19
"independent sovereign", 19
Indian Civil Service, 95
India's Special Frontier Force, 57
Indo-Pakistan Military Conflict of 1971, 765–766
Indo-Tibetan Border Police (ITBP), 765
Indo-Tibetan Buddhist Cultural Institute School, 15
Indo-Tibetan Buddhist Cultural School, 160
Inji khudum, 250
'Inner Chamber Regiment', 359
"inner seal proclamations", 24
Intelligence Bureau (IB), 160, 176, 765
International Association of Tibet Studies conference, 58

International Commission of
    Jurists (ICJ), 262, 301
International Tibetan Studies, 126
involuntary memory, xxii
Istanbul: Memories and the City, 330

J
Jha-do Monastery, 458
Jhapo-Jhakay, 465
JIAOCHANG, 539
jijifenzi, 236
Journal of the Maha Bodhi Society,
    161–162

K
Kabru I & II peaks, 7
Kalimpong
    big wool warehouses in, 184
    Dodge City in, 5
    Europeans in, 12
    Gandhi Ashram at, 181
    how to approach, 7
    market location, 6
    mean elevation of, 6
    pilgrims to, 13
    St. Augustine's School in, 184
    Tibetan Christian Church of, 9
    Tibetan Refugee School in,
        169, 184
    Tibetan scholars in, 15
    Tibetan Trade Agency in, 17
    via Teesta River, road to, 8
    watch agency, 4
Kalimpong, British resident agent
    in, 161
Kalimpong, Communist Chinese
    in, 160

Kalimpong, red agents in, 174
Kanchenjunga, 2
Kanchenjunga range, 7
"Kangding revolt", 375
Kangya Drakar Monastery, 484
Kapre Tsatok, 394, 420
"khabingchang", 250
Kham, great forests of, 624–643
Khampa folk song, 196
Khampa militia, 72
Khampa refugees, 378
Khampa Uprising, of 1956, 510
khata scarves, 223
khenchen, 87
Khochang, 230
khyuk cursive signatures, of Tibet,
    101
"Kodak enthusiast", 31
Korean War, 87
    Stalin's support for, 118
    Western public, 117
Kumbum Monastery, 173, 286
Kundeling Monastery, 530, 571

L
"Ladies, Patterson of Tibet", 170
lak-tey, 319
Lama, Dalai, 87
    accept *Tenshuk* offering, 399
    administration, xv
    autobiography, 117, 517
    biography, 521
    blessing to Robert Ford, 59
    bodyguards, 65
    to Chinese government, 88
    Compassion in Exile, 410
    conversion to Marxism, 507

desire to be member of the
    Communist Party, 509
exile court in Darjeeling, 22
fears about "Lukhangwa's
    personal safety", 371
Fifth, 19
First, 18
flight from Lhasa, 153
forming "National Party", 20
Fourteenth, 95
Ganden Lhagya teachings in
    Bodh Gaya, 409
and Gelugpa church, 133
Gyurme Gyatso meet, 24
and his brother-in-law, 529
ill health, 127
to Lhasa, escorting, 20
Lord Chamberlain, 156
meeting with Chairman Mao,
    507
Mönlam Festival, 501
older brother, 70
and the Panchen Lama
    photograph, 692
and Panchen Lama's arrival at
    Willingdon Airport, 406
representative in Delhi, 767
return to Lhasa, 509
in Samding Monastery, 154
Second National People's
    Congress, 511
Seventh, 19
signature, 101
summer palace, 44
Thirteenth, 16, 19–23, 26, 27,
    40, 42, 53, 122, 125, 132,
    152, 153, 157

and the Tibetan government, 96
"Lama Tomden", 234
Lama Wangden peak, 7
Laogai labour camps, 354, 786
Laogai slavelabour camps, 300
Latthakin, Prince K. M., 10
"Lawrence of Tibet", 170
.303 Lee Enfield cartridges, 256
Lee Enfield rifles, 250
Lenin on the Tribune, 16
Le Sacre du Printemps, 11
Lewis guns, 65
"Lhakpa Bookie", 178
"Lha-mak", 45
Lhasa
    Andrugtsang house in, 388
    British mission in, 352
    Chinese Secret Police in, 197
    Convair CV-240-401 landing
        in, 376
    first military airport in, 376
    Great Prayer (Mönlam) Festival
        in, 388
    Ilyushin Il-12 landing in, 376
    Khampa and Amdo community
        in, 433
    Khampa refugees left, 441
    Khampa traders and refugees
        in, 397
    Kyichu River at, 496
    Manchu Imperial, 20
    Municipal Office, at the
        Tsuglakhang, 389
    "People's Organization" in, 176
    PLA march in, 345
    private schools in, 338–339
    Special Police Unit in, 341

Tibetan high command in, 60
Tibet Military Area
    Headquarters at, 631
twilight, 501–532
uprising, 550–589
Lhasa Medical and Astrological
    Center, 320
goals of, 321
    "Routine Child Care and
        Welfare" (chipa nyerchö)
        project, 321–322
Lhasa, memory songs of, 328–343
Lhasa Mentsikhang School, 320
"Lhasa rebellion", 299
Lhasa, Sera Monastery in, 242
Lhasa, street fighters in, 492
Lhasa, Tibetan population of, 381
Lhasa, Tibetans in, 353
Lhasa Uprising, 57
    of March 1959, 129
"Liberation Committee", 627
Liber Chronicarium, 46
"Lidé-Nari-Shingkham", 245
LIFE magazine, 277
Life Magazine, 591
lingchí, 20
"lingering death", 20
LINGKA SARPA, 539
Lingkashi, bombing in, 271
Lithang
    drop zone, 419–425
    forests of, 208
    Great Monastery of, 208, 377
    great monastery of, 210
    manufacture of silver jewellery,
        272
    tribes of, 214

Lithang Monastery, 198, 255
    bombing of, 202
    "Democratic Reforms" in, 241
    destruction of, 420
    dronyer of, 247
    fear and concerns of tribal
        chiefs, 242
    foundation, 210
    lamas in, 240
    monk of, 205
    pilgrims from eastern Tibet
        visit, 241
    steward of, 262
    Tibetan opera at, 219
Lithang uprising
    first battle of, 252
"Little Taiwan", 289
"long-haired star", 47
"Luo diabiao", 220

M
MAGAR SARPA, 537
Mago-la Pass, 609
makhar
    Chatreng, 493
    Ganden, 493
    Lithang, 493
    Nyarong, 493
    Sandhu, 493
Manchu dynasty, 281
Mao
    and Dharamshala, 787
    died on 9 September 1976, 786
Markham
    mission to, 644–668
    operation, 619
    resistance leader in, 625

Martial law, in Chamdo, 88
"Martyrs Memorial" cemetery, 639
McLeod Ganj, Rangzen Gym at, 305
"Meadow of Joy", 43
Mekong River, 49
Mighty Lama peak, 7
Mila Gurbum, 12
Military History, 84, 570, 581
Military History of Tibet, 57
military tax, 310
"Mimang Movement", 350
"Mimang Tsongdu", 374
Minyak Rabgang range, 226
Mirror of Beryl, 320
Missamari refugee camp, 610
Molla, xii
Molwa, xii
Mongol military power, 210
Mongol recurve bow, 222
"*mönlam chumae shay*", 105
Mönlam Festival, 375, 555
Moon Peak, 192
"*mosa*", 250
muleteers
   dress up of, 5
   journey across the mountains, 5
Mullick, B.N.
   visited Darjeeling, 176
Mustang, Guerrilla Trails to, 716–745
My Land and My People, 283, 542

N
Namgyal Monastery, at Potala palace, 322
Nangra, 288–294

"rebels" of, 289
   Red Army in, 288
"national conference", 522
National Geographic Magazine, 46, 213
National Geographic Society, 158
Nationalist troops, 232
Nehru, Jawahar Lal
   on Tibetan revolt, 174–175
"neo-colonialism", 159
Nepal Frontier Road, 36
New York Times, xviii
Ngadang (Gyantsé) Regiment, 85
Ninth Tadang regiment, 86
Noël Coward song, 65
Norbulingka defences, 535
NORTÖLINGKA, 537
Novelty Bioscope Theatre, 5
Nyarong uprising, 300
Nyarong War (1865), 134
Nyemo Machu River, 449
Nyemo uprising (1969), 310
Nyingma monasteries, 227

O
"October 1950: the Battle of Chamdo", 58
One Hundred Thousand Songs of Milarepa, 12
"Operation Caravan", 4
Oracles and Demons of Tibet, 11
"Origin Chronicles of Tibet", 50
Orphans of the Cold War, 412

P
"*pamaling*", 249
Pandim peak, 7

Pangdatsang, Rabga, 16
Pangdatsang rebellion, 128
"parachutes", 238
"parlour game", 54
P. A. system, 190
Patriotic Women's Association,
    528
Patterson of Tibet, 170
"Peaceful Suppression of Rebels",
    300
peak Natrar Jodh, 192
People's Bank of China, 579
"People's Conference", 374
People's Daily, 82
People's Liberation Army, 367
"People's Liberation" Army, 120
People's Liberation Army (PLA),
    297, 364
    Artillery Regiment, 155, 537
    Regiment #159
        second battalion of, 540
    Tibet Military Command, 540
People's Republic of China (PRC),
    35, 86
Phagpa, Drogön Chögyal, 33
phowa ritual, 263
Political History of Tibet, 329
Pomé song, 49
Popular Science magazine, 202
Population Atlas of China, 299
Puborgang range, 207
Pulger, Tenduk, 36

Q

Qing dynasty, in 1912, 214
Qinghai, revolt in, 287
Qinghai-Tibet highway

depot, 529, 538
opening of, 375

R

RANGKYONGJONG, 538
Rani, Devika, 10
"Rashomon" factor, xviii
'reactionary clique', 526
Reader's Digest, 186, 378
"rebel bandits", 631
Red Army, 59
    in Qinghai, 68
    at Shaanxi, 274
'Red Chinese Enemies of the
    Dharma', 254
Red Chinese soldier, 114
"red herring", 54
"reform through labor" camp, 626
Research and Analysis Wing
    (RAW), 718, 765
Resistance Force, at Nyemo, 454
Reting Monastery, 339
revolution, of 1911, 41
Rigya Monastery, 586
Ripin chakshup, 249
Roerich, Nicolas, 11
Rolex Company, in Kalimpong, 4
Rubicon moment, 117
Russian Moisin-Nagant rifle, 250,
    469
Russian Revolution, 55

S

Saga Dawa festival, 436
Sakya Monastery, 125
Samding Monastery, 154
Sampheling Monastery, 274, 275

Samye, drop zone, 415–419
Sangpo, Amdo Lama, 40
sangsöl ceremony, 219
Santa Claus beards, manufacture
    of, 45
Scottish Universal Mission, 9
sea of inhumanity, 696–715
*Sea of Inhumanity: Tibet in the
    Cultural Revolution*, 708
Second Drapchi, 86
Second Drapchi Regiment, 690
"Second Great Famine", 712
"second outbreak of fighting in
    1957–58", 297
"Second Tibetan Rebellion", 709
Secrets of Tibet, 342
*Selections from China Mainland
    Magazines* (SCMM), 776
"Self-Strengthening Movement",
    507
"*Senge Lemba*", 249
Sera Monastery, 43, 380
Serdung Chenmo, 404
Service de Documentation
    Extérieure et de Contre-
    Espionnage (SDECE), 768
The Seven Samurai, xviii
Seventeen Point Treaty, 90, 116
Seventh Jhadang, 86
Seven Years in Tibet, 56
Shakya Thubpa Phodrang temple,
    263
Shan Hai Ching, 46
Shigatsé regiment, 27
shoshi gambu, 266
Shoton Opera Festival, 332
Shotön opera festival, 44

SHUGTRI LINGKA, 538–539
"Sichuan" bridge, 50
Sichuan Frontier Force, 28
Sichuan-Tibet Highway, 371
Sichuan-Tibet highway, opening
    of, 375
Sierra de Guadarrama mountains,
    185
Sigmo Chenmo, 43
Sikkim
    British intrusion into, 36
    Tibet frontier, 38
Simla Conference, 211
Simla Convention, of 1914, 101
Singapore
    British surrender of, 110
    'monster' guns, 110
"Singing the Erlang-Shan
    Mountain", 375
Siniolchhu peak, 7
Sino-Japanese war, 591
Sino-Soviet split, 353
Sino-Tibetan frontier, 6, 60
Sino-Western friendship, 204
sisi lendu, 251
Sixth Artillery, 86
"Slave China", 12
Smiley, George, 590
"smokey long-tail star", 47
"Socialist Transformation", 235
Songs in Remembrance of Lhasa,
    328
*Sources on Culture and History of
    Tibet*, 57
South West Military Command,
    218
Spanish Civil War, 494

Special Frontier Force (SFF), 765
Spy on the Roof of the World, 161
stakhanovites, 236
State Intelligence Bureau (SIB),
    160
Statesman, 180
Sten guns, 65
Stepping-Stones, 161
"*Stille Nacht, Heilige Nacht*", 337
Stockholm syndrome, 91
"Straight Arrow", 153
String Theory, 55
Summa Theologica, 240
Sung dynasty, 35
Survey of China Mainland Press
    (SCMP), 776
Swiss Technical Cooperation, 187

T
Tagore, Rabindranath, 10
    in Kalimpong, 12
Tagtra Regent, 87
Taiwan, Nationalist
    (Guomindang) government in,
    94
Tamgenma, xii
"Tank Man", xvii
Tantric Buddhism, 13
Tashi, Gonpo, 386
    arrived at Tsethang, 474
    and Athar's Calcutta meeting,
        446
    attacked Khyungpo Tengchen,
        472
    attacked Powo Tramo, 471
    created resistance army, 444

direct contact with the Chinese,
    391
at Dowa Dzong, 438
Drepung Monastery, 399
to Drigu base, escort, 454
in Driguthang, 467
at Driguthang with guns and
    rifles, 443
expedition to Nyemo Machu
    River, 449
expedition to Shang Ganden
    Chökor monastery, 448
at founding ceremony, 439
on four rivers six ranges, 430
and Golden Throne ceremony,
    428
hand-written receipts to
    donors, 402
inventory of the gold and silver,
    404
left Lhasa on 1 June 1958, 437
in Lharigo settlement, 465–466
in Lho Dzong, 472
at Lhoka, 441
personal contingent of, 429
platoons attack Chinese, 450
ride north to Yangpachen, 456
rode to Kongtse la, 464
sent Khampas to Kalimpong,
    395
sent messenger to Lhoka, 471
on set up new resistance army
    base, 431
and Tenzin Tsultrim, 460
and Tibetan government, 427
trip to Tsari, 391
Tashi Lhunpo Monastery, 43

Tashi, Lobsang
    arrested in March 1959, 372
    at *Laogai* camp, 372
Tashi Ta-ring, 250
Tears of the Lotus, 412
Te Deum Laudamus, 403
Teesta River, 7
    naming of, 7
    road to Kalimpong, 8
    trees around, 8
Tenth Phagpala Rinpoche, 52
Tenth Thadang, 86
Tethongs, ancestors of, 18
thangka paintings, 243
18th Army's Tibet Invasion Force, 67
"The Battle of Dartsedo," 228
The Chinese Horse, 196, 306
The CIA's Secret War in Tibet, 412
The Cultural Monuments of Tibet, 404
The Golden Grain of the History of Do-Kham Chatreng, 278
"The Great Snows Volunteer Army of the Defenders of the Dharma", 630
"The Honorable Secretary", 184
"The Iliad or the Poem of Force", xix
"The Key to China and Tibet", 226
"The Litang Horse Festival", 223
The Ocean Annals, 283
'the Old Lama's Abode', 315
"Theory of Everything", xxiii
"The Peaceful Liberation of Tibet", 74

"The Pistol Shot," 10
"the Red Lama", 82
"the Red Ulan", 44
The Road to Serfdom, 236
The Romance of the Three Kingdoms, 290
The Sorrow and the Pity, 351
The Spy, 24
The Tantra of Secret Instructions on the Eight Branches, the Essences of the Elixir of Immortality, 326
The Timely Rain: Travels in New Tibet, 565
The Tragedy of My Homeland, 286
"The Volunteer Army to Defend the Dharma", 429
The Weapon of the Fearless One, 321
The White Annals, 209, 284
The White Haired Girl, 352
The Wounds of Three Generations, 287
"The Yak-Tail Mission", 44
The Year of the Fire Monkey, 204
Third Shigatsé Regiment, 539
Third Shigatsé regiment, 86
Thirteenth Drongdrak, 86
Thomas, Anthony, xvii
Thomas, F.W., xiii
Thondup, Karchung Tsering, 107
Thönpa Mansion
    Chinese soldiers broke, 312
    description of, 316
    in Lhasa, 315
    old medieval Lhasa of, 318
"Three Big Feudal Land-Owning Classes", 234

Tiananmen Square, xvii
Tibet
    army, 56
    British military intrusion into,
        38
    China's military occupation of,
        189
    Chinese invasion in, 72–85
    civil war in, 20
    Communist threat to, 172
    Cultural Revolution in, 130,
        131
    Declaration of Independence in
        1913, 26
    Dingri Regiment, 63
    Drapchi Regiment, 63
    encounter with Qing (Manchu)
        Empire, 19
    Gyantsé Regiment, 63
    individualized signatures, 101
    Jhadang Regiment, 63
    magar regiment in, 62
    Manchu occupation army in,
        19
    Minyak in, 35
    Nyadang Regiment, 63
    "peaceful liberation" of, 119
    Red Army in, 67
    Shigatsé Regiment, 63
    signed the Seventeen Point
        Treaty, 410
    Tadang Regiment, 64
    thangka painting in, 19
    "The Peaceful Liberation" of,
        58
    trade with, 6
    victory of 1918, 30

western visitor to, 14
Tibetan
    defeat at Chamdo, 111
    u-chen print script, 100
Tibetan army, Sixth (Chadang)
    Regiment of, 123
Tibetan Autonomous Region Sub-
    Committee, 297
Tibetan Bulletin, 203
Tibetan Communist Party, 55
Tibetan Foreign Bureau, 44
Tibetan government signed, Simla
    Accord, 580
Tibetan History, 76
Tibetan Institute of Performing
    Arts (TIPA), 183, 817
Tibetan military headquarters, in
    Lhasa, 119
Tibetan Office of Research and
    Analysis (TORA), 396
Tibetan Refugee Self-Help Center,
    183
Tibetan Review, 4, 55, xiv
Tibetan "telecode" system, 593
Tibetan Trade Agency, 17
Tibetan Trade Agent, 124
Tibetan Youth Conference, 196
Tibetan Youth Congress (TYC),
    717, 788
Tibet Autonomous Region (TAR),
    129, 236, 676, 677
    Public Security Bureau, 690
Tibet, Buddhist monastery in, 415
Tibet, Chinese occupation
    authorities in, 407
Tibet, drop zone, 406–415
Tibet Freedom Alliance, 503

Tibet, Gelugpa institutions in, 51
Tibet Improvement Association,
    16, 127
Tibet, *laissez-passer* to enter, 14
Tibet Military Area Headquarters,
    182
Tibet Mirror, 9, 32, 163, 164, 277
    closed in 1963, 169
    editorial office of, 166
    first issue of, 164
    published Bible stories, 165
Tibeto-Burman stock, 6
Tibet, raids into, 746–764
Tibet, Rebel-Alliance fighting in,
    708
Tibet Task Force, 444
*Tibet, Tibet: A Personal History of a
    Lost Land*, 302
Tibet Welfare Society, 393, 408,
    444
"Tibet Welfare Society", 175
Time magazine, 277
Times of India, 200
*Travels of a Consular Officer in
    Eastern Tibet*, 133
"Treaty of Friendship", 26
"Triumph of the Dharma", 546
Tsechokling Monastery, 437
Tsering, Tashi, xxi
Tsering, Tsongkha Lhamo, 590
    birth of, 590
    settled in Kalimpong, 592
Tunisian street vendor, self-
    immolation of, 829

U
"Uncle Baldy", 244
UN Command, 111

"un-equal treaties", 90
UN Genocide Convention, 304
United Nations General Assembly,
    94
United Nations Information
    Center, 791
United Tibetan Society, 503
"Universal Incense Offering", 332
University of Vienna, 13
Uprising of March 1959, 196
urusu bura, 250
U.S. army Colt automatic pistol,
    250
U.S. Consulate in Calcutta, 3
U.S. defence budget, 118

V
Vietnam War, 117
Voice of Tibet, 385

W
War and Peace, 11
"War on Tibet", 58
"warrior's topknot", 25
Water Dragon Lhasa People's
    Association, 350
"Water Mouse Chinese War", 26,
    492
Western Front, in World War
    One, 60
West Tibet Improvement
    Association, 16, 124
We Tibetans, 136
When Iron Gates Yield, 140
White Bird-Poop Mountain, 555
White Crystal Monastery, 177
Whitehall's scheme of things, 156

X

Xinhua News agency, 541

Y

Yellow Earth Pass, 251
Young Men's Buddhist
    Association, 161
"Yunnan" bridge, 49, 50

Yunru, 209
Yushu Tibetan Autonomous
    Prefecture, 300

Z

Zemu glacier, 7
zompa, 359